The Routledge Companion to Financial Accounting Theory

Financial accounting theory has numerous practical applications and policy implications. For instance, international accounting standard setters are increasingly relying on theoretical accounting concepts in the creation of new standards, and corporate regulators are increasingly turning to various conceptual frameworks of accounting to guide regulation and the interpretation of accounting practices.

The global financial crisis has also led to a new-found appreciation of the social, economic and political importance of accounting concepts in general and corporate financial reporting in particular. The fundamentals of capital market theory (i.e. market efficiency) and measurement theory (i.e. fair value), for example, have received widespread public and regulatory attention.

This comprehensive, authoritative volume contains the current scholarship and practice in the established field of financial accounting theory. It is a prestige reference work and a valuable resource for students, academics, regulators and practitioners.

Stewart Jones is Professor of Accounting at the University of Sydney, Australia. He is co-author of the bestselling textbook *Financial Accounting Theory, Third Edition* (2009, Cengage) and edits the prestigious accounting journal *Abacus*.

Routledge Companions in Business, Management and Accounting

Routledge Companions in Business, Management and Accounting are prestige reference works providing an overview of a whole subject area or sub-discipline. These books survey the state of the discipline, including emerging and cutting-edge areas. Providing a comprehensive, up-to-date, definitive work of reference, each Routledge Companions can be cited as an authoritative source on the subject.

A key aspect of these Routledge Companions is their international scope and relevance. Edited by an array of highly regarded scholars, these volumes also benefit from teams of contributors which reflect an international range of perspectives.

Individually, Routledge Companions in Business, Management and Accounting provide an impactful one-stop-shop resource for each theme covered. Collectively, they represent a comprehensive learning and research resource for researchers, postgraduate students and practitioners.

Published titles in this series include:

The Routledge Companion to Fair Value and Financial Reporting
Edited by Peter Walton

The Routledge Companion to Nonprofit Marketing
Edited by Adrian Sargeant and Walter Wymer Jr

The Routledge Companion to Accounting History
Edited by John Richard Edwards and Stephen P. Walker

The Routledge Companion to Creativity
Edited by Tudor Rickards, Mark A. Runco and Susan Moger

The Routledge Companion to Strategic Human Resource Management
Edited by John Storey, Patrick M. Wright and David Ulrich

The Routledge Companion to International Business Coaching
Edited by Michel Moral and Geoffrey Abbott

The Routledge Companion to Organizational Change
Edited by David M. Boje, Bernard Burnes and John Hassard

The Routledge Companion to Cost Management
Edited by Falconer Mitchell, Hanne Nørreklit and Morten Jakobsen

The Routledge Companion to Digital Consumption
Edited by Russell W. Belk and Rosa Llamas

The Routledge Companion to Identity and Consumption
Edited by Ayalla A. Ruvio and Russell W. Belk

The Routledge Companion to Financial Accounting Theory

Edited by Stewart Jones

Routledge
Taylor & Francis Group

LONDON AND NEW YORK

First published 2015
by Routledge
2 Park Square, Milton Park, Abingdon, Oxon OX14 4RN

Simultaneously published in the USA and Canada
by Routledge
711 Third Avenue, New York, NY 10017

Routledge is an imprint of the Taylor & Francis Group, an informa business

British Library Cataloguing in Publication Data
A catalogue record for this book is available from the British Library

Library of Congress Cataloging in Publication Data
The Routledge companion to financial accounting theory / edited by Stewart Jones. —
1 Edition.
pages cm. — (Routledge companions in business, management and accounting)
Includes bibliographical references and index.
1. Accounting. I. Jones, Stewart, 1964- editor.
HF5636.R684 2015
657.01—dc23
2014038304

ISBN: 978-0-415-66028-0 (hbk)
ISBN: 978-0-203-07425-1 (ebk)

Typeset in Bembo
by Swales & Willis Ltd, Exeter, Devon, UK

Printed and bound in the United States of America by Publishers Graphics,
LLC on sustainably sourced paper.

Contents

Contents

Figures

Tables

Contributors

Max Aiken has been Professor of Accounting at Victoria University of Wellington, La Trobe University and the Royal Melbourne Institute of Technology (RMIT). Professor Aiken is particularly well known for his work in public sector financial reporting and auditing, accounting theory and Chinese accounting history. He has published extensively in a wide range of leading international journals.

Amir Amel-Zadeh is an Assistant Professor at the University of Cambridge, Judge Business School. His research interests include the interaction of fair value accounting with bank capital regulation, accounting disclosure and mergers and acquisitions. In 2010, Amir received the Salje Medal for the best PhD thesis in the Arts, Humanities and Social Sciences 2008–2009 at Clare Hall, University of Cambridge. He was a scholar with the Gates Cambridge Trust and Economic and Social Research Council, UK, and received an award for academic excellence from Haas Business School, University of California at Berkeley. Amir's research has been published in accounting journals such as *The Accounting Review*, *Abacus*, and the *Journal of Business Finance and Accounting*. He has held visiting positions at Harvard Business School, Columbia Business School, New York University Stern School of Business and Bologna University.

Muhammad Junaid Ashraf is an Associate Professor of Accounting at the Suleman Dawood School of Business, Lahore University of Management Sciences, Pakistan. His current research focus is on studying management control changes in public-sector organizations operating in developing countries.

Jeremy Bertomeu is an Assistant Professor of Accountancy at Baruch College at the City University of New York. He previously held an appointment at Northwestern University. He received an MS from Hautes Etudes Commerciales in Paris and a PhD from Carnegie Mellon University. Professor Bertomeu teaches courses in managerial and financial accounting at both the undergraduate and graduate levels and conducts an analytical PhD course in accounting. He received the Alexander Henderson Award in 2008 for excellence in economic theory from Tepper Business School at Carnegie Mellon University. His research articles on financial accounting appear in *The Accounting Review*; *Journal of Accounting and Economics*; *Journal* *of Accounting Research*; *Contemporary Accounting Research*; *Journal of Accounting, Auditing & Finance*; *Review of Accounting Studies*; *Economic Letters*; *Management Science* and *International Journal of Industrial Organization*. He is a co-organizer for the Junior Accounting Theory Conference and co-editor for the SSRN e-journal *Accounting Theory*.

R.J. Chambers The late Professor Ray Chamber's career as an academic accountant was characterised by a prodigious research output attuned to deeply held convictions as to what accounting was, what it should be and how it should be done. His major work, *Accounting Evaluation and Economic Behaviour* (1966), set the theme for much of the work that followed. He authored 11 major books and produced over 230 articles during his career. He was an early proponent of fair values and was ever willing to pronounce on the difficulties associated with historical costs, often in the face of trenchant opposition. As an educator, Ray Chambers was arguably without peer, having taught and mentored at least eight professors of accounting together with a legion of others who have made their names in academia or the wider profession. Although a first-class scholar, Ray Chambers also recognised a duty to contribute in a tangible way to the accounting profession. He did this through service as the national president of the then Australian Society of Accountants. He was also founder and foundation editor of the prestigious accounting research journal, *Abacus*. Ray Chamber's status was recognised early with membership in the Social Science Research Council, the forerunner to the present day Academy of the Social Sciences in Australia. He was also the sole Australian to be honoured with membership in the Ohio Accounting Hall of Fame. His contribution to accounting in Australia was further recognised with his appointment as an officer in the Order of Australia. On retirement from the University of Sydney, Ray Chambers was accorded the honour of Emeritus Professor.

Edwige Cheynel is an Assistant Professor of Accounting at Columbia Business School in New York City. Prior to joining Columbia University, Edwige completed her doctorate in business administration at Carnegie Mellon University in 2010 and obtained a master's degree in finance from Hautes Etudes Commerciales in Paris. She previously worked for Deloitte in the financial services division in Paris. She received the 2010 Alexander Henderson Award for excellence in economic theory from Tepper Business School at Carnegie Mellon University for her dissertation. She is the co-editor for the SSRN e-journal *Accounting Theory*. Professor Cheynel's research on accounting theory has been published in *The Accounting Review* and *Review of Accounting Studies*. She teaches financial accounting to MBA students and the analytical accounting seminar in the PhD program at Columbia Business School.

Frank Clarke is Emeritus Professor of Accounting at the University of Newcastle and Honorary Professor of Accounting at the University of Sydney. He has held visiting appointments at the Universities of Sydney, Glasgow, Canterbury (NZ) and Lancaster. He is a past editor and currently a consulting editor of *Abacus* and the author or joint author of nine books and over 100 refereed journal articles.

Graeme Dean is Emeritus Professor at the University of Sydney. He has also held visiting appointments at several overseas universities in Canterbury (NZ), Cardiff, Glasgow, Hohenheim, Munich, Stuttgart and Graz. A long-time editor (1994–2009) and currently consulting editor of *Abacus*, the fourth-oldest and one of the leading Anglo-American accounting academic journals, he has published over a dozen books as well as more than 60 refereed journal articles.

Contributors

Michael Dempsey joined RMIT University as a Professor and Head of the Finance discipline in early 2013. Prior to this, he was an Associate Professor at Griffith University and at Monash University, having previously been at Leeds University, UK. He also has many years' experience working for the petroleum exploration industry in the Middle East, Egypt, Aberdeen and London. His teaching expertise includes corporate and investment finance, international finance, derivatives and financial engineering. He is an active researcher and research supervisor across financial markets, about which he has published articles that have appeared in leading international journals, including *Journal of Banking and Finance (2)*, *Financial Analysts Journal (2)*, *European Financial Management (1)*, *Abacus (2)*, *Journal of Investment Management (1)*, *Australian Journal of Management (1)*, *Journal of Business Finance and Accounting (3)*, *Accounting and Business Research (3)*, *Critical Perspectives on Accounting (3)*, *Journal of Asset Management (1)* and *Accounting and Finance (1)*.

John Richard Edwards is a Research Professor of Accounting at Cardiff University. He has published papers on accounting history in numerous academic journals. Book publications include *The History of Financial Accounting* (1989) and joint authorship of *The Priesthood of Industry: The Rise of the Professional Accountant in British Management* (1998), *The Routledge Companion to Accounting History* (2009) and *A History of Management Accounting: The British Experience* (2013).

Dale L. Flesher is a Professor in the Patterson School of Accountancy at the University of Mississippi and holds the Roland and Sheryl Burns Chair; he also serves as Associate Dean of the School of Accountancy. He received both a bachelor's and master's degree from Ball State University and a PhD from the University of Cincinnati. He has authored over 400 articles for more than 100 professional journals throughout the world, including *The Accounting Review*; *Journal of Accountancy*; *The CPA Journal*; *Abacus*; *The Accounting Historians Journal*; *Accounting and Business Research*; and *Accounting, Organizations and Society*. He is also the author of 50 books (in 89 editions), including the 50th anniversary history of the Institute of Internal Auditors, the centennial history of NASBA, and the 75th anniversary history of the American Accounting Association. Dr Flesher has served as editor of The *Accounting Historians Journal*, a position he held from 1989 through 1994. He previously edited *The Accounting Historians Notebook* for 10 years.

Geoff Frost is an Associate Professor in the discipline of Accounting at the University of Sydney Business School. His current research interests include reporting and accounting of sustainability activities, the accountant's role in the environmental management system, and the use of alternative reporting mediums by reporting entities. Geoff has published extensively in the field of sustainability reporting.

Trevor Hopper is Emeritus Professor of Management Accounting at Sussex University, UK; Adjunct Professor at Victoria University of Wellington, New Zealand; and a Visiting Professor at Stockholm School of Economics, Sweden. Previously he was a Cost Accountant in Industry, a Lecturer at Wolverhampton and Sheffield Universities, and Professor at Manchester Business School. His visiting positions include the University of Michigan, Ann Arbor, USA; Queen's University, Canada; Griffith University, Gold Coast, Australia; and the Universities of Kyushu and Fukuoka, Japan. His major interests lie in the social, organisational and political aspects of management accounting, especially with respect to ERPs, developing countries and contemporary accounting changes. Professor Hopper was a co-editor of *British Accounting Review* and is the consulting editor for the *Journal of Accounting in Emerging Economies*. He has co-edited eight books, including *A Handbook of Accounting in Developing Countries* and *Issues in Management Accounting*, and has published extensively in professional journals, books and international research journals including *Accounting and Business Research*; *Accounting, Organizations and Society*; *the Auditing, Accounting and Accountability Journal*; *British Accounting Review*; *Critical Perspectives on Accounting*; *European Accounting Review*; *Journal of Management Studies*; and *Management Accounting Research*.

David Johnstone is a PhD graduate from the University of Sydney. After completing his doctorate, David spent one year at Lancaster University as a British Commonwealth post-doctoral fellow and two years as an Assistant Professor in the School of Business at the University of California Berkeley. David's research is in the statistical foundations of financial valuation and markets. He has published on topics concerning statistical inference and decision theory in prestigious international journals in the philosophy of science, statistics, decision theory, accounting and finance. Recent papers have extended his work to include behavioural models of decision making which underpin the emerging field of behavioural finance. David has completed major consulting tasks in the private and public sectors in Australia. A recent research project on infrastructure valuation for the purposes of tariff regulation formed the basis for a review of Australian regulatory practices by the Productivity Commission.

Stewart Jones is a Professor of Accounting at the University of Sydney and was previously a Professor of Accounting and Finance at Deakin University and an Associate Professor at Monash University. His specialist research area is corporate financial reporting. Over the past decade he has published more than 100 scholarly research pieces in the field of financial reporting and accounting, including over 60 refereed articles, 10 books, and numerous book chapters, working papers and short monographs. Stewart's most recent books are *Advances in Credit Risk Modelling and Corporate Bankruptcy Prediction*, published by the Cambridge University Press, UK; the third edition of *Financial Accounting Theory*, published by Cengage Learning, Sydney; and *The Reality and the Rhetoric: Sustainability Reporting within the Organisation*, published by Sydney University Press in 2013. Stewart's research interests cover such topics as accounting theory, credit risk and corporate distress analysis, standard setting, international standards harmonization, financial analysis and research methodology. He has published in many leading journals, including *The Accounting Review*, *Accounting Horizons*, *The Journal of the Royal Statistical Society*, *Journal of Business Finance and Accounting*, *The British Accounting Review*, *Accounting and Business Research*, *The Journal of Behavioral Finance* and *The Economic Record*. Stewart is currently editor-in-chief of the prestigious international quarterly, *Abacus*. Stewart's industry experience includes the interpretation of accounting standards, financial analysis and regulation, credit risk modelling and corporate performance analysis.

Tom Lee is Emeritus Professor of Accountancy at the University of Alabama, USA, and Honorary Professor of Financial Reporting and Corporate Governance at the University of St Andrews, UK. He has made numerous contributions to the literatures of financial reporting, auditing and accounting history. He is best known for research on cash flow reporting and the professionalization of public accountancy.

Geoff Meeks has been a Professor of Financial Accounting at Cambridge Judge Business School since 2003. He was previously employed by Price Waterhouse, the University of Edinburgh and the Faculty of Economics at Cambridge, and he has held visiting positions at Harvard Business School, INSEAD and the London School of Economics. At CJBS he has served as Director of Teaching, Head of the Finance and Accounting Group, and Acting Director.

His research interests include financial reporting about major events in business finance (especially takeover and bankruptcy), creative accounting and accounting regulation, and the relation between company accounting and national accounting.

Chris Nobes is a Professor of Accounting at Royal Holloway (University of London) and at the University of Sydney. He was a member of the Accounting Standards Committee of the UK and Ireland from 1987 to 1990 and was one of two UK representatives on the Board of the International Accounting Standards Committee from 1993 to 2001. He was the 'Outstanding International Educator' of the American Accounting Association in 2002.

Stephen Penman is the George O. May Professor in the Graduate School of Business, Columbia University, where he is also Co-Director of the Center for Excellence in Accounting and Security at Columbia. His research is concerned with the valuation of equity and the role of accounting information in security analysis. He has published widely in finance and accounting journals and has conducted seminars on fundamental analysis and equity evaluation for academic and professional audiences. He has won numerous awards, including the Notable Contribution to Accounting Literature Award, the Wildman Medal for his book *Financial Statement Analysis and Security Valuation*, the Institute for Quantitative Investment Research (INQUIRE) Prize, and the Roger F. Murray Prize from the Institute for Quantitative Research in Finance. His new book, *Accounting for Value*, was published by Columbia University Press in January 2011.

Gary John Previts is the E. Mandell de Windt Professor, Weatherhead School of Management, Case Western Reserve University. He is co-author of *A History of Accountancy in the United States* (1998, Ohio State University Press) and is editor of *Research in Accounting Regulation* (Elsevier). He has served as a member of the American Institute of CPA's Board of Directors and conducted research for the AICPA Special Committee on Financial Reporting (Jenkins Committee) and the FASB's Business Reporting Research Project. He is a member of the Public Company Accounting Oversight Board Advisory Council, the Accountability Advisory Council of the US Government Accountability Office and a past president of the American Accounting Association. In 2007 and 2008, Previts served as a member of the Advisory Committee on the Auditing Profession of the US Department of the Treasury and chaired the Subcommittee on Human Resources. In October 2007, he received the AICPA's Gold Medal for Distinguished Service. In 2010 he received the American Accounting Association's Outstanding Educator Award. At CWRU he holds the rank of Distinguished University Professor. He was inducted into the Ohio State University Accounting Hall of Fame in 2011. He is currently concluding his term of service as the technical advisor to the United States representative of the International Accounting Education Standards Board of the International Federation of Accountants.

Janek Ratnatunga is Chief Executive Officer of the Institute of Certified Management Accountants. He has held senior professional academic appointments at Monash University, the University of Melbourne and the Australian National University in Australia, and the Universities of Washington, Richmond and Rhode Island in the USA. He is currently the editor of the *Journal of Applied Management Accounting Research*. He has authored or co-authored 25 books on strategic cost management, entrepreneurship, financial accounting, accounting theory, financial modelling and sustainability reporting and over 200 academic and professional papers. He has worked in the profession as a chartered accountant with KPMG and as a consultant for the World Bank. He is also a world authority on the business and accounting implications of global warming and carbon trading and has worked with the senior management of the United Nations Framework Convention for Climate Change.

Joshua Ronen is a Professor of Accounting at New York University Stern School of Business. His primary research areas include capital markets, disclosure, earnings management, economic impact of accounting rules and regulations, financial reporting, legal liability of firms, transfer pricing, agency theory, corporate governance and fair valuation. Professor Ronen has written numerous books including *Accounting and Financial Globalization*; *Off-Balance Sheet Activities*; *Entrepreneurship*; *Smoothing Income Numbers: Objectives, Means and Implications*; and *Earnings Management*. He has been published in many academic journals and publications including *The New York Times*; *The Accounting Review*; *Journal of Accounting Research*; *Journal of Accounting, Auditing and Finance*; *Abacus*; *Management Science*; *Journal of Public Economics*; *Journal of Organizational Behavior and Human Performance*; *Stanford Journal of Law, Business, and Finance*; and *Journal of Financial Markets*.

Nuno Soares is an Assistant Professor at the School of Engineering, University of Porto, Portugal, where he teaches masters and undergraduate courses in financial accounting and economics. He holds a PhD in accounting from the Manchester Business School, UK, and a BSc in management and an MSc in finance from the School of Economics of the University of Porto. His research focuses on company valuation, mergers and acquisitions, the impact of IFRS adoption in earnings information, share issuance and firm cash holdings. He has published in leading academic journals and presented at the main research conferences in the area.

Andrew Stark is the Coutts Professor of Accounting and Finance at the Manchester Business School, a part of the University of Manchester. He has a BA in mathematics from Cambridge University and an MBA and PhD from the Manchester Business School. He previously held faculty positions at the Yale School of Management, the University of Essex, the University of Ulster at Jordanstown, the University of Maryland at College Park and the Victoria University of Manchester. He has published over 40 papers in refereed research journals. He is a past editor of the *British Accounting Review* and is a current editor of the *Journal of Business Finance and Accounting*. He is a fellow of the Academy of Social Sciences and has been a recipient of the Distinguished Academic Award of the British Accounting and Finance Association.

Sir David Tweedie was educated at Edinburgh University (BCom 1966, PhD 1969) and qualified as a Scottish Chartered Accountant in 1972. After teaching at Edinburgh University, he became technical director of the Institute of Chartered Accountants of Scotland (ICAS) in 1978. In 1982 he was appointed national technical partner of Thomson McLintock & Co and later of KPMG. In 1990 he became the chairman of the UK Accounting Standards Board, and in January 2001 he was appointed the first chairman of the International Accounting Standards Board. He then led the Board for ten years, retiring in June 2011. He is a fellow of the Judge Business School at Cambridge University and a visiting professor of accounting in the Management School at Edinburgh University. He has received honorary degrees from nine British universities. He was knighted in 1994 and has been presented with a number of awards from the accounting profession. He was inducted into the Accounting Hall of Fame in 2013. Sir David became President of the Institute of Chartered Accountants of Scotland in April 2012 (until April 2013) and Chairman of the International Valuation Standards Council in October 2012. He chairs the Royal Household Audit Committee for the Sovereign Grant and is also Chairman of the Board of Trustees of the Scottish Charities, Leuchie House and the ICAS Foundation.

Contributors

Shahzad Uddin is a Professor of Accounting and the Director of the Essex Accounting Centre. He is a qualified cost and management accountant and fellow member of the Institute of Cost and Management Accountants. Prior to Essex, he was at Queen's University, Belfast, UK. Shahzad moved to the University of Essex in 2002 as a lecturer prior to becoming a Professor of Accounting at Essex Business School in 2010. Shahzad has had a number of visiting academic positions at universities in Japan, China, Denmark, France, Malaysia, Oman and Bangladesh. Shahzad's main research interest includes accounting and economic development, governance and poverty alleviation. Shahzad has received funding from the Commonwealth Commission in the UK, CIMA, the British Academy, JSPS and the Nuffield Foundation for his research projects. Professor Uddin has published in top accounting and development journals. In addition, he has established a journal and book series published by Emerald. Shahzad is the co-editor of the *Journal of Accounting in Emerging Economies (JAEE)* and *Research in Accounting in Emerging Economies (RAEE)*.

Alfred Wagenhofer is a Professor at the University of Graz, Austria. He is the Chair of the Institute of Accounting and Control and Director of the Center for Accounting Research. His research interests include financial and management accounting, international accounting and corporate governance. He has authored and co-authored seven books and many publications in leading international accounting journals.

Geoffrey Whittington is currently Emeritus Professor of Financial Accounting at the University of Cambridge; a Life Fellow of Fitzwilliam College; a Senior Associate of the Judge Business School, attached to the Centre for Financial Analysis and Policy; and an Honorary Professor at the University of Sussex. From 2001 to 2006, he was a full-time member of the International Accounting Standards Board with responsibility for liaison with the Accounting Standards Board for the UK and Ireland (ASB). He was a part-time member of the ASB from 1990 to 2001 and from 2006 to 2009. He graduated from the London School of Economics and subsequently qualified as a chartered accountant. He also has a doctorate in economics from Cambridge University. His early academic career was as a Researcher at the Department of Applied Economics in Cambridge, where he also became a Fellow and Director of Studies in Economics at Fitzwilliam College. He subsequently held chairs in financial accounting at the Universities of Edinburgh (1972–1975), Bristol (1975–1988) and Cambridge (1988–2001) and served as a part-time member of the UK Monopolies and Mergers Commission (1987–1996). He was a part-time economic advisor to the Office of Fair Trading on the Stock Exchange case (which led to the 'Big Bang' reforms). He has also served on many other public, professional and academic committees and as an expert witness in legal and regulatory cases. Current activities include membership on the academic panels of the Competition Commission and the Accounting Standards Council and of the Accounting Standards Council's advisory committee on accounting for public benefit entities. He is also a Governor of the National Institute of Economic and Social Research and a member of the editorial boards of four academic journals.

Danture Wickramasinghe is a Professor and the Chair of Management Accounting at the University of Glasgow, UK. He has published in a number of international accounting journals including *Accounting, Auditing and Accountability Journal*; *Critical Perspectives on Accounting*; and *Qualitative Research in Accounting and Management*. Previously, he taught management accounting over a period of 30 years in various universities, including the Universities of Colombo (Sri Lanka); Manchester (UK) and Hull (UK), and had visiting assignments at the universities of Colombo (Sri Lanka), Paris Dauphine (France) and Norland (Norway). He is the co-author of *Management Accounting Change: Approaches and Perspectives*, published by Routledge, and the co-editor of *Handbook of Accounting and Development*, published by Edward Elgar. His research interest broadly lies in critical accounting and management accounting in less developed countries.

Varda Yaari finished his PhD degree at New York University and since then has published in accounting, finance, and economics journals. In particular, he uses game theory tools to solve issues that involve earnings management. He has worked in universities in Israel and the USA. In recent years, Varda Yaari served as CEO of a family firm in Israel.

1

Development of financial accounting theory

Stewart Jones

This volume traces aspects of the development of financial accounting theory from its historical antecedents in the UK and USA to the many thriving debates we see today, particularly in the areas of accounting measurement, the role of the conceptual framework and accounting concepts, the trend toward a globalised set of accounting standards, and the politicisation of the standard setting process, particularly at the international level. This volume explores a wide range of financial accounting theory topics, including early 'practice descriptive' theories, which were influential from the 1930s to the late 1950s; the normative research traditions of the 1960s and 1970s, which focused primarily on alternative asset valuation models for income determination; positive accounting theory, which came to dominate accounting research from the 1980s and embraces capital markets research; agency theory; earnings management; the impacts of disclosure on the cost of capital and other empirical topics; and the emergence of critical accounting theory, which also emerged in the 1980s and has taken a radically different standpoint from positive theory on many important methodological, ontological and epistemological issues. The classification of accounting research into competing schools of thought covering a discrete chronology is convenient but somewhat arbitrary. One limitation is that it ignores significant points of commonality and interrelationship in accounting research over time. The accounting literature is replete with recycled ideas resurfacing under different methodological and theoretical guises at different chronological junctures. For instance, the concept of fair value accounting (in one form or another) was explored in early accounting writings, but it was developed with much greater conceptual rigour in the 'normative' literature of Chambers, Sterling and others. After a long period in the wilderness, the importance of fair value accounting has now enjoyed something of a renaissance, being incorporated into various international financial reporting standards (IFRS) and resurrected in new (testable) empirical contexts, particularly following the fallout of the Global Financial Crisis (GFC). In another example, the staunch theoretical defence of historical cost accounting (HCA) and accounting conservatism by earlier theorists such as Littleton (1953) parallels the rationalisation of these concepts in agency theory many decades later. This volume also explores emerging areas of accounting measurement and reporting, such as carbon accounting and corporate sustainability reporting, where recent research has exhibited normative, empirical and critical accounting theory elements.

While the development of financial accounting theory and testable propositions is clearly important to establishing the scientific status of accounting research, this volume also recognises that there is no coherent or generally accepted body of accounting theory. A theory can be defined as 'a set of interrelated constructs (concepts), definitions, and propositions that present a systematic view of phenomena by specifying relations among variables with the purpose of explaining and predicting the phenomena'.[1] If this is the litmus test of theory, the accounting discipline has some distance to travel yet. Rather than having a comprehensive accounting theory, different theories continue to be proposed in the literature, each using different approaches to theory construction and verification. Even within the narrow confines of some well-established theoretical fields, there appears to be little consensus on the essential elements making up a theory. For instance, the conceptual framework and accounting measurement issues have continued to be debated and re-debated over many decades, often with a failure to achieve general consensus on fundamental theoretical concepts or antecedent conditions for theory development. Across many fields of accounting, there appears to be wide diversity on the core assumptions and methodological foundations of the accounting discipline, which has impeded the development of a comprehensive accounting theory.

This volume also picks up on important contemporary themes and events which are proving influential in shaping the development of accounting theory and practice. For example, following the turmoil of the GFC which so severely shattered global financial markets, there has been a new-found appreciation of the socio-economic and political importance of accounting. For instance, the fundamental assumptions of capital market efficiency and measurement theory (i.e. fair values) has received widespread public and regulatory attention, much of it critical, in the aftermath of the GFC. Another important theme in recent years is the rise of IFRS and the growing trend towards globalised accounting standards. These developments have also ushered in an age of intensifying politicisation of the standard setting process at the international level. Several chapters of this volume will address accounting topics within the context of these important themes.

The following provides a brief introduction to each chapter. Chapters 1–3 explore the early development of accounting theory and practice in the UK and USA. The study of the history of accounting concepts and practices is a useful guide to understanding and interpreting current and potential future practices and forming a better appreciation of the social, economic and political forces which have shaped accounting thought over time. In Chapter 2, Richard Edwards examines the British contribution to the development of financial accounting theory, starting with the Companies Act, which introduced limited liability in 1855. Edwards explores a variety of topics which came to dominate accounting practice over the historical period he covers, including the early development and influence of HCA and depreciation accounting, the use and abuse of secret reserves, cash flow reporting, the evolution of group accounts, price level accounting, the relevance and impact of statutory regulation, early conceptual framework initiatives, and the early development of empirical research initiatives in the UK. Edwards concludes that financial accounting theory and financial regulation in the UK have developed rather haphazardly with no consistent evolutionary pattern. History is rife with contradictions, and accounting ideas tend to be recycled at different times. For example, attitudes towards secret reserves changed from cautionary approval to eventual illegalisation. Further, while HCA was firmly entrenched in early UK accounting practices, there was occasional discussion and debate in the early accounting treatises and publications (from various sources) about the relevance of market values for assets. An insight of Edwards is that many accounting thinkers with innovative ideas – what he terms Baxter's 'countless anonymous innovators' – remain unknown. However, it is possible to identify some influential thinkers who have dramatically impacted accounting practice, such as through the British judiciary. Edwards concludes that ideas about how accounting should best be done might well advance financial transparency, but history has shown us that improvements can be ephemeral. This could in part be a consequence of lack of congruence between the priorities of preparers and users of accounting information.

In Chapter 3, Gary J. Previts and Dale L. Flesher outline historical, regulatory, socio-economic and political factors which have shaped accounting thought and practice in the United States over nearly two hundred years. The chapter covers the transformation of the American economy from a predominantly agricultural to an industrial one and from a developing and mainly debtor economy to a major creditor nation. The chapter explores several themes and events that have influenced the evolution of US accounting thought and practice, from the early accounting emanating from popular books and manuals, to the regulatory phase involving the development of large railroads, to a period of common law influence, and then on to the current period, in which codification has been adopted in the form of the accounting standards and concepts statements issued by the Financial Accounting Standards Board (FASB). Previts and Flesher conclude that over the past two hundred years, the form and format of disclosure have significantly changed, from the locked proprietor's ledger balance of accounts, to crude railroad balance sheets, to the modern corporate financial statements that we know today. The authors also point out how the focus shifted during this period, from financial statements to a 'Trueblood Report' style, decision usefulness orientation for financial reports to the current, broader, business reporting model as envisioned by the Jenkins Committee and influenced by modern web-based technology and the instant global communication culture. Previts and Flesher also identify the philosophy of 'American pragmatism' in accounting thought and the regulatory maxim of 'sunshine' or disclosure (or publicity) as dominant ideas in the development of accounting thought and practice. They conclude that the central assumption or belief evolving from the sunshine era of the post–Civil War period was the 'full and fair disclosure' concept and the modern, growing views about 'transparency', which include the trend towards sustainability reporting. This assumption is that disclosure will impact decisions in a way that is consistent with economic and social well-being. However, the authors conclude that disclosure assumes that stakeholders are capable of understanding and acting upon this information, which is a tenuous assumption at best. Previts and Flesher also address the issue of a globalised set of accounting standards as originally promised by the Norwalk Agreement in 2002. More than a decade later, the SEC's endorsement of IFRS seems increasingly improbable (having repeatedly failed to meet its self-imposed deadlines to support IFRS adoption). While Previts and Flesher conclude that the failure to achieve convergence should not be a particular surprise to anyone, the continued efforts to develop *the* conceptual framework continue to occupy the attention of standard setters globally.

In Chapter 4, Stewart Jones and Max Aiken explore early accounting developments in the UK and USA. Their focus is on the development and influence of 'practice descriptive' theories of accounting. These early theories came into prominence from the 1930s to the early 1950s. This theoretical movement, as put forward in the words of Gilman (1939), May (1936), Paton and Littleton (1940), Littleton (1953) and others, attempted to develop coherent propositions and concepts which could justify, explain and articulate accounting regulations and conventional accounting procedures, principles and doctrines as advanced by professional accountants, regulators and policy makers. Littleton (1953) became the most influential and prolific writer in this field. His theories emphasised the importance of unadjusted HCA as the basis of accounting measurement, the primary importance of income determination as the 'centre of gravity' in accounting thought, and the dominance of the income statement over the balance sheet. Littleton's theoretical position used observations from history and accounting practices to both build and corroborate theoretical propositions, many of which may still hold currency in today's accounting world. However, Littleton's ideas sharply contrasted with other emerging scholars of the 1950s, particularly R.J. Chambers. Debate over accounting measurement and valuation approaches, and how the history of accounting has shaped these debates (or provides evidence for different theoretical approaches), continues unabated, as we see in other chapters of this volume.

In Chapter 5, Tom Lee examines the objectives and qualitative characteristics of financial reporting currently prescribed by accounting standard setters in the conceptual framework (CF), particularly the CF of the International Accounting Standards Board (IASB). Chapter 5 is timely, as the FASB in the US and the IASB have agreed to harmonise their CFs. Although the CF harmonisation project is still incomplete (and may be for some time), the FASB (2010) and the IASB (2010) have issued identical statements on the objectives and qualitative characteristics of financial information. Lee is largely critical of FASB/IASB efforts on the CF to date. A key concern is that the concept of decision usefulness articulated in the CF is divorced from reality, as it fails to address the many different types of financial decisions possible in practice. Further, Lee believes the concept of relevance is only vaguely defined in terms of *potential* rather than actual influence on economic decisions, and, similarly, faithful representation is defined without full appreciation of the ambiguous nature of the economic phenomena being represented. Lee sees the most obvious omission in the IASB CF (2010) to be the lack of focus on the nature of the economic phenomena interpreted by accountants to be useful for decisions. However, economic reality represented in accounting terms consists mainly of socially constructed institutional facts that, to date, have been identified without common agreement as to their meaning and function. Lee concludes that the construction of a CF that will be effective and have authority as a body of professional knowledge must involve an appropriate and detailed analysis of the ontology and epistemology of economic reality for accounting purposes.

In Chapter 6, the late Ray Chambers reviews competing concepts of income and capital maintenance, particularly replacement cost accounting versus the exit price system (more particularly, *continuous cotemporary accounting* or CoCoA). Chambers observes that by the 1980s, two concepts of capital maintenance yielding two distinct concepts of income had developed a strong following in the literature. These concepts are *financial* and *physical* capital maintenance. Chambers' position is clear and uncompromising: only financial capital maintenance and the exit price system can avoid the variant valuation rules of HCA, the multiplicity of calculations of the Edwards and Bell replacement cost approach, and the 'arithmetical solecisms of both'. According to Chambers, the CoCoA system captures the effects of 'all rises and falls in specific prices' and has the added advantage relative to other current value systems of both simplicity and understandability. Under CoCoA, non-monetary assets are valued at their selling prices and dated cash equivalents are valued at balance date. Cash equivalents can then legitimately be added together and related to the amounts of monetary items. According to Chambers, the differences between book values and the observed selling prices of assets at balance date, whatever their 'causes', would be accumulated in a 'price variation account'. Valuation at cash equivalents would yield a net asset amount (equal to the equity or capital account balance) that is a homogenous aggregate of uniformly dated values, creating an interpretable and understandable concept of financial position. Chambers then suggests that a general price index be applied to the opening balance so that general purchasing power is maintained. As a disciple of the 'true income' approach, Chambers is quick to dismiss the pronouncements of standard setting bodies which would permit optional treatments of different valuation models. He rejects the prevailing professional view that a single serviceable concept of income is not feasible or practicable and that it should be permissible (even a pragmatic necessity) to publish financial statements using more than one valuation method.

In Chapter 7, Sir David Tweedie takes a personal perspective of the standard setting process from his unique vantage point as a former chairman of the IASB. Sir David provides unique insight into the political factors and controversies which have shaped standard setting in the international arena, particularly the development of the IASB–US convergence program. As Sir David observes, a major triumph of the IASB to date is that more than one hundred countries globally now use IFRS. However, Sir David argues that countries moving to IFRS are faced with the three issues of cost, change and loss of control or autonomy in standard setting. In the context of the IASB–US convergence program, the loss of sovereignty or autonomy in standard setting has been the main sticking point for US regulators in shifting to IFRS. The issues have been different in Europe. For instance, some governments in Europe have regretted the decision to move from national to international standards – according to Sir David, it was a decision made by the EU 'with great courage and almost certainly in complete ignorance of some of the consequences of the International Accounting Standards Europe proposed to adopt'. Sir David indicates that the IASB's first decade was characterised by a constant juggling act to engender greater European confidence in IFRS while also engaging the US FASB in the challenging process of securing US acceptance of IFRS. Despite the tardiness of the US to embrace IFRS, the momentum behind IFRS as the de facto global accounting standards seems irreversible. Looking to the future, the IASB's vision appears to be different from that of the US, whose standard setting approach is to limit the number of standards to be issued and, ideally, to have very short standards dealing with major points of principle. Sir David concludes that, ultimately, we are back to the issue of fair presentation and the willingness of preparers, auditors and regulators to accept judgement in accounting.

In Chapter 8, Chris Nobes explores empirical research evidence about the adoption of IFRS across different countries. He notes that the literature appears to give the misleading impression that IFRS is now widely used for most corporate financial reporting and by most companies in the world. But Nobes finds significant variations in how IFRS is actually applied across many reporting jurisdictions. Related to this issue, Nobes discusses two regulatory issues which vary significantly across these reporting jurisdictions: translations of IFRS and enforcement of IFRS. Nobes observes several important caveats on IFRS adoption, including that the requirement or permission to use IFRS is restricted in most jurisdictions to certain types of reporters (e.g. listed companies) or types of reporting (e.g. consolidated statements) or both; that most of the so-named IFRS adoptions do not require the direct application of IFRS as issued by the IASB; and that, in several countries, companies and auditors do not refer to compliance with IASB-IFRS even when such compliance is being achieved. After examining the regulatory environments of the sixteen countries with the largest stock markets in the world, Nobes concludes that none of them requires IASB-IFRS for all types of regulated reporting, and most of them do not even *allow* (let alone require) even some local version of IFRS for unconsolidated reporting. Nobes also finds empirical evidence that the most powerful single explanatory variable for a company's IFRS policy choices is its pre-IFRS policies. Since a company's pre-IFRS policies were mostly determined by the accounting requirements or other institutional features of its country, then country can be used as a proxy variable for pre-IFRS practices. Country is also a major explanatory variable for the amount of IFRS policy *change* over time.

In Chapter 9, Amir Amel-Zadeh and Geoff Meeks explore the role of fair value accounting during the GFC. Did fair value contribute to the banking crisis that led to the near collapse of the global financial system? In the search for culprits for the GFC, bankers, journalists and politicians have been quick to point the finger at the accounting profession for insisting on inappropriate (fair value) measures of financial assets which ostensibly distorted the financial position of major investment banks. At the height of the GFC, political pressures on standard setters (particularly on the FASB from the US Congress and the SEC) led to a major re-thinking of fair value requirements under accounting standards, culminating in a series of guidelines and amendments to existing fair value accounting rules. In reviewing the relevant literature, Amel-Zadeh and Meeks focus on three particular issues relating to the solvency of banks and the stability of the financial system: procyclicality, feedback and contagion, and bank failure. Amel-Zadeh and Meeks conclude that if there had been a pure fair value system in place in the crisis, then it is quite likely that fair value accounting could have exacerbated the GFC, as many critics have contended. However, because so much of the corporate balance sheet was exempt from fair valuation, and because accounting regulators softened fair value requirements as the banking crisis developed, the authors conclude that it is unlikely that fair value measurement was the real culprit behind the GFC. However, the authors conclude that the GFC has increased our understanding of some important limitations of fair value accounting applied in practice.

In Chapter 10, Geoff Whittington analyses the IASB's approach to fair value accounting. He discusses the definition of fair value, the arguments for and against fair value in IFRS, the early support and adoption of fair values by the IASB in various IFRS from 2001 to 2006, and the IASB's process of retreat and retrenchment from fair values over the period from 2006 to 2013. Whittington also provides important insight as to why the IASB fundamentally changed its position on fair value measurement. The IASB has already had significant achievements in regulating financial reporting, notably in persuading more than a hundred countries to make use of its standards. However, it has also attracted significant criticism and controversy, and a focus for this negativity has been its alleged support for fair value accounting as the basis of measurement in financial reports. Whittington explores four aspects of fair value in the IASB's standards programme: the definition of fair value; the case for using fair value as the measurement basis; the degree of support for fair value in the IASB's standards and other pronouncements and the way this has changed over the first twelve years of the IASB's existence; and the forces that have influenced the IASB's attitude towards fair value, including the effects of the GFC. Whittington concludes that the future of fair value measurement is both assured and limited, as the IASB moves towards a more mixed measurement framework. Whittington further concludes that there is a need to provide more precise standard setting guidance to prevent future standards being reduced to a mere series of political compromises without any underlying theoretical coherence. In the measurement area, for example, Whittington finds that there is a need to articulate the precise criteria upon which the choice of accounting measurements will be made; however, this will necessitate a more detailed and careful review of the conceptual framework moving forward.

In Chapter 11, Stephen Penman observes that significant progress has been made over the past two decades in the development of valuation models. However, the dominant model in the literature until the 1990s was the discounted cash flow model. More recently, alternative models based on earnings and book values (particularly the residual earnings model and the abnormal earnings growth model) have become influential in accounting research. This observation is valid despite growing scepticism that valuation models simply do not work in practice. This scepticism may have led some investment professionals to revert back to simple schemes such as multiple pricing that Penman regards as theoretically unsatisfactory. This scepticism emanates partly from a failure to understand what valuation models tell us. Hence, Penman reviews several valuation models and the features that differentiate them. He views valuation fundamentally as an accounting issue, and valuation models are differentiated by how they account for value. Despite the development of so-called accrual accounting models in recent years, Penman believes they still lack theoretical rigour. For instance, the form of the accounting to go into those models is not well developed, which presents a major challenge for accounting research.

According to Penman, accounting theory and valuation theory should ideally come under the same discipline, as should empirical research in accounting and asset pricing. Standard setters will then be better guided in pursuing their objective of providing information about future cash flows to investors, and investors ultimately will be able to access valuations that provide a sound basis for evaluating the present value of expected cash flows.

In Chapter 12, Joshua Ronen and Varda Yaari provide a comprehensive survey of the earnings management (EM) literature, including a review of empirical research relating to earnings management and earnings management models. An important conclusion of their chapter is that there is an inclination by practitioners, regulators and researchers to regard EM as pernicious and associated with manipulation, dishonesty or deception. In their extensive bibliography, Ronen and Yaari identify over 435 research studies which treat EM practices as inherently pernicious. Only eleven of the listed studies take the position that EM was purely beneficial. These findings suggest that regulators need to be vigilant in finding ways to curb EM practices. According to Ronen and Yaari, the easiest way to manage earnings is through the choice of accounting estimates, such as the estimated life of a depreciable asset or the recognition of revenue. This type of choice can be made close to the time of the preparation of the financial reports. The most difficult EM tactic is real production, because it requires making decisions early in the operating cycle, long before the financial report is released. For example, a firm may reduce the cost of goods sold by increasing production so that the inventory will absorb a higher proportion of fixed manufacturing expenses. In this way, overproduction results in higher earnings. This EM tactic, however, is subject to constraints of production capacity: production should increase as long as possible before the end of the fiscal period. Ronen and Yaari also assess the effectiveness of various forms of regulation in reducing EM, such as IFRS and the Sarbanes-Oxley Act, but the empirical results are largely mixed. EM presents a continual challenge to standard setters and regulators. In particular, the IASB's principles-based approach to accounting standards (requiring more reliance on accounting judgements) and a wider use of fair values (requiring more reliance on estimates) can lead to more opportunistic behaviour by unscrupulous corporate managers who engage in pernicious EM.

In Chapter 13, Alfred Wagenhofer outlines typical agency problems and the mechanisms that can be put in place to mitigate them. Arguably the most important of these mechanisms is financial accounting and reporting, which provides information to reduce information asymmetry among conflicting interests and to control the decisions of the contracting parties. Agency theory provides a framework for understanding and predicting the incentives of managers to provide information, the use of information in contracts, and the usefulness of the accounting concepts that underlie financial accounting standards. Wagenhofer argues that analytical research in agency theory draws heavily from the theory of information economics and other fields and has generated many useful results showing how accounting information can help resolve or reduce agency problems. It does so by providing contractible information that improves contracting efficiency and by enhancing recognition of contracting and information costs. According to Wagenhofer, a particular characteristic of financial accounting information is its credibility, which is assured by several other institutions, such as auditing, corporate governance, enforcement and litigation. Another characteristic of accounting information is the high degree of aggregation, which reduces the information content relative to the disaggregated signals but lowers the costs of contracting and can even have desirable incentive effects. Wagenhofer also reviews the application of agency theory to stewardship and valuation objectives of financial accounting, to fair values and conservatism, and to the politics of standard setting. Wagenhofer concludes that empirical research has found a substantial amount of evidence that is consistent with agency theory predictions, suggesting that agency theory is useful for explaining and predicting real phenomena in financial accounting. However, as in other empirical and theoretical fields in financial accounting, there are many other interesting problems requiring investigation.

In Chapter 14, Jeremy Bertomeu and Edwige Cheynel provide a review of the literature on financial disclosure and the cost of capital, including various definitions of the cost of capital used in empirical and theoretical research and empirical issues relating to timing of the measurement of cost of capital (i.e. whether the cost of capital should be measured post- or pre-release of information or over time in a dynamic trading model). They note that the cost of capital is the observable outcome of a 'complex set of phenomena and, therefore, how one interprets measurements of the cost of capital is deeply engrained in the working assumptions made about those phenomena'. Using this theme, they provide a framework for evaluating competing theories about disclosure and the cost of capital. They conclude that there is significant agreement in the literature on some of the basic insights surrounding the cost of capital and the disclosure debate, including the notions that (1) disclosure does affect the cost of capital; (2) the disclosure effect on the cost of capital is not diversifiable; (3) the disclosure effect can be ambiguous and does not necessarily imply that information can be a priced risk factor that (theoretically) has explanatory power beyond other factors connected to real decisions; and (4) the cost of capital is a proxy for risk in the economy, not a proxy for welfare. However, Bertomeu and Cheynel conclude that many challenges remain for this area of research. For instance, they conclude that there is no consensus as to whether some measure of accounting quality should be a priced risk factor, above and beyond other factors based on economic outcomes. A second area of contention concerns the appropriate measure of the cost of capital. Measurement needs to address what is meant by the cost of capital and whether it should refer mainly to the risk premium or, more generally, to the extra return required by investors in informed markets. Future research is needed to resolve these issues.

In Chapter 15, David Johnstone provides a different perspective on debates relating to financial disclosure and the cost of capital. While the conventional literature typically associates higher corporate disclosure (or more information) with lower cost of capital, Johnstone maintains that the cost of capital implied by a capital asset pricing model (CAPM) can actually increase even in circumstances where better information brings greater certainty. He concludes that a characteristic of better information is that it can reveal previously unforeseen or unexpected negative signals, which can provide a basis for either greater uncertainty or greater certainty in a *negative* direction, thus driving market returns down and the cost of capital up. Johnstone argues that the role of financial reporting should be understood not in terms of its effect on the cost of capital *per se*, but as a decision tool to help investors assess the probability distributions of future cash flows more accurately, thereby leading to higher expected utility portfolios. Johnstone argues that this is a technical restatement of the traditional view in accounting theory that financial disclosure should provide decision useful information for asset valuation and other investment decisions. Importantly, Johnstone observes that more accurate probabilities are not always closer to zero or one; hence, information disclosure does not always leave users with greater certainty. However, more accurate probabilities are still desirable because on average they lead to higher realised payoffs and, thus, utility.

In Chapter 16, Nuno Soares and Andrew Stark consider the issue of controlling for risk in capital markets research. The need to control for risk occurs in a number of settings in accounting research, such as in the accruals anomaly which asserts that markets systematically misjudge the persistence of the accruals and cash components of earnings, and as a consequence, the market reaction to earnings announcements is biased. Another context is the post-earnings announcement drift phenomenon whereby the future abnormal returns after a firm's earnings announcement tend to follow the sign of the earnings surprise. Soares and Stark conclude that at the heart of such studies is the issue of adjusting, or controlling, for risk in generating estimates of risk-adjusted returns for firms and portfolios. In order to assess whether a firm or portfolio is making an 'abnormal' return once risk effects are taken into account, the researcher must be able to come up with a reliable estimate of the appropriate expected 'normal' risk-adjusted return to which the achieved return can be compared. According to Soares and Stark, this is one of the most problematic methodological issues that researchers have to deal with in capital markets research. If risk is not properly controlled for in the assessment of the 'normal' risk-adjusted return, it can lead to erroneous conclusions that firms or portfolios constructed on the basis of accounting (or other) characteristics are incorrectly priced when in fact they are not, or vice versa. Soares and Stark suggest that a wide variety of firm characteristics are candidates for jointly explaining firm excess returns in the UK. Further, the conventionally accepted firm characteristics that tend to be used in UK asset pricing factor models – firm size, book-to-market ratio and past stock returns – are not the strongest amongst such candidates, although there is evidence in their favour. The empirical findings presented by Soares and Stark suggest that risk-control methods need to be carefully worked out, and importing conventional wisdom from other jurisdictions is likely to result in low-power, mis-specified tests. More particularly, Soares and Stark advise using a regression approach where variables that have been proven to explain future excess returns are included as proxies for risk control. Such an approach is likely to provide the most useful insights on the phenomena being studied, particularly in countries with a limited number of firms available for constructing control portfolios or with under-developed factor models.

In Chapter 17, Mike Dempsey and Stewart Jones review our understanding of asset pricing and market efficiency as upheld in modern finance theory. The role of fair values and HCA are considered in the context of this literature. Their review of asset pricing theory leads to a discussion of the GFC and the destruction of individual and corporate wealth that had relied on price discovery in orderly markets. Dempsey and Jones highlight the adverse reaction to the concept of efficient markets as an outcome of the GFC and the subsequent academic and practitioner debates that ensued. This is followed by a review of economic theory that had warned of the innate dynamic of unsustainable asset bubbles and dysfunctional cycles in the economy, which modern finance theory has either overlooked or chosen to ignore. The final section of this chapter concludes with a consideration of the implications of accounting measurement seeking to use market pricing as an arbiter of value in corporate financial reports.

In Chapter 18, Trevor Hopper, Junaid Ashraf, Shahzad Uddin and Danture Wickramasinghe review the underlying tenets and assumptions of critical accounting theory, with a particular focus on the role of social theory in accounting thought. Much critical theory shares a common philosophical perspective on the nature of subjective ontology, the use of a social constructivist epistemology, and research methods based on intensive case studies. Clearly, these perspectives contrast sharply with positive accounting theory and related empirical research traditions such as capital markets research. Hopper et al. conclude that there is considerable scope for advancing social research in accounting thought through 'theoretical triangulation', but given fundamentally different assumptions between accounting theories, the methodology for achieving this needs to be carefully considered and articulated by the researcher. Hopper et al. observe that a common criticism of social theory research is that, while it has provided some interesting insight on accounting, it has been weak on prescription or application. However, the authors contend that the social theory perspective is more process oriented than output oriented. That is, the social theory perspective serves a unique purpose as it aims to enhance understanding by serving a broad range of constituencies and 'puncturing claims to absolute truth by those in privileged positions of power'. Hence, social theory research is often offered as a prelude and contribution to better informed and more 'democratic debate' rather than as a source of technical or prescriptive answers to particular accounting issues or problems.

In Chapter 19, Frank Clarke and Graeme Dean discuss the role of business ethics and the 'true and fair view' concept in accounting. In defining the true and fair view concept, they draw on Malloch's thesis, which explains that the onus for ensuring trust in accounting should return to individual accounting practitioners. According to Clarke and Dean, practitioners should not be bound by rules (standards) capable of being 'ticked off', but rather they should follow a principled approach that includes such ideas as ensuring that financial reporting is serviceable to users. Their concept of 'serviceability' encompasses the much-contested qualitative characteristics of financial information from the conceptual framework, including relevance, reliability, neutrality, verifiability and understandability. Importantly, these concepts provide an operational meaning or benchmark based on audit and financial outputs rather than on inputs or processes. Finding indirect support for their concept of serviceability from many sources, Clarke and Dean argue that accountants, particularly in the British tradition, are the custodians of the oldest surviving professional ethic enshrined in legislation. The 'true and fair' concept is a business ethos 'par excellence', one that they argue is the province of individual practitioners to determine on the basis of their accumulated knowledge and wisdom.

In Chapter 20, Janek Ratnatunga and Stewart Jones discuss the challenges of a carbon constrained economy and the many new questions this could present for the accounting profession. They show that the economic decisions of organisations operating within a carbon trading scheme (and within a carbon constrained economy more generally) will impact the accounting profession significantly. Whilst there is some literature on how best to report the income statement effects of CO_2 trading, there has been no discourse as to how to value the underlying assets that produce or use carbon allowances on the balance sheet. The chapter focuses on organisations that have the capability of generating renewable energy credits (i.e. those that have not only an emissions liability but also an emissions intangible carbon sequestration asset capability), although their valuation model can be used to fit into more conventional scenarios. Ratnatunga and Jones state that there is no controversy within the field of accounting and financial reporting that issuers of financial statements should provide the users of financial statements with all material information that is both relevant and reliable. The relevance of organisational capabilities (especially via intangibles such as carbon sequestration assets) has not usually been doubted, but the reliability of the valuations of these intangibles has often been questioned. This chapter illustrates techniques that make these valuations more relevant and contextual, while also showing how tangible and intangible asset combinations provide true capability values for the organisation. However, a paradigm shift from the current conceptual accounting framework is required before the profession could accept such new accounting treatments.

In Chapter 21, Geoff Frost and Stewart Jones review the fast-growing literature on the corporate reporting of environmental, social and sustainability performance of organisations. Corporate sustainability reporting (CSR) is now a key area of public concern and, consequently, an explicit component of the relationship between the firm and society. Corporate sustainability reporting emerges from the perception of an increased need for external stakeholders to understand the underlying performance of the organisation, and in recent years there has been a remarkable transformation in the expectations of an organisation's social and environmental performance. Through a 'social contract' lens, organisations now need to engage more comprehensively in social and environmental performance to prove their value to society and meet the demands of various stakeholders. Corporate managers have responded by reporting on their organisation's CSR performance. Initially, such reporting was typically on an ad hoc basis undertaken by a limited number of organisations. As societal performance expectations have increased, so has the volume of CSR information being reported. Today the majority of global corporations disclose on CSR at varying levels of detail and comprehensiveness. The information content reported has also evolved, from ad hoc general disclosures to compliance with comprehensive sustainability guidelines. What was implicit has now become an explicit expression of the organisation's performance. However, recent debates about the need for sustainability reporting standards (on par with financial reporting standards) have engendered commentary suggesting there is still a considerable distance to travel before we are ready to accept mandatory sustainability reporting.

Stewart Jones
The University of Sydney
September 2014

Note

1 Kerlinger, F.N., *Foundations of Behavioral Research* (New York: Holt, Rinehart & Winston, 1964), p. 11.

References

FASB (2010) Conceptual framework for financial reporting, *Statement of Financial Accounting Concepts 8* (Norwalk, CT. FASD).

Gilman, S., *Accounting Concepts of Profit*, New York, Ronald Press (1939).

IASB (2010) *Conceptual Framework for Financial Reporting 2010* (London: IASB).

Littleton, A.C., *Structure of Accounting Theory*, Sarasota, American Accounting Association (1953).

May, G.O., 'The Influence of Accounting on Economic Development', *Journal of Accountancy*, January, pp. 11–12; February, pp. 92–105; March, pp. 171–184 (1936; three articles).

Paton, William A. and Littleton, A. C. *An Introduction to Corporate Accounting Standards*. Ann Arbor, MI: American Accounting Association, 1940 (1957 revision).

2

History of financial accounting theory in Britain[1]

John Richard Edwards

Overview

This chapter focuses on British contributions[2] to the development of financial accounting theory,[3] commencing with the creation of the limited liability company by registration under the Companies Act in 1855. Up to the 1930s, Britain's accounting thinkers continued to support historical cost-based accounting, and their principal contribution was to seek new ways of making it a more effective instrument for reporting financial performance and position to shareholders and creditors. Starting in the late 1930s, attention turned to the examination of proposals for the more fundamental revision of published corporate reports. It is shown that ideas about how accounting should be done are by no means the prerogative of accountants. Contributions from businessmen, engineers, lawyers and economists are highlighted. This exploration of Britain's accounting history also recognises the social, economic and institutional factors that have affected the development of ideas designed to advance external reporting practices.

Scope and coverage

Parker defines financial accounting as '[t]hat part of accounting which is concerned mainly with external reporting' (1984: 120), while the accounting literature includes the following definition of theory: 'the coherent set of hypothetical, conceptual, and pragmatic principles forming the general frame of reference for a field of inquiry' (Hendriksen 1977: 1). Few authors have attempted to construct an all-embracing theory of financial accounting,[4] and a wider definition will be employed for the purpose of this chapter. Financial accounting theory is defined as attempts made by accounting thinkers to explain, influence and improve financial reporting practice. The principal focus is therefore on ideas, though there will inevitably be references to the practices which accounting thinkers focus upon.

This chapter does not intend to rehearse contributions to the development of financial accounting thought by *all* known British writers, though this is the approach adopted in a number of valuable works (e.g. Mattessich 2008). To do so, given the breadth of the topic and the long time span addressed, would require the presentation of a vast amount of detail and run the risk of conveying the impression of an unproblematic programme of improvement through to the present day. Instead, the aim will be to (i) cover the major issues in financial accounting thought where British commentators have made a contribution, and (ii) supply an awareness of social, economic and institutional factors which have affected, both positively and negatively, the formulation of ideas concerning the development of financial reporting practices.[5]

The period covered starts with the creation of the limited liability company in 1855 by registration under the Companies Act. British chartered and statutory companies date from the sixteenth century, of course, and these organisations raised finance from the general public, particularly with the development of the canal system in the latter half of the eighteenth century and the railway network beginning in about 1830. The year 1855 was significant, however, because it saw the creation of an organisational structure that greatly facilitated the separation of ownership from management and, in due course, led to an unprecedented rise in the demand for external financial reports. This chapter therefore studies the provision of financial information within a principal and agent relationship, where a lack of goal congruence can have significant implications for the quality of published financial reports. It is also important to be mindful of the fact that during the period studied major changes have occurred in the objectives of financial reports; and this naturally has important implications for the kind of information they should contain. At the start of the period studied, published financial reports were principally intended as records of managerial stewardship of shareholders' money, whereas today there is a growing focus on the usefulness of such data as the basis for decision-making. This is important because, in very broad terms, a bias towards prudence is considered a desirable characteristic of financial reports used to assess stewardship, whereas the faithful representation of events is today considered a fundamental qualitative characteristic of decision-useful data. Similar differences can be seen in the information requirements of providers of debt compared with equity finance.

Writings designed to influence and improve financial accounting practice predate the creation of the limited liability company. Bookkeeping texts published from the second half of the sixteenth century through to the nineteenth century invariably contained instructions about how information should be presented in both the profit and loss account and balance sheet. Usually these didactic treatises also devoted some attention to the valuation of assets and liabilities, and occasionally the relative benefits of alternative measures – for example, whether to value inventories at full cost or prime cost, or whether to use market value instead – were debated (Edwards *et al.* 2009). But to the extent that these early authors sought explanations for what was being done, attention was mainly confined to what has been described as 'theories of accounts'. These, as Mattessich (2003: 129) put it, 'aimed at finding the basic rules of keeping books, [and] sought to disentangle the "mystery" of double-entry'.

Sources of ideas about how external reports are and should be prepared are numerous. Principal among these are published textbooks, monographs and articles. There are also the submissions made to government-appointed committees charged with the responsibility for amending and improving existing company law. A third venue focuses on the efforts made by professional bodies and other institutions to improve financial reporting practice by formulating new recommendations or standards for the reporting entity to comply with. Finally, ideas expressed in the courts about the acceptability of prevailing practices are not overlooked.

Given our broad definition of financial accounting theory, it is probably reasonably safe to say that the vast majority of accounting thinkers remain unknown. Anyone working in business who is involved in the process of financial reporting can have an idea about how the informative value of accounting statements might be improved. But, as Baxter pointed out, there will probably be no public record of the contributions which they make. Reflecting on the growing impact of regulatory bodies on financial reporting practice in 1980, he offered the following:

> Hitherto, accounting has been pushed forward by forces internal to firms. Obscure people, bent on improving their existing methods or meeting new needs, have continually made minor experiments. If an experiment failed, it was abandoned and forgotten; if it was a success, it was kept and in time copied in other firms. Accounting has thus grown by small steps, and is the creation of countless anonymous innovators.
>
> *(Baxter 1981a: 6)*

Baxter's assessment has much to commend it. Businessmen and women are at least as much pre-occupied with the image portrayed by published financial reports as are accountants – perhaps more so. Often pilloried for engaging in schemes of unparalleled deception, it is difficult not to imagine that they have often also been the instigators of new reporting methods intended to more effectively portray financial progress and position.

The thinkers whose contributions to the development of accounting thought are captured in this chapter were primarily academics and accountants in public practice, though ideas expressed by accountants working in business also receive some attention. Featured individuals from other walks of life include engineers, economists and judges.

The remainder of this paper comprises two main sections. The first examines developments up to the 1930s when contributions from accountants were mainly made by practitioners. The second focuses principally on contributions made by academics as accounting became a main-stream subject taught at universities.

Improving historical cost accounting

Early British accounting thinkers were almost without exception practitioners. A few did hold academic posts, but there were limited opportunities in this direction given the slow development of accounting as a university subject in Britain until after World War 2. Indeed, it was not until the 1970s that university accounting courses 'took off'. Those who did hold teaching posts – such as Dicksee at Birmingham University and the London School of Economics (LSE), Lisle at Heriot-Watt College in Edinburgh, and de Paula, also at the LSE – were usually also in practice. Perhaps it was proximity to how accounting was being done at the time that caused writers to concentrate on how the existing historical cost-based financial reporting model might be improved. In the main, British writers up to the 1930s were not radical thinkers in the mould of, say, Theodore Limperg (the Netherlands), Kenneth MacNeal (USA), Martti Saario (Finland), Eugen Schmalenbach (Germany) or Gino Zappa (Italy).[6] To the extent that they addressed theoretical issues, the British writers did so from a predominantly practical viewpoint.

Early British accounting thinkers such as Cooper, Cutforth, de Paula, Dickinson, Dicksee, Guthrie, Garnsey and Pixley adopted an 'empirical inductive' approach (Whittington 1986: 6) to develop their ideas about how accounting should be done. That is, they observed and analysed financial reporting practice in order to identify 'best' methods and, having done so, recommended their widespread adoption. In essence, their objectives were to justify, rationalise and improve reporting practices. Working as practising accountants, these think-ers naturally had a great deal of practical knowledge and experience to draw upon. But, also, there was the risk that their thinking could be constrained by close association with what was already being done.

In the next two subsections, some of the main measurement issues that occupied the minds of accounting thinkers up until the 1930s are considered.

Measurement concepts

The development of the accounting profession in Britain accelerated during the second half of the nineteenth century with the establishment of professional bodies in Scotland in the 1850s and England in the 1870s. The Institute of Chartered Accountants in England and Wales (ICAEW) was formed from the merger in 1880 of five existing bodies based south of the River Tweed. *The Accountant*, first published in London in 1874, and *The Accountants' Magazine*, which was inaugurated in Edinburgh in 1897, were important forums for accountants to discuss pressing accounting and auditing issues. An early issue of *The Accountant* raised a fundamental issue that persists to the present day: 'What is profit of a company' (Cooper 1888). In attempting to formulate an answer, Ernest Cooper (one of the four original Cooper Brothers) and other thinkers reflected on such notions as accruals, going concern, realisation and prudence.

Cooper was an implicit advocate of the going concern concept: 'It is not, I think, necessary for a Company in valuing any of its assets to consider the effect of liquidation . . . if, as is usual, the permanent continuance of the business is what is contemplated' (Cooper 1888: 745). The use of estimated residual value when deciding on the appropriate rate for writing off fixed assets[7] caused the Manchester accountant Edwin Guthrie to consider why 'the principle of valuation' might not be used at each accounting date. He concluded: 'A large, irrecoverable outlay is generally expended in the preparation of [say] a factory, and unless speedy destruction overtakes any certain business, the method of treatment for annual accounting is as of a "going concern"' (Guthrie 1883: 7). Explicit reference to the term 'going concern' was also made by Dicksee in the fourteenth edition of *Auditing*, published in 1928.

> As a general rule, the amount at which *all* assets are stated in the Balance Sheet − except where a special statutory provision to the contrary obtains − should be regulated by the realisable value of such assets on the basis of a going concern.
>
> *(quoted in Kitchen and Parker 1994: 215)*

Cooper (1888: 745) also favoured a prudent approach to profit measurement when advocating recognition of 'the fall in value . . . when the asset is of a marketable nature', such as government stock. Dicksee (1927: 38) agreed that it was 'always far better that the published statement should be conservative rather than optimistic'.

An interest in the conceptual basis for financial reporting is evident in discussions of the appropriate treatment of stock-in-trade. The recommended treatment, early on, was consistent with the rule that survives to the present day, that it should be stated at the lower of cost and net realisable value.[8] Pixley (1908: 164–5) was very clear on the matter:

> [W]hile 'cost price' may be regarded as the basis for arriving at the value to be placed upon the 'Stock-in-Trade' at the date of closing the books, any ascertained diminution of the value which has taken place should be dealt with in a businesslike manner.

15

The prudent approach towards asset valuation was explained as follows:

> [C]redit should not be taken in the Trading Account for any sum in anticipation of the profit which may eventually be made when the goods are actually sold and which profit belongs to the period in which the sale takes place.
>
> *(Pixley 1908: 163; see also Dicksee 1892: 121)*

The inter-relationship between the prudence concept and the realisation concept was made clear by Dickinson (1913: 93),[9] a practitioner who served in both the London and New York offices of Price, Waterhouse & Co.:

> The mere increase in the market value of an article which is not actually sold, can not be considered as a profit; for the reason that the article may never be sold at that price, and the paper profit may never be realised.

However, 'if there is any possibility that what remains unsold may not realize its cost, a proportion of the realized profits on sales which have been made, should be carried forward to cover these possible losses' (Dickinson 1913: 94; see also p. 101).

Fixed assets and depreciation

The valuation of fixed assets was a central issue in some of the many 'dividend cases' (French 1977) that came before the courts during the last quarter of the nineteenth century. The most famous of these is Lee v. Neuchatel Asphalte Co. (Law Reports 1889), where at Court of Appeal it was decided that there was no obligation on the directors to amortise the company's principal asset – a quarry – when computing profits available for dividends. In delivering his judgement, Lord Justice Lindley observed: 'If it is said that such a course involves payment of dividends out of capital the answer is that the [Companies] Acts nowhere forbid such a payment as is here supposed' (Law Reports 1889: 28). He continued: 'It has been very judiciously and properly left to the commercial world to settle how the accounts were to be kept'.

The Lee decision was the subject of critical comment in the professional press. The leader writer for *The Accountant* claimed: 'The principles it lays down are simply startling' (Leading article 1889: 89). This may have been so, but the further comment that the decision was 'opposed to general usage' (ibid.: 89) placed depreciation accounting practices in Britain in 1889, and much later, on too high a pedestal. The judicial attitude to depreciation when calculating divisible profits was the subject of further comment from Lindley five years later. After pointing out that 'the word "profits" is by no means free from ambiguity', he continued, 'the distinction which I am endeavouring to explain is to say that fixed capital may be sunk and lost . . . but that floating or circulating capital must be kept up' (Law Reports 1894: 71). The significance of decisions in the dividend cases for the development of accounting thought concerning the treatment of depreciation may be inferred from the amount of attention devoted to them in accounting texts published well into the twentieth century.

The central role of depreciation in making a proper distinction between capital and income ensured that the topic received a great deal of attention in the accounting literature (Brief 1976, 1993). As Pixley (1908: 199) put it, perhaps with a hint of hyperbole, 'if the construction of Profit and Loss Accounts could be carried out without reference to this difficult but interesting subject, Accountancy might certainly be described as one of the exact sciences'. The first in-depth study of depreciation had already been authored by the civil engineer, Ewing Matheson, who warned that 'any neglect of error in "writing off" will, according to its extent, render calculations of cost and profit fallacious' (Matheson 1893: 1). The kind of problems auditors were up against when attempting to ensure a proper charge – problems which continue to the present day – were made clear by the ICAEW council member who contributed an introduction to Matheson's book: '[W]here the remuneration of the management is made wholly or partly dependent upon declared Profits, [auditors] know in what varied forms resistance to an adequate Charge against profits for Depreciation is presented' (ibid.: vii–viii).

Kitchen and Parker (1980: 14) believe that the first article on the subject of depreciation was authored by Guthrie, who was a partner in the first British accounting firm to open an office in New York. Guthrie (1883: 6) pointed out that it was the subject 'in connection with accounts . . . most open to controversy'. He distinguished between different classes of fixed assets and considered which depreciation method and depreciation rate might be suitable in each case. The appropriate treatment of 'permanent assets', according to Dicksee (1892: 121) in his highly acclaimed book *Auditing*, depended on the nature of the fixed asset. Freehold lands should be retained at cost because 'they suffer no depreciation' (ibid.: 126). Goodwill was deemed 'liable to fluctuation, both continual and extreme' (ibid.: 127), and retention at cost seems to have been a common practice for this item, as was writing it off out of profits. Dicksee considered the treatment of goodwill unimportant, given widespread agreement that the amount reported 'is absolutely meaningless' (ibid.).[10] Most other assets, in his estimation, should be reported at cost less depreciation (ibid.: 126–31). Dicksee also wrote one of the earliest books to focus primarily on financial reporting – *Advanced Accounting*,[11] first published in 1903. This naturally devoted space to the issue of depreciation, with Dicksee (1905: 238) insisting that 'during the life of an asset its original cost . . . is a charge against Revenue', although this treatment did not become general practice until well into the twentieth century (Edwards 1981: 21–5). Concerning the favoured methods of depreciation, Pixley (1908: 205; see also Dickinson 1913: 77) agreed that the 'correct value from an accountancy point of view' of fixed assets with a finite useful life was to report them at 'cost price less the proper amount of depreciation' charged against profit. De Paula (c.1918:[12] 111–4; see also Dicksee 1905: 238–9) recommended the following depreciation methods: 'fixed instalment [straight-line] system', 'reducing instalment [balance] system', and 'annuity system'.

Authors also explored the possible connection between measurement practices and financing arrangements. For example, Guthrie (1883), in common with writers well into the twentieth century (de Paula c.1918: 112–3; Jones 1964: 41–6), discussed the need to invest an amount of cash equal to the depreciation charge, which together with interest should accumulate to a figure sufficient to replace the asset at the end of its economic life.

The question of whether enhancements in current worth should receive recognition in published reports was not absent from discussion. The issue came to the fore in Bolton v. Natal Land and Colonisation Company, 1891. This led Dicksee to reflect on its appropriate treatment for financial reporting purposes. His conclusion was that 'there is no legal objection to a re-valuation of assets caused by a fluctuation (upwards) in value', but on no account should such 'accidental variation (owing to external causes) in the value of certain property owned, but not traded in . . . affect the Profit and Loss Account' (Dicksee 1892: 121, 135–6). Dickinson (1913: 82) also emphasised the need for any revaluation surplus to be 'clearly distinguished from earnings from operations'. Where a capital profit had been realised, he advised retaining it as a capital reserve to meet 'possible losses from further sales or ultimate realization' (ibid.). But he did envisage a scenario where 'a surplus exists beyond all reasonable doubt and [in such a case] no objection can be taken to treating at any rate a substantial portion thereof as realized and divisible' (ibid.).

Writers also reflected on the relevance of market price when fixing a figure for depreciation. Dicksee (1905: 239) acknowledged the possibility of basing the depreciation charge on the difference between successive revaluations made 'by an expert valuer'. But although he judged this method to be 'theoretically the most perfect, as enabling the assets to be brought into the Balance Sheet at a more theoretically correct basis of valuation', he rejected the 'balance sheet' approach towards income measurement, today embedded in the International Accounting Standards Board's *Conceptual Framework for Financial Reporting* (2010), as 'very defective in practice, on account of the uneven sums that it charges against Revenue from year to year in respect of practically identical services rendered to Revenue by the asset in question' (ibid.). But Dicksee (ibid.) found it difficult to completely disconnect depreciation charges from changes in market value, commenting: 'As a check upon the rate of Depreciation employed, it is, however, very useful occasionally' to compare book value with 'a revaluation made by an expert valuer'. De Paula (c.1918: 104) further explained why 'fluctuations' in market value should usually be ignored when accounting for fixed assets: '[T]hese fluctuations are caused by outside factors in no way affecting either the earning capacity or the actual revenue earnings of such assets'.

In the remainder of this section, general attitudes towards publicity up to World War 2 are first examined, followed by a consideration of the following key issues that occupied the minds of accounting thinkers during that period: secret reserves, standardisation and group accounts.

Publicity

It was not until 1948 that significant statutory requirements for financial accountability were imposed on British companies in general.[13] The matter had occupied the attention of successive government committees over the previous century, but the usual conclusion was that excessive disclosure requirements would hamper rather than encourage corporate development. Such accounting requirements that were imposed on directors were based on the philosophy of 'minimum disclosure' (Aranya 1974: 7; Edwards 1996: 50), i.e. the conviction that legislation should require disclosure of the minimum amount of detail compatible with contemporary conceptions of stewardship responsibilities. Anything beyond that was to be left to the market. The rationale for non-intervention was laid bare. In the estimation of the Davey Committee (1895: para. 4), '[r]estrictive provisions, which may have the effect of . . . deterring the best class of men from becoming Directors, are not to be lightly entertained', while the Greene Committee (1926: para. 9) concluded:

> It appears to us, as a matter of general principle, most undesirable, in order to defeat an occasional wrongdoer, to impose restrictions which would seriously hamper the activities of honest men and would inevitably re-act upon the commerce and prosperity of the country.

Given the *laissez faire* attitude towards financial reporting communicated in government reports, it is perhaps unsurprising that Dickinson (1924: 477) should observe: 'In the majority of cases it may be said that the information given [by companies] is on principle as little as possible'. Further, the tendency has been in recent years and continues to be 'to reduce rather than to increase the very inadequate information which is given with regard to earnings and costs' (ibid.: 477–8; *cf.* Edwards 1981: 33–46). The statistician and business administrator Sir Josiah Stamp (1925: 686) also drew attention to the 'more or less obscurantist method' of financial reporting that was in vogue; an approach which resulted in the publication of 'the condensed balance sheet' (de Paula 1925: 801). In de Paula's (ibid.: 802) estimation, secrecy in financial reporting was 'a survival of the past', and he 'seriously' questioned whether it was 'a sound policy to-day, or a possible one in the near future'. But the business community was not quite yet ready for change.

The level of publicity in company accounts was examined by the Greene Committee (1926) on company law amendment, and one of its members, the prominent professional accountant Sir William McLintock, described published balance sheets as, sometimes, *'models of obscurity'*, (quoted in Samuel 1933: 251). He commented on the practice of using omnibus items to cover a wide range of disparate assets or liabilities: 'Take one instance, a large Company in London whose total assets amount to £14,700,000, and they have only one heading for the whole lot' (ibid.). The Senior Official Receiver pleaded for greater disclosure as follows:

> If you could have some directions as to the way in which the assets should be described, the way in which stocks and shares and so on should be described, and the way in which liabilities should be described, so that the truth could be ascertained by an *ordinary person of ordinary capacity*, that is all I require.
>
> *(quoted ibid.: 251–2)*

These pleas fell on deaf ears. Dicksee (1927: 53) described the accounting provisions contained in the Greene Committee's report as 'disappointingly meagre'. He also made the further scathing comment: 'It would have been interesting to know precisely why the Committee considered that shareholders and others concerned "have little ground for complaint"' (ibid.: 2–3). But attitudes towards publicity remained equivocal. Another of Kitchen and Parker's (1980) pioneers of 'Accounting thought and education', Edwin Cutforth (1930: 175), considered it a matter for the directors

> to decide as to how far in regard to this matter of disclosure they should take Shareholders into their confidence. It must be remembered that it is, practically speaking, impossible to afford the information to Shareholders without giving it also to competitors.

Leaders of the accounting profession, including Cutforth, began to express support for greater publicity in the aftermath of the Royal Mail case (Rex v. Kylsant), which receives attention in the next subsection.

Secret reserves

Contemporary authors drew on the term 'reserve' to describe an amount set aside for specific purposes. For example, the definition of a 'specific reserve' – today a provision – as 'a sum *charged* against profits to provide for a known contingency, the exact amount of which, however, cannot be ascertained' (de Paula, c.1918: 116) has a distinctly modern ring about it. In contrast to other widely used terms such as general reserve (an amount retained within the business for no specific purpose) and reserve fund (an equivalent amount of money invested outside the business to ensure the ready availability of an equivalent amount of money), it was the phenomenon of 'secret reserves' that became increasingly problematic. As early as 1888, Cooper (1888: 744) referred to undervaluation of property as 'a common practice . . . The Bank of England for many years has excluded the premises in Threadneedle Street, which were estimated in 1832 as worth a million sterling, altogether from their accounts'. He also acknowledged the fact that some companies actively 'create secret contingency funds' but, in contrast with what for many years became the conventional wisdom, seemed uncomfortable with this practice: '[I]t is not easy to see why . . . an outgoing shareholder whose paid agent in a sense the directors are, is not entitled to recover the loss occasioned by having sold his shares below their real value' (ibid.).

Secret reserves were the subject of masterly analysis by de Paula (c.1918: 122). First, he outlined two of their main purposes: (i) 'to provide a fund out of which heavy losses can be met, without disclosing the fact to the shareholders and general public', and (ii) 'to avoid disclosing information to trade rivals'. Secret reserves were classically created through an undisclosed transfer from the profit and loss account to a reserve which did not appear on the face of the balance sheet. De Paula (ibid.) identified the following additional ploys: writing down assets of all types 'below their true value'; making excessive provisions for outstanding liabilities; and charging capital items against revenue. He acknowledged the fact that the auditors' responsibility 'with reference to secret reserves is one of some little difficulty' (ibid.: 123). He also stated that, in theory, the use of secret reserves could not be justified and that 'the auditor cannot report that the Balance Sheet shows a true and correct view'. But theory does not translate to practice, as de Paula (ibid.) explained: '[I]n the case of large public companies, these reserves are of such considerable practical value that they are adopted extensively, and in practice, auditors do not invariably refer to such reserves in their audit reports.'

Dicksee (1927: 38) expressed identical sentiments when concluding, 'one must in all cases (at all events up to a point) concede the propriety, indeed, the desirability – of Internal, or Secret, Reserves, even though their existence *ipso facto* invalidates the accuracy of the published accounts'. The Greene Committee collected a great deal of evidence testifying to the utility of secret reserves. For example, Francis D'Arcy Cooper, formerly a partner in Cooper Brothers and, at the time, chairman of probably the largest conglomerate in Britain, Lever Brothers, commented: 'Otherwise, in 1921 you would not have had a Company in England which was solvent' (quoted in Edwards 1976: 292). A few years later, in a lecture delivered to the Bristol Society of Chartered Accountants (1929), William Cash, ICAEW President 1921–3, echoed those sentiments, saying, 'we know the strength of a commercial undertaking lies in its hidden reserves' (quoted ibid.: 293).

The history of secret reserves is a further illustration of the contribution of the judiciary to the development of ideas about how accounting should be done. In Newton v. Birmingham Small Arms Co. Ltd (1906), the court rejected an action brought by a shareholder seeking to restrain the directors from creating an 'internal' (i.e. secret) reserve. In the course of delivering judgement, Mr Justice Buckley made it clear that it was perfectly sound commercial practice to take a prudent view when valuing assets, and that a degree of confidentiality was often in the interests of shareholders (Edwards 1989: 148). This decision was subsequently described as a 'charter for the creators of secret reserves' (Samuel 1933: 278).

A quarter of a century later, secret reserves again came under the judicial microscope in the well-known case of Rex v. Kylsant (1931). There, the Royal Mail Steam Packet Co.'s chief executive, Lord Kylsant, and its auditor, Harold Morland of Price, Waterhouse & Co., were charged under the Larceny Act 1861 with publishing a balance sheet that was false and fraudulent. For the year 1926, the company had suffered a loss of about £240,000, whereas the published accounts contained the following description of profit for the period: 'Balance for the year, including dividends on shares in allied and associated companies, adjustment of taxation reserves, less depreciation on the fleet, etc. . . . . £439,212: 12:1' (Kitchen and Parker 1980: 96). The company had succeeded in reporting this 'balance' by making an undisclosed transfer from taxation reserves. The defence claimed that the wording was technically accurate, which it was. The prosecution argued that the impression conveyed by the accounts was grossly misleading, which was also the case. The key to acquittal of the two defendants was evidence presented by the senior partner of Deloitte, Plender, Griffiths & Co., Lord Plender, who was the leading figure in the accounting profession for much of the inter-war period. Plender confirmed that the phrase 'adjustment of taxation reserve', inserted on the auditors' insistence, ensured that the accounts complied with contemporary best practice (Edwards 1989: 151–2).[14] Despite acquittal, Mr Justice Wright took the opportunity to criticise both the auditors and the reporting practices of the company:

> If the accounts . . . were being fed by undisclosed reserves, it seems very difficult to see how an auditor could discharge his duty of giving a true and accurate view of the correct state of the company's affairs without drawing attention to those facts, which were vitally important.
>
> *(quoted in Bigg 1951: 437)*

Writing two years after Wright issued this admonition, de Paula (quoted in Kitchen and Parker 1980: 96), assessed the significance of the case as follows:

> [T]he accountancy profession has been shocked by the *Royal Mail Steam Packet Case*. There is no single event in my memory that has made so profound an impression upon the accountancy world, and that case, in my opinion, is destined to influence accountancy practice in a marked degree.

De Paula was right; twenty or so years later Jones (1964: 265) observed: 'Mainly as a result of the *Royal Mail Steam Packet Co.* case the creation of secret reserves ceased to be a respectable company practice.' Its impact on accounting thought was dramatically demonstrated by the decision of the ICAEW, in 1943, to recommend discontinuance of secret reserves[15] and for the Companies Act 1948 to outlaw the practice.

Standardisation

The 'want of uniformity in accounts' (Parker 1980b) became the subject of debate in the press when Guthrie (1882: 8) authored a paper criticising 'the frequency of inconsistency between the title and subject matter of published accounts, and the employment of non-correlative terms in accounts'. He continued: 'It is to these irregularities, – which by our clients the public are justly complained of, – that I desire the attention of the [Manchester] Society [of Chartered Accountants].' The arguments presented by Guthrie aroused interest in the columns of *The Accountant* (Kitchen and Parker 1980: 12–4). Nearly half a century later, Dicksee (1927: 1, see also pp. 4–11) insisted that 'uniformity is always desirable where practicable', and this was the general opinion of most critical observers of contemporary practice. They had to contend, however, with an institutional philosophy that continued to favour non-intervention.

The standardisation issue was addressed by a number of company law amendment committees over the years, and it was evidence taken before the government Select Committee of 1877 that set the tone for future discussions. The professional accountant and company promoter David Chadwick had been for some time an enthusiastic proponent of 'uniform' accounts and, as a member of the Select Committee (having been returned as an MP for Macclesfield), he was in a strong position to propagate his ideas. Chadwick prepared for consideration by the Committee a draft Companies Bill containing a statutory form of profit and loss account and balance sheet. Full standardisation of accounts involves setting out rules concerning what items are to be reported in the accounts, where they are to be disclosed and how they should be measured. Chadwick's *pro forma* profit and loss account and balance sheet tackled the first two issues but not the third. The absence of valuation requirements was probably a conscious decision and perfectly understandable given the absence of generally accepted measurement practices. Chadwick's proposals gained support from a number of witnesses but not from the Master of the Rolls, Sir George Jessel.

Chadwick suggested to Jessel that it would be an advantage to frame company balance sheets 'on the same model'. Jessel would have none of it: 'It is not only the same model in form but the same theory that is needed; you cannot compare the balance sheets of two life insurance companies unless you know the theory on which they have been framed' (Select Committee 1877, minutes of evidence: 2242). The following further comment indicates that Jessel should be acknowledged as an early advocate of substance over form as a fundamental concept for financial reporting: 'It is not sufficient to put it [the balance sheet] in form; it is the substance [that matters]' (ibid.). Jessel's objection to the imposition of a standardised balance sheet was also based on quite different considerations. In his judgement, the whole issue of accountability was a matter best left to market forces: '[W]hy you should compel directors to issue accounts to their own shareholders, which their own shareholders can call for, whenever they like by resolution at a general meeting, I do not quite understand' (ibid.: 2192).

Jessel may therefore be remembered not only as a thinker who had ideas about how accounting should be done, but also as someone who affected what actually happened. Certainly, despite Chadwick's best efforts, the ensuing Companies Act 1877 contained no accounting requirements whatsoever. Indeed, it was not until company legislation became subservient to European Directives that British companies in general were obliged (Companies Act 1981) to publish accounts conforming to a prescribed format.

A further issue that received increasing attention in the early decades of the twentieth century was whether the growing practice of conducting business activity through the medium of subsidiary companies required radical revision of the form and content of published accounts.

Group accounts

The Pearson & Knowles Coal and Iron Company is the first known British company to publish a set of consolidated accounts, and it did so more than a decade before the topic became the subject of significant debate (Kitchen 1972). The episode comprises an example of accounting change based on the ideas of a businessman, in this case John J. Bleckly. The initiative to publish a consolidated balance sheet first surfaced in 1907, with its purpose being 'to make clear to the Shareholders the exact position of the Company at the present time' (Edwards 1991: 117). Ironically, the chairman of the board, the prominent professional accountant J. S. Harmood Banner (Tweedale 2004),[16] resisted Bleckly's initial proposal to publish a '"joint" balance sheet' (Edwards 1991: 117) but supported publication when the plan was revived three years later. Its purpose then was to enable the publication of a stronger balance sheet at a time when the directors were planning a substantial share issue. The newly created financial statement was captioned 'General Balance Sheet Incorporating the Assets and Liabilities of Rylands Bros. Ltd'; Rylands Bros. Ltd was Pearson & Knowles' main (but not only) subsidiary company (ibid.: 118). The failure of other companies to follow Pearson & Knowles' lead is unexplained, though it might be partly a consequence of the fact that it was not a high-profile company. Neither would the lack of a British literature on group accounting have helped. This lacuna was not to be remedied for some time.

A dozen years later, one of Price Waterhouse's senior partners, Sir Gilbert Garnsey, caused quite a stir when he presented to the London members of the ICAEW a lecture entitled 'Holding companies and their published accounts'. The talk was subsequently published in *The*

Accountant and in book form.[17] It was greeted by *The Accountant* as the 'first serious examination given to the subject on this side of the Atlantic' (quoted in Edwards and Webb 1984: 36). Garnsey pointed out that the holding company form of business organisation, by this time quite common in Britain, presented new problems for accountants. He questioned whether the publication of a holding company's balance sheet alone, which satisfied the legal requirement for publication contained in the Companies Act 1908, 'really gives the shareholders the information to which they are entitled' (Garnsey 1923: 18). He argued that the information appearing in the statutory balance sheet should be supplemented by sufficient additional information to enable users of accounts to assess the financial position of the group as a whole.

The procedures Garnsey described were not new; there was already a significant English-language literature on the subject in the US to which his partner, Dickinson, had made a significant contribution. Garnsey's lecture was an important milestone in the development of group accounting in Britain, however, because it forced the profession's leaders to acknowledge a potentially important limitation of published accounting practices. This was because Garnsey was a partner in the then leading firm of chartered accountants, and his ideas were presented, centre stage, to the London members of the ICAEW in a lucid and forceful manner. Although Garnsey could not be ignored, his ideas were not welcomed by an accounting establishment which interpreted them as an implicit criticism of contemporary reporting practices. In a climate of professional conservatism and general complacency with the standard of financial reporting, pre–Rex v. Kylsant, his efforts had little immediate effect (Kitchen 1972).

The case for group accounts was taken up by Sir Josiah Stamp (1925: 687; see also de Paula 1925) who declared,[18] 'It seems to me that there can be nothing to be said against the publication of consolidated balance sheets in conjunction with the legal balance sheet, and everything to be said for it.' It is thought that Stamp had already taken the opportunity to put his ideas into practice as secretary of Nobel Industries, which in 1922 published a supplementary statement that combined the assets and liabilities of its subsidiaries with those of the holding company (Edwards and Webb 1984: 37–9). De Paula also fulfilled the role of leadership by example at the Dunlop Rubber Company which he had joined as chief accountant in 1929, soon becoming its controller of finance. He persuaded the directors of Dunlop to make a number of innovations in the accounts for 1929, and in the aftermath of the Royal Mail Case significant further improvements were made, including the publication of consolidated accounts. These revisions attracted glowing comments from the financial press, being welcomed by the *Daily Telegraph* as 'a joy to its own shareholders and the envy of all others' (quoted in Edwards 2004). In Edwards' (2004) estimation, 'Dunlop undoubtedly blazed a trail for other companies to follow'.

In developing their ideas about how accounting should be done, these early accounting thinkers focused on existing best practice. The empirical inductive approach which they adopted was principally directed towards developing a coherent package of accounting practices based on the historical cost accounting model. The process saw the distillation of theoretical principles based on agreed best accounting practice as a means of rationalising what was already being done. The procedures that they recommended for widespread adoption have proved exceptionally resilient, and their evolutionary philosophy continues to dominate the thinking of regulatory bodies (Whittington 1986: 6).

A feature of early texts was an implied assumption that published accounting information would satisfy user requirements. Cutforth was unusual in focusing explicitly on the utility of published financial statements, though his attention was confined to the absentee shareholder. In *Public Companies and the Investor*, Cutforth (1930: Preface) acknowledged that balance sheets, prospectuses and other public documents 'are subjects which every investor should know something about: yet to the uninitiated they seem difficult to understand'. His book was designed to address this issue, given the '[e]normous sums [that] are invested each year by the general public in this country . . . through the medium of the Public Company' (ibid.: 2). A greater focus on users is a feature of the second main section of this chapter.

Academics enter the fray

Up to the mid-1930s in Britain, accounting thinkers came primarily from outside academe. This then changed, with contributions from professional accountants becoming less prominent in the public domain. However, we will see that accountants working in practice and in industry continued to play important roles 'behind the scenes'. Contributions made by accounting thinkers during this more recent period sometimes displayed a deductive approach to problem solving rather than relying entirely on inductive reasoning. By definition, such an approach was not constrained by current practice and left room for the development of more radical solutions to external financial reporting problems.

Early institutional initiatives

It was primarily academics associated with the LSE that made contributions to accounting thought prior to World War 2. Dicksee had of course held a part-time post at the LSE for much of the first quarter of the twentieth century (Kitchen and Parker 1980: 60), but it was the appointment of Ronald S. Edwards as an assistant lecturer in 1935 that started their 'tradition of scholarly study of accounting, *rooted in economic theory*' (Dev 1980: 5, emphasis added). In Mumford's (1994: 279) estimation: 'For thirty years, academic accounting in Britain survived as a small and sickly plant, a small LSE fiefdom only broken up in the late 1960s.' A year after his appointment Edwards was instrumental in the creation of the Accounting Research Association (Mumford 2007: 8), which consisted of a small group of LSE scholars and practitioners, among whom was Eric Hay Davison of Courtaulds. The Association held seminars and discussions and built up a close working relationship with *The Accountant*.

It was in the columns of *The Accountant* that Edwards (1938) published a series of articles which, in common with earlier thinkers in the United States and Continental Europe, adopted deductive reasoning in the endeavour to identify 'true income' (Whittington 1986: 11). Edwards also turned 'to economic theory for inspiration' when confronting the problem of 'measuring such concepts as income, value and cost' (ibid.). Edwards' articles gave rise to a furore which starkly revealed an inability of even one of his academic colleagues to countenance radical new ideas. 'The nature and measurement of income' criticised traditional profit measurement procedures and advocated a forward-looking concept of income measurement. This brought Edwards into conflict with his head of department, the chartered accountant Stanley Rowland, who, 'apparently playing to a gallery of the most intransigent backwoodsmen on the Council of the English Institute' (Mumford 1994: 278), publicly criticised his younger colleague. Rowland was a traditional accountant, and, according to Will Baxter, his overreaction resulted from the fact that Edwards' ideas were completely 'at odds with everything that Rowland was teaching' (Mumford 2007: 6).

Another institution-related initiative occurred in the mid-1930s, when the Society of Incorporated Accountants and Auditors created a Research Committee which mounted a project that culminated in the publication of *Design of Accounts* (Bray and Sheasby 1944). The standardisation of accounts was proceeding apace in some European continental countries – Frank Sewell Bray was in Parker's (1980a: 312) estimation 'obviously influenced by H. W. Singer's analysis of *Standardised Accountancy in Germany*' – but had always been resisted in Britain except by selected industries such as the railways (Parker 1980b: 210–11). The concern of the Society to encourage the theoretical as well as the practical led also to the establishment of a journal, *Accounting Research*, in 1948 and the creation of the Stamp-Martin[19] chair, to be held at Incorporated Accountants' Hall (Garrett 1961: 283–4). Bray was the first and only occupant of the chair and the instigator and co-editor of *Accounting Research*, which he intended should make 'a real contribution to the practical and theoretical development of the accounting art' (Bray 1949: 275).

Bray's enthusiasm for design and standardisation extended to central government accounts, and through the columns of *Accounting Research*, a British literature on national accounting briefly flourished (see also Edey and Peacock 1954). Indeed, the inaugural issue of that journal opened with 'The presentation of central government accounts', authored by Bray in collaboration with the eminent economist Richard Stone (Bray and Stone 1948). *Accounting Research* did not survive the merger of the Society with the chartered institutes in 1957. Its discontinuance has been put down 'to the belief by many members of the Institute's Council that its articles, most of which were written by academics, were abstruse and of no practical value' (Parker 1980a: 309).[20]

British accounting thinkers and institutions grappled with the problem of how to account for the effects of inflation from World War 2 onwards. Some of the major contributions are considered in the next section.

Price-level accounting and income measurement

The issue of price-level accounting received significant attention from continental scholars during the inter-war period (Tweedie and Whittington 1984: chapter 2; Mattessich 2008: 46–8, 118–22), but it was not until a rise in the rate of general inflation to between 7 and 8 per cent in 1947–8 that it became a prominent topic of debate in Britain. Focusing on price-level accounting, Tweedie and Whittington (1984: 1) drew attention to the political dimension of attempts to reform and improve financial reporting practices:

> [T]he inflation accounting debate is merely one example of the problems facing accounting. There is a lack of generally accepted accounting principles because a changing environment has made traditional principles obsolete, and the process of evolving new principles is essentially political, involving the reconciliation of the conflicting interests of various groups of preparers and users of accounts.

The Council of the ICAEW issued two Recommendations on Accounting Principles (RoAPs) dealing with price-level accounting between 1949 and 1952. RoAP No. 12, 'Rising price levels in relation to accounts', 1949 (reproduced in Zeff 2009: 70–3), provided unreserved support for the continued use of historical cost accounting. In response to criticism, the ICAEW re-examined the issue, and RoAP No. 15[21] was a little more circumspect in advocating the continued use of historical cost accounting '[u]nless and until a practicable and generally acceptable alternative is available' (reproduced ibid.: 90).

These pronouncements fail to reveal a radical divergence of ideas between members of the Taxation and Research Committee that studied the issue on behalf of the ICAEW's Council. There, industrial members such as Eric Hay Davison[22] of Courtaulds and P. M. Rees of Unilever[23] by and large supported the adoption of some form of current cost accounting, whereas practising members presented practical and theoretical arguments advocating retention of the historical cost model. What the industrialists objected to – a concern particularly well articulated by Davison – was the 'rapacious "effective rate" of corporate taxation' (Zeff 1972: 17). They further argued that inflation-adjusted accounts provided a more meaningful measurement of profit and were better placed to fulfil the Companies Act requirement for published accounts to show a true and fair view. It has been shown that '[t]he arguments raised by the industrial members were labelled "extreme" and marginalized by exclusion from the authoritative channel for the formulation of the RoAPs on inflation and accounts by the over-riding power of the practitioner-dominated' Parliamentary and Law Committee (Noguchi and Edwards 2004: 312). Continuing internal conflict between practising and industrial members prevented the ICAEW from formulating further RoAPs on inflation accounting through to the late 1960s, when a renewed upturn in the general price level re-focussed attention on the issue.

Accounting for Stewardship in a Period of Inflation was published by the Research Committee of the ICAEW in 1968. W. E. Parker of Price Waterhouse and, at the time, the President of the ICAEW, is described by Whittington (1994b: 264) as its 'principal author'. Prepared by a prac-titioner, the pamphlet, perhaps unsurprisingly, advocated and illustrated the general index-based adjustment of historical cost accounts called current purchasing power accounting. It formed the basis for the Provisional Statement of Standard Accounting Practice issued by the Accounting Standards Steering Committee (ASSC)[24] in 1974.

Within academe, the 1950s and 1960s have been described as 'a golden age for norma-tive accounting research' (Lee 2004: 64). Such researchers, in Beattie's (2002: 101) estimation, endeavoured 'to derive measures of income which, on the one hand, conformed to economic theory, and, on the other hand, also satisfied the requirement of existing accounting practices'. It was within this *milieu* that the 'LSE Triumvirate' of Baxter, Edey and Solomons made their contribution to the debate on income measurement generally and price-level accounting in particular, starting with Baxter's 1949 paper, 'Accountants and the inflation'. The broad intel-lectual framework for their ideas was that published accounts should be decision-oriented,[25] that the opportunity cost concept was particularly important, and that practical problems should be acknowledged (i.e. proposals should be workable). Their prescriptions have been summarised by Whittington (1994b: 267) as follows:

1   Assets (and liabilities) should be measured at current values.
2   The basis of current valuation should be deprival value,[26] otherwise known as value to the business or value to the owner.
3   For income measurement purposes, opening capital should be adjusted by the change in a general price index over the period to reveal real income, where 'real' is used in the economist's sense of implying constant command over goods and services undistorted by inflation.

It was current value which gained favour with the government-appointed Sandilands Committee, whose report (1975) sunk the ICAEW's decision to embrace current purchasing power account-ing. The story of Britain's current cost accounting experiment that then followed is given by Tweedie and Whittington (1984: chapters 5 and 6; see also Rutherford 2007: chapter 4).[27]

External financial reporting post–World War II has been the subject of burgeoning regula-tion. This discontinuity is now considered.

Regulations

In Britain, statutory requirements for financial accountability for registered companies were intro-duced in 1844, abandoned for reasons that are not altogether clear in 1856, and reintroduced in 1900. It was not until 1942 that the accounting profession began to provide formal guidance concerning financial reporting practices through the ICAEW's series of RoAPs, some of which have been considered above, while the publication of accounting standards dates from 1970. Early recommendations focused principally on taxation matters, whereas RoAP No. 6 and following addressed more general financial reporting issues. De Paula was chairman of the ICAEW's Taxation and Financial Relations Committee during the period (1943–5) when RoAP Nos. 6–10 laid down the main valuation bases to be used in published accounts. These five RoAPs 'followed exactly the list of subjects identified by de Paula' in his preface to the sixth edition (1933) of *The Principles of Auditing* (Kitchen and Parker 1980: 111) and for which, in his estimation, 'some form of uniform practice should be adopted by the profession' (quoted ibid.: 111).

The RoAPs initiative was broadly welcomed by the business community but not by Baxter, who set out the case against 'cut and dried pronouncements' (Baxter 2005: 29) in an article published in *The Accountant* in 1953. In his assessment, quoting Judge Oliver Wendell Holmes, 'the best test of truth is the power of the thought to get itself accepted in the competition of the market' (Baxter 1953: 410). As intended, Baxter's typically forthright views attracted attention and, as he acknowledged, 'aroused a good deal of derision among accountants' (Baxter 2005: 29). The low regard for academic contributions among the ICAEW's leadership might be gauged from the following satirical contribution made by Bernhard Heymann Binder (1953: 437), a member of council and a previous (1948–9) president of the ICAEW:

Oh! Professor Baxter whatever shall we do
With the Recommendations disapproved by you?
Must we withdraw them, in deference to your ban
Or ignore the views unpractical of an academic man?

Many years later, by which time Recommendations had transmogrified into Standards, Baxter (1981b) continued to question the widespread belief that more and more regulations were the solution to financial reporting's problems. A broader study of the pros and cons of accounting regulation with a particular focus on its economic consequences is provided by Taylor and Turley (1986).

A series of 'accounting scandals' (Rutherford 2007: 2) in the 1960s meant that the time was ripe for those who believed in regulatory control to voice their concerns. As Mumford (1994: 280) puts it: '[Edward] Stamp happened to be the right person in the right place to translate public concern into action.' In 1969, this 'crusader for standards' (ibid.: 274) received a telephone call from an editorial writer at *The Times* who had read an academic article written by Stamp (1969a) critical of the state of accounting practice and of the accountancy profession for failing to do anything about it. Stamp was invited to comment on contemporary events. His famous letter to *The Times* published on 11 September 1969 attracted interest among the business community and created horror within the accounting profession. The publication in the 'establishment' newspaper of a communication alleging lack of auditor independence and criticising use of the 'word principle [which] lends a spurious air of authority and accuracy to a situation which is in fact almost chaotic' (Stamp 1969b: 156) was taken seriously by the leaders of the profession. The letter set in train a sequence of events supported by influential practitioners such as Henry Benson of Cooper Brothers and Sir Ronald Leach of Peat, Marwick, Mitchell that led to the ICAEW's setting up the ASSC a year later (Rutherford 2007: 8–14, 22–7).

As the ASSC/ASC got into its stride, there was no shortage of ideas concerning the effectiveness of accounting standards. Baxter apart, most of the critical comment was directed at the content of the standards rather than at standard setting *per se* (see papers cited in Bromwich

1981: 41). One constructive contribution was made by Edey, who served as a founding member of the ASSC. It has been suggested that Edey's paper on 'Accounting standards in the British Isles' (1977) had 'a major influence' on the ASC's decision to draw a 'distinction between those users' objectives which are "legally oriented, in which certainty . . . is the main aim" and "those needs which are oriented more towards economic factors, in which case judgement may be more important than certainty"' (Bromwich 1981: 41). Edey favoured standards, not because they provided perfect answers, but because they improved accounting communication so long as they were generally accepted. Despite plenty of academic interest in accounting standards, Anthony Carey, undersecretary to the ASC in the late 1980s, felt justified in drawing attention to the failure of academics to mount major research studies that might influence the standard setting process (Rutherford 2007: 114). Thus, in Rutherford's estimation (2007: 114), '[e]arly optimism that fundamental research could provide a rigorous underpinning for the improvement of financial reporting rapidly dissolved'.[28] Such 'underpinning' that exists today has been a product of the conceptual framework project which is now considered.

Conceptual framework initiatives

The first British book with the term 'accounting theory' as its title, or even *in* its title, was authored by the practising accountant Harry Norris when working for Deloittes. He began with the following encouraging observation: 'It is possible to derive "first principles" by a process of reasoning more or less abstractly, and then to compare existing usage in accountancy with a theoretical model' (Norris 1946: 1). The contents of Norris' text, however, mainly focused on improving the coherence of financial reports conforming to the historical cost model. Norris was heavily influenced by Paton and Littleton's *An Introduction to Corporate Accounting Standards* (1940), which has been described by Zeff (1999: 90) as 'an elegant explication and rationalization of the historical cost accounting model'.

A more promising study of the fundamental issues of financial reporting was contained in *The Corporate Report*, a discussion document prepared for public comment by the ASSC in 1975. The report, which focused on the decision–useful dimension of published financial statements, has been described as the 'first real attempt by the accounting profession in Europe to develop a conceptual framework' (Financial Reporting Group of Ernst & Young 2004: 102). Edward Stamp was 'the academic consultant to the project, and he undertook a major part of the drafting of the report' (Mumford 1994: 283). *The Corporate Report* set out the user-decision-oriented approach that became central to the conceptual framework project. It also emphasised a duty to report to the full range of potential user groups – not just shareholders and creditors – and explored the possible publication of a wide variety of financial statements reflecting Stamp's concern 'to ensure that [company] affairs were conducted in as open and democratic a manner as possible' (ibid.: 284).[29] As intended, *The Corporate Report* attracted a great deal of interest, but it was pushed into the background by the publication of the Sandilands Committee's report a few months later, whose crushing comments concerning the utility of current purchasing power accounting required the full attention of the professional accounting bodies. The government did publish a Green Paper endorsing proposals put forward in *The Corporate Report* for recognising a broader conception of corporate social responsibility, but May 1979 saw the election of Margaret Thatcher's 'Conservative government with a very different philosophy' (Rutherford 2007: 110).

Consistent with the philosophy of *The Corporate Report,* a focus on the usefulness of financial reports as a means of looking forward as well as backwards caught the attention of academics at Manchester University. Carsberg, Arnold and Hope (1977: 411) placed emphasis on the idea of predictive value: '[F]inancial accounting reports may be valuable if they help users to make improved predictions of variables which are relevant to their decisions.' It is an approach that is central to the International Accounting Standards Board (IASB)/Financial Accounting Standards Board (FASB) endeavour to develop a more effective conceptual framework. The recently revised *Conceptual Framework for Financial Reporting* highlights 'relevance' as one of the two 'fundamental qualitative characteristics' of published financial reports, with such reports deemed relevant if they possess '*predictive value*, confirmatory value or both' (IASB 2010: 17, emphasis added).

At the end of the 1970s, Richard Macve was invited by the ASC to review the pertinent US and UK literature with a view to advising on the potential for developing a British conceptual framework to underpin the standard setting process that was then well underway. In the light of Macve's report (1981), the ASC decided not to go down the line followed by the FASB in formulating a conceptual framework (Macve 1997: xi). Macve's critique was further developed in 'The FASB's conceptual framework – vision, tool or threat?' (Macve 1983). A few years later the Research Committee of the Institute of Chartered Accountants of Scotland, which included among its membership David Tweedie, who later served as chair of the Accounting Standards Board (ASB) and the IASB, produced a report that favoured net realisable value on the grounds that it provided a superior measure for assessing financial wealth compared with historical or replacement cost (McMonnies 1988). In the following year, the ICAEW published a paper prepared for its Research Board by David Solomons (1989). Solomons' approach was almost identical to that taken by the FASB, which is unsurprising given that he had served as an academic consultant on its conceptual framework project (Financial Reporting Group of Ernst & Young 2004: 114). Thus, Solomons favoured the asset and liability approach to financial reporting on the grounds that the revenue and expenditure basis provided scope 'for all kinds of income smoothing' (Solomons 1989: 18).[30]

According to Macve (1997: xi), it was pressure 'to demonstrate the coherence of the British standards programme' that led the ASB to renew its interest in developing a conceptual framework. Work began in 1991 (see Arnold *et al.* 1991) and culminated in publication of the *Statement of Principles* in 1999 (ASB 1999). More recently, Macve re-entered the fray with two colleagues (Bromwich *et al.* 2005). Together they challenged the FASB/IASB's claim (Bullen and Crook 2005: 7–8) that the superiority of the 'asset/liability' notion of profit over the 'revenue and expense view' was derived from Sir John Hicks' (1946) definition of income.

Two papers contained in a festschrift in honour of Edward Stamp tackled the idea of a conceptual framework from an 'explicitly philosophical' viewpoint (Whittington 1994a: 279). Power (1993) employed Rawls' model of reflective equilibrium to produce the following conclusion: 'A conceptual framework is not an ultimate foundation in any classical sense but a point of reference in the network of accounting standards and practices that serves to "organise" thinking about them' (quoted in Whittington 1994a: 279). Archer (1993: 91) criticised the FASB's conceptual framework project on the grounds that it 'was intended to provide "comfort and reassurance to some body of believers" (Ravetz 1971: 360) rather than effective intellectual guidance and authority for the development of accounting thought and practice'. He also engaged heavily with the literature on jurisprudence to justify his conviction that acceptance of the process through which standards are derived is more important that any concern with the conceptual framework they are supposed to comply with. A different but equally interesting philosophical dimension was provided by Bryer (1999), who concluded that 'whereas the FASB's framework, based on the marginalist idea of economic value, is subjective and vague, the Marxist theory of financial accounting derived [in this paper] provides critical accounting with a scientific foundation'. Further thoughtful contributions were made by Willett (1987, 1988), who put forward an axiom-grounded conceptual framework to be used as a basis for deriving accounting measurement practices.

Cash flow accounting

The development of ideas favouring the publication of cash-based accounting information confronted the fundamental problem of allocation inherent in an accruals-based system and recognised the all-important role of cash flow in the survival and success of business entities. Significant contributions to the literature on cash flow accounting were made by British authors in the period leading up to the introduction of requirements to publish a Statement of Source and Application of Funds (1976) and its successor, the Cash Flow Statement (1991).[31]

Starting in 1971, Tom Lee consistently advocated cash flow accounting based on a model that reports both actual and future cash flows. In the middle of the following decade, Lee drew together his ideas on cash flow accounting and exit-value accounting to create 'a unified system of cash flow reporting' employing a range of inter-related accounting statements (Lee 1984: 50). Lee's Statement of Financial Position classifies assets according to the ease with which they can be realised, commencing with cash. Liabilities are listed in order of date of maturity. The model contains three further financial statements:

- The Statement of Realized Cash Flows, which sets out information broadly equivalent to the content of today's Financial Reporting Standard (FRS) 1;
- The Statement of Realizable Earnings which reports (i) realised earnings derived from an entity's operating cash flow and (ii) unrealised earnings comprising potential cash flows that have accrued during the period as the result of changes in the realisable value of assets and liabilities;
- The Statement of Changes in Financial Position, which has been described as 'a conventional funds statement presented on an exit value basis' (Financial Reporting Group of Ernst & Young 2004: 109).

The second of Britain's principal promoters of cash flow reporting is G. H. Lawson, 'who advocates the reporting of actual and forecast cash flows but in combination with the market value of enterprise capital in order to assist internal management and investors in assessing enterprise performance' (Lee 2009: 153). Lee (ibid.) points out that 'Lawson's arguments take F[inancial] A[ccounting] T[heory] into the macro-economic areas of dividend policy, inflation, and taxation' (see Lawson 1997).

The final subsection draws attention to distinctive British contributions to financial accounting theory development based on empirical investigations.

Empirical research

Equity valuation models based on accounting figures are today widely used by investors, particularly professional investors, in their financial decision-making (Cascino *et al.* 2013). It is important to engage with empirical research initiatives to elucidate academic contributions to the construction of accounting-based valuation models in investment decisions.

The rise of what its proponents claim to be a more scientific approach to financial accounting research dates from the 1960s and has involved the 'increasing use of formal empiricism and mathematical model building' (Zeff 1989: 169). From the outset some of its advocates sought to legitimise their favoured research paradigm by attacking the previously ascendant normative approach (see, for example, Dopuch and Revsine 1973; Whittington 1986: 25). Mattessich (1996: 16) summed up the change as follows: 'Empirical accounting research, on one side, and agency-information research, on the other, began to dominate academic accounting and assumed during the 1970s the character of normal science – in contrast to the *revolutionary* accounting research of the 1960s.'

The rise of empirical research and the denigration of alternative approaches did not go unanswered. Indeed, it provoked a storm of controversy, with British researchers making prominent critical contributions (Peasnell and Williams 1986; Puxty 1985; Whittington 1987).

Most of the key contributions in the areas of empirical research have originated outside Britain, often in the United States. One area where British researchers have made a major contribution, however, is in the theoretical literature on residual income valuation, which has helped to frame much of the empirical market-based accounting research that has blossomed in the last two decades or so.

Peasnell (1981, 1982) challenged conventional pessimism concerning the feasibility of valuing businesses on the basis of accounting data rather than future cash flows by showing mathematically 'how both a firm's economic value and its economic yield can be derived from accounting numbers in a very simple fashion' (Peasnell 1982: 361). As with most 'new' ideas, of course, it is possible to find people thinking along similar lines earlier on (Cascino *et al.* 2013; Pope 2010: 92). Indeed, Peasnell and Brief (1996) draw attention to a diverse literature that features aspects of residual income dating from the early twentieth century. These include contributions from Dickinson and Dicksee, who have featured prominently in this chapter.

Peasnell's own pioneering initiatives remained 'neglected' (Pope 2010: 92) until Jim Ohlson's (1995) seminal contribution helped spawn a plethora of market-based accounting research. There, the influence of Peasnell's earlier work was duly recognised. Post-Ohlson, market-based research includes theoretical and empirical contributions from Peasnell as well as other British academics (e.g. Ashton *et al.* 2011; Bromwich and Walker 1998; Landsman *et al.* 2006, 2011; O'Hanlon and Peasnell 2000, 2004; Pope and O'Hanlon 1999; Stark 1997; Stark and Thomas 1998; Walker 1997; Walker and Wang 2003).

Concluding remarks

This chapter shows that the history of financial accounting theory in Britain is not a story of continuous improvement or even of consistent movement in a particular direction. For example, the attitude towards secret reserves changed from one of caution concerning its use to a situation where it was considered the cornerstone of financial stability and, in turn, to it being the subject of critical re-evaluation, and, finally, to secret reserves being outlawed. Also, the early part of the period covered by this survey saw writers sympathetic to the idea of taking some account of market prices when measuring fixed assets. As the historical cost model became firmly entrenched, however, writers increasingly presented the measurement of fixed assets at historical cost less depreciation as entirely unproblematic. In Watts and Zimmerman's parlance, thinkers provided the excuses required to rationalise the continued use of existing practices. Recent decades have seen the cost versus value debate flourish with the virtues of fair value extolled by both regulators and researchers.

It has been argued that many of those with new ideas about how accounting should be done and, indeed, those who have put those ideas into practice – Baxter's 'countless anonymous innovators' – remain unknown. Where accounting thinkers have impacted on practice in a dramatic fashion, it is the contribution of judges that can sometimes be more easily identified, such as Mr Justice Buckley's legitimisation of secret reserves in Newton v. Birmingham Small Arms (1906) and Mr Justice Wright's criticism of accounting practices which complied with contemporary best practice but completely misled external stakeholders (Rex v. Kylsant 1931). We have also seen that the 'medium of the message' (Edwards 1996: 62) can be important in the effective communication of new ideas. Thus, Garnsey's advocacy of group accounting in the 1920s attracted attention because of who he was – a partner in a leading firm of accountants – and where his views were expressed – at a lecture to members of the ICAEW that was reported in the leading professional journal of the day, *The Accountant*. Forty or so years later, Stamp's detailed critique of accounting and accountants published in an academic journal attracted little attention, but similar sentiments expressed in a letter to *The Times* a few months later are recognised as the catalyst for the ICAEW's conversion to accounting standard setting in 1970.

New ideas about how accounting should be done might well advance financial transparency, but history shows us that improvement might be short-lived; a consequence, of course, of lack of congruence between the priorities of preparers and users of accounting information. Thus the reaction against secret reserves that culminated in their prohibition in 1948 did not put an end to income smoothing. In Britain, FRS 12 'Provisions and Contingencies', issued in 1998, had as its objective to prevent provisions being used to achieve a similar outcome to that of secret reserves, and there is an extensive empirical literature testifying to the fact that earnings management is not a thing of the past. Similarly, the development of a consensus in favour of requiring holding companies to publish group accounts did not succeed in stamping out the financial machinations that had become a cause for concern in the 1920s. British management subsequently used the associated company to smooth reported profit through the 'timing' of inter-company dividend transfers in the 1960s, and the quasi-subsidiary was created to keep external finance off the balance sheet in the 1980s.

It is important to remember that such practices do not necessarily signify a desire on the part of management to be dishonest, though this might be the case. Edey (1977: 303) summed up the problem as follows:

> It is very easy [for management] to argue . . . that the non-disclosure of X or Y, or its presentation in such and such a way, or a change in the basis of its presentation, will in the end bring benefit to 'the company' that will outweigh any temporary disadvantage to the shareholder and others from the treatment in question – in short to regard accounting statements as tactical or strategic weapons of management instead of as intelligence reports for the world at large.

One of the many challenges for accounting thinkers is to resolve this conundrum as part of an effective endeavour to devise a better way of doing accounting.

Notes

1 The preparation of this chapter has benefited from advice provided by Mark A. Clatworthy, Robert H. Parker and Kenneth V. Peasnell.
2 British writers include those mainly working and writing in Britain, so George O. May, for example, although British, is excluded.
3 General studies of this topic which adopt a broader international focus include Beattie (2002), Lee (2009), Mattessich (2003, 2008) and Whittington (1986).
4 One example is R. J. Chambers' Continuously Contemporary Accounting.
5 Differences in the information requirements of external users are not specifically examined. A useful discussion and analysis of this issue is provided by Cascino *et al.* (2013).
6 For profiles of these and other accounting thinkers see Edwards (1994).
7 Terms in use for most of the period covered by this study will be used, e.g. fixed assets rather than non-current assets, stock-in-trade instead of inventories and holding company instead of parent company.
8 Parker (1965: 170) asserts that the 'rule was never seriously challenged' in Britain.
9 Echoing Malcolm (1731: 89) who stated:

> Yet it seems more reasonable to value them as they cost you; for otherwise you bring in Gain and Loss into your Accounts, which has not yet actually happened, and may, perhaps, not happen; because you may not dispose of them at those Rates.

Many other parallels could be drawn between eighteenth- and twentieth-century thinkers.

10 For more on goodwill, see Dicksee and Tillyard (1906) and Cooper (2007).
11 Parker (1994: 73) points out that '[f]ew even of late nineteenth- and early twentieth-century books had either "accounting" or "accountancy" in their titles'. Other exceptions were authored by Francis W. Pixley (1908) and George Lisle (1899).
12 Neither the date of publication nor the edition of this text, first published in 1914, is stated. References to dates, e.g. of Companies Acts, indicate 1918 as a reasonable approximation.
13 The reporting practices of companies in certain industries were the subject of closer regulation, commencing with the railways in 1868 (Parker 1990).
14 In a paper delivered to the International Congress of Accountants at Amsterdam five years earlier, Plender had argued that the reputation of a professional accountant depended not just on the adherence to legal principles, but on his 'much wider moral duty and responsibility' (quoted in Edwards 1985: 739).
15 Recommendation on Accounting Principles (RoAP) No. 6 entitled Reserves and provisions, 1943 (reproduced in Zeff 2009: 52–3).
16 Harmood Banner served as president of the ICAEW, 1904–5.
17 Much of the material in this and the following paragraph is taken from Edwards and Webb (1984).
18 This was part of an address to the London members of the ICAEW chaired by Garnsey.
19 Named after an honorary member of the Society, Sir Josiah Stamp, and its former Secretary and President, Sir James Martin.
20 A more enlightened attitude towards academic endeavour on the part of the ICAEW marked the resurrection of *Accounting Research* as *Accounting and Business Research* in 1970.
21 Accounting in relation to changes in the purchasing power of money, 1952 (reproduced in Zeff 2009: 85–91).
22 Davison had helped Edwards set up the Accounting Research Association in 1936.
23 Practising members such as G.F. Saunders, partner in Harmood Banner, Lewis & Mounsey of Liverpool and F. S. Bray supported the stance of the industrialists.
24 Shortened to Accounting Standards Committee (ASC) in 1976.
25 For a well-informed discussion of the contribution of LSE scholars, including Ronald Coase, to the development of the decision-useful concept, see Napier (2011).
26 Weetman (2007) contains a range of assessments of the long-term significance of Baxter's work on deprival value.
27 For other discussions of price-level accounting, see Mumford (1994) on Stamp's advocacy of current cost accounting and Whittington (1983). For contributions to the broader debate on income measurement, see Whittington (1981).
28 For contributions to our understanding of the politics of standard setting, see for example Solomons (1983) and Rutherford (2007: 116–19).
29 Additional proposed financial reports included the value added statement. The social context within which ideological support for publication of that statement emerged, briefly blossomed and evaporated is examined by Burchell *et al.* (1985).
30 See Mumford (1989) and Whittington (1989) for reviews of McMonnies (1988) and Solomons (1989).
31 The usefulness of cash flow data is recognised in reports prepared for the British government (Sandilands Committee 1975, para. 518) and for the Institute of Chartered Accountants of Scotland (McMonnies 1988).

References

Aranya, N. (1974) The influence of pressure groups on financial statements in Britain, *Abacus*, 10 (1): 3–12.
Archer, S. (1993) On the methodology of constructing a conceptual framework for financial reporting, in M. J. Mumford and K. V. Peasnell (eds) *Philosophical Perspectives on Accounting. Essays in Honour of Edward Stamp*, pp. 62–122 (London: Routledge).
Arnold, J., Boyle, P., Carey, A., Cooper, M. and Wild, K. (1991) *The Future Shape of Financial Reports* (London: Institutes of Chartered Accountants in England and Wales and of Scotland).

ASB (1999) *Statement of Principles for Financial Reporting* (London: Accounting Standards Board).

Ashton, D., Peasnell, K. and Wang, P. (2011) Residual income valuation models and inflation, *European Accounting Review*, 20 (3): 459–83.

Baxter, W. T. (1949) Accountants and the inflation, *Proceedings of the Manchester Statistical Society*, 9 February: 1–19.

_____ (1953) Recommendations on accounting theory, *Accountant*, 129 (4112): 405–10.

_____ (1981a) Accounting history as a worthwhile study, *Accounting Historians Notebook*, Spring: 5–8.

_____ (1981b) Accounting standards: boon or curse? *Accounting and Business Research*, 12 (45): 3–10.

_____ (2005) Interview, in S. P. Walker (ed.) *Giving an Account: Life Histories of Four CAs*, pp. 9–54 (Edinburgh: Institute of Chartered Accountants of Scotland).

Beattie, V. (2002) Traditions of research in financial accounting, in B. Ryan, R. W. Scapens and M. Theobald (eds) *Research Method and Methodology in Finance and Accounting*, 2nd edn, pp. 94–113 (London: Thomson).

Bigg, W. W. (1951) *Spicer and Pegler's Practical Auditing*, 10th edn (London: H.F.L.).

Binder, B. H. (1953) Recommendations on accounting theory, *Accountant*, 129 (4113): 437.

Bleckly, J. J. (n.d.) *The History of the Pearson and Knowles Coal and Iron Co. Ltd. 1873–1920*, unpublished manuscript, Shotton Records Centre.

Bray, F. S. (1949) The English universities and the accounting profession, *Accounting Review*, 24 (3): 273–6.

Bray, F. S. and Sheasby, B. H. (1944) *Design of Accounts* (Oxford: Oxford University Press).

Bray, S. and Stone, R. (1948) The presentation of central government accounts, *Accounting Research*, 1 (1): 1–12.

Brief, R. P. (1976) *The Late Nineteenth Century Debate over Depreciation, Capital, and Income* (New York: Arno Press).

_____ (1993) *The Continuing Debate over Depreciation, Capital, and Income* (New York & London: Garland Publishing).

Bromwich, M. (1981) The setting of accounting standards: the contribution of research, in M. Bromwich and A. Hopwood (eds) *Essays in British Accounting Research*, pp. 33–58 (London: Pitman).

Bromwich, M. and Walker, M. (1998) Residual income past and future, *Management Accounting Research*, 9 (4): 391–419.

Bromwich, M., Macve, R. and Sunder, S. (2005) FASB/IASB revisiting the concepts: a comment on Hicks and the concept of 'income' in the conceptual framework. Available: www2.lse.ac.uk/accounting/pdf/MacveComment_on_FASB_IASB_July05.pdf (accessed 23 November 2012).

Bryer, R. A. (1999) A Marxist critique of the FASB's conceptual framework, *Critical Perspectives on Accounting*, 10 (5): 551–89.

Bullen, H. G. and Crook, K. (2005) Revisiting the concepts (Financial Accounting Standards Board/International Accounting Standards Board). Available: www.fasb.org/project/communications_paper.pdf (accessed 23 November 2012).

Burchell, S., Clubb, C. and Hopwood, A. G. (1985) Accounting in its social context: towards a history of value added in the United Kingdom. *Accounting, Organizations and Society*, 10 (4): 381–413.

Carsberg, B., Arnold, J. and Hope, A. (1977) Predictive value: a criterion for choice of accounting method, in W. T. Baxter and S. Davidson (eds) *Studies in Accounting*, pp. 403–23 (London: ICAEW).

Cascino, S., Clatworthy, M., García Osma, B., Gassen, J., Imam, S. and Jeanjean, T. (2013) *The Use of Information by Capital Providers* (Edinburgh: Research Committee of The Institute of Chartered Accountants of Scotland and European Financial Reporting Advisory Group).

Cooper, E. (1888) What is profit of a company? *Accountant*, 14 (727): 740–6.

Cooper, J. (2007) Debating accounting principles and policies: the case of goodwill, 1880–1921, *Accounting, Business & Financial History*, 17 (2): 241–64.

Corporate Report, The (1975) (London: Accounting Standards Steering Committee).

Cutforth, A. E. (1930) *Public Companies and the Investor* (London: G. Bell).

Davey Committee (1895) *Report of the Departmental Committee*, C. 7779 (London: HMSO).

Dev, S. (1980) *Accounting and the L.S.E. Tradition* (London: London School of Economics and Political Science).

Dickinson, Sir A. L. (1913) *Accounting Practice and Procedure* (New York: Ronald Press). Reprinted by Scholars Book Co., Houston, TX, 1975.

_____ (1924) Publicity in industrial accounts. With a comparison of English and American methods, *Accountant*, 71 (2600): 469–90.

Dicksee, L. R. (1892) *Auditing: A Practical Manual for Auditors* (London: Gee). Reprinted by Arno Press, New York, NY, 1976.

_____ (1905) *Advanced Accounting*, 2nd edn (London: Gee).

_____ (1927) *Published Balance Sheets and Window Dressing* (London: Gee). Reprinted by Arno Press, New York, NY, 1980.

Dicksee, L. R. and Tillyard, F. (1906) *Goodwill and its Treatment in Accounts* (London: Gee).

Dopuch, N. and Revsine, P. (eds) (1973) *Accounting Research 1960–1970: A Critical Evaluation* (Urbana, IL: Center for International Education and Research in Accounting).

Edey, H. C. (1977) Accounting standards in the British Isles, in W. T. Baxter and S. Davidson (eds) *Studies in Accounting*, pp. 294–305 (London: ICAEW).

Edey, H. C. and Peacock, A. T. (1954) *National Income and Social Accounting* (London: Hutchinson).

Edwards, J. R. (1976) The accounting profession and disclosure in published reports, 1925–1935, *Accounting and Business Research*, 6 (24): 289–303.

_____ (1981) *Company Legislation and Changing Patterns of Disclosure in British Company Accounts, 1900–1940* (London: Institute of Chartered Accountants in England and Wales).

_____ (1985) William Plender, Lord Plender of Sundridge, Kent, (1869–1946) Accountant, in D. J. Jeremy (ed.) *Dictionary of Business Biography, Vol. 4 (M–R)*, pp. 736–44 (London: Butterworths).

_____ (1989) *A History of Financial Accounting* (London: Routledge).

_____ (1991) The process of accounting innovation: the publication of consolidated accounts in Britain in 1910, *Accounting Historians Journal*, 18 (2): 113–32.

_____ (ed.) (1994) *Twentieth-Century Accounting Thinkers* (London: Routledge).

_____ (1996) Financial accounting practice 1600–1970: continuity and change, in T. A. Lee, A. Bishop and R. H. Parker (eds) *Accounting History from the Renaissance to the Present: A Remembrance of Luca Pacioli*, pp. 31–70 (London & New York: Garland Publishing).

_____ (2004) Paula, Frederic Rudolph Mackley de (1882–1954), *Oxford Dictionary of National Biography*, Oxford University Press. Available: www.oxforddnb.com/view/article/46874 (accessed 12 October 2004).

Edwards, J. R. and Webb, K. M. (1984) The development of group accounting in the United Kingdom to 1933, *Accounting Historians Journal*, 11 (1): 31–61.

Edwards, J. R., Dean, G. and Clarke, F. (2009) Merchants' accounts, performance assessment and decision making in mercantilist Britain, *Accounting, Organizations and Society*, 34 (5): 551–70.

Edwards, R. S. (1938) The nature and measurement of income, *Accountant*, July–October.

Financial Reporting Group of Ernst & Young (2004) *International GAAP 2005* (London: Ernst & Young).

French, E. A. (1977) The evolution of the dividend law of England, in W. T. Baxter and S. Davidson (eds) *Studies in Accounting*, pp. 306–31 (London: ICAEW).

Garnsey, Sir Gilbert (1923) Holding companies and their published accounts, *Accountant*, 108 (2509): 13–26, 108 (2510): 53–68.

Garrett, A. A. (1961) *History of the Society of Incorporated Accountants 1885–1957* (Oxford: Oxford University Press).

Greene Committee (1926) *Company Law Amendment Committee 1925–6. Report*. Cmd. 2657 (London: HMSO).

Guthrie, E. (1882) The want of uniformity in the mode of stating accounts, *Accountant*, 8 (412): 8–13.

_____ (1883) Depreciation and sinking funds, *Accountant*, 9 (437): 6–10.

Hendriksen, E. S. (1977) *Accounting Theory*, 3rd edn (Homewood, IL: Richard D. Irwin).

Hicks, J. R. (1946) *Value and Capital*, 2nd edn (Oxford: Clarendon Press).

IASB (2010) *The Conceptual Framework for Financial Reporting* (London: International Accounting Standards Board).

Jones, F. H. (1964) *Guide to Company Balance Sheets and Profit and Loss Accounts*, 6th edn (Cambridge: W. Heffer).

Kitchen, J. (1972) The accounts of British holding company groups: development and attitudes to disclosure in the early years, *Accounting and Business Research*, 2 (6): 114–36.

Kitchen, J. and Parker, R. H. (1980) *Accounting Thought and Education: Six English Pioneers* (London: Institute of Chartered Accountants in England and Wales).

_____ (1994) Lawrence Robert Dicksee (1864–1932), in J. R. Edwards (ed.) *Twentieth-Century Accounting Thinkers*, pp. 206–44 (London: Routledge).

Landsman, W. R., Miller, B. L., Peasnell, K. V. and Yeh, S. (2011) Do investors understand really dirty surplus? *Accounting Review*, 86 (1): 237–58.

Landsman, W. R., Peasnell, K. V., Pope, P. F. and Yeh, S. (2006) Which approach to accounting for employee stock options best reflects market pricing? *Review of Accounting Studies*, 11 (2–3): 203–45.

Law Reports (1889) Lee v. Neuchatel Asphalte Company, *Accountant Law Reports*, 15 (741): 26–8.

35

_____ (1894) Verner v. The General and Commercial Investment Trust, *Accountant Law Reports*, 20 (1010): 70–2.

Lawson, G. H. (1997) *Aspects of the Economic Implications of Accounting* (New York: Garland Publishing).

Leading article (1889) The payment of dividends out of capital, *Accountant*, 15 (742): 89–90.

Lee, T. A. (1984) *Cash Flow Accounting* (Wokingham: Van Nostrand Reinhold).

_____ (2004) Accounting and auditing research in the United States, in C. Humphrey and B. H. K Lee (eds) *The Real Life Guide to Accounting Research*, pp. 57–71 (Oxford: Elsevier).

_____ (2009) Financial accounting theory, 2009, in J. R. Edwards and S. P. Walker (eds) *The Routledge Companion to Accounting History*, pp. 139–61 (London: Routledge).

Lisle, G. (1899) *Accounting in Theory and Practice: A Text-Book for the Use of Accountants* (Edinburgh: William Green).

Macve, R. (1981) *A Conceptual Framework for Financial Accounting and Reporting: The Possibilities for an Agreed Structure* (London: Institute of Chartered Accountants in England and Wales).

_____ (1983) The FASB's conceptual framework – vision, tool or threat, reproduced in R. Macve (1997) *A Conceptual Framework for Financial Accounting and Reporting, Vision, Tool, or Threat*, pp. 167–217 (New York & London: Garland Publishing).

_____ (1997) *A Conceptual Framework for Financial Accounting and Reporting, Vision, Tool, or Threat* (New York & London: Garland Publishing).

Malcolm, A. (1731) *A Treatise of Book-keeping or Merchants Accounts* (London).

Matheson, E. (1893) *The Depreciation of Factories, Mines and Industrial Undertakings and their Valuation*, 2nd edn (London: E & F N Spon). Reprinted by Arno Press, New York, NY, 1976.

Mattessich, R. (1996) Academic research in accounting: the last 50 years, *Asia-Pacific Journal of Accounting*, 3(1): 3–81.

_____ (2003) Accounting research and researchers of the nineteenth century and the beginning of the twentieth century: an international survey of authors, ideas and publications, *Accounting, Business & Financial History*, 13 (2): 125–70.

_____ (2008) *Two Hundred Years of Accounting Research* (London: Routledge).

McMonnies, P. (ed.) (1988) *Making Corporate Reports Valuable* (London: Kogan Page).

Mumford, M. J. (1989) The search for a British conceptual framework: a review essay, *British Accounting Review*, 21 (4): 381–90.

_____ (1994) Edward Stamp (1928–86): a crusader for standards, in J. R. Edwards (ed.) *Twentieth-Century Accounting Thinkers*, pp. 274–92 (London: Routledge).

_____ (2007) Interview with William T. Baxter. Available: www.icas.org.uk/mumford/ (accessed 23 November 2012).

Napier, C. (2011) Accounting at the London School of Economics: opportunity lost? *Accounting History*, 16 (2): 185–205.

Noguchi, M. and Edwards, J. R. (2004) Accounting principles, internal conflict and the State: the case of the ICAEW, *Abacus*, 40 (3): 280–320.

Norris, H. (1946) *Accounting Theory* (London: Sir Isaac Pitman).

O'Hanlon, J. F. and Peasnell, K. V. (2000) Residual income and EVA, *Economic and Financial Computing*, 10 (2): 53–95.

_____ (2004) Residual income valuation: are inflation adjustments necessary? *Review of Accounting Studies*, 9 (4): 375–98.

Ohlson, J. A. (1995) Earnings, book values, and dividends in equity valuation, *Contemporary Accounting Research*, 11 (2): 661–87.

Parker, R. H. (1965) Lower of cost and market in Britain and the United States: an historical survey, *Abacus*, 1 (2): 156–72.

_____ (1980a) Memorial. Frank Sewell Bray 1906–1979, *Accounting Review*, 55 (2): 307–16.

_____ (1980b) The want of uniformity in accounts: a nineteenth century debate, in D. M. Emanuel and I. C. Stewart (eds) *Essays in Honour of Trevor R. Johnson* (Auckland: Department of Accountancy, University of Auckland and The New Zealand Society of Accountants).

_____ (1984) *Macmillan Dictionary of Accounting*, 2nd edn (London: Macmillan).

_____ (1990) Regulating British corporate financial reporting in the late nineteenth century, *Accounting, Business & Financial History*, 1 (1): 51–71.

_____ (1994) Finding English words to talk about accounting concepts, *Accounting, Auditing & Accountability Journal*, 7 (2): 70–85.

Paton, W. A. and Littleton, A. C. (1940) *An Introduction to Corporate Accounting Standards. Monograph No. 3.* (Chicago, IL: American Accounting Association).

de Paula, F. R. M. (c.1918) *Principles of Auditing* (London: Sir Isaac Pitman).

_____ (1925) Accountants' problems of to-day, *Accountant*, 73 (2659): 801–12.

Peasnell, K. V. (1981) On capital budgeting and income measurement, *Abacus*, 17 (1): 52–67.

_____ (1982) Some formal connections between economic values and yields and accounting numbers, *Journal of Business Finance and Accounting*, 9 (3): 361–81.

Peasnell, K. V. and Brief, R. P. (1996) *Clean Surplus: A Link between Accounting and Finance* (London & New York: Garland Publishing).

Peasnell, K. V. and Williams, D. J. (1986) Ersatz academics and scholar-saints: the supply of financial accounting research, *Abacus*, 22 (2): 121–35.

Pixley, F. W. (1908) *Accountancy* (London, Bath & New York: Sir Isaac Pitman).

Pope, P. F. (2010) Bridging the gap between accounting and finance, *British Accounting Review*, 42 (2): 88–102.

Pope, P. F. and O'Hanlon, J. F. (1999) The value-relevance of UK dirty surplus accounting flows, *British Accounting Review*, 31(4): 459–82.

Power, M. K. (1993) On the idea of a conceptual framework for financial reporting, in M. J. Mumford and K. V. Peasnell (eds) *Philosophical Perspectives on Accounting: Essays in Honour of Edward Stamp*, pp. 44–61 (London: Routledge).

Puxty, A. G. (ed.) (1985) *Reductionism ad Absurdum. Critiques of Agency Theory in Accountancy* (Glasgow: Strathclyde Convergencies).

Rutherford, B. A. (2007) *Financial Reporting in the UK: A History of the Accounting Standards Committee, 1969–1990* (London: Routledge).

Samuel, H. B. (1933) *Shareholders' Money* (London: Pitman).

Sandilands Committee (1975) *Report of the Inflation Accounting Committee. Inflation Accounting*, Cmnd. 6225 (London: HMSO).

Select Committee (1877) *Report from the Select Committee on the Companies Acts, 1862 and 1867: Together with the Proceedings of the Committee, Minutes of Evidence, and Appendix*. (Ordered, by the House of Commons, to be Printed, 26 July 1877).

Solomons, D. (1983) The political implications of accounting and accounting standard setting, *Accounting and Business Research*, 13 (50): 107–18.

_____ (1989) *Guidelines for Financial Reporting Standards* (London: Institute of Chartered Accountants in England and Wales).

Stamp, E. (1969a) The public accountant and the public interest, *Journal of Business Finance*, 1 (1): 32–42.

_____ (1969b) Auditing and auditors, *Times*, 11 September, reproduced in E. Stamp and C. Marley (1970) *Accounting Principles and the City Code: The Case for Reform*, pp. 155–9 (London: Butterworths).

Stamp, Sir Josiah (1925) Accountants' problems of to-day, *Accountant*, 73 (2656): 685–7.

Stark, A. (1997) Linear information dynamics, dividend irrelevance, corporate valuation and the clean surplus relationship, *Accounting and Business Research*, 27 (3): 219–28.

Stark, A. and Thomas, H. M. (1998) On the empirical relationship between market value and residual income in the UK, *Management Accounting Research*, 9 (4): 445–60.

Taylor, P. and Turley, S. (1986) *The Regulation of Accounting* (Oxford: Basil Blackwell).

Tweedale, G. (2004) Banner, Sir John Sutherland Harmood, first baronet (1847–1927), *Oxford Dictionary of National Biography*, Oxford University Press. Available: www.oxforddnb.com/view/article/47601 (accessed 12 October 2004).

Tweedie, D. P. and Whittington, G. (1984) *The Debate on Inflation Accounting* (Cambridge: Cambridge University Press).

Walker, M. (1997) Clean surplus accounting models and market-based accounting research: A review, *Accounting and Business Research*, 27 (4): 341–55.

Walker, M. and Wang, P. (2003) Towards an understanding of profitability analysis within the residual income valuation framework, *Accounting and Business Research*, 33 (3): 235–46.

Weetman, P. (ed.) (2007). Comments on deprival value and standard setting in measurement: from a symposium to celebrate the work of Professor William T. Baxter, *Accounting and Business Research*, 37 (3): 233–42.

Whittington, G. (1981) The British contribution to income theory, in M. Bromwich and A. Hopwood (eds) *Essays in British Accounting Research*, pp. 1–29 (London: Pitman).

_____ (1983) *Inflation Accounting: An Introduction to the Debate* (Cambridge: Cambridge University Press).

_____ (1986) Financial accounting theory: an overview, *British Accounting Review*, 18 (2): 4–41.

_____ (1987) Positive accounting theory: a review article, *Accounting and Business Research*, 17 (68): 327–36.

_____ (1989) Accounting standard setting in the UK after 20 years: a critique of the Dearing and Solomons Reports, *Accounting and Business Research*, 19 (75): 195–205.

_____ (1994a) Review of: Philosophical Perspectives on Accounting. Essays in Honour of Edward Stamp. M. J. Mumford and K. V. Peasnell (eds), *Accounting and Business Research*, 24 (95): 279–80.

_____ (1994b) The LSE Triumvirate and its contribution to price changes accounting, in J. R. Edwards (ed.) *Twentieth-Century Accounting Thinkers*, pp. 252–73 (London: Routledge).

Willett, R. J. (1987) An axiomatic theory of accounting measurement (Part 1), *Accounting and Business Research*, 17 (66): 155–71.

_____ (1988) An axiomatic theory of accounting measurement (Part 2), *Accounting and Business Research*, 19 (73): 71–91.

Zeff, S. A. (1972) *Forging Accounting Principles in Five Countries: A History and an Analysis of Trends* (Champaign, IL: Stipes Publishing).

_____ (1989) Recent trends in accounting education and research in the USA: some implications for UK academics, *British Accounting Review*, 21 (2): 159–76.

_____ (1999) The evolution of the conceptual framework for business enterprises in the United States, *Accounting Historians Journal*, 26 (2), 89–131.

_____ (2009) *Principles before Standards: The ICAEW's 'N series' of Recommendations on Accounting Principles* (London: ICAEW Financial Reporting Faculty).

3

Financial accounting and reporting in the United States of America – 1820 to 2010

Toward sunshine from shadows

Gary J. Previts and Dale L. Flesher

Foreword

The Treaty of Ghent (Belgium) signed on the eve of Christmas in 1814 and the contemporaneous battle of New Orleans and victory attributed to General Andrew Jackson ended an episode in United States history that can be considered an anticlimax to the American Revolution. To many who doubted the ability of the fledging republic to survive another contest with Great Britain, the outcome of the War of 1812 made further apparent the ability of the young nation to survive and, soon, to prosper. The acquisition of territories under the Louisiana Purchase of 1803 laid out a country that would be a continental one. These defining events of the early nineteenth century, along with developments such as the opening of the Erie Canal (1825) and the chartering of the Baltimore and Ohio (B&O) Railroad (1827), shaped the beginning of a distinctive American Business System. For these reasons, 1820 becomes a meaningful choice to begin this writing.

This essay explicates and discusses historical, regulatory, socioeconomic, and political factors that are considered to have influenced the changes in accounting thought and practice in the United States over nearly two centuries. These factors, including the key role of individuals, will be roughly subdivided into two broad periods – namely the period before 1920 and the period thereafter. The choice of 1920, while arbitrary, reflects changes in the aftermath of World War I, wherein the US economy was transformed from a mainly agricultural one to an industrial one and the US became a creditor nation in contrast to its previous status as a debtor developing economy. Between 1820 and 1920, the country's demographics changed from a population of slightly under 10 million, including 1.6 million slaves, with voting limited to males, to a population of 308 million individuals, the adult population of which had the right to vote. Many measures were developed during this period to determine the size, direction, and scope of the economy. From an investment perspective, perhaps none has gained more attention than the Dow Jones Industrial Average (DJIA), established in May 1896, which serves as a broad barometer of the prospects and mood of the equity markets, if not the entire economy.

The DJIA is both a metric and a symbol of the equity portion of an investment culture that has been a dynamic component of the American business system and capital formation. The DJIA forms and shapes the demand for information provided by a profession of preparers, auditors, and analysts who have similar, common, or licensed education attainments; a certified professional credential is involved as well as a claim toward public responsibility. Just as the economy has changed, so too have the DJIA components changed dozens of times over the years since its inception. At its inception, it included twelve stocks; today it includes thirty, and only one, General Electric, remains from the original group. On its first day, the DJIA closed at 40.94, and by August of that year it was down to 28.48, a 30 percent decline (Gordon, 2000, p. 171). At the end of 2010, the DJIA closed at 11,577. At the trough of its post-2008 period, at the end of February 2009, the index was just above 7000. During a decade-long period of "irrational exuberance" during the 1990s, the DJIA sprinted from a 1990 opening of 1,273 to a December 1999 month-end close of just under 11,500. Indeed, the DJIA and the market capitalizations of bonds and stocks have grown substantially over the period in question and provide background for why the controversy over the purpose of accounting and financial disclosure has become so vibrant and challenging a topic.

This essay identifies and describes episodes in the development of US accounting thought and practice, including events and activities from a time when accounting was based on the content of early popular books and manuals through a period of original regulatory activity involving the development of large railroads, to a period of common law influence up to the current period when codification has been adopted as a central form of organizing accounting thought – that is, wherein accountancy may be seen as a regulated activity with its own form, seeking a type of conceptual coda. The time frame of this chapter concludes at the end of the year in which the Financial Accounting Standards Board (FASB) issued its most recent non-authoritative statement of conceptual guidance, Financial Accounting Concepts Statement No. 8 (September 2010). Over the preceding two-century period, the United States emerged from its infancy as a commercial and industrial nation and a federation of individual states to become demonstrably the most successful sovereign national economic colossus of any era, affecting the lives and livelihood of not only its citizens but also a global community of billions.

And so, what are the important episodes and aspects of accountancy in this period? Is a philosophy of "American pragmatism" in accounting thought an explanatory element in this development? Is a regulatory maxim of "sunshine" a prominent framework as a social remedy between the public and large economic entities that deploy major amounts of capital in the economy? While this essay does not seek to respond specifically to such framing questions, they serve a valuable point from which to begin any consideration of the development of accounting thought during this period.

The notion of "sunshine" or "disclosure" – or as it is more popularly called today, "transparency" – implicitly provides an objective for the discipline, which leads over time to public reporting, beginning in the post–Civil War period as a response to corporate industrialism and continuing to today's global capital sourcing and markets. Accounting itself, however, precedes this emphasis on publicity and was focused principally on stewardship or control over assets, with the information being proprietary to the individual or a limited group of individuals in ownership roles. Broad public participation in capital markets over the period of study has shifted sentiment as to the role of both financial accounting and reporting. As well, the role and identity of the community of practitioners who provide accountancy services and claim the status of a profession has transformed in significant ways. Awareness of how a "sense of purpose" of this group is understood in previous and current political and economic times seems important to the intellectual identity of accountancy as a discipline. For example, the initial legal recognition and licensure of the Certified Public Accountant (CPA) under state law in New York in 1896 fostered a movement that includes similar legislation in all other US states and territories and corollary non-licensed certifications in specialty areas. Until the 1920s, a high school diploma was sufficient to meet the educational requirement, and over the ensuing decades the requirement has changed first to a college degree and now to a post-baccalaureate degree, most commonly a professional fifth-year degree. During this time, the population of CPAs has grown from a handful to fewer than 10,000 at the time of World War II to over 400,000 today. Similar growth in non-licensed certifications, identified prominently with the post-1970s period, has also taken place.

American accountancy thought, 1820–1920: merchants and countinghouses (Cronhelm, Marsh, Bennett, Jones, and Foster)

The purpose of this chapter is to establish a common and dominant set of ideas about what might be identified as stages through which financial accounting and financial reporting developed in the United States. No single attempt can be complete or comprehensive, of course, since no single expression of a complicated past can be told from all points of view at one point in time. The story begins during the early period of the American republic when the physical domain was only beginning to reflect the added geography of the Louisiana Purchase of 1803, which enlarged the dimensions of the nation as a country that was now developing on a major continent. By the 1730s, the activities of the merchant in the American colonies were identified with the "countinghouse" or "compting house," wherein the merchant directed many operations (Previts and Sheldahl, 1977). At the end of the eighteenth century, the focus shifted to the earliest known US published book on accounting, Benjamin Workman's *The American Accountant* (1789).[1] However, since that publication was somewhat of an outlier, a more appropriate starting point is deemed to be 31 years later in the period of "rote" bookkeeping based on double entry. This was a time of pioneering writers such as James Arlington Bennett, who is identified as an early influence due to a visual device, the "balance chart," provided as a fold-out, double-page illustration in his 1820 work, *The American System of Practical Book-Keeping: Adapted to the Commerce of the United States.* The chart is a framework depicting the manner in which debit and credit accounts were kept and the details of the merchant's "leger" of an organization. Pages ix to xi describe the classes of accounts and the "General rules for Dr. and Cr.," identifying those actions for "real accounts," such as, "When a thing becomes mine it is a Dr.; When it costs me any thing it is a Dr.; When it ceases to be mine it is a Cr.; When it brings me in any thing it is a Cr.," and so on. These rules are the basis for the lectures captured in the book and are indicative of the rote guidance, or what might now be called a "rule-based" system, for how to treat transactions in the setting of the mercantile economy of the early American system of business. At the chosen point of departure, Bennett's work is representative of this era of mercantile/proprietary capitalism and is arguably sufficient, but there were many other important authors, including Turner (1804), Sheys (1818), Jackson (1801), Lee (1797), Marsh (1831), and Colt (1838). Scholarly reviews of many of the works of this Mercantile Era are found in the 25-volume set covering the years from 1796 to 1887 edited by Williard E. Stone and published in 1982 in the Yushodo American Historic Accounting Literature Collection. Stone provides an introduction to each of the 25 volumes, placing their content in perspective and adding to the understanding of how early practices were written about and taught throughout the nineteenth century.

"Two-account series" era, proprietary books, and schools

The development of the technical double entry system of transaction accounting in the early nineteenth century permitted accounting activity to be redefined, as the proprietor's counting-house evolved into the office of the business in a more open, albeit still non-public, manner. In particular, Thomas Jones (1841) and his copying-synthesizing contemporary, Benjamin Franklin Foster (1836), are recognized as beginning the period of defining recognition of "primary" and "secondary" accounts, which evolved into the process that differentiates the balance sheet (primary) and income (secondary) statements. In a paper by Henry Rand Hatfield translated from an early German-language writing, Jones' advocacy of the two-account series view of record keeping is identified as predating similar work being undertaken by prominent writers in Germany and Switzerland in the mid-nineteenth century (Homburger and Previts, 1977). This simple but profound distinction in accounts by Thomas Jones of the United States (*Book-keeping and Accountantship*, 1849) and the advocacy of Foster in promoting the notion in propriety textbooks of the time advanced the preparation of balance sheet and income statement forms to support the process of external communication beyond the domain of the individual proprietor. And as Chatfield (1974, p. 72) observes, it was when the preparation of statements became the main purpose of bookkeeping, supplanting the owner's private use of ledger information, that amounts became further "refined to more closely approximate current market prices." The phrase "keeping the books" henceforth would denote an increased expectation for financial statements that resulted from a broader, more publicly responsive thought pattern or, to use a contemporary term, a "framework" as to an expected end product of the accounting process. Bryant, Stratton, and Packard, who were active promoters of early so-called proprietary schools of business, as universities had not yet extended academic recognition to the field, taught the rules or rote of this process and reached not only all the major cities in the United States but also overseas areas, including Japan. The language of "For" and "By" to indicate which account received which entry evidenced the emphasis toward a rote approach to teaching bookkeeping. This was a slight advance from Bennett's "General Rules for Dr. and Cr." of the Mercantile Era.

Algebraic foundations, sunshine, and uniformity (Adams, Sprague, Dickinson, and Hatfield)

Bryant, Stratton, and Packard's texts in the 1860s explicated and advanced these general rules and other notions within the commercial education establishment needed to support the new accounting workforce and to deal with the business and capital market developments instigated by the industrialization of the Civil War and post–Civil War era. Charles Ezra Sprague's four-part series in exposition of "The Algebra of Accounts," first published in *The Book-keeper* in July and August of 1880, presented the beginnings of a proprietary theory by establishing the mnemonic rationale for a *transaction-based accounting* "equation" as a foundation of practice, expressed then as "What I Have + What I Trust = What I Owe + What I am Worth" or "Assets = Liabilities + Proprietorship." A fuller expression of proprietary theory's "conceptual framework," as it would today be called, was Sprague's privately published work, *The Philosophy of Accounts* (1907). As a faculty member of the newly formed School of Commerce, Accounts and Finance of New York University, Sprague was ideally situated to propagate this important intellectual view. His influence was not limited to the commercial center of New York; his *Philosophy* was read by other early accounting academics, including Henry Rand Hatfield and William A. (Bill) Paton, and application and debate about proprietary theory expanded rapidly.

Both Hatfield and Paton provided testaments to this influence in the foreword to the 1922 Ronald Press reprint of Sprague's *Philosophy of Accounts*.

These advances in the stewardship role of accounting and the subsequent developments in reporting within the proprietary view were significantly affected by the expanding network of capital sources beyond the resources of a single capital provider and by the increasing influence of state agencies that began to oversee the numerous corporate entities that were enlarging the industrial base of the economy with their highly scaled activities, with railroads being a prominent example. From the mid-nineteenth century forward, Chatfield (1974, p. 72–73) identified "American Financial Reporting" as being in a nascent stage demonstrating a pronounced liquidity and banker doctrine. In 1894, the predecessor of the American Institute of CPAs (AICPA) adopted a resolution that seems to be the first professional standard; it required that the balance sheet should be presented in order of the quickest realization, thereby achieving a focus of liquidity (AIA, 1938, p. 6). Railroad regulation, notably by state commissions, began to involve matters of public safety, but due to the influence of Charles Francis Adams, Jr., the grandson of one president and the great-grandson of another, the economic impact of these large corporations soon became a focus. Adams, as the head of the Massachusetts Railroad Commission in the years following the War Between the States, prominently championed the concept of full disclosure. He called the concept sunshine, and his agency became known as the Sunshine Commission. Adams called for railroads to report information, including non-financial disclosures that might involve issues of public safety, in a manner that would improve the general public's understanding of the function and performance of these entities. In the ensuing years, Adams marshaled and supported an expanding effort among regulators from many other key states and, as reported in the *New York Times* (November 13, 1878), agitated for a "special committee" to be appointed to consider the subject of accounts and . . . a system of "uniform railroad book-keeping" (Brearey and Previts, 2013).

These efforts eventuated from the growing popular unrest as to the nature of corporations and the belief that disclosure would provide some remedy for concerns by way of informing the general public. Indeed in 1887, upon the establishment of the first major federal regulatory agency, the Interstate Commerce Commission (ICC), the reporting requirements established for interstate carriers followed those developed by the states, resulting in volumes of information prepared and ultimately utilized as the basis for early attempts at security analysis by individuals including Benjamin Graham (Graham, 1986, p. 50). The recognition of such a special role for publicly available information and use of disclosure as a social response and remedy for secretive corporate activity subtly and perhaps silently exists as a fundamental objective of contemporary corporate reporting. "Uniformity" was one of the most desirable aspects of sunshine, a notion that the ICC experimented with throughout the early progressive years of the Woodrow Wilson administration in the twentieth century. The concept of disclosure would be adapted following the writings of Berle and Means in the 1930s (*The Modern Corporation and Private Property*, 1933). The British view of "True and Fair Disclosure" was displaced by the ideal of "Full and Fair Disclosure" to address agency problems once the Securities Acts of the 1930s were enacted.

Contributions of the railroads

Miranti and Goodman point out that the "railroad accounting model" developed in the nineteenth century as a response to the information needs of three groups (1996, p. 487). The first group was management – the railroad managers who utilized cost data to operate the railroads, controlling people and equipment across a wide geographical area in which a close schedule and a single-track system required careful coordination. The second set of users of accounting information were the investors who had provided unprecedented amounts of capital to build the rail lines. This group needed information to evaluate stock and bond investments. Given their outside position, these providers of capital also had to monitor the railroad managers. Finally, railroad accounting was shaped by regulators at the state and national levels, who sought accounting information in order to understand costs and thereby address rates charged for freight and passengers. The railroad accounting model dominated the nineteenth century and influenced capital-intensive industries, such as the steel industry, utilities, and manufacturers, that were seeking capital to develop.

Previts, Samson, and Flesher have extensively examined the US railroads prior to the Civil War for their contributions to the development of accounting and auditing. In a 2000 *Accounting Historians Journal* article, the authors analyzed the content of 25 years of B&O annual reports to trace the development of annual reports, their content, and the evolution of financial statement format (Previts and Samson, 2000). A similar article in 2006 addressed the same issue at the Illinois Central Railroad (Flesher et al., 2006). Papers that explore auditing of American railroads include "The Origins of Value-for-Money Auditing" (Flesher et al., 2003) and "Auditing in the United States: A Historical Perspective" (Previts et al., 2005). These papers examine the use of the audit committee by directors of railroads. The public interest dimension of US railroads was examined in "Accounting, Economic Development and Financial Reporting: The Case of Three Pre-Civil War US Railroads," published in *Accounting History* (Previts et al., 2003). The problems of income measurement of nineteenth-century railroads was examined in "Quality of Earnings: The Case of the Mobile and Ohio Railroad," published in *Issues in Accounting Education* (Samson et al., 2003). In another case, also published in *Issues in Accounting Education*, the authors examined corporate governance and the raising of capital from external investors during the early years (1831) of the B&O Railroad (Samson et al., 2006). In "Reporting for Success," published in *Business and Economic History*, the managerial accounting information developed and utilized during the developmental stage of the B&O is described (Samson and Previts, 1999). This issue is further explored for its cost accounting contributions in "Using Accounting to Manage" in *Accounting and History* (Flesher et al., 2000). In "The First CPAs of 1896–97," published in *Business and Economic History*, Flesher, Previts, and Flesher profiled the early CPAs that started the US accountancy profession, a group that included C. W. Haskins and E. W. Sells, both of whom were former railroad accountants (1996). With respect to financial statements, an article by Rosen and DeCoster (1969) attributed the invention of the cash flow statement to the nineteenth-century railroads. These citations provide examples of railroad innovations, including the format and content of annual reports; the measurement of income with depreciation of long-lived assets becoming not only a theoretical but also a pragmatic issue; the standardization of accounting methods and accounts to aid regulators; the concept of retained earnings being a source of capital; and the use of internal auditors, controllers, audit committees, vouchers, and controls over cash. The managerial accounting concepts of fixed costs and variable costs and the impact of efficiency (throughput) on the profitability of large-scale, capital-intensive businesses were learned at the railroads and later applied in heavy manufacturing. The essence of the preceding articles and others is that the railroads played a major role in the development of accounting in America. Detailed historical study of railroading involving primary archival records as to practice and policy has been a development of recent decades.

Uniform accounts

Seeking uniformity in sunshine reporting began with the railroads following the Civil War and was accepted perhaps because it was deemed as desirable, achievable, and beneficial. Meetings in Columbus, Ohio, and Saratoga, New York, in the 1870s and 1880s led to considerable uniformity among railroads. This pursuit of uniformity was abetted by the passage in 1887 of the Interstate Commerce Commission Act, which later adopted uniform reporting requirements for railroads and other means of transportation. The ICC was influenced by the "Saratoga Classification" of state regulators until 1907, when ICC regulations ended the significance of that classification (Berger, 1947, Ch. XII). Nevertheless, accounting's "framework" – if that is what it is called – continued its trend toward uniformity.

A set of events in the early twentieth century signaled the developing influence of Arthur Lowes Dickinson, head of Price Waterhouse in the United States. In an address to the First World Congress of Accountants in St. Louis in 1904 on the subject of a profit and loss statement, he presented his outline of what was to become the income statement format recommended a decade later as part of a set of uniform information guidelines to be required by banks. In an action taken by the newly initiated Federal Reserve Board (FRB) in the April 1917 *Federal Reserve Bulletin*, the Board members identified the characteristics of Uniform Accounts to be used to guide banks in making financial lending decisions and also as guidance for the Federal Trade Commission in its pursuit of uniform information from corporations regarding managing its mandate to assure a competitive economy. The income statement format found in this release mirrored the profit and loss statement outlined by Dickinson; indeed the disclosures were heavily influenced by his firm in its advice to the FRB (Allen and McDermott, 1993, p. 51).

Uniformity of disclosure to benefit bankers won support, but also contending for importance was the model of annual reporting influenced, if not developed, by George O. May, also of Price Waterhouse & Co., in the reports of United States Steel. The depth and breadth of detail disclosed in these annual reports can be described as iconic. They exemplify, according to Carduff, the stewardship model of reporting, reflecting the view of the Morgan Bank that the first US billion-dollar corporation would best serve its own interests by providing a model for appropriate industrial disclosure (2013). For decades thereafter, until the 1990s when institutional investors firmly and finally displaced individual investors as the principal source of direct equity capital, US Steel was looked to as a leader in such reports.

In the wake of the commercial expansion following World War I, the United States became a global source of capital and Wall Street arguably replaced Lombard Street as the major capital center of the world. The influx of the public or main street investors as capital providers and the exuberant formation of capital on Wall Street during the 1920s, combined with a rapidly maturing community of accounting practitioners directed largely by leaders of the CPA movement, led the discipline of financial accounting to become engaged and then married to the notion of financial reporting – continuing a reality that has been so ever since. The penchant for uniformity in accounting previously alluded to would diminish following the Great Crash of 1929 and the subsequent destabilizing "Ivar Kreuger Crash" of March 1932. The regulation of the capital markets and the introduction of the securities acts into the domain of professional accounting would have untold consequences upon the role of accounting and disclosure (Flesher and Flesher, 1986). The world of financial accounting and reporting was to evolve as a facet of the information age, wherein, as Walter Wriston (1919–2005) observed, "Information about money has become almost as valuable as money itself" (Bass, 1996). Moving into that "age" would not be simple or direct. It would be a series of disconnected episodes, perhaps only discernible to those with the time and perspective to ponder the changes of the past as a prologue.

1920 and after: principles to postulates

Early in his career, William A. Paton included a chapter in his *Accounting Theory* textbook on the basic postulates underlying the structure of accounting (Paton, 1922). Another author, John B.

Canning, in *The Economics of Accountancy*, developed a conceptual framework for asset valuation and measurement based on future expectations (Canning, 1929). The works of both Paton and Canning influenced many future theoreticians (Zeff, 1999, p. 90). An early organizational attempt to develop a conceptual framework for accounting came in 1936, when the American Accounting Association (AAA) published a committee report entitled "Tentative Statement of Accounting Principles Affecting Corporate Reports." The objective of the "Tentative Statement" was to provide the Securities and Exchange Commission (SEC) with guidance regarding what should appear in financial statements. Since the passing of the Securities Acts in the 1930s, there had been pressure for companies to provide more and better publicly available information. There was in the minds of some academic accountants a view that practitioner organizations, such as the American Institute of Accountants (now AICPA), would not want to openly address such guidance. Therefore, the AAA initiated what would become a series of attempts to develop a fuller expression of accounting principles. The objective was to make a tentative declaration of what principles should underlie financial statements without being held back by concerns about conflicting with existing practice. Three main points were contained in the first document, the last two of which were controversial: (1) transactions were to be recorded at historical cost and not at "value"; (2) the all-inclusive concept should be used in the preparation of the income statement rather than the current operating view, which excluded non-recurring and similar items from income statements; and (3) there should be a distinction between paid-in capital and retained earnings. The 1936 document was revised in 1941, 1948, and 1957. The first two revisions were based upon the historical cost principle, matching, and existing practice, and represented little change from the 1936 pronouncement. The 1957 revision, however, deviated from established practice and was not widely accepted. The 1957 version introduced the term "standards" in place of the word "principles" that had been used in 1936 and 1941 and "concepts" that had been used in 1948. The 1957 pronouncement also recommended some form of price-level adjustments – a controversial position.

Sanders, Hatfield, and Moore: Statement of Accounting Principles

The 1936 AAA "Tentative Statement" was followed in 1938 by a publication authored by Thomas H. Sanders, Henry Rand Hatfield, and Underhill Moore entitled *A Statement of Accounting Principles*. This too was designed to provide guidance to the new SEC. The American Institute of Certified Public Accountants and the predecessor firm of today's Deloitte sponsored the project. It was a survey of "what was being done" in practice intended to provide authoritative guidance about existing practice, as opposed to the AAA pronouncement that had offered a more normative view, including suggestions for improved reporting. Together these documents constituted an early example of positive versus normative thought developments. To say that the 1938 volume represented a conceptual framework would be true only to the extent that current practice represented the conceptual framework.

John R. Wildman, who had been the first president of the American Accounting Association in 1916, was by then a Haskins & Sells partner and New York University professor who was closely associated with the development of *The Statement of Accounting Principles*. Arthur Foye, a future managing partner of the firm, noted that when the

> Haskins & Sells Foundation projected *The Statement of Accounting Principles* in July, 1935, Mr. Wildman through his knowledge of and acquaintance with distinguished educators arranged for Professor Thomas H. Sanders . . . and Professor Henry Rand Hatfield . . . to be two of the three independent authorities.
>
> *(Previts and Taylor, 1978)*

Regarding Wildman's role in the project, Sanders added:

> The work which the Foundation has entrusted to the committee has required frequent and intimate association between Mr. Wildman and myself. Although I have for years known and admired his ability and character . . . I have been constantly surprised by his penetration, understanding and unfailing sound judgment.
>
> *(Previts and Taylor, 1978)*

Studies of contemporary and acceptable accounting principles seemed to gain attention during the years of the Great Depression. Previously, accounting reports had been used by internal management and outside investors and creditors. But with the establishment of the SEC in 1934, the role of general-purpose financial statements became broader. Accountants preparing financial statements were to produce statements that achieved full and fair disclosure, a more common-law objective than the prescriptive uniformity of an earlier era. All of this was now subject to federal law. The writings of George O. May, arguably one of the most influential accountants of his age, in 1943 suggested at least ten major uses of financial statements, many of which could not be achieved by general purpose statements (May, 1943). A perceived violation of generally accepted accounting principles in such disclosures could have dire results. In addition, the federal government's increasing role in regulation in all areas of the economy under President Franklin D. Roosevelt led to more emphasis on financial statements.

The Haskins & Sells Foundation and John Wildman recognized that need by funding the research of Sanders, Hatfield, and Moore. The Foundation urged the authors to observe accounting practice and identify a body of principles that could become useful in unifying thought and helping to standardize practice. It was stated by the Foundation:

> The need for the kind of study suggested has become increasingly apparent, particularly during the past three years. Sharp variations among the statutes of the different jurisdictions have existed for some time. These statutes collectively are not only inconsistent and contradictory, but in some instances they permit practices which are difficult to reconcile with dutiful business management. Federal agencies have issued regulations involving accounting principles which have resulted in contradiction between agencies, and federal regulations involving such matters conflict frequently with those of state regulatory bodies. The stock exchanges in their efforts to promote greater publicity of corporate financial information, the federal government in its administration of the Securities Act of 1933, as amended, designed to afford adequate disclosure with respect to new issues of securities, and through the Securities Exchange Act to insure the same information to the holders of and prospective investors in listed securities, have raised sharply the question as to what are accepted principles of accounting. Notwithstanding the difficulties involved, accountants who certify to financial statements filed with the Securities and Exchange Commission have been required by the regulations of that Commission to express an opinion concerning such financial statements and the practices of the registrant in the light of accepted principles of accounting.
>
> *(Foye, 1970, pp. 87–88)*

The three authors saw their assignment as a rational identification and classification of current accounting practice rather than as a re-examination of any specific practices. Thus, the published volume represented an extensive inventory that would become an uncritical acceptance of existing accounting methods. Copies of the final report (116 pages, plus 22 pages of notes regarding legal provisions of concern to accountants) were distributed in 1938 to all members of the American Institute of Accountants. In 1970, Foye summarized the volume in the following words:

> It was clearly a broad-based and logical approach, new to the field of accountancy literature and uniquely valuable to the profession. Coupled with the merits of their research method, the acknowledged competence and impartiality of the Committee members gave to *A Statement of Accounting Principles* persuasiveness and weight never previously enjoyed by any pronouncement of comprehensive scope in the annals of accountancy. The book has been widely quoted by courts and commissions and by writers on accounting subjects generally. Without doubt judicial and other governmental authorities, as well as bankers, other business executives, and investors, derived from it a better understanding of the unwisdom of trying to oversimplify some of the inherent complexities of accounting. To many such persons the report made it clearer than before that accounting is far from being an exact science.
>
> *(Foye, 1970, p. 88)*

The volume was reprinted by the American Accounting Association in 1959. This episode occurred during the first years when the identification of a body of authoritative accounting principles, known as generally accepted accounting principles (GAAP), was beginning. Thus, the Sanders, Hatfield, and Moore volume was a pioneer study activity of a positive nature attempting to inform the establishment of GAAP.

As the economy transitioned from economic emergency to the war effort, Victor H. Stempf of Touche, Niven & Co., while serving as president of the American Institute in 1944, provided his view of the growing and essential importance of accounting:

> With startling speed, particularly during the last two decades, accounting has become a potent social force in the interpretation, direction, and control of our evolving national economy. As the government has extended its control and supervision over economic activities, it has become more and more apparent that accounting is an important instrument of regulation. It has clearly demonstrated its value as a management device under a free-enterprise system. It is equally evident that it will continue to be of great importance under any system of relationship between government and business. Through one emergency after another it has manifested its ability to meet new tasks and new conditions promptly and satisfactorily.
>
> *(Stempf, August 1944, p. 102)*

The theoretical background and framework of such a "potent social force" requires study to guide whatever may be proposed to regulate or oversee it.

Paton and Littleton

Also during this era, in 1940, the AAA published a monograph that proved to be highly influential – Paton and Littleton's *An Introduction to Corporate Accounting Standards*. The Paton and Littleton volume was income statement oriented and presented a strong rationalization of the historical cost and matching principles that were becoming widely used. Because of the academic renown of the authors, the monograph was widely used in college classrooms, and it popularized and perpetuated historical cost as a value measure. According to Accounting Hall of Fame member Reed K. Storey, the Paton and Littleton monograph had its major impact on accounting practice because it was so widely used in classrooms and because its two signature principles found their way into nearly all textbooks. Generations of students were directly or indirectly influenced by Paton and Littleton's writing as a gospel for accountants. It was this gospel, Storey noted, to which the early members of the Financial Accounting Standards Board (FASB) had been exposed during the 1970s. Thus, regardless of the changing environment, especially as to capital sourcing where institutional investors supplanted individual/retail investors, the early Board members were often unwilling to vary from the historical cost principle and the concept of matching revenues and expenses (Storey, 1999).

The post–World War II era

In the late 1940s and into the 1950s, disagreements arose over several controversial issues in accounting. Inflation following World War II led some accountants to argue that current costs or price-level adjusted figures should be shown in the financial statements. Furthermore, the treatment of deferred taxes and the reporting of extraordinary and unusual items did not seem to fit with the accepted concepts of the time. The environment was changing, and the concepts of the 1930s and 1940s did not always seem applicable. In 1958, AICPA president Alvin R. Jennings sought the establishment of an entity to conduct research on basic accounting concepts, and the managing partner of Arthur Andersen & Co., Leonard Spacek, publicly criticized the profession for not establishing the premises upon which accounting standards were based. The result was the establishment of the Accounting Principles Board (APB) in 1959 to replace the previous, initial authoritative body, the Committee on Accounting Procedure (CAP). CAP had been hastily assembled in the late 1930s in an opportunistic response to the SEC's Accounting Series Release No. 4, which recognized that efforts by such a group would constitute "substantive authoritative support" as to the basis of acceptable principles. Unfortunately, most of the CAP's efforts over its 20-year lifespan were directed at narrow issues and were never based on a conceptual framework of any kind.

In response to Jenning's efforts, respected professor Maurice Moonitz of the University of California at Berkeley was hired by the AICPA as Director of Accounting Research. Moonitz took it upon himself to write a research study, *The Basic Postulates of Accounting*, which was published in 1961 as the APB's Accounting Research Study No. 1. From the contents, readers could not discern whether Moonitz was supporting historical cost or some other basis of valuation, and there was criticism that the study was too vague and unrelated to practice.

In 1962, Moonitz joined with future FASB charter member Robert T. Sprouse to conduct a follow-up study that was published as APB Accounting Research Study No. 3 under the title *A Tentative Set of Broad Accounting Principles for Business Enterprises*. Based on Moonitz's earlier postulates, Moonitz and Sprouse argued for greater use of current values in accounting and less reliance on the realization concept. The use of discounted present values for receivables and payables was also advocated, which was a little-known concept in 1962. Accounting Research Study No. 3 was thought to be too radical, and the work was not well received in the practice community.

> Moonitz and Sprouse had thought their assignment was to develop a rational argument for a sound approach to financial reporting. Most members of the APB and other leaders of the accounting profession, by contrast, looked upon basic research as an instrument for rationalizing the *status quo* (in the tradition of the Paton and Littleton monograph), rather than as a normative argument for fundamental change in accounting. Above all, the SEC was at that time a conservative regulator, which regarded departures from the "objectivity" of historical cost accounting as possessing the potential to deceive the readers of financial

statements. In the 1960s, the SEC saw its mission chiefly as one of guarding against misleading financial statements rather than of improving the information content of the statements. As a result of the APB's rejection of the postulates and principles studies, the cause of basic accounting research as a foundation stone for pronouncements on specific subjects suffered a severe setback, and the board instead began to deal with specific issues, much as had the CAP before it, without a body of underlying concepts on which to draw.

(Zeff, 1999, pp. 94–95)

The APB issued two additional publications relating to accounting concepts. In 1965, Accounting Research Study No. 5, by retired Price Waterhouse partner Paul Grady, was issued under the title *Inventory of Generally Accepted Accounting Principles for Business Enterprises*. As in the case of the 1938 Sanders, Hatfield, and Moore monograph, Grady felt that theoretical explanations should be derived inductively from observing existing practice (Zeff, 1999, p. 95). Grady did show how concepts were included in current practice, but his study offered little that sought to improve practice. Accounting Research Study No. 5 was, however, a popular resource in other countries where individuals were seeking a catalogue of then current US practices; it sold briskly for many years after its publication.

In 1964 and 1965, the APB was under attack because of the debacle that arose over its issuance of Opinions No. 2 and No. 4 on the investment tax credit. The AICPA Council formed a special committee chaired by J. S. Seidman to (1) review the status of APB opinions and (2) assess the development of accounting standards. In May 1965, the Seidman Committee reported on its second charge with the recommendation that there should be an authoritative identification of generally accepted accounting principles and that the APB should

1   Set forth the purposes and limitations of published financial statements;
2   Enumerate and describe the basic concepts that accounting principles should follow; and
3   Define the key terms used in the profession.

In 1970, in response to the Seidman Committee, the APB issued Statement No. 4, entitled *Basic Concepts and Accounting Principles Underlying Financial Statements of Business Enterprises*. Statement No. 4 was not an authoritatively required document and was often described as a disappointment since it provided little guidance for the future development of accounting principles. Reed Storey stated that the APB "gave every indication of having issued it primarily to comply, somewhat grudgingly, with the Seidman Committee's recommendations" (Storey, 1999, pp. 2-28).

As global influences began to make themselves felt in the post–World War II era, one particular group of scholars, headed up by Foundation Chair Professor of Accounting Ray Chambers at the University of Sydney (an indelible influence on the reputation of what has come to be called the Sydney School of Accounting), made itself known. By the early 1970s, Chambers was a regular visitor at leading American universities, lecturing about the intrinsic superiority of what he had identified as "continuously contemporaneous accounting," also called COCOA or exit-price value measurement. Chambers debated and argued effectively in the domain of historical cost and matching communities, and long before it became better known due to the efforts of others in the late twentieth and early twenty-first centuries, Chambers remained an ardent supporter of COCOA. His success, however, was limited to being recognized as a superior theorist while few converts were found in practice. Nevertheless, the stage was set for more debate, and his influence continues to be recognized and felt despite his retirement in 1982 and his death in 1999 (Clarke et al., 2012). Indeed, the influence of Chambers and his association with Robert Sterling and Stephen Zeff culminated in many important intellectual activities and papers, particularly during the period of debates involving the appropriate accounting for the difficult inflationary period of the 1980s in the United States.

ASOBAT and SATTA

In 1966, a committee of the AAA chaired by Charles T. Zlatkovich published a monograph entitled *A Statement of Basic Accounting Theory* (*ASOBAT*). *ASOBAT* was based on supporting the objective of decision usefulness, which had been identified and promoted in an *Accounting Review* paper by H. Justin Davidson and Robert Trueblood in 1961 (p. 582). Their thesis promoted the integration of stewardship and decision making. *ASOBAT* defined accounting as "the process of identifying, measuring, and communicating economic information to permit informed judgments and decisions by users of the information" (AAA, 1966, p. 1). In other words, the emphasis was not on stewardship but on information that would benefit decision making regarding the future by users of financial statements. Besides the emphasis on decision usefulness, *ASOBAT* also argued in favor of a dual reporting system wherein both historical costs and current values would be reported. Stephen Zeff later called *ASOBAT* "one of the most important studies ever issued by the Association, both in terms of impact on the literature and on standard setting" (Zeff, 1991). *ASOBAT* was widely distributed; all members of the AAA received a free copy, and an additional 9,000 copies were printed to be sold to non-member practitioners. If Zeff's evaluation is correct, it is telling because the emphasis on decision making would have significant conceptual design implications for the future of accounting and the search for guidance and the development of frameworks.

Decision making is, after all, an idiosyncratic function, one that, like leadership, is unique to individuals and tempered by their values and experiences; decision making falls under the classic "black-box" term, *judgment*. Further, in the American business system, pragmatism, not merely of a make-a-buck nature but of a more deeply philosophical nature, as captured in the writings of John Dewey and others associated with the academy, would now require consideration. It would be more than a decade before another academic committee would attempt to sort through the philosophical implications of such an "integration" of stewardship and decision making. Richard Mattessich once pointed out the role of the scientific method to one of the authors of this essay as to resolving such intellectual challenges. He noted the writings of P. W. Bridgman, the 1946 Nobel Laureate in Physics, who had taken part in the project that resulted in the discovery of atomic energy and the weapon it created. Bridgman noted: "The scientific method, as far as it is a method, is nothing more than doing one's damnedest with one's mind, no holds barred" (1945). Bridgman's admonition suggests a form of American pragmatism that is not in conformity with a rigid structure of research observing merely logical consistency or similar forms of positive or normative influences.

However, adherence to the norms of logic and science seems evident in the 1977 AAA *Statement on Accounting Theory and Theory Acceptance* (*SATTA*). The committee's charge, developed in 1973, was to prepare a statement that would provide the same type of survey of current thinking on accounting theory as *ASOBAT* had done in 1966. However, the committee was unable to align the various schools of thought identified in the literature. It never directly addressed the philosophical aspects of accounting theory, including the implications of pragmatic decision making and accounting judgments. *SATTA* was, however, a useful summary and digest of the major legacy views of positive and negative epistemologies and of the recently developed information economics. However, the committee could not achieve the consensus needed to address theoretical problems facing accounting, leading to a view that under these circumstances a disparate appointed committee was ill suited to conduct research (AAA, 1977, p. 49). Hakansson summarized the contributions of *SATTA* as follows:

> It does bring a number of seemingly disparate threads together in a way which is, on balance, helpful. It reflects faithfully the recent broadening of the accounting horizon and the gradual lifting of scholarly standards that is currently in motion. It suggests, if only indirectly, that careful attention to less ambitious slices of the accounting problem is essential to further progress.
>
> *(Hakansson, 1978, p. 724)*

The Trueblood Committee

The AICPA's Study Group on the Objectives of Financial Statements, better known as the Trueblood Committee, issued its report in October 1973. The Trueblood Committee was formed by the AICPA in 1971 at the same time that the Wheat Committee was established to consider the institutional process by which authoritative pronouncements were to be undertaken in the wake of the demise of confidence in the Accounting Principles Board and the Supreme Court decision in the Continental Vending case. The Trueblood Committee was composed of practitioners, academics, and users of financial statements. The chairman, Robert Trueblood, was a practitioner and professional leader who had coauthored the 1961 *Accounting Review* article on "decision usefulness." The charge to the committee was to determine the objectives of financial statements. George H. Sorter, a professor at the University of Chicago, was appointed the research director of the Trueblood Committee. Sorter had been a member of the AAA *ASOBAT* Committee. Both Trueblood and Sorter were influential in orienting the committee toward the decision-usefulness concept. The origin of the decision-usefulness concept, which now has been adopted as a central objective, is attributed to former FASB director of research George Staubus, who developed the concept in his 1954 University of Chicago dissertation and in later articles in *The Accounting Review*. Sorter had also studied at the University of Chicago and while there had read Staubus' work (Staubus, 2003, pp. 165–166). Sorter had also reviewed Staubus' 1961 book on the subject (*A Theory of Accounting to Investors* [Staubus, 1961; Sorter, 1963]). Because of these prior exposures, the articulate Sorter was able to convince both the *ASOBAT* Committee and the Trueblood Committee of the importance of emphasizing the needs of the growing community of what today is known as institutional investors. The Trueblood report, entitled *Objectives of Financial Statements*, focused on future cash flows. Yet a key audience for financial statements was also viewed as "those users who have limited authority, ability, or resources to obtain information and who rely on financial statements as their principal source of information about an enterprise's economic activities" (*Objectives . . .* , 1973, p. 17). The basic emphasis was on investors and creditors, but employees were also included in the definition of users.

As with *ASOBAT*, the Trueblood report enumerated qualitative characteristics of financial reporting and concluded that a single valuation basis was not sufficient in the preparation of effective financial statements; mixed attributes were necessary. Several valuation bases were recommended and examples given of when each basis would be relevant. There was also a suggestion that measurements in terms of single numbers that do not include ranges do not effectively describe events that are subject to uncertainty. Ranges of precision and reliability should be included in the financial statements. The Trueblood report also advocated a form of social reporting (*Objectives . . .* , 1973, pp. 54–55). The Trueblood report was forward thinking, identified departures from past accounting practice, and would serve as a model for future FASB activities. It was based to some extent on previous conceptual studies by the AAA and APB, but it was not tied to any of the predecessor pronouncements entirely. Zeff summarized the Trueblood Committee's work as follows:

> The Trueblood report was remarkable for the freshness of its approach. It did much to refocus discussions in the accounting policy arena from stewardship reporting to providing information useful for decision makers. The report became a kind of blueprint for the conceptual framework project that the newly established FASB was just beginning.
>
> *(Zeff, 1999, p. 101)*

Unfortunately, there was one paragraph near the end of the Trueblood report that, while connecting with the future FASB Concepts Statements, was not a positive attribute:

> Members of the Study Group disagree on whether value changes . . . should be included in earnings. Some believe the objective should be to reflect current value changes in earnings. Others believe that inclusion of unrealized value changes in earnings may be desirable but is not now practicable. Still others believe that their inclusion is neither desirable nor practicable.
>
> *(Objectives . . . , 1973, p. 64)*

The above paragraph would foretell much of the debate that the FASB would undertake in the ensuing decades.

The FASB conceptual framework

When the FASB began operations in 1973, the Board considered twenty-seven initial agenda items, but it quickly decided to pursue only seven. Of those seven, two could be considered elements of what later came to be called the conceptual framework project.[2] One of these two projects was initially called "broad qualitative standards for financial reporting" and the other was "materiality." Nothing ever came of the materiality project, but there were ten paragraphs on the subject in the second Concepts Statement issued in 1980. It was the "broad qualitative standards" project that subsequently, in late 1973, came to be known as the conceptual framework project. The purpose of the project was to set forth fundamentals upon which financial accounting and reporting standards were to be based. According to the introduction to the first statement, the "Concepts are intended to establish the objectives and concepts that the Financial Accounting Standards Board will use in developing standards of financial accounting and reporting" (SFAC No. 1, FASB, 1978, p. i). The introduction went on to say that the Board itself was likely to be the major user and most direct beneficiary of the guidance provided in the series of publications. Nevertheless, all individuals affected by financial accounting standards were foreseen to benefit to some extent from the conceptual framework. It was also noted that Concepts Statements were not GAAP, and therefore accountants did not have to comply with the ideas expressed in the Concepts Statements. When something in a Concepts Statement was inconsistent with current standards, accountants were not to deviate from the standards currently in place (SFAC No. 1, FASB, 1978, p. ii).

The objectives of the conceptual framework project did not include resolving accounting issues but were intended to set the stage for solving such problems in the future. Marshall Armstrong, the FASB's first chairman, stated in 1976:

> The conceptual framework project will lead to definitive pronouncements on which the Board intends to rely in establishing financial accounting and reporting standards . . . . Though the framework cannot and should not be made so detailed as to provide automatically an accounting answer to a set of financial facts, it will determine bounds for judgment.

Reed Storey, an FASB staff member who became extensively engaged in the project, later wrote:

> The Board undertook the self-imposed task of providing accounting with an underlying philosophy because Board members had concluded that to discharge their standards-setting responsibilities properly they needed a set of fundamental accounting concepts for their own guidance in resolving issues brought before the Board.
>
> *(Storey, 1999, pp. 1–47)*

Has this happened? One study conducted after the issuance of the sixth Concepts Statement found that of several standards approved after the completion of the project, none were entirely consistent with the framework. This disconnect was attributed to the fact that the conceptual framework did not take into account the social and political environment in which standards are promulgated (Gore, 1992).

In many people's minds, a conceptual framework for accounting was needed, if for no other reason than that accountants had never agreed on the objectives of financial reporting. As attractive as a conceptual framework sounds in theory, there are critics who charge that the FASB framework is not useful. For example, writing in 1987, Dale Gerboth, then a partner with Arthur Young & Company and a former AICPA and FASB staff member, concluded:

> For better or for worse, the accounting profession seems irrevocably committed to under-girding its standards with the strongest – or at least the most expensive – methodological foundation that money can buy. Yet, as the dust settles around what seems to be the completed conceptual framework, there is an unmistakable sense of disappointment with what the profession got for its money. Lee Seidler spoke for many when he dismissed the draft of what later became FASB Concepts Statement No. 5 as "doing nothing but consuming paper and words." Not a few among Seidler's fellow accountants would apply that description to the conceptual framework as a whole.
>
> *(Gerboth, 1987, p. 1)*

Actually, Seidler blamed the problems on the fact that there were no conceptual frameworks in the social sciences and felt that the FASB was ignorant to think that one could be developed.

Despite the objections to a conceptual framework, the majority of accountants were initially supportive of such an undertaking by the FASB (as they had been in earlier years with earlier standard-setting bodies). Given that the conceptual framework project was implemented for the benefit of the Board itself, it might not be relevant that outsiders have been critical; only the Board members themselves are in a position to know whether the framework has accomplished the purposes that were set out for it. The views of Donald Kirk, a former FASB chairman and partner at PWC, were perhaps typical of other Board members; he stated after leaving the Board:

> I accepted the conceptual framework project in the early years on faith. It was faith in the belief that something needed to be done beyond just the structural changes that had resulted in the independent, full-time FASB. If the development of objectives of financial statements, definitions of the elements thereof, and other concepts would help show the way by logical deduction to sound and consistent standards, I was all for it.
>
> *(Kirk, 1988, p. 12)*

Over time, the conceptual framework also has raised issues regarding pedagogical coverage and consistency. Intermediate accounting textbooks typically include a chapter or major section on concepts. However, one early study on how widespread the teaching of the framework was concluded that coverage in intermediate accounting classes was superficial and that Concepts Statements No. 1 and No. 2 were covered more often than were the later statements. Apparently, time limitations are one of the reasons that the concepts are not always taught; those instructors who had more class hours available for intermediate accounting (in excess of six semester hours for the subject) were more apt to teach the concepts (Smith, 1986).

The conceptual framework has been widely noticed by other standard-setting organizations throughout the world. Because of the efforts of the FASB, standard-setting bodies in other countries, including the International Accounting Standards Committee, implemented similar projects. In some cases, the FASB framework was adopted with little modification (Beresford, 1998, p. 159). However, one could question whether this was a good thing, given that the cultural complications of the conceptual framework in the United States was likely to differ from the political and economic environment and traditions in other nations.

The efforts to establish the conceptual framework has had an impact on the FASB. In the early years, acceptance of the need for a framework made for slower progress on standards until some consensus was reached; later it was slowed by the time that the Board was forced to devote to the framework project. The amount of Board and staff time spent on the Concepts Statements was considerable. Van Riper estimated that in the early 1980s the technical staff spent 40 percent of its time on the conceptual framework (1994, p. 81). As Britain's Edward Stamp pointed out in a 1983 interview, "The U.S. Supreme Court doesn't realize how lucky it is that it was given a Constitution by the founding fathers instead of having to frame one of its own" (Stamp, 1984, p. S3). The efforts of the *SATTA* developers and the Trueblood Committee were considerable, but the result was not a [fully formed] conceptual framework of accounting.

The FASB Concepts Statements

Through the end of 2012, the FASB has issued eight Concepts Statements. Together, these statements comprise the conceptual framework of financial accounting. One of these, No. 4, deals with not-for-profit entities; the remainder are considered below. The FASB issued its first publication associated with the conceptual framework project in mid-1974 in the form of a Discussion Memorandum. However, that memorandum was little more than a reprint of the 1973 report of the Trueblood Study Group (Van Riper, 1994, p. 20). The first formal Concepts Statement was published in 1978, followed by five others through the end of 1985. The seventh statement was issued in February 2000 and the eighth in September 2010.

Concepts Statement No. 1: Objectives of Financial Reporting

Five years after it was founded, the FASB finally decided upon the objectives of financial reporting. The first Statement of Financial Accounting Concepts (SFAC), entitled *Objectives of Financial Reporting by Business Enterprises,* was issued in November 1978. The pronouncement had been preceded by a Discussion Memorandum in June 1974 and a public hearing in September 1974. It was over two years later, in December 1976, that the Board issued an analysis of the public hearing under the title *Tentative Conclusions on Objectives of Financial Statements of Business Enterprises.* Another public hearing followed in June 1977.

SFAC No. 1 included the following two basic elements, which had also appeared in the Trueblood Report:

1   Financial reporting should provide information that is useful to present and potential inves-
     tors and creditors and other users in making rational investment, credit, and similar decisions.
     The information should be comprehensible to those who have a reasonable understanding
     of business and economic activities and are willing to study the information with reasonable
     diligence.
2   Financial reporting should provide information to help present and potential investors and
     creditors and other users in assessing the amounts, timing, and uncertainty of prospective cash
     receipts from dividends or interest and the proceeds from the sale, redemption, or maturity of
     securities or loans.

Thus, the target audience is present and potential investors and creditors, who have a reasonable
understanding of business; the information presented should help that audience assess future
cash flows from their investments. The specific identity of an investor, however, was likely
to be itself a matter of later dispute, as the idea of "user needs" prevailed in determining the
content of disclosures. Publicly available equity capital sourcing information for recent years
suggests that direct investment funds from individual/retail investors are declining rapidly. To
some, this could signal a shift in "user needs." Since investors' and creditors' cash flows are
related to enterprise cash flows, financial reporting should provide information to help investors, creditors, and others assess the amounts, timing, and uncertainty of prospective net cash
inflows to the enterprise. Also, SFAC No. 1 stated that financial reporting should provide information about the economic resources of an enterprise, the claims to those resources, and the
effects of transactions, events, and circumstances on the resources and claims to those resources.
"Investors" and "creditors" were terms that were used broadly and included not only those
who have or contemplate having a claim to enterprise resources, but also those who advise
or represent them. Although investment and credit decisions reflect expectations about future
enterprise performance, those expectations are commonly based at least partly on evaluations
of past enterprise performance. The primary focus of financial reporting is information about
earnings and its components. Information about enterprise earnings based on accrual accounting generally provides a better indication of an enterprise's present and continuing ability to
generate favorable cash flows than information limited to the financial effects of cash receipts
and payments. Unlike the Trueblood Report, SFAC No. 1 did not address the wider role of
financial reporting, including such elements as social reporting. Broader social issues as a whole,
beyond entity economic operations, were not seen by the Board as meeting the definition of a
need for users of financial statements.

     As straightforward as the first statement's contents seem to have been, there was not universal
agreement on those objectives among the Board's constituency, which explains in part why
SFAC No. 1 was slow to come to fruition. According to Chairman Marshall Armstrong, there
was little agreement among surveyed constituents on the provision that "the basic objective of
financial statements is to provide information useful for making economic decisions." This was
taken word for word from the Trueblood Report, but less than 40 percent of surveyed respondents were in agreement. For those who objected, the primary view was that the basic function
of financial statements was to report on management's stewardship of corporate assets and the
information needs of investors were secondary (Armstrong, 1977, p. 77). Many of those who
objected were managers, while the supporters were investors or their representatives. Auditors,
too, would have been opposed to a wider audience for financial statements, since that might
be accompanied by greater exposure to the risk of litigation without any corresponding benefits to the audit firm (Dopuch and Sunder, 1980). Overall, about 10 percent of the comment
letters were from academics, just under 10 percent from public accountants, about 20 percent

from banks and other financial institutions, and the remainder from industry preparers. Many accountants were strongly aligned with the importance of the stewardship function, which was fundamental to what they had learned in college, and were not ready to accept a decision-usefulness objective for accounting, especially if it was seen as being superior to stewardship and meant shifting away from the matching concept and the message of the income statement.

The opposition to the decision-usefulness concept was well organized under the leadership of Robert K. Mautz of Ernst & Ernst. Mautz was on the FASB's Conceptual Framework Task Force and had access to all materials being developed. He and his firm were fully supported by the Financial Executives Institute. The reason for opposition was the fear that the acceptance of decision usefulness as an objective would lead to the adoption of current value accounting and a balance sheet focus to reporting. If that happened, management could lose its discretion over earnings, the management of which was of importance to their own performance evaluations. Managers might be less able to select from choices about historical cost values and convert them into realized gains or losses as the need arose. Managers, critics charged, did not care about the needs of investors; they were most concerned with reporting that would reflect positively on their own careers. Mautz and his firm's position coincided with that of the management teams of their clients (Staubus, 2003, p. 184). Their opposition slowed the process, but gradually a decision-usefulness orientation prevailed. Recently, in a letter to former FASB chairman Donald Kirk, George Staubus opined that "I still think that that period when it stood up to fierce resistance from Bob Mautz, Ernst & Ernst, and the FEI was the Board's finest hour" (Staubus, November 15, 2009). Given the consolidation of capital providers that occurred in the wake of the Financial Modernization Act of 1999, wherein investment banks, commercial banks, insurance companies, mutual funds, and other capital sources were able to combine into single powerful capital provider entities, and when liquidity would once again become a focus, the decision usefulness that would prevail would be dictated by the "golden rule" of capital markets, namely, "Those who have the gold (i.e., capital) set the rules." Oversight of the FASB would evolve toward representation by institutional investors and bankers as the Financial Accounting Foundation became increasingly represented not by auditors or preparers but by capital providers. But this was an episode yet to come, many years in the future. What SFAC No. 1 was to represent in that coming period would be a shift from the primacy of the income statement and the process of matching to a twenty-first-century focus on the balance sheet once again as the principal financial statement, with income being measured not in Patonian matching terms but in Hicksian terms, namely determining how much "better off" a business would be between the beginning and the end of the measurement period in value terms.

Don Kirk's views regarding the delays in issuing SFAC No. 1 related that an objection to an emphasis on the decision needs of investors and other external users was also seen as a defense against current value accounting and in support of historical cost and matching. Kirk went on to conclude:

> With hindsight, most observers will think the Objectives Concepts Statement says the obvious, but at the time it was not widely accepted to acknowledge the preeminence of external users in the determination of accounting standards. Some of the opposition was blunted when the Board accepted the suggestion that it focus on the objectives of financial reporting, not just financial statements. It was thought by this broadening that, as under the securities laws, the needs of users could be satisfied through disclosures, possibly even separate from the financial statements, and, therefore, not require the type of income measurement changes that opponents feared.
>
> *(Kirk, 1988, p. 13)*

SFAC No. 1 did make official what audience the Board, and preparers of financial statements, was addressing – namely external users. According to most sources, the objectives in SFAC No. 1 have been highly influential in the setting of accounting standards. A necessary and fundamental criticism was the amount of time it took for SFAC No. 1 to come to fruition and the costs involved, given that the FASB had the benefit of the work previously done by the Trueblood Committee. According to Reed Storey:

> It may be unfortunate that it took five years and substantial cash for FASB to get the objectives accepted, but that's the way the real world works. *Changing peoples' minds takes time* [emphasis added]. When you consider that acceptance of the objectives involved reversing long-held attitudes, five years is not so long. Rather than a basis for criticism, those five years practically produced a miracle.
>
> *(1981)*

Even the Business Roundtable, a group that was pervasively critical of the FASB, had few criticisms of SFAC No. 1. In a background paper prepared by staff at General Motors, the members of the Business Roundtable were told that "Statement #1 is so broadly written that little quarrel can be taken with its general comments and conclusions" (Smith, March 29, 1982). However, later in the same year, members of a Business Roundtable task force seemingly did object to some of the objectives in SFAC No. 1.

Today, many years after its adoption, parts of SFAC No. 1 remain the subject of debate. In fact, it was superseded by SFAC No. 8 in September 2010. Former Board member David Mosso, who served on the Board when the first six Concepts Statements were approved, recently made the following statement with respect to the contents of SFAC No. 1:

> Those are good objectives, but they are too broad to give sharp focus to an accounting system suitable for twenty-first century economies. At the time they were adopted, those broad objectives were ground breaking and forward looking. They turned the GAAP model away from the then prevalent stewardship notion of accounting and re-oriented it toward economic decision making. The objectives paved the way for many subsequent improvements in GAAP. But they were not strong enough to be translated into a coherent accounting model with consistent recognition criteria and a single measurement method – they left us with vague recognition criteria and multiple measurement methods, in short, a choice-based model.
>
> *(Mosso, 2009b)*

Mosso's intent when stating the above was to point out that the Concepts Statements do not support fair value accounting, which he observes to be a weakness of all of the Concepts Statements.

Concepts Statement No. 2: Qualitative Characteristics

In May 1980, a year and a half after the issuance of the first Concepts Statement, the FASB issued Concepts Statement No. 2, entitled *Qualitative Characteristics of Accounting Information*. Much of the work of developing SFAC No. 2 was contributed by David Solomons, an accounting professor at the University of Pennsylvania. Solomons believed strongly that neutrality was central to the effectiveness of the standard-setting process. Decision usefulness was also accepted as a major goal of SFAC No. 2, with emphasis on the qualitative elements of relevance, reliability, and comparability.

SFAC No. 2 was perhaps the least controversial of the Concepts Statements because, according to past Board Chairman Donald Kirk, "readers did not see implications that portended current value accounting" (1988, p. 13). Also, the clarity of SFAC No. 2, largely attributed to Solomons, made it less controversial. The criticisms that did arise included the fact that the idea of decision usefulness was so vaguely stated as to be of little practical use (Sweeney and Yaari, 1998, p. 42). David Mosso, who was, as noted above, involved with the first six Concepts Statements, did not object to SFAC No. 2, but neither did he applaud it. He stated that he was supportive because he thought that it brought a "good bit of order to the GAAP accounting model. It was the best we could do at the time and I am a believer in moving forward as long as there is a net gain" (Mosso, 2009c). He explained his current views as follows:

> The framework implicitly endorsed alternative methods by devoting one whole concepts statement, CON 2, to so-called qualitative characteristics: " . . . the qualities to be sought when accounting choices are made." Unfortunately, the ten or so qualitative characteristics described in CON 2 are truisms. They are essential qualities of any good measurement system but they are consequences not causes. My butchers' scale has all of the CON 2 characteristics, the current accounting model has none. The difference is that the butchers' scale has a clear objective, a design to achieve it, and an inspection process to maintain its integrity. The accounting model does not. The moral is: Establish a clear measurement objective and the characteristics will follow naturally.
>
> *(Mosso, 2009a, p. 34)*

One of the elements addressed in SFAC No. 2 was the importance of standard setters weighing the relative costs versus benefits of adopting new standards. The cost/benefit ratio had been a hotly debated aspect of SFAS No. 33 on inflation accounting, and that discussion carried over to the discussions about the conceptual framework. The notion of a demonstrated cost benefit of a new standard continues to be raised in present-day regulatory settings, most recently with the Public Company Accounting Oversight Board's standards for auditing and in the contents of recent legislation (i.e., the JOBS Act of 2012).

Concepts Statement No. 3: Elements of Financial Statements

In December 1980, the FASB issued SFAC No. 3: *Elements of Financial Statements of Business Enterprises*. The contents of SFAC No. 3 were among the earliest addressed by the Board, dating back to the discussions of assets, for purposes of issuing SFAS No. 2 (research and development costs), and liabilities, at the time of the issuance of SFAS No. 5 (on contingencies). Two exposure drafts were issued before SFAC No. 3 was approved. The main criticism of the first exposure draft was the emphasis on a balance sheet approach, as opposed to the then preferred income statement, or matching, approach. In a 1978 comment letter to the Board from Thomas A. Murphy of General Motors Corporation, himself an accounting graduate of the University of Illinois, it was noted that the anti-matching bias was apparent throughout the draft but was summed up in paragraph 66, where the comment was made:

> In other words, there is no place in articulated financial statements for items that do not fit the definitions in this statement but are sometimes said to be "required to match costs and revenues properly to measure periodic earnings" or "required to avoid distorting periodic earnings."
>
> *(Murphy, April 19, 1978)*

Murphy went on to articulate the orthodoxy, or credo, held by many accountants of the time:

> We believe that in view of the long history of the use of the matching concept, the historical emphasis on the income statement in the financial field, the use of the balance sheet as a statement of costs not values in this same field, and the overwhelming support for the matching concept expressed in the written and oral responses the Board received to the DM [Discussion Memorandum] covering the conceptual framework project, that the Board should withhold the establishment of a new balance sheet oriented concept until the entire conceptual framework study has been completed.
>
> *(Murphy, April 19, 1978)*

Because of this and other similar letters, the Board did delay issuance of a final statement until after a second exposure draft had been issued and discussed. Despite all of the support for the matching principle, the Board countered that position, suggesting that the responses of the letter writers did not completely reflect the outcomes that matching sought or permitted.

> Many of the responses indeed were vague, and it soon became clear that proper matching and distortion of periodic net income were largely in the eye of the beholder. Respondents said eventually that although they had difficulty in describing proper matching and distorted income, they knew them when they saw them and could use professional judgment to assure themselves that periodic net income was determined without distortion in individual cases. The thinking and practice described in the comment letters and at the hearings seemed to make income measurement primarily a matter of individual judgment and provided no basis for comparability between financial statements. To Board members, the arguments for including in balance sheets items that could not possibly qualify as assets or liabilities – what-you-may-call-its – sounded a lot like excuses to justify smoothing reported income, thereby decreasing its volatility. The experience generally strengthened Board members' commitment to a broad conceptual framework – one beginning with objectives of financial statements and qualitative characteristics (the Trueblood Report) and also defining the elements of financial statements and including concepts of recognition, measurement, and display – and affected the kind of concepts it would comprise.
>
> *(Storey, 1999, pp. 2–38)*

Although Concepts Statements No. 3 and No. 6 did not explicitly endorse the asset-and-liability view nor castigate the income statement view, it was clear by the definitions given which view the Board was adopting (Storey, 1999, pp. 1–85). Assets and liabilities are defined "as the most fundamental elements." The Board had become convinced that definitions of assets and liabilities that depended on definitions of revenues and expenses produced by an orientation to the income statement and matching simply would not achieve an optimal decision-useful financial reporting outcome. The Board had actually come to this conclusion much earlier when it promulgated Statements No. 2 and No. 5 on research and development and contingent liabilities. Thus, the conceptual definitions of assets and liabilities had their roots in the Board's earliest pronouncements.

Supporters of the matching principle were not the only critics of SFAC No. 3. The Business Roundtable, a group typically critical of FASB actions in the 1980s, noted that SFAC No. 3 contained some "troublesome areas, notably the introduction of the concept of 'comprehensive income'" (Smith, March 29, 1982). The Roundtable members were informed that although the definition of comprehensive income was vague, it seemed that it would consist of the changes in stockholders' equity that went beyond net income as then known. Thus, they observed, "It appears that the concept was introduced to permit current value measurement of assets to be introduced without disturbing the traditional net income concept." The group perceived that historical–cost-based financial statements would thus be replaced by fair value reporting.

Concepts Statement No. 5: Recognition and Measurement

SFAC No. 5, *Recognition and Measurement in Financial Statements of Business Enterprises* (December, 1984) has been criticized for being nothing new. As Donald Kirk pointed out, "Development of the first three Concepts Statements was time consuming, and at times controversial, but nothing compared to what preceded the issuance of FASB Concepts Statement No. 5" (1988, p. 15). In July 1981, a noted academician, Robert R. Sterling, was recruited as a senior fellow at the FASB to lead the campaign to develop the statement on recognition and measurement. After two years, Sterling gave up in disgust and returned to his professorship at Rice University. Sterling later stated that "No. 5 was not a Concepts Statement" (2009). He claims the failure of SFAC No. 5 was attributable to the cleavage between historical cost and the use of fair values. Three Board members, Block, Morgan, and March, were firmly opposed to the use of fair values – under any circumstance; they would not even agree that the then current uses of fair values, such as the lower of cost or market, were acceptable. Sterling gave the example of a farmer's corn inventory, which traditionally was valued at fair market value; corn was a fungible product with a ready market and could be sold at any time. Therefore, accountants have always valued such inventories at fair market values, but the three Board members would not agree that this treatment was acceptable and thus would not allow such mention in the Concepts Statement (Sterling, 2009). The antipathy toward anything other than valuation at historical costs was too strong for progress to be made. In fact, Kirk was so sure that nothing meaningful would come from the completion of SFAC No. 5 that he admitted in 1983 that he was ready to set the project aside. "My views at that time were colored . . . by the frustrations of trying to find common ground among a group of very different thinking Board members" (Kirk, 1988, p. 16).

Sterling came aboard at a restive time. The earlier phases of the conceptual framework had focused on the more basic aspects of accounting. Those Statements had been passed unanimously, a condition that the Board had set as a goal for itself in approving the Concepts Statements (Johnson, 1997, p. xlii). While the third Concepts Statement was delayed because of the noted objections and the need to issue a second exposure draft, it was nevertheless unanimously approved. Some Board members, however, were becoming concerned that future concepts were being put in place so as to move away from the old historical cost/matching approach toward value accounting. Although Board members may not have known initially what Sterling's views on fair values were,[3] he had long been a noted accounting conceptualist and had even presented a paper at the FASB's June 1980 Conceptual Framework Symposium in New York. Chairman Kirk and Michael Alexander, the FASB's Director of Research and Technical Activities, were impressed with Sterling and created a position for him, with his assignment being to work on the conceptual framework project. Sterling could not refuse the opportunity to help shape accounting's conceptual framework and the subsequent standards that would be based on the framework.

The Board had commissioned two research reports designed to contribute to the Discussion Memorandum on recognition criteria (measurement was to have been addressed in a later phase of the project because of the Board's concern that the issue would be more contentious). In December 1980, Yuji Ijiri's study, *Recognition of Contractual Rights and Obligations*, was published. A month later, Henry Jaenicke published *Survey of Present Practices in Recognizing*

Revenues, Expenses, Gains, and Losses. Upon his arrival in July 1981, Sterling convinced the Board that recognition could not be effectively addressed without also addressing the issue of measurement. Thus, the project was expanded to include measurement. Sterling's definition of measurement criteria was simple – use fair values in the form of current exit values (Sterling, 1981; Johnson, 1997, p. xliv). Three members of the Board would not accept a proposal that would supplant the historical cost principle, and one or two others who were in favor of fair value were not enthusiastic about the use of exit prices. With Sterling and other staff members working toward a fair value approach, the three opposing Board members pressed to hire a researcher who would support the historical cost approach. That person was the noted academic Robert K. Mautz, who was by then working for Ernst & Whinney as a consultative partner. There was such an impasse among Board members that the fair value concept simply could not be adopted. Sterling left the FASB in June 1983, and SFAC No. 5 was eventually approved in December 1984. The final document was little more than a recap of the concepts that had been approved in earlier statements. As later noted by another FASB staff member, H. Todd Johnson, "It is not a document with which Bob would have wanted to be associated" (1997, p. xliv).

Sterling, it would seem, must have gone into the project without a full awareness of the concerns. As early as the summer of 1980, before he was ever invited to join the FASB, he observed the following:

> As the framework gets nearer completion the likely changes will be more easily anticipated, and therefore it will be easier to anticipate real or imagined adversely affected vested interests. Thus, progress toward completion will be accompanied by a crescendo of perceived adversely affected vested interests, which in turn will be accompanied by a crescendo of resistance and criticism. The resistance may become so great that the board will find it impossible to complete the framework. If so, it may be forced to return to the procedure of putting out brush fires and abandon the project. I am not forecasting that outcome, but I do think that it is a possibility that shouldn't be lightly dismissed. In short, in looking at the history I see the glass to be half full in that the board has made much more progress than its predecessors, but in forecasting the future I see the glass to be half empty in that each step in filling it is going to be increasingly difficult.
>
> *(Sterling, 1982, p. 105)*

One of the reasons that some Board members were not enthusiastic about the acceptance of fair values in SFAC No. 5 was the experience that was then being noted with regard to the requirements of SFAS No. 33 on inflation accounting. While considering SFAC No. 5, the Board learned that the current cost information required under the inflation standard was not being widely used and that there were serious questions about the reliability of the information. According to Kirk, "I could find little reason to endorse on a conceptual level a current value or current cost measurement system for future standards when it appeared that the utility of such a system in Statement 33 was going to be seriously challenged" (1988, p. 16). Eventually, SFAS No. 33 was rescinded because its requirements failed to meet the cost/benefit test, primarily because studies showed that users saw little benefit, especially after inflation rates became lower and of less concern.

Eventually, through compromise, SFAC No. 5 was approved by a 6–1 vote in December 1984. The reasons for the dissent included the facts that (a) the statement did not adopt measurement concepts oriented toward what was the most useful attribute for recognition purposes, namely the cash equivalent of recognized transactions reduced by subsequent impairments or loss of service value – instead the statement suggested selecting from several different attributes (i.e., a mixed-attribute approach) without providing sufficient guidance for the selection process; (b) it used a concept of income that was based on measurements of assets and liabilities and changes in them, rather than adopting the concept of earnings as the definition of income (i.e., it recommended the publication of a statement of comprehensive income); and (c) it failed to provide sufficient guidance for initial recognition and derecognition of assets and liabilities. Finally, the dissent noted the following:

> Disregarding the foregoing objections, Mr. March believes this Statement offers insufficient guidance for the near-term future work of the Board. To be useful, it needs to be supplemented with more specific guidance for selecting measurement attributes for specific assets, liabilities, and transactions and for deciding when the criteria require recognition or derecognition of an asset or a liability.
>
> *(SFAC No. 5, 1984, para. 91)*

March's dissent was the only dissent on any of the first six Concepts Statements.

David Mosso, a member of the FASB who voted in favor of SFAC No. 5, apparently had second thoughts about the document, although not for the reasons enunciated by March. In a recent book, Mosso noted:

> The conceptual framework did nothing to establish operable recognition criteria. More importantly, the framework did not even try to eliminate choice of methods . . . . The FASB identified five "measurement attributes" in the then-current accounting model and said: "The Board expects the use of different attributes to continue." That was in 1984. The attributes are still with us. The five attributes listed were: Historical cost, current cost, current market value, net realizable value, and present value of future cash flows. But five understates the problem. There are many variations of each. I have noted before that the most explosive choice in standard setting has been between historical cost allocation and fair value measurement. FASB wrestled with this issue throughout the development of its conceptual framework, but it concluded with this statement in CON 5: "Information based on current prices should be recognized if it is sufficiently relevant and reliable to justify the costs involved and more relevant than alternative information." This is not a concept. It is a waffle.
>
> *(2009a, p. 34)*

Concepts Statement No. 6: Elements of Financial Statements, again

Perhaps the most lauded of the seven Concepts Statements was No. 6, entitled *Elements of Financial Statements*, which was issued by unanimous vote in December 1985 as a supersession of SFAC No. 3. The reason for the updated statement was to expand its coverage to not-for-profit organizations. One article stated that the strength of SFAC No. 6 was its definitions: "[O]f all the Board's concepts, the definitions in Statement No. 6 are the most robust" (Gerboth, 1987, p. 2). The essence of SFAC No. 6 was similar to SFAC No. 3, but there were many new paragraphs describing how the elements of financial statements that had been described in SFAC No. 3 also applied to not-for-profit organizations.

Concepts Statement No. 7: Using Cash Flow Information and Present Value

After a decade-and-a-half hiatus, the FASB issued another Concepts Statement in February 2000 entitled *Using Cash Flow Information and Present Value in Accounting Measurements*. Initially, SFAC No. 7 was supposed to define "fair value," but the Board quickly determined that fair value was too much of an issue and agreement would be difficult in achieving. Eventually, the Board decided that a fair value statement would be impossible. Since present value was a major component of many fair value judgments, it was decided that a present value project would be helpful and was doable. Two Board members dissented to SFAC No. 7 because of its adoption of fair value as the sole objective of using cash flow information and present value in accounting measurements.

Concepts Statement No. 8: Conceptual Framework for Financial Reporting

In September 2010, SFAC No. 8 was issued as a replacement for SFAC No. 1 and SFAC No. 2. This document began as a joint project with the International Accounting Standards Board (IASB) with the objective of converging the respective frameworks of the two organizations. According to SFAC No. 8, the objective of general purpose financial reporting is "to provide financial information about the reporting entity that is useful to existing and potential investors, lenders, and other creditors in making decisions about providing resources to the entity," which is consistent with what appeared in SFAC No. 1. However, SFAC No. 1 viewed potential investors and creditors as the primary user groups, while SFAC No. 8 considered this group to be resource providers and not necessarily the primary user group. This view indicates that there is a wide separation between business entities and the owners of those businesses. From a conceptual point of view, SFAC No. 8 is based more on the entity theory of accounting than the earlier owner-emphasis proprietary theory.

Another change appearing in SFAC No. 8 – one that emanated from the joint efforts with the IASB – was a reorganizing of some of the qualitative characteristics of financial information. The changes were small and perhaps subtle. Under the new view, materiality, for example, was changed from a quantitative characteristic relating to whether an item would influence investor decisions to being a subsidiary of the relevance concept.

Summary of the FASB conceptual framework

The FASB as an institution needed a conceptual framework. A framework is desirable, but not sufficient, for effective standard setting. According to Donald Kirk, "Sound concepts are essential guides for standard setters beset by lobbying and political pressures to distort what must be, to serve the public interest, an even-handed measurement system" (1988, p. 17). Thus, in addition to being a planning tool for the Board, a conceptual framework can be a defensive tool against the slings and arrows of the political process. The FASB's conceptual framework is based on a number of sources, including the 1973 Trueblood Report, the APB's Accounting Research Studies No. 1 and No. 3, and on Board members' experiences in attempting to establish standards in the absence of a conceptual framework. Altogether, the framework is a body of concepts that were developed at different times and put together to form a whole. One British writer noted that the conceptual framework project gave birth to 60 documents totaling over 4,000 pages, which made it the most ambitious attempt to establish financial reporting guidelines ever undertaken (Gore, 1992). That writer also concluded that the results had been the subject of extensive criticism and little acclaim.

The verdict on the FASB conceptual framework has been mixed; even former Board members are often critical, or at least not enthralled with the results. As early as 1986, Board Chairman Donald Kirk mentioned in a speech that "Board members who were not involved in developing the conceptual statements seem to have less attachment to them or proprietary interest in them" (quoted in Gerboth, 1987, p. 6). Why has there been disappointment with the Concepts Statements? The FASB itself, in a December 1983 issue of its newsletter, *Status Report*, suggested that its constituents had "false hopes" that the framework would produce instant answers to the problem areas of accounting. Others, including several former Board members, argued that accounting already had all of the conceptual framework that it needed, and the FASB simply gave new expression to old ideas. Another argument that has been put forth is that the fundamental error of the conceptual framework is the mistaken idea that it is possible to avoid or control debate on a subject by prior agreement on abstract principles (Gerboth, 1987, p. 2). Other criticisms have included that the project was internally inconsistent, failed to take the economic environment into account, and was of little use to present or future practice (Gore, 1992). The political environment was also ignored; the framework does not recognize that standard setting is of a political nature. One 1992 study concluded that the successes had been limited to issues that were not controversial in the first place, and successful usage of the framework had not been evident with the more complex issues (Nussbaumer, 1992, p. 235). Former Board member Arthur Wyatt has stated that the framework is incomplete, and he wanted further revisions. Abraham Briloff, often a critic of the accounting profession, stated that the framework lacks any claim to being conceptual at all and has resulted in reduced academic input into the standard-setting process (Sweeney and Yaari, 1998, p. 41).

Although the idea that prior agreement on principles has intuitive appeal, such agreement has not always been true when the FASB begins discussing whether an item meets the definition of an asset or liability. Unfortunately, the result has often been an argument that the conceptual framework was incomplete; the item in question is an asset or liability despite the fact that it does not seem to meet the definition. The contributions of the FASB conceptual framework were summarized by one former staff member as follows:

> In fairness, it cannot be said that the conceptual framework adds nothing. It may have failed to deliver on some of its promises, and it is almost certainly not worth the big bundle of bucks the FASB spent on it. Nevertheless, it did a reasonably good job of drawing together, organizing, and articulating the basic concepts of accounting, and that is no mean accomplishment. Used properly, the conceptual framework can enhance the process of setting accounting standards.
>
> *(Gerboth, 1987, pp. 7–8)*

In 2005, the FASB decided to revisit the conceptual framework and added a new project to its agenda. The goal of the still-in-process project is to update and improve existing concepts and to fill in gaps in areas such as measurement, disclosure, and financial statement presentation. The project is being conducted jointly with the IASB with the objective of producing a single conceptual framework that can be used anywhere in the world. The progress of the new project is open to debate. In April 2009, Robert Bloomfield posted the following lines on a website:

> Sometimes I think that differences of opinion on the importance of the Conceptual Framework are as wide as differences of opinion on the appropriateness of Fair Value Accounting. The debate isn't as loud, though, because those who think Fair Value Accounting is inappropriate argue vehemently against it, while many who think the Conceptual Framework is not important just quietly ignore it.
>
> *(Bloomfield, April, 2009)*

Quietly ignoring the conceptual framework has been an easy way to deal with controversial issues. Alternatively, some critics argue that it is not that the framework is being ignored, but rather that the framework is too generalized to be useful in specific situations. According to one Board member, the framework is too vague to guide standard setting in any meaningful way. Alternatively, a staff member argued that the framework is widely used by staff members in framing their analyses for the benefit of Board members (Bloomfield, 2009). Such disparate views were first noted as early as 1981. In a November 24, 1981, memo, FASB Director of Research and Technical Activities, Michael Alexander, made the following observation about the conceptual framework:

> The last pensions Board meeting indicated to us that the staff have a much better work-ing knowledge of the conceptual framework than the Board do. The staff work with the conceptual framework on a day-to-day basis – some staff more than others. But the Board have difficulty remembering it even though they were the ones that passed it. Part of the reason for this is that concepts are hard to internalize when they require a change in fixed values or concepts that already exist. For many of the Board members, the new concepts in the conceptual framework replaced or contradicted or were different from their concepts of accounting that they had held for many years. So even though they were the architects and legislators of the new conceptual framework, without using it on a day-to-day basis they quickly forgot the detailed concepts that they had originated. The staff, on the other hand, had few prior biases to inhibit them and saw their job as accepting the concepts as stated and started to work with them as tools to do their job.
>
> At this Board meeting, the conceptual framework was put out in front of the Board as a way of guiding the analysis of the pension accounting question. Board members again and again demonstrated their lack of familiarity and comfort with the framework. Some had forgotten that a liability could meet the definition of the liability and still remain unre-corded. That is, it needn't be recognized even though it could be defined as a liability. Others claimed that there wasn't any sense in defining a liability if you weren't going to record it. The question of decision usefulness seemed paramount to some Board members but they forgot that they had produced a statement on qualitative characteristics of deci-sion usefulness. Somehow the term had come to mean something other than relevance and reliability, comparability, cost benefit and so on. The whole meeting seemed to degenerate into disarray. The discussion resembled the Biblical tale of the tower of Babel. Those build-ing the tower one day realized that they spoke so many different languages that they could no longer communicate to finish the job.
>
> Needless to say, this is worrisome. Many Board members would like to choose to forget the framework or apply it in their own way. Their focus is naturally on the final solution. This kind of behavior does not auger well for the success of the FASB in developing a framework or making it stick as a useful tool in standard setting. There could be hope that the observers at this Board meeting were sufficiently confused by the discussion that they would not notice what was going on. But, unfortunately there were a few who well understood the problem. A representative of a large industrial corporation was later over-heard to say, "Now that we have demonstrated that the conceptual framework isn't good for anything, we can get back to the real questions."
>
> *(Alexander, November 24, 1981)*

Alexander concluded from the above that "you cannot teach old dogs new tricks; teaching Board members new concepts, or concepts that differ from the way they are accustomed to doing things, appears impossible." About seven months later, Alexander shared another view of the Board:

> The prospects for changing the positions of Board members are probably nil and yet to admit this openly seems to be a rejection of conventional wisdom – that is that all people are malleable, fluid, or flexible in their thinking and open minded. It seems from watching this operation that the opposite is true. People are generally quite fixed in their thinking and like grain in a piece of wood, it is almost impossible to change them. There are, however, a few exceptions and this seven man Board has two of them.
>
> *(Alexander, June 18, 1982)*

Although all members of the Board may not always use the framework, some observers have also suggested that constituents testifying before the Board or commenting on exposure drafts often do use the framework, "partly at least because they have discovered that they are more likely to influence the Board if they do" (Storey, 1999, pp. 1–110). The area of vagueness has opened up new opportunities for opponents and supporters of particular standards under discussion. The framework now serves as a tool that can be used to argue for or against proposed accounting standards. Terminology in the concepts is often so ambiguous as to support widely divergent views.

The old generation grew up with matching and historical cost. As a new generation becomes comfortable with fair values and a balance sheet oriented view of accounting, the FASB concepts could become more acceptable, and more fluid. Indeed, acceptance of new theories in the social sciences is usually a slow process. When writing about his own decision-usefulness concept, George Staubus wrote that "publishing a new theory in accounting is like dropping a rose petal in the Grand Canyon and waiting for the echo. An early start and good health increase the chances of seeing results in one's lifetime" (2003, p. 163). Alternatively, perhaps David Mosso best summed up many individuals' views of the conceptual framework project with the following lines: "My conclusion is that the conceptual framework was a useful step in accounting development but it has done all that it can. It is an anachronism and it is time to recognize that and move on to something better" (2009c).

Principles and standards

Over the years there has been criticism that US accounting standards are more detailed and complex than standards in other countries. The explanation offered is that US standards are more rules based, while those in other countries, including those promulgated by the IASB, are principles based. According to critics, rules-based standards have made it difficult for both preparers and auditors to stay current and have led to a "check-the-box" mentality "that encourages financial and accounting engineering to structure transactions around the rules to attain form-over-substance results" (Herz, 2003, p. 251). Also, many standards include numerous exceptions to the rules, which resulted from Board members adding compromises to assure an adequate number of votes or to accommodate the interests of particular constituent groups. As a result of the criticism over standards overload, the Sarbanes-Oxley Act of 2002 mandated that the SEC evaluate the feasibility of implementing principles-based standards.

The problem is that the FASB's constituents have typically requested rules-based standards. It has been pointed out that the American economy is more litigious than in other nations. As a result, goes the argument, the US needs rules-based standards to stave off lawsuits. Rules-based standards create clarity; there are bright lines between right and wrong. With principles-based standards, the lines are not as clear. Principles-based standards do not try to provide specific guidance or rules for every possible situation. The asserted potential advantages of a principles-based approach include enhanced professionalism in both the reporting and auditing of financial statements, easier-to-understand standards, reduced opportunity for form–over–substance structuring of rules since there would be fewer rules, and convergence with IASB standards that already use a more principles-based approach. Alternatively, there are disadvantages. One disadvantage might be reduced comparability, which could come about because of different good faith judgments about the correct accounting treatment. Even with the same facts, accountants could conceivably come up with alternative conclusions. Another disadvantage would be more difficult enforcement of standards. The SEC would be put in the position of having to make judgments about firm-specific interpretations of general standards. This would make the enforcement job more difficult, lengthier, and more subject to controversy than if the SEC could simply check to be sure that a registrant had followed a clear rule.

Many auditors and preparers recognize that to some extent they are protected from lawsuits if they follow the rules in rules-based accounting (Previts and Merino, 1998, p. 277). The rules-based standards provide a safe-harbor provision to auditors and preparers who make a good faith effort to apply accounting principles. A corollary to this is that with principles-based standards managers may feel less pressure to be constrained in their choices in the preparation of financial statements. There will be more opportunity for earnings management, and managers will likely seize these opportunities. Auditors will be put in the position of being unable to override management's assertions unless the misstatement is so egregious that it produces evidence that can be used in court. Principles-based standards will result in greater professional judgment, but "professional judgment," according to former Board member David Mosso, is a euphemism for "client choice," and that is motivated by self-interest. Thus, the issue is not really rules versus principles, but choice versus restriction of choice and the degree of discretion that is left to management (Ketz, February 2008).

Some supporters of principles-based standards have gone so far as to suggest that rules-based standards lead to accounting scandals. In 2006, Graham Ward, the president of the International Federation of Accountants, claimed that detailed rules were "conducive to promotion of dishonesty," whereas principles-based accounting led to "integrity, transparency and expertise." In an op/ed piece, J. Edward Ketz called Graham's comments "rubbish" (Ketz, March 2006). Ketz suggested that one reason for Graham's perception was that fewer scandals were uncovered in other countries than in the US, and the reason for this was because the perpetrators in other countries were getting away with their frauds due to the lack of rules-based accounting. American perpetrators were more apt to be caught because of the availability of accounting rules. Ketz concluded his article with the following lines:

> This discussion on principles-based accounting and its marvelous abilities to heal economic maladies remains unreasonable and indeed preposterous. U.S. society has some good forces that lead to greater apprehension of the bad guys, and it also has some dysfunctional aspects that tempt managers to commit securities fraud via accounting manipulation. As Graham Ward and others ignore these economic realities, they overlook social and economic variables that explain the incidence of accounting fraud in America versus the rest of the world. They overlook the explanatory variables and replace them with some dogma to justify their own agenda.
>
> *(Ketz, March 2006)*

The question of principles versus rules is not a new issue; it is something that the FASB has been grappling with since its founding. Charter Board member Walter Schuetze addressed the subject in a 1978 speech. Schuetze stated that all entities face this question – whether you are setting standards for a government agency, a private business, or your own home. He concluded that proceeding in either direction brings problems. The FASB examples he gave included the following:

> If they write a very general standard, such as FASB Statement No. 14 on segment reporting, it is very difficult for preparers of financial statements and their auditors to interpret it uniformly. If they write a very specific standard, such as FASB Statement No. 13 on leases, inevitably some ingredient is left out or an extraneous ingredient is stuck in. Furthermore, people like to use their judgment and are averse to cookbooks that tell them what to do . . . . Some balance, some sense of proportion, is needed when acting in the real world, and those who set rules have to find the concepts that are consistent with the limitations the real world imposes. Well-formulated rules are somewhere between the very general and the very specific. I hope the Board will be able to find this middle ground.
>
> *(Schuetze, 1978, p. 8)*[4]

Another 1978 supporter of principles-based standards was former Board member Ralph Walters. In a memo to other Board members, Walters wrote:

> Standards should flow from concepts, economic logic, practice, and may even contain a dash of aspirations. But we, like regulators, tend to concern ourselves that people not be allowed to exercise judgment to implement a standard – judgment that might differ from ours. Therefore, we concern ourselves with heading off the perceived evil-doer, with plugging possible loopholes; and we get all tangled up in how-to when we should be concerned with what and why. We end up writing regulations . . . . Let the standard-setting body set standards. Let the regulators regulate.
>
> *(Walters, December 8, 1978)*

Walters was of the opinion that the FASB should write standards and not worry about how those standards were interpreted by management; the SEC should write regulations and should worry about how management interpreted the FASB's standards. In a 1983 speech, Walters questioned whether American accountants could even survive in anything other than a rules-based system:

> We find regulators and standard setters whose attitudes and actions reflect the effects of thirty years of fire fighting and loophole plugging. They have become accustomed to it – like Brazilians have become accustomed to inflation and New Yorkers to noisy, dirty subways – it has become the norm and one seldom hears screams of outrage or see signs of resistance. Government regulators, in particular, are conditioned to press for more rules, more uniformity, less flexibility (read less judgment). Their frequent oversight attitude to the private standard setters, expressed or implied, is "if you don't, we will." . . . One result is that we have trained a generation or two who are conditioned to detailed rules. We have learned how to live with the letter rather than the spirit of the rules. We have learned that detailed rules can usually be subverted by a careful structuring of transactions. We have bred a generation of extremely sophisticated and talented loopholers. The typical reaction of standard setters, when loopholing (politely referred to as diversity of practice) is detected is to write more detailed rules to plug the loophole. But, it's a losing battle – for loopholers are more creative and agile than standard setters – so we have an endless cycle.

In late 2002, the FASB and the SEC began working on the idea of moving toward principles-based standards. A request for comments on the subject was issued in October 2002, and public roundtable discussions were held in December. One conclusion was that a movement toward principles-based standards could not be accomplished by the FASB by itself; it would also require major behavioral changes among other parties:

> It requires preparers, auditors, audit committees, and boards to be willing to exercise professional judgment, to resist the urge to seek specific answers and rulings on every implementation issue, and to view accounting and reporting as an exercise in good communication that goes beyond mere compliance. It requires that investment bankers and the accountants and lawyers that work with them stop trying to invent ways to create products and structures to "loophole" standards, and it may require that the SEC staff temper their demands for bright lines to facilitate their review and enforcement activities. Moreover, it may require some changes to the legal and litigation framework surrounding financial reporting and auditing.
>
> *(Herz, 2003, p. 251)*

By 1991, Schuetze's views on principles versus rules had not changed much:

> We have tried the simple approach that requires judgment. For example, in APB Opinion 5, the Accounting Principles Board said that lessees should recognize in their balance sheet those leases that are in substance installment purchases of property – those that result in creation of a material equity in the property. That was a general standard, requiring judgment to implement. It did not work. Very few leased assets and corresponding lease obligations were recognized by lessees. As a result, the Financial Accounting Standards Board issued very detailed, complex rules on accounting for leases in FASB Statement 13. But now, Statement 13, even with all its amendments and interpretations does not work. And, to make things worse, the Securities and Exchange Commission's staff and the Emerging Issues Task Force keep adding layers of complexity to it.

Ketz attempted to summarize the issue of rules versus principles in his February 2008 article:

> FASB and the SEC continue to take steps to implement a principles-based accounting standards-setting system. But questions and concerns still abound. What exactly is an accounting rule and what is an accounting principle? Why is complexity viewed as a problem but managerial lying and thievery are not? Where is the evidence that principles-based accounting will help investors? For some strange reason, FASB and the SEC ignore these annoying questions and continue with religious fervor to support their idol.

In a more recent article, Ketz verbalized what many observers have thought about the principles-based standards of the IASB:

> I also find it ludicrous for so many practitioners to claim the superiority of IFRS [International Financial Reporting Standards] over U.S. standards. Such individuals should read and compare (say) lease accounting under these two systems. If they undertake this simple exercise, they will see that there is little difference . . . . As I have said in many columns, principles-based accounting is superior to rules if and only if these so-called accounting principles are implemented by principled managers. As too many managers don't exhibit principles as

evidenced in their financial reports, I shall continue to believe U.S. rules-based standards are superior to principles-based ambiguities.

(Ketz, December 2009)

Perhaps a sometimes wearisome debate over principles versus standards was addressed sufficiently, if not resolved, in November 2003 at the 103rd American Assembly meeting, sponsored by Columbia University, where it was noted that the

> current debate about the future of accounting swirls around the issue of whether or not the profession should replace the rules-based system . . . . with the so-called principles-based system favored by the IASB. . . . The either/or debate over principles and rules-based accounting is, we believe, simply a proxy for a more important and subtle issue: to what degree do we expect the preparers and auditors of financial statements to exercise judgments?

With this to frame the discussion, the attendees favored fewer rules and more judgments. The discussion was summed up as follows: "The debate over rules-based and principles-based accounting is based on a false premise that the two systems are mutually exclusive. We believe they are tied together inextricably" (The American Assembly, 2003).

The Jenkins Committee report

Financial Reporting and Standard Setting, a symposium sponsored by the AICPA at the Wharton School of the University of Pennsylvania on October 25–26, 1990, was the event that served as the catalyst for the forming of the Special Committee on Financial Reporting chaired by Edmund Jenkins, then the senior technical partner of Arthur Andersen & Co. (Previts, 1991).

By 1994, the committee and its study groups had ranged widely into investigations of various practices and issues that were emerging in the capital market reporting environment of public companies. Innovative financial instruments, off-balance-sheet financing, separate highlighted reports being provided to institutional investors by public companies, and communication technologies with increasing global and instant reach had all combined to suggest that the old emphasis in both education and mainstream practice toward producing "financial statements" had passed. Innovative structures for the content of financial reports were developed at a never before considered level, namely as broader business reports reflecting non-financial performance or key performance indicators as well as traditional financial metrics.

The Jenkins Committee report included a ten-point information model, of which only one point was identified with traditional "financial statements and related disclosures." Coming some twenty years after the Trueblood Report and being derived and hosted by a Wharton School Dean, Russell Palmer, who had previously served as the managing partner of the Touche firm, which Trueblood had also served in a similar capacity, seems like curious historical coincidence.

The ten elements of the Jenkins Business Reporting Model were parts of five major categories:

1   Financial and non-financial data
2   Management's analysis of the financial and non-financial data
3   Forward-looking information
4   Information about management and shareholders
5   Background about the company

Not unexpectedly, the preparer community received the Jenkins model with coolness, seeing the proposal perhaps at best as another unfunded mandate, despite the research support that indicated a growing need for expansion of the information content of communications between corporations, capital providers, and society. Later, the Financial Executives Research Foundation produced an executive research report, issued in November 1999, indicating that sufficiency of such data, especially in the non-financial area, appeared to be based on comparative reports of key companies over the years. The study identified the manner by which management selects themes, the level of detail, and the structure of annual reports with the intention of conscientiously communicating with its constituents.

The Jenkins Committee report preceded and likely led to the appointment of Jenkins as chair of the FASB, following the two-term chairmanship of Dennis R. Beresford. At this point the Board initiated, under the watchful eye of FAF member Paul Kolton, former chair of the American Stock Exchange, and Board member Joseph V. Anania, a business reporting research project to study in depth and detail the reporting practices and information flow needs of financial analysts. The project, however, failed to gain broad support, and Jenkins left the Board position after one five-year term. The business reporting model's inability to win support was but another example of the difficulty of bringing together the broad and various constituencies of the reporting community, preparers, auditors, analysts and investors, and regulators to support an agenda of change.

Fair value accounting

Some have blamed the disappointment over the outcomes of the conceptual framework project on the Board's unwillingness to abandon historical cost accounting, "an ideological heresy that in some circles bears blame for everything from nuclear Armageddon to spastic colitis" (Gerboth, 1987, p. 1). Several former Board members have commented that the mongrelization of accounting makes it impossible to come up with an effective conceptual framework, since some accounts are shown at historical cost and others are reported at fair market values. Mosso summarized the relationship between the conceptual framework and fair value accounting:

> I was supportive of the conceptual framework in its entirety because I thought, and still think, that it brought a good bit of order to the GAAP accounting model. It was the best we could do at the time and I am a believer in moving forward as long as there is a net gain. Also at the time, I was still enamored of the FAF-FASB model and thought we could make real improvements in accounting. Experience with the process – the inability to get anything done in a reasonable time frame and the continuing largely successful resistance to fair values and retention of the ability to manage earnings – reinforced by my experience with federal accounting, gradually eroded my support for both the accounting model and the standard setting process.
>
> *(2009c)*

Statement No. 157, *Fair Value Measurements*, issued by unanimous Board vote in September 2006, defines fair value, establishes a framework for measuring fair value, and expands disclosures about fair value measurements. SFAS No. 157 applies under other accounting pronouncements that require or permit fair value measurements. Therefore, this statement does not require any new fair value measurements, and SFAS No. 157 does not represent a radical departure from previous accounting standards. Prior to the issuance of SFAS No. 157, there were several different definitions of fair value and little guidance for applying those definitions. These differences in guidance created inconsistencies that added to the complexity of applying GAAP. In developing SFAS No. 157, the Board considered the need for increased consistency and comparability in fair value measurements and for expanded disclosures about fair value measurements. A fair value standard was 30 years in the making, albeit the concept itself is nearly ageless as noted below. Despite the fact that SFAS No. 157 introduced little in the way of new standards, it did amend, supersede, or otherwise affect more than 40 areas of accounting guidance, beginning with SFAS No. 13 on leasing. That was the first FASB pronouncement to introduce the fair value concept. Following SFAS No. 13, many other statements continued the move away from historical cost toward fair value, including SFAS No. 87 on pensions, SFAS No. 106 on other post-retirement benefits, and SFAS No. 133 on derivatives. However, many of these standards used the concept of fair values in different contexts. SFAS No. 157 was designed to provide a uniform definition of fair value that would apply in all cases. In summary, SFAS No. 157 did not require any new transactions to be accounted for at fair value, but it stipulated the framework to be used when other standards require the use of fair values.

In February 2007, the Board issued SFAS No. 159, *The Fair Value Option for Financial Assets and Financial Liabilities – Including an Amendment of FASB Statement No. 115*. This statement permits entities to choose to measure financial instruments and certain other items at fair value. The objective was to improve financial reporting by providing organizations with the opportunity to mitigate volatility in reported earnings caused by measuring related assets and liabilities differently without having to apply complex hedge accounting provisions. SFAS No. 159 was expected to expand the use of fair value measurement. This Statement applies to all entities including not-for-profit organizations. The portion that is an amendment to FASB Statement No. 115, *Accounting for Certain Investments in Debt and Equity Securities*, applies to all entities with available-for-sale and trading securities. Some requirements apply differently to entities that do not report net income. The vote on SFAS No. 159 was not unanimous; both dissenters doubted that the statement represented a cost-beneficial interim step toward measuring all financial instruments at fair value – a long-term goal expressed by the Board in Statement 133. Instead, they believed users of financial statements would be better served by accelerating efforts to issue a statement requiring all financial instruments to be measured at fair value each reporting period with changes in those fair values reported in earnings.

Although fair value accounting, as professed in Statements of Financial Accounting Standards No. 157 and 159, is hardly addressed in the conceptual framework (although it was originally to have been a major part of Concepts Statement No. 7 and was what made Statement No. 5 so controversial), it is discussed here because fair value has been a part of the personal conceptual framework of some past and current Board members. For example, one of the charter Board members, Walter Schuetze, claimed that he resigned from the Board because not enough of the other Board members shared his penchant for fair values. However, more recent Board members have included fair value in their personal conceptual frameworks. In particular, since the early 1990s the Board has accepted the responsibility of moving toward the use of fair values to the extent possible. Unfortunately, fair value is sometimes difficult to determine. One advantage of historical cost is that it is an objective measure (albeit not after the date of purchase), but fair values can also be objective. With the issuance of Statements No. 157 and 159, the FASB officially moved to fair value reporting. However, with the decline in the mortgage market in 2007–2008, criticism arose that fair values do not work in illiquid markets. Arguments against fair values have included the fact that fair values in an illiquid market understate the "true value" of assets (but critics have not defined true value).

The concept of fair value accounting did not grow in a vacuum; it has been around in a conceptual mode for decades. Henry Rand Hatfield mentioned the use of current costs in a

1909 book but suggested that historical costs were a more appropriate valuation method in most circumstances. Economist J. B. Canning supported the use of exit prices for valuing assets in his classic 1929 book, and in 1939 Kenneth MacNeal went so far as to say that truth in accounting can only be achieved when financial statements report the current value of assets and the income or loss from changes in those asset values. Similarly, the Paton and Littleton monograph mentioned the topic in Chapter 7. Edwards and Bell had argued for the use of replacement costs in their 1961 book, while George Staubus advocated in his 1961 book the use of the present values of future cash flows. Chambers' 1960 exposition of continuously contemporaneous accounting (COCOA) led to him being viewed by many as the apostle of fair value accounting. Chambers (1966) and Sterling (1970) had somewhat similar theoretical proposals involving the use of exit prices for valuation purposes. Even the Trueblood Committee report that came out in 1973 mentioned that current values should be used if they differed significantly from historical costs. Thus, even though the typical practitioner might have been unfamiliar with fair value accounting, academic accountants and the FASB staff and Board were aware of the many proposals.

As early as 1977, the Business Roundtable lobbying group made up of corporate executives campaigned against fair value accounting. In a letter from Thomas A. Murphy of General Motors Corporation commenting on the first Conceptual Framework Discussion Memorandum, a section entitled "Cause for Concern," the Roundtable noted:

> We are particularly interested in a full discussion of the subject because we perceive an apparent drift toward the avocation of the incorporation of some type of current value accounting within the formal audited financial statements. This causes concern on our part because we believe such a change in the financial statements would, among other things, have a detrimental effect on the capital markets . . . . We fear that if the basis for reporting financial results is changed to some type of current value accounting, the result would be highly subjective financial statements, subject to different interpretations and possible abuse by various individuals with the result being a reduction in investor confidence.
>
> *(Murphy, June 24, 1977)*

The 1977 Murphy letter went on in an attempt to educate the Board as to why current values were a bad idea. Murphy noted that:

> except for the problem of inflation, we don't believe this old accounting debate (which was decided nearly forty years ago in favor of the matching of revenues and expenses by such renowned accountants as Paton and Littleton) would have been raised again.

Murphy pointed out that businessmen and people in general are transaction oriented: "Selling a product or a service is the purpose of an enterprise, not holding assets or liabilities for a future 'gain' dependent upon the effect of inflation." He went on:

> We don't believe that the balance sheet of a company was ever intended to be a representation of the market price of a company, which seems to be what some of the most vocal critics of accounting want. This can only be determined by a willing buyer and a willing seller through negotiation and even then the price might turn out to have been incorrect based on subsequent events. Certainly none of the current value methods which have been proposed can be considered to be a realistic representation of the supposed value of a company on a going concern basis.
>
> *(Murphy, June 24, 1977)*

The Board issued an exposure draft of the first Concepts Statement in December 1977, which led to a July 26, 1978, Board meeting on the topic. In a letter to senior management at General Motors, Eugene Flegm reported that the FASB had adopted the so-called asset/liability view of the measurement of income instead of the matching concept, in spite of "overwhelming testimony and papers" in favor of the continuation of the matching concept. Flegm noted that the purpose of the meeting seemed to be "to assure people that the change to the asset/liability view does not represent the revolution in accounting that it has been presented to be" (July 31, 1978). Flegm concluded that the Board believed that in the next ten to fifteen years historical cost would remain the basis for financial statements, but in the long run accounting would at some point be valued based. "Therefore, in viewing the conceptual framework of accounting today the concepts must be based on an asset/liability view as opposed to revenue/expense view because a valuation-based system cannot be supported under the revenue/expense view." Flegm also observed that the Board understood that the asset/liability view and the revenue/expense view were not mutually exclusive; they often give the same results. However, if there was a conflict between the two, the emphasis on the balance sheet view would be selected over the income statement view. Flegm reported that in his testimony before the Board, he had concluded with the line that the Board "could not improve upon Paton and Littleton's work of 40 years ago."

The Business Roundtable campaign against fair value accounting had become even more aggressive by 1982. The minutes of the September 13, 1982, Business Roundtable Accounting Principles Task Force, held in New York City under the leadership of Roger Smith and Eugene Flegm of General Motors, indicate that the group had two specific areas of concern: "One was the apparent trend toward some type of value based accounting while the other was the emphasis on specific rule making as opposed to more general guidelines" (Business Roundtable, 1982). The basic conclusion was that the fair value approach was hurting the effectiveness of the accounting system, was unproven, and was difficult to implement. The financial statements would no longer measure the stewardship of management. The Roundtable must have thought that something had been accomplished at the meeting; Roger B. Smith, then the Chairman of General Motors Corporation, sent a letter afterward to Walter B. Wriston, Chairman of Citicorp, thanking him for his participation in the meeting and stating, "I believe we have laid the foundation for a greater appreciation on their (the FASB) part of the problems we in business face with financial accounting standards for reporting" (Smith, September 20, 1982).

Flegm was still arguing against fair values in 2005 when he wrote a letter to the Board commenting on fair value measurements. His contention was that fair values were to blame for some of the recent accounting frauds. He pointed out fair values were not auditable. This would be okay in a Utopian world, but in the real world some people are dishonest. According to Flegm, fair values place auditors in the untenable position of assessing management's estimates of fair values. In a 2005 article Edward Ketz stated:

> FASB likely will ignore Flegm's comment. Indeed, the Board has become more or less immune to criticism as it lives in some toy universe in Connecticut. But, in the real world, investors must worry about the scruples of corporate managers and directors. After all, investors do not know which managers are ethical and who are crooks. Fair value measurements exacerbate the problem because they make it virtually impossible to discern the honest from the dishonest executives until it is too late.
>
> *(July 2005)*

Illustrating the other point of view, in a speech delivered at the August 2009 American Accounting Association annual meeting in New York City, former Board member David

Mosso made the following statement: "FAS 157 is the only thing I will praise in the universe of generally accepted accounting principles (GAAP). FAS 157 is like the lone gold nugget in a miner's pan of mud and gravel" (2009b). Mosso is not alone; more and more accountants are beginning to recognize that historical–cost–based financial statements are not the end-all that they once appeared to be.

What caused the change between the time when SFAC No. 5 and No. 7 were being studied and 2006, when SFAS 157 was approved? The FASB in 2006 was composed of people who had begun to employ and believe in approaches other than historical cost and the matching principle to a greater extent than the Board members of the 1970s and 1980s; the twenty-first-century Board members were more open to change. Also, the discussions of the early 1980s may have helped pave the way for some of the Board's more recent standards. Even in 1984, there were only three Board members opposed to fair values. Perhaps the efforts of Robert Sterling and other academics, especially Robert Sprouse, who served on the FASB as a long-standing advocate of positions first outlined in ARS No. 3, as noted previously, seeking to establish fair values into the conceptual framework were not a failure; as times changed, new Board members became less protective of the historical cost concept and more willing to accept relevance and its value implication as a goal.

David Mosso, who was on the FASB Board during the promulgation of the first six Concepts Statements, summarized the situation this way:

> I helped build the conceptual framework model. It was a giant step forward in the development of the theory and practice of accounting. But the framework was built in word-to-word combat with the business community and the framework came out of combat with a bit of post-traumatic stress disorder, which is manifested by nightmares in the form of contorted accounting standards.
>
> Every accounting standard adopted before and after the conceptual framework has gone through the same kind of combat as the framework itself. FAS 157 could be called the Iwo Jima of accounting warfare. It planted a flag on top of a hotly contested fair value hill symbolizing what should be, I contend, the beginning of a transition from an undisciplined legislative style accounting model to a disciplined economic measurement-based accounting model.
>
> *(2009b, pp. 2–3)*

Some critics, mostly commercial bankers, have blamed fair value accounting, particularly the requirements of SFAS 157 and 159, for the market distress of 2008 and 2009. Some argued that fair value measures were not reflective of reality in that market prices would eventually rise and the written-down assets would eventually recover their original values. Historical cost, they contended, would allow the market time to recover, while writing down the assets under fair value accounting only served to make the business cycle deeper. In other words, the argument was that fair value accounting resulted in the financial statements being an influencer on the economy rather than merely a neutral measuring tool. The reaction from bankers was perhaps indicative that they did not know their own regulatory history. Prior to 1938, banks were required to use fair value reporting; the 1938 Interagency Accord abolished the use of current value accounting for investment securities in bank examination reports. The justification for the change was that the use of current market values caused banks to operate in ways that hindered economic growth. The use of fair values for reporting caused bankers to trade securities in such a way that interest rates fluctuated and markets became depressed. The argument was that the use of fair values causes banks to buy securities for short-term price appreciation (Johnson and Swieringa, 1996, p. 156).

Perhaps concerns were more about volatility or change than about the valuation model. On conceptual grounds, a 2007 article questioned whether financial statements should report the value of a firm, concluding that financial statements are never capable of truly showing the value of a firm, and therefore they should not be expected to do so.

> Financial statements are of course an essential input into analysis for decisions of many kinds, including investment decisions – but they constitute only one input. Their goal should not be to measure the value of the firm, but something more modest and achievable: to make a historical record of transactions and then to present as accurately as possible a summary representation of the financial results of these transactions. As Robert A. Healy, the longest-serving commissioner in the SEC's history, said in the 1930s, the purpose of accounting is "to make a historical record of events," and further that "the purpose of accounting is to account – not to present opinions of value."
>
> *(Pollock, January 18, 2007)*

Such conceptual arguments also bolstered the position of the banks. Despite the criticisms, the FASB and many accountants advocating the concept of fair value accounting argued that to ignore current market conditions only serves to hide problems. Investors want the financial statements to report the current fair values of financial assets, whereas preparers whose assets might have to be written down would blame the cyclicality and the outcome. In the past, the use of historical cost reporting has aided management's use of discretion to plan when losses would be reported (i.e., when an asset is disposed of), but Statements 157 and 159 challenged the process of managing earnings and, thus, the bonuses based on earnings.

Big GAAP and Little GAAP

The accounting profession has long struggled with the idea that the financial reporting needs of smaller closely held businesses might differ from those required by large publicly traded companies. The work of the FASB supposedly focuses on the financial reporting of companies of all sizes. There is a popular belief that the FASB's standards are developed primarily to affect the reporting requirements for larger publicly owned companies because the FASB's source of cash is linked to recognition by the SEC. However, the *AICPA Rules of Conduct* specifies that the FASB is the purveyor of accounting standards for all businesses – large and small. Small companies, however, argue that they should not be held to the same standards as large publicly held companies because the cost of such compliance is disproportionate when compared to larger entities. Smaller companies, and their smaller audit firms, have regularly suggested the need for differential standards for their purposes.

For decades, it has been proposed that the same accounting standards should not have to be required for both groups. In the December 1972 edition of the *Journal of Accountancy*, even before the FASB began operations, two CPAs expressed frustration with GAAP requirements being applied to smaller organizations. A small-firm practitioner pointed out that local practitioners are aware that requiring smaller organizations to prepare a long list of noncompliance with GAAP can be so confusing to clients and users of their reports that they can become meaningless. A partner with a large regional firm suggested that clients are reluctant to pay for services that they see as providing no value to them or the related capital providers or the public. The partner went on to suggest that certain closely held companies should be exempt from GAAP requirements that are prepared primarily for the readers of publicly held company financial statements. In 1974, while discussing the necessity of duality in accounting standards for public and private organizations, Max Block, a former editor of *The CPA Journal*, stated that "the accounting standards should not have been made mandatory to public and private companies without exception." Block argued that, in some instances, later exemplified in his article, they should have been made *optional* for private companies. A few years later, Block (1977) quoted John Burton, a former chief accountant of the SEC, to point out that public accounting is actually two professions. In one profession, the primary relationship is between the accountant and the client. In this situation, attestation is not as important because it is limited to capital providers who have a personal or direct relationship with the client. In the other profession, the capital is provided by the public and other outsiders. Burton had suggested that although a basic accounting model is appropriate for all preparers of financial statements, this is different from the need for specific detailed disclosures and comparability between financial statements. In referring to Burton's statements, Block clarified his perspective that public corporations and non-public companies are actually more like *two types* of clients that should be sharply distinguished within the profession.

In contrast to the preceding opinions generally supporting separate GAAP for closely held businesses, James Naus presented the case for not allowing separate rules for public and private companies. First, he pointed out that allowing alternative treatments may weaken the position of the CPA in achieving fair presentation and full disclosure. A second point is that a private company may still interact with the public environment. For example, an organization may wish to compare itself with larger competitors or may later become a public corporation. Naus implied that CPAs associated with non-public organizations would do better to influence GAAP in a way that meets all reporting needs (Naus et al., 1974). As a result of the interest in the subject, the AICPA had several committees study the issue between 1976 and 1983.

A compromise position

In the mid-1970s, the accounting standards division of the AICPA studied the application of GAAP to smaller and/or closely held businesses. In reporting its findings, the committee distinguished between two sets of principles. First, there are principles that are used in the measurement process. The committee believed that this process should not be affected by the nature of the user of the information since confusion would result from similar transactions being reported on an inconsistent basis. Secondly, there are principles that regulate disclosure practices. The committee supported the idea that particular disclosures may depend upon the needs of the user or on other factors (Chazen and Benson, 1978).

The opposing perspectives described above received significant attention in the 1970s, leading to a comprehensive study supported by the FASB to provide detailed empirical data to aid in determining the possibility of having different accounting principles govern reporting by public and private companies. The findings from the study indicated that although accountants believed that a separate GAAP would be beneficial, bankers found GAAP-based statements useful for decision making and favored the continued reliance of all companies on one set of GAAP. No consistent opinion was found among managers (Abdel-Khalik, 1983). The Board finally concluded that it had entered an area that was long on complaints and strongly held beliefs but short on facts. The FASB followed in 1981 with a call for public comment on the matter and also commissioned a research study. The study was carried out by a University of Florida team headed by Rashad Abdel-Khalik and was published in 1983 under the title *Financial Reporting by Private Companies: Analysis and Diagnosis*. Contrary to the general argument that small businesses should be treated differently was the alternative view that small businesses should not be treated as "second-class" citizens; they should have the same standards as big companies. In addition, the FASB special report included a principal finding that most lenders and other creditors feel "that their financial information needs and decision making practices are essentially the same for private as for public companies" (Abdel-Khalik, 1983). This latter view was borne out by a 1985 poll by Louis Harris and Associates that found a relatively high level of acceptance of FASB standards by executives of small companies. The small companies saw in the standards "a level playing field" on which they could compete for capital against larger organizations (Van Riper, 1994, p. 94). The FASB established a Small Business Advisory Group in 1984 and agreed to explicitly examine the implications to small businesses of all future standards projects. In 2004, the Small Business Advisory Committee was founded to meet twice a year to allow members to share their thoughts with the FASB. In 2007, the Private Company Financial Reporting Committee (PCFRC) was formed to represent all non-public business entities, regardless of size. The PCFRC gets its administrative support from the AICPA.

The 1983 study by Abdel-Khalik settled the issue for a few years, until 1995 when the AICPA's Private Companies Practice Executive Committee (PCPEC) concluded that standards overload is one of the most significant concerns of members practicing in small firms (Burke, 1997). However, the issue of separate GAAP for private companies was again rejected when the conclusion was reached that allowing a new basic accounting method would only contribute to the perceived standards overload problem. It was therefore recommended that the best approach at that time would be to have "the Financial Accounting Foundation (FAF) make a concerted effort to recruit and select trustees, FASB board members, and FASB staff persons who have experience with and understanding of the needs of small non-public entities" (AICPA, 1996). In fact, *The CPA Journal* had reported just a few years earlier in 1989, that the Private Companies Practice Section of the AICPA Division for CPA Firms promoted other comprehensive bases of accounting (OCBOA) as an alternative for small businesses to meet financial reporting needs in certain situations, but not as an alternative form of GAAP. After the turn of the twenty-first century, the AICPA (2005) noted that no in-depth study of the issue has been conducted in recent years. This concern led to the 2004 study described below.

Despite the above-mentioned support from the small business community, the FASB has occasionally addressed the issue of whether the same standards should apply to both small businesses and large corporate entities, and FASB decided that differential reporting would be acceptable. In some cases, the Board has limited the applicability of a standard to only larger entities. For example, under the provisions of SFAS No. 21, small non-public companies were exempted from the requirements to report earnings per share. Similarly, SFAS No. 14 on segment reporting did not apply to smaller companies. SFAS No. 14 defined a non-public company as one whose debt or equity securities do not trade on a stock exchange or in the over-the-counter market or one that does not have to report to the SEC. When SFAS No. 131 superseded No. 14, non-public companies were again exempted from segment reporting. Small companies, including some public companies, were also exempted from the requirements of SFAS No. 33 on inflation accounting. That Statement applied to only about the 1,500 largest companies according to certain size criteria.

SFAS No. 79, *Elimination of Certain Disclosures for Business Combinations by Nonpublic Enterprises – An Amendment of APB Opinion No. 16*, was specifically issued to relieve small companies from some of the disclosure requirements of APB Opinion No. 16 on business combinations. That statement eliminated the obligation of non-public companies to disclose pro forma information for business combinations accounted for under the purchase method. Disclosure requirements for public companies were not affected by the pronouncement. SFAS No. 79 was the result of FASB research and a survey of practitioners on financial reporting by private companies. Participants in the studies often mentioned requirements that they felt should not apply to non-public enterprises, including the pro forma information required by APB Opinion 16.

The FASB decided that the costs of providing the pro forma disclosures normally exceeded the benefits for the typical users of small company financial reports.

Another example of differential reporting for large and small entities is illustrated by SFAS No. 126, approved in December 1996, which exempted non-public entities from the market value disclosure requirements of SFAS No. 107. To qualify, a non-public entity must have less than $100 million of assets and no derivative financial instruments outstanding. This was a standard wherein the FASB was experimenting with differing disclosure standards for smaller entities. Disclosures about financial instruments were made optional for entities that met the criteria. Most Board members did not think the issue particularly important.

The issue of Big GAAP/Little GAAP has been a pervasive issue throughout the history of the FASB but has never been properly solved in the minds of smaller constituents. Yet the FASB has addressed the issue and has typically made the decision that small companies should subscribe to the same accounting principles as larger entities. Board Chairman Robert Herz was asked whether there should be a defining line based on some factor such as size of equity or amount of revenue. His response serves as a summary of the issue:

> I'm not in favor of wholesale big GAAP/little GAAP. Any differences should be based on user needs and cost/benefit considerations. We don't need a two-tiered system for the sake of having one; it only creates more complexity. The FASB is primarily interested in the delineation between public and private companies.
>
> ("FASB Chair . . . ," 2008, p. 17)

The controversy of Big GAAP versus Little GAAP arose again in the twenty-first century. The AICPA's Private Company Financial Reporting Task Force began comprehensive research in early 2004 to consider whether:

- The general purpose financial statements of private companies, prepared in accordance with GAAP, meet the financial reporting needs of constituents of that reporting; and whether
- The cost of providing GAAP financial statements is justified compared with the benefits they provide to private company constituents.

The AICPA Task Force concluded that some of the constituencies in the 2004 study are of the opinion that it would be useful if the underlying accounting for public versus non-public (private) companies were different in certain situations. This may be attributed to the fact that some GAAP requirements for public companies are perceived to lack relevance or decision usefulness for private companies. However, the Task Force also found that although respondents rated certain GAAP requirements as being low on decision useful-ness or relevance, respondents appear to believe that the benefits of complying with GAAP outweigh the costs. This apparent conflict may be explained by the feeling that favorable ratings are given regarding the overall value of GAAP (AICPA, 2005). The Task Force also concluded that allowing GAAP exceptions and other bases of accounting are not the appropriate response to addressing the unique needs of private company financial reporting. Task Force members believed that such an approach would erode the overall recognized value of GAAP, while other bases of accounting might not adequately serve the needs of the constituents of private companies.

The issue is still being considered. In December 2009, a blue-ribbon panel of eighteen members was organized as a joint effort by the Financial Accounting Foundation, the AICPA, and the National Association of State Boards of Accountancy to provide recommendations on the future of US standard setting for private companies. In December 2010, the panel announced a recommendation to the Financial Accounting Foundation that a new private company standard-setting board be established. The mission of the new board would be "to establish exceptions and modifications to US GAAP for private companies, while ensuring that such exceptions and modifications provide decision-useful information to lenders and other users of private company financial reports" (Defelice, 2010). In the event that such a board is eventually created, there arises the problem of how it would be financed, since money from the PCAOB could not be used to finance standard setting limited only to private companies.

As stated by Robert Herz, "Private companies are a vital force in the nation's economy and it is, therefore, critical that their financial reporting be conceptually sound, cost effective, and provide relevant, reliable and useful information" (Zanzig and Flesher, 2006). This does not mean that there should be two sets of GAAP requirements that do not share some common components. Although there have been some standards that differentiated between private and public companies, most standards apply universally to firms of all sizes and organizational structures. The question of Big GAAP versus Little GAAP has often been considered by the Board in its deliberations, but only in a few cases have separate reporting standards been recommended. As the FASB learned in the 1970s, this is an area with occasional loud complaints but little in the way of organized agreement across all constituencies. In general, the FASB and its constituencies seem to have agreed that a single inclusive set of standards was best for users of financial statements. Then came the post-2008 "great recession" cost-benefit perfect storm, leading to the creation in May 2012 of the Private Company Council within the institutional framework of FAF to address concerns about unwarranted reporting and disclosure requirements for small and medium-sized entities (SMEs). The focus now seems to be shifting toward a debate about a conceptual framework for SMEs.

With respect to international standards, the IASB in July 2009 published an International Financial Reporting Standard (IFRS) designed for use by SMEs. That standard was the result of a five-year development process and extensive consultation with SMEs worldwide. The reason given in support of the standard was that since full IFRSs were designed to meet the needs of equity investors in companies in public capital markets, they contain a sizeable amount of implementation guidance and include disclosures appropriate for public companies. Users of the financial statements of SMEs do not have those needs. Also, many SMEs say that full IFRSs impose a burden on them that has grown as IFRSs have become more detailed and as more countries have begun to use them. Thus, in developing the proposed IFRS for SMEs, IASB's twin goals were to meet user needs while balancing costs and benefits from a preparer perspective. The objective of the project was to develop an IFRS to meet the reporting needs of entities that do not have public accountability. Future IFRSs for SMEs will be derived from full IFRSs with modifications based on the needs of users of SME financial statements and on cost-benefit considerations.

Twenty-first century political developments (Gramm, Leach, Bliley): Financial Services Modernization Act of 1999

In the belief that scaled-up financial institutions would benefit the position of the United States in global capital market activity, and that the proliferation of smaller financial institutions was a bane to efficiency, President Clinton signed into law in November 1999 a sweeping deregulation bill sponsored by three Republican members of Congress. The Gramm-Leach-Bliley Act (GLB), also known as the *Financial Services Modernization Act of 1999*, rescinded the limitations on combination of financial institutions prohibited since the passage of the 1933 Glass Steagall

(GS) banking law during the early days of the Great Depression. GS had divided the investment banking and commercial banking sectors under the view that each of these institutions had different missions in the capital market, and the degree of risk related to each sector warranted separation of their functions.

GLB, coming upon the conclusion of arguably the greatest period of market wealth creation in history, the 1990s (when the equity market indices increased by a multiple of several times from the decade opening level in 1990), suggested that it was time to consolidate financial institutions in a manner that would take fullest advantage of incentives to properly place resources in their respective marketplace. The institutional changes in the financial sector that followed had in many ways already manifested themselves due to lax enforcement of GS and seem to have become more clearly reflected in the considerations of the conceptual framework. As previously noted, SFAC No. 8 (2010) indicated a preference for the entity versus the proprietary view or orientation.

This may reflect a view toward providing information that portrays the assets of the entity in a manner that serves the short-term versus longer-term investment horizons of larger, diversely invested financial institutions, which are often selected as intermediaries for their ability to demonstrate short-term versus long-term performance gains. A focus on the short term versus the long term, with an emphasis more on liquidity than operating performance, as noted by Rappaport (*Saving Capitalism from Short Termism*, 2011) seems reflective of institutional behavior, especially in the wake of the strife of the marketplace in the latter half of the first decade of the twenty-first century. The emphasis is on immediate, liquidity-related value versus performance metrics from operations and, as observed by the *Economist* as early as May 1990, institutional investors demonstrate limited interest in serving on boards of directors of investees and behave more like "punters" than proprietors. In SFAC No. 8, the FASB signaled a position in support of the entity view, which considers the sourcing of capital to be indistinguishable – that is, the distinction between debt or equity is mostly a legal distinction. In a proprietary model, on the other hand, the focus is longterm risks and rewards to the residual risk holder who is the equity or proprietary capital contributor. Thus, there are important distinctions between the entity and the proprietary view. *By staking out an entity view, SFAC No. 8 in 2010 established the conceptual groundwork for adjustments to disclosure consistent with the former, and not the latter, orientation. The issue then becomes, "What are those differences and how do they affect preparation, auditing, disclosure, and analysis?"*

Sarbanes-Oxley Act (2002)

The Sarbanes-Oxley Act (SOX) of July 30, 2002, was transformative for the FASB and possibly for standard setting per se in that the funding previously provided by private sources is now undertaken by means of an annual fee assessed upon publicly traded companies. The FASB's budget is subject to review and approval by the US SEC. This shift in sourcing was hailed by many as a reduction of the influence of private-sector constituencies who could apply pressure on the FASB in exchange for financial support – a factor affecting the appearance if not the fact of its ability to act independently. A competing criticism is that an agency supported by public funding is even more directly under the aegis and influence of the SEC, the federal government, and public and political processes. In indirect but important ways, the Financial Accounting Foundation, the parent organization of the FASB, is subjected to oversight, for example, in the vetting of candidates for seats on the FAF, where finalists are "interviewed" by one or more members of the Commission.

SOX also established the Public Company Accounting Oversight Board (PCAOB), which for the first time placed a private entity outside the CPA profession's direct influence in the position of reviewing the work of public company auditors. The PCAOB, while not a governmental agency, submits its proposed standards to the SEC as a part of the protocol for final adoption.

These changes seemed likely to influence the activities of standard setters and auditors, given the explicit role played by the SEC. As well, additional requirements were placed on preparers to affirm financial reports and for the review of internal controls. The post-SOX standard-setting and auditing environment is now arguably a domain not dominated by the private sector. For while the SEC has always been an influential observer at FASB meetings since its inception, formal budget involvement explicitly relates the FASB's actions to the political process and the public policy direction of the Commission, whose members are appointed by the President. The implications of this may not be easily or even readily identifiable in particular standards but, as noted in the case of GLB legislation, may be supportive of the rationale supporting an entity versus proprietary view of reporting as indicated in SFAC No. 8. As yet however, it is not apparent that SFAC No. 8 has explicitly affected standard setting. As former Representative Michael Oxley stated in public forums in the years following the Act, with full agreement from his coauthor colleague, retired Senator Paul Sarbanes, the principal objective of SOX was to "restore" confidence in the public capital markets. With such a broad public policy objective, how its provisions are interpreted and enforced leaves substantial room for discussion as to implications for standard setting.

Dodd-Frank Act (2010), conflict materials, and political use of reporting rules

A mammoth legislative undertaking during the first years of the first term of President Barack Obama was the Dodd-Frank Wall Street Reform and Consumer Protection Act of 2010 (DF). DF mandates an unprecedented multiyear rule-making process involving over 200 new regulations for as many as a dozen regulatory agencies. A novel disclosure requirement enacted in DF affects publicly traded companies under the oversight of the SEC and creates a so-called EXTRA GAAP disclosure, one not established or endorsed by the FASB. The SEC rules mandated by the Dodd-Frank Act require disclosures by public companies concerning conflict minerals that originated in the Democratic Republic of the Congo or an adjoining country. The concern is that miners of these minerals in that region have adopted abusive labor practices. One study suggested that the aggregate cost to comply with the Dodd-Frank Act's conflict minerals rule could run close to $8 billion, much greater than the SEC's $71.2 million estimate.

In this way, indirectly, Congress has preempted FASB in a matter of social disclosure, consistent with the so-called triple-bottom-line framework advanced by many who are concerned about corporate social responsibility as well as financial or economic measures. These disclosures will require involvement of company auditors as to the processes by which such information has been gathered in order to substantiate that the representations being provided about the sources of conflict minerals are properly identified. Given that the FASB's conceptual framework is narrowly focused on financial and similar metrics, since it failed to adopt a broader business reporting model as recommended by the Jenkins Committee, the SEC's final rules released in November 2012 affirm that the standards for disclosure regarding conflict minerals is the responsibility of the US Government Accountability Office. Another consideration is the definition of the "user" of such disclosures. Presumably, the user will not be investors or financial analysts, but probably the US Department of State. Thus, financial reporting, and therefore financial reporting standards, are being taken over by politicians who are trying to promote an agenda of which corporate financial statements were never designed to be a part.

The codification project

Given the great number of standards that have emanated from the FASB, AICPA, and the Emerging Issues Task Force (EITF) over the years, many on similar topics, it is obvious that users have been a major beneficiary of the recent standards codification project. Before the codification project began, it was noted that there were at least 180 different pronouncements dealing with revenue recognition – many of which had emanated from the EITF. Determining which pronouncement was relevant in a particular circumstance was nearly impossible. This difficulty led to the onset of the project to codify all pronouncements of the FASB, APB, CAP, EITF, the AICPA's Accounting Standards Executive Committee (AcSEC), and the SEC. In the summer of 2004, the trustees of the FAF approved the largest and most expensive project ever undertaken by the Board – the codification of all accounting standards. A computer-based searchable codification was completed in early 2008 and became official on July 1, 2009. A wide variety of viewpoints have developed about this technological application, from facilitating and supporting effective research to dumbing down judgmental processes to a level of mechanical dependency.

While the codification project did not "change" accounting standards, it has reordered and re-identified them by a classification scheme that uses section numbers, and not topics, to identify the subject under consideration. The availability of the codification may reduce criticisms related to standards overload. There are still as many standards as ever, but the overload, it can be argued, may be less noticeable with the organization and simplification provided by the efficient and searchable codification. Prior to the codification, many accountants thought all they had to do to solve a problem was to look to the previously approved FASB statements; they often ignored, or were not aware of, all of the other sources of GAAP. Codification may foster research; indeed, familiarity with the Code may afford facility in responding to some computer-based CPA examination questions. The codification of standards resembles in some ways the codification of the law, and it may be an indication that knowledge about principles is less of a focus than mastering the techniques of searching a "Code Structure."

At the outset of this essay a number of questions were posed: What are important episodes and aspects of accountancy in this period? Is a philosophy of American pragmatism in accounting thought an explanatory element in these episodes? Is a regulatory maxim of sunshine or disclosure a prominent framework as an effective social remedy for the tension between the public and large economic entities that deploy major amounts of capital in the economy? These questions may now be further summarized into a single query: What are the signature aspects of American financial accounting and reporting that you as a reader have discerned about this period?

Summary and observations

Over the past two centuries, perhaps scores of millions of words have been written by individuals who would profess to be associated with the development or instruction of accounting thought and process in the United States. So it is ambitious, to say the least, to attempt to condense or distill so much in so brief an essay as this one. And yet proper summaries are needed to provide perspective for an appreciation of those events that occur outside the bounds of one's own memory and experience. Furthermore, institutions in the accounting discipline, as is often the case in the peculiarly future-oriented American social fabric, tend to be forward looking and somewhat dismissive of history. Perhaps that is why there is a taste of *rechauffe*, or recooking, of the variety of flavors of the so-called framework debate over long decades of change in technology and technique that makes one impatient for – or worse, truly expectant of – a resolution to the quest for *the* conceptual framework instead of *a* conceptual framework. The term itself, framework, invades the senses with a preconception of form and solid purpose, which betrays the subjective nature of the process of providing information that both protects those who have invested capital in an enterprise and those who might soon do so. What can be said is that the form and format of disclosure over the period has indeed changed, from the locked proprietor's ledger balance of accounts, to the crude balance sheets found in antebellum railroads, the first large capitalizations in the US, to the iconic examples found in the multiple eras of US Steel annual reports, wherein the income statement and, ultimately, "matching" dominated an era of large industrials and their financial statements. Thereafter, the focus shifted from financial statements to a Trueblood Report orientation focused on financial reports to a broader business reporting model, as envisioned by the Jenkins Committee, which was influenced by web-based technology and instant global communication. There is in all of this perhaps one central assumption or belief that traces back to the sunshine era of the post-Civil War period, which first sought uniformity in what was to be disclosed. Thereafter the SEC sought not uniform disclosure but full and fair disclosure. Currently there are viewpoints which widely proclaim that disclosure should be "transparent" and concerned about "sustainability". These evolving states presume that disclosure will affect decisions in a way that is consistent with economic and social well being. Belief in sunshine (or disclosure or transparency) as a social remedy assumes that the parties whose investment capital is ultimately at risk and who are given such information are capable of understanding and acting upon it. The frequently affirmed low levels of popular financial literacy seem to make this a tenuous premise.

Does a conceptual framework exist that will meet the needs of a complex global multicultural society? Will an eventual consensus or intellectual alignment occur as to the objectives and purpose of standard setting in the United States? And will it eventually be "condorsed" by other sovereign nations in some form? In 2002, the Norwalk Agreement between the FASB and IASB held forth the bright promise of "a single set of high-quality accounting standards" to be used globally. But over a decade later, following a July 2012 non-decision by the SEC – the agency that gives voice to the sovereign US government in such matters, no basis exists for expecting a mandate to adopt IFRS. The failure to achieve convergence probably surprises no one, and yet the expectation of discovering *the* conceptual framework continues to tantalize those engaged in discharging the substantial responsibilities of constructing standards for reporting that have the potential of casting out the shadows of darkness and opening up the full light of disclosure sunshine, the hope of which has been so brightly promised for over a century.

An orientation postulate and the framework

The first level of D. R. Scott's (1931) framework is an orientation postulate that articulates between the environment in which accounting operates and accounting principles. While an orientation postulate as an essential element of a theoretical framework is becoming acknowledged, the need for an orientation postulate was not widely recognized in the 1930s. Scott, in his *Cultural Significance of Accounts*, contended that unity in accounting comes from a broad consideration of the social, political, and economic environment in which accounting serves. Years later, Zeff (1962), DePree (1989), and Stewart (1989) provided a similar argument that an essential element of a theoretical accounting framework is an orientation postulate. Zeff and, later, Lawrence and Stewart (1993), seem to argue that a conceptual framework must include the perspective from which accounting reports are to be prepared. Separating a reporting framework from the accounting framework may seem specious to some, but the distinction between the goal of accounting to meet stewardship and fiduciary roles and the goal of reporting to assist decision making seems necessary if not vital. Writing in 1961, Davidson and Trueblood, Staubus and others, made an argument for the importance of decision making as a key to a disclosure framework. Davidson and Trueblood also noted that decision making shared prominence with "stewardship." Can stewardship and decision making be reconciled in a single conceptual framework?

Could it be that this integration confounds what might better be structured as a separable accounting framework? And could it also be that the Lee (2006) and the MacIntosh (2006) commentaries on the saga of conceptualizing are most helpful in recognizing that a framework must first be considered as a socially constructed exercise?

John Kenneth Galbraith, a noted economist who passed away in the first decade of the twenty-first century, can be called upon to assist in understanding why the levels of frustration are so high and yet the effort toward a conceptual framework continues unabated. He said, "There is certainly no absolute standard of beauty. That precisely is what makes its pursuit so interesting."

Lamenting the frustration of such pursuits does not serve us well. Recall again, that a conceptual framework is not authoritative. *Perhaps in seeking and assessing frameworks, we should recognize that the value is not in achieving them but in undertaking and perfecting their pursuit.* That is, the value of these efforts is to be found as much in the PROCESS, as in the PRODUCT.

Notes

1 Workman's book is widely available in libraries in reprint form. The Yushodo American Historic Accounting Literature Series (1982) contains 25 selected and complete reprint volumes from this early period (1796–1887). It also contains edited commentary by Williard E. Stone, University of Florida, and represents an excellent resource for further investigation.
2 The other five projects were (1) foreign currency translation, (2) accounting for leases, (3) segment reporting, (4) accounting for contingencies, and (5) accounting for research and development and similar costs.
3 Board members should have known Sterling's views. He had published a 1970 book wherein he extolled the virtues of using exit prices for a company as a basket of goods, an aggregate valuation, as opposed to other writers such as Raymond Chambers (1966), who advocated individual asset valuation using exit prices.
4 It is interesting to note that Schuetze gave SFAS No. 14 on segment reporting as an example of a general standard. Two decades later, another Board viewed SFAS No. 14 as too rules based and opted for an even more general standard when it approved SFAS No. 131. Thus, one person's general standard might be another individual's idea of a rules–based standard.

References

Abdel-Khalik, A. Rashad. *Financial Reporting by Private Companies: Analysis and Diagnosis*. Research Report. Stamford, CT: FASB, 1983.

Alexander, Michael O. Memo to self, November 24, 1981; also, June 18, 1982 (both documents in the possession of the authors).

Allen, David G. and McDermott, Kathleen. *Accounting for Success: A History of Price Waterhouse in America 1890–1990*. Boston, MA: Harvard Business School Press, 1993.

American Accounting Association. *A Statement of Basic Accounting Theory*. Evanston, IL: American Accounting Association, 1966.

_____. *Statement on Accounting Theory and Theory Acceptance*. Sarasota, FL: American Accounting Association, 1977.

American Institute of Accountants. *Fiftieth Anniversary Celebration*. New York, NY: American Institute of Accountants, 1938.

American Institute of Certified Public Accountants. *Report of the Private Companies Practice Section, Special Task Force on Standards Overload*. New York, NY: AICPA, 1996.

_____. *AICPA Council Endorses Dedicated Effort to Explore Potential Changes to GAAP for Private Companies*. News Release. New York, NY: AICPA, May 2005.

Armstrong, Marshall S. "The Politics of Establishing Accounting Standards," *Journal of Accountancy* (Vol. 143, No. 2, February 1977), pp. 76–79.

Bass, Thomas A. "The Future of Money," *WIRED* (October 1996), http://www.wired.com/wired/archive/4.10/wriston.html (accessed May 27, 2013).

Bennett, James. *The American System of Practical Book-keeping: Adapted to the Commerce of the United States*. New York, NY: ABM Paul, 1820.

Beresford, D. R. "The FASB's Accomplishments to Date: One Participant's View," *Accounting Historians Journal* (December 1998), pp. 151–166.

Berger, R. O. Sr. *The History of Price, Waterhouse & Co. and Jones, Caesar & Co. 1890 to June 30, 1901*. Typescript: Columbia University Library PWC Collection, 1947.

Berle, A. and Means, G. *The Modern Corporation and Private Property*. New York, NY: Macmillan, 1933.

Block, M. "Trend to Duality in Accounting Standards," *The CPA Journal* (March 1977), pp. 11–15.

Bloomfield, Robert. "Office Hours: Conceptual Framework Project," *Financial Accounting Standards Research Initiative* (April 10, 2009), http://fasri.net/index.php/category/standard-setting-projects/ (accessed March 13, 2015).

Brearey, C. and Previts, G. "Charles Francis Adams Jr. Pioneer U.S. Accounting Regulator," Working Paper, 2013.

Bridgman, Percy Williams. "The Prospect for Intelligence," *The Yale Review* (Vol. 14, No. 19, 1945), pp. 444–461.

Burke, John F. "Report on Standards Overload," *The CPA Journal* (March 1997), p. 11.

Business Roundtable. Minutes of Meetings, September 13, 1982.

Canning, John B. *The Economics of Accountancy*. New York, NY: Ronald Press, 1929.

Carduff, K. C. "Stewardship in Corporate Reporting: The Annual Reports of U.S. Steel (1938–1969)," Working Paper, May 2013.

Chambers, Raymond J. *Accounting, Evaluation and Economic Behavior*. Englewood Cliffs, NJ: Prentice-Hall, Inc., 1966.

Chatfield, Michael. *A History of Accounting Thought*. Hinsdale, IL: The Dryden Press, 1974.

Chazen, C. and Benson, B. "Fitting GAAP to Smaller Businesses," *Journal of Accountancy* (Vol. 145, No. 2, February 1978), pp. 46–51.

Clarke, F., Dean G., and Wells, M. *The Sydney School of Accounting: The Chambers Years*. Revised. Sydney, Australia: The University of Sydney, 2012.

Colt, John C. *The Science of Double Entry Book-keeping*. Cincinnati, OH: N. G. Burgess & Co., 1838.

Davidson, H. Justin and Trueblood, R. "Accounting for Decision-Making," *The Accounting Review* (Vol. 36, No. 4, October 1961), pp. 577–582.

Defelice, Alexandra. "Panel Moves Forward with Recommendations for a Separate Private Company Financial Reporting Board," *Journal of Accountancy Online* (December 10, 2010).

DePree, Chauncey M. Jr. "Testing and Evaluating a Conceptual Framework for Accounting," *Abacus* (Vol. 25, No. 2, September 1989), pp. 61–73.

"Discussing Railroad Men's Duties," *The New York Times* (November 13, 1878), http://query.nytimes.com/mem/archive-free/pdf?res=F40713FB3E5A137B93C1A8178AD95F4C8784F9. (accessed March 13, 2015).

Dopuch, Nicholas and Sunder, Shyam. "FASB's Statements on Objectives and Elements of Financial Accounting: A Review," *Accounting Review* (Vol. 55, No. 1, January 1980), pp. 1–21.

Edwards, Edgar O. and Bell, P. W. *The Theory and Measurement of Business Income*. Berkeley, CA: University of California Press, 1961.

"FASB Chair Thinks Globally," *New Jersey CPA* (September–October 2008), pp. 16–17.

Financial Accounting Standards Board. Statement of Financial Accounting Concepts No. 1, *Objectives of Financial Reporting by Business Enterprises*. Stamford, CT: FASB, November, 1978.

Flegm, Eugene. Letter to General Motors, Inc. Management, July 31, 1978.

Flesher, Dale L. and Flesher, Tonya K. "Ivar Kreuger's Contribution to U.S. Financial Reporting," *The Accounting Review* (Vol. 61, No. 3, July 1986), pp. 421–434.

Flesher, Dale L., Previts, Gary J., and Flesher, Tonya K. "Profiling the New Industrial Professionals: The First CPAs of 1896–97," *Business and Economic History* (Vol. 25, No. 2, Fall 1996), pp. 252–266.

Flesher, Dale L., Previts, Gary J., and Samson, William D. "Using Accounting to Manage: A Case of Railroad Managerial Accounting in the 1850s," *Accounting and History: A Selection of Papers Presented at the 8th World Congress of Accounting Historians*. Madrid: Asociacion Espanola de Contabilidad y Administration de Empresas, 2000, pp. 91–126.

_____, "Early American Corporate Reporting and European Capital Markets: The Case of the Illinois Central Railroad, 1851–1861," *Accounting Historians Journal* (Vol. 33, No. 1, June 2006), pp. 3–24.

Flesher, Dale L., Samson, William D., and Previts, Gary J. "The Origins of Value-for-Money Auditing: The Baltimore and Ohio Railroad: 1827–1830," *Managerial Auditing Journal* (Vol. 18, No. 5, 2003), pp. 374–386.

Foster, B. F. *A Concise Treatise on Commercial Book-keeping*. Boston, MA: Perkins & Marvin, 1836.

Foye, Arthur B. *Haskins & Sells: Our First Seventy-Five Years*. New York: Haskins & Sells, 1970.

Gerboth, Dale L. "The Conceptual Framework: Not Definitions, But Professional Values," *Accounting Horizons* (Vol. 1, No. 3, September 1987), pp. 1–8.

Gordon, John Steele. *The Great Game: The Emergence of Wall Street as a World Power, 1653–2000*. New York, NY: Touchstone, 2000.

Gore, Pelham. *The FASB Conceptual Framework, 1973–1985: An Analysis*. Manchester, UK: Manchester University Press, 1992.

Grady, Paul. *Inventory of Generally Accepted Accounting Principles for Business Enterprises*. New York, NY: AICPA, 1965.

Graham, Benjamin, "A Prophet on Wall Street," *Audacity* (Vol. 5, No. 2, Fall 1996), pp. 50–61.

Hakansson, Nils H. "Where We Are in Accounting: A Review of 'Statement of Accounting Theory and Theory Acceptance,'" *The Accounting Review* (Vol. 53, No. 1, July 1978), pp. 717–725.

Hatfield, Henry Rand. *Modern Accounting*. New York, NY: D. Appleton & Co., 1909.

Herz, Robert H. "A Year of Challenge and Change for the FASB," *Accounting Horizons* (Vol. 17, No. 3, September 2003), pp. 247–255.

Homburger, R. H. and Previts, G. J. "The Relevance of 'Zwei Pfadfinder,'" *Accounting Historians Journal* (Vol. 4, No. 1, Spring 1977), pp. 9–13.

Jackson, William. *Book-keeping in the True Italian Form of Debtor and Creditor by Way of Double Entry*. Philadelphia, PA: H. & P. Rice, 1801.

Johnson, L. Todd. "Sterling at the FASB," in Lee, Thomas A. and Wolnizer, Peter W. (eds.) *The Quest for a Science of Accounting: An Anthology of the Research of Robert R. Sterling*. New York, NY: Garland Publishing, Inc., 1997.

Johnson, L. Todd and Swieringa, R. "Anatomy of an Agenda Decision: Statement No. 115," *Accounting Horizons* (Vol. 10, No. 2, June 1996), pp. 149–179.

Jones, Thomas. *The Principles and Practice of Book-keeping*. New York, NY: John Wiley, 1841.

_____. *Book-keeping and Accountantship*. New York, NY: John Wiley, 1849.

Ketz, J. Edward. "The Accounting Cycle: Let's Quit Enabling Accounting Frauds," *SmartPros*, (July 2005), http://accounting.smartpros.com/x48974.xml. (accessed March 13, 2015).

_____. "The Accounting Cycle: Debunking the Supposed Link Between Rules and Accounting Scandals," *SmartPros* (March 2006), http://accounting.smartpros.com/x51840.xml. (accessed 3/13/2015).

_____. "The Accounting Cycle: Demand for Principles-Based Accounting: The American Accounting Idol," *SmartPros* (February 2008), http://accounting.smartpros.com/x60866.xml. (accessed March 13, 2015).

_____. "The Accounting Cycle: 200th Column: Retrospection," *SmartPros* (December 2009), http://accounting.smartpros.com/x68360.xml. (accessed March 13, 2015).

Kirk, Donald J. "Looking Back on Fourteen Years at the FASB: The Education of a Standard Setter," *Accounting Horizons* (Vol. 2, No. 1, March 1988), pp. 8–17.

Lawrence, Carol and Stewart, J. P. "DR Scott's Conceptual Framework," *Accounting Historians Journal* (Vol. 20, No. 2, Fall 1993), pp. 93–118.

Lee, Chauncey. *The American Accomptant*. Lansingburgh, NY: William W. Wands, 1797.

Lee, T. "The FASB and Accounting for Economic Reality," *Accounting and the Public Interest* (Vol. 6, 2006), pp. 1–21.

MacIntosh, N. "The FASB and Accounting for Economic Reality: Accounting – Truth, Lies, or 'Bullshit'? A Philosophical Investigation," *Accounting and the Public Interest* (Vol. 6, 2006), pp. 22–36.

MacNeal, Kenneth. *Truth in Accounting*. Philadelphia, PA: University of Pennsylvania Press, 1939.

Marsh, C. C. *The Science of Double Entry Book-keeping*. Baltimore, MD: Geo. M'Dowell & Son, 1831.

May, George O. "The Nature of the Financial Accounting Process," *The Accounting Review* (Vol. 18, No. 1, July 1943), pp. 189–193.

Miranti, Paul and Goodman, L. "Railroad Accounting (U.S.)," in Chatfield, M. and Vangermeersch, Richard (eds.) *The History of Accounting: An International Encyclopedia*. New York, NY: Garland Publishing Inc., 1996.

Mosso, David. *Early Warning and Quick Response: Accounting in the Twenty-First Century*. London, UK: Emerald Group Publishing Limited, 2009a.

_____. "Transparency Unveiled: Financial Crisis Prevention Through Accounting Reform," Presentation to the American Accounting Association Financial Accounting and Reporting Section, August 3, 2009b.

_____. Letter to G. J. Previts, August 10, 2009c.

Murphy, Thomas A. Letter (on Business Roundtable stationery) to the FASB Director of Administration, June 24, 1977.

_____. Letter (on Business Roundtable stationery) to the FASB Director of Research and Technical Activities, April 19, 1978.

Naus, J., McGill, B. and Arnstein, P. "Practitioners Forum: Unaudited Financial Statements Revisited," *Journal of Accountancy* (Vol. 134, No. 6, January 1974), pp. 77–80.

Nussbaumer, N. "Does the FASB's Conceptual Framework Help Solve Real Accounting Issues?" *Journal of Accounting Education* (Vol. 10, No. 1, 1992), pp. 235–242.

Objectives of Financial Statements. Report of the Trueblood Committee. New York, NY: AICPA, 1973.

Paton, William A. *Accounting Theory: With Special Reference to Corporate Enterprise*. New York, NY: Ronald Press, 1922.

Paton, William A. and Littleton, A. C. *An Introduction to Corporate Accounting Standards*. Ann Arbor, MI: American Accounting Association, 1940 (1957 revision).

Pollock, Alex J. "Has the FASB Outlived Its Usefulness?" *Financial Services Outlook* (January 18, 2007).

Previts, Gary J., ed. *Financial Reporting and Standard Setting: A Symposium . . . October 25–6, 1990*. New York, NY: AICPA, 1991.

Previts, Gary J. and Merino, Barbara. *A History of Accountancy in the United States*. Columbus, OH: The Ohio State University Press, 1998.

Previts, Gary J. and Samson, W. "Exploring the Contents of the Baltimore and Ohio Railroad Annual Reports: 1827–1856," *Accounting Historians Journal* (Vol. 27, No. 1, June 2000), pp. 235–254.

Previts, Gary J. and Sheldahl, T. K. "Accounting and 'Countinghouses': An Analysis and Commentary," *Abacus* (Vol. 13, No. 1, June 1977), pp. 52–59.

Previts, Gary J. and Taylor, Richard. *John R. Wildman, Pioneer Professional of American Accounting*. Monograph No. 2, The Academy of Accounting Historians, 1978.

Previts, Gary J., Flesher, D. L., and Samson, W. "Accounting, Economic Development and Financial Reporting: The Case of Three Pre-Civil War US Railroads," *Accounting History* (November 2003), pp. 61–77.

_____. "Auditing in the United States: A Historical Perspective," *Abacus* (February 2005), pp. 21–39.

"Punters or Proprietors: A Survey of Capitalism," *The Economist* (May 5–11, 1990), pp. 21–23.

Rappaport, A. R. *Saving Capitalism from Short Termism*. New York, NY: McGraw-Hill, 2011.

Rosen, L. S. and DeCoster, Don T. "Funds Statements: A Historical Perspective," *The Accounting Review* (Vol. 44, No. 1, January 1969), pp. 124–136.

Samson, William D. and Previts, Gary, J. "Reporting for Success: The Baltimore and Ohio Railroad and Management Information, 1827–1856," *Business and Economic History* (Vol. 28, No. 2, 1999), pp. 236–254.

Samson, William D., Flesher, Dale L., and Previts, Gary J. "Quality of Earnings: The Case of the Mobile and Ohio Railroad in the 19th Century," *Issues in Accounting Education* (Vol. 18, No. 4, 2003), pp. 335–357.

_____. "Corporate Governance and External and Internal Controls: The Case of the Baltimore and Ohio Railroad, Circa 1831," *Issues in Accounting Education* (Vol. 21, No. 1, 2006), pp. 45–62.

Sanders, Thomas H., Hatfield, Henry Rand, and Moore, Underhill. *A Statement of Accounting Principles*. New York, NY: American Institute of Accountants, 1938.

Schuetze, Walter P. "Reflections of a Former Member of the FASB," *Stanford Lectures in Accounting 1978*. Stanford, CA: Stanford University Graduate School of Business, 1978.

_____. "Keep It Simple," *Accounting Horizons* (Vol. 5, No. 2, June 1991), pp. 113–117.

Scott, D. R. *Cultural Significance of Accounts*. New York, NY: H. Holt & Co., 1931.

Sheys, B. *The American Book-keeper*. New York, NY: Collins & Co., 1815, 1818.

Smith, Nancy E. "The Impact of the FASB's Conceptual Framework Project on Intermediate Accounting," Unpublished Ph.D. dissertation, University of Nebraska, 1986.

Smith, Roger B. Letter to members of the Business Roundtable Accounting Principles Task Force, March 29, 1982.

_____. Letter to Walter B. Wriston, September 20, 1982.

Sorter, George. "Review of 'A Theory of Accounting to Investors,'" *The Accounting Review* (Vol. 38, No. 1, January 1963), pp. 223–224.

Sprague, C. E. "The Algebra of Accounts," *The Book-keeper* (July 20, 1880), pp. 2–4; and (August 17, 1880), pp. 34ff.

_____. *The Philosophy of Accounts*. New York, NY: Privately Published, 1907 (Reprint New York: Ronald Press, 1922).

Stamp, Edward. "Accounting Regulation in the US: The Growing Debate," *International Accounting Bulletin* (Supplement, January 1984), pp. S1–S14.

Staubus, George J. *A Theory of Accounting to Investors*. Berkeley, CA: University of California Press, 1961.

_____. "Autobiography: An Accountant's Education," *Accounting Historians Journal* (Vol. 30, No. 1, June 2003), pp. 155–196.

_____. Letter to Donald Kirk, November 15, 2009.

Stempf, Victor H. "The Post-Victory Challenge," *Journal of Accountancy* (Vol. 78, No. 2, August 1944), pp. 99–105.

Sterling, Robert R. *Theory of the Measurement of Enterprise Income*. Lawrence, KS: University Press of Kansas, 1970.

_____. "Costs (Historical Versus Current) Versus Exit Values," *Abacus* (Vol. 17, No. 2, 1981), pp. 93–129.

_____. "The Conceptual Framework: An Assessment," *Journal of Accountancy* (Vol. 154, No. 5, November 1982), pp. 104–107.

Stewart, J. P. "The Significance of an 'Orientation Postulate,'" *Abacus* (Vol. 25, No. 2, September 1989), pp. 97–115.

_____. Telephone interview with G. J. Previts, July 13, 2009.

Stone, Williard E. *Yushodo American Historic Accounting Literature*. Tokyo, Japan: Yushodo Co., 1982.

Storey, Reed K. "Conditions Necessary for Developing a Conceptual Framework," *Journal of Accountancy* (Vol. 151, No. 6, June 1981), pp. 84–96.

_____. "The Framework of Financial Accounting Concepts and Standards," in Carmichael, D. R., Lilien, Steven B., and Mellman, Martin (eds.) *Accountants Handbook, Ninth Edition*. New York, NY: John Wiley & Sons, 1999, pp. 1–114.

Sweeney, Jan and Yaari, Varda. "The FASB at 25: A Critical Appraisal," *Journal of Corporate Accounting and Finance* (Vol. 10, No. 1, Autumn 1998), pp. 37–49.

The American Assembly. *The Future of the Accounting Profession*. New York, NY: The American Assembly, 2003.

Turner, Thomas. *An Epitome of Book-keeping by Double Entry*. Portland, ME: Jenes & Shirley, 1804.

Van Riper, Robert. *Setting Standards for Financial Reporting: FASB and Struggle for Control of A Critical Process*. Westport, CT: Quorum Books, 1994.

Walters, Ralph E. Memorandum to Board members, December 8, 1978.

_____. "Standards Overload," File copy of speech, Audience Unknown, 1983.

Workman, Benjamin. *The American Accountant*. Philadelphia, PA: William Young, 1789.

Zanzig, J. and Flesher, D. F. "GAAP Requirements for Nonpublic Companies," *CPA Journal* (Vol. 76, No. 5, May 2006), pp. 40–44.

Zeff, S. A. *A Critical Examination of the Orientation Postulate in Accounting, with Particular Attention to Its Historical Development*. Ph.D. dissertation, University of Michigan, 1962.

_____. Letter to Dale L. Flesher, April 15, 1991.

_____. "The Evolution of the Conceptual Framework for Business in the United States," *Accounting Historians Journal* (December 1999), pp. 89–131.

4

Evolution of early practice descriptive theory in accounting

Stewart Jones and Max Aiken

This chapter examines the development and influence of 'practice descriptive' theories of accounting.[1] These early theories of accounting came into prominence in the 1940s and 1950s. This theoretical movement, as developed in the words of Gilman (1939), May (1936), Littleton (1953) and others, attempted to develop coherent propositions and concepts which could explain and articulate accounting regulations and conventional accounting procedures, principles and doctrines as developed by professional accountants, law and policy makers. Among the practice descriptive theoreticians, Littleton (1953) was to become the most prominent. The first two sections of this introduction briefly explore the history of accounting regulations in the UK and the USA. In many respects, these historical developments provided the genesis of today's traditional financial accounting practices. Furthermore, many theorists of this period, particularly Littleton (1953), used observations from history to both build and corroborate theoretical propositions.

1 Corporate regulation in the UK

Most historians acknowledge that modern financial regulations had their most recent origins in nineteenth-century Britain. The British Companies Acts of this period exercised a decisive influence on the development of professional accounting practice in Britain (Littleton, 1953; Littleton and Zimmerman, 1962). While companies legislation in the US produced similar effects on accounting practice and professionalism, comprehensive statutory regulation did not arrive in the US until the 1930s. The most important British Companies Acts of the nineteenth century included the Joint Stock Companies Acts (1844, 1944); the Joint Stock Banks Act (1844); the Companies Clauses Consolidation Act (1845); the Limited Liability Acts (1855, 1856); the Regulation of Railways Act (1868); the Life Assurance Companies Act (1870); the Building and Friendly Societies Acts (1874); the Companies Acts (1879, 1900); and the public utilities acts of the 1870s and 1880s covering water, gas and electricity companies.

As the British accounting profession grew in size, legal importance and social prestige in the last decades of the nineteenth century, accounting debates and publications through official accounting outlets, such as *The Accountant*, became far more frequent and numerous. Many of the articles appearing in *The Accountant* in the later nineteenth century were particularly concerned with developing professional solidarity, forging best accounting practices, defining the scope of auditing responsibility and professional ethics, and interpreting the legal and procedural requirements of the Companies Acts. However, one of the most pressing issues of the age related to the measurement and determination of profit available for distribution as dividends. In many instances, British statutes had imposed heavy civil and criminal liabilities on auditors if they sanctioned the payment of dividends out of capital. Jones and Aiken (1994) observed that two different concepts of profit were applied at different times during the nineteenth century. One school of thought interpreted distributable profit to mean the excess of total valued assets less total valued liabilities, with the remainder being distributable surplus. Under this 'surplus' method, the main accounting issues related to which particular assets and liabilities, and their valuation bases, should be included in the rule to determine distributable surplus. This concept of profit stressed the importance of the corporate balance sheet and was underpinned by asset valuation and capital maintenance objectives. Another school of thought interpreted distributable profit to mean the excess of realised revenues less all expenses properly chargeable to the period's revenues. This transaction-based approach, known as the profit and loss method or the 'net profits' test, emphasised the primacy of nominal accounts summarised in the profit and loss account.

The fundamental nature of measurement was not only at the heart of professional and legal debate in the later nineteenth century, but it has dominated much twentieth-century accounting theory. Since 1889, the British judiciary, particularly the Court of Appeal, had come to favour, for a variety of legal, ethical and commercial reasons, the profit and loss account method for determining a company's distributable profit (Jones and Aiken, 1994).

While similar conclusions were being forged, the accounting profession was developing accounting measurement conventions more or less independently of the judicial decisions. The objective of the professional development of accounting conventions was to seek, often unsuccessfully, universal guidelines for determining how corporate profits were to be reckoned and under what constraints (Yamey, 1978).

The existence of a general body of accounting principles or conventions can be detected from the later part of the nineteenth century and onwards (Yamey, 1978). The most frequently mentioned conventions or rules surfacing in nineteenth-century journals and texts include the revenue realisation convention, the historical cost convention in relation to fixed assets, the lower of cost or market rule for current assets such as inventory and marketable securities, and the going concern convention. Other conventions that were rather uncommonly mentioned in the later nineteenth century were consistency, disclosure and materiality.

These measurement principles, whilst having clear implications for the balance sheet, were primarily used to afford objective and verifiable constraints upon the determination of periodic corporate profits. There is strong evidence from articles appearing in *The Accountant* that the determination of profits and the profit and loss account was treated to be of high significance by professional auditors and accountants.[2] Many of the important balance sheet items which were seen to be of primary importance by late-nineteenth-century British auditors – including the valuation of non-current and current assets, depreciation of non-current assets, doubtful debt reserves, irregularities in the treating of expense items as assets, foreign exchange transactions, and goodwill – were viewed primarily with respect to the determination of corporate profits, particularly with avoiding the *overstatement* of profit.

There has been much theoretical debate on the continuing validity of conventional accounting principles in modern accounting theory (see Chambers, 1966; Sterling, 1970). Nevertheless, the measurement principle and conventions which were emerging in the closing decades of the nineteenth century have proved to be remarkably resilient, and they still appear to dominate accounting practices today.

2 Corporate regulation in the USA

The British system of regulatory control through the succession of Companies Acts was virtually absent in the USA prior to the 1930s. Nor was there any system of regulation in America which resembled the British Companies Acts. The absence of business regulation in the US can be explained in part by the influence of the *laissez-faire* principle in American culture, economic and social policy and political thought (Lukes, 1973). Regulation over companies and commercial activities was particularly resisted in the US, as America's political institutions have always attempted to preserve the sanctity of the business institution and the free market economy (Pole, 1980; Clews, 1900). The *laissez-faire* principle was not finally compromised by the US government until the economic and social chaos of the Great Depression threatened the stability of the country.

While US cultural and political thought was poorly disposed towards federal regulation of companies, certain dilemmas continued to plague legislators at the turn of the twentieth century. After the Civil War, the character of American commerce changed rapidly (see Sutton et al., 1956). The business corporation, with its concomitant divorce of ownership from control, began to dominate American commerce. The emergence of pools, trusts and business consolidations was partly fuelled by harshly competitive conditions in the US. By the beginning of the twentieth century, the phenomenon of giant corporations (also known as 'trusts') had emerged as the dominant form of business corporation in the US. However, these giant and substantially unregulated corporations were creating much public concern and anxiety in the first decades of the century. Doubtful financial activities, unethical trade activities and anti-competitive behaviour were frequent points of complaint (Sutton et al., 1956). Effective regulation of the trusts was the centrepiece of the business reform controversy until the 1930s. Business reformers and legislators pursued conflicting regulatory programs. One program was to combat the trusts by redefining and strengthening the competition laws. Such laws would prevent the formation of large companies possessing oligopoly or monopoly powers over the market. This option had considerable public support because the approach was envisaged to be consistent with basic cultural tenets of competition, equality of opportunity and individualism (Pole, 1980).

To appease public opinion, the Sherman Antitrust Act was passed in 1890, which made the restraint of trade illegal in interstate commerce (Armentano, 1982). The competition laws were an attempt to maintain competitive trading conditions under the theory that smaller firms in open competition would prevent extortionate prices because of the competitive checks on these firms (Bork, 1978, p. 57). The legislation was loosely drafted and proved to be easily manipulated by business interests (Armentano, 1982). Ironically, the great era of business consolidation, the years between 1897 and 1904, came after the Sherman Act was passed (Hawley, 1966). In the wake of persistent public hostility towards the trusts, coupled with the ineffectiveness of the Sherman Act, the US Congress appointed a Congressional Industrial Commission between 1901 and 1902. The Commission was established to consider the need for the federal regulation of companies.[3] The Commission produced a voluminous report which considered many aspects of American commerce and industry. After having considered the 'stringent requirements' of the British regulatory system at some length, the most important conclusion of the Commission was that the present state of corporate regulation embodied in the competition laws was inadequate. The Commission also concluded that any attempt to 'turn the clocks back' by maintaining the ideals of the competitive model would be impractical given the economic realities of industry concentration. Public demands to dismantle large corporations through a strengthening of the competition laws was considered too destructive to the commerce of that nation. After considering the British experience in some detail, the Commission also concluded that the competition laws were not only inadequate in their own right but were an insufficient measure for securing the social control of business. The Commission concluded:

> A summary of the results of . . . legislation and decisions may be stated as follows; . . . Practically all of these statutes were formed with the same purpose in view: To prevent the formation of combinations in trade which might become dangerous to the public . . . It is a striking fact that not one of these statutes aims at especially securing publicity regarding the business of the large industrial combinations, through detailed reports in order that publicity itself may prove a remedial measure.
>
> *(pp. 641–642)*

The Commission argued that federal regulation over corporations was justified on two accounts: 'The evils of combination, remedial by regulative legislation, come chiefly from two sources: (1) the more or less complete exercise of monopoly power (2) deception (to) the (public) through secrecy or false information' (p. 645).

In dealing with the issue of publicity of corporate affairs for effective regulation of business concerns in the US, the Commission made no changes to initial recommendations in 1900. Echoing the British regulator experience, the Commission concluded that publicity, through the disclosure of company financial statements, was the substantive remedy for controlling large and unchecked corporations in the interests of public welfare. The Commission had recommended the disclosure as follows:

> The larger corporations – the so-called trusts – should be required to publish annually a properly audited report showing in reasonable details their assets and liabilities, with profit or loss; such reports and audit under oath to be subject to Government inspection. The purpose of such publicity is to encourage competitions when profits become excessive, thus protecting consumers against higher prices and to guard the interest of employees by knowledge of the financial condition of the business in which they are employed.
>
> *(pp. 649–650)*

While the Commission's recommendations resulted in the establishment of the Bureau of Corporations by President Theodore Roosevelt in 1903, they failed to convince Congress of the need for legislation. The recommendations were shelved for further debate. One major dilemma politicians had to face at this time was that popular opinion and numerous politicians were strongly in support of competition as the effective social control of business (Burn, 1936; Wilson, 1913).

The American regulatory program before the New Deal of the 1930s remained confused and inconsistent. Regulation was reduced to little more than the piece-meal supervision of certain industries and the employment of ad hoc regulations, such as the Pure Food and Drug Act (1906), to combat the more flagrant abuse of ethical and commercial standards by certain industries.

3 New Deal politics and the Federal Securities Acts

Following the Wall Street Crash of 1929 and the Great Depression of the 1930s, the long reign of *laissez-faire* came to a somewhat abrupt end in the USA. During the 1930s, Franklin

Roosevelt's administration combatted the Depression with the initiation of numerous highly controversial legislative reforms in the social and economic arena (Fetter, 1933; Burn, 1936). One of the most pressing issues which New Deal administrators wanted to resolve was the business reform controversy which had dogged American politics for over thirty years. Since the competition laws first came into operation, enforcement had vacillated under confused and sporadic policies (Thorelli, 1955). Roosevelt was determined that corporations should be regulated at the federal level with a broad national legislation. As noted by Previts and Merino (1979, pp. 243–245), Roosevelt, in a message to Congress in 1932, had pledged to the public the prompt adoption of laws 'to provide for the furnishing of information and the supervision of traffic in investment securities in Interstate commerce'. The push for legislation was further precipitated by the US Senate hearings in 1932, which extensively investigated banking, currency, stock exchange practices and business regulation generally. The revelations of widespread corporate corruption, financial abuse and substandard accounting practices made the Senate's recommendations for legislation more palatable to the American public.

The philosophy behind the Federal Securities Acts (1933, 1934) is beyond question. These 'disclosure statutes' (Benston, 1976) cannot be interpreted outside of the context of New Deal politics and strategies of the 1930s. The New Deal was intended to alleviate some of the worst afflictions of the Great Depression through planned government intervention. The passing of the Securities Acts was an attempt by the Roosevelt administration to restore broken investor confidence in the nation's depressed capital markets. Mandatory provisions requiring companies to disclose a reasonable amount of auditing financial information were expected to instil renewed confidence by investors in company securities (Stewart, 1938). Phillips and Zecher (1981, pp. 9–10) noted:

> By the passing of the 1933 Act, sometimes called the truth-in-securities law, Congress opted for a disclosure approach to securities regulation: issuers of securities were required to disclose the financial underpinning of stock and bond issues. It was believed that disclosure in the glaring light of publicity would provide investors with sufficient information to be able to make informed investment decisions that would serve to self-regulate the allocation of capital. The 1933 Act had two basic purposes: to provide investors with sufficient material information to enable informed investment decisions and to prohibit fraud in connection with the sale of securities.

Previts and Merino (1979, p. 245) noted that after the passing of the Securities Acts, the accounting profession 'acquired a legally defined social obligation – to assist in creating and sustaining investor confidence in the public capital markets'.

3.1 Professional accountancy developments before and after the advent of the Securities Acts

As noted by Berle (1938, p. 370), prior to the passing of the Securities Acts (1933, 1934), professional accounting was largely a private entrepreneurial convenience. In the absence of statutory regulations, professional accounting services were largely determined by demand and supply forces. One of the most important developments to emerge from America's *laissez-faire* era was the prominence given to 'balance sheet audits' by US accounting practitioners. The demand for balance sheet audits came mainly from banking and credit institutions. Littleton and Zimmerman (1962, pp. 109–113) made this remark when comparing the development of US and British accounting regulations:

In the United States similar motivating forces were not present; legislation in the same spirit of public interest, such as requiring the audit of commercial accounts, did not appear. Nevertheless, a profession of public accounting also developed in America . . . . The strongest motivating factor seemed to have been the needs of creditors, particularly banks, for dependable financial information as basis of their extension of credit to businessmen . . . The financial practice was peculiarly American. The financial information desired by bankers was inherently different from that needed by stockholders, the parties of chief importance in Britain . . . These . . . methods of financing business strongly favoured 'balance sheet audits', and through them, the American profession of public accounting grew . . . The pattern of American audits . . . evolved under the influence of [the] bankers . . . [T]he central concern of the banker was the ability of the borrower to repay the loan when it matured. The most useful quantitative evidence available on this question was the relation between the total of short-term obligations that the borrower would soon have to face and the total current assets now under his control which, in the normal course of business would produce a cash flow to apply to the loan. Since this relationship did not raise a question of enterprise solvency (the relation of total assets to total liabilities) a complete audit was not needed. The important question was a safe margin of working capital, that is, the excess of current assets over current liabilities.

Littleton and Zimmerman (1962, p. 117) further wrote: 'The presence of compelling influences, such as the need of certified statements for credit purposes, clearly was primary in the development of an American public profession.'

America's early emphasis on the balance sheet contrasted sharply with UK practice, which had given considerable emphasis to income determination issues and the profit and loss account (Jones and Aiken, 1994).

Accounting academics and practitioners such as Wilkinson, Beckett, Staub and Montgomery had a vital part to play in the development of the early American balance sheet audit. They drew attention to methods of selective testing, of critical analysis of the content of the balance sheet items, and also of the verification of assets, liabilities and surplus.

Although the exact date of the first mention of the 'balance sheet audit' is unknown, it was fully developed in Montgomery's 'Auditing Theory and Practice' (1912). The principles of the balance sheet were enumerated as follows:

GENERAL PRINCIPLES. The underlying principles of a balance sheet audit may be reduced to writing and are not subject to fit particular businesses or special systems of account. They are few in numbers and can be applied generally.

The principles upon which all balance sheet audits are based are as follows:

1   The auditor must ascertain that all of the assets shown by the books to have been on hand at a certain date were actually on hand.
2   He must ascertain whether any other assets, not on the books, should be on hand.
3   He must ascertain that the liabilities shown by the books to be owing at a certain date were actual liabilities.
4   He must ascertain whether or not all liabilities were in fact shown by the books.
5   He must ascertain whether or not the liabilities as shown were properly incurred.

(Montgomery, 1912, p. 82,87)

Gilman (1939, p. 31) ascribed the first mention of the balance sheet audit to Montgomery. Further, he said: 'The balance sheet audit, which was first heard of in 1910 or thereabouts, had a powerful and rather extraordinary influence upon accounting.' However, mention of the 'balance sheet audit' became far more frequent after 1910. In 1913, J. C. Scobie, connected with Price Waterhouse & Co., prepared for private distribution a memorandum entitled 'General Remarks on the Balance Sheet Audit'. In 1917, the Federal Reserve Bulletin (Vol. III, No. 4) noted, 'probably more than 90 per cent of the statements certified by public accountants are what are called balance sheet audits' (see Gilman, 1939, p. 34). This indicates the general acceptance of this form of audit by accountants in general. From 1918 on, references to the balance sheet audit were increasingly numerous, and the form became firmly established among professional accountants in the United States. Indicative of this was the Federal Reserve Board publication of May 1929. A revision of its 'Approved Methods for the Preparation of Balance Sheet Statements' was condoned under the new title of 'Verification of Financial Statements'. Furthermore, an editorial in the *Journal of Accountancy* claimed that the publication of 'Verification of Financial Statements' had received universal approval – from bankers, credit institutions and accountants.[4] The strong emphasis on the balance sheet in US practice prior to the 1930s was emphasised in US dividend law (Weiner, 1928) and by accounting theoreticians, including Hatfield (1928) and Paton (1922).

Without doubt, the Wall Street Crash of 1929 and the ensuing Great Depression were the most vital factors which ended the period of the balance sheet audit. Many intellectuals and politicians during the late 1920s and early 1930s had a profound conviction that the capitalist system had broken down. Picking up the threads of the breakdown of the 'old' American capitalism and recognising the generally felt hopelessness about restoring the old days of free competition, the US government ushered in an age of increasing regulation and economic planning. Many writers perceived a greater importance for accounting in this new age of social and economic regulation. For instance, Schluter (1938, pp. 278–280) wrote:

> The experiences of the late 'twenties' and the early 'thirties' have led public opinion to the conviction that unrestrained individualism in the pursuit of profit has proved detrimental to general social welfare. The result of this conviction has been the appearance of numerous plans for the better control of economic and business affairs . . . There is a general discontent with the economic system, with the political system, and with the relation between the two . . . Already the 'public interest' in the accounting methods and procedures of private enterprise is marked. Accounting from the stand point of profit seeking, as practised by competitive individual enterprises, is slowly giving way to the employment of accounting and accounting facts with a view of controlling and guiding private enterprises in the interest of social and economic stability . . . Considering the fact that private, individualistic and competitive business enterprises, as we have known it, had to do the best it could with the accounting methods and procedures in a turbulent economic world, the results achieved, judged on the basis of the profit motive, are all that could have been expected. It can also be readily understood why accounting has become more of an instrument rather than a basis for policy.

In an age of regulation, Rorem (1928, p. 261) perceived financial statements to be powerful instruments for social control. Such statements should be a basis for guiding economic activity in the interests of the public welfare. However, he observed: 'Little has been said . . . about the uses of accounting beyond the confines of an individual profit seeking business enterprise.' Scott (1931, pp. 201–206) also perceived a changing emphasis between the respective roles of economics and accountancy in the midst of social change:

The history of accounting developments discloses a growth of accounting functions, an increasing dependence of business administration upon accounts and the absorption of accounting technique into the body of social machinery through which conflicting economic interests are adjusted . . . [W]e can safely generalise to the effect that in a competitive system accounting must always remain thus dependent on the market. It must look to the market as a superior authority. However, the market, as we have seen, is losing its authority. Accounts, on the other hand, are steadily increasing in importance. What will happen if regulation becomes the rule rather than the exception and the authority of the competitive market dwindles into relative insignificance?

It was previously mentioned that before this time, and especially during the 1920s, accounting services in the US were largely a private convenience. Services were offered widely and indiscriminately to those who desired them. The 'evils' of the 1920s were described by George O. May (1936, pp. 15–16):

Capital assets . . . have traditionally been recorded by the accountant at costs . . . [I]t [is] neither a practical nor a useful undertaking to attempt to determine the value of assets not intended to be sold and for which there is no ready market, especially as the concept of value differ; . . . [D]uring 1920's accountants fell from grace and took to readjusting capital values on the books . . . to an extent never before attempted. In extenuation they might plead unsound laws, unpractical economics and a widespread but unfounded belief in the new order of things combined to recommend such a course, but the wiser course is to admit the error and to determine not to be mislead into committing it again.

One of the important accounting developments during the 1930s was a shift in emphasis from the importance of balance sheet valuation to the significance of the profit and loss account by practitioners. One important theorist of the 1930s who had a substantial influence on the development of accounting standards and principles in this period was Eric Kohler. Kohler had become a leading spokesman of the 'revenue-expense' income orientation, which came to dominate accounting theory during the 1930s and beyond. In 1936, as President of the American Accounting Association, he was the most prominent person involved in the publication of a monograph entitled 'A Tentative Statement of Accounting Principles Affecting Corporate Reports'. The monograph contained three notable propositions which indicated the direction the profession would take on accounting measurement issues:

1   Accounting is essentially a process of cost allocation rather than valuation.
2   The all-inclusive concept of income should be applied to financial reporting.
3   A clear distinction should be maintained between paid-up capital and accumulated earnings.

Kohler articulated the profession's new-found commitment to the historical cost model. The 1936 'Tentative Statement' expressed these views as follows:

The fundamental basis of asset-and-expense valuation is price: the amount of money or objectively established money's worth paid in an exchange between independent parties. Arm's length practice is the only objective basis of value; being the consequence of actual transactions it is comprehensible to and serves the interests of management, investor and consumer. Further it is an operable medium for the application of a wide variety of internal and external controls and for portraying the degree of responsibility attained in the discharge of management accountability.

Kohler and other theorists of the historical cost school maintained that it was bankers and credit institutions that had led accountants to stress liquidating values and the importance of balance sheets prior to the 1930s. To Kohler, this had greatly reduced the worth of accounting services. If accountants attempted to trace values rather than costs they would find no satisfactory solution. Kohler noted that 'the intent of management must play a prominent role in the definition of assets and liabilities'. Hence, Kohler argued that since an accountant should not substitute his judgement for management 'the profession must focus on objective measures – such as revenue and expense'.

Evidence that the vogue of the balance sheet audit was coming to an end in the 1930s comes from a variety of other sources. In January 1936, the American Institute of Accountants published 'Examinations of Financial Statements by Independent Public Accountants'. This was a revision of the 1929 bulletin, and great pains were taken to eliminate references to the balance sheet audit, with the term 'examination of the financial statements' being submitted from the original title. Stephen Gilman (1939, p. 25) perceived a 'new emphasis' on profits in American accounting thought after the long reign and dominance of the balance sheet: 'Within the last few years accounting emphasis has shifted somewhat to the profit and loss viewpoint with numerous effects, some not yet evaluated.' George O. May (1937) in 'Improvements in Financial Accounts' was to announce that the determination of income 'is now generally recognised as the most important single problem in the field of financial accounting'.

4 Practice descriptive theories

The importance of income determination and the profit and loss account was central to most practice descriptive theorists. Most of these academics made special reference to the transition from the balance sheet to the profit and loss account by US practitioners and professional bodies during the 1930s. Furthermore, practice descriptive theorists tended to place much emphasis on the growing social and public interest significance of accountancy following the regulatory events of the 1930s. These theoretical developments in accountancy will now be reviewed, particularly from the viewpoint of the controversy between the balance sheet versus the income statement emphasis to financial accounting.

One of the most influential practice descriptive theorists of the twentieth century was A.C. Littleton (1953). More than any other theorist of his age, Littleton provided a theoretical orientation and justification for the social importance of the income statement and income determination in modern financial accounting thought. Littleton was well known for defending conventional accounting principles that were forged in the US during the 1930s and in Britain in the late nineteenth century. Of particular relevance to Littleton's thesis was the 'matching' principle. In assessing the matching concept in accounting, where revenues are related to costs, Littleton (1953) indicated that this process involved more than the essential problems concerned with the distinction between capital and income. Matching as his 'central purpose' of accounting did not rest upon a sharp distinction between producer (capital) and product (income), as if one were 'separating principal from interest' (p. 32). The matching principle treated capital as a means and income as an end. *Gross* income was then defined under this approach to be 'in part a recovery of costs advanced, a fruition of a future now become the present, a measure of accomplishment secured' (ibid.). It is not surprising, given this end, that Littleton also addressed the question of capital maintenance, an issue central to the balance sheet emphasis to financial accounting:

> The maintenance of capital is indeed important, but maintenance is not an objective of a statistical methodology like accounting. The proper matching of costs and revenues carries the relation of capital and income further than does the relation of principal and interest.

> *(ibid.)*

It is noteworthy that in supporting the primacy of the income statement, Littleton (1953) did not emphasise the significance of the bottom line or net income. Littleton's attention was focused on 'gross income' being a detailed measurement and disclosure process (p. 32). This related the integrity of distributions of revenue to the 'end' to be served by accounting principles. The end was stated to be 'lack of deception' (p. 15). We are thus introduced to an understanding of 'gross income' disclosure by professional accountants. This reveals 'distributional morality', the cultural objective of Littleton's theory. His dismissal of concepts which others found to be compelling was apparent in that Littleton's concept of 'net income', or the bottom line, had a distinctly subsidiary role in his theory:

> net income is merely a plus or minus result of subtracting a smaller total from a larger . . . [It could be as usefully computed from a comparison of the proprietorship figures of two different dates as by any other method.
>
> *(p. 23)*

The use of Littleton's work to examine the impact of practice descriptive research on financial accounting and theory formation is deliberate, for Littleton himself was much interested in issues of history and philosophy (Bedford and Ziegler, 1975, pp. 436–439). Furthermore, Littleton was well acquainted with the historical and cultural differences that were influential in the formation of the fundamental philosophical perspectives that characterised the evolution of accounting practice in both countries from the middle of the nineteenth century.

In Britain, a parliamentary network had been building since the Middle Ages. Commoners were protected from the ravages of advantaged elitism through the sovereignty of Parliament; and the public interest, being general to parliamentary rule, was thus attached to the formation of joint companies legislation. The requirement for audit was identified by Littleton (1953, p. 106):

> The British Parliament, particularly in 1845 and 1862 . . . acknowledged the fact that accounting could be used in the public interest. It was in the public interest that men should be permitted again to form joint stock companies after a prohibition that had lasted for a century . . . [T]he formation of business companies would not be in the public interest if old abuses were not prevented from reappearing. Accounting and auditing were the preventative medicine prescribed to safeguard the investing public.

The sovereignty of Parliament was stressed in the British jurisdiction even more strongly through the Exchequer and Audit Departments Acts of 1866 and 1921, which provided powers to the Controller and Auditor General. Such powers monitored governmental appropriations on behalf of the Parliament.

In the USA, the effects of public interest criteria on accounting regulations were more belated and occurred through the influence of such American writers as Littleton and through traditions of public sovereignty. In addition, there was the importation from Britain into America of men of practice, of whom George O. May was to become the most influential.

4.1 Role of the balance sheet in early accounting thought

The writings of Littleton can be contrasted with those of Henry Rand Hatfield (1928) in order to provide a perspective for the early development of American accounting thought. A private interest thrust more in tune with a strong cultural emphasis in the US on the sovereignty of individual freedom and equality of opportunity in market places has permeated research in that country, especially after the Second World War. This emphasis has also been noticeable in public sector writings, especially in the 1970s and beyond.

Littleton pointed out that auditing in America did not develop under statutory requirements as it did in Britain. During the 1880s audits for management quickly developed, especially as mergers and consolidations came into vogue. During the first two decades of the twentieth century, the banker's need for analytical support to verify decisions about loans and credit-worthiness came to dominate auditing. Verification of balance sheet items became the central focus, with the bank lender being the principal party at interest. This situation contrasted with the British audit where, under the company act, 'the stockholder', actual or potential, was considered to be the principal party at interest (1953, pp. 108–109). Littleton (1953, p. 110) noted further:

> In connection with those sections of the public consisting of investors (because of securities holdings and bank loans) and government (because of income taxes), accounting is being called upon to render public service as clearly as it was in Great Britain as a result of audits required by Statute.

Littleton went on to examine the reporting problem, embracing credit assessment, income tax specifics, and governmental requirements. By the middle of the twentieth century, regulatory reports about financial issues were being transmitted to agencies including the Securities and Exchange Commission, the Interstate Commerce Commission, the Federal Power Commission and also to central government departments.

Even before Littleton entered accounting academia in 1915, many of the ideas he and others were to develop had been identified by Hatfield (1928). Hatfield noted the recent (1906) requirement by the Interstate Commerce Commission for all railroads to prepare balance sheets and also the 1903 requirement for other businesses to do likewise under Massachusetts Corporation Law (p. 41). Hatfield (1928, p. 54) noted:

> The purposes of the Balance Sheet are two fold: Primarily it shows the financial status of the concern, giving information as to its solvency, and in less degree it exhibits profits which have been made. The first purpose is on the face the most evident one . . . [S]ome writers . . . maintain that the prime function of the Balance Sheet is to show the profits of the year and serve as the basis for the declaration of dividends.

While Hatfield himself was a proponent of the primacy of the balance sheet, he felt obliged to comment upon operational problems which could leave the accounts open to distortion and ultimately to misleading interpretations and deception. This included conservatism or under-valuation as a 'safeguard' against overstatement of profits: 'the understatement of profits and establishment of a secret reserve, if the lesser of the two evils, nevertheless falls far short of the ideal standard of accounting' (p. 85).

Hatfield was an advocate for the objectivity of cost price measurement except in the case of investments, where the value was listed in the stock exchange quotation for the day (p. 90). In conjunction with this valuation philosophy, Hatfield noted Marshall's warning that all machinery is on 'an irresistible march to the junk heap' (p. 121). Hatfield then defended use of the concept of depreciation because this 'obvious economic fact is of momentous import to accountancy, although full recognition has not been given to it in accounting practice' (p. 121). However, under Littleton's income statement emphasis, 'depreciation' was a question in practice of a justifiable policy for a distribution from revenues to the entity. This may or may not coincide with economic concepts of depletion service potential.

With respect to the profit and loss account, Hatfield envisaged it as 'a temporary, collective account, recording the changes in net wealth due to the business operations of a stated period' (p. 195). In his view, the balance sheet was of more interest to the creditor; the profit and loss account, to the proprietor or stockholder (p. 196). All of this seems conventional enough in the setting of that period in the USA until his discussion of the accounting emphasis sparked off in the famous British dividend decision in Lee V. Neuchatel Ashpalts Company Limited of 1889 (L.R. 41 Ch. Div 1). In this decision, no allowance was made for the exhaustion of 'wasting' assets before a dividend was paid (p. 205). Hatfield pointed out that creditors would be on guard in such speculative ventures (p. 206), but that the quality of the dividend decisions by the courts over the next decade had been confused both in Britain and the USA. He saw the principle involved to be predicated on a distinction between 'fixed' and 'wasting' capital: 'Dividing the income of a company without the replacement of circulating capital consumed in producing the income, is a payment of a dividend out of capital, such as is prohibited by law' (p. 208).

Where there has been a loss of 'circulating capital,' no dividend should be paid (p. 218). However, Hatfield noted that a loss of capital need not prevent payment of a dividend (p. 217). This would depend upon the prospects for continuity. Also, in Littleton's (1953, pp. 19–23) view, as previously mentioned, maintenance was a question of managerial policy to be approved by the shareholders, not an assumption to be held as a constant in financial accounting models.

It is not supposed here that Hatfield was relaxing the notion of capital maintenance as a fundamental maxim. That is, he would not have agreed with Littleton (1953, p. 23) that capital maintenance was simply an issue for managerial policy. For him, the concept of profit as the periodic difference between the two statements of wealth (p. 197) appeared real and reflected the cultural emphasis of the time and place.

Flexibility as to dividend payments appears more to be reflected in his apparent resignation about continuing imperfections in judgements by the courts:

> But for a more perfect rationalisation of the legal dicta concerning profits, it will probably be necessary to await the day when the growing identity of the profession of accounting shall cause its principles to permeate the ranks of bench and bar.
>
> *(p. 231)*

Hope tinged with resignation was replaced by a more forceful approach to progress in the face of legal rigidity when Edwards and Bell (1961, pp. 282–283) confronted this issue half a century later.

In addressing the need for perception to be applied to accounting at the turn of the century, Charles E. Sprague was both parsimonious in expression and direct in substance: 'As a branch of mathematical or classificatory science, the principles of accounting may be determined by a priori reasoning, and do not depend upon the customs and traditions which surround the art' (1907, p. ix).

Here is an early exposition of hope that accounting as a measurement system can be understood and analysed separately from the customary mode of the environment which surrounds it. We pause to consider the continuing existence of financial accounting as a reasonably primitive measurement system. The double entry system has survived enormous technological change, including the invention of negative numbers centuries ago. Can justification for such continuity be embodied in the measurement process itself? If not, the very edicts of a rational 'measurement' focus may be suspect. With this caution in mind, we may pursue the ideas of Sprague. He noted, 'The balance sheet may be considered as groundwork of all accountancy, the origin and the terminus of every account' (p. 30).

From this base Sprague considered the 'elements which constitute the wealth of some person or collection of persons' (ibid.). They included '1. The value of assets . . . 2. The values of the claims existing against assets . . . 3. The value of the residue . . . ' (ibid.).

It is not surprising that a straightforward adopting of Irving Fisher's idea that all assets are capital was accompanied by a variety of conceptions of the nature of assets, any of which may be useful in accounting practice:

1   As things possessed . . . ;
2   As rights over things and persons, for use, for services, or for exchange;
3   As incomplete contracts . . . or contractual assets;
4   As the result of services previously given or *cost*;
5   As the present worth of expected services to be received;
6   As capital for the conduct of business operations;
7   As investments in the hands of another who uses it as capital.

(Sprague, 1907, pp. 47–48)

Sprague then identified the 'reservoir' of proprietorship. Because this would be changed during the period by many positive and negative items, a summary of results was useful. This 'account of the second degree' had a resultant available for distribution to the proprietary interests (p. 78). In discussing this profit and loss account, Sprague pointed out that debits were not losses; rather, when more than returned, they were values laid out with the expectation that they would later come in (p. 80). This fundamental concept underlying the income statement was then tied to the bottom line. 'Wealth' theorists advocating the primacy of the balance sheet, both before and since, have seen this to be a logical necessity in order to reconcile inventories of values or service potential over time. Sprague (1907, p. 80) stated:

We may consider the title 'Profit and Loss account' however, as referring, not to the items composing it, but to the final outcome, which is either a Profit or a Loss. In this sense the time-honoured title is entirely justified.

This view was opposite to Littleton (1953, p. 95), who stressed verification criteria of gross profit statements.

Also with respect to Monograph B entitled 'The Merchandise Account', Sprague followed the valuation philosophy to the point of attributing 'profit', the difference between sales at cost and sales at selling price, to the sales account (p. 183). One is not hard pressed to interpret elements of Sprague in the work of R.J. Chambers (1966) some fifty years later.

W.A. Paton followed the Hatfield tradition in *Accounting Theory* (1922). He observed, 'The two classes of the balance sheet, in a sense, are merely different aspects of the same situation' (Ch.20). He further stated:

The assets represent a direct statement of the value of the properties of the enterprise; the liabilities represent an indirect statement of the same values. In one sense the accountant is listing the objective properties; in the other he is recording the proper distribution of the asset total among the various individuals or interests having claims therein.

(ibid.)

Two other issues raised by Paton have come to occupy the attention of accounting theorists over many decades. The first is that the accountant 'assumes that the value or significance of the measuring unit remains unchanged. This postulate is, of course, not sound . . . ' (ibid.). A second point not stressed so strongly is, 'if it immediately became evident in any case that real values were greater or less than cost, the profit or loss could be recognised at once' (ibid.). While this was a tentative step, Paton was aware of the potential of fair market value as a continuing basis for asset valuation over time. Furthermore, in cost accounting for work-in-process, the value of inputs 'utilised in production passes over into the object . . . and attaches to the result, giving it its value' (ibid.).

Paton's preoccupation with the then existing postulates of accounting would be taken up by other theorists in future years, presumably for the reasons which he offered: 'Accounting has taken long strides in recent years . . . [T]he pillars of theory and practice [should] be occasionally scrutinised and assayed, with a view to discovering precisely how firmly they are grounded.'

4.2 Role of the income statement

George O. May (1936, p. 407) stated: 'Where accountancy treatment diverges from economic theory, it is usually because economic theory has diverged from business practice. To accountants, as to businessmen, income is essentially a money concept, and the idea of psychic income leaves them cold.'

This direct view of May is taken from his review of J.B. Canning's 1929 book, *The Economics of Accountancy*. It gains in importance when one encounters further discussions by May in the same year. Commenting upon legislation in Delaware and other states which had become so legally convoluted as 'to destroy the significance of such terms as dividends' (1936, p. 68), May noted that identification of profits had become the central focus of the auditor's responsibilities. Were there any profits in any meaningful sense from which dividends could be appropriated and paid? Then comes the revelation of a changing focus among men of practice:

> Modern developments have tended also to reduce the importance of the balance sheet, and they seem to me to necessitate reconsideration of the methods of preparation of corporate reports. As business grows more complex it becomes more impractible to present a single picture and representation of the position of any important corporation which will be accurate . . . and will tell an intelligible story to the average investor. A series of pictures, rather than a single one is needed – and in such a series the balance sheet will perhaps be (the) least significant.
>
> *(pp. 71–72)*

In May's view, the annual report should contain (1) a 'well-arranged' income statement and surplus account; (2) quick assets and liabilities; (3) summaries of capital assets and capital obligations; and (4) a list of the acquisition and disposal of resources.

The question of 'the nature of business income from the accountant's view point', was discussed by May in 1950. He referred back to the post–World War I price recession of 1920, which started a renewed emphasis on the balance sheet. However, in the ensuing years there was a 'major shift of emphasis from the balance sheet to the income statement, and from credit grantors to the stock exchange as an influence upon financial accounting practices' (1962, p. 220). Commenting upon the 1920s, when price levels were 'fairly constant' May (1962, pp. 221–222) noted a contradiction:

> It has been said on the one hand that there were great (and pernicious) write-ups of assets in the 1920's. At the same time . . . no consideration was then given to the change of price level . . . Having been in active practice during the decade I believe that there was more consideration given to the last mentioned point than is commonly recognised and that write-ups . . . were not of major significance.

Whether his view can be sustained on the basis of no valuations being the ultimate 'ideal' is today open to question. Companies themselves are bought and sold frequently. However, under the income statement emphasis, which tends towards practicality rather than towards the theoretically difficult concept of wealth measurement in imperfect and incomplete markets (Beaver and Demski, 1979), May's (1962, p. 228) conclusions were quite direct:

> I believe the so-called 'cost principle' in its present form is of modern origin and calls for re-examination . . . [A]ccounting has an interpretative as well as a recording function and must, therefore, take cognisance of economic events . . . And, if accounting is to render the full service of which it is capable, it must in my view accept . . . [that] the monetary unit – is unstable.

Stephen Gilman (1939) expressed admiration (p. 610) for Canning's (1929) definition of income:

> what is set out as a measure of net income can never be supposed to be a fact in any sense at all except that it is the figure that results when the accountant has finished applying the procedure which he adopts.
>
> *(1929, p. 98)*

There should be no apology, according to Gilman, for the fact that it is 'in his role as interpreter that the accountant excels' (p. 610). The role of interpreter had been growing during Gilman's long association with practice. He had witnessed the balance sheet or ownership emphasis in his earlier days. Roy B. Kester had stated, in a manner that promised further intellectual growth by accountants in the area of production, exchange and distribution of 'equitable' returns to all those in the business arena: 'The record, then, of the value of the rights of the various parties to this product, is the special field of work assigned to accountancy' (1918, p. 13).

Gilman conceded that it had seemed reasonable to construct sets of accounts as a conventionalised statistical scheme translating non-homogenous items into homogenous expressions. When the accounting period convention was applied, reporting then 'naturally developed as a mechanism having an asset and liability rather than an income and expense viewpoint' (Gilman, 1939, p. 27). Kester's view, however, had emphasised the product. Gilman continued:

> Four influences have so profoundly affected this simple accounting mechanism as to require brief consideration. These four are: (1) the introduction and growth of the corporate form of organisation, (2) the development of large-scale manufacturing, (3) taxation of income, and (4) the balance sheet audit.
>
> *(ibid.)*

He also observed that until the New York Stock Exchange asked the American Institute to shift emphasis to the profit and loss statement in 1930, there had been a long tradition of verifying investors' rights through the balance sheet audit (1939). As has been mentioned previously, this type of audit had come into prominence at the turn of the century and then persisted until finally and formally rejected in the American Institute of Accountants' bulletin, 'Examinations of Financial Statements by Independent Public Accountants' (January, 1936). Gilman (1939, p. 37) stated:

> In looking back upon the balance sheet audit, it is mere hindsight to note that it was inadequate or that its emphasis was wrongly placed. It required the sharp lesson of 1929 to reveal the discrepancies of this audit . . . [which] temporarily counteracted those forces which normally would have shifted accounting emphasis to the profit and loss statement much sooner.

After the pronouncement by the profession, Gilman noted with approval the statement by George O. May (1937, p. 346) that the determination of income 'is now generally recognised as the most important single problem in the field of financial accounting'. Perhaps this view in the American context reflects the introduction of income tax legislation in 1913 as well as the lack of effectiveness of balance sheet valuation (historical or otherwise) to ensure the protection of investors' rights. It should be noted that the 'income' emphasis in Britain had possibly reflected the introduction of income tax legislation in 1842 as well as the cultural differences examined previously. Also the earlier *statutory* emphasis on shareholders' rights was important. This British tradition carried through to pronouncements in Westminster countries in the 1960s. For example, the Institute of Chartered Accountants in Australia discounted the role of the balance sheet as compared with the profit and loss statement:

> A balance sheet is therefore mainly an historical document which does not purport to show the realisable value of assets such as goodwill, land, buildings, plant or machinery; nor does it normally purport to show the realisable value of assets such as stock-in-trade. Thus a balance sheet is not a statement of net worth of the undertaking and this is normally so even when there has been revaluation of assets and the balance sheet amounts are based on the revaluation *instead of on cost.*
>
> *(D1.1 Presentation of the Balance Sheet, December 1963)*

4.3 A.C. Littleton (1953)

The 'income' emphasis stressing integrity and morality in financial accounting found its strongest advocate among intellectuals in the person of Littleton (1953). It appeared to Littleton, who supported the primacy of the income statement, that morality or integrity in accounting was more at ease with objective verification of transactions and prices than with confirmation of subjective asset valuations.

The 'structure' of Littleton's theory was enunciated in his *Structure of Accounting Theory* (1953), which emphasised 'income' determination as the 'centre of gravity' in accounting (Ch.2). The matching concept which has received wide acceptance among practitioners for half a century was identified as follows (1953, p. 24, 67): 'The idea of enterprise suggests a desirable contribution to society and it implies, by and large, the contribution is worth what it costs. Suitability as to costs means assigning costs according to their relevancy to service efforts made.'

Under this perception, 'income' will vary somewhat in its determinants across entities. This is in order to capture the stewardship qualities of each firm, which are to some extent unique (1953, p. 55). Moral and cultural issues are emphasised, even in the identification of the purpose of accounting in relation to financial disclosure: 'Obviously a moral obligation rests upon accounting to produce figures and reports that will avoid deception as much as possible. The principles of accounting and the procedures are directed towards that end' (1953, p. 15).

These ideas were displayed further under Littleton's concept of the role and nature of theory in accounting. Littleton (1953, p. 1) acknowledged that in order to understand practice, we need to understand theory as well. However, in order to know something of the *totality* of accounting, it is necessary to note its historical setting in relation to other fields of knowledge and its service to society (ibid.). From this 'navigational' perspective, Littleton indicated that 'capital' was not the most fundamental item in accounting. 'Capital is not as fundamental as "income" since an understanding of production and income is a necessary antecedent to the understanding of property (capital) used to produce income; and income (capitalised) is a primary basis for judging property value' (p. 19). As to social emphasis, Littleton (1953, p. 21) was firmly on the production thrust:

The modern emphasis on enterprise income rather than solvency suggests that reporting on management's stewardship is now better done through the income statement than the balance sheet. The one statement tells something of what stewardship is doing to make the owner's investment productive, the other statement reports the form in which the entrusted investments stand at the moment.

In emphasising his historical interest, Littleton confronted the reader with the spectre of double entry book-keeping without income determination. For him this was the heart and soul of the system. The result could not be called 'double entry ("enterprise accrual accounting") without overthrowing the connotations that have been accumulated through five centuries' (1953, p. 27). On the basis of his historical research, he concluded that 'income determination by matching cost and revenue has, for 500 years, been the central feature of double entry' (ibid.). This perspective was now institutionalised by Littleton within the structure of his theory: 'The central purpose of accounting is to make possible the periodic matching of costs (efforts) and revenues (accomplishments). This concept is the nucleus of accounting theory, and a benchmark that affords a fixed point of reference for accounting discussions' (1953, p. 30).

Before identifying Littleton's clarification of this issue (p. 32), it is necessary to explain Littleton's theoretical focus, which provided meaning and understanding for his 'structure' to be built upon practice in order to explain such practice. This theoretical focus set Littleton apart from other intellectuals in accounting (1953, p. 132):

> accounting practice is neither purely expedient, wholly individualistic, nor merely customary. For practice is integrated with a body of rational beliefs, useful intuitions, known objectives. It should be clear . . . theory is practice-created and practice-conditioning. Finally, whenever evidence of integration among accounting ideas is found it . . . will strengthen the conviction that accounting doctrine contains the possibility of being built into a system of coordinated explanations and justifications of what accounting is and what it can become.
>
> *(1953, p. 131)*

According to Littleton, accounting doctrine contains the seeds of feasibility, and theory is devoted to understanding the world as it is and the constraints upon the world's improvement in practical affairs. Morality and doctrine point to issues of distribution rather than allocation as the focus of accounting. The point was made by Littleton as follows (1953, p. 32):

> Reduced to its barest essentials, an income statement is a calculation (1) of the revenue produced by the operations of an enterprise and (2) of the way that total has been divided among the claimants. Although the dividing of revenue is usually controlled by statute or contract, and although many claims are settled in advance of determining gross revenue, it is still an economic fact that revenue is shared. It is also a fact that a complex and unending struggle goes on with change in sharing as its object. The independent public accountant is not party to these contracts, nor is he a critic of their objectives. But his professional opinion supports the income statement in his report.

With this notion of the professional auditor's social responsibility in mind, Littleton could not move away from a myopic fixation on the need to use unadjusted historical cost, even though May had claimed that abuses of valuation during the 1920s were less serious than was often stated. Littleton believed that few people wished to see accounting 'tangle again with the revaluation approach' often used in the 1920s. He also mentioned that little discussion had favoured a general use of appraised values (1953, p. 213). Also, he observed that there were no strong opinions among professional accountants in favour of 'adjusting balance sheet assets and liabilities for higher price levels' (1953, p. 213). While professional accountants have remained disinterested in current value accounting, the 1960s and 1970s evidenced a strong academic movement in support of alternative valuation concepts, particularly current value accounting and exit price systems. Furthermore, fair values have been adopted more extensively by the International Accounting Standards Board (IASB) in the first decade of the twenty-first century. However, following the political fallout from the global financial crisis, there has been some evidence of a change in direction of the IASB away from a pure fair value approach to a mixed model approach. Other chapters in this volume explore the use of fair values by the IASB and the role of fair values in the global financial crisis.

Notes

1 This chapter is a revised version of 'The Emergence of Practice Descriptive Research in Accounting', previously published in S. Jones, J. Ratnatunga and R.A. Romano (1996) *Accounting Theory: A Contemporary Review*, Harcourt Brace, Sydney. Reprinted with permission.
2 See the article by Arthur Lowes Dickenson, 'The Duties and Responsibilities of the Public Accountant', published in *The Accountant*, March 1, 1902, reprinted in Chatfield, p. 156ff.
3 US Congress, 1902. House. 'Final Report of the Industrial Commission', H. Doc. 380, 57th Congress, 1st Session.
4 *Journal of Accountancy*, Vol. 48, 1929, p. 448.

References

American Accounting Association, 'A Tentative Statement of Accounting Principles Affecting Corporate Reports', *Accounting Review* (June 1936), pp. 187–192.

Armentano, D.T., *Anti-trust and Monopoly: Anatomy of a Policy Failure,* New York, Wiley (1982).

Beaver, W.H. and Demski, J.S., 'The Nature of Income Measurement', *Accounting Review* (January 1979), pp. 38–46.

Bedford, N.M. and Ziegler, R.E., 'The Contributions of A.C. Littleton to Accounting Thought and Practice', *Accounting Review* (July 1975), pp. 435–443.

Benston, G.S., *Corporate Financial Disclosure in the UK and the USA*, Farnborough, Hants, Saxon House (1976).

Berle, A.A., 'Accounting and the Law', *Journal of Accountancy* (May 1938), pp. 368–378.

Bork, R.H., *The Antitrust Paradox: A Policy at War with Itself*, New York, Basic Books (1978).

Burn, A., *The Decline of Competition*, New York and London, McGraw Hill (1936).

Canning, J., 'Some Divergences of Accounting Theory from Economic Theory', *Accounting Review* (April 1929), pp. 1–8.

Chambers, R.J., *Accounting, Evaluation and Economic Behaviour*, Englewood Cliffs, NJ, Prentice-Hall (1966).

Clews, H., *The Wall Street Point of View*, New York, Greenwood Press (1968; first published 1900).

Dickenson, A.L., 'The Duties and Responsibilities of the Public Accountant', *The Accountant* (March 1902).

Edwards, E. and Bell, P., *The Theory of the Measurement of Business Income*, Berkeley, CA, University of California Press (1961).

Fetter, F.A., 'The Truth about Competition', *Annals of the American Academy of Political and Social Science*, Vol. 165 (1933), pp. 93–100.

Gilman, S., *Accounting Concepts of Profit*, New York, Ronald Press (1939).

Hatfield, H.R., *Modern Accounting*, New York, Arno Press (1976; first published 1928).

Hawley, H., *The New Deal and the Problem of Monopoly: A Study in Economic Ambivalence*, Princeton, NJ, Princeton University Press (1966).

Jones, S. and Aiken, M., 'The Significance of the Profit and Loss Account in Nineteenth Century Britain: A Reassessment', *Abacus*, Vol. 30 (1994), pp. 196–230.

Kester, R.B., *Accounting Theory and Practice*, New York, Ronald Press (1918).

Littleton, A.C., *Structure of Accounting Theory*, Sarasota, American Accounting Association (1953).

Littleton, A.C. and Zimmerman, V.K., *Accounting Theory: Continuity and Change*, Englewood Cliffs, NJ, Prentice-Hall (1962).

Lukes, S., *Individualism*, New York, Harper and Row (1973).

May, G.O., 'The Influence of Accounting on Economic Development', *Journal of Accountancy*, January, pp. 11–12; February, pp. 92–105; March, pp. 171–184 (1936; three articles).

———, 'Improvements in the Financial Statements', *Journal of Accountancy* (May 1937).

———, *Memoirs and Accounting Thought of George O. May*, ed. by P. Grady, New York, Ronald Press (1962).

Montgomery, R.H., *Auditing Theory and Practice*, New York, Ronald Press (1922; first published 1912).

Paton, W.A., *Accounting Theory*, New York, Ronald Press (1922).

Phillips, S.M. and Zecher, J.R., *The SEC and the Public Interest*, Cambridge, MA, MIT Press Series on the Regulation of Economic Activity (1981).

Pole, J.R., *American Individualism and the Promise of Progress* (Inaugural Lecture), Oxford, Clarendon University Press (1980).

Previts, G. and Merino, B.P., *A History of Accounting in America: A Historical Interpretation of the Cultural Significance of Accounting*, New York, Wiley (1979).

Rorem, C.F., 'Social Control Through Accounts', *Accounting Review* (September 1928).

Schluter, W., 'Accountancy Under Economic Self-Government', *Accounting Review* (December 1938), pp. 278–284.

Scott, D.R., *The Cultural Significance of Accounts,* Columbia, MO, Lucas Brothers (1931).

Sprague, C.E., *The Philosophy of Accounts*, Lawrence, Kansas, Scholars Book Co. (1972; first published 1907).

Sterling, R., *Theory and Measurement of Enterprise Income*, Houston, TX, Scholars Book Co. (1970).

Stewart, A., 'Accounting and Regulatory Bodies in the United States', *Journal of Accountancy* (January 1938), pp. 33–60.

Sutton, F.X., *The American Business Creed*, Cambridge, MA, Harvard University Press (1956).

Thorelli, H., *The Federal Antitrust Policy*, Baltimore, MD, Johns Hopkins Press (1955).

Weiner, J., 'Theory of Anglo-American Dividend Law: English Cases', *Columbia Law Review*, Vol. XXVIII (1928), pp. 1046–1060.

Wilson, W., *The New Freedom: A Call for the Emancipation of the Generous Energies of the People*, New York, Doubleday, Page and Co (1913; reprint 1961).

Yamey, B.S., 'Development of Company Accounting Conventions' (1978), reprinted in Yamey, B.S., *Essays on the History of Accounting*, New York, Arno Press (1978), pp. 3–8.

5

Accounting and the decision usefulness framework

Thomas A. Lee

Overview

This chapter examines the objectives and qualitative characteristics of financial reporting cur-rently prescribed by accounting standard-setters in their conceptual framework (CF). The CF is that of the International Accounting Standards Board (IASB 2010). In 2002, following account-ing scandals and a Securities and Exchange Commission proposal for principles-based account-ing standards (PBAS), the Financial Accounting Standards Board (FASB) in the US and the IASB agreed to harmonise their CFs and PBAS (FASB 2002a and 2002b).[1] Although the pro-ject is incomplete,[2] that part relating to the objective and qualitative characteristics of financial reporting is contained in identical statements from the FASB (2010) and the IASB (2010). This chapter initially considers the nature and role of the CF and issues relating to it. The objec-tive and qualitative characteristics in IASB 2010 are then outlined and assessed using research published predominantly since the 2002 harmonisation agreement. Accounting for economic reality is particularly emphasised.

Conceptual framework

A relevant context for the objective and qualitative characteristics in IASB 2010 is the nature and role of the CF. The first statement of purpose for a CF was made by the FASB (1976: 2):

> A conceptual framework is a constitution, a coherent set of interrelated objectives and fundamentals that can lead to consistent standards and that prescribes the nature, function, and limits of financial accounting and financial statements. The objectives identify the goals and purposes of accounting. The fundamentals are the underlying concepts that guide the selection of events to be accounted for, the measurement of these events, and the means of summarising and communicating them to interested parties.

Other than 'fundamentals' being replaced by 'qualitative characteristics', this statement remains relevant to IASB 2010. It asserts that the CF is the conceptual foundation from which consistent accounting standards can be produced. As Schipper (2003: 62; emphasis in original) states, the 'desire to achieve *comparability* and its over-time counterpart, *consistency*, is the reason to have reporting standards'. IASB 2010 is therefore not intended as a normative theory of accounting such as in Chambers (1966) and Sterling (1979), although the objective and qualitative characteristics are similar to those in such theories. Instead, according to the IASB (2010: 6), the CF exists to assist standard-setters to review existing standards, promulgate new standards, and reduce variety in practice; and to assist preparers to apply standards, auditors to give opinions, and users to interpret financial statements. In other words, the CF is a knowledge-based tool for the regulation of reporting quality.[3] Thus, as Walker (2003: 342) argues, if the CF has a 'clear view' about the function of accounting, commercial practice, and user needs, it can provide a 'coherent and consistent set of statements' as a basis to improve practice rather than 'legitimise existing (and unsatisfactory) practices'. Whether such a 'clear view' exists in IASB 2010 is a theme of this chapter.

The first CF appeared in the US in the late 1970s (FASB 1978). It had origins in an American Institute of Certified Public Accountants (AICPA) study of reporting objectives intended to influence the newly formed FASB in its program to identify standards capable of increasing consistency in accounting practice (AICPA 1973: 4). The CF therefore has a relatively short history as a constitution to assist accounting regulation. However, as Christensen (2010: 297) remarks: 'A constitution should have long-term validity and it should not be changed in response to small changes in the workings of society.' In contrast to this ideal, standard-setters such as the IASB appear to revise their CF whenever there is significant failure in accounting practice (Hines 1989: 85; Moore 2009: 337; see also Dean and Clarke 2003). Reasons for revision are offered by standard-setters, as, for example, when Bullen and Crook (2002: 2) argue that:

> Although the current concepts have been helpful, the IASB and FASB will not be able to realise fully their goal of issuing a common set of principles-based standards if those standards are based on the current FASB Concepts Statements and IASB *Framework*. That is because those documents are in need of refinement, updating, completion, and convergence.

FASB (2010) and IASB (2010) contain the most recent CF in the current program of refinement, updating and convergence. Whether this framework addresses the general need of a profession for social legitimacy through ownership and control of an authoritative body of knowledge, and more specifically addresses issues raised by CF critics, is debatable. The following section outlines briefly the professionalisation argument in relation to the CF.

Professionalisation

The argument of Larson (1977) concerning the ownership and control by professions of authoritative bodies of knowledge in market settings is well recognised in the sociology of professions literature (Macdonald 1995: 7–14). More specifically, Larson (1977: 180–1) argues:

> The main instrument of professional advancement, much more than the profession of altruism, is the capacity to claim esoteric and identifiable skills – that is, to create and control a cognitive and technical basis. The claim of expertise aims at getting social recognition and collective prestige which, in turn, are implicitly used by the individual to assert his authority and demand respect in the course of every-day transactions within specific role-sets.

The CF should be assessed in this context because it is a principal means by which professional accountants lay claim to the authority of the technical skills they use in the preparation, presentation and audit of financial information. In the absence of a generally accepted theory of accounting, the CF attempts to provide a cognitively authoritative basis for these skills. If it fails in this mission, then the authority of the skills is in doubt and, in turn, so too is the professional status of accountants.

Conceptual framework issues

In a historical review of the construction of accounting knowledge in which she states that the knowledge core of financial accounting is a significant problem as it is not unique to accountants and cannot be differentiated from other domains such as law, Hines (1989: 89; emphasis in original) observes from criticisms of the CF project: 'The major rationale for undertaking CFs was not functional or technical, but was a *strategic manoeuvre* for providing legitimacy to standard-setting boards and the accounting profession.' She is arguing that, in the absence of a theory of accounting, accountants use the CF to justify their social status as professionals – that is, the CF is an example of a professional community projecting an image of the cognitive authority underlying their practices and standards. In a further study of criticisms of the specific failure of the FASB CF to provide satisfactory accounting standards, Hines (1991: 327) concludes that a major reason for this is the presumption in the CF's qualitative characteristics of a concrete and objective world that actual accounting standards do not reflect or represent. Consistent with Hines, West (2003: 80) perceives the CF to be a failed project because its concepts statements are prescriptive and appear to be the consequence of an attempt to match concepts to existing rules. Walker (2003: 341) agrees when he states that the content of some concepts statements virtually predetermines the preservation of flawed accounting practices. Dean and Clarke (2003: 292–3; emphasis in original) go much further:

> It is reasonable to contemplate whether there is a *unique CF of accounting*. That the projects have, indeed, stalled and frustration has out-gunned progress, that agreement on key issues has been so elusive, may well be the consequence of searching for what does not exist.

Lee (2006: 435) characterises the current project to harmonise the CF and PBAS as an example of what Fogarty et al. (1991) label the strategy of doing 'nothing' – or the strategy of professionalisation that appears to have potential to improve reporting quality but which in fact maintains the status quo in order to meet the needs of vested interests such as managers, auditors and regulators.[4]

These ongoing issues with the CF undermine, rather than enhance, the professional status of accountants, as do cognitive weaknesses identified in the CF. Loftus (2003), for example, identifies persistent discrepancies between CF prescriptions of user needs and the provisions of individual accounting standards. Walker (2003) demonstrates that the CF lacks clarity, is inconsistent with commercial practice and user behaviour, has internal inconsistencies, and is not comprehensive as a guide to financial reporting. Further to Walker, Booth (2003) evidences the CF as not only internally inconsistent but also reliant on circular reasoning, and as inconsistent with the legal framework regulating business entities.[5] More generally, Penno (2008: 349–50) concludes that rules-based accounting standards are inevitably vague and that the qualitative characteristics underlying PBAS are also necessarily vague in order to cope with the complexity of report preparation, use and regulation. Thus, implicitly accepting the current system of the CF and related standards, Penno (2008: 350) further argues that this vagueness should be acknowledged and accepted by standard-setters, and the degree of vagueness to be tolerated in standards production should be determined.

Christensen (2010) argues that, as a constitution to regulate accounting, the IASB CF is too detailed and does not reflect the diversity of information needs, variety of private and public information sources, and comparative advantage of financial reports as a verified information source. Staunton (2003: 411–12) criticises the Australian CF for its failure to adequately define the role of financial reports – particularly the separate functions of accountability (and stewardship), and decision-making. In a similar vein, O'Connell (2007) argues that the recent FASB and IASB decision not to designate stewardship as a separate reporting objective in the CF and, instead, to subsume it as part of decision usefulness, assumes the latter has potential to cover the stewardship function for investors and other users, and ignores the importance of stewardship in relation to corporate governance and social and environmental reporting.

Jones and Wolnizer (2003; see also Dean and Clarke 2003) question whether the IASB is capable of constructing an internationally relevant and generally acceptable CF to guide globally compatible accounting standards. West (2003: 193) goes much further when he concludes: 'The authority of the accounting profession will lack justification until professional accounting knowledge is sufficiently well-developed to provide a robust framework for mediating the conflicting interests and differential capacities of actors within the accounting domain.' West challenges the idea that the current system of rules-based standards guided by an ambiguous and inconsistent CF is an adequate basis for accountants to claim professional authority. For this reason, the following sections analyse the robustness of the framework as it concerns the reporting objective and related qualitative characteristics prescribed in IASB 2010.

Reporting objective

According to its introduction in the CF, the IASB is concerned with financial statements prepared for the purpose of providing information useful in economic decision-making (IASB 2010: 5). No detailed rationale is offered by the IASB for this function other than that such statements are intended to meet the common needs of most users making decisions for purposes of investment, stewardship, benefits, security, taxation, dividends, statistics and regulation (IASB 2010: 5).[6] The specific purpose of financial reporting is stated as follows (OB2):

> The objective of general purpose financial reporting is to provide financial information about the reporting entity that is useful to existing and potential investors, lenders and other creditors in making decisions about providing resources to the entity. Those decisions include buying, selling or holding equity and debt instruments, and providing or settling loans and other forms of credit.

The term 'general purpose' is not explained, but it presumably refers to the aforementioned common needs of most users. However, the term 'common needs' is also undefined, although the reporting objective refers to investors, lenders and other creditors having an interest in expected returns and a consequential need to assess the amount, timing and uncertainty of future net cash inflows to the reporting entity (OB3). Interest and need are regarded by the IASB as similar for each designated user group, following similar assertions in previous frameworks from AICPA (1973) onwards. Ignored in the CF are differences between user groups in terms of risk, reward, timing and security. Indeed, the IASB regards users as one group – that is, as primary users who need information about the resources of and claims against the entity and about how efficiently and effectively the entity's management and governing board have discharged their responsibilities to use the entity's resources (OB4). The IASB also claims without explanation that its responsibilities compel it to focus on the needs of participants in capital markets (BC1.16). Thus, even though the CF does not yet specify the reporting entity, it is clear that the framework is intended to regulate the financial reports of corporate organisations whose equity, loans and other credits are managed in capital markets. In the context of the private and public sectors of an economy, this is a significant restriction in reporting focus.

The IASB states the limitations of general purpose financial reports, including an inability to satisfy all information needs, to be used for entity valuation, and to provide exact depictions as distinct from estimates, judgments and models (OB6, OB7, OB11). Nevertheless, general purpose financial reports are claimed to provide information about the reporting entity's financial position and changes in that position (i.e. in economic resources and claims) and to assist users in identifying the reporting entity's financial strengths and weaknesses, including its liquidity, solvency and financing (OB13). The specific function of such information is to permit users to assess entity financial performance and predict future entity cash flows as returns on managed economic resources and claims, with financial performance reflected in accrual accounting and past cash flows, distinguishing between resources provided from operations and external sources (OB14–OB21). This reporting structure is consistent with that inherent in reported financial statements over several past decades.

The IASB also provides additional commentary in support of the reporting objective of decision usefulness (BC1.1–BC1.35). This principally relates to the harmonisation project with the FASB, changes from the IASB CF of 1989, and responses received on a previous discussion document. Specific comments relate to IASB decisions to focus on (1) financial reporting rather than financial statements in order to broaden the scope of the CF and cover information other than financial statements; (2) general purpose reporting as the most effective, efficient and economic means of meeting the information needs of different user groups; (3) the entity rather than its owners in order to reflect the separation of owners and managers; (4) designated users who make decisions about resource provision; (5) the most critical, immediate and common needs of those requiring information for use in capital markets (excluding management and regulators); (6) investment decisions (including those relating to whether management has made efficient and effective use of resources); and (7) not regarding one type of information as more important than another or directing one type of information at a specific user group.

Qualitative characteristics

The qualitative characteristics of financial reports are presented by the IASB as a set of reporting qualities founded on the basic prescription that to be useful for decisions, the information must be relevant and must faithfully represent what it claims to represent (QC4). Relevance and faithful representation are advocated as the fundamental qualities of reported financial information, and they are supported by other qualitative characteristics that the IASB claims enhance the decision usefulness of relevant and faithfully represented information – comparability, verifiability, timeliness and understandability (QC19). None of these additional characteristics are to be used by preparers in substitution for the absence of relevance and faithful representation (QC34). In other words, relevance and faithful representation are qualities that must be present in financial information if 'good' decisions are to be made (QC17) and must apply to both financial statements and financial information provided in other ways (QC3). Achievement of relevance and representational faithfulness is subject to the benefits from these characteristics exceeding the costs of attempting to achieve them (QC35). Relevance and faithful representation are described by the IASB as the most critical characteristics, whereas enhancing characteristics are less critical but highly desirable (BC3.8).

Relevance refers to financial information which has the capacity to make a difference to decisions, irrespective of whether it is used or not (QC6). Capacity is claimed to be a condition that is determinable as distinct from the actual relevance of information to a particular decision, which is deemed to be indeterminable (BC3.12, BC3.13). The IASB offers no evidence in support of this assertion and therefore prescribes decision usefulness in terms of relevance as a potential rather than an achieved quality. The relevance of financial information is further asserted in terms of its predictive value in the decision process relative to future outcomes; its confirmatory value as feedback confirming or changing previous evaluations; or both values when they are interrelated (QC7). More specifically, the IASB states that predictive value is present if the information can be used to make or modify predictions about returns, as distinct from predictability in the statistical sense of forecasting accuracy (BC3.16). Thus, relevant financial information according to the IASB is that which can assist a decision-maker to predict, modify or confirm returns.

The CF goes on to state that relevant financial information is material information if its omission or misstatement could influence decisions that users make on the basis of financial information about a reporting entity (QC11). Materiality is regarded as entity-specific and concerned with the nature or magnitude, or both, of the items to which the information relates in the context of the entity's financial report (QC11). In other words, the IASB asserts that relevant financial information is material information. Conversely, immaterial information is irrelevant to decisions. Neither of these assertions is tested by the IASB, nor are criteria offered regarding materiality cut-off points (QC11).

Faithful representation is the other main qualitative characteristic advocated by the IASB. It has appeared in previous CFs as 'reliability'. The IASB believes the past use of the term reliability created ambiguity and confusion about its meaning in relation to decision usefulness (BC3.20–BC3.25). Faithful representation, by contrast, is presented in terms of a proposition that financial information is decision useful if it not only represents relevant economic phenomena but also faithfully represents them as completely, neutrally and free from error as possible (QC12). Faithfully represented financial information depicts the economic substance rather than legal form of the relevant economic phenomenon (BC3.26). No comment is offered regarding the meaning of 'economic substance' and 'legal form' in this context.

A complete representation of an economic phenomenon means the representation contains all the information necessary for a user to understand the phenomenon, including descriptions and explanations (QC13). A neutral representation of a phenomenon means there has been no bias in the selection or presentation of the financial information depicting it (QC14). To be neutral, the relevant phenomenon is not depicted in a conservative or prudent way (BC3.27), because according to the IASB, conservative accounting is likely to introduce representational bias (BC3.28). Freedom from error means there has been no error or omission in the process of depicting the phenomenon (QC15). This prescription is not intended to provide complete accuracy, because the IASB believes estimation is an inevitable part of accounting representation. The aim in this respect is to maximise these qualities to the extent possible (QC12). Faithful representation is also stated to be a quality that, if achieved, does not necessarily provide decision-useful information, as the latter also must have a credible level of relevance for its intended users (QC16). In addition, according to the IASB, faithful representation is a reporting quality that researchers have failed to determine by empirical measurement, whereas relevance has been empirically tested by means of stock market price reactions (BC3.30–BC3.31).

Comparability is the first enhancing characteristic prescribed by the IASB to produce relevant and faithfully represented financial information; it is the condition whereby reported financial information can be compared to similar information for another entity or the same entity for another period, with consequential similarities and differences identifiable by the user (QC20). This enhancing characteristic relates directly to the stated primary reason for accounting standards of increasing the comparability of financial information (BC3.33). However, the IASB warns that comparability does not mean consistency – although use of consistent accounting practices is regarded as a means of achieving comparability (QC22) – nor does it mean uniformity – because different things should look different (QC23). Comparability is, at least in part, perceived as possible by the IASB because of adherence to the fundamental characteristics of relevance and faithful representation (QC24). But such an enhancing characteristic does not of itself create relevant and faithfully represented information (BC3.33). None of these assertions are supported by evidence or detailed argument.

Verifiability is the next enhancing characteristic advocated by the IASB. It is stated as the quality of financial information that gives users assurance that consensus is possible among knowledgeable and independent observers about the faithful representation of an economic phenomenon (QC26). It is also believed to provide confidence to users that the financial information is free from material error and bias and can be depended on to be relevant and faithfully represented (BC3.36). This prescription is presumably intended as a basis for the independent audit. Thus, the IASB claims that verifiable information can be used with confidence, although unverifiable information may be used, but with caution because it is more risky to use (BC3.34). Verifiability is perceived by the IASB to be a reporting characteristic that is very desirable but not necessarily required (BC3.36). Again, no evidence is offered about these distinctions.

The remaining characteristics claimed by the IASB to enhance the relevance and faithful representation of financial information are timeliness (i.e. reported financial information needs to be available to users in sufficient time to be capable of influencing their decisions) (QC29) and understandability (i.e. reported financial information is classified, characterised and presented as clearly and concisely as possible) (QC30). According to the IASB, understandability does not mean financial information that is difficult to understand should be omitted, but that it should be disclosed in a manner maximising understanding and preventing misunderstanding, assuming users with reasonable financial knowledge and willingness to apply reasonable diligence to its use (BC3.40). No evidence is offered by the IASB about varying levels of understandability associated with financial information nor about what constitutes reasonable financial knowledge and user diligence.

Assessing objective and characteristics

Reporting objectives and qualitative characteristics have been a significant part of the regulation of financial reporting quality for several decades. Their prescription in the CF provides accounting researchers with opportunities to seek evidence of their nature and role in standard-setting, and this section assesses research over the last decade on the reporting objective and qualitative characteristics in IASB 2010 outlined above. The assessment starts with the decision usefulness objective and is followed by the qualitative characteristics. The research is taken mainly from leading research journals from 2002 onwards.

Decision usefulness

The IASB prescription of decision usefulness as the only objective of financial reporting is simultaneously rational and problematic. On the one hand, the rationality of the objective is its consistency with a common-sense argument that financial information is a potential input to investment, lending and credit decisions. On the other hand, the problem with the objective is its consistency with previous criticisms of the CF that it consists of prescriptions by assertion rather than empirical evidence and depends on vague and unexplained language (e.g. Penno 2008: 349–50; Walker 2003: 344–51). For example, as outlined in the previous section, the IASB asserts that the primary users of financial information from a reporting entity are capital market participants such as actual and potential investors, lenders and other creditors, and that these participants have common information needs that can be satisfied by general purpose financial statements. The reporting entity has not yet been identified by the IASB, but the inference in IASB 2010 is that it is a corporate organisation in which equity, loans and other forms of credit are determined, managed and regulated in capital markets.

Specific terms such as decision, usefulness, general purpose, common need, reporting entity, and future return are used throughout IASB 2010 with little or no definition or explanation. This makes the decision usefulness objective ambiguous. In particular, IASB 2010 does not explicitly consider the nature of decisions associated with organisations. For example, decision topics such as rationality, uncertainty, ambiguity, risk preference and rules are not mentioned. This neglect of the nature of decisions by the IASB contrasts with accounting theories such as those advanced by Chambers (1966: 40–58) and Sterling (1979: 95–115), in which the subject is explained and discussed at length. Thus, rather than explicitly seeking to improve reporting practice by providing an authoritative and coherent conceptual statement in relation to decisions and decision-makers, the IASB appears to perpetuate the use of the CF as a device to project a normative platform capable of justifying existing rules prescribed in accounting standards and satisfying the diversity of reporting entities and report users affected by these rules (Dean and Clarke 2003: 293; West 2003: 80–3; see also Hines 1989, 1991). By asserting that general purpose financial statements meet the common information needs of a variety of decision-makers, the IASB advocates a reporting objective, contrary to the argument of West (2003: 184–6) that the CF must explain the specific conditions in which decision usefulness is achieved. In other words, the decision usefulness objective makes sense only when it is stated in the context of evidence about the nature and variety of economic decisions commonly made in relation to specific reporting entities, and the role, timeliness and veracity associated with specific financial information and statements applied in these decisions. To be authoritative, the CF must recognise that each identifiable type of economic decision needs a specific informational input related to the objectives, options, evaluations, constraints and judgments of the type of decision-maker associated with it. Unless this is done, general purpose financial statements encompassing different time dimensions, subjective and arbitrary judgments, and varying degrees of veracity remain an incoherent and unintelligible means of achieving decision usefulness (West 2003: 186; see also Moore 2009: 328–30).

Because of a long-term bias in the accounting research community in favour of the capital market paradigm in relation to financial accounting, decision usefulness is typically researched from the perspective of the influence of financial information on the decisions of equity investors and on equity prices in a market setting (see Beaver 2002) rather than from a perspective of the nature and role of accounting (Kaplan 2011; see also Parker 2007). The capital market paradigm is described by Sterling (1990: 107, 126) as anthropology, in which the researcher focuses predominantly on the reactive behaviour of users of financial information in equity markets. This means, however, that although price reactions can be considered evidence of financial information use, they cannot be interpreted as evidence of usefulness (Walker 2003: 348).

Empirical studies of the reporting objective of decision usefulness in recent times have typically been presented under the generic research label of value relevance (Francis and Schipper 1999: 319; Wyatt 2008: 217); financial information is value relevant when it is associated with investors' valuation of the reporting entity as reflected in its stock price. Most capital market researchers focus on value relevance rather than decision usefulness because their interest is predominantly with investment valuation and stock price rather than stewardship or other decision-related functions (Francis and Schipper 1999: 319). Value relevance studies effectively capture both relevance and reliability (now termed faithful representation under IASB 2010), but they create the attendant problem of separating the effects of relevance from reliability (Wyatt 2008: 222).[7] Reviews of specific value relevance studies are presented in the next sub-section of this chapter. Meanwhile, there are a number of studies that imply or explicitly observe the decision usefulness objective.

Tucker and Zarowin (2006: 267–8) find the informativeness of earnings and cash flows for equity valuation increases when income smoothing is present because, compared to unsmoothed information, subsequent changes in equity prices reflect more information about future earnings and cash flows. This study suggests the decision usefulness of smoothed information is greater than that of unsmoothed information. Dichev (2008) provides an assessment of the long-standing predilection of standard-setters for the balance-sheet-based model of financial reporting. He argues that this approach has reduced the usefulness to investors of earnings information because such numbers have more volatility, less persistence and less predictability because they reflect changes due to accounting rather than economics (Dichev 2008: 464–5). Kothari et al (2009) report that the magnitude of negative equity price reactions to disclosure of bad news concerning dividend changes and earnings forecasts is greater than that for positive equity price reactions to disclosure of good news, leading to a conclusion that, on average, managers have incentives to withhold bad news and leak good news (Kothari et al. 2009: 273). This study provides strong evidence of the potential effect on the decision usefulness of financial information of managerial judgments and interventions. Penman (2007) observes the conceptual and practical merits of fair values on financial reporting quality from the demand perspective of equity valuation and stewardship[8] and concludes that these accounting measurements work well for both objectives at the conceptual level, although there are significant practical implementation issues (Penman 2007: 42). Relevance and reliability are not mentioned in this study, but the overall conclusions can be linked to the decision usefulness objective.

There are also several non-market-based studies focusing on decision usefulness. Koonce et al. (2005) report on a behavioural experiment to detect how investors perceive financial risk from accounting disclosures. They use the decision theory variables of probabilities and outcomes and the behavioural variables of worry and control. They conclude that both sets of variables provide more explanatory power than conventional decision theory alone, and that they are dependent on one another in their effects on perceived risk (Koonce et al. 2005: 238–9). The study concludes that regulators need to consider the effect of risk disclosures by first understanding the factors that users consider when judging risk. These conclusions relate to earlier comments in this chapter concerning the IASB's neglect of the nature of decisions. Sharma and Iselin (2003) use a behavioural field experiment with professional bankers to examine the relative decision usefulness of cash flow and accrual information reported by companies. The context is solvency assessment, and their findings reveal cash flow data to be more accurate than accrual data, particularly for insolvent companies, thus supporting prior normative arguments about the decision usefulness of cash flow information. Hitz (2007) examines theoretically the desirability of reporting fair values by comparing their decision usefulness from a measurement perspective of accounting inputs to valuation models and an information perspective of signals capable of revising expectations underlying decisions. The study concludes that fair values are useful for decisions from both perspectives (with reservations about reliability issues) and that standard-setters should use theoretical perspectives to construct standards (Hitz 2007: 354–5). Gassen and Schwedler (2010) use an online survey of professional investors and find that they regard fair values determined by market prices as more useful for their decisions than fair values determined by financial models in the absence of market prices. The researchers specifically asked investors to judge decision usefulness in terms of several qualitative characteristics including relevance and reliability (Gassen and Schwedler 2010: 501–2). Bailey and Sawers (2012), in a behavioural experiment with non-professional investors, reveal that, compared to those who are less trusting, investors who trust the current system of rules-based reporting are more likely to use information based on PBAS. Although decision usefulness is a term not used in the study, it is addressed indirectly when participants are asked to rate information quality in terms of relevance, reliability, verifiability, neutrality, comparability and understandability, with a mean quality rating calculated (Bailey and Sawers 2012: 33, 39).

Value relevance

The value relevance of financial information is central to contemporary research of the influence of financial information on decisions associated with reporting entities. These studies typically focus on information relevance in relation to stock market price and do not always refer to reliability or faithful representation, contrary to the testable proposition that to be value relevant, financial information must have some degree of reliability – that is, a significant statistical association with stock price suggests the information is reliable enough to be relevant (Wyatt 2008: 218, 222–3).

According to Francis and Schipper (1999: 325–7), the value relevance of financial information can be observed from four perspectives of stock price. Financial information (a) precedes the intrinsic stock price to which the market price drifts, assuming accounting numbers capture intrinsic value before the stock price does (an approach offering no scope for improving financial reporting); (b) contains variables used in valuation models or predictions of these variables (an approach also offering no scope for report improvement); (c) causes investors to change prior expectations of stock prices (typically, this does not happen); and (d) correlates with stock price changes and returns (thus allowing for the influence of information sources other than financial statements). Testing for the value relevance of financial information reported by quoted companies between 1952 and 1994 and using perspective (d), Francis and Schipper (1999: 349–51) reveal evidence of some decline in value relevance for earnings to explain stock market returns and some increase for earnings and book values of assets and liabilities to explain stock market values. They infer that this research improves understanding of the decision usefulness of financial statements (Francis and Schipper 1999: 351).

Holthausen and Watts (2001) deal with inadequacies in the theoretical foundations underpinning value relevance studies such as Francis and Schipper (1999), particularly their inability to adequately reflect actual relationships between financial information, accounting standard-setting and investor valuation (e.g. because of reliance on tests of stock market efficiency). They argue that the results of value relevance research describe statistical association between relevant variables rather than causation. Barth et al. (2001) take a more relaxed view of the worth of value relevance research, arguing that it reflects the primary focus of financial statements as input to equity investment rather than reflecting other uses of financial information such as contracting, and therefore extant valuation models are useable despite their theoretical frailty.

In contrast to reviews such as Holthausen and Watts (2001) and Barth et al. (2001) that focus predominantly on information relevance, Maines and Wahlen (2006) examine the nature of reliability from extant research. Their review includes the characteristics of neutrality, freedom from error and representational faithfulness, and it reveals the complex nature of reliability as a qualitative characteristic and the difficulties in precisely specifying reliability in accounting standards. Preparer incentives to manipulate reported information are identified as one significant factor affecting reliability, as is the danger of relying on audit verification (alternative comparisons with economic benchmarks and future cash flows are recommended). Maines and Wahlen (2006: 419–20) conclude that there needs to be adequate disclosure of underlying economic factors, judgments and estimates, as users are sensitive to the issue of reliability and to the factors that most affect it.

Wyatt (2008) examines the value relevance of financial and non-financial information about intangible assets from a sample of pertinent research studies. Intangibles include research and development, brands and advertising, customer loyalty, competitive advantage, human capital and goodwill. Wyatt (2008: 243–7) concludes that these studies are predominantly about research and development expenditure and, particularly, its influence on stock price levels. Different types of intangibles involve different information metrics, such as management reports and output measures, but most studies capture the relevance of financial information from the perspective of stock prices. Also, most studies have little to say directly from their results about the reliability of information sources and numbers, although there are attempts to empirically test the unreliability of measures of research and development and brands and advertising expenditures. Landsman (2007) reviews the capital market literature to judge the decision usefulness of fair values in terms of relevance and reliability. The findings are that fair values have relevance to report users but are characterised by reliability issues such as measurement error and source authority. Landsman (2007: 208–9) identifies the history of fair value disclosure and reveals the need for general consensus regarding reliability in the context of minority support for 'financial reality' in reporting supplanting the traditional focus on 'legal reality'. Ronen (2008: 205–7), on the other hand, argues that fair values do not satisfy the informativeness objective (in the sense of reflecting future cash flows), nor are they useful regarding stewardship (in the sense of reflecting added shareholder value), although they do give some insight into risk by reflecting abandonment values. The unreliability of fair values is also noted. Unlike other researchers and reviewers, Ronen takes a normative stance by suggesting an alternative report framework of expected and realised cash flows (thus allowing reliability to be judged over time) using a combination of historical transactions, exit values and use values in terms of opportunity costs and abandonment values.

Dye and Sridhar (2004) use a simple analytical model to demonstrate the relevance-reliability trade-off with respect to aggregated financial information. A summary report is produced from two information sources (one highly relevant but potentially unreliable and the other less relevant but more reliable). The effect of the report on investor behaviour related to stock price is modelled mathematically, assuming investor awareness of information sources. A conclusion is that aggregation increases the reliability of the more relevant information as it tempers incentives to misreport (Dye and Sridhar 2004: 78). Horton (2007) provides an empirical assessment of the value relevance of voluntary disclosures by life insurance companies of embedded value (i.e. discounted present value) to shareholders of existing life policies. These values provide report users with an estimate of the value of future profits from policies and contrast with the solvency focus of the current legally required reporting in the insurance industry. Horton (2007: 193–6) finds that embedded value disclosures are value relevant and further considers implications for this finding for accounting standard-setters – particularly whether these disclosures should be mandatory, thus raising questions about their reliability. Barton et al. (2010) examine the individual usefulness of performance measures commonly used by investors around the world, including sales, earnings and operating cash flows. They find that the most value relevant measures are those that directly and quickly capture information about the reporting entity's cash flows. More specifically, Barton et al. (2010: 786–7) find that value relevance peaks for measures above the line in the income statement, although no one measure is dominant, and value relevance varies from country to country. Their concluding advice is that accounting standard-setters should focus on measures that consider the properties of sustainability and articulation with cash flows. Kadous et al. (2012) use several behavioural experiments to test whether report users' evaluation of the relevance of an accounting measurement are affected by factors underlying its reliability in terms of potential for bias and error. The measurements used in the experiments are fair values. The findings demonstrate that report users use reliability assessments, such as the competence of the source of the fair value measurement and whether the basis is a market transaction or a model (Kadous et al. 2012: 1353–5). The findings are also unidirectional in that reliability issues affect assessments of relevance but not vice versa. The authors conclude that reliability issues dominate relevance.

Other characteristics

There is relatively little recent research that focuses on characteristics other than relevance and reliability, although a small number of studies examine the related but not identical topics of consistency and comparability. For example, in relation to consistency, Wüstemann and Wüstemann (2010) examine accounting standard-setting in the US and Germany, arguing that the quest for consistent practice means little if there are inconsistencies in standards. Inconsistent standards and PBAS provide preparers with opportunities to choose between different accounting methods. In relation to comparability, Yip and Young (2012) reveal that cross-country comparability in financial reporting is improved by increased quality through mandatory IASB standards. In a study of the current movement in accounting standards from rules-based to principles-based, Bennett et al. (2006: 201) argue that standard-setters need to reduce the weighting they explicitly give to consistency and comparability and increase the weighting given to relevance and reliability, thus suggesting the need for more professional judgment in relation to reporting overrides such as the true and fair view.

The only other reporting characteristic specified in the CF and observed in recent research is understandability. Courtis (2004) observes the writing condition of obfuscation, in which the writer intentionally or unintentionally writes in a manner that obscures the intended message. Courtis examines the external reporting of a set of public companies and discovers the level of reading ease to be difficult and readability variability to be pervasive. He concludes, however, that there is no systematic evidence of deliberate obfuscation by preparers (Courtis 2004: 308).

Economic reality

Associated with the objective of decision usefulness and the characteristics of relevance and faithful representation is the notion of economic reality. In this context, economic reality is a generic label used by accountants to identify reportable economic phenomena such as resources, obligations, sales and expenses arising from the economic behaviour of a reporting entity. The accounting function inherent in IASB 2010 is concerned explicitly with the recognition of economic phenomena when they are judged to have potential to be relevant inputs to user decisions and capable of being faithfully represented as reportable financial information. More specifically, in relation to the accounting recognition of an entity's assets, liabilities or equity, the IASB (2010: B.6) states that what needs to be recognised is the underlying substance and economic reality as well as the legal form. Achieving this in practice, however, is not straightforward, as Moore (2009) demonstrates. Although she does not address economic reality specifically in terms of decision usefulness, relevance or faithful representation, Moore (2009: 328–30)

Thomas A. Lee

acknowledges that there is a representational problem in accounting for economic reality when she asks why accountants, regulators and users fixate on a mythical accounting bottom line that involves mixed scales of measurement, lack of consensus about the meaning of income, incorrigible allocations and transfer pricing, and counter-intuitive, unauditable and opportunistic accounting measurements. She argues that while scientists and philosophers address reality in terms of relative rather than ultimate truth, accountants pursue a determinate truth based on a Western societal bias that every issue has an answer (Moore 2009: 331–3). Thus, Moore (2009: 336–7) believes that accountants are trapped in a 'cycle of constant revision' because, by seeking a determinate accounting truth, they oversimplify problems associated with the recognition and representation of economic phenomena in accounting terms.

Moore's paper relates to this chapter because she believes that accountants face similar problems to physicists and philosophers when recognising and representing reality. She argues in relation to physical phenomena that it is only in recent times that physicists, with quantum theory, began to understand the indeterminate, probabilistic, random and non-existent nature of these phenomena at the subatomic level (Moore 2009: 331). Further, in Buddhist philosophy, the ambiguity of reality is explicitly recognised (e.g. the interdependence of observable phenomena in which boundaries and separations are difficult to determine, limits to descriptions of phenomena, consequential lack of distinction between subject and object, and objectives becoming irrelevant in the long-term) (Moore 2009: 332). Accountants have similar problems when accounting for interrelated and interdependent economic phenomena like assets, liabilities, revenues, expenses, income and capital over defined past periods of time and within legally constructed entities (Moore 2009: 328–30). Moore (2009: 334–6) goes on to criticise the misplaced faith of capital market researchers that there is sufficient market efficiency to deal with the limitations of accounting and the inability of these researchers to debate with public interest researchers who have attempted to address the issue of accounting for economic reality. However, she fails to review specific public interest studies with potential to provide understanding of the ontology and epistemology of economic reality.

When committing to the notion of accounting for substance and economic reality, standard-setters implicitly accept the realism argument of philosophers such as Searle (1995) and public interest researchers such as Mattessich et al. (2003), Alexander and Archer (2003), Mouck (2004), Baker (2006) and Lee (2006). Searle's perception of reality is that the world comprises a combination of objective physical facts, governed by the laws of nature and independent of humans, and subjective social facts, constructed by humans through observation, consensus and communication. Social facts are often multi-layered and multi-dimensional, and knowledge about their truth requires a linguistic correspondence between fact and representation. According to Searle, institutional facts are a subset of social facts created within human institutions such as markets, governments, corporations and professional associations by means of collective agreement about their status function in society.[9] Consequently, as human creations, institutional facts are ontologically subjective. They can also be epistemologically objective if there is consensus about the constitutive rules of their representation. Searle's (1995, 7–9) overall conception of reality is summarised as follows:

Table 5.1 Conception of reality

Reality	Ontology	Epistemology
Objective	1	3
Subjective	2	4

Scientists typically seek to observe and research reality in quadrants 1 and 3, but they often find they are in quadrants 2 and 3. Philosophers and social scientists recognise and work with combinations from all four quadrants. However, as implied in their CFs and standards, accountants appear to believe they are dealing with quadrants 1 and 3, when, to the contrary, they effectively cope with a combination of quadrants 2 and 3 (if there can be a neutral representation) (Mouck 2004: 529–30) or 2 and 4 (if there is a self-referential relationship between phenomena and representation) (see Macintosh et al. 2000).

Thus, although it may have bases in objective physical reality (see Mattessich 2003), economic reality consists of institutional facts such as money, exchange, asset, liability, revenue, expense, income and capital. According to researchers such as Alexander and Archer (2003), Mouck (2004), Baker (2006) and Lee (2006) who have adopted the realism argument of Searle to investigate the nature of accounting, the latter is a technical function that recognises subjective institutional facts and numerically represents them with as much epistemological objectivity as possible by means of agreed rules such as PBAS. In other words, according to these researchers, relevant economic reality is ontologically subjective, but representations of it are epistemologically either objective or subjective, depending on the degree of consensus about the rules of representation. Accounting numbers are faithful representations when they correspond to relevant economic reality with sufficient accuracy. The principal issues for accounting standard-setters are which aspects of economic reality are relevant to the decisions of specific types of report users and which accounting standards provide sufficient accuracy for faithful representation. Unfortunately, neither issue is identified or discussed in CFs such as IASB 2010. For this reason, they are examined here from the perspective of recent research.

Alexander and Archer (2003) argue ontologically that the principal objects of accounting such as income and capital are socially constructed institutional facts dependent on their accounting representation and therefore not externally real. As a consequence, epistemologically, Alexander and Archer argue that if there is no external realism, there can be no correspondence between object and representation (i.e. no faithful representation) and no overriding of accounting standards by mandates such as the provision of a true and fair view. However, they concede that by adopting a pragmatic, inter-subjective and consensus view of economic reality, for accounting purposes it can be regarded ontologically as a form of 'internal realism' consisting of socially constructed objects and epistemologically as a 'coherent representation' for which there is a rational acceptance of coherence in beliefs held about socially constructed objects (Alexander and Archer 2003: 6, 7, 13).

When considering the possibility of successfully achieving the reporting quality of neutral representation, Mouck (2004) follows similar reasoning to Archer and Alexander when observing that accounting numbers can appear epistemologically objective yet represent an ontologically subjective economic reality; that is, the rules of accounting standards provide numbers reflecting an objectivity that does not exist in the underlying reality represented. For example, representations of income and capital are, according to Mouck (2004: 540), 'fuzzy' indicators of economic reality rather than 'foolproof' representations, and there is therefore a need for a coherent theory of accounting based on a convincing explanation of how income and capital represent economic reality.

Macintosh et al. (2000) go further than either Alexander and Archer or Mouck when observing that certain accounting numbers do not refer to real objects or events and that accounting does not function according to the logic of transparent representation, stewardship or information economics. Instead, they argue that accounting models are only models, consistent with a post-modern society in which 'signs, images, models, pretences, and shadowy likenesses' gradually merge and implode into an ontologically and epistemologically subjective hyperreality (Macintosh et al. 2000: 14–16). This is an argument based on historical evidence that accounting has altered its focus from physical reality to hyperreality over many centuries; it no longer refers to an objective reality but instead to a hyperreality of self-referencing human constructs such as income and capital, which nevertheless influence daily human behaviour (Macintosh et al. 2000: 16–39).

Mattessich (2003) challenges this perspective by arguing that, ontologically and epistemologically, accounting represents socially constructed facts, such as income and capital, that have some referents in an objective reality. More specifically, using the metaphor of an onion, Mattessich portrays economic reality as a layered construct that builds from an objective core of ultimate reality (as in physics, chemistry and biology) through successive outer layers of subjective, socially constructed reality (including law and economics) that can be represented with sufficient approximation in accounting terms to be useful. In this sense, Mattessich's arguments are consistent with the internal realism/sufficient coherence observation of Alexander and Archer and the fuzzy indicators argument of Mouck. Moreover, Mattessich (2003: 466–9) believes there are pragmatic grounds for an accounting practice based on honest intention and general consensus that produces purpose-orientated representations of social facts such as income and capital (i.e. where standards produce numbers that are useful for some purposes and not for others).

Lee (2006) brings together the philosophical arguments of Searle (1995) and the accounting-related arguments of Macintosh et al. (2000), Alexander and Archer (2003), Mattessich (2003) and Mouck (2004) to examine the issue of accounting for economic reality in the context of the FASB's use of the CF to produce PBAS. Lee's conclusion is that unless the FASB addresses the ontology and epistemology of socially constructed economic reality, little progress will be made in improving financial accounting by use of PBAS. He bases his conclusion on an analysis of the history of the search for PBAS using the CF as a foundation, believing the project has more to do with reducing options in order to achieve consistency and comparability than seeking an understanding of socially constructed economic reality (Lee 2006: 4–10). Consistent with Mouck, Lee (2006: 16–19) concludes that standard-setters need to explain the ontology and epistemology of economic reality associated with specific standards; spell out and obtain consensus regarding the function, collective intentionality and constitutive rules of the institutional facts inherent in these standards; provide better ways of representing institutional facts with the maximum of objectivity and minimum of fuzziness; and diminish the current focus on consistency and comparability in favour of an approach that seeks to improve the quality of accounting representations.

Tollington and Spinelli (2012) examine issues associated with an aspect of economic reality concerned with recognising and representing intangible assets. The latter's inherent nature and status create problems about what to recognise as an asset (e.g. purchased goodwill or customer loyalty or brand name) prior to deciding how best to faithfully represent it in accounting terms. According to Tollington and Spinelli, the 'surface' construction of an intangible's accounting representation may appear to provide a concrete reality of a financial fact. However, the 'deep' structure of its existence creates the need to recognise a subjective, socially constructed artefact (e.g. purchased goodwill) to make sense of the representation. This distinction is consistent with Searle's argument about social facts becoming institutional facts when there is collective agreement about the meaning and status function of social facts. Baker (2006) shows a concern similar to Tollington and Spinelli in relation to internet accounting when he considers issues regarding the nature of institutional facts such as revenue, software, prepayments, expenses and financial instruments associated with internet retailers and service providers.

Summary and conclusions

The purpose of this chapter is to examine accounting standard-setters' prescriptions of a main objective and several qualitative characteristics for reported financial information. The specific prescriptions are contained in IASB 2010. The CF prescribes decision usefulness as the reporting objective, supported by relevance and faithful representation as the qualitative characteristics. An analysis of IASB 2010 reveals that the objective and qualitative characteristics are asserted rather than logically argued with support of empirical evidence. Decision usefulness is advocated as the reporting objective without consideration of the diversity of financial decisions; relevance is advanced in terms of potential rather than actual influence on decisions; and faithful representation is argued without regard to the ambiguous nature of the economic phenomena represented. Nor is there consideration of what is meant by faithful representation in accounting. These absences in the CF mean that its prescriptions are vague and ambiguous normative statements, suggesting that the CF is an attempt to provide a conceptual underpinning to existing accounting rules through PBAS rather than a theory of accounting capable of producing improved financial information. Thus, a conclusion is that the CF is part of accounting's attempt to project itself to the public as a profession with an authoritative body of knowledge.

The decision usefulness objective is advocated without consideration of the nature of specific decisions in relation to factors such as risk and uncertainty, timing, return and security. The related assertion of the usefulness of general purpose financial statements to meet common needs is particularly problematic. The function of accounting is stated as the provision of financial information for decisions, with stewardship having been subsumed. This raises an important question about the validity of merging reporting functions given the contemporary focus on corporate governance and managerial accountability. Relevance is prescribed in terms of potential rather than actual use, and faithful representation is advanced with no regard to the inherent issues of recognising and representing subjective, socially constructed economic phenomena.

There are a few recent research studies that explicitly test for the decision usefulness of accounting data (e.g. earnings, cash flows and fair values). The majority are behavioural rather than empirical experiments. Thus, relevance and reliability receive most of the research attention, particularly with respect to value relevance, where relevance is judged by the association of financial information with stock prices or stock price changes or returns. These empirical studies focus on capital market behaviour, information use rather than usefulness, and association rather than causation. Reliability is often considered in terms of difficult-to-determine representations such as fair values. The trade-off between relevance and reliability is also observed, with relevance being the dominant characteristic.

The most obvious omission in IASB 2010 is its lack of focus on the nature of the economic phenomena judged by accountants to be useful for decisions because of their relevance and faithful representation in accounting terms. Economic reality represented in accounting terms consists mainly of socially constructed institutional facts that, to date, have been identified without common agreement as to their meaning and function. The principal social constructs in this regard are income and capital, and these, by their nature, are self-referencing (what has been described as hyperreality). The construction of a CF that has authority as a body of professional knowledge must involve a proper and detailed analysis of the ontology and epistemology of economic reality for accounting purposes. Until this is done, what is relevant and faithfully represented remains ambiguous.

Key works

Hines (1989) is an essay that explores the nature and role of the CF from the perspective of the search by public accountants for professional status.

Kadous et al. (2012) is an empirical study that seeks to determine the nature, role and interrelatedness of relevance and reliability in relation to decision-useful financial information.

Lee (2006) is a review based on Searle's notion of social reality and how the FASB is dealing with the notion of economic reality in its CF and PBAS.

Moore (2009) contrasts the approaches of scientists, philosophers and accountants to the representation of reality within the context of a flawed financial reporting system.

Walker (2003) is a study of the objectives of financial reporting prescribed by accounting standard-setters that uses the CF as an evidential source.

Notes

1 According to standard-setters, principles-based accounting standards (PBAS) rely on the CF, including its objective and qualitative characteristics (FASB 2002b: 6; Schipper 2003: 62). PBAS are intended to reduce the rules-based nature of accounting standards and increase the need for professional judgment when applying standards (see Bradbury and Schröder 2012). However, as argued by Dennis (2008: 270), this approach creates an ambiguous situation in which PBAS can be interpreted as principles-based using principles in the CF or as rules-based using rules with particular characteristics (Dennis 2008: 270).

2 To date, the CF project is incomplete. The reporting objective (IASB 2010: chapter 1) and related qualitative characteristics (chapter 3) have been determined. However, the reporting entity (chapter 2) is unspecified, and the elements of financial statements (including recognition and measurement, and capital and capital maintenance) (chapter 4) remain as stated in the previous IASB CF of 1989.

3 The IASB CF is explicitly intended to assist in the regulation of financial reporting generally rather than of financial statements particularly (IASB 2010: 43).

4 The importance of improving the quality of reported financial information has been identified in a recent study of the effect of mandatory IASB accounting standards. Florou and Pope (2012) demonstrate that in the countries where such standards are made mandatory, there is a corresponding increase in institutional investor demand for equities, thus ensuring a means by which these standards become impounded in market outcomes.

5 The studies of the CF by Booth (2003), Loftus (2003) and Walker (2003) refer to the CF then in use in Australia. However, each study acknowledges similarities with the CFs of the FASB and the IASB.

6 Hereafter, any reference to the objective (OB), qualitative characteristics (QC) or basic concepts (BC) in IASB 2010 is denoted by the relevant alpha-numeric stated in the latter.

7 IASB 2010 uses the term faithful representation instead of reliability. Most recent research studies use the term reliability. The latter will be used in all cases when the specific study uses the term.

8 These are separate user functions collapsed by the IASB into the single perspective of decision usefulness (BC1.28).

9 Searle (1995: 40) uses the term 'status function' in the sense of the status and function humans give to recognised, accepted and acknowledged phenomena.

References

AICPA (1973) *Objectives of Financial Statements* (New York, NY: AICPA).

Alexander, D. and Archer, A. (2003) On economic reality, representational faithfulness and the 'true and fair override', *Accounting and Business Research*, 33 (1): 3–17.

Bailey, W.J. and Sawers, K.M. (2012) In GAAP we trust: examining how trust influences nonprofessional investor decisions under rules-based and principles-based standards, *Behavioural Research in Accounting*, 24 (1): 25–46.

Baker, C.R. (2006) Epistemological objectivity in financial reporting: does internet accounting require a new model? *Accounting, Auditing & Accountability Journal*, 19 (5): 663–80.

Barth, M.E., Beaver, W.H. and Landsman, W.R. (2001) The relevance of the value relevance literature for financial accounting standard-setting: another view, *Journal of Accounting and Economics*, 31 (1): 77–104.

Barton, J., Hansen, T.B. and Pownall, G. (2010) Which performance measures do investors around the world value the most – and why? *The Accounting Review*, 85 (3): 753–89.

Beaver, W.H. (2002) Perspectives on recent capital market research, *The Accounting Review*, 77 (2): 453–74.

Bennett, B., Bradbury, M. and Prangnell, H. (2006) Rules, principles and judgments in accounting standards, *Abacus*, 42 (2): 189–203.

Booth, B. (2003) The conceptual framework as a coherent system for the development of accounting standards, *Abacus*, 39 (3): 310–24.

Bradbury, M.E. and Schröder, L.B. (2012) The content of accounting standards: principles versus rules, *British Accounting Review*, 44 (1): 1–10.

Bullen, H.G. and Crook, K. (2002) *A New Conceptual Framework Project* (Norwalk, CT: FASB).

Chambers, R.J. (1966) *Accounting, Evaluation, and Economic Behaviour* (Englewood Cliffs, NJ: Prentice Hall).

Christensen, J. (2010) Conceptual frameworks of accounting from an information perspective, *Accounting and Business Research*, 40 (3): 287–99.

Courtis, J.K. (2004) Corporate report obfuscation: artefact or phenomenon? *British Accounting Review*, 36 (3): 291–312.

Dean, G.W. and Clarke, F.L. (2003) An evolving conceptual framework, *Abacus*, 39 (3): 279–97.

Dennis, I. (2008) A conceptual enquiry into the concept of a 'principles-based' accounting standard, *British Accounting Review*, 40 (3): 260–71.

Dichev, I.D. (2008) On the balance sheet-based model of financial reporting, *Accounting Horizons*, 22 (4): 453–70.

Dye, R.A. and Sridhar, S.S. (2004) Reliability-relevance trade-offs and the efficiency of aggregation, *Journal of Accounting Research*, 42 (1): 51–88.

FASB (1976) *Scope and Implications of the Conceptual Framework Project* (Stamford, CT: FASB).

_____ (1978) Objectives of financial reporting of business enterprises, *Statement of Financial Accounting Concepts 1* (Stamford, CT: FASB).

_____ (2002a) *The Norwalk Agreement* (Norwalk, CT: FASB).

_____ (2002b) *Proposal: Principles-Based Approach to US Standard Setting* (Norwalk, CT: FASB).

_____ (2010) Conceptual framework for financial reporting, *Statement of Financial Accounting Concepts 8* (Norwalk, CT: FASB).

Florou, A. and Pope, P.F. (2012) Mandatory IFRS adoption and institutional investment decisions, *The Accounting Review*, 87 (6): 1993–2025.

Fogarty, T.J., Heian, J.B. and Knutson, D.J. (1991) The rationality of doing 'nothing': auditors' response to legal liability in an institutionalised environment, *Critical Perspectives on Accounting*, 2 (2): 201–226.

Francis, J. and Schipper, K. (1999) Have financial statements lost their relevance? *Journal of Accounting Research*, 37 (2): 319–52.

Gassen, J. and Schwedler, K. (2010) The decision usefulness of financial accounting measurement concepts: evidence from an online survey of professional investors and their advisors, *European Accounting Review*, 19 (3): 495–509.

Hines, R.D. (1989) Financial accounting knowledge, conceptual framework projects and the social construction of the accounting profession, *Accounting, Auditing & Accountability Journal*, 2 (2): 72–92.

_____ (1991) The FASB's conceptual framework, financial accounting, and the maintenance of the social world, *Accounting, Organisations and Society*, 16 (4): 313–31.

Hitz, J-M. (2007) The decision usefulness of fair value accounting – a theoretical perspective, *European Accounting Review*, 16 (2): 323–62.

Holthausen, R. and Watts, R. (2001) The relevance of the value relevance literature for financial accounting standard setting, *Journal of Accounting and Economics*, 31 (1): 3–75.

Horton, J. (2007) The value relevance of 'realistic reporting': evidence from UK life insurers, *Accounting and Business Research*, 37 (3): 175–97.

IASB (2010) *Conceptual Framework for Financial Reporting 2010* (London: IASB).

Jones, S. and Wolnizer, P.W. (2003) Harmonisation and the conceptual framework: an international perspective, *Abacus*, 39 (3): 375–87.

Kadous, K., Koonce, L. and Thayer, J.M. (2012) Do financial statement users judge relevance based on properties of reliability? *The Accounting Review*, 87 (4): 1335–56.

Kaplan, R.S. (2011) Accounting scholarship that advances professional knowledge and practice, *The Accounting Review*, 86 (2): 367–83.

Koonce, L., McAnally, M.E. and Mercer, M. (2005) How do investors judge the risk of financial items? *The Accounting Review*, 80 (1): 221–41.

Kothari, S.P., Shu, S. and Wysocki, P.D. (2009) Do managers withhold bad news? *Journal of Accounting Research*, 47 (1): 241–76.

Landsman, W.R. (2007) Is fair value accounting information relevant and reliable? Evidence from capital market research, *Accounting and Business Research*, 37, special issue: 19–30.

Larson, M.S. (1977) *The Rise of Professionalism: A Sociological Analysis* (Berkeley: University of California Press).

Lee, T.A. (2006) The FASB and accounting for economic reality, *Accounting in the Public Interest*, 6: 1–21.

Loftus, J.A. (2003) The CF and accounting standards: the persistence of discrepancies, *Abacus*, 39 (3): 298–309.

Macdonald, K M. (1995) *The Sociology of Professions* (London: Sage Publications).

Macintosh, N.B., Shearer, T., Thornton, D.B. and Welker, M. (2000) Accounting as simulacrum and hyperreality: perspectives on income and capital, *Accounting, Organisations and Society*, 25 (1): 13–50.

Maines, L.A. and Wahlen, J.M. (2006) The nature of accounting information reliability: inferences from archival and experimental research, *Accounting Horizons*, 20 (4): 399–425.

Mattessich, R. (2003) Accounting representation and the onion model of reality: a comparison with Baudrillard's orders of simulacra and his hyperreality, *Accounting, Organisations and Society*, 28 (5): 443–70.

Moore, L. (2009) Economic 'reality' and the myth of the bottom line, *Accounting Horizons*, 23 (3): 327–40.

Mouck, T. (2004) Institutional reality, financial reporting and the rules of the game, *Accounting, Organizations and Society*, 29 (5/6): 525–41.

O'Connell, V. (2007) Reflections on stewardship reporting, *Accounting Horizons*, 21 (2): 215–27.

Parker, L. (2007) Financial and external reporting research: the broadening corporate governance challenge, *Accounting and Business Research*, 37 (1): 39–54.

Penman, S.H. (2007) Financial reporting quality: is fair value a plus or a minus? *Accounting and Business Research*, 37, special issue: 33–44.

Penno, M.C. (2008) Rules and accounting: vagueness in conceptual frameworks, *Accounting Horizons*, 22 (3): 339–51.

Ronen, J. (2008) To fair value or not to fair value: a broader perspective, *Abacus*, 44 (2): 181–208.

Schipper, K. (2003) Principles-based accounting standards, *Accounting Horizons*, 17 (1): 61–72.

Searle, J.R. (1995) *The Construction of Economic Reality* (New York, NY: The Free Press).

Sharma, D.S. and Iselin, E.R. (2003) The decision usefulness of reported cash flow and accrual information in a behavioural field experiment, *Accounting and Business Research*, 33 (2): 123–35.

Staunton, J. (2003) A statement of accounting concepts for level 1 of the conceptual framework? *Abacus*, 39 (3): 398–414.

Sterling, R.R. (1979) *Toward a Science of Accounting* (Houston, TX: Scholars Book Company).

———— (1990) Positive accounting: an assessment, *Abacus*, 26 (2): 97–135.

Tollington, T. and Spinelli, G. (2012) Applying Wand and Weber's surface and deep structure approaches to financial reporting systems, *Abacus*, 48 (4): 502–17.

Tucker, J.W. and Zarowin, P.A. (2006) Does income smoothing improve earnings informativeness? *The Accounting Review*, 81 (1): 250–71.

Walker, R.G. (2003) Objectives of financial reporting, *Abacus*, 39 (3): 340–55.

West, B.P. (2003) *Professionalism and Accounting Rules* (London: Routledge).

Wüstemann, J. and Wüstemann, S. (2010) Why consistency of accounting standards matters: a contribution to the rules-versus-principles debate in financial reporting, *Abacus*, 46 (1): 1–27.

Wyatt, A. (2008) What financial and non-financial information on intangibles is value-relevant? A review of the evidence, *Accounting and Business Research*, 38 (3): 217–56.

Yip, R.W.Y. and Young, D. (2012) Does mandatory IFRS adoption improve information comparability? *The Accounting Review*, 87 (5): 1767–89.

6

Price variation and inflation accounting research

R.J. Chambers

The period 1950–1980 was marked by an unprecedented flurry of prescription, argument and invention in accounting practice and discourse.[1] It inherited a variety of conflicting principles on almost every matter in or adjacent to the domain of accounting.

The balance sheet had long been held to represent a dated financial position of an identified entity. But it had also been held to be merely a list of account balances or residues from whatever devices were used to calculate income. Income had been held to be the periodical increment in capital. It had also been held to be the difference between revenues and costs, however those components were calculated. Assets had been said to be exchangeable property. They had also been described as unrecovered, unamortised and unexpired costs.

Value had been held to subsist in values in exchange or selling prices of assets. It had also been said by some to subsist in unrecovered costs, and by others in the service capacities or potential of assets. Depreciation had been said to be the fall in price of durable goods from whatever cause. It had also been described as the fall in usefulness of such goods, and as the product of amortisation rules, neither of which corresponds with a fall in price. Prices of assets were known to rise and fall over time. But some held that these rises and falls should be ignored in accounting, and others endorsed occasional revaluations. That the purchasing power of money changes from time to time was known, but it was generally held that those changes and their effects could be ignored in accounting. This cluster of contradictories and others like them were to be the concern of practitioners and teachers for the next four decades.

In the deliberate pursuit of any end in view, if one course of action is found to be unfruitful it is abandoned and another is adopted in its place. Canning (1929) had observed that accountants had no established and agreed idea of financial position or income. There was thus no clear end in view. Instead of one idea or rule being abandoned when considered defective, there was no test of what was defective; conflicting rules survived in parallel. Occasionally it had been suggested by non-accountants that accounting should be subject to firm principles as other technologies are. But accountants held that accounting was a practical art. 'it is left to each individual [practitioner] to be a law unto himself' (Walton, 1909, 39). 'Each one of us, having passed our final examinations, went our several ways, and built up our own individual code of principals' (de Paula, 1946, 39). 'the result is a mass of conflicting opinions on many subjects, each one of which

129

receives its value from the reputation of the person holding it, or the more of less convincing way in which he can express it' (Walton, 1909, 452).

Long before, Mill had written: 'Now the reasons of a maxim policy or of any other rule of art, can be no other than the theorems of the corresponding science' (1865/1925, 616). But accountants recognised no 'corresponding science', no body of reliable knowledge, as a source of principles. Scientific knowledge provides a systematic account of the manner in which observable objects and events are related. It is observable that people and firms buy and sell, and determine their ability to exploit opportunities, on the basis of prices as they stand from time to time. By inference, then, 'the accounts should be as sensitive as possible to all price and value changes' (Paton & Stevenson, 1916/1976, 103). But that inference was not generally drawn. The prevalent belief was that asset values in periodical financial statements should be, or be based on, costs. In the course of an examination of accounting assumptions, Paton (1922/1962, 491) observed that, on a 'cost theory of value', the accountant 'assumes that in some mysterious manner the values of [commodity and service inputs] . . . pass over into and inhere in the object for which they were utilised'. This 'cost doctrine' was basic to the conventional disregard of appreciation, the calculation of depreciation charges by reference to expected physical outputs and capacities, and the common disregard of changes in prices and in the value of money – the propriety of all of which Paton disputed. He maintained the importance of up to date accounting, and advocated the use of replacement prices in the process. He described many of the assumptions he noticed as 'largely assumptions of expediency' (499).

Hatfield (1927, 272–3) pointed out the value of 'comprehensive and significant' theories in the progress of other sciences, giving astronomy, chemistry, biology and engineering as examples. 'Accounting . . . needs above all else the formulation of sound theories.' But expediency prevailed. Conflicting opinions inevitably gave rise to diversity of practices. This became of concern to the banking and the securities industries. A committee of the American Institute of Accountants responded (AIA, 1932). It acknowledged that assets had been periodically valued in earlier times. Periodical asset valuation would bring balance sheet values up to date. Indicators of solvency, rate of return, debt dependence and asset composition would be based on up-to-date information, and for that reason useful to managers, investors and creditors. But the AIA committee contended that periodical valuation was no longer possible. The central problem of financial accounting was said to be: how expenditures incurred in one period, in the expectation of profits in the future, shall be dealt with in accounts. The cost (= expenditure) doctrine and cost allocation were made the dominant features of accounting. It has remained a major source of confusion and complaint ever since.

It cut the linkage between accounting and up to date values. That linkage was supplanted by a variety of recognition, allocation and matching rules, advocated on a variety of quite different and often inconsistent grounds, making the indicators mentioned above no longer fair indicators of the financial conditions of firms. But that drawback was set aside, for it had come to be held that the income account and the net income figure were of greater interest to managers and investors than features of financial position. The rise in taxation of business incomes also made income calculation a matter of increased concern.

The 1932 AIA committee did not even consider the possibility of deriving principles or rules from observation of how the world works, after the manner of Mill (see above). The problem of diversity in practice was skirted by a proposal that led to use of the phrase 'generally accepted accounting principles' later in the 1930s. There was not then, nor has there been since, a comprehensive statement of those principles. The phrase simply meant practices commonly used or endorsed among accountants, regardless of their logical incompatibility, and their diverse and misleading consequences.

Shifting prices and income calculation

When the prices of specific goods bought and sold are rising, historical cost-based account-ing (HCA) results in the lower prices of inputs at the time of their purchase being charged against the higher prices at the time of sale. If depreciation and inventory charges are regarded as providing the means of maintaining, by replacement, a physical stock of goods for use or sale, cost-based charges are inadequate for that purpose. Profits could be said to be 'overstated'; business incomes could be said to be 'overtaxed', and investors would be given excuse for demanding higher dividends – effects which might imperil replacement and growth opportu-nities. These effects, said some, might be mitigated by charging revenues with the replacement costs of inputs.

The idea seems to derive some support from macroeconomics. In macroeconomics, the capi-tal of a community is considered to be its stock of privately owned and publicly owned property together with the knowledge and skills of its inhabitants. If that capital stock is not maintained, the standard of living may be expected to fall. Money and interpersonal and interfirm debts are not regarded as parts of capital, since across a whole community they would be offsetting. Also, insolvency of persons or firms would not reduce the capital stock, for it only effects a redistri-bution of the community's capital. Items of property are wanted, of course, for their physical or instrumental properties, of which there is no common denominator; economists have never attempted to calculate national capitals as defined. Nevertheless, academic accountants familiar with economics were influenced by the general idea of maintaining a physical capital. Income calculation on a replacement cost basis came to be endorsed. The movement had strong propo-nents in Germany and in the Netherlands in the 1920s.

Though many of these proposals arose in the context of general inflation, they were not directed at the effects of inflation *per se*. Generally they disregarded the effects of inflation on monetary items; focussed on adjustments in accounts for non-monetary items only; and in some cases granted that adjustments for inflation could be made to the products of replacement price accounting (RPA) if desired.

By contrast with macroeconomics, in microeconomics, the economics of consumers and firms, public property and human skills are not regarded as parts of private capital; money and debts are significant parts of the properties of persons and firms; solvency, debt dependence and rates of return are important considerations; and gains and losses arise from changes in the value of money as well as from shifts in the prices of particular assets. Business accounting is, of course, within the ambit of microeconomics, and might therefore be expected to embrace all of these factors in a systematic way.

The general purchasing power of money

Under inflation (or deflation) the value of money, its general purchasing power, is the reciprocal of the general level of prices. If all prices rise at the same rate, the holder of a given set of goods (any set) would gain by the rise in price and lose by the fall in the value of the money unit in which prices are expressed; the gain and loss would be offsetting. But nothing would offset the loss in the purchasing power of money in respect of net monetary items (cash and receivables less payables), which are commonly exchangeable at their nominal amounts.

In the more general case, the prices of non-monetary assets do not vary uniformly or con-sistently with changes in the value of money; and the asset compositions of firms, as between monetary and non-monetary assets, vary. These variations have differential impacts on firms. Further, a change in the price of any good may be in part due to a change in the relativities of the prices of goods, and in part due to a change in the general purchasing power of money. To what extent those changes affect severally any price is unknown, even to buyers and sellers; and they, in any case, deal on the basis of prices as they stand from time to time whatever their 'causes'. But periodical income calculation was a different matter. To know what persons *could* consume or firms *could* distribute in a period without impairing their financial capital would be a guide to prudent behaviour. Simply to deduct an opening capital from a closing capital would be arithmetically improper and practically misleading if the two capitals were stated in money units of different purchasing power. The nominal increment would have to be reduced by an amount representing the fall in the purchasing power of money. A new item so designated would have to be introduced into the income statement to cope with this.

Drawing on European experiences and proposals of the early 1920s, Sweeney advanced 'stabilised accounting' for that purpose (various papers, and, in 1936, *Stabilised Accounting*). Stabilised accounting dealt with income calculations by reference to the maintenance of real capital, dated general purchasing power, deriving the 'stabilised' accounts from customary HCA accounts by the use of a general price index. Such schemes would later be called 'current purchasing power, or CPP, accounting'. Sweeney also considered, and preferred, replacement cost stabilisation. He suggested a two-step calculation – original cost stabilisation, and replacement cost stabilisation, where replacement costs of non-monetary assets were approximated by appraisal or replacement costs index numbers for particular classes of assets. He regarded the 'inflation' gain or loss as an integral part of income calculation. Appreciation and depreciation of assets (changes in replacements costs) would also be brought into the asset accounts and the income account, though the two terms ordinarily refer to changes in selling prices. Though not endorsed in general practice, general indexation ideas persisted in the discursive literature. Sweeney was to observe, on publication is 1963 of ARS6, *Reporting the Financial Effects of Price-Level Changes*, that its ideas were substantially the same as his of 1936. But there were solecisms.

HCA does not yield a balance sheet representing the money's worth of non-money assets. Where depreciation charges are based on calculations and inventory charges are based on any such rule as valuation at the lower of cost and market, neither of those charges nor the resulting asset balances are prices indicative of money's worth. Neither therefore is the derived balance of the capital account. The same objection applies to RPA. Only to dated selling prices and dated amounts of net monetary assets may a price index be applied, if the object is to discover a present purchasing power equivalent of an opening stock of general purchasing power, and thence a gain or loss on the change in the value of money. This seems to have been generally overlooked. The propriety of HCA was almost universally unquestioned. And the advocates of RPA overlooked the fact that a dated replacement cost does not represent a capacity to spend or to pay debts. The use of dated market prices for periodical valuations, advocated by MacNeal (*Truth in Accounting*, 1939), would have gone far to eliminate these defects, but it seems to have been generally disdained.

Diverse income concepts

Gilman's *Accounting Concepts of Profit* (1939) put under inquiry the diverse ideas said by others to underlie practice. Notice that it was not 'profit' or income as the commercial world would have understood it, but what *accountants represented* as profit, that concerned Gilman – as it had concerned Paton and would concern Littleton and others later.

Drawing on books and articles published, mainly in the United States and mainly in the then recent past, Gilman dealt with a wide range of transaction and valuation problems. He sought what seemed to be the main general ideas behind practices and their justification. Some of those ideas were designated conventions; others, doctrines, 'general statements of accounting or reporting policy'. Conflicts or inconsistencies between some of these ideas were noticed. Gilman concluded that 'the significance of accounting profit is ... the algebraic sum of the separate significances of the various conventions, doctrines, rules and practices which at any particular time constitute the common law of accounting' (605). 'Algebraic sum', a figure of speech borrowed from the more exacting field of mathematics, could scarcely be applied to a set of ideas whose mutual consistency or legitimacy was in question. And, 'common law' could scarcely be used of a set of ideas the interpretation of which was far from common. These terms, like 'generally accepted accounting principles', masked the problem of giving a coherent general account of what accountants were doing. Certainly, the significance of 'accounting profit' bears no conceivable relationship to the significance of actual profits or incomes of persons or firms earning them.

To Gilman, accounting was essentially eclectic; only 'embarrassment and awkwardness' would result from 'trying to justify a proposition as a principle of accounting because it is based upon a principle of mathematics, or because it is derived from a principle of economics, or because it is required by statute or edict' (257). However, concentration on what accountants thought and said about what they did disregarded the cleavage between the products of accounting and the factual states and incomes which financial statements were expected to depict. Many before and after Gilman would claim that accounting should represent facts truly; evidence that financial statements did not do was abundant. Yet nowhere in the many lists of doctrines, conventions, principles, postulates or basic ideas – as they were variously described – was there an unequivocal proposition to the effect that true representations of the financial facts, as they could be discovered from time to time, were the dominant aims of practice.

Inflation and replacement cost

Inflation in the post-war years prompted many companies to revalue assets where the practice was permitted. In the United States, the Securities and Exchange Commission (SEC) stood firmly against the practice. A number of companies argued the case in their annual reports for more realistic income calculation. But the AIA Committee on Accounting Procedure rejected increased depreciation charges as a means of meeting the effects of rising prices (ARB 33, 1947). In 1947 the AIA sponsored a Study Group on Business Income. Alexander, an economist, in a monograph commissioned by the Study Group, concluded that the 'differences among the bewildering number of concepts of income' could be 'narrowed down to the three major issues ... the real versus the money measure, inclusion versus exclusion of capital gains, and accrual versus realisation as the criteria for timing of a gain or loss' (1950, 54). The Study Group in the upshot considered that 'methods could, and should, be developed ... so that the results of activities, measured in units of equal purchasing power, and effects of changes in the value of the monetary unit would be reflected separately in an integrated presentation which would also produce statements of financial position more broadly meaningful than the orthodox balance sheet of today' (1952, 105). But no indication was given of the processes by which the two desired improvements might be attained systematically and simultaneously.

Replacement price continued to be the kernel of suggestions for dealing with rising prices – in proposals of the Institute of Cost and Works Accountants (*The Accountancy of Changing Price Levels*, 1952), of the Association of Certified and Corporate Accountants (*Accounting for Inflation*, 1952), of Mathews and Grant (*Inflation and Company Finance*, 1958), of Edwards and Bell (*The Theory and Measurement of Business Income*, 1961), of Sprouse and Moonitz (*A Tentative Statement of Broad Accounting Principles for Business Enterprises*, 1962), of the Committee of Inquiry into Inflation and Taxation (the Mathews committee, Australia, 1975), and of proposals under the general rubric 'current cost accounting' (CCA).

By origin, 'replacement cost' was associated with actual replacement of physical stocks. The logic of setting off against the current selling prices of outputs the current buying prices of inputs (instead of original costs) seemed to have merit independently of the physical replacement consideration. 'Current cost' came to be used in place of replacement cost (e.g. by Mathews & Grant, 1958). 'Current value accounting' (CVA) was also used of some proposals of the same kind.

Current value accounting

The best known exposition of CVA in the Anglo-American literature is that of Edwards and Bell (1961). The authors were economists. They were concerned with the different orientations of economists and accountants towards income calculation – economists with future expectations as inputs to decisions (and therefore with subjective notions), accountants with the past (and therefore, in principle, with objective magnitudes). They suggested 'therefore, that a principal function of accounting data is to serve as a fundamental tool in the evaluation of past decisions' (3). The economic concept of income (the difference between successive subjective valuations – net present values, NPVs, or discounted expected net cash inflows) – they said, is not objectively measurable and would not serve the purposes of managers or investors (15). They also rejected HCA and CPP, in favour of recording particular price changes as they occur (17).

They considered firms as adaptive entities in an uncertain world, adjusting their operations and arrangements to shifts in the price-indications of changes in internal and external conditions. The options for discovering the consequences of past decisions they considered to be the exit prices and the entry prices (current costs) of assets at the terminal dates of successive periods. Both were considered at length. The use of exit prices would yield a 'realisable profit'; the use of entry prices would yield a 'business profit'. They confessed to a 'feeling that a strong case can be made for the inclusion of both sets of data in the accounting records' (97). But the fact that the realisable profit concept 'represents a more substantial departure from accepted accounting principles than does the business profit concept' was considered 'a weighty argument in favour of the accumulation of data on a current cost basis' (109). Their exposition followed the latter course.

Edwards and Bell proposed the separation of gains (or losses) into operating and holding gains. Holding gains, said to be capital gains, are the differences between selling prices while goods are held. Current operating profit is the difference between the prices at which goods are sold and their current costs is at the time of sale, aggregates of both of which are said to be expressed in average of the year dollars. The distinction was made necessary by the determination to distinguish current operating profit, realisable cost savings, realised costs savings and capital gains; and to calculate realised profit and business profit, two concepts of money profit. Given the occurrence of inflation, price level changes were considered to play a 'subsidiary role'. Inflation gave rise to 'fictional' gains or losses which had to be eliminated to obtain real realised profit and real business profit.

The varieties of 'profit' are, thus, many; and the processes of calculating them complicated, making use at many points of averages and at some points of indexes to obtain and adjust experienced prices and intermediate elements in the calculations. But in the whole exercise some significant considerations were set aside or overlooked. Neither current costs nor their calculated derivatives represent dated stocks of money and money's worth. So, first, the arithmetical fallacy of adding such amounts to dated amounts of monetary items in balance sheets is perpetrated. Second, the resulting amounts of net assets and capital do not represent the financial outcome of operations, nor the stake with which a firm faces a succeeding period, the amount available to redeploy. In the context of judgement of the past and decision making for the future, the products of CVA of the Edwards and Bell variety are irrelevant and misleading. No budget can properly proceed except from an up to date statement of the amounts of money's worth available to enter the budget period. No solvency ratio, rate of return, leverage ratio or asset combination analysis represents what in ordinary parlance it is expected to represent. The extent of the deviations from dated factual indications of these matters is unknowable without going back to dated exit prices, which Edwards and Bell had rejected. However, the scheme had so many similarities to conventional accounting that its main features attracted widespread attention and advocacy.

Past, present and future

The Accounting Research Division of the AICPA, set up in 1960, published a 'tentative statement of accounting principles' in 1962 (Sprouse & Moonitz, ARS3). It seems to have attempted to accommodate some views of Canning, Sweeney, and Edwards and Bell, all of whom had alluded to differences between the viewpoints of accountants and economists. Fisher (1906/1965) had suggested that, given perfect foreknowledge and perfect markets, the dated values of assets would be equal to their net present values (NPVs). The 'equality' breaks down in the universal absence of the 'perfect' conditions. Canning (1929) had endorsed the idea, as a method of 'direct valuation'. Sweeney had advocated the use of replacement costs, with indexation for the effects of inflation. Edwards and Bell had endorsed CVA.

'Assets', said Sprouse and Moonitz (54), 'represent future economic benefits'; the problem of measuring assets is the problem of measuring the future services. NPVs of future services can be calculated for fixed money contracts; but for other assets, the calculation would entail speculation about future demands and prices in a world marked by uncertainties. Sprouse and Moonitz proposed the use of net present values for receivables and payables. For other assets they endorsed the use of replacement costs. The 'undepreciated cost' of depreciating assets 'should reflect a reasonable estimate of unused service units'. What was meant by 'future benefits' and 'service units' was not made clear. 'Future benefits' looks very much like the outcome of the speculative calculations mentioned above; 'service units' seems to be a physical notion, not at all a financial notion. The shift to future benefits in the definition of assets was prompted perhaps by the widespread contention that accounts based on past (often long past) costs were of little use in appraising performance or choosing future courses of action. The future is inevitably uncertain; but that uncertainty would only be compounded by an accounting based on speculation about the future while purporting to represent a dated present. In common usage, asset values in balance sheets are expected to represent the dated money's worth of assets, the means of paying debts and doing other things, not the prospective outcome of their use and sale into some distant future.

The 'future benefits' idea had antecedents. By the 1930s, Limperg (Amsterdam) had formulated the following valuation rule: 'The value of a commodity is its realisable value or its replacement value, but always the lower of the two. As to the realisable value a distinction should be made with regard to factors of production between the direct and the indirect realisable value [proceeds to be realised in the normal course of business]; of these two the higher is always relevant' (Burgert, 1972, 112). Using NPV as 'indirect realisable value', Solomons (1966) described this compound or derivative of the three values as 'value to the owner'. As 'value to the business' (VTB) it would later be described thus: 'the value of an asset to a company is its written down replacement cost (current purchase price), except in situations where the written down replacement cost is higher than both the economic value [NPV] and the net realisable value in which case the value of the asset to the company is the economic value or the net realisable value, whichever is the higher' (Sandilands, 1975). It was said that valuation under the formula would turn out to be, in most cases, replacement cost, or current cost. But no one would know from the stated value itself whether or if the other options had influenced the stated value. In any case, if a balance sheet were expected to represent a dated financial position, consequential upon past transactions and events, replacement cost (or current cost) is irrelevant. It would arise from no past transaction, but from speculation about a singular future action from the many possible future actions available to a firm.

NPVs are, of course, valuations of prospects, prospective and hypothetical valuations, not dated and independently verifiable valuations of property such as the amounts appearing in balance sheets were supposed to be. It is difficult to imagine what such a calculated valuation might have to do with the payment of debts or the means available to fund ongoing or variant operations as from a balance date. The practical importance of that kind of information seemed to have dropped from sight.

A purchasing power accounting

Canning (1929, 196) had said: 'Accountants are fully aware of the differences between dollar accounting and a conceivable purchasing power accounting, and would prefer, just as economists do, a purchasing power accounting.' Such an idea had been at the root of Sweeney's and other CPP proposals, and seems to have been implicit in the 1952 conclusion of the Study Group indicated above. However, if general price indexes were to be applied to basic data to obtain an income based on the maintenance of capital, interpreted as a stock of general purchasing power, the basic data – opening and closing balance sheets of a period – would have to be dated purchasing power data. Only balance sheets based on dated money amounts and dated selling prices of non-monetary assets would serve. That meant a return to something like the periodical valuation that was common before HCA became popular.

Selling price had long been used for valuing inventories of primary products. Sporadic but widespread revaluations were evidence of the need for more up to date information than HCA provided. Knowledge of up-to-date buying and selling prices is always necessary in estimating the prospects of gain from any contemplated activity. Dated buying prices and dated selling prices would provide an accounting that could deal with price variations and the effects of inflation in a coordinated manner, without suppositions and differential valuations, and could yield financial statements that would correspond with the outcomes of the conduct of the affairs of firms.

Inflation and price variation problems are only part of the general context of accounting. Over several centuries, the information provided by bookkeeping had been held to be a valuable guide to the prudent conduct of financial affairs. A similar object is served by all instrumentation systems in settings where prudent responses to the effects of variables are necessary. If financial statements are regarded as guides to the rectification of disadvantageous drifts and the exploitation of advantageous drifts in solvency and profit, the information they contained would necessarily be up to date and would correspond, in particulars and in total, with observable financial facts.

These things suggested replacement of the prevalent accounting conception of the ongoing concern. The 'going concern' had long been depicted as a firm that continued and would continue to carry on its business in the same fashion and with the same functions and policies more or less indefinitely, in an environment that would not interfere with the firm's plans. By contrast, the literature of microeconomics postulated an adaptive firm responding to shifts in its own state and in the world about it. The histories of firms and the daily reported changes in the tactics, plans and intentions of companies confirmed that adaptation, rather than the 'static' going concern idea postulated by accountants, was the typical characteristic of commercial and financial ventures. In a money economy of interdependent persons and firms, adaptation depends on up to date information on the money and money's worth of other exchangeable property available to each party from time to time. Since to pay debts, to take advantage of opportunities, and to meet other exigencies, any item of non-money property may be exchanged, the values in exchange or selling prices of non-money property are pertinent to all deliberate and informed choice and action.

Further, examination of the process of decision making (or responding to circumstances at a stated date), suggests that there are three kinds of input – past (historical) factual information up to the stated date, as indicative of past experience; present factual information on financial position at the stated date, as indicative of the consequences of the recent past, and as point of departure into the future; and future speculations, based on past and present factual information and on expectations of the outcomes of alternative courses of action. These three inputs are logically different, and have logically different functions. It is therefore logically fallacious to mix any two or more of such past, present and future magnitudes, or to regard them as optional alternatives, if the aim is to obtain a presently dated magnitude – which is what dated balance sheets purport to indicate. And, if logically fallacious, then practically misleading, as to the past, present and future. Such invalid mixtures are a widespread feature of all styles of accounting other than an accounting using exit prices as periodical values.

Further still, the outputs of selling price accounting would be verifiable. Valuation by reference to an observed selling price is just as objective as valuing any purchase at its purchase price. On the other hand, the numerous and diverse valuation rules applied in processing original prices (recognition rules, conservatism, and so on) make the products of other systems almost entirely subjective. 'Verification' can be nothing more, then, than agreeing (or disagreeing) with the calculations made, never testing for correspondence with facts.

There was, thus, a set of conditions that should be met by a serviceable style of accounting – namely, correspondence with the amounts of transactions, correspondence of dated financial statements with dated valuations, accommodation of changes in prices and in the value of the money unit, and independent verifiability of all inputs to the accounting.

Exit price accounting

It seemed possible, by examining the context of financial arrangements and calculations, to devise an accounting that would meet all of these conditions, a system that would be based on reliable knowledge in related fields of expertise. Accounting is concerned with money and prices and exchanges. No one would know better than economists the features and functions of money and exchanges. Accounting is concerned with quantified aggregates, differences and relations. No one would know better than experts in applied mathematics the rules governing quantification. Accounting is a form of communication, initially by accountants to owners and managers of property, but in due course to a wide but unknown audience. No one would know better than linguists and social psychologists the conditions of and the impediments to fruitful communication. Accounting is concerned with rights in property and rights to information. No one would know more about those things than legal scholars. And so on. It seemed possible to develop a serviceable accounting if notice was taken of what could be regarded as reliable knowledge in related fields of expertise.

The intention to proceed in that fashion was foreshadowed in Chambers' 'Blueprint for a theory of accounting' (1955). The pieces were put together over the next decade, culminating in *Accounting, Evaluation and Economic Behaviour* (1966). Working independently, about the same time, by a different route, but relying on substantially similar premises, Sterling (*Theory of the Measurement of Enterprise Income*, 1970) reached substantially the same conclusion: 'the present [selling] price is the proper and correct valuation coefficient for the measurement of wealth at a point in time' and income is the difference between dated wealths so calculated (189).

The system was called continuously contemporary accounting, CoCoA for short, or exit price accounting. It would capture the effects of all rises and falls in specific prices. Non–monetary assets would be valued at their net selling prices, dated cash equivalents, at balance date. Cash equivalents could legitimately be added to and related to the amounts of monetary items. The differences between book values and the observed selling prices of assets at balance date, whatever their 'causes', would be accumulated in a price variation account. Valuation at cash equivalents would yield a net asset amount (equal to the equity or capital account balance) that was a homogenous aggregate of uniformly dated values. A general price index applied to such an opening balance (derived in the same way) would indicate the amount by which the opening balance must be augmented if a stock of general purchasing power were to be maintained.

Deduction of that amount, a capital maintenance or inflation adjustment, from the nominal difference between opening and closing capitals, would give the net increment in purchasing power, the real income, of a period. The inflation adjustment would automatically cover gains and losses in purchasing power from net holdings of money and money's worth. Net real income would then be the algebraic sum of (a) net realised revenues based on consummated transactions, or net cash flows, (b) the aggregate of price variation adjustments, the unrealised changes in value for assets on hand at balance date, and (c) the inflation adjustment. The amount of the inflation adjustment would be added proportionately to the opening balances of contributed capital and undivided surplus, giving closing amounts in units of up to date purchasing power. All ratio analysis of financial statements so derived would yield up to date indicators; all additions and relations of aggregates would be mathematically valid. It would be unnecessary to 'up date' previous financial statements, which would be true for their dates; for ratios and percentages could be compared across periods, since they are expressed in pure numbers derived from genuine dated valuations.

Selling price based accounting is essentially simple. All entries in accounts for transactions are the same as under any other system of accounting for transactions. At balance dates, accountants would be not be valuers, but discoverers of the values generated in the markets for particular classes of property; and that information is commonly at the fingertips of buying and selling officers of firms.

The scheme would satisfy the expectations of the 1952 Study Group. It would avoid the variant valuation rules of HCA, and the multiplicity of calculations of the Edwards and Bell variety of CVA, and the arithmetical solecisms of both. A series of inquiries in the early eighties provided evidence of the utilitarian propriety of the conclusions of Sterling and Chambers (Chambers, 1985). The logical, mathematical and empirical propriety of the system was demonstrated in Chambers, 1991.

Current cost accounting – the seventies

CPP accounts attracted short-lived attention in the late sixties and early seventies. In Britain, a proposal to publish an accounting standard along those lines provoked the government to appoint a committee (the Sandilands committee) to consider proposals for inflation accounting. The committee reported in 1975. It recommended a variety of CCA. In effect, it proposed to substitute 'value to the business' (VTB) as described by Solomons in 1966, for replacement cost of the Edwards and Bell proposal. VTB is, of course, an individualistic valuation, not a sum available to a firm to pay debts, taxes or dividends, and therefore unrelatable to the actual solvency, debt dependence, asset composition and capacity to redeploy money or money's worth.

To take the VTB of assets severally ignores the fact that no single asset has a unique value to the business, since all assets and debts are part of an interlocked and variable set, only the conjunction of which yields revenues and hence profits.

That apart, profit, described as current cost profit, was to be regarded as gains other than holding gains. There were to be two 'current cost operating' adjustments to HCA income, a depreciation and a cost of sales adjustment. 'So far as the profit and loss account is concerned we think that these two adjustments to historic cost accounts, and these two alone, constitute a comprehensive system of accounting for inflation' (Sandilands Report, 1975, para 535). The proposal was said to be based on a physical capital maintenance notion of profit.

The professional association committees which considered the Sandilands proposal disagreed. An additional adjustment was suggested, for net working capital. Further debate led to a fourth adjustment for borrowing companies, a gearing adjustment which would abate the current cost operating adjustments proportionately to the relationship between average net borrowings and the average of total shareholders' and creditors' interests of the year. The Accounting Standards Committee's SSAP16 (*Current Cost Accounting*, 1980) provided for accounting along these lines.

In the United States events took similar turns over the period. Jones had made studies of the application of price level adjustments to small groups of companies in 1949 and 1955. The American Accounting Association (AAA) published his monograph, *Effects of Price Level Changes on Business Incomes, Capital and Taxes,* in 1956, and Mason's *Price Level Changes and Financial Statements, Basic Concepts and Methods* in the same year. In 1963, the Accounting Research Division of the AICPA produced a Staff Study, *Reporting the Financial Effects of Price Level Changes* (ASR6). The general direction of these exercises was the production of financial statements, supplementary to conventional statements, based on indexation after the manner of Sweeney. The AICPA study provoked Mathews, advocate of CCA, to respond with 'Price-level changes and useless information' (1965). That prompted Chambers to improve a formal notation developed in 1961; differences in the purchasing power of the money unit were signified by subscripts identifying the specific dates to which prices referred (Chambers, 1965); the inflationary element was shown to be separable from shifts in prices, and both could be incorporated in one system using selling prices as balance date values.

There were now two AICPA Research Division studies, Moonitz and Sprouse (1962) advocating replacement cost valuation for some inventories and for durable assets, and ARS6 dealing in a general way with indexation. In 1971 the AICPA appointed a Study Group (the Trueblood Committee) to consider afresh the objectives of financial statements. The committee contended that users of accounts were concerned with forecasting future cash-flow potentials of firms. But, after considering four different valuation bases (historical cost, exit value, current replacement post and discounted cash flows), it concluded that its stipulated objectives 'cannot be best served by the exclusive use of a single valuation base' (AICPA, 1973, 41). Given the committee's main contention and its conclusion, the problems of dealing with asset price variations and inflation could not be resolved. They were apparently set aside.

The Financial Accounting Standards Board, established in 1973, issued an exposure draft on CPP accounting (FASB, 1974). In 1976, the SEC, by Accounting Series Release 190, required companies under its jurisdiction to provide information, supplementary to conventional accounts, based on the current cost of inventories and productive capacity at balance dates. In the light of the conflict of opinions, the FASB undertook an examination of the whole setting of accounting, the conceptual framework project considered below. In 1979 the FASB published FAS33, *Financial Reporting and Changing Prices*, which required supplementary information on both current cost and indexed cost bases.

In Australia, as elsewhere, competing proposals were advanced. The Australian Accounting Standards Committee (AASC) issued a proposal on CPP accounting in 1974. The government, concerned with the impact of inflation on the incidence of taxation, in late 1974 appointed a committee (the Mathews Committee) to consider the matter. Taxation policy is, of course, a macroeconomic matter. The committee held that 'the overriding criterion in the selection of a tax base must be its compatibility with long run business stability and continuity of existence' (Mathews Committee, 1975, para 11.23). The adoption of a current value concept of income would secure that the 'operating capacity' of a firm would be preserved (para 12.64). Two adjustments would suffice to produce such an income figure, a cost of sales adjustment and a depreciation adjustment. The proposal was thus similar to earlier replacement value proposals, and as indicated already, it would entail the use of a macroeconomic notion in a microeconomic setting. In late 1975, the AASC issued a draft on *A Method of Current Value Accounting*. It advocated an income measure based on maintenance of the operating capability of physical assets. Assets were to be valued at replacement cost if 'essential' to the continuance of operations, at realisable value if not essential. Inflationary gains and losses on monetary items would be the subject of later revisions of earlier documents.

Meanwhile, in New Zealand, at least five public companies had published, in the years 1974, 1975 and 1976, supplementary statements based on CoCoA (Chambers, 1986, V:269–87). They included the then largest and most diversified New Zealand company. They had apparently acted on their own initiatives. These exercises were abandoned when professional sentiment swung towards CCA on publication of the Richardson report. In 1975 the government had appointed a committee (the Richardson Committee) with much the same brief as the Sandilands (UK) Committee. The committee reported in 1976, recommending a variety of CCA similar to the Australian proposal of 1975.

The variety of proposals and the complexity of many of them is daunting. In most cases, the adjusted accounts were required as supplementaries to conventional HCA accounts, the fallacies of which would not be eliminated. That the coexistence of basic and supplementary statements would breed confusion in the minds of their readers was only occasionally noticed. In most cases the adjusted accounts were required only of large companies whose securities were publicly traded; the vast number of other companies and firms would have neither the skills, nor the interest nor the time to digest or to employ the complex processes advocated; most of the proposals could not therefore be regarded as general in application. The differential treatments of classes and subclasses of assets and debts overlooked the fact that an integral treatment of financial affairs in financial statements required a single uniform basis of valuation. The idea that the maintenance of a physical or a financial capital could be advanced by a system of accounting which did not yield statements representing genuine dated money amounts, was mistaken. And, as already indicated, 'physical capital' is not an idea germane to the conduct of the financial affairs of persons or firms; it was a confusing intruder. Further, the amounts of the piecemeal adjustments generally required are individually and collectively incomprehensible to any person but the calculator; the resulting statements therefore fail to meet the elementary condition of intelligibility in communications.

The focus of attention was to shift from these matters in the 1980s, on the establishment of standards boards and committees engaged in restatement, as accounting standards, of much of the existing corpus of traditional rules with increasing attention to detail.

Diversity in practice

So long as bookkeeping remained a matter of private interest to owners and managers of property, bookkeeping rules might pardonably be a matter of choice, though the association, since

Pacioli, of bookkeeping with the prudent conduct of affairs should have given some structure to the ideas that would underlie it.

The growth of the use of partnerships and corporate forms of business, and of the trade in shares and bonds, however, made accounts a matter of multipersonal, or public, interest. Owners, managers and financial supporters would have common interests in the survival and growth of firms, but divergent interests in the conduct and the division of the financial outcome of their affairs. Managers would become the agents of owners and shareholders, owing to them a true accounting for the funds entrusted for business use. That true accounts should be kept, and true summaries prepared periodically was provided for in partnership agreements and in the first UK companies act (1844). True accounts would be accounts that corresponded with experienced and observed facts, events and prices. Deeds and articles of association about the middle of the nineteenth century would specify that balance date values of property would be selling prices, not costs. Audits would be expected to ensure that the accounts were true and correct. And, of course, the contents of periodical accounts would be expected to be generally intelligible. These circumstances and considerations might have been expected to lead to substantially uniform and factual (true) accounting, at least for companies issuing securities to the investing public.

However, as the opening paragraphs of this chapter pointed out, variant and often contradictory ideas had come to be accepted as rules or guides in practice. Diversity was perhaps the inevitable consequence of uncoordinated or *ad hoc* responses to circumstances from time to time. *Ad hoc* responses became precedents, and thence 'principles'. By the 1960s diversity of practices had for decades been characteristic of the profession, and the butt of complaints by eminent people within and beyond the profession. But it had not been regarded as worthy of notice, as an underlying idea, until Grady (*Inventory of Generally Accepted Accounting Principles*, 1965) included 'diversity in accounting among independent entities' in what he described as basic concepts. Grady's inventory was a compilation of utterances of committees of the AIA (by then the AICPA) over preceding decades. It made obvious the variety of ways in which financial affairs could be represented in published reports since the phrase 'generally accepted accounting principles' had been introduced in the thirties. A minority of the advisory committee for the project pointed out the impediments to analysis and comparison that diversity imposed; one recalled that the elimination of obscurity and diversity had been one of the intentions underlying the establishment of the SEC in the thirties. Much later the AICPA was to indicate a vast range of pronouncements and utterances including 'other accounting literature' which could be regarded by auditors as sources of established accounting principles (AICPA, 1975).

The stock exchanges and allied information services and the financial press had long used the ratios, percentages and trends derived from the financial statements of companies. But those indicators would necessarily be misleading if the statements were diverse in kind and not factual as at the dates they bore. Through the decades to which this chapter relates, financial columnists would comment on discrepancies between real and reported asset values, and differences between the products of alternative, optional rules. Discrepancies would come to light on the occurrence of revaluations, mergers, bankruptcies and official inquiries into the affairs of failed companies. The general professional response to such things was to lay the blame elsewhere than on accounting. Over decades it was suggested that investors and others should be 'educated' to understand the 'limitations' of accounting. But the limitations had been imposed by the dicta of accountants themselves.

Repeatedly, and in different countries, professional organisations would set up committees to examine the then prevalent corpus of rules or principles, with the avowed object of reducing diversity – without success. Processes disciplined by experienced or observable facts could replace the overlay of conventions and doctrines that seriously impaired the factual representation of financial affairs. A theory of accounting, which would link its products with the ways persons and firms go about their business, would help. However, as indicated earlier, accountants have generally been dubious, even suspicious, of the value of theoretical inquiry, and of suggestions that their technology could be based on reliable knowledge as were other technologies. Scarcely a reference occurs in the literature to the modes of development of other sciences and arts.

A conceptual framework

Perhaps that attitude would change. Storey (1964, 60) suggested the necessity of a conceptual framework as a basis for judging the merits of prevalent and proposed principles and rules. The idea of a conceptual framework was as old as the earliest attempts to understand or 'explain' the elements of the physical world and their relationships. These explanations had long been called theories. A theory, said Caws (1965, 86), is 'as nearly as we can make it so a replica, in constructs and language, of the real world'. The term 'conceptual framework' is of more recent vintage than 'theory', but it meant substantially the same thing: 'The first conceptual scheme for all the sciences is the common sense world' (Homans & Curtis, 1934/1970, 27).

Countless people manage private or commercial financial affairs for the greater part satisfactorily, by reference to the constraints of the institutions and circumstances that surround them. They understand that the prices of things they possess and of things they wish to possess determine what they can and cannot do, financially. They earn incomes; they engage in exchanges at money prices. They know that prices rise and fall, that the value of money varies from time to time, and that both may affect their wealth and prospects. They understand the uses of debt and the dangers of insolvency. They share a conceptual framework, an understanding of 'how the wold works' in financial matters, simply by their ordinary engagement in buying, selling, saving, investing, and so on. A formal conceptual framework would ideally make explicit and systematic the elements of that implicit framework, leading to an accounting that would play a definable part in the way the world goes about its business.

That it would be desirable, as the 'grounds' for standards, prompted the FASB to launch, in 1976, a conceptual framework project, the fruit of which was a series of statements of accounting concepts over the next decade. However, the FASB's first statement of intention described a conceptual framework, not as a systematic account of how the common sense world works, but as a constitution, a term that in common usage means an agreement among certain parties to be bound by stated rules of behaviour. If rules promulgated by the FASB could be accepted by agreement or made obligatory, they could be described as a constitution in that sense. It resembled the old idea of 'generally accepted principles', except that the Board was given explicit authority by the AICPA to determine rules to be followed. This would be no drawback if the concepts and principles underlying promulgated rules were to be based on knowledge of the common sense world of commerce and finance. But they were not.

Passing notice was given to the 'real world' at a point where the distinction between facts and their representation was crucial. It was said that the common practice would be followed 'of calling by the same names both the financial representations in financial statements and the resources, claims, transactions, events, or circumstances that they represent' (FASB, SFAC6, 1985, paras 6,7). This confusion of the 'word' with the 'thing' had long been denounced by linguists and logicians. The Board noted five different amounts by which assets could be represented; it excluded none of them. If things can have any one of five, or any combination of the five, representations, no one can be assured of what 'representations' means, nor understand what the differences between dated summaries of the assets of different firms would mean, nor compare the states or results represented by the dated summaries of different firms – all of them necessary conditions of the reasoned conduct of financial affairs.

In the common sense conduct of affairs, an asset is an exchangeable item of property, its value in interpersonal dealing being its value in exchange or selling price. But a vastly different 'concept' was endorsed. Assets were defined as 'probable future benefits obtained or controlled . . . as a result of past transactions or events' (FASB, SFAC6, 1985, para 25). 'Obtained or controlled' clearly relates to the past or the present; but future benefits will be neither obtained nor controlled until some future date. The confusion of tenses virtually allows values to be assigned having past, present and future referents indiscriminately. Liabilities were likewise defined, as 'probable future sacrifices of economic benefits'. Dated balance sheet valuation had been the most disputed element of accounting for a century. But the Board left it in limbo. It declined to choose between the methods of valuation 'used in present practice' – historical cost, replacement cost, market value, net realisable value and net present value – and expected their use to continue (FASB, SFAC5, 1984).

If there is no singular, specified, 'standard' concept of valuation for the representation of dated financial positions, there can be no 'standard' notion of income. In the absence of firm, unambiguous concepts of these fundamental determinants of choice in financial matters, there can be no conceptual framework for accounting. In particular, there can be no unambiguous increment that could be augmented or diminished by changes in prices and changes in the value of money – the most vexing problem of the preceding four decades. Indeed, in the treatment of gains and losses (FASB, 1985, SFAC6, paras 82–89), changes in asset prices and in foreign exchange rates are mentioned, but only in passing, and no mention whatever is made of purchasing power gains and losses on the occurrence of changes in the purchasing power of money. A matter of pressing private and public concern over two generations, that had produced volumes of inquiry and debate, was thus passed over as if it were of no consequence. The project was virtually scuttled by its own constructors. Prevalent practices prevailed. Complaints of legal scholars and the courts, of analysts and observers, of public officials, and of many accountants, about the quality of the products of those practices were ignored.

Most choices are made on the basis of more criteria than one. The choice of an accounting system is no different. Are the inputs and outputs factual (and therefore verifiable)? Are derived aggregates and relationships of aggregates mathematically valid? Are dated outputs (balance sheets) indicative of factual states of firms at the specified dates? Do the amounts of assets correspond with the legitimate rights and claims of the firms and its creditors, respectively, at balance sheet dates? Is the calculated income indicative of a factual increase in the means available for any legitimate purpose? These are some of the tests that should be satisfied. A 'test battery' along these lines would show which of the optional valuation bases satisfied most of the criteria. And if a given battery did not discriminate sufficiently, additional tests (like demonstrable relevance to action, and intelligibility) could be applied. That is common procedure in day-to-day affairs as well as in technical and scientific matters. But in the course of the project, no such test battery was applied to the five valuation systems noticed.

The works of Chambers (1966) and Sterling (1970) had illustrated the process of proceeding from a conceptual framework. They presented, as premises, positive statements descriptive of a course of commercial and financial affairs, leading to conclusions on the nature of rules of practice that, they expected, would yield information comprehensible and relevant, equally to tradesmen and tycoons. The treatment of price variations and changes in the value of money were made integral parts of the system. The premises may have been inadequate, and the inferences may have been mistaken; many theories or frameworks have had to be abandoned in the history of advancement of knowledge. But the conceptual framework projects of the eighties, in the United States and elsewhere, made no attempt to extend or refine (or even dispute) the practical pertinence, or the empirical foundations, or the logic, of the exit price framework.

Dated wealths, financial positions and periodical incomes are the dominant products of accounting, and the dominant considerations in the management of financial affairs – both in appraising the past and in planning the future. Clear and unambiguous descriptions of what those terms stand for in the world of commerce, not in the minds of accountants, would provide the only firm foundation on which a serviceable technology could rest. But those ideas remained unexamined. In accounting, said Hatfield (1927, 271), 'the ordinary language of the market place has been used in senses the market place knew not of, and in senses varying with different accountants'. It remained the same sixty years later.

The prospect

It would be hazardous indeed to speculate on future development and debate on changes in the prices of assets and in the value of money. Said Einstein, of disciplined inquiry: 'We are seeking for the simplest possible systems of thought which will bind together the observed facts' (1935, 40). William of Occam had enunciated the principle (Occam's razor) in the fourteenth century. Peirce expressed it thus: 'a few clear ideas are worth more than many confused ones . . . far happier they . . . whose ideas are meagre and restricted . . . than such as wallow in a rich mud of conceptions' (1877/1958, 117). Simplicity and clarity, essential to the development and production of communications to a numerous, diverse and unknown readership, had clearly been disregarded in the debate over principles and standards.

By the eighties two antithetical ideas of capital maintenance – physical and financial – yielding two distinct notions of income, had had staunch advocates. Those general notions of income had come to be qualified by diverse subsidiary considerations. Pronouncements of standards boards and committees continued to permit optional treatments of many matters, as their antecedents had done. It came to be claimed by some that a single, serviceable notion of income could not be devised, and that is was permissible, even necessary, to prepare and publish accounts on two or more different sets of ideas. That such multivalent accounting would confuse rather than enlighten was set aside, as were the mathematical and logical fallacies underlying much of prevalent and proposed accounting. Implicitly and sometimes explicitly, it had been held that the possibility of a systematic set of clear and self-consistent ideas could not be entertained.

Dissatisfaction with the outcome of inquiries of, and of standards promulgated by, standard-setting bodies persists (e.g. Burton & Sack, 1990). Critical attention has been drawn to the diversity of ideas underlying utterances of the FASB; and the suggestion that assets need not be exchangeable nor the subject of legally enforceable rights (SFAC6, para 26) has been challenged (e.g. Schuetze, 1991, 1993). 'Mark to market' has become an advocated recipe for the valuation of some assets. But observations such as these had been made at other times before and during the period under present notice.

Old and customary ideas in cosmology, biology, physics and mathematics survived for centuries before advances in knowledge of how the world works led to their replacement by now prevalent ideas. 'The Copernican revolution', used of one such switch, is almost a trite term. But knowledge of the course and the facts of financial affairs is far more readily accessible and abundant than knowledge of the course of the planets. It should not take generations to effect a rationalising and unifying change in accounting ideas. But will it? Who knows?

Note

1 This chapter was originally published in S. Jones, J. Ratnatunga and R.A. Romano (1996) *Accounting Theory: A Contemporary Review*, Harcourt Brace, Sydney. Reprinted with permission.

References

AASC (Australian Accounting Standards Committee), *A Method of Current Value Accounting*, Melbourne (1975).

ACCA (Association of Certified and Corporate Accountants), *Accounting for Inflation*, London, Gee (1952).

AIA (American Institute of Accountants), Report of a Special Committee of the American Institute of Accountants to the Committee on Stock List of the New York Stock Exchange, reproduced in G.O. May, 1943, *Financial Accounting*, New York, Macmillan (1932).

_____, *Accounting Research Bulletin*, 'Depreciation and high costs', ARB33 (1947).

_____, Study Group on Business Income, *Changing Concepts of Business Income*, New York Macmillan (1952).

AICPA (American Institute of Certified Public Accountants), Staff on the Accounting Research Division, *Reporting the Financial Effects of Price-Level Changes* (ARS6), New York, AICPA (1963).

_____, Study Group on Objectives of Financial Statements (the Trueblood Committee), *Objectives of Financial Statements*, New York, AICPA (1973).

_____, 'The meaning of "present fairly in conformity with generally accepted accounting principles . . ."', AICPA Auditing Standards, AU411 (1975).

Alexander, S.S., 'Income measurement in a dynamic economy' in *Five Monographs on Business Income*, New York, AICPA (1950).

ASC (Accounting Standards Committee), UK, *Current Cost Accounting*, SSAP16, London (1980).

Burgert, R., 'Reservations about "replacement value" accounting in the Netherlands', *Abacus* (December 1972).

Burton, J.C. & R.J. Sack, 'Standard setting process in trouble (again)', *Accounting Horizons* (December 1990).

Canning, J.B., *The Economics of Accountancy*, New York, Ronald (1929).

Caws, P., *The Philosophy of Science*, Princeton, Van Nostrand (1965).

Chambers, R.J., 'Blueprint for a theory of accounting', *Accounting Research* (January 1955).

_____, 'The price level problem and some intellectual grooves', *Journal of Accounting Research* (Autumn 1965).

_____, *Accounting Evaluation and Economic Behaviour*, Englewood Cliffs, Prentice-Hall (1966).

_____, 'The functional utility of resale price accounting', *International Journal of Accounting Education and Research* (Fall 1985).

_____, *Chambers on Accounting*, Chambers & G.W. Dean (eds), Vol V, New York, Garland (1986).

_____, 'Metrical and empirical laws in accounting', *Accounting Horizons* (December 1991).

Edwards, E.O. & P.W. Bell, *The Theory and Measurement of Business Income*, Berkeley, University of California Press (1961).

Einstein, A., *The World As I See It*, London, Lane & Bodley Head (1935).

FASB (Financial Accounting Standards Board), *Financial Reporting in Units of General Purchasing Power*, FASB, Stamford (1974).

_____, *Statement of Financial Accounting Concepts*, No 5, FASB (1984).

_____, *Statement of Financial Accounting Concepts*, No 6, FASB (1985).

Fisher, I., *The Nature of Capital and Income*, reprint, 1965, New York, Kelley (1906/1965).

Gilman, S., *Accounting Concepts of Profit*, New York, Ronald (1939).

Grady, P., *Inventory of Generally Accepted Accounting Principles* (ARS7), New York, AICPA (1965).

Hatfield, H.R., 'What is the matter with accounting?', *Journal of Accountancy* (October 1927).

Homans, G.C. & C.P. Curtis, *An Introduction to Pareto, His Sociology*, 1970, New York, Fertig (1934/1970).

ICWA (Institute of Cost and Works Accountants), *The Accountancy of Changing Price Levels*, London, ICWA (1952).

Jones, R.C., *Effects of Price Level Changes on Business Income, Capital and Taxes*, American Accounting Association (1956).

MacNeal, K., *Truth in Accounting*, Philadelphia, University of Pennsylvania Press (1939).

Mason, P., *Price Level Changes and Financial Statements, Basic Concepts and Methods*, American Accounting Association (1956).

Mathews, R.L., 'Price-level changes and useless information', *Journal of Accounting Research* (Spring 1965).

Mathews, R.L. & J.M. Grant, *Inflation and Company Finance*, Sydney, Law Book Company (1958).

Mathews Committee, Committee of Inquiry into Inflation and Taxation, *Inflation and Taxation*, Australian Government Publishing Service (1975).

Mill, J.S., *A System of Logic*, London, Longmans Green (1865/1925).

Paton, W.A., *Accounting Theory*, reprint, 1962, Accounting Studies Press (1922/1962).

Paton, W.A. & R.A. Stevenson, *Principles of Accounting*, reprint, 1976, New York, Arno Press (1916/1976).

de Paula, F.R.M., 'Accounting principles', *The Accountant* (July 27, 1946).

Peirce, C.S., in P.P. Wiener (ed.), *Values in a Universe of Chance*, New York, Doubleday (1877/1958).

Richardson Committee, *Report of the Committee of Inquiry into Inflation Accounting*, Wellington, New Zealand Government Printer (1976).

Sandilands Committee, *Inflation Accounting: Report of the Inflation Accounting Committee . . .* , London, HMSO (1975).

Schuetze, W., 'Keeping it simple', *Accounting Horizons* (June 1991).

_____ 'What is an asset?', *Accounting Horizons* (September 1993).

Solomons, D., 'Economic and accounting concepts of cost and value', in M. Backer (ed.), *Handbook of Modern Accounting Theory*, Englewood Cliffs, Prentice-Hall (1966).

Sprouse, R.T. & M. Moonitz, *A Tentative Statement of Broad Accounting Principles for Business Enterprises* (ARS3), New York, AICPA (1962).

Sterling, R.R., *Theory of the Measurement of Enterprise Income*, Lawrence, University of Kansas Press (1970).

Storey, R.K., *The Search for Accounting Principles*, New York, AICPA (1964).

Sweeney, H.W., *Stabilised Accounting*, New York, Holt Rinehart & Winston (1936/1964).

Walton, S., 'Earnings and income', *Journal of Accountancy* (April 1909).

7

Standard setting, politics and change management

A personal perspective

Sir David Tweedie

When I began to train as an accountant, the UK had no accounting standards. Accounting at that time was a collection of practices bolstered by a few recommendations (of no binding force) issued by the Institute of Chartered Accountants in England and Wales, but guided above all by adherence to the overriding objective of a true and fair view. I was fortunate to be apprenticed to Professor David Flint,[1] Senior Partner in Mann Judd Gordon & Co. and part-time professor at Glasgow University. It was he who took the new apprentices out for lunch once a month and plied them with accounting issues. I remember vividly him asking us how we would calculate our wealth (not that there was much of it at that time) and why we thought in terms of the value of our house rather than the cost of its purchase. Suddenly what I had been taught in my fairly basic accounting classes at university was called into question – David started me thinking about how accounting could be improved. He also taught me the ethics and integrity required of a professional accountant and the need for calm and reflective professional judgement when there was no clear written guidance or established practice.

In 1969, just as I entered my Chartered Accountant apprenticeship (as it was then), the Accounting Standards (Steering) Committee was created following a very public row between Professor Edward Stamp, then of the University of Edinburgh, and Mr (later Sir) Ronald Leach, President of the Institute of Chartered Accountants in England and Wales and Senior Partner of Peat Marwick Mitchell and Co.[2]

The genesis of this public debate was two famous cases in the UK – the AEI-GEC takeover battle and the Pergamon Press–Leasco affair – which led Stamp to comment that generally used accounting principles could be combined in a million different ways all combinations of which would be said under the then prevailing practices to show a true and fair view – the ultimate legal requirement for company financial reports.[3]

Some twenty years later the problems were different in the UK, but British financial reporting was again in disrepute. Polly Peck went into liquidation shortly after reporting pre-tax profits of £161m. Coloroll also disappeared shortly after the acquisition of Crowther. In accounting for that acquisition, Coloroll wrote off goodwill and provisions amounting to £224m (£11m more than the total cost of the purchase). In 1989 Coloroll's pre-tax profits amounted to £55m, of which £52m were unused provisions utilised from the acquisition.[4]

By this time, the late 1980s, I was National Technical Partner of KPMG and was horrified by many of the practices in the UK. Merchant banks were marketing schemes that were disguising the true financial position of a company. Once such a scheme had been accepted by a couple of major accounting firms, if it was not against the law or UK accounting standards, a third auditor who opposed it would be told by the lawyers that the scheme was now part of accepted practice and he could not qualify the financial statements. That scheme would then be developed further, and what the technical partners termed the 'creeping crumple' was under way.

Additionally, British profits tended to be on the high side. A Touche Ross study, *Accounting for Europe 1989*, which required practising accountants in various European Commission (EC) countries to prepare accounts under national accounting policies based on a similar series of transactions, resulted in British accountants showing the highest profits when producing 'the most likely result', and Britain still showed the highest profits when the policies were strained to their limits to obtain the 'maximum achievable result'.

Something had to be done to strengthen the hand of the auditor and to ensure UK Accounting Standards were improved.

A realisation that all was not well had led to the Dearing Committee[5] being set up by the British accounting institutes to review and make recommendations on the standard-setting process. Various problems were identified by the Committee:

1   The absence of a conceptual framework – inconsistencies existed in the extant accounting standards.
2   The lack of precision – options existed in standards allowing a variety of interpretations. The absence from individual standards of a full explanation of the reasoning behind them, and of the reasons for rejecting alternative solutions, added to the difficulties of the profession in capturing the spirit of a standard.
3   Timeliness – delays were caused in the production of standards by a Committee (the then Accounting Standards Committee) operating on a part-time basis.
4   Emerging issues – the problems of the precedent; once an interpretation had been adopted, especially if it was deemed to give an advantage in commercial terms, there was pressure on others (finance directors and auditors) to follow suit. True and fair is not only progressive; it is also regressive. As mentioned above, once bad practice which did not conflict with company law or accounting standards had been accepted, it became part of the corpus of the true and fair view and could not be challenged.
5   Competitive pressures – the desire to maintain and enhance listed company share price to safeguard against or to launch takeovers and the trend towards rewarding management through profit sharing and share option schemes must, in the Committee's view, have tended in some cases to influence judgement. The Committee had also been advised that companies were increasingly prepared to challenge auditors, to shop for options, to seek Counsel's opinion on the auditors views and to change auditors. It would have been idealistic of the Committee to assume that all auditors at all times were unmindful of the risk of losing business.
6   The problem of compliance – the pressure on auditors from time to time to accept interpretations of accounting standards which conformed with the interests of the preparers rather than with the spirit of a standard led to fears that it was unreasonable and unrealistic to leave the burden of securing sound financial reports entirely or mainly with the accountancy profession.

The Committee's conclusions were accepted, leading in 1990 to the introduction of the Financial Reporting Council, the Accounting Standards Board, the Urgent Issues Task Force and the Financial Reporting Review Panel. The new institutional arrangements led to major changes in the UK standard-setting process:

1   Directors were required by law to state in the notes to the accounts whether the accounts were drawn up in accordance with applicable accounting standards. Attention had to be drawn to material departures from standards.
2   The Financial Reporting Council covered a wide constituency of interests, both to guide the standard-setting body in its work programmes and issues of public concern and to ensure that it was properly financed. Previously this had been left to the six UK and Irish accounting institutes.
3   The Accounting Standards Board (ASB) would have two full-time members and up to eight part-time members and the right to publish its own authoritative standards. (Previously the Accounting Standards Committee had to obtain the agreement of all six UK and Irish accounting institutes before it could publish a standard.) Similarly, the ASB would have the capability of creating an Urgent Issues Task Force to tackle the problem of poor interpretation of standards or what was deemed to be bad practice.
4   The Financial Reporting Review Panel, a part-time body mainly consisting of company directors, auditors and lawyers, could ensure that accounts did obey the standards if non-observance with these standards failed to show a true and fair view. Accounts could be withdrawn by the company directors and re-issued to ensure that a true and fair view was shown. If the accounts were not altered on a voluntary basis, the Panel had the power to take companies to court to seek enforcement of changes.[6]

The Chairman of the Review Panel, Edwin Glasgow QC, was an experienced lawyer whose previous experience with accountants had been defending them in court, attempting to explain, as he put it,

> to wholly unreasonably disgruntled creditors and ridiculously pernickety judges that it might not have made much difference even if the auditor had noticed the odd £20m that had slipped from the balance sheet into the profit and loss account; or that the goodwill in the Saudi Arabian igloo time share subsidiary had indeed seemed very substantial at the time when the auditor had considered it; or that the igloos were melting so surprisingly slowly that it would have been positively misleading to depreciate them!

He added:

> The Review Panel has not had to take any company to court. Indeed it is quite amusing to witness spokesmen of the companies or even auditors who had already appeared before the Panel arguing for a tougher approach and the Court action to be taken – not quite their attitude at the time of their appearances before the Panel! The Panel had of course been criticised by those who have agreed to put their mistakes to rights, no matter how obsequious the companies and their representatives might have been at the time of visiting the Panel. The inmates of British gaols are not known for their unstinting praise of the judicial system either!

The ASB operated within the overall boundaries of the true and fair view and consequently was constrained by the general perception of what was, at the time, acceptable practice. Whilst some commentators wished the Board to break the mould of accounting completely and abruptly, the Board proceeded by evolution not revolution, to avoid destroying familiar markers in financial reports and obliterating well-known frames of reference of their users. That does not mean to say, however, that the Board did not have a mission for change. By the late 1980s financial reports in the United Kingdom had fallen seriously behind standards in other Anglo-Saxon countries. UK reporting, however, did have some virtues. In terms of presentation to the equity markets, UK accounting most certainly ranked ahead of many European countries where regulations were strongly influenced by tax considerations and where finance for companies tended to come not from the equity markets but from bank finance. In such countries there was not the same need to report a fair presentation of financial performance or position; instead the intention was to emphasise prudence to minimise the tax bill or to give minimal disclosure to avoid endangering commercial interests.

The Board's aim was to ensure British accounting came in line with the best in the world and, on the basis of increased international respect, acted as a catalyst for improved accounting worldwide. When the Board's work commenced in 1990, the UK had policies which were quite different from those in other countries. For example, the British policy on accounting for acquisition provisions was far more liberal than in other Anglo-Saxon countries; for goodwill, the standards allowed a write-off against reserves, a practice which hardly existed elsewhere and which was shortly afterwards rejected by the (then) International Accounting Standards Committee (IASC).

The Board, at the outset of its work, considered both the UK's existing accounting standards and the state of financial reporting as a whole. The Board's future work programme was derived from those early meetings. The ASB resolved to tackle subjects of pressing urgency in the first stage of its programme, designed to last some five years, while at the same time tackling the problem of the underlying inconsistencies of the (then) existing accounting standards. These accounting standards had been produced by different working parties on behalf of the Board's predecessor body, the Accounting Standards Committee. As the working parties consisted of different individuals, the working parties' views about accounting not surprisingly were on occasion at variance with each other, and different working parties adopted different frames of reference in attacking various problems, leading to inconsistencies between standards. The Board, therefore, resolved to correct this problem by producing a Statement of Principles on which its standards would be based and which would form the underlying core of its work. It determined that there were several basic areas to be tackled, namely:

1 the objectives of accounting,
2 qualitative characteristics of financial reports,
3 the elements of financial statements,
4 recognition,
5 valuation,
6 presentation, and
7 the reporting entity.

The Statement of Principles, which was generally in line with the conceptual frameworks of the IASC and the standard setters in Australia, Canada, New Zealand and the United States, had a major effect on the Board's thinking.[7] In particular, in line with the other standard setters, assets were defined as resulting from past events leading to a stream of benefits in the future, while liabilities were deemed to be obligations which had arisen from past events and would lead to resources leaving the entity. One of the Board's most controversial standards, FRS5, *Reporting the Substance of Transactions*, dealt with the off-balance-sheet problem. It relied heavily on the definitions of assets and liabilities requiring that if obligations did exist, then liabilities must be shown on the balance sheet, and it stated that if benefits do accrue to a company, then clearly it has an asset and that too must be displayed.

While concentrating primarily on national issues, the ASB was looking to other national standard setters to benefit from their experience. Initially these contacts were spasmodic, but from 1992 such meetings began to occur on a regular basis. The initial discussions were with the US Financial Accounting Standards Board (FASB). Later, the issue of provisions led to a meeting of the Chairmen of the American, Canadian and UK standard-setting boards. An invitation was issued to other standard setters to join the North Americans and the British to debate this and other issues of concern. This was accepted initially by the Australians and the Dutch, but after only a meeting or two, the Dutch fell away. The IASC was invited to partake in these meetings, which began to occur three times a year, and the G4+1 group was born. (Towards the middle of the decade the New Zealand standard setter also joined the group.)[8]

The G4+1 group probably gave most of us participating in standard setting our most enjoyable moments. The issues we considered were contentious – there were either no established solutions or the existing solutions were hopelessly antiquated. We had the freedom to think outside the box since the final product of each debate would be a research paper rather than a standard for which acceptance had to be sought. Subjects covered included future events, provisions, performance reporting, share options and leases. As the decade wore on, members of the G4+1 began to discuss whether this group of standard setters should issue joint standards. This was clearly a threat to the IASC, which since 1973 had been producing International Accounting Standards (IAS), increasingly with the support of multinational companies that had problems in dealing with various accounting regimes to which their subsidiaries were subject. In 1997, the collapse of companies in Asia, which under national accounting standards had seemed sound, led to a flight of short-term capital, rising interest rates, a reduction in investment and rising unemployment. It was believed that the lack of trust in local accounting standards could not be easily restored, and the only solution was to move to standards accepted by the international community.

This major problem and the obstruction in the way of globalisation of the capital markets caused by differing national accounting rules led the IASC to examine its own future and structure by setting up a strategy committee. The process of change and the creation of the IASC Foundation and the International Accounting Standards Board (IASB) are superbly examined in Camfferman and Zeff's seminal work on the subject.[9]

At the time of the IASC's debate on its future, there were two sets of accounting standards used internationally – the leader, US GAAP (Generally Accepted Accounting Principles), and to a much lesser extent, International Accounting Standards. The latter had defects (not that the former were perfect!), and generally speaking the standards (frequently based on the US GAAP) were an amalgam of national standards which often included many options and were often outdated. It was possibly for that reason that a group of global regulators gave their support to a restructured IASC. Out of the restructuring, a newly selected board of trustees of the IASC Foundation (IASCF; later the IFRSF), chaired by the esteemed Paul Volcker, former Chairman of the US Federal Reserve, selected a board consisting primarily of experienced national standard setters with clear objectives:

1   to improve the existing standards; and
2   through an independent and high-quality process, to develop a set of standards commanding the same level of respect of those of the FASB.

Initially the IASB[10] looked upon itself as more of a think tank. It would take over the role of the G4+1 (which, at the instigation of Ed Jenkins, the FASB Chairman, was disbanded just weeks after the IASB was formed) and produce standards which could be adopted by national standard setters on an individual basis. Shortly after the Board's work began, that aim disappeared as a result of the EC's announcement of June 2002 that the new International Financial Reporting Standards (IFRS) should be used in consolidated financial reports of listed European companies beginning in 2005.[11] In many ways this decision was inevitable, as it would be difficult to create a single unified capital market with multiple national versions of accounting. While the EU could have set out to produce its own suites of standards, this would clearly have taken about a decade. Furthermore, the adoption of British or US standards was almost certainly unacceptable on nationalistic grounds!

The EU's decision was quickly followed by that of the Financial Reporting Council in Australia, leading to a chain reaction in other jurisdictions, notably New Zealand, Hong Kong and South Africa. Suddenly the IASB was the standard setter for Europe, Australasia and other parts of the Commonwealth. The Australasian decision had important effects. First, the Australian and New Zealand standard setters were at the leading edge of accounting thought – if they were to switch to IFRS, why shouldn't other countries in the Asian Pacific region do the same? We shall discuss this issue later. Second, Europe was perhaps surprised to discover that the IASB was not working solely for European companies, and this led to many arguments between the Board and the EC – the IASB's biggest 'client' (as the EC seemed to perceive itself!) could not be allowed to dominate at the expense of other countries.

There were other areas of contention between the Board and the European Commission. Senior members of the Commission argued in public that a fourteen-man board with six North American members was too heavily loaded towards countries not presently using international standards. The IASCF trustees dismissed this argument on the grounds that the Foundation's constitution did not require that geography be a basis of selection and that while international standards could exist without the United States, global standards would not become a reality until they were adopted by the Americans – and the Americans certainly would not adopt the new standards if they had no say in drafting them.

Furthermore, the realisation dawned on European companies, especially financial institutions, that some of the existing IAS and proposed new IFRS would involve major, unpopular changes to national accounting practice, especially as regards financial instruments. Finally, there were concerns that an independent Board was just too independent, and that it had a responsibility to moderate its views to accommodate national interests.

In moving to IFRS, countries are faced with the three issues of cost, change and loss of control. The IASB-US convergence programme, which resulted in US standards and IFRS moving ever closer, meant that the change and cost would have incurred in US GAAP regardless of whether the USA moved to IFRS. The loss of complete sovereignty – the willingness to lose national power over standards – would be the only, albeit a major, issue.

With Europe the issue was different. Some governments in Europe regretted the decision to move from national to international standards – a decision made by the EU with great courage and almost certainly in complete ignorance of some of the consequences of the International Accounting Standards Europe proposed to adopt. Some governments resented, the, as they saw it, undue Anglo-Saxon influence within the Board and would rather have had a European standard setter.[12]

The IASB's first ten years were a constant balance act of trying to increase European confidence in IFRS amidst some significant pressures to alter the standards and the structure and methods of the Foundation and Board, while at the same time engaging the US FASB in an often challenging process to bring about US acceptance of IFRS. In addition, the Board members, trustees and the Foundation's Chief Operating Officer, Tom Seidenstein, spent a considerable amount of time in Asia-Oceania, South America, Canada and Africa, selling, with a certain amount of success, the vision of one single set of global accounting standards.

Standard setting is the art of the possible and largely involves change management. It is possible to lead some yards ahead but impossible to do it miles ahead, as in the latter situation the followers are liable to break ranks and scatter. Standard setting involves floating new ideas and gradually gaining acceptance for them. A first standard that takes the community only part of the way to the ideal answer has more of a chance of acceptance than a completely revolutionary approach, however frustrating that might be to idealistic theorists. The way ahead should, however, be mapped out to allow constituents to see where the standard setter intends to go and enable the former to become accustomed to the idea of future change.

In one respect the EU did have a point about the Board's accountability; the IASB and the IASC Foundation were modelled on the structure of the FASB and the Financial Accounting Foundation. There was, however, a difference. In the United States the power of the FASB and its trustees ultimately derived from the fact that the Securities and Exchange Commission (SEC) had delegated accounting standard-setting power to them, and only on very rare occasions would it intervene in the standard-setting process – for example, in the debates on accounting for share options and oil and gas. The SEC Commissioners were appointed by the President with the advice and consent of Congress.

Complaints arose from certain European governments backed by the EC that the IASB suffered from a deficit of accountability. Fourteen board members in London were effectively setting laws for European countries. While almost all other laws had to be debated in parliament by democratically elected members, this group of accountants bypassed the process.[13] It was therefore no surprise when, towards the end of the first decade of the IASB's existence, the trustees and major national regulators agreed to set up a Monitoring Board to oversee the trustees' supervision of the IASB and the selection of the trustees' successors. The initial Monitoring Board was formed by the Chairmen of the SEC and the Japanese Financial Services Authority, the European Commissioner for the Internal Market, and the Chairmen of the International Organisation of Securities Commission's (IOSCO) Technical Committee and Emerging Markets Committee. Not surprisingly, other nations wished to be involved, and in a recent report the Monitoring Board has accepted that security regulators from other countries should form part of its membership. The Monitoring Board consists of publicly accountable officials appointed by governments, thereby dealing with the accountability deficit. The IASB's trustees, however, would not allow its Monitoring Board to intervene in technical decisions, although it could give its views to the Chairman of the IASB. A later meeting would explain whether the Monitoring Board's views had been accepted by the IASB and, if not, the reasons for rejection.

The IASB's first ten years were focused on its stated objective to deliver one single set of high-quality global standards. To do that, as mentioned earlier, it needed to encourage the USA to adopt IFRS and to keep countries, and particularly the EU, from abandoning IFRS or adapting them to accommodate local concerns. The first five years of its existence involved a time-consuming programme to improve the inherited IAS by removing options, ambiguities or redundant or antiquated parts of the standards. This was not a particularly satisfying experience, but it was necessary if the standards were to be accepted worldwide.

The second stage focused on encouraging the United States to join the IFRS family. The IASB had been fortunate in 2002 when one of its part-time members, Bob Herz, was appointed Chairman of the FASB. Bob was a firm believer in international standards, and while the Board was sorry to lose his invaluable contribution, they were delighted to have such a friend at the head of the American standard setter. At the time of Herz's appointment, the US capital markets were reeling from the effects of the collapse of Enron and other major corporate scandals involving poor accounting practices. While in a relatively small way certain US accounting standards had proved to be open to abusive behaviour, the real culprits were fraud, poor corporate governance and weak auditing.

Very quickly the two boards signed the Norwalk Agreement by which they agreed to improve each other's set of standards while moving closer together. The method adopted was simple. Any company using IFRS and listing in the United States had to reconcile to US GAAP. By looking at the reconciliations it was easy to see where the major differences between the two sets of standards lay. The aim was for the boards to debate which had the better standard and for the other simply to adopt the standard without attempting to improve it. The boards determined that attempts to improve an adopted standard would delay the convergence of the two sets of standards; while desirable, such improvements had to be left for a later date.

The motivation for the Norwalk Agreement was to remove the need for overseas registrants using IFRS to reconcile to US GAAP. Many on the IASB hoped that this might be the first step towards IFRS use by US corporations, although this was a long shot at the time.

By 2006 many changes had been made by both boards, but the quantum of changes and the potential length of the programme were leading to protests. In particular, there was increasing resentment at the reconciliation requirement and calls for Europe and other countries to require US companies listed outside the United States to reconcile to IFRS or to the relevant national standards. The SEC was aware of this concern, and in 2006, with the support of the SEC and the European Commission, a Memorandum of Understanding was signed by the FASB and the IASB. This agreement stated that, in essence, word-for-word convergence of existing standards was not necessary so long as the principles were broadly the same. There was no point in trying to converge outdated or overly complicated standards, and in these cases the boards should consider writing joint new standards. Eleven subjects were highlighted, of which ten were put on the programme for new standards. The SEC made it clear that this programme did not have to be completed for reconciliation to be discontinued, but that satisfactory progress towards convergence would be regarded positively. In 2007 the SEC determined that sufficient progress had been made and the reconciliation requirement was removed.

Despite the rate of progress being slower than many of us would have wished in developing new standards, delay was inevitable when two boards with different objectives and with constituents with different interests and sophistication levels worked together. Progress was made in many areas and accelerated in early 2008, when the then Chairman of the SEC, Christopher Cox, indicated privately through his Chief Accountant to the Chairmen of the FASB and IASB that he wished to see the programme finished by 2011 to give the US a prospect of adopting the Standards in 2013/2014. This led to an examination of the programme and the cutting back of some of the projects to the main essentials.[14] It is likely that without the global financial crisis, the SEC may well have made a decision in 2011 to adopt IFRS. The crisis, however, derailed Chairman Cox's ability to make IFRS adoption a reality. There were concerns expressed in the USA that at a time of great uncertainty in markets, with companies fighting for survival, this was not the time to change the accounting frame of reference or to incur costs of change.

Further concerns arose when, at the height of the crisis in October 2008, the European Commission proposed changing EU law to prevent European companies from being 'disadvantaged' compared to their US competitors by enabling them to cease showing certain assets at fair value (which was tumbling in many illiquid markets) and to revert to cost for these assets.[15] Reclassification from fair value was allowed under US GAAP under exceedingly rare circumstances. The Board's initial reaction was to stand firm and let the law be passed. It quickly became apparent, however, that if the law were pushed through in a matter of days, already fragile market confidence could be damaged even further, since, unlike in the USA, there were no rules or disclosures around the EC's proposed reclassification process. The IASB, with only a few days to react and encouraged by the securities regulators, felt obliged to move ahead of the EC law change and allow reclassification, but only at fair value (albeit the fair value of a few months earlier).[16] The effect on the profit and loss account and balance sheet had to be shown until the asset was derecognised in order to enable users to calculate the effect of the change of accounting policy.

The Board felt tainted by the fact that it had, albeit with the support of its trustees, been forced to act within days to prevent the law from being passed.[17] For the first and only time (and hopefully the last) in the Board's history, due process did not take place. The Board was roundly criticised for the omission, but the alternative was to take weeks for due process while the markets imploded as companies added back, without disclosure, fair value losses incurred in the early days of the crisis. The latter was not deemed to be an option by either the Board or security regulators who helped behind the scenes to draft the amendment to the financial instruments standard.[18]

The IASB had been subject to intense political pressure, believed to be at the instigation of French President Sarkozy. His predecessor, President Chirac, had earlier (2003) written to the European Commission complaining that IAS39, with its fair value requirements, would 'destabilise the economy'. Following the 2008 amendment to IAS39, the European Commission wrote demanding that three other issues should be dealt with in time for the year's reporting season. With assistance from evidence gathered from a series of roundtables and support from national standard setters and IOSCO, the IASB declined to act without appropriate due process. (This due process culminated the following year in the issue of IFRS9.) Despite further pressure from some European members of the G20 to attempt to force the IASB to pay more account to financial stability, the G20 largely supported the IASB's position, although at its summit the final communiqué proposed that the governance of the international standard-setting body should be further enhanced.[19]

Shortly afterwards, the FASB came under political pressure from Congress and was forced to make changes diminishing the effect on income statements of falls in asset values. These incidents showed the need for international regulators and standard setters to stand together. Some academics argue that where there are differences in accounting standards, companies will naturally gravitate to the higher level.[20] My cynical view is that the opposite will take place, and the crisis did nothing to dispel that view. The only way to prevent a retreat to the lowest level is to move towards one single set of accounting standards to ensure a level playing field.

Even if the world were to have only IFRS, political pressure on the standard setter would continue. The role of the Monitoring Board, instituted in 2009 and foreseen in the G20 communiqué referred to above, is therefore critical. Had the Monitoring Board been in place at the time of the reclassification debate, it is possible that the US and Japanese members might have been able to contain European demands.

Some have argued that the Monitoring Board should have formed part of the initial structure of the international standard-setting process, yet there was then (and still is) no international SEC equivalent. If, given its early adoption of IFRS, the EC had assumed such a role, the IASB would clearly have been seen as simply part of the European corporate governance structure and not as an international organisation.

At present among the five (shortly to be seven) members of the Monitoring Board, the European Union is the only major economy requiring the use of IFRS – a fact about which the Board and its trustees are frequently reminded![21] This situation gives greater political weight to the European Commissioner, who can, when complaining about proposed standards, always claim that his constituents have a greater interest in the outcome than those Monitoring Board participants, who at present do not require IFRS for domestic companies. Acceptance of IFRS particularly by the United States and Japan (and China and India) and the inclusion of other IFRS adopters in the Monitoring Board are needed to offset the European regional claim.

In the second half of the IASB's existence, other countries began to move towards IFRS. In 2007 China changed to standards which were designed to get the same answers as IFRS. These new Chinese standards were not word-for-word identical to the international standards, but would generally, with a few exceptions, deliver the same result. Obviously word-for-word adoption can remove the arguments over whether the Chinese versions interpret IFRS correctly.

In 2008 Israel adopted IFRS, followed by Chile in 2009, Brazil in 2010, Canada and South Korea in 2011, and Malaysia, Indonesia and Mexico in 2012. Taiwan adopted IFRS in 2013. From a handful of countries using IFRS at the beginning of the IASB's existence, over 120 now either require or allow the use of the international standards. The move to global standards, however, still depends, up to a point, on the SEC making a positive decision requiring listed US domestic companies to move to international standards. Until that decision is made it is likely that Japan will initially hold back from compulsory adoption (although it allows an option for domestic companies), and that China will not move to word-for-word adoption and India will continue to seek to argue that it has special circumstances (which in the main it has not!) which require IFRS to be amended.

It is into this situation that the IASB was delighted to see the formation of the Asian–Oceanian Standard-Setters Group (AOSSG). Under the dynamic leadership first of China, Malaysia, and Japan and latterly of the Chairman of the Australian Accounting Standards Board, Kevin Stevenson, AOSSG is likely to become a major force in developing international standards. If IFRS are simply a product of the debate between America and Europe, the global accounting experiment will fail. The IASB is at present determining its new agenda. It has spent its first five years dealing with issues having to do with European adoption, whilst the last five have been concerned with the convergence with US GAAP. It is now the turn of the rest of the world to determine which subjects should be considered. The Board knows that many Asian countries are concerned about foreign currency translation under an outdated standard based on the American standards that assume a reserve currency rather than a foreign currency used for trade.

Latin America has been watching developments in Asia, and in 2011 it formed its own regional standard-setters group, the Group of Latin American Accounting Standard Setters (GLASS).[22] These developments are extremely healthy and indicate a growing assertiveness by regional standard setters. The IASB will welcome this development of international standards as a partnership. It should ensure that international standards mirror the economic effects of transactions throughout the world – and in some parts of the world there are transactions different from those found elsewhere. For example, New Zealand farming co-operatives and major German companies proved to the Board that its definition of a liability was far too strict and did not take into account partnerships where the stakes have to be sold back to the partnership itself.[23]

The growth of regional standard-setting partnerships is a source of strength to the IASB. The commitment of the USA to adopting IFRS is being questioned in some quarters, as the SEC has repeatedly missed its self-imposed deadlines for making a decision to move to international standards.[24]

Nevertheless, the momentum behind IFRS as the de facto global accounting standard is irreversible. IFRS have already established a critical mass. Two-thirds of the G20 countries have already adopted the standards, and half of Global Fortune 500 companies (including those using Chinese standards) now use the standards. The SEC and the US government, as well as successive G20 communiqués, have all committed to the implementation of global standards. IFRS remain best placed to fill this role.

The question then is, will those major economies still to adopt IFRS continue to wait for the USA? Alternatively, will Australia, China and Japan (and possibly India) within the leadership of the AOSSG (and possibly other regional standard-setting groupings), noting the growing scepticism about the American commitment to the global accounting experience despite the years of the IASB's agenda being devoted to the US GAAP-IFRS convergence programme, take a greater role in shaping the new IFRS than in the past? The future direction of international standards is at a turning point. With enthusiasm in the USA for global standards perceived to be waning, will its already declining influence in the international equity markets[25] be reflected in a corresponding diminution in FASB influence over the development of IFRS? And will the influence on these standards increasingly come from the burgeoning economies of Asia-Oceania and Latin America? Indeed, will the major economies who have not already adopted IFRS decide to take a leadership role and put pressure on the USA by moving to adoption rather than continuing to wait for a positive SEC decision?

Frustrations

As my time at the IASB came to an end, my sense of frustration at having been involved in standard setting for over twenty years and having to walk away while major issues still existed concerned me greatly. Putting aside the disappointment that the USA has not moved more quickly towards IFRS adoption, I now turn to some issues indicating that accounting standard setting is by no means near the end of the road. Accounting is still a primitive subject and there is much still to do. It also, like many activities, requires crisis to engender change.

Financial reporting is still facing some major questions. Rather than looking specifically at the subjects tackled by the IASB, I would like to explore some of these issues and give some personal reflections upon them. These issues are pervasive to financial reporting internationally and, depending on their resolution, could result in major changes in the manner in which companies report.

1 Measurement

While there are various measurement techniques in accounting, there are two obvious major candidates – cost and value. Is it possible to agree on which is the better of the two? Ray Chambers would have had no doubts, although he may have disagreed with the definition of fair value! I remember well coming to the University of Sydney in 1985 and at Ray Chamber's invitation giving a lecture in which I attacked his adherence to Continuously Contemporary Accounting. He sat back with an amused smile at the certainty of youth and was gentle in his comments. The difference between us was that I was arguing from the point of view of change management and what might be possible at that time (and even now!), not what might be a superior solution in the future. The world does not appear to be ready to accept the volatility associated with a value model.

It is hard to imagine that at the height of the global financial crisis senior European political leaders were privately analysing (unfavourably) IAS39 and its successor, IFRS9. In particular, their concern was that fair values were leading to volatility in the markets and were not showing the 'true' value.

Many, however, argue that all financial instruments should be marked to market. Andrew Haldane notes that a clear historical pattern has emerged – fair value principles have waxed when asset prices and banks are rising and waned when both are falling.[26] He points out that if UK banks had been required, in addition to their trading book, to mark the banking books to market over the period from 1999 to 2008, UK bank profits would have been around eight times more volatile. Between 2001 and 2006, the cumulative profits of UK banks would have been around £100b higher than recorded profits as the expected future returns to risky projects were brought forward. However, hypothetical losses during 2008 would then have totalled in excess of £300b as the risks from these projects were realised. Even where liabilities were perfectly matched with assets – there is no necessity for the bank to liquidate the assets to make good its liabilities as they fall due – problems can arise with fair value accounting. The market price of assets might be affected by liquidity considerations. In times of stress, these liquidity premia are large and can overshoot, lowering asset prices below what could be deemed to be their longer-term economic value. If large enough, these losses could even generate insolvency during a crisis. If the UK banking books had been marked to market, Haldane estimated the loss in value would have peaked at over £400b during the early months of 2009. The total capital resources of UK banks at that time were around £280b.[27] In other words, the UK banking system in aggregate would have been technically insolvent on a marked-to-market basis. Most major global banks were in a similar position – recovery in asset prices meant that UK banks were back in the black within a matter of months.[28]

In reconsidering IAS39 and in developing IFRS9, the IASB believed that the only financial instruments that could be carried at cost were those whose cash flows were known and for which the institution's business model was designed to hold those assets to achieve those cash flows. In other words, only loans and debt instruments with unknown cash flows and debt instruments held for trading would have to be at fair value. The argument was not so much about the insolvency or liquidity issues mentioned above but about the fact that bringing in the market value of debts and loans as interest rates moved would lead to noise in the income statement not reflected by the actual cash flows. For example, a £100 debt instrument yielding 5 per cent per annum would lose half its value if interest rates rose to 10 per cent, yet (assuming the instrument was not impaired) the organisation would still receive its 5 per cent per annum, provided it continued to hold the instrument, and would receive £100 at the end of its life.[29] Users of financial statements, however, should be aware of the current state of the value of the portfolio, and therefore fair values would have to be shown in the notes. This discussion leads to another – what is the role of the statement of financial position?

2 The role of the statement of financial position

As a result of limitations stemming from reliability of measurement and cost–benefit considerations, not all assets and not all liabilities are included in a balance sheet (e.g. some contingent liabilities are not included), and some assets and liabilities that are included may be affected by events, such as price changes or other increases or decreases in value through time, that are not recognised or are only partially recognised. Even if all recognised assets and liabilities were to be included at up-to-date values, the total of assets less the total of liabilities would not, except by coincidence, equal the value of the business. However, together with other financial statements and other information, statements of financial position should provide information that is useful to those who wish to make their own assessments of the enterprise's value.

The statement of financial position records the assets available to the company to conduct its business in the future. How then should these assets be valued? The answer lies in what will be most useful to readers of accounts who have to make decisions based on this information. Would they be satisfied with assets shown at original cost? In many cases I suspect the answer will be in the affirmative, provided price changes are not at a high level. In such a situation, would the costs of revaluation of assets such as specialist plant be worth the additional benefit of knowing the replacement cost of that plant, especially if it were unlikely that it would be sold or even replaced? Would additional depreciation charges in a low inflationary environment be of much use to users of accounts? The information may be helpful in assessing the current operating margins of a business, but despite allowing for recognition of cost-saving gains from holding the present asset, they may have little impact on a user's decision. The plant presumably will gradually become outdated and be fully depreciated.[30]

On the other hand, would information about assets that are not central to the business and of an investment nature, which can easily be sold, be more useful if it were valued at current values? Commodity traders already value stocks at market prices. They clearly believe their gains and losses are reflected by the value of their portfolio of assets. Similarly, as discussed above, financial companies trading in stocks and shares are required to mark their dealing assets to market. It is not a big step to take to suggest that other investment assets with relatively liquid markets should also be marked to market.

The properties of investment property companies are valued annually, but is there any difference between an investment property and the identical head office owned by the same company? In IFRS, the latter has to be depreciated over its life whilst the investment property is adjusted to market values and not depreciated as such. How can we justify the different treatment? The assets are identical – both could be sold and profits realised – so should they not both be treated the same way?

Similar considerations arise in the case of stocks of long-term items, such as land banks, which are in the nature of an investment and can be sold without affecting the day-to-day trading of a company. Should assets such as these be valued to reflect the potential cash flow available to a company at any time? Similarly, if the performance of a company's investment assets is poor, should this not be reflected in the year when these assets fall in value, leaving it to management to explain why it continues to hold such assets rather than realising them at an opportune moment for the benefit of the shareholders? (Hence the requirement to display in the notes the fair value of financial assets shown at cost in the financial statements!)

In essence, at a time of low inflation, if only evolutionary change is required, it would seem sensible to preserve 'the engine' of the company's productive processes at historical cost while showing investment assets at current values. As I suggest below, it would be possible to show such gains and losses on these non-traded investment assets in other comprehensive income, leaving the trading account to deal purely with operations for which the key 'operating' assets of a company would be used. In this way the statement of financial position would have a consistent rationale: 'investment' assets at current values, operating assets at historical cost.

If inflation or input prices rose to material levels, however, the situation would well change, and demands could arise for a better guide to a company's future prospects. This could be achieved by showing a company's current operating profits so that its performance was not artificially enhanced by the use of relatively cheap assets bought either some time ago or at times of lower demand and which would have to be replaced at much higher cost.

The so-called windfall gains of the oil dealing companies during the Gulf War soon disappeared when the oil price fell. Suppose the oil price had been $60 per barrel prior to the war and the oil companies made an additional $2 margin. If this $2 operating margin had been maintained when the oil price rose to $100, the accounts would have shown an historical cost profit of $42. Yet the profit of $42 would have consisted of two components, an operating margin of $2 and a windfall holding gain of $40. The holding gain in an active company would presumably be ploughed back into reinvestment of oil at $100, leaving 'free' cash of $2. Once the price returned to (say) $60, a loss of $38 would have been shown on sale – that is, operating margin gain of $2 less holding loss of $40. Accounts based on historical costs reflecting transactions fail to record events (price changes) in a timely way that many would see as more relevant.

To some, the suggestion of looking at current cost operating profits smacks of the inflation accounting debate of the 1970s – where much of the original thinking came from Australia.[31] Many of the problems with previous attempts at showing current costs in accounts had to do with over-complication of the issues and adjustments concerned with monetary working capital and gearing. In many ways this turned accounting from reflecting performance to mere arithmetic. There are relatively simple ways for an historical cost trading profit ($42) to be split in a division between short-term holding gains ($40) and current operating margins ($2) without doing any damage to existing practice. When we become more sophisticated, such holding gains could be taken to other comprehensive income, and the profit and loss account would then simply show the trading margin.

3 Presentation of performance

At present the income statement is a jumble of gains and losses. Some items are shown in other comprehensive income without any apparent reason. Net profit includes capital gains in certain situations and not in others. A key future objective of the IASB is to look at the criteria for determining whether a gain or loss should go to other comprehensive income or to the income statement. There has always been a suspicion that, as our American friends would say, other comprehensive income is being used as a 'dumpster' to avoid items affecting net income.

At present, the main items shown in other comprehensive income are gains and losses on the revaluation of properties, actuarial gains and losses on pension funds, and (until IFRS9) changes in the value of available sale securities. The main feature of the first two items is their term nature. If this is to be the determining criterion (but see 2 above), the income statement would largely consist of trading gains and losses. Part of our problem is that net income is often thought to encompass all that is important to a company's performance. Yet a company's performance consists of components such as profit on sales of traded items, holding gains from assets, and changes in the pension obligation – a very long-term liability. To give a very simple example, if a company bought an asset in 1930 for $1,000 and sold it in 2012 for $10,000, is the $9,000 gain a profit of the year 2012 or should we measure the gain accruing each year? The latter annual gain or loss would obviously be unrealised, but this could be reported with a warning that the change in value was not available as cash until the final sale based on a market transaction.

The Board adopted the position of measuring gains or losses on disposal of assets on the basis of their carrying value in the accounts. Capital gains have little to do with a disposal transaction in a particular year and a lot to do with the past. Holding gains should be recorded through the medium of other comprehensive income when the assets are revalued or sold. To return to our example, if the asset in question had been revalued in 1985 from $1,000 to $7,000, $6,000 would have appeared in other comprehensive income in 1985. On sale, a gain of $3,000 would appear in the profit and loss account in 2012. The answer is clearly a hybrid and unsatisfactory – a partial measure. For an asset of an investment nature, showing the total gain or loss in value at the time of sale does not reflect fairly the performance of a company in a period – but neither do irregular valuations. An inexpensive way has to be found to revalue such assets on an annual basis and gradually move all such changes in value, including the final gain or loss on disposal, into the statement of recognised gains and losses, thereby reflecting the performance of the investment asset portfolio and leaving the profit and loss account as a measure of trading performance.[32]

This leads to a further question of whether gains and losses shown in other comprehensive income should be transferred on the disposal of the asset to the income statement ('recycling').

The answer depends on whether you believe net profit should encompass every single gain and loss recorded by an entity or whether components of income are more important. At present we have a mixture. The gain and loss on the disposal of a revalued property is shown in profit and loss, yet this only records the change in value since the last valuation. The revalued amount is not recycled. Gains and losses in pension funds are recorded only once in other comprehensive income. Yet for those still using IAS39, realised gains and losses on available-for-sale instruments are transferred to the income statement. Clearly, a decision has to be made on whether the income statement is going to be more of a trading statement whilst the longer-term gains and losses are shown elsewhere; that is, are the components of performance more important than a net profit through which all gains and losses must eventually pass? I belong in the components camp!

4 The profit and loss account – cash flow based?

Ignoring unrealised changes in the value of traded items, it is well accepted that the profit and loss account is, broadly speaking, a cash flow statement adjusted by accrual accounting to smooth out the lumpiness of transactions having effects over many years. Consequently, depreciation is charged over a period of an asset's life rather than the total cost of the asset being charged against income in the year of purchase. The cash flow statement itself can show how the profits reflected in the profit and loss account are in fact turned into cash, and it can thereby give a guide to the quality of the profit. For example, it has been shown[33] that, in Polly Peck's final year of existence (1990), while its pre-tax profits were stated as £161m and its funds flow from operations (as shown by the [then] source and application of funds statement) was £172m, if a standard requiring cash flows had been in existence in the UK,[34] cash flow from operations would have been revealed as a negative figure of £129m. The quality of the company's profit, to put it mildly, was very poor.

If it is accepted that the profit and loss account is in essence an adjusted cash flow statement, then what role is there for equity accounting? Equity accounting is applied to show the share of profits in an associated company, that is, a company over which the investing company has significant influence. (Significant influence is defined by IAS28 as 'the power to participate in the financial and operating policy decisions of the investee but is not control or joint control of those policies'.) The notion of partnership and joint control is critical. In a partnership or joint venture everyone is entitled to their share of the profits, which are either paid out or, by agreement of the partners, reinvested in the business. With associated companies, however, where the investing company may have (say) 20 per cent of the equity holding, is the nature of this investment really that of a partner? In most such situations there will not be a cash flow reflecting the share of profit. Equity accounting should not be permitted unless such a form of partnership exists. In such a situation, there must be some agreement, formal or informal, which enables an investing company to extract its share of profits. At present, however, some companies that have failed in a hostile takeover bid have used equity accounting for their so-called profit share even though the investor and investee companies may not even be on speaking terms!

Associated company accounting is a relic of the past.[35] In the period before standard setters began to require controlled and non-legal subsidiaries to be consolidated, the standard had its uses. It now has its abuses. If all a company can receive from its investment are dividends and the gain or loss on sale, why should the accounting not reflect this and treat the investment like any other financial instrument, rather than show a share of profits which almost certainly will never be realised?

Conclusion

The issues above indicate there is still much to debate in accounting. The second part of this chapter has considered measurement, the role of the statement of financial position, and the presentation and determination of profit. Most of these issues are major matters of contention and will be hotly debated over the next few years. Accounting is an expanding yet underdeveloped subject, and the IASB does not have a monopoly of wisdom. It is therefore vital for all countries to be involved in the debate as the Board determines in terms of cost and benefits what users of financial statements wish to see and what accounting policies management believe fairly reflect the performance of their businesses. One of the most telling arguments that can ever be given against a proposal of the IASB is that the proposed requirement would not reflect reality. The Board's intention has always been that accounts should be an appropriate mirror of the real business world. Sometimes, of course, despite the proposed standard reflecting the reality of the situation, it can be attacked by those who would rather the facts not be shown. Transparency and vested interest can also instigate opposition!

The Board would like to limit the number of standards to be issued. Ideally it would like to have extremely short standards dealing with points of principle. In the USA, it is clear that this situation does not prevail. On each issue, the Board is attempting to deal with about 80 per cent of the problem, leaving the other 20 per cent on trust to the skill and judgement of companies and their auditors, tempered always by the true and fair view/fair presentation objective.

A danger is that, whilst almost all preparers genuinely seek to obey the rules and to produce financial statements which fairly reflect their companies' situation, a tiny minority may be tempted to seek competitive advantage and to play at the edges of a standard. Inevitably, if a competitor produces a rather dubious accounting policy and this is accepted by his auditor, other companies and auditors, not unnaturally, may feel obliged to follow. A regulator may step in and force companies to reissue their accounts, or perhaps the IASB or the Interpretation Committee may feel the need has arisen to ban a particular practice. A further concern is the request for certainty by both preparer and auditor – a move towards lengthy standards. In that way accounting heads for the rule book and 'search engine' accounting. This is an overriding issue affecting all parties interested in financial reporting.[36] The Board will have to make tough decisions in deciding between competing choices for accounting standards. It will not wish to produce long standards. Inevitably it has been asked to explain and to go into detail where the issues are complex. The Board would rather not tackle issues in that manner. Ultimately we are back to the issue of fair presentation and the willingness of preparers, auditors and regulators to accept judgement.[37] Good behaviour and an appropriate 'tone at the top' are the best defences against the encroachment of regulation.[38]

Can the Board rely on such behaviour, however – or will it continually have to make adjustments to the course of practice? This is a challenge to the professionalism of those involved, and on this professionalism hangs the form of accounting standards of the future.

In the late 1980s, UK accounts had hidden much. The issues described above indicate some of the problems still to be overcome and debates to be settled before accounts provide what is truly required by the financial community – a fair presentation of the reality of a company's trading performance, its economic stewardship of its assets, and its potential obligations. We all have much still to do.

In introducing the Management Commentary, the IASB attempted to hand back accounts to senior management. The intention is to enable directors to escape from the rigidities of accounting standards, statutory formats, and regulation and to describe the accounts to the user, emphasising points of importance and showing what management believes are the underlying trends reflected in the information. It is then up to the user to decide whether he accepts management's story or wishes to investigate further by doing additional analysis.

The narrative statement has been introduced to enable management to explain the volatility of the company's profit, to explain which items that have occurred this year will not be there next year (and vice versa), and to disclose how future financing will be achieved. In other words, management is invited to go beyond the raw accounting numbers and tell the story of their company's performance and financial position; that is, to become involved in *financial communication* rather than simply *financial reporting*. Clear, honest information will ultimately lead to reducing costs as lenders of capital reduce interest rates as a reflection of their increased confidence in the company's account of its own performance. It is the accountant's job to present what happened in the year, warts and all – to tell it as it is – and let management explain this away if it can. That is ultimately what presentation is all about, presenting numbers that relate to actual events – not numbers management or what the financial community want to see – and then explaining what lies behind these figures. The motto of the Institute of Chartered Accountants of Scotland says it all: 'Quaere Verum' – Seek the truth! That is how it should be in accounting – the truth, plain and unadorned! We are not there yet!

Notes

1 Later author of the New Zealand Society of Accountants Invitation Research Lecture, *The Significance of the Standard 'True and Fair View'* (1980) and *A True and Fair View in Company Accounts* for the Institute of Chartered Accountants of Scotland (1982).

2 See letters in *The Times*, 11, 22 and 26 September 1969, also reproduced in Stamp and Marley's *Accounting Principles and the City Code: The Case for Reform* (1970).

3 See also *The Economist*, 30 August 1969, which observed:

> Accountants do not have, nor do they believe in, written rules. Apart from the information and method of presentation required by the Companies Act, they rely on integrity and common sense, guided by occasional statements issued by the various professional institutions. They carry none of the legal weight that similar recommendations from institutions of American accountants do. They merely represent the evolving concept of what constitutes 'best practice' and the need to define this only arises when accountants find themselves increasingly meeting situations that defeat their common sense . . . Playing the game is all very well and most accountants do. But the system that has been exposed so lamentably this week in the City's handling of this mess-up (see Pergamon affair) simply is not good enough.

4 See Smith 1992, pp. 23–27.

5 *The Making of Accounting Standards: Report of the Review Committee under the Chairmanship of Sir Ron Dearing CB* (1988).

6 The Dearing Proposals introduced an ingenious disincentive for companies contemplating fighting the Panel's conclusion in court. If the Panel won the case, the court could hold the company directors personally liable for the costs of the court action and the subsequent republication of the accounts.

7 Not all agreed with the Statement of Principles. The ASB was involved in a long-running argument with Ernst and Young concerning the primacy of the matching principle and the income statement over the ASB's definition of assets and liabilities with (as the firm saw it) the primacy of the balance sheet. The ASB saw it differently. If only defined assets and liabilities could be shown in the balance sheet rather than deferred gains or losses, the income statement would better reflect a company's performance.

8 The history of the G4+1 is given by Donna Street in *Inside G4+1: The Working Group's Role in the Evolution of the International Accounting Standard Setting Process* (2005).

9 Camfferman and Zeff, *Financial Reporting and Global Capital Markets: A History of the International Accounting Standards Committee 1993–2000* (2007). See also Zeff's 'The Evolution of the IASC into the IASB, and the Challenges it Faces' in *Accounting Review* (2012).

10 Of which I was the Chairman from January 2001 to June 2011.

11 The EC had earlier indicated that the EU should use IFRS. See *EU Financial Reporting Strategy: The Way Forward* (2000).

12 Part of the problem was French attitudes to the Anglo-Saxon model of standard setting. For an insight into the conflict between the Anglo-Saxon model of standard setting based on economics and the French 'social model', see J. Jennings' 'France and the "Anglo-Saxon" Model: Contemporary and Historical Perspectives' in *European Review* (2006).

13 The EU's endorsement process does, however, include the option for parliament to debate and ultimately reject an IFRS.

14 See IASB/FASB paper, *Information for Observers: Update on the Status of the Memorandum of Understanding – Suggestions for MOU II Technical Plan*, IASB-FASB Meeting, 21 April 2008, which outlines the choices deemed to be available and makes recommendations for the curtailed programme to meet a mid-2011 completion date.

15 The EU IAS Regulation (2002/1606) requiring use of IFRS in the EU includes a requirement that IFRS as endorsed by the EU must not disadvantage European companies as compared to those in other major markets.

16 Many companies and politicians in the EU were pressing for the ability to restate the assets at cost with perhaps some impairment provision. Despite the intense pressure, the Board refused to acquiesce. Instead, in an attempt to reflect potential corporate action if reclassification had always been possible but to avoid undue backdating so that financial institutions had to take losses, the effective date of the IAS39 amendment was 1 July 2008. Any reclassification taking place after 1 November 2008 would involve the institution using the fair value at the date of reclassification.

17 See IASCF Press Release, 'Trustees Support IASB's Accelerated Steps on the Credit Crisis', 9 October 2008 (http://www.iasplus.com/en/news/2008/October/news4477), and IASB Press Release, 'IASB Amendments Permit Reclassification of Financial Instruments', 13 October 2008 (http://www.ifrs.org/News/Press-Releases/Pages/IASB-amendments-permit-reclassification-of-financial-instruments.aspx).

18 The Board did try to obtain some comments in the limited time available. It took some comfort from the informal 'fatal flaw' responses of senior technical and audit partners in certain firms to drafts of the proposed amendments.

19 For a very perceptive and more detailed analysis of the political machinations of this period, see 'Fair Value Accounting and the Banking Crisis in 2008: Shooting the Messenger' by Andre et al. in *Accounting in Europe* (2009). Note that despite all the pressure from the EU to change IAS39 in time for the 2009 reporting season, when IFRS9 was issued in November 2009 the EU did not endorse it for use in the EU! The French government had been persuasive once again!

20 See for example, Dye and Sunder's 'Why Not Allow the FASB and IASB Standards to Compete in the US?' in *Accounting Horizons* (2001).

21 As mentioned earlier, two seats on the Monitoring Board are reserved for IOSCO members. They represent committees many of whose members do use IFRS.

22 In Africa, a new body, the Pan-African Federation of Accountants, has been formed, which one hopes will become the forerunner of the African regional standard-setters group.

23 Technically the partnership had an obligation to buy out its partners (a liability), but the ownership interest was, in essence, equity. The New Zealand partnership was restricting its membership to its national farmers and protecting itself from being bought by outsiders. Consequently, the 'share exchange' market was run by the partnership itself. In Germany, the motivation was frequently to keep the ownership in the hands of the inside/family group.

24 The US Treasury, which has not attempted to impose any pressure on the US institution charged with making the decision on US adoption of IFRS, has long supported the notion of one set of global standards and has defended the notion in international fora such as G20 meetings.

25 When the IASB started work in 2001, the USA's domestic market capitalisation amounted to 52% of the world total (EU, Africa and the Middle East, 30%; Asia, 15%; and the Americas excluding the USA, 3%). By 2010 the situation had changed, with the share of global capitalisation being as follows: USA, 31%; EU, Africa and the Middle East, 27%; Asia, 33%; and the Americas excluding the USA, 9%. Source: World Federation of Exchanges.

26 A. Haldane, *Accounting for Bank Uncertainty* (2011). In his speech Haldane raises the issue for giving ranges of asset values where significant valuation uncertainly exists. This, he argues, would not only help investors but may lead to banks restricting exposure to such assets.

27 A. Haldane, *Fair Value in Foul Weather* (2009).

28 To see the effect of fair value declines on industry and countries, see Bini and Penman's *Companies with Market Values Below Book Values Are More Common in Europe than in the US: Evidence, Explanations and Implications* (2013).

29 The use of such cost measures instantly puts pressure on the impairment methods used – a major source of contention during the financial crisis.

30 As discussed later, in a period of higher inflation, however, the situation could easily change as investors seek information on the necessary capital expenditure required to maintain the business model.

31 See *The Debate on Inflation Accounting* by Tweedie and Whittington (1984).

32 For depreciating assets this treatment could tempt companies to use artificially low depreciation rates to boost net income while reducing the ultimate gain on sale. Accounting, however, cannot be based on anti-avoidance measures – this would clearly be an area for discussion between the auditor and the company.

33 County NatWest, 'What Can You Learn from a Dead Parrot?', *Equity Briefing*, 8 April 1992.

34 As a result of the Polly Peck collapse, the ASB's first standard, FRS1, dealt with cash flow and abolished the Source and Application of Funds Statement.

35 Statement of Standard Accounting Practice (SSAP) 1, 'Accounting for Associated Companies', was the UK's first accounting standard – but only because the newly created Accounting Standards Steering Committee, under pressure from the government, was looking for a quick win and seized upon a nearly completed Institute of Chartered Accountants in England and Wales (ICAEW) research report on the subject. See 'Standards, Objectives and the Corporate Report' (Tweedie, 1981).

36 But see the SEC's *Work Plan for the Consideration of Incorporating International Financial Reporting Standards into the Financial Reporting System for US Issuers: Final Staff Report* of 13 July 2012. Feedback included a comment that 'the IASB's interpretative function needs to be much more active than it has been'. Here we go! I would point out that US GAAP contains more than five times as many pages as IFRS. The profession has to decide which way it wishes to go and it will get the standards it deserves!

37 For further discussion on this issue, see my 2007 lecture, *Keep it Simple, Stupid! Can Global Standards be Principle-based?*

38 See Douglas Flint's 2012 lecture, *Highlight of a Crisis: An Opportunity to Improve or Deceive?* Douglas, the Chairman of HSBC, is the son of Professor David Flint, to whom I was apprenticed. The genes have been passed on!

References

Andre, P., A. Cazavan-Jeny, W. Dick, C. Richard and P. Walton, 'Fair Value Accounting and the Banking Crisis in 2008: Shooting the Messenger', *Accounting in Europe*, Vol. 6, No. 1, 2009.

Bini, M. and S. Penman, *Companies with Market Values Below Book Values Are More Common in Europe than in the US: Evidence, Explanations and Implications*, Global Valuation Institute, KPMG, 2013.

Camfferman, K. and S. A. Zeff, *Financial Reporting and Global Capital Markets: A History of the International Accounting Standards Committee 1993–2000*, Oxford University Press, 2007.

Consultative Committee of Accountancy Bodies, *The Making of Accounting Standards: Report of the Review Committee under the Chairmanship of Sir Ron Dearing CB*, ICAEW, 1988.

Dye, R. A. and S. Sunder, 'Why Not Allow the FASB and IASB Standards to Complete in the US?' *Accounting Horizons*, Vol. 15, No. 3, September 2001.

European Commission, *EU Financial Reporting: The Way Forward*. Communication from the Commission to the Council and the European Parliament, 13 June 2000.

Flint, D., *The Significance of the Standard 'True and Fair View'*, New Zealand Society of Accountants Invitation Research Lecture, 1980.

———, *A True and Fair View in Company Accounts*, Gee & Co. for the Institute of Chartered Accountants of Scotland, 1982.

———, *Highlight of a Crisis: An Opportunity to Improve or Deceive?* Aileen Beattie Memorial Lecture, ICAS, 2012.

Haldane, A., *Fair Value in Foul Weather*, speech given at the Royal Institution of Chartered Surveyors, London, 10 November 2009.

———, *Accounting for Bank Uncertainty*, Better Markets Conference, ICAEW, 2011.

Jennings, J., 'France and the "Anglo-Saxon" Model: Contemporary and Historical Perspectives', *European Review*, Vol. 14, No. 4, 2006.

Smith, T., *Accounting for Growth*, Century, 1992, pp. 23–27.

Stamp, E. and C. Marley, *Accounting Principles and the City Code: The Case for Reform*, Butterworth, 1970.

Street, D., *Inside G4+1: The Working Group's Role in the Evolution of the International Accounting Standard Setting Process*, ICAEW, 2005.

Tweedie, D. P., 'Standards, Objectives and The Corporate Report', in R. Leach and E. Stamp (eds), *British Accounting Standards: The First 10 Years*, Woodhead and Faulkner, 1981, pp. 168–189.

_____, Keep It Simple, Stupid! Can Global Standards Be Principle-based? Ken Spencer Memorial Lecture, Melbourne, IASB, 2007.

Tweedie, D. P. and G. Whittington, *The Debate on Inflation Accounting*, Cambridge University Press, 1984.

US Securities and Exchange Commission, *Work Plan for the Consideration of Incorporating International Financial Reporting Standards into the Financial Reporting System for U.S. Issuers: Final Staff Report*, Securities and Exchange Commission, 2012.

Zeff, S. A., 'The Evolution of the IASC into the IASB, and the Challenges It Faces', *Accounting Review*, Vol. 87, 2012, pp. 807–837.

8

International differences in IFRS adoptions and IFRS practices[1]

Christopher Nobes

1 Introduction

Many publications give the impression that International Financial Reporting Standards (IFRS) are now used for most reporting by most companies in the world. The first objective of this chapter is to provide an antidote to these exaggerations. This involves looking in some detail at the many different ways in which major jurisdictions have adopted or adapted IFRS. Related to this, there are two other regulatory issues which differ by jurisdiction: translations of IFRS and enforcement of IFRS. This chapter's second aim is to summarise and update the discussion of these issues.

In addition to adapting the standards, or not adopting them at all, there is a further, quite different way in which international accounting differences have survived the arrival of IFRS. Even among companies which are fully compliant with IFRS as issued by the International Accounting Standards Board (IASB), there is scope for, and evidence of, variety of accounting practice. This variety is associated with such factors as firm size, industry, and country. Nobes (2006) divided the scope for different IFRS practice into five aspects of the content of IFRS, such as overt options and covert options. The next tasks of this chapter are to update and go beyond the earlier discussion of these aspects in two ways: (i) by taking account of the many changes to the content of IFRS from 2005 to 2012, and (ii) by summarising the empirical findings based on IFRS annual reports of 2005 onwards.

The next four sections examine the above four sets of issues: different national implementations of IFRS; language and enforcement; the scope for variations in IFRS practice; and the empirical search for those variations. Relevant literature is included section by section. The author apologises to readers for the amount of self-citation, but that is inherent in the nature of the task because this has been my field of research for many years. Section 6 concludes, and also asks whether any other set of standards (particularly US GAAP [generally accepted accounting principles]) would have faced the same challenges if adopted widely.

When examining national implementations, reference is made to the requirements for financial statements relating to accounting periods ending on 31 December 2013, unless otherwise stated. For variations allowed within IFRS (in Section 4), it is possible[2] to go one year further, to the requirements in force for 31 December 2014 year ends.

2 National implementations of IFRS

It is a commonplace that International Financial Reporting Standards have spread to over 100 countries (e.g. SEC, 2011; IASB, 2012, p. 11). Examples of reports about this process are as follows:

- IFRS is the official reporting standard which was recently adopted by over 100 countries (Benzacar, 2008, p. 26).
- To date, more than 12,000 companies in over 100 countries have adopted IFRS (Interfacing, 2012).
- The global rollout of International Financial Reporting Standards is gaining momentum, with more than 100 countries now using IFRS and all of the world's major countries anticipated to be on board within the next few years (BDO, 2012).
- The number of countries requiring International Financial Reporting Standards (IFRS) for public companies has grown from a relative handful to over 100 (Pacter, 2012).
- Approximately 120 nations and reporting jurisdictions permit or require IFRS for domestic listed companies, although approximately 90 countries have fully conformed with IFRS as promulgated by the IASB and include a statement acknowledging such conformity in audit reports (AICPA, 2013).

This section contains a reminder that such reports should not be taken to imply the imminent death of international accounting differences. I present data on the variety in national implementations of IFRS, stressing where implementation is partial or non-mandatory, in order to provide an antidote to the lack of caution in some of the quotations above. Therefore, my inaugural proposition is this: ask not what a company in a country *can* do; ask what the company is *required* to do. More specifically, ask not which country allows some version of IFRS for some purpose; ask which country requires 'IFRS as issued by the IASB' (IASB-IFRS) for all purposes.

As noted above, the literature (academic, professional and journalistic) contains many references to widespread or almost universal adoption of IFRS. However, four caveats should be entered. First, in several major capital markets, IFRS is either not *required* for any purpose (e.g. in Japan or Switzerland) or not even *allowed* for domestic reporters (e.g. for SEC registrants in the USA). Secondly, even in jurisdictions where IFRS is required or allowed, this is often restricted in some way (e.g. to listed companies or to consolidated statements). I am not suggesting that these restrictions on IFRS are inappropriate, merely that they cause an unadorned statement about 'adoption' to be misleading. In the quotations at the start of this section, Pacter (2012) carefully refers to 'public companies' (which are a very small percentage of companies, although economically important), whereas the other authors do not. Thirdly, for many of the 'more than 100 countries', it is not IASB-IFRS that is required or allowed (for some purposes), but national (e.g. Australian) or regional (e.g. EU) versions of IFRS. Fourthly, in many countries where IFRS adoption is alleged to have taken place (e.g. several EU countries), no companies or auditors refer to compliance with IASB-IFRS. Whether companies *are* complying with IASB-IFRS is a different issue from whether IASB-IFRS is required or whether it is referred to. I deal with those issues separately below, but it should be noted immediately that some versions of IFRS do not necessarily imply (and some do not even allow) compliance with IASB-IFRS.

Zeff and Nobes (2010) investigated a number of national implementations of IFRS. They asked, for example: 'Has Australia adopted IFRS?', concluding that there is no simple answer. Strictly speaking, Australia has not adopted IASB-IFRS because, in Australian IFRS (AIFRS), (i) early adoption[3] as allowed by most new or amended IASB standards is not allowed, (ii) some disclosure requirements have been added, (iii) many paragraphs have been amended to extend application to not-for-profit entities, and (iv) references are added. The lack of permission to early adopt is a major issue: for example, for accounting periods ending on 30 June 2012 or 30 June 2013, a large amount of IFRS was allowed in South Africa or Switzerland but not allowed[4] in Australia. This included, *inter alia*, IFRSs 9 to 13 and important amendments to International Accounting Standard (IAS) 19. This material occupied over 500 pages of IFRS, including vital issues such as the definition of a subsidiary.

On the other hand, those for-profit entities which comply with AIFRS should automatically thereby be complying with IASB-IFRS. Thus, in terms of comparability, the result is the same as if IASB-IFRS had been required in Australia. Figure 8.1 illustrates these points. Starting from the top, various versions of implementation are shown. Starting from the bottom, there is an assessment of the likelihood of compliance by companies with IASB-IFRS. More recently, there has been another relevant development in Australia, in that companies without public accountability[5] are allowed to follow a special version of AIFRS which contains reduced disclosure requirements, so is clearly not IASB-IFRS.

EU-adopted IFRS is also not IASB-IFRS in that (i) it has a more permissive version of IAS 39 (Whittington, 2005), and (ii) early adoption is not allowed until EU endorsement.[6] Despite this, at least up to the time of writing, EU companies can easily arrange[7] to comply with IASB-IFRS, and most are probably[8] doing so even though few *acknowledge* that they are (Nobes and Zeff, 2008). By contrast, Chinese or Venezuelan versions of IFRS would probably not normally allow compliance with IASB-IFRS. Zeff and Nobes (2010) concluded that very few countries with significant stock markets require direct compliance with IASB-IFRS. They mentioned Israel and South Africa, but even in those countries, compliance is only required for listed companies.

The impression of widespread IFRS adoption can be created or dispelled by careful choice of the questions being asked. Table 8.1 asks questions, at the head of its columns, designed as

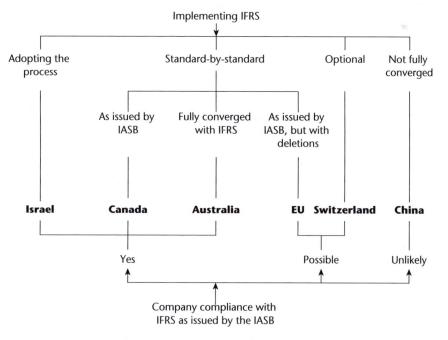

Figure 8.1   Methods of implementing IFRS (for consolidated statements of listed companies)
Source: Zeff and Nobes (2010)

an antidote to the conventional wisdom outlined at the start of this section. The table reports on IFRS implementations in the 16 jurisdictions which have the world's largest stock markets.[9] The table deals with the regulated reporting of domestic companies. It deals only with requirements, not with options (except in column 8). So, various *permissions* to use IFRS are not mentioned such as (i) permission in the US for foreign SEC registrants, or (ii) permission in Japan for Japanese companies. A table which tried to deal with permissions would be very complex and would not be relevant for the purpose here.

Column 2 of Table 8.1 records that IASB-IFRS is not required in any of the 16 countries for the reporting of all types of entities which are regulated. There would be a more efficient way of conveying this information, but that display suits the purpose outlined in the previous paragraph. Column 3 reports on countries where IASB-IFRS is required for at least some types of reporting (e.g. the consolidated statements of all listed companies). Only Russia and South Africa are recorded as 'Yes'. I treat the Russian translation of IFRS as IASB-IFRS because it has been approved by the IASB. Whether Russian companies are fully complying with this recent requirement to use IFRS is a different (empirical) matter. In comparison to Table 8.1, Figure 8.1 relates only to the consolidated statements of listed companies. Therefore, for example, South Africa was shown as fully adopting the IFRS process in Figure 8.1, but because this does not apply to unlisted companies, South Africa is in column 3 (not column 2) of Table 8.1.

Canada is not included in column 3 because it does not require IFRS for Canadian companies which are rate-regulated or are also listed in the USA; for example, of the 60 members of the main stock market index (TMX S&P), only 49 companies used IFRS for 2011.[10] A similar analysis of 2012 annual reports shows the same position.[11]

Columns 4 and 5 concern versions of IFRS which are intended by regulators to lead to compliance with IASB-IFRS. No additional countries appear with a 'Yes' in column 4. Those three countries appearing for the first time in column 5 require, for some reporting, a version of IFRS that is not 'as issued by the IASB' because, for example, it does not allow early adoptions of new or amended standards. Columns 6 and 7 concern versions of IFRS which currently *allow* companies to achieve compliance with IASB-IFRS. No extra countries appear in column 6, but column 7 contains the EU countries.

Column 8 concerns unconsolidated statements. No version of IFRS is required for this purpose for all regulated companies in any of the jurisdictions. It is not generally the topic of this chapter to investigate the many jurisdictions where versions of IFRS are *allowed*. However, relaxing the strict approach, column 8 also records any cases where a version of IFRS is allowed for unconsolidated reporting. The UK is the only EU country of Table 8.1 which is recorded as '(A)' because the others require national GAAP to be used for the unconsolidated statements from which tax and distribution are calculated.

In summary, because of the way the questions are asked, there is little 'Yes' in Table 8.1. Only 9 of the 16 countries have any 'Yes' at all. It would be easy to reduce the number of 'Yes' answers further by deleting the three countries with the smallest of the 16 stock markets (South Korea, South Africa and Spain).

As we move to the right across Table 8.1, a date is inserted for the first appearance of 'Yes' for any country. The date refers to the earliest accounting period ending on 31 December for which the 'Yes' applies. As may be seen, there are no such implementations before 2005, and three out of nine implementations are recent, relating to 2010 or later.

Researchers might find it valuable to consider Table 8.1 when assessing the reliability of reports about IFRS adoption. For example, Francis *et al.* (2008) presented a table showing that most *unlisted* companies in a majority of 56 countries (including many EU countries) had 'adopted'[12] IFRS by 1999/2000. This cannot have been the case (see columns 6 or 8 of Table 8.1) if 'adopted' means compliance, as it generally does in the empirical and other literature (e.g. Ashbaugh, 2001; Ashbaugh and Pincus, 2001; Leuz, 2003; Jermakowicz, 2004; Cuijpers and Buijink, 2005; Gassen and Sellhorn, 2006; Hoogendoorn, 2006; Christensen *et al.*, 2007; Barth *et al.*, 2008). Country of domicile is by no means a complete predictor of which GAAP will be adopted by a company, but it does make some answers unlikely or (without dual reporting) legally impossible.

Research work on national implementations has taken many different directions. For example, Leuz (2010) sought to explain clusters of countries with similar IFRS implementations; Goncharov *et al.* (2009) examined the economic functions of the dual (IFRS/national) accounting system in Germany.

Nothing in this chapter should be read as implying that the International Accounting Standards Committee (IASC) and IASB have not succeeded in reducing international differences in financial reporting, and therefore in increasing comparability. The consolidated statements of thousands of listed companies are complying with IASB-IFRS, even if many (e.g. nearly all EU companies) do not acknowledge this. It is clear, for example, that German and UK listed companies now publish consolidated statements which are much more similar than before IFRS was adopted, and that both German[13] and UK[14] national rules have been changed towards IFRS.

3 Language and enforcement

Introduction

As discussed in Section 2, the jurisdiction in which an entity operates will determine the version of IFRS with which the entity is required or allowed to comply. However, there are other aspects of nationality that will also affect IFRS practices. Ball (2006) and Nobes (2006) have explained how, even if all entities are apparently complying with IFRS, the incentives of preparers and enforcers remain 'primarily local' (Ball, 2006, p. 15). Wysocki (2011) showed how the determinants and outcomes of IFRS and non-accounting institutions are intertwined. Section 4 focuses on issues of judgement and choice with respect to policies on recognition, measurement and presentation.

Before that, this section looks at two other national issues: language and enforcement. From here on, a large number of accounting standards are referred to. In order to avoid clutter, they are referred to by their numbers only, but the full title of each of these standards is shown in an Appendix to this chapter.

The issues of language and enforcement can be introduced with the aid of a typical[15] audit report on IFRS financial statements in the EU. This one relates to a German company's[16] consolidated statements, as follows:

> We conducted our audit in accordance with §317 HGB and German generally accepted standards for the audit . . . promulgated by the Institut der Wirtschaftsprüfer . . . .
> According to §322 Abs. 3 Satz 1 HGB, we state that our audit . . . has not led to any reservations. In our opinion, . . . the consolidated statements comply . . . with IFRSs, as adopted by the EU, and the additional requirements of German commercial law pursuant to §315a Abs. 1 HGB and give a true and fair view . . . in accordance with these requirements.

The auditors reveal (or imply) at least eight 'national' (or EU) aspects of the reporting: (i) the audit is required by German law and its quality would be assessed under German law; (ii) the auditors use German professional audit standards (although these are now closely based on

Table 8.1 IFRS implementations for regulated reporting by domestic companies, 31 December 2013 year ends

1	2	3	4	5	6	7	8
Jurisdiction	Is IASB-IFRS required for all regulated reporting?	Is IASB-IFRS required for consolidated statements of all listed companies?	Is a version of IFRS which is intended to ensure compliance with IASB-IFRS required for all regulated reporting?	Is a version of IFRS which is intended to ensure compliance with IASB-IFRS required for consolidated statements of all listed companies?	Is a version of IFRS which allows compliance with IASB-IFRS required for all regulated reporting?	Is a version of IFRS which allows compliance with IASB-IFRS required for consolidated statements of all listed companies?	Is a version of IFRS which allows compliance with IASB-IFRS required (or allowed; A) for all regulated unconsolidated reporting?
Australia	N	N	N	Y[1] (2005)	N	←Y	N (A)
Brazil	N	N	N	Y[2] (2010)	N	←Y	N
Canada	N	N[3]	N	N	N	N	N[4] (A)
China	N	N	N	N	N	N	N
France	N	N	N	N	N	Y (2005)	N
Germany	N	N	N	N	N	Y (2007)[5]	N[6]
Hong Kong[7]	N	N	N	N	N	N	N
India	N	N	N	N[8]	N	N	N
Japan	N	Y (2012)[9]	N	N	N	N	N
Russia	N	Y (2005)[10]	N	←Y	N	←Y	N
South Africa	N	N	N	←Y	N	←Y	N (A)
South Korea	N	N	N	Y[11] (2011)	N	←Y	N (A)
Spain	N	N	N	N	N	Y (2005)	N
Switzerland	N	N[12]	N	N	N	N	N (A)
UK	N	N	N	N	N	Y (2005)	N
US	N	N	N	N	N	N	N[13]

Sources: http://www.iasplus.com/country/useias.htm and http://www.pwc.com/us/en/issues/ifrs-reporting/country-adoption/index.jhtml (both accessed 2 June 2013).

Key: Y = Yes. ←Y = Yes, as follows from a column to the left.

N = No.

A = Allowed.

Notes:

[1] Many additions to IASB-IFRS. See text for explanation.

[2] Some IFRS options have been deleted and some disclosures added.

[3] Rate-regulated companies are exempted. Companies which are also listed in the US are allowed to use US GAAP.

[4] Private entities are allowed to use the Accounting Standard for Private Enterprises.

[5] US GAAP was allowed for certain companies until 2007.

[6] No, unless statements prepared according to the Commercial Code are also prepared.

[7] Hong Kong Financial Reporting Standards have been converged with IFRS, but differences remain, primarily in transitional provisions.

[8] The Deloitte and PwC websites concur that the status of IFRS in India is sufficiently unclear that 'N' is the answer.

[9] Japan allows IASB-IFRS for the consolidated statements of listed companies.

[10] The Deloitte and PwC websites concur that IFRS (with an IASB-approved translation into Russian) is required for listed companies.

[11] IASB-IFRS in Korean translation, and without early adoptions permitted.

[12] IFRS or US GAAP are allowed.

[13] Unconsolidated reporting is not generally required in the US. To the extent that it is required, US GAAP is mandated.

international standards); (iii) the auditors comply with particular German legal requirements for what must be stated; (iv) the accounting standards are 'IFRS, as adopted by the EU', which (as explained above) is not the same thing as IASB-IFRS, even though the company might be complying with IASB-IFRS; (v) because the reporting is under German law, it is the German-language version of EU-adopted IFRS that applies legally; (vi) German law contains extra accounting requirements; (vii) the auditors apparently[17] report on 'true and fair' rather than on the 'fair' required by IAS 1 (see below); and (viii) German law contains particular references to 'true and fair' which weaken the 'override' (see below). The audit points contained here could affect the quality of reporting because they might affect compliance (see below).

Language

Evans (2004) examined language difficulties in detail in the context of accounting. She points out the inevitability that some meaning will be lost in translation. Zeff (2007) included problems of translation and terminology in his survey of obstacles to global comparability of financial reporting. The translations of 'true and fair view' and 'fair presentation' were investigated in detail for several languages by Nobes (2009, pp. 417–419). The various official translations have rendered 'true and fair' and 'fair' identically, although the German translations use different words for 'view' and 'presentation'.[18] When translating German documents the other way, into English, the translators have to remember to use 'true and fair view' in a legal context (e.g. for the audit report quoted above) but 'fair presentation' in the context of IAS 1.

German law does not include the 'true and fair override', despite its being required by the EU's Fourth Directive on company law (Nobes, 1993). However, the German version of EU-adopted IFRS does include the 'fair presentation override' of IAS 1. Nobes (2009) investigated the use of the override in the context of IFRS, including the famous case of *Société Générale* in which, on its 2007 financial statements, the company received a clean audit report from two Big-4 firms after explaining that it had departed from IASs 1, 10 and 37. To the extent that this would have been less likely to happen in Germany or the UK, cultural rather than linguistic explanations might be needed (Standish, 2003; Burlaud and Colasse, 2011; Danjou and Walton, 2012).

More simply, there are some clear errors of translation. To give a German example, the discount rate required by IAS 19 (para. 83) for pension obligations is the interest rate on 'corporate bonds'. However, the official EU German text renders this as *'Industrieanleihen'*. Such industrial bonds are a subset of corporate bonds, perhaps with different, or differently volatile, average interest rates. The IASB's approved German translation (but not the EU's) was corrected to *'Unternehmensanleihen'* in 2010.

Baskerville and Evans (2011) examined the complex issues to be considered when translating IFRS. Dahlgren and Nilsson (2012) give many detailed examples of translating IFRS into Swedish, noting several straight-forward errors. However, they make the more general point that because conceptual structures in different languages do not match perfectly, some accounting concepts are 'simply not translatable' (p. 57).

Monitoring and enforcement

The quality of audit and of other compliance monitoring is a national issue, although there is some co-ordination and exchange of information on enforcement at the EU level through the European Securities and Markets Authority. Efforts have been made to avoid national or European 'interpretations' of IFRS, but that topic takes us into the following section of this chapter, which is concerned with IFRS policies. Ball *et al.* (2000) suggest that the strength of enforcement is related to a country's position in the common/code law classification. Brown and Tarca (2005) examined the varying strengths of the enforcement agencies of some countries.

If auditors and companies are weakly monitored or subjected to little enforcement in a particular country, non-compliance with IFRS is likely to occur. Non-compliance is one cause of different practices even within jurisdictions which apparently require IFRS. At one stage, for example, it was suggested that non-compliance with IFRS disclosure requirements by German companies was substantial (Street and Bryant, 2000; Street and Gray, 2001; Glaum and Street, 2003). German compliance might now have greatly improved (Berger, 2010; Meyer, 2011; Hitz *et al.*, 2012), but doubts remain about how fully companies in other countries, such as Russia (Krylova, 2003), will comply with IFRS. A pan-European survey is provided by Glaum *et al.* (2013), who reveal differential compliance with IFRS disclosures related to factors of both country and company (e.g. listing status and auditor).

4 IFRS policies of recognition, measurement and presentation

Comparability

In this section, it is assumed that all the companies being considered are properly complying with IASB-IFRS. That is, we set aside any differences in practice caused by different national versions of IFRS, by translations of IFRS or by non-compliance with IFRS.

IFRS (even the original English version of IASB-IFRS) contains different types of scope for varied practice. One context in which to think about varied practice, and why it matters, is comparability. This quality is central to the objectives of IFRS financial reporting (IASC, 1989, paras. 39–42; IASB, 2010, paras. QC 20–25). In Nobes (2006) and several subsequent papers, it was assumed that comparability is undermined by any differences in IFRS practices which are associated with the nationality[19] of a company. However, Jaafar and McLeay (2007) and Stadler and Nobes (2014) point out that apparently country-driven differences might be connected to internationally different mixes of industries, and that some accounting policies might be industry-specific. For example, the use of weighted average inventory measurement (as opposed to first-in, first-out [FIFO]) might be common among a sample of German companies because it is appropriate for a particular industry whose members are numerous in the sample. If that industry is less important in other countries, then the resulting international difference in inventory measurement does not necessarily suggest a lack of comparability.

Apart from the issues discussed in Sections 2 and 3 above, the types of scope for varied IFRS practice identified by Nobes (2006) were (i) overt options, (ii) covert options or vague criteria, (iii) gaps in the requirements, (iv) estimations, and (v) first-time adoption issues. Later in this section, the examples of types (i) and (ii) will be updated and expanded, focussing on what might be useful for researchers. Before that, let us deal briefly with the other three types.

Gaps in IFRS, measurement estimations and first-time adoption

Gaps in any GAAP are, of course, inevitable. IAS 8 deals with the selection of accounting policies when IFRS does not deal with an issue. This leaves much room for judgement and therefore for different solutions. For example, at the time of writing, IFRSs 4 and 6 do not provide requirements on several major issues of accounting for insurance contracts and for oil and gas exploration, respectively. Indeed, those standards allow *more* flexibility than IAS 8 normally does (see Table 8.2). The same approach is being planned by the IASB in 2013 for rate-regulated entities. The gaps in IFRS were mentioned by the SEC (2011) as one reason for wariness about implementing IFRS in the United States. US GAAP does have requirements in the above areas.

Table 8.2 Examples of overt options in IFRS in 2013*

IAS 1	No format requirements for balance sheets or income statements (paras. 54, 82).
IAS 1	Choice of by-nature or by-function income statement (para. 99).
IAS 1	Permission to show comprehensive income in two statements (para. 81).
IAS 2	Permission to measure certain types of inventories at net realisable value, with gains and losses to profit and loss (para. 3).
IAS 2	FIFO or weighted average for the determination of the cost of inventories (para. 25).
IAS 7	Choice of direct or indirect calculation of operating cash flows (para. 18).
IAS 7	Net basis allowed for some cash flows (para. 21).
IAS 7	Choice of classification for interest and dividend flows (para. 31).
IAS 8	When developing an accounting policy, an entity 'may also consider' the rules of certain other standard-setters (para. 12).
IAS 16	Cost or fair value measurement for classes of property, plant and equipment (para. 29).
IAS 19	Inclusion of defined benefit interest cost as finance expense or as operating expense (BC para. 202)
IAS 20	Asset grants can be presented as a deduction from the asset or as deferred income (para. 24).
IAS 21	Choice of presentation currency (para. 38).
IAS 27	In 'separate' statements, investments in subsidiaries, joint ventures and associates may be shown at cost or as available-for-sale financial assets (para. 10).
IAS 28	In consolidated statements, certain investments in joint ventures and associates may be measured at fair value through profit and loss (para. 18).
IAS 38	Cost or fair value measurement for some types of intangible assets (para. 72).
IAS 39	Choice of cost basis or marking to market for some 'designated' financial assets and liabilities (para. 9). (Other choices are also available within para. 9.)
IAS 39	Trade date or settlement date accounting for 'regular way' transactions in financial assets (para. 38).
IAS 39	Permission to re-classify financial assets out of trading in 'rare circumstances' (para. 50 (c)).
IAS 39	Hedge accounting based on the designation of a hedging relationship (para. 71).
IAS 40	Permission to classify a property held under an operating lease as an investment property (para. 6).
IAS 40	Entity-wide choice of cost or fair value for measurement of investment property (para. 30).
IFRS 3	For measurement of a non-controlling interest, a choice of fair value or the share of the acquiree's net assets (para. 19).
IFRS 4	Permission for insurers not to separate certain embedded derivatives (para. 8).
IFRS 4	Permission to unbundle components of an insurance contract (para. 10).
IFRS 4	Permission to depart from IAS 8 when developing certain accounting policies for insurance contracts (para. 14).
IFRS 6	Permission to depart from aspects of IAS 8 when developing accounting policies for exploration assets (para. 6).
IFRS 6	Cost or fair value measurement for exploration assets (para. 12).
IFRS 9	Trade date or settlement date accounting for 'regular way' transactions in financial assets (para. 3.1.2).
IFRS 9	Option to designate certain financial assets and liabilities at fair value through profit or loss (paras. 4.1.5 and 4.2.2).
IFRS 9	Option to present fair value changes on non-trading financial assets in OCI (para. 5.7.5).

*For accounting periods beginning on or after 1 January 2013. Paragraph numbers as at 30 April 2013.

Nobes (2006, Table 8.4) recorded a number of areas in IFRS which require measurement estimations, such as assessing an asset's useful life, its pattern of wearing out and its residual value (in order to calculate depreciation). The examples in that table all remain in IFRS in 2013. An important recent addition is several estimations needed for the disclosures on financial instruments required by IFRS 7, such as exposures to risks (paras. 33 and 36). These remarks are not a particular criticism of IFRS, because any GAAP would require many of these measurement estimations. However, they are part of the scope for international variations in practice.

First-time adoption issues relate to the many choices in IFRS 1. For example, in its pre-IFRS accounting, a company might have treated goodwill in one of several ways: (i) held at zero, with a corresponding deduction from reserves; (ii) held on a cost basis, amortised over 5, 20 or 40 years; or (iii) held on a cost basis but checked for impairment every year. Although IFRS 3 requires method (iii), a company is allowed, on first-time adoption of IFRS, to retain the goodwill amount resulting from any other method in its first opening IFRS balance sheet. The large differences between goodwill numbers prepared under the various bases can last for many years[20] after first IFRS adoption.

Overt options

An IFRS option is called 'overt' here if it is plainly specified as a choice[21] within a standard. By contrast, 'covert' options (discussed in the next subsection) exist where no choice is explicitly offered but where the degree of judgement involved might allow scope for the preferences of the preparers of financial statements.

Table 8.2 expands and updates the list of overt options found in Nobes (2006). Researchers might wish to divide these into 'presentation' and 'recognition/measurement' topics. However, this is sometimes ambiguous. For example, it is clear that the IAS 1 options in Table 8.2 relate to 'presentation' and that the IAS 16 or IAS 40 options are 'measurement'. However, the IAS 20 option, which is expressed in the standard as an issue of presentation, affects the measurement of assets. The IAS 7 options, again expressed as having to do with presentation, change totals such as 'operating cash flows'.

IFRS has historically contained more options than most national GAAPs, because of the negotiations involved in setting standards internationally (e.g. Camfferman and Zeff, 2006, p. 269). For example, US GAAP contains considerably fewer options,[22] although still allowing last-in, first-out (LIFO), which has been removed from IFRS. Over time, the IASB has removed options in order to improve comparability. Researchers would need to check which options were available for which period. Table 8.3 shows the options which have been removed for various periods after 2004. However, the IASB has not been able to avoid[23] *adding* options, such as that related to IFRS 3 in Table 8.2. At the time of writing (middle of 2013), extra options are expected in the standard on revenue recognition (for the measurement of contingent revenue) and in the exposure draft on leases (for short-term leases).

Although all the overt options are clearly visible in the standards (and the resulting choices are clearly visible in annual reports), this does not mean that they are all well-suited to research. This is because (i) some topics occur infrequently (e.g. in Table 8.2, the first IAS 2 choice, the IAS 8 choice, the IAS 38 choice and the first IAS 40 choice); and (ii) some relate to specific industries which the researcher might not be studying (e.g. the second IAS 39 choice and the IFRS 4 and IFRS 6 issues).

Removing the rare issues leads us to a set of easily researched choices, as set out in Table 8.4. These have formed the basis of the recent empirical research discussed in Section 5. Table 8.4 includes four items (shown with daggers) which are no longer options in 2013, but it excludes some items which have proved difficult to assess in practice.[24]

Table 8.3 Former overt options in IFRS*

Until (and including) 2004

IAS 2   LIFO basis allowed (para. 23).

IAS 8   Policy changes and error corrections could be taken through the income statement (para. 38).

IAS 21   Certain exchange differences from 'severe devaluation' could be capitalised (para. 21).

IAS 27   Option to present minority interests outside of equity (para. 26).

Until (and including) 2008

IAS 1   Choice of two types of presentation of OCI (para. 10).

IAS 23   Choice of capitalising or expensing interest costs on construction contracts (paras. 7 and 10).

Until (and including) 2012

IAS 19   Actuarial gains and losses could be taken (a) immediately in full to OCI, (b) immediately in full to profit or loss, (c) in full to profit or loss over the remaining useful lives of employees in the plan, (d) in part to profit or loss over that period (corridor method), (e) in full or in part to profit or loss over a shorter period (paras. 92–93A).

IAS 31   In consolidated statements, there was a choice of proportional consolidation or equity accounting for joint venture entities (para. 30).

---

*Paragraph numbers relate to the last versions of the IASs before the removal of the relevant option.

Covert options

Turning to 'covert' options, Table 8.5 presents a list which is an expanded and updated version of that provided in Nobes (2006, Table 2). An example of an important covert option is the degree to which development costs are capitalised, which depends on the interpretation of several somewhat vague criteria. As with overt options, IFRS contains more of them than some other GAAPs. For example, the one in the previous sentence does not apply generally[25] in US GAAP, and neither do several others.[26]

Not only are covert options hidden from view in the standards, the exercise of such options is also generally hidden from view in financial statements. For example, it is usually impossible for outside users of the statements to assess whether or how a company exercised its preferences when capitalising (or not) development costs. One exception to this is the depreciation method, which is often disclosed. IASs 16, 38 and 41 make it clear[27] that selecting the depreciation method is not a policy choice, because it should rely on estimating the pattern of consumption of the asset's benefits.

Just as the list of overt options has changed over time, so has the list of covert options. For example, until the 2003 version of IAS 1, entities were required to present any 'extraordinary items' in their income statements, and the determination of whether an item was extraordinary involved judgement. Given that it is much more difficult to research covert options, the treatment of them here is not as detailed as for overt options.

Scope for country differences

The scope for variation in IFRS practices, as examined in this section, could undermine comparability. This would be the case even if the scope were exercised randomly by companies, but it has been suggested (e.g. Ball, 2006; Nobes, 2006) that there will be systematic country-based differences in practice. These might be influenced by the same forces which drove national GAAPs to be different in the first place, such as different tax systems and different prime purposes of accounting, linked to different owners and financiers of companies. The influence can be indirect.

Table 8.4 IFRS policy choices that are or were† easily observed

1*	(a)	Balance sheet shows assets = credits
	(b)	Balance sheet shows net assets
2*	(a)	Liquidity decreasing (cash at top)
	(b)	Liquidity increasing
3*	(a)	Income statement by function
	(b)	Income statement by nature
	(c)	Neither
4*	(a)	Equity accounting results included in 'operating' profit
	(b)	Results immediately after operating profit
	(c)	Results after finance
5†	(a)	Statement of changes in equity, including dividends and share issues
	(b)	Statement of recognised income and expense/other comprehensive income, not including dividends and share issues
6*	(a)	Direct calculation of operating cash flow
	(b)	Indirect calculation of operating cash flow
7*	(a)	Interest paid shown as operating cash outflow
	(b)	Interest paid shown as financing
8	(a)	Only cost for property, plant and equipment
	(b)	Some fair value for property, plant and equipment
9	(a)	Investment property at cost
	(b)	Investment property at fair value
10*	(a)	Some designation of financial assets at fair value
	(b)	No designation of financial assets at fair value
11†	(a)	Capitalisation of interest on construction
	(b)	Expensing of interest on construction
12*	(a)	FIFO for inventory cost
	(b)	Weighted average for inventory cost
13†	(a)	Actuarial gains and losses to OCI
	(b)	Actuarial gains and losses to income in full
	(c)	Corridor method
14†	(a)	Proportional consolidation of joint ventures
	(b)	Equity method

*Non-financial companies only.
†Options removed for 2013 statements or before; see Table 8.3.

For example, tax considerations could influence a company's accounting policies (e.g. choosing weighted average inventory costing) or estimations (e.g. maximising the size of impairments or provisions) in unconsolidated statements under a national GAAP; and these might flow through to IFRS consolidated statements. Even if such forces are no longer relevant, companies might prefer to continue with previous practices for administrative ease or to provide continuity for users.

5 Empirical studies of variations in IFRS practice

Introduction

Several studies have collected data on IFRS practices, mostly relating to 2005 financial statements or later. Some of these studies record the overt IFRS options chosen by companies on some topics (e.g. KPMG and von Keitz, 2006; ICAEW, 2007; European Commission, 2008). Those

Table 8.5 Examples of covert options or vague criteria in IFRS in 2013*

IAS 1	Departure from the requirements of IFRS when necessary to comply with the objective of financial statements (para. 19).
IAS 1	Determination of whether a liability is current on the basis of expected date of settlement or purpose of holding (para. 60).
IAS 8	Determination of materiality for various purposes (para. 5).
IAS 11	Use of stage of completion method for construction if contract outcome can be estimated reliably (para. 22).
IAS 12	Recognition of deferred tax asset for a loss carry forward only if future taxable profit is probable (para. 34).
IAS 12	Recognition of deferred tax liability on unremitted profits from subsidiaries only if dividends are probable in the foreseeable future (para. 39).
IAS 16	Depreciation method (paras. 60 to 62).
IAS 17	Lease classification based on 'substantially all the risks and rewards' with no numerical criteria (para. 8).
IAS 18	Use of stage of completion method for services if contract outcome can be estimated reliably (para. 38).
IAS 21	Determination of functional currency based on a mixture of criteria (paras. 9–12).
IAS 28	The identification of an associate on the basis of 'significant influence' (para. 2).
IAS 32	Offsetting of financial asset and liability when there is intent to settle on a net basis (para. 42).
IAS 36	Identification of an indication of impairment based on a mixture of criteria (paras. 12–14).
IAS 37	Recognition of a provision based on probability of outflow of resources (para. 14).
IAS 38	Capitalisation of development costs when all of various criteria are met (para. 57).
IAS 38	Amortisation of intangible assets only if useful life is assessed as finite (para. 88).
IAS 39	Classification of financial assets based on intention to trade, hold to maturity or neither (para. 9).
IAS 39	Use of cost basis where equity instruments cannot be measured reliably (para. 46).
IAS 39	Estimation of hedge effectiveness as a condition for use of hedge accounting (para. 88).
IAS 40	Use of cost basis, despite entity-wide choice of fair value, for an investment property whose fair value cannot be measured reliably (para. 53).
IAS 41	Use of cost basis for a biological asset whose fair value cannot be measured reliably (para. 30).
IFRS 3	Identifying the acquirer in a business combination presented as a merger of equals (para. 20).
IFRS 5	Treatment of assets as held-for-sale if expected to be sold within one year (para. 8).
IFRS 8	Identification of operating segments based on whether results are reviewed internally (para. 5).
IFRS 9	Classification of financial assets based on the entity's business model (para. 4.1.1).
IFRS 10	Identification of a subsidiary based on assessing power over an investee (para. 17).
IFRS 11	Identification of a joint venture based on assessing relevant activities (para. 7).

*For accounting periods beginning on or after 1 January 2013. Paragraph numbers as at 30 April 2013.

studies mix large and small companies, have small samples per country, and they generally do not report data by country. However, several empirical studies have systematically collected data for a formal sample of companies on a country-by-country basis, using lists of overt options for which company choice is easily observable, similar to that in Table 8.4. These studies are now discussed in the next five subsections, followed by a subsection containing new analogous data on Canada.

IFRS policy choices in 2005/6: national patterns

Kvaal and Nobes (2010, hereafter K&N) examined the 2005/6 practices of 232 large, listed companies from the five IFRS-using countries with the largest stock markets: Australia, France,

Table 8.6 Country and sector* distribution of companies, 2008/9 data (Canada, 2011)

	Australia	Canada	UK	Germany	France	Spain	NL	Italy	Sweden
0 Oil and gas	3	2	4	0	1	1	1	2	0
1 Basic materials	5	21	10	3	1	2	0	0	3
2 Industrials	5	2	3	5	7	7	5	5	6
3 Consumer goods	1	2	9	6	7	0	4	0	5
4 Health care	2	0	5	1	2	0	0	0	1
5 Consumer services	6	4	22	4	6	4	2	1	1
6 Telecommunications	1	3	3	1	1	1	1	1	2
7 Utilities	1	1	7	2	3	5	0	5	0
8 Financials	16	10	21	7	4	7	3	13	7
9 Technology	0	0	1	1	2	1	1	0	1
Total companies	40	45	85	30	34	28	17	27	26

*Sectors according to Industry Classification Benchmark.

Germany, Spain and the UK. As in all the papers discussed in this section, foreign companies[28] are excluded. For 16 overt IFRS options,[29] K&N's general hypothesis (based on the reasoning outlined at the end of the previous section) was not that country would determine policy but that any particular company would continue to follow its own individual pre-IFRS national practice on each particular optional topic. This motivated K&N to collect data on the pre-IFRS policies of the 232 companies for the topics without pre-IFRS national requirements.

K&N then hand-picked the data on the IFRS policy choices made by the companies. They found very strong statistical evidence that these choices followed pre-IFRS practices, and therefore that there are national patterns of IFRS practice which undermine comparability. K&N noted that some of their 16 topics are of little importance in this context but that they all bolster the findings on the importance of nationality in explaining policy choice. This increases the probability that there are national differences in other important areas which cannot be easily observed, such as the covert options related to impairment or to the capitalisation of development costs (see Table 8.5).

K&N did not examine the potential importance of a company's sector in explaining IFRS policy choice, although they excluded financial companies on topics for which a sector-specific choice is likely. Table 8.4 shows these topics with asterisks. K&N disclose the sectoral mix of their sample, which is approximately[30] as in Table 8.6 of this chapter. They note that (apart from financial companies) there is a broad sectoral spread for all of the five countries. Sector is discussed further below.

Studies of particular IFRS policy areas also uncover a national effect. Morais (2008) and Fasshauer *et al.* (2008) looked at the treatment of actuarial gains and losses in the 2005 IFRS reports of European companies. Both studies found an influence of nationality; for example, UK and Irish companies use different methods from continental companies. Cairns *et al.* (2011) focused on the use of fair value (including options to use it) in Australia and the UK around the time of transition to IFRS. They did not find great difference between the two countries, and this is not surprising given the similarities of background. Verriest *et al.* (2012) examined first-time adoption of IFRS and discovered national variations, possibly due to varying quality of corporate governance.

IFRS policy changes from 2005/6 to 2008/9

For most of the 232 companies in Kvaal and Nobes' sample, the financial statements examined were the first to be prepared under IFRS. This raises the question of whether the influence of pre-IFRS practices (and the resulting patterns of national IFRS practice) was mostly a feature of transition to IFRS and might therefore dissipate over time. In order to investigate that, Kvaal and Nobes (2012) examined the IFRS policy choices of the same companies as in K&N but three years later. They expected the influence of pre-IFRS policies (and therefore nationality) to continue, not least because IAS 8 discourages[31] policy change.

Kvaal and Nobes (2012) examined the 126 policy changes over the three-year period. They discovered little change among Australian and UK companies but significantly greater change by French and Spanish companies. Remarkably, the French and Spanish companies changed their policies more after transition (despite the constraints of IAS 8) than they had done at transition (when IFRS 1 imposes no constraints). For Australian and UK companies, the reverse was the case.

Kvaal and Nobes (2012) asked what might explain this. They suggest that French and Spanish companies had been the furthest away from the culture, ethos and requirements of the IASB, so they were least aware of the possibilities for change at transition. Kvaal and Nobes tested this idea by recording for each post-transition policy change whether the change was towards or away from the pre-IFRS requirement under national GAAP. They found that most of the few Australian and UK changes were towards the pre-IFRS national requirement, suggesting that the companies were not learning from foreign companies but were perhaps interested in comparability among their national peers. However, the many French and Spanish post-transition changes were mostly away from the pre-IFRS national norms, suggesting some learning, perhaps from the practices of companies listed on the London stock exchange as the largest in the world to be based on reporting under IFRS.

As part of this exercise, Kvaal and Nobes checked whether any amendments or proposed amendments to standards could explain the policy changes. There were no relevant amendments to IFRS requirements in the period and, on average, companies took no policy action in response to amendments *proposed* by the IASB. For example, there was no net movement away from the proportional consolidation of joint ventures after the IASB announced plans to abolish the method; and there was no increase in the move towards taking actuarial gains and losses to other comprehensive income (OCI) after the IASB announced plans to require this.

Haller and Wehrfritz (2013) also used the research of Nobes (2006) as a starting point. They examined the IFRS policy changes of German and UK companies from 2005 to 2009. Like Kvaal and Nobes (2012), they found few policy changes among companies of those countries.

Australia presents a special case because the initial Australian implementation of IFRS had deleted certain non-Australian options, such as the indirect method of calculating operating cash flows (topic 6 in Table 8.4). However, for 2007 onwards, the options were reinserted. Bond *et al.* (2012) found that less than 1 per cent of all Australian listed companies had changed from the direct to the indirect method by 2009. This confirms the strong influence of pre-IFRS practices.

Country, sector, firm and topic influences on IFRS policies

As mentioned in Section 4, Jaafar and McLeay (2007) investigated whether sector-specific policy choices lay behind some of the international differences in pre-IFRS practices. They found only a small effect of sector compared to that of nationality. However, they studied pre-IFRS practices, which means that some (perhaps most) of the effect of nationality was caused by international differences in requirements rather than in policy choice.

Cole *et al.* (2011) and Stadler and Nobes (2014) studied the influence of various factors in the context of IFRS. Cole *et al.* (2011) looked at 34 IFRS options (expanded from the list in Nobes, 2006) relating to 79 companies in four EU countries. They found that country was the most important determinant of policy choice, but that formats and disclosures were somewhat related to which audit firm the company used.

Stadler and Nobes (2014) note that, despite the strong association of policy choice and country, the IFRS practices within a country are not uniform. They therefore investigated the degree to which IFRS policy choices are driven by sector-, firm- or policy-specific factors, as well as by country. They used the 2008/9 data relating to 323 large non-financial companies of ten major countries. Their firm-specific factors included size and leverage. The policy-specific factors related to the effects on accounting numbers of the policy choice; for example, if a company already has high gearing, it might be disinclined to choose proportional consolidation of joint ventures, which would increase gearing.

Stadler and Nobes found that the very strong association of policy choice and country (found by K&N) largely survived the inclusion of variables for sector, firm and topic. They found that country factors were particularly influential when the choice did not affect an important accounting number; industry and topic factors influenced the choice on some topics; overall, country factors had the greatest influence on IFRS policy choice; and industry factors had more influence than topic factors.

Do smaller firms choose different policies?

Kvaal and Nobes had suggested that the study of the very largest listed companies meant that their findings were robust. That is, K&N expected that smaller firms would be less interested in international comparability and would therefore exhibit even clearer country-related patterns of policy choice. Indeed, some of the IFRS choices made by the large companies seemed out of line with pre-IFRS national traditions. For example, the large German companies mostly chose by-function income statements, presumably to be in line with the majority practice on the New York and London exchanges, whereas the by-nature format had been traditional German practice and, until 1987, the legal requirement.[32]

Nobes and Perramon (2013) investigated this issue. They took the 2008/9 data of Kvaal and Nobes (2012) as it relates to non-financial companies. Then they hand-picked data on the IFRS policy choices made in 2008/9 by a sample of the smallest listed companies of the same five countries. For 12 of their 15 topics,[33] they found that the policy choices were significantly different between the small and large companies for at least some countries. This included the German choices related to the income statement, noted above, in that the small German companies mostly chose the traditional by-nature format.

Classification of countries based on IFRS practices

Another major theme in the international accounting literature is closely related to the above discussions: classification of accounting systems. Attempts at classification go back more than a century, to Hatfield (1911). This and the other early classifications (i.e. Seidler, 1967; AAA, 1977; da Costa et al., 1978; Frank, 1979; Nair and Frank, 1980) had three or four groups, and all put the UK and the US in different groups. However, all the writers and all the data[34] were based in North America. They were more likely to be informed about UK and US accounting details than those of other countries.

By contrast, Mueller (1967), whose origins were German, put the US and the UK together in one class, with the other three classes each typified by different continental European countries. Nobes (1983) followed Mueller's lead, but added more countries (14 rather than Mueller's 5 example countries) and created a hierarchical classification (see Figure 8.2), which was then tested with somewhat informal data[35] according to proposed key topics in accounting practice. Doupnik and Salter (1993) confirmed the classification with more extensive data.

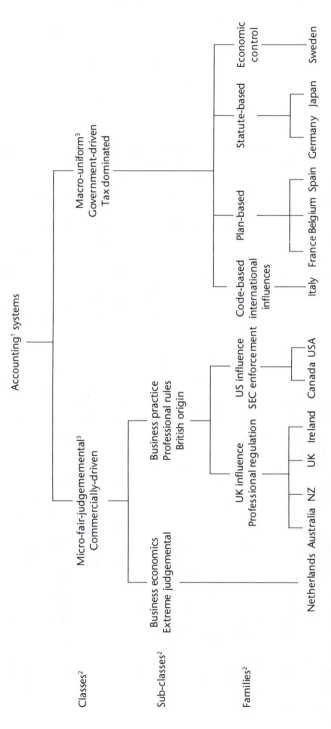

Figure 8.2 A suggested classification of accounting 'systems' in some developed Western countries in 1980

Notes:
[1]This is an abbreviated term for corporate financial reporting.
[2]These terms, borrowed from biology, should be interpreted merely as loose labels.
[3]The terms at these and other branching points are merely labels to be used as shorthand to try to capture some of the attributes of the members of the accounting systems below them. This classification was prepared by a UK researcher and may contain usage of terms that will mislead those from other cultures.

Source: Nobes (1983)

Christopher Nobes

Grouping the US and UK together is also overwhelmingly backed up by common sense concerning the two countries (in contrast to France or Germany, for example): shared language and legal system; old and powerful accountancy professions; private-sector standard-setters; strong equity markets; and major disconnections between tax and financial reporting. Despite this, many writers have continued to deny the existence of Anglo-American or Anglo-Saxon accounting (Shoenthal, 1989; Cairns, 1997; Alexander and Archer, 2000; d'Arcy, 2001). The first and the third of those papers consider the US and the UK only, note that they have differences and conclude that they cannot be classified together. This is an extreme version of the start-with-the-US-and-UK method discussed above. Nobes (1992, 1998, 2003 and 2004) disagrees with all these denials.

If the thesis of this chapter is accepted (namely that international differences continue to survive even within IFRS practice), then classification of countries by their IFRS policy choices should reveal groupings, perhaps even groupings similar to those proposed 30 years earlier for pre-IFRS practices (see Figure 8.2). In order to examine this, Nobes (2011) used the 2008/9 data of Kvaal and Nobes (2012) on five countries and added data for the same period on the same IFRS policy choices of the largest listed companies of Italy, the Netherlands and Sweden. This set of eight countries comprises all the major[36] countries included in Figure 8.2 and which required IFRS for the consolidated statements of listed companies in 2008/9.

Table 8.6 shows the sample used for the eight countries (plus Canada, which is discussed later). Table 8.7 shows the data on the 14 IFRS policy topics of Table 8.4. For classification purposes; attention must be paid to which policy topics are included and how they are weighted because the data on the various topics are added together. This is not a problem for the main

Table 8.7 Policy choices (percentages of companies by country)

		Aus	Can	UK	Ger	Fra	Spa	NL	Ita	Swe
1 (b)*	Balance sheet shows net assets	100.0	0.0	85.2	0.0	0.0	0.0	14.3	0.0	0.0
2 (a)*	Cash at top of balance sheet	100.0	100.0	0.0	30.4	0.0	4.8	14.3	21.4	0.0
3 (a)*	Income statement by function	58.3	87.5	82.1	82.6	62.1	4.8	50.0	7.1	95.0
4 (a)*	Equity profit in 'operating'	68.8	30.8	40.4	23.3	10.7	0.0	0.0	0.0	93.3
5 (b)†	Only SORIE/OCI presented	67.5	–	90.6	33.3	14.7	32.1	41.1	18.8	23.1
6 (b)*	Indirect operating cash flows	8.3	100.0	100.0	100.0	100.0	95.2	100.0	100.0	100.0
7 (a)*	Interest paid as operating flow	81.5	74.3	65.1	60.9	80.0	42.9	78.5	85.7	90.0
8 (b)	Some PPE at fair value	15.4	7.9	13.4	0.0	0.0	0.0	11.8	0.0	3.8
9 (b)	Investment property at fair value	73.3	40.0	72.7	10.0	12.5	6.3	75.0	0.0	100.0
10 (a)*	Some fair value designation	29.2	35.3	12.7	17.4	33.3	19.0	75.0	12.5	52.6
11 (a)†	Interest capitalisation	87.1	–	57.4	41.7	44.4	100.0	66.6	33.3	33.3
12 (b)*	Weighted average only	52.9	63.0	30.0	76.2	50.0	83.3	41.7	78.6	10.0
13 (a)	Actuarial gains/losses to OCI	86.7	79.6	85.4	63.3	50.0	57.8	31.3	24.0	20.0
14 (a)	Proportional consolidation of JV	11.5	63.0	22.6	15.8	75.8	88.0	46.0	40.0	33.3

The table shows the companies choosing a particular policy as a percentage of the companies exhibiting a policy for the topic. For several topics, the N is the total from Table 8.6. In a few cases (e.g. topic 9), the N is much smaller.
Notes:
*Non-financial companies only.
†Options removed for 2011 statements or before; see Table 8.3.
SORIE = Statement of recognised income and expense.
OCI = Other comprehensive income.
PPE = Property, plant and equipment.
JV = Joint ventures.
– = Not applicable.

purpose of papers like those by Kvaal and Nobes, which seek to use as much evidence of policy differences as is observable. However, for classification, Nobes (2011) excluded certain less important presentation differences,[37] although all the remaining 13 topics were given equal weight, as with all previous classification exercises.

Three different statistical techniques of classification all show that Australia and the UK form one group and the six continental European countries another. Incidentally, Nobes (2011) points out something rather surprising: the paper's classification of countries using data on IFRS policy choices is the first and only classification based on the observed *practices* of companies, as opposed to a classification based on rules, opinions about practices, or mixtures of the two, as found in the 11 previous accounting classifications referenced in the paper.

New data on Canadian IFRS practices

The above classification of countries based on IFRS choices excludes three countries with major capital markets which are shown in Figure 8.2: Canada, Japan and the US. In 2008/9, none used IFRS. For research carried out on data available in 2013, this remains a reason for excluding Japan and the US and for excluding other countries shown in Table 8.1, such as China and India. However, data have become available for Canada, as now explained.

IFRS was required in Canada for the majority of listed companies for accounting periods beginning on or after 1 January 2011. Following the techniques of the papers discussed above, the IFRS policies of the companies in Canada's TSX 60 index are now examined for year ends of 31 December 2011 or nearest after (e.g. 31 October 2012 year ends for banks). As Table 8.6 shows, after eliminating exempted companies and a few others which had non–December year ends[38] from the TMX index, a sample of 45 companies remains. As may be seen from Table 8.6 (sectors 0 and 1), 53 per cent of the sample are basic materials or oil and gas companies (with all but two of them in the extractives sector).[39]

Table 8.7 shows the policy choices of the Canadian companies. Given the warning from Jaafar and McLeay (2007) concerning the possible idiosyncratic policies of extractive companies, the data are segmented into three sets: extractive, financial and other. Two IFRS policy issues (shown with asterisks) no longer involved choices for 2011 and so are blank for Canada.

Inspection of the Canadian data reveals several interesting points which add to the evidence from other countries on the persistence of pre-IFRS policies. Following the line of Mueller (1967) and Nobes (1983 and 2011), one might expect Canadian companies to make choices similar to those of Australian and UK companies. Therefore, it is instructive to examine the topics of Table 8.7 for which this expectation is clearly refuted – topic 1 on the structure of the balance sheet and topic 14 on the treatment of joint venture entities. Following the logic of Kvaal and Nobes, there is a simple explanation for the fact that the Canadian policies on these topics are so far out of line with those of the Australian and UK companies: the Canadian companies are following pre-IFRS national practices.[40]

For topic 14, the Canadian choices are especially interesting because before the end of 2011, the IASB had already[41] issued a standard outlawing the predominant Canadian choice from 2013 onwards. This is spectacular evidence of the influence of previous policies: the companies adopted the pre-IFRS policy at the time of transition to IFRS even though it would very soon have to be abandoned.

For topic 2, Australian and Canadian national balance sheet formats began with cash, whereas the British Companies Act format has cash as the last asset. The IFRS policies follow those pre-IFRS practices closely. For topic 6, UK and Canadian national rules allowed the indirect method, whereas the Australian did not.

Christopher Nobes

Table 8.8 Canadian policy choices by sector (percentages*)

		Extractive	Other	Financial
4 (a)	Equity accounting profit in 'operating'	33.3	28.6	–
4 (b)	Immediately after	44.4	14.3	–
4 (c)	Below finance items	22.2	57.1	–
9 (b)	Investment property at fair value	–	0.0	66.7
13 (c)	Corridor method	15.4	0.0	88.9
14 (a)	Proportional consolidation of JVs	77.7	44.4	37.5

Notes:
*The percentages are calculated as in the note to Table 8.7.
– = No data.

Preliminary evidence about the special accounting policies of the extractive industries[42] is shown in Table 8.8, which gives data on the topics which had the largest inter-sectoral variation. Clearly, the averages shown in Table 8.7 hide important differences on some topics between extractives, financials and others. As noted earlier, extractive companies comprise most of the Canadian sample. This suggests that the Canadian averages should not be used for cross-country comparison, especially with the continental European countries which have few extractive companies (see Table 8.6). For statistical research, a control variable for the extractive sector should be included.

Other findings

Work has also begun in other research areas which stem from the lists of options and estimations in Nobes (2006). Wehrfritz *et al.* (2012) investigated, using questionnaires, whether German and UK accountants make different choices when faced with IFRS estimations on provisions and contingent assets. However, they discovered more variation within the countries than between them.

André *et al.* (2012) investigated, for 187 European companies, whether comparability of financial reports changed from 2003 (pre-IFRS) to 2005 (first IFRS) to 2010 (mature IFRS). They report increased comparability of practices on transition to IFRS but little change after that. They studied 25 policy topics (referred to as choices, policies or options). These included 13 of the 16 topics used by Kvaal and Nobes (2010). However, many of the others they included are not policy choices in IFRS: some are covert options (which only allow choice at the margin),[43] and some result from different transactions (which might not allow any policy choice).[44] It is not clear how these choices affect their findings or the interpretation of them.

Kvaal and Nobes (2013) studied an issue which does not easily fit into the categories of overt options, covert options, or the others mentioned above. They examined the quality of IFRS disclosures related to taxation for five countries in 2008/9. IAS 12 is not detailed about how the disclosures should be achieved. The research found significantly different practices across countries that cannot be explained by sectoral differences.

6 Summary and conclusions

Jurisdictions

Many academic and other writings refer to widespread adoption of IFRS. This chapter points out a number of caveats: (i) several major capital markets do not require or do not allow any

186

version of IFRS for any regulated reporting; (ii) the requirement or permission to use IFRS is restricted in most jurisdictions to certain types of reporters (e.g. listed companies) or types of reporting (e.g. consolidated statements) or both; (iii) most adoptions do not require the direct application of IFRS as issued by the IASB; and (iv) in several countries, companies and auditors do not refer to compliance with IASB-IFRS even when it is being achieved. After examining the regulatory environment in the jurisdictions which harbour the world's largest 16 stock markets, I conclude that none of them requires IASB-IFRS for all types of regulated reporting and that most of them do not even *allow* (let alone require) even some local version of IFRS for unconsolidated reporting. This is not necessarily a criticism of the IASB or of the jurisdictions, although the EU's approach seems cumbersome, and the general lack of reference to IASB-IFRS by EU listed companies and their auditors misses a major objective of international harmonisation. The common restriction of IFRS to the consolidated statements of listed companies is also not necessarily a matter for criticism; it is those statements for which IFRS was primarily intended. However, the caveats do imply a criticism of some claims about IFRS adoption.

The author's own assessment of the spread of IFRS follows. Key words are in italics.

i   The *majority* of *listed* companies in about *90* countries are *either required to comply* with *IASB-IFRS* for their *consolidated* statements, or *choose* to do so.

ii In many of the above countries (e.g. the 27 countries of the EU), IASB-IFRS is *not required* for the above purpose, although most companies probably choose to comply with IASB-IFRS, with the clearest *exception* being a number of EU banks. Most EU companies (and their auditors) *do not state compliance with IASB-IFRS*.

iii In some of the countries in (i) above (e.g. Australia), it is not IASB-IFRS that is *required*, but a version of it that is *intended to ensure compliance* with it.

iv In some of the countries in (i) above (e.g. Canada), there is a requirement to follow the content of IASB-IFRS (or a translation of it), except that *several important companies are exempted*.

v   In some further countries, IASB-IFRS is *allowed* for the *consolidated* statements of *listed* companies. In some of these countries (e.g. Switzerland), *many companies comply with IASB-IFRS*, but in others (e.g. Japan) *few companies comply*.

vi In some further countries (e.g. China and Venezuela), considerable convergence with IASB-IFRS has been achieved, but companies do not state compliance and are *probably not achieving it*.

vii In a majority of the countries in (i) above, IASB-IFRS (or something intended to ensure compliance with it) is *not required* for any reporting by unlisted companies.

Readers are encouraged to note the distinction between *de jure* matters (requirements or permissions) and *de facto* matters (company practice). I have noted that some researchers have not been clear about their regulatory setting, and others have made claims about IFRS adoption which are implausible once the regulatory setting is considered.

Country-related differences in IFRS practices

When examining a typical IFRS audit report for an EU company, eight 'national' aspects of regulation have been identified, which include language and enforcement issues. Similar issues apply more widely across the world, and they can lead to international differences in IFRS practice. In addition, five aspects of the content of IFRS can lead to international differences in the application of IFRS. Of these, this chapter updates and expands the earlier discussion of covert options and focuses in detail on overt options. The gradual change in the list of overt options since 2001 is charted as a guide for researchers. The empirical literature relating to IFRS practices from 2005 is also synthesised.

There is overwhelming evidence that the most powerful single explanatory variable for a company's IFRS policy choices is its pre-IFRS policies. Since the latter were mostly determined by the accounting requirements or other institutional features of a country, then country can be used as a proxy variable for pre-IFRS practices. The findings also mean that there are clear national profiles of IFRS practices and that countries can be classified into the same groups as suggested decades earlier for pre-IFRS national practices. Recent data on Canadian IFRS practices, reported in this chapter, confirm the persistence of pre-IFRS national practices, even when the IASB has already issued standards which will soon outlaw them. Country is also a major explanation for the amount of IFRS policy *change* over time.

However, sector is also relevant in explaining IFRS policy choice. It has been clear to all researchers that financial companies are likely to have sector-specific policies on certain topics. In IFRS, there are no sector-specific differences in the rules for financial companies (or for any others), but the pre-IFRS sector-specific national rules clearly influence IFRS practice. This chapter has summarised and (relating to Canada) added to the evidence that extractive companies also have idiosyncratic policies. One conclusion is that researchers should separately record data on these companies.

Most of the empirical papers on IFRS policy choices relate to very large listed companies. Within that context, size as a variable has been included, but it has not revealed much explanatory power. However, when the largest listed companies are compared to the smallest, highly significant differences are found within any country. This finding related to size does not reduce the importance of country. By contrast, the IFRS practices of the smaller listed companies are even closer to pre-IFRS national practices and are more homogeneous within a country, and therefore show even clearer national profiles. A conclusion is that researchers who study the largest companies need to insert caveats about the generalisability of their findings, though not about the importance of country.

One reason for being interested in policy differences is the effect that they might have on the comparability of financial statements. There is some evidence that large and multi-listed companies gradually move towards more uniform practices internationally and within their sector. Many of the policy differences associated with country or size seem to be unrelated to differences in underlying transactions. For example, the researchers have been unable to identify such reasons for differences in policies with respect to the treatment of actuarial losses or of joint ventures. Even where sector could perhaps affect the underlying transactions (e.g. in inventory flows), the policy differences on most topics are still better explained by a country variable (e.g. caused by the effect of tax on the unconsolidated components of the consolidated statements). A conclusion is that the standard-setters should continue the process of removing options in standards. This is not a call for a type of uniformity which masks economic differences. If there are different types of transactions, a standard can set out different practices for the different economic circumstances.

Being fair to IFRS

As explained earlier, the discussion about the diverse methods of adoption of IFRS by jurisdictions should not generally be taken as criticism of those jurisdictions or of the IASB. Turning to other aspects of the scope for country-based differences in IFRS practices, should these remarks be taken as critical of the IASB? On enforcement, of course, the IASB has no powers. If any other GAAP (e.g. US GAAP) had been adopted globally, similar enforcement problems would follow, unless the content of IFRS is inherently more difficult to enforce (see below). Similarly, if the EU had adopted US GAAP, there would have been a need to produce an official translation in (for example) Bulgarian which, given the much greater volume of US GAAP, would have been even more troublesome.

Would an adoption of US GAAP (instead of IFRS) have lessened the scope for choice and judgement? Section 4 suggests that despite a few counter-examples (e.g. permission to use LIFO), US GAAP generally involves fewer options and less judgement. Whether this would have implied greater comparability (or better accounting) is a different question. However, the research surveyed above suggests that the choice of IFRS options is largely driven by country and is little affected by sector or by differing economic circumstances.

Nothing in this chapter should be read as implying that the IASB and its predecessor have not succeeded in harmonising accounting, especially in the field that really matters: the consolidated statements of listed companies. Harmonisation is a process, not a state. Although many differences (from IFRS and within IFRS) remain, it is quite clear that the practices of German and UK companies (for example) are now much more similar than they were before German companies began to adopt international standards. Even in countries which have not adopted IFRS (e.g. Japan and the USA), the differences from IFRS have been greatly reduced. There is also a great deal of evidence about the positive economic effects of IFRS. This is not directly the topic of this chapter but is summarised in Brüggemann et al. (2013) and discussed in other chapters of this book.

7 Further research

The final section of Nobes (2006) presented a research agenda in the form of hypotheses related to the eight types of scope for international differences in IFRS practice, generally using Germany and the UK as example countries. This is shown here as Table 8.9. Some specific suggestions for carrying out such research follow.

Of these hypotheses, H_1 could be checked for banks to see if the EU 'carve out' is an important issue in practice. H_2 could be checked to see, for example, if the error in the German translation of IAS 19 (referred to above) affects discount rates. H_3 could be examined by comparing IFRS-using insurance companies around the world. H_4 is the main topic of the papers discussed in Section 5 above. Especially for less weighty research (e.g. for masters' degree dissertations), there are almost endless opportunities for replication of the study of the overt options for different countries and in later years.

On H_5, there has been little research on the international differences in the use of covert options. These differences might have much greater effects (than those of overt options) on

Table 8.9 Summary of main hypotheses

H_1	International differences in practice exist among IFRS companies due to differences in the version of IFRS being used.
H_2	For some topics, different translations of IFRS lead to different practices.
H_3	For topics on which there are no specific rules in IFRS, German practice is different from UK practice.
H_4	The choice of IFRS options by UK and German groups is different.
H_5	Covert options in IFRS are exercised differently by UK groups than by German groups.
H_6	Estimations under IFRS are biased differently in German than in UK groups.
H_7	Pre-IFRS differences between national practices have a significant effect on IFRS financial statements.
H_8	Compliance with IFRS by German groups is lower than compliance by UK groups.

assets, earnings, and so forth. Researchers have begun to investigate this important issue through case studies, for example, by utilising interviews in major IFRS-using companies of the same industry from several countries. For H_6, a study of estimations would be difficult to pursue using published financial statements, but the same approach as used for H_5 might succeed.

H_7 is difficult to examine: the *direction* of international differences on transitional issues can be worked out, but quantification would rely on knowing what financial statements would have looked like if IFRS had been fully applied retrospectively. This is likely to be impossible for researchers to discover; the difficulties of doing so, even within companies, are what led to the inclusion of the exemptions from retrospection in IFRS 1. On H_8, several studies on compliance with disclosures have been noted above. There is scope for similar studies on a wider group of countries. A study of compliance relating to aspects other than disclosures would be potentially more interesting, but previous studies (e.g. ICAEW, 2007) have discovered little non-compliance; studies of the audited financial statements of listed companies are unlikely to discover substantial amounts of non-compliance by looking at stated accounting policies.

There are several more specific opportunities for research. First, the policy choices of financial companies are under-researched. This is despite their importance: of the companies in Table 8.6, financial companies comprise 40 per cent of the Australian, 48 per cent of the Italian, and 25 per cent of the UK companies. Yet most of the papers examined above exclude financials entirely, and the remaining papers exclude them for most policy topics. Secondly, it is now clear that extractive industries also make sector-specific policy choices. This could be investigated further, perhaps to assess, for example, whether international comparability is the driver. Using quite different approaches, there is plenty of scope for looking into the economic effects of the different policy choices, and some such research has begun.

Appendix
IASB statements referred to in the chapter (titles as at 1 January 2014)

IAS	1	Presentation of financial statements
IAS	2	Inventories
IAS	7	Statement of cash flows
IAS	8	Accounting policies, changes in accounting estimates and errors
IAS	10	Events after the reporting period
IAS	11	Construction contracts
IAS	12	Income taxes
IAS	16	Property, plant and equipment
IAS	17	Leases
IAS	18	Revenue
IAS	19	Employee benefits
IAS	20	Accounting for government grants and disclosure of government assistance
IAS	21	The effects of changes in foreign exchange rates
IAS	23	Borrowing costs
IAS	27	Separate financial statements[a]
IAS	28	Investments in associates and joint ventures[b]
[IAS	31	Interests in joint ventures][c]
IAS	32	Financial instruments: presentation
IAS	36	Impairment of assets
IAS	37	Provisions, contingent liabilities and contingent assets
IAS	38	Intangible assets
IAS	39	Financial instruments: recognition and measurement
IAS	40	Investment property
IAS	41	Agriculture
IFRS	1	First-time adoption of International Financial Reporting Standards
IFRS	2	Share-based payment
IFRS	3	Business combinations
IFRS	4	Insurance contracts
IFRS	5	Non-current assets held for sale and discontinued operations
IFRS	6	Exploration for and evaluation of mineral resources
IFRS	7	Financial instruments: disclosures
IFRS	8	Operating segments
IFRS	9	Financial instruments
IFRS	10	Consolidated financial statements
IFRS	11	Joint arrangements
IFRS	12	Disclosures of interests in other entities
IFRS	13	Fair value measurement

Notes:
[a]Formerly, 'Consolidated and separate financial statements'.
[b]Formerly, 'Investments in associates'.
[c]Standard not applicable from 2013.
Source: Nobes (1983).

Christopher Nobes

Notes

1 This chapter is an updated and expanded version of 'The continued survival of international differences under IFRS', which was published in *Accounting and Business Research*, 43(2), 2013.

2 These are easy to track and are generally announced by the IASB well in advance, whereas changes in national regulations are less easy to track. Sometimes announcements of IFRS adoption do not eventuate.

3 That is, adoption after the publication of a standard but before its date of compulsory application.

4 Except to the extent that it is compatible with Australian IFRS, which IFRSs 12 and 13 might be.

5 Basically, those that are unlisted and do not hold assets in a fiduciary capacity (e.g. a bank).

6 A list of unendorsed standards like those for Australia mentioned in the previous paragraphs applied, for example, for 31 December 2011 or 30 June 2012 year ends.

7 To take the two points at the start of the paragraph, compliance could have been achieved for 31 December 2011 year ends by (i) not taking advantage of EU-IFRS's permission for more hedge accounting, and (ii) not early adopting IFRSs 9 to 13, which had not been endorsed but also had not yet reached their 'effective dates'.

8 That is, few companies are taking the permission to do an extra type of hedge accounting that the EU version of IAS 39 allows (ICAEW, 2007), and companies are not early adopting unendorsed standards.

9 By market capitalisation on 31 January 2012, as found in the monthly statistics of the World Federation of Stock Exchanges.

10 That is, for 31 December 2011 year ends or nearest after.

11 Carried out in May 2013, therefore not including one company with a 31 May year end.

12 Francis *et al.* (2008) sometimes refer to 'use' of IFRS (e.g. p. 334 and in the description of the variable on p. 342), but otherwise they refer almost exclusively to 'adoption' (e.g. in the title, the abstract and the conclusions).

13 The *Bilanzrechtsmodernisierungsgesetz* of 2009 made various adjustments compatible with IFRS (Gee *et al.*, 2010).

14 Financial Reporting Standards (FRSs) 12, 20 to 26 and 29 are copies of IASB standards.

15 Very similar points are made, *mutatis mutandis*, in other EU countries. For example, UK auditors refer to 'International Standards on Auditing (UK and Ireland)', to EU-IFRS and to the requirements of the British Companies Act.

16 These words are taken from the English-language version of the audit report by PricewaterhouseCoopers AG (a German company) on the annual report for 2012 of Bayer AG (a German company), pp. 283–284.

17 In the original German, the audit report uses the same words as the German translation of IAS 1. See further discussion below.

18 The Fourth Directive and the law have 'ein den tatsächlichen Verhältnissen entsprechendes Bild'. IAS 1 has 'eine den tatsächlichen Verhältnissen entsprechende Darstellung'.

19 This term means here the location of a company's registration, head office and lead auditor.

20 For example, much goodwill of UK companies is held at zero under IFRS because it was generally held at zero under UK GAAP if purchased before IFRS 10 came into force in 1998. With analogous facts, a French company would generally show goodwill under IFRS at the amount of amortised cost on 1 January 2004. This difference will last forever unless the French company's goodwill becomes impaired.

21 The first item of Table 8.2 is not expressed as a choice between two possibilities, but companies have to choose a format for the specified lists of items which are required, by IAS 1, to be presented. A similar point relates to the IAS 19 topic.

22 For example, in terms of Table 8.2, US GAAP does not have the first IAS 1 option, the last of IAS 7, or those of IAS 16, IAS 38, IAS 40 or IFRS 3.

23 For example, because of disagreements with the Financial Accounting Standards Board of the USA on joint standards.

24 For example, Kvaal and Nobes (2010) included two such items: (i) whether a line item for 'operating profit' is included in the income statement, and (ii) how dividends paid are treated in a cash flow statement. Issue (i) overlaps somewhat with items 3 and 4 of Table 8.4, and it requires assessing whether descriptions other than 'operating profit' count. Also, this is not a specifically stated policy choice in IAS 1. For issue (ii), dividends received are generally not visible in cash flow statements, so assumptions have to be made.

25 Except for software costs.

26 The first IAS 1 point in Table 8.5, and those relating to IASs 17, 38, 40 and 41 and IFRS 10 where US GAAP does not allow fair value or has clearer 'rules'.

27 For example, IAS 16 (paras. 60 and 62) and IAS 8 (para. 32 (d)). It could be argued that this topic should be seen as an estimation rather than as a covert option. However, since the estimation determines a method, not just a number, I include it as a covert option.

28 Those registered abroad or with the prime head office abroad.

29 The 14 topics of Table 8.4 plus the two referred to in footnote 24.

30 Table 8.6 relates to 2008/9 data, as used in Nobes 2011, discussed below. A few companies had ceased to report since 2005/6 (e.g. because of mergers).

31 IAS 8 (paras. 14, 19, 29) allows policy change, but only under certain conditions and if accompanied by disclosures.

32 The amended *Handelsgesetzbuch* which came into force in 1987 as a result of the *Bilanzrichtliniengesetz* of 1985 introduced the option of the by-function format as part of EU harmonisation.

33 Nobes and Perramon (2013) included the 14 topics of Table 8.4, plus the topic of whether a company displays a line for operating profit or earnings before interest and tax.

34 The first four classifiers used informal data. The last three used surveys by Price Waterhouse (1973 and 1976). These had begun as a list of detailed differences between US and UK accounting, so they were good at picking up Anglo-American differences, but not others.

35 The measures in Nobes (1983) were not based directly on a formal sample of company practices but on rules and on general observations of practices in the countries concerned.

36 Belgium, Ireland and New Zealand have much smaller stock markets than the eight other countries and were excluded.

37 These are the two topics of footnote 24, and topic 2 of Tables 8.4 and 8.7.

38 There were three rate-regulated companies, four non-bank companies with non-December year ends, and eight companies using US GAAP.

39 One of the 'basic' companies was in agriculture.

40 For the two issues, these can be found, respectively, in the *Handbook of the Canadian Institute of Chartered Accountants:* HB 1521 and 3055.

41 IFRS 11 was issued in May 2011.

42 For this purpose, sectors 0 and 1 have been combined. Sector 1 contains certain chemical companies which researchers might prefer to add to 'Industrials'. However, for Canada this was only one company.

43 Depreciation methods, criteria for capitalisation of development costs, currency translation method, and identification of whether the company has reportable segments.

44 Classification of leases and, to some extent, the use of hedge accounting (which rests, *inter alia*, on whether the company has purchased a hedging instrument).

References

AAA, 1977. *Accounting Review, Supplement to Vol. 52:* 65–132. Sarasota, FL: American Accounting Association.

AICPA, 2013. *IFRS Resources: IFRS FAQs.* At www.ifrs.com/ifrs_faqs.html#q3, accessed 1 January 2013.

Alexander, D. and Archer, S., 2000. On the myth of Anglo-Saxon financial accounting. *International Journal of Accounting*, 35(4), 539–557.

André, P., Dionysiou, D. and Tsalavoutas, I., 2012. Mandatory adoption of IFRS by EU listed firms and comparability: determinants and analysts' forecasts. Paper presented at the European Accounting Association Conference, Ljubljana.

Ashbaugh, H., 2001. Non-US firms' accounting standard choices. *Journal of Accounting and Public Policy*, 20(2), 129–153.

Ashbaugh, H. and Pincus, M., 2001. Domestic accounting standards, international accounting standards, and the predictability of earnings. *Journal of Accounting Research*, 39(3), 417–434.

Ball, R., 2006. International Financial Reporting Standards (IFRS): pros and cons for investors. *Accounting and Business Research, International Accounting Policy Forum*, 36(1), 5–27.

Ball, R., Kothari, S.P. and Robin, A., 2000. The effect of international institutional factors on properties of accounting earnings. *Journal of Accounting and Economics*, 29(1), 1–51.

Barth, M., Landsman, W. and Lang, M., 2008. International accounting standards and accounting quality. *Journal of Accounting Research*, 46(3), 467–498.

Baskerville, R. and Evans, L., 2011. *The Darkening Glass: Issues for Translation of IFRS*. Edinburgh: The Institute of Chartered Accountants of Scotland.

BDO, 2012. *How IFRS can add value to your information.* At www.bdo.ca/library/publications/aboriginal/articles/how_IFRS_can_add_value.cfm, accessed 5 May 2013.

Benzacar, K., 2008. IFRS: the next accounting revolution. *CMA Management*, June/July, 26–30.

Berger, A., 2010. The development and status of enforcement in the European Union. *Accounting in Europe*, 7(1), 15–35.

Bond, D., Bugeja, M. and Czernkowski, R., 2012. Did Australian firms choose to switch to reporting operating cash flows using the indirect method? *Australian Accounting Review*, 22(1), 18–24.

Brown, P. and Tarca, A., 2005. A commentary on issues relating to the enforcement of international financial reporting standards in the EU. *European Accounting Review*, 14(1), 181–212.

Brüggemann, U., Hitz, J.-M. and Sellhorn, T., 2013. Intended and unintended consequences of mandatory IFRS adoption: a review of extant evidence and suggestions for future research. *European Accounting Review*, 22(1), 1–37.

Burlaud, A. and Colasse, B., 2011. International accounting standardisation: is politics back? *Accounting in Europe*, 8(1), 23–47.

Cairns, D., 1997. The future shape of harmonization: a reply. *European Accounting Review*, 6(2), 305–348.

Cairns, D., Massoudi, D., Taplin, R. and Tarca, A., 2011. IFRS fair value measurement and accounting policy choice in the United Kingdom and Australia. *British Accounting Review*, 43(1), 1–21.

Camfferman, K. and Zeff, S.A., 2006. *Financial Reporting and Global Capital Markets*. Oxford: Oxford University Press.

Christensen, H.B., Lee, E. and Walker, M., 2007. Cross-sectional variation in the economic consequences of international accounting harmonization: the case of mandatory IFRS adoption in the UK. *International Journal of Accounting*, 42(4), 341–379.

Cole, V., Branson, J. and Breesch, D., 2011. Determinants influencing the *de facto* comparability of European IFRS financial statements. *Accountancy and Bedrijfskunde*, 32(1), 21–40.

Cuijpers, R. and Buijink, W., 2005. Voluntary adoption of non-local GAAP in the European Union: a study of determinants and consequences. *European Accounting Review*, 14(3), 487–524.

d'Arcy, A., 2001. Accounting classification and the international harmonisation debate: an empirical investigation. *Accounting, Organizations and Society*, 26(4), 327–349.

da Costa, R.C., Bourgeois, J.C. and Lawson, W.M., 1978. A classification of international financial accounting practices. *International Journal of Accounting*, 13(2), 73–85.

Dahlgren, J. and Nilsson, S.-A., 2012. Can translations achieve comparability? The case of translating IFRSs into Swedish. *Accounting in Europe*, 9(1), 39–59.

Danjou, P. and Walton, P., 2012. The legitimacy of the IASB. *Accounting in Europe*, 9(1), 1–15.

Doupnik, T.S. and Salter, S.B., 1993. An empirical test of a judgemental international classification of financial reporting practices. *Journal of International Business Studies*, 24(1), 41–60.

European Commission, 2008. *Evaluation of the Application of IFRS in the 2006 Financial Statements of EU Companies.* At http://ec.europa.eu/internal_market/accounting/docs/studies/2009-report_en.pdf, accessed 5 May 2013.

Evans, L., 2004. Language translation and the problem of international communication. *Accounting, Auditing and Accountability Journal*, 17(2), 210–248.

Fasshauer, J.D., Glaum, M. and Street, D.L., 2008. *Adoption of IAS 19 by Europe's Premier Listed Companies*, ACCA Research Report No. 100. London: Association of Chartered Certified Accountants.

Francis, J.R., Khurana, I.K., Martin, X. and Pereira, R., 2008. The role of firm-specific incentives and country factors in explaining voluntary IAS adoptions: evidence from private firms. *European Accounting Review*, 17(2), 331–360.

Frank, W.G., 1979. An empirical analysis of international accounting principles. *Journal of Accounting Research*, 17(2), 593–605.

Gassen, J. and Sellhorn, T., 2006. Applying IFRS in Germany: determinants and consequences. *Betriebswirtschaftliche Forschung und Praxis*, 58(4), 365–386.

Gee, M., Haller, A. and Nobes, C., 2010. The influence of tax on IFRS consolidated statements: the convergence of Germany and the UK. *Accounting in Europe*, 7(1), 97–122.

Glaum, M. and Street, D.L., 2003. Compliance with the disclosure requirements of Germany's new market: IAS versus US GAAP. *Journal of International Financial Management and Accounting*, 14(1), 64–100.

Glaum, M., Schmidt, P., Street, D. and Vogel, S., 2013. Compliance with IFRS 3- and IAS 36-related required disclosures across 17 European countries: company- and country-level determinants. *Accounting and Business Research*, 43(3), 163–204.

Goncharov, I., Werner, J.R. and Zimmerman, J., 2009. Legislative demands and economic realities: company and group accounts compared. *International Journal of Accounting*, 44(4), 334–362.

Haller, A. and Wehrfritz, M., 2013. The impact of national GAAP and accounting traditions on IFRS policy selection: evidence from Germany and the UK. *Journal of International Accounting, Auditing and Taxation*, 22(1), 39–56.

Hatfield, H.R., 1911. Published 1966, Some variations in accounting practice in England, France, Germany and the United States. *Journal of Accounting Research*, 4(2), 169–182.

Hitz, J.-M., Ernstberger, J. and Stich, M., 2012. Enforcement of accounting standards in Europe: capital-market-based evidence for the two-tier mechanism in Germany. *European Accounting Review*, 21(2), 253–281.

Hoogendoorn, M., 2006. International accounting regulation and IFRS implementation in Europe and beyond: experiences with first-time adoption in Europe. *Accounting in Europe*, 3, 23–26.

IASB, 2010. *Conceptual Framework for Financial Reporting*. London: International Accounting Standards Board.

———, 2012. *IFRSs as the Global Standards: Setting a Strategy for the Foundation's Second Decade*. London: International Accounting Standards Board.

IASC, 1989. *Framework for the Preparation and Presentation of Financial Statements*. London: International Accounting Standards Committee.

ICAEW, 2007. *EU Implementation of IFRS and the Fair Value Directive*. London: Institute of Chartered Accountants in England and Wales.

Interfacing, 2012. *International Financial Reporting Standards (IFRS)*. At www.interfacing.com/ComplianceSOX-ISO-BASEL-Six-Sigma-Risk/IFRS-International-Financial-Reporting-Standards, accessed 16 May 2012.

Jaafar, A. and McLeay, S., 2007. Country effects and sector effects on the harmonization of accounting policy choice. *Abacus*, 43(2), 156–189.

Jermakowicz, E.K., 2004. Effects of adoption of International Financial Reporting Standards in Belgium: the evidence from BEL-20 companies. *Accounting in Europe*, 1, 51–70.

KPMG and von Keitz, I., 2006. *The Application of IFRS: Choices in Practice*. London: KPMG.

Krylova, T., 2003. Book review of Enthoven *et al.* (2001), in *International Journal of Accounting*, 38(3), 389–391.

Kvaal, E. and Nobes, C.W., 2010. International differences in IFRS policy choice. *Accounting and Business Research*, 40(2), 173–187.

———, 2012. IFRS policy changes and the persistence of national patterns of IFRS practice. *European Accounting Review*, 21(2), 343–371.

———, 2013. International variations in tax disclosures under IFRS. *Accounting in Europe*, 10(2), 241–273.

Leuz, C., 2003. IAS versus U.S. GAAP: information asymmetry-based evidence from Germany's new market. *Journal of Accounting Research*, 41(3), 445–472.

———, 2010. Different approaches to corporate reporting regulation: how jurisdictions differ and why. *Accounting and Business Research*, 40(3), 229–256.

Meyer, H., 2011. Audit and enforcement of IFRS. Paper presented at the European Financial Reporting Conference, Bamberg, September.

Morais, A.I., 2008. Actuarial gains and losses: the choice of the accounting method. *Accounting in Europe*, 5(1/2), 127–139.

Mueller, G.G., 1967. *International Accounting, Part I*. New York: Macmillan.

Nair, R.D. and Frank, W.G., 1980. The impact of disclosure and measurement practices on international accounting classifications. *Accounting Review*, 55(3), 426–450.

Nobes, C.W., 1983. A judgmental international classification of financial reporting practices. *Journal of Business Finance and Accounting*, 10(1), 1–19.

———, 1992. Classification of accounting systems using competencies as a discriminating variable: a comment. *Journal of Business Finance and Accounting*, 19(1), 153–155.

———, 1993. The true and fair view requirement: impact on and of the Fourth Directive. *Accounting and Business Research*, 24(Winter), 35–48.

———, 1998. The future shape of harmonization: some responses. *European Accounting Review*, 7(2), 323–333.

———, 2003. On the myth of 'Anglo-Saxon' accounting: a comment. *International Journal of Accounting*, 38(1), 95–104.

———, 2004. On accounting classification and the international harmonisation debate. *Accounting, Organizations and Society*, 29(2), 189–200.

———, 2006. The survival of international differences under IFRS: towards a research agenda. *Accounting and Business Research*, 36(3), 233–245.

_____, 2009. The importance of being fair: an analysis of IFRS regulation and practice. *Accounting and Business Research*, 39(4), 415–427.

_____, 2011. IFRS practices and the persistence of accounting system classification. *Abacus*, 47(3), 267–283.

Nobes, C.W. and Perramon, J., 2013. Firm size and national profiles of IFRS policy choice. *Australian Accounting Review*, 23(3), 208–215.

Nobes, C.W. and Zeff, S.A., 2008. Auditor affirmations of compliance with IFRS around the world: an exploratory study. *Accounting Perspectives*, 7(4), 279–292.

Pacter, P., 2012. Stop and smell the roses. *Australian Accounting Review*, 22(3), 246–247.

Price Waterhouse, 1973. *Accounting Principles and Reporting Practices: A Survey in 36 Countries*. New York: Price Waterhouse.

_____, 1976. *A Survey in 46 Countries: Accounting Principles and Reporting Practices*. London: Institute of Chartered Accountants in England and Wales.

SEC, 2011. *Work Plan for the Consideration of Incorporating International Financial Reporting Standards into the Financial Reporting System for U.S. Issuers*. Washington, DC: Securities and Exchange Commission.

Seidler, L.J., 1967. International accounting: the ultimate theory course. *Accounting Review*, 42(4), 775–781.

Shoenthal, E., 1989. Classification of accounting systems using competencies as a discriminatory variable: a Great Britain–United States study. *Journal of Business Finance and Accounting*, 16(4), 549–563.

Stadler, C. and Nobes, C.W. 2014. The influence of country, industry and topic factors on IFRS policy choice. *Abacus*, 50(4), 386–421.

Standish, P., 2003. Evaluating national capacity for direct participation in international accounting harmonization: France as a test case. *Abacus*, 39(2), 186–210.

Street, D.L. and Bryant, S.M., 2000. Disclosure level and compliance with IASs. A comparison of companies with and without US listings and filings. *International Journal of Accounting*, 35(3), 305–329.

Street, D.L. and Gray, S.J., 2001. *Observance of International Accounting Standards: Factors Explaining Noncompliance*. London: Association of Chartered Certified Accountants.

Verriest, A., Gaeremynck, A. and Thornton, D., 2012. The impact of corporate governance on IFRS adoption choices. *European Accounting Review*, 22(1), 39–77.

Wehrfritz, M., Haller, A. and Walton, P., 2012. National influences on the application of IFRS: interpretations and accounting estimates by German and British accountants. Working paper of the University of Regensberg.

Whittington, G., 2005. The adoption of international accounting standards in the European Union. *European Accounting Review*, 14(1), 127–153.

Wysocki, P., 2011. New institutional accounting and IFRS. *Accounting and Business Research*, 41(3), 309–328.

Zeff, S.A., 2007. Some obstacles to global financial reporting comparability and convergence at a high level of quality. *British Accounting Review*, 39(4), 290–302.

Zeff, S.A. and Nobes, C.W., 2010. Has Australia (or any other jurisdiction) 'adopted' IFRS? *Australian Accounting Review*, 20(2), 178–184.

9

Fair value and the great financial crisis

Amir Amel-Zadeh and Geoff Meeks

1 The debate

Adjustments to valuations in bank balance sheets during the Great Financial Crisis (GFC) have been estimated to be at least $2 trillion for the world (IMF, 2010). The cost of government bank rescues and aid to the financial sector in response to these adjustments transformed the public finances in countries with large financial sectors. In the UK, funding the rescue programme raised the ratio of government debt to GDP from some 40 per cent to around 150 per cent (IFS, 2014), a level not seen since the aftermath of the Second World War. The fiscal policies adopted in response to these worsening public finances have produced results reminiscent of the Great Depression which preceded World War 2: it has been estimated that for the world economy, the long-run total output loss will be at least $60 trillion (Haldane, 2010). Much of the cost has been borne by innocent and vulnerable groups: youth unemployment has risen to exceed 20 per cent in the UK and 50 per cent in Spain (Eurostat, 2014).

In the search for culprits for this highly damaging institutional failure, bankers, journalists and politicians have been quick to point the finger at the accounting profession – for insisting on inappropriate (fair value) measures of financial assets which, it is held, have grossly distorted financial decision-making. The American Bankers Association (2008) describes the consequences of fair value accounting: '[C]apital is artificially eroded . . . the lending capability of a bank is [massively] reduced . . . the accounting formula is driving economic outcomes . . . and does not reflect economic reality.' A leading journalist, Anatole Kaletsky, wrote in *The Times* (of London): 'Much of the damage in the financial crisis was caused by forcing banks to use mark to market accounting rules' (9 July 2009). Political leaders joined the condemnation. For example, European Commissioner for Internal Market Services Charlie McCreevy announced:

> [T]here is growing concern among Finance Ministers at the perceived slowness of the International Accounting Standards Board in responding to the systemic crisis we have endured . . . [M]any Ministers have complained about what they see as an 'over-academic' approach to standard setting, which many see as 'out of touch' with today's reality.[1]

And the communiqué from the April 2009 G20 summit of world leaders joined the implicit criticism with a call (paragraph 15) on the accounting standard setters to work urgently with supervisors and regulators to improve standards on valuation and provisioning.

The political pressure on accounting standard setters and regulators at the height of the GFC led to investigations of the potential role of fair value accounting in the financial crisis. The investigations ultimately culminated in a series of guidelines and amendments to existing fair value accounting rules. In the European Union, the International Accounting Standards Board (IASB) issued amendments to International Accounting Standard (IAS) 39 *Financial Instruments: Recognition and Measurement* (IASB, 2008a) and International Financial Reporting Standard (IFRS) 7 *Financial Instruments: Disclosures* (IASB, 2008b) that permitted financial institutions to reclassify investments – in some cases retroactively to 30 June 2008 – out of categories requiring fair value measurement into categories measured at amortised cost.

In the US, the Emergency Economic Stabilization Act of 2008 included a provision that required the Securities and Exchange Commission (SEC) to conduct a study of the potential effects of Statement of Financial Accounting Standards (SFAS) No. 157 *Fair Value Measurements* (FASB, 2006) on the financial position of the major financial institutions. The SEC's report (SEC, 2008) endorsed fair value accounting, but it recommended that the Financial Accounting Standards Board (FASB) readdress accounting for financial asset impairment and develop implementation guidelines for SFAS No. 157. Thereupon, the FASB issued several FASB Staff Positions that effectively allowed firms to minimize the impact of fair value losses on income and equity (FASB, 2009).

In this chapter we provide a review of the debate and the academic literature on the role and consequences of fair value accounting in the GFC and its effect on the stability of banks. We discuss the theoretical literature and review the empirical evidence in support of the theoretical arguments. Where appropriate, we refer to available research prior to the GFC and provide additional evidence of our own. This chapter focuses on three particular issues related to the solvency of banks and stability of the financial system – procyclicality, feedback and contagion, and bank failure – and is therefore deliberately selective in its review. For different perspectives and more comprehensive discussions of the role of fair value accounting and financial reporting in the GFC, we refer the reader to excellent discussions in Barth and Landsman (2010), Laux and Leuz (2009, 2010) and Ryan (2008) and to other contributions in this volume.

2 The importance of fair value in banking[2]

The prevailing accounting regime during the GFC followed a so called 'mixed attribute model', which stipulates a different accounting treatment and measurement model for different types of assets. Particularly relevant for the banking industry are the accounting standards for the measurement and disclosure of financial instruments (FASB, 1991, 1993, 2006; IASB, 2003a, 2003b). Both the IASB and the FASB require that financial instruments be classified according to management's intended use of the asset; those classified as held-for-trading (HFT) and available-for-sale (AFS) securities, or assets for which the fair value option (FVO) has been chosen, must be measured at fair value. Of these, only changes in the fair value of trading securities and those securities for which the FVO was exercised are recognized in net income. Fair value changes of AFS securities are instead recorded in other comprehensive income as part of equity. For all other financial assets (e.g., those classified as held-to-maturity (HTM) or loans and receivables (L&R)), fair value only becomes relevant if the value of these assets is deemed other than temporarily impaired, in which case these assets are written down to fair value with the resulting impairment charge booked against income.

Special attention has been devoted to mortgage assets, in particular those related to subprime mortgages, due to their role during the GFC. Mortgage loans are classified as either held for investment or held for sale. Held-for-sale mortgages are accounted for at the lower of cost or market value subject to an impairment test (FASB, 1982). Securitized mortgages, on the other hand, are classified into one of the three financial instruments categories, HFT, AFS or HTM, depending on management intent.

Laux and Leuz (2010) report that more than 90 per cent of commercial bank balance sheets consist of financial instruments; and of these the majority consist of loans, which are not continuously marked to market. Nevertheless, Laux and Leuz (2010) show that, at least for investment banks and large bank holding companies, up to 33 per cent and 12 per cent, respectively, of assets are reported as HFT and that another large fraction of the balance sheet is made up of AFS securities (around 15 per cent).

In Table 9.1 we report summary statistics for the population of bank holding companies that filed FR Y-9C reports with the US Federal Reserve between 1994 and 2010. Panel A shows that on average around 9 per cent of all bank assets are HFT securities, and around 19 per cent are AFS securities, with a large variation across banks. The panel reveals a heavy skewness to the right tail of the distribution for these two categories in particular, suggesting that HFT and AFS securities are more relevant for larger banks. More than 50 per cent of the assets in bank balance sheets are loans. The fraction of HFT assets increases with the size of the bank as reported in Panel B of the table. Banks with more than $100 billion in assets on average report more than 13 per cent of their assets in the HFT category. These figures are also economically significant in absolute terms, with the average large bank holding more than $100 billion in HFT and AFS securities.

Table 9.1 Summary statistics

Panel A: Entire sample

	Mean	(% of assets)	SD	p25	Median	p75
Total assets	5,399	(100)	53,300	202	360	927
Trading securities	462	(9)	9,804	0	0	0
Available-for-sale securities	1,010	(19)	9,328	36	73	180
Loans	2,849	(53)	24,200	122	226	610
Held-to-maturity securities	103	(2)	776	0	3	33

Panel B: Large banks with assets greater than $100 billion

	Mean	(% of assets)	SD	p25	Median	p75
Total assets	389,000	(100)	428,000	141,000	215,000	426,000
Trading securities	51,400	(13)	93,300	1,845	10,300	54,600
Available-for-sale securities	56,000	(14)	66,900	16,400	30,400	64,000
Loans	179,000	(46)	189,000	67,100	112,000	196,000
Held-to-maturity securities	1,571	(0)	5,582	0	30	890

Note:

This table reports summary statistics for the population of bank holding companies that filed FR Y-9C reports with the US Federal Reserve between 1994 and 2010. Panel A shows averages and dispersion of total assets and the different accounting categories for financial instruments for the entire sample. Panel B shows the equivalent figures for large banks with more than $100 billion in assets. All figures in US$ million.

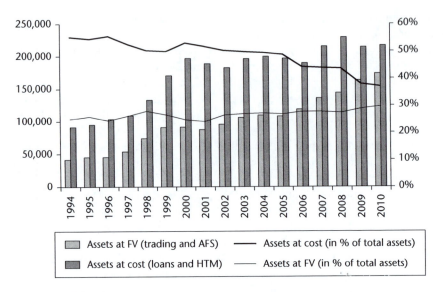

Figure 9.1 Bank holding company assets measured at fair value (FV) and assets measured at cost in absolute terms and as a fraction of total bank assets

Note: FV, fair value; AFS, available-for-sale; HTM, held-to-maturity.

The figures in Table 9.1 are somewhat smaller than those reported in Laux and Leuz (2010), who sampled banks between 2004 and 2006. That is, bank holdings of assets measured at fair value have most likely increased over the years as banks have expanded their trading and market-making operations. Figure 9.1 confirms this trend. The figure shows an increasing trend of securities measured at fair value in absolute and relative terms. For the average bank the fraction of fair value financial assets increased from around 25 per cent to 30 per cent of total assets, while the fraction of financial assets measured at cost decreased from more than 50 per cent to less than 40 per cent.

The trend of increasing trading activity is particularly evident for larger bank holding companies. Figure 9.2 shows that the average trading books for banks with assets of more than $100 billion have increased threefold between 1995 and 2009. In particular, mortgage loans traditionally held in the banking book, and thus at amortized cost, have increasingly been held in the form of mortgage-backed securities (MBS) as part of trading assets. Specifically, the fraction of MBS held for trading increased sixfold, from about 5 per cent of total trading assets in 1995 to about 30 per cent by 2007, just before the GFC. Thus, it is no surprise that the accounting recognition and measurement for these assets has been at the heart of the debate on fair value accounting during the GFC.

3 The role of fair value in the GFC: theoretical underpinnings

The main criticism directed towards fair value accounting by policy makers and the banking industry alleges that the accounting rules have exacerbated the financial crisis and increased systemic risks in the banking sector. Specifically, it is believed that during financial crises, fair value accounting introduces procyclicality and feedback in financial markets and exacerbates contagion among financial institutions. Procyclicality refers to excessive asset sales by financial institutions in response to accounting (mark-to-market) losses during crises such that their leverage

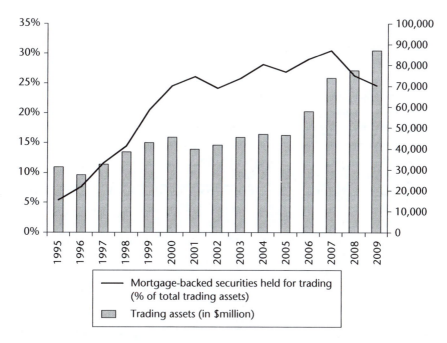

Figure 9.2 Trading assets and mortgage-backed securities held as a proportion of trading assets of large bank holding companies (with total assets greater than US$100 billion)

decreases, denying the wider economy vital credit supply during a downturn. Excessive asset sales also 'feed back into' further market price declines, which in turn require the same financial institutions to recognize further losses. This downward spiral might create contagion if the price pressure through large sales of one bank requires other banks to mark down similar assets to lower market values, in particular if the market does not exhibit sufficient liquidity to absorb these large asset sales. In a financial crisis, these effects might also reinforce each other. Thus, critics argue, fair value accounting amplifies asset price declines and deleveraging in the banking sector and leads to accelerated bank failures, with all their attendant costs for the real economy.

We will discuss the theoretical arguments and empirical evidence on the role of fair value in introducing procyclicality and feedback/contagion and on accelerating bank failure in sections 4 and 5. In this section we clarify the theoretical underpinnings that are prerequisites for the above-mentioned negative effects to prevail. Specifically, the theoretical models cited in support of the criticisms of fair value often rely on four elements – two regulatory and two economic assumptions:

1   Accounting standards: accounting standards stipulate that financial assets be recorded at fair value – preferably marked to current market price.[3]
2   Bank regulation: prudential banking regulators who set lower limits on the ratio of equity to assets – the capital ratio – use accounting fair values in their assessment of the capital ratio.
3   Bank behaviour: banks will seek to maximise their return on equity by holding as many assets as possible yielding a higher return than the interest rate the bank has to pay on its borrowing.
4   Market conditions: markets may be – and in the financial crisis were – illiquid, so that participants were not price-takers, implying that large asset sales would depress prices.

In what follows we discuss each of these four elements in more detail.

Accounting standards

The IASB and the FASB define fair value as the price that would be received to sell an asset or paid to transfer a liability in an orderly transaction between knowledgeable market participants. In measuring financial assets and liabilities at fair value, both accounting bodies outline a three-level hierarchy. In its pure form, fair value relies on exit, (i.e., quoted market) prices in active markets (Level 1). Financial instruments subject to fair value measurement are marked to market if such market prices are observable from orderly transactions. If market prices are not available, then other observable market inputs are used to determine fair value (Level 2). In the absence of any observable data points, management estimates can be used as unobservable inputs into valuation models to derive fair value (Level 3).

Most theoretical models that analyze the effects of fair value accounting in times of market stress typically assume that all financial assets on bank balance sheets are measured at fair value and that all changes in fair value are recorded in net income. However, as discussed in section 2, both the IASB and the FASB require only a subset of assets to be measured at fair value and only part of the changes in the fair value of that subset to be included in net income.

One of the main criticisms during the GFC of fair value accounting relates to the difficulty of measuring fair values of assets in illiquid markets in which only a few transactions are observed – and there are particular concerns over whether asset sales at fire-sale prices in those markets constitute orderly market transactions. Specifically, the financial services industry objected to the use of Level 1 quoted market prices for financial assets, in particular MBS, which traded in increasingly illiquid markets at the height of the crisis. It was argued that financial institutions were required to use quoted market prices that were (a) based on very few distressed transactions and (b) reflected market over-reaction due to the opacity and complexity of many products and transactions. Thus, so the argument goes, observable market prices were far below the fundamental value of these assets. As a consequence, financial institutions had to recognize higher unrealized fair value losses beyond those reflecting reasonable default expectations of these assets, even though, they argued, they did not intend to sell these assets at such low prices and they expected valuations to recover in the future. Losses would have been much lower if institutions had been allowed to use their own internal models in Level 3 fair valuations instead of Level 1 market prices or if they had not been required to apply fair values to these assets at all – for example, by being allowed to transfer assets from the fair value categories HFT and AFS to the categories measured at amortized cost, such as HTM and L&R. It was further argued that even assets in the latter categories were subject to excessive loss recognition as the declines in value were often deemed to be other-than-temporary by the accountants, who then required these assets to be written down to fair value.

Moreover, as banks increasingly recognized losses in their income statements from their trading assets and from other-than-temporary impairments, markets adjusted prices for these assets further downwards, initiating further markdowns on bank balance sheets. These so called feedback effects also spilled over to other assets unrelated to subprime as institutions had to sell liquid assets to raise cash. Thus, it was argued, fair value accounting introduces feedback effects and ultimately leads to contagion and systemic failures in the banking sector.

The political pressure on the accounting regulators on both sides of the Atlantic ultimately led to a series of amendments to the fair value rules. The FASB issued further guidance about when to use unobservable estimates when measuring fair values and modified the rules on other-than-temporary impairment losses (FASB, 2009). The IASB issued amendments allowing the reclassification of financial assets (IASB, 2008a) and also provided measurement and disclosure guidance for financial instruments that trade in inactive markets (IASB, 2008c). The amendments relate to problems in determining fair values when there is no active market and allow management to apply more judgment where the price inputs that are being used otherwise represent distressed sales; the amendments also reduce the effect of fair value losses by allowing reclassifications of HFT and AFS assets into categories measured at cost or by relaxing the requirements on the measurement and recognition of other-than-temporary impairments.

Bank regulation

Bank regulators use financial statement information in their calculation of regulatory capital measures when assessing the solvency of financial institutions. Value changes on the financial statements of banks will therefore also have consequences for the banks' regulatory solvency. However, contrary to the criticism voiced during the GFC and to the widely adopted assumptions in theoretical models, financial reporting information is not adopted at face value for regulatory purposes. Rather, in calculating regulatory capital ratios, so called prudential filters are used to adjust accounting numbers for regulatory purposes. For example, among all unrealized fair value gains and losses, only those of HFT securities and of AFS equity securities are recognized in the calculation of regulatory capital – unrealized gains in the case of the latter, however, are recognized only with substantial discount.[4] Nevertheless, accounting losses that affect regulatory capital have been shown to initiate deleveraging if they lead to breaches of regulatory constraints as banks seek to comply with capital adequacy regulation and shrink their balance sheets to avert failure.

The impact of regulatory constraints can be illustrated with a simple numerical example. In this example, a bank may operate under three different regulatory systems, one crude leverage constraint and two risk-based capital rules. Under the first system, banks have to hold a minimum ratio of equity capital to total assets irrespective of differences in the economic risk of these assets. Risk-based capital rules, on the other hand, weight assets by their risk, where the risk weights can either be static – fixed by type of asset, as is the case for example under Basel I capital adequacy rules (BIS, 1988) – or they can be dynamic – changing with some predefined measure of credit risk (e.g., credit ratings) or market risk (e.g., value-at-risk), as is the case for instance under Basel II (BIS, 2004).

Now consider a bank which holds only loans on its balance sheet, with equity of 10 and a regulatory capital ratio of 10 per cent under each of the three regimes, which is above the minimum regulatory capital ratio of 8 per cent. Assume that the average risk weight of the assets on the bank balance sheet under the risk-based regimes is 50 per cent. Further, assume all loans are marked to market and, due to a deterioration of economic conditions, are worth only 97 cents on the dollar.

First, consider the change in the bank's balance sheet under the regime with the crude leverage constraint. Initially, the bank made loans valued at 100 (10 equity with a capital ratio of 10 per cent). These loans are marked down 3 per cent and are now worth 97. Since equity is reduced by 3, the bank now has a capital ratio of $(10 - 3)/0.97 \star 100 = 7.2\%$. If no capital can be raised, the bank has to reduce its balance sheet by $97 - (7/0.08) = 9.5$ to reach the minimum capital ratio requirement of 8 per cent.

Now consider the case for a bank operating under Basel I. Because the average risk weight of assets is 50 per cent, the bank can now make 200 in loans in order to have a 10 per cent capital ratio to risk-weighted assets. After a 3 per cent write-down, the assets are now worth 194 and equity is reduced by 6. The new risk-weighted capital ratio is now only $(10 - 6)/(0.5 \star 194) = 4.1\%$. Hence, the bank has to reduce its balance sheet by $194 - (4/0.5 \star 0.08) = 94$ to be able to maintain a minimum risk-weighted capital ratio of 8 per cent.

Recall that Basel II differs from Basel I in that the risk weights are not static but depend on (external or internal) credit ratings of the loans. It is likely that due to the deterioration of the economic conditions, default probabilities increase such that the risk weights under dynamic risk-based capital rules such as Basel II increase. Assume for simplicity that average risk weights have increased from 0.5 to 0.6. Although the bank has incurred the same loss of 6 and holds loans worth 194, it now must raise $194 - (4/0.6 \times 0.08) = 110.7$, or almost 20 per cent more than under Basel I.

We can conclude, then, that banks did face binding regulatory constraints, and that by the time of the GFC, the impact of these constraints on the balance sheet adjustments required of banks in response to a change in asset valuations was much greater than it had been under earlier prudential regulation.

Bank behaviour

It is of course a duty of executives – as agents of shareholder principals – to maximise the returns to shareholders, allowing for risk. Their fulfilment of this duty – to a fault – is documented by Admati and Hellwig (2013, ch. 8), who illustrate the preoccupation of senior bankers with targeting the return on equity (ROE), even at the expense of undue risk. They report the 25 per cent target for ROE set (though rarely achieved) by the CEO of Deutsche Bank, Josef Ackermann, as well as the CEO of Barclays recording his rising target for ROE, noting the bank's readiness to increase its risk appetite in pursuit of increased earnings. Admati and Hellwig also report the incentives to pursue the ROE goal embodied in performance-related systems of executive compensation. As an example, achieving Fannie Mae's goal of doubling earnings brought its CEO $52 million of extra pay in the period 1993–2003.

We would argue then that it is reasonable to assume that, other things being equal, banks will exploit opportunities to increase their ROE.

Market conditions

The literature has explored the relationship between prices and liquidity in stressed financial markets. If, for instance, markets become illiquid during financial crises and prices reflect investors' demand for liquidity rather than expected future cash flows (Allen and Carletti, 2008; Plantin et al., 2008), realizable (market) values will fall substantially below values in use because market participants will require a premium to give up liquidity and hold the illiquid asset. As liquidity dries up in markets, creditors demand liquid assets or charge higher premia to hold illiquid assets as collateral, forcing debtors to turn assets into cash with a substantial discount (Gorton and Metrick, 2012). Short-term funding in wholesale markets freezes. This may result in procyclical adjustments of balance sheets with negative feedback effects, as explained in Adrian and Shin (2010). Worse still, if creditors anticipate each other's moves, all will demand cash almost simultaneously as everyone tries to pre-empt the other's move, even though collectively it might prove beneficial to forbear (Epstein and Henderson, 2009).

The role of illiquidity is well illustrated by the two landmark bank failures in the GFC: Northern Rock in the UK, the target of the first UK bank run in 150 years, and Lehman Brothers in the US, whose failure was the iconic event of the GFC.

In normal times, when markets are orderly, banks with positive equity can raise cash via the short-term lending markets. However, in Northern Rock's case, 'on August 9, 2007, the short-term market and interbank lending all but froze' (Shin, 2009, p.102). Northern Rock was unable to renew its short- and medium-term paper; as Shin's analysis shows, by the December

2007 balance sheet, the funding from this wholesale market had shrunk to £11.4 billion from £26.7 billion a year earlier. News leaked of the bank's request to the central bank for substitute funding, and the famous run developed in the following month. The retail deposits market also became inaccessible for Northern Rock, and these liabilities fell by a similar sum to the shrinkage of wholesale sources – by some £14 billion over the year to December 2007. Although Northern Rock was balance sheet solvent and compliant with prudential regulation (Amel-Zadeh and Meeks, 2013), it became cash flow insolvent.

Similar to the Northern Rock case, Lehman Brothers became a victim of the capital and term structure of its balance sheet. Lehman was extremely reliant on short-term funding and high levels of leverage (Zingales, 2008). As opposed to commercial banks, Lehman Brothers as a broker-dealer had no access to retail deposits and only limited access to liquidity from the Federal Reserve Bank, and it relied heavily on the repo market. In the days immediately before the bankruptcy filing, Lehman faced collateral calls on its secured loans and was denied access to wholesale funds. Even though Lehman's assets exceeded its liabilities based on fair values, the collateral value of these mostly illiquid and hard to value assets pledged for liquidity in repo markets required steep haircuts. Due to the uncertainty surrounding the value of the collateral in highly volatile markets, lenders generally demanded higher haircuts for all types of non-cash collateral – in the extreme case of up to 100 per cent for mortgage-related assets (i.e., these assets were not accepted as collateral at all any more) (Gorton and Metrick, 2012). Liquidity previously accessible in abundance froze almost instantaneously as haircuts on assets used as collateral became prohibitive and suitable collateral became scarce (Morris and Shin, 2008; Brunnermeier, 2009). Lehman Brothers, too, was balance sheet solvent and compliant with prudential regulations, but it too failed when it became cash flow insolvent.

4 The consequences in theory

Procyclicality

Banks' leverage will be procyclical

Procyclical bank leverage suggests that when the price of a financial asset held in the bank's balance sheet changes, it will adjust the size of its balance sheet using debt. If the price rises, equity and assets will rise by the same dollar amount, so the ratio of equity to assets increases; and, consistent with returning to the minimum capital ratio allowed by the prudential regulators, the bank can then increase the return on equity by buying more assets, financed by extra borrowing. If the price falls, the bank will sell assets and repay borrowings in order to restore the capital ratio prescribed by the prudential regulators.

Adrian and Shin (2008, 2010) assert that because asset price changes are immediately recorded in income and equity of financial institutions under fair value accounting, the actions financial institutions take to offset the mechanical fall in leverage in boom times, and to offset the increase in leverage in economic downturns, will cause leverage to move procyclically. Adrian and Shin (2010) show that procyclical leverage is a direct consequence of banks targeting a predefined ratio of value-at-risk to economic capital as they adjust their leverage in response to market value changes of their economic capital.

In contrast, Amel-Zadeh et al. (2014) show that bank actions taken in response to fair value gains and losses can only result in procyclical leverage when banks exploit differences in regulatory risk weights of the assets that are being bought and sold. Differences in risk weightings of bank assets lead to differences between leverage as measured by the accountants, on the one hand, and leverage as measured by prudential regulators, on the other. Observed procyclical *accounting* leverage in their analytical description is only possible because banks take actions to remain at a targeted optimal *regulatory* leverage. Amel-Zadeh *et al.* (2014) show that, absent these differences, accounting leverage cannot be procyclical irrespective of the magnitude of fair value gains and losses.

Analytical models in Allen and Carletti (2008) and Plantin *et al.* (2008) also rely on asset sales in response to fair value losses to generate procyclical balance sheet adjustments. In Allen and Carletti (2008), procyclical selling of assets by banks arises due to solvency constraints set by regulators. A key ingredient of their model is market depth of bank assets that are valued at market prices. They argue that if market depth is low (i.e., if there is not enough liquidity to absorb a sudden large supply of the asset), prices will be depressed due to selling from an insurance sector hit by an exogenous shock. In order to remain solvent, banks too will be forced to sell assets, resulting in further downward pressure on prices. Similarly, in Plantin *et al.* (2008), procyclicality results from pre-emptive selling of assets by banks as a strategic response to expected low prices (below fundamental value) in illiquid markets because of selling by other banks. This in turn amplifies asset price movements, causing further rounds of selling.

A similar destabilizing (i.e., amplifying) role to capital requirements in Amel-Zadeh *et al.* (2014) is played by the bank's retained interest in securitizations in Shleifer and Vishny (2010). Their model generates procyclical leverage because banks participate in profitable securitization activities to cater to investor sentiment for securitized assets and does not rely on mark-to-market accounting.

Feedback and contagion

The banking system will suffer contagion, with circular and cumulative processes of contraction triggered by an initial downward change in the price of an asset

The theoretical reasoning in Allen and Carletti (2008) and Plantin *et al.* (2008) not only shows that banks adjust balance sheets procyclically, but also that these procyclical adjustments generate feedback effects and contagion among banks. When an asset price changes and banks enter the illiquid market to buy or sell assets to restore their capital ratio, their purchases or sales will increase or decrease the market price, magnifying the initial price change. With their own assets marked to the new market price, other banks will wish to buy or sell assets to restore their capital ratio. An expansionary or contractionary spiral will ensue. During market downturns in particular, when market liquidity and funding liquidity is low, procyclical balance sheet adjustments can lead to self-reinforcing loss spirals (Brunnermeier and Pedersen, 2009).

Similar to Allen and Carletti (2008), Cifuentes *et al.* (2005) investigate the destabilizing effects of the combination of mark-to-market accounting and externally imposed solvency constraints for banks in markets that are less than perfectly liquid. Their model results suggest that asset price changes that elicit breaches of regulatory solvency controls generate endogenous responses by financial institutions that amplify the initial shock, leading to contagion in the banking sector overall.

While most theoretical models emphasize the impact of illiquidity on market prices that are used in fair valuations of bank assets, destabilizing effects of regulatory solvency regimes based on accounting fair values can also arise due to market fluctuations caused by changes in fundamental risk. Heaton *et al.* (2010) show that bank capital requirements based on market values might affect banks' risk-taking in environments of high volatility, leading to inefficiently high regulatory interventions, bank reorganizations and systemic risk.

Following a different line of reasoning from the studies above, von Peter (2009) shows that within a dynamic macroeconomic model, feedback and contagion among banks due to asset price declines can occur through the lending channel irrespective of fair value accounting. In this model, contagion occurs because banks are indirectly exposed to asset price declines through their borrowers, and not through direct mark-to-market losses.

Insolvency and bank failure

In a contractionary spiral, some banks will see their equity fall not just below the level required to satisfy the prudential regulators, but below zero; they will be balance sheet insolvent and fail

Freixas and Tsomocos (2004) compare the expected bankruptcy cost of fair value accounting and book value accounting in a banking model in which banks allow for intertemporal consumption smoothing by facilitating transfer of resources. Their model generates higher expected bankruptcy costs under fair value accounting due to a higher probability of bankruptcy when unrealized capital gains are reflected in equity values. In a related study, Burkhardt and Strauz (2006) concur that fair value accounting increases the failure risk of banks due to risk shifting. Their analysis suggests that because fair value accounting reduces adverse selection costs between the banks and investors, it allows banks to pursue riskier investment opportunities, thereby increasing the probability of default.

Amel-Zadeh and Meeks (2013) discuss the effects of fair value on the potential and actual failure of banks under four different failure criteria covering economics, regulation and bankruptcy law. Their theoretical analysis reveals that fair value accounting becomes relevant only in two of the failure conditions, neither of which have been the prevailing conditions in two of the prominent bank failures during the GFC. The authors conclude that at least the two most notorious bank failures of the crisis, Northern Rock and Lehman Brothers, cannot be attributed to fair value accounting.

5 The empirical evidence

As a matter of logic, the theoretical models show how the damaging downward spirals which bankers, journalists and politicians have attributed to accounting rules on fair value could have occurred. However, whether fair value actually played this leading role in the crisis is an empirical matter. We therefore review in turn the available evidence on the regulatory rules, the economic assumptions, and the claimed results for the banking system.

Procyclical leverage

Adrian and Shin (2010) provide evidence of a positive relationship between quarterly leverage growth and quarterly asset growth for a small sample of investment banks and attribute this procyclicality to banks' leverage adjustments in response to fair value gains and losses. Figure 9.3 replicates Adrian and Shin's (2010) analysis and plots quarterly asset growth over leverage growth for the sample periods 1980–1994 and 1995–2008 for a sample of commercial banks, savings institutions and broker-dealers drawn from Compustat. Consistent with Adrian and Shin (2010), the figure shows signs of procyclical leverage, in particular for broker-dealers as indicated by the strong positive relationship between changes in total assets and changes in leverage. The graphs for commercial banks and savings institutions show a somewhat similar

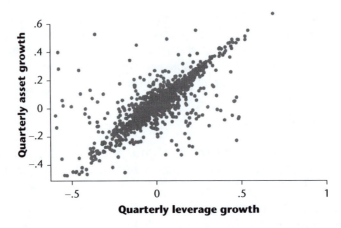

Figure 9.3a   The relationship of asset growth and leverage growth for broker-dealers, 1980–1994

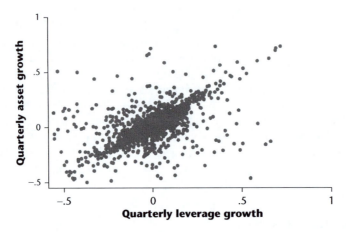

Figure 9.3b   The relationship of asset growth and leverage growth for broker-dealers, 1995–2008

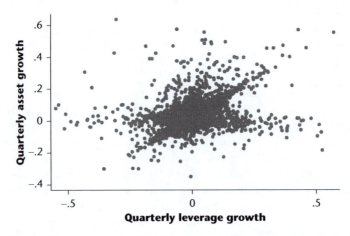

Figure 9.3c   The relationship of asset growth and leverage growth for commercial banks, 1980–1994

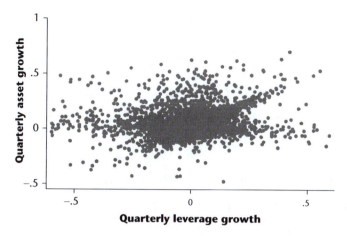

Figure 9.3d The relationship of asset growth and leverage growth for commercial banks, 1995–2008

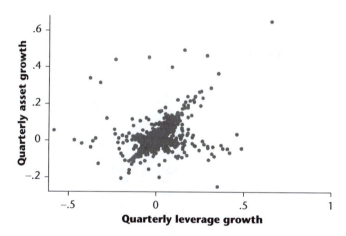

Figure 9.3e The relationship of asset growth and leverage growth for savings institutions, 1980–1994

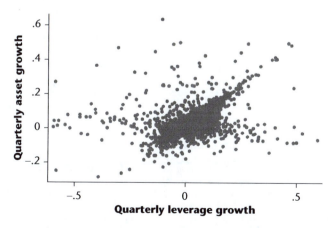

Figure 9.3f The relationship of asset growth and leverage growth for savings institutions, 1995–2008

pattern, albeit not as pronounced. However, contrary to Adrian and Shin's (2010) supposition that this phenomenon is the main behavioural feature of banks under a fair value accounting regime, there is no indication of differences in this pattern in the period before 1995, under predominantly historical cost accounting, and after, when fair value accounting was introduced.[5]

To investigate this further, we regress quarterly leverage growth on asset growth and include an indicator variable for the change in the accounting regime and its interaction with asset growth. We estimate the following model in a pooled regression over the entire sample period 1980–2008:

$$\Delta LEV_{it} = \delta_1 + \delta_2 \Delta TA_{it} + \delta_3 FVA_t + \delta_4 \Delta TA_{it} * FVA_t + \gamma_i + \varphi_t + \varepsilon_{it} ,$$

where ΔLEV is the growth in quarterly leverage ratio; ΔTA is the quarter-on-quarter growth in total assets; and FVA is a dummy variable representing the accounting regime, which is equal to 1 for the fiscal years after 1994 when fair value accounting became predominant for financial institutions in the US and zero otherwise. The regression includes time and firm fixed effects, and standard errors are clustered by firm. If fair value accounting introduced procyclical leverage, we would expect the regression coefficient on the interaction term to be positive and significant.

The regression results are summarized in Table 9.2. The regression is also run for the different types of banks separately. Although we confirm a positive association between changes in total assets and changes in leverage, the evidence does not suggest that leverage became more procyclical with the introduction of fair value accounting; rather, the empirical evidence points in the opposite direction. Almost all coefficients on the interaction term are significantly negative. For example, for the entire sample, the coefficient on ΔTA is positive and statistically

Table 9.2 Regression results (dependent variable: quarterly leverage growth)

	All	Commercial banks	Savings institutions	Broker-dealers
ΔTA	0.652	0.507	0.555	0.827
	(20.25)***	(15.16)***	(6.61)***	(18.29)***
FVA	0.005	−0.002	0.030	0.039
	(1.41)	(−0.81)	(0.78)	(1.23)
ΔTA*FVA	−0.197	−0.155	0.018	−0.210
	(−5.45)***	(−3.75)***	(0.20)	(−3.14)***
Fixed effects				
Year	yes	yes	yes	yes
Firm	yes	yes	yes	yes
Firm clusters	1801	1126	524	151
Observations	42621	29962	9133	3526
Adj. R-squared	0.243	0.157	0.223	0.481

Note:
This table presents coefficients and t-statistics of pooled regressions of quarterly growth in leverage (measured as the ratio of total assets to equity) on quarterly growth in total assets (*ΔTA*), a dummy variable (*FVA*) for the prevailing accounting regime which is equal to 1 for a fair value accounting regime (in the years after 1994) and 0 otherwise, and their interaction. The regression is pooled over the sample period 1980–2008 and run over the entire sample and for different types of financial institutions separately. Robust standard errors clustered at the firm level were used to calculate *t*-statistics (in parentheses). ***, **, * denote statistical significance at the 0.01, 0.05, and 0.1 levels, respectively.

significant at 0.652 (t-stat = 20.25), and the interaction effect $\Delta TA \ast FVA$ is negative and statistically significant at −0.197 (t-stat = −5.45). The results suggest that the marginal effect of asset growth was smaller in the years with fair value accounting compared to before, indicating that procyclical leverage in financial institutions is not encouraged by a fair value accounting regime but rather is reduced. The results also indicate that the procyclical relationship of leverage is generally higher for savings institutions compared to commercial banks and even higher for broker–dealers, as shown in the larger coefficient on ΔTA, although the differences are not statistically significant. The evidence further suggests that the diminished effect of procyclical leverage in the fair value accounting environment is particularly evident for broker–dealers and commercial banks, whereas there is no difference in procyclical leverage for savings institutions after 1994. The regression results presented here stand in contrast to the widely expressed criticism that fair value accounting introduces procyclical leverage in bank balance sheets and hence intensifies boom and bust cycles.

Further evidence for rejecting the role of fair value accounting as a contributor to procyclical leverage is provided in Amel-Zadeh *et al.* (2014). The authors find that the procyclical association between change in leverage and change in assets can be fully explained by the change in the average regulatory asset risk weight of the banks' balance sheets. Their results suggest that banks change the asset composition on their balance sheet by buying lower-risk-weighted assets during booms and selling these assets during downturns, thereby changing the average risk weight of their balance sheets countercyclically. They further find that all changes in assets that come from fair value components in equity are negatively associated with changes in leverage, and that there is no interaction effect between fair value gains and asset purchases. The authors conclude that any procyclicality in leverage originates from banks targeting an optimal regulatory leverage.

Badertscher, Burks and Easton (2012) investigate the effects of fair value losses on bank regulatory capital and on the selling behaviour of commercial banks. They find no evidence that other-than-temporary fair value impairment charges significantly depleted bank regulatory capital or that they caused significant procyclical selling behaviour (results which are consistent with Shaffer (2010)).

Feedback and contagion

The evidence above suggests that mark-to-market accounting played a very limited role in contributing to procyclical leverage. But the literature discussed above also suggests that liquidity problems were a powerful force in contagion and that asset sales in illiquid markets might introduce feedback effects that are amplified by the use of fair values on balance sheets.

Bhat, Frankel and Martin (2011) examine the selling behaviour of banks in response to declines in market values of MBS and feedback effects on market prices of MBS before and after the FASB's guidance on fair value measurements in April 2009. The study did find a positive association between changes in MBS holdings and changes in prices, which is consistent with the existence of feedback effects. But this relationship weakened after the rule clarification. Badertscher, Burks and Easton (2012), on the other hand, do not find any economically significant increase in sales in response to fair-value-related impairments.

Several studies also investigate contagion effects of fair value accounting by analysing bank stock returns. Notably, Khan (2010) examines the co-movements of extreme negative stock returns of individual banks when a few large money centre banks perform poorly. The study finds that under a more fair value-oriented accounting regime, the probability that more banks will experience extreme negative stock returns, when money centre banks are under stress, increases. Bowen *et al.* (2010) further find that around key events in the GFC in which policy makers signalled that the fair value accounting rules would be relaxed, banks susceptible to contagion experienced higher abnormal stock returns, suggesting that market participants viewed fair value accounting as increasing the likelihood of contagion.

In sum, direct evidence on the feedback and contagion effects of fair value accounting is mixed. However, event study evidence on stock market reactions suggests that the market – at least during the GFC – perceived fair value accounting as contributing to feedback and contagion in the banking sector, ultimately increasing the failure risk of banks.

Bank failure

The empirical evidence gives little support to the contention that banks were chiefly brought down by erosion of equity through mark-to-market accounting. Rather, illiquidity – leading to cash flow insolvency – was the dominant factor in the landmark failures of the GFC.

The literature now includes a series of studies of the actual impact of fair value rules on bank balance sheets and on the likelihood of bank failure. The literature also examines the impact of regulators' relaxation of accounting rules relating to fair value during the crisis.

Early research suggests that banks violate regulatory solvency requirements more frequently under fair value accounting than under historical cost accounting, but this increased risk of regulatory intervention is not reflected in the stock market's assessment of the economic failure risk of the bank (e.g., Barth *et al.*, 1995). The SEC (2008) concluded from an analysis of 50 financial institutions that failed during the crisis that assets whose fair value losses diminished regulatory capital did not generally play a major role; where they did, the failures tended to be precipitated by losses on loans (which were not reported at market value) rather than from marking assets to market.

Laux and Leuz (2010) develop materiality arguments similar to those of the SEC. They show that for banks at this time, much of the balance sheet was actually measured not by fair value, but with measures where declines in the market prices of assets did not lead to a shrinkage of equity, and so did not actually lead to a vicious loss spiral. Around half the assets took the form of loans and leases which were not fair valued (but included at cost less impairments proposed by management). Approximately a fifth were in the form of HTM securities (again mostly not fair valued) and AFS securities (reported at fair value, but with temporary changes in fair values not generally included when calculating equity for prudential regulation).

The potential impact of fair value changes was further limited by rule changes introduced by the accounting regulators during the GFC. One relaxation of the fair value regime introduced by IASB and FASB concerns the fair values to be used when the markets in which the relevant instruments are to be priced have become very thin and illiquid. One notorious example of a financial instrument being sold in large quantity in an illiquid market at a massive discount was Merrill Lynch's disposal of its ABS CDO portfolio, with a face value of $30.6 billion, at a price of $6.7 billion in the summer of 2008. Amel-Zadeh and Meeks (2013) find that this did have a negative short-term effect on share prices for the banking sector overall at the time of the announcement. However, the subsequent relaxation of the accounting regime seemed to dampen fears that such asset sales would impact other banks' balance sheets; that is, the relaxation relieved the indicator of bankruptcy risk.

A further relaxation of the accounting regime during the crisis – the amendment of IAS 39 in 2008 – allowed banks to reclassify certain financial instruments from the trading category into categories measured at cost. This partial suspension of fair value accounting may have reduced for some banks the probability of regulatory failure with all its attendant costs, and such a benefit would show in share prices. Amel-Zadeh and Meeks (2013) conclude that this benefit for the banking sector's market valuation does, at first sight, seem to have accompanied the IASB announcement (results that are confirmed in Bischof *et al.*, 2011).

The recurrent theme of this literature, then, is that the actual accounting regime was far from one of pure fair value, with most assets falling outside the scope of fair value in practice. The actual impact of fair value was further muted by relaxations of the accounting regime during the crisis.

6 Conclusion

In principle, if there had been a pure fair value system in place during the Great Financial Crisis, along with the other features of the fair value model and of actual experience – Basel II, illiquid markets, and ROE maximization – then it is likely that the accounting system would have exacerbated the crisis as critics have complained it did. But in practice, the transmission mechanism for fair value to drive the crisis was very much weaker than suggested by the critics, both because so much of the balance sheet was exempt from fair valuation and because of the relaxation of the fair value regime by the accounting regulators as the crisis developed. So fair value was not the main culprit in the GFC.

However, the GFC has increased our understanding of the limitations of fair value. At first sight, financial assets seem a prime candidate for fair valuation: they are more homogeneous than many asset categories and they are frequently traded, so there are many more markets with regularly published price data. But as Ryan (2008) pointed out early in the crisis, the very trigger for the crisis was that the market had got prices hopelessly wrong: '[T]the market as a whole woke up to the fact that underwriting in the subprime mortgage industry had been lax and losses on subprime mortgages would likely considerably exceed those expected by the market and accrued for by firms' (p. 1619), yet the US fair value accounting standard, FAS 157, 'does not contemplate the idea that information asymmetry between the current holder of a position and a potential purchaser or assumer of the position is so severe that markets break down altogether, as they have for many subprime positions' (p. 1626). Sometimes the only transactions were fire sales, as in Merrill Lynch's massive sale of assets at 22 cents to the dollar. And as we have shown, this problem spread more widely as the crisis developed: major wholesale markets froze, producing cash flow insolvencies at Lehman and Northern Rock, and FASB and the IASB were pressured into relaxing the fair value regime.

Of course the fair value regime allows preparers of accounts who do not have reliable market data to resort to Level 3 inputs – firm-supplied, mark-to-model estimates using the assumptions that participants in the market would employ. But the fact that they are, in Ryan's words, 'largely undisciplined by market information' (p. 1627) is a special drawback in times of crisis and financial distress. It is precisely at times of stress that managers face the greatest temptations to manage earnings or do business off balance sheet (Schilit and Perler, 2010). But it is also precisely at times of liquidity crisis that current market values, however far removed from fundamentals, tell the accounts user the crucial information – what cash the assets will fetch now. And so current market values are most relevant to whether the firm will avoid cash flow insolvency and survive to recover the fundamental value of its assets.

Those nostalgic for earlier accounting rules might argue that at least historic cost was 'disciplined by market information' – the original purchase transaction in the market. But this valuation basis was blamed for perpetuating and compounding the previous major financial crisis in the US, the savings and loans crisis in the 1980s through the early 1990s. Although total liabilities of the savings and loans institutions exceeded their total assets by $118 billion on a fair value basis, effectively leaving most institutions insolvent, this deficit did not appear in their balance sheets, which were based on historical costs. At the same time, no mark-to-market losses from rising interest rates were recognized in income even though the funding costs of these institutions had surpassed their mortgage rates (Enria *et al.*, 2004). At that time, the historic cost accounting regime concealed inefficiencies in the savings and loans institutions and was said to have contributed to the length and severity of the crisis to the detriment of stakeholders and taxpayers (Kane, 1987, 1989; Michael, 2004). It was in the wake of the savings and loans crisis that fair value accounting for financial institutions was advocated as a remedy against such a prolonged credit crisis.

This is not to deny that historic cost still serves a very important role in accounts. For stewardship purposes – principals holding their agents to account – does it make sense to ignore the use of shareholders' funds by managers to pay for the assets in the first place, their historic cost? Comparing current values with the sums originally paid for assets is a fundamental activity of effective governance (Whittington, 2008), one that, as the debates on purchased goodwill show (Zeff, 2002), executives who have presided over large capital losses are often eager to avoid.

We would argue, therefore, that the GFC has neither fundamentally undermined nor strengthened the case for fair values in balance sheets. Market value is not the Holy Grail of asset measurement, but it assumes crucial importance when liquidity is tight and assets have to be turned into cash very quickly. It is also relevant to many business decisions outside of crises, as an indicator of the opportunity cost of holding assets in current conditions that can be compared with a second asset measure, the present value of the assets in their current use. These two measures can then be combined with the historic cost to inform principals' evaluation of the stewardship of their executive agents.

Notes

1 www.iasplus.com/europe/0905mccreevy.pdf.
2 Whittington (2014) in this volume provides a fuller discussion of fair value in accounting regulation.
3 For simplicity we use fair value and mark-to-market pricing interchangeably. We discuss cases below where the two diverge.
4 See CEBS (2007) report for an overview of prudential filters in bank regulation in the EU.
5 In the US, fair value accounting for financial assets was introduced with SFAS 107 *Disclosures about Fair Value of Financial Instruments*, which became effective in 1993, and SFAS 115 *Accounting for Certain Investments in Debt and Equity Securities*, which became effective in 1994. The IASB followed its US counterpart swiftly with IAS 32 and IAS 39 in the following years.

References

Admati, A. and M. Hellwig (2013), *The Bankers' New Clothes*, Princeton and Oxford, Princeton University Press.
Adrian, T. and H.S. Shin (2008), 'Liquidity and financial contagion', *Banque de France, Financial Stability Review* 11, pp. 1–7.
———— (2010), 'Liquidity and leverage', *Journal of Financial Intermediation* (July) 19, pp. 418–437.
Allen, F. and E. Carletti (2008), 'Mark-to-market accounting and liquidity pricing', *Journal of Accounting and Economics* 45, pp. 358–378.
Amel-Zadeh, A. and G. Meeks (2013), 'Bank failure, mark-to-market and the financial crisis', *Abacus* 49, pp. 308–339.
Amel-Zadeh, A., M. Barth and W. Landsman (2014), 'Does fair value accounting contribute to procyclical leverage?', Working paper.
American Bankers Association, ABA (2008), Letter to Robert H. Herz, Chairman, Financial Accounting Standards Board (November 13).

Badertscher, B., J. Burks and P. Easton (2012), 'A convenient scapegoat: fair value accounting by commercial banks during the financial crisis', *Accounting Review* 87, pp. 59–90.

Bank for International Settlements, BIS (1988), *International Convergence of Capital Measurement and Capital Standards*, Basel, Basel Committee on Banking Regulations and Supervisory Practice.

———— (2004), *International Convergence of Capital Measurement and Capital Standards: A Revised Framework*, Basel, Basel Committee on Banking Regulations and Supervisory Practice.

Barth, M. and W. Landsman (2010), 'How did financial reporting contribute to the financial crisis?' *European Accounting Review* 19, pp. 399–423.

Barth, M., W. Landsman and J. Wahlen (1995), 'Fair value accounting: effects on banks' earnings volatility, regulatory capital, and value of contractual cash flows', *Journal of Banking and Finance* 19, pp. 577–605.

Bhat, G., R. Frankel and X. Martin (2011), 'Panacea, Pandora's box, or placebo: feedback in bank mortgage-backed security holdings and fair value accounting', *Journal of Accounting and Economics* 52, pp. 153–173.

Bischof, J., U. Bruggemann and H. Draske (2013), 'Fair value reclassifications of financial assets during the financial crisis', Working paper, University of Mannheim.

Bowen, R., U. Khan and S. Rajgopal (2010), 'The economic consequences of relaxing fair value accounting and impairment rules on banks during the financial crisis of 2008–2009', Working paper, http://ssrn.com/abstract=1498912 (accessed 19 February 2014).

Brunnermeier, M.K. (2009), 'Deciphering the liquidity and credit crunch 2007–2008', *Journal of Economic Perspectives* 23, pp. 77–100.

Brunnermeier, M. and L.H. Pedersen (2009), 'Market liquidity and funding liquidity', *Review of Financial Studies* 22 (6), pp. 2201–2238.

Burkhardt, K. and Strauz, R. (2006), 'The effect of fair vs. book value accounting on banks', Working paper, Free University of Berlin.

Cifuentes, R., G. Ferrucci and H.S. Shin (2005), 'Liquidity risk and contagion', *Journal of the European Economic Association* 3, pp. 556–566.

Committee of European Banking Supervisors, CEBS (2007). *Analytical Report on Prudential Filters for Regulatory Capital*, http://www.eba.europa.eu/documents/10180/16094/145Final_Analytical_report_on_prudential_filters.pdf (accessed 19 February 2014).

Enria A., L. Cappiello, F. Dierick, S. Grittini, A. Haralambous, A. Maddaloni, P. Molitor, F. Pires and P. Poloni (2004), 'Fair value accounting and financial stability', *European Central Bank Occasional Paper Series No. 13*, Frankfurt, European Central Bank.

Epstein R.A. and M.T. Henderson (2009), 'Marking to market: can accounting rules shake the foundations of capitalism?' *University of Chicago Law School John M. Olin Law & Economics Working Paper No. 458.*

Eurostat (2014), *Unemployment Statistics*, http://ec.europa.eu/eurostat/tgm/refreshTableAction.do?tab=table&plugin=1&pcode=tsdec460&language=en (accessed 19 February 2014).

Financial Accounting Standards Board, FASB (1982), *Statement of Financial Accounting Standards 65, Accounting for Certain Mortgage Banking Activities*. Norwalk, CT, FASB.

———— (1991), *Statement of Financial Accounting Standards 107. Disclosures about Fair Value of Financial Instruments*. Norwalk, CT, FASB.

———— (1993), *Statement of Financial Accounting Standards 115, Accounting for Certain Investments in Debt and Equity Securities*. Norwalk, CT, FASB.

———— (2006), *Statement of Financial Accounting Standards 157, Fair Value Measurements*. Norwalk, CT, FASB.

———— (2009), 'FASB issues final staff positions to improve guidance and disclosures on fair value measurements and impairments', Press release, Norwalk, CT, April 9, http://www.fasb.org/news/nr040909.shtml. (accessed 19 February 2014).

Freixas X. and D. Tsomocos (2004), 'Book vs. fair value accounting in banking, and intertemporal smoothing', Working paper.

Gorton, G. and A. Metrick (2012), 'Securitized banking and the run on repo', *Journal of Financial Economics* 104, pp. 425–451.

Haldane, A. (2010), 'Regulation or prohibition: the \$100 billion question', *Journal of Regulation and Risk North Asia* 2, pp. 101–122.

Heaton J.C., D. Lucas and R.L. McDonald (2010), 'Is mark-to-market accounting destabilizing? Analysis and implications for policy', *Journal of Monetary Economics* 57, pp. 64–75.

Institute for Fiscal Studies, IFS (2014), *Fiscal Facts*, http://www.ifs.org.uk/fiscalFacts/fiscalAggregates (accessed 19 February 2014).

International Accounting Standards Board, IASB (2003a), *International Accounting Standard 32, Financial Instruments: Presentation*, London, IASB.

_____ (2003b), *International Accounting Standard 39, Financial Instruments: Recognition and Measurement*, London, IASB.

_____ (2008a), *Reclassification of Financial Assets: Amendments to IAS 39 Financial Instruments: Recognition and Measurement and IFRS 7 Financial Instruments: Disclosures*, London, IASB.

_____ (2008b), *Reclassification of Financial Assets: Effective Date and Transition: Amendments to IAS 39 Financial Instruments: Recognition and Measurement and IFRS 7 Financial Instruments: Disclosures*, London, IASB.

_____ (2008c), *Measuring and Disclosing the Fair Value of Financial Instruments in Markets That Are No Longer Active*, London, IASB Expert Advisory Panel.

International Monetary Fund, IMF (2010), *Global Financial Stability Report*, http://www.imf.org/External/Pubs/FT/GFSR/2010/01/index.htm (accessed 19 February 2014).

Kaletsky, A. (9 July 2009) 'Five golden rules for regulating the banks: the government's financial plans have worked – so far', *The Times*.

Kane, E. (1987), 'Dangers of capital forbearance: the case of the FSLIC and "zombie" S&Ls', *Contemporary Policy Issues* 5(1), pp. 77–83.

_____ (1989), *The S&L Mess: How Did It Happen?* Washington, DC, Urban Institute Press.

Khan, U. (2010), 'Does fair value accounting contribute to systemic risk in the banking industry?' Working paper, Columbia Business School.

Laux, C. and C. Leuz (2009), 'The crisis of fair-value accounting: making sense of the recent debate', *Accounting, Organizations and Society* 34, pp. 826–834.

_____ (2010), 'Did fair value accounting contribute to the financial crisis?', *Journal of Economic Perspectives* (Winter) 24, pp. 93–118.

Michael, I. (2004), 'Accounting and financial stability', *Financial Stability Review* 16, pp. 118–128.

Morris, S. and H.S. Shin (2008), 'Financial regulation in a system context', *Brooking Papers on Economic Activity*, Fall, pp. 229–261.

Plantin, G., H. Sapra and H.S. Shin (2008), 'Marking-to-market: panacea or Pandora's box?' *Journal of Accounting Research* 46, pp. 435–460.

Ryan, S.G. (2008), 'Accounting in and for the subprime crisis', *The Accounting Review* 83, pp. 1605–1638.

Schilit, H.M. and J. Perler (2010), *Financial Shenanigans*, New York, McGraw Hill.

Securities and Exchange Commission, SEC (2008), *Report and Recommendations Pursuant to Section 133 of the Emergency Economic Stabilization Act of 2008: Study on Mark-to-Market Accounting*, Washington, DC, SEC.

Shaffer, S. (2010), 'Fair value accounting: villain or innocent victim: exploring the links between fair value accounting, bank regulatory capital and the recent financial crisis', Working paper, Federal Reserve Bank of Boston Quantitative Analysis Unit.

Shin, H.S. (2009), 'Reflections on Northern Rock: the bank run that heralded the global financial crisis', *Journal of Economic Perspectives* 23, pp.101–119.

Shleifer, A. and R. Vishny (2010), 'Unstable banking', *Journal of Financial Economics* 97, pp. 306–318.

Von Peter, G. (2009), 'Asset prices and banking distress: a macroeconomic approach', *Journal of Financial Stability* 5, pp. 298–319.

Whittington, G. (2008), 'Fair value and the IASB/FASB conceptual framework project: an alternative view', *Abacus* 44 (2), pp. 139–168.

_____ (2015), 'Fair value and IFRS', *The Routledge Companion to Financial Accounting Theory*, ed. Stewart Jones, London: Routledge, pp. 217–235.

Zeff, S. (2002), 'Political lobbying on proposed standards: a challenge to the IASB', *Accounting Horizons* 16, pp. 43–54.

Zingales, L. (2008), 'Causes and effects of the Lehman Brothers bankruptcy', Testimony before the Committee on Oversight and Government Reform, United States House of Representatives, 6 October 2008.

10

Fair value and IFRS

Geoffrey Whittington[1]

Introduction

The International Accounting Standards Board (IASB) replaced the International Accounting Standards Committee (IASC) in 2001. During its short career, the IASB has already had significant achievements in regulating financial reporting, notably in persuading more than a hundred countries to make use of its standards. However, it has also attracted criticism and controversy, and a focus for this has been its alleged support for fair value as the basis of measurement in financial reports. In this chapter, we explore four aspects of fair value in the IASB's standards programme: first, the definition of fair value; second, the case for using fair value as the measurement basis; third, the degree of support for fair value in the IASB's standards and other pronouncements, and the way this has changed over the first twelve years of the IASB's existence; and fourth, the forces that have influenced the IASB's attitude to fair value, including the effects of the financial crisis. We conclude with some observations on the implications of the IASB's recent experience for future developments in International Financial Reporting Standards (IFRS).

The definition of fair value

The term 'fair value' has a long history in accounting, dating back at least to the late nineteenth century, when the term was used in regulatory and legal cases. It was used to describe the amount of consideration that would be required if a particular asset (or liability) were exchanged in an 'arm's length' transaction between willing and informed parties. Hence, it was an exchange value in a competitive market. This remained the common meaning of fair value throughout the twentieth century. For example, the IASC's definition of fair value was:

> *Fair value* is the amount for which an asset could be exchanged, or a liability settled, between knowledgeable, willing parties in an arm's length transaction.
>
> *(International Accounting Standard [IAS] 2, 1993)*

This definition was inherited by the IASB when it adopted the IASC's standards in 2001 and continued to be the standard definition in IFRS until it was changed by IFRS 13 (based on the

Financial Accounting Standards Board's Statement of Financial Accounting Standard [FASB SFAS] 157) in 2011.

This early concept of fair value is intuitively appealing, but it contains three important ambiguities.

First, it refers to the *amount* rather than to the *price*, so that it is unclear as to whether *transaction costs* are included. For example, if the item concerned is real property, there are likely to be professional fees, registration costs and transfer duties that must be paid in addition to the nominal price in order to exchange the asset, so that the total cost of the transaction is greater than the price.

Second, the definition does not specify *which perspective* is assumed to be involved in the transaction, that of a buyer or of a seller – an *entry* value or an *exit* value. These terms were first introduced, and their significance explored, by Edwards and Bell (1961). If transaction costs are included in 'the amount', the purchase cost (entry value) would be higher than the value realisable from sale (exit value). In some dealer markets, transaction costs are included in the price through a buy/sell 'spread', so there would be a difference between entry and exit prices. In other markets, a single price is quoted but the dealer levies commission charges to cover the cost of dealer services. However, the economic substance of the transaction may be identical to that in a dealer market, there still being a difference between the amount paid by the buyer and the amount received by the seller. Differences between the entry and exit perspectives are not confined to transaction costs. When markets are imperfect, the price required to induce a transaction may be different for a buyer and a seller. For example, the owner of a large block of shares in a listed corporation may have to offer a discount to the current share price (which will typically be based on relatively small, marginal trades) in order to dispose of the entire holding, whereas a prospective take-over bidder will typically have to offer a premium to the current price in order to acquire a controlling interest (the 'control premium').

Third, the definition does not specify *which market* is to be used as the reference point. This might be the most advantageous price available anywhere, or the most advantageous price available to the specific holder of the asset, or the price in the market in which the holder is expected to deal. The 'which market' problem adds a further dimension to the problem of perspective, because a business is likely to deal in different markets for buying and selling. For example, in the case of the inventory of a retailer, the entry value will be purchase cost in the wholesale market, whereas the exit value will (in a going concern business) be its sale value (net of selling costs) in the retail market. Clearly, if price were the basis of fair value, the retail price would typically be higher than the wholesale price, but even if transaction costs were taken into account (including all costs to sell) it seems unlikely that net realisable value would exactly equal replacement cost.

In the early days, replacement costs ('entry' values) were often taken to be fair value, particularly in rate regulation cases, such as the important case of Smyth v. Ames (1898), which concerned railway charges in the USA (Boer, 1966). Replacement cost could be interpreted to include the full cost of replacement, including transaction costs (Bonbright, 1937), rather than merely the contract price for replacement. These ambiguities persisted when the term 'fair value' was used by the IASC. Historical cost remained the measurement base used for most IASC standards, but fair values were used to modify this in certain special circumstances, such as impairment testing (as in the 'lower of cost or market value' rule for inventory measurement), and to clarify the measurement of an item on initial recognition when historical cost consideration was absent (as in the case of donated assets) or when the consideration did not have a specified monetary value (as in barter transactions).

It was the deliberations of working parties of the IASC in the 1990s that drew attention to the need for a more precise definition of fair value, particularly in the context of accounting for financial instruments. In its 1997 discussion paper, the Steering Committee on Financial Instruments advocated fair value for the measurement of the consideration paid on initial recognition of an asset (4.2.1) and persisted with the IASC definition of fair value given above (4.3.1). The discussion of transaction costs (4.3.12) suggested that transaction costs should be included in the measurement of fair value of consideration paid on initial recognition but eliminated subsequently when the asset is re-measured at fair value. Three years later, the Joint Working Group of Standard Setters (JWG, 2000) produced a draft standard on financial instruments. This defined fair value in a new way, as an exit price rather than an entry price, and explicitly excluded transaction costs from fair value:

> For the purposes of measuring a financial instrument, fair value is an estimate of the price an enterprise would have received if it had sold the asset or paid if it had been relieved of the liability on the measurement date in an arm's length exchange motivated by normal business considerations.
>
> (JWG, 2000, 70)

> An enterprise should not adjust the estimated market exit price to reflect expected costs it would incur to sell a financial asset or obtain relief from a financial liability.
>
> (JWG, 2000, 72)

These definitions were explicitly related to the measurement of financial instruments, and the JWG's draft standard was not adopted by the IASC or its successor, the IASB: its requirement (in paragraph 69) for universal measurement of financial instruments at fair value on initial recognition and at subsequent measurement was very controversial and aroused strong opposition, particularly from the banking sector. The standard on recognition and measurement of financial instruments, IAS 39, issued as an 'interim standard' in 1999 (but which, subject to subsequent revisions, has remained the IASB's standard for more than a decade), retained the original IASC definition of fair value, with all of its ambiguities. The same ambiguities remained in other IFRS. However, despite this ambiguity and the apparent inability of the IASB to choose a clear universal definition of fair value, the JWG draft of 2000 had introduced a new and more precise definition into the deliberations of standard setters, and the measurement of financial instruments, for which the definition was specifically designed, was one of the more important issues that the IASB had to address in the following decade. Hence, although the proposals of the JWG's draft standard were not adopted in 2000, its definition of fair value was influential in future developments.

Fair value continued to be used in new standards by both the FASB and the IASB, notably in their projects on business combinations, which were coordinated by the two boards as part of their convergence process. There was an obvious need to clarify the definition of fair value. The initiative to do this was taken by the FASB, culminating in SFAS 157 (2006), which defined fair value as an exit value, ignoring transaction costs, in the manner of the JWG draft standard. The IASB immediately initiated a project to adopt the proposals of SFAS 157 in the cause of convergence. This move encountered criticism from IASB constituents, particularly those in Europe who were concerned by the apparent influence of the USA (as represented by FASB) in the international standard-setting process, and it was not until 2011 that convergence was achieved in FRS 13. The FRS 13 definition of fair value is

> the price that would be received to sell an asset or paid to transfer a liability in an orderly transaction between market participants at the measurement date.
>
> (IFRS 13, May 2011, 9)

This is clearly an exit price ('the price that would be received to sell'), as in the JWG (2000) definition. It also follows the JWG definition in emphasising that fair value is determined by market participants rather than utilising the subjective expectations of the reporting entity. It is this definition that we shall adopt in the subsequent discussion of the merits of fair value and its role in IFRS. It is the current authoritative IASB definition of fair value, and it reflects a particular theoretical stance which has supported the adoption of practices based upon what we shall call the 'fair value view'.

The case for (and against) fair value in IFRS

Measurement is an essential part of the financial accounting process, and the choice of measurement method has proved to be one of the most difficult issues in accounting theory. Amongst academics there has been a long-standing debate which was particularly fierce in the 1960s. This became an equally fierce debate amongst policy-makers, regulators and practitioners during the inflation accounting debate of the 1970s, during which standard setters attempted unsuccessfully to impose current cost accounting as a solution (Tweedie and Whittington, 1984). This debate subsided when inflation rates declined in the 1980s, allowing the problem to be ignored as immaterial in the world of practice and allowing academics to turn their attention to empirical studies of the economic impact of different accounting practices whilst avoiding normative judgements about the relative merits of alternative methods. The conceptual frameworks of the FASB and the IASB, which are intended to make prescriptive statements about the desirable properties of accounting information, have failed to resolve the measurement issue, and it is one of the topics still being addressed in the IASB's conceptual framework project. The framework has decision usefulness as a primary objective, and this suggests that up-to-date values might be preferred as a supplement to or even as a substitute for the traditional historical cost measures. However, entry values, based on replacement cost, became very controversial during the inflation accounting debate and were widely considered to be impractical. It was natural, therefore, that, in seeking to extend the use of current values, standard setters should seek to avoid the controversy created by cost-based measures and look to market-based exit values. Fair value is such a measure, and during the first decade of the twenty-first century the IASB's perceived preference for fair value has been much discussed and criticised. We shall consider later the extent to which the perception of a preference for fair value is accurate; many members of the IASB would reject the claim, and there have certainly been recent changes that suggest a different emphasis. For the present, we shall consider the theoretical case for using fair value in financial accounts, where fair value is defined as in current IFRS: a selling price in an orderly market, excluding selling costs.

Fair value is intuitively an appealing concept. The owner of an asset tends to think of its worth as being what it could be sold for (exit value), and selling price is an obvious single monetary measure of this. Selling costs may be ignored because they may be immaterial, uncertain and sometimes difficult to measure in monetary terms. Replacement costs are less appealing because they refer to an asset that the owner does not yet own (the replacement asset) and a decision that has not yet been made (the replacement decision). Historical cost reflects past transactions rather than the current position. The intuitive preference for exit values was evident in a study of beginning accounting students who thought that realisable values were the best representation of current financial position (Tweedie, 1977: the author subsequently became Chairman of the IASB from 2001 to 2011).

This intuitive preference for fair value can be made more sophisticated by defining the market setting in which it can be supported by economic theory. This has been done by Barth and

Landsman (1995), who identify a situation of complete and perfect markets as one in which fair value is an ideal measure. In this setting, all assets (and liabilities) have observable market values and there are no transaction costs.

In this situation (which assumes a perfect market for some intangible assets that are not currently recognised in accounts), the sum of the net assets recorded in the balance sheet is equal to the market value of the firm's equity capital. Thus, the fair values of the individual assets and liabilities give a complete picture of the present financial position of the firm, and as Beaver and Demski (1979) have demonstrated, the measurement of income is no longer useful because income is simply the value of the equity multiplied by the cost of capital. The choice of current value measures is simplified in this world because entry values equal exit values (the 'law of one price' in perfect markets), and there are assumed to be no transaction costs. Fair values are then objective market measurements, not specific to the entity holding the asset and free of the problem of choosing a specific market in which fair value is to be measured (because price is the same in all markets).

Clearly, the assumptions of this ideal world are unrealistic. Markets are not complete (e.g. some intangible assets cannot easily be traded) or perfect (e.g. as Beaver and Demski point out, not all market participants have full information, which is why financial accounts are useful in relieving some of the information asymmetry that exists between internal managers and external providers of finance), and there are significant transaction costs which drive a wedge between entry and exit values. Furthermore, issues of accountability and stewardship arise, because the feedback from investors in response to accounting information may affect the firm's future policies and prospects in a world of imperfect markets (Whittington, 2010). For example, a failure to meet profit expectations may result in pressure on management from leading shareholders, resulting in policy changes that affect future profitability.

Thus, in the world of less than perfect or complete markets, accounting information, including accounting measurement, has a different role from that in the idealised economy. Beaver and Demski (1979) describe this as the 'informational perspective' on accounting, as opposed to the 'measurement perspective' that exists in the world of perfect and complete markets where the balance sheet might measure the value of the equity. The informational perspective regards accounting information as an input into the individual decision models of users of accounts rather than as an objective evaluation that is a substitute for users' own decisions. Thus, in valuing the equity of a firm, the informational approach would hope to provide relevant information to investors, such as indications of the amount of sales or assets employed, which would be combined with other information, such as the state of the economies in which the firm operates, by users to form their own subjective estimates of value. Such an approach would not aspire to providing a 'bottom line' measure of value that required no further processing by investors. In the world of imperfect and incomplete markets, the informational perspective implies a process of what Beaver and Demski describe as 'noisy communication', where 'noisy' is used in the statistical sense to imply the inclusion of error in the information.

In the world of 'noisy communication', fair value (as defined earlier) is only one of a number of alternative measurement methods that may be useful. Entry values, based on current or historical cost may be useful (Penman, 2007); value in use (the discounted present value of future returns obtainable by continuing use in the business), although dependent on the ('entity-specific') expectations of current management, may also be informative, and there will be variants of exit value that might be more relevant than selling price. In the presence of transaction costs, there will be differences between entry and exit prices that may be material, and the realisable value will be less (by the amount of selling cost) than the amount obtainable from sale (net realisable value), which might seem more relevant to economic decisions than the price. The difference between entry and exit values will be due not simply to transaction costs but also to the choice of market. Typically, a business buys in one market and sells (hopefully at a profit) in another. If an asset is measured with reference to the selling market (exit value, commonly referred to as 'mark-to-market'), it will show an instant profit as soon as an asset is acquired (known as a 'day 1 profit') reflecting the difference between the entry price and the exit price. The reporting of such profits has been controversial and has been a difficult area for IFRS. Such gains may well be useful information where the selling market is deep and liquid, approaching the ideal of a perfect market (as may be the case in some organised commodity exchanges), but they are less so when a significant selling effort is required (as in the case of a conventional retail business). Furthermore, they are not realised and may be eliminated by future price changes, especially where prices are volatile, and they will cease to be realisable when markets are illiquid. These concerns were apparent in the recent financial crisis.

The IASB has not yet managed to articulate its own theoretical position on measurement in general or fair value in particular; this awaits the forthcoming revision of the conceptual framework, the due process for which was initiated by the discussion paper issued in July 2013. However, IFRS 13, on fair value measurement, does acknowledge that fair value is one of the measures used in current IFRS and it explains how fair value should be measured in IFRS. In doing so, the standard deals with such problems as the choice of market and the estimation of fair value when a relevant market is not available. Hence, it acknowledges that the world in which IFRS are used is one of imperfect and incomplete markets, which implies that the informational perspective is more relevant than the measurement perspective. Equally, its latest drafts on measurement for the conceptual framework suggest a mixed measurement approach – that is, different measurement methods might be used in different market settings or for different types of assets, depending upon the circumstances. This too is consistent with the informational perspective, as opposed to a measurement perspective in which fair value is the universal ideal measurement method. This represents a degree of moderation in the IASB's views during recent years. Until 2006 or so, it was reasonable to believe that the fair value view, based on universal fair value principles, was becoming a dominant element in the thinking of a majority of IASB board members (Whittington, 2008). A summary of that view (as subjectively perceived by the present author) is given in the Appendix to this chapter. It will be seen that the implications of adopting the fair value view of the world extend to all of the important aspects of financial reporting, including the basic objectives and such important issues as the role of stewardship, the relevance of prudence (or conservatism) and the extent to which financial accounts should reflect the subjective estimates of management rather than the objective (but not necessarily fully informed) estimates of the market. We explore the evidence for this, and the recent apparent change of direction, in the following section.

Support for fair value in IASB pronouncements: the early years, 2001–2006

It has been suggested that the belief that fair value was ever a predominant factor in the IASB's thinking or standards is misplaced (Cairns, 2007). It is true that recently the IASB has made a number of decisions that reject the opportunity of using fair value, but there was a time, around 2006, when the IASB first proposed to adopt the American standard on fair value measurement and fair value seemed to be the preference of the majority of the Board. Alexander (2007), who gives an account of the development of fair value at the IASB up to this time, asserts that 'there is overwhelming evidence that the IASC/B is favourably disposed towards the use of fair values' (p. 72). However, even at that time, IFRS required the majority of transactions to be accounted for at historical cost, and the IASB's own framework (IASC, 1989) embraced a mixed measurement method approach. Fair value was not included in the list of possible methods considered in the 1989 framework; this demonstrates the rapidity of the subsequent emergence of fair value in the Board's thinking. That framework document is still in place today (as of July 2013) despite many discussions of possible revision by the IASB, and the latest IASB pronouncement (IASB, July 2013) suggests that the mixed measurement approach will continue to be supported. In this section, we explore the role of fair value in the IASB's work up to about 2006, when it seems to have reached its highest prominence.

Cairns (2007) gives a thorough and authoritative account of the place of fair value in IFRS in 2006. He points out that the extant uses of fair value at that time were natural extensions of practice that had developed over many years within a mixed measurement framework, which might broadly be described as modified historical cost. The most obvious use of fair value in this context was on initial recognition of an item in the accounts, where the fair value of the consideration for acquisition of the item was the usual basis (in an 'arm's length' transaction) for determining historical cost. Cairns cites IAS 16 (Property, Plant and Equipment, 1982) as the first example of this in IASC standards. This was followed by IAS 17 (Leases, 1982), which required fair value as the initial measurement of assets held under finance leases. Fair value was also used on initial recognition as a means of allocating a single amount of purchase consideration between individual assets and liabilities acquired. The obvious example of this was in allocating the purchase cost of a business combination under the acquisition method of accounting (IAS 22, 1983). A different use of fair value was in impairment testing: the process of writing down an asset to recoverable amount where that was lower than carrying amount (which would typically be historical cost). Fair value was one basis upon which recoverable amount would be measured. Impairment tests are essentially an application of the prudence principle, which has strong roots in what might be termed the traditional view of accounting, rather than the fair value view. Hence, there could be little reason to regard the use of fair value in impairment testing as a revolutionary change.

There was, however, another strand in the development of IFRS (and their predecessors up to 2001, the IAS issued by the IASC) which was more revolutionary. This was the use of fair value for re-measurement of assets and liabilities in periods subsequent to initial measurement. Cairns reports that this practice developed in some IASC standards from the 1980s onwards, the first instance being the requirement for annual re-measurement at fair value of investments of post-retirement benefit plans (IAS 26, 1986). The use of fair value for re-measurement in the standards of the IASC seemed to gather some momentum. In particular, its final three standards, IAS 39, 40 and 41, all required or allowed significant fair value revaluations. IAS 39 (1998), on financial instruments (issued originally as a 'provisional' standard), required certain (but not all) categories of financial instruments (both assets and liabilities) to be carried in accounts at current fair value. IAS 40 (2000), on investment property, had current fair value as the basis of its preferred model, although there was a historical cost alternative. IAS 41 (2000), on agriculture, prescribed fair value (less point-of-sale costs) for biological assets up to the point of harvesting, but with an exemption where fair value was not reliably measurable. Hence, by the time that the IASB took over from the IASC in 2001, there was some indication of a preference among standard setters for fair value and a degree of indignation in the industries affected, notably banking (IAS 39) and agriculture (IAS 41).

The anxiety about fair value was compounded when the IASB adopted all of the standards inherited from the IASC (subject to an 'improvements programme' which addressed details rather than principles), including the recent IAS 39 and 41. It also embarked upon its own programme of developing new standards which were regarded by many constituents as favouring fair value. For example, in revising IAS 39, it introduced the 'fair value option', which allowed any financial instrument to be carried at fair value, with gains and losses passing through the profit and loss account. This change was intended to address the 'mismatch' problem which arose because, under IAS 39, some industries, such as insurance, would carry investments at market value but the liabilities that financed them would be at amortised cost, thus creating artificial volatility in the net amount reported when certain market conditions (such as interest rates) changed. However, the European Central Bank, in particular, saw this discretionary extension of the use of fair value as a potentially destabilising development allowing more extensive use of an unreliable measure (fair value) in bank balance sheets. The result was a European Commission 'carve-out' of the fair value option when the revised IAS 39 was first adopted as part of European Union law in 2004. The disagreement was resolved in the following year by restricting the circumstances in which the fair value option could be exercised, but it demonstrated the anxiety that the IASB was giving too much support to the use of fair value. There was a second EU 'carve-out' of IAS 39 in 2004 relating to hedge accounting rather than fair value, and this has still not been resolved. Ironically, the sticking point in negotiations has been the view of the European Banking Federation that demand deposits should be measured at fair value for hedging purposes, whereas the IASB wishes to maintain the amount redeemable on demand as the minimum value (the 'deposit floor'), even when it is anticipated that the full redemption option will not be exercised immediately. Thus, in this case, the IASB appears to prefer an approach that incorporates prudence, whereas the allegedly prudent European bankers are advocating an approach that is consistent with the fair value view. This should serve as a warning against over-simplification of the views of the two groups: in practice, theoretical consistency is often sacrificed to pragmatism.

Another unpopular standard which made use of fair value was IFRS 2 (2004), on share-based payments. The central issue here was really whether employee stock options should be recognised as an expense. If they were so recognised, in the absence of cash consideration, some form of market value was the only measurement option for initial recognition, and the IASB chose to describe this as 'fair value', although when it later issued IFRS 13 (2011) on fair value, it decided that IFRS 2 was not strictly advocating fair value according to the new definition (IFRS 13, para. 6). Hence, the core of the unpopularity of IFRS 2 was not really its use of fair value, but the fact that the standard used the term helped to add to the impression that the IASB was proposing to extend the use of fair value in unpopular directions. The business combinations standard, IFRS 3 (2004), was also an early controversial standard which appeared to support greater use of fair value. Most obviously, it removed the possibility of merger ('pooling of interests') accounting, so that all combinations would be accounted for using the acquisition method, which requires the assets and liabilities of the acquired firm to be revalued at fair value at the point of acquisition. It also seemed to extend the use of fair value in various detailed aspects of acquisition accounting. For example, it required that all intangible assets and contingent liabilities of acquired firms should be recognised at fair value, asserting that the usual recognition criterion of reliable measurement was not relevant because fair value was always reliably measurable. Also, it required a surplus of the fair value of net assets acquired over the purchase consideration (a bargain purchase) to be recognised immediately in profit, whereas many constituents wished to continue the earlier, more prudent, practice of recognising the gain over the life of the assets acquired. This appeared to be further evidence either of the IASB's confidence in the reliability of fair value measurement or its belief that any deficiencies in reliability were compensated for by the superior relevance of fair value.

Apart from specific fair value requirements in standards issued, fair value was prominent in a number of ongoing projects that were active but not completed in 2006. It was so prominent in the discussions at IASB board meetings in 2002 and 2003 that Walton (2009, Tables 7 and 8) found that it was by far the most frequently mentioned topic. The broader fair value view (an environment in which fair value appeared to be the appropriate measurement basis) appeared to be favoured by the early stages of the conceptual framework revision on which the IASB embarked jointly with the FASB in 2005. The draft of the first two chapters of the revised framework emphasised decision usefulness and the estimation of future cash flows as the central objective of accounting, according no distinctive role to stewardship and the recording of past transactions and events. They also replaced reliability with faithful representation as one of the two primary characteristics of good accounting information, with faithful representation implying that the information measured an 'economic phenomenon'. Critics feared that a representationally faithful depiction of an economic phenomenon would be interpreted as being necessarily a current market price (probably fair value) rather than historical cost, which has traditionally played an important part in accounting for stewardship (Whittington, 2008). This fear was reinforced by the early papers prepared on measurement (section C of the proposed new framework) by the FASB staff as part of the joint conceptual framework project. These appeared to reflect two important assumptions: first, that there should be a closely defined measurement objective which would favour a single measurement method, and, second, that fair value was a possible choice to be that method, whereas deprival value, the principle underlying current cost, was dismissed as a hybrid.

The IASB's interest in introducing more fair value measurement was apparent in a number of other ongoing projects which had not been completed in 2006 and which, in the majority of cases, have not yet (as of July 2013) achieved a final standard. This support for fair value measurement was not confined to assets: in three projects (in addition to the financial instruments project), the IASB appeared to be about to adopt fair value for measuring liabilities. One of these was insurance, where it was considering proposing the measurement of insurance obligations at the price which an independent third party (a reinsurer) would charge to take on the obligation (i.e. fair value, as confirmed in the 2007 IASB discussion paper on insurance). This raises the possibility of 'day 1 profits', when the premium received is higher than the estimated cost of transferring the obligation. A similar issue arose in the revenue recognition project, where the IASB was considering recognising revenue as sale proceeds receivable less the cost of the obligation to perform under the contract, where the latter was measured on the basis of what a competitive third party would charge to fulfil the obligation (i.e. fair value). Finally, the IASB was conducting a project to develop a standard on liabilities (the revision of IAS 37, on provisions), intended to deal with all liabilities not covered by other standards, including such issues as environmental obligations and legal damages. In this project, too, the IASB seemed to be leaning towards a preference for a fair value measure of the liability, a market-based estimate of what a third party would charge to assume the obligation.

Opposition to the IASB's apparent adoption of the fair value view, as opposed to specific fair value measurement, was apparent in the reaction to the IASB project on reporting financial performance (i.e. the structure of the income statement). The IASB proposed a statement of comprehensive income, including all gains and losses, which included revaluations, in income. This produced a sharp reaction from some constituents, such as the European Round Table of financial executives, who were keen to preserve an operating income measure which would be free of the effects of revaluations and would, they believed, better capture current operating performance. Underlying their view was the type of theoretical framework, articulated later by Penman (2007), in which operating flows rather than fair value balance sheets are a critical element in appraising and valuing the firm.

The other indication in 2006 that the IASB might have a preference for the fair value view was its enthusiastic initial reaction to the new FASB standard on fair value measurement, SFAS

157 (2006). As explained earlier, this standard removed the earlier ambiguity about the definition of fair value by defining it clearly as a sale (exit) price (with no allowance for transaction costs). It thus removed the possibility that fair value could embrace other measurement techniques, such as replacement costs, in appropriate circumstances. Alternative measurement techniques were allowed only if they were the best available proxies for sale prices. The FASB had gone beyond the IASB's more inclusive definition, but the IASB had already (in 2005) started a project to define fair value more precisely, and in 2006 it resolved, as part of its convergence agreement with FASB, to coordinate its work on this topic with that of FASB. It proposed to issue SFAS 157 as an IASB exposure draft, and this was eventually achieved in 2009. Following exposure and amendment, it became a standard (IFRS 13) in 2011. The IASB claimed that the new standard did not extend the use of fair value, and this was strictly correct. SFAS 157 and IFRS 13 defined fair value in those cases in which fair value measurement was already required by a standard. They did not require any additional use of fair value measurement, and in this sense they could be regarded as welcome clarification of a definition that had previously been a little too ambiguous for consistent application. However, by imposing a new definition and implementation guidance on existing practice, these standards were clearly changing existing practice; where fair value was already required, it had to conform with what might be described as a 'hard line' definition of fair value (exit prices with no allowance for transaction costs or 'entity-specific' assumptions) rather than with the looser definition (some relevant current market value, preferably supported by market evidence) that may have been applied at the time of the original requirement. The IASB tried to meet this criticism by considering, standard by standard, whether the new definition of fair value was compatible with the original intention of the standard. In the first discussion of this issue, the majority of the IASB took a very strong line in asserting compatibility, even, for example, suggesting that it should apply to finance leases under IAS 17, but this view was eventually reversed in IFRS 13 (para. 7).

Hence, in its first period of operation, from 2001 to 2006, the IASB did show some clear signs of preferring fair value as the measurement base for financial reporting. Also, in some respects, such as its strong emphasis on comprehensive income and its revisions of the conceptual framework, it showed a preference for some aspects of the fair value view, based on a measurement rather than an informational perspective on accounting. However, these were mainly signs of intent rather than concrete enactments in the form of revised standards. In the subsequent period (to 2013), few of these intentions have been transformed into reality, and the IASB seems to be set upon a much more pragmatic course associated with a mixture of measurement methods and more consistent with the informational approach.

Retreat and retrenchment, 2006–2013

In the more recent period of the IASB's operations, fair value has not disappeared from the Board's pronouncements, but it has had less prominence (hence, 'retreat') both in proposed standards and in discussions of the conceptual framework. In one respect – the issuance of IFRS 13 (2011) – the period has seen fair value more clearly defined as a component of IFRS (hence, 'retrenchment').

The retreat has been most obvious in the treatment of liabilities, including performance obligations, where the IASB appears to be moving towards the type of entry value approach proposed by Lennard (2002) for revenue recognition, the measurement of insurance obligations and the measurement of other performance liabilities.

The revenue recognition project has seen a retreat from measuring the performance obligation under a contract as the fair value (market cost of transfer to a third party). Instead, the latest exposure drafts (2010 and 2012) prefer a model that reflects the traditional performance-based approach, based on performance by the entity rather than a third party and measuring an unper-formed obligation by reference to the consideration received (an entry value) rather than a notional market cost of fulfilment (an exit value). Essentially, the contract is divided into sepa-rate performance stages and the consideration is allocated to each stage. The relevant proportion of the consideration is subsequently recognised as revenue whenever a stage is completed. 'Day 1 profits' are ruled out by this model (because the obligation equals the contract price), but 'day 1 losses', due to taking on onerous contracts, are recorded. This introduces an element of prudence consistent with the traditional stewardship objective but not with the fair value view.

A similar model of revenue recognition has been adopted by the insurance project. The current exposure draft on insurance (2013) adopts the premium received (entry value) as the initial measure of the insurer's obligation under the contract rather than as a market-based cost of transferring the obligation, and the obligation is written off (creating revenue) over the life of the contract as insurance services are provided.

The project on revising IAS 37's treatment of liabilities made no further progress towards fair value. In 2010, the IASB issued an exposure draft that continued to propose that liabilities arising from service obligations should be measured at 'what the entity would rationally pay' to discharge them. This would ideally be fair value, based on the amount that would be charged by an independent external contractor. It also retained the proposal to abolish the probability test for recognition of a liability. Both proposals would have supported a fair value view. However, there was opposition from some constituents and within the Board (six members opposing the measurement proposal), and, following the exposure period, the proposed revision of IAS 37 was suspended in 2010. This removed one of the apparent fair value threats of 2006.

A standard in which the IASB appears to have retreated from the fair value view of the con-text of financial reporting, rather than the specific use of fair values for measurement, is IAS 1 with respect to the presentation of financial performance, more specifically income. The revi-sion to IAS 1 (2011) emphasises the importance of reporting the components of comprehensive income rather than concentrating on the total. In particular, it acknowledges the central role of a profit subtotal and of providing a more informative dis-aggregation of items classified as 'other comprehensive income'. This could be interpreted as a concession to those in business who feared that the 'balance sheet approach' to income reporting was drawing attention away from core operating performance and towards an aggregate comprehensive income measure.

The other area of obvious retreat is in the measurement section of the conceptual framework project. Little progress was made from 2006 to 2012, when the IASB struggled to finalise the basic chapters on objectives and qualitative characteristics of financial reports, but IASB discussions of measurement during this period, until the project was paused in 2010, did not focus on a single measurement method, such as fair value. The conceptual framework discussion paper issued in July 2013 states a clear preference for a mixed measurement model, with the measure chosen to suit the specific opportunities and circumstances of the reporting entity. This clearly represents an informational approach rather than the measurement approach that would be required to under-pin a pure fair value view, in which fair value was the preferred objective of measurement in all circumstances. However, the informational approach would still allow the use of fair value when circumstances were appropriate, such as in the case of financial instruments that are held for sale in markets that are competitive, deep and liquid. The discussion paper offers a variety of alternatives, but the preference for mixed measurement methods is clear. The rest of the discussion paper might be regarded as retrenchment rather than retreat. The IASB's earlier revisions, which emphasised, amongst other things, decision usefulness, the prediction of cash flows, and the importance of faithful representation, have been retained but not developed further. This is also the situation of most of the IASB standards that in 2006 contained elements of fair value measurement.

The one instance of a clear advance in the importance of fair value in IFRS during this period is the adoption of IFRS 13 on fair value measurement (2011). As explained earlier, the IASB emphasised that this standard did not extend the use of fair value but rather clarified how it should be defined and calculated. In this sense, IFRS 13 could be regarded as a necessary step to the adoption of a mixed measurement approach (as proposed in the recent conceptual framework discussion paper) in which fair value was one of the methods used. The greater clarity of definition and guidance on such issues as the 'which market' question would improve the consistency with which fair value was applied in such an approach, and the 'hard line' definition (exit values only and no adjustment for transaction costs) would help to distinguish it from other current values (such as 'fair value, less cost to sell', where transaction costs were considered to be important) that might be used in appropriate circumstances. However, IFRS 13 did impose the new 'hard line' fair value definition on the fair value measures required by previous standards which had been devised when the definition was looser.

The other important area that attracted much discussion during the period and in which fair value was applied was financial instruments. The marketability of financial instruments and the fact that many are actively traded makes them natural candidates for fair value measurement. The standard on accounting for financial instruments (IAS 39) required fair value measurement for all derivatives and for instruments held for sale or available for sale. Instruments held to maturity were accounted for on an amortised cost basis. Hence, IAS 39 was (and is) a mixed measurement standard. It has proved to be very controversial, mainly because complex financial transactions are becoming more common and because of the increasing interest of financial regulators, which culminated during the banking crisis of 2007 and its aftermath. A Financial Crisis Advisory Group (FCAG) was established in 2008 by the IASB and the FASB to guide future work on financial reporting standards, particularly with reference to problems which were identified in the financial crisis. The subsequent IASB developments in the financial instruments area reflect the recommendations of the *Report of the Financial Crisis Advisory Group* (2009).There have been a number of amendments to IAS 39, and a project is currently active to replace it with a simpler standard (IFRS 9), eventually including the simplification of the current complex hedge accounting requirements. The first stage of IFRS 9, classification and measurement, was approved in 2009.

These recent developments in accounting for financial instruments have tended to confirm the view that mixed measurement rather than universal fair value will be the basis of future standards, although the complete IFRS 9 (which will include a simplified treatment of hedge accounting) is still to come and views may change.

The first significant change in standards in response to the financial crisis was an amendment to IAS 39 in 2008 which relaxed the restrictions on the reclassification of certain fair valued financial instruments ('available for sale') to the amortised cost category ('held to maturity'). Advocates of this change argued that the lack of liquidity during the crisis rendered market prices of some financial assets unreliable and very volatile or even unavailable, so that a more realistic alternative to sale would be to hold the assets to maturity. The amendment to IAS 39 allowed this alternative to be reflected in the accounting method. The contrary view might be that the entity had chosen on initial recognition to report the asset as available or held for sale, and discretionary reclassification might give preparers of accounts undue leeway to hide their mistakes by switching to a more favourable valuation basis that did not necessarily reflect their intentions. This change certainly allowed a move away from fair value, but it did not signify a change of view by the IASB, because it was forced on the IASB by political pressure from within the European Union, as documented by Andre et al. (2009).

Another issue arising from the financial crisis is the measurement of loan loss provisions. The IASB's current approach is to use the 'incurred loss' approach to loan impairment. This records only those losses which will result from events that have already occurred. The alternative approach is the 'expected loss' method, which measures losses on loans on the basis of what present knowledge suggests could be expected to occur over the future life of the loan. The expected loss method has been advocated by regulators, particularly banks, as being more prudent, because it allows for expected future losses and thus gives an earlier indication of the risk of default. The fair value view usually rejects prudence in favour of unbiased market measures, but in this case there might seem to be no conflict, because expected loss anticipates the same cash flows that would determine a market price. However, as Barth and Landsman (2010) point out, the expected loss method is not full fair value because it does not change its discounting factor to reflect changes in market interest rates. Also, expected loss is used in conjunction with amortised cost (at which loans are typically carried under IAS 39), so it is part of a mixed measurement framework. The IASB has proposed to change to the expected loss method as part of its response to the financial crisis. It started its due process on the subject in 2009, working in collaboration with the FASB, and its latest proposals appear in an exposure draft published in March 2013.

A final development in relation to the fair value of financial instruments has been the IASB's discussion of own credit risk, which is another issue that arose from the financial crisis. If liabilities are valued at fair value (which is possible for some financial instruments), an increase in the issuer's probability of non-payment (a rise in credit risk) will lower the market value (and hence fair value) of the instrument, so the amount of the liability will decrease. This will result in an apparent gain to the issuing entity, which some find counter-intuitive. It may seem odd, particularly from a stewardship perspective, that an entity appears to gain from the market's perception that it has become a poor credit risk, but supporters of fair value see no difficulty here. They argue that increased credit risk does lower the burden of a liability because it can now be redeemed, by purchase in the market, at a lower amount than before. Moreover, credit risk is included in the initial amount at which a liability is recorded, and it would seem to be inconsistent to ignore it when revaluing the item. This creates a conundrum for standard setters: how can they design accounts so that both the fair value purists and their critics can obtain the information that they require? The IASB attempted to deal with this problem in its October 2010 amendments to IFRS 9, which introduced a requirement that the 'gain' arising from an increase in own credit risk should be reported separately in other comprehensive income, rather than with other gains as part of profit and loss. This reflects the general tenor of the IASB's recent decisions: it makes a clear concession to the informational perspective but maintains the use of fair value where it believes that it is a useful measure.

In summary, the IASB's work since 2006 suggests a more pragmatic approach to fair value, which is now treated as one measurement option among others in a mixed measurement model. This is consistent with the informational view of financial reporting rather than the measurement view, although the IASB has not explicitly acknowledged this. Certainly there has been little recent sign of the enthusiasm for the wider fair value view which characterised the IASB's earlier approach to such topics as revenue recognition and the recognition of liabilities. In the following section, we consider the factors that have led to the IASB's apparent change of position.

Why has the IASB's position changed?

When the IASB was established in 2001, the main criterion for appointment was technical expertise. Inevitably, this led to the initial membership being dominated by those who had experience as participants in the work of the previous IASC either as members of IASC or as participants in associated working groups, such as the G 4+1 (the IASC plus national standard setters in the USA, Canada, the UK, Australia and New Zealand) and the JWG. They therefore shared a common culture which, in continental Europe particularly, was often criticised as being Anglo-Saxon (i.e. based on English-speaking cultures and institutions). The USA, for example, provided five of the initial fourteen members, although it had not committed to adopting IFRS domestically (still not achieved) or for foreign registrants in the USA (subsequently achieved). As individuals the Board members were fiercely independent, but many shared certain prior beliefs, such as that accounts should aid investors' decisions and that market prices were relevant to this. Moreover, many had debated current standard-setting issues before and achieved a degree of consensus on their solution. For example, there was a remarkably high consensus on the Board that employee stock options should be accounted for as an expense.

It was against this background that the IASB's early decisions may have created the impression that a majority of the Board favoured what has been called the fair value view. As the membership of the Board changed, the apparent shared culture eroded. This was partly because a deliberate effort was made, as a result of constitutional change, to broaden the geographical origins of members to include, for example, Chinese and Brazilian members. The 'independent expert' model of Board membership was modified to take account of the need for wide experience of different business environments in order to ensure that the IASB would be truly international. It is not surprising that the new IASB (the last of the original members retired in 2011) would tend to favour a more pragmatic theoretical framework, as represented by the informational perspective, rather than pursuing the 'Holy Grail' of fair value.

However, the change of board membership was as much a symptom as a cause of the change. The change of structure of the IASB and of the IASC Foundation (amended to IFRS Foundation in 2010) of which it is a part was a response to pressure from constituents. As IFRS became more widely adopted, there was natural pressure for the operations of the IASB to be seen as truly international and not dominated by a small group of countries. The European Union 'carve-outs' of IAS 39 have already been referred to and were a symptom of the feeling that the IASB was an alien body, unsympathetic to the local problems of the EU. The EU had adopted IFRS in 2005, but other countries (including the USA) were still considering adoption and so had even greater bargaining power. Hence, the IASB had to adapt its programme to satisfy these countries that it could meet their needs. Such needs were often perceived as being contrary to the fair value view; for example, in many countries there was a strong tradition of accounting serving a stewardship objective.

These underlying pressures to make the IASB serve a wider world with less emphasis on decision usefulness in the context of deep and liquid markets (the hallmarks of the fair value view) were expressed very clearly during the banking crisis, which started in 2007, and the subsequent recession.

The possible role of financial reporting, particularly fair value, in causing the banking crisis has been much debated. A series of papers by Shin and various co-authors (for example Plantin, Sapra and Shin, 2008) has demonstrated the possibility that fair value could interact with regulatory requirements to destabilise the banking system. The process assumes that fair value has an element of artificial volatility due to illiquid markets and that this measurement error is amplified by the regulatory system, which applies accounting ratios based on fair value so that lower fair values force further 'fire sales' of assets, which cause fair values to fall further. Even if this were the case, it might reasonably be argued that the process assumes that regulators are at fault in using accounting data inappropriately (a view implicit in the FCAG's 2009 report, which refers to the need to be aware of the limitations of financial accounts). However, more important is the empirical question as to whether fair value did actually have this effect. Empirical studies, such as those by Laux and Leuz (2010) on large US banks and by Amel-Zadeh and Meeks (2009) on the Northern Rock bank failure in the UK and the collapse of Lehman Brothers in the USA, do not suggest that the recording of financial instruments at fair value could have been a critical factor in the crisis. It seems more likely that accounting provided a convenient scapegoat for bankers and their regulators who sought to deflect attention from their own deficient decision-making. Laux (2012) provides a useful survey of the evidence for this conclusion.

However, accounting may have played a subsidiary role in the financial crisis. For example, Barth and Landsman (2010) identify asset securitisations, derivatives and loan loss provisions as possible areas where accounting could provide better information. The securitisation issue is one of recognition (potential off–balance sheet accounting). Derivatives are carried at fair value, and Barth and Landsman recommend better disclosure (e.g. sensitivity analysis). Loan loss provisions are a measurement issue, although not a fair value issue, and as we have seen, this topic is currently being addressed by the IASB. Another issue related to the financial crisis is the incentive effects of 'day 1 profits' recognised by fair value accounting. This may well have encouraged speculative behaviour and optimistic valuations of the outcome when management bonuses were based on fair value profits. The evidence on this is, at present, mainly anecdotal. In all of these areas, further and more comprehensive empirical evidence may be hoped for in the future.

The implications of the financial crisis for the IASB were important. Irrespective of the justice of the criticisms of IFRS that were made in the aftermath of the crisis, the IASB (and the Trustees of the Foundation) were made acutely aware of their responsibility to the international community and of their vulnerability to political pressure. The establishment of the FCAG was the IASB's immediate response. The fact that the IASB accepted and implemented its recommendations (IASB, 28 January 2010) is evidence that this was not merely a token response. Indeed, the fact that the joint chairman of the FCAG (Hans Hoogervorst, an economist, regulator and politician rather than a technical accounting expert) subsequently (2011) became chairman of the IASB demonstrates the changing character of the whole organisation.

With respect specifically to fair value, the financial crisis encouraged critics of the fair value view and discouraged its supporters. The 'deep and liquid markets' that had previously been seen to justify fair value measurement, particularly for financial instruments, had demonstrated an alarming degree of vulnerability. They had done so in the area that had once been regarded as the natural home of fair value: financial instruments. This did not rule out the use of fair value in a clearly defined role within a mixed measurement system, but it did rule out the all-embracing fair value view which had appeared earlier to be dominating the thinking of the IASB.

The present and the future

As of July 2013, with the discussion paper on the conceptual framework just released, the place of fair value in IFRS seems to be assured but limited. It appears that the IASB will choose a mixed measurement framework which will include fair value (as do the present standards) as one of the measures to be used in appropriate circumstances. The broader fair value view, embracing the whole of the financial reporting process and affecting such issues as revenue recognition, seems unlikely to prevail. The IASB seems to be on a more pragmatic course, intended to balance the competing needs of different constituencies and nationalities and to maintain and enhance its position as a world-wide standard setter.

Although the fair value view may not have been appropriate for the IASB, there is some danger of adopting a pragmatic course without developing a conceptual framework that will add rigour and consistency to its decisions. The 'alternative view', as articulated in the Appendix, is more a critique of the fair value view than a coherent framework to help the standard setter. There is a need to provide more precise guidance to prevent future standards from becoming merely a series of political compromises without any coherence. In the measurement area, for example, there is a need to articulate the precise criteria upon which the choice of measurements will be made. It is for this reason that the review of the conceptual framework promised for 2015 (with an exposure draft in 2014) is so important.

Appendix
Summary of the 'fair value view' and the 'alternative view'

Extracted from Whittington, 2008, pp. 157–160

A summary of the two perspectives

The 'fair value view' emphasizes the role of financial reporting in serving investors in capital markets. It seeks accounting information that has forward-looking content, impounding future cash flows from a non-entity-specific market perspective. It is most likely to achieve this when the reference markets are complete and competitive; ideally, perfect markets would be accessible.

The 'alternative view' also seeks to serve investors, broadly defined, but it gives priority to existing shareholders and regards stewardship as an important and distinct function of financial reporting. It too seeks accounting information that is relevant to forecasting future cash flows, but it assumes that this will often be achieved by providing information that is useful input to investors' valuation models, rather than by direct valuation of future cash flows. Such information may be entity specific. This approach assumes that information asymmetry and imperfect and incomplete markets are common.

The author's own subjective interpretation of the main assumptions and implications of the two views is given below.

The fair value view

Assumptions

- *Usefulness for economic decisions* is the sole objective of financial reporting.
- *Current and prospective investors and creditors* are the reference users for general purpose financial statements.
- *Forecasting future cash flows*, preferably as directly as possible, is the principal need of those users.
- *Relevance* is the primary characteristic required in financial statements.
- *Reliability* is less important and is better replaced by *representational faithfulness*, which implies a greater concern for capturing economic substance and less concern for statistical accuracy.
- Accounting information needs ideally to reflect the *future*, not the past.
- Market prices should give an informed, *non-entity-specific* estimate of cash flow potential, and *markets* are generally sufficiently complete and efficient to provide evidence for representationally faithful measurement on this basis.

Implications

- *Stewardship is not a distinct objective* of financial statements, although its needs may be met incidentally to others.

- *Present shareholders have no special status* amongst investors as users of financial statements.
- *Past transactions and events* are relevant only insofar as they can assist in predicting future cash flows.
- *Prudence* is a distortion of accounting measurement, violating *faithful representation.*
- *Cost* (entry value) is an inappropriate measurement basis because it relates to a *past* event (acquisition), whereas future cash flow will result from future exit, measured by *fair value.*
- *Fair value,* defined as market selling (exit) price, as in SFAS 157 (FASB, 2006), should be the measurement objective.
- *The balance sheet* is the fundamental financial statement, especially if it is fair valued.
- *Comprehensive income* is an essential element of the income statement: it is consistent with changes in net assets reported in the balance sheet.

The alternative view

Assumptions

- *Stewardship,* defined as accountability to present shareholders, is a distinct objective ranking equally with decision usefulness.
- *Present shareholders* of the holding company have a special status as users of financial statements.
- *Future cash flows* may be *endogenous:* feedback from shareholders (and markets) in response to accounting reports may influence management decisions.
- Financial reporting relieves *information asymmetry* in an uncertain world, so *reliability* is an essential characteristic.
- *Past transactions and events* are important both for stewardship and as *inputs* to the prediction of future cash flows (as indirect rather than direct measurement).
- The economic environment is one of *imperfect and incomplete markets* in which market opportunities will be *entity specific.*

Implications

- The information needs of *present shareholders,* including *stewardship* requirements, must be met.
- *Past transactions and events* are *relevant* information and, together with *reliability of measurement* and *probability of existence*, are critical requirements for the *recognition* of elements of accounts, in order to achieve *reliability.*
- *Prudence,* as explained in the current IASB framework and in the *Statement of Principles* of the UK's Accounting Standards Board, can enhance *reliability.*
- *Cost* (historic or current) can be a *relevant* measurement basis, for example as an input to the prediction of future cash flows, as well as providing information for stewardship purposes.
- The financial statements should reflect the financial performance and position of a specific entity, and *entity-specific* assumptions should be made when these reflect the real opportunities available to the entity.
- *Performance* statements and *earnings* measures can be more important than balance sheets in some circumstances (but there should be arithmetic consistency – articulation – between flow statements and balance sheets).

Note

1 The author thanks Richard Barker, Andrew Lennard and Geoff Meeks for helpful comments on an earlier draft. They are not responsible for any errors that remain.

Bibliography

Alexander, D. (2007) 'Recent history of fair value', Chapter 6, pp. 71–90 of Walton (2007) *The Routledge Companion to Fair Value and Financial Reporting*, New York, Routledge.

Amel-Zadeh, A. and G. Meeks (October 2009) 'Bank failure, mark-to-market and the financial crisis', *Abacus*, 49:3, pp. 308–339.

Andre, P., A. Cazavan-Jeny, W. Dick, C. Richard and P. Walton (2009) 'Fair value accounting and the banking crisis: shooting the messenger', *Accounting in Europe*, 6:1, pp. 3–24.

Barth, M. and W. Landsman (1995) 'Fundamental issues related to using fair value accounting for financial reporting', *Accounting Horizons*, 9:4, pp. 97–107.

_____ (2010) 'How did financial reporting contribute to the financial crisis?' *European Accounting Review*, 19:3, pp. 399–423.

Beaver, W. and J. Demski (1979) 'The nature of income measurement', *The Accounting Review*, 54:1, pp. 38–46.

Boer, G. (1966) 'Replacement cost: a historical look', *The Accounting Review*, 41:1, pp. 92–97.

Bonbright, J. C. (1987) *The Valuation of Property*, New York, McGraw-Hill.

Cairns, D. (2007) 'The use of fair value in IFRS', Chapter 2, pp. 9–23, of Walton (2007).

Edwards, E. and P. Bell (1961) *The Theory and Measurement of Business Income*, California, University of California Press.

FASB (September 2006) SFAS 157: *Fair Value Measurements*, Stamford, CT.

FCAG (July 2009) *Report of the Financial Crisis Advisory Group*. Available at http://www.ifrs.org/News/Press-Releases/Documents/FCAGReportJuly2009.pdf (accessed 17 March 2015).

IASB (2004) IFRS 2: *Share-based Payment*, IASB Publications, London.

_____ (2004) IFRS 3: *Business Combinations*, IASB Publications, London.

_____ (2007) *Preliminary Views on Insurance Contracts*. Discussion paper, IASB Publications, London.

_____ (13 October 2008) *Amendment to IAS 39: Reclassification of Certain Financial Instruments*, IASB Publications, London.

_____ (2009) IFRS 9: *Financial Instruments: Classification and Measurement*, IASB Publications, London.

_____ (2010) Exposure draft: *Measurement of Liabilities in IAS 37*, IASB Publications, London.

_____ (2010) *Amendments to IFRS 9: Financial Liabilities*, IASB Publications, London.

_____ (28 January 2010) *A Comprehensive Overview of the Measures Taken by the IASC Foundation and the IASB in Responding to the Recommendations of the Financial Crisis Advisory Group*. Available at http://www.ifrs.org/About-us/IASB/Advisory-bodies/FCAG/Documents/FCAGlettertoG20January10AttachmentB.pdf (accessed 17 March 2015).

_____ (2010) Exposure draft: *Revenue from Contracts with Customers*, IASB Publications, London.

_____ (2011) IFRS 13: *Fair Value Measurement*, IASB Publications, London.

_____ (2011) *Revision to IAS 1: Presentation of Financial Statements. Presentation of Items of Other Comprehensive Income*, IASB Publications, London.

_____ (2012) Revised exposure draft: *Revenue from Contracts with Customers*, IASB Publications, London.

_____ (July 2013) *A Review of the Conceptual Framework for Financial Reporting*. Discussion paper DP/2013/1, IASB Publications, London.

_____ (2013) Exposure draft: *Financial Instruments: Expected Credit Losses*, IASB Publications, London.

_____ (2013) Exposure draft: *Insurance Contracts*, IASB Publications, London.

IASC (1982) IAS 16: *Accounting for Property, Plant and Equipment*, IASB Publications, London.

_____ (1982) IAS 17: *Accounting for Leases*, IASB Publications, London.

_____ (1983) IAS 22: *Accounting for Business Combinations*, IASB Publications, London.

_____ (1986) IAS 26: *Accounting and Reporting for Retirement Benefit Plans*, IASB Publications, London.

_____ (1989) *Framework for the Preparation and Presentation of Financial Statements*, IASB Publications, London.

_____ (1993) IAS 2: *Inventories* (revised), IASB Publications, London.

_____ (1997) *Accounting for Financial Assets and Liabilities*. Discussion paper issued for comment by the Steering Committee on Financial Instruments, IASB Publications, London.

_____ (1998) IAS 37: *Provisions, Contingent Liabilities and Contingent Assets*, IASB Publications, London.

_____ (1998) IAS 39: *Financial Instruments: Recognition and Measurement*, IASB Publications, London.

_____ (2000) IAS 40: *Investment Property*, IASB Publications, London.

_____ (2000) IAS 41: *Agriculture*, IASB Publications, London.

JWG (2000) Draft standard: *Financial Instruments and Similar Items,* International Accounting Standards Committee.

Laux, C. (2012) 'Financial instruments, financial reporting, and financial stability', *Accounting and Business Research*, 42:3, pp. 239–260.

Laux, C. and C. Leuz (2010) 'Did fair-value accounting contribute to the financial crisis?' *Journal of Economic Perspectives*, 24:1, pp. 93–118.

Lennard, A. (2002) *Liabilities and How to Account for Them*, Accounting Standards Board, ASB, London.

Penman, S. (2007) 'Financial reporting quality: is fair value a plus or a minus?' *Accounting and Business Research*, Special Issue, pp. 33–44.

Plantin, G., H. Sapra and H. Shin (2008) 'Marking-to-market: panacea or Pandora's box?' *Journal of Accounting Research*, 46:2, pp. 435–460.

Tweedie, D. (1977) 'Cash flows and realisable value: the intuitive accounting concepts? An empirical test', *Accounting and Business Research*, 8:29, pp. 2–13.

Tweedie, D. and G. Whittington (1984) *The Debate on Inflation Accounting*, Cambridge, Cambridge University Press.

Walton, P. (2007) (ed) *The Routledge Companion to Fair Value and Financial Reporting*, New York, Routledge.

_____ (2009) 'Les deliberations de l'IASB en 2002 et 2003: une analyse statistique'm *Comptabilite, Controle, Audit*, 15:1, pp. 35–53.

Whittington, G. (2008) 'Fair value and the IASB/FASB conceptual framework project: an alternative view', *Abacus*, 44:2, pp. 139–168.

_____ (2010) 'Measurement in financial reporting', *Abacus*, 46:1, pp. 104–110.

11

Valuation models
An issue of accounting theory

Stephen H. Penman

The last 20 years has seen significant development in valuation models. Up to the 1990s, the premier model in both textbooks and practice was the discounted cash flow model. Now, alternative models based on earnings and book values – the so-called residual earnings model and the abnormal earnings growth model, for example – have come to the fore in research and have made their way into the textbooks and into practice. At the same time, however, there has been a growing skepticism, particularly in practice, that valuation models do not work. This finds investment professionals reverting to simple schemes such as multiple pricing that are not really satisfactory.

Part of the problem is a failure to understand what valuation models tell us. This chapter lays out the models and the features that differentiate them. Understanding also exposes the limitations of the models, so skepticism remains – indeed, it becomes more focused. The chapter therefore identifies issues that have yet to be dealt with in research.

The skepticism about valuation models is not new. Benjamin Graham, considered the father of value investing, was of the same view:

> The concept of future prospects and particularly of continued growth in the future invites the application of formulas out of higher mathematics to establish the present value of the favored issue. But the combination of precise formulas with highly imprecise assumptions can be used to establish, or rather justify, practically any value one wishes, however high, for a really outstanding issue.
>
> *(The Intelligent Investor, 4th rev. ed., 315–316)*

One might hesitate in calling a valuation model a "formula out of higher mathematics," but Graham's point is that models can be used to accommodate any assumption about the future. This is what is behind current skepticism: valuations are very sensitive to assumptions about the cost of capital and growth rates – the "continued growth" that Graham highlights. Valuation is about reducing uncertainty about what to pay for an investment, but given the uncertainty about these and other inputs, how certain can valuation models be?

This chapter lays out alternative valuation models and evaluates their features. Three themes underlie the discussion. First, we require that the models be consistent with established theory of finance. Second, valuation involves accounting, so accounting theory as well as finance theory comes into play. Third, valuation models are a tool for practical valuation, so the respective models are judged on how they perform or do not perform (as a practical matter), with an emphasis on *caveat emptor*.

1 Valuation models

All valuation models start with the idea that the value of an investment is based on the cash flows it is expected to deliver. This idea is noncontroversial in economics because it ties back to the premise that individuals are concerned with consumption and cash buys consumption. An investment is current consumption deferred to buy future consumption, and it is future cash that buys that consumption. So the value of an investment is the present value of the cash that it is expected to deliver. Cash given up to buy the investment has a time value, so expected future cash must be discounted for the time value of money. Further, if there is a risk of not receiving the expected cash, the expectation must be discounted for that risk. Accordingly, value is the present value of (discounted) expected cash flows.

This perspective puts valuation theory on the same rationalist foundations as neo-classical economics, and it is on this basis that we proceed here. That, of course, introduces a qualification: the criticisms of standard economics apply here also. In particular, the view that consumption is the end-all of investing can be questioned. We do not entertain this question and so ignore the recent work of "behavioral economics" that attempts to bring in other factors to explain why traded prices may not conform to values predicted by rationalist valuation principles.

1.1 The dividend discount model

For the most part, our discussion will be couched in terms of equity valuation, although the principles are quite general, including investments in real assets rather than paper claims. Dividends, d, are the cash flows to equity holders, so a (noncontroversial) equity valuation model is the dividend discount model (DDM):

$$Value_0 = \sum_{t=1}^{\infty} \frac{d_t}{\rho^t} \qquad \text{(DDM) (1)}$$

where ρ is one plus the discount rate (also known as the required return or the cost of capital). Here and elsewhere in the chapter, amounts subscripted $t > 0$ are expected values. Equities (and the businesses behind them) are considered to be going concerns, and thus the infinite summation in the expression. While this is a valuation model, it is also a statement of no-arbitrage: for a given expectation of future dividends, value is the amount paid for an investment that yields the required return.

In the theory of finance, value must be a no-arbitrage value (otherwise another value is implied). As a practical matter, the (active) investor wishes to discover the no-arbitrage value in order to compare that value with price, and so discover an "inefficient" price (that is subject to arbitrage). The constant discount rate in the model is thus suspect, because with stochastic discount rates this model is inconsistent with no-arbitrage. This issue is dealt with by discounting for risk in the numerator, then discounting for the time value of money in the denominator, as in Rubinstein (1976). Formally, given no-arbitrage,

$$Value_0 = \sum_{t=1}^{\infty} \frac{d_t - Cov(d_t, Y_t)}{R_{Ft}^t} \qquad (1a)$$

where R_{Ft} is the term structure of (one plus) the spot riskless interest rates for all t, Y_t is a random variable common to all assets, and the covariance term that discounts for risk is the covariance of dividends with this random variable. All valuation models below can accommodate this modification. However, the Y_t variable is unidentified – it is a mathematical construct whose existence is implied by the no-arbitrage assumption and with no economic content (without further restrictions) – so the model is difficult to apply in practice. Accordingly, we maintain the constant discount rate assumption with the model (1) that is so familiar in texts and in practice. In should be recognized, however, that working with a constant discount rate is inconsistent with no-arbitrage valuation (though, as we will see, this is not at the top of the investor's problem with valuation models). Christensen and Feltham (2009) lay out models along the lines of the more general model (1a), and Nekrasov and Shroff (2009) and Bach and Christensen (2013) attempt to bring empirical content to them.

While model (1) with its generalization in (1a) is theoretically correct under the no-arbitrage assumption underlying the theory of modern finance, it runs into a practical problem that ties back to another foundational proposition in the theory. The practical problem arises from the infinite summation in the model; the investor has to forecast dividends "to infinity," and this is not practical. He or she requires a model where forecasting for a finite period gives a reasonable handle on the value, and the shorter the period the better. For a company that does not pay dividends, this problem is acute. The theoretical problem is the Miller and Modigliani (1961) (M&M) dividend irrelevance proposition, also based on no-arbitrage (and some additional assumptions). This says that even if a firm pays dividends, dividend payout up to the liquidating dividend is irrelevant to value – and going concerns are not expected to liquidate. To see this, restate the DDM for a finite-horizon forecast to year T:

$$Value_0 = \sum_{t=1}^{T} \frac{d_t}{\rho^t} + \frac{P_T}{\rho^T}$$

$$= \frac{1}{\rho^T} \left[\sum_{t=1}^{T} \rho^{T-t} d_t + P_T \right] \tag{1b}$$

Here the terminal cash flow is the expected price at which the investment will be sold at T. The valuation merely states the no-arbitrage condition for prices between two points of time and so serves to demonstrate the M&M principle with no-arbitrage. Dividends reduce value, dollar-for-dollar (at least where there are no frictions like taxes); otherwise there would be arbitrage opportunities. Accordingly, any dividend paid up to point T reduces P_T by the same present-value amount; dividend payout is a zero–net–present–value activity. Frictions may modify this statement, but they are presumed to be of second order, best dealt with in valuation by understanding the cost of the frictions – liquidity discounts and control premiums, for example – rather than designing a valuation model with frictions as the main driver.

The DDM presents a conundrum: value is based on expected dividends, but forecasting dividends is irrelevant to valuation. This conundrum must be resolved. The resolution must design a practical approach to valuation while still honoring the theory of modern finance. Clearly, another model is needed, but that model must maintain the no-arbitrage property that value is the discounted value of expected dividends forecasted to infinity. That is, the model must yield the equivalent valuation to the DDM for infinite-horizon forecasts.

We proceed now to investigate alternative models. As we do so, the reader will become aware that the solution to the valuation problem is an accounting problem. And a valuation model is really an accounting model, a model of how one accounts for value.

1.2 The discounted cash flow model

The M&M dividend irrelevance proposition assumes that firms' investment activities are not affected by dividend payments. Thus dividends are a distribution of value rather than the creation of value. This implies that value comes from investment activities, and so a valuation model captures the value generated from investments. A popular alternative is the discounted cash flow (DCF) model, where value is based on the expected free cash flows coming from investments. The equivalence to the DDM is clear from the cash conservation equation (otherwise referred to as the sources and uses of funds equation):

$$FCF_t = d_t + F_t$$

That is, the net cash from the firm, free cash flow (FCF), is applied as cash payout to shareholders, d_t, or to net debt holders, F_t. This is an accounting identity; as a practical matter, the accountant's bank reconciliation will not reconcile without uses of cash equal to sources. Substituting for $d_t = FCF_t - F_t$ in equation (1) for all t, the DDM is restated as

$$Value_0 = \sum_{t=1}^{\infty} \frac{FCF_t}{\rho_f^t} - V_0^{ND} \qquad \text{(DCF) (2)}$$

where V_0^{ND}, the value of the net debt, is the present value of expected cash flows to debt, F_t. The required return, ρ_f, now pertains to "the firm" (or "the enterprise") rather than the equity and reconciles to the required return for equity, ρ, via the Miller and Modigliani (1961) weighted-average cost of capital formula implied by no-arbitrage. The valuation also involves infinite-horizon forecasting, so the (practical) finite-horizon version of the model is implemented in practice:

$$Value_0 = \sum_{t=1}^{T} \frac{FCF_t}{\rho_f^t} + \frac{FCF_{T+1}}{\rho_f^T (\rho_f - g_{FCF})} - V_0^{ND} \qquad \text{(2a)}$$

where g_{FCF} is (one plus) the expected growth rate for free cash flow after period $T+1$ (and $g_{FCF} < \rho_f$).

Is this model an improvement over the DDM? If the firm has no net debt, $FCF_t = d_t$, so the model forecasts the same dividends as the DDM (with its inherent problems). So nothing is being put on the table; pure substitution is not theory. If the firm has net debt, then $FCF_t = d_t + F_t$, but under the Miller and Modigliani (1961) debt irrelevance principle, trading in financing debt is a zero-net-present-value activity. One can recognize frictions where issuing and redeeming debt affect value, but, again, building a valuation model around frictions misses a central point: value comes primarily from investing in businesses.

If $d_t + F_t$ is not a valuation metric, neither is free cash flow, for $FCF_t = d_t + F_t$. This is best demonstrated by an example:

Over the period 1996–2000, the share price for Starbucks, the retail coffee chain, increased 423 percent, so investors saw value generated. However, the free cash flows over the same period were negative. How can a firm with negative cash flow add so much to its market price? The answer lies with the free cash flow metric. Free cash flow is cash flow from operations minus cash invested in the business, as in the exhibit. Firms invest to generate value, but free cash flow treats investment as a negative; firms increasing investment reduce free cash flow and those liquidating investments increase it, *ceteris paribus*. This is perverse. Value-adding firms generate cash, but they also consume cash to do so.[1]

Table 11.1 Starbucks Corporation (in thousands of dollars)

	1996	1997	1998	1999	2000
Cash from operations	135,236	97,075	147,717	224,987	314,080
Cash investments	148,436	206,591	214,707	302,179	363,719
Free cash flow	(13,200)	(109,516)	(66,990)	(77,192)	(49,639)
Earnings	42,127	57,412	68,372	101,693	94,564

The problems with DCF valuation are evident if one applies the model to a valuation of Starbucks at the beginning of 1996 with expected free cash flows for 1996–2000 set equal to the actual numbers in the exhibit. Using the actual cash flows for expected cash flows removes uncertainty, but the resulting valuation is not at all helpful. All free cash flows to the forecast horizon in 2000 are negative, but value must be positive (assuming limited liability). Thus more than 100 percent of the value must be in the continuing value, and that rides on the assumed growth rate. Benjamin Graham's concern about valuations that put a lot of weight on "continued growth in the future" (in the quote in the introduction) weighs heavily here. Of course, the valuation can be completed by forecasting the long run (when the cash flows from the investments will be realized), but that puts the investor into long-horizon forecasting where he or she is most uncertain. In short, the model is not very practical.

DCF valuation forecasts cash that will flow through the cash flow statement in the future. In accounting terms, DCF is a valuation approach that employs cash accounting. To the point that a valuation model is an accounting model, DCF valuation is a cash accounting model for valuation.

1.3 Accrual accounting models

Every beginning accounting student is told that cash accounting is not appropriate for businesses. Rather, business employs accrual accounting. Correspondingly, alternative models focus on the income statement and balance sheet and thus involve accrual accounting. (Accrual) earnings reconcile to free cash flow according to the accounting equation,

$$Earnings_t = FCF_t - i_t + Investment_t + Additional\ accruals_t$$

where i_t is accrued net interest expense. So the investment that was so troubling in the Starbucks example is added back to free cash flow, along with added accruals for non-cash flows (sales on credit, accrued expenses, pension liabilities, depreciation, and the like). Correspondingly, the investment and additional accruals are added to the balance sheet as net operating assets, NOA:

$$Change\ in\ NOA_t = Investment_t + Additional\ accruals_t$$

The balance sheet is thus comprised of net operating assets involved in the business and net debt involved in the financing of the business, with the difference, the book value of equity, B, governed by the balance sheet equation:

$$B_t = NOA_t - ND_t$$

While free cash flows are negative in the Starbucks exhibit, earnings are positive, and the difference is due to the accounting for investment and accruals. The identification of investment and accruals is governed by accounting theory. Treating investment as an asset rather than a deduction from the flow variable "looks right" and indeed is supported by extant accounting theory. But will valuation based on earnings and book values work?

1.3.1 The Gordon model

The Gordon model begins (appropriately) with the dividend discount model, with expected dividends after the forward year represented by a constant growth rate (given here by one plus the growth rate, g):

$$Value_0 = \frac{d_1}{\rho - g}$$

(The model can be extended to any forecast horizon, with constant growth assumed after that horizon.) Recognizing that forecasting dividends is impractical, the Gordon model substitutes earnings for dividends with an assumed payout ratio, $k = d_t/Earnings_t$, all t. Thus, substituting for d_1,

$$Value_0 = \frac{k.Earnings_1}{\rho - g_{Earn}}$$

and the growth rate is now the expected earnings growth rate.

The case of zero payout is clearly an issue here. But, more generally, rescaling by a constant, k, adds little as a matter of theory, so nothing has been put on the table. Indeed, this valuation violates the M&M dividend irrelevance property. Payout reduces subsequent earnings growth and retention increases it, so the earnings growth rate becomes a function of payout as well as the firm's ability to generate earnings. An extension of the Gordon model, the Gordon-Shapiro model sets the earnings growth rate equal to $1 - ROE$, where ROE is the (book) rate of return on equity. But $1 - ROE$ reflects the retention rate, that is, the dividend payout. To be M&M consistent, one requires a valuation model where earnings growth represents the ability of the business to grow earnings, rather than earnings growth as a representation of irrelevant payout/retention.

1.3.2 The residual income model

A further accounting equation – the so-called clean-surplus equation – reconciles earnings, book values, and dividends:

$$B_t = B_{t-1} + Earnings_t - d_t$$

where $Earnings_t$ is comprehensive ("clean-surplus") earnings, and d_t is the net dividend to equity holders. Substituting $d_t = Earnings_t - (B_t - B_{t!1})$ for dividends in model (1) and iterating over future periods,

$$V_0^T \equiv B_0 + \sum_{t=1}^{T} \frac{RE_t}{\rho^t} \qquad \text{(RIM) (3)}$$

$\rightarrow Value_0$ in model (1) as $T \rightarrow \infty$, provided that $\dfrac{B_T}{\rho^T} \rightarrow 0$ as $T \rightarrow \infty$.

Accordingly, this model is equivalent to the DDM for infinite forecasting horizons. $RE_t \equiv$ $Earnings_t - (\rho - 1)B_{t-1}$ is called residual earnings or residual income, so this model is known as the residual income model (RIM).[2]

Equivalently, by iterating out earnings, book values, and dividends from the future stream of forecasted residual earnings,

$$V_0^T = \frac{1}{\rho^T}\left[\sum_{t=1}^{T} \rho^{T-t} d_t + B_T\right] \tag{3a}$$

and

$$V_0^T = \frac{1}{\rho^T}\left[B_0 + \sum_{t=1}^{T} Earnings_t^C\right] \tag{3b}$$

where $\sum_{t=1}^{T} Earnings_t^C = \sum_{t=1}^{T} Earnings_t + \sum_{t=1}^{T}\left(\rho^{T-t} - 1\right) d_t$, that is, total earnings forecasted to T with dividends reinvested at the discount rate (known as cum-dividend earnings). Both expressions depict value as the present value of expected cum-dividend book value.[3]

The RIM has a desirable property: it is M&M consistent. Ohlson (1995) shows that, if dividends are paid out of book value (and do not affect contemporaneous earnings) – as prescribed by the clean-surplus equation – then the RIM valuation is insensitive to payout. A proviso comes in Feltham and Ohlson (1995): dividends must be paid out of zero-net-present-value assets (for example, excess cash). Under M&M assumptions, current dividends reduce current value dollar-for-dollar but also reduce V_0^T in (3) in the same way by reducing B_0 dollar-for-dollar with no effect on subsequent residual earnings. Further, any anticipated future payout in equation (3a) reduces future book value B_t by the same present value amount to leave V_0^T unaffected. Note that this is an accounting property; M&M properties are built into clean-surplus accounting as a matter of accounting principle.[4]

We noted that the finite-horizon DDM in equation (1b) was circular because it requires an expectation of the terminal price to find the current price. However, a comparison of equation (3a) with (1b) shows that the RIM supplies a terminal value for the finite-horizon dividend discount model, a point emphasized in Penman (1998). That is, in accumulating earnings in book values, the accounting system projects an expected terminal payoff in book value at time T. Dividends are paid out of book value, so expected book value at any point in time, T, is an estimate of the expected dividends to be paid from T onwards. Thus we see how forecasting using accounting numbers potentially reduces an infinite forecasting problem to a finite one, a feature much desired for practical valuation.

However, the comparison of equations (3a) and (1b) shows the error that remains from forecasting for a given forecast horizon:

$$Value_0 = V_0^T + \frac{1}{\rho^T}\left(P_T - B_T\right) \tag{3c}$$

The error, $P_T - B_T \rightarrow 0$ as $T \rightarrow \infty$, but for finite T, the error is value not yet booked to book value by time, T. As the difference between price and book value is given by subsequent expected residual income, value can be expressed as

$$Value_0 = B_0 + \sum_{t=1}^{T} \frac{RE_t}{\rho^t} + \frac{P_T - B_T}{\rho^T}$$

$$= B_0 + \sum_{t=1}^{T} \frac{RE_t}{\rho^t} + \frac{RE_{T+1}}{\rho^T (\rho - g_{RE})} \qquad (3d)$$

This standard textbook formula plugs for the error with a growth rate in residual income after $T+1$, $g_{RE} < \rho$. Like the DCF model, the application of the model requires a speculative long run growth rate. Thus any practical advantage of the model over the DCF model must focus on the weight that has to be given to speculative growth rates, and that, in turn, depends on the amount of value expected to be booked to book value prior to T. We return to this issue in section 2.

Like the DCF model, RIM can be unlevered to separate the value of the business, the enterprise, from the value of the net debt.[5]

1.3.3 The abnormal earnings growth model

Define abnormal earnings growth for period t as $AEG_t \equiv Earnings_t + (\rho - 1)d_{t-1} - \rho Earnings_{t-1}$. That is, AEG_t is earnings for the period in excess of earnings for the prior period growing at the required return rate, but with dividends reinvested. Given clean-surplus accounting, $AEG_t = \Delta RE_t$, where Δ indicates changes. Substituting in RIM (3),

$$V_0^T = \frac{Earnings_1}{\rho - 1} + \frac{1}{\rho - 1} \sum_{t=2}^{T} \frac{1}{\rho^{t-1}} AEG_t \qquad (4)$$

This is the so-called AEG model or the Ohlson-Juettner model from Ohlson and Juettner-Nauroth (2005). That paper shows that the model, like the RIM, is consistent with M&M dividend irrelevance. While this derivation demonstrates the equivalence with the RIM given clean-surplus accounting, there are subtle differences. First, this model does not involve book value; the model is based on expected earnings and expected earnings growth. As such, it can be seen as the M&M-consistent version of the Gordon model. Second, for finite-horizon applications, the forecasted growth rate in the continuing value has a different interpretation from that for the RIM. Indeed, while the two models are equivalent for infinite-horizon forecasting (and equivalent to the DDM), they are not necessarily equivalent valuations for finite-horizon forecasting.

The first point is demonstrated by a derivation of both models that is more general than that for the RIM, as in Ohlson and Juettner-Nauroth (2005). An algebraic, zero-sum equality

$$0 = y_0 + \sum_{t=1}^{\infty} \frac{1}{\rho^t} \left(y_t - \rho y_{t-1} \right)$$

holds given the transversality condition, $\lim_{t \to \infty} \rho^{-t} y_t = 0$. Adding this series to DDM in equation (1),

$$Value_0 = y_0 + \sum_{t=1}^{\infty} \frac{1}{\rho^t} \left(y_t + d_t - \rho y_{t-1} \right)$$

A valuation model then becomes an issue of specifying the y variable. Setting $y_0 = B_0$ and assuming clean-surplus accounting, we have the RIM. Setting $y_0 = \dfrac{Earnings_1}{\rho - 1}$, we have the AEG model, but without the requirement of clean-surplus accounting (and without book value).[6]

As the AEG model does not require clean-surplus accounting, it is more general. That is probably of little consequence in practice. However the second difference mentioned is more consequential. For finite-horizon forecasting, the AEG model with a constant growth rate (for just two forward periods here) is

$$Value_0 = \frac{Earnings_1}{\rho - 1} + \frac{1}{\rho - 1} \cdot \frac{AEG_2}{\rho - g_{AEG}} \tag{4a}$$

$$= \frac{Earnings_1}{\rho - 1} \left[\frac{g_2 - (g_{AEG} - 1)}{(\rho - 1) - (g_{AEG} - 1)} \right] \tag{4b}$$

where $g_{AEG} < \rho$ and $g_2 \equiv (\Delta Earnings_2 + (\rho - 1)d_1)/Earnings_1$, that is, the expected growth rate in cum–dividend earnings two years ahead. While $AEG_t = \Delta RE_t$, given clean-surplus accounting, it is not the case that $g_{AEG} = g_{RE}$. This follows simply from the mathematical statement that if the level of a variable grows at the rate, g, so do its changes, but the converse is not true. So valuations (3a) and (4a) (for the same forecast horizon) are not equivalent. Indeed, a constant growth rate for AEG implies a declining rate for RE. One might suggest that a declining rate is more likely, but that is an empirical matter. The g_{AEG} rate in the model equals the long run (asymptotic) growth rate in expected earnings, provided dividend payout meets a minimum. This long run rate is likely to be the same for all firms (the average gross domestic product growth rate?), but that means than g_{AEG} (the rate at which AEG is expected to grow) is the same for all firms in the cross section. Value is then driven solely by forward earnings, growth in the second period, g_2, and the discount rate. While that might be doubtful for a two-period horizon (as in model (4a)), the model presumably calibrates better with longer forecast horizons.

1.4 Empirical evidence

Empirical research compares valuation models is three ways. First, a set of papers compares the models on their ability to explain current prices. Second, a number of papers ask whether the models work to determine "value," which is then compared to traded prices to identify mispriced securities. Third, papers apply the models in reverse engineering fashion to estimate the "implied cost of capital." This chapter does not cover the latter; the literature is long and rather inconclusive, in part because there is no objective benchmark for the "true" observable cost of capital. And, disappointingly, these papers have had difficulty in showing that their estimates of the cost of capital actually predict average stock returns, though Nekrasov and Ogneva (2011) and Fitzgerald, Gray, Hall, and Jeyaraj (2013) are recent exceptions. For a survey, see Easton (2009).

Penman and Sougiannis (1997) examined whether valuations based on accrual accounting numbers exhibit the M&M properties of dividend displacement and dividend irrelevance, with an answer in the affirmative. Then followed a number of papers that compared RIM valuation with DDM and DCF valuation, with the metric being the relative error of model values in approximating observed prices.[7] While it is recognized that all models provide the same valuation for infinite forecasting horizons, the emphasis in these papers is on comparing the valuations over varying finite horizons. The consistent result is that residual income models provide more accurate valuations than cash flow models when US GAAP (generally accepted accounting principles) accrual accounting is used. However, the RIM does not perform particularly well when price-earnings ratios and price-to-book ratios are high. This might be expected, for these are cases where the continuing-value growth rate contributes heavily to the valuation.

For a discussion of these papers, follow the debate in Lundholm and O'Keefe (2001a and 2001b) and Penman (2001).[8]

Two papers have compared the RIM with the AEG model. In his comments on the AEG model, Penman (2005) documents that RIM values approximate traded prices better than AEG. In a more extensive analysis, Jorgensen, Lee, and Yoo (2011) demonstrate the same.

These papers take traded prices as a benchmark with the assumption that prices express value. This "efficient market" assumption is common in much empirical research in accounting and finance, but a second set of papers takes the alternative view: do valuation models yield values that identify mispricing? Using analysts' consensus earnings forecasts as inputs along with assumptions on the continuing value, Frankel and Lee (1998) show that, while the RIM values track prices, they also predict future stock returns in the cross section, an indicating of mispricing. Lee, Myers, and Swaminathan (1999) conduct a similar analysis for the portfolio of Dow stocks and find that value relative to the price of the Dow index (V/P) leads the price in a way that is consistent with V/P identifying mispricing. As in all empirical studies that forecast stock returns, the conclusions of these studies must be qualified because the predicted returns may be due to differences in risk. Ali, Hwang, and Trombley (2003) investigate whether returns predicted by the RIM are explained by risk or mispricing.

2 Accounting theory and valuation

The legitimacy of valuation models rests on their equivalence to the DDM. However, that equivalence holds only for infinite forecast horizons and then via a substitution that simply involves a mathematical relation. With the DCF model, the relation is the cash conservation equation; for the RIM, the clean–surplus equation; and the AEG model uses a mathematical equivalence that identifies a y variable that is then simply nominated as capitalized forward earnings, by fiat. This is hardly satisfactory as a matter of theory, for substitution without additional structure puts little on the table. The equivalence to DDM necessarily holds only for infinite horizons, but practical valuation must involve finite horizons. So the theorist (and practitioner) might well ask how far we have come.

The point is driven home by recognizing that the RIM works for random numbers for earnings, provided one forecasts "to infinity." This is because the clean–surplus relation forces a reconciliation of the accounting to dividends, but only necessarily so with the final payout; book value must go to zero as the final dividend is paid in liquidation. Indeed, without further structure, accrual accounting models exhibit a value-irrelevance property with respect to the accounting. This is demonstrated with the finite-horizon RIM in equations (3a) and (3b):

$$V_0^T = \frac{1}{\rho^T}\left[\sum_{t=1}^{T}\rho^{T-t}d_t + B_T\right] = \frac{1}{\rho^T}\left[B_0 + \sum_{t=1}^{T}Earnings_t^C\right]$$

Accrual accounting is a matter of allocating earnings to periods under the constraint that total, life-long earnings equal total cash flows. The allocation to earnings expected before T can be anything and the asymptotic property still holds; an infinite horizon is needed to correct the "errors" in the accounting. That allocation determines the expected book value at T, and that, in turn, determines the error for the horizon T, $P_T - B_T$ in equation (3c). At one extreme, the allocation could be zero earnings recognized before T. At the other extreme, all expected earnings could be recognized immediately such that $T = 0$ and $Value_0 = B_0$. Though the RIM handles the problem of the DDM being insensitive to dividends, it replaces it with the problem of the valuation being insensitive to the accounting. Added structure that specifies the accounting that goes into the model is required for accrual accounting models to have an advantage over the DDM for finite (practical) finite horizons. Again, a practical valuation model is really an accounting model (that specifies the accounting involved).

The point is further illustrated by recognizing that the difference between the DCF model and the RIM is simply an issue of the accounting. DCF valuation uses cash accounting and thus forecasts what will come through the cash flow statement, whereas the RIM uses accrual accounting and thus forecasts future income statements and balance sheets. Indeed, the DCF model is just a special case of the RIM, a case that uses a particular accounting (cash accounting). This can be shown by separating the balance sheet and income statement into operating and financing activities, as in Feltham and Ohlson (1995). So, $B_t \equiv NOA_t - ND_t$ (for all t), where ND is net debt and NOA is net operating assets in the business (as earlier). Set $B_t \equiv -ND_t$ (that is, omit any accounting for business operations). The cash conservation equation implies a clean-surplus relation such that $ND_t = ND_{t-1} - (FCF_t - i_t) + d_t$, where i_t is net cash interest paid on the debt. Here $FCF_t - i_t$ is earnings ("cash flow earnings"). Substituting for dividends in the DDM via the clean-surplus equation,

$$V_0^T(DCF) = -ND_0 + \sum_{t=1}^{T}\frac{1}{\rho^t}\left(FCF_t - i_t + (\rho - 1)ND_{t-1}\right)$$

If net debt is measured at its present value by accruing interest such that $i_t = (\rho_D - 1)ND_{t-1}$ (for all t, with ρ_D the required return for net debt), then

$$V_0^T(DCF) = \sum_{t=1}^{T}\frac{FCF_t}{\rho_f^t} - V_0^{ND}$$

which is DCF model (2) for a forecast horizon of T. So, the DCF model is a residual income model with cash accounting for operations and accrual accounting for net debt. Lücke (1955) provides a similar demonstration. Note from equation (3c) that the error for the DCF model for a finite horizon is $\frac{1}{\rho^T}(P_T - B_T)$, but $B_T = -ND_T$ in this case, so the error is quite large (equal to or greater than P_T). This might point to the superiority of accrual accounting (which typically reports positive book values), but there is no necessity that accrual accounting work well without further specification on the type of accrual accounting.

This discussion serves to emphasize that much research needs to be done before we have a satisfactory valuation model. Recognizing the point that a valuation model is really an accounting model – a model for accounting for value – the issue is one for accounting research. It is an issue for accounting theory, and in a valuation context, that theory is also valuation theory. This is a challenge for accounting theory and one with potentially big payoffs, for it provides a framework for research to address the normative issues of accounting policy faced by accounting standard setters.

2.1 Accounting research to date

The empirical research on valuation models, summarized above, points to the superiority of accrual accounting models over cash flow models with US GAAP accounting. But US GAAP accounting is not necessarily the ideal accrual accounting for the purpose. The question is open, but regrettably research to date has done little to answer the question. However, while there has been little normative work, there has been some modeling of how different accounting principles affect accounting numbers and, thus, of how one infers value under those accounting principles. We summarize this research with the aim of promoting more thought on the normative accounting question.

The clean-surplus operation

In the derivation of the RIM, there is one aspect of the accounting that does bite. The clean-surplus relation is not an identity but rather a prescriptive accounting procedure; accounting starts with book value, calculates earnings, closes the earnings to book value (in the "closing entry"), and then pays dividends out of book value. Unlike the cash conservation equation for the derivation of the DCF model, this procedure does not have to be so; it is part of the design of an accounting system, an accounting principle. Indeed, it is violated by the practice of recognizing "other comprehensive income" in equity rather that in earnings per share under GAAP and International Financial Reporting Standards (IFRS).

As we have seen, it is this principle that renders a valuation model consistent with a fundamental principle in the theory of finance, dividend irrelevance; the clean-surplus accounting principle impinges directly on the use of accounting numbers for valuation. Valuation theory therefore suggests a normative accounting principle: accounting should be clean surplus, at least in expectation. From the point of view of valuing the common (ordinary) shareholders' claim, that rules out preferred dividends going through equity rather than earnings, for example. It also says that GAAP and IFRS fail in not recognizing the loss on the conversion of contingent claims to equity (such as convertible bonds and preferred stock and employee stock options). From a practical point of view, it says that an investor using GAAP and IFRS earnings is in danger of overvaluing the equity.[9]

The cancelling error property

Given clean-surplus accounting, one can substitute $d_t = Earnings_t - (B_t - B_{t-1})$ for dividends in the stock return, $P_t + d_t - P_{t-1}$, such that

$$E(P_t + d_t - P_{t-1}) = E(Earninigs_t + P_t - B_t - (P_{t-1} - B_{t-1}))$$

That is, the expected stock return is equal to expected earnings plus the expected change in premium of price over book value. In the case of no expected change in premium, earnings equal the stock return. This expression, found in Easton, Harris, and Ohlson (1992), has two implications for valuation.

First, it is not necessary to have a "correct" balance sheet to infer expected returns, and thus value, if the expected error in the balance sheet is a constant. In this case, value is expected earnings capitalized with the required return, and accounting in the balance sheet is irrelevant. Omitted assets, for example, are not a problem if they result in a constant premium, a point made in Penman (2009) in evaluating the accounting for intangible assets. In short, valuation tolerates error in the balance sheet up to a constant. Second, finite-horizon valuation is completed (without error) for a forecast horizon, T, if $P_{T+1} - B_{T+1} - (P_T - B_T) = 0$. In this case,

$$P_T = \frac{Earnings_{T+1}}{\rho - 1}$$

so the terminal value for the DDM in equation (1b) is supplied by the accounting, as is the valuation error for the RIM, $\frac{1}{\rho^T}(P_T - B_T)$, in equation (3c). For the AEG model, valuation reduces to capitalized forward earnings, the first term in equation (4), if the expected change in premium in the forward year is zero. More generally, finite-horizon valuation is completed (without error) for any horizon, T, where the condition is satisfied. For the AEG model, it is easy to see that expected $AEG = 0$ for periods after T in this case.

The case of no change in premium has a close resemblance to the canceling error property in accounting theory: earnings are unaffected by the accounting errors in the balance sheet provided the errors in the opening and closing balances cancel. Research and development (R&D) accounting provides an example. GAAP accounting (and IFRS, in part) leaves R&D investment off the balance sheet such that price is greater than book value. But earnings are the same whether one capitalizes and amortizes R&D expenditures or expenses them immediately, provided there is no growth in R&D expenditure. So the accounting treatment of R&D does not matter in this case. Similarly, depreciation and earnings are the same, irrespective of depreciation method, if there is no growth in depreciable assets. The growth qualification makes a point: expected growth in expenditures with error in the balance sheet implies an increase in expected premiums. It is the growth case that accounting theory has to grapple with. This leads us into the properties of accounting numbers under conservatism.

Conservative accounting

The valuation theory in Ohlson (1995) involves "unbiased accounting," where $P_T - B_T \rightarrow 0$ as $T \rightarrow \infty$. That, of course, facilitates finite-horizon valuation. If, for a given T, $P_T = B_T$, the valuation is made without error, and the horizon, T, depends on how quickly book value catches up with price. Feltham and Ohlson (1995) explore an alternative accounting, conservative accounting, where carrying values are systematically below value such that $P_T - B_T > 0$ for all T. Zhang (2000) and Cheng (2005) explore this accounting further. If the expected premium is given by a constant (that is, there is no expected change in premium), then a finite valuation is also satisfied, as we have just seen. However, Feltham and Ohlson (1995) show that, with growth in investment, premiums expand under conservative accounting, and, correspondingly, there is expected growth in earnings and residual earnings, and thus g_{RE} in model (4b) is greater than 1. As $AEG = \Delta RE$, there is corresponding expected growth in AEG.

GAAP accounting and IFRS accounting are conservative accounting systems where the price-to-book ratio is typically above 1. The understanding of conservative accounting brings warnings about how to handle accounting numbers. First, book rates of return, like ROE, are typically above the required return in expectation because of low carrying value for assets in the denominator. This challenges any theory and valuation model that assumes that ROE is expected to revert to the required return in the long run, as many models do – for example, the Vuolteenaho (2002) model and the many finance and accounting papers that build on that model. That assumption requires that $P_T - B_T$ reverts to zero in the long run (unbiased accounting). Second, there are also numerator effects when conservative accounting affects earnings, so conservative accounting can both increase and decrease ROE. Consequently, it is a mistake to take the accounting rate of return as the economic rate of return, as also is often done when evaluating a firm's "profitability"; a firm earning normal economic returns (and adding no value above the required return) may report ROE greater than the required return under conservative accounting. The effect of conservative accounting on book rate of return is further explored in Livingstone and Salamon (1970); Brief and Lawson (1992); Danielson and Press (2003); Rajan, Reichelstein, and Soliman (2007); and Penman and Zhang (2014).

Accounting methods

Some papers have investigated alternative metrics and their properties. While not always focused on valuation, these papers are relevant because they involve different accounting for book rate of return and residual earnings. Liu, Ohlson, and Zhang (2013) propose profitability measures based on modified cash accounting as an alternative to book rate of return under GAAP, and in so doing highlight the difficulties with the standard measures. Rogerson (1997 and 2008) and Dutta and Reichelstein (2005) propose alternative accounting for depreciation. McNichols, Rajan, and Reichelstein (2013) propose alternative price-to-book ratios based on accounting that "corrects" for conservatism.

3 Accounting, risk, and the required return

With all the valuation models examined, one component has gone unmentioned: the required return, ρ. Practitioners well know the sensitivity of a valuation to this input. Discount rates are compounded in many valuations – for period t ahead, the discount rate is ρ^t – so error in the rate has a significant effect. What is the required return?

The accounting theorist might dodge this question by saying that the number is supplied by asset pricing research; models such as the capital asset pricing model (CAPM) and the Fama and French multifactor model supply the required return. Generalized asset pricing theory has indeed led to a better understanding of the theory of the required return, but it is fair to say that research has not produced an operational model that supplies the number. After 60 years of research in asset pricing, we still do not have a handle on the problem.[10]

This chapter closes with some thoughts about how accounting theory might be brought to the issue. Accounting principles determine the allocation of earnings to periods, and, as noted, that bears on finite-horizon valuation. But does it also bear on risk?

A key accounting principle ties the inter-period allocation to risk (and potentially to the required return): under uncertainty, earnings are not booked until the uncertainty has largely been resolved. In most cases, this "realization principle" requires receipt of cash to be relatively certain, usually indicated by a sale and a (collectible) accounts receivable. In asset pricing terms, earnings are not recognized until the firm has a low-beta asset. This deferral principle is operative throughout GAAP and IFRS, with revenue recognition rules (and consequent deferred revenue) and associated expense matching producing a number that is indicative of expected cash (with some certainty). Even the expensing of R&D expenditures and advertising, seen by many as a mismatching of revenues with expenses, involves a deferral of earnings recognition until uncertainty has been resolved; R&D is risky and may not generate revenues against which (capitalized and amortized) R&D can be matched.

Deferral of earnings is an application of conservative accounting, but now with conservative accounting tied to risk. (The label "conservative accounting" is appropriate, for it refers to accounting under risk.) Deferral of earnings recognition produces expected earnings growth, so the accounting principle ties risk to expected earnings growth: growth is risky (as, indeed, the investor buying a start-up growth company appreciates). Conservative accounting produces expected earnings growth with investment (above), and thus earnings growth is tied to risky investment. In the Feltham and Ohlson (1995) conservative accounting paper, the required return is ignored – it is a constant unrelated to the accounting – but now we have a basis of tying the accounting to the required return.

The implications for valuation are important. In all the valuation models we have referred to, the finite-horizon valuation is completed with a terminal value calculation, as in equations (2a), (3d), and (4b). The capitalization rate, $\rho - g$, is usually applied by first finding the required return and then adjusting this for the expected growth. Typically, ρ and g are seen as independent inputs, with g increasing the calculated value for a given ρ. But what if growth were risky? Then r would increase with g, yielding a lower valuation. The practice of adding value for growth may not be correct. Penman and Reggiani (2013b) show how failure to recognize this point can lead value investors into a value trap.

The relationship between growth and risk is clear with financing leverage. Penman (2012, chapter 4) shows that increased leverage adds to expected earnings growth deterministically, provided leverage is favorable. But it also adds to (financing) risk such that, under Modigliani and Miller (1958) conditions, price is unaffected; risk and growth cancel with no value added to price. It is not unreasonable that this might also be so for business operations, at least to some extent; one cannot buy more earnings growth without taking on more risk, at least on average.

The connection of accounting numbers to risk via the realization principle suggests that accounting theory might have something to contribute to solving the problem of the required return. Just as accounting valuation models must be consistent with the theory of finance, so must this accounting theory be consistent with the theory of risk and return in asset pricing. The difficulty is tying the deferral accounting to priced risk, that is, systematic risk priced under asset pricing.

A few papers show promise. First, Ohlson (2008) shows that an accounting system can be designed with the expected earnings growth rate tying one-to-one to the risk premium. Second, Penman and Reggiani (2013a) show empirically that expected earnings growth from the deferral principle is risky and is associated with higher average returns. Significantly, it is a combination of a firm's earnings-to-price (E/P) and book-to-price (B/P) that provides this indication, thus providing an explanation of why B/P appears so prominently in asset pricing models such as the Fama and French three-factor model and its relatives. Penman, Reggiani, Richardson, and Tuna (2013) take up the idea to develop a simple characteristic model for asset pricing, where, in predicting the expected return, E/P is sufficient when there is no growth but the weight shifts to B/P when there is expected growth. While empirical finance has had trouble documenting that financing leverage adds to expected returns – most papers document a negative relationship – this paper shows that leverage is priced positively under the model. Penman and Zhu (2013) show that a number of accounting "anomalies" – accruals, asset growth, investment, and more – can be explained by these accounting variables predicting risky expected earnings growth. Penman and Zhang (2014) show explicitly how conservative accounting (and the earnings deferral it implies) connects to risk and return. Konstantinidi and Pope (2014) use quantile regressions to predict the full distribution of ex ante earnings outcomes, a promising approach to identifying risk in earnings.

Penman (2012) proposes ways for the investor to finesse the problem of the indeterminacy of the cost of capital and to incorporate the idea that growth is risky into valuation and stock selection. However, there is a pressing need for accounting and finance theory to develop these ideas more rigorously. That holds great promise, with the possibility of developing an accounting-based asset pricing model. In doing so, accounting theory will deal not only with the accounting issues in the numerator of a valuation model, but also with a denominator that involves the discount rate. That will truly be a contribution to establishing a practical valuation model. The two are connected: valuation is based on expected accounting outcomes but also on the risk that those expectations will be realized, transmitted via the realization principle.

4 Conclusion

The conclusion is very short. Valuation is an accounting issue; valuation models are differentiated in how they account for value. However, the so-called accrual accounting models developed in recent years still lack substance; the form of the accounting to go into those models is not well developed. That presents a challenge to accounting research. The promise is that accounting theory and valuation theory will come under the same discipline, as will empirical research in accounting and asset pricing. Financial accounting standard setters will be guided in pursuing their goal of providing information about future cash flows to investors, and investors will be served with valuations that provide a sound basis for evaluating the present value of expected cash flows.

Notes

1 For further demonstration of the problems with DCF valuation, see Penman (2013, chapter 4).
2 Ang and Liu (2001) modify the model to accommodate stochastic discount rates, and Feltham and Ohlson (1999) derive the model in the form of equation (1a), that is, with the discount for risk in the numerator.
3 The residual earnings model has had a long history. In the early part of the twentieth century, the idea that a firm's value is based on "excess profits" was firmly established in the United Kingdom. The model is in the German literature of the 1920s and 1930s, particularly in the writings of Schmalenbach. In the US, Preinreich (1936 and 1938) wrote on the model. In a 1941 paper, Preinreich recognizes the model in a prize essay by a student, J. H. Bourne in *Accountant*, London, 22 September 1888, pp. 605–606. Strangely, the model was ignored for many years. Williams (1938) promoted dividends as the fundamental for equity valuation, and academics have followed that tradition up to recently. Some relatively recent expositions of the residual earnings model are in Edwards and Bell (1961, pp. 48–54 and 66–69), Peasnell (1982), and Brief and Lawson (1992). Ohlson (1995) parameterizes the evolution of residual earnings to arrive at propositions about how accounting relates to value.
4 Dividends may provide information about value if they are correlated with variables that pertain to value. (This is the so-called "signaling" feature of dividends.) For more discussion of dividend irrelevance and accounting, see Gao, Ohlson, and Ostaszewski (2013), Clubb (2013), and Rees and Valentincic (2013).
5 Feltham and Ohlson (1995) unlever the RIM model. See Penman (2013, chapter 14) for the practical application.
6 See Ohlson and Gao (2006). Penman (2005) evaluates the AEG model against the RIM.
7 See Francis, Olsson, and Oswald (2000); Courteau, Kao, and Richardson (2001); and Penman and Sougiannis (1998).
8 Other papers have examined RIM under the linear information dynamics imposed on the evolution of residual earnings by Ohlson (1995), but these dynamics are not implied by the model in its more general form. See, for example, Dechow, Hutton, and Sloan (1999).
9 The normative prescription for the accounting for contingent equity claims is in Ohlson and Penman (2004). A full coverage of "dirty surplus" accounting is in Penman (2013, chapter 8).
10 Penman (2012, chapter 1) assesses the current state of asset pricing for the purpose of valuation.

References

Ali, A., L. Hwang, and M. Trombley. 2003. Residual-income-based valuation predicts future stock returns: evidence on mispricing vs. risk explanations. *The Accounting Review* 78, 377–396.

Ang, A., and J. Liu. 2001. A general affine earnings valuation model. *Review of Accounting Studies* 6, 397–425.

Bach, C., and P. Christensen. 2013. Consumption-based equity valuation. Unpublished paper, Aarhus University.

Brief, R., and R. Lawson. 1992. The role of the accounting rate of return in financial statement analysis. *The Accounting Review* 67, 411–426.

Cheng, Q. 2005. What determines residual income? *The Accounting Review* 80, 85–112.

Christensen, P., and G. Feltham. 2009. Equity valuation. *Foundations and Trends in Accounting* 4, 1–112.

Clubb, C. 2013. Information dynamics, dividend displacement, conservatism, and earnings measurement: a development of the Ohlson (1995) valuation framework. *Review of Accounting Studies* 18, 360–385.

Courteau, L., J. Kao, and G. Richardson. 2001. Equity valuation employing the ideal versus ad hoc terminal value expressions. *Contemporary Accounting Research* 18, 625–661.

Danielson, M., and E. Press. 2003. Accounting returns revisited: evidence of their usefulness in estimating economic returns. *Review of Accounting Studies* 8, 493–530.

Dechow, P., A. Hutton, and R. Sloan. 1999. An empirical assessment of the residual income valuation model. *Journal of Accounting and Economics* 26, 1–34.

Dutta, S., and S. Reichelstein. 2005. Accrual accounting for performance evaluation. *Review of Accounting Studies* 10, 527–552.

Easton, P. 2009. Estimating the cost of capital implied by market prices and accounting data. *Foundation and Trends in Accounting* 2, 241–364.

Easton, P., T. Harris, and J. Ohlson. 1992. Accounting earnings can explain most of security returns: the case of long-event windows. *Journal of Accounting and Economics* 15, 119–142.

Edwards, E., and P. Bell. 1961. *The Theory and Measurement of Business Income*. Berkeley, CA: University of California Press.

Feltham, G., and J. Ohlson. 1995. Valuation and clean surplus accounting for operating and financial activities. *Contemporary Accounting Research* 12, 689–731.

————. 1999. Residual income valuation with risk and stochastic interest rates. *The Accounting Review* 74, 165–183.

Fitzgerald, T., S. Gray, J. Hall, and R. Jeyaraj. 2013. Unconstrained estimates of the equity risk premium. *Review of Accounting Studies* 18, 560–639.

Francis, J., P. Olsson, and D. Oswald. 2000. Comparing the accuracy and explainability of dividend, free cash flow, and abnormal earnings equity value estimates. *Journal of Accounting Research* 38, 45–70.

Frankel, R., and C. Lee. 1998. Accounting valuation, market expectation, and cross-sectional stock returns. *Journal of Accounting and Economics* 25, 283–319.

Gao, Z., J. Ohlson, and A. Ostaszewski. 2013. Dividend policy irrelevancy and the construct of earnings. *Journal of Business Finance and Accounting* 40, 673–694.

Jorgensen, B., Y. Lee, and Y. Yoo. 2011. The valuation accuracy of equity value estimates inferred from conventional empirical implications of the abnormal earnings growth model: US evidence. *Journal of Business Finance and Accounting* 38, 446–471.

Konstantinidi, T., and P. Pope. 2014. Forecasting risk in earnings. *Contemporary Accounting Research*, forthcoming.

Lee, C., J. Myers, and B. Swaminathan. 1999. What is the intrinsic value of the Dow? *Journal of Finance* 54, 1693–1741.

Liu, J., J. Ohlson, and W. Zhang. 2013. A comparison of Chinese and US firms' profitability. Unpublished paper, Cheung Kong Graduate School of Business and New York University.

Livingstone, J., and G. Salamon. 1970. Relationship between the accounting and the internal rate of return measures: a synthesis and an analysis. *Journal of Accounting Research* 2, 199–216.

Lücke, W. 1955. Investitionsrechnung auf der grundlage von ausgaben oder kosten? *Zeitschrift für Betriebswirtschaftliche Forschung*, 310–324.

Lundholm, R., and T. O'Keefe. 2001a. Reconciling value estimates from the discounted cash flow model and the residual income model. *Contemporary Accounting Research* 18, 311–335.

————. 2001b. On comparing residual income and discounted cash flow models of equity valuation: a response to Penman. *Contemporary Accounting Research* 18, 693–696.

McNichols, M., M. Rajan, and S. Reichelstein. 2013. Conservatism correction for the market-to-book ratio and Tobin's *q*. Paper, Stanford University. *Review of Accounting Studies* 19, 1393–1435.

Miller, M., and F. Modigliani. 1961. Dividend policy, growth and the valuation of shares. *Journal of Business* 34, 411–433.

Modigliani F., and M. Miller. 1958. The cost of capital, corporation finance and the theory of investment. *American Economic Review* 48, 261–297.

Nekrasov, A., and M. Ogneva. 2011. Using earnings forecasts to simultaneously estimate firm-specific cost of capital and long-term growth. *Review of Accounting Studies* 16, 414–457.

Nekrasov, A., and P. Shroff. 2009. Fundamentals-based risk management in valuation. *The Accounting Review* 84, 1983–2011.

Ohlson, J. 1995. Earnings, book values, and dividends in equity valuation. *Contemporary Accounting Research* 12, 661–687.

————. 2008. Risk, growth, and permanent earnings. Unpublished paper, New York University.

Ohlson, J., and Z. Gao. 2006. Earnings, earnings growth and value. *Foundations and Trends in Accounting* 1, 1–70.

Ohlson, J., and B. Juettner-Nauroth. 2005. Expected EPS and EPS growth as determinants of value. *Review of Accounting Studies* 10, 349–365.

Ohlson, J., and S. Penman. 2004. *Debt vs. Equity: Accounting for Claims Contingent on Firms' Common Stock Performance, with Particular Attention to Employee Compensation Options*. Center for Excellence in Accounting and Security Analysis, Columbia Business School, White Paper No. 1.

Peasnell, K. 1982. Some formal connections between economic values and yields and accounting numbers. *Journal of Business Finance and Accounting* 9, 361–381.

Penman, S. 1998. A synthesis of equity valuation techniques and the terminal value calculation for the dividend discount model. *Review of Accounting Studies* 2, 303–323.

———. 2001. On comparing cash flow and accrual accounting models for use in equity valuation: a response to Lundholm and O'Keefe. *Contemporary Accounting Research* 18, 681–692.

———. 2005. Discussion of "On accounting-based valuation formulae" and "Expected EPS and EPS growth as determinants of value." *Review of Accounting Studies* 10, 367–378.

———. 2009. Accounting for intangible assets: there is also an income statement. *Abacus* 45, 359–371.

———. 2012. *Accounting for Value*. New York: Columbia University Press.

———. 2013. *Financial Statement Analysis and Security Valuation*, 5th ed. New York: The McGraw-Hill Companies, Inc.

Penman, S., and F. Reggiani. 2013a. Returns to buying earnings and book value: accounting for growth and risk. *Review of Accounting Studies* 18, 1021–1049.

———. 2013b. The value trap: value buys risky growth. Unpublished paper, Columbia University and Bocconi University.

Penman, S., and T. Sougiannis. 1997. The dividend displacement property and the substitution of anticipated earnings for dividends in equity valuation. *The Accounting Review* 72, 1–21.

———. 1998. A comparison of dividend, cash flow, and earnings approaches to equity valuation. *Contemporary Accounting Research* 15, 343–383.

Penman, S., and X. Zhang. 2014. Connecting book rate of return to risk: the information conveyed by conservative accounting. Unpublished paper, Columbia University and University of California, Berkeley.

Penman, S., and J. Zhu. 2014. Accounting anomalies, risk and return. *The Accounting Review* 89, 1835–1836.

Penman, S., F. Reggiani, S. Richardson, and Í. Tuna. 2013. An accounting-based characteristic model for asset pricing. Unpublished paper, Columbia University, Bocconi University, and London Business School.

Preinreich, G. 1936. The fair value and yield of common stock. *The Accounting Review* 11, 130–140.

———. 1938. Annual survey of economic theory: the theory of depreciation. *Econometrica* 6, 219–241.

Rajan, M., S. Reichelstein, and M. Soliman. 2007. Conservatism, growth, and return on investment. *Review of Accounting Studies* 12, 325–370.

Rees, B., and A. Valentincic. 2013. Dividend irrelevance and accounting models of value. *Journal of Business Finance and Accounting* 40, 646–672.

Rogerson, W. 1997. Intertemporal cost allocation and managerial investment incentives: a theory explaining the use of economic value added as a performance measure. *Journal of Political Economy* 105, 770–795.

———. 2008. Intertemporal cost allocation and investment decisions. *Journal of Political Economy* 116, 931–950.

Rubinstein, M. 1976. The valuation of uncertain income streams and the pricing of options. *The Bell Journal of Economics* 7, 407–425.

Vuolteenaho, T. 2002. What drives firm-level stock returns? *Journal of Finance* 57, 233–264.

Williams, J. 1938. *The Theory of Investment Value*. Cambridge, MA: Harvard University Press.

Zhang, X. 2000. Conservative accounting and equity valuation. *Journal of Accounting and Economics* 29, 125–149.

12

Earnings management

Implications and controversies

Joshua Ronen and Varda Yaari

1 Introduction

In April 2007, after five years of hard work, we submitted our book, *Earnings Management: Emerging Insights in Theory, Practice, and Research*, to Springer's Series in Accounting Scholarship. Initially, we expected to follow the footsteps of Ronen and Sadan (1981) and write a short manuscript focusing on the developments in earnings management since 1981. We soon realized, however, that the volume of research on this topic had expanded dramatically, so we changed the year cutoff to 1990, and the final product is a 623-page book. The references list alone is 123 pages long, covering over 2,000 citations. Since our goal was to maximize the longevity of the book's relevance, we made the decision to include yet unpublished working papers.

When invited to prepare this chapter for Routledge, our first task was to examine how many new entries have been added to the Social Science Research Network (SSRN) since we submitted the book. To our surprise, the original list yielded about 800 entries from April 2007 to October 24, 2012. Some were double entries, either paper revisions submitted as new entries or manuscripts entered both as working and accepted papers; some were papers already cited in the book; and some contained just the abstract or addressed issues that were too far removed from the main earnings management theme to be of interest to the readers. We also discarded three papers written in French, one in Polish, and one in Chinese for obvious reasons. After all of the eliminations we had 583 new entries left, which can be found in the bibliography of this chapter.

The recommended use of this survey, especially for graduate students and researchers doing empirical or analytical work, is to start with the relevant part in the book, where we present the accounting scene for each earnings management (henceforth referred to as EM) incidence. This allows the reader to better understand the role of EM.

The organization of this chapter loosely follows that of our four-part book. The first part ends with Section 2, which sets up the philosophy of accounting. It also presents the definition of EM and discusses briefly the methods through which firms manage earnings. Sections 3, 4, and 5 review the main themes in the empirical research and correspond to Part 2 of the book. Parts 3 and 4 are covered in Section 6, which presents the innovations in theoretical contributions, and Section 7, which presents the empirical methodology. Section 8 offers parting remarks.

2 Definition

At the very basic level, earnings are managed whenever decisions are made to report an earnings number that differs from net cash flows of a given period. This means that any accrual or deferral is an EM decision. Put differently, EM, consisting of accruals and deferrals, is the collection of decisions to allocate past, present, and expected cash flows across accounting periods where the resulting re-allocated cash flows are labeled "earnings."

Since expected cash flows are uncertain, EM requires predictions by management. If management incorporates its genuine cash flow expectations into the periodic allocation process, we say that EM is beneficial. Otherwise, it is pernicious.

The managed earnings result from taking production or investment actions before earnings are realized, or making accounting choices that affect the earnings numbers and their interpretation after the true earnings are realized.[1]

2.1 Discussion

In a world where transactions were recorded mechanically, without any room for judgment, there would be no room for EM. There is no dispute, however, that accounting includes estimates: allowance for uncollectible accounts, depreciation, pension liability, post-retirement benefits liability, tax valuation allowance, insurance claims, impairment of assets, loan loss reserves in financial institutions, and so forth.[2] All of these estimates constitute accruals that affect earnings and are, to a large degree, within management's discretion. Hence, accruals and earnings – that are simply operating cash flows plus accruals – perforce are "managed," that is, decided on by the manager. Of course, management is not restricted to accruals. Cash flows can be managed by choices about transactions and their timing (real EM); classification of items in the financial statements can be managed to change investors' inferences regarding future estimates of cash flows (classificatory smoothing); and rounding schemes can impact the calculation of earnings per share.

These decisions require planning and might consume costly economic resources. Hence, "EM," broadly seen as encompassing all these decisions, is likely to serve some goal.[3] It is the nature of this goal that determines what we can say about EM. The goal referred to here is endogenous: it is dictated by management's incentives as created by its compensation package – broadly construed to include both explicit and implicit performance-based rewards and penalties. Incentives are designed to drive measureable performance, which in turn depends on both unobservable effort, factors beyond the control of management (labeled "Nature") that determine the actual performance. Specifically, the explicit rewards and penalties include the contractual measures of performance that trigger the reward, and implicit rewards and penalties refer to the perceived (by the manager) probabilities of contract renewal, being fired, and the like.

Ultimately, these incentives are determined by the board of directors (BOD), representing shareholders' interests. Suppose controlling shareholders – controlling in the sense of having the power to dictate the compensation package created by the BOD – wish to maximize the long-term value of the firm. Such shareholders will cause compensation contracts to be designed to induce the manager to invest in value maximizing projects and to report his genuine expectations truthfully through the accruals component of earnings. Suppose, on the other hand, the controlling shareholders have a short horizon such that they wish to sell their shareholdings at the maximum possible price in the short run in order to maximize their profits. In this case, the designed compensation contract will contain provisions that induce the manager to choose short-term projects (sacrificing long-term value) and to convey to the market biased expectations through inflated reported earnings – including "managed accruals" to maximize the short-term price.[4]

It is clear therefore that in the first case described above – where the manager maximizes value and truthfully reports his expectations through the "managed earnings" – the goal is aligned with both the interest of the *value* maximizing shareholders and of investors at large: the financial report is transparent and truthful. In this case, EM is not only innocuous, it is also *beneficial* regardless of whether accruals are high or low and, importantly, regardless of whether so-called discretionary accruals, from whatever model they are derived, are high or low.[5]

In the second case, where expectations are reported with a bias, EM is clearly a bad thing; it is *pernicious*. Hence, EM can be either *beneficial* or *pernicious,* depending on the circumstances.[6]

It becomes obvious from the preceding discussion that EM can be simply defined as accrual accounting; EM and accrual accounting are isomorphic. It is beneficial when accrual-accounting-based earnings truthfully convey management's expectations, and pernicious otherwise. Since management's (private) expectations presumptively constitute new information relative to the existing publicly available information, there is almost surely no room for "neutral" EM – the probability that the managed earnings provide no fresh news to the market approaches zero. Hence EM, or, equivalently, accrual accounting, is either beneficial or pernicious almost all of the time. It is important to note, however, that EM can be pernicious if it shortchanges the interest of pre-existing long-horizon shareholders even if it serves the interests of pre-existing short-horizon shareholders, and it can be beneficial when it serves the interests of pre-existing long-horizon shareholders even if it shortchanges the interests of pre-existing short-horizon shareholders.

The question we need to address now is how the literature to date fares in terms of helping us identify, on the basis of available observations, whether and under what circumstances EM is beneficial or pernicious.

The empiricist's difficulty is that the manager's true expectations are neither observable nor ex-post verifiable: ex-post realizations may diverge from honestly reported expectations just as they could diverge from dishonestly reported expectations. Hence, whether EM is beneficial or pernicious is not an observable datum! For example, suppose exceptionally high accruals or discretionary accruals (assuming so-called non-discretionary accruals were correctly estimated – a heroic assumption given the myriad problems surrounding a Jones-like model discussed in Chapter 10 of the book) are observed to be associated with a subsequent profitable insider-sale (or IPO) in turn followed by negative earnings surprises and reversals of accruals. Does this imply pernicious EM? Not necessarily, although we may conclude otherwise because these circumstances may lead to inferences of *motive and opportunity.* Provided the manager has enough reporting discretion to inflate earnings (pernicious EM) before the insider-sale (i.e., opportunity), then, since the profitable sale is consistent with motive to mislead, motive and opportunity can perhaps be established. Indeed, motive and opportunity – referred to in the securities laws as scienter – are necessary for plaintiffs to prevail in securities class action suits in general and for judging EM as pernicious in particular.

The analogy with what the courts require plaintiffs to prove in securities litigation is apt. Scienter is not a sufficient condition to establish fault leading to the compensation of investors who suffered losses. There must also be proof of an omission or misrepresentation. This implies the need to show that the manager-defendant knew or should have known, under the circumstances, that the report contained misrepresentations. Through information discovery, plaintiffs can endeavor to establish that the reports contain misrepresentations. This is feasible for the plaintiffs only when they obtain access to proprietary information contained in the company's internal documents. That is, the plaintiffs, through access to internal information, can point to discovered proxies for what should have been the "correct" accrual or, equivalently, the manager's true expectation. If the actual accrual differs from this inferred expectation, plaintiffs may claim that the manager misrepresented, thus establishing pernicious EM. The researcher-empiricist is not placed in such a favored position, because he or she lacks access to internal information. There is no reason to expect a researcher without access to privileged information to be able to establish pernicious EM any better than plaintiffs can. Without sufficient information about the manager's true expectations, pernicious EM cannot be distinguished from beneficial EM.[7]

At this point, a digression is in order. Recall that EM and accrual accounting are one and the same. Researchers often associate accruals ("Acc") or discretionary accruals ("DAcc") with earnings quality: the higher the Acc or DAcc, the lower the earnings quality. In fact, empiricists view high Acc or DAcc as proxies for EM, which in turn is assumed to be pernicious and hence an indication of lower accounting quality. But we have just seen that EM can be either pernicious or beneficial and that, in any case, empiricists cannot easily distinguish between the two. Hence, the presumed correspondence between Acc and quality is simply false: if EM is beneficial, then clearly we cannot say that the accounting quality is low. Indeed, other things being equal, when EM is beneficial we would have to conclude that accounting quality is high. To see this, we need to define the concept of "accounting quality." The definition of accounting quality must be derived from the objectives of financial reporting, including features such as persistence and predictability. If we accept the Conceptual Framework's statement that the objective of financial reporting is to help investors predict, evaluate and compare future cash flows and their timing and uncertainty, then accounting is of higher quality the better it accomplishes this objective. In other words, accounting is of higher quality if earnings along with other accounting numbers better predict future cash flows; timing and uncertainty can be incorporated by properly discounting the flows and testing whether earnings better predict the discounted cash flows. Correspondingly, the quality of accruals can be evaluated by testing the accruals' incremental (to cash flows) ability to predict aggregates of future cash flows. It is important to note, however, that the predictive ability of earnings or accruals by itself sheds little light on whether EM is beneficial or pernicious. This is so because accounting quality – measured by predictive ability – is a joint product of several causes: (1) the inherent economic uncertainty associated with the firm's transactions – the higher the uncertainty, the poorer the predictive ability; (2) the manager's skill and effort directed to acquiring information that helps make accruals more precise and hence better predictors; (3) the manager's incentives to misrepresent by conveying false expectations; and (4) audit quality. Hence, EM, even when seen by researchers as reflecting intent to mislead or manipulate, cannot and should not be seen alone as reflecting quality.

Continuing the digression, other commonly used measures of accounting quality can be just as misleading. Consider, for example, the observation of "too high" a frequency of small positive earnings compared with small negative earnings (discontinuity around a zero threshold), or a frequency of small excess earnings compared with a small earnings shortfall (around a target such as analysts' consensus forecast). Empiricists have viewed such discontinuities as an implication of pernicious EM or, alternatively, poor accounting quality. To see how this conclusion can be false, consider a manager facing a potential loss or an earnings shortfall relative to analysts' consensus forecast. As we know, such shortfalls can be very damaging by triggering precipitous price declines. It certainly would be rational for such a manager to take corrective actions that increase his or her (genuinely believed) expectations of future cash flows and to truthfully signal this by increasing positive accruals. Thus, while these studies may infer pernicious EM, the data could also reflect beneficial EM, which, other things being equal, also points to higher earnings quality.

Consider next the Dechow and Dichev (2002) measure of accrual quality based on the deviation of actual working capital accruals from the working capital accruals predicted by current, one-lagged period and one-following period cash flows from operations. The measure can be seen as a reflection of the degree to which accruals closely approximate current, preceding, and succeeding cash flows. This measure may reflect the predictive ability of working capital accruals with respect to the next period's operating cash flows. But this falls short of meeting the objective of predicting *aggregate* future cash flows over the long run, including total cash flows and cash flows from operations. Yet another measure of quality – the ability of stock returns to predict next year's income – while somewhat closer to the correct notion of predictive ability, fails to reflect the true performance because returns are also a function of private information acquired by investors and public information contained in financial statements.

Returning to our main theme of EM, note that our definition says nothing about how the market or various constituents react to financial reports. This is deliberate. How external (to the firm) entities, including the market, react to information contained in financial reports cannot and should not change the definition of EM, which addresses an inherent quality of earnings. The reaction to earnings characteristics depends on the nature of the market and the particular capital market equilibrium that prevails. The reaction depends on whether the market is efficient, the cost of acquiring private information about whether EM is beneficial or pernicious, and other factors. To illustrate, under a signal jamming equilibrium, the manager inflates earnings because otherwise the market may erroneously attribute earnings to the firm lower than the earnings that faithfully convey the manager's true expectations. In this case, we would observe no market reaction to the pernicious EM, but this does not alter the definition of EM. It is still pernicious even though the manager's motive was not nefarious; the EM still misreported the true expectations.

The inclination of practitioners and researchers is to regard EM as pernicious. "Creative Accounting is normally portrayed as [a] maligned and negative act. As soon as these words 'Creative Accounting' are mentioned, the image that emerges in one's mind is that of manipulation, dishonesty and deception" (Ali Shah et al. 2011, p. 531). In our bibliography, we denote next to each paper if the researcher treats EM as pernicious [P], beneficial [B], or both [P, B]. In most cases (435 papers), EM is treated as pernicious; in 25 studies it could be either pernicious or beneficial (especially when informative smoothing is considered). Only in 11 papers is EM seen as purely beneficial.[8]

2.2 The EM toolkit

The definition describes EM as a collection of decisions. This collection can be quite rich. Chapter 2 of our book collects research evidence of the following activities:

- A choice from a menu of treatments that are accepted under generally accepted accounting principles (GAAP), such as inventory evaluation method and depreciation (Ali Shah 2011).
- A decision on the timing of the adoption of a new standard.
- A judgment call when GAAP requires estimates, such as depreciation.
- A classification of items as above or below the line of operating earnings (Cain et al. 2012; Bhojraj et al. 2009; Cheng et al. 2010).
- Structuring transactions to achieve desired accounting outcomes (such as the finding of Cohen et al. 2009 that firms decrease their advertising expenses in the third and fourth quarter, when the products near the end of the life cycle, to meet or beat market expectations; the finding of Kama and Melumad 2012 that firms factor receivables to camouflage accruals EM; and the finding of Zechman 2010 that cash-constrained firms finance asset purchases off balance sheet with synthetic leases).

- Timing the recognition of revenues and expenses (Du and Zhang 2011).
- A real production investment decision (such as a decrease in research and development (R&D) [Brown and Krull 2008 and García et al. 2009]).
- Managing the transparency of the presentation (Cohen et al. 2012a).
- Managing the informativeness of earnings through various means (such as pro-forma earnings [Black et al. 2011] and ethnostatistics[9] [Davidson et al. 2009]).

The easiest means to manage earnings is through the choice of estimates, such as the estimated life of a depreciable asset, and such a choice can be made close to the time of the preparation of the financial reports. The most difficult tactic is real production because it requires making decisions early in the operating cycle, long before the financial report is released. For example, a firm may reduce cost of goods sold by increasing production so that the inventory will absorb a higher proportion of fixed manufacturing expenses. That way, overproduction results in higher earnings. This tactic, however, is subject to the constraints of production capacity: production should increase as long as possible before the end of the fiscal period.

From a bird's eye view, the search for novelties in empirical research in this area over the last couple of years has been promising. On a paper-by-paper basis there is little novelty, but the field did advance collectively, as seen, for example, in the increased diversity of modeling EM econometrically and in relying on the findings of prior research to formulate new approaches, such as refining previous answers by partitioning the sample between the subsample to which the previous answer applies and the subsample to which it does not. Still, we find that there are some unanswered questions.

In the book, we identified thirteen incidences of blatant EM. We classified them by the key player that induces (or hampers) EM: the firm's management, with a focus on the CEO; plain vanilla users that are the audience of the financial information but exert no control over the report, such as investors; and monitors, also known as gatekeepers, who provide an attestation function, such as auditors, or function as information intermediaries, such as analysts. This classification parallels the discussion in our book. Chapter 3 discusses instances that are associated with a direct benefit to the manager, such as his or her compensation. Chapter 4 is concerned with instances that involve the users of financial information: investors, creditors, employees, customers, and suppliers, such as seasoned equity offering, debt issuance, and regulation. Chapter 5 discusses controlling owners, boards of directors, auditors, and the media.

3 Management

In the book, we identified four incidences associated with senior management as follows (the number of papers in the references list that make a contribution to this category are given in parentheses):

3.1 Compensation and tenure (57)
3.2 Insider trading (6)
3.3 Turnover (7)
3.4 Management buyout (3)

In addition to the book's coverage, we created a new category based on the more recent work, henceforth denoted:

3.5 Culture, legal environment, corporate culture, religion, gender, ethics and social norms, and other social issues (27)

3.1 Compensation and tenure

Incentives are supposed to align the interests of managers with those of shareholders. Since managers are given bonuses that are based on accounting earnings, it is little wonder that the common wisdom is that management manipulates reported earnings to optimize its lifetime compensation. The salary component and the equity component of compensation also induce managers to manage earnings. Salary is important for the manager's fringe benefits and post-retirement benefits. A firm that did not report higher earnings would be reluctant to award its managers a salary increase; unless a firm reports improvement over the previous year, it would be hard pressed to justify this kind of bonus. At the same time, since the exercise price of options is set to the stock price at the time of the grant for a variety of reasons (McAnally et al. 2008), it is better to report lower earnings or accelerate bad news just before the grant (e.g., Baker et al. 2008). When it is time to exercise options, however, the manager prefers to report aggressively (Kuang 2008) and take other measures such as a share buyback to increase the stock price (Balachandran et al. 2008). It is not surprising, therefore, that some studies focus on the components of compensation and some on total compensation (e.g., Barth and Taylor 2009; García-Meca and Sánchez 2009).

We know that the relationship between stock ownership and EM is nonlinear (see, for example, the UK study of Bos et al. 2011, the US study of Hutchinson and Leung 2007, and the Japanese study of Teshima and Shuto 2008).[10]

The regulatory scene changed in the US when the Sarbanes–Oxley Act (SOX) was enacted in July 2002 in the wake of WorldCom's huge restatements. Section 304 authorizes the Securities and Exchange Commission (SEC) to enforce the recovery from the CEO and CFO of their "bonus or other incentive-based or equity-based compensation" or "any profits received from the sale of securities" when there is a financial restatement "due to the material noncompliance of the issuer, as a result of misconduct, with any financial reporting requirement under the securities laws." Referring to this clause as a "clawback," Babenko et al. (2012) examine the reports of S&P 1,500 firms on the voluntary adoption of clawback policy. Interestingly, the adoption rate rose from 1 percent in 2001 to almost 70 percent of S&P 500 firms by 2011. Some of this has to do with misconduct or violation of no competition policy. Triggering events include earnings restatements (70 percent) and fraud (32 percent), but also extend beyond the intent of SOX and Dodd-Frank to include misconduct and negligence of fiduciary duty (48 percent) and "misrepresentation" (18 percent).

Because of the importance of compensation as a driver of managerial behavior, the research that is classified under Section 3.1 has four more dimensions. One is to find situations or managerial decisions that exacerbate the association between EM and compensation (e.g., Ali and Zhang 2012 and Demers and Wang 2010, who examine managers' tenure, or the Canadian study of Boubakri et al. 2008, who examine the decision to purchase liability insurance coverage for officers and directors).[11]

The second dimension deals with the economics of EM and with the internal organization of the firm. Examples for the economic aspects are found in studies that examine investment. For example, the Malaysian study of Chu and Song (2012) finds that EM is associated with over-investment that destroys shareholders' wealth. As noted by the studies on real EM, EM leads to deviation from efficient production (see also Cook et al. 2012a, 2012b). Another economic implication is the cash sacrifice when the firm faces a class action suit by previous shareholders. Wu and Jones (2010) find that larger equity compensation results in higher probability of settlement, and more extensive EM is associated with a higher settlement amount. An interesting study by Faleye et al. (2010) illustrates the difficulty in distinguishing between pernicious and beneficial EM when the financial reports fulfill two goals – informativeness and resource alloca-tion. This study reports that better monitoring by the board not only depresses compensation and EM, but it also results in lower innovation and poorer decisions on acquisitions that destroy shareholders' value. Is it the case that good intentions by a conscious board suppress beneficial EM? Issues of internal organizational design include R&D decentralization (Dhaoui 2010), corporate general counsel (Hopkins et al. 2012), and transfer pricing (Lo et al. 2010). The third dimension is to tie EM to governance using, for example, a comparison between the impact of equity ownership on EM when the award is given to directors and when it is given to managers (e.g., Boumosleh et al. 2012).

The fourth dimension relates to using compensation as a control variable in the regression analysis. The compensation is added as a control in order to explore alternative explanations for the research hypotheses (e.g., Guthrie and Sokolowsky 2010), mostly motivated as a governance mechanism component (e.g., Bowen et al. 2008).

3.2 Insider trading

Insider trading is not completely divorced from compensation and tenure, because it too affects the wealth of the manager and hence determines his or her incentives to manage earnings. Since compensation is awarded by options and shares, managers typically sell shares to pay the strike price in order to convert options to stock. Furthermore, to avoid class action suits, managers will submit trading plans to the SEC wherein they commit to a certain level of future sales. We refer to the means by which the profits are increased by selling shares as "pump and dump." That is, earnings are inflated to increase the price and then shares are sold at an inflated price. However, since managers can also purchase shares, Sawicki and Shrestha (2008) predictably find that firms with heavy insider sales manage earnings aggressively, while the EM strategy of insiders with heavy purchases is to deflate earnings. What we still do not know is whether the EM strategy triggers the insider trading policy or if it is the other way around (see the discussion in the book).[12]

3.3 Turnover

Turnover involves two decision makers, the outgoing CEO and the incoming one. If compen-sation and insider trading are the carrot, then forced separation is the stick. Forced departure is typically triggered by failing to meet analysts' expectations (Hwang et al. 2010), dismal perfor-mance (see, e g., Faleye et al. 2010[13]), or aggressive upward EM by a good performer (Hazarika et al. 2012). In all instances, the firm manages earnings upwards before the turnover event. When the CEO's departure is amicable, as is the case where he or she reaches retirement age, there is a good likelihood that the CEO retains a position on the board and thus controls the incoming CEO.

It is well known that when a new CEO takes over, the first order of business is to "take a bath" (see, e.g., Wilson and Wu 2011). In this strategy, reported earnings are hoarded in order to present strong future performance. The ability to manage earnings upwards to present stronger performance depends, however, on whether the board does not block such a move (Davidson et al. 2009; Wilson and Wang 2010). Davidson et al. (2009), for example, find that positive EM is stronger when the new CEO is also nominated to be the chairman of the board.

Specific country aspects of EM are also evident in the study of turnover. In a Chinese study, Chen et al. (2011) show that when state-owned firms are privatized, the government officials who ran the business before privatization are more likely to retain their managerial position after privatization and the more aggressively earnings are managed downwards. The reason is that the Chinese rule that investors cannot buy the firm for less than its book value means that managing earnings downwards is likely to afford the grateful new owners more profitable transactions and make them indebted to those that helped them acquire the firm.

3.4 Management buyout

We find three new studies on EM when managers conduct a buyout (Davidson et al. 2011; Fischer and Louis 2008; Zhu et al. 2012), confirming that firms report lower earnings during the year prior to the announcement of a management buyout (MBO), with some evidence that the phenomenon was more pronounced before the enactment of SOX in 2002 (Davidson et al. 2011). This strategy is tempered, however, when the buyout requires external financing, because then the managers have incentives to inflate earnings in order to obtain external financing for the MBO and lower their financing costs (Fischer and Lewis 2008).

4 Instances associated with external users that exert little control over financial reporting

The list of incidences that are associated with external users and the number of studies that contribute to each category, given in parentheses, is as follows:

4.1 Influencing the stock price and engaging in threshold meeting or beating (120)
4.2 Initial public offerings, seasoned equity offerings, convertible bond offers, and spin-offs (47)
4.3 Mergers and acquisitions (12)
4.4 Debt (20)
4.5 Regulation and regulation change, including the impact of SOX and the change to international financial reporting standards (IFRS) (89)
4.6 Tax (28)
4.7 Regulated industries such as insurance companies, banks, privately sponsored US defined benefit pension plans, utilities, demutualizing thrifts, regulated not-for-profit hospitals, and real estate investment trusts (47)
4.8 Employees (3)
4.9 Suppliers and customers; competitors (4)

4.1 The stock market

The objective of accounting is to enable investors to predict, evaluate, and compare the magnitude, timing, and uncertainty of future cash flows. Public firms are likely to meet their investors in the stock market, wherein the "stock prices are visible signals that summarize the implications of internal decisions for current and future net cash flows. This external monitoring exerts pressure to orient a corporation's decision process toward the interests of residual claimants" (Fama and Jensen 1983, p. 313). Because of the sensitivity of the stock price to reported earnings, firms include EM in their arsenal of tools to impact the price. The research in this category, broadly speaking, addresses the following questions:

- Question 1: Are stock investors able to detect EM and understand its consequences? (See, e.g., Ambrose and Bian 2009; Bradshaw et al. 2010; Callao and Jarne 2008; Chen et al. 2007; Cready et al. 2011; and Dinh et al. 2009.)

- Question 2: How do changes in stock prices (e.g., Ambrose and Bian 2009), liquidity of the stock (e.g., Bardos 2011), or information already in the market price (e.g., Bratten et al. 2012) affect managers' incentives to manage earnings?
- Question 3: Is the phenomenon of reporting earnings that meet or beat thresholds, such as zero earnings and earnings with some growth factor of the same period last year, evidence of EM (Cohen et al. 2009; Donelson et al. 2013; Du et al. 2011; Harris et al. 2010; Jia 2012; Mosebach and Simko 2009)?

4.1.1 Question 1: Are stock investors able to detect EM?

In an ideal word, we would like the answer to be positive. If EM is pernicious, investors are not fooled, and if EM is beneficial, it conveys to investors value-relevant information. Research findings are not unequivocal. In some cases, the market anticipates pernicious EM, understands beneficial EM, and even uses EM to judge other value-relevant information. For example, Eames and Kim (2012) and Davidson et al. (2011) provide evidence that the market sees through pernicious EM. Kee (2010) and Linck et al. (2012) show that high discretionary accruals (i.e., high EM) are a signal of strong future performance.[14]

Still, there is also evidence that the market is fooled by pernicious EM (e.g., Hardouvelis et al. 2012; Hsu and Kross 2010; Zhao et al. 2012). There are two types of cases: (1) where the market fails to notice red flags of pernicious EM (Cohen et al. 2012) and (2) where the market understands that the firm engages in EM but it does not evaluate it correctly (see, e.g., Ang et al. 2012; Bhojraj et al. 2009). This is consistent with the existence of lemons and peaches in the market. That is, firms that employ EM perniciously gain at the expense of the good firms who do not because the market cannot separate lemons from peaches (Ronen and Yaari 2002).

4.1.2 Question 2: What is the impact of the market price on EM?

Since valuation increases in reported earnings, firms have incentives to perniciously inflate earnings to have overvalued stock (Chi and Gupta 2009; Chu and Song 2010; Coulton et al. 2012; Fernandes and Ferreira 2007; Houmes and Skantz 2010)[15] or deflate earnings to beneficially correct over-optimistic market expectations (Duong 2010). Overvaluation through pernicious EM traps the firm into escalating the costly EM over time. Badertscher (2011) finds that at the beginning of the overvaluation periods, firms use the less costly accruals EM; then they use the more costly, real EM; and then, if the overvaluation continuous, they violate GAAP.

Another aspect of how the market impacts EM is that it also has an effect on the EM strategy. Some firms that do not have a myopic horizon prefer to smooth earnings. That is, the volatility of reported earnings is deliberately lower than the volatility of economic earnings. Figure 12.1 depicts the difference between truth-telling and smoothing.[16] When economic income is low, the firm overstates earnings, and when it is high, it understates them. That way, the volatility of the reported earnings is lower than that of economic earnings.

In Ronen and Sadan (1981), smoothing could be beneficial EM when it signals long-term performance. But it could also be a means to hide undesired information perniciously, such as by reducing the perceived riskiness of the firm's performance and facilitating the ability of the firm to meet or beat expectations (Harris and Shi 2012b).

Using different measures for smoothing, most studies explore smoothing as a methodological tool. That is, smoothing is regarded as evidence for EM. Not surprisingly, this methodology is likely to be used when the research question involves a situation where the riskiness of reported earnings is important,[17] such as when attempting to get a better credit rating or when

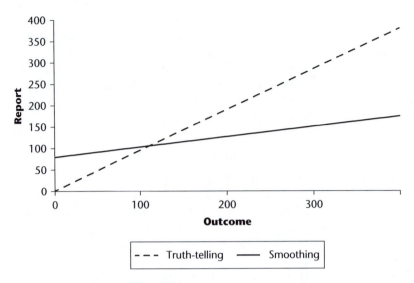

Figure 12.1 Smoothing versus truth-telling

scrutinizing the risk-taking behavior of managers, but it can also go beyond that. We also notice that some studies detect smoothing without labeling their finding as such (e.g., Harris and Shi 2012b; Rath and Sun 2007).[18]

4.1.3 Question 3: Meeting or beating expectations?

Meeting or beating expectations (MBE) encompasses a plethora of phenomena; the common denominator is that there is a threshold earnings figure that represents the expectations of the investors. In response, the firm's goal is to publicize a report that meets or beats the figure. The market induces firms to MBE by rewarding these firms (Jiang 2008) and penalizing firms that do not MBE (see the discussion of Payne and Thomas 2011).

The three best-known thresholds are zero income, zero change in earnings, and consensus analysts' forecast (further discussed in Section 5.1.2.3). That is, firms attempt to report small profits and avoid reporting a loss. Alternatively, firms want to show either no decline or stable growth relative to the same quarter of the previous year. These two phenomena fall within the scope of Section 3.2 (insider trading). The discussion of the threshold of analysts' consensus forecast is provided in Section 3.3.1. Clearly, there are other thresholds. For example, firms that issue bonds are keen to report earnings that exceed minimum levels specified by debt covenants, and firms need to report enough income to avoid cutting dividend payments (Bennett and Bradbury 2010; Naveen et al. 2008). Another example of a threshold is evident in China, where firms face the benchmark used by regulation (Gul and Ma 2012; Jian and Wong 2010; Lai 2009; Zou et al. 2008).[19]

From a historical perspective, the research into MBE started with the observation that the distribution around zero earnings and zero change in earnings is irregular (Jorgensen et al. 2010; Lahr 2011). Unlike the expected bell-shaped distribution, the actual distribution has a kink around the threshold (see Figure 12.2).[20]

The kink raises the question as to whether firms manage earnings to MBE. Two studies that claim that the kink does not indicate EM are by Durtschi and Easton (2009 and 2005). They claim that discontinuities in earnings distributions are driven by the research methodology – that is,

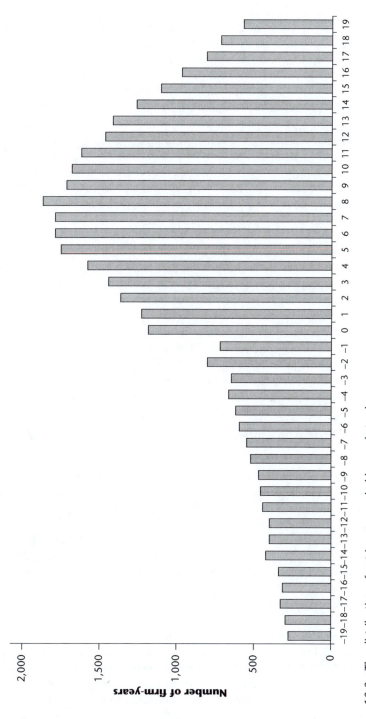

Figure 12.2 The distribution of net income scaled by market value

"by sample selection bias and scaling" (p. 1250) of the threshold and by the systematic relation between the sign of earnings and market prices. When these issues are resolved, the kink disappears. The debate, however, is not settled. The study that responds directly to Durtschi and Easton's claims was conducted by Burgstahler and Chuk (2012). They explain that the research design choices of Durtschi and Easton mechanically obscure discontinuities, and that the only plausible explanation for the kink is that firms indeed manage earnings.[21]

Other research provides evidence that MBE leads to pernicious EM (Cohen et al. 2009; Donelson et al. 2013; Du and Zhang 2011; Harris et al. 2010; Jia 2012; Li 2010; Mosebach and Simko 2009). Indeed, the EM research views MBE as an indication for EM (which is why Section 3.2 is so rich, with 113 new papers). That is, when the research question calls for a choice of a sample of firms that are likely to manage earnings, a good option is to use a sample of MBE firms (e.g., Cassel et al. 2012; Chi et al. 2011; Cook et al. 2012a, 2012b; Dunn et al. 2011; Fan et al. 2010; Hwang and Kim 2012; Krishnan et al. 2011; Srivastava 2011; Wagener and Watrin 2012; Yen 2008; Zhao et al. 2012). The advantage of such a strategy is that, unlike with smoothing, MBE encompasses many EM strategies. Fogel-Yaari and Ronen (2011) study the reporting strategy of MBE firms with two types of firms: (1) firms that must MBE in the short run to survive, such as growth firms (short-term MBE firms) and (2) firms like those in Mosebach and Simko's 2009 study, which must MBE in the long run even at the sacrifice of failing to MBE in the short run, such as value firms (long-term MBE firms). Fogel-Yaari and Ronen (2011) show that MBE results in a rich menu of EM strategies. The chosen strategy depends on the firm's type and the actual performance. When the true performance is low, MBE is associated with "taking a bath" and "cookie jar reserve" policy by a long-term MBE firm. These strategies allow the firm to hoard reported earnings. The short-term NBE firm engages in "meeting a threshold" and "marginally beating it." That way, the short-term MBE firm attempts to dampen the aggressiveness of an MBE report in the previous period. When, however, the true performance is so high that management is confident of being able to MBE throughout the reporting horizon, the firm "beating the threshold" by a large margin or "smoothing."

4.2 Initial public offerings, seasoned equity offerings, convertible bond offers, and spin-offs

While Section 4.1 treats valuation in general, specific events where valuation determines the proceeds from an equity offering are detailed in this section, which focuses mainly on initial public offering (IPO), seasoned equity offering (SEO), and other equity-impacting events such as issuing convertible bonds (Chou et al. 2009) and conducting spin-offs (Lin and Yung 2011).

On the one hand, there is overwhelming evidence that firms use EM around the offerings event through total accruals (e.g., Armstrong et al. 2008; Guthrie and Sokolowsky 2010), specific accruals (e.g., Cecchini et al. 2012), both total accruals and real activities (e.g., Cohen and Zarowin 2010; Roychowdhury et al. 2012; Wongsunwai 2011), structuring transactions such as related-party transactions between the parent and the firm (see the Chinese study of Aharony et al. 2010), and classification by moving items that are income-decreasing from core earnings to special items in the fourth quarter (Siu and Faff 2012). The presence of large owner-outsiders (Guthrie and Sokolowsky 2010) and high business complexity that enhances information asymmetry, as in the case of a diversified firm (Lim et al. 2008), intensify the incentives to manage earnings.

On the other hand, there are mitigating factors, such as (a) having private equity sponsorship (Katz 2009) and the involvement of venture capitalists (Gioielli and De Carvalho 2008; Jaemin and Lee 2012; Lee and Masulis 2011; Wongsunwai 2011), (b) engaging high-quality financial intermediaries such as investment banks (Lee and Masulis 2011; Lewis 2008) and a more reputable underwriter (Chen et al. 2010; Lee and Zhou 2012), (c) higher auditor quality in terms of experience and ability (Chi et al. 2011; Chu et al. 2010; Siu and Faff 2012; Zhu et al. 2010), and (d) better governance (Boubakri et al. 2008; Chang et al. 2010; Cormier et al. 2012; Zhu et al. 2010).

The papers that initiated the research into EM by IPO and SOE firms are Teoh et al. 1998a and 1998b. They investigated whether the long-run underperformance of SEO and IPO relative to similar firms that did not raise capital is explained by the issuing firm inflating earnings perniciously to mislead the market. New studies claim that when performance is measured as the return on assets (ROA), then, as expected, pernicious accrual EM is associated with lower future ROA. If performance is measured as abnormal returns from holding the stock, then the results are mixed. Armstrong et al. (2008) and Lewis (2008)[22] find no relationship between EM and post-event returns, whereas Lim et al. (2008) report that buy-and-hold abnormal returns, measured by the cumulative monthly stock returns of SEO firms relative to matched firms over a three-year holding period, are more negative for diversified firms with complex operations.

We view EM that misleads the market as pernicious, but what if EM helps raise capital, and the firm uses this capital to make investments that increase the profits of the firm? Can pernicious EM be economically beneficial? On the other hand, it can be argued that firms that use EM perniciously are unlikely to invest profitably. Aharony et al. (2010) and Lee and Masulis (2009) provide support for the latter conjecture. For example, Aharony et al. (2010) show that the parent of a Chinese IPO firm that structured transactions to boost the IPO price also siphoned proceeds of the equity offering by taking loans from the IPO firm that it did not attempt to pay back.[23]

The pernicious EM that is associated with the equity offering is by now so well understood and accepted that some studies use this event as a methodological tool in their research to identify samples when they need to have a sample of firms engaging in pernicious EM. For example, Kothari et al. (2005), the Canadian study of Boubakri et al. (2008), and the two studies of Chi et al. (2011) and Chu et al. (2010) use SEO to test for the impact of audit quality on real and accruals EM.[24]

4.3 Mergers and acquisitions

With the exception of Ben-David and Roulstone (2008), who provide evidence that the EM phenomenon is driven by small acquirers, not by large ones, the consensus in the literature is that firms that acquire other firms using stock manage earnings upwards before the acquisition in order to boost the price of their stock, while cash acquirers do not (Ardekani et al. 2012; Baik et al. 2007; Botsari and Meeks 2008; Gong et al. 2008; Higgins 2012; Kravet et al. 2012; Pungaliya and Vijh 2009). When the transaction is a merger, both parties manage earnings (Meisel 2007). Anilowski Cain et al. (2012) contribute to the research on the economic consequences of accounting by documenting a correlation between EM and making the acquisition through an auction. The intuition is that auctions are more profitable to the target when there is high information asymmetry; and because EM is pernicious, the more aggressive the EM, the more profitable the auction becomes.

The only study that addresses EM after the acquisition is Hsu et al. (2009), which shows that firms write off R&D of the target after acquisition as a means of boosting future profitability measures such as ROA.[25]

4.4 Debt

Shareholders and debt holders are the two major stakeholders of the firm, and they share many similarities. Also, there are certain classes of stock whose features render them similar to debt, and there are debt instruments that share the features of equity. Furthermore, bankrupt firms may offer their creditors stock to settle the debt (see, e.g., Kodak 2013).

While shareholders use the research of analysts to alleviate information asymmetry between them and management, debt holders rely on credit agencies. These agencies rank each public debt issuance, or the firm overall, on the basis of their credit risk (the anticipation that the debt will be paid in full), with the highest grade of long-term debt given the grade of AAA. The lowest grade is C for Standard and Poor's (S&P) and D for the others. So, for example, the S&P ranking is AAA, AA, A, BBB, BB, B, CCC, CC, and D.[26]

Since the firms that issue the debt are those that pay the credit rating agencies to research and certify their grade (in the US, the market is dominated by S&P, Moody's, and Fitch[27]), their ratings may be affected by conflict of interest.[28] Understandably, therefore, SOX in July of 2002 called for more research into what credit agencies do. Indeed, in the 17 new papers in this category, credit rating and credit rating agencies and EM occupy a large space. See, for example, Ali and Zhang (2008); Boubakri and Ghouma (2008); Demirtas and Cornaggia (2012); Jung et al. (2013); and Martinez and Rivera (2010).[29] Ali and Zhang (2008) find that firms in the plus and minus rating in their category (e.g., B+ or B−) that are vulnerable to the threat of being down-graded inflate earnings. Boubakri and Ghouma (2008) analyze the impact of EM on the cost of debt and credit rating of bond issuances. They find that bondholders charge higher cost and that credit rating is lower for firms with aggressive EM. This raises the question of why firms manage earnings if they are penalized for it. Demirtas and Cornaggia (2012) sampled firms that issued straight corporate debt for the first time between 1980 and 2003 and received credit ratings from Moody's Investors Service. They find that firms engage in aggressive EM, which confirms their premise that acquiring the most favorable *initial* credit rating is strategically important because (i) initial ratings become the benchmark for ratings of future debt issues and credit rating agencies prefer stability in rating, and (ii) because ratings are not continuously updated (they are potentially "sticky").[30]

Jung et al. (2013) and the Brazilian study of Martinez and Rivera (2010) examine smoothing *cum* credit rating. Beneficial smoothing as an EM strategy has the advantage of reducing information asymmetry so that the smoothers can separate themselves from the "lemons" more clearly and get the higher rating they deserve. When smoothing is pernicious, it reduces perceived volatility, and hence the perceived riskiness of earnings, and favorably impacts the perception of the credit risk of the firm. Jung et al. (2013) show that a subsequent upgrade in rating is positively related to an increase in smoothing. Martinez and Rivera (2010) find that Brazilian companies that engage in smoothing receive better ratings.

Gupta et al. (2008) find that borrowers of short-term debt use EM aggressively.[31] The rationale of this study is that one means for lenders to monitor the borrower is to issue short-term debt that needs to be renewed periodically. In response, short-term borrowers attempt to look good.[32] This raises the question of why the lender, anticipating this response, tacitly colludes with the borrower.

4.5 Regulation and regulation change

The research in this section falls into several categories: first, the enactment of SOX in 2002; second, studies of the European requirements that EU members adopt International Financial Reporting Standards (IFRS) in 2005; third, the set of studies that examine new accounting promulgations in the US; and fourth, the analysis of similar issues for countries outside of the US.

4.5.1 Sarbanes-Oxley Act (SOX)

For the SOX category, we summarize the studies in a table given in the Appendix. The big picture indicates that SOX led to reduced EM. There are some exceptions, as listed in the table. Since this conclusion is conditional on the specific sample, we describe the sample of each study (omitting Compustat and ExecuComp when it is obvious that they were used). Note, however, that causality, as expected, is difficult to establish. As described in the book, SOX was enacted with some haste in the wake of major accounting scandals. Thus, when a study finds that SOX is associated with the alleviation of pernicious EM, is SOX the cause, or were there market mechanisms triggered by the same events that led to SOX, suggesting that the correlation between SOX and EM may be spurious?

4.5.2 IFRS

In 2005, members of the European Union were directed to shift their generally accepted accounting principles (GAAP) to International Financial Reporting Standards (IFRS). Since this directive followed a reform of the International Accounting Standards (IAS) structure and improvement in international GAAP, the expectation was that the shift to IFRS would improve the quality of accounting information by reducing pernicious EM. The studies indicate that the evidence of improvement is mixed. Cai et al. (2008) find in their sample of 102,636 firm–years across 32 countries from 2000–2006 that EM declined in countries that adopt IFRS. Some studies find that the improvement depends on additional factors, such as the EM level before IFRS adoption (Aussenegg et al. 2008); the existence of a legal infrastructure, for example to provide for investor protection (Elbannan 2008; Ernstberger et al. 2011; Houqe et al. 2012); and the capital market environment and the economic cycle during the adoption period (Günther et al. 2009). A mixed picture is also revealed by Günther et al. (2009) in their German study and by Outa (2011) in his Kenyan study. One plausible explanation for Günther et al. (2009) is provided by Christensen et al. (2008), who find that the shift of German firms to IFRS reduces EM when those firms have incentives to do so. A negative answer is provided by Bentwood and Lee (2012), Capkun et al. (2012), Ipino and Parbonetti (2011), Lin et al. (2012),[33] and Pronobis et al. (2008). Bentwood and Lee (2012) find that Australian firms exploited the transition to manage earnings. Capkun et al. (2012) and Pronobis et al. (2008) find that the shift to IAS/IFRS is associated with more EM. Ipino and Parbonetti (2011) document an increase in real EM (but a decrease in accrual-based EM) for mandatory IFRS adopters only under a strict investor protection regime.

4.5.3 Accounting promulgations

This category includes studies that examine the impact on EM of the following US-based promulgations:

- Auditing standards (when the audit industry was self-regulated before the establishment of PCABO) – Statement of accounting standard (SAS). See the study of SAS 53 on red flags for auditors by Feroz et al. (2000).
- The Financial Accounting Standards Board's (FASB) statements of financial accounting standards (SFAS) process. See the study of SFAS 87 on pensions by Asthana (2007); the study of SFAS on earnings per share by Jorgensen et al. (2010); the study of SFAS 131 on segment reporting by Hann and Lu (2009); the study of SFAS 142 on goodwill impairment by Jordan and Stanley (2011); the studies of SFAS 133 on Accounting for the Impairment or Disposal of Long-Lived Assets by Barua et al. (2009) and Curtis et al. (2010); and the studies of SFAS 146 on restructuring by Anantharaman et al. (2012) and Bhojraj et al. (2009).
- FASB interpretations (FIN), such as the study of FIN 45 on warranties by Cohen et al. (2011) and of FIN 48 on tax liability by Cazier et al. (2011), Gupta et al. (2011), and Graham et al. (2012).

- Statements of Opinion (SOP) of the American Institute of Certified Public Accountants, such as the study of SOP 97-2 on revenue recognition by Srivastava (2011).
- Studies of an accounting principle, such as conservatism, by Garcia et al. (2012).
- Studies of acts of congress, such as the study on the Taxpayer Relief Act of 1997 by Albring et al. (2011).[34, 35]

The big picture is that if promulgation restricts EM, then EM takes place either in another way, such as through the use of real EM instead of accruals-based EM, or in a different account. Overall, when firms have incentives to engage in EM, they will do so by hook or by crook.

Studies outside of the US that are not concerned with the banking industry include the German studies of Böcking et al. (2012) on enforcement investigations and of Duecker (2009) on KonTraG (the German parallel of SOX); the Chinese studies of Chen et al. (2011) on possible collusion of government officials with private investors during privatization, of Gul et al. (2009) and Gul and Ma (2012) on audit quality, and of Sami and Zhou (2008) on auditing standards; the Spanish study of De las Heras et al. (2012) on the impact of the Spanish Financial Act (44 | 2002) on audit quality; the Canadian study of Geremia et al. (2010) on options expensing as per Handbook Section 3870; the Australian study of Herbohn et al. (2010) on Australian Accounting Standards Board ruling of 2010 on deferred taxes; the Korean study on auditor designation of Kim and Yi (2009); the Taiwanese study of Lin and Hsu (2008) on asset impairment; the Brazilian/Mexican study of compliance with the Code of "Best" Corporate Practices of Price et al. (2011); and the Malaysian study of Sahlan (2011) on listing requirement reforms.

4.6 Tax expense and deferred tax

We have already touched on taxes when discussing regulators (see Albring et al. 2011; Gupta et al. 2011). Still, there is much to discuss from the perspective of accounting for taxes. As noted in our book, tax expense, deferred tax, and deferred tax allowance are among the last accounts to be closed before the financial reports are publicized. By the time these accounts are prepared, firms know whether they can reach their target reported earnings. They therefore have incentives to flex the accounts to achieve the desired level of EM (Lisic 2012), and they do so (Cazier et al. 2011; Chen et al. 2012; Lisic 2012).

From an EM-research perspective, an important factor is whether the firm reports in a country, such as the US, that has two separate reporting regimes: one for financial reporting and one for taxes. A dual system creates a difference between the reported expense and the actual payment – a book-tax difference. The differences are either permanent (such as amortization of goodwill, acquired R&D, dividend received deductions, nondeductible acquisition costs, regulatory disallowances, domestic production deductions, and tax-exempt income) or temporary (such as depreciation, tax credit carry-forwards, foreign sales, and merger and acquisition activities) that even out in the long run. Firms have incentives to report low earnings for taxes and high earnings for investors. When they are not under pressure to use EM, they would lower earnings or smooth them (see, e.g., the Slovenian study of Garrod et al. 2007). When firms are under pressure to report higher performance, they inflate earnings and pay higher taxes. The excessive tax payment becomes an economic sacrifice which renders EM a costly endeavor (Badertscher et al. 2009).

The belief that EM is achieved through tax accounting has led researchers to investigate deferred taxes and the book-tax difference, or the effective tax rate (ETR), in order to detect EM (see Ghosh et al. 2010; Hanlon et al. 2011; the Chile/Malaysia study of Mahenthiran et al. 2008; Wagener and Watrin 2012). The question is whether such an approach is valid. One viable criticism of this approach is that there are two competing explanations for large positive book-tax differences. Differences could be attributed either to *tax avoidance* in order to reduce tax payments or to EM in order to inflate reported earnings.[36]

As expected, the answer to this issue is mixed. The research of Dhaliwal et al. (2008), Gleason et al. (2012), and Graham et al. (2012) supports the EM theory. For example, Dhaliwal et al. (2008) theorize that tax avoidance should be rewarded by a low cost of capital, and EM should be penalized by a high cost of capital. They find that firms are indeed penalized. Several studies indicate that both explanations hold (Blaylock et al. 2010; Chen et al. 2012; Frank et al. 2009; Plesko 2007; Steijvers and Niskanen 2011; Tang and Firth 2011). In their Chinese study, Tang and Firth (2011) find that EM and tax avoidance explain 7.4 percent and 27.8 percent of abnormal book-tax differences, respectively, and their interaction explains 3.2 percent of abnormal book-tax differences. There are also studies that cast doubt on using tax accounting as an EM methodology, such as Blaylock et al. (2012) and Gupta et al. (2011), as well as Blaylock et al. (2012), who study a panel of 141,389 firm-year observations across 35 countries from 1996–2007 and find that high levels of book-tax conformity are associated with more EM. Gupta et al. (2011) find that managers timed tax cushion reversals to meet analysts' forecasts in the pre-FIN 48 period only.[37]

4.7 Regulated industries

The main regulated industries are financial institutions such as bank and insurance companies that fall within Standard Industrial Classification (SIC) 6000–6999. These deserve separate attention because their accounting is different and the pressure to report under the regulatory eye is high. Our book covers these industries. A regulated industry that was not considered in the book is the real estate investment trust (REIT). To maintain their favorable tax status, REITs must pay out 90 percent of their taxable income as dividends. The mandatory dividend payout creates incentives to report lower profits by deflating income (Ambrose and Bian 2009; Edelstein et al. 2008).

4.8 Employees

Employees are important stakeholders of the firm. In this chapter, we cover two papers that examine the direct impact and one paper that examines the indirect impact[38] of this constituency on EM. Hamm et al. (2012) document that firms with stronger labor unions smooth more. They contend that smoothing is a vehicle to protect management when there is a conflict of interest between management and labor. When earnings are high, the deflation of earnings dampens demand for raises by labor unions. When earnings are low, inflating earnings does not invite demand for a raise (that, if declined, leads to a costly strike). Furthermore, because salary increases are sticky, weaker pressure to raise salaries makes the firm's survival more likely when earnings are indeed low.

The perspective of conflicts is also adopted by Bova (2009). Bova argues that firms with labor unions will signal bad news by missing analysts' forecasts more frequently. Indeed, this study finds that managers of unionized firms take less action than their non-unionized counterparts to guide forecasts downward when estimates are too high, and they take more action to deflate earnings when expectations are too low.

It is interesting to note that the available anecdotal evidence on egregious accounting scandals suggests that EM is a collusive behavior between upper management and the managers below. It could be that the collusion is enforced by upper management under the threat that if low management does not play ball, it will be booted out; or it might be collusive behavior to share the spoils of "the cake." The research so far has not documented collusion empirically.

4.9 Suppliers, customers, and competitors

If we had to pinpoint an area where there are many research opportunities, we would choose this section. Tinaikar and Xue (2009) comment, "We acknowledge at the outset that existing theories that directly correlate product market competition to our specific nature of financial reporting (e.g., excessive earnings smoothing) are scarce or at best, incomplete" (p. 3).

4.9.1 Suppliers and customers

Suppliers that make a single sale or immaterial sales, or one-time customers that do not purchase durable goods, are unlikely to read the financial reports of a firm to see if it is a strong performer or to exercise their financial analysis skills to decipher whether the firm practices EM. Clearly, EM matters when the horizon of the relationship is longer. Raman and Shahrur (2008) examine supplier and customer relationships when the horizon of their relationship exceeds the operating cycle, because the supplier has to make costly investments that are specific to the demands of that customer (hence, if their relationship is terminated, the supplier cannot take advantage of the investment in relation to another customer). Since the supplier wants assurance that the cost of investment will be covered by profitable future sales, the customer-firm has conflicting incentives to engage in EM. On the one hand, it has incentives to inflate earnings and MBE to appear solid to the supplier. On the other hand, it has incentives to make the supplier apprehensive that its investment has become a sunk cost and increase the supplier's willingness to make greater price concessions in future sales.

4.9.2 Competition

The 10-Ks of large S&P 500 firms reveal that every successful firm is threatened by competition. In this chapter, we cover nine papers that examine the impact of competitors on EM. The presence of competition has a dual effect. On the one hand, the firm wishes to beat the competition by appearing strong and intimidating. Hence, it inflates earnings or smoothes them to reduce the perceived riskiness of its profits. On the other hand, the firm has incentives to collude with its competitors to set a limit on those actions that reduce profits, such as price discounts at the ends of quarters (Chapman 2011).

Two studies examine the competition from the perspective of a threat that needs to be eliminated. Tinaikar and Xue (2009) examine the strength of the threat by using, as a proxy, the intensity of import penetration and how low the price–cost margins are. Employing an international sample of 14,213 observations from 1990–2007 from 21 countries, they document the result that competition increases EM. We suggest that this result is intuitive. Firms are under pressure to report at least threshold earnings (see the MBE phenomenon discussed in Sections 4.1 and 5.1). They will do so either because it is the truth or because they utilize EM perniciously. More intense competition makes it harder to benignly meet the threshold. In contrast, Marciukaityte and Park (2009), who measure the impact of competition by the US Census Herfindahl–Hirschman index that is calculated (for all public and private firms) by adding the squares of the individual market shares of the fifty largest firms in each industry,[39] find that firms in more competitive industries are less likely to engage in accrual-based EM and are more likely to engage in smoothing that improves earnings informativeness about future cash flows.[40]

5 Gatekeepers

An underlying theme in Sections 3 and 4 is that the users of accounting information attempt to alleviate the information asymmetry between firms' insiders and themselves by focusing on accounting earnings as a performance measure. This, in turn, induces management to use EM, mostly perniciously. The users then need intermediaries or other mechanisms to monitor management – that is, the accounting scene must also include gatekeepers. The main gatekeeper is the auditor, who attests to financial information and the strength of the internal controls that impact the integrity of the accounting process. In this chapter, we observe that the list of gatekeepers includes the following:

5.1 Analysts (88)
5.2 External governance (75)
5.3 Internal governance (81)
5.4 Auditors (61)
5.5 The media and whistle-blowers (1)

A frequently voiced lament is that these gatekeepers sometimes fall asleep on their watch, collude with management, or, even worse, become another trigger of pernicious EM.

5.1 Analysts

5.1.1 Introduction

Broadly, analysts are divided into buy-side analysts, who work in-house for institutional investors such as hedge funds, and sell-side analysts, who work for brokerage firms. The latter make a living by earning commissions on helping brokerage firms sell stock and providing service to investment banking. We restrict discussion to the sell-side analysts because they conduct research and publicize forecasts and recommendations that provide value-relevant information to investors. Since pernicious EM tends to be opaque, these analysts become a governance mechanism (e.g., the International study of DeGeorge et al. 2012; Hall and Trombley 2011; Hwang et al. 2010; Li et al. 2009; the Indonesian study by Murhadi 2010; Sun 2009). As a result, some studies use the number of analyst followings as a control for the informational environment of the firm. See, for example, Allayannis and Simko (2009); the European study of Beuselinck et al. (2010); and Wolfe (2012). Others use forecast dispersion and forecast error as a measure of information asymmetry (Marciukaityte and Park 2009).

5.1.2 Three questions

We now organize the discussion parallel to Section 4.1 by addressing the same three questions. In this section, however, instead of focusing on the interplay between stock market participants and firms, the players are firms and analysts.

5.1.2.1 Question 1: Are analysts able to detect EM?

The rationale for this question is that pernicious EM contaminates the data on which analysts base their research, and hence they can fulfil their monitoring role efficiently only if they correct for pernicious EM in their evaluations. We observe that the design of a study that answers this question is tricky. One the on hand, how can analysts detect EM that is done behind closed doors, such as real EM? On the other hand, how can they be blind to EM when the incentives to use EM are obvious, such as when a new CEO is appointed (see the Australian study of Wilson and Wu 2011)?

The answer provided by the empirical research is mixed. Billings and Morton (2008) and Givoly et al. (2011) find that analysts fail to detect pernicious EM. Givoly et al. note that analysts are unaware of EM because the managed earnings component of earnings is correlated with their subsequent earnings forecasts; that is, EM that inflates earnings is associated with upward forecast revisions and upgraded stock recommendations, which are contradicted by the firms' subsequent operating performance. In contrast, Louis et al. (2012) show that analysts correct for EM in their forecasts, and Ma and Markov (2012) find that the market correctly understands incentives to MBE. Wilson and Wu (2011) find that the analysts' forecast error is smaller in the year that a new CEO is appointed. A more complete answer is provided by De Jong et al. (2012). On the basis of a survey of analysts that work for 11 of the world's largest investment banks, supplemented by 21 interviews, they find that analysts suspect EM when a firm MBE but are unable to detect EM when it is accomplished by real transactions rather than by an obvious signal such as stock repurchase. Analysts prefer smoother earnings but are unable to distinguish between pernicious and beneficial smoothing.

5.1.2.2 Question 2: What is the impact of analysts on EM?

The dark side of having analysts as monitors is that because the market pays attention to analysts' forecasts, there is pressure on the firm to report earnings that do not fall below the forecast. That is, their forecasts become another threshold that leads to the phenomenon of firms meeting or beating analysts' expectations, or MBE (e.g., He and Tian 2012; McAnally et al. 2008). Furthermore, the market rewards firms that MBE (Mirciov 2010) and seems to penalize firms that fall short of analysts' expectations after a long series of successful MBE (Payne and Thomas 2011). However, the reward is smaller for a firm that meets the forecast or beats it marginally by one penny or less (Keung et al. 2010).

Notably, the pressure can be mitigated when the industry's leader fails analysts' expectations (Bratten et al. 2012) or when firms wish to convey bad news to their employees' labor union (Bova 2009).

A recurrent question in the EM literature concerns how MBE is achieved. The two earliest ways, discussed extensively in our book, are accrual-based EM[41] and expectations guidance. See the UK study of Athanasakou et al. (2008, 2011); the European study of Beccalli et al. (2011); Brown and Pinello (2007); Call et al. (2011); Chen et al. (2010); Das et al. (2011); Harris and Shi (2012b); Hsu (2012); Koch et al. (2012); and Zhao (2011). There are other means of MBE, as well: Cohen et al. (2007), Cook et al. (2012a, 2012b), and Chen et al. (2010) document the exercise of real EM (notably, Chen et al. prove that MBE firms that use real EM only outperform those that MBE by accrual-based EM). Xu and Taylor (2007) find that firms use stock repurchase to boost earnings per share in order to MBE; Athanasakou et al. (2008, 2011), Barua et al. (2009), Fan et al. (2010), and Zhao (2011) find EM through classification – the firm classifies items to or from core earnings in the income statement; and Grundfest and Malenko (2011) document the "rounding the numbers strategy" (see Chapter 11 in our book for a discussion of this strategy). Interestingly, while we associate inflating earnings with the EM strategy to MBE, this is not always the case. Du and Zhang (2011) find that firms "take a bath" when they change their fiscal year date to hoard reported earnings. Harris and Shi (2012b) note that EM can also be used to deflate income when the true earnings are too high because firms then hoard reported earnings to MBE in the future quarters.

Finally, the thresholds discussed in Section 4.1 are set exogenously, while meeting or beating analysts' forecasts is endogenous. Indeed, Hong et al. (2012) and Mirciov (2010) find that the phenomenon of MBE is a waltz between the firms and analysts. For example, Hong et al. use a simultaneous equations analysis to show that analysts prefer to follow firms with low EM, and in return, firms followed by analysts employ less EM.

5.1.2.3 Question 3: Meeting or beating expectations?

The current understanding in research is that MBE is pernicious EM (Harris et al. 2010; Keune and Johnstone 2012; Wolfe 2012; and others). As a matter of fact, the understanding that firms use EM perniciously is so well entrenched that the MBE phenomenon has become a methodological tool. That is, when their research question requires a sample fraught with pernicious EM, researchers use a sample of firms that MBE by a penny or less. In the bibliography, we added the footnote "MBE is a methodology" to such studies. For further discussion of these questions, consult Cohen et al. (2009), Davidson et al. (2009), Elliott et al. (2010), Keskek et al. (2011), and Li (2010).

5.2 and 5.3 Governance

A summary of the research on the relationship between EM and governance is so rich that had we attempted a thorough coverage this chapter would have been at least twice as long. Interestingly, though, the main insights in this area that are summarized in our book are unchanged. Better governance reduces pernicious EM, but not when the gatekeepers collude with management, as is the case, for example, when the institutional shareholders are transient – an indication of a short-term perspective. Section 5.2 applies to external governance (i.e., to the type of ownership) and Section 5.3 applies to internal governance (i.e., to the board of directors). We treat the type of ownership as external governance because most shareholders are outsiders to the firm. The literature distinguishes among the following types: shareholders in general, where shareholder activism impacts EM; institutional owners who are divided between those with a long-term horizon and those who are transient; a controlling shareholder; family ownership, which is divided between firms where the family is merely the owner and firms where the family takes a more active role in management); and venture capitalists. Within this category, we also classify studies on state-owned enterprises in China, yet another aspect of governance. From an EM perspective, the issue is two dimensional because whether owners control EM depends on their own incentives and on their ability to influence management.

Internal governance is determined mostly by the characteristics of the board of directors. It encompasses issues such as CEO entrenchment. when, for example, the CEO is also the chairman of the board, or whether the board is staggered – such as when only one third of the directors may be replaced each year, hampering the ability to change the make-up of the board and, for example, overthrow the CEO. Other issues include the ability of the board to control management as proxied for by its size, the composition of directors that are loyal to management, independent directors, and the gray issues: the composition of the audit and compensation committee, including the size and financial expertise of the audit committee members; and incentives of directors to antagonize management as is proxied, for example, by the interlocking of directors, where the CEOs of two different firms serve as directors in the other firms.

The big picture from the research is that when the firm is doing well and there is no demand for pernicious EM, collusion between management and the board is good because it guarantees teamwork, but when the economic position of the firm deteriorates, better governance reduces pernicious EM. There are also international studies that link governance to EM: Australia (Coulton et al. 2007); Pakistan (Ali Shah et al 2009).

5.4 Auditors[42]

The foremost issue associated with this gatekeeper is his or her independence. Accounting standards require, among other things, that auditors have "independence in mental attitude" and that they exercise due professional care in performing the audit and preparing the auditor's report. Independence requires an impartial attitude in evaluating evidence and the absence of bias in reports rendered; investors must be able to access credible information to mitigate the hazards of misrepresentation. Unfortunately, independence has proved to be elusive for the primary reason that when auditors are hired and paid by the companies they audit, they are tempted at a minimum to shade gray-area judgments to please management. Lack of independence has been suspected as an important factor in the major accounting scandals. Consider, for example, the questioning of Arthur Andersen's independence in the case of Enron; allegedly, shredded documents would have implicated the firm in either knowing that it misleadingly issued unqualified audit opinions or that it knowingly neglected to gather evidence that would have caused it not to issue a clean opinion.

The Sarbanes-Oxley Act, in attempting to improve the independence of auditors, required first that audit committees, rather than management, appoint auditors and decide on their pay, and second, that audit firms not provide certain non-audit services. The use of audit committees, however, does not eliminate the conflict of interest; committee members are paid out of the company's coffers and depend on management for a variety of benefits. As to proscribing non-audit services, evidence is contradictory regarding any link between audit quality and the level of non-audit fees (Ronen 2010).

A successful reform of the audit profession should mitigate the agency problem created by the fact that auditors are hired and paid by the client firms. Furthermore, audit quality should become visible enough so that firms providing better audits can command a premium for their services. Proposals for reform include more independent state boards of accountancy, requirements for more transparency by audit firms, better internal governance mechanisms in the audit firms, and similar suggestions (The Advisory Committee on the Auditing Profession 2008); mandating rotation of audit firms (Arrunada 1997); a voucher financing proposal for intermediaries (Choi and Fisch 2003); auditors being hired by stock exchanges (Healy and Palepu 2003); and increased liability (Talley 2006). As suggested by commentators, while possibly mitigating some of the independence-related problems, these proposals do not effectively eliminate conflict of interest.

An alternative proposal utilizing a market mechanism to align auditors' and managers' incentives with those of investors was suggested by Ronen (2002) (see also Dontoh et al. 2013). Companies would solicit from insurance carriers offers of coverage for their security holders against losses caused by omissions and misrepresentations in financial statements that occur during the covered year. Underwriting reviewers would assess the risk of misrepresentation by examining a firm's internal controls, management incentive structures, and other factors. Based on this review, insurance carriers would decide whether to offer coverage and, if so, under what conditions. Managers would decide whether to purchase such coverage, and if they did, both the coverage and the premium would be publicized. Companies that opted for zero coverage would revert to the existing auditing regime. Companies would then select an external auditor from the list of firms approved by their insurance carrier. The auditor would be hired and paid by the insurance carrier, but the audit fees would be reimbursed by the insured and separately publicized. Once an insurer has underwritten a financial statement insurance policy, its objective would be to minimize the cost of claims, and thus its incentives would be aligned with those of investors. Toward this end, the insurer would incentivize its hired auditor to exert optimal effort, improving the quality of the financial statement in the process.

Managers of firms with high-quality financial statements would likely wish to buy insurance and pay small premiums relative to other companies to credibly signal their higher-quality financial statements, thus initiating a race to a higher quality of financial reports overall. Auditors –agents of the insurers – would want to build a reputation for high quality, and thus their independence, both real and perceived, would be enhanced. Finally, investors and financial markets would benefit from a higher quality of information. Audits would be more accurate, and public information on premiums and coverage for financial statements insurance would provide an index of quality or reliability for investors.[43] There are also international studies that link the auditor and audit quality to EM: Spain (Amat 2008).

5.5 The press

In our book, we cite a few papers showing that revelations in the press expose EM. For this survey, we find one paper whose main focus is whistle-blowing. It documents that when whistle-blowing is revealed in the press, there is a higher likelihood of improvement in governance thereafter (Bowen et al. 2010).

5.6. Summary of the empirical research

We summarize the empirical research referred to in Sections 3, 4, and 5 in the following table, which follows the format of a similar table in the postscript of our book. We use our judgment to classify the EM incidences according to the player in the accounting scene that is most associated with these incidences: senior management; plain users such as creditors and investors; or an audience that exerts influence on the report, such as auditors. For each category, we provide an example for a player in the accounting scene that is the focus of the study and, in parentheses, a sample citation.

6 Theory

6.1 The four dimensions of EM

To organize the analytical research in a meaningful way, we follow the scheme in our book in which we draw attention to the fact that EM has four dimensions. The two best known are the capital market perspective, wherein EM impacts the stock price, and the governance perspective, associated with the principal-agent relationship between management and investors. Two additional dimensions that explain EM are regulation due to the involvement of accounting-rule bodies and, much less known, the economics of EM.

6.1.1 The capital market dimension

Capital market incentives are determined by the rationality of the market. We illustrate this issue through the following example, taken from Bolton et al. (2007). Bolton et al. consider a three-date model where the privately held, owner-managed firm seeks to go public at date $t = 1$. Since the owner-manager of the firm reports the firm's earnings in period 1 before putting the company up for sale, the goal is to create a report that maximizes the price. In period 2, earnings are reported by whoever is then in charge of the company.

The owner-manager can use EM in period 1 at a cost that reduces the firm's value. That is, suppose the firm could optimally produce earnings of $20 million each period. The firm can also report higher earnings in period 1 of $25 or $35 million by moving forward earnings from

Table 12.1 Summary of empirical research by user/supplier of information

Provider of Earnings Numbers		Receivers/Audience of Earnings Information		
Senior Management		Plain Users*		Gatekeepers**
(3.1)	*Compensation* (Armstrong et al. 2013; Baker et al. 2008; Barth and Taylor 2009; Cheng et al. 2009; Eckles et al. 2011; Jayaraman and Milbourn 2010) *and tenure* (Ali and Zhang 2012; Demers and Wang 2010; Hazarika et al. 2012)	(4.1)	*Valuation for non-controlling investors: influencing the stock price and threshold meeting or beating* (Badertscher 2011)	(5.1) *Analysts* (Badertscher et al. 2012; Bratten and Thomas 2012; Brown and Pinello 2008)
(3.2)	*Insider trading* (Armstrong et al. 2013; Sawicki and Shrestha 2008; Yu and Bricker 2007)	(4.2)	*IPOs* (Aharony et al. 2010; Armstrong et al. 2009; Chang et al. 2010), *seasoned equity offerings* (Teoh et al. 1998b), *convertible bond offers* (Chou et al. 2009; Lewis and Verwijmeren 2009), *and spin-offs* (Lin and Yung 2011)	(5.2) *External governance: ownership by shareholders in general* (Martin 2011) *and shareholder activism* (Banko et al. 2012), *or institutional owners* (Ayers et al. 2011;
(3.3)	*Turnover* (Chen et al. 2011; Davidson et al. 2009; Faleye et al. 2010; Hazarika et al. 2012; Hwang et al. 2010; Jiang 2008; Wilson and Wang 2010; Wilson and Wu 2011)	(4.3)	*Mergers and acquisitions* (Anilowski Cain et al. 2012; Baik et al. 2007; Gong et al. 2008)	Beuselinck et al. 2010), *controlling shareholder* (Bona-Sánchez et al. 2011), *family ownership* (Bhaumik and Gregoriou 2010), *venture capitalist involvement* (Chen et al.
(3.4)	*Management buyout* (Davidson et al. 2011; Fischer and Louis 2008; Zhu et al. 2012)	(4.4)	*Debt, such as credit rating* (Ali and Zhang 2008)	2012b; Cho et al. 2012; Lee and Masulis 2011), *or stated-owned enterprises in China* (Charoenwong and Jiraporn 2008; Nelson and
(3.5)	*Culture* (Desender et al. 2011; Doupnik 2008; Han et al. 2010; Jha 2011; Li et al. 2012; Zhang 2010), *legal system* (Ben Othman et al. 2005; Dyreng et al 2011; Enomoto et al. 2012; Francis and Wang 2008), *corporate culture* (Diego et al. 2008; Frank et al. 2011; Kim et al. 2011; Mohamad et al. 2010; Salewski and Zülch 2012), *religion* (Callen et al. 2010; Grullon et al. 2009; Hanif 2010; McGuire 2012; Ismail et al. 2012), *gender* (Ittonen et al. 2012; Mohamad et al. 2010; Niskanen et al. 2011), *ethics and social norms* (Fischer and Huddart 2007; Jha 2011; Labelle 2009), *and other social issues* (Francoeur et al. 2010)***	(4.5)	*New accounting release* (Anantharaman et al. 2012; Barua et al. 2009), *the Sarbanes-Oxley Act* (Ang 2011; Aono and Guan 2008; Boubakri and Ghouma 2008), *and the change to IFRS* (Aussenegg et al. 2008)	Jamil 2012)
		(4.6)	*Tax* (Albring et al. 2011; Chen et al. 2012)	(5.3) *Internal governance, such as composition and size of the board of directors* (Babenko et al. 2012;
		(4.7)	*Regulated industries such as insurance companies and banks* (Anandarajan et al. 2007; Beck and Narayanamoorthy 2012), *privately sponsored U.S. defined benefit pension plans*, (Addoum et al. 2010), *utilities* (Alam and Fu 2008), *demutualizing thrifts* (Adams et al. 2009), *regulated not-for-profit hospitals* (Ballantine et al. 2007; Newton and Thomas 2011), *and Real Estate Investment Trusts* (Ambrose and Bian 2009; Edelstein et al. 2008)	Cheng et al. 2012), *number of meetings* (Davidson et al. 2011), *etc.*
		(4.8)	*Employees* (Bova 2013)	(5.4) *Auditors* (Boone et al. 2011)
		(4.9)	*Suppliers and customers* (Raman and Shahrur 2008), *and competitors* (Chapman 2011)	(5.5) *The press and whistleblowers* (Bowen et al. 2010)

*Suppliers, investors, employees, consumers, creditors, regulators.
**Boards of directors, analysts, investment banks, credit agencies, auditors, attorneys, the press.
***A new addition; no such category in the book.

Table 12.2 Efficient markets

	Reporting Policy		
	Truthful	Inflated	Aggressively Inflated
Reported Earnings in $t = 1$	$20 million	$25 million	$35 million
Realized Earnings in $t = 2$	$20 million	$14.5 million	$0 million
Firm's Value at $t = 1$	$40 million	$39.5 million	$35 million

Table 12.3 "Bubble" with naïve investors (10 percent chance)

	Reporting Policy		
	Truthful	Inflated	Aggressively Inflated
Reported Earnings in $t = 1$	$20 million	$25 million	$35 million
Realized Earnings in $t = 2$	$20 million	$14.5 million	$0 million
Stock's Value at $t = 1$	$40 million	$50 million	$70 million

period 2. If the firm reports $25 million, the firm can only generate earnings of $14.5 million in period 2, and if it reports $35 million, the firm makes a profit of zero in the second period.

To appreciate the importance of the market's rationality, consider the benchmark case wherein the stock market is perfectly efficient. That is, investors are able to see through any form of manipulation. Since manipulation is costly, this means that the market value of the firm is maximized when there is no manipulation.

Next, suppose now that stock markets are not efficient and that differences of opinion may emerge because some naïve investors actually take reported numbers at face value.[44] The presence of irrational investors induces EM to boost the short-term stock price.

Specifically, suppose that with a 10 percent chance, a sufficient number of naïve investors would be fooled and believe that the same earnings will be realized in period 2. This mistake is consistent with behavioral finance literature claiming that investors are subject to a combination of overconfidence and inattention. Upon observing an earnings report of $25 million in period 1, these investors are then prepared to pay a price of $50 million for the company in period 1, and if a profit of $35 million is announced, they will pay $70 million. The stock price will be overvalued in period 1 when (with a 10 percent chance) a sufficient number of naïve investors appear in the market, misinterpret the firm's reported earnings, and create a "bubble." The sophisticated investors then stay out of the game.

Although this situation only occurs with a 10 percent chance, it may still induce the firm to engage in pernicious EM. A truthful report yields a price of $40 million. A report of $25 million is a gamble between a 90 percent chance of selling the firm for $39.5 million and a 10 percent chance of selling the firm for $50 million. Hence, its expected value is $0.9 \times \$39.5$ million $+ 0.1 \times \$50$ million $= \$40.55$ million. A report of $35 million yields an expected price of $0.9 \times \$35$ million $+ 0.1 \times \$70$ million $= \$38.5$ million.

Clearly, the owner is better off by choosing to bring $5 million forward even though the true present value of the stock is then lower.

6.1.2 Governance

The main insight of this dimension is that EM can be pernicious and that the principal-owners would contract with the manager-agent in such a way as to induce EM. This insight can be summarized by a simple binary example. Suppose that the true earnings of the firm are either 1 or zero. The probability of each outcome is determined by the effort of the manager. High effort costs the manager a disutility of 0.05, the probability of high profits is 0.7, and with low effort the probability of high profits falls to 0.3. The manager is paid a salary, S, and upon realization of profits of 1, a bonus, B. So he or she is willing to exert high effort only if

$$0.7 \times (B + S) + 0.3 \times S - 0.05 \geq 0.3 \times (B + S) + 0.7 \times S.$$

The left (right) hand side is the expected reward for exerting high (low) effort. Rearranging and solving this relationship as a strict equality in order to find the minimum bonus that makes the agent indifferent to exerting high effort yields $0.4 \times B = 0.05$, so that $B = 0.0125 > 0$. So, the agent has incentives to inflate the report. If EM is costly, then the agent may not engage in EM, because if he or she reports 1 when true earnings are zero, the bonus is achieved, but if the expected cost of EM exceeds 0.0125, the benefit to use EM does not justify the cost.

Suppose that EM is costless. The agent will then attempt to inflate the report. The report is audited. There is probability of π, $1/2 < \pi < 1$, that the auditor will discover the proof. The expected payoff upon exerting high effort and engaging in EM is

$$[0.7 + 0.3 \times (1 - \pi) \times (B + S) + 0.3 \times \pi \times S - 0.05 = [0.3 + 0.7 \times (1 - \pi) \times (B + S) + 0.7 \times \pi \times S.$$

The difference is that now there is some chance that the agent receives the bonus when the true earnings are zero because the audit did not discover the truth. Rearranging yields $0.4\pi B = 0.05$. It is immediately apparent that since π is less than one, the bonus is higher. Economically, EM has no impact. The agent exerts high effort with and without EM. Still, EM is pernicious because the agent misleads the principal when his or her performance is low.

Note that we employed here a rather simple example, wherein the agent is risk neutral and the principal therefore does not incur the higher cost of incentives associated with incentive contracts being more risky. When the agent is risk neutral, a higher bonus translates to a lower salary. However, when the agent is risk averse, a higher bonus also translates to a higher cost of incentives and economic loss to the principal, because the contract with EM becomes more risky.

6.1.3 Regulation

The regulation dimension opens up many research opportunities. Recent developments in research on the impact of regulation on EM include the following studies: Caskey (2012), who examines the effects of the litigation environment and litigation insurance on the value of the firm and the frequency of litigation; Chen et al. (2007), who study the conservatism mandate; Köenigsgruber (2009), who studies the impact of dual listing when the second stock market regulates EM better; and Murakami and Shiiba (2009), who have an interesting study on the impact of regulation and enforcement and EM on each other. However, while there has been progress in this vast area, there exist more opportunities for research.

6.1.4 Economics of EM

The economics of EM is largely unexplored. In fact, we had to provide our own examples in the book because we were not aware of any accounting paper addressing this important front. On the one hand, any principal-agent game which investigates effort or investment has economic consequences. On the other hand, there is a lot we do not know. Lambert (2007) observes:

... earnings management is viewed as an activity that is widely practiced by managers. Even though the agency framework seems to be a natural one to use to study earnings management, the agency literature to date has not made much progress in helping us understand how, why, and when earnings management takes place.

(p. 260)

A tentative step towards filling up this gap is provided in Elitzur et al. (2013). We study a decentralization decision in a binary model that is similar to the example of real EM above. The organizational design involves the centralization/decentralization dimension, that is, the choice of the party that generates the profits of a division. Either headquarters runs the operations – a centralized design – or the operations are delegated to division managers who receive both autonomy and incentives to exert effort – a decentralized design. This problem is not trivial, because the intervention of the headquarters is costly and this cost increases in the cultural distance between headquarters and division. For example, consider a US firm with a division in Canada and a division in India. Clearly, it is easier to communicate procedures and make decisions for the Canadian subsidiary at the headquarters in the US than for the culturally distant Indian division. So, in the absence of EM, there is a cutoff cultural distance such that for all lower (higher) levels, the division is perfectly centralized (decentralized). In the centralized design, managers receive a salary. When the headquarters wants the division to manage earnings in order to reap the premium for presenting strong performance by the firm to its external constituency (i.e., to the stock market), there are now a number of new consequences. First, for some distances for which a centralized design was optimal in the absence of EM, a centralized design will be replaced by a decentralized design with EM. Second, and more surprisingly, a new hybrid design appears wherein economic earnings are generated by the headquarters (i.e., the organizational design is centralized), but the subsidiaries' managers receive a bonus as in the decentralized organization design. The only purpose of the bonus is to induce the subsidiaries' managers to manage earnings. Hence, the bonus is designed so that it is not high enough to induce effort to increase economic earnings. This is an interesting result because whenever critics are outraged over excessive compensation of top management, the defenders appeal to the necessity for providing incentives. This result shows that EM may introduce bogus incentives as a product of collusion between headquarters and division managers to engage in EM perniciously.

6.2 The theoretical developments

In the book, Chapters 5–8 cover theoretical developments in the analytical accounting research. Not surprisingly, this section was much shorter than Section 2 of the book that covers empirical research. The same is true for this chapter as well. There are 37 theoretical papers, excluding our own. We summarize them in the following table, where the orientation of each study (according to the four dimension of EM) is given in the last column.

The state of EM in most of the studies is as follows. In a one-shot game, the propagator of EM wants to inflate earnings. When the propagator is the privately informed manager, this strategy increases his earnings-based bonus, the stock price, and, hence, the value of the stocks in his compensation contract. When the propagator is an entrepreneur looking for a financier, this strategy increases the chance of finding financing and the size of the entrepreneur's equity. The manipulation is executed either through accruals management or through real EM. In both cases, the amount of EM is constrained by its cost. Some model the cost as personal. Others treat the cost indirectly through the unfavorable impact of EM on the firm's value. In fact, this strategy explains the demand for accounting conservatism. Conservatism is a vehicle used to alleviate aggressive EM.

Table 12.4 Recent developments in analytical EM research

Study	Research question	Answer	Orientation
Amir, Einhorn, and Kama(2008)	Components of earnings that are used in ratio analysis can be manipulated differently; e.g., estimated depreciation and amortization are more easily managed than sales. The question is whether an examination of the components of earnings, not just earnings, allows the market to detect and deter EM.	When different components have similar economic fundamentals and different abilities to be manipulated, the market can monitor EM by examining the components of earnings.	Capital market (NREE) and agency
Bachman and Hens (2008)	The paper examines the reporting strategy of a firm that wants to meet or beat the consensus analysts' forecasts (MBF). The binary-outcome game features analysts who wish to mimic the consensus forecast and a manager whose payoff is proportional to the price in a two-period model when the market rewards MBF and penalizes failure to MBF.	If the manager is indifferent between the present stock price and future price, the goal of EM is to MBF, and EM is pernicious. Otherwise, the manager's incentives to manipulate earnings vary with investor preferences, his or her compensation, and the analysts' forecasts. The market can then undo EM to learn the truth.	Capital market
Bagnoli and Watts (2010)	How does competition in the product market impact EM, and how does EM impact the production quantities when two firms compete within the framework of a Cournot competition (i.e., in quantities) with privately known unit cost?	Firms underestimate the rivals' cost. Hence, each firm cuts its production below the full-information level, which in turn increases the market price and profit. These effects are smaller when firms compete in more profitable product markets or when they use reasonably similar technologies. The firm with lower cost of misreporting manages earnings more.	Economics
Beyer (2008)	What is the equilibrium reporting strategy and analysts' earnings forecasts accuracy? The framework is a one-shot game between analysts and firms wherein misreporting is costly.	The analysts issue optimistic reports, and firms manage reports upwards when the true report falls short of the analysts' forecast and report the truth if not.	Capital market
Beyer (2009)	What is the equilibrium management's forecast and EM strategy? The framework is a two-period model wherein the mean and variance of the distribution of firms' cash flows is unknown to the market. The market price is the sum of expected cash flows in both periods minus discount for the variance of the sum to reflect investors' risk-aversion. The manipulation of forecast and report are personally costly to the firm's manager-owner; the cost is unknown to the market.	In equilibrium, the firm both (i) issues pessimistic forecasts and (ii) manipulates earnings; (iii) the stock price is more sensitive to the actual earnings announcement than to the forecast; (iv) the capital market values firms with positive earnings surprises at a premium; and (v) the expected stock price reaction to earnings surprises increases as the cost to the manager of manipulating earnings declines.	Capital market

Study	Question / Framework	Findings	Category
Beyer, Guttman, and Marinovic (2012)	What is the optimal performance-based compensation contract that allows firms to attract more productive personnel (adverse selection) and also to incentivize its employees to exert more unobservable effort (moral hazard) when the employee can manage the reported performance?	(1) the optimal compensation contract is (i) convex in reported earnings, (ii) more convex the less costly it is for the manager to use EM, and (ii) less sensitive to reported earnings than it would be if the manager were not able to use EM; and (2) the manager's cost of EM affects EM, the manager's productive effort, and firm value.	Agency
Bolton and Xiong (2007)	Can the recent corporate scandals associated with CEO pay be explained by the irrationality of the investors, which creates a speculative bubble (the price deviates from the fundamental value of the firm)?	When some investors are sometimes (or always) *overconfident* or *inattentive*, and when stock markets are undergoing a speculative phase, then pernicious EM will drive up short-term stock performance.	Capital market and agency
Camara and Henderson (2009)	How does performance-based compensation impact real EM? The framework is an agency model where the firm's stock is traded publicly. Risk-neutral shareholders grant the risk-averse manager stock options. The manager controls the first two moments of the distribution of the accounting earnings.	Real EM increases with the level of the earnings-per-share performance threshold. The incentive to undertake direct EM is stronger when the options are further "out-of-the-money." The manager may choose not to employ EM when the earnings-per-share threshold is low.	Agency and capital market
Caskey (2012)	What are the effects of the litigation environment and litigation insurance on the value of the firm and the frequency of litigation? The framework extends Fischer and Verrecchia (2000).	When it is revealed that earnings were previously inflated, the price plummets by the update of the firm's fundamental value and the incremental litigation cost. Insurance has a favorable impact on the firm's value.	Capital market regulation
Chen, Hemmer, and Zhang (2007)	Consider conservatism as an accounting system with downward bias. Then, under what conditions is conservatism in accounting standards so effective in reducing incentives to manage earnings upwards that it is better than an accounting system that is bias-free?	The likelihood of EM is lower in the conservative regime.	Capital market,* agency, regulation
Demers and Wang (2010)	What are the relationships between tenure and accrual and real EM? The manager, whose productivity is unobservable, chooses costly EM to bias his or her performance measure to maximize lifetime compensation.	The model generates a "signal jamming" equilibrium (Stein 1989). Young executives do not use EM because accruals reverse, and real EM is value-destroying in the long run. Older executives engage in income-increasing EM in order to get directorship offers after retirement.	Agency

(continued)

Table 12.4 (continued)

Study	Research question	Answer	Orientation
Dutta and Fan (2012)	What is the impact of EM on pay/performance sensitivity in a multi-period model?	With EM, the optimal pay/performance sensitivities across the two periods would be closer to each other.	Agency and economics
	A two-period model wherein the productivity of the manager is time-specific and he or she can engage in EM by shifting reported earnings intertemporally. EM is costly.	Also, sometimes, EM alleviates the problem of underinvestment caused by the information asymmetry between managers and owners.	
Ewert and Wagenhofer (2011)	What do earnings quality metrics measure, and how are different ones related?	Value relevance and persistence are the best. In general, however, there are no metrics that perfectly respond to the requirement that the metrics reveal (i) managerial incentives, (ii) operating risk, and (iii) accounting noise.	Capital market
	EM is costly to the manager who wishes to increase both the stock price and the smoothness of reported earnings.		
Ewert and Wagenhofer (2012)	How does the choice of capitalization, and the precisions of financial and non-financial information, as well as the personal cost of EM, affect earnings quality (i.e., the ability of investors to predict future cash flows)?	EM is beneficial because it allows the firm to convey value-relevant, non-financial information; the quality of the report is independent of the cost of EM.	Capital markets
		Higher capitalization may lower earnings quality because it suppresses the inclusion of non-financial information.	
Fedyk (2007)	What is the rational explanation for the kink in the distribution of earnings around zero?	The optimal contract includes a threshold beyond which the project is terminated.	Agency
	The manager has private information about his own effort and about the firm's expected cash flows. Shareholders prefer early termination of a negative net present value (NPV). The manager can engage in real EM at personal cost. EM is value-destroying	Shareholders induce overinvestment to reduce managerial surplus and real EM to reduce severance pay upon termination of employment. Hence, for some parameters, the manager aggressively engages in real EM, which creates discontinuity in the distribution of earnings.	
Friebel and Guriev (2012)	To the extent that whistleblowing is a valuable mechanism of corporate governance, the question is whether it enhances a firm's value.	Whistle-blowing has negative effects on productive efficiency of division managers because they are bribed not to be whistle-blowers by top management when outcome is low, which thus reduces their incentives to exert effort.	Agency regulation
Gao (2012a)	Is there demand for conservatism as an accounting measurement rule that requires more verification of good news, alleviates pernicious EM to counter pernicious aggressive EM?	Conservatism, as a measurement rule that requires more verification of good news, alleviates pernicious EM to hide poor performance.	Agency

Gao (2012b)	What is the optimal threshold in the application of accounting standards (such as the threshold for recognizing contingent liability) when the manager can utilize EM to meet or beat the threshold?	A threshold that partitions raw evidence to a binary classification serves as a commitment mechanism that renders the accounting report more value-relevant.	Agency
Hofmann (2008)	Will the optimal contract be based on a stochastic signal that indicates that the agent spent costly effort on non-productive EM tasks?	A penalty may be designed to perfectly eliminate EM, but it may have an unfavorable impact on the agent's effort. Hence, in equilibrium, the principal may prefer the noisy measure of managed earnings for contracting.	Agency
Köenigsgruber (2009)	What is the impact of dual listing on EM when an entrepreneur can signal the high quality of its project by cross-listing in a jurisdiction with stricter enforcement of financial reporting regulation?	(i) For some parameters, cross-listing reduces EM by dual listing firms, and for others, cross-listing increases EM. (ii) The entrance of firms with dual listing induces domestic firms to decrease EM.	Capital market
Lai (2011)	For a given income generation process, what is the impact of EM on performance measures (net income, book value of equity, accounting return on equity, and residual income) and growth measures (growth in book value of common equity, growth in comprehensive net income, growth in residual income, growth in net operating assets, growth in operating revenue)?	First, different measures of growth are not equivalent. Second, the real growth rate of a particular performance measure can be exacerbated or attenuated by varying the level of accounting bias. In the extreme case, growth can be fictitiously created even though real growth is zero. Third, the departure of P/B ratio from one is not a good proxy for accounting conservatism or aggressiveness.	Accrual process
Lai, Debo, and Nan (2010)	What is the optimal "channel stuffing"*** strategy for EM when:(a) the firm manages inventory levels, (b) the manager has private information on second-period demand when the first-period inventory level is determined, and (c) falling short of demand is costly?	There is a threshold first-period demand, such that when the first-period demand is lower than the threshold, the firm engages in channel stuffing that is proportional to the demand, and hence the report reveals the true second-period demand. When demand exceeds the threshold, the firm rids itself of all excess inventory through channel stuffing.	Capital market, agency, and economics
Laux and Laux (2009)	What are the relationships between the board's monitoring, CEO compensation in the form of saleable equity, and EM?	Investors are not fooled by EM. Since an audit committee increases oversight to control EM when the compensation committee increases the link between CEO pay and performance, the board can credibly signal to the CEO that it will take its oversight function seriously. In equilibrium, more powerful incentives may be associated with less EM.	Agency

(continued)

Table 12.4 (continued)

Study	Research question	Answer	Orientation
Laux (2010)	What is the impact of the emerging practice of making directors personally liable to shareholders in the wake of an accounting scandal on compensation of the management, the board's oversight, and the firm's value?	Directors can reduce EM by designing less powerful incentives for managers who engage in EM. The new practice of liability of directors induces a lower level of board oversight, lower CEO incentive pay, and, consequently, lower shareholder value.	Agency
Laux and Stocken (2011)	Is it true that if managers paid for damages related to EM when class-action suits were filed, they would not engage in EM?	The anticipation of damages may decrease the cost of capital. In equilibrium, then, it may be the case that an increase in expected legal penalties paid privately may lead to more EM, overinvestment, and a reduction in expected social welfare.	Capital market, economics
Levine and Smith (2009)	Is a clawback clause in the compensation contract of the manager (that specifies that the manager must return previously awarded bonuses), better than a contract without such a clause?	The no-clawback contract dominates the clawback contract if the cash realization is relatively noisy, EM is difficult, or when the agent is very impatient.	Agency
Murakami and Shiiba (2009)	How does regulation impact EM and how does current EM impact future regulation?	Depending on parameters, an increase in the tightness of regulations may increase EM presently; while increased relaxation of regulations decreases the level of EM at present, it increases EM in the future.	Regulation
Nan (2008)	What is the interaction between hedging and EM?	When the decision to hedge is contractible, the contract alleviates both the risk premium paid to the manager and the equilibrium amount of EM because it allows better monitoring of EM. When hedging is not contractible, in some situations discouraging hedging but allowing EM is efficient. In others, the principal can induce hedging and truth revelation.	Agency
Schultze and Weiler (2011)	What is the impact of tightening accounting standards on an impatient manager's long-term investment decisions under earnings-based performance evaluation?	Tighter accounting regulation leads to underinvestment and pernicious real EM.	Agency, regulation, and economics

Study	Research question	Summary / Findings	Theory
Stratopoulos and Vance (2009)	Consider the decision to employ EM when the firm must meet or beat a stochastic threshold (analysts' forecasts). The manager must first forecast future reported performance. If expected performance exceeds the target, no EM is necessary. If not, the manager can then weigh the benefits of achieving the target against the likelihood of detection and the associated costs, given the amount of manipulation deemed necessary.	As the uncertainty (variance) associated with a prediction of future earnings declines, managers who want to maximize their payoffs are more likely to use EM, but the magnitude of EM is smaller.	Agency
Strobl (2009)	What is the impact of EM on a firm's cost of capital in a market with multiple firms whose cash flows are correlated?	Managers are more inclined to engage in EM during periods of economic expansion. EM reduces the correlation between the firms' cash flows and thus lowers the risk premium required by investors	Agency, capital market
Sun (2011)	What is the role of EM in the properties of asset prices and stock market participation?	EM causes excess volatility. Investors require a risk premium for EM. When investors have heterogeneous beliefs about EM, EM reduces stock market participation.	Capital market
Teshima and Shuto (2008)	What is the relationship between managerial ownership and pernicious EM?	The relationship between ownership and EM is nonlinear. EM decreases in ownership for both high and low levels of the managerial ownership range, while it increases for the intermediate range for certain parameters.	Agency
Trueman and Versano (2011)	Considering security analysts as experts in the industries they follow, what is the impact of such expertise on market prices and returns when earnings are decomposed into two parts: an industry component, common to all firms in the same industry, and a firm-specific component when the persistence of these two components is different?	A firm's post-earnings announcement price is a function of the analyst's prior earnings forecast, even though that forecast does not contain any incremental information about current period earnings. When facing the choice between expectations management and EM, EM is a better means to impact the price, but for some parameters it is too costly.	Capital market
Xin (2007)	Why does missing an earnings target trigger a large and disproportionate negative stock price response, while exceeding it meets with only a moderate response?	In equilibrium, there is a kink in the distribution of reported earnings around the earnings forecast. The equilibrium stock price schedule is much steeper when reported earnings lie below the forecast than when reported earnings lie above the forecast.	Capital market

(continued)

Table 12.4 (continued)

Study	Research question	Answer	Orientation
Yim (2012)	What is the relationship between EM that violates generally accepted accounting principles to meet/beat a threshold, and auditor-client interaction in a two-round audit?	A "cookie jar reserve" policy is equilibrium. Simulation results indicate that the model can accommodate the earnings distribution discontinuity phenomenon, as well as the volcano shape of the distributions of earnings change and earnings surprise. Potential applications are suggested, including the construction of an EM measure distinct from but complementary to abnormal accruals.	Capital market
Yu (2012)	Why do firms take a "big bath" when the CEO changes?	When an earnings report issued by the outgoing CEO is sufficiently low, the incoming CEO will adopt the "big bath" policy despite its adverse effect on his or her earning, since investors require a risk premium for the perceived volatility of earnings-based compensation.	Agency

*Capital market through the participants, but the model is binary without the LEN (linear contract, exponential utility, normal distribution) that are common to this type of work.

**Channel stuffing is a strategy wherein the firm records future sales in the in the current period by offering customers discounts.

In repeated games, the optimal strategy is either aggressive EM or smoothing. Smoothing is value enhancing because it reduces the temporal riskiness of the contract and thus reduces the cost of the incentives.

Two studies depart from the aggressive/smoothing strategy profile. Yim (2012) shows that the threat of an audit discovery of the truth and reversing EM may lead to a "cookie jar reserve" strategy to ensure meeting or beating a threshold in the future. Yu (2012) shows that an incoming CEO may adopt a "big bath" policy. These studies are the exception, not the rule. This is a curious state of research because, in reality, EM policy features a rich menu of strategies, and the same firm may vary its policy across performance levels and over time. The empirical research recognizes the following policies, given in the following definitions adapted from Fogel-Yaari and Ronen (2011):

Definitions:

- A "truth-telling" report: the report equals economic earnings (henceforth also referred to as outcome).
- A "smoothing" strategy: the report overstates low and understates high economic earnings.
- An "aggressive" report: the report overstates the truth.
- A "conservative" report: the report understates the outcome.
- A "taking a bath" report: a conservative strategy where the report equals the minimum outcome.
- A "cookie jar reserves" report: a conservative strategy where the report equals the true outcome minus a reserve.
- Meeting/beating the threshold: the report equals or exceeds the threshold:

  o A "threshold meeting" report: the report equals the threshold.
  o A "marginal threshold beating" report: the report exceeds the threshold by a very small margin.[45]
  o A "threshold beating" report: the report exceeds the threshold by more than the margin under the "marginal threshold beating" report.

With the exception of a 2000 study that is cited in our book explaining when a firm smoothes and when it takes a bath, there has been little progress in understanding the richness of the phenomenon. A first step towards filling the gap is Fogel-Yaari and Ronen (2011). In this study, the firm is a two-period, principal-agent contract between the manager and the board, in which neither the effort of the manager (the agent) nor the economic earnings in each period are observable. The board observes only the accumulated earnings at the end of the second period. Hence, the agent can manipulate earnings in the first period by shifting reported earnings intertemporally. Not surprisingly, in this setting the agent likes to smooth and the principal designs a contract that induces smoothing.

What differentiates this study from others is that the firm is under pressures to meet or beat thresholds that represent the market's expectations (MBT) repeatedly.[46] There are two types of firms: those that must MBE in the first period more than in the second period (short-run MBT firms), and those that must MBE in the second period more than in the first (long-run MBT firms).

Figure 12.3 depicts the reporting strategy of a short-run MBT firm when the first-period threshold is 60 and the second is fixed at 100 when the truth varies from the minimum of zero and maximum of 350.

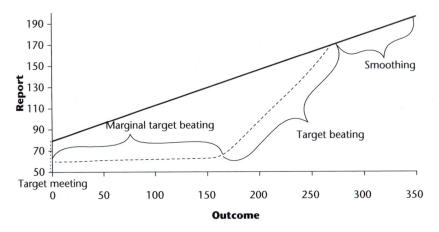

Figure 12.3   The reporting strategy of a short-run MBT firm

The reporting strategy divides the range of the true outcomes into four regions. The firm reports meet the threshold only at the minimal outcome of zero (Region I^R). It marginally beats the threshold thereafter (in Region II^R). That is, upon denoting the reporting strategy of the short-run MBT firm $M^R(x_1) = 60 + 0.025x_1$ and by x_1 the truth. The reason that marginal beating dominates meeting lies in the impact of a revealing report on the cost of incentives. The marginal beating strategy affords the principal the ability to vary pay with performance and, hence, provide more powerful incentives to exert effort from the manager. This region ends when true earnings reach the level of 164.1. Beyond $x_1 = 164.1$ (Region III^R), it beats the threshold, $M^R(x_1) = 56 + 0.9636 \times (x_1 - 160)$ until the outcome is 260. The firm can now increase the margin between the report and the truth, because the first-period outcome suffices to MBT in both periods even in the worst-case scenario when the second-period economic earnings are zero. Beating a threshold need not be uniform. For example, the reporting strategy changes to $M^R(x_1) = 20 + 1.3636 \times (x_1 - 160)$ between 260 and 270. At $x_1 = 270$, the firm shifts to smoothing (Region IV^R) by reporting $M_1{}^R(x_1) = 80 + 1/3x_1$. It does not smooth for lower outcomes because the smoothed report is too high to enable it to MBT in the second period. For example, when $x_1 = 210$, the smoothed report is 150 (= $80 + 1/3 \times 210$), leaving an inadequate reserve of unreported earnings of 60 (= $210 - 150$) for the second period, and when the second period outcome is lower than 40, the firm fails to MBT in the second period. The threshold-beating report is 108.18 (= $56 + 0.9636 \times (210 - 160)$), leaving a reserve of 101.82 >100.[47]

Figure 12.4 divides the set of outcomes into five regions. Up to a first-period outcome of 100 (Region I^L), the firm "takes a bath" by reporting the minimum outcome of zero, hoarding all first-period earnings for beating the more important second-period threshold. In Region II^L, between 100 and 160 (= reserve of 100 + first-period threshold of 60), the firm creates a "cookie jar reserve" of 100 for the second-period report. That is, when the outcome is 110, 120, or 130, the firm reports 10, 20, or 30, respectively, hoarding the remaining 100 for reporting in the second period. Region III^L is a single point at an outcome of 160: the firm meets the first-period threshold by reporting 60, thus hoarding the minimum reported earnings of 100. Region IV^L contains those higher outcomes, up to 270, for which the smoothed message is too high; here, similar to region III^R, the firm replaces smoothing with beating the threshold. In the figure, $M^L(x_1) = 55 + 0.9636(x_1 - 160) + k$. Variable k is a scalar that ranges from -0.5 at $x_1 = 170$ to 9 at $x_1 = 270$, and because the difference between the outcome and first-period threshold is proportional to the first-period outcome, the report reveals the truth. In Region V^L

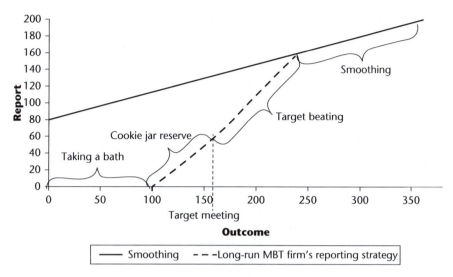

Figure 12.4 The reporting strategy of a long-run MBT firm

(it starts at $x_1 = 270$, at which point the smoothed report is 170), the firm smoothes just as the short-run MBT firm does.

In general, the studies in the table explore whether EM is pernicious or not depending on whether investors can figure out the choice of the optimal bias of the report. When they do, EM has no impact on their expectations because investors undo the report in order to learn the truth. If, however, the private demand of the manager for EM is unknown, then EM is pernicious because it fools the market. The incentives of managers to manage earnings are closely related to the impact of EM on the perceptions of investors. A criticism of EM studies when the managed report reveals the truth is leveled by appealing to the revelation principle. This principle states that in games with information asymmetry, there is no loss of generality in studying them as a game that induces the privately informed agents to reveal the truth. The intuition is that the agent is paid the same for telling the truth as for misrepresenting and would therefore not EM. For an explanation of when the revelation principle does not hold, consult Foget-Yaari and Ronen (2002).

In EM research, the researcher first characterizes the optimal report. The revelation mechanism is a tool (used in the mechanism design literature) to avoid calculating the optimal reporting strategy. It employs a two-stage process. The mechanism designer first calculates the optimal lie and then recalculates the payments that provide the sender the same payoff for telling the truth. Implementing the second step in the EM context is unnecessary *and* not parsimonious. Why would a rational decision maker spend precious time and effort on calculating payoffs for truth-telling when he or she already knows enough and stands to gain nothing for exerting extra effort?

7 Methodology

7.1 Introduction

Nowadays, there is a plethora of measures of EM. In a way, the question is not how to measure EM, but rather which method provides the best and strongest results. Some methods use regression models, such as those that attempt to detect EM by decomposing accruals into those that are necessitated by operations and those that arise from discretionary EM. An example of an EM that does not use regression is the matching procedure of Kothari et al. (2005). At the risk of sounding overcritical, we note that most studies make a choice on the EM methodology in an ad-hoc manner. That is, if an EM methodology is popular in previous studies, then it is likely to be used in the next one.

7.2 The Jones model

7.2.1 Issues in detecting EM through accruals

Most of the empirical research measures EM by abnormal accruals. The test has two stages (see our book, p. 406 and also the next subsection). In the first stage, the researcher models the relationships between accruals and changes in sales plus other regressors and then uses the coefficients derived from the first stage for each regressor to calculate the normal accruals in the test period/subsample. The difference between accruals and estimated accruals – abnormal accruals – indicates EM if the null hypothesis of zero is rejected at the accepted significance levels.

It is readily seen that an important aspect of this design is to define the proxies for accruals, since unlike sales and property, plant, and equipment (PP&R), accruals are not provided by Compustat or a similar database. There is no unique way to define accruals. Broadly, there are two by two dichotomies. The first differentiates between the balance sheet approach and the statement of cash flows approach. The balance sheet approach follows Jones (1991): total (current) accruals are defined as non-cash working capital changes (plus depreciation and loss/gain on sale of assets) less the adjustments for income tax payable and the portion of long-term debt that is classified as short-term debt because it matures before the next balance sheet date (see our book, pp. 405–407). The statement of cash flows approach is associated with Hribar and Collins (2002): the accruals are calculated as the difference between net income before extraordinary items and cash flows from operations. This definition of accruals is considered cleaner because it is immune to noise in the accruals measures introduced by transactions such as mergers and acquisitions and foreign currency translations. However, there are no data for cash flow from operations before 1988, and at times this measure is more volatile than the accruals measure calculated from the balance sheet.[48] Barton and Simko's study (2002) draws attention to the fact that when EM is considered cumulatively, in each period that the EM is not reversed, the cumulative EM constrains the firm from engaging easily in EM in the same direction (see the discussion in Baber et al. 2010). The measure of this loss of flexibility is the net operating assets from the balance sheet. Hence, the balance sheet approach is more consistent with this constraint.

The other approach for classifying accruals differentiates between total accruals and current accruals. Current accruals are derived from total accruals by adding back loss/gain on sale of assets and the depreciation expense (some studies ignore the loss/gain on sale of assets). The current accruals approach is appropriate when the model for estimating normal accruals does not contain regressors that are associated with long-term accruals, such as Property, Plant and Equipment (PPE), which are responsible for the depreciation expense.

A scrutiny of the new references reveals that most studies in our references list use the total accruals approach. Exceptions that use current accruals include Ahmad-Zaluki et al. (2009); Anilowski Cain et al. (2012); Baber et al. (2010); Chang et al. (2010); Choi and Young (2012); Davidson et al. (2011); DeGeorge et al. (2012); Espenlaub et al. (2009); Gioielli et al.

(2008); Greco (2012); Houmes and Skantz (2010); Houqe et al. (2012); Lim et al. (2008); Liu et al. (2010); Oberholzer-Gee and Wulf (2012); and Sengupta and Shen (2007). Some use both (e.g., Aussenegg et al. 2008; Oberholzer-Gee and Wulf 2012).

Another difference in the test of EM arises from choosing between signed abnormal accruals or unsigned abnormal accruals. If the sign is considered, then the less negative the abnormal accruals, the more aggressive the EM policy. If the unsigned abnormal accruals are considered, then a larger absolute value of abnormal accruals provides stronger evidence for EM. Hribar and Nichols (2007) examine EM by considering the absolute value of discretionary accruals. They note that such an examination has two implications. The first is that the null hypothesis of no EM is not supposed to be rejected by examining the probability that abnormal accruals are different from zero by chance, because unmanaged absolute accruals are positive.[49] So, the use of absolute discretionary accruals introduces type I error. Second, the variability of the absolute variable is lower (because, intuitively, the values in support of the distribution density function spread over a smaller range). This again affects the interpretation of the results: firms that have greater underlying accrual volatility or for which the regression line poorly fits their accruals (i.e., low R^2) are subject to type I error.

The variety in research design is much larger: one of the criticisms of the accruals methodology is that identifying abnormal accruals as an EM measure is wrong because abnormal accruals may reflect changes induced by economic shocks and not by EM, or that EM arises from incentives that lie outside of the scope of the paper. So, when the research question tests the theory that factor/event A causes firms to engage in EM, the regression model should include controls for both alternative explanations and for changes in economic conditions. The most commonly used controls are leverage and size-related variables that control for the informational environment of the firm. For some interesting examples, consult the South Korean study of Cho and Lee (2012) on IPO and Venture Capital; Roychowdhury et al. (2012) on SEO; the International study of Leuz et al. (2003); and the Brazilian/Mexican study of Price et al. (2011) on governance.

7.2.2 The Jones procedure

The basic model is the Jones model. That is, since estimation of EM is a two-stage process, the current–accruals version is:

Observe that the Jones model lacks an intercept because each variable and the intercept are deflated by lagged assets. Hence, when one wishes to compare models by their econometric fit, R^2, an intercept would be added to the model (see, e.g., Aaker and Gjesdal 2010.)

We present here the bare essentials of the Jones model, but it has been refined and enriched as discussed in Section 7.3.2.

7.2.3 The theory behind the Jones model

There is so far no theoretical foundation for the Jones model. In a recent paper, Fogel-Yaari et al. (2014) outline the assumptions that justify the Jones model.

Consider a firm whose accruals are all short-term accruals. Normal short-run accruals (denoted NA) are generated from sales (denoted $Sales$) and expenses (denoted $Expenses$) transactions. Sales generate accounting receivable and expenses generate accounts payable. Assuming that for any given year short-run accruals constitute a fixed fraction of sales and all expenses (excluding depreciation and other non-operating expenses), the accruals can be represented by the following linear *decomposed model*:

$$NA_{i,t} = \beta_1\, Sales_{i,t} - \beta_2\, Sales_{i,t1} - \beta_3\, Expenses_{i,t} - \beta_4\, Expenses_{i,t-1} \qquad \text{(DM)}$$

Joshua Ronen and Varda Yaari

Table 12.5 The Jones Procedure

Stage 1	
Estimation of the coefficients of the regressors that drive current unmanaged accruals (CA)	Regression of unmanaged accruals on reciprocal of lagged assets and the change in sales, deflated by the beginning-of-the-period assets, $$CA_{it} / A_{it-1} = \alpha_i[1 / A_{it-1}] + \beta_{1i}[\Delta REV_{it} / A_{it-1}]$$ Where: CA_{ip} are current accruals obtained by adding depreciation expense and loss on sale of assets to earnings from continuing operations from the statement of cash flows of firm i in period p, ΔREV_{ip} is the change in sales, and A is total assets.*

Stage 2	
Find normal accruals given the new lagged assets and the deflated change in sales	Denote by hat the estimated coefficients of stage 1: $\hat{\alpha}_i$ and $\hat{\beta}_{1i}$, and estimated unmanaged current accruals, $C\hat{A}$, $$C\hat{A}_{ip} / A_{ip-1} = \hat{\alpha}_i[1 / A_{ip-1}] + \hat{\beta}_{1i}[\Delta REV_{ip} / A_{ip-1}]$$
Discretionary current accruals	Equal to actual current accruals minus normal current Accruals: $$EM_{ip1} = CA_{ip-} C\hat{A}_{ip-}$$

i stands for firm i, and t for period in the estimation period in a time-series analysis, and for industry/year in a cross-sectional sample when the research creates cohorts by industry and year; p denotes period in the estimation period in a time-series analysis, and for industry/year in the sample of firms suspected for EM in a cross-sectional design.
*The total accrual version:

$$TA_{ip} / A_{ip-1} = \hat{\alpha}_i[1/A_{ip-1}] + \hat{\beta}_{1i}[\Delta REV_{ip} / A_{ip-1}] + \hat{\beta}_{2i}[PPE_{ip} / A_{ip-1}]$$

Where: TA_{ip} and PPE are total accruals and property, plant, and equipment, respectively.

where i and t denote a firm and a period. In an empirical investigation, the coefficients are derived from either the history of the financial performance and accruals of a given firm in a time-series analysis, or from financial performance and accruals of other firms in the same industry and year within a cross-sectional research design.

By the matching principle, expenses are correlated with revenues. Denoting by $\pi_{i,t}$ the t-period expenses expressed as a fraction of the t-period sales of firm i, $Expenses_{i,t} = \pi_{i,t} Sales_{i,t}$. (DM) can be written in terms of sales and lagged sales in the following *unrestricted model:*

$$NA_{i,t} = \gamma_1 Sales_{i,t} - \gamma_2 Sales_{i,t-1} \tag{UM}$$

where $\gamma_1 = \beta_1 - \pi_{i,t} \beta_3$, and $\gamma_2 = \beta_2 - \pi_{t,t-1} - \beta_4$

In its current version, the Jones model relates current accruals to the change in sales (e.g., Teoh et al. 1998a, 1998b). That is, the Jones model is the following *restricted model:*

$$NA_{i,t} = \delta[Sales_{i,t} - Sales_{i,t-1}]. \tag{RM}$$

(RM) and (DM) are equivalent only if $\delta \equiv \beta_1 - \pi_{i,t} \beta_{3j} \equiv \beta_2 - \pi_{i,t-1}\beta_4$. This identity (1) requires three stationarity conditions to hold:

i   Sales in consecutive periods contribute the same proportion to accruals, $\beta_1 = \beta_2$.

ii   The expenses as a fraction of sales for firm i are stationary, $\pi_{i,t} = \pi_{i,t-1}$.

iii   Expenses in consecutive periods contribute the same proportion to accruals, $\beta_3 = \beta_4$.

These stationarity conditions are questionable (for example, credit policy is sensitive to volume, and sales in consecutive years are not likely to be identical). Hence, accounts receivable as a proportion of sales in period t are likely to be different from the proportion in period $t - 1$. The instability of the coefficients also arises from their sensitivity to changes in business conditions, such as changes in the supply of goods by new entrants to the industry, or exogenous shocks that change demand patterns, such as the timing of sales, the mix of customers, or sales growth, which affect the credit policy of both the firm and its suppliers.

7.3 The new methodologies

The discussion in the previous section inspired an alternative approach to measure EM, which we discuss in Section 7.3.1. We then provide a discussion of the most popular designs and a summary table for the recent developments in Section 7.3.2.

7.3.1 The alpha (conundrum) model

7.3.1.1 The conundrum

To ease the presentation and streamline the discussion, we depart from the paper. That is, the stationarity assumptions underlying the Jones model also determine the relationship between earnings (denoted *Earnings*) and accruals. Specifically, accruals should comprise the fixed portion of change in earnings, α. The *alpha model* is

$$NA_{i,t} \cong \alpha \Delta Earnings \left\| I \right\|_{i,t} \tag{AM}$$

If α were indeed constant, as postulated by the Jones model, the covariance profile of earnings, cash flows, and accruals conditional on lagged earnings, would differ from the observed profile. Specifically, if normal accruals are loosely a constant fraction α of earnings, the cash flows from operations (*CF*) component varies with earnings at a constant fraction $1 - \alpha$ of earnings. The finding that the covariance of each component of earnings with earnings is positive implies that both α and $1 - \alpha$ are positive. This implies that both components move in the same direction with a change in earnings. Therefore, the covariance of accruals and cash flows should also be positive. Prior research, however, documents a negative covariance between cash flows and accruals. We conclude then that the Jones model represents a conundrum.

7.3.1.2 The alpha model

Fogel et al. (2014) offer an alternative model. The accrual conundrum can be resolved if the assumption that α is a constant will be replaced with the assumption that the fraction of earnings constituting accruals has two components: a stationary component, α, and a stochastic zero-mean variable, η. That is, the fraction of accruals is $\alpha + \eta$, and the fraction of cash flows is $1 - \alpha - \eta$. Because η affects cash flows and accruals in opposite directions, it introduces a substitution effect between them. It is shown that α is the ratio of the sum of the variance of accruals and the covariance of cash flows, and accruals divided by the variance of earnings. Using the notation of NA for normal accruals, X for earnings, and F for cash flows, and considering the general case where η is correlated with the noise in earnings, this study calculates the variance (Var)/covariance (Cov) of earnings and its components. The algebra shows that the stationary component of accruals as a fraction of earnings, α, is

$$\alpha = [\text{Var}(NA) + \text{Cov}(NA, F)]/\text{Var}(X).$$

7.3.2 Recent developments

The discussion so far indicates that there is a plethora of EM methods. For example, Aussenegg et al. (2008) employ 15 EM measures that are categorized into five groups. Group 1 is based on discretionary total and current accruals estimated using the modified Jones model of Dechow et al. (1995), as described below; Group 2 treats the kink in the distribution of net income as a manifestation of EM (see Section 4.1.3), and considers the number of profit/loss firms in the neighborhood of small profits and small losses (see discussion above); Groups 3 and 5 focus on the relationships between accrual measures and cash flow from operations and changes in these variables, respectively; and Group 4 measures are based on smoothing by comparing the volatility of earnings to the volatility of cash flow from operations, both scaled by lagged total assets.

Despite the rich menu of EM methodologies, there is still room for improvement. An examination of recent contributions reveals that while some studies examine the efficiency of existing models in a special sample, the majority of them seek to improve the testing for EM. Broadly, the improvements are of three types: better modeling of normal accruals, better ways of measuring key variables, and improved econometric methods. It is notable, however, that even in 2013, the three most popular refinements of the Jones model were the modified Jones model, the performance-matching Jones model of Kothari et al. (2005), and the timely recognition of loss model of Ball and Shivakumar (2006). The modified Jones model considers the fact that reported revenues are composed of cash sales and credit sales that are reflected in accounts receivable. Because firms tend to manage earnings by inflating credit sales, the modified Jones model in a time-series design estimates normal accruals by using as a regressor the total change in reported revenues, and then applies the coefficient for normal accruals to the change in cash revenues (change in sales minus change in accounts receivable) in the test period, while in a cross-sectional design, the modified Jones model considers only change in a cash revenues regressor (i.e., in both stages). See the valuable discussion of Kothari et al. (1994) and Dechow et al. (2003). To sharpen the distinction between the Jones and the modified Jones models, observe that in the Jones model, the first regressor for estimating normal accrual and for testing for EM is the change in total sales.

The other two refinements add controls to the normal accruals model. The performance-matching Jones model adds either ROA or lagged ROA. Ball and Shivakumar (2006) refine the Jones model to consider the asymmetry in recognizing gains and losses. That is,

$$ACC_t = a_0 + a_1 \Delta REV_t + a_2 GPPE_t + a_2 VAR_t + a_3 DVAR_t + a_4 DVAR_t + VAR_t + v_t,$$

where ACC is accruals in year t; the first three regressors are those used in the Jones model – a deflated intercept, deflated change in revenues, and deflated gross property, plant, and equipment ($GPPE$); VAR_t stands for fiscal year gain or loss (VAR is run with five different proxies: cash flows from operations, change in cash flows from operations, industry-adjusted cash flows that compare cash flows to the industry's median variable, and, following Basu (1997), abnormal returns (see table on p. 216). $DVAR_t$ is a (0, 1) dummy variable that takes the value 1 if VAR_t implies a loss in year t. v_t is the customary error term in year t.

In Fogel et al., the authors offer the improvement of decomposing the change in sales regressor into sales and lagged sales. Another suggested improvement is adding both expenses and lagged expenses. It is shown that this decomposition can triple the power of the test.

The following table summarizes the recent contributions to methodology (with the exception for obvious reasons of studies that made contributions to the methodology that related EM to tax accounting, such as Tang and Firth 2011; Hanlon et al. 2011; Plesko 2007; and Seidman 2010).

Table 12.6 Recent developments in EM methodology 2

Study	The New Methodology	Comments
Aaker and Gjesdal (2010)	The innovation is that when inventory is a tool for EM, EM can be detected by decomposing inventory accruals into volume (nondiscretionary) and price (discretionary) components.	Need evidence to rule out that real EM does not drive the volume component, which is viewed as unmanaged accrual.
Baber, Kang, and Li (2010)	Discretionary accruals must reverse. Hence, the difference between reported and unmanaged earnings in period t equals $d_t^{new} - d_t^{reverse}$, where d^{new} and $d^{reverse}$ denote discretionary accruals initiated in period t, and past discretionary accruals that reverse in period t, respectively. This difference accumulates in net operating assets on the balance sheet. The accumulated past bias in net operating assets at the beginning of a quarter constrains present EM in the same direction when the reversal of prior discretionary current accruals occurs quickly.	The paper makes an interesting contribution to understanding the constraints on EM in the same direction as in prior periods that is caused by the reversal of prior discretionary accruals. The paper implies that empirical studies should control for the speed of the reversal. It is not possible, however, to know if adding lagged accruals as a control mitigates this omitted-variable issue.
Cardoso, Mendes, Poueri, Martinez, and Ferreira (2010)	This paper introduces a new variable (*DIF*) to replace discretionary accruals in the detection of EM, derived from data mining techniques.	*DIF* is the discrepancy in ending balances. An interesting approach.
Cheng, Liu, and Thomas (2012)	This paper compares the modified Jones model (MJ), MJ with operating cash flows (MJOCF), and MJ with return on assets (MJROA), with two estimation procedures: industry-specific (cross-sectional) and firm-specific (time-series) regressions. The performance criterion is the relation between current estimates of abnormal accruals and future price movements (see the mispricing phenomenon explained in Chapter 9 of the book). The best models are the firm-specific MJOCF and the industry-specific MJROA. When the recursive firm-specific procedure is used, MJOCF's performance diminishes, while there is no difference in the performance of MJROA.	The theory: the industry-specific MJOCF generates a measurement error because firms in the same industry have different operating cycles; including ROA reduces the measurement error.

(continued)

Table 12.6 (continued)

Study	The New Methodology	Comments
Cohen, Pandit, Wasley, and Zach (2011)	This study (i) provides systematic evidence on the time-series and cross-sectional properties of alternative measures of real EM by documenting the type I error rates of alternative measures. (ii) Since the measures are misspecified because they exhibit type I error rates far in excess of the nominal (1% or 5%) significance level of the test, this study proposes alternative performance-matching measures of real EM, wherein EM is detected as the difference in the measure between two firms, matched by industry and by the property that the return on assets (ROA) lies in the ±10% of the treatment firm.	The procedure is to form lowest and highest quartiles of subsamples from samples that are obtained by drawing 250 random samples of 100 Compustat firms. The performance measures are book-to-market, past sales growth, earnings-to-price, market value of equity, and operating cash flow. Since extreme performance generates extreme EM measures (because of the non-linear relationship between them), the evidence does not shed light on EM. It is better to consider non-extreme subsamples.
Collins, Pungaliya, and Vijh (2012)	This study shows that accrual tests of EM in quarterly earnings should control for both performance (ROA) and growth.	See McNichols (2000) and Dechow et al. (2003).
Dabo and Laux (2012)	This study builds a probability model for predicting the likelihood of restatements by analyzing ROA, accounts receivable turnover, net profit margin, and operating cash flow to net income measures. The findings are that accounts receivable turnover above the industry average and a downward trend in cash flow to net income are associated with a higher likelihood of a restatement.	See Badertscher (2011) and Ettredge, Scholz, Smith, and Sun (2010).
Dechow, Hutton, Kim, and Sloan (2012)	This study incorporates the reversal of discretionary accruals in the estimation of accrual EM.	Very thorough, but a highly complicated model. The paper also compares the performance of different models. See Gerakos (2012).
Di Narzo, Freo, and Mattei (2010)	This study proposes a new econometric approach to estimate the accrual model parameters. It clusters the firms into a finite number of groups that are automatically determined by an expectation-maximization algorithm.	An interesting approach to avoid the unreasonable homogeneity assumptions that justify the cross-sectional research design.

Reference	Description	Comment
Durtschi and Easton (2009); Burgstahler and Chuk (2012)	Durtschi and Easton claim that the kink is the distribution of earnings around zero is not an indication of EM, but rather the product of sample selection and scaling. The scaling by market capitalization drives the kink because the relation between earnings and prices differs according to the magnitude and sign of the earnings.	Burgstahler and Chuk (2012) provide a rebuttal.
Ettredge, Scholz, Smith, and Sun (2010)	This study documents that high balance sheet bloat, or unusually high levels of working capital, account balance predict pernicious EM that leads to restatements due to fraud.	See Badertscher (2011) and Dabo and Laux (2012).
Feroz, Kwon, Pastena, and Park (2000)	The paper uses artificial intelligence (Artificial Neural Network) to identify which red flags in SAS 53 anticipate fraudulent, pernicious EM. The authors provide evidence of a successful prediction rate of 81%.	A contribution to the independence of the audit industry. It performs well without further regulation.
Harris and Shi (2012a)	This paper proposes a new research design for investigating potential EM that relies only on conservative rank-based variables and utilizes indicator variables, in addition to a bootstrap.	This study resolves the difficulties in detecting EM around benchmarks when more than one strategy is employed.
Hribar and Nichols (2007)	The test of EM by absolute discretionary accruals might be biased. (1) There are economically small (large) correlations between the signed (absolute-unsigned) measures and size and operating volatility metrics. (2) The typical firm that has high absolute discretionary accruals tends to be smaller, with lower operating cash flows but better growth prospects and substantially higher volatility of cash flows and revenues, than the typical firm with low absolute discretionary accruals. (3) Omitting operating volatility in tests based on absolute discretionary accruals creates an omitted-variable problem and heteroskedasticity.	Important contribution that needs further examination.
Jones, Krishnan, and Melendrez (2010)	This study examines whether the following models predict fraudulent restatement: the Jones model, the modified Jones model, the modified Jones model with book-to-market ratio and cash flows as additional regressors, the modified Jones model with either current year or prior year ROA, and performance-matched discretionary accruals estimated from the modified Jones model (in addition to two measures of accrual quality and the Beneish unweighted and weighted probabilities of earnings manipulation). The only model that works is the hybrid of the Jones model with the Dechow and Dichev (2002) earnings quality work.	Small sample issues as well as problematic application of linear regression models to situations involving abnormal performance. Nor did this study control for cumulative EM.
Kama and Melumad (2012)	Firms camouflage EM to make it difficult to detect pernicious EM by manipulating cash flows, too, such as by factoring accounts receivable.	Important to understand the cost of pernicious EM. Points to possible connection between real and cosmetic EM.

(continued)

Table 12.6 (continued)

Study	The New Methodology	Comments
Kirk, Reppenhagen, and Tucker (2012)	This study replaces the benchmark of consensus analysts' forecasts in the MBT literature with two alternatives: (1) the percentage of individual analysts' forecasts met, and (2) whether a forecast of a key individual analyst is met. These benchmarks better explain the market rewards to MBT.	Provides insight into the game between firms and analysts. For example, firms meet every analyst in 47% of firm-quarters and miss every analyst in 13% of firm-quarters.
Lahr (2011)	This study proposes a test procedure based on bootstrap density estimation to test for EM around the kink in the distribution of earnings, earnings changes, and analysts' earnings forecast errors. Test results confirm earlier findings of discontinuities in the whole sample of earnings and earnings changes, but not in all subsamples.	This study improves upon previous studies that use a similar approach.
Larcker and Rusticus (2010)	This is a general methodology paper that offers a better choice of instrumental variables in the research design.	
Pae (2005)	This study examines whether the incorporation of cash flows from operations (CFO) both in the current period and the previous period, in addition to lagged accruals, improves the power of the Jones model, and it examines the association between abnormal accruals and returns. Cash flows from operations improve the Jones model while lagged accruals do not.	
Paulo and Martins (2009)	This study proposes a normal accruals model that encompasses both accruals and real EM. Specifically, total accruals of company i in period t are regressed on its net revenues, operational costs, and expenses in period t, excluding financial expenses and depreciation, exhaustion and amortization expenses; fixed assets at the end of period t; deferred assets at the end of period t; operating cash flow in period t; accounting income in period t; variation in net accounting profit from year $t - 2$ to year $t - 1$; a dummy variable to indicate whether a negative variation exists in the net accounting profit of company i from year $t - 2$ to year $t - 1$, equal to 1 for negative change and 0 otherwise; lagged total accruals; abnormal behavior of production costs, operational expenses, and operating cash flows in period t.	A commendable attempt to provide a comprehensive model with the caveat of endogeneity between accruals and income and cash flows measures. See also Kang and Sivaramakrishnan (1995) and Ye (2006).

Study	Description	Comment
Pungaliya, and Vijh (2009)	After finding that (1) ROA-matched discretionary accruals are misspecified for both high-growth and low-growth firms, and (2) the median sales growth rate equals 12.1% for cash acquirers and 38.5% for stock acquirers, this study proposes a new discretionary accrual measure that controls for both ROA and sales growth. The finding of EM disappears with the new measure.	See the above for discussion of growth measures.
Shan, Taylor, and Walter (2010)	This study argues that when the firm makes a non-EM economic decision that has a big impact on financing activity that affect assets and accruals, the current models would likely detect the finance-related accruals as abnormal accruals arising from EM.	The criticism that abnormal accruals may be driven by other factors beyond EM is not new. See, e.g., Kaplan (1985) and Healy (1996).
Shih (2011)	This study shows that performance-matched discretionary accruals for firms matched on ROA as proposed by Kothari et al. (2005) may increase type II error (the null hypothesis is no EM).	A good study that indicates our lack of understanding of the economics of EM, which will determine if matching by ROA is indeed a good methodology.
Stubben (2009)	This study proposes that discretionary revenues provide a better methodology for detecting EM than discretionary accruals. The normal accruals model focuses on the change in annual receivables as a linear function of (1) change in reported revenues of the first three quarters and (2) change in reported fourth-quarter revenues.	The paper identifies a measurement error in annual data, but it addresses it imperfectly and focuses on accounts receivable only.
Welc (2011a)	Since overstatement results in assets growth surpassing revenues growth, this study examines investment strategy based on assets turnover. The investment strategy is profitable.	This strategy is limited to cases when EM is aggressive.
White (2012)	This paper challenges the practice of using the change in working capital rather than the ending balance, because the change captures the impact of the previous period's EM. Substituting the ending balance for the change in balance improves estimation.	Good point that needs more evidence.

7.4 Real earnings management

A non-accrual EM strategy that has attracted attention in recent years is real EM, as attributed to Roychowdhury (2006) and Gunny (2005, 2010), with the adaptation of cost stickiness of Anderson et al. (2003).

Roychowdhury (2006) focuses on the following dimensions of real EM:

1   Cash flows from operations (CFO);
2   Advertising expenses (ADV), plus
3   Research and development expenses (R&D), plus
4   Selling, general, and administrative expenses (SG&A);
5   Production costs, defined as the sum of the cost of goods sold (COGS) and change in inventory (INV) during the period.

The abnormal cash flows from operations is de facto a summary statistic of all real EM activities that affect earnings from operations, because by definition earnings minus accruals equal cash flows. Consider the manipulation of sales. Firms increase earnings by accelerating the timing of sales; by offering large discounts; or by channel stuffing, which is the practice of offering excessive price discounts or more lenient credit terms in order to induce customers to hasten their orders so that they can be reported in the current fiscal period. EM then decreases the cash flows from operations. A decrease in discretionary expenses, such as advertising and R&D, boosts earnings, with an opposite effect on cash flows from operations.

Firms can also inflate earnings by reducing the discretionary components of their advertising, R&D, and SG&A expenses. When one observes that SG&A expenses include investment in intangible assets such as employee training costs, it is immediately apparent that advertising, R&D, and SG&A expenses are capital expenditure. US GAAP recognizes these expenses in full in the period they are incurred, even though they create assets and hence should be capitalized.

The challenge is how to estimate the normal, unmanaged activities of cash flows from operations, discretionary expenditures, and production costs. Dechow et al. (1998) show that under plausible assumptions, cash flows from operations are related to sales and the shock to sales (sales in period t minus sales in period $t - 1$) linearly, depending on the profit margin and on the operating cash cycle, respectively; production costs, through inventory changes, also depend on the prior year change in sales, while discretionary expenses depend on current sales only.

To estimate the model in a cross-sectional research design, Roychowdhury (2006) runs the following regression for every industry and year:

$$CFO_t / A_{t-1} = \alpha_0 + \alpha_1 \times (1 / A_{t-1}) + \beta_1 \times (S_t / A_{t-1}) + \beta_2 \times (\Delta S_t / A_{t-1}) + \varepsilon_t$$
$$PROD_t / A_{t-1} = \alpha_0 + \alpha_1 \times (1 / A_{t-1}) + \beta_1 \times (S_t / A_{t-1}) + \beta_2 \times (\Delta S_t / A_{t-1}) + \beta_3 \times (\Delta S_{t-1} / A_{t-1}) + \varepsilon_t$$
$$DISEXP_t / A_{t-1} = \alpha_0 + \alpha_1 \times (1 / A_{t-1}) + \beta \times (S_{t-1} / A_{t-1}) + \varepsilon_t$$

Where CFO is cash flows from operations, A_t = total assets at the end of period t, S_t = sales during period t, and $\Delta S_t = S_t - S_{t-1}$; $PROD$ is the sum of cost of goods sold (COGS) and change in inventory (INV); and $DISEXP$ is the sum of advertising expenses, R&D expenses, and SG&A expenses.

The regression includes an intercept and a scaled intercept for econometric expediency. The intercept ensures that the mean abnormal CFO for every industry-year is zero, and the scaled intercept, $\alpha \times (1/A_{t-1})$, avoids a spurious correlation between scaled CFO and scaled sales, due to variation in the scaling variable, total assets.

Gunny (2005) has some similarities and some differences with Roychowdhury (2006). Gunny focuses on four types of real EM:

1 R&D expense (R&D RM),
2 SG&A expense (SG&A RM),
3 Timing the sale of fixed assets to report gains (asset RM), and
4 Overproduction reflecting an intention to cut prices or extend more lenient credit terms to boost sales or overproduction to decrease COGS expense (production RM).

Gunny uses the following model to estimate the normal expenses and the timing of sales of fixed assets:

$$\frac{RD_t}{A_{t-1}} = \alpha_0 + \frac{a_1}{A_{t-1}} + \beta_1 MV_t + \beta_2 Q_t + \beta_3 \frac{INT_t}{A_{t-1}} + \beta_4 \frac{RD_{t-1}}{A_{t-1}} + \varepsilon_t^{R\&D}$$

$$\frac{SGA_t}{A_{t-1}} = \alpha_0 + \left(\frac{a}{A_{t-1}}\right) + \beta_1 MV_t + \frac{INT_t}{A_{t-1}} + \beta_2 Q_t + \beta_3 + \beta_3 \frac{INT_t}{A_{t-1}} + \beta_4 \left(\frac{\Delta S_t}{S_{t-1}}\right) + \beta_5 \left(\frac{\Delta S_t}{S_{t-1}}\right) DD + \varepsilon_t^{SG\&A}$$

$$\frac{GainA_t}{A_{t-1}} = \alpha_0 + \left(\frac{a}{A_{t-1}}\right) + \beta_1 MV_t + \beta_2 Q_t + \beta_3 + \beta_4 \left(\frac{ASales_t}{S_{t-1}}\right) + \beta_5 \frac{ISales_t}{S_{t-1}} + \varepsilon_t^{Assets}$$

$$\frac{PROD_t}{A_{t-1}} = \alpha_0 + \left(\frac{a}{A_{t-1}}\right) + \beta_1 MV_t + \beta_2 Q_t + \beta_3 \left(\frac{S_t}{S_{t-1}}\right) + \beta_4 \left(\frac{\Delta S_t}{S_{t-1}}\right) + \beta_5 \frac{\Delta S_{t-1}}{S_{t-1}} + \varepsilon_t^{Production}$$

Where:

RD	Research and development expense [Data46] [#46/#6]
A	Total assets [Data6], [#6]
MV	Log of market value of equity [Data199 × Data25]
Q	Tobin's Q: firm's market value divided by the replacement cost of its assets [((Data199 × Data25) + Data130 + Data9 + Data34)/Data6]
INT	Internal funds available for investment [Data18 + Data46 + Data14]
S (ΔS)	Sales (change in sales) [Data12]
DD	Indicator variable equal to 1 when sales revenue decreases between $t - 1$ and t, zero otherwise
GainA	Income from asset sales [Data213 × (-1)[50]]
ISales	Long-lived investment sales [Data109]
PROD	COGS plus change in inventory [Data41 + Data303]

The modeling of the R&D normal expense is based on previous research and is used consistently for estimating the other real EM strategies. The modeling of SG&A decomposes this item into the fixed component and the variable component that varies with change in sales. As Anderson et al. (2003) have shown, these costs are sticky in the sense that firms are reluctant to cut them down in parallel with a downward change in sales in the same proportion as the increase upon a sales increase. Consequently, when sales decrease, the sensitivity of SG&A to change in sales is lower, and the costs then exhibit stickiness. The variety in the ways researchers estimate normal gains from sales of assets and production costs also rely on findings of previous research.

We discuss these two papers because they pave the way to testing for real EM. Other researchers adopt different methods. For example, Albring et al. (2011) ignore cash flows from operations and examine abnormal revenues instead; they focus on cost of goods sold rather than on total production costs (defined as the sum of cost of goods sold and change in inventory). We draw attention to the fact that unlike the research that focuses on a single item of the income statement (see Ronen and Yaari 2008, Chapter 11), this kind of research employs a number of categories. To be precise, Roychowdhury (2006) uses six line items and Gunny (2005), four. The advantage of using more than one item is that firms are likely to engage in a portfolio of means to achieve their ends, but the sad fact is that we do not have a theory on their selection hierarchy.

8 Parting remarks

When we summarized the research on EM in our book, we noted that the field is not adequately addressing the economics of EM. At that time, what we knew was that firms that report aggressively may have to overpay taxes, and that pernicious EM is costly because it increases the cost of capital. For a recent study that shows that a high cost of capital may drive the firm to making inefficient decisions, such as leasing assets instead of purchasing them, see Beatty et al. (2010). We are happy to report that more attention has been given to this front recently; there are 50 papers in the references list, some of which offer new insights. For example, He and Tian (2012) find that MBE to meet analysts' forecasts is associated with reduced innovation. Since innovation is crucial to a firm's survival, EM is pernicious both in terms of the quality of information and the role of accounting in influencing resource allocation in the economy. Another example is Wu and Yan (2010), who examine litigation and find that while EM has no impact on the likelihood of a settlement, it impacts the settlement amount: the higher the EM, the higher the settlement amount. Further analysis on the association between EM and innovation is pursued in Fogel-Yaari's dissertation (2015).

Notes

1 The alert reader will notice that we depart from the definition of Healy and Wahlen (1999), which states:

> Earnings management occurs when managers use judgment in financial reporting and in structuring transactions to alter financial reports to either mislead some stakeholders about the underlying performance of the company or to influence contractual outcomes that depend on reported accounting numbers.

(p. 368)

2 Estimates are necessitated by the need to report the financial results for an arbitrarily defined standard period length (such as a year or a quarter) that does not coincide with the operating/investment cycle.

3 For ease of exposition, we refer interchangeably to "earnings management" and "accrual management" to mean management by any of the means employed to accomplish the goal of management.

4 See Ronen and Yaari (2002).

5 Note the implication of this conclusion for studies that use "accruals" or "discretionary accruals" as proxies of accounting quality. Specifically, high accruals or discretionary accruals need not imply bad accounting quality when they convey truthful expectations; in fact, they reflect good accounting quality.

6 An example that illustrates beneficial EM is the following episode from Pakistan's cement industry (Ali Shah et al. 2001). In the mid-1990s, Pakistan suffered an acute shortage of cement. The government induced the creation of seven new plants. The combined production of these and existing plants was expected to meet the demand for cement and leave a surplus for export. It takes three years for a cement plant to start production, and by the time the new plants came into production in the late

1990s, the country was in a recession and construction had virtually come to a halt. With tremendous overcapacity, cement prices started falling precariously. The companies got together and slashed production. Plants started operating at an average of around 22 percent production capacity to ensure that prices did not fall. The price-drop stopped, but it still did not help much.

Because cement is an industry where the largest slice of costs is fixed and time related, rather than operations related, as much as 72 percent of annual costs of a new cement plant may comprise only two items: depreciation and interest. Both of these are fixed and computed on the basis of time. As a result, low capacity utilization meant higher cost per ton of cement produced in any period, leading to huge losses. EM, in this case, was beneficial. The industry changed from straight-line to units-of-production depreciation. This drastically curtailed the periodic charge to the income statement and improved the profitability figures, which in turn enabled the companies to keep the investors reasonably comforted and the staff relaxed.

7   An example that illustrates this point is Bhojraj et al. (2009), who studied the market reaction to the Sarbanes-Oxley Act and Financial Accounting Standard 146 on new rules for recognizing restructuring charges. They conclude that uncertainty regarding managers' objectives in taking restructuring charges affects the markets' ability to distinguish between EM and economically driven charges.

8   We draw attention to the difference between the good practice of managing earnings and the bad, pernicious one because it is a factor that affects empirical results. For example, Bhojraj et al. (2009), who investigated restructuring charges, conclude that uncertainty regarding managers' objectives in taking restructuring charges affects the markets' ability to distinguish between EM and economically driven charges.

9   Ethnostatistics is the study of how statistics are produced and managed.

10 Bos et al. (2011) examine the relationship between discretionary accruals and equity ownership by executive directors as a percentage of total equity. They find a negative association when the ownership stakes are below 5 percent and above 10 percent of equity capital and a positive association for managerial equity stakes in the 5 percent to 10 percent range. A similar U-shape is documented by Teshima and Shuto. A positive relationship is also found for firms that perform so poorly that their EM practice constitutes fraud. This latter finding is not explained by poorly performing firms giving managers more options instead of the cash they do not have, because boards of directors are likely to reduce equity awards in poorly performing firms, especially when there is a concern of accounting fraud (Cazier and Folsom 2010). In comparison, Hutchinson and Leung (2007) find positive or negative associations for high or low holding, respectively.

11 For additional examples, consult Bozanic (2010), Naveen et al. (2008), and Schrand and Zechman (2012) on the optimism of overconfident managers that allowed their firms to bias the report aggressively.

12 In essence, insider trading is profitable because insiders possess superior private information. Yu and Bricker (2007) examine the information asymmetry in depth by focusing on the market's misestimation of the persistence of accruals and operating cash flows. This approach allows for the plausibility of managers selling (buying) following managerial negative (positive) EM when the misestimation of operating cash flows is in the opposite direction to that of accruals.

13 Performance is measured as the annual stock return less the same period value-weighted return on a portfolio of firms in the same size and book/market deciles.

14 Eames and Kim (2012) show that the market is better than analysts in avoiding an erroneous prediction of EM to avoid small losses. Davidson et al. (2011) find that EM of MBO firms does not appear to fool the stock market because there is no association between the announcement-period abnormal returns and EM. Kee (2010) finds that in firms with good governance that are likely to control pernicious EM, a higher level of EM is associated with positive portfolio returns (and in poorly governed firms, with negative portfolio returns). Linck et al. (2012) find that financially constrained firms with valuable projects use discretionary accruals to credibly signal positive prospects, enabling them to raise the necessary capital.

15 In an international study, Fernandes and Ferreira (2007) find that a move from the seventy-fifth to the twenty-fifth percentile of EM is associated with an increase in Tobin's Q of 16 percent.

16 The figure is copied from Ronen and Fogel-Yaari (2011). (Smoothing is reflected in the linear equation $m_1 = 80 + 0.25x_1$.)

17 Gunny et al. (2011) show that fourth quarter earnings exhibit higher volatility than other interim quarters, because EM to produce the desired year-end reported earnings – compensation and lending contracts are based on fiscal year earnings – lead to a concentration of EM in the fourth quarter (see also Givoly and Ronen 1981).

18 The following studies (including the originating countries of the samples) examine smoothing, explicitly demonstrating that smoothing is a worldwide phenomenon: *International:* Barth and Taylor 2009; Biurrun and Rudolf 2010a; Capkun et al. 2012; Fernandes and Ferreira 2007; Gopalan and Jayaraman 2012; Hamm et al. 2012; LaFond et al. 2007; Zhang 2010. *Asian countries:* Shen and Chih 2007. *Australia:* Rath and Sun 2007. *Brazil:* Martinez 2005; Martinez and Rivera 2010; Price et al. 2011; Torres et al. 2010. *China:* Cheng and Han 2012. *Europe:* Aussenegg et al. 2008; Capkun et al. 2011; Quagli and Ricciardi. 2010. *Germany:* Bornemann et al. 2012; Duecker 2009; Günther et al. 2009; Paananen and Lin 2007; Pronobis et al. 2008. *Italy:* Prencipe et al. 2008. *Japan:* Shuto and Iwasaki 2012. *Kenya:* Outa 2011. *Malaysia:* Mohamad et al. 2010. *Mexico:* Price et al. 2011. *Slovenia:* Garrod et al. 2007. *Spain:* Perez et al. 2011. *UK:* Kuang 2008. *US:* Allayannis and Simko 2009; Ambrose and Bian 2009; Barth and Taylor 2009; Bowen et al. 2008; De Jong et al. 2012; Dechow et al. 2010; Doupnik 2008; Eckles et al. 2011; Elshafie 2007; Fiechter and Meyer 2011; Grant et al. 2009; Gunny et al. 2011; Harris and Shi 2012b; Hsu and Kross 2010; Jung et al. 2013; Louis and Sun 2008; Marciukaityte and Park 2009; Raman and Shahrur 2008; Servaes and Tamayo 2009.

19 We classify MBE under section 4.1, and not under the regulations subsection, because the ultimate users of the information are investors.

20 Source: Fogel-Yaari et al. (2014), Figure 3.

21 The MBE phenomenon is documented worldwide: *Australia:* Bentwood and Lee 2012. *Brazil:* Martinez 2005. *China:* Lai 2009; Wang and Wu 2009. *Germany:* Bornemann et al. 2012. *Greece:* Caramanis and Lennox 2008. *Japan:* Shuto 2009. *Kenya:* Outa 2011. *New Zealand:* Bennet and Bradbury 2010; Coulton et al. 2012. *Poland:* Welc 2011b. *Singapore and Thailand:* Charoenwong and Jiraporn 2008. *UK:* García et al. 2009. See also the international study of Lingxiang et al. 2011.

22 Lewis (2008), who measures the relationships between EM and proceeds from issuance of IPO, finds that EM is beneficial given that the market correctly rewards EM when the IPO is conducted by more prestigious investment bankers as one observes a positive correlation between EM and proceeds (and no such association is observed in the case of poor-quality investment banks).

23 The setting: In China, most firms are owned by the state (state-owned enterprises [SOE]). Before the IPO, the SEO has three main components: profitable units, unprofitable units, and not-for-profit units such as schools and hospitals. The IPO firm tends to be spun as a profitable unit from an existing SEO, and the unprofitable and not-for-profit units remain part of the original firm (now the parent company of the IPO firm). The newly listed companies typically continue in the post-IPO period to share with their parent company certain personnel (such as the chairperson of the board of directors), brand names, and certain assets, remaining as a part of a business group with their parent. This study examined 185 Chinese Shanghai-listed firms that conducted an IPO during the period 1999–2001, with a footnote disclosure on related-party transactions with the parent, such as sales, expenses, assets sales, and leases. The researchers find that the parent company designs transactions to boost the IPO price.

24 Finally, we note that EM in the context of equity offering is not unique to the US scene. Consult studies of SEO in Bangladesh (Islam et al. 2002), IPO in Brazil (Gioielli and De Carvalho 2008), IPO in Canada (Cormier et al. 2012), IPO in China (Aharony et al. 2010; Chen et al. 2010), SEO in India (Sapar 2008), equity offerings in Japan (Bae et al. 2009), SEO in Malaysia (Ahmad-Zaluki et al. 2009), IPO in Malaysia (Ismail and Weetman 2008), IPO in South Korea (Jaemin and Lee 2012), and SEO in the UK (Espenlaub et al. 2009).

25 This circumstance provides an opportunity to re-examine the question regarding when the market recognizes EM. Servaes and Tamayo (2009) find that firms in the same industry treat a hostile takeover attempt of their peer as a threat and take measures to improve their standing with their stockholders, including engaging in less aggressive EM. This dynamic provides the market with a valuable clue about the level of EM. The importance of such clues is also evident in Baik et al. (2007), who find that at the time of an acquisition, investors price the bidder's EM.

26 The rating of short-term debt utilizes different letters.

27 Additional credit rating agencies are Dominion Bond Rating Services and A.M. Best.

28 Apparently, the cost of credit rating is high enough to deter young and unprofitable firms from paying for a rating. See Lam and Wei (2012), for example, who show that the negative association between external financing and future stock returns is driven by small, young, unprofitable, and, hence, underperforming firms that are also unrated despite their large borrowings.

29 In the book, we relegated credit rating to Chapter 5 because credit rating agencies are supposed to be the monitors. In this chapter, we cover them in this section.

30 Interestingly, looking good at the time of the first borrowing extends beyond the credit agency realm. Huyghebaert et al. (2007) detect a similar EM pattern for Belgian start-ups seeking bank loans for the first time.

31 As noted in our book, firms inflate earnings to avoid a violation of debt covenants. See Dyreng (2009) and the Italian study of family firms by Prencipe et al. (2008).

32 As in Section 4.1, we ask whether the market sees through EM. Most studies suggest that EM is misleading, especially when information asymmetry is high, as is the case when rating the first public debt (Demitras and Comaggia 2012). Two exceptions are Boubakri and Ghouma (2008) and Prevost et al. (2008).

33 Lin et al. (2012) find that those high-tech German firms that shifted from US GAAP to IFRS in 2005 use EM more, use less timely loss recognition, and produce less-value-relevant numbers compared to those remaining under US GAAP.

34 Ramanna and Roychowdhury (2010) find that firms that outsourced jobs internationally during the 2004 election (when this issue was subject to much public scrutiny), deflated earnings. In this study, it is the concern with impending regulation rather than regulation already in place that seemed to induce EM.

35 There are also studies on banks. See Beck and Narayanamoorthy (2012) (Staff Accounting Bulletin 102); Dunn et al. (2011) (SFAS 141R); the Chinese study of Hsieh and Wu (2012); the international study of Laghi et al. (2012) (SFAS 157 and IFRS 7); the European study of Quagli and Ricciardi (2010) (IAS 39); and Song (2008) (FAS 159).

36 For a valuable discussion on these opposing views from the perspective of the auditor who also supplies tax services, consult the Korean study of Choi et al. (2009).

37 For additional studies in this category, consult Brown and Krull (2008) on R&D tax credits; Diehl (2010); Durnev et al. (2011); and Herbohn et al. (2010).

38 Ramanna and Roychowdhury (2010).

39 When an industry has fewer than fifty firms, all firms are included in the calculations. The US Census uses four-digit SIC codes to identify industries in the surveys from 1992 and earlier and North America Industry Classification System (NAICS) codes in the later surveys.

40 For a study that has the potential to shed light on the impact of competition on EM, consult the Bangladesh study of 14-firm textile industry by Razzaque et al. (2006).

41 Most studies are concerned with total accruals. Two exceptions that restrict attention to specific accruals are Caylor (2010), who examines gross accounts receivable and deferred revenues, and Jackson and Liu (2010), who show that firms decrease the bad debt expense to MBE.

42 Most of this material is based on Ronen (2010).

43 The idea of financial statements insurance was first floated in an op-Ed article by Joshua Ronen in the *New York Times* (March 8, 2002). On July 10, 2002, a column by Susan Lee presented the idea in the *Wall Street Journal*.

44 Suppose, in addition, that investors cannot take short positions in the stock.

45 In the empirical literature, this strategy is beating the threshold by up to a penny.

46 The table above details studies that are concerned with MBT, but all study a one-shot game.

47 Except for the smoothing strategy depicted in Figures 12.1 and 12.2, the policies in Figure 12.2 are independent of the utility functions and the technology.

48 This explains why some studies use the balance sheet approach, such as Dechow et al. (2012); Lim et al. (2008); and Sengupta and Shen (2007). The statement of cash flows approach is more common, however.

49 To illustrate, suppose that abnormal accruals are distributed according to the normal distribution around a mean of zero. Since absolute abnormal accruals are positive, their expected mean exceeds zero because zero is the minimum value of discretionary accruals in support of the distribution of the absolute variable.

50 Data213 is coded negative for gains and positive for losses by Compustat.

51 MBE is a methodology.

52 MBE is a methodology.

53 Austria, Belgium, Denmark, France, Finland, Germany, Greece, Ireland, Italy, Luxemburg, Netherlands, Portugal, Spain, Sweden, and the UK, plus Switzerland and Norway.

54 MBE is a methodology.

55 MBE is a methodology.

56 This study challenges Dechow et al. 2010.

57 MBE is a methodology.

58 MBE is a methodology.

59 MBE is a methodology.

60 MBE is a methodology.
61 MBE is a methodology.
62 MBE is a methodology.
63 MBE is a methodology.
64 MBE is a methodology.
65 MBE is a methodology.
66 MBE is a methodology.
67 MBE is a methodology.
68 MBE is a methodology.
69 MBE is a methodology.
70 Book-tax difference is an EM methodology.
71 Deferred tax ratios are an EM methodology.
72 Aggressive tax reporting is a methodology.
73 EM methodology: absolute performance-adjusted discretionary accruals, special items, and deferred tax expense.
74 MBE is a methodology.
75 MBE is a methodology.
76 MBE is a methodology.
77 MBE is a methodology.
78 MBE is a methodology.
79 MBE is a methodology
80 Example that EM is beneficial to the firm but regarded as pernicious by the researcher.
81 MBE is a methodology.
82 MBE is a methodology.
83 Estimate of discretionary accruals by Kang and Sivaramakrishnan (1995).
84 Estimate of discretionary accruals by Kang and Sivaramakrishnan (1995).
85 EM is measured by abnormal working capital accruals.
86 Section 6 develops a model for EM.
87 Book-tax difference is an EM methodology.
88 Distinguishes between short-term accruals and long term accruals.
89 MBE is methodology.
90 An example that EM is beneficial, but the authors' point of view is that it is not.
91 Uses Leuz et al. 2003 methodology for EM.
92 MBE is a methodology.
93 Chapter 9 in our book models the accrual process and examines the impact of EM on the pattern of the series of reported earnings. We usually ask our students to do a simulation with Excel when we teach this material.
94 MBE is a methodology.
95 MBE is a methodology.
96 MBE is a methodology.
97 MBE is a methodology.
98 EM is measured as in Leuz et al. (2003).

Appendix notes

i   We do not mention the common filters in every accruals EM of deleting firms in the financial and/or utility sectors and deleting observations with missing financial data (Compustat) and stock prices data (CRSP).
ii   This study also establishes that alternative governance mechanisms can substitute for the SOX requirements concerning the audit committee.
iii   The online version of this paper is incomplete.

Bibliography

We employ the following notation: [M], methodology; [B, P] for beneficial and/or pernicious EM; [R, C] for real or cosmetic accrual-based EM when the study examines real earnings management; and [Economics] if the study contributes to the economics of EM. [Accounting] is a study that is appropriate to Chapter 2. [Specific transaction] when the research deals with specific income statement item and not some subset or total income statement items. [Classification] is EM achieved through moving items across categories in the income statement because income from continuing operations is more persistent than lower items. [Review] is a category of papers that are a survey papers. [Theory] are analytical papers to distinguish them from pure archival studies. For a random sample of firms, we also use [D], deflating, and [U], unsigned if the study uses absolute values of discretionary accruals, and [I] for Industry-specific. In the footnotes, we describe studies that select a sample of firms that meet or beat expectations for their methodology. Categories in square brackets follow the numbering in the book, as given in the summary table of Section 3.

[M] [I] [P] Aaker, Harald and Gjesdal, Frøystein. 2010. Do Models of Discretionary Accruals Detect Actual Earnings Management Via Inventory? A Comparison of General and Specific Models. ssrn.com/abstract=1402663.

[4.7] [D] [P] Adams, Brian John, Carow, Kenneth A., and Perry, Tod. 2009. Earnings Management and Initial Public Offerings: The Case of the Depository Industry. ssrn.com/abstract=1397390.

[4.7] [R,C] [P] Addoum, Jawad M., Van Binsbergen, Jules H., and Brandt, Michael W. 2010. Asset Allocation and Managerial Assumptions in Corporate Pension Plans. ssrn.com/abstract=1710902.

Advisory Committee on the Auditing Profession. 2008. Advisory Committee on the Auditing Profession Final Report, October 6. Washington.

[4.2] [China] [Specific transaction] [P] Aharony, Joseph, Wang, Jiwei, and Yuan, Hongqi. 2010. Tunneling as an Incentive for Earnings Management During the IPO Process in China. *Journal of Accounting and Public Policy*, Vol. 29, No. 1, January–February, pp. 1–26.

[4.2] [Malaysia] [P,B] [C] Ahmad-Zaluki, Nurwati A., Campbell, Kevin, and Goodacre, Alan. 2009. Earnings Management in Malaysian IPOs: The East Asian Crisis, Ownership Control and Post-IPO Performance. ssrn.com/abstract=963085.

[4.7] [I] [P] Alam, Pervaiz and Fu, Liang. 2008. Earnings Management and Mispricing of Allowance for Funds During Construction in the Electric Utility Industry. ssrn.com/abstract=1264842.

[4.5] [4.6] [B] Albring, Susan, Dhaliwal, Dan S., Khurana, Inder K., and Pereira, Raynolde. 2011. Short Term Incentive Effects of a Reduction in the NOL Carryback Period. *The Journal of the American Taxation Association*, Vol. 33, No. 2, Fall, pp. 67–87.

[4.4] [P,B] Ali, Ashiq and Zhang, Weining. 2008. Proximity to Broad Credit Rating Change and Earnings Management. ssrn.com/abstract=1163003.

[3.1] [P,B] Ali, Ashiq and Zhang, Weining. 2012. CEO Tenure and Earnings Management. ssrn.com/abstract=2060119.

[Review] [P,B] Ali Shah, Syed Zulfiqar, Butt, Safdar A., and Bin Tariq, Yasir. 2011. Use or Abuse of Creative Accounting Techniques. *International Journal of Trade, Economics and Finance*, Vol. 2, No. 6, pp. 531–536. ssrn.com/abstract=2009823.

[5.2] [5.3] [5.4] [Pakistan] [P] Ali Shah, Syed Zulfiqar, Butt, Safdar A., and Hassan, Aarshad. 2009. Corporate Governance and Earnings Management an Empirical Evidence from Pakistani Listed Companies. *European Journal of Scientific Research*, Vol. 26, No. 4, pp. 624–638. ssrn.com/abstract=1732510.

[Smoothing] [B] [5.1] Allayannis, George and Simko, Paul J. 2009. Earnings Smoothing, Analyst Following, and Firm Value. ssrn.com/abstract=1361228.

[5.4] [Spain] [P] Amat, Oriol. 2008. Earnings Management and Audit Adjustments: An Empirical Study of IBEX 35 Constituents. ssrn.com/abstract=1374232.

[4.1] [Smoothing] [P] [R,C] Ambrose, Brent W. and Bian, Xun. 2009. Stock Market Information and REIT Earnings Management. ssrn.com/abstract=1397313.

[Theory] [P] Amir, Eli, Einhorn, Eti, and Kama, Itay. 2008. The Role of Disaggregated Accounting Data in Detecting and Suppressing Earnings Management. ssrn.com/abstract=1126145.

[4.7] [Australia] [P] Anandarajan, Asokan, Hasan, Iftekhar, and McCarthy, Cornelia. 2007. Use of Loan Loss Provisions for Capital, Earnings Management and Signalling by Australian Banks. *Accounting and Finance*, Vol. 47, No. 3, pp. 357–379.

[4.5] [SFAS 146] [Classification] [P] Anantharaman, Divya, Darrough, Masako N., and Lee, Yong Gyu. 2012. Do Firms Shift within Non-Recurring Items to Manage Earnings under SFAS 146? ssrn.com/abstract=2065554.

Anderson, M., Banker, R.D., and Janakiraman, S.N. 2003. Are Selling, General, and Administrative Costs "sticky"? *Journal of Accounting Research,* Vol. 41, No. 1, pp. 47–63.

[4.1] [5.3] [P] Ang, James S., Jiang, Zhiqian, and Wu, Chaopeng. 2012. Good Apples, Bad Apples: Sorting Among Chinese Companies Traded in the US. ssrn.com/abstract=2024826.

[4.5 SOX] [P] Ang, Rachel. 2011. Sarbanes Oxley Effectiveness on the Earning Management. ssrn.com/ abstract=1791766.

[Accounting] [Classification] [P] Anilowski Cain, Carol, Kolev, Kalin S., and McVay, Sarah E. 2012. A Comprehensive Analysis of the Use of Special Items to Manage Earnings. AAA 2009 Financial Accounting and Reporting Section (FARS) Paper. ssrn.com/abstract=1267022.

[4.3] [Economic consequences] [P] Anilowski Cain, Carol, Macias, Antonio J., and Sanchez, Juan Manuel. 2012. Do Targets Benefit From Auctions? The Role of Private Information. ssrn.com/ abstract=1339963.

[4.5 SOX] [Methodology of rounding] [P] Aono, June Y. and Guan, Liming. 2008. The Impact of Sarbanes-Oxley Act on Cosmetic Earnings Management. *Research in Accounting Regulation,* Vol. 20, pp. 205–215.

[5.3] [Restatements] [P] Archambeault, Deborah S., Dezoort, F. Todd, and Hermanson, Dana R. 2008. Audit Committee Incentive Compensation and Accounting Restatements. *Contemporary Accounting Research,* Vol. 25, No. 4, Winter, pp. 965–992.

[4.3] [Malaysia] [P] Ardekani, Aref Mahdavi, Younesi, Nejat, and Hashemijoo, Mohammad. 2012. Acquisition, Earnings Management and Firm's Performance: Evidence from Malaysia. *Journal of Business Studies Quarterly,* Vol. 4, No. 1, pp. 91–110.

[3.1] [3.2] [4.2] [P,B] Armstrong, Chris S., Foster, George, and Taylor, Daniel J. 2008. Earnings Management around Initial Public Offerings: A Re-Examination. Rock Center for Corporate Governance Working Paper No. 23. ssrn.com/abstract=1147328.

[3.1] [Accruals, restatements, Accounting and Auditing Enforcement Releases (AAERs); also uses matching] [P] Armstrong, Chris S., Larcker, David F., Ormazabal, Gaizka, and Taylor, Daniel J. 2013. The Relation between Equity Incentives and Misreporting: The Role of Risk-Taking Incentives. *Journal of Financial Economics,* Vol. 109, August, pp. 327–350.

[5.4] [Spain] [P] Arnedo, Laura, Sánchez, Santiago, and Lizarraga, Fermín. 2008. Discretionary Accruals and Auditor Behaviour in Code-Law Contexts: An Application to Failing Spanish Firms. *European Accounting Review,* Vol. 17, No. 4, pp. 641–666.

Arrunada, Benito. 1997. Mandatory Rotation of Company Auditors: A Critical Examination. *International Review of Law and Economics,* Vol. 17, No. 1, pp. 31–61.

[Definition for Chapter 2] [P] Asien, Etumudon Ndidi. 2010. It Is Not Earnings Management if It Is Not Earnings Management: An Epistemological Dialectic in Accounting. ssrn.com/abstract=1570029.

[4.5 SFAS 87] [5.1 SFAS 87] [P] Asthana, Sharad. 2007. Expected Returns on Pension Assets, and Resource Allocation Decisions. *Journal of Pension Economics and Finance,* Vol. 7, No. 1, March, pp. 1–22.[51]

[5.1] [5.4] [P] Asthana, Sharad. 2012. Diversification by the Audit Office and Its Impact on Audit Quality. ssrn.com/abstract=2157681.[52]

[5.1] [United Kingdom] [P] [Classification, C] Athanasakou, Vasiliki E., Strong, Norman C., and Walker, Martin. 2008. Earnings Management or Forecast Guidance to Meet Analyst Expectations? *Accounting and Business Research,* Vol. 39, No. 1, pp. 3–35.

[5.1] [United Kingdom] [R,C] [P] Athanasakou, Vasiliki E., Strong, Norman C., and Walker, Martin. 2011. The Market Reward for Achieving Analyst Earnings Expectations: Does Managing Expectations or Earnings Matter? *Journal of Business Finance and Accounting,* Vol. 38, Nos. 1–2, pp. 58–94.

[4.5 IFRS] [17 countries in Europe][53] [Smoothing and other measures] [P] Aussenegg, Wolfgang, Inwinkl, Petra, and Schneider, Georg Thomas. 2008. Earnings Management and Local vs. International Accounting Standards of European Public Firms. ssrn.com/abstract=1310346.

[5.2] [P,B] Ayers, Benjamin C., Ramalingegowda, Santhosh, and Yeung, Eric. Hometown Advantage: The Effects of Monitoring Institution Location on Financial Reporting Discretion. 2011. *Journal of Accounting and Economics,* Vol. 52, No. 1 pp. 41–61.

[3.1] [P] Babenko, Ilona, Bennett, Benjamin, Bizjak, John M., and Coles, Jeffrey L. 2012. Clawback Provisions. ssrn.com/abstract=2023292.

[5.1] [M] [P] Baber, William R., Kang, Sok-Hyon, and Li, Ying. 2011. Modeling Discretionary Accrual Reversal and the Balance Sheet as an Earnings Management Constraint. *The Accounting Review,* Vol. 86, No. 4, pp. 1189–1212.[54]

[Theory] [P] Bachman, Kremena, and Hens, Thorsten. 2008. The Earnings Game with Behavioral Investors. ssrn.com/abstract=1101505.

[4.1] [C,R] [P] Badertscher, Brad. 2011. Overvaluation and the Choice of Alternative Earnings Management Mechanisms. *The Accounting Review,* Vol. 86, No. 5, September, pp. 1491–1518.

[5.1] [Restatements] [P,B] Badertscher, Brad, Collins, Daniel W., and Lys, Thomas Z. 2012. Discretionary Accounting Choices and the Predictive Ability of Accruals with Respect to Future Cash Flows. *Journal of Accounting and Economics,* Vol. 53, Nos 1–2, February-April, pp. 330–352.[55]

[4.6] [Restatements] [P] Badertscher, Brad, Phillips, John D., Pincus, Morton P.K., and Rego, Sonja O. 2009. Earnings Management Strategies and the Trade-Off between Tax Benefits and Detection Risk: To Conform or Not to Conform? *The Accounting Review,* Vol. 84, No. 1, January, pp. 63–97.

[4.2] [4.4] [Japan] [P] Bae, Gil S., Hamao, Yasushi, and Kang, Jun-Koo. 2009. Bank Monitoring Incentives and Borrower Earnings Management: Evidence from the Japanese Banking Crisis of 1993–2002. ssrn. com/abstract=1357834.

[Theory] [P] Bagnoli, Mark E. and Watts, Susan G. 2010. Oligopoly, Disclosure, and Earnings Management. *The Accounting Review,* Vol. 85, No. 4, pp. 1191–1214.

[4.3] [P] Baik, Bok, Kang, Jun-Koo, and Morton, Richard M. 2007. Earnings Management in Takeovers of Privately Held Targets. ssrn.com/abstract=1013639.

[4.7 deregulation] [I] [P] Baik, Yoon-Suk and Lee, Jaywon. 2007. Earnings Management Dynamics and Deregulation: Case of the US Airline Industry. KAIST Business School Working Paper No. 2007-008. ssrn.com/abstract=989690.

[3.1] [P] Baker, Terry A., Collins, Denton, and Reitenga, Austin L. 2008. Incentives and Opportunities to Manage Earnings around Option Grants. *Contemporary Accounting Research,* Vol. 26, No. 3, pp. 649–672.

[3.1] [4.1] [C] [P,B] Balachandran, Balasingham, Chalmers, Keryn, and Haman, Janto. 2008. On-Market Share Buybacks, Exercisable Share Options and Earnings Management. *Accounting and Finance,* Vol. 48, No. 1, March, pp. 25–49.

Ball, Ray and Shivakumar, Lakshmanan. 2006. The Role of Accruals in Asymmetrically Timely Gain and Loss Recognition. *Journal of Accounting Research,* Vol. 44, No. 2, May, pp. 207–242.

[4.7] [I] [England] [P] Ballantine, Joan Amanda, Forker, John, and Greenwood, Margaret J. 2007. Earnings Management in English NHS Hospital Trusts. *Financial Accountability and Management,* Vol. 23, No. 4, November, pp. 421–440.

[3.1] [4.5 SOX] [5.2] [5.3] [P] Banko, John, Frye, Melissa B., Wang, Weishen, and Whyte, Ann Marie. 2012. Earnings Management and Annual General Meetings: The Role of Managerial Entrenchment. *The Financial Review,* Vol. 48, No. 2, pp. 259–282.

[4.1] [Restatements] [P] Bardos, Katsiaryna Salavei. 2011. Quality of Financial Information and Liquidity. *Review of Financial Economics,* Vol. 20, No. 2, May, pp. 49–62.

[3.1] [4.1] [5.3] [Smoothing] [P,B] Barth, Mary E. and Taylor, Daniel J., 2009. In Defense of Fair Value: Weighing the Evidence on Earnings Management and Asset Securitizations. *Journal of Accounting and Economics,* Vol. 49, Nos 1–2, pp. 26–33.[56]

Barton, Jan and Simko, Paul J. 2002. The Balance Sheet as an Earnings Management Constraint. *The Accounting Review,* Vol. 77 (supplement), pp. 1–27.

[4.5 SFAS 144] [5.1] [Classification] [P] Barua, Abhijit, Lin, Steve W.J., and Sbaraglia, Andrew M. 2009. Earnings Management Using Discontinued Operations. ssrn.com/abstract=1245863.

Basu, Sudipta. 1997. The Conservatism Principle and Asymmetric Timeliness of Earnings. *Journal of Accounting and Economics,* Vol. 24, pp. 3–37.

[5.3] [Australia] [P] Baxter, Peter and Cotter, Julie. 2009. Audit Committees and Earnings Quality. *Accounting and Finance,* Vol. 49, No. 2, pp. 267–290.

[M] [P] Bayley, Luke and Taylor, Stephen L. 2007. Identifying Earnings Overstatements: A Practical Test. ssrn.com/abstract=995957.

[4.4] [P] Beatty, Anne, Liao, S., and Weber, J., 2010. Financial Reporting Quality, Private Information, Monitoring, and the Lease-versus-Buy Decision. *The Accounting Review,* Vol. 85, No. 4, July, pp. 1215–1238.

[4.7] [5.1] [Europe] [P] Beccalli, Elena, Bozzolan, Saverio, Menini, Andrea, and Molyneux, Philip. 2011. Earnings Management, Forecast Guidance and the Banking Crisis. ssrn.com/abstract=1953843.

[4.5 Staff Accounting Bulletin 102] [4.7] [P] Beck, Paul J. and Narayanamoorthy, Ganapathi S. 2012. Did the SEC Impact Banks' Loan Loss Reserve Policies and Their Informativeness? ssrn.com/abstract=1904441.

[5.4] [Canada] [P] Bédard, Jean and Courteau, Lucie. 2010. Value and Costs of Auditor's Assurance: Evidence from the Review of Quarterly Financial Statements. ssrn.com/abstract=1701038.

[4.3] [P] Ben-David, Itzhak and Roulstone, Darren T. 2008. Why Do Small Stock Acquirers Underperform in the Long-Term? AFA 2009 San Francisco Meetings Paper. ssrn.com/abstract=1108418.

[Culture] [3.5] [Canada, France] [P] Ben Othman, Hakim, Zeghal, Daniel, and El Younsi, Bechir. 2005. A Comparative Study of Earnings Management Practice between Canada and France. ssrn.com/abstract=990264.

[4.1] [New Zealand] [R] [P] Bennett, Bruce K. and Bradbury, Michael E. 2010. An Analysis of the Reasons for the Asymmetries Surrounding Earnings Benchmarks. *Accounting and Finance,* Vol. 50, No. 3, September, pp. 529–554. ssrn.com/abstract=1661368.

[4.1] [4.5] [IFRS] [Australia] [P] Bentwood, Sophie and Lee, Philip J. 2012. Benchmark Management during Australia's Transition to International Accounting Standards. *Abacus,* Vol. 48, No. 1, pp. 59–85.[57]

[5.1] [5.2] [Europe] [P] Beuselinck, Christof, Deloof, Marc, and Vanstraelen, Ann. 2010. Earnings Management Contagion in Multinational Corporations. ssrn.com/abstract=1599678.

[Theory] [P] Beyer, Anne. 2008. Financial Analysts' Forecast Revisions and Managers' Reporting Behavior. *Journal of Accounting and Economics,* Vol. 46, Nos 2–3, pp. 334–348.

[Theory] [P] Beyer, Anne. 2009. Capital Market Prices, Management Forecasts, and Earnings Management. *The Accounting Review,* Vol. 84, No. 6, November, pp. 1713–1747.

[Theory] [P] Beyer, Anne, Guttman, Ilan, and Marinovic, Ivan. 2012. Optimal Contracts with Performance Manipulation. ssrn.com/abstract=2040986.

[5.2] [Review] [P] Bhaumik, Sumon Kumar and Gregoriou, Andros. 2010. "Family" Ownership, Tunneling and Earnings Management: A Review of the Literature. *Journal of Economic Surveys,* Vol. 24, No. 4, September, pp. 705–730.

[4.1] [4.5] [FAS 146 and SOX] [P] Bhojraj, Sanjeev, Sengupta, Partha, and Zhang, Suning. 2009. Restructuring Charges, Regulatory Changes and the Accruals Anomaly. Johnson School Research Paper Series No. 33-09. ssrn.com/abstract=1413210.

[5.1] [P] Billings, Bruce K. and Morton, Richard M. 2008. Managerial Discretion and Bias in Annual Forecast Errors. ssrn.com/abstract=1265813.

[5.4] [Italy] [D] [B] Bisogno, Marco. 2012. Audit Quality of Italian Industrial Non-Listed Firms: An Empirical Analysis. *International Journal of Business Research and Development,* Vol. 1, No. 1, pp. 32–47. ssrn.com/abstract=2157448.

[4.1] [4.7] [International] [Smoothing] [P] Biurrun, Valeria and Rudolf, Markus. 2010a. The Costs of Bank Earnings Management. ssrn.com/abstract=1569496.

[4.7] [International] [P] Biurrun, Valeria and Rudolf, Markus. 2010b. Mitigating Bank Earnings Management – The Role of Regulation and Supervision. ssrn.com/abstract=1600703.

[3.1] [4.1] [5.4] [P] Black, Dirk E., Black, Ervin L., Christensen, Theodore E., and Waegelein, James F. 2011. The Effects of Executive Compensation Contracts and Auditor Effort on Pro Forma Reporting Decisions. ssrn.com/abstract=1312562.

[4.6] [International] [P] Blaylock, Bradley S., Gaertner, Fabio B., and Shevlin, Terry J. 2012. The Association between Book-Tax Conformity and Earnings Management. ssrn.com/abstract=1983107.

[4.1] [4.6] [Economics] [P] Blaylock, Bradley S., Shevlin, Terry J., and Wilson, Ryan J. 2010. Tax Avoidance, Large Positive Book-Tax Differences and Earnings Persistence. ssrn.com/abstract=1524298.

[Economics] [P] Blouin, Jennifer L., Krull, Linda K., and Robinson, Leslie A. 2012. Is US Multinational Dividend Repatriation Policy Influenced by Reporting Incentives? *The Accounting Review,* Vol. 87, No. 5, September, pp. 1463–1491.

[4.5 enforcement investigations] [Germany] [P] Böcking, Hans-Joachim, Gros, Marius F., Wallek, Christoph, and Worret, Daniel. 2012. Earnings Management and Enforcement of Accounting Standards – Evidence from Germany. ssrn.com/abstract=1755122.

[Theory] [P] Bolton, Patrick, Scheinkman, Jose, and Xiong, Wei. 2007. Pay for Short-Term Performance: Executive Compensation in Speculative Markets. NBER Paper 12107. http://www.nber.org/papers/w12107.pdf.

[5.2] [Spain] [P] Bona-Sánchez, Carolina, Pérez-Alemán, Jerónimo, and Santana-Martín, Domingo J. 2011. Defense Measures and Earnings Management in an Owner Dominant Context. *Journal of Business Finance and Accounting,* Vol. 38, Nos 7–8, pp. 765–793.

[5.4] [P] Boone, Jeff P., Khurana, Inder K., and Raman, K.K. 2011. Litigation Risk and Abnormal Accruals. *Auditing: A Journal of Practice and Theory,* Vol. 30, No. 2, May, pp. 231–256.

[5.1] [5.4] [P] Boone, Jeff P., Khurana, Inder K., and Raman, K.K. 2012. Audit Market Concentration and Auditor Tolerance for Earnings Management. *Contemporary Accounting Research,* Vol. 29, No. 4, Winter, pp. 1171–1203.[58]

[4.1] [4.7] [Germany] [Smoothing] [P] Bornemann, Sven, Kick, Thomas K., Memmel, Christoph, and Pfingsten, Andreas. 2012. Are Banks Using Hidden Reserves to Beat Earnings Benchmarks? Evidence from Germany. *Journal of Banking and Finance,* Vol. 36, No. 8. ssrn.com/abstract=2085276.

[3.1] [UK] [P] Bos, Sebastian, Pendleton, Andrew, and Toms, Steve. 2011. Earnings Management in the UK: The Nonlinear Relationship between Managerial Share Ownership and Discretionary Accruals. ssrn.com/abstract=1747919.

[4.3] [UK] [P] Botsari, Antonia and Meeks, G. 2008. Do Acquirers Manage Earnings Prior to a Share for Share Bid? *Journal of Business Finance and Accounting,* Vol. 35, Nos 5–6, June/July, pp. 633–670.

[4.4] [4.5 SOX] [P] Boubakri, Narjess and Ghouma, Hatem. 2008. Managerial Opportunism, Cost of Debt Financing and Regulation Changes: Evidence from the Sarbanes-Oxley Act Adoption. ssrn. com/abstract=1127351.

[3.1] [4.2] [5.3] [Canada] [P] Boubakri, Narjess, Ghalleb, Nabil, and Boyer, M. Martin. 2008. Managerial Opportunism in Accounting Choice: Evidence from Directors' and Officers' Liability Insurance Purchases. ssrn.com/abstract=1109254.

[5.3] [P] Boumosleh, Anwar S. 2009. Director Compensation and the Reliability of Accounting Information. *Financial Review,* Vol. 44, No. 4, November, pp. 525–539.

[3.1] [5.3] [P] Boumosleh, Anwar S., Cline, Brandon N., and Yore, Adam S. 2012. Should the Outsiders Be Left Out? Director Stock Options, Expectations and Earnings Management. ssrn.com/abstract=1928166.

[4.8] [5.1] [P] Bova, Francesco. 2013. Labor Unions and Management's Incentive to Signal a Negative Outlook. *Contemporary Accounting Research,* Vol. 30, No. 1, Spring, pp. 14–41.

[5.5] [Economics] [SOX] [P] Bowen, Robert M., Call, Andrew C., and Rajgopal, Shivaram. 2010. Whistle-Blowing: Target Firm Characteristics and Economic Consequences. *The Accounting Review,* Vol. 85, No. 4, pp. 1239–1271.

[3.1] [5.3] [5.4] [4.1] [Smoothing] [P,B] Bowen, Robert M., Rajgopal, Shivaram, and Venkatachalam, Mohan. 2008. Accounting Discretion, Corporate Governance and Firm Performance. *Contemporary Accounting Research,* Vol. 25, No. 2, Summer, pp. 351–405.

[3.1] [5.3] [Canada] [P] Boyer, M. Martin and Amandine, Hanon. 2009. Protecting Directors and Officers from Liability Arising from Aggressive Earnings Management. CIRANO – Scientific Publications 2009s-35. ssrn.com/abstract=1504208.

[3.1] [Economics] [P] Bozanic, Zahn. 2010. Managerial Motivation and Timing of Open Market Share Repurchases. *Review of Quantitative Finance and Accounting,* Vol. 34, No. 4, pp. 517–531. ssrn.com/abstract=1979781.

[4.1] [P] Bradshaw, Mark Thomas, Hutton, Amy P., Marcus, Alan J., and Tehranian, Hassan. 2010. Opacity, Crash Risk, and the Option Smirk Curve. ssrn.com/abstract=1640733.

[4.7] [5.4] [P] Bratten, Brian, Causholli, Monika, and Myers, Linda A. 2012. Fair Value Accounting, Auditor Specialization, and Earnings Management: Evidence from the Banking Industry. ssrn.com/abstract=2151635.

[4.1] [5.1] [Classification] [P] Bratten, Brian, Payne, Jeff L., and Thomas, Wayne B. 2012. Earning Management: Do Firms Play "Follow the Leader"? ssrn.com/abstract=2120859.

[4.6] [R] [P] Brown, Jennifer L. and Krull, Linda K. 2008. Stock Options, R&D, and the R&D Tax Credit. *The Accounting Review,* Vol. 83, No. 3, pp. 705–734.

[5.1] [P] Brown, Lawrence D. and Pinello, Arianna S. 2007. To What Extent Does the Financial Reporting Process Curb Earnings Surprise Games? *Journal of Accounting Research,* Vol. 45, No. 5, December, pp. 947–981.

[5.3] [5.4] [P] Bruynseels, Liesbeth and Cardinaels, Eddy. 2012. The Audit Committee: Management Watchdog or Personal Friend of the CEO? ssrn.com/abstract=2014613.

[4.1] [Methodology] [P] Burgstahler, David C. and Chuk, Elizabeth. 2012. What Have We Learned About Earnings Management? Correcting Disinformation about Discontinuities. ssrn.com/abstract=1866008.

[4.5 regulators] [I] [P] Byard, Donal A., Hossain, Mahmud, and Mitra, Santanu. 2007. US Oil Companies' Earnings Management in Response to Hurricanes Katrina and Rita. *Journal of Accounting and Public Policy,* Vol. 26, No. 6, November–December, pp. 733–748.

[5.4] [New Zealand] [P] Cahan, Steven F., Emanuel, David M., Hay, David, and Wong, Norman. 2008. Non-Audit Fees, Long-Term Auditor-Client Relationships and Earnings Management. *Accounting and Finance,* Vol. 48, No. 2, pp. 181–207.

[M] [International] [P] Cai, Lei. 2009. A Multivariate Study on Earnings Management. ssrn.com/abstract=1473608.

[4.5 IFRS] [International sample from 32 countries] [P] Cai, Lei, Rahman, Asheq Razaur, and Courtenay, Stephen M. 2008. The Effect of IFRS and Its Enforcement on Earnings Management: An International Comparison. ssrn.com/abstract=1473571.

[5.1] [R] [P] Call, Andrew C., Chen, Shuping, Miao, Bin, and Tong, Yen H. 2011. Short-Term Earnings Guidance and Earnings Management. ssrn.com/abstract=1879254.

[4.1] [5.2] [Eleven European countries] [P] Callao, Susana and Jarne, José Ignacio. 2008. Country Factors and Value Relevance of Discretionary Accruals in the European Union. ssrn.com/abstract=1154993.

[3.5] [Culture, religion] [International] [P] Callen, Jeffrey L., Morel, Mindy, and Richardson, Grant A. 2010. Do Culture and Religion Mitigate Earnings Management? Evidence from a Cross-Country Analysis. *International Journal of Disclosure and Governance,* Vol. 8, No. 2, pp. 103–121.

[Theory] [P] Camara, Antonio and Henderson, Vicky. 2009. Performance Based Compensation and Direct Earnings Management. ssrn.com/abstract=763325.

[3.1] [4.1] [4.5 IFRS] [Smoothing] [Nine European countries] [P] Capkun, Vedran, Cazavan, Anne, Jeanjean, Thomas, and Weiss, Lawrence A. 2011. Setting the Bar: Earnings Management during a Change in Accounting Standards. ssrn.com/abstract=1870007.[59]

[4.5 IFRS] [Smoothing] [International] [P] Capkun, Vedran, Collins, Daniel W., and Jeanjean, Thomas. 2012. Does Adoption of IAS/IFRS Deter Earnings Management? ssrn.com/abstract=1850228.

[4.1] [5.4] [Greece] [P] Caramanis, Costas and Lennox, Clive S. 2008. Audit Effort and Earnings Management. *Journal of Accounting and Economics,* Vol. 45, No. 1, March, pp. 117–138.

[4.5 SOX] [5.2] [5.3] [R,C] [P] Carcello, Joseph V., Hollingsworth, Carl W., and Klein, April. 2006. Audit Committee Financial Expertise, Competing Corporate Governance Mechanisms, and Earnings Management. NYU Working Paper No. APRIL KLEIN-6. ssrn.com/abstract=1280676.

[4.7] [I] [Brazil] [M] [P] Cardoso, Ricardo Lopes, Mendes, Alexandre, Mário, Poueri Do Carmo, Martinez, Antonio Lopo, and Ferreira, Felipe Ramos. 2010. Accounting Information Inconsistencies and Their Effects on Insolvency Prediction Models. ssrn.com/abstract=1567754.

[4.4] [4.5 SOX] [US and Canada] [Economics] [P] Carter, Kelly. 2011. Capital Structure Behavior of Domestic and Cross-Listed Firms: Evidence from the Sarbanes-Oxley Act of 2002. ssrn.com/abstract=1664204.

[Theory] [P] Caskey, Judson. 2012. The Pricing Effects of Securities Class Action Lawsuits and Litigation Insurance. ssrn.com/abstract=1660162.

[4.1] [5.4] [P] Cassell, Cory A., Myers, Linda A., Seidel, Timothy A., and Zhou, Jian. 2012. The Effect of Lame Duck Auditors on Management Discretion: An Empirical Analysis. ssrn.com/abstract=1957323.[60]

[4.1] [4.5 SOX] [5.1] [Specific accruals] [P] Caylor, Marcus L. 2010. Strategic Revenue Recognition to Achieve Earnings Benchmarks. *Journal of Accounting and Public Policy,* Vol. 29, No. 1, pp. 82–95.

[3.1] [P] Cazier, Richard A. and Folsom, David. 2010. Incentives to Misreport Earnings and Adjustments to CEO Equity Pay. ssrn.com/abstract=1532255.

[4.5 FIN 48] [4.6] [5.1] [P] Cazier, Richard A., Rego, Sonja O., Tian, Xiaoli (Shaolee), and Wilson, Ryan J. 2011. Did FIN 48 Limit the Use of Tax Reserves as a Tool for Earnings Management? ssrn.com/abstract=1656012.[61]

[4.2] [Specific accruals] [P] Cecchini, Mark, Jackson, Scott B., and Liu, Xiaotao Kelvin. 2012. Do Initial Public Offering Firms Manage Accruals? Evidence from Individual Accounts. *Review of Accounting Studies,* Vol. 17, No. 1, March, pp. 22–40. ssrn.com/abstract=1873956.

[4.5 SOX] [Accruals persistence] [P] Chambers, Dennis J. and Payne, Jeff L. 2011. Audit Quality and Accrual Persistence: Evidence from the Pre- and Post-Sarbanes-Oxley Periods. *Managerial Auditing Journal,* Vol. 26, No. 5, pp. 437–456.

[4.5 SOX] [P] Chan, Kam C., Farrell, Barbara R., and Lee, Picheng. 2008. Earnings Management of Firms Reporting Material Internal Control Weaknesses under Section 404 of the Sarbanes-Oxley Act. *Auditing: A Journal of Practice and Theory,* Vol. 27, No. 2, November, pp. 161–179.

[4.2] [P] Chang, Shao-Chi, Chung, Tsai-yen, and Lin, Wen-Chun. 2010. Underwriter Reputation, Earnings Management and the Long-Run Performance of Initial Public Offerings. *Accounting and Finance,* Vol. 50, No. 1, March, pp. 53–78.

[4.9] [5.1] [Economics] [R] [P] Chapman, Craig J. 2011. The Effects of Real Earnings Management on the Firm, Its Competitors and Subsequent Reporting Periods. ssrn.com/abstract=1747151.[62]

[4.1] [Singapore and Thailand] [P] Charoenwong, Charlie and Jiraporn, Pornsit. 2008. Earnings Management to Exceed Thresholds: Evidence from Singapore and Thailand. ssrn.com/abstract=1104523.

[4.2] [Economics] [P] Chemmanur, Thomas J., He, Shan, and Nandy, Debarshi K. 2010. The Going-Public Decision and the Product Market. *Review of Financial Studies,* Vol. 23, No. 5, pp. 1855–1908.

[4.2] [China] [P] Chen, Chao, Shi, Haina, and Xu, Haoping. 2010. Earnings Management, Underwriter Reputation, and Marketization: Evidence from IPO Market in China. ssrn.com/abstract=1540283.

[3.3] [4.5 regulation] [China] [D] [P] Chen, Charles J.P., Du, Jun and Xijia, Su. 2011. A Game of Accounting Numbers in Asset Pricing: Evidence from the Privatization of State-Owned Enterprises. ssrn.com/abstract=1917302.

[5.2] [5.4] [P] Chen, Hanwen, Chen, Jeff Zeyun, Lobo, Gerald J., and Wang, Yanyan. 2010. Effects of Audit Quality on Earnings Management and Cost of Equity Capital: Evidence from China. *Contemporary Accounting Research,* Vol. 28, No. 3, September, pp. 892–925.

[5.1] [R,C] [B] Chen, Jeff Zeyun, Rees, Lynn L., and Sivaramakrishnan, Shiva. 2010. On the Use of Accounting vs. Real Earnings Management to Meet Earnings Expectations – A Market Analysis. ssrn.com/abstract=1070122.

[4.2] [5.2] [5.3] [Taiwan] [P] Chen, Jengfang, Liao, Woody M., and Lu, Chiachi. 2012. The Effects of Public Venture Capital Investments on Corporate Governance: Evidence from IPO Firms in Emerging Markets. *Abacus,* Vol. 48, No. 1, pp. 86–103.

[5.4] [Ethics] [China] [P] Chen, Jiandong, Cumming, Douglas J., Hou, Wenxuan, and Lee, Edward. 2011. Executive Integrity, Audit Opinion, and Fraud in Chinese Listed Firms. ssrn.com/abstract=183944.

[4.2] [P] Chen, Jie, Gu, Zhaoyang, and Tang, Yi. 2008. Causes or Consequences? Earnings Management around Seasoned Equity Offerings. AFA 2009 San Francisco Meetings Paper. ssrn.com/abstract=1108063.

[5.3] [D] [P] Chen, Kung H. 2008. The Influence of Takeover Protection on Earnings Management. *Journal of Business Finance and Accounting,* Vol. 35, Nos 3–4, April/May, pp. 347–375.

[4.6] [P] Chen, Linda H., Dhaliwal, Dan S., and Trombley, Mark A. 2012. Consistency of Book-Tax Differences and the Information Content of Earnings. *Journal of the American Taxation Association,* Vol. 33, No. 2, pp. 93–116.

[Theory] Chen, Qi, Hemmer, Thomas, and Zhang, Yun. 2007. On the Relation between Conservatism in Accounting Standards and Incentives for Earnings Management. *Journal of Accounting Research,* Vol. 45, No. 3, June, pp. 541–565.

[4.1] [China] [P] Chen, Shimin, Wang, Yuetang, and Zhao, Ziye. 2007. Evidence of Asset Impairment Reversals from China: Economic Reality or Earnings Management? ssrn.com/abstract=998234.

[M] [P] Cheng, C.S. Agnes, Liu, Cathy Zishang, and Thomas, Wayne B. 2012. Abnormal Accrual Estimates and Evidence of Mispricing. *Journal of Business Finance and Accounting,* Vol. 39, Nos 1–2, pp. 1–34. ssrn.com/abstract=2015150.

[4.1] [China] [Economics] [R,C] [Classification] [P] Cheng, Peng, Aerts, Walter, and Jorissen, Ann. 2010. Earnings Management, Asset Restructuring, and the Threat of Exchange Delisting in an Earnings-Based Regulatory Regime. *Corporate Governance: An International Review,* Vol. 18, No. 5, September, pp. 438–456.

[5.2] [5.3] [Organizational design] [R] [P] Cheng, Qiang, Lee, Jimmy, and Shevlin, Terry J. 2012. Internal Governance and Real Earnings Management. ssrn.com/abstract=2162277.

[3.1] [4.7] [P] Cheng, Qiang, Warfield, Terry D., and Ye, Minlei. 2009. Equity Incentives and Earnings Management: Evidence from the Banking Industry. CAAA Annual Conference 2009 Paper. ssrn.com/abstract=1326558.

[4.1] [Smoothing] [China] [P] Cheng, Yuan and Han, Xuehui. 2012. Nasty or Naughty: Predictability of Cash Flow and Earnings Management. ssrn.com/abstract=2027738.

[4.1] [P] [Dynamics] Chi, Jianxin Daniel and Gupta, Manu. 2009. Overvaluation and Earnings Management. *Journal of Banking and Finance,* Vol. 33, No. 9, September, pp. 1652–1663.

[4.1] [4.2] [5.1] [5.4] [R] [P] Chi, Wuchun, Lisic, Ling Lei, and Pevzner, Mikhail. 2011. Is Enhanced Audit Quality Associated with Greater Real Earnings Management? *Accounting Horizons,* Vol. 25, No. 2, pp. 315–335.[63]

[5.3] [Restatements] [P] Chiu, Peng-Chia, Teoh, Siew Hong, and Tian, Feng. 2010. Board Interlocks and Earnings Management Contagion. ssrn.com/abstract=1723714.

[4.2] [5.2] [5.4] [South Korea] [P] Cho, Jaemin and Lee, Jaeho. 2012. Initial Public Offerings, Earnings Management and Venture Capital: Evidence in Bull and Bear Market Conditions. ssrn.com/abstract=2065670.

[4.7] [I] [D] [P] Cho, Seong-Yeon Y. and Sachs, Kevin D. 2008. Earnings Management and Deregulation: The Case of Motor Carriers. ssrn.com/abstract=1081334.

[5.4] [P] Choi, Jong-Hag, Kim, Jeong-Bon, and Zang, Yoonseok. 2010. Do Abnormally High Audit Fees Impair Audit Quality? *Auditing: A Journal of Practice and Theory,* Vol. 29, No. 2, November, pp. 115–140.

[3.4] [5.2] [5.3] [5.4] [Korea] [R,C] [D] [P] Choi, Jong-Seo, Kwak, Young-Min, and Choe, Chongwoo. 2012. Earnings Management Surrounding CEO Turnover: Evidence from Korea. ssrn.com/abstract=2128362.

Choi, Steven J. and Fisch, Jill E. 2003. How to Fix Wall Street: A Voucher Financing Proposal for Securities Intermediaries. *Yale Law Journal,* Vol. 113, November, pp. 269, 336–338.

[4.6] [5.4] [Korea] [Economics] [P,B] Choi, Won-Wook, Lee, Ho-Young, and Jun, Byung Wook. 2009. The Provision of Tax Services by Incumbent Auditors and Earnings Management: Evidence from Korea. *Journal of International Financial Management and Accounting,* Vol. 20, No. 1, Spring, pp. 79–103.

[5.1] [UK] [P] Choi, Young-Soo and Young, Steven. 2012. Transitory Earnings Components and the Two Faces of Non-GAAP Earnings. ssrn.com/abstract=2115466.[64]

[4.2] [P] Chou, De-Wai, Wang, C. Edward, and Tsai, Sandra. 2009. Earnings Management and the Long-Run Underperformance of Firms Following Convertible Bond Offers. *Journal of Business Finance and Accounting,* Vol. 36, Nos 1–2, January/March, pp. 73–98.

[4.5 IFRS] [Germany] [P] Christensen, Hans Bonde, Lee, Edward, and Walker, Martin. 2008. Incentives or Standards: What Determines Accounting Quality Changes around IFRS Adoption? AAA 2008 Financial Accounting and Reporting Section (FARS) Paper. ssrn.com/abstract=1013054.

[Theory] [P] Christensen, Peter O., Frimor, Hans, and Sabac, Florin. 2011. The Stewardship Role of Analyst Forecasts, and Discretionary versus Non-Discretionary Accruals. ssrn.com/abstract=1786621.

[4.1] [Economics] [Malaysia] [P] Chu, Ei Yet and Song, Saw-Imm. 2010. Information Asymmetry and Earnings Management: Causes of Inefficient Investment in Malaysia. *Capital Market Review,* Vol. 18, Nos 1–2, pp. 1–21. ssrn.com/abstract=1589429.

[3.1] [5.3] [Economics] [Malaysia] [P] Chu, Ei Yet and Song, Saw-Imm. 2012. Executive Compensation, Earnings Management and Over Investment in Malaysia. ssrn.com/abstract=2050862.

[4.2] [5.4] [Standard deviation of key accruals] [P] Chu, Ling, Dai, Jie, and Zhang, Ping. 2010. The Impact of Auditors' Experiences with Their Clients on the Consistency and Bias in Earnings Reporting and Auditors' Independence. ssrn.com/abstract=1533946.

[4.2] [R,C] [P] Cohen, Daniel A. and Zarowin, Paul. 2010. Accrual-Based and Real Earnings Management Activities around Seasoned Equity Offerings. *Journal of Accounting and Economics,* Vol. 50, No. 1, May, pp. 2–19.

[4.1] [4.5 SOX] [5.1] [R,C] [P] Cohen, Daniel A., Dey, Aiyesha, and Lys, Thomas Z. 2007. Real and Accrual-Based Earnings Management in the Pre- and Post-Sarbanes Oxley Periods. AAA 2006 Financial Accounting and Reporting Section (FARS) Meeting Paper. ssrn.com/abstract=813088.[65]

[4.1] [Economics] [R] [P] Cohen, Daniel A., Mashruwala, Raj, and Zach, Tzachi. 2009. The Use of Advertising Activities to Meet Earnings Benchmarks: Evidence from Monthly Data. *Review of Accounting Studies,* Vol. 15, No. 4, pp. 808–832. ssrn.com/abstract=1398788.

[4.1] [4.5] [I] [P] Cohen, Daniel A., Darrough, Masako N., Huang, Rong, and Zach, Tzachi. 2011. Warranty Reserve: Contingent Liability, Information Signal, or Earnings Management Tool? *The Accounting Review,* Vol. 86, No. 2, March, pp. 569–604.

[M] [P] Cohen, Daniel A., Pandit, Shail, Wasley, Charles E., and Zach, Tzachi. 2011. Measuring Real Activity Management. ssrn.com/abstract=1792639.

[5.3] [Restatements and discretionary accruals] [P] Cohen, Jeffrey R., Hoitash, Udi, Krishnamoorthy, Ganesh, and Wright, Arnold. 2012. Audit Committee Industry Expertise and Financial Reporting Quality. ssrn.com/abstract=1567453.

[5.1] [5.3] [P] Cohen, Lauren, Frazzini, Andrea, and Malloy, Christopher J. 2008. Hiring Cheerleaders: Board Appointments of "Independent" Directors. NBER Working Paper No. w14232. ssrn.com/abstract=1230856.

[4.7] [P] Cohen, Lee J., Cornett, Marcia Millon, Marcus, Alan J., and Tehranian, Hassan. 2012. Bank Opacity and Tail Risk during the Financial Crisis. ssrn.com/abstract=2064928.

[M] [P] Collins, Daniel W., Pungaliya, Raunaq S., and Vijh, Anand M. 2012. The Effects of Firm Growth and Model Specification Choices on Tests of Earnings Management in Quarterly Settings. ssrn.com/abstract=1823835.

[3.1] [4.1] [5.1] [5.2] [5.3] [R] [P] Cook, Kirsten A., Huston, George Ryan, and Kinney, Michael R. 2012a. Cross-Sectional Variation in Inventory-Based Earnings Management. ssrn.com/abstract=1454794.[66]

[4.1] [5.1] [R] [P] Cook, Kirsten A., Huston, George Ryan, and Kinney, Michael R. 2012b. Managing Earnings by Manipulating Inventory: The Effects of Cost Structure and Valuation Method. ssrn.com/abstract=997437.

[4.2] [5.3] [Canada] [P] Cormier, Denis, Lapointe-Antunes, Pascale, and McConomy, Bruce J. 2012. Forecasts in IPO Prospectuses: The Effect of Corporate Governance on Earnings Management. CAAA Annual Conference 2012 Paper. ssrn.com/abstract=1985762.

[5.3] [Australia] [P] Coulton, Jeffrey J., Ruddock, Caitlin M.S., and Taylor, Stephen L. 2007. Audit Fees, Non-Audit Services and Auditor-Client Economic Bonding. ssrn.com/abstract=964792.

[4.1] [Australia] [P] Coulton, Jeffrey J., Saune, Naibuka, and Taylor, Stephen L. 2012. Overvalued Equity, Benchmark Beating and Unexpected Accruals: Australian Evidence. UNSW Australian School of Business Research Paper No. 2012 ACCT 08. ssrn.com/abstract=2141700.

[4.1] [5.1] [P] Courteau, Lucie, Kao, Jennifer L., and Tian, Yao. 2010. The Impact of Earnings Management on the Performance of Earnings-Based Valuation Models. ssrn.com/abstract=1707056.[67]

[4.1] [Classification] [P,B] Cready, William M., Lopez, Thomas J., and Sisneros, Craig A. 2011. Negative Special Items and Future Earnings: Expense Transfer or Real Improvements? ssrn.com/abstract=1799990.

[4.5 SFAS 144 and APB 30] [Classification] [P] Curtis, Asher, McVay, Sarah E., and Wolfe, Mindy. 2010. An Analysis of the Implications of Discontinued Operations for Continuing Income. ssrn.com/abstract=1270861.

[M] [Economics] [P] Dabo, Abdoulaye and Laux, Judith A. 2012. A Probability Model for Earnings Restatement. Colorado College Working Paper No. 2012-05. ssrn.com/abstract=2060430.

[4.1] [5.1] [Economics] [P] Das, Somnath, Kim, Kyonghee, and Patro, Sukesh. 2011. An Analysis of Managerial Use and Market Consequences of Earnings Management and Expectation Management. *The Accounting Review,* Vol. 86, No. 6, November, pp. 1935–1967.

[3.3] [P] Davidson, Wallace N., Jiraporn, Pornsit, Kim, Young Sang, and Nemec, Carol. 2009. Earnings Management Following Duality-Creating Successions: Ethnostatistics, Impression Management and Agency Theory. ssrn.com/abstract=1483765.

[3.4] [4.1] [4.5 SOX] [5.1] [5.3] [P] Davidson, Wallace N., Jiraporn, Pornsit, Ning, Yixi, and Sakr, Ahmed. 2011. Boards, Audit Committees, Earnings Management and Shareholder Returns in MBO's. ssrn.com/abstract=1884464.

[4.5 SOX] [5.1] [5.3] [P] Davis, Larry R., Soo, Billy S., and Trompeter, Gregory M. 2009. Auditor Tenure and the Ability to Meet or Beat Earnings Forecasts. *Contemporary Accounting Research,* Vol. 26, No. 2, Summer, pp. 517–548. ssrn.com/abstract=1014601.[68]

Dechow, Patricia M. and Dichev, Ilia D. 2002. The Quality of Accruals and Earnings: The Role of Accrual Estimation Errors. *The Accounting Review,* Vol. 77 (supplement), pp. 35–59.

[Review of methodology] [P] Dechow, Patricia M., Ge, Weili, and Schrand, Catherine M. 2010. Understanding Earnings Quality: A Review of the Proxies, Their Determinants and Their Consequences. *Journal of Accounting and Economics,* Vol. 50, Nos 2–3, December, pp. 344–401.

Dechow, Patricia M., Kothari, S.P., and Watts, Ross L. 1998. The Relation between Earnings and Cash Flows. *Journal of Accounting and Economics,* Vol. 25, No. 2, May, pp. 133–168.

[3.1] [4.1] [5.3] [Smoothing] [P] Dechow, Patricia M., Myers, Linda A., and Shakespeare, Catherine. 2010. Fair Value Accounting and Gains from Asset Securitizations: A Convenient Earnings Management Tool with Compensation Side-Benefits. *Journal of Accounting and Economics,* Vol. 49, Nos 1–2, February, pp. 2–25.

Dechow, Patricia M., Richardson, Scott Anthony, and Tuna, Irem A. 2003. Why Are Earnings Kinky? An Examination of the Earnings Management Explanation. *Review of Accounting Studies,* Vol. 8, June–September, pp. 355–384.

Dechow, Patricia M., Sloan Richard, and Sweeney, Amy P. 1995. Detecting Earnings Management. *The Accounting Review,* Vol. 70, No. 2, April, pp. 193–225.

[M] [P] Dechow, Patricia M., Hutton, Amy P., Kim, Jung Hoon, and Sloan, Richard G. 2012. Detecting Earnings Management: A New Approach. *Journal of Accounting Research,* Vol. 50, No. 2, pp. 275–334.

[5.1] [I] DeGeorge, Francois, Ding, Yuan, Jeanjean, Thomas and Stolowy, Hervé. 2012. Analyst Coverage, Earnings Management and Financial Development: An International Study. *Journal of Accounting and Public Policy,* Vol. 32, No. 1, pp. 1–25.

[5.1] [Smoothing] [P,B] De Jong, Abe, Mertens, Gerard, Van der Poel, Marieke, and Van Dijk, Ronald. 2012. Does Earnings Management Affect Financial Analysts? Survey Evidence. ssrn.com/abstract=1476762.

[4.5] [5.4] [Spain] [P] De las Heras, Elena, Canibano, Leandro, and Moreira, Jose. 2012. The Impact of the Spanish Financial Act (44|2002) on Audit Quality. *Revista Española de Financiación y Contabilidad (REFC)/Spanish Journal of Finance and Accounting,* Vol. 41, No. 156, pp. 521–546.

[4.7] [Brazil] [P] De Medeiros, Otavio Ribeiro, Dantas, Jose Alves, and Lustosa, Paulo Roberto B. 2012. An Extended Model for Estimating Discretionary Loan Loss Provisions in Brazilian Banks. ssrn.com/abstract=2030847.

[3.1] [5.1] [Theory] [R,C] [P] Demers, Elizabeth A. and Wang, Chong. 2010. The Impact of CEO Career Concerns on Accruals Based and Real Earnings Management. INSEAD Working Paper No. 2010/13/AC. ssrn.com/abstract=1562428.[69]

[5.2] [5.3] [Economics] [P] Demirkan, Sebahattin and Platt, Harlan D. 2009. Financial Status, Corporate Governance Quality, and the Likelihood of Managers Using Discretionary Accruals. *Accounting Research Journal,* Vol. 22, No. 2, pp. 93–117.

[4.4] [I] Demirtas, K. Ozgur and Cornaggia, Kimberly Rodgers. 2012. Initial Credit Ratings and Earnings Management. *Review of Financial Economics*, Vol. 22, No. 4, pp. 135–145.

[5.2] [5.4] [India] [P] Desai, Renu, Desai, Vikram, Munsif, Vishal, and Singhvi, Meghna. 2012. The Effect of Nonaudit Fees and Family Owned Businesses on Earnings Management in the Indian Industry. ssrn.com/abstract=2020267.

[3.5] [Culture] [P] Desender, Kurt A., Castro, Christian E., and Escamilla de Leon, Sergio Antonio. 2011. Earnings Management and Cultural Values. *American Journal of Economics and Sociology,* Vol. 70, pp. 639–670. ssrn.com/abstract=1026000.

[4.6] [Economics] [P] Dhaliwal, Dan S., Huber, Robert E., Lee, Hye Seung "Grace," and Pincus, Morton P.K. 2008. Book–Tax Differences, Uncertainty about Fundamentals and Information Quality, and Cost of Capital. ssrn.com/abstract=1127956.[70]

[3.1] [5.2] [Economics] [R,C] [P] Dhaoui, Abderrazak. 2010. MNCs' Strategy in R&D: The Effect of the Decentralization on the Performance and on the Earnings Management. *Global Review of Business and Economic Research,* Vol. 6, No. 1, January–April, pp. 83–97.

[Survey for Chapter 3] Dichev, Ilia D., Graham, John R., Harvey, Campbell R., and Rajgopal, Shivaram. 2012. Earnings Quality: Evidence from the Field. ssrn.com/abstract=2103384.

[5.3] [Italy] [P] Di Donato, Francesca and Fiori, Giovanni. 2012. The Relation between Earnings Management Independent Directors and Audit Committee: A Study of Italian Listed Companies. ssrn.com/abstract=1991232.

[4.6] [P] Diehl, Kevin A. 2010. Ratio of Deferred Tax Liabilities to Shares as a Predictor of Stock Prices. *Accounting and Taxation,* Vol. 2, No. 1, pp. 95–105.[71]

[M] [France, Germany, Italy, UK] [P] Di Narzo, Antonio Fabio, Freo, Marzia, and Mattei, Marco Maria. 2010. Improving the Power of Accrual Models in Europe: The Mixture Approach. ssrn.com/abstract=1685623.

[5.2] [China] [P] Ding, Yuan, Zhang, Hua, and Zhang, Junxi Jack. 2007. Private vs. State Ownership and Earnings Management: Evidence from Chinese Listed Companies. *Corporate Governance: An International Review,* Vol. 15, No. 2, March, pp. 223–238.

[4.1] [Germany] [R,C] [P,B] Dinh Thi, Tami, Kang, Helen, and Schultze, Wolfgang. 2009. Discretionary Capitalization of R&D – The Trade-Off between Earnings Management and Signaling. AAA 2009 Mid-Year International Accounting Section (IAS) Meeting Paper. ssrn.com/abstract=1275785.

[4.1] [5.1] [Restatements] [P] Donelson, Dain C., McInnis, John M., and Mergenthaler, Richard Dean. 2013. Discontinuities and Earnings Management: Evidence from Restatements Related to Securities Litigation. *Contemporary Accounting Research,* Vol. 30, No. 1, Spring, pp. 242–268.

Dontoh, Alex, Ronen, Joshua, and Sarath, Bharat. 2013. *Abacus,* Vol. 49, No. 3, September, pp. 269–307.

[5.2] [5.3] [European countries] [P] Doukakis, Leonidas C. and Bekiris, Fivos V. 2011. Corporate Governance and Accruals Earnings Management. *Managerial and Decision Economics,* Vol. 32, No. 7, pp. 439–456.

[3.5] [Culture] [Smoothing] Doupnik, Timothy S. 2008. Influence of Culture on Earnings Management: A Note. *Abacus,* Vol. 44, No. 3, September, pp. 317–340.

[3.1] [4.1] [5.1] [5.2] [5.2] [D] [P] Du, Kai and Zhang, Frank. 2011. Orphans Deserve Attention: Financial Reporting in the Missing Months When Corporations Change Fiscal Year. ssrn.com/abstract=1618598.

[4.5 KonTraG] [Germany] [Smoothing] [P] Duecker, Hannes. 2009. The Effects of KonTraG on Earnings Quality in Germany. ssrn.com/abstract=1405245.

[4.1] [4.5 SFAS 141R] [Classification] [P] Dunn, Kimberly A., Kohlbeck, Mark J., and Smith, Thomas Joseph. 2011. Bargain Purchase Gains and the Acquisitions of Failed Banks. ssrn.com/abstract=1800883.

[4.1] [UK] [R] [B] Duong, Chau Minh. 2010. Highly Valued Equity and Real Operation Management: Long-Term "Detoxification." ssrn.com/abstract=1662535.

[5.2] [5.3] [International] [Economics, political] [P] Durnev, Art and Fauver, Larry. 2011. Stealing from Thieves: Expropriation Risk, Firm Governance, and Performance. Second Annual Conference on Empirical Legal Studies Paper. ssrn.com/abstract=970969.

[4.6] [International] [R,C] [P] Durnev, Art, Li, Tiemei, and Magnan, Michel. 2011. Beyond Tax Sheltering: Offshore Firms' Institutional Environment and Financial Reporting. CAAA Annual Conference 2009 Paper; AFA 2011 Denver Meetings Paper. ssrn.com/abstract=1325895.

[M] Durtschi, Cindy and Easton, Peter D. 2005. Earnings Management? The Shapes of the Frequency Distributions of Earnings Metrics Are Not Evidence Ipso Facto. *Journal of Accounting Research,* Vol. 43, No. 4, September, pp. 557–592.

[M] [P] Durtschi, Cindy and Easton, Peter D. 2009. Earnings Management? Erroneous Inferences Based on Earnings Frequency Distributions. *Journal of Accounting Research,* Vol. 47, No. 5, pp. 1249–1281.

[Theory] [P,B] Dutta, Sunil and Fan, Qintao. 2012. Equilibrium Earnings Management and Managerial Compensation in a Multiperiod Agency Setting. ssrn.com/abstract=2116555.

[4.4] [Economics] [P] Dyreng, Scott. 2009. The Cost of Private Debt Covenant Violation. ssrn.com/abstract=1478970.

[3.5] [Culture] [Economics] [P] Dyreng, Scott, Hanlon, Michelle, and Maydew, Edward L. 2011. Where Do Firms Manage Earnings? ssrn.com/abstract=1849244.

[4.1] [5.1] [P] Eames, Michael and Kim, Yongtae. 2012. Analyst vs. Market Forecasts of Earnings Management to Avoid Small Losses. *Journal of Business Finance and Accounting,* Vol. 39, Nos 5–6, pp. 649–674.

[5.2] [Japan] [P] Ebihara, Takashi, Kubota, Keiichi, Takehara, Hitoshi, and Yokota, Eri. 2012. Quality of Accounting Disclosures by Family Firms in Japan. ssrn.com/abstract=1996505.

[3.1] [5.3] [I] [Smoothing] [P] Eckles, David L., Halek, Martin, He, Enya, Sommer, David W., and Zhang, Rongrong. 2011. Earnings Smoothing, Executive Compensation, and Corporate Governance: Evidence from the Property-Liability Insurance Industry. *Journal of Risk and Insurance,* Vol. 78, No. 3, pp. 761–790.

[4.7] [R] [I] [P] Edelstein, Robert H., Liu, Peng, and Tsang, Desmond. 2008. Real Earnings Management and Dividend Payout Signals: A Study for US Real Estate Investment Trusts. CAAA Annual Conference 2008 Paper. ssrn.com/abstract=1079984.

[4.5 IAS-based standards] [Egypt] [P] Elbannan, Mohamed A. 2008. Earnings Quality and Firm Market Valuation Following the Implementation of Mandatory Accounting Standards in an Emerging Country: The Egyptian Experience. ssrn.com/abstract=1277223.

Elitzur, Ramy, Ronen, Joshua, Shoham, Amir, and Yaari, Varda. 2013. On The Economics of Earnings Management: Earnings Management, Cultural Gaps and Organizational Design. Working paper, University of Toronto.

[5.1] [5.2] [P] Elliott, W. Brooke, Krische, Susan D., and Peecher, Mark E. 2010. Expected Mispricing: The Joint Influence of Accounting Transparency and Investor Base. *Journal of Accounting Research,* Vol. 42, No. 2, May, pp. 343–381.

[3.5] [4.7] [Smoothing] [P] Elshafie, Essam. 2007. A Comparison of Earnings Management between Not-for-Profit and For-Profit Hospitals. ssrn.com/abstract=1013935.

[3.5] [Culture] [International] [R,C] [P] Enomoto, Masahiro, Kimura, Fumihiko, and Yamaguchi, Tomoyasu. 2012. Accrual-Based and Real Earnings Management: An International Comparison for Investor Protection. ssrn.com/abstract=2066797.

[5.3] [P] Epps, Ruth W. and Ismail, Tariq Hassaneen. 2009. Board of Directors' Governance Challenges and Earnings Management. *Journal of Accounting and Organizational Change,* Vol. 5, No. 3, pp. 390–416.

[4.5 IFRS] [Germany] [P] Ernstberger, Jürgen, Stich, Michael, and Vogler, Oliver. 2011. Economic Consequences of Accounting Enforcement Reforms: The Case of Germany. *European Accounting Review,* Vol. 21, No. 2, pp. 217–251.

[4.2] [UK] [P] Espenlaub, Susanne, Iqbal, Abdullah, and Strong, Norman C. 2009. Earnings Management around UK Open Offers. *The European Journal of Finance,* Vol. 15, No. 1, pp. 29–51.

[M] [Restatements] [R,C] [P] Ettredge, Michael L., Scholz, Susan, Smith, Kevin R., and Sun, Lili. 2010. How Do Restatements Begin? Evidence of Earnings Management Preceding Restated Financial Reports. *Journal of Business Finance and Accounting,* Vol. 37, Nos 3–4, April/May, pp. 332–355.

[Theory] [Smoothing] [B,P] Ewert, Ralf and Wagenhofer, Alfred. 2011. Earnings Quality Metrics and What They Measure. ssrn.com/abstract=1697042.

[Theory] [Smoothing] [B] Ewert, Ralf and Wagenhofer, Alfred. 2012. Accounting Standards, Earnings Management, and Earnings Quality. ssrn.com/abstract=2068134.

[3.1] [3.3] [5.3] [Economics] [P] Faleye, Olubunmi, Hoitash, Rani, and Hoitash, Udi. 2010. The Costs of Intense Board Monitoring. *Journal of Financial Economics,* Vol. 101, No. 1, July, pp. 160–181.

Fama, Eugene F. and Jensen, Michael C. 1983. Separation of Ownership and Control. *Journal of Law and Economics,* Vol. 26, No. 2, June, pp. 301–325.

[4.1] [5.1] [Classification] [P] Fan, Y., Barua, A., Cready, W.M., and Thomas, W.B. 2010. Managing Earnings Using Classification Shifting: Evidence from Quarterly Special Items. *The Accounting Review,* Vol. 85, No. 3, July, pp. 1303–1323.

[5.4] [Indonesia] [P] Febrianto, Rahmat and Sugiri, Slamet. 2012. Does Mandatory Auditor Rotation Increase Audit Quality? A Test of Indonesian Ministry of Finance's Decree Effectiveness. ssrn.com/abstract=2093250.

[Theory] [P] Fedyk, Tatiana. 2007. Discontinuity in Earnings Report and Managerial Incentives. ssrn.com/abstract=899680.

[4.1] [Economics] [International] [Smoothing] [P] Fernandes, Nuno G. and Ferreira, Miguel A. 2007. The Evolution of Earnings Management and Firm Valuation: A Cross-Country Analysis. EFA 2007 Ljubljana Meetings Paper. ssrn.com/abstract=965636.

[4.5] [M] [P] Feroz, Ehsan H., Kwon, Taek M., Pastena, Victor, and Park, Kyung Joo. 2000. The Efficacy of Red Flags in Predicting the SEC's Targets: An Artificial Neural Networks Approach. *International Journal of Intelligent Systems in Accounting, Finance, and Management,* Vol. 9, No. 3, September, pp. 145–157.

[4.7] [Smoothing] [P] Fiechter, Peter and Meyer, Conrad. 2011. Discretionary Measurement of Financial Assets during the 2008 Financial Crisis. ssrn.com/abstract=1522122.

[4.4] [P] Fields, L. Paige, Gupta, Manu, and Wilkins, Michael S. 2012. Refinancing Pressure and Earnings Management: Evidence from Changes in Short-Term Debt and Discretionary Accruals. ssrn.com/abstract=2069076.

[3.5] [Culture, social norms] [P] Fischer, Paul E. and Huddart, Steven J. 2007. Optimal Contracting with Endogenous Social Norms. *American Economic Review,* Vol. 98, No. 4, pp. 1459–1475.

[3.4] [4.4] [P] Fischer, Paul E. and Louis, Henock. 2008. Financial Reporting and Conflicting Managerial Incentives: The Case of Management Buyouts. *Management Science,* Vol. 54, No. 10, October, pp. 1700–1714.

[3] [Economics] [B,P] Fogel-Yaari, Hila. 2014–2015. CEO Characteristics, Information Asymmetry, and Innovation. Dissertation, University of Toronto.

Fogel-Yaari, Hila and Ronen, Joshua. 2011. The Reporting Strategy to Meet or Beat Thresholds. CAAA Annual Conference 2011 Paper.

Fogel-Yaari, Hila, DaDalt, Peter, and Ronen, Joshua. 2014. An Exploration into the Jones Model. American Accounting Association Meeting, Atlanta.

Francis, Jennifer, LaFond, Ryan, Olsson, Per, and Schipper, Katherine. 2005. The Market Pricing of Accruals Quality. *Journal of Accounting and Economics,* Vol. 39, No. 2, June, pp. 295–327.

[Culture] [5.3] [International] [P] Francis, Jere R. and Wang, Dechun. 2008. The Joint Effect of Investor Protection and Big 4 Audits on Earnings Quality around the World. *Contemporary Accounting Research,* Vol. 25, No. 1, pp. 157–191.

[3.5] [Culture, social] [Canada] [P] Francoeur, Claude, Makni Gargouri, Rim, and Shabou, Ridha Mohamed. 2010. The Relationship between Corporate Social Performance and Earnings Management. *Canadian Journal of Administrative Sciences,* Vol. 27, No. 4, pp. 320–334. ssrn.com/abstract=1723207.

[4.6] [P] Frank, Mary Margaret, Lynch, Luann J., and Rego, Sonja O. 2009. Tax Reporting Aggressiveness and Its Relation to Aggressive Financial Reporting. *The Accounting Review,* Vol. 84, No. 2, pp. 467–496.

[4.5 SOX] [4.6] [Culture] [3.5] [P] Frank, Mary Margaret, Lynch, Luann J., Rego, Sonja O., and Zhao, Rong. 2011. Are Aggressive Reporting Practices Indicative of an Aggressive Corporate Culture? ssrn.com/abstract=1066846.[72]

[Theory] [P] Friebel, Guido and Guriev, Sergei M. 2012. Whistle-Blowing and Incentives in Firms. *Journal of Economics and Management Strategy,* Vol. 21, No. 4, pp. 1007–1027.

[4.2] [China] [P] Fung, Hung-Gay, Leung, Wai K., and Zhu, Jiang. 2008. Rights Issues in the Chinese Stock Market: Evidence of Earnings Management. *Journal of International Financial Management and Accounting,* Vol. 19, No. 2, Summer, pp. 133–160.

[Theory] [P] Gao, Pingyang. 2012a. A Measurement Approach to Conservatism and Earnings Management. Chicago Booth Research Paper Nos 11–35. ssrn.com/abstract=1918339.

[Theory] [P] Gao, Pingyang. 2012b. A Measurement Approach to Binary Classifications and Thresholds. Chicago Booth Research Paper Nos 12–51. ssrn.com/abstract=2166039.

[4.1] [UK] [Economics] [R,C] [P] García Lara, Juan Manuel, Garcia Osma, Beatriz, and Neophytou, Evi. 2009. Earnings Quality in Ex-Post Failed Firms. *Accounting and Business Research,* Vol. 39, No. 2, pp. 119–138. ssrn.com/abstract=1311806.

[4.5 conservatism] [R,C] [P] García Lara, Juan Manuel, Garcia Osma, Beatriz, and Penalva, Fernando. 2012. Accounting Conservatism and the Limits to Earnings Management. ssrn.com/abstract=2165694.

[3.1] [5.3] [International] [P] García-Meca, Emma and Sánchez-Ballesta, Juan Pedro P. 2009. Corporate Governance and Earnings Management: A Meta-Analysis. *Corporate Governance: An International Review,* Vol. 17, No. 5, September, pp. 594–610.

[5.3] [UK] [Economics] [P] Garcia Osma, Beatriz. 2008. Board Independence and Real Earnings Management: The Case of R&D Expenditure. *Corporate Governance: An International Review,* Vol. 16, No. 2, March, pp. 116–13.

[5.2] [5.3] [Spain] [P] Garcia Osma, Beatriz and Noguer, Belén Gill-de-Albornoz. 2007. The Effect of the Board Composition and Its Monitoring Committees on Earnings Management: Evidence from Spain. *Corporate Governance: An International Review,* Vol. 15, No. 6, November, pp. 1413–1428.

[4.1] [UK] [R] [P] Garcia Osma, Beatriz and Young, Steven. 2009. R&D Expenditure and Earnings Targets. *European Accounting Review,* Vol. 18, No. 1, pp. 7–32. ssrn.com/abstract=1095699.

[4.6] [Slovenia] [Economics] [Smoothing] [P] Garrod, Neil W., Ratej, Pirkovic Sonja, and Valentincic, Aljosa. 2007. Political Cost (Dis)Incentives for Earnings Management in Private Firms. ssrn.com/abstract=969678.

[M] Gerakos, Joseph J. 2012. Discussion of "Detecting Earnings Management: A New Approach." *Journal of Accounting Research,* Vol. 50, No. 2, pp. 335–347. ssrn.com/abstract=2002090.

[3.1] [4.5 Handbook Section 3870] [Canada] [P] Geremia, Karrie, Carnaghan, Carla, and Nelson, Toni. 2010. Exploring Changes in Management Compensation Structure in Canada: Evidence on the Consequences of Requiring Options Expensing. CAAA Annual Conference 2010 Paper.ssrn.com/abstract=1534381.

[3.1] [4.6] [4.5 SOX] [5.3] [P][73] Ghosh, Aloke, Marra, Antonio, and Moon, Doocheol. 2010. Corporate Boards, Audit Committees, and Earnings Management: Pre- and Post-SOX Evidence. *Journal of Business Finance and Accounting,* Vol. 37, Nos 9–10, pp. 1145–1176.

[4.2] [5.2] [Brazil] [P] Gioielli, Sabrina Ozawa and De Carvalho, Antonio Gledson. 2008. The Dynamics of Earnings Management in IPOs and the Role of Venture Capital. ssrn.com/abstract=1134932.

Givoly, Dan and Ronen, Joshua. 1981. Smoothing Manifestations in Fourth-Quarter Results of Operations: Some Empirical Evidence. *Abacus,* December.

[4.1] [P] Givoly, Dan, Hayn, Carla, and Katz, Sharon P. 2009. Does Public Ownership of Equity Improve Earnings Quality? Harvard Business School Research Paper No. 09–105. ssrn.com/abstract=981426.

[5.1] [Economics] [Also restatements] [P] Givoly, Dan, Hayn, Carla, and Yoder, Timothy R. 2011. Do Analysts Account for Earnings Management? ssrn.com/abstract=1260032.[74]

[Review] [P] Glaum, Martin. 2009. Pension Accounting and Research: A Review. *Accounting and Business Research,* Vol. 39, No. 3, pp. 273–311. ssrn.com/abstract=1336965.

[4.6] [P] Gleason, Cristi A., Pincus, Morton P.K., and Rego, Sonja O. 2012. Consequences of Material Weaknesses in Tax-Related Internal Controls for Financial Reporting and Earnings Management. ssrn.com/abstract=1509765.

[5.4] [Germany] [P] Gold, Anna, Lindscheid, Friederike, Pott, Christiane, and Watrin, Christoph. 2012. The Effect of Engagement and Review Partner Tenure and Rotation on Audit Quality: Evidence from Germany. ssrn.com/abstract=1631947.

[4.3] [P] Gong, Guojin, Louis, Henock, and Sun, Amy X. 2008. Earnings Management, Lawsuits, and Stock-for-Stock Acquirers' Market Performance. *Journal of Accounting and Economics,* Vol. 46, No. 1, September, pp. 62–77.

[5.2] [International] [Smoothing] [P] Gopalan, Radhakrishnan and Jayaraman, Sudarshan. 2012. Private Control Benefits and Earnings Management: Evidence from Insider Controlled Firms. *Journal of Accounting Research,* Vol. 50, No. 1, pp. 117–157.

[3.5] [Culture, reputation] [4.5 SOX, FIN 48] [Survey] [P] Graham, John R., Hanlon, Michelle, Shevlin, Terry J., and Shroff, Nemit. 2012. Incentives for Tax Planning and Avoidance: Evidence from the Field. ssrn.com/abstract=2148407.

[Review] [P] Graham, John R., Raedy, Jana Smith, and Shackelford, Douglas A. 2011. Research in Accounting for Income Taxes. ssrn.com/abstract=1312005.

[3.1] [Smoothing] [P] Grant, Julia, Parbonetti, Antonio, and Markarian, Garen. 2009. CEO Risk-Related Incentives and Income Smoothing. AAA 2009 Financial Accounting and Reporting Section (FARS) Paper. ssrn.com/abstract=1106096.

[5.2] [5.3] [I] [Europe] [P] Greco, Giulio. 2012. Ownership Structures, Corporate Governance and Earnings Management in the European Oil Industry. ssrn.com/abstract=2015590.

[3.1] [UK] [P] Grey, Colette, Stathopoulos, Konstantinos, and Walker, Martin. 2012. The Impact of Executive Pay on the Disclosure of Alternative Earnings per Share Figures. ssrn.com/abstract=2147646.

[3.5] [Culture, religion] [P] Grullon, Gustavo, Kanatas, George, and Weston, James Peter. 2009. Religion and Corporate (Mis)Behavior. ssrn.com/abstract=1472118.

[5.1] [Rounding the numbers] [P] Grundfest, Joseph A. and Malenko, Nadya, Quadrophobia. Strategic Rounding of EPS Data. Rock Center for Corporate Governance at Stanford University Working Paper No. 65; Stanford Law and Economics Olin Working Paper No. 388. ssrn.com/abstract=1474668.[75]

Guay, Wayne R. 2008. Discussion of Accounting Discretion, Corporate Governance, and Firm Performance. *Contemporary Accounting Research,* Vol. 47, No. 2, Summer, pp. 407–413.

Guay, Wayne R. 2010. Discussion of Ramanna and Roychowdhury (2010): Elections and Discretionary Accruals: Evidence from 2004. *Journal of Accounting Research,* Vol. 48, No. 2, May, pp. 477–487.

[4.5 target report] [5.4] [China] [Allegations of EM] [P] Gul, Ferdinand A. and Ma, Mark (Shuai). 2012. Auditing Multiple Public Clients and Audit Quality. ssrn.com/abstract=2156399.

[4.5] [5.4] [China] [Classification] [P] Gul, Ferdinand A., Sami, Heibatollah, and Zhou, Haiyan. 2009. The Auditor Disaffiliation Program in China and Auditor Independence. *Auditing: A Journal of Practice and Theory,* Vol. 28, No. 1, May, pp. 29–51.

Gunny, Katherine. 2010. The Relation between Earnings Management Using Real Activities Manipulation and Future Performance: Evidence from Meeting Earnings Benchmarks. *Contemporary Accounting Research,* Vol. 27, No. 3, September, pp. 855–888.

[4.1] [Smoothing] [P] Gunny, Katherine, Jacob, John, and Jorgensen, Bjorn N. 2011. Implications of the Integral Approach and Earnings Management for Alternate Annual Reporting Periods. AAA 2008 Financial Accounting and Reporting Section (FARS) Paper. ssrn.com/abstract=992068.

[4.5 IFRS] [5.2] [Germany] [Smoothing] [P] Günther, Nina, Gegenfurtner, Bernhard, Kaserer, Christoph, and Achleitner, Ann-Kristin. 2009. International Financial Reporting Standards and Earnings Quality: The Myth of Voluntary vs. Mandatory Adoption. CEFS Working Paper No.2009–09. ssrn.com/abstract=1413145.

[4.4] [International] [Economics] [P] Gupta, Manu, Khurana, Inder K., and Pereira, Raynolde. 2008. Legal Enforcement, Short Maturity Debt, and the Incentive to Manage Earnings. *Journal of Law and Economics,* Vol. 51, No. 4, September, pp. 619–639.

[4.5 FIN 48] [4.6] [5.1] [P] Gupta, Sanjay, Laux, Rick C., and Lynch, Dan. 2011. Do Firms Use Tax Cushion Reversals to Meet Earnings Targets? Evidence from the Pre- and Post-FIN 48 Periods. ssrn.com/abstract=1163842.[76]

[3.1] [4.2] [5.2] [P] Guthrie, Katherine and Sokolowsky, Jan. 2010. Large Shareholders and the Pressure to Manage Earnings. *Journal of Corporate Finance,* Vol. 16, No. 3, June, pp. 302–319.

[Review] [P] Habib, Ahsan and Hansen, James C. 2008. Target Shooting: Review of Earnings Management around Earnings Benchmarks. *Journal of Accounting Literature,* Vol. 27, pp. 25–70.

[5.3] [Malaysia] [Economics] [Compliance with regulations: AAERs and qualified opinion] [P] Haji-Abdullah, Noor Marini and Wan-Hussin, Wan Nordin. 2009. Audit Committee Attributes, Financial Distress and the Quality of Financial Reporting in Malaysia. ssrn.com/abstract=1500134.

[5.1] [5.2] [P] Hall, Curtis and Trombley, Mark A. 2011. Accounting Responses to Hedge-Fund Activism. ssrn.com/abstract=1912279.

[5.3] [Jordan] [P] Hamdan, Allam Mohammed Mousa, Al-Hayale, Talal, and Aboagela, Emad Mohamed. 2012. The Impact of Audit Committee Characteristics on Earnings Management: Additional Evidence from Jordan. European Business Research Conference Proceedings 2012. ssrn.com/abstract=2130354.

[4.8] [US and International] [Smoothing] [R,C] [P] Hamm, Sophia J. W., Jung, Boochun, and Lee, Woo-Jong. 2012. Labor Unions and Income Smoothing. ssrn.com/abstract=2158081.

[3.5] [Culture] [P] Han, Sam, Kang, Tony, Salter, Stephen B., and Yoo, Yong Keun. 2010. A Cross-Country Study on the Effects of National Culture on Earnings Management. *Journal of International Business Studies,* Vol. 41, No. 1, January, pp. 123–141.

[3.5] [Culture] [P] Hanif, Muhammad. 2010. Implications of Earnings Management for Implementation of Sharia Based Financial System. *Interdisciplinary Journal of Contemporary Research in Business.* ssrn.com/abstract=1507022.

[4.6] [5.4] [Methodology] [P] Hanlon, Michelle, Krishnan, Gopal V., and Mills, Lillian F. 2011. Audit Fees and Book-Tax Differences. *Journal of the American Taxation Association,* Vol. 34, No. 1, Spring, pp. 55–86.

[4.5 SFAS 131] [Economics] [P] Hann, Rebecca N. and Lu, Yvonne Y. 2009. Earnings Management at the Segment Level. Marshall School of Business Working Paper No. MKT 04–09. ssrn.com/abstract=1138164.

[4.1] [P] Hardouvelis, Gikas A., Papanastasopoulos, Georgios, Thomakos, Dimitrios D., and Wang, Tao. 2012. External Financing, Growth and Stock Returns. *European Financial Management,* Vol. 18, No. 5, pp. 790–815. ssrn.com/abstract=2164036.

[4.1] [5.1] [M] [P] Harris, David G. and Shi, Linna. 2012a. A General Differences-in-Differences Research Design for Evaluating Firms Deviations from Expectations. ssrn.com/abstract=1866354.

[4.1] [5.1] [Smoothing] [D] [P] Harris, David G. and Shi, Linna. 2012b. A General Examination of Earnings Management around Financial Benchmarks. ssrn.com/abstract=1950745.

[4.1] [5.1] [P] Harris, David G., Shi, Linna, and Xie, Hong. 2010. Is Meeting and Beating Earnings Benchmarks Associated with Accounting Fraud? Working paper, Syracuse University. http://www2.binghamton.edu/som/files/DavidHarris-Syracuse.pdf.

[5.2] [5.3] [5.4] [Malaysia] [Firms that committed fraudulent EM] [Economics, politics] [P] Hasnan, Suhaily, Abdul Rahman, Rashidah Abdul, and Mahenthiran, Sakthi. 2008. Management Predisposition, Motive, Opportunity, and Earnings Management for Fraudulent Financial Reporting in Malaysia. ssrn.com/abstract=1321455.

[3.1] [3.3] [5.3] [P] Hazarika, Sonali, Karpoff, Jonathan M., and Nahata, Rajarishi. 2012. Internal Corporate Governance, CEO Turnover, and Earnings Management. *Journal of Financial Economics,* Vol. 104, No. 1, April, pp. 44–69.

[5.1] [5.2] [Economics] [P] He, Jie and Tian, Xuan, 2012. The Dark Side of Analyst Coverage: The Case of Innovation. ssrn.com/abstract=1959125.

[Review] [P] He, Luo, Labelle, Réal, Piot, Charles, and Thornton, Daniel B. 2009. Board Monitoring, Audit Committee Effectiveness, and Financial Reporting Quality: Review and Synthesis of Empirical Evidence. *Journal of Forensic and Investigative Accounting,* Vol. 1, No. 2, July–December. ssrn.com/abstract=1159453.

Healy, Paul M. 1985. The Effect of Bonus Schemes on Accounting Decisions. *Journal of Accounting and Economics,* Vol. 7, Nos 1–3, April, pp. 85–107.

Healy, Paul M. 1996. Discussion of a Market-Based Evaluation of Discretionary Accrual Models. *Journal of Accounting Research,* Vol. 34, No. 3 (supplement), pp. 107–115.

Healy, Paul M. and Palepu, Krishna G. 2003. How the Quest for Efficiency Corroded the Market. *Harvard Business Review,* Vol. 81, July, pp. 76–85.

Healy, Paul M. and Wahlen, James Michael. 1999. A Review of the Earnings Management Literature and Its Implications for Standard Setting. *Accounting Horizons,* Vol. 13, No. 4, December, pp. 365–383.

[5.4] [Australia] [P,B] Herbohn, Kathleen and Ragunathan, Vanitha. 2008. Auditor Reporting and Earnings Management: Some Additional Evidence. *Accounting and Finance,* Vol. 48, No. 4, December, pp. 575–601.

[4.5 AASB 1020] [4.6] [Australia] [P,B] Herbohn, Kathleen, Tutticci, Irene, and Khor, Pui See. 2010. Changes in Unrecognised Deferred Tax Accruals from Carry-Forward Losses: Earnings Management or Signalling? *Journal of Business Finance and Accounting,* Vol. 37, Nos 7–8, July/August, pp. 763–791.

[4.3] [Japan] [P] Higgins, Huong N. 2012. Do Stock-for-Stock Merger Acquirers Manage Earnings? Evidence from Japan. *Journal of Accounting and Public Policy,* Vol. 32, No. 1, January, pp. 44–70.

[Theory] [P] Hofmann, Christian. 2008. Earnings Management and Measurement Error. 2008. *BuR Business Research,* Vol. 1, No. 2, December, pp. 149–163. ssrn.com/abstract=1330338.

[4.5 SOX] [5.1] [R,C] [P] Hong, Yongtao, Huseynov, Fariz, and Zhang, Wei. 2012. Earnings Management and Analyst Following: A Simultaneous Equations Analysis. ssrn.com/abstract=2139559.

[3.1] [Chapter 5] [Internal] [Organizational design] [P] Hopkins, Justin, Maydew, Edward L., and Venkatachalam, Mohan. 2012. Corporate General Counsel and Financial Reporting Quality. Darden Business School Working Paper No. 2060437. ssrn.com/abstract=2060437.

[3.1] [4.1] [P] Houmes, Robert and Skantz, Terrance R. 2010. Highly Valued Equity and Discretionary Accruals. *Journal of Business Finance and Accounting,* Vol. 37, Nos 1–2, January/March, pp. 60–92.

[3.1] [5.2] [5.3] [5.4] [Bangladesh] [P] Houqe, Nurul, Van Zijl, Tony, Dunstan, Keitha L., and Karim, A.K.M. Waresul. 2010. Does Corporate Governance Affect Earnings Quality: Evidence from an Emerging Market. *Academy of Taiwan, Business Management Review,* Vol. 7, No. 3, pp. 48–57.

[3.5] [Culture, investor protection] [4.5 IFRS] [International] [P] Houqe, Nurul, Van Zijl, Tony, Dunstan, Keitha L., and Karim, A.K.M. Waresul. 2012. The Effect of IFRS Adoption and Investor Protection on Earnings Quality around the World. *International Journal of Accounting,* Vol. 47, No. 3, September, pp. 333–355.

Hribar, Paul and Collins, Dan. 2002. Errors in Estimating Accruals: Implications for Empirical Research. *Journal of Accounting Research,* Vol. 40, No. 1, March, pp. 105–134.

[M] [P] Hribar, Paul and Nichols, D. Craig. 2007. The Use of Unsigned Earnings Quality Measures in Tests of Earnings Management. *Journal of Accounting Research,* Vol. 45, No. 5, December, pp. 1017–1053.

[4.5 bank reform] [4.7] [China] [P] Hsieh, Chia-Chun and Wu, Shing-Jen. 2012. Monitoring the Monitors: The Effect of Banking Industry Reform on Earnings Management Behavior in an Emerging Market. *Corporate Governance: An International Review,* Vol. 20, No. 5, pp. 451–473.

[4.1] [Smoothing] [Classification] [P,B] Hsu, Charles and Kross, William. 2010. The Market Pricing of Special Items that Are Included versus Excluded from "Street" Earnings. *Contemporary Accounting Research,* Vol. 28, No. 3, pp. 990–1017.

[4.3] [R] [P] Hsu, Kathy Hsiao Yu, Kim, Young Sang, and Song, Kyojik "Roy." 2009. The Relation Among Targets' R&D Activities, Acquirers' Returns, and In-Process R&D in the US. *Journal of Business, Finance, and Accounting,* Vol. 36, pp. 1180–1200.

[5.1] [5.3] [P,B] Hsu, Pei H. 2012. How Does Financial Expert Director Affect the Incidence of Accruals Management to Meet or Beat Analyst Forecasts? ssrn.com/abstract=2070897.

[3.1] [5.3] [China] [P] Humphery-Jenner, Mark. 2012. The Governance and Performance of Chinese Companies Listed Abroad: An Analysis of China's Merits Review Approach to Overseas Listings. *Journal of Corporate Law Studies,* Vol. 12, No. 2, pp. 333–365.

[3.1] [5.2] [5.4] [P] Hutchinson, Marion R. and Leung, Sidney. 2007. An Investigation of Factors Influencing the Association between Top Management Ownership and Earnings Management. ssrn.com/abstract=1077467.

[4.1] [4.5 SOX] [P] Hutton, Amy P., Marcus, Alan J., and Tehranian, Hassan. 2008. Opaque Financial Reports, R–Square, and Crash Risk. ssrn.com/abstract=1115967.

[4.4] [Belgian start-ups] [P] Huyghebaert, Nancy, Vander Bauwhede, Heidi J.C., and Willekens, Marleen. 2007. Bank Financing as an Incentive for Earnings Management in Business Start-Ups. ssrn.com/abstract=967386.

[4.1] [5.3] [P] Hwang, Byoung-Hyoun and Kim, Seoyoung. 2012. Social Ties and Earnings Management. ssrn.com/abstract=1215962.

[3.4] [5.1] [Restatements] [P] Hwang, Chuan-Yang, Li, Yuan, and Tong, Yen H. 2010. Are Analysts Whose Forecast Revisions Correlate Less with Prior Stock Price Changes Better Information Producers and Monitors? Finance and Corporate Governance Conference 2010 Paper. ssrn.com/abstract=1742669.

[4.5 SOX] [P] Iliev, Peter. 2009. The Effect of SOX Section 404: Costs, Earnings Quality and Stock Prices. *Journal of Finance,* Vol. 65, No. 3, pp. 1163–1196.

[4.5 IFRS] [International] [Economics] [R,C] [P] Ipino, Elisabetta and Parbonetti, Antonio. 2011. Mandatory IFRS Adoption: The Trade-Off between Accrual and Real-Based Earnings Management. ssrn.com/abstract=2039711.

[4.2] [Bangladesh] [P] Islam, Mohammad Sadiqul, Uddin, Muhammad Mosfique, and Ahmad, Shabbir. 2002. The Operating Performance of Firms Conducting Seasoned Equity Offerings in Bangladesh. *Dhaka University Journal of Business Studies,* Vol. 23, No. 2, December, pp. 205–217. ssrn.com/abstract=1083672.

[4.2] [4.7] [Malaysia] [P] Ismail, Norashikin and Weetman, Pauline. 2008. Regulatory Profit Targets and Earnings Management in Initial Public Offerings: The Case of Malaysia. *Journal of Financial Reporting and Accounting,* Vol. 6, No. 1, pp. 91–115.

[3.5] [Culture, religion] [P] Ismail, Wan Adibah, Kamarudin, Khairul Anuar, and Sarman, Siti Rahayu. 2012. The Management of Reported Earnings in Shariah-Compliant Companies: A Panel Data Analysis of Accrual Quality. ssrn.com/abstract=2055145.

[3.5] [Culture, gender] [Finland, Sweden] [P] Ittonen, Kim, Peni, Emilia, and Vähämaa, Sami. 2012. Female Auditors and Accruals Quality. ssrn.com/abstract=2060797.

[3.1] [P] Iyengar, Raghavan J. and Zampelli, Ernest M. 2010. Does Accounting Conservatism Pay? *Accounting and Finance,* Vol. 50, No. 1, March, pp. 121–142.

[5.1] [P] Jackson, Scott B. and Liu, Xiaotao (Kelvin). 2010. The Allowance for Uncollectible Accounts, Conservatism, and Earnings Management. *Journal of Accounting Research,* Vol. 48, No. 3, pp. 565–601.

[3.2] [5.3] [Hong Kong] [P] Jaggi, Bikki and Tsui, Judy S.L. 2007. Insider Trading, Earnings Management and Corporate Governance: Empirical Evidence Based on Hong Kong Firms. *Journal of International Financial Management and Accounting,* Vol. 18, No. 3, Autumn, pp. 192–222.

[5.2] [5.3] [Hong Kong] [P] Jaggi, Bikki, Leung, Sidney, and Gul, Ferdinand A. 2009. Family Control, Board Independence and Earnings Management: Evidence Based on Hong Kong Firms. *Journal of Accounting and Public Policy,* Vol. 28, No. 4, pp. 281–300.

[5.2] [Europe] [P] Jara, Mauricio and Lopez, Felix J. 2011. Earnings Management and Contests for Control: An Analysis of European Family Firms. *Journal of CENTRUM Cathedra,* Vol. 4, No. 1, pp. 100–120.

[3.1] [I] [P] Jayaraman, Sudarshan and Milbourn, Todd T. 2010. Financial Misreporting and Executive Compensation: The Qui Tam Statute. ssrn.com/abstract=1550348.

[3.1] [5.4] [P] Jayaraman, Sudarshan and Milbourn, Todd T. 2012. The Effect of Auditor Expertise on Executive Compensation. ssrn.com/abstract=1955488.

[5.1] [Class action suit filings] [P] Jennings, Jared N. 2012. The Role of Sell-Side Analysts after Accusations of Managerial Misconduct. ssrn.com/abstract=2128122.

[3.5] [Culture, social capital] [4.5 SOX] [R,C] [P] Jha, Anand. 2011. Earnings Management and Social Capital. American Accounting Association Annual Meeting, Denver, Colorado. ssrn.com/abstract=1893011.

[4.1] [5.1] [3.5] [Culture, ethics] [Backdating firms] [P] Jia, Yuping. 2012. Meeting or Missing Earnings Benchmarks: The Role of CEO Integrity. ssrn.com/abstract=2154169.[77]

[5.2] [China] [P] Jian, Ming and Wong, T.J. 2010. Propping Through Related Party Transactions. *Review of Accounting Studies,* Vol. 15, No. 1, March, pp. 70–105.

[4.1] [5.1] [Economics] [B] Jiang, John (Xuefeng). 2008. Beating Earnings Benchmarks and the Cost of Debt. *The Accounting Review,* Vol. 83, No. 2, March, pp. 377–416.

[3.1] [5.1] [P] Jiang, John (Xuefeng), Petroni, Kathy R., and Wang, Isabel Yanyan. 2010. CFOs and CEOs: Who Have the Most Influence on Earnings Management? *Journal of Financial Economics,* Vol. 96, No. 3, pp. 513–526.[78]

[4.1] [UK] [R,C] [P] Jiang, Wei and Stark, Andrew. 2011. Accounting and Economic Determinants of Loss Reversals. ssrn.com/abstract=1619173.

[4.1] [P] Jiao, Tao, Roosenboom, Peter, and Mertens, Gerard. 2007. Industry Valuation Driven Earnings Management. ERIM Report Series Reference No. ERS-2007-069-F&A. ssrn.com/abstract=1032748.

[5.2] [P] Jiraporn, Pornsit and DaDalt, Peter J. 2007. Does Founding Family Control Affect Earnings Management? An Empirical Note. ssrn.com/abstract=1017856.

[5.3] [P] Jiraporn, Pornsit and Liu, Yixin. 2010. Staggered Boards, Accounting Discretion, and Firm Value. ssrn.com/abstract=1684676.

Jones, Jennifer J. 1991. Earnings Management during Import Relief Investigations. *Journal of Accounting Research,* Vol. 29, No. 2, Autumn, pp. 193–228.

[M] [Restatements] [P] Jones, Keith L., Krishnan, Gopal V., and Melendrez, Kevin D. 2010. Do Models of Discretionary Accruals Detect Actual Cases of Fraudulent and Restated Earnings? An Empirical Analysis. *Contemporary Accounting Research,* Vol. 25, No. 2, Summer, pp. 499–531.

[4.5 SFAS 142] [P] Jordan, Charles E., and Clark, Stanley, J. 2011. Big Bath Earnings Management: The Case of Goodwill Impairment Under SFAS No. 142. *Journal of Applied Business Research,* Vol. 20, No. 2, pp. 63–70.

[4.1] [4.5 SFAS 128] [Rounding numbers] [P] Jorgensen, Bjorn N., Lee, Yong Gyu, and Rock, Steve Karl. 2010. Numbers Games? A Natural Experiment Investigating Three (Ir)Regularities in Reported Earnings Per Share. ssrn.com/abstract=1665290.

[4.4] [Smoothing] [P,B] Jung, Boochun, Soderstrom, Naomi S., and Yang, Yanhua Sunny. 2013. Earnings Smoothing Activities of Firms to Manage Credit Ratings. *Contemporary Accounting Research,* Vol. 30, No. 2, June, pp. 645–676.

[3.1] [P] Kalyta, Paul. 2009. Accounting Discretion, Horizon Problem, and CEO Retirement Benefits. *The Accounting Review,* Vol. 84, No. 5, pp. 1553–1574.

[M] [P] Kama, Itay and Melumad, Nahum D. 2012. Camouflaged Earnings Management. ssrn.com/abstract=1733107.

[4.7] [5.4] [I] [P] Kanagaretnam, Kiridaran (Giri), Krishnan, Gopal V., and Lobo, Gerald J. 2010. An Empirical Analysis of Auditor Independence in the Banking Industry. *The Accounting Review,* Vol. 85, No. 6, pp. 2011–2046.

[5.4] [5.1] [I] [International] [P] Kanagaretnam, Kiridaran (Giri), Lim, Chee Yeow, and Lobo, Gerald J. 2010. Auditor Reputation and Earnings Management: International Evidence from the Banking Industry. *Journal of Banking and Finance,* Vol. 34, No. 10. ssrn.com/abstract=1568866.[79]

[4.1] [P] Kang, Qiang, Liu, Qiao, and Qi, Rong. 2010. Predicting Stock Market Returns with Aggregate Discretionary Accruals. *Journal of Accounting Research,* Vol. 48, No. 4, pp. 815–858.

Kang, Sok-Hyon and Sivaramakrishnan, K. 1995. Issues in Testing Earnings Management and an Instrumental Variable Approach. *Journal of Accounting Research,* Vol. 33, No. 2, Autumn, pp. 353–367.

Kaplan, Robert. 1985. Evidence of the Effect of Bonus Schemes on Accounting Procedure on Accruals Decisions. *Journal of Accounting and Economics,* Vol. 7, Nos 1–3, April, pp. 109–113.

[Review] [P] Kassem, Rasha H. 2012. Earnings Management and Financial Reporting Fraud: Can External Auditors Spot the Difference? *American Journal of Business and Management,* Vol. 1, No. 1, pp. 30–33. ssrn.com/abstract=2121218.

[4.2] [5.2] [P] Katz, Sharon P. 2009. Earnings Quality and Ownership Structure: The Role of Private Equity Sponsors. *The Accounting Review,* Vol. 84, No. 3, May, pp. 623–658.

[Economics] [P] Kedia, Simi and Philippon, Thomas. 2009. The Economics of Fraudulent Accounting. *The Review of Financial Studies,* Vol. 22, No. 6, pp. 2169–2199.

[4.1] [5.2] [5.3] [P] Kee, Koon Boon. 2010. Why "Democracy" and "Drifter" Firms Can Have Abnormal Returns: The Joint Importance of Corporate Governance and Abnormal Accruals in Separating Winners from Losers. 23rd Australasian Finance and Banking Conference 2010 Paper. ssrn.com/abstract=1646783.

[4.1] [4.5 SOX] [5.1] [P] Keskek, Sami, Myers, Linda A., Omer, Thomas C., and Sharp, Nathan Y. 2011. Exploring the Accrual-Related Optimism in Management Earnings Forecasts. ssrn.com/abstract=1975122.

[5.1] [5.3] [5.4] [Misstatements constrained in SAB 108] [P] Keune, Marsha B. and Johnstone, Karla M. 2012. Materiality Judgments and the Resolution of Detected Misstatements: The Role of Managers, Auditors, and Audit Committees. *The Accounting Review,* Vol. 87, No. 5, September, pp. 1641–1677.

[4.1] [5.1] [Economics] [P] Keung, Edmund C., Lin, Zhi-Xing, and Shih, Michael S.H. 2010. Does the Stock Market See a Zero or Small Positive Earnings Surprise as a Red Flag? *Journal of Accounting Research,* Vol. 49, No. 1, March, pp. 81–121.

[3.1] [5.3] [Australia] [P] Khan, Arifur, Mather, Paul R., and Balachandran, Balasingham. 2012. Managerial Share Ownership and Operating Performance: Do Independent and Executive Directors Have Different Incentives? *Australian Journal of Management,* Vol. 39, No. 1, pp. 47–71.

[Review] [P,B] Kheng Soon, Kelly Wee. 2011. Earning Management: Is It Good or Bad? ssrn.com/abstract=1775400.

[4.1] [Economics] [P] Kim, Hyo Jin and Yoon, Soon Suk. 2009. Firm Characteristics and Earnings Management of Different Types of Security Issuers. ssrn.com/abstract=1325952.

[4.1] [R,C] [Economics] [P] Kim, Jeong-Bon and Sohn, Byungcherl Charlie. 2011. Real versus Accrual-Based Earnings Management and Implied Cost of Equity Capital. ssrn.com/abstract=1297938.

[4.1] [5.2] [Korea] [Economics] [P] Kim, Jeong-Bon and Yi, Cheong H. 2006. Ownership Structure, Business Group Affiliation, Listing Status, and Earnings Management: Evidence from Korea. *Contemporary Accounting Research,* Vol. 23, No. 2, Summer, pp. 427–464.

[4.5 auditor designation] [Korea] [P] Kim, Jeong-Bon and Yi, Cheong H. 2009. Does Auditor Designation by the Regulatory Authority Improve Audit Quality? Evidence from Korea. *Journal of Accounting and Public Policy,* Vol. 28, No. 3, pp. 207–230.

[Corporate culture] [R,C, AAERs] [P] Kim, Yongtae, Park, Myung Seok, and Wier, Benson. 2011. Is Earnings Quality Associated with Corporate Social Responsibility? *The Accounting Review,* Vol. 87, No. 3, May, pp. 761–796.

[5.1] [Methodology-measurement] [P] Kirk, Marcus, Reppenhagen, David A., and Tucker, Jenny Wu. 2012. Meeting Individual Analyst Expectations. ssrn.com/abstract=2102920.[80]

[5.1] [P] Koch, Adam S., Lefanowicz, Craig E., and Shane, Philip B. 2012. Earnings Guidance and Earnings Management Constraints. ssrn.com/abstract=2161762.

[Theory] [P] Köenigsgruber, Roland. 2009. An Economic Analysis of Cross-Listing Decisions and Their Impact on Earnings Quality. *Schmalenbach Business Review,* Vol. 61, July, pp. 310–330. ssrn.com/abstract=1514439.

[3] [4.1] [Economics] [P] Koh, Kevin. 2011. Value or Glamour? An Empirical Investigation of the Effect of Celebrity CEOs on Financial Reporting Practices and Firm Performance. *Accounting and Finance,* Vol. 51, No. 2, pp. 517–547.

[5.4] [B] Koh, Kevin, Rajgopal, Shivaram, and Srinivasan, Suraj. 2011. Non-Audit Services and Financial Reporting Quality: Evidence from 1978–1980. *Review of Accounting Studies,* Vol. 18, No. 1, pp. 1–33.

Kothari, S.P., Leone, Andrew L., and Wasley, Charles E. 2005. Performance Matched Discretionary Accrual Measures. *Journal of Accounting and Economics,* Vol. 39, No. 1, February, pp. 163–197.

[4.3] [Restatements] [Economics] [P] Kravet, Todd D., Myers, Linda A., Sanchez, Juan Manuel, and Scholz, Susan. 2012. Do Financial Statement Misstatements Facilitate Corporate Acquisitions? ssrn.com/abstract=2029953.

[4.1] [4.5 SOX] [5.1] [5.3] [P] Krishnan, Gopal V., Raman, K.K., Yang, Ke, and Yu, Wei. 2011. CFO/CEO-Board Social Ties, Sarbanes Oxley, and Earnings Management. *Accounting Horizons,* Vol. 25, No. 3, September, pp. 537–557.[81]

[4.5 SOX] [5.3] [5.4] [P] Krishnan, Gopal V., Sun, Lili, Wang, Qian, and Yang, Rong. 2011. Client Risk Management: A Study of Earnings Management, Audit Fees, and Auditor Resignations. ssrn.com/abstract=1578441.

[4.1] [5.4] [P] Krishnan, Gopal V. and Visvanathan, Gnanakumar. 2011. Is There an Association Between Earnings Management and Auditor-Provided Tax Services? *Journal of American Taxation Association,* Vol. 33, No. 2, Fall, pp. 111–135.

[3] [R,C] [P] Krishnan, Gopal V., Visvanathan, Gnanakumar, and Su, Lixin (Nancy). 2009. Does Accounting and Financial Expertise in the C-Suite Aid or Mitigate Earnings Management? ssrn.com/abstract=1420182.

[4.5 SOX] [5.4] [D] [P] Krishnan, Jayanthi, Su, Lixin (Nancy), and Zhang, Yinqi. 2011. Nonaudit Services and Earnings Management in the Pre-SOX and Post-SOX Eras. *Auditing: A Journal of Practice and Theory,* Vol. 30, No. 3, August, pp. 103–123.

[3.1] [UK] [Smoothing] [P] Kuang, Yu Flora. 2008. Performance-Vested Stock Options and Earnings Management. *Journal of Business Finance and Accounting,* Vol. 35, Nos 9–10, November/December, pp. 1049–1078.

[2.3] [P] Kuang, Yu Flora, Qin, Bo, and Wielhouwer, J.L. 2012. Survival Expectations and Discretionary Accruals over CEO Tenure: Evidence from Inside versus Outside CEOs. ssrn.com/abstract=2105651.

[Review] [Japan] [P] Kurokawa, Yasuyoshi. 2009. M&A for Value Creation in Japan. Monden Institute of Management: Japanese Management and International Studies. ssrn.com/abstract=1588623.

[3] [5.2] [5.3] [Norway] [P] Kvaal, Erlend, Langli, John Christian, and Abdolmohammadi, Mohammad J. 2012. Earnings Management Priorities of Private Family Firms. ssrn.com/abstract=1532824.

[4.7] [Japan] [P] Kwak, Wikil, Lee, Ho-Young, and Eldridge, Susan W. 2009. Earnings Management by Japanese Bank Managers Using Discretionary Loan Loss Provisions. *Review of Pacific Basin Financial Markets and Policies,* Vol. 12, No. 1, pp. 1–26.

[3.5] [Culture, ethics] [P] Labelle, Réal, Makni Gargouri, Rim, and Francoeur, Claude. 2009. Ethics, Diversity Management and Financial Reporting Quality. *Journal of Business Ethics,* Vol. 93, No. 2, May, pp. 335–355.

[5.2] [5.3] [International] [Smoothing] [P,B] LaFond, Ryan, Lang, Mark H., and Skaife, Hollis Ashbaugh. 2007. Earnings Smoothing, Governance and Liquidity: International Evidence. ssrn.com/abstract=975232.

[4.5 SFAS 157 and IFRS 7] [I] [International] [P] Laghi, Enrico, Pucci, Sabrina, Tutino, Marco, and Di Marcantonio, Michele. 2012. Fair Value Hierarchy in Financial Instruments Disclosure – Is Transparency Well Assessed for Investors? Evidence from the Banking Industry. *Journal of Governance and Regulation,* Vol. 1, No. 3. ssrn.com/abstract=2153645.

[4.1] [M] [P] Lahr, Henry. 2011. Identifying Discontinuities in Distributions of Earnings by Kernel Density Estimation. ssrn.com/abstract=1587969.

[M] [P] Lai, Cheng Y. 2010. Modelling the Accruals Process and Assessing Unexpected Accruals. ssrn.com/abstract=1428171.

[Theory] [P] Lai, Cheng Y. 2011. The Impact of Accounting Distortions on Performance and Growth Measures. ssrn.com/abstract=1428202.

[Theory] [P] Lai, Guoming, Debo, Laurens G., and Nan, Lin. 2010. Channel Stuffing with Short-Term Interest in Market Value. ssrn.com/abstract=1126778.

[4.1] [5.2] [5.3] [China] [P] Lai, Liona. 2009. Managing Earnings to Meet Critical Thresholds and the Role of Corporate Governance: A Case Study of China. CAAA Annual Conference 2009 Paper. ssrn.com/abstract=1326191.

[3] [4.1] [P] Lail, Bradley E. 2007. Manipulation of Internal Performance Measures: Evidence from SFAS No. 131 Disclosures. ssrn.com/abstract=1014107.

[4.1] [4.4] [R,C] [P] Lam, F.Y. Eric C. and Wei, K.C. John. 2012. The External Financing Anomaly beyond Real Investments and Earnings Management. ssrn.com/abstract=1360677.

Lambert, Richard A. 2007. Agency Theory and Management Accounting. In Chapman, C.S., Hopewood, A.G., and Shields, M.D. *Handbook of Management Accounting,* Vol. 1. Elsevier, Amsterdam.

[M] [P] Larcker, David F. and Rusticus, Tjomme O. 2010. On the Use of Instrumental Variables in Accounting Research. *Journal of Accounting and Economics,* Vol. 49, No. 3, pp. 186–205.

[Theory] [P] Laux, Christian and Laux, Volke. 2009. Board Committees, CEO Compensation, and Earnings Management. *The Accounting Review,* Vol. 84, No. 3, May, pp. 869–891.

[Theory] [P] Laux, Volker. 2010. Effects of Litigation Risk on Board Oversight and CEO Incentive Pay. *Management Science,* Vol. 56, No. 6, June, pp. 938–948.

[Theory] [P] Laux, Volker and Stocken, Phillip C. 2011. Managerial Reporting, Overoptimism, and Litigation Risk. Tuck School of Business Working Paper No. 2011-87. ssrn.com/abstract=1616276.

[4.2] [Economics] [P] Lee, Gemma and Masulis, Ronald W. 2009. Seasoned Equity Offerings: Quality of Accounting Information and Expected Flotation Costs. *Journal of Financial Economics,* Vol. 92, No. 3, June, pp. 443–469.

[4.2] [5.2] [P] Lee, Gemma and Masulis, Ronald W. 2011. Do More Reputable Financial Institutions Reduce Earnings Management by IPO Issuers? *Journal of Corporate Finance,* Vol. 17, No. 4, pp. 982–1000.

[4.1] [4.2] [4.5 SOX] [P] Lee, Hei Wai, Xie, Yan Alice, and Zhou, Jian. 2012. Role of Underwriters in Restraining Earnings Management in Initial Public Offerings. *Journal of Applied Business Research,* Vol. 28, No. 2, July/August, pp. 709–723.

[4.1] [R] [P] Leggett, Denise, Parsons, Linda M., and Reitenga, Austin L. 2009. Real Earnings Management and Subsequent Operating Performance. ssrn.com/abstract=1466411.

[5.4] [AAERs] [P] Lennox, Clive S. and Pittman, Jeffrey A. 2010. Big Five Audits and Accounting Fraud. *Contemporary Accounting Research,* Vol. 27, No. 1, March, pp. 209–247.

Leuz, Christian, Nanda, Dhananjay and Wysocki, Peter D. 2003. Earnings Management and Investor Protection: An International Comparison. *Journal of Financial Economics,* Vol. 69, pp. 505–527.

[4.1] [4.2] [Restatements] [B] Lewis, Melissa Fay. 2008. When are IPO Firms' Income-Increasing Accruals Informative? ssrn.com/abstract=1012362.

[4.7] [P] Leverty, J. Tyler and Grace, Martin F. 2010. Property-Liability Insurer Reserve Error: Motive, Manipulation, or Mistake. ssrn.com/abstract=964635.

[Theory] [P] Levine, Carolyn B. and Smith, Michael J. 2009. The Relative Efficiency of Clawback Provisions in Compensation Contracts. Finance and Corporate Governance Conference 2011 Paper. ssrn.com/abstract=1531203.

[3] [4.2] [P] Lewis, Craig M. and Verwijmeren, Patrick. 2009. Convertible Security Design and Contract Innovation. ssrn.com/abstract=1352503.

[3.5] [Culture] [International] [P] Li, Kai, Griffin, Dale W., Yue, Heng, and Zhao, Longkai. 2012. How Does Culture Influence Firm Risk-Taking? ssrn.com/abstract=2021550.

[4.1] [International] [R,C] [P] Li, Lingxiang, Francis, Bill B., and Hasan, Iftekhar. 2011a. A Cross-Country Study of Legal Environment and Real Earnings Management. CAAA Annual Conference 2011 Paper. ssrn.com/abstract=1740036.

[4.1] [4.5 SOX] [R] [P] Li, Lingxiang, Francis, Bill B., and Hasan, Iftekhar. 2011b. Firms' Real Earnings Management and Subsequent Stock Price Crash Risk. CAAA Annual Conference 2011 Paper. ssrn.com/abstract=1740044.

[4.1] [5.1] [P] Li, Sherry Fang. 2010. Determinants of Management's Preferences for an Earnings Threshold. *Review of Accounting and Finance,* Vol. 9, No. 1, pp. 33–49.

[5.2] [5.3] [P] Li, Tegang. 2009. Accounting Quality and Corporate Governance. ssrn.com/abstract=1447225.

[4.1] [P] Li, Xi. 2010. Real Earnings Management and Subsequent Stock Returns. ssrn.com/abstract=1679832.

[5.1] [P] Li, Yinghua, Rau, Raghavendra, and Xu, Jin. 2009. The Five Stages of Analyst Careers: Coverage Choices and Changing Influence. ssrn.com/abstract=1460382.

[Review] [P] Libby, Robert and Seybert, Nicholas. 2009. Behavioral Studies of the Effects of Regulation on Earnings Management and Accounting Choice. Accounting, Organizations, and Institutions: Essays for Anthony Hopwood, Oxford University Press; Johnson School Research Paper Series No.#16–09. ssrn.com/abstract=1366425.

[4.2] [P] Lim, Chee Yeow, Ding, David K., and Thong, Tiong Yang. 2008. Firm Diversification and Earnings Management: Evidence from Seasoned Equity Offerings. *Review of Quantitative Finance and Accounting,* Vol. 30, No. 1, pp. 69–92.

[5.3] [5.4] [International] [P] Lin, Jerry W. and Hwang, Mark I. 2010. Audit Quality, Corporate Governance, and Earnings Management: A Meta-Analysis. *International Journal of Auditing,* Vol. 14, No. 1, pp. 57–77.

[4.5 US GAAP IFRS] [Germany] [P] Lin, Steve W.J., Riccardi, William, and Wang, Changjiang (John). 2012. Does Accounting Quality Change Following a Switch from US GAAP to IFRS? Evidence from Germany. *Journal of Accounting and Public Policy,* Vol. 31, No. 6, pp. 641–657.

[4.5 Taiwan SFAS 35] [5.3] [Taiwan] [P] Lin, Wei-Heng and Hsu, Joseph C.S. 2008. Corporate Governance and Asset Impairments: Evidence from the Adoption Choice of SFAS No. 35 in Taiwan. ssrn.com/abstract=1325068.

[4.1] [4.2] [P] Lin, Ying Chou and Yung, Kenneth. 2011. Earnings Management and Corporate Spin-Offs. ssrn.com/abstract=1759594.

[4.1] [5.4] [China] [P] Lin, Z. Jun, Liu, Ming, and Wang, Zhemin. 2009. Market Implications of the Audit Quality and Auditor Switches: Evidence from China. *Journal of International Financial Management and Accounting,* Vol. 20, No. 1, pp. 35–78.

[4.1] [Economics] [B] Linck, James S., Netter, Jeffry M., and Shu, Tao. 2012. Can Managers Use Discretionary Accruals to Ease Financial Constraints? Evidence from Discretionary Accruals Prior to Investment. ssrn.com/abstract=1573147.

[4.6] [5.3] [5.4] [P] Lisic, Ling Lei. 2012. Auditor-Provided Tax Services and Earnings Management in Tax Expense: The Importance of Audit Committees. ssrn.com/abstract=2150374.

[4.4] [Economics] [P] Liu, Yixin, Ning, Yixi, and Davidson, Wallace N. 2010. Earnings Management Surrounding New Debt Issues. *Financial Review,* Vol. 45, No. 3, August, pp. 659–681.

[3.1] [5.2] [China] [Economics] [P] Lo, Agnes W.Y., Wong, Raymond M.K., and Firth, Michael. 2010. Tax, Financial Reporting, and Tunneling Incentives for Income Shifting: An Empirical Analysis of the Transfer Pricing Behavior of Chinese-Listed Companies. *Journal of the American Taxation Association,* Vol. 32, No. 2, Fall, pp. 1–26.

[Introduction] [P] Lo, Kin. 2008. Earnings Management and Earnings Quality. *Journal of Accounting and Economics,* Vol. 45, Nos 2–3, August, pp. 350–357.

[4.1] [Smoothing] [P] Louis, Henock and Sun, Amy X. 2008. Earnings Management and the Post-Earnings Announcement Drift. ssrn.com/abstract=1010103.

[5.1] [P] Louis, Henock, Sun, Amy X., and Urcan, Oktay. 2012. Do Analysts Sacrifice Forecast Accuracy for Informativeness? *Management Science,* Vol. 59, No, 7, pp. 1688–1708.

[5.1] [P] Ma, Guang and Markov, Stanimir. 2012. The Market's Assessment of the Probability of Meeting or Beating the Consensus. ssrn.com/abstract=1734484.

[3] [Organizational design] [P] Maas, Victor S. and Matejka, Michal. 2009. Balancing the Dual Responsibilities of Business Unit Controllers: Field and Survey Evidence. *The Accounting Review,* Vol. 84, No. 4, July, pp. 1233–1253.

[4.6] [Chile, Malaysia] [5.2] [P] Mahenthiran, Sakthi, Blanco, María, and Cademartori, David. 2008. Effects of Accruals, Cash Flows, and Taxes on Earnings Management: Evidence from Chile and Malaysia. ssrn.com/abstract=1272435.

[3] [5.1] [P] Mande, Vivek and Son, Myungsoo. 2012. CEO Centrality and Meeting or Beating Analysts' Earnings Forecasts. *Journal of Business Finance and Accounting,* Vol. 39, Nos 1–2, January, pp. 82–112.[82]

[5.4] [P] Manry, David, Mock, Theodore J., and Turner, Jerry L. 2008. Does Increased Audit Partner Tenure Reduce Audit Quality? *Journal of Accounting, Auditing and Finance,* Vol. 23, No. 4, pp. 553–572.

[4.1] [4.9] [5.1] [Economics] [Smoothing] [Restatements] [P,B] Marciukaityte, Dalia and Park, Jung Chul. 2009. Market Competition and Earnings Management. ssrn.com/abstract=1361905.

[5.3] [P] [Italy] Markarian, Garen and Parbonetti, Antonio. 2009. Financial Interlocks and Earnings Management: Evidence from Italy. ssrn.com/abstract=1396299.

[4.5 SOX] [5.2] [P] Martin, Gregory W. 2011. Trends in Financial Reporting: Shareholder Rights as a Poor Solution to Financial Reporting Abuses. ssrn.com/abstract=1773845.

[4.1] [Brazil] [Smoothing] [P] Martinez, Antonio Lopo. 2005. Earnings Management in Brazil: Motivation and Consequences. ssrn.com/abstract=1652499.

[5.1] [Brazil] [P] Martinez, Antonio Lopo. 2010a. Analysts as Gatekeepers in Brazil: Analysts' Coverage and Earnings Management. ssrn.com/abstract=1595086.[83]

[4.1] [5.4] [Brazil] [R,C] [P] Martinez, Antonio Lopo. 2010b. Corporate Governance, Auditing and Earnings Management through Accounting Choices and Operational Decisions in Brazil. ssrn.com/abstract=1595089.[84]

[5.4] [Brazil] [P] Martinez, Antonio Lopo and Reis, Graciela Mendes Ribeiro. 2010. Audit Firm Rotation and Earnings Management in Brazil. ssrn.com/abstract=1640260.[85]

[4.4] [Brazil] [Smoothing] [B] Martinez, Antonio Lopo and Rivera, Miguel Angel. 2010. Risk Agencies, Bond Ratings and Income Smoothing in Public Bond Offering in Brazil. ssrn.com/abstract=1677470.

[3.1] [4.1] [5.1] [P] McAnally, Mary Lea, Weaver, Connie D., and Srivastava, Anup. 2008. Executive Stock Options, Missed Earnings Targets and Earnings Management. *The Accounting Review,* Vol. 83, No. 1, January, pp. 185–216.

[3.5] [Culture, religion] [R,C] [P] McGuire, Sean T., Omer, Thomas C., and Sharp, Nathan Y. 2012. The Impact of Religion on Financial Reporting Irregularities. *The Accounting Review,* Vol. 87, No. 2, March, pp. 645–673.

McNichols, Maureen F. 2000. Research Design Issues in Earnings Management Studies. *Journal of Accounting and Public Policy,* Vol. 19, Nos 4–5, Winter, pp. 313–345.

[4.3] [4.7] [P] Meisel, Scott I. 2007. Detecting Earnings Management in Bank Merger Targets Using the Modified Jones Model. *Journal of Accounting, Ethics and Public Policy,* Vol. 7, No. 3, p. 301. ssrn.com/abstract=2164504.

[Regulation] [P] Mergenthaler, Richard Dean. 2009. Principles-Based versus Rules-Based Standards and Earnings Management. ssrn.com/abstract=1528524.

[5.1] [P,B] Mirciov, Ioan. 2010. Meeting Analyst Forecasts and Stock Returns. ssrn.com/abstract=1507962.[86]

[4.5 SOX] [5.4] [P] Mitra, Santanu and Hossain, Mahmud. 2010. Auditor's Industry Specialization and Earnings Management of Firms Reporting Internal Control Weaknesses under SOX Section 404. ssrn.com/abstract=1599748.

[4.1] [4.2] [R,C] [P] Mizik, Natalie and Jacobson, Robert. 2007. Earnings Inflation through Accruals and Real Activity Manipulation: Its Prevalence at the Time of an SEO and the Financial Market Consequences. ssrn.com/abstract=1031006.

[3.5] [4.1] [5.3] [Culture, social responsibility, director gender] [Malaysia] [Smoothing] [P] Mohamad, Nor Raihan, Abdullah, Shamsul, Zulkifli Mokhtar, Mohd, and Kamil, Nik Fuad Bin. 2010. The Effects of Board Independence, Board Diversity and Corporate Social Responsibility on Earnings Management. Finance and Corporate Governance Conference 2011 Paper. ssrn.com/abstract=1725925.

[4.5 SOX] [4.6] [5.2] [5.3] [P] Moore, Jared A. 2010. Empirical Evidence on the Impact of External Monitoring on Book-Tax Differences. *Advances in Accounting,* Vol. 28, No. 2, December, pp. 254–269.[87]

[Organizational design] [P] Morris, John J. and Laksmana, Indrarini. 2010. Measuring the Impact of Enterprise Resource Planning (ERP) Systems on Earnings Management. *Journal of Emerging Technologies in Accounting,* Vol. 7, No. 1, November, pp. 47–71.[88]

[4.1] [P] Mosebach, Michael and Simko, Paul J. 2009. Discretionary Accruals and the Emergence of Profitability. ssrn.com/abstract=1360893.

[Theory] [P] Murakami, Yutaro and Shiiba, Atsushi. 2009. Earnings Management in Dynamic Settings. ssrn.com/abstract=1435992.

[5.1] [5.2] [5.3] [Indonesia] [P] Murhadi, Werner Ria. 2010. Good Corporate Governance and Earning Management Practices: An Indonesian Cases. ssrn.com/abstract=1680186.

[Theory] [P] Nan, Lin, 2008. The Agency Problems of Hedging and Earnings Management. *Contemporary Accounting Research,* Vol. 25, No. 3, pp. 859–890. ssrn.com/abstract=1022218.

[5.3] [Korea] [P] Nasev, Julia, Black, Bernard S., and Kim, Woochan. 2012. Does Corporate Governance Affect Earnings Management? Evidence from an Exogenous Shock to Governance in Korea. Northwestern Law and Econ Research Paper 12-13; ECGI – Finance Working Paper. ssrn.com/abstract=2133283.

[3.1] [4.1] [4.5 SOX] [Dividend smoothing] [P] Naveen, D. Daniel, Denis, David J., and Naveen, Lalitha. 2008. Do Firms Manage Earnings to Meet Dividend Thresholds? *Journal of Accounting and Economics,* Vol. 45, No. 1, March, pp. 2–26.

[5.2] [5.3] [Malaysia] [P] Nelson, Sherliza Puat and Jamil, Nurul Nazlia. 2012. An Investigation on the Audit Committee's Effectiveness: The Case for GLCS in Malaysia. Second Accounting Research Education Conference (AREC). ssrn.com/abstract=2020184.

[4.7] [5.4] [Classification] [P] Newton, Ashley N. and Thomas, Wayne B. 2011. Cost Shifting in Nonprofit Hospitals. ssrn.com/abstract=1953837.

[3.1] [5.2] [5.3] [P] Nguyen, Van Thuan and Xu, Li. 2010. The Impact of Dual Class Structure on Earnings Management Activities. *Journal of Business Finance and Accounting,* Vol. 37, Nos 3–4, April/May, pp. 456–485.

[3.5] [Culture, gender] [Finland] [P] Niskanen, Jyrki, Karjalainen, Jukka Tapani, Karjalainen, Jussi, and Niskanen, Mervi. 2011. Earnings Cosmetics and Auditor Gender: Evidence from Finnish Private Firms. ssrn.com/abstract=1773623.

[3.1] [Class actions suits] [P] Oberholzer-Gee, Felix and Wulf, Julie M. 2012. Earnings Management from the Bottom Up: An Analysis of Managerial Incentives below the CEO. Harvard Business School Strategy Unit Working Paper No.12-056. ssrn.com/abstract=1982528.

[4.1] [4.5 IFRS] [Kenya] [Smoothing] [P] Outa, Erick Rading. 2011. The Impact of International Financial Reporting Standards (IFRS) Adoption on the Accounting Quality of Listed Companies in Kenya. ssrn.com/abstract=1976146.[89]

[4.5 IFRS] [Smoothing] [P] [Germany] Paananen, Mari and Lin, Cecilia. 2007. The Development of Accounting Quality of IAS and IFRS Over Time: The Case of Germany. ssrn.com/abstract=1066604.

[M] [P] Pae, J. 2005. Expected Accrual Models: The Impact of Operating Cash Flows and Reversals of Accruals. *Review of Quantitative Finance and Accounting,* Vol. 24, No. 1, February, pp. 5–22.

[3] [4.7] [Survey] [R,C] [P] Parsons, Linda M., Pryor, Charlotte, and Roberts, Andrea Alston. 2012. The Use of Real Ratio Management or Accounting Discretion to Manage Efficiency Ratios: Evidence from Nonprofit Managers. ssrn.com/abstract=2079304.

[5.2] [International] [P] Pathak, Jagdish and Sun, Jerry Y. 2010. International Investor Protection Regime and the Effectiveness of Outside Directorship on the Board: An Empirical Essay. ssrn.com/abstract=1520456.

[M] Paulo, Edilson and Martins, Eliseu A. 2009. A Theoretical and Empirical Analysis of Discretionary Accrual Estimation Models in Earnings Management Research. ssrn.com/abstract=1439836.

[4.1] [5.1] [P] Payne, Jeff L. and Thomas, Wayne B. 2011. The Torpedo Effect: Myth or Reality? *Journal of Accounting, Auditing and Finance,* Vol. 26, No. 2, April, pp. 255–278. ssrn.com/abstract=1321712.

[4.7] [Spain] [Smoothing] [P] Perez, Daniel, Salas-Fumás, Vicente, and Saurina Salas, Jesus. 2011. Do Dynamic Provisions Reduce Income Smoothing Using Loan Loss Provisions? Banco de Espana Working Paper No. 1118. ssrn.com/abstract=1926668.[90]

[4.6] [M] [P] Plesko, George A. 2007. Estimates of the Magnitude of Financial and Tax Reporting Conflicts. ssrn.com/abstract=1001476.

[Complexity of accounting standards] [Restatements] [P] Plumlee, Marlene A. and Yohn, Teri Lombardi. 2009. An Analysis of the Underlying Causes Attributed to Restatements. ssrn.com/abstract=1104189.

[4.4] [5.3] [R] [Italy] [Smoothing] [P] Prencipe, Annalisa, Markarian, Garen, and Pozza, Lorenzo. 2008. Earnings Management in Family Firms: Evidence from R&D Cost Capitalization in Italy. *Family Business Review,* Vol. 21, No. 1, March, pp. 71–88.

[4.4] [Economics] [P] Prevost, Andrew K., Rao, Ramesh P., and Skousen, Christopher J. 2008. Earnings Management and the Cost of Debt. ssrn.com/abstract=1083808.

[4.5 mandatory report of compliance with the Code of "Best" Corporate Practices] [5.2] [Brazil, Mexico] [Smoothing] [P] Price, Richard A., Román, Francisco J., and Rountree, Brian Robert. 2011. The Impact of Governance Reform on Performance and Transparency. *Journal of Financial Economics,* Vol. 99, No. 1, pp. 76–96.[91]

[3.5] [Culture, corporate social responsibility] [International] [P] Prior, Diego, Surroca, Jordi, and Tribo, Josep A. 2008. Are Socially Responsible Managers Really Ethical? Exploring the Relationship between Earnings Management and Corporate Social Responsibility. *Corporate Governance: An International Review,* Vol. 16, No. 3, May, pp. 160–177.

[4.5 IFRS] [Germany] [Smoothing] [P] Pronobis, Paul, Schwetzler, Bernhard, Sperling, Marco O., and Zülch, Henning. 2008. The Development of Earnings Quality in Germany and Its Implication for Further Research: A Quantitative Empirical Analysis of German Listed Companies between 1997 and 2006. ssrn.com/abstract=1266589.

[4.3] [M] [P] Pungaliya, Raunaq S. and Vijh, Anand M. 2009. Do Acquiring Firms Manage Earnings? ssrn.com/abstract=1273464.

[4.1] [P] Qian, Yiming and Yu, Xiaoyun. 2009. Business Cycles, Firm Size and Market Reactions to News. ssrn.com/abstract=891403.

[4.5 IAS 39] [4.7] [I] [Europe] [Smoothing] [P] Quagli, Alberto and Ricciardi, Maurizio. 2010. The IAS 39 October 2008 Amendment as Another Opportunity of Earnings Management: An Analysis of the European Banking Industry. ssrn.com/abstract=1639925.

[3.1] [Italy] [P] Quagli, Alberto, Avallone, Francesco, and Ramassa, Paola. 2006. Stock Option Plans in Italy: Does Earnings Management Matter? ssrn.com/abstract=955469.

[4.1] [5.1] [P] Rajgopal, Shivaram, Shivakumar, Lakshmanan, and Simpson, Ana Vidolovska. 2007. A Catering Theory of Earnings Management. ssrn.com/abstract=991138.

[4.1] [4.9] [Smoothing] [Economics] [B,P] Raman, Kartik and Shahrur, Husayn K. 2008. Relationship-Specific Investments and Earnings Management: Evidence on Corporate Suppliers and Customers. *The Accounting Review,* Vol. 83, No. 4, July, pp. 1041–1081.[92]

[4.5] [4.8] [P] Ramanna, Karthik and Roychowdhury, Sugata. 2010. Elections and Discretionary Accruals: Evidence from 2004. *Journal of Accounting Research,* Vol. 48, No. 2, May, pp. 445–475.

[4.1 industry- and firm-specific characteristics] [Australia] [Smoothing] [D] [P] Rath, Subhrendu and Sun, Lan. 2007. Do Australian Firms Engage in Earnings Management? ssrn.com/abstract=1009121.

[5.2] [P] Rauch, Christian, Umber, Marc P., and Furth, Sven. 2012. Private Equity Shareholder Activism. ssrn.com/abstract=1929159.

[4.9] [I] [P] [Bangladesh] Razzaque, Rusdi Md. Rezaur, Rahman, Muhammad Zahedur, and Salat, Amirus. 2006. Earnings Management: An Analysis on Textile Sector of Bangladesh. *Cost and Management,* Vol. 34, No. 5, September, pp. 5–13.

[4.1] [Economics] [Classification] [P] Robinson, Leslie A. 2010. Do Firms Incur Costs to Avoid Reducing Pre-Tax Earnings? Evidence from the Accounting for Low-Income Housing Tax Credits. *The Accounting Review,* Vol. 85, No. 2, March, pp. 637–669.

Ronen, Joshua. 2002. Post-Enron Reform: Financial Statement Insurance and GAAP Re-visited. *Stanford Journal of Law, Business & Finance,* Vol. 8, No. 1, pp. 1–30.

Ronen, Joshua. 2010. Corporate Audits and How to Fix Them. *Journal of Economic Perspectives.* Vol. 24, No. 2, Spring, pp. 189–210.

Ronen, Joshua and Sadan, Simcha. 1981. *Smoothing Income Numbers: Objectives, Means, and Implications.* Addison-Wesley Publishing Company, Reading, MA.

Ronen, Joshua, and Yaari, Varda Lewinstein. 2002. Incentives for Voluntary Disclosure. *Journal of Financial Markets,* Vol. 5, No. 3, July, pp. 349–390.

Ronen, Tavy and Yaari, Varda. 2002. On the Tension Between Full Revelation and Earnings Management: A Reconsideration of the Revelation Principle. *Journal of Accounting, Auditing and Finance,* Vol. 17, No. 4, pp. 273–294.

Roychowdhury, Sugata. 2006. Earnings Management through Real Activities Manipulation. *Journal of Accounting and Economics,* Vol. 42, No. 3, pp. 335–370.

[4.2] [R,C] [P] Roychowdhury, Sugata, Kothari, S.P., and Mizik, Natalie. 2012. Managing for the Moment: The Role of Real Activity versus Accruals Earnings Management in SEO Valuation. ssrn.com/abstract=1982826.

[4.5 Bursa Malaysia Listing Requirement reforms] [5.3] [5.4] [Malaysia] [P] Sahlan, L.A. 2011. The Malaysian Listing Requirement Reforms and Earnings Management Practices of Public Listed Firms. *The IUP Journal of Corporate Governance,* Vol. 10, No. 2, April, pp. 7–36.

[3.5] [Culture, social] [Europe] [P] Salewski, Marcus and Zülch, Henning. 2012. The Impact of Corporate Social Responsibility (CSR) on Financial Reporting Quality – Evidence from European Blue Chips. HHL Working Paper Series No. 112. ssrn.com/abstract=2141768.

[4.5 auditing standards] [China] [P] Sami, Heibatollah and Zhou, Haiyan. 2008. Do Auditing Standards Improve the Accounting Disclosure and Information Environment of Public Companies? Evidence from the Emerging Markets in China. *International Journal of Accounting,* Vol. 43, No. 2, pp. 139–169.

[3] [5.2] [Spain] [P] Sánchez-Ballesta, Juan Pedro P., and García-Meca, Emma. 2007. Ownership Structure, Discretionary Accruals and the Informativeness of Earnings. *Corporate Governance: An International Review,* Vol. 15, No. 4, pp. 677–691.

[4.2] [India] [P,B] Sapar, Narayan Rao. 2008. Earnings Management and Performance of Indian Equity Rights Issues. 21st Australasian Finance and Banking Conference 2008 Paper. ssrn.com/abstract=1155027.

[5.1] [5.2] [P] Sapra, Haesh. 2010. Discussion of Expected Mispricing: The Joint Influence of Accounting Transparency and Investor Base. *Journal of Accounting Research,* Vol. 48, No. 2, pp. 383–391.

[5.2] [5.3] [India] [P] Sarkar, Jayati, Sarkar, Subrata, and Sen, Kaustav. 2008. Board of Directors and Opportunistic Earnings Management: Evidence from India. *Journal of Accounting, Auditing and Finance,* Vol. 23, No. 4, pp. 517–551.

[3.2] [4.1] [P,B] Sawicki, Julia and Shrestha, Keshab. 2008. Insider Trading and Earnings Management. *Journal of Business Finance and Accounting,* Vol. 35, Nos 3–4, April/May, pp. 331–346.

[3.2] [4.1] [P] Sawicki, Julia and Shrestha, Keshab. 2011. Overvalued Equity and the Accruals Anomaly: Evidence from Insider Trades. ssrn.com/abstract=1804498.

[3.1] [5.2] [5.3] [AAERs] [P] Schrand, Catherine M. and Zechman, Sarah L.C. 2012. Executive Overconfidence and the Slippery Slope to Financial Misreporting. *Journal of Accounting and Economics,* Vol. 53, Nos 1–2, February, pp. 311–329.

[Theory] [P] Schultze, Wolfgang and Weiler, Andreas. 2011. Earnings Management, Time Preferences, and Long Term Decisions. ssrn.com/abstract=1603464.

[M] [P] Seidman, Jeri K. 2010. Interpreting the Book-Tax Income Gap as Earnings Management or Tax Sheltering. McCombs Research Paper Series No. ACC-02-10. ssrn.com/abstract=1564253.

[5.4] [P] Sengupta, Partha and Shen, Min. 2007. Can Accruals Quality Explain Auditors' Decision Making? The Impact of Accruals Quality on Audit Fees, Going Concern Opinions and Auditor Change. ssrn.com/abstract=1178282.

[4.1] [4.3] [4.9] [Economics] [Smoothing] [P] Servaes, Henri and Tamayo, Ane Miren. 2009. Intra-Industry Effects of Control Threats on Investment, Financing, and Financial Reporting Quality. ssrn.com/abstract=1092796.

[M] [P] Shan, Yaowen, Taylor, Stephen L., and Walter, Terry S. 2010. Errors in Estimating Unexpected Accruals in the Presence of Large Changes in Net External Financing. ssrn.com/abstract=1572164.

[5.2] [Asian countries] [Smoothing] [P] Shen, Chung-Hua and Chih, Hsiang-Lin. 2007. Earnings Management and Corporate Governance in Asia's Emerging Markets. *Corporate Governance: An International Review,* Vol. 15, No. 5, September, pp. 999–1021.

[M] [P] Shih, Michael S.H. 2011. ROA-Matched Discretionary Accruals Models vs. the Original Jones Type Models: A Cost and Benefit Analysis. ssrn.com/abstract=1836208.

[4.1] [Japan] [P] Shuto, Akinobu. 2009. Earnings Management to Exceed the Threshold: A Comparative Analysis of Consolidated and Parent-Only Earnings. *Journal of International Financial Management and Accounting,* Vol. 20, No. 3, Autumn, pp. 199–239.

[4.1] [5.2] [Japan] [Smoothing] [P,B] Shuto, Akinobu and Iwasaki, Takuya. 2012. Stable Shareholdings, the Decision Horizon Problem, and Patterns of Earnings Management. ssrn.com/abstract=2052243.

[4.2] [Classification] [P] Siu, David T.L. and Faff, Robert W. 2012. Management of Core Earnings Using Classification Shifting around Seasoned Equity Offerings. ssrn.com/abstract=1928578.

[3.1] [4.5 SOX] [5.1] [5.4] [R,C] [P] Sohn, Byungcherl Charlie. 2011a. The Effect of Accounting Comparability on Earnings Management. ssrn.com/abstract=1927131.

[4.5 SOX] [5.4] [R] [P] Sohn, Byungcherl Charlie. 2011b. Do Auditors Care About Real Earnings Management in Their Audit Fee Decisions? ssrn.com/abstract=1899189.

[4.5 FAS 159] [5.7] [I] [P] Song, Chang Joon. 2008. An Evaluation of FAS 159 Fair Value Option: Evidence from the Banking Industry. ssrn.com/abstract=1279502.

[4.1] [Foreign listing] [Restatements] [P] Srinivasan, Suraj, Wahid, Aida Sijamic, and Yu, Gwen. 2012. Admitting Mistakes: Home Country Effect on the Reliability of Restatement Reporting. ssrn.com/abstract=2065892.

[4.1] [4.5 SOP 97-2] [5.1] [I] [P] Srivastava, Anup. 2011. Selling-Price Estimates in Revenue Recognition and Earnings Informativeness. ssrn.com/abstract=1078584.

[4.6] [5.2] [5.3] [Finland] [Economics] [P] Steijvers, Tensie and Niskanen, Mervi. 2011. Tax Aggressive Behaviour in Private Family Firms – The Effect of the CEO and Board of Directors. ssrn.com/abstract=1937651.

[Theory] [P] Stratopoulos, Theophanis C. and Vance, Thomas W. 2009. Uncertainty and the Decision to Manage Earnings. CAAA Annual Conference 2009 Paper. ssrn.com/abstract=1328479.

[Theory] [P] Strobl, Günter. 2009. Earnings Manipulation and the Cost of Capital. ssrn.com/abstract=1364282.

[M] [P] Stubben, Stephen. 2009. Discretionary Revenues as a Measure of Earnings Management. ssrn.com/abstract=1135811.

[Theory] [P] Sun, Bo. 2011. Limited Market Participation and Asset Prices in the Presence of Earnings Management. FRB International Finance Discussion Paper No. 1019. ssrn.com/abstract=1893042.

[5.1] [International] [P] Sun, Jerry Y. 2009. Governance Role of Analyst Coverage and Investor Protection. *Financial Analysts Journal,* Vol. 65, No. 6, pp. 52–64.

[Review] Sun, Lan and Rath, Subhrendu. 2010. Earnings Management Research: A Review of Contemporary Research Methods. *Global Review of Accounting and Finance.* Vol. 1, No. 1, September, pp. 121–135

[4.1] [Economics] [P] Sun, Qian, Yung, Kenneth, and Rahman, Hamid. 2012. Earnings Quality and Corporate Cash Holdings. *Accounting and Finance,* Vol. 52, No. 2, pp. 543–571.

Talley, Eric. 2006. Cataclysmic Liability Risk among Big 4 Auditors. *Columbia Law Review,* Vol. 106, No. 7, pp. 1641–1697.

[4.2] [4.6] [5.2] [M] [China] [P] Tang, Tanya Y.H. and Firth, Michael. 2011. Can Book-Tax Differences Capture Earnings Management and Tax Management? Empirical Evidence from China. *The International Journal of Accounting,* Vol. 46, No. 2, June, pp. 175–204.

[4.1] [R] [Economics] [P] Taylor, Gary K. and Xu, Zhaohui Randall. 2010. Consequences of Real Earnings Management on Subsequent Operating Performance. *Research in Accounting Regulation,* Vol. 22, No. 2, pp. 128–132.

[Review] [Australia] [3.1] [5.3] [5.4] [P] Teo, Eu-Jin. 2007. Some Thoughts on Performance-Based Pay, Earnings Management and Corporate Law from an Antipodean Perspective. *Corporate Ownership and Control,* Vol. 4, No. 3, pp. 173–195.

Teoh, Siew Hong, Welch, Ivo, and Wong, T.J. 1998a. Earnings Management and the Underperformance of Seasoned Equity Offerings. *Journal of Financial Economics,* Vol. 50, No. 1, October, pp. 63–99.

Teoh, Siew Hong, Welch, Ivo, and Wong, T.J. 1998b. Earnings Management and the Long-Run Market Performance of Initial Public Offerings. *Journal of Finance,* Vol. 53, No. 6, December, pp. 1935–1974.

[3.1] [Theory] [Japan] [P] Teshima, Nobuyuki and Shuto, Akinobu. 2008. Managerial Ownership and Earnings Management: Theory and Empirical Evidence from Japan. *Journal of International Financial Management and Accounting,* Vol. 19, No. 2, Summer, pp. 107–132.

[5.1] [Chapter 9][93] [P] Tian, Yao, Courteau, Lucie, and Kao, Jennifer L. 2011. The Impact of Earnings Management on the Performance of Earnings-Based Valuation Models. CAAA Annual Conference 2011 Paper. ssrn.com/abstract=1736346.[94]

[3] [4.9] [5.2] [International] [Economics] [P] Tinaikar, Surjit and Xue, Song. 2009. Product Market Competition and Earnings Management: Some International Evidence. ssrn.com/abstract=1466319.

[3.1] [China] [P] Ting, Wei, Yen, Sin-Hui, and Huang, Sheng-Shih. 2009. Top Management Compensation, Earnings Management and Default Risk: Insights from the Chinese Stock Market. *The International Journal of Business and Finance Research,* Vol. 3, No. 1, pp. 31–46.

[5.2] [Brazil] [Smoothing] [P] Torres, Damiana, Bruni, Adriano Lea, Martinez, Antonio Lopo, and Rivera, Miguel Angel. 2010. Ownership and Control Structure, Corporate Governance and Income Smoothing in Brazil. ssrn.com/abstract=1651991.

[Theory] [P] Trueman, Brett and Versano, Tsahi. 2011. The Impact of Analyst Industry Expertise on Market Prices. ssrn.com/abstract=1762131.

[4.1] [4.4] [P] Ujah, Nacasius U. and Brusa, Jorge O. 2011. Earnings Management, Financial Leverage, and Cash Flow Volatility: Do Economic Conditions Matter? ssrn.com/abstract=1929550.

[4.7] [Brazil, China, India, Mexico, Nigeria, Russia, South Africa] [P] Ujah, Nacasius U. and Okafor, Collins Emeka. 2011. Is Bank Performance What It Is, in Light of Bank Earnings Management and Bank Market Structure? – Evidence from the Emerging and the Frontier Markets. ssrn.com/abstract=1930634.

[3.5] [Culture, gender] [P] Vähämaa, Emilia and Vähämaa, Sami. 2010. Female Executives and Earnings Management. *Managerial Finance,* Vol. 36, No. 7, pp. 629–645.

[4.7] [P] Vansant, Brian A. 2011. The Effect of Regulatory Pressures on Earnings Management by Nonprofit Hospitals. AAA 2011 Management Accounting Section (MAS) Meeting Paper. ssrn.com/abstract=1658483.

[3.1] [3.2] [P] Veenman, David, Hodgson, Allan C., Van Praag, Bart J., and Zhang, Wei. 2011. Decomposing Executive Stock Option Exercises: Relative Information and Incentives to Manage Earnings. *Journal of Business Finance and Accounting,* Vol. 38, Nos 5–6, pp. 536–573.

[4.1] [4.5 SOX] [Theory] [P] Vojtech, Cindy M. 2012. The Relationship between Information Asymmetry and Dividend Policy. FEDS Working Paper No. 2012-13. ssrn.com/abstract=2051018.

[4.1] [4.6] [P] Wagener, Tim and Watrin, Christoph. 2012. GAAP ETR Management to Beat Relevant Thresholds. ssrn.com/abstract=2121373.

[5.2] [China] [P] Wang, Liu and Yung, Kenneth. 2011. Do State Enterprises Manage Earnings More than Privately Owned Firms? The Case of China. *Journal of Business Finance and Accounting,* Vol. 38, Nos 7–8, pp. 794–812.

[4.1] [5.2] [P] [China] [Restatements] [P] Wang, Xia and Wu, Min. 2009. Quality of Financial Reporting in China. ssrn.com/abstract=1653278.

[4.6] [Europe] [P] Watrin, Christoph, Ebert, Nadine, and Thomsen, Martin. 2012. One-Book versus Two-Book System: Learnings from Europe. 2012 American Taxation Association Midyear Meeting: JATA Conference. ssrn.com/abstract=2001714.

[3.1] [5.3] [5.4] [Germany] [P] Watrin, Christoph, Pott, Christiane, and Tebben, Tobias. 2009. Outside Director Independence, Auditor Independence and Executive Cash Bonus Compensation. ssrn.com/abstract=1518317.

[M] [Poland] [P] Welc, Jacek. 2011a. Corporate Assets Turnover as the Proxy for Earnings-Quality on the Polish Stock Market. Second International Accounting and Business Conference Proceedings, Johor Bahru, Malaysia. ssrn.com/abstract=1784189.

[4.1] [Poland] [P] Welc, Jacek. 2011b. Are Polish Public Companies "Cooking the Books"? The Evidence from Annual Earnings Thresholds. *International Business and Economics Research Journal,* Vol. 10, No. 3, pp. 83–90.

[4.7] [5.2] [I] [P] Wen, Yuan and Zhang, Rongrong. 2012. Institutional Investors and Earnings Management by Bank Holding Companies. ssrn.com/abstract=2142143.

[3.5] [4.7] [5.3] [I] [Netherlands] [P] Westerduin, Peter, Wouterson, Jerry, and Langendijk, Henk P.A.J. 2012. Pension Funds and the Required Minimum Funding Ratio: A Research on Earnings Management in Dutch Pension Funds. ssrn.com/abstract=2163732.

[M] [P] White, Hal D. 2012. Accruals, Deferrals, Cash Flows and Earnings: Articulation Implications for Earnings Management Models and a Suggested Alternative. ssrn.com/abstract=2038813.

[3.3] [5.3] [Australia] [P] Wilson, Mark David and Wang, Liang Wui. 2010. Earnings Management Following Chief Executive Officer Changes: The Effect of Contemporaneous Chairperson and Chief Financial Officer Appointments. *Accounting and Finance,* Vol. 50, No. 2, June, pp. 447–480.

[3.3] [5.1] [Australia] [P] Wilson, Mark David and Wu, Yi (Ava). 2011. Do Publicly Signalled Earnings Management Incentives Affect Analyst Forecast Accuracy? *Abacus,* Vol. 47, No. 3, pp. 315–342.

[5.1] [P,B] Wolfe, Mindy. 2012. The Capitalization of Intangibles and Managerial Information. CAAA Annual Conference 2012 Paper. ssrn.com/abstract=1985664.

[4.2] [5.2] [R,C] [Restatements] [P] Wongsunwai, Wan. 2011. The Effect of External Monitoring on Accruals-Based and Real Earnings Management: Evidence from Venture-Backed Initial Public Offerings. *Contemporary Accounting Research,* Vol. 30, No. 1, Spring, pp. 296–324.

[3.1] [4.1] [Economics] [P] Wu, Yan and Jones, Robert A. 2010. Executive Compensation, Earnings Management and Shareholder Litigation. *Review of Quantitative Finance and Accounting,* Vol. 35, No. 1, July, pp. 1–20.

[Theory] [P] Xin, Baohua. 2007. Earnings Forecast, Earnings Management, and Asymmetric Price Response. AAA 2008 Financial Accounting and Reporting Section (FARS) Paper. ssrn.com/abstract=1013461.

[5.1] [Economics] [R] [P] Xu, Zhaohui Randall and Taylor, Gary K. 2007. Economic Cost of Earnings Management through Stock Repurchases. ssrn.com/abstract=982165.

[Review] [P] Xu, Zhaohui Randall, Taylor, Gary K., and Dugan, Michael T. 2007. Review of Real Earnings Management Literature. *Journal of Accounting Literature,* Vol. 26, pp. 195–228.

[Review] [P] Yang, Jingjing, Chi, Jing, and Young, Martin R. 2012. A Review of Earnings Management in China and Its Implications. *Asian-Pacific Economic Literature,* Vol. 26, No. 1, pp. 84–92.

[5.4] [Japan] [P] Yazawa, Kenichi. 2011. Does Audit Partner Rotation Enhance Audit Quality? Evidence from Japan. 23rd Asian-Pacific Conference on International Accounting Issues 2011. ssrn.com/abstract=1839363.

Ye, Jianming. 2006. Accounting Accruals and Tests of Earnings Management. Working paper, Baruch College.

[4.1] [Economics] [R] [P] Yen, Airu. 2008. The Influence of Myopic R&D Investment Decisions on Earnings Growth. ssrn.com/abstract=1266345.[95]

[Theory] [P] Yim, Andrew. 2012. Earnings Distribution Discontinuity from a Continuous Model of Earnings Management. ssrn.com/abstract=2061381.

[Theory] [P] Yu, Chia-Feng. 2012. CEO Turnover, Earnings Management, and Big Bath. ssrn.com/abstract=2165123.

[3.2] [5.1] [P] Yu, Wen and Bricker, Robert J. 2007. Earnings Valuation and Insider Trading. ssrn.com/abstract=1014252.[96]

[Economics] [R,C] Zang, Amy Y. 2012. Evidence on the Trade-Off between Real Activities Manipulation and Accrual-Based Earnings Management. *The Accounting Review,* Vol. 87, No. 2, pp. 675–703.

[4.1] [5.1] [P] Zarowin, Paul and Cohen, Daniel A. 2012. Do "Firms Lean Against the Wind"? Earnings Management and Stock Market Returns. ssrn.com/abstract=1987153.[97]

[4.4] [4.5 FIN 46] [Economics] [P] Zechman, Sarah L.C. 2010. The Relation between Voluntary Disclosure and Financial Reporting: Evidence from Synthetic Leases. *Journal of Accounting Research,* Vol. 48, No. 3, June, pp. 725–765.

[4.5 SOX] [5.3] [P] Zhang, Wei, Zhou, Jian, and Lobo, Gerald J. 2007. The Impact of Corporate Governance on Discretionary Accrual Changes around the Sarbanes-Oxley Act. ssrn.com/abstract=1011844.

[3.5] [Culture] [International] [Smoothing] [P] Zhang, Xu. 2010. Individual-Collectivism, Private Benefits of Control, and Earnings Management: A Cross-Culture Comparison. ssrn.com/abstract=1572272.[98]

[4.5 SOX] [5.1] [5.2] [R,C] [Classification] [P] Zhao, Jianxin (Donny). 2011. The Association between Corporate Governance and Earnings Surprises Games. Finance and Corporate Governance Conference 2010 Paper. ssrn.com/abstract=1534005.

[3] [5.3] [AAERs] [P] Zhao, Yijiang and Chen, Kung. 2008. Staggered Boards and Earnings Management. *The Accounting Review,* Vol. 83, No. 1, September, pp. 1347–1381.

[3] [4.1] [R] [P,B] Zhao, Yijiang, Chen, Kung, Zhang, Yinqi, and Davis, Michael. 2012. Takeover Protection and Managerial Myopia: Evidence from Real Earnings Management. *Journal of Accounting and Public Policy,* Vol. 31, No. 1, January–February, pp. 109–135.

[4.5 SOP 97-2] [I] [R,C] [P] Zhong, Ke, Welker, Robert B., and Gribbin, Donald W. 2010. Method-Shifting in Aggressive Earnings Reporting: The Case of the US Software Industry's Response to New US Regulation. *Journal of Business Finance and Accounting,* Vol. 37, Nos 7–8, July/August, pp. 792–814.

[4.5 SOX] [P] Zhou, Jian. 2008. Financial Reporting after the Sarbanes–Oxley Act: Conservative or Less Earnings Management? *Research in Accounting Regulations,* Vol. 20, pp. 187–192.

[3.4] [4.1] [5.2] [D] [R,C] [P] Zhu, Julie Lei, Qian, Jun, and Li, Xi. 2012. Do Investors Understand "Operational Engineering" before Management Buyouts? ssrn.com/abstract=2022091.

[4.2] [5.2] [5.4] [I] [P] Zhu, Yuan Wei, Ong, Seow Eng, and Yeo, Wee Yong. 2010. Do REITs Manipulate Their Financial Results around Seasoned Equity Offerings? Evidence from US Equity REITs. *Journal of Real Estate Finance and Economics,* Vol. 40, No. 4, pp. 412–445.

[5.2] [5.3] [China] [P] Zou, Hong, Wong, Sonia, Shum, Clement, Xiong, Jun, and Yan, Jun. 2008. Controlling–Minority Shareholder Incentive Conflicts and Directors' and Officers' Liability Insurance: Evidence from China. *Journal of Banking and Finance,* Vol. 32, No. 12, pp. 2636–2645.

[5.2] [P] [International] Zouari, Anis and Rebaï, Iskandar. 2009. Institutional Ownership Differences and Earnings Management: A Neural Networks Approach. *Research Journal of Finance and Economics,* Vol. 34, December, pp. 42–55.

Appendix

The impact of SOX on EM[i]

Study	Sample and findings	Did SOX reduce EM?
Ang (2011)	217 domestic *Fortune 500* companies filing internal control financial reports from 2000–2006, from Mergent Online database. 60 firms had only internal control before SOX. The market value of sample firms increases after SOX.	Yes
Aono and Guan (2008)	10,413 observations for the pre-SOX period (2000–2001) and 9,809 observations for the post-SOX period (2003–2004), taken from S&P Research Insight database, chosen to enable a comparison of the distribution of the number zero as the second digit of net income between the pre- and the post-SOX periods. The practice of rounding earnings upwards has decreased since SOX.	Yes
Banko, Frye, Wang, and Whyte (2012)	10,228 observations from S&P 1500, with annual and third and fourth quarterly data from 1996–2005, with managers' entrenchment index and director data obtained from Investor Responsibility Research Center (IRRC) and RiskMetrics. The RiskMetrics database also provides the number of shareholder proposals voted on at the annual meeting. The positive returns preceding an annual meeting are lower after SOX. Abnormal accruals in firms with entrenched managers are positive in the two quarters preceding the annual meeting and are negative in the two quarters following it. Abnormal accruals are lower after SOX.	Yes
Bhojraj, Sengupta, and Zhang (2009)	5,006 firms with restructuring charges on Compustat from 2001–2006. SOX was not an improvement because it increased investors' uncertainty about whether restructuring is a means of pernicious EM or an economically optimal decision.	No
Boubakri and Ghouma (2008)	1,018 American corporations with bond issues from 1995–2006 drawn from the Fixed Investment Securities database.	Yes. See Section 4.4.
Carcello, Hollingsworth, and Klein (2006)	283 non-financial domestic firms from *Compact D/SEC* with fiscal years ending between July 15, 2003, and December 31, 2003, where financial expertise of the members of the audit committee is obtained by reading the biographical sketch of each member in the proxy statement and categorized by whether the director is currently or was previously engaged as a CPA, CFO, controller, treasurer, or vice president of finance. SOX's strengthening of the audit committee is valuable in reducing pernicious EM.[ii]	Yes

(continued)

Study	Sample and findings	Did SOX reduce EM?
Carter (2011)	579 Canadian and 2,324 US firms/quarters from 2000–2004. SOX impacts capital structure. Post-SOX, US firms have higher debt and tend to issue less stock than Canadian firms.	Earnings management prior to SOX is used as a control.
Caylor (2010)	15,193 (7,284) firm-year observations for the loss and earnings decrease (earnings surprise) benchmarks for fiscal years 2001–2005 to test for gross accounts receivable, and 4,846 (2,664) firm-year observations for the loss and earnings decrease (earnings surprise) benchmarks for fiscal years 2001–2005 for testing deferred revenues. Firms used discretion in deferred revenue before SOX but not afterwards.	Yes
Chambers and Payne (2011)	18,451 company-years, representing 4,439 companies, from 1998–2001 and 2003–2006. Accruals persistence increased after SOX.	Yes
Chan, Farrell, and Lee (2008)	149 internal-control-weakness (ICW) firms and 908 non-ICW firms whose 10-K filings cover the fiscal year ended December 31, 2004. Since firms reporting ICW manage earnings more, Section 404 of SOX is likely to reduce EM.	Yes
Cohen, Dey, and Lys (2007)	87,217 firm-year observations (8,157 firms) from 1987–2005 for firms that meet or beat threshold. Cosmetic (real) EM decreased (increased).	Yes and no
Davidson, Jiraporn, Ning, and Sakr (2011)	197 MBOs that were not preceded by a takeover attempt from 1980–1999 and a sample of 46 MBOs from 2002–2003 (after SOX).	Yes. See Section 4.3.
Davis, Soo, and Trompeter (2009)	23,748 firm-year observations from 1988–2006 with data on auditor's tenure. The positive relationship between tenure and EM (positive discretionary accruals) disappears after SOX.	Yes
Frank, Lynch, Rego, and Zhao (2011)	49,944 non-regulated, non-financial firm-years (8,499 firms) from 1994–2007. SOX dampens previously aggressive corporate cultures.	Yes
Ghosh, Marra, and Moon (2010)	9,290 firm-year observations from S&P 1500 from 1998–2005 with governance information on board characteristics (composition, size, and structure) and audit committee characteristics (composition, size, and activity) from RiskMetrics (financial expertise, stock ownership, and tenure) and *Corporate Library* (formerly IRRC). The correlation of EM with board size and audit committee characteristics (size, activity, and tenure) is weaker after SOX, but the overall level of EM has not declined since SOX.	Yes and no
Graham, Hanlon, Shevlin, and Shroff(2012)	Survey responses from nearly 600 corporate tax executives on firms' incentives and disincentives for tax planning. 28% of respondents who began using different audit and tax service providers due to SOX indicate that they would limit their tax planning because of the additional scrutiny from a service provider that is not their auditor.	Yes

Hong, Huseynov, and Zhang (2012)	Over 35,522 firm-year observations from 1989–2010, with sell-side analyst data from the Institutional Brokers Estimate System (I/B/E/S) database. Before (after) SOX, absolute discretionary accruals reduce analysts' following with the same (twice as much) impact as abnormal cash flows – a measure of real EM.	Yes
Hutton, Marcus, and Tehranian (2008)	40,882 firm-years from 1991–2005 (the sample includes 43 of the 49 Fama/French industry). Pernicious EM does not predict stock-price crashes in the post-SOX period.	Yes
Iliev (2009)	301 companies with 2004 public float between $50 and $100 million in 2004. Section 404 led to conservative reported earnings, but SOX compliance reduced the market value of small firms.	Yes and no
Jha (2011)	12,196 observations from US firms from 1989–2005 with known social capital (level of altruism, honesty, and social norms) given zip code. EM declined after SOX, especially for firms with low social capital.	Yes
Keskek, Myers, Omer, and Sharp (2011)	5,649 firm-years from 1996–2009 drawing their annual management earnings forecasts from First Call's Company Issued Guidance database. Accrual-related optimism in management earnings forecasts (i.e., firms both manage earnings upwards and issue overly optimistic management forecasts) disappears after SOX.	Yes
Krishnan, Raman, Yang, and Yu (2011)	12,430 firm-years for meeting expectations of analysts, 15,437 for "avoid a loss" analyses, and 14,874 for "avoid an earnings decline" analyses from 2000–2007 (excluding 2002), with data on social ties between the CFO/CEO and the board obtained from BoardEx. EM declined after SOX but CFOs/CEOs picked more socially connected directors after SOX.	Yes and no
Krishnan, Sun, Wang, and Yang (2011)	8,513 firm-year observations consisting of 141 auditor resignations and 8,372 auditor-retaining observations, from August 1, 2002, to 2008, available in Audit Analytics database, for clients of Big 4 auditors. Auditors price EM risk by charging more, and when the riskiness of the client is higher, they resign. However, the analysis starts after SOX enactment.	No answer
Krishnan, Su, and Zhang (2011)	1,768 firms and 7,072 observations from Audit Analytics database in the fiscal years 2000, 2001, 2004, and 2005, with data on fees and non-audit services. The positive correlation between aggressive and non-audit services is weaker after SOX.	Yes
Lee, Xie, and Zhou (2012)	2,880 IPO firms from 1991–2005. The finding that IPO firms engage in less EM if they are underwritten by prestigious investment bankers is not sensitive to the passage of SOX, and the finding that EM is lower after SOX is attributed to changing objectives of venture capitalists.	No

(continued)

(continued)

Study	Sample and findings	Did SOX reduce EM?
Li, Francis, and Hasan (2011)	44,932 firm-years from 1994–2009. On the one hand, the predictive power of real EM on stock price crash in the margin tripled after SOX. On the other hand, the predictive power of accrual-based EM on stock price crash in the margin is halved after SOX.	Yes and no
Martin (2011)	20,953 firm-years for GIM-index and 23,322 firm-years for E-index from 1990–2009, where these shareholder rights measures are drawn from IRRC and RiskMetrics database available on WRDS. SOX may not reduce the positive relationships between stronger shareholders' rights and EM magnitude measured by absolute discretionary accruals.	No
Mitra and Hossain (2010)	4,538 firms with effective internal controls and 1,064 firms with ineffective internal controls from 2004–2006. When the auditor has strong industry expertise, Section 404 is less effective in mitigating EM – that is, SOX effectiveness is conditional on the auditor's capabilities.	Conditional yes
Moore (2010)	7,070 firm-year observations for 1,161 firms from 1998–2009 with data from Compustat, ExecuComp, RiskMetrics (ISS) Directors databases, and Thomson-Reuters Institutional Holdings (13F) database for institutional holdings. Post-SOX, the negative association between institutional holding and book-tax difference is stronger.	Yes
Naveen, Denis, and Naveen (2008)	16,922 firm-years from 1992–2005 with data on ExecuComp (i.e., S&P 1500 firms). The pressure to use EM after SOX to pay dividends is weaker.	Yes
Sohn (2011a)	32,211 firm-year observations (4,486 firms) from 1980–2009, drawn from CRSP, I/B/E/S, Thomson-Reuters for institutional ownership data, ExecuComp, and audit fee data from Audit Analytics.	Similar to Cohen et al. (2007) above.
Sohn (2011b)	14,678 firm-years from 2000–2008 with data from Compustat and CRSP, and audit fee, auditor, and internal control deficiencies drawn from Audit Analytics. The positive relation between real EM and audit fees is stronger (weaker) than the positive relation between accrual-based EM and audit fees in the post- (pre-) SOX period.	Unclear
Vojtech (2012)	12,334 firm-years from 1998–2005 drawn from Compustat and CRSP. After SOX, the negative relationship between (costly) dividend paying and EM is weaker.	No
Zhang, Zhou, and Lobo (2007)	963 firm-years from 2000–2002 drawn from the IRRC database. The effect of SOX in reducing pernicious EM is weaker for firms with strong governance.	Yes
Zhao (2011)	5,179 firm-year observations (of meeting/beating analysts' expectations) from 1998–2006 drawn from RiskMetrics, Compustat, Thomson Financial I/B/E/S, Thomson-Reuters Institutional Holdings (13F), and ExecuComp.	Yes
Zhou (2008)	15,852 observations (7,926 in the pre-SOX period and 7,926 in the post-SOX period).[iii]	Yes

13

Agency theory

Usefulness and implications for financial accounting

Alfred Wagenhofer

1 Introduction

Financial accounting is a heavily regulated area in modern economies. Financial accounting standards have grown steadily and describe in great detail the financial statement representation of transactions that firms undertake and events that affect their net worth. The financial statements are audited by independent accounting experts who attest that they present fairly the financial condition of the firm. Auditors themselves are subject to auditing standards and to oversight by their peers and government institutions. The audit committee in the board of directors oversees the accounting processes and the audit of the financial statements. Many countries operate accounting enforcement institutions to ensure compliance of the audited financial statements with the rules and to impose sanctions. Finally, investors and other parties can sue firms before court if they made decisions based on erroneous financial information by the firm.

These detailed requirements, checks, and double checks are in place to assure the credibility of financial information. Agency theory explains the existence of these institutions and why credibility of information is so important that substantial resources are spent to ensure its integrity. The basic element of agency theory is the existence of an agency relationship, which is pervasive in business. Essentially every business contract creates an agency relationship between the contracting parties. Agency relationships are characterized by two main ingredients: (potential) conflicts of interest between the parties and information asymmetries between them. Contracting costs, including the costs of information, preclude complete contracts that would prescribe in detail the desired outcomes conditional on every conceivable future circumstance. Agency costs arise because each of the contracting parties aims at maximizing its own expected utility under the arrangement, which is often referred to as "opportunistic" behavior. Financial accounting produces information that is useful for contracting and, thus, helps to reduce agency costs and to improve the efficiency of contracts.

The term agency theory is often used interchangeably with terms such as economic theory of the firm, contract theory, and positive accounting theory, albeit there are some differences. Economic theory relates to the micro-economic theory of the firm, which provides the base economy in which agency problems arise, and to information economics as a special area. Contract theory is concerned with optimal contracting in more general settings than business and finance, and positive accounting theory describes a mostly empirical-based paradigm that derives its hypotheses from agency theory. While many disciplines in business address agency problems, accounting focuses on the role of asymmetric information and the design and features of accounting information in an agency setting.

This chapter provides a non-technical overview and a discussion of agency theory in financial accounting theory. It embodies both the analytical agency theory, which generates rigorous statements of the use of accounting information in optimal contracting, and the empirical agency theory, which examines economic effects of accounting standards predicted by agency theory.

The rest of the chapter is organized as follows. Section 2 starts with a description of agency problems in firms that are at the core of financial accounting and then puts financial accounting in perspective by describing mechanisms to mitigate agency problems. In section 3, I discuss analytical agency models in more detail, but still informally, to present the breadth of different uses of accounting information in agency settings. The application of agency theory to fundamental conceptual issues in financial accounting is the focus of section 4, which examines contentious issues in the Conceptual Framework of the International Accounting Standards Board (IASB), including stewardship versus valuation objectives, fair values, and conservatism in accounting. A brief look at the politics of standard setting from an agency perspective concludes this section. In section 5, I discuss the empirical testing of agency predictions. Section 6 critiques agency theory mainly regarding its main assumptions about individual decision makers, and section 7 concludes.

There exists a large body of literature on agency theory. This paper makes no attempt to cover this broad literature but uses specific examples to highlight main features of agency theory in financial accounting theory. Lambert (2001) provides a survey of analytical agency theory, and Christensen and Demski (2003) and Christensen and Feltham (2003, 2005) are comprehensive books based on analytical agency theory. Watts and Zimmerman (1986) is a standard reference for the empirical branch of agency theory; and Fields, Lys, and Vincent (2001); Kothari, Ramanna, and Skinner (2010); and Shivakumar (2013) survey the empirical literature.

2 Agency relationships in firms

2.1 Agency problems

Agency theory has been developed on the basis of the property rights theory (Coase 1937) and the theory of the firm, which views firms as institutions that "serve as a nexus for a set of contracting relationships among individuals" (Jensen and Meckling 1976, p. 310). Firms exist because in many settings contracts can be written more efficiently with the firm as an intermediary between parties than in markets in which all parties contract individually. The theory explains existing institutions and arrangements as those that minimize the contracting costs of doing business. Contracting costs include a wide array of direct cash outflows or opportunity costs from contracting, such as transaction costs, information and monitoring costs, bonding costs, contract enforcement costs, opportunity costs of dysfunctional decisions, negotiation and renegotiation costs, or bankruptcy costs.

Agency problems arise in an agency relationship if it is too costly (or even impossible) to write a contract that covers each and every conceivable circumstance. In circumstances not covered by contract requirements, the parties make decisions that maximize their expected utility regardless of the effect on the welfare of the other parties. The most common agency problem results from the separation of ownership and control of a firm (Fama and Jensen 1983). Growing firms are in need of external financing, and many investors are unable or unwilling to participate in the management of the firm, so they delegate business decisions to a manager (or an executive board) to make decisions on their behalf. Ownership is associated with the residual claims in the firm, which creates powerful incentives for owners to make efficient decisions. As long as the manager holds less than 100 percent of the firm's stocks, incentives and the personal inclinations of the manager lead to decisions that can deviate from those the owners would prefer. For example, the manager may under-supply effort or over-consume perks. Management compensation contracts that are contingent on firm performance are used to align management incentives with those of the shareholders. However, such contracts and other measures are usually not a perfect means to resolve agency conflicts.

Another important agency problem arises between owners and creditors. Creditors provide debt financing to the firm, which usually includes a fixed claim to repayment of the face value of the debt plus interest.[1] A standard debt contract creates a conflict of interest between owners and creditors, as debt capital has the features of a written put option and equity capital those of a call option. Thus, owners have incentives to over-invest in risky projects, to sell off assets and distribute the proceeds, and to make similar dysfunctional decisions.

Figure 13.1 depicts these two agency relationships, both of which arise from financing. However, agency problems are not limited to financing firms. Customer and supplier relationships are another source of agency problems. Suppliers know better than their customers the quality of the products and services they provide. Since both parties want to maximize their respective profits, a sourcing contract naturally generates a conflict of interest between supplier and customer. The agency problem can become so severe that the market breaks down (as in the "market for lemons," Akerlof 1970). Another friction is the hold-up problem, in which the supplier invests an inefficient level of upfront capacity if its cost is (at least partly) sunk, in order to avoid being subsequently exploited by the customer.

Besides arising from voluntary contracts, agency relationships arise from legal requirements, such as tax collection, prudential regulation, rate regulation, and other regulatory actions. Just like contracts, laws contain provisions that determine the rights and obligations of the government institution and of the firms that are subject to the regulation. Regulation provides incentives for firms to adapt their economic decisions to minimize the disadvantage (maximize the

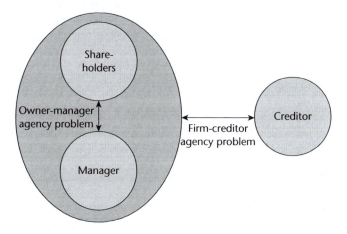

Figure 13.1   Agency problems from financing

advantage) from the requirements. For example, in order to minimize their income tax burden, firms may choose to relocate business activities to other business or geographical areas if the tax savings outweigh the costs of doing so. The effect of the tax on economic decisions is also a reason for the existence of a particular tax rule; think of investment incentives through tax exemptions.

2.2 Mechanisms to mitigate agency problems

A broad set of mechanisms has been developed to mitigate or eliminate particular agency problems. One set of mechanisms aims at increasing the generation and disclosure of information. For example, capital markets laws require firms that raise capital from investors and creditors to disclose financial statements, prospectuses, and to make other disclosures. In addition, shareholders request information on their own to assess how management has discharged its duties ("monitoring"). Information is also produced by other capital markets participants, including analysts, investment bankers, and the media.

Another set of mechanisms are restrictions of decision rights ("bonding") of managers. For example, company law provides constraints on the distribution of profits and repayment of equity to owners. Corporate governance regulation by law or by comply-or-explain rules requires that firms establish oversight bodies over management, including boards and board committees, and it allocates decision rights back to shareholders' meetings, as in the case of executive compensation contracts. Contracts allocate decision rights, for example through debt covenants, to control management behavior. Threat of litigation constrains the flexibility of management to make decisions, and it makes self-serving behavior very costly. For example, the business judgment rule focuses on management's duty to obtain sufficient information to justify business decisions.

The optimal mix of mechanisms employed to control agency problems in a firm depends on the incremental costs and benefits of the mechanisms, which are again contingent on the kind of agency problems that are most pertinent, the economic and information environments, and other factors. A change in the use of one mechanism may have an effect on the optimal mix of mechanisms; hence, optimization of a single mechanism must consider the implications on the set of other mechanisms in place.

It is worth emphasizing that most of the mechanisms to mitigate agency problems rely on information provided by financial accounting. Accounting is an institution that generates a particular set of information, which is used to reduce information asymmetry (increase transparency) and to determine restrictions of the decision rights of managers (see, e.g., Benston et al. 2006).

Financial accounting information is publicly available information, which reduces the information costs for its users regardless of whether or not they have a contractual relationship with the firm. For example, financial information is useful to potential shareholders, whose interest conflicts with that of existing shareholders, and to competitors, who can infer valuable business information from financial reports. Firms' disclosure strategies consider such effects even if there are no contracts that govern the usage of published information at that time. However, a contract originates once a potential shareholder actually invests in a share.

3 Agency models

3.1 A generic agency model

This section provides a non-technical discussion of analytical agency theory and the usefulness of accounting information in agency models. This theory explains the rise of certain agency problems and characterizes optimal contracts that maximize the utility of the residual claimant. Since the focus is on accounting systems, the theory seeks to identify desirable properties of accounting information that serve to attain this outcome.

A generic agency model consists of at least the following components:

1   A production technology that requires the input of an agent (and possibly other inputs) and yields a risky outcome that has value in the market the firm operates.
2   A principal who owns the production technology or provides capital to invest in the production technology.
3   An agent who is hired by the principal to manage the firm or to provide other input in the production technology, including effort, managerial skills or experience, among others.

The principal and the agent write a contract that specifies their respective duties and returns. The principal aims at maximizing his or her expected utility received from the returns of the production or capital provision. The manager aims at maximizing his or her expected utility from the compensation paid by the principal, other benefits, or the residual return of the production after payment for the capital. Additionally, either the principal or the agent, or both, have alternative options to invest or work; that is, in order for them to agree to the contract it must provide them with at least the expected utility of their best alternative.

An agency problem arises if the following two conditions are simultaneously met:

1   A conflict of interest between the principal and the agent; and
2   Asymmetric information, when one party to the contract has more information than the others (and the other parties know this fact) about the uncertain outcome of the production process either before agreeing to the contract or during its execution.

If there is no conflict of interest, then both parties maximize the same expected utility and agree in the evaluation. This situation is equivalent to a single-person decision-making setting and no agency problem arises in the first place. If there is no asymmetric information, the parties are able to specify in the contract the optimal decisions and the mechanism to enforce them. Then they distribute the return conditional on their respective outside opportunities. Here an agency problem arises, but it can be solved directly. The solution to these problems is called a first-best solution.

If there are both a conflict of interest and asymmetric information, then the first-best solution cannot be achieved and there is a loss in welfare (except in very special circumstances). The solution is called a second-best solution in which both parties maximize their expected utilities, taking into account the decisions made by the other party. The difference in the outcome from the first-best and the second-best solution is called agency costs and reflects the loss in welfare arising due to the conflict of interest and information asymmetry.

The generic agency model described above can be easily adapted to describe an owner-manager agency problem (see again Figure 13.1): the principal owns the production technology and the agent provides managerial input that is privately costly and not observable to the principal (what creates the basic information asymmetry). The principal has the bargaining power and offers the agent a contract that matches the agent's expected utility from alternative employment (reservation utility) and offers incentives to provide the desired input. The key element of the contract is the compensation promised to the manager. It is based on performance measures that are contractible, which means they are observable by the two parties to the contract and an enforcement institution (e.g., a court).[2] Typically, performance measures are noisy and do not capture all aspects of the manager's effort. Moreover, making the manager's compensation contingent on the performance measures affects the risk sharing of the returns to the owner and the manager, which generally differs from optimal risk sharing and thus reduces welfare.

The generic agency model also accommodates the firm–creditor agency problem: here, the agent is the firm represented by the manager (assuming no owner–manager agency problem) who seeks external debt financing.[3] The manager invests the funds into a project with features that are not observable or contractible. The creditor is the principal who is interested in maximizing the expected return of the loan. The creditor is usually assumed to have a fixed reservation utility – the expected return from alternative financing activities in the capital market, for example. In a standard debt contract, a conflict of interest arises if there is a possibility that the firm may become bankrupt, in which case the creditor receives less than the agreed upon repayment and, hence, carries some risk from the production process. The parties are aware of this potential event and take measures in the debt contract to minimize its costs. Such measures often use accounting numbers, such as debt covenants or performance pricing agreements.

Several observations are in order. One is that managers behave "opportunistically," which means that under the contract they make decisions that maximize their own expected utility and these decisions are not necessarily in the best interest of the principal. Opportunistic behavior is undesirable but either cannot be avoided through the mechanisms that mitigate agency problems or it would be too costly to avoid them. It should be noted that the principal also maximizes its own expected utility. The distinction is that the principal is usually modeled as the party that does not take any specific actions after writing the contract, so there is simply no room for opportunistic behavior. There exists a class of agency models known as double moral hazard models in which both the principal and the agent take actions and, of course, both act opportunistically in such a setting.

A second observation relates to the role of the reservation utility constraint in agency models. In the owner–manager agency problem, it is usually assumed that the manager's (the agent's) expected utility is no less than what he or she would earn from outside employment opportunities. The manager accepts the contract if it promises this minimum expected utility, and the residual claimant is the principal.[4] Conversely, in the firm–creditor agency problem it is usually the creditor (the principal) who is subject to the reservation utility constraint. The assumption is that creditors compete with other creditors for financing the firm, and in order to offer financing the creditor must expect to earn a return greater or equal to alternative investments in the capital market. The residual claimant is the agent. The assumption of whether the principal or the agent is effectively bound by a reservation utility does not matter for the optimal design of the contract.[5] It merely reflects an assumption about the bargaining power of the parties. However, the reservation utility constraint does protect a party from being exploited by the opportunistic behavior of the other party. It ensures that that party earns at least the reservation utility by agreeing to the contract after considering and anticipating potential opportunistic behavior by the other party. In a sense, this party is "price-protected." It is the other party that bears the residual loss from agency costs, and this party has an incentive to take measures to minimize the agency costs.

Third, the promises in the optimal contract are usually not efficient ex post. That is, in order to achieve the optimal (second-best) outcome, the parties precommit to courses of action that they would not optimally take after the contract unfolds. For example, assume the optimal contract imposes compensation risk to a risk-averse agent to provide incentives to take the decision desired by the principal. After the agent has made the decision, the parties have an incentive to renegotiate the contract to provide an expected compensation that would result under optimal risk allocation, ignoring the incentive effect because the decision has been made already.

Naturally, anticipation by the parties that such a possibility exists eliminates the very incentive effects the contract aims to provide in the first place. Hence, optimal contracts require strong commitment by both parties.

3.2 Other model structures

The generic agency model described above includes moral hazard as a source of an agency problem. Moral hazard is opportunistic behavior that occurs after the contract is signed. Therefore, moral hazard models are also known as hidden action models. There are many extensions of this type of agency model. Besides double moral hazard and renegotiation, which have been mentioned already, staggered agency relationships, multiple actions, multiple periods, and multiple agents and principals each create additional concerns that are addressed in the optimal contract. Staggered agency relationships arise if there are several layers of agency relationships. For example, shareholders install a board of directors and write a contract with them, whereas the board writes contracts with executives. Multiple actions introduce another agency problem besides motivating effort, because the allocation of effort across the various actions becomes important as well. In multi-period settings, the agent's intertemporal utility function may differ from that of the principal. The agent may be "impatient," that is, he or she discounts future compensation at a higher rate than the principal or stays with the firm for only for a limited time. Such an agent prefers activities that lead to higher short-term results even if this means foregoing long-term benefits. The availability or preclusion of writing and enforcing long-term contracts generates additional concerns if information from prior periods is informative about subsequent performance. This can create a "ratchet effect" if the principal utilizes such information to provide stronger incentives in future contracts, which again leads the agent to take different actions in earlier periods to influence the early information. In a setting with multiple agents, the performance of one agent can be informative about the performance of other agents (e.g., used in relative performance measurement and promotion), or agents can collude to their mutual benefit at the cost of the principal. Multiple principals create a tension about what actions they desire and how the outcome distribution affects the principals' utilities.

Moral hazard models are at the core of agency theory, but there exist several other model structures that rest on conflict of interest and asymmetric information. One class is adverse selection models, also known as hidden information models. In these models, information asymmetry already exists prior to signing the contract. For example, the principal may be better informed about the economic situation of the firm, or the agent may know more about his or her skills in management or risk attitudes. In technical parlance, such characteristics of parties or the circumstances in which they operate are referred to as their "type." For example, a firm that is looking for a particularly able manager can offer compensation that heavily depends on the outcome of the production process (e.g., by offering a low fixed salary and a large stock options package), which is calibrated such that able managers are willing to take the risk and accept working for the firm but less able managers do not expect to earn their reservation utility and refuse the contract.[6] If different types of agents accept the contract, the usual solution of adverse selection problems consists of a "menu" of contracts that the informed party is free to choose from directly or indirectly through communicating its type. The menu of contracts is designed so that each appeals to a certain type, and selecting a particular contract reveals (some of) the party's private information of its type. Again, once the type is known the parties would have an incentive to renegotiate the contract, which would destroy the self-selection property of the original contract.

In an adverse selection problem, the informed party has an incentive to take costly actions to signal its type through the creation of a signal. Suppose a "good" type can produce a high signal at a lower cost than a "bad" type. Communicating a high signal would then inform about the type if it is too costly for the "bad" type to imitate the high signal in equilibrium. Thus, signaling is a mechanism to communicate private information about the type that could not be credibly communicated otherwise. Anything that has this cost property can be a signal; hence, the signal need not tell anything directly about the underlying type. In financial accounting, though, interest centers on signals that come from accounting choices, such as from a recognition of a measurement option that generates a particular cost.

The possibility of renegotiation usually reduces the set of feasible contracts. It is difficult to commit not to renegotiate: if both parties agree to renegotiate, why would a court uphold such an agreement? Considering renegotiation adds (renegotiation-proof) constraints that ensure the ex post efficiency of a contract at every point in time. Respecting such constraints leads to a solution that reduces welfare (a "third-best" solution). However, there are settings in which renegotiation improves the efficiency of a contract. An example is if the parties anticipate that new information will arise during the execution of the contract, but they cannot contract on it in the original contract either because the information is non-contractible or because writing a contingent contract is too costly. Via renegotiation, the parties are able to incorporate such information into the agency problem, and the original contract can be designed so as to give them the incentives to renegotiate it.

There are other ways to take advantage of non-contractible information in an agency relationship. One example is the creation of bonus pools in which the principal determines the amount of bonus that he or she commits to pay out to the agents or, if the agents are not eligible, to an independent third party (e.g., a charity organization). The fixed payment removes any incentive of the principal to hold back part of the bonus and makes it credible for the principal to use non-contractible information to reward the agents.

In many cases contracts do not prescribe every consequence, but there is a common understanding among the parties that they deliver as stipulated for other reasons. Self-enforcing contracts are designed to give parties the incentives to continue to deliver, given that the other party has performed previously. Such incentives often follow from other economic consequences of not fulfilling a contract (outside of a direct breach of contract). Examples are reputation effects or economic punishment, particularly in case of expected future agency relationships with the same party. These contracts are often referred to as implicit contracts, in contrast to explicit contracts that prescribe all relevant circumstances. Of course, if the economic environment in which a party operates changes drastically, the cost of reneging may decrease and make the implicit contract ineffective.

Many users of accounting information do not have a contractual relationship with the firm, but they still use the information in financial statements to inform their decisions, which potentially affect the utility of the firm. While one can argue that, in a strict sense, non-contractual relationships are not covered by agency theory, the boundary is less clear-cut than it appears. Incomplete contracts prescribe some rights and obligations of parties, but not all of them, which provides room for decisions not covered by the contract. Indeed, many considerations for contractual settings carry over to non-contractual settings because these situations are still characterized by conflict of interest and information asymmetry. Rather than designing an optimal contract ex ante, the parties act in a game-theoretic model structure for which the Nash equilibrium is the solution concept. It stipulates that each party maximizes its expected utility given that the other party plays its equilibrium strategy. Such strategies determine an equilibrium if no party has a unilateral incentive to deviate, and therefore they are sequentially rational.

Disclosure models, used to examine voluntary financial disclosure by firms, are a typical example. A common assumption here is that disclosure, when made, must be truthful. The firm can therefore decide only whether to disclose or not. If it discloses, a symmetric information situation obtains with respect to this information; otherwise, users make rational inferences as to the set of signals the firm would not disclose in equilibrium and act on that (partial) information. In equilibrium, the user can usually infer some information despite the lack of disclosure.[7] If the firm is not restricted to truthful disclosures, then disclosure becomes "cheap talk" and the firm can transfer information only if the conflict of interest is sufficiently small.[8] In the case that disclosure need not be truthful but biasing is costly, in equilibrium some information is transferred, although the disclosure is biased, because investors understand the equilibrium.

It should be noted that contractual relationships are usually preferable to non–contractual relationships, although contracts restrict the parties' courses of actions to those agreed in the contract, which is intuitively unfavorable to the parties. The reason is that the equilibrium strategies without a contract are feasible solutions in a contracting setting, but the parties can usually do better than that by committing to other strategies.

3.3 Role of accounting information

Accounting information is useful for mitigating agency problems because it reduces the information asymmetry among the parties. Agency theory research in accounting analyzes the effect of accounting information on incentive problems and on the welfare of the parties in an agency relationship. Since accounting information and other contractual provisions are interdependent, ideally they should be considered together. In particular, a role of accounting is to substitute for an inflexibility or constraint of contracting. Most of the constraints arise from information and contracting costs, which are often substantial. Since financial accounting is highly regulated, agency theory can aid understanding of the incentive and welfare effects of different accounting requirements. Further, standardized equity (stock) and debt contracts prevail in capital markets. Given such contract constraints, the interesting question is what properties a useful accounting system should exhibit.

Financial accounting information is communicated via mandatory or voluntary disclosures; hence, it provides contractible information. The special feature of this information is that it provides the ultimate information about the firm's performance; there is usually no other information system that generates contractible signals about the same period later. In contrast, there are several other information sources that provide early information, including the firm's own forecasts and disclosures, analyst forecasts, media news, and the like. The quality of such information is evaluated against the firm's financial reports that become available later. Financial accounting thus has a disciplining and confirmatory role for early information that is usually not regulated or verified.

In the following two subsections, I emphasize two special characteristics of accounting information: credibility and aggregation of information. Credibility is important in making accounting information valuable for contracting, and aggregation is a pervasive element of accounting because all key performance measures are aggregates.

3.4 Credibility of accounting information

Information is credible, trustworthy, or objective if it does not (fully) depend on one party's discretion. Consider, for example, playing roulette over the phone. It is unlikely that rational people would participate in such a gamble because they cannot verify the actual result. Information that is useful for contracting must have measures in place that prevent one party from arbitrarily manipulating the signal. However, credibility is not a dichotomous attribute, and information can be more or less credible – with obvious effects on its (relative) usefulness to improve contract efficiency.

The accounting system tracks transactions and events in a particular manner determined by the application of accounting standards as implemented by the firm. In many cases, applying the standards requires professional judgment, which can be used to manage earnings. Earnings management is the intentional intervention by management to modify or manipulate the outcome of the accounting system, and it is of great concern in contracting (as well as in decision making more generally, as it renders signals less informative).

Agency theory provides a fundamental result on earnings management, which is called the revelation principle (Myerson 1982). It states that for any contract that induces the manager to manage earnings, there exists another contract that induces truth-telling by the manager, which results in the same outcome as the original contract. Intuitively, if the manager benefits from reporting particular earnings that deviate from the true earnings, the new contract promises the same compensation if the manager reports true earnings directly. If the revelation principle applies, there is no use in studying earnings management because it can simply be avoided by a truth-inducing contract. However, the revelation principle relies on many strong assumptions, including full commitment, full communication, and full contracting flexibility (Arya, Glover, and Sunder 1998). Full commitment is important because under the truth-inducing contract, the firm learns the true earnings but must commit to not make full use of that knowledge. Notice that commitment is not possible in non-contracting settings such as disclosure to anonymous users. Full communication is necessary to be able to convey all aspects of the private information held by the manager. Finally, to tailor a truth-inducing contract that matches another contract, the contract space must not be restricted. So, for example, standardized stock and debt contracts, "simple" contracts, and the like do not satisfy this requirement. If these strong assumptions do not apply, earnings management incentives must be considered in designing an optimal contract.

An accounting system that provides no room for earnings management appears to be optimal, but eliminating any discretion can be very costly or can preclude conveying important aspects of the private information held by management (thus limiting communication). In practice, accounting standards provide some flexibility as a result of a tradeoff between the qualitative characteristics of relevance and reliability. Management can use the discretion to convey more information to users, but it can also (try to) mislead them by engaging in earnings management. These two objectives are in conflict with each other, but self-interest can actually help to reveal additional information. A simple, abstract example illustrates this point (Penno 1990). Suppose a manager observes several independent signals of similar statistical quality but is required to disclose exactly one of them truthfully. A rigid accounting system would prescribe disclosure of, say, the third signal observed. A lenient accounting system offers the manager a choice of which signal to disclose, and assuming the manager benefits from high signals, he or she will disclose the highest signal from those observed. Interestingly, the lenient accounting system is more informative than the rigid one because while both convey information about one signal (it does not matter ex ante which one is disclosed), the lenient one implicitly conveys the additional information that all other signals are lower than the one reported. In more general terms, the observation of management's accounting choice is telling about the underlying private information (a revealed preferences argument).

Making signals more reliable generally increases contract efficiency. There are several institutions in place to make accounting information trustworthy. These institutions, including corporate governance, auditing, enforcement, and litigation, consume substantial resources, and their mere existence suggests that their benefits outweigh their costs. However, they rarely prevent earnings management completely; they just make it more costly to the manager (or the firm) to succeed in earnings management. Consider, for example, disclosure of forward-looking information in management reports. In countries with a litigious environment, managers are reluctant to disclose any meaningful information, so safe harbor rules have been put in place to constrain excessive litigation based on forward-looking information to encourage informative disclosures.

Earnings management in an agency model can be seen as the manager deciding on the effort spent on two activities; one is productive and the other affects only the performance measure but not the principal's utility (window dressing activity). The latter action can be interpreted as real or as accrual earnings management. Both actions are costly to the manager. Feltham and Xie (1994) show that if the principal has only a single performance measure available for compensation contracting, the only way to provide incentives for the productive activity is to make compensation increasing in the performance measure. However, this also induces the manager to engage in earnings management because the effects of the two activities cannot be disentangled. As a consequence, the optimal incentive rate is lower than the one without an earnings management opportunity, so the principal optimally dampens both activities. Although the principal anticipates the equilibrium level of earnings management, there is nothing he or she can do to prevent it. Note that in this setting, earnings management not only reduces the productive activity, but it must be compensated for to meet the agent's reservation utility. Suppose now that that more effective auditing or enforcement increases the cost of earnings management. Then the reduction of earnings management is less than the direct effect because the principal increases the incentive rate, thus inducing more earnings management, which partially offsets the initial reduction.

If there is no way that earnings management can be controlled through the means of the contract, the situation becomes similar to one with no contract. Assuming the manager can bias reported earnings at a cost that increases in the bias, the users (e.g., the capital market) rationally infer the average bias and adjust the market price accordingly (see Fischer and Verrecchia 2000). In equilibrium, rational users are not fooled by earnings management on average and earnings management does not provide a benefit to the manager (as long as there is no additional asymmetric information). An interesting feature of this equilibrium is that even though users correct for the earnings management bias, the manager still engages in earnings management in equilibrium. Therefore, this equilibrium is dubbed a "shoot-yourself-in-the-foot" equilibrium.

There exist situations in which explicitly allowing earnings management is beneficial to the contracting parties. The mechanisms leading to this result are subtle. For example, if communication is limited and the availability of earnings management depends on the manager's action, then allowing for earnings management can facilitate motivating the manager to take the desired actions (Demski 1998). The fact that a manager that took the desired action can avoid certain outcomes, whereas he or she cannot avoid these outcomes for a different action, can be exploited to improve contracting. Another example is a multi-period setting with a persistent earnings component. In this case, the observation of prior earnings is informative about future expected earnings. If the parties cannot write and enforce long-term contracts, or are able to renegotiate a long-term contract, they will increase the incentive rates in subsequent periods. Anticipating that, the manager has an incentive to provide inefficiently low effort in earlier periods. Allowing the manager to manage earnings mitigates the information content of earnings in interim periods, thus avoiding too strong adjustments of the incentives, which improves welfare (Christensen, Frimor, and Şabac 2013). Earnings management is the lesser evil here.

Empirical research provides pervasive evidence of earnings management in a variety of economic contexts.[9] Whatever the particular reasons are that earnings management occurs in a contractual setting, it is obvious from the above discussion that earnings management is part of the optimal solution of the agency problem. Therefore, it is difficult to label earnings management as undesirable or "bad" – it is bad only relative to an unattainable first-best world. Earnings management is a consequence of an ex ante efficient contract, despite its being ex post undesirable. This distinction between ex ante and ex post emphasizes the important role of commitment in contracting.

3.5 Aggregation of accounting information

A contract is an efficient mechanism for aggregating the signals that it includes to specify the rights and obligations between the parties. For example, a compensation contract aggregates multiple managerial performance measures into the compensation pay.[10] In the extreme, a contract could be written on each single transaction of the firm with third parties and each event that affects the net worth of the firm, thus mirroring, and including, the accounting system. This would grant the contracting parties the most flexibility in determining the desired consequences, but it would obviously make contracting costly. In reality, most contracts are based on very few performance measures, which suggests that the costs of highly specific contracts are substantial. Using accounting signals that aggregate transactions and events in a predetermined way saves contracting costs but reduces the flexibility of using the individual information. The optimal level of aggregation trades off these costs and benefits.

Financial accounting systems include many detailed rules that prescribe how transactions and events are aggregated. Aggregation requires quantification of the large variety of transactions and events into single summary measures such as earnings, net income, and equity. There is much discussion about the use of non-financial performance indicators besides financial information; these are also aggregates of underlying transactions and events, but they normally capture only part of the firm's performance because of the difficulty of aggregating different non-financial measures. Financial performance is designed to portray the total performance.

Accounting standards induce very special aggregations. First, financial accounting is not based on a single consistent set of recognition and measurement principles but follows a mixed-attribute approach. Some assets are recognized, others are not. If they are recognized, they are measured at cost; others at fair value, and still others at discounted cash flow measures. In some cases profit is recorded only if a transaction took place; in other cases the mere change in value of an asset gives rise to a profit. Second, some information is recognized, whereas other information is only disclosed in the notes. Information that is only disclosed does not flow into the key summary measures. Third, accounting simply sums up monetary equivalents; that is, the aggregation applies equal weights to individual items and is insensitive to different qualities, such as their level of credibility. Indeed, this special aggregation procedure may explain the existence of accounting principles, such as conservatism,[11] or the demand for and supply of pro-forma or adjusted earnings.

Aggregation of signals always comes with a loss of information content relative to the individual signals (except for the special case in which the aggregate is a sufficient statistic of those signals). In a single decision-making context, this loss of information is always welfare reducing. In an agency setting, however, there can be a strict benefit from using aggregate information. One case is multi-period contracting if long-term contracts cannot be written or enforced. As mentioned earlier, if information from early periods is also informative about future periods, a ratchet effect arises, which reduces welfare. Contracting on aggregate performance can substitute for the lack of long-term commitment because it prevents the principal from receiving "too much" information that can be used to fine-tune subsequent contracts (Feltham, Indjejikian, and Nanda 2006). Another benefit of aggregation is preventing the agent from receiving too much information, which makes motivating a subsequent action less costly (Arya, Glover, and Liang 2004). In a non-contracting setting, Dye and Sridhar (2004) find that aggregation is beneficial because it mitigates earnings management incentives of a manager; this is because aggregate information prevents capital market participants from using information too aggressively in pricing the firm's shares in equilibrium.

4 Implications for financial accounting standards

Agency theory provides a framework to better understand and evaluate the usefulness of the fundamental concepts that underlie financial accounting standards (see also Christensen 2010). In this section, I discuss the application of agency theory to three contentious themes as discussed in the development of the Conceptual Framework by the IASB: valuation and stewardship objectives of financial accounting, fair value measurement, and conservatism. The section ends with a brief discussion of the implications of agency theory when it is applied to standard setters themselves, that is, by viewing standard setters as self-interested institutions as well.

4.1 Valuation and stewardship

A fundamental, and recurring, issue in financial accounting standard setting is the objective, or the objectives, of financial reporting. In 2010, the IASB and the US Financial Accounting Standards Board (FASB) published the first part of a joint Conceptual Framework, which states that the objective of financial reporting is the usefulness to (primarily) investors and creditors for capital allocation decisions (IASB 2010, OB4). It mentions stewardship only indirectly, suggesting it is already comprised in decision usefulness.

A general result of agency theory is that the ranking of information systems differs according to their use in contracting and in valuation (Gjesdal 1982). This result follows from the general insight that the value of information systems depends on the specific decision context. To illustrate, assume a simple one-period owner-manager agency problem in which the manager provides effort in a production process. Effort and the stochastic economic environment jointly determine the outcome. For valuation purposes the most important piece of information is the outcome itself; information about either the action or the economic environment is less useful. Conversely, for motivating the manager to exert the desirable effort, it is preferable to obtain information on the effort directly rather than on the outcome, which is just another noisy measure of effort. This insight can explain why, for example, firms remove non-recurring items that the manager cannot control from the performance measure (Christensen, Feltham, and Şabac 2005).

The fact that the *ranking* of information systems can differ according to their purposes does not imply that the value of information for stewardship and valuation would not be closely related. In fact, Drymiotes and Hemmer (2013) construct an agency model with accruals that reverse in future periods; they find that in this setting the ranking of information for motivating the manager and for valuation of the firm coincides. A close relation of the objectives also arises from the fact that meeting each objective depends on the relevance and reliability of the information. Differences arise mainly in specific details and the weights attached to different pieces of raw information.[12]

The IASB is of the view that contracting parties can define whatever information they consider useful in individual contracts, so the purpose of financial statements is to serve those users that cannot write specific contracts (IASB 2010, OB5). While this is a valid point, it is an empirical issue whether it leads to an efficient solution when contracting costs are taken into account. For example, Ball and Shivakumar (2008) examine the news content of earnings announcements and find that they convey little information to the market. They interpret this finding to suggest that the main benefit of accounting information lies in its use for contracting purposes, not in providing timely information to capital market participants. Under the assumption that (at least in the long run) only optimal institutions survive, this finding indicates that the costs of adjusting individual contracts are very high indeed.

Another role of financial reporting that is consistent with the low news information content at the time of disclosure is that financial reporting disciplines earlier voluntary disclosure by firms (e.g., Ball, Jayaraman, and Shivakumar 2012). The fact that credible information will be available later creates a cost for earnings management in prior disclosures, even though biasing such prior disclosures appears costless initially.

4.2 Fair value measurement

International accounting standards require measurement of increasingly more assets and liabilities at fair value. This trend started with financial instruments and extended to other assets, such as investment property, and to initial measurement of most assets acquired in a business combination. However, the move towards increased fair value measurement has been highly contentious for several reasons, which I discuss from an agency theory perspective.

Fair value measurement is appealing to the IASB because it matches the requirement in the Conceptual Framework that capital providers need information about the amount, timing, and risk of expected future cash flows (IASB 2010, OB3). Fair values apparently fulfill these needs because they are a contemporaneous aggregate of this raw information. This suggests that they provide more relevant information than historical cost, or cost and impairment measures.[13] It is no coincidence that the trend to fair values started with financial instruments. Over the last decades, financial instruments grew in importance, plenty of new and complex instruments were created, and financial markets boomed. The cost of a derivative instrument does not provide much, if any, information about its current value and about the risk that is involved in holding the derivative, whereas fair values, preferably in the form of market prices, are much more useful. Moreover, fair value measurement (with fair value changes in profit or loss) preempts real earnings management that a manager could engage in by boosting reported earnings by selectively selling financial instruments whose market price exceeds their carrying amount.

Kothari, Ramanna, and Skinner (2010, p. 260) argue that "the primary role of the balance sheet is to provide information on the values of the entity's separable assets and liabilities." They suggest that verifiable fair values can be more useful than cost-based measures for creditors who are particularly interested in assessing the value of net assets that are available to satisfy their claims in case of default of a firm. This should hold particularly for fair values if they are defined as exit values (as in International Financial Reporting Standard [IFRS] 13), although liquidating values are usually lower than fair values.

The main concern with fair values is that they are based on estimates made by management (level 3 inputs) if there is no active market for the asset or liability. Although accounting standards include detailed requirements (e.g., IFRS 13), the determination of fair values is ultimately based on inputs that are subjective and difficult, or impossible, to verify. Management has significant discretion in determining fair values, which provides ample room for earnings management. Since credibility is an important attribute of financial information used in contracts, fair values that are not based on market prices diminish their usefulness for contracting purposes.[14] Empirical evidence is consistent with this effect. For example, Demerjian (2011) documents a declining use of debt covenants based on balance sheet numbers and suggests that this is due to increased fair value measurement.

Fair values based on market prices do not raise strong credibility concerns, but they can cause other disadvantages in contracting. One is that market prices are driven by a variety of factors, many of which are not useful for contracting and as such increase the risk parties have to bear. For example, using market price for management compensation may be a performance measure that is congruous to shareholders' interests, but it usually contains much noise that is uninformative about the manager's performance and the manager must be compensated for the compensation risk. Another issue is that market prices are unlikely to provide the right amount of incentive for management to act in the interest of the shareholders. The reason is subtle: market prices are based on market participants' *expectations* of the manager's decisions, besides other factors. The manager, considering the benefits and costs of effort, now incurs the full costs but little benefit as the anticipated benefit is already included in the market price. This curbs the incentive to actually perform and increases the agency problem.[15]

To summarize, agency theory identifies several advantages and disadvantages of fair value compared to cost measurement.[16] Ultimately, it is an empirical question whether fair values lead to net benefits for contracting, and the conclusion is likely to differ across different classes of assets, which is in line with the current mixed-attribute measurement approach under international accounting standards.

4.3 Conservatism

Financial accounting standards typically include several rules that induce conservative financial reporting. Conservative accounting leads to a downward biased book value of the firm's net assets. Examples of such rules are the full expensing of research and (many) development costs and other self-constructed intangibles, recognizing provisions for bad debt, early loss recognition in onerous contracts, lower-of-cost-or-market measurement, and impairment of assets. With its emphasis on decision usefulness, the Conceptual Framework of the IASB defines faithful representation of economic phenomena as a fundamental qualitative characteristic of financial reporting, and this characteristic includes a neutral depiction (IASB 2010, QC14). The Conceptual Framework 2010 explicitly eliminates conservatism as it contradicts neutral information. Since conservatism has a very long tradition in accounting, this move by the standard setters is highly contentious.[17]

Agency theory gives several explanations for why and how conservatism can be preferable to neutrality (Watts 2003a, b). Conditional conservatism, which comprises asymmetric timeliness of gains and losses, is considered useful, whereas unconditional conservatism, which leads to unconditional understatement of net assets, is viewed as undesirable because it eliminates information about events that affect the value of the asset.

Agency theory shows that conservatism can mitigate the adverse effects of several frictions in owner–manager agency problems. Earnings usually constitute a major component of the manager's compensation contract. The desire to increase compensation creates an incentive for the manager to overstate (rather than understate) earnings. Accounting standards that restrict the potential to overstate earnings are useful for mitigating earnings management.[18] While this argument is intuitive, Chen, Hemmer, and Zhang (2007) point out that there is also a cost to conservatism: it reduces the information content of earnings, so the benefit from mitigating earnings management must offset this cost to make conservative accounting desirable. Conservatism also interacts with the motivation of managers to voluntarily disclose information about earnings. For example, Gigler and Hemmer (2001) find that the incentive for disclosure is greater if the accounting system is *less* conservative; they also show that the earnings response pattern that is used to measure conditional conservatism (Basu 1997) obtains due to voluntary disclosure in their model.

Another friction arises from a short-term horizon or the "impatience" of a manager relative to shareholders (Ball 2001). By recognizing losses early, the manager is more likely to internalize a possible future expected loss from projects, which reduces the manager's incentive to invest in projects that yield positive returns in early periods but have a negative net present value. It also induces the manager to abandon projects early that are expected to lose value. While these incentives are again intuitive, they come at a cost. For example, a cost of early loss recognition is that it may induce underinvestment in a positive net present value project that yields early losses. Chen, Mittendorf, and Zhang (2010) find that conservative accounting is useful to motivate the manager to exert outcome-increasing effort, but motivating him or her to both increase outcome and reduce its risk calls for non-conservative (aggressive) accounting.

Conservatism can also be useful in a debt contracting setting. The standard arguments are that conservatism provides timely warning signals that can lead to a violation of debt covenants earlier, and that conservatism reduces incentives to make investments that divert value from creditors to shareholders, thus enhancing contract efficiency (see, e.g., Armstrong, Guay, and Weber 2010). Rigorous analyses show that these arguments do not apply generally, but there are settings in which a non-conservative bias is actually preferable. The reason is that a conservative bias increases the probability with which low earnings are reported *and* at the same time reduces the conditional information content of low earnings. A debt covenant that allocates a project's ownership rights to either the manager or the creditor (who may then want to continue with the project or abandon it to recover the liquidation value of the asset) is subject to type I and type II errors – that is, violating the covenant even though the actual outcome is likely favorable, or not violating the covenant even though the actual outcome is likely unfavorable. The expected costs of these two errors depend on the probability of the signals and their information content, and these costs determine whether a conservative or non-conservative accounting system is preferable. Gigler et al. (2009) show that under plausible conditions, an aggressive bias is preferable.

In this formalization, conservatism increases the type I error and decreases the type II error. This is descriptive for revenue recognition, where in case of doubt no revenue is recognized and the evidence that lends to recognition must be strong. An alternative formalization of conservatism is based on the (early) recognition of bad news, whereas no news or good news are not recognized until later. An example is the impairment of assets (Göx and Wagenhofer 2009). Here recognition serves as a disclosure device, making it a precise signal, whereas no recognition pools good news and no news and thus is less precise. These two formalizations yield somewhat differing conclusions about the preferability of conservative accounting.

The takeaway from this discussion is that a neutral accounting system is almost never preferable in an agency context. The optimal bias results from a tradeoff between different economic effects of decisions, and therefore conservatism is beneficial under some circumstances but detrimental in others. Additionally, the discussion makes clear that the results depend on the exact articulation of conservatism in a model.

Interestingly, accounting has always been conservative (see, e.g., Watts 2003b), but not intentionally aggressive. From a perspective of the survival of the best standards, this suggests that the benefits of conservatism prevail. Further, when contracting parties can modify the degree of conservatism, they tend to favor more conservatism. For example, Beatty, Weber, and Yu (2008) document that the majority of their sample contracts include conservative modifications, but they also find that earnings conservatism and contract modifications are complements rather than substitutes, so contracts do not make up for a perceived lack of conservatism. Pervasive modifications of accounting numbers are an indicator that the accounting standards are not efficient and need fixing.[19]

In their study of debt covenants, Beatty, Weber, and Yu (2008) consider income escalators that introduce asymmetric effects of earnings on the tightness of covenants and modifications that exclude purchased intangibles from the calculation of net worth. Interestingly, the exclusion of intangibles generates unconditional conservatism, which systematically eliminates information rather than providing early warning information. From a contracting perspective, one might argue that unconditional conservatism is unnecessary because the same contract consequences could be achieved through an appropriate adjustment of the covenant threshold. However, the elimination of investment in intangibles has an economic effect in that it induces a penalty to investment in intangible relative to tangible assets that do not affect the covenant. Creditors are likely to favor investment in tangible assets because they represent a higher liquidation value than intangibles in case of default.[20]

4.4 Politics of accounting standard setting

Ideally, financial accounting standards that survive in the long run are a best response to the underlying agency problems. Traditionally, the evolution of Generally Accepted Accounting Principles (GAAP) suggests such a trial-and-error process in striving for an efficient outcome. However, most modern accounting standards do not evolve from such a process but are the product of an institution that develops them, a standard setter. The standard setter can be considered as a benevolent institution that is purely interested in contracting efficiency, capital market efficiency, and social welfare maximization. This requires trading off all economic effects of particular standards, which is a difficult task. Changes in standards also imply wealth redistributions across affected parties (as long as the parties are not price protected). Consequently, the standard setter must strike a balance between these effects.

Agency theory, as applied to standard setting, recognizes that standard setters, like firms, managers, auditors, and other interested parties, act as economic agents – they produce standards in pursuit of their own interests (capture theory of regulation). The continuous reforms of the governance of the International Financial Reporting Standards Foundation are an example of the importance interest groups attribute to standard setting. These reforms are intended to result in a particular representation and a "voice" in standard setting through the channels of monitoring and financing the standard setter. Moreover, the board members that actually make the decisions on accounting standards may have individual interests, similar to agents in an agency relationship. This similarity suggests that agency theory can provide insights into standard setting as well (Watts and Zimmerman 1986).

There is some literature that models the particular incentives of a standard setter and examines the effects of the incentives on the resulting accounting standards. For example, Bertomeu and Magee (2011) assume a standard setter that sets the disclosure standard preferred by the majority of firms and banks that finance the firms, over other possible disclosure standards. They show that the quality of disclosure in the resulting standard is driven by the economic condition that is present at that time. If the expected profitability of projects is high, disclosure quality is high as well. If profitability declines, the disclosure quality suddenly drops to a minimum but increases again if the economy becomes recessionary. The demand for the varying quality is a consequence of the changing ability to finance projects through banks.

Bertomeu and Cheynel (2013) consider an economy with firms that make investments and are interested in maximizing their market prices. They compare the resulting disclosure standards for three different regulatory regimes. In the first, two politicians who are up for election propose standards and the winning politician's proposal is implemented. The second is a self-regulated environment in which the owners of the firms collectively decide on the standard through majority voting. The third regime allows for competition among standard setters, who want to maximize adoption of their respective standards. The researchers show that the first regime leads to low-quality standards because the politicians have an incentive to underbid each other. The self-regulatory regime tends to lead to excessively high quality because it does not fully reflect the costs of disclosure. Finally, they find that competition among standard setters also tends to lead to overly high quality, but it is the most efficient regime if voluntary disclosure is possible.

An agency perspective of standard setting suggests that accounting standards are affected by the self-interest of the standard setters. Hence, the organization of the standard setting institution matters for the outcome. The same view may call into question the assumption maintained in empirical studies that observed accounting standards are a best response to the needs of those regulated. However, there is no contradiction if one takes the analysis one step further by asking which standard setting institutions are efficient. Unfortunately, there is little work in accounting that addresses this broader question.

5 Empirical tests of agency theory

Agency theory provides a rich set of predictions that can be empirically tested, and there is an extensive literature that tests hypotheses derived from agency theory. Empirical tests are as important as theory building for the evolution of accounting research (see, e.g., Watts and Zimmerman 1986). While analytical models can discover new effects, they cannot answer the question of how important the results they identify are in practice. Empirical research complements analytical research because of its ability to generate insights into the magnitude of effects and to distinguish between competing hypotheses. In this section, I discuss some issues that arise in testing agency theory predictions.

Many empirical papers in the agency theory realm examine incentives for earnings management, including accounting choices. Early research often tested three basic hypotheses formulated by Watts and Zimmerman, which have been refined over time:[21]

> "Bonus plan hypothesis: Ceteris paribus, managers of firms with bonus plans are more likely to choose accounting procedures that shift reported earnings from future periods to the current period."

> "Debt/equity hypothesis: Ceteris paribus, the larger a firm's debt/equity ratio, the more likely the firm's manager is to select accounting procedures that shift reported earnings from future periods to the current period."

> "Size hypothesis: Ceteris paribus, the larger the firm, the more likely the manager is to choose accounting procedures that defer reported earnings from current to future periods."

Other work attempts to discriminate between the "opportunistic management" hypothesis and the "information signaling" hypothesis. The opportunistic management hypothesis derives from agency theory and assumes opportunistic behavior of managers (in both owner-manager and firm-creditor agency relationships). As emphasized earlier, if earnings management occurs in a contracting setting, it is part of an ex ante efficient contract. Yet it typically reduces the information content of financial information relative to a situation in which no earnings management is possible. The information signaling hypothesis presumes that a manager makes financial information more informative than unmanaged financial statement information through earnings management. An opportunistic manager has an incentive to make accounting information more informative if it provides an expected benefit to him or her (or to the firm). For example, more informative accounting can make earnings more predictive of future earnings, an aspect valued by capital providers. Smoothing incentives may do the same if smoothing is based on the manager's private information and, thus, indirectly conveys that information. Strategic decisions for voluntary disclosure can signal private information because it reveals part of the information that is not voluntarily disclosed. The information signaling hypothesis can also be derived from other theories about management behavior (see below). Finding out which hypothesis is more consistent with the data should be helpful for standard setters in deciding whether to allow more options or discretion in standards.

An example of such work is Ramanna and Watts (2012), who examine the impairment of goodwill. Impairment rules provide management with significant discretion in determining whether impairment needs to be recognized and what amount is appropriate. Ramanna and Watts test whether impairment is motivated by providing more information about future cash flows or whether it is used opportunistically to maximize managers' utility, including compensation, reputation, violation of debt covenants, and others. Using a sample of firms that recognized goodwill and had a book-to-market ratio of greater than one (which is an indicator for necessary impairment), they find no evidence for the information signaling hypothesis, but they do find evidence for the opportunistic management hypothesis. Badertscher, Collins, and Lys (2012) study a sample of firms that restated financial statements. The advantage of this sample is that the difference between originally reported and restated earnings is known ex post. They find that if originally reported earnings meet or beat certain benchmarks, they are less informative about future cash flows than restated earnings, while the converse is true for those firms whose originally reported earnings did not meet or beat benchmarks.

The analytical agency theory is based on models, which are simplifying descriptions of reality. While the virtue of models is that the assumptions and the mechanisms that generate the results are explicitly laid out, the disadvantage is that they cannot (and are not supposed to) capture the richness of reality.[22] Since the model predictions follow logically from the model, an empirical test of an analytically derived prediction is essentially a test of whether the assumptions that underlie the model are valid in reality. If the assumptions are considered descriptive for reality, then not finding the predicted association can have two main reasons: (i) it suggests that the effects are not of first-order importance, or (ii) it raises concerns about the empirical design, including the sample and the proxies used to measure the constructs. Another possible reason is the implicit assumption in archival empirical research that observed contracts are optimal, at least on average. This need not hold, for example, if the economic environment is dynamic and there are frequent innovations. It may be too costly or take time to move to the optimum, so satisfactory rather than optimal solutions prevail.

There exist a number of practical problems in testing agency theory. First, deriving predictions can be difficult since agency theory results are often not robust but hinge on many specific assumptions. A slight variation of an assumption about the environment or the characteristics of decision makers can even reverse a result. Further, there are situations in which multiple equilibria arise as possible solutions. In this case, theory does not give a clear prediction. Archival empirical research mainly looks at the average rather than at the extremes, so it may help to distinguish between possible equilibria, but it may also overlook particular circumstances necessary for a theoretical result. In the best case, the empirical design can control for such assumptions either by selecting an appropriate sample or by adding control variables. Experimental research is often in a better position to test analytical agency theory because it offers a clean environment in which variation of a single parameter can help identify its effect. But it has other relative disadvantages, such as external validity.

Second, agency theory is based on optimal decisions made by the parties in an agency relationship. Therefore, all decisions are endogenous and – even more complicated – they are based on endogenous expectations (Demski 2004). For example, if a contract induces the manager to manage earnings, this behavior is part of a contract that is most efficient among a set of other feasible contracts. Empirically finding that some firms manage earnings more than others does not tell much about the efficiency of the respective arrangements. Ideally, empirical research would examine a situation in which there is an exogenous shock, such as a regulatory change, and test for the change in financial reporting this shock induces. But even then, the shock likely induces changes in decisions other than financial reporting choices, which jointly influence the change in financial reporting.

Third, many aspects of a contract are not observable. Demski and Sappington (1999) show that omitting certain variables leads to variation in the observed features of contracts, which can lead to a misinterpretation of the results. Examples are the omission of additional performance measures or multiple compensation components in an empirical analysis of compensation-based incentives, or omission of multiple tasks and multiple periods, all of which affect the observed intensity of variable compensation in each individual period. A related issue is that some theoretical results rely on out-of-equilibrium strategies, that is, strategies that are never played in equilibrium but are used as threat points to establish the equilibrium strategies. By definition, out-of-equilibrium strategies are never observed, although they affect the observed behavior. Further, predicting efficient accounting standards (or their change) requires a sense of the costs and benefits of accounting standards, few of which are observable.

Fourth, empirical tests require choosing proxies that capture the constructs used in the predictions. An example is the measurement of earnings quality (e.g., Dechow, Ge, and Schrand 2010), for which many proxies have been developed in the empirical literature, but for which it is still an open issue about what attributes they measure and how the proxies are related to each other (see, e.g., Ewert and Wagenhofer 2011). One particular proxy for earnings quality that is often used in empirical studies is earnings management. As discussed earlier, it is not clear if earnings management is "good" or "bad" in the sense that it increases or reduces earnings quality. Moreover, the most effective earnings management is not observable or inferable from a proxy. Hence, what proxies capture is perhaps something other than actual earnings management or only a minor occurrence.

6 Critique of agency theory

The main criticism of agency theory lies in the assumption of rational, purely self-interested parties. This assumption has been challenged by theories that describe human behavior in general and in organizations. The self-interest criticism consists of two distinct parts: one is rationality in general and the other is the objective of the parties, particularly opportunistic management.

The rationality assumption says that all parties are fully rational in the sense that they are fully aware of the situation and make use of all information available to them when they make their decisions. Agency models make heavy use of this assumption, as the solution concept, an equilibrium, is based on the strategic interactions between the contracting parties' strategies. It is obvious that real people do not behave fully rationally in many situations. Psychological research has identified many biases in human decision making and many circumstances that can affect those decisions, such as overconfidence, emotions, stressful situations, and the like. A large body of experimental research shows that the decisions people make are affected by envy, inequity, fairness, and other considerations that make other parties' utilities important for decision making. From an economic perspective, some deviations from fully rational decision making can be explained by explicitly inserting into the model the costs and disutility of thinking and reasoning or understanding the information that is available.[23] In such cases, rational behavior prevails, although it may not appear as such to observers. The assumption of full rationality is justified as a benchmark because it is difficult to imagine that any decision maker would *intentionally* decide irrationally.[24] Moreover, financial accounting decisions are made in a business context, which is likely to foster "more" rational decision making.

Another aspect of the rationality assumption is that the parties in an agency relationship fully understand the asymmetric information situation they face. The fact that one party has more information or is likely to receive more information than another party must be common knowledge to allow application of the standard solution concepts of game theory (e.g., Sunder 2002). This means the parties deal with "known unknowns," but not with "unknown unknowns." If the parties unknowingly make decisions on different information sets, they do not interact strategically as the models require.

The rationality assumption does not specify the arguments in the parties' utility functions. Agency theory typically assumes that parties maximize their expected utility, which includes their (monetary) net worth and other factors. For example, the standard owner–manager agency problem assumes that agents are effort-averse (i.e., more effort is personally costly to them), which is the main source of conflict of interest in this type of model. Other factors are, for example, empire building (a benefit from controlling a larger business), power, consumption of perquisites on the job, impatience (a higher discount rate or a short-term horizon), career concerns (e.g., tenure, promotion, increasing the value on the manager market), liability and litigation threats, and many more. Even if there is no direct conflict of interest in a particular task, induced moral hazard may arise from a separate task that has a spill-over effect on other tasks, thus creating an agency problem.

Another critique is the fundamental assumption of opportunistic behavior by managers. However, agency theory requires only the determination of well-defined utility functions for all parties in the agency relationship. Maximization of the utilities (under constraints) serves as the objective function for the optimal solution. From a modeling perspective, it does not really matter what the assumed behavior looks like. Factors that are viewed as important can easily be added to the utility function. Eventually, which factors a useful theory should consider is an empirical question.

Organizational research argues that people in organizations are not driven so much by self-interest as by joint objectives of the organization. For example, stewardship theory (Davis, Schoorman, and Donaldson 1997) – not to be confused with the stewardship objective in agency theory – assumes that the behavior of managers is motivated by the organizational, collectivistic goals of the organization rather than by self-serving behavior. Managers are stewards whose interests are aligned with those of the principal and accounting information is purely informative, like in a single decision making context. From an agency theory perspective, eliminating the conflict of interest resolves the agency problem, and this would make predictions from agency theory consistent with those from stewardship theory. In fact, mechanisms to mitigate agency problems include the selection of persons that fit the organization or the creation of a strong corporate culture and common values.

Finally, it should be noted that because agency theory is at the core of positive accounting research, there is also methodological criticism that focuses on the *positive* theory and argues that it actually is a normative, value-laden theory.[25] While positive accounting theory does not prescribe what principals and agents *should* do, it makes assumptions about their behaviors to derive testable hypotheses. Setting these assumptions can be considered normative, but it is subjected to empirical tests. In a sense, similar methodological issues arise in other scientific disciplines that study human behavior, particularly in the humanities.

7 Conclusions

The cover of the book *Principals and Agents* by Pratt and Zeckhauser (1985) displays a puppet controlling a marionette using strings attached to its movable parts. This illustration is a nice depiction of agency theory, which is about principals who write contracts to control and constrain agents' behavior. Agency conflicts arise in situations of potential conflict of interests and asymmetric information. This chapter discusses typical agency problems and the mechanisms in place to mitigate them. Arguably, one of the most important of such mechanisms is financial accounting and reporting, which provides contractible information that reduces information asymmetry and helps to control the decisions of the contracting parties. Indeed, the heavy regulation of financial reporting is evidence of its importance in practice.

Analytical research in agency theory has generated many useful results about how accounting information can help to resolve or reduce agency problems. A particular characteristic of financial accounting information is its credibility, which is assured by several other institutions, such as auditing, corporate governance, enforcement, and litigation. Another characteristic of accounting information is the high degree of aggregation, which reduces the information content relative to the disaggregated signals but lowers costs of contracting and can even have desirable incentive effects.

Agency theory provides a framework for explaining the incentives of managers to provide information in the first place, the use of information in contracts, and the existence of concepts that underlie financial accounting standards. The chapter specifically examines the application of agency theory to stewardship and valuation objectives of financial accounting, to fair values and conservatism, and to the politics of standard setting. It also discusses issues that arise in empirically testing predictions from agency theory and critical fundamental assumptions, such as the full rationality of the parties involved in a contract.

Often, agency theory is associated with blunt hypotheses about the opportunistic behavior of managers, who are narrowly self-interested and manage earnings to the detriment of firms and creditors. This chapter shows that this view is inappropriate and that agency theory is sufficiently sophisticated to explain behavior and institutions. In particular, ex post incentives of managers for earnings management are part of ex ante efficient contracts, trading off costs and benefits of a variety of mechanisms to mitigate agency costs. Theories become more refined and generate more and more interesting effects that can inform empirical studies. So far, empirical research has found ample evidence that is consistent with agency theory predictions, but there is definitely no scarceness of possibilities for further interesting analyses. Of course, a theory cannot be verified, but the evidence suggests that agency theory is useful for explaining and predicting real phenomena in financial accounting.

Acknowledgment

I acknowledge useful comments by Ralf Ewert, Sebastian Kronenberger, and David Windisch.

Notes

1 Of course, there are many hybrid forms of financing that contain features of both equity and debt capital. They create their own agency problems but can resolve other agency problems (see, e.g., Green 1984).
2 Contract enforcement is usually not considered in the contract design (or is assumed to be costless).
3 If the firm wants to raise equity capital, agency problems arise between existing and new owners.

4   The principal may also have a minimum expected utility, e.g., whether investing in the firm provides a positive net present value. Otherwise he or she would shut down the firm. In typical agency models it is usually simply assumed that this condition holds; otherwise the agency problem disappears.

5   Under mild regularity assumptions the efficient frontier is convex, and varying the reservation utility of one party swipes out all feasible solutions. See, e.g., Arya, Fellingham, and Young (1993).

6   Note that optimal contracts under moral hazard or adverse selection may have several common characteristics, which makes it difficult to empirically distinguish between the underlying agency problems.

7   Indeed, if there are no costs of disclosure, unraveling induces full voluntary disclosure because the user will hold skeptical beliefs in the sense that he or she assumes the most unfavorable signal for the firm in case of non-disclosure. These beliefs induce full disclosure.

8   See Crawford and Sobel (1982).

9   See Dechow, Ge, and Schrand (2010) for a recent survey.

10 The compensation may include monetary payments, other benefits, and stock and stock options. But still they can be, and are, converted into a monetary value.

11 For example, Beyer (2013) shows that if the performance measure linearly aggregates two signals, then conservative accounting (i.e., recognizing losses but not gains) distinguishes particular events better than fair value measurement, and thus it can be preferable depending on the circumstances. Dye (2002) analyzes standards that require binary classification and shows the evolution of shadow standards (that result from earnings management).

12 For example, Paul (1992) shows an agency model in which the weights attached to signals optimally differ by whether they are used for contracting or valuation purposes.

13 It should be noted that there exist other measurement bases that have their own advantages and disadvantages.

14 While a similar concern holds for the determination of impairment under cost measurement, earnings management under fair value measurement can also serve to increase net asset values over their historical cost.

15 See, e.g., Dutta and Zhang (2002).

16 A similar conclusion arises from disclosure models. See, e.g., Liang and Wen (2007) for an analysis of the effects of cost and market-based measurement on investment efficiency and Plantin, Sapra, and Shin (2008) for the emergence of procyclical effects under fair value measurement.

17 It is worth noting that despite the abolishment of conservatism, there continue to exist many individual requirements in old and recent IFRSs that induce conservative information.

18 Gao (2013) models conservatism as requiring a higher level of verification for recognizing gains than for losses. Given the manager's incentives to maximize reported earnings, there is less need for verification when he or she reports a loss, whereas if the manager reports a gain, the anticipation of earnings management increases verification requirements. Nevertheless, there may also be reasons to verify reported losses; e.g., a manager may take a "big bath" if compensation is bounded from below, as it allows the reporting of overstated earnings in future periods.

19 For example, the overhaul of the standards for leases by the IASB (and the FASB) has been largely motivated by the fact that analysts and debt contracts add operating lease obligations to liabilities. Similarly, the use of pro forma earnings numbers indicates that performance reporting standards could be improved.

20 There is evidence that creditors do not systematically deduct goodwill from covenant calculations, which appears to contradict the elimination of purchased intangibles. See Armstrong, Guay, and Weber (2010) for a discussion.

21 The following quotes are from Watts and Zimmerman (1986), pp. 208, 216, and 235.

22 Further discussion of models of agency theory can be found in Wagenhofer (2004).

23 Just imagine reading a typical analytical agency theory paper, which takes many people quite some time to comprehend and is, therefore, costly.

24 Erratic (i.e., randomized) behavior may be an intentional strategy in equilibrium.

25 See, e.g., Christenson (1983), Watts and Zimmerman (1990), and for an overview Mattessich (1984).

References

Akerlof, G.A. (1970): The Market for "Lemons": Quality Uncertainty and the Market Mechanism, *Quarterly Journal of Economics* 84: 488–500.

Armstrong, C.S., W.R. Guay, and J.P. Weber (2010): The Role of Information and Financial Reporting in Corporate Governance and Debt Contracting, *Journal of Accounting and Economics* 50: 179–234.

Alfred Wagenhofer

Arya, A., J.C. Fellingham, and R.A. Young (1993): Preference Representation and Randomization in Principal-Agent Contracts, *Economics Letters* 42: 25–30.

Arya, A., J. Glover, and P.J. Liang (2004): Intertemporal Aggregation and Incentives, *European Accounting Review* 13: 643–657.

Arya, A., J. Glover, and S. Sunder (1998): Earnings Management and the Revelation Principle, *Review of Accounting Studies* 3: 7–34.

Badertscher, B.A., D.W. Collins, and T.Z. Lys (2012): Discretionary Accounting Choices and the Predictive Ability of Accruals with Respect to Future Cash Flows, *Journal of Accounting and Economics* 53: 330–352.

Ball, R. (2001): Infrastructure Requirements for an Economically Efficient System of Public Financial Reporting and Disclosure, *Brookings-Wharton Papers on Financial Services*: 127–169.

Ball, R., and L. Shivakumar (2008): How Much New Information Is There in Earnings? *Journal of Accounting Research* 46: 975–1016.

Ball, R., S. Jayaraman, and L. Shivakumar (2012): Audited Financial Reporting and Voluntary Disclosure as Complements: A Test of the Confirmation Hypothesis, *Journal of Accounting and Economics* 53: 136–166.

Basu, S. (1997): The Conservatism Principle and the Asymmetric Timeliness of Earnings, *Journal of Accounting and Economics* 24: 3–37.

Beatty, A., J. Weber, and J.J. Yu (2008): Conservatism and Debt, *Journal of Accounting and Economics* 45: 154–174.

Benston, G., M. Bromwich, R.E. Litan, and A. Wagenhofer (2006): *Worldwide Financial Reporting: The Development and Future of Accounting Standards,* Oxford University Press: Oxford and New York.

Bertomeu, J., and E. Cheynel (2013): Toward a Positive Theory of Disclosure Regulation: In Search of Institutional Foundations, *The Accounting Review* 88: 789–824.

Bertomeu, J., and R.P. Magee (2011): From Low-Quality Reporting to Financial Crises: Politics of Disclosure Regulation Along the Economic Cycle, *Journal of Accounting and Economics* 52: 209–227.

Beyer, A. (2013): Conservatism and Aggregation: The Effect on Cost of Equity Capital and the Efficiency of Debt Contracts, Working paper, Stanford University.

Chen, Q., T. Hemmer, and Y. Zhang (2007): On the Relation between Conservatism in Accounting Standards and Incentives for Earnings Management, *Journal of Accounting Research* 45: 541–565.

Chen, Q., B. Mittendorf, and Y. Zhang (2010): Endogenous Accounting Bias when Decision Making and Control Interact, *Contemporary Accounting Research* 27: 1063–1091.

Christensen, J. (2010): Conceptual Frameworks of Accounting from an Information Perspective, *Accounting and Business Research* 40: 287–299.

Christensen, J., and J.S. Demski (2003): *Accounting Theory: An Information Content Perspective,* McGraw-Hill Irwin: New York.

Christensen, P.O., and G.A. Feltham (2003): *Economics of Accounting, Volume I: Information in Markets,* Kluwer: Boston, Dordrecht, London.

Christensen, P.O., and G.A. Feltham (2005): *Economics of Accounting, Volume II: Performance Evaluation,* Springer: New York.

Christensen, P.O., G.A. Feltham, and F. Şabac (2005): A Contracting Perspective on Earnings Quality, *Journal of Accounting and Economics* 39: 265–294.

Christensen, P.O., H. Frimor, and F. Şabac (2013): The Stewardship Role of Analyst Forecasts, and Discretionary Versus Non-Discretionary Accruals, *European Accounting Review* 22: 257–296.

Christenson, C. (1983): The Methodology of Positive Accounting, *The Accounting Review* 58: 1–22.

Coase, R.H. (1937): The Nature of the Firm, *Economica* 4: 386–405.

Crawford, V.P., and J. Sobel (1982): Strategic Information Transmission, *Econometrica* 50: 1431–1451.

Davis, J.H., F.D. Schoorman, and L. Donaldson (1997): Toward a Stewardship Theory of Management, *Academy of Management Review* 22: 20–47.

Dechow, P., W. Ge, and C. Schrand (2010): Understanding Earnings Quality: A Review of the Proxies, Their Determinants and Their Consequences, *Journal of Accounting and Economics* 50: 344–401.

Demerjian, P.R. (2011): Accounting Standards and Debt Covenants: Has the "Balance Sheet Approach" Led to a Decline in the Use of Balance Sheet Covenants? *Journal of Accounting and Economics* 52: 178–202.

Demski, J.S. (1998): Performance Measure Manipulation, *Contemporary Accounting Research* 15: 261–285.

Demski, J.S. (2004): Endogenous Expectations, *The Accounting Review* 79: 519–539.

Demski, J.S., and D.E.M. Sappington (1999): Summarization with Errors: A Perspective on Empirical Investigations of Agency Relationships, *Management Accounting Research* 10: 21–37.

Drymiotes, G., and T. Hemmer (2013): On the Stewardship and Valuation Implications of Accrual Accounting Systems, *Journal of Accounting Research* 51: 281–334.

Dutta, S., and X.-J. Zhang (2002): Revenue Recognition in a Multiperiod Agency Setting, *Journal of Accounting Research* 40: 67–83.

Dye, R.A. (2002): Classification Manipulation and Nash Accounting Standards, *Journal of Accounting Research* 40: 1125–1162.

Dye, R.A., and S.S. Sridhar (2004): Reliability-Relevance Trade-Offs and the Efficiency of Aggregation, *Journal of Accounting Research* 42: 51–88.

Ewert, R., and A. Wagenhofer (2011): Earnings Management, Conservatism, and Earnings Quality, *Foundations and Trends in Accounting* 6: 65–186.

Fama, E.F., and M.C. Jensen (1983): Separation of Ownership and Control, *Journal of Law and Economics* 26: 301–325.

Feltham, G.A., and J. Xie (1994): Performance Measure Congruity and Diversity in Multi-Task Principal/Agent Relations, *The Accounting Review* 69: 429–453.

Feltham, G., R. Indjejikian, and D. Nanda (2006): Dynamic Incentives and Dual-Purpose Accounting, *Journal of Accounting and Economics* 42: 417–437.

Fields, T.D., T.Z. Lys, and L. Vincent (2001): Empirical Research on Accounting Choice, *Journal of Accounting and Economics* 31: 255–307.

Fischer, P.E., and R.E. Verrecchia (2000): Reporting Bias, *The Accounting Review* 75: 229–245.

Gao, P. (2013): A Measurement Approach to Conservatism and Earnings Management, *Journal of Accounting and Economics* 55: 251–268.

Gigler, F., and T. Hemmer (2001): Conservatism, Optimal Disclosure Policy, and the Timeliness of Financial Reports, *The Accounting Review* 76: 471–493.

Gigler, F., Kanodia, C., Sapra, H., and R. Venugopalan (2009): Accounting Conservatism and the Efficiency of Debt Contracts, *Journal of Accounting Research* 47: 767–797.

Gjesdal, F. (1982): Information and Incentives: The Agency Information Problem, *Review of Economic Studies* 49: 373–390.

Göx, R.F., and A. Wagenhofer (2009): Optimal Impairment Rules, *Journal of Accounting and Economics* 48: 2–16.

Green, R.C. (1984): Investment Incentives, Debt, and Warrants, *Journal of Financial Economics* 13: 115–136.

IASB (2010): *The Conceptual Framework for Financial Reporting 2010,* London.

Jensen, M.C., and W.H. Meckling (1976): Theory of the Firm: Managerial Behavior, Agency Costs, and Ownership Structure, *Journal of Financial Economics* 3: 305–360.

Kothari, S.P., K. Ramanna, and D.J. Skinner (2010): Implications for GAAP from an Analysis of Positive Research in Accounting, *Journal of Accounting and Economics* 50: 246–286.

Lambert, R.A. (2001): Contracting Theory and Accounting, *Journal of Accounting and Economics* 32: 3–87.

Liang, P.J., and X. Wen (2007): Accounting Measurement Basis, Market Mispricing, and Firm Investment Efficiency, *Journal of Accounting Research* 45: 155–197.

Mattessich, R. (ed.) (1984): *Modern Accounting Research: History, Survey, and Guide,* Canadian Certified General Accountants' Research Foundation: Vancouver.

Myerson, R.B. (1982): Optimal Coordination Mechanisms in Generalized Principal-Agent Problems, *Journal of Mathematical Economics* 10: 67–81.

Paul, J.M. (1992): On the Efficiency of Stock-Based Compensation, *Review of Financial Studies* 5: 471–502.

Penno, M. (1990): Auditing for Performance Evaluation, *The Accounting Review* 65: 520–536.

Plantin, G., H. Sapra, and H.S. Shin (2008): Marking-to-Market: Panacea or Pandora's Box? *Journal of Accounting Research* 46: 435–460.

Pratt, J.W., and R.J. Zeckhauser (eds.) (1985): *Principals and Agents: The Structure of Business,* Harvard Business School Press: Boston.

Ramanna, K., and R.L. Watts (2012): Evidence on the Use of Unverifiable Estimates in Required Goodwill Impairment, *Review of Accounting Studies* 17: 749–780.

Shivakumar, L. (2013): The Role of Financial Reporting in Debt Contracting and in Stewardship, *Accounting and Business Research* 43: 362–383.

Sunder, S. (2002): Knowing What Others Know: Common Knowledge, Accounting, and Capital Markets, *Accounting Horizons* 16: 305–318.

Wagenhofer, A. (2004): Accounting and Economics: What We Learn from Analytical Models in Financial Accounting and Reporting, in: Leuz, C., D. Pfaff, and A.G. Hopwood (eds.): *The Economics and Politics of Accounting,* Oxford University Press: Oxford 5–31.

Watts, R.L. (2003a): Conservatism in Accounting Part I: Explanations and Implications, *Accounting Horizons* 17: 207–221.

Watts, R.L. (2003b): Conservatism in Accounting Part II: Evidence and Research Opportunities, *Accounting Horizons* 17: 287–301.

Watts, R.L., and J.L. Zimmerman (1986): *Positive Accounting Theory,* Prentice-Hall: Englewood Cliffs, NJ.

Watts, R.L., and J.L. Zimmerman (1990): Positive Accounting Theory: A Ten Year Perspective, *The Accounting Review* 65: 131–156.

14

Disclosure and the cost of capital

A survey of the theoretical literature

Jeremy Bertomeu and Edwige Cheynel

The objective of this chapter is to provide an accessible and concise review of advances on disclosure of accounting information as a determinant of the cost of capital. The effect of information on the cost of capital is a broad question that spans the areas of accounting, economics and finance. To guide and organize research about this question, this chapter will follow a general guiding theme: the cost of capital is the observable outcome of a complex set of phenomena, and, therefore, how one interprets measurements of the cost of capital is deeply engrained in the working assumptions made about those phenomena. In this spirit, the reader should find here a primer to organize the various competing theories about disclosure and the cost of capital.

Historically, the terminology of cost of capital is not new. By means of a brief introduction, records from the 19th century indicate that the cost of capital was occasionally used in trade publications. The vignette reproduced in Figure 14.1 is extracted from the September 13, 1869, issue of *The American Railway Times* and examines the profitability of manufacturing in the state of Ohio from data supplied by the US census bureau.

The record presents the remarkably modern practice of applying a standard rate on a stock of capital to calculate profitability net of a capital charge. Yet the analyst shies away from considering the opportunity cost on the capital used by the firm and the rate of 6 percent appears to be primarily meant to capture various accounting expenses missing from the census data:

> It will be observed that there are two important elements of cost left out – rents and wear and tear. Perhaps both of these may be balanced by the 6 per cent interest on capital we have added in. In that case the actual profit on capital in 1850 was 40 per cent, and in 1860 was 45 percent. The census tables for 1850 made the profit 49 per cent, but this was obviously wrong, for no allowance was made for rent, repairs, etc.
>
> *(p. 300)*

Over the following century, the cost of capital started to become a popular tool for economic analysis as a result of various innovations to accounting and financial transactions. First, the set of accounting practices in double-entry book-keeping prescribed the expensing of interest paid on debt instruments, thus motivating interest as a cost analogous to the rental of a tangible asset.

	1850	1860	(Increase per cent)
Capital invested	$29,019,538	$57,295,303	.96
Raw materials	$34,677,937	$69,800,270	1.0
Hands employed	51,489	75,602	.24
Annual wages	$13,467,660	$22,302,989	.70
An. val. of products.	$62,607,859	$121,691,148	.95

According to this, the actual cost of the products announced to this:

	1850	1900
Cost of capital (6 per cent)	$1,700,000	$3,400,000
Raw materials	$34,677,937	$69,800,270
Wages	$13,467,660	$22,303,989
Total cost	$49,875,597	$95,504,259
Value of products	$62,647,859	$121,691,148
Apparent profits	$12,772,262	$26,186,889

Figure 14.1 Manufacturing in Ohio (period 1850–1860)

Second, the development of financial markets and, with it, the spread of different forms of interest-bearing instruments more complex than standard debt (debentures, certificates, etc.) required new language that gradually extended the terminology of cost of debt toward a broader concept of capital. A representative example is found in an excerpt from H. Dureau in the February 1927 issue of the *Journal of Land and Public Utility Economics*, reproduced in Figure 14.2 below. For the most part, the measures assigned to the cost of capital correspond to debt-like instruments, but the *"return earned on stock"* offers an interesting precursor to measuring the cost of equity capital.

The development of equity markets during the interwar period made apparent the need to broaden the notion of cost of capital to other non–debt financing alternatives, but some important questions needed to be answered first: (i) If only interest-bearing instruments are to be costed, can the corporation raise equity capital at no cost? (ii) If not, when does the corporation meet the compensation demanded by (but not guaranteed to) its equity investors? (iii) How should managers calculate a capital charge to select which investments to engage in? In practice, an answer to these three questions ran approximately as follows: (i) no, (ii) non-negative returns, and (iii) the average of cost of debt. Naturally, these answers were somewhat inconsistent with each other: why were returns on new investments evaluated against the cost of debt if they were partially paid for with equity, and, if so, should equity investors receive a return that is on par, if not greater, than the return given to debt providers? As equity capital became scarce during the great depression of the 1930s, economists began to think about an extended concept of cost of capital that would involve the cost of equity as a key component.

The modern approach to the cost of capital largely evolved from the classic 1958 text, "The cost of capital, corporation finance and the theory of investment," by Franco Modigliani and Merton Miller, then two researchers at the Carnegie Institute of Technology. This text offered a now classic paradigm to define and measure the cost on *all* forms of capital used by the firm, inclusive of debt and equity capital, in environments with uncertain returns. Modigliani and Miller famously concluded that, in a frictionless market, the type of securities issued by the firm is irrelevant (or, colloquially, "it does not matter how you slice a cake").[1] Since then, a large body of research has tried to explain what determinants can affect the corporation's cost of capital.

Table xiv   Comparison of total cost of capital with ratio of operating income to investment
and net income to stock of operating steam railway companies

| YEAR | COST OF CAPITAL SECURED BY ISSUANCE OF: | | | | RETURN EARNED | |
	All Securities	Bonds	Equip. Trust Certificates	Misc. Securities	On Investment	On Stock
1920	7.29	7.34	7.28	7.01	.06	5.45
1921	7.21	7.23	6.76	7.64	2.96	3.94
1922	5.86	5.92	5.71	6.00	3.74	4.85
1923	5.61	5.38	5.72	6.45	4.50	6.95
1924	5.54	5.61	5.27	6.11	4.44	6.74
1925	5.45	5.60	5.04	5.18	5.01	8.20
1926	5.15	5.27	4.95	5.27	–	–
1920–1926	5.82	5.87	5.50	6.24	3.37	5.99

Figure 14.2   Cost of capital in the railway industry (1920–1926)

This family of theories of the cost of capital emphasizes the risk premium demanded by risk-averse investors trading the firm's securities. Because this approach is the most widely studied in the existing literature, it will occupy most of this chapter. It traces its origins from the Arrow-Debreu utility theory and, later on, its application in portfolio theory by Harry Markowitz and in the capital asset pricing model (CAPM) of Lintner-Mossin-Sharpe. The theory emphasizes that risk-averse investors require a premium to hold risky payoffs relative to sure ones, and hence from a portfolio perspective, only those individual risks that cannot be insured by holding other assets should be considered risky. Hence, the model concludes that the risk premium is not directly a function of the variance (or risk) of an individual asset but rather is a function of its covariance with other assets. Markowitz is one of the first to formally identify undiversifiable risks as the primary determinant of a risk premium, and the CAPM provided the first practical theory to derive the cost of capital for various classes of assets. An introduction to this model is given in section 1.1.

Asset pricing theory poses a number of questions, some of which are answered in the following sections.

a   When and how does information affect the risk premium? (sections 1.2 and 1.3)
b   Does information affect the risk premium differently in environments with asymmetric information? (section 2.1)
c   How does disclosure affect a firm's investor base? (section 2.2)
d   How does disclosure affect investors' subjective beliefs? (section 2.3)
e   What is the effect of voluntary disclosure on the risk premium? (section 2.4)
f   And, when do changes in the risk premium proxy for risk-sharing efficiency, productive decisions, and welfare implications? (section 3)

Once these questions are answered within the baseline model, we will develop richer models that extend some of the insights of the CAPM to more complex environments. A brief introduction to other asset pricing models is offered, which includes the consumption CAPM, the asset pricing model, and models of markets with imperfect liquidity.

g   When do accounting frictions, in the form of earnings management, affect the risk premium? (section 4.2)

h   How does the cost of capital interact with the stewardship value of information? That is, do characteristics of measurement used to resolve agency problems affect the risk premium? (section 4.3)

i   How should we identify, theoretically and empirically, an accounting-based risk factor? (section 5.1)

j   When does disclosure affect the cost of capital in liquidity-constrained environments? (section 5.2)

1 Overview of asset pricing

A fundamental determinant of the cost of capital defined in Modigliani and Miller's theory is the risk premium demanded by investors for holding securities whose payoffs are uncertain. The capital asset pricing model provides the foundations to predict the discount demanded by investors to hold such uncertain claims. The focus of this section will be the component of the cost of capital represented by the *risk premium* when risk-averse investors and traders make portfolio choices in a competitive market. This section formalizes the notion of diversification and the pricing of uncertain claims in competitive markets.

1.1 The CARA-Normal model

Before we analyze the risk premium as an abstract concept, it is helpful to illustrate its formation within a parsimonious model of an economy with risk-averse investors making simple trading decisions. There are two dates $t = 0, 1$ such that investors trade at date $t = 0$ and asset payoffs realize at date $t = 1$. The economy is composed of $i = 1, \ldots, I$ investors and $j = 1, \ldots, J$ different assets with normally distributed payoffs $\mathbf{x} \sim N(\mathbf{m}, \mathbf{V})$ where $\mathbf{x}$ and $\mathbf{m}$ are $J \times 1$ vectors, and $\mathbf{V}$ is a $J \times J$ definite positive variance-covariance matrix. In what follows, a sub-index refers to a component of a vector or matrix and a prime indicates the transpose operation.[2]

Assets are in exogenous supply $\mathbf{b}$, a $J \times 1$ vector. Each investor has an exponential (i.e., CARA) utility function $u_i(w) = -e^{-\alpha_i w}$, which depends only on the end-of-period payoff w and where $\alpha_i > 0$ represents the investor's Arrow-Pratt coefficient of absolute risk-aversion. Investors can borrow at date $t = 0$ at an interest rate normalized to zero.[3] Let $\mathbf{p}$ denote the $J \times 1$ vector of prices for each asset, while $\mathbf{k}$ denotes the $J \times I$ matrix of units of each asset purchased by each investor.

A competitive (Walrasian) equilibrium is represented by a choice of $(\mathbf{p}^*, (\mathbf{k}_i^*))$ that satisfies two conditions. First, each investor is price-taking and chooses a portfolio $\mathbf{k}_i^*$ to maximize his expected utility $\mathbf{E}(u_i(\mathbf{k}_i'(\mathbf{x}-\mathbf{p}^*)))$, taking the equilibrium price $\mathbf{p}^*$ as a given. This problem can be restated in terms of maximizing the following mean-variance objective:

$$u_i = \mathbf{k}_i'(\mathbf{m} - \mathbf{p}*) - \frac{\alpha_i}{2}\mathbf{k}_i'\mathbf{V}\mathbf{k}_i.$$

The optimal portfolio choice is then given by:

$$\mathbf{k}_i^* = \frac{1}{\alpha_i}\mathbf{V}^{-1}(\mathbf{m} - \mathbf{p}*). \tag{1}$$

Second, the equilibrium must be such that the total demand for assets equals the supply; hereafter, this condition is referred to as market–clearing. This is mathematically stated by noting the cumulative demand of all investors must equal the supply of each asset; that is,

$$\mathbf{b} = \sum \mathbf{k}_i^* = \mathbf{V}^{-1}\left(\mathbf{m} - \mathbf{p}^*\right)\underbrace{\sum \frac{1}{\alpha_i}}_{\equiv 1/\alpha}, \tag{2}$$

where $\dfrac{1}{\alpha} = \dfrac{1}{I}\sum 1/\alpha_i$ is a geometric average of investors' risk aversion.

Solving equations (1) and (2),

$$\mathbf{p}^* = \mathbf{m} - \alpha \mathbf{V}\mathbf{b}/I, \tag{3}$$

$$\mathbf{k}_i^* = \frac{\alpha}{\alpha_i}\frac{\mathbf{b}}{I}. \tag{4}$$

Equation (3) is a fundamental result stating that the price of an asset is equal to its expected pay-off minus a premium measured as the covariance of the asset payoff with the market portfolio.

Equation (4) states that each investor owns a share of the same *market portfolio*, a result also known as two–fund separation.[4] Hereafter, assume that $\mathbf{m}$ is sufficiently large so that no asset would trade at zero or negative price.

The model lends itself well to illustrating the standard capital asset pricing model. Let $r^M = \mathbf{b}'(\mathbf{x} - \mathbf{p})/\mathbf{b}'\mathbf{p}$ denote the return of the market portfolio. The risk premium on the market, denoted $RP^M = \mathbb{E}(r^M)$ is given, in matrix form, by:

$$RP^M = \mathbf{b}'(\mathbf{m} - \mathbf{p}^*)/\mathbf{b}'\mathbf{p}^* \tag{5}$$

Let $\mathbf{e}_i$ denote the $J \times 1$ vector where the ith component is one and the other components are zeros. For any of J assets, the risk premium RP^i for asset i is given by:[5]

$$RP^i \equiv \frac{\mathbf{e}_i'\left(\mathbf{m} - \mathbf{p}^*\right)}{\mathbf{e}_i'\mathbf{p}^*} = \frac{\alpha \mathbf{e}_i'\mathbf{V}\mathbf{b}/I}{\mathbf{e}_i'\mathbf{p}^*} = \underbrace{\frac{co\mathbf{V}\left(r^i, r^M\right)}{Var\left(r^M\right)}}_{\beta^i} RP^M, \tag{6}$$

where $r^i = \mathbf{e}_i'(\mathbf{x} - \mathbf{p}^*)/\mathbf{e}_i'\mathbf{p}^*$ is the return of asset i.

The risk premium of an asset is a function of the exposure of the asset return to the market portfolio return (its "beta," denoted here β_i). From a statistical perspective, the expected return on an asset can thus be predicted by estimating the beta from a linear regression of the realized return of the asset on the realized return of the market.

1.2 Comparative statics on information and the cost of capital

The asset pricing relationship given in equation (6) yields several comparative statics on the effect of additional information on the predicted cost of capital. To obtain such results, let us add to the model slightly by assuming that a random variable $\tilde{s}$ is observed before any trade is made. Then, let the posterior distribution of all assets be normally distributed with mean $\mathbf{m}^s$ and variance–covariance matrix V^s. We know from equation (6) that the risk premium demanded by investors after information is released is:

$$RP^i\left(s\right)\equiv\frac{\alpha\mathbf{e}_i'\,\mathbf{V}^s\,\mathbf{b}\,/\,I}{\mathbf{e}_i'\mathbf{m}^s-\alpha\mathbf{e}_i'\mathbf{V}^s\,\mathbf{b}\,/\,I}=\frac{1}{\dfrac{\mathbb{E}\left(\mathbf{x}_i\,|s\right)}{\alpha\,cov\left(\mathbf{x}_i\,,\,x^M\,|s\right)/\,I}-1}\,,\tag{7}$$

where $x^M=\mathbf{b}'\mathbf{x}$ indicates the payoff of the market portfolio.

Information can have two effects on the cost of capital, which Richard Lambert, Christian Leuz, and Robert Verrecchia called direct and indirect effects in several of their research papers.[6] The *direct effect* of information is to alter the covariance of the asset with other assets in the economy, as captured by the term $cov(\mathbf{x}_i, x^M|s)$, which measures the contribution of a firm's cash flow to total risk. Second, the *indirect effect* of information is to change the expected cash flow of the asset, as captured by the term $\mathbb{E}(x_i|s)$. The greater the posterior expectation about the cash flow, the lower the risk premium on the asset. In general, information has an ambiguous effect on both the direct and the indirect effect. An informative signal might increase the covariance of the asset with the total market payoff, if this signal indicates that the firm carries a greater share of total risk. Similarly, a signal could increase or decrease the posterior mean cash flow, thus having an ambiguous effect on the cost of capital for a given variance.[7]

A clear intuition is best obtained by placing a factor structure on the model.[8] Assume that each firm's cash flow is driven by a single factor; that is,

$$\mathbf{x}_i=a_iF+\in_i,\tag{8}$$

where $\in_i$ is white noise with mean zero and variance σ_i^2 and F has mean m_F and variance σ_F^2.

Assume also that the signal on the firm's cash flow has the additive form $s=\mathbf{x}_i+u$ where u is normally distributed white noise with mean zero and variance σ_u^2. By Bayesian updating,

$$\mathbb{E}\left(\mathbf{x}_i\,|\,s\right)=\frac{\sigma_u^2}{\sigma_u^2+a_i^2\sigma_F^2+\sigma_i^2}\,m_i+\frac{a_i^2\sigma_F^2+\sigma_i^2}{\sigma_u^2+a_i^2\sigma_F^2+\sigma_i^2}\,s$$

$$cov\left(\mathbf{x}_i\,,x_M\,|s\right)=cov\left(\mathbf{x}_i\,,x_M\right)\frac{\sigma_u^2}{\sigma_u^2+a_i^2\sigma_F^2+\sigma_i^2}\,,$$

where $m_i=\alpha_i m_F$ is the prior expectation about the asset return.

Equation (9) illustrates the indirect effect of releasing information. When the signal is more favorable, the cash flow is greater, thus implying fewer units of systematic risk per unit of expected cash flow and reducing the risk premium. Equation (9) reveals an unambiguous direct effect of information on the risk premium (within this factor specification). Because it partially realizes the firm's terminal cash flow, information reduces the covariance between all assets, causing a reduction in the risk premium.

The value of this model is also in terms of *what it does not say,* and unfortunately many of its fundamental insights are often distorted. First, the indirect effect is plausibly quite large relative to the direct effect because the indirect effect is an update on the firm's expected cash flow,

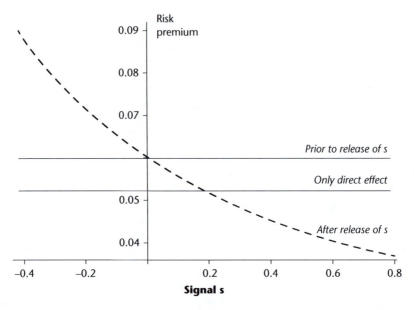

Figure 14.3   Effect of information on the risk premium

while the direct effect largely works via an update on the entire economy.[9] Information reduces the risk premium only to the extent that the indirect effect is ignored. To compare direct and indirect effects, consider the following numerical example. Set $m_F = 0.18$, $\sigma_F = 0.1$, $a_i = 1$, and $\sigma_i = 0.2$ for all i (these imply an ex-ante risk premium of approximately 6 percent). Finally, let the signal have variance $\sigma_u = 0.6$.

In Figure 14.3, the bold line represents the risk premium before any information is released. The dotted curve represents the risk premium after information is released and, due to the indirect effect, is a function of the realized signal. For comparison, the lower line corresponds to the direct effect only (holding s at its unconditional mean). The direct effect does indeed reduce the risk premium, but the variation due to the indirect effect is quite large. For a variation of minus a standard deviation, the indirect effect can cause the risk premium to *increase,* and its magnitude is greater than the direct effect at one standard deviation. Furthermore, these observations are likely to be understating the true direct effect because this calibration would imply that the disclosure of a single firm would reduce the total market risk premium by almost one percentage point, probably overstating the magnitude of the indirect effect contained in one firm's disclosure. To summarize this first point, information can reduce the risk premium, but this claim can only be made unambiguously *at the portfolio level,* when the diversification across elements of a portfolio will neutralize the direct effect.

Second, information does not necessarily reduce the firm's beta. Ignoring the indirect effect (setting the realized signal close to $s = a_i\, m_F$), one can use equation (3) to write:

$$RP^i\left(a_i m_F\right) = \mathbb{E}\left(\mathbf{x}_i \mid s = a_i m_F\right) - \frac{\alpha}{I}\mathrm{cov}\left(\mathbf{x}_i, x_M \mid s = a_i m_F\right)$$

$$= \underbrace{\frac{\sigma_u^2}{a_i^2 \sigma_F^2 + \sigma_i^2 + \sigma_u^2}\left(\mathbb{E}\left(\mathbf{x}_i\right) - \frac{\alpha}{I}\mathrm{cov}\left(\mathbf{x}_i, x_M\right)\right)}_{= \beta_i RP^M} + \frac{a_i^2 \sigma_F^2 + \sigma_i^2}{a_i^2 \sigma_F^2 + \sigma_i^2 + \sigma_u^2}a_i m_F, \tag{9}$$

where β_i is the theoretical beta before any information is released and RP^M is the risk premium on the market portfolio.[10]

The first part of equation (9) above implies a reduction of the beta due to the revelation of some firm-specific information. Because the average beta in the economy must average to one, the second term captures the overall reduction of total risk in the market, implying that less total risk is shared among all the firms.[11] Whenever the payoff of firm i tends to correlate more with market payoffs (a_i is large), this effect can imply a greater beta for firm i.

Third, the model provides support for a *time-series* analysis of the risk premium examined before versus after a disclosure has been made. Ignoring the indirect effect, a firm making a disclosure will tend to see its risk premium decrease after the disclosure. However, no claim is made about cross-sectional differences in the risk premium between firm i (or a group of firms producing more transparent financial statements) and other firms that do not disclose. To illustrate this point with a basic example, consider the simplifying assumption of $\sigma_i^2 = \sigma_i^2 \approx 0$ where two assets i and j are mainly driven by the factor realization. Equation (9) will imply that:

$$RP^i\left(a_i m_F\right) = \frac{\sigma_u^2}{a_i^2 \sigma_F^2 + \sigma_u^2} \beta_i RP^M + \frac{a_i^2 \sigma_F^2}{a_i^2 \sigma_F^2 + \sigma_u^2} a_i m_F \tag{10}$$

$$RP^j\left(a_i m_F\right) = \frac{\sigma_u^2}{a_i^2 \sigma_F^2 + \sigma_u^2} \beta_j RP^M + \frac{a_i^2 \sigma_F^2}{a_i^2 \sigma_F^2 + \sigma_u^2} a_j m_F. \tag{11}$$

Hence, in this example, the difference $RP^j\left(a_i\, m_F\right) - RP^i\left(a_i\, m_F\right)$ will be positive, implying a higher risk premium for the non-disclosing firm, if and only if firm j is more exposed to the common factor than firm i. Put differently, the public disclosure by firm i does not change the relative ranking of risk premia between these two firms.

Fourth, and continuing this idea further, the effect of information on the cost of capital (typically) does not occur through a firm's beta, since betas in the economy must average to one. Instead, information affects the cost of capital because it reduces the expected return on the market portfolio $RP^M = E\left(r^M\right) - r_f$ where r_f is the risk-free rate (normalized to zero in the model). A necessary condition for information to affect the cost of capital is, therefore, that it reduces the market risk premium. That is, if a firm's disclosure has no effect on the market premium, the theoretical mechanism will not operate and the firm's disclosure, being mostly about the firm's idiosyncratic risk, will have no effect on its own cost of capital.

1.3 Ex-ante versus ex-post risk premium

The model presented earlier provides a measurement of the risk premium after information has been released. However, for practical purposes, a time series of stock returns and accounting disclosures will, more plausibly, feature some data points before information is released (say, before a major earnings release) and some data points after information is released. For obvious reasons, it is difficult to analyze a fully dynamic market model with repeated arrival and release of new information, but a simpler question is to ask whether the same implications as those derived after information is released would carry over even in a market open before the disclosure stage.

To examine this question in more detail, we formally specify the period of trade before any information is released. As the multi-asset setting plays no special role for this question, we assume that there is a single representative investor, with exponential utility function and absolute risk-aversion $\alpha > 0$, and a single risky security in initial supply equal to b and which pays x at date $t = 2$, normally distributed with mean m and variance σ^2. Denote p_0 the price at date $t = 0$, prior to any information being released and d_0 the demand at date $t = 0$. At date $t = 1$, a signal $s = x + u$ is observed where u is white noise with variance V. Then, denote $p1$ the price at date $t = 1$, and d_1, the demand at date $t = 1$. Extending the previous definitions slightly, we now refer to a dynamic trading equilibrium as $(d_t^*, p_t^*)_{t=0,1}$ such that markets clear and the representative investor trades to maximize his utility, taking prices as given, in both periods of trade.

Consider the market-clearing condition at date $t = 1$. Since there is no further supply of asset, this market-clearing condition is that $d_1^* = 0$. Consider next the portfolio choice problem of the representative investor at date $t = 0$,

$$d_0^* \in argmax \qquad \mathbb{E}_0(-e^{-\alpha c}),$$

where:

$$c = (d_0 + d_1^*)x - p_0^* d_0 - p_1^* d_1^* = d_0 x - p_0^* d_0.$$

Note that the solution d_0^* does not depend on characteristics of the signal $\tilde{s}$ and, indeed, is the same as in a one-period model where no information is released. It follows that the *ex-ante* risk premium $(E(x) - p_0^*)/p_0^*$ cannot be a function of properties of the interim information.

A key element of this argument is, of course, that there is no trading at $t = 1$ so that information does not change final endowments and is not priced in the ex-ante problem. This intuition extends to a more general economy in which heterogeneous investors are endowed with private information and may find it useful to rebalance their portfolio decisions. This claim is formally demonstrated by Peter Christensen, Enrique de la Rosa, and Gerald Feltham.[12] A simple intuition for this observation is that the additional information amounts to a shock to the wealth of all agents, which, within exponential preferences, does not change risk tolerance. Indeed, this implies that the investors subject to this private wealth shock do not change how much premium they demand.

2 Applications and empirical implications

2.1 Asymmetric information

The model we have presented until this point has the general property that investors are equally informed about the cash flows from each asset. A growing set of results suggests that the insights of the basic model (by and large) extend to environments with asymmetric information. This section briefly introduces some of the primary findings that emerge from models with asymmetric information.[13]

We extend next the previous model to one in which investors may have public and private information. This section follows the multi-asset economy described in section 1. Let the information set of each investor be denoted ϕ^i, which, by assumption, collects all information that this investor can use to make an assessment about future cash flows.[14] We superscript all variables by i to refer to their analogue according to investor i's information set; that is, investor i believes that assets have cash flows $\mathbf{x}|\phi^i \sim N(\mathbf{m}^i, \mathbf{V}^i)$. In addition, as is usual in such models, we assume that the supply of assets $\mathbf{b}$ is a random variable realized prior to trade, uncorrelated to all other variables, and not privately observable.[15] We simplify notations by assuming that all investors have the same absolute risk-aversion coefficient.

Within this economy, investor demands are similar to the baseline model that is,

$$\mathbf{k}_i^* = \frac{1}{\alpha}\left(\mathbf{V}^i\right)^{-1}\left(\mathbf{m}^i - \mathbf{p}*\right) \tag{12}$$

Then, summing over all i, applying the market-clearing relation and solving for $\mathbf{p}^*$,

$$\mathbf{p}^* = \left(\Sigma\left(\mathbf{V}^i\right)^{-1}\right)^{-1}\left(\Sigma\left(\mathbf{V}^i\right)^{-1}\mathbf{m}^i - \alpha\mathbf{b}\right) \tag{13}$$

Because of the non-linearities present in this type of model, existing literature uses an alternative definition of the risk premium written in gross payoff terms rather than returns;

$$RP' = \mathbb{E}(\mathbf{p} - X). \tag{14}$$

We make the following assumptions: (a) investors' variance-covariance matrices are not a function of signal realizations (a property that typically holds in models with normally distributed random variables), (b) investors' signals are drawn from a common-knowledge prior distribution (i.e., $\mathbf{E}(\mathbf{m}^i) = \mathbf{m}$), and (c) investors share the same belief about the supply of assets. Then, taking expectations over equation (13).

$$RP' = \frac{\alpha}{I}\underbrace{\left(\frac{\Sigma\left(V^i\right)^{-1}}{I}\right)^{-1}}_{V^0}\mathbb{E}(\mathbf{b}). \tag{15}$$

The key to equation (15) is that the risk premium depends only on an average of the precision of each investor's variance-covariance matrix V^0. While asymmetric information may affect this average (in a possibly non-linear manner), it does not channel into the risk premium in a manner that is inherently different from models with only public information.

Interestingly, a few fundamental implications can be "read" directly from this equation. As is entirely intuitive, more public information increases the precision of all investors and reduces the risk premium. In addition, if more investors are endowed with incremental private signals, this will tend to make their information more precise, increasing the average precision and, thus, reducing the risk premium. On the other hand, if some previously public signals become private, this will tend to reduce average precision and thus increase the risk premium.

There is still some debate about more subtle implications of this pricing relationship, two of which are worth mentioning (and probably will be further clarified through continuing research). First, the model presented above relies on the assumption that all investors are price-takers and, thus, do not consider how their trades reveal their private information. If investors are not price takers, this mechanism might be weakened, causing less information to be revealed and thus – possibly – higher risk premia. There is still debate as to whether a similar interpretation in terms of a modified average precision would still hold in these settings, in part because models with non-price-taking investors are considerably more cumbersome.[16] Second, there is no consensus as to whether asymmetric information should lead to a new informational risk factor. To be sure, asymmetric information may affect the construction of a factor, creating a deviation from the capital asset pricing model, but as long as the economy is sufficiently large and any information is potentially diversifiable, only the systematic shocks should be priced.[17] Third, there is still debate as to whether, empirically, factors or their loading are known or easy to estimate. If this is not the case, information quality may still play a role as part of an estimation procedure of an underlying procedure within an empirical asset pricing model.[18]

2.2 Investor base

A property of the baseline model is that the presence of more investors increases the collective risk-bearing capacity, thus decreasing the overall risk premium. In most models, the number of investors is assumed to be exogenous. Yet only a fraction of individuals invest their savings in stock, suggesting that equity investing might involve a personal cost (from trading costs to education, time, or psychic costs). The question discussed here is how information changes participation, which in turn might affect the risk premium.[19]

To answer this question, consider the single-asset economy with payoff $x \sim N(m, \sigma^2)$. There are a large number of potential investors, all with identical exponential utilities, but each investor incurs a monetary cost $C > 0$ if he wants to trade in the risky asset. Abusing the language slightly, denote I as the number of investors choosing to trade. None of the investors initially owns any of the asset (e.g., this is a new security offering by an outside party).

Let us conjecture a given participation I. We already know that each investor will hold a portfolio of $1/I$ of the risky asset, and the price is given by:

$$p^* = m - \frac{\alpha}{I}\sigma^2$$

This implies a certainty equivalent for each investor equal to:

$$CE^{buy} = \frac{m - p^*}{I} - \frac{\sigma}{2}\frac{1}{I^2}\sigma^2 - C.$$

By not buying, an investor obtains a certainty equivalent normalized to zero.

In equilibrium, free-entry should make the $CE^{buy} = 0$, which implies that:

$$I^* = \frac{\alpha\sigma^2 + \sqrt{\alpha\sigma^2\left(\alpha\sigma^2 - 2C\right)}}{2C}. \tag{16}$$

Plugging equation (16) into the risk premium, we have:[20]

$$RP = \frac{m - p^*}{p^*} = \frac{2\alpha C\sigma^2}{\alpha\sigma^2\left(m - 2C\right) + m\sqrt{\alpha\sigma^2\left(\alpha\sigma^2 - 2C\right)}}.$$

Interestingly this risk premium is *decreasing* in the quality of the information σ^2, so that noisier information leads to a lower risk premium. The reason for this counter-intuitive finding is as follows. New buyers participate (by paying the cost C) because they expect to earn some trading surplus from owning the risky security. However, in a competitive market where information is nearly perfect, assets are priced very close to their correct value and there is no opportunity for earning any excess surplus. On the one hand, with endogenous participation, this causes few investors to participate and hence increases the risk premium. On the other hand, when information is noisier, investors acquire a higher trading surplus and thus are more willing to participate.

2.3 Investor disagreement

So far, we have made the simplifying assumption that investors share common beliefs about the distribution of cash flows. This assumption is usually motivated by the fact that beliefs should share a common Bayesian structure if there is common knowledge of rationality. Yet little is known about models without this assumption, where investors do not agree about the future payoffs of an asset. Fortunately, independent work by Paul Fischer and Robert Bloomfield, as well as by Peter Christensen and Zhenjiang Qin, clarifies the effect of disagreement on the risk premium.[21]

We simplify the previous model by assuming that there is a single asset that delivers a random cash flow x in total supply normalized to one. The price of this asset is denoted p. As before, a competitive equilibrium is defined such that traders buy a quantity of the risky asset optimally and the price p is set such that the total demand for the risky asset equals the supply of one. For simplicity, there are two investors $i = 1, 2$ with identical exponential preferences and absolute risk aversion $2\alpha > 0$.

First, consider an economy with heterogeneous beliefs about the mean payoff of the asset. Assume that investor 1 believes that $x \sim N(m+k, \sigma^2)$ and investor 2 believes that $x \sim N(m-k, \sigma^2)$, where $k \geq 0$ is a measure of disagreement. Let d_i^* denote the demand of each investor:

$$d_1^* = \frac{m+k-p}{2\alpha\sigma^2}, \ d_2^* = \frac{m-k-p}{2\alpha\sigma^2}.$$

Applying the market-clearing condition,

$$1 = d_2^* + d_2^* = \frac{m-p^*}{\alpha\sigma^2}.$$

It follows that the risk premium does not depend on the degree of disagreement about the mean and simply reflects the average belief in the economy.

Yet disagreement can affect the risk premium, as the following alternative specification will show. Assume that investors disagree about the riskiness of the asset: investor 1 believes that $x \sim N(m, \sigma^2 + k)$ and investor 2 believes that $x \sim N(m, \sigma^2 - k)$, where $k \in [0, \sigma^2)$. It must hold that:

$$d_1^* = \frac{m-p}{2\alpha(\sigma^2 + k)}, \ d_2^* = \frac{m-p}{2\alpha(\sigma^2 - k)}.$$

Applying the market-clearing condition and solving for the price p^*,

$$p^* = m + \frac{\sigma(k^2 - \sigma^4)}{\sigma^2}.$$

Note that greater disagreement about the variance now increases the price and reduces the risk premium. An intuition for this is that the person with lower risk perception absorbs a greater share of the asset, and thus his belief is over-weighted in the determination of the total risk premium.

A key implication of disagreement models is that information can affect the degree of disagreement because it changes how different investors would interpret the signal. In fact, more disagreement is, all other things being equal, a desirable property because it facilitates trade and a value-creating transfer of the asset from the least to the most optimistic trader.

In connection to the previous observation about the ex-ante risk premium (section 1.3), information can affect the ex-ante risk premium in a two–date trading model through the mechanism described above. In particular, information systems that cause the greatest variation in posterior beliefs, thus causing more disagreement and greater ex-ante risk premia, are typically socially desirable.[22]

2.4 Voluntary disclosure

As we have seen in section 1, the direct effect of disclosure on the risk premium is generally ambiguous, as unfavorable disclosure increases the risk premium. In addition, the basic model does not speak about differences in risk premia between disclosing versus non–disclosing firms. To address these limitations, one approach, advocated by the trio of researchers Michael Kirschenheiter, Bjorn Jorgensen, and Edwige Cheynel, is to narrow the analysis of the risk premium to releases of information that are *voluntary* and thus, by construction, tend to convey favorable news.[23]

In what follows, we slightly simplify the previous factor model by assuming that the economy is sufficiently large so that the market portfolio (approximately) does not depend on each firm's individual cash flow realizations.[24] We follow here the factor model given in equation (8) where the firm $i's$ cash flow is $x_i = a_i F + \varepsilon_i$. To save on notation, we set $a_i = a$ for all firms.

Assume now that, as in voluntary disclosure models, each manager in a firm may receive information about ε_i with probability $1 - p \in (0, 1)$ and, then, can either withhold or truthfully disclose in a voluntary manner. An uninformed manager cannot disclose that he is uninformed and must withhold. Conditional on disclosing ε, the value of firm i is:

$$P_i(\varepsilon) = \varepsilon_i + aP_M, \tag{17}$$

where P_M is the price of the market portfolio.

Conditional on not disclosing and under the assumption that only informed firms with $\varepsilon_i \geq \tau_i$ disclose, the price of a non–disclosing firm $P_i(ND)$ is:

$$P_i(ND) = \mathbb{E}(\varepsilon|ND) + aP_M, \tag{18}$$

where ND is the event that the manager is uninformed or $\varepsilon_i \leq \tau_i$.

There is a single threshold τ_i above which informed managers, decide to disclose voluntarily, and it is given by $P_i(ND) = P_i(\tau_i^*)$. Eliminating P_M on both sides, the threshold is given by $(\tau_i^* = \mathbb{E}(\varepsilon_i |ND)$ and is identical to the Dye-Jung-Kwon model.[25] Importantly, the probability of a voluntary disclosure is unrelated to the risk premium and does not depend on the exposure of firm i to the factor or its factor beta.

Vice-versa, however, the existence of voluntary disclosures creates cross-sectional differences in risk premia between disclosing and non-disclosing firms. To see this, note that, for any disclosing firm $P_i(\varepsilon) > P_i(ND)$. In particular, the risk premium from a diversified portfolio of firms choosing to disclose is given by:

$$RP_D = \frac{\mathbb{E}\left(\varepsilon_i \middle| \varepsilon_i \geq \tau_i^*\right) + am_F}{\mathbb{E}\left(\varepsilon_i \middle| \varepsilon_i \geq \tau_i^*\right) + aP_M} < \frac{\mathbb{E}\left(\varepsilon_i \middle| ND\right) + am_F}{\mathbb{E}\left(\varepsilon_i \middle| ND\right) + aP_M} = RP_{ND}.$$

Therefore, firms that do not disclose will exhibit a greater risk premium (all other things being equal) than firms that do disclose. The intuition for this result is that the endogenous nature of the voluntary disclosure implies that a disclosure must always lead to a more favourable posterior about the expected cash flow, leading to a favorable *indirect* effect.

3 Welfare considerations

3.1 Risk-sharing efficiency

Several regulators have presented the reduction of the cost of capital as one of the primary objectives of financial transparency. As Arthur Levitt, then chairman of the US Securities and Exchange Commission, put it in his September 29, 1997, speech: "The truth is, high standards lower the cost of capital. And that's a goal we all share."[26] Unfortunately, these remarks are often taken literally, leading to a "reductio ad cost of capital" where complex welfare questions are reduced to a measurement of the risk premium. This question is formally discussed in the dissertation work of Pingyang Gao, then at Yale School of Management.[27] His work and much of the follow-up literature emphasize that risk premia cannot be used as a proxy for welfare, and therefore risk premia should not be used as an input for policy evaluation.

We illustrate here a few welfare considerations within a simple economy with a single asset $x \sim N(m, \sigma^2)$ and two agents with the same exponential utility function with absolute risk aversion coefficient $\alpha > 0$. Assume that agent 1 holds a fraction $b_1 = b$ of the asset while agent 2 holds the remaining fraction $b_2 = 1 - b$.

Consider an economy with no disclosure. Each agent will trade to hold half of the market portfolio, investing all remaining wealth in the risk-free asset. We know from equation (3) that the price of the asset is:

$$P_M = m - \frac{\alpha\sigma^2}{2} . \tag{19}$$

Hence, each agent achieves an expected utility given by:

$$u_j = \mathbb{E}\left(-e^{-\alpha\left(.5(x - P_M) + b_j P_M\right)}\right)$$

$$CE_j = \frac{\alpha\sigma^2}{8} + b_j\left(m - \frac{\alpha\sigma^2}{2}\right), \tag{20}$$

where CE_j is the certainty equivalent of agent j (i.e., $\mathbb{E}u_j = u_j(CE_j)$).

Consider now an economy in which trade occurs after a signal $s = x + u$ is released, where $u \sim N(0, \sigma_u^2)$. Note that if the direct effect is sufficiently large (see section 1.2), this signal will tend to reduce the risk premium.

$$x|s \sim N\left(m + \underbrace{\frac{\sigma^2}{\sigma^2 + \sigma_u^2}(s - m)}_{m_1}, \underbrace{\frac{\sigma^2\sigma_u^2}{\left(\sigma^2 + \sigma_u^2\right)}}_{V_1}\right) \tag{21}$$

Rewriting the expected utility function with disclosure:

$$CE_j^d = \frac{\alpha V_1}{8} + b_j \left(m_1 - \frac{\alpha \sigma^2}{2} \right)$$

Following some basic (but cumbersome) steps of algebra, the ex-ante certainty equivalent CE_j^0 can be formally derived.[28]

$$CE_i^0 = CE_j - \frac{\alpha}{8} \frac{\sigma^4}{\sigma^4 + \sigma_u^2} \left(1 - 2b_j \right)^2$$

(22)

As long as there is some effective trade (i.e., $b_j \neq .5$), this result shows that more information always hurts the two agents. This is a version of what is known as the "Hirshleifer effect."[29] The standard interpretation of this effect is that the purpose of markets (in this type of model) is to share risks among risk-averse agents. Information given publicly prior to trade precludes this benefit because the risk is realized before the market opens.

Although this interpretation is correct, it is slightly incomplete. A seller clearly benefits from greater risk-sharing without information because information generates uncertainty about the selling price. But consider the case in which $b_j = 0$, and therefore agent j does not pre-own any quantity of the asset, and, therefore, because $CE_j^d = \alpha V_1/8$, is not exposed to any risk related to the actual realized s. Noting that $CE_j^0 = CE_j^d = \alpha V_1/8$, it can be observed that such a "buyer" still prefers less disclosure, even though less disclosure implies that there is more residual risk left on the asset. Why, then, does a risk-averse investor prefer to trade over more risky assets?

The reason for this somewhat counter-intuitive side of the Hirshleifer effect is that, in a competitive market, buyers obtain their surplus based on their contribution to the economy's risk-bearing capacity. In the limit, buyers earn no surplus if no risk is left and all assets trade at their true value. On the other hand, their contribution to risk-bearing capacity increases when more risk is left. In this sense, and this is a point that could not be emphasized more strongly, in a competitive pure-exchange economy, *all* investors (whether buyers or sellers) benefit from less information.[30]

3.2 Value of information under pure-exchange and an application to conservatism

The previous analysis suggests that information is welfare-reducing under pure-exchange. But to be precise, this claim only holds true provided all investors can make their optimal trade and are not constrained to sell the asset, consume the proceeds, and exit the economy (e.g., as in the case of retirement motives). As we will show next, information can have value under pure-exchange within a generational model where one generation sells to the next generation. As an application of this idea, we shall then show that a conservative measurement, where more precise information is reported conditional on low fundamentals, is typically optimal in this setting.[31]

We adopt here a modified version of the model in Section 3.1. The asset is now fully owned by agent 1 (the seller) who must sell the entire asset to agent 2 (the buyer). We assume that buyer and seller have (possibly) different risk-aversions $\alpha_i > 0$.

Absent any information, the market has a single asset and a single agent. Therefore the asset price is:

$$P_M = m - \alpha_2 \sigma^2.$$

The seller sells at the price P_M and achieves a certainty equivalent:

$$CE_1 = P_M = m - \alpha_2 \sigma^2.$$

As before, there is a signal $s = x + u$ and we derive the seller's certainty equivalent after the disclosure has occurred:

$$CE^d_1 = m_1 - \alpha_2 V_1.$$

This implies an ex-ante expected utility given by:

$$u_1 = \mathbb{E}\left(-e^{-\alpha_1 CE^d_1}\right)$$
$$= -e^{-\alpha_2\left(m + G\left(\sigma_u^2\right)\right)}, \tag{23}$$

where:

$$G\left(\sigma_u^2\right) = \frac{\sigma^2\left(\alpha_1\sigma^2 + 2\alpha_2\sigma_u^2\right)}{2\left(\sigma^2 + \sigma_u^2\right)}. \tag{24}$$

The function $G(\sigma_u^2)$ represents the value of information to the seller. Unlike in section 3.1, the seller is not necessarily worse off with more information. Specifically, if $\alpha_1 < 2\alpha_2$ and the seller is not too risk averse relative to the buyer, $G(.)$ is decreasing in σ_u^2 and the seller is better off with a perfect signal $\sigma_u = 0$. If $\alpha_1 < 2\alpha_2$, as in the previous section, information is detrimental to the seller.

This observation has an important implication in terms of the information system preferred by the seller. Assume here that $\alpha_1 < 2\alpha_2$. Further, to avoid a solution with a perfect signal, reducing the noise in the signal is costly and reduces the utility of the seller by $C(\sigma_u^2)$ where $C(.)$ is decreasing and convex with $C(0) = \infty$ and $C(\infty) = 0$. Assuming that the seller controls the choice of σ_u^2, the optimal precision of the signal is given by taking the first-order condition on the seller's expected utility $u_1 - 1/\sigma_u^2$

$$\Gamma\left(\sigma_u^2\right) = G'\left(\sigma_u^2\right) - e^{-\alpha_2\left(m - G\left(\sigma_u^2\right)\right)} - C'\left(\sigma_u^2\right) = 0. \tag{25}$$

In what follows, we assume that the solution $\sigma_u > 0$ is interior and for this solution to be a regular local maximum, the second-order condition must be satisfied as well that is,

$$\frac{\partial \Gamma}{\partial \sigma_u^2} < 0.$$

Consider now how this choice varies as a function of the fundamental value of the asset m. Because the solution σ_u is defined implicitly in terms of equation (25), we need to obtain this comparative static using the implicit function theorem,

$$\frac{\partial \sigma_u^2}{\partial m} = -\frac{\partial \Gamma / \partial m}{\partial \Gamma / \partial \sigma_u^2} = Sign\left(-\alpha_2 G'\left(\sigma_u^2\right)\right) > 0. \tag{26}$$

It then follows that the signal s is chosen to be more precise, with lower σ_u, when the fundamentals of the asset are more favorable (i.e., when m is larger). To explain this result, note that the seller trades off a benefit in higher prices versus a cost in utility terms. By concavity of the utility function, the agent tends to be more willing to increase prices relative to the utility cost when expected payoffs are low, as in the case of low fundamentals. Thus, a conservative measurement that produces more information for low m tends to be desirable for risk-sharing purposes.[32]

3.3 Production and real effects

Before a formal model of investment is presented, consider a fable that best illustrates the disconnection between welfare and risk premia. Consider an economy that produces two consumption goods, one that is produced underground and is deterministic (say, mushrooms) and the other whose output depends on the amount of rain (say, fruit). If it is prohibited to cultivate fruit, the economy will enjoy a predictable stream of mushrooms and with risk nearly absent, the risk premium will be zero. If investors in this economy can voluntarily cultivate fruit, the economy will now include risky weather-dependent fruit production, causing a higher risk premium. In this example, the fruit and mushroom economy features a higher risk premium and greater welfare relative to the mushroom-only economy. To summarize, the risk premium is a measure only of risk, not of whether the risk is on the upside – and might give rise to welfare gains – or on the downside.

We illustrate next this basic point with an example featuring production; for a discussion featuring other specifications of production, the reader may consult the extensive literature in this area.[33] We use here an extension of the one-asset economy in section 3.1 and simplify the model to a single representative agent. Assume that $x = \tau y - k\tau^2$, where $k > 0$ and $\tau \geq 0$ is a scale parameter to be chosen and y has variance V_y and mean m_y. The certainty equivalent under no information is given by:

$$CE^0 = \tau m_y - \frac{\alpha}{2}\tau^2 V_y - k\tau^2. \tag{27}$$

The optimal choice τ^* is then given by:

$$\tau^* = \frac{m_y}{2k + \alpha V_y}. \tag{28}$$

In the economy without information, let us compute the risk premium RP^0_M and the certainty equivalent of the representative agent CE^0.

$$RP^0_M = \frac{\alpha V_y}{k} \tag{29}$$

$$CE^0 = \frac{m_y^2}{4k + 2\alpha V_y} \tag{30}$$

Note that the lower k is, implying that increasing the scale of investment is cheaper, the higher the certainty equivalent (as is intuitive) and the *higher* the risk premium because the economy features more risk overall. It is unfortunately cumbersome to fully solve this model with an additional signal prior to the investment stage. But a heuristic argument can aid in perception of how information can increase the ex-ante risk premium. To see this, consider a signal structure of the form discussed earlier with $y \,|s = N \,(m_y^1,\, V_y^1)$ where:

$$m_y^1 = m_y + \frac{V_y}{V_y + \sigma_u^2}\left(s - m_y\right) \tag{31}$$

$$V_y^1 = \frac{V_y \sigma_u^2}{V_y + \sigma_u^2}. \tag{32}$$

Note that the risk premium post-disclosure is now $RP_M^1 = \alpha V_y^1 / k$, which is lower than absent information. However, note that the scale of investment is now:

$$\tau^* = \frac{m_y^1}{2k + \alpha V_y^1} = \frac{m_y \sigma_u^2 + s V_y}{\alpha \sigma_u^2 + 2k\left(\sigma_u^2 + V_y\right)}. \tag{33}$$

If we evaluate this expression at the benchmark of the average signal $s = m_y$,

$$\tau^* = \frac{m_y}{2k + \alpha V_y \dfrac{\sigma_u^2}{\sigma_u^2 + V_y}}. \tag{34}$$

From an ex-ante perspective, total investment tends to increase, which induces a greater ex-ante risk premium. This effect also implies that it is possible for such a production economy to observe a situation in which better information causes more investment, and hence higher welfare and higher risk premia. Clearly, this link cannot be ignored because a fundamental purpose of accounting is to allocate capital to profitable investments – a purpose that is not explicitly modeled under pure-exchange. Then, an information system that facilitates investment would tend to increase upside risk and, in turn, cause higher risk premia and higher welfare.[34]

4 Consumption-based CAPM (CCAPM)

4.1 Overview

While the exponential-Normal model is still frequently used because it provides clarity and simplicity to the analysis, the stylized trading model used to derive (and apply) the standard capital asset pricing model makes it difficult to use in conjunction with models of individual consumption. We present here a version of the consumption-based capital asset pricing model and then derive some incremental accounting implications of this model. The model presented here will address two notable limitations of the standard approach, namely that (a) assets may not be normally distributed, and (b) experimental evidence shows that investors do not have exponential preferences.[35]

To develop this model, let us represent uncertainty between the two dates as a random variable $\tilde{s}$ that is unknown at date $t = 0$ and realizes at date $t = 1$, taking its values in a finite set S. For any $s \in S$, let the event "$\tilde{s} = s$" have probability $h_s > 0$ and indicate that the state of the world is s. The total amount of resource available at date 1 conditional on state s is denoted $\phi(s)$.

Assume that markets are complete; that is, there exists a vector of state prices $(p_s)_{s \in S}$ such that the price of a security that pays contingent cash flows $X = (x_s)$ is given by:

$$P_X = \sum_{s \in S} p_s x_s. \tag{35}$$

Equation (35) can be equivalently in terms of two stochastic processes:

$$P_X = \sum_{s \in S} h_s \frac{p_s}{h_s} x_s = \mathbb{E}(\widetilde{M}\widetilde{X}), \tag{36}$$

where $\widetilde{M} = p_{\tilde{s}} / h_{\tilde{s}}$ and $= x_{\tilde{s}}$.

In the asset pricing literature, the random variable $\widetilde{M}$ is referred to as the pricing kernel or stochastic discount factor because it prices uncertain returns by discounting certain kinds of future cash flows. Evaluating this equation in the special case of the risk-free security $\widetilde{X}_{rf} = 1$, the risk-free rate r_0 can be easily expressed in terms of the first moment of the stochastic discount factor, that is, $1 + r_0 = 1 / \mathbb{E}(\widetilde{M})$. To simplify notations, we normalize r_0 to zero, so that $\mathbb{E}(\widetilde{M}) = 1$.

Denoting RP_X as the risk premium of an asset with payoff $\widetilde{X}$, equation (36) can be decomposed to make the role of the covariance with the pricing kernel apparent:

$$1 + RP_X = \frac{\mathbb{E}(\widetilde{X})}{P_X} = \frac{1}{1 + \text{cov}(r_X, \widetilde{M})}, \tag{37}$$

where $r_X = \widetilde{X} / P_X$ is the asset's return.

In other words, an asset yields a higher expected return when its return covaries negatively with the pricing kernel. The CCAPM then asks the following questions: Which economic variable is informative on the pricing kernel? And, once such a variable has been found, what characteristics of individual preferences drive the relationship between this variable and the pricing kernel?

To address these questions, we can modify the previous model as follows. Assume that preferences exhibit linear risk tolerance (LRT),

$$u_i(c) = \frac{1}{d_2(1-\gamma)}(d_1 + d_2 c)^{1-\gamma}. \tag{38}$$

This class of functions is convenient because it nests most commonly used preferences, from quadratic, constant relative risk aversion to even (in the limit) constant absolute risk aversion.[36] Each investor owns an initial portfolio of assets $l_i(.)$, which can be traded in period 0 and such that, absent trading, $l_i(s)$ is received conditional on state s. As in section 1, an equilibrium is given by prices p^* and portfolios $(k^*_i(s))$ such that investors maximize their utility and markets clear. The first condition implies:

$$k^*_i(.) \in argmax_{k_i(.)} \sum_s h_s u(k_i(s))$$

$$s.t. \quad \sum_s p^*_s l_i(s) = \sum_s p^*_s k_i(s), \tag{39}$$

where equation (39) is investor i's budget constraint.

The first-order condition of the problem can be rearranged as follows:

$$k^*_i(s) = (u')^{-1}\left(\lambda_i \frac{p^*_s}{h_s}\right) = \frac{\left(\lambda_i \frac{p^*_s}{h_s}\right)^{-1/\gamma} - d_1}{d_2}, \tag{40}$$

where $\lambda_i > 0$ is the Lagrange multiplier associated to the constraint.

It is convenient, at this point, to focus on a large economy by making the assumption that there is a large number of atomistic investors with index $i \in [0, 1]$.[37] Then, if markets clear, the total demand for the aggregate endowment must equal the supply $\tilde{s} = s$ for any realization of the state of the world, implying that:

$$\phi(s) = \int k_i^*(s) di = \frac{1}{d_2} \left(\frac{p_s^*}{h_s} \right)^{-1/\gamma} \sum_{i=1}^{I} \lambda_i^{-1/\gamma} - \frac{d_1}{d_2}.$$

The pricing kernel simplifies to the following pricing equation:

$$m_s^* = \frac{p_s^*}{h_s} = \left(\frac{d_2 \phi(s) + d_1}{\Sigma \lambda_i^{-1/\gamma}} \right)^{-\gamma}. \tag{41}$$

Note, finally, that under the normalization the risk-free rate is zero that is, $\mathbb{E}(\tilde{M}) = \Sigma p_s^* = 1$, we have that:

$$\left(\left(\Sigma \lambda_i \right)^{-1/\gamma} \right)^{\gamma} = \Sigma h_s \left(d_2 \phi(s) + d_1 \right)^{-\gamma}. \tag{42}$$

This implies the following representation for the pricing kernel,

$$m_s^* = \frac{h_s U'\left(\phi(s) \right)}{\Sigma h_s U'\left(\phi(s') \right)}, \tag{43}$$

where $U(c) = \frac{1}{d_2(1-\gamma)} (d_1 + d_2 c)^{1-\gamma}$ is the utility function of a representative agent.

This pricing equation has a fundamental implication for asset pricing. In this model, investors price claims in terms of the correlation of their returns to the marginal utility of (aggregate) wealth, $u'(\phi(\tilde{s})) = \phi(\tilde{s})^{-\gamma}$. By concavity of the utility function, the pricing kernel discounts assets that pay more in states with high aggregate endowment $\phi(s)$, implying a risk premium for securities that pay less in states with low aggregate endowment. A key difference from the CARA-Normal model is that no assumption has been made here about the nature of a market portfolio, and in this more general model, a factor that correlates to aggregate wealth can be used for asset pricing.

4.2 Earnings management

We can easily illustrate the usefulness of pricing equation (43) to examine the impact of (economy-wide) earnings management activities on the risk premium. Assume next that firms are operated by risk-neutral owner-managers ("managers") who own a proportion of the shares $s \in (0,1)$. The firm will deliver a future cash flow that, absent earnings management, is denoted $e \in \{0,1\}$, where $e = 1$ indicates a success and $e = 0$ indicates a failure. We now model a state of the world as the probability that the cash flow is successful and denote it by the state $q \in (0,1)$. For simplicity, this state is publicly observable before any earnings management decision is made (the earnings management occurs after the state is known). At this point, there is no residual aggregate uncertainty and all assets are priced at their expected value.[38]

The realized cash flow e is privately observable to the manager but not to outside investors. The manager must sell his equity stake and, before the sale, issues an accounting report $r \in \{h,l\}$ to investors, which can be high (h) or low (l). A success manager always issues the high report

385

$r = h$. A failure manager, on the other hand, can choose to manage earnings by $K \geq 0$ and then issues $r = h$ with probability K for a personal cost $c\,K^2/2$, where $c > 0$ is an exogenous parameter assumed large enough to avoid corner solutions.[39] There are also *real* costs of earnings management and, conditional on failure, the cash flow is reduced from 0 (absent earnings management) to $-K$.

Investors are competitive and price the firm at its expected cash flow minus earnings management costs conditional on the accounting report. The manager chooses K to maximize the sale value of his equity minus any earnings management costs.

Denote $P\left(r;\hat{k}\right)$ as the market value of the entire equity conditional on a public accounting report r and anticipated earnings management $\hat{k}$, then:

$$P\left(l;\hat{k}\right)=-\hat{k}.$$

Consider now a success firm. By Bayesian updating, we know that:

$$\mathrm{Prob}\left(e=1\middle|r=h\right)=\frac{q}{q+\left(1-q\right)\hat{k}}.$$

Therefore:

$$P\left(h;\hat{k}\right) = \underbrace{\frac{q}{q+\left(1-q\right)\hat{k}}}_{\text{Success firm reports } r=h} - \underbrace{\frac{\left(1-q\right)\hat{k}}{q+\left(1-q\right)\hat{k}}\hat{k}}_{\text{Faliure firm manages its earnings}}. \tag{44}$$

The objective of the manager is then given by:

$$\mathrm{K} \in \mathit{argmax}_k\ v\,(kP(h;\ \hat{k}) + (1-k)\,P\,(1\,;\ \hat{k})) - ck^2/2,$$

where v is the share of equity owned by the manager.

Taking the first-order condition on this problem, it follows that:

$$K=v/c\,(P\,(h;\ \hat{k}) - P(l\,;\ \hat{k})). \tag{45}$$

In equilibrium, market expectations must coincide with the actual choice, which implies that $\hat{k} = K$. After some simplifications, we can write the total social cost of earnings management $\Lambda^* = \hat{k}^*(1 - q)$ as a second-order polynomial,

$$c(\Lambda^*)^2 + q(c-s)\,\Lambda^* - q(1-q)s = 0.$$

This function is inverse U-shaped in s, zero when s is small or large (since in the latter case there is almost complete information that all firms fail and, thus, no purpose in managing earnings).

Let us turn to the analysis of the risk premium conditional on earnings management. Our previous discussion emphasizes that the risk premium is greater in the presence of more volatile aggregate consumption. The effect of earnings management is to reduce aggregate consumption in moderate states, that is, $\phi(q) = q-\Lambda^*$ is lower with earnings management when q is intermediate. This, in turn, tends to "convert" moderate states into low states, which will reduce total risk (reducing the risk premium) when low states are likely but increase total risk (increasing the risk premium) when high states are likely. We thus observe that the effect of earnings management on the risk premium is likely to be cyclical, and, in general, the relationship between the amount of earnings management and the risk premium is ambiguous.

4.3 Agency frictions

We have so far analyzed economies in which investors solely make portfolio choices but bear no other sources of income risk. The assumption, however, stands in contrast to the insights of agency theory, which states that if effort is unobservable, firms must expose their workers to uninsurable risk. In other words, agency frictions make markets endogenously incomplete because some of the risk of a worker cannot be diversified by that employee (for example, a manager will not be permitted to fully insure his exposure to the company's risk).[40]

We build on the model of section 4.1 by assuming that each firm needs one worker. Without loss of generality, let us assume that each investor is employed in a firm.[41] Each agent now has a utility function $u(c) - a B$ where c is final consumption, $a \in \{0, 1\}$ is a privately observed effort decision, and $B > 0$ is the cost of effort. The function u (.) is in the LRT class described in equation (38). Each agent requires an expected utility of R to participate in a contract.

The firm produces a cash flow $\phi(s, \in)$, which depends on the aggregate state s and a firm specific performance metric $y \in Y$, drawn from a finite set. Conditional on effort a, the probability of $\tilde{y} = y$ is given by $f_a(y) > 0$, which is assumed independent of s (i.e., the state of the world does not change the nature of agency frictions). As is usual in such models, the monotone likelihood ratio property holds, that is, $(f_1(y) - f_0(y))/f_1(y)$ is strictly increasing in y. Assume that inducing the effort $a = 1$ is desirable. All agents and firms are identical and receive a compensation contract $w(s, y)$ in addition to their own wealth $l(s)$.

The contracting program is stated next:

$$(P) \quad \max_{\omega(..)} \Sigma p_s f_1(y) \, (\phi(s,y) - w(s,y))$$

subject to:

$$\Sigma \, h_s f_1(y) \, u(l(s) + w(s,y)) - B \geq R, \tag{46}$$

$$\Sigma \, h_s \, (f_1(y) - f_0(y)) u(l(s) + w(s,y)) \geq B. \tag{47}$$

Equations (46) and (47) are standard participation and incentive-compatibility constraints; that is, the agent should be willing to accept the contract and prefers high effort over low effort. Consistent with the asset pricing approach developed earlier, the firm values a stream of cash flow using the price vector (p_s).

Taking a first-order condition and rearranging:

$$\frac{1}{u'(l(s)+w(s,y))} = \underbrace{\left(\lambda + \mu \frac{f_1(y) - f_0(y)}{f_1(y)}\right)}_{Inc(y)} \frac{h_s}{p_s}. \tag{48}$$

where the two Lagrange multipliers $\lambda, \mu > 0$ are associated with constraints (46) and (47).

Then, using the fact that $u(.)$ is in the LRT class and market-clearing:

$$\phi(s) = l(s) + \mathbb{E}_y \left(w(s,y)\right) = (u')^{-1} \left(\frac{p_s}{h_s} \frac{1}{Inc(y)}\right). \tag{49}$$

where $\phi(s) = \mathbb{E}_y(\phi(s, y))$ is the aggregate endowment.

Rewriting this equation,

$$\left(G(s)+\frac{d_1}{d_2}\right)^{-\gamma}=\frac{p_s}{h_s}\left(\underbrace{\frac{\mathbb{E}_\gamma\left(Inc(\gamma)^{-1/\gamma}\right)}{d_2}}_{I^{agg}}\right)^{-\gamma} \tag{50}$$

Multiplying both sides of this equation by h_s and summing with respect to s,

$$\Sigma h_s\left(G(s)+D\right)^{-\gamma}=I^{agg}.$$

Therefore, substituting I^{agg} in equation (50) yields that:

$$\frac{\pi_s}{h_s}=\frac{\left(G(s)+D\right)^{-\gamma}}{\Sigma h_{s'}\left(G(s')+D\right)^{-\gamma}}, \tag{51}$$

The right-hand side of equation (51) depends only on parameters that are specific to the risk aversion of agents in the economy and the total endowment; the risk premium, then, does not directly depend on the agency problem. In fact, to be complete, the agency problem may only affect the risk premium indirectly through any potential effect on the aggregate endowment $\phi(s)$ if, for example, the aggregate effort level is a function of the agency problem. This aspect is not specific to the agency problem and has already been discussed in the production economy of section 3.3.

5 Other asset pricing models

5.1 The arbitrage pricing model (APT)

The standard and consumption-based capital asset pricing models have been widely used to provide intuition as to key determinants of the cost of capital, but they require fairly heavy handed assumptions about the nature of the economy. Indeed, these models have had relatively low predictive power – if they are testable at all – in explaining the cross-section of expected returns. An alternative approach to these models is the arbitrage pricing model (or APT), which makes much weaker assumptions about the economy; yet these assumptions are sufficient to provide minimal conditions that must be satisfied by a risk factor.

Consider the stochastic discount factor $\tilde{M}$ as defined in equation (36). We make no further assumption about investors or assets and only assume at this point that there exist n observable uncorrelated factors $\left(\tilde{F}_i\right)_n^{i=1}$ such that:

$$\tilde{M}=a_0\sum_{i=1}^n a_i\tilde{F}_i+\tilde{\varepsilon}, \tag{52}$$

where $\tilde{\varepsilon}$ is white noise.

Note that in equation (52), the stochastic discount factor might not be observable, and therefore the linear regression implied by this relationship cannot be implemented. However, some statistical relationships can help unravel the usefulness of this decomposition.

Consider any security with gross payoff $\tilde{X}$ and return per value invested at date $t=0$ written $\tilde{R}_X=\tilde{X}/P_X$. Plugging (52) into (36),

$$\mathbb{E}\left(\tilde{R}_X\right)=\left(1+r_f\right)\left(1-\sum_{i=1}^n a_i \operatorname{cov}\left(\tilde{F}_i,\tilde{R}_X\right)\right). \tag{53}$$

If we evaluate the above expression for the security being one of the factors, that is, $X = F_i$, some tedious algebra implies the following expression for a_i:

$$a_i = \frac{1}{Var\left(\tilde{F}_i\right)P_{Fi}}\left(1 - \frac{\mathbb{E}\left(\tilde{R}_{Fi}\right)}{1 + r_f}\right). \tag{54}$$

Plugging the result of (54) into (53), the following relationship can then be made apparent:

$$\mathbb{E}\left(\tilde{R}_X\right) = 1 + r_f + \sum_{i=1}^{n} \underbrace{\frac{cov\left(\tilde{R}_{Fi}, \tilde{R}_X\right)}{Var\left(\tilde{R}_{Fi}\right)}}_{\beta_i}\left(\mathrm{E}\left(\tilde{R}_{Fi}\right) - 1 - r_f\right), \tag{55}$$

where β_i is the beta of the security to the factor i.

The intuition for this relation is, in fact, immediate. As long as an investor knows the determinants of the stochastic discount factor ("the risk factors") and the residual noise is uncorrelated to the assets being priced, then the risk factors can be used to price the cross section of assets without actual knowledge of the pricing kernel. Because only factors yield an excess return above the risk-free rate, the asset can be priced in terms of a linear regression on each factor.

Another precious aspect of equation (7) is that it gives researchers the characteristics to be empirically expected from a factor. First, a factor should explain the returns of certain types of assets (have non-zero beta) above and beyond other factors; this condition is, obviously, very easy to satisfy given the large number of potential assets to be priced. Second, the factor should carry a non-zero premium, that is $\mathrm{E}\tilde{R}_{Fi} - 1 - r_f > 0$. This feature is generally more difficult to satisfy and led to the now well-known conclusion originally made by Eugene Fama and Kenneth French that the market return fails this condition after controlling for a book and size risk factor. Third, the equation presented in (4) should not have its error term correlated to the returns of certain assets; this last condition is what generally drives the search for new factors.[42]

5.2 Imperfect liquidity

We have so far focused on the risk premium component of the cost of capital, but this approach is somewhat reductive because a cost may be incurred when issuing capital because of future potential liquidity costs borne by the financier supplying capital. A study by Jeremy Bertomeu, Anne Beyer, and Ronald Dye demonstrates that liquidity shocks in situations of asymmetric information cause the firm to experience higher cost of capital, even absent any of the risk-sharing motives discussed earlier.[43] This investigation is of some importance given that the standard capital asset pricing model does not predict that the cost of capital should be fundamentally affected by the presence of asymmetric information if liquidity is perfect (see section 1.2).

To illustrate this point, consider a manager with an investment project that requires an investment infusion normalized to one. This capital is obtained from a competitive investor. Conditional on financing the project, the product will generate one of the three equally likely cash flows $\theta \in \{\mu - e, \mu, \mu + e\}$ where $e > 0$, $\mu - e > 0$ and $\mu > 1$. The manager has probability $p \in (0, 1)$ to observe θ and then discloses his information if $\theta \geq \mu$. A manager not receiving information or observing $\theta = \mu - e$ stays silent.[44]

In order to compensate the investor for providing the unit of capital, the manager gives the investor a portion of the equity α, retaining the remaining portion $1 - \alpha$. This occurs after the public disclosure. We then model imperfect liquidity as follows. After the manager sells the equity, the investor may be subject to a liquidity shock with probability 0.5 and, in this case, must sell the equity (absent the shock the investor keeps the equity and achieves θ). The liquidity sale occurs in a market with an additional informed trader who knows the true realized $\tilde{\theta}$. It is clear that the trader buys only when observing favorable private information relative to the non-disclosure prior. Hence, the optimal trading decision is to buy when $\theta \geq \mu$.

A competitive market-maker observes the net order flow z, which is the sum of the trader's order and the investor's trade, if any. We write, then, $P(z) = \mathbb{E} (\theta | z, \text{no-disclosure})$ as the price of the entire equity conditional on a non-disclosure and net order flow z.

(i) If $z = -1$, the market-maker knows that the trader did not place a buy order, implying that $P(-1) = \mu - e$.

(ii) If $z = 1$, the market-maker knows that the trader placed a buy order, implying that $\theta \in \{\mu, \mu + e\}$. This also implies that the manager was uninformed (or, else, he would have disclosed), so that $P(1) = \mu + e/2$.

(iii) If $z = 0$, the market-maker infers that two possible events could have occurred: (a.i) the trader placed a buy order and the investor received the liquidity shock, or (a.ii) the trader placed a sell order and the investor did not receive the liquidity shock. Using Bayes rule,

$$P(0) = \mu - e \frac{p}{3 - 2p} < \mu. \tag{56}$$

By backward induction, we consider next the amount of equity that the manager must issue to the investor conditional on non-disclosure. At this point, the investor does not yet know whether he will receive a liquidity shock and can only infer that conditional on non-disclosure, there is a probability 0.5 that he keeps the equity (no shock) and realizes θ and a probability 0.5 that he must sell and realizes a price $P(z)$. Taking expectations, the expected surplus of the investor per unit of equity is given by:

$$K = \mathbb{E}\left(\theta | \text{ no - disclosure} \right) - e \underbrace{\frac{3(1-p)}{2(3-2p)^2}}_{CoC} \tag{57}$$

where $CoC > 0$ indicates the additional cost of capital caused by the liquidity shock.

The term CoCs is positive, which means that the investor recuperates less than the average value of the asset conditional on non-disclosure. The problem here is that the lack of disclosure forces the investor to trade for liquidity reasons against a more informed trader, implying that the investor will trade at a disadvantage and forfeit some surplus to the informed trader. This, in turn, will imply that the manager will have to issue more equity $\alpha = 1/K$ conditional on non-disclosure. This cost of capital has some further comparative statics worth mentioning. First, the greater the volatility of the cash flow e, the greater the cost of capital, as volatility increases the value of the information of the informed trader. Second, the cost of capital is inverse U-shaped in the probability p of the manager being informed. In particular, situations in which the market is unsure of what information the manager had (at intermediate levels of p) make the information of the informed trader incrementally more valuable.

6 Conclusion and some remaining debates

By and large, there is a fair amount of agreement on some of the basic insights of the theory on disclosure and the cost of capital; much of what may sometimes appear as "disagreement" reflects a focus on the different components of the cost of capital rather than a fundamentally different perspective about the underlying economic model. These areas of agreement are as follows: (a) information does affect the cost of capital, (b) this effect is not diversifiable, (c) this effect can be ambiguous and does not mean that information can be a priced risk factor that (theoretically) has explanatory power beyond other factors connected to real decisions, and (d) the cost of capital is a proxy for risk in the economy, not a proxy for welfare.

This noted, a few questions are yet unsolved and present open challenges for both theorists and empiricists. First, there is no consensus as to whether some measure of accounting quality should be a priced risk factor, above and beyond other factors based on economic outcomes. This debate is both a theoretical and empirical one given that, as shown theoretically, the pricing kernel is a function of choices made by the agent, and if these choices can be proxied, there should be no further explanatory power in the informational determinants of these choices (accounting quality). Accounting researchers have not yet articulated a convincing testable model where a specific construction of an accounting factor could predict the cross-section of expected returns.

A second area of contention is about the appropriate measure of the cost of capital. This in part refers to the definition of the cost of capital, and we have seen in this chapter various definitions of the cost of capital (which, to be fair, are not nearly as diverse as those used empirically). It also refers to the timing of the measurement, whether the cost of capital should be measured post- or pre-release of information or over time in a dynamic trading model. Lastly, the measurement might refer to what is meant by the cost of capital, whether it should refer mainly to the risk premium or, more generally, to the extra return demanded by investors in informed markets. Hopefully, the growing body of research in this area will provide more clarity about these remaining issues.

Notes

1 To be fair, these ideas were not unknown at the time they were published, and Merton Miller, originally trained as an economic historian, was well aware of the existing debate in the area of project financing. But Modigliani and Miller were undoubtedly the first to develop a *proof* that linked their claim to clearly stated assumptions and clarified the general debate for decades to follow.

2 Because asset pricing often applies to economies with multiple correlated assets, the theory of asset pricing in the CARA-Normal environment is greatly simplified by the use of (simple) matrix algebra. The interested reader will find a complete presentation of matrix algebra in Christensen and Demski (2003) or any introductory finance or econometrics textbook.

3 This assumption is not innocuous and implies that the model is solved in partial equilibrium; that is, we take the amount of available funds (and, hence, the interest rate) as exogenously given, but more research is certainly needed to understand the link between the interest rate and accounting measurement in general equilibrium. In a recent working paper, we provide some first steps toward finding such a link in a model of collateralized lending.

4 These properties are known to hold under more general conditions, provided that preferences are in the class of utilities with hyperbolic absolute risk aversion (HARA); see Stiglitz and Cass (1970).

5 Proving the last equality below is straightforward, but the curious reader may find it easier to develop the term $\dfrac{cov(r_i, r_m)}{Var(r_m)} RP_m$ in the right-hand side, i.e.,

$$\frac{cov(r_i, r_m)}{Var(r_m)} RP_m = \frac{\mathbf{e}_i' \mathbf{Vb}(1/\mathbf{e}'\mathbf{p}^*)(1/\mathbf{b}'\mathbf{p})}{\mathbf{b}'\mathbf{Vb}/(\mathbf{b}'\mathbf{p})^2} \frac{\mathbf{b}'(\mathbf{m}-\mathbf{p}^*)}{\mathbf{b}'\mathbf{p}^*}$$

$$= \frac{\mathbf{e}_i' \mathbf{Vb}(1/\mathbf{e}'\mathbf{p}^*)}{\mathbf{b}'\mathbf{Vb}} \mathbf{b}'(\alpha \mathbf{Vb}/I)$$

$$= \mathbf{e}_i' \mathbf{Vb}(1/\mathbf{e}'\mathbf{p}^*)\frac{\alpha}{I},$$

where the second equality follows from rewriting $\mathbf{m} - \mathbf{p}^*$ from equation (3).

6 For more details on these comparative statics and discussion of economies with asymmetric information and market power, see Lambert, Leuz, and Verrecchia (2007); Armstrong, Core, Taylor, and Verrecchia (2011); and Lambert, Leuz, and Verrecchia (2012).

7 A discussion of these two effects in the case of general information structures is examined in the comprehensive study by David Johnstone ("The effect of information on uncertainty and the cost of capital") in which he suggests that, absent strong assumptions on the information structure (which we make in what follows), the interaction between information and the cost of capital is ambiguous.

8 Such factor structures are commonly used to clarify in the model the sources of common risks. See, among other examples, Hughes, Liu, and Liu (2007); Caskey, Hughes, and Liu (2015); and Cheynel (2013). As shown by Caskey et al. (2015), similar results can also be obtained with a (more general) approach in which the covariance matrix can be written in terms of an "approximate" factor structure.

9 In recent studies ("What do management earnings forecasts convey about the macroeconomy?"), Samuel Bonsall, Zahn Bozanic, and Paul Fischer and Ayung Tseng ("Investors' demand for disclosures: the case of bellwether Firms") argue that tests of the theory should be conducted with bellwether firms that indicate trends in the economy.

10 The attentive reader may note that we are not being rigorous here as we are using for β_i^{pre} the equation for the beta in a one-shot market with no information but interpreting as the beta in an ex-ante market that precedes a second trading date after information has arrived (which, as interpreted, would then feature two trading dates: a market before the signal s is released and a market after the signal s is released). In the environment that we study here, these two approaches coincide (a heuristic argument is given in section 1.3, and a more formal argument can be found in Christensen, de la Rosa, and Feltham (2010)).

11 This observation predates the literature on disclosure and the cost of capital since it was the main object of research in the finance area on estimation risk.

12 See Christensen et al. (2010), Theorem 2(a), p 832.

13 This section offers only an introduction, as models with asymmetric information nearly always involve cumbersome algebra. For rigorous treatments, one may read Christensen et al. (2010), Caskey et al. (2015), and Lambert et al. (2012) among others.

14 Naturally, the information set could include information that is inferred from the market price, consistent with rational expectations equilibria (Grossman and Stiglitz (1980)).

15 This assumption is made to avoid a situation that would occur in rational expectations models, where prices become sufficient statistics that perfectly reveal all private information.

16 Two teams of researchers lay at each side of this debate. This effect is informally presented in Lambert et al. (2012) and analyzed in Lambert and Verrecchia (2014). At the other side of the debate, Caskey et al. (2015) argue that, in a large economy, imperfect competition can only affect the construction of the risk factors. Perhaps a reconciliation of these two approaches might be that imperfect information could affect risk premia in relatively shallow markets (on which the empirical tests of Armstrong et al. (2011) focus).

17 This debate is rigorously examined in Hughes et al. (2007), who show that, in a large-economy model of a model with asymmetric information where information risk is diversifiable, information risk is not priced.

18 These arguments are along the lines of estimation risk and, within the context of accounting, are presented in Armstrong, Banerjee, and Corona (2013) and Bertomeu (2013).

19 This section is largely adapted from Heinle and Verrecchia (2012), who further examine the problem of a firm making such a disclosure to induce participation.

20 In what follows, assume that this is well defined (otherwise, if C is too large there is no participation) and that Γ is large enough so that we can ignore integer constraints.

21 See Bloomfield and Fischer (2011) and Christensen and Qin (2014).

22 We refer to Christensen and Qin (2014) for a formal treatment of disagreement in a dynamic trading model.

23 See Jorgensen and Kirschenheiter (2003), Jorgensen and Kirschenheiter (2009), and Cheynel (2013). See also Clinch and Verrecchia (2013) for a recent study of this question within a model in which the private information is not fully diversifiable.

24 This simplification is entirely innocuous and equivalent to taking the limit when $I, J \to \infty$.

25 See Dye (1985) and Jung and Kwon (1988). Note that, here, the risk premium is measured *after* the disclosure has or has not been made. If we were to proxy for the risk premium using the stock return during the period of disclosure in these models, we would see a higher return for disclosing firms, suggesting a higher risk premium for a disclosing firms'. This interpretation is, however, somewhat deceptive because such a return would be an "unexpected" return that would not capture the risk premium.

26 See Levitt (1998) for a reprint of the speech.

27 See Gao (2010) for a published version of the dissertation.

28 This equation can be derived by noting that CE^d_j is normally distributed and, hence, $CE^0_j = E(CE^d_j) - \alpha/2\ Var(CE^d_j)$.

29 See, e.g., Hirshleifer (1971) and various discussions of this effect in accounting by Dye (2001) and Verrecchia (2001).

30 General conditions to obtain this property can be found in the classic text by Hakansson, Kunkel, and Ohlson (1982), and an application in accounting appears in Dye (1990).

31 This section is largely adapted from Armstrong, Taylor, and Verrecchia (2014); see also Bertomeu and Magee (2015) for a different valuation rationale for a reporting asymmetry. Other studies such as Gigler, Kanodia, Sapra, and Venugopalan (2009); Goex and Wagenhofer (2009); Bertomeu, Darrough, and Xue (2013); or Caskey and Laux (2013) provide a rationale for the asymmetry based on stewardship concerns.

32 We refer to Kirschenheiter and Ramakrishnan (2009) for a related approach that emphasizes consumption smoothing decisions over time; they show that a measurement system that is more conservative achieves more desirable consumption streams for preferences that exhibit prudence (e.g., such as exponential preferences).

33 See Gao (2010), Beyer (2012), Zhang (2013), and Cheynel (2013) for comprehensive treatments of the relationship between the risk premium, welfare, and investment choices.

34 While this simple example suggests that public disclosure should increase productive efficiency, the linkage between efficiency and (pre-decision) disclosure is often context specific, and we refer to Arya, Glover, and Sivaramakrishnan (1997); Kanodia, Sapra, and Venugopalan (2004); Arya, Glover, Mittendorf, and Narayanamoorthy (2005); and Suijs and Wielhouwer (2014) for various examples in which information can reduce efficiency.

35 To see why exponential preferences are "unreasonable," note that a property of such preferences is that an investor would buy exactly the same dollar amount of risky asset regardless of his personal wealth, investing what remains in the risk-free asset (see Rubinstein (1975) for a discussion of the right preferences for asset pricing). Empirical asset pricing models, for example, generally use constant relative risk-aversion preferences (Mehra and Prescott (1985)).

36 This formulation nests most commonly used preferences, such as risk-neutrality ($\gamma = 0$), constant absolute risk-aversion ($d_2 = 1/\gamma$ and $\gamma \to 0$), quadratic preferences ($\gamma = -1$), or constant relative risk-aversion ($d_1 = 0, \gamma > 0$).

37 This formulation is mathematically equivalent to assuming that the number of investors I is large and then writing the market-clearing condition on a per-capita basis.

38 For more on this question, see Bertomeu (2013) and Strobl (2013); the model developed here is largely inspired from the latter.

39 We follow here the standard model of costly misreporting; for other examples, see Liang (2004); Guttman, Kadan, and Kandel (2006); Einhorn and Ziv (2012); and Laux and Stocken (2012).

40 The nature of optimal contracts with systematic risk is introduced in Fischer (1999) and Christensen and Feltham (2005) (pp. 125–135). A more general treatment of this problem is given in section 2 of Bertomeu (2014). See also Gao and Verrecchia (2012) for an analysis of this problem in an exponential-Normal setting with optimal investment choices.

41 For individuals that are "not" employed, we can always choose their performance signal to be extremely informative, so that they would bear almost no effective exposure to diversifiable risks.

42 We refer to Core, Guay, and Verdi (2008) for a recent application of APT to empirically test whether an aggregate factor pertaining to accounting quality is a priced risk factor.

43 See Bertomeu, Beyer, and Dye (2011); we present here a version of this model where the manager must finance using equity, while the study derives the optimal financing structure (which involves risky debt financing and some cross-sectional variation in the optimal voluntary disclosure policy).

44 This disclosure strategy will be optimal in any voluntary disclosure model à la Dye-Jung-Kwon (Dye (1985), Jung and Kwon (1988)) since in these models any average or above-average signal is disclosed and the worst signal is never disclosed.

Bibliography

Armstrong, Christopher S., Snehal Banerjee, and Carlos Corona (2013) "Factor-loading uncertainty and expected returns." *Review of Financial Studies* 26(1), 158–207.

Armstrong, Christopher S., John E. Core, Daniel J. Taylor, and Robert E. Verrecchia (2011) "When does information asymmetry affect the cost of capital?" *Journal of Accounting Research* 49(1), 1–40.

Armstrong, Christopher S., Daniel J. Taylor, and Robert E. Verrecchia (2014) "Asymmetric reporting". Wharton School Working Paper.

Arya, Anil, Jonathan C. Glover, Brian Mittendorf, and Ganapathi Narayanamoorthy (2005) "Unintended consequences of regulating disclosures: the case of Regulation Fair Disclosure." *Journal of Accounting and Public Policy* 24(3), 243–252.

Arya, Anil, Jonathan C. Glover, and K. Sivaramakrishnan (1997) "Interaction between decision and control problems and the value of information." *The Accounting Review* 72(4), 561–574.

Bertomeu, Jeremy (2013) "Discussion of earnings manipulation and the cost of capital." *Journal of Accounting Research* 51(2), 475–493.

——(2014) "Incentive contracts, market risk and cost of capital." *Contemporary Accounting Research*, forth.

Bertomeu, Jeremy, and Robert P. Magee (2015) "Mandatory disclosure and asymmetry in financial reporting." *Journal of Accounting and Economics*, 59(2–3), 284–299.

Bertomeu, Jeremy, Anne Beyer, and Ronald A. Dye (2011) "Capital structure, cost of capital, and voluntary disclosures." *The Accounting Review* 86(3), 857–886.

Bertomeu, Jeremy, Masako Darrough, and Wenjie Jason Xue (2013) "Optimal conservatism with earnings manipulation." *Conference of Contemporary Accounting Research*, Fall 2013.

Beyer, Anne (2012) "Conservatism and aggregation: the effect on cost of equity capital and the efficiency of debt contracts." Rock Center for Corporate Governance at Stanford University Working Paper No. 120.

Bloomfield, Robert, and Paul E. Fischer (2011) "Disagreement and the cost of capital." *Journal of Accounting Research* 49(1), 41–68.

Bonsall, Samuel B., Zahn Bozanic, and Paul E. Fischer (2013) "What do management earnings forecasts convey about the macroeconomy?" *Journal of Accounting Research* 51(2), 225–266.

Caskey, Judson, and Volker Laux (2013) "Effects of corporate governance and managerial optimism on accounting conservatism and manipulation." Austin McCombs School of Business Working Paper.

Caskey, Judson, John Hughes, and Jun Liu (2015) "Strategic informed trades, diversification, and cost of capital."

Cheynel, Edwige (2013) "A theory of voluntary disclosure and cost of capital." *Review of Accounting Studies* 18(4), 987–1020.

Christensen, John, and Joel S. Demski (2003) *Accounting Theory: An Information Content Perspective* (McGraw-Hill Companies).

Christensen, Peter O., and Gerald A. Feltham (2005) *Economics of Accounting: Performance Evaluation. Vol. 2,* (Springer).

Christensen, Peter O., and Zhenjiang Qin (2014) "Information and heterogeneous beliefs: cost of capital, trading volume, and investor welfare." *Accounting Review,* 89(1), 209–242.

Christensen, Peter O., Enrique L. de la Rosa, and Gerald A. Feltham (2010) "Information and the cost of capital: an ex-ante perspective." *The Accounting Review* 85(3), 817–848.

Clinch, Greg, and Robert Verrecchia (2013) "Voluntary disclosure and the cost of capital." Unpublished Working Paper, Wharton.

Core, John E. Wayne R. Guay, and Rodrigo Verdi (2008) "Is accruals quality a priced risk factor?" *Journal of Accounting and Economics* 46(1), 2–22.

Dye, Ronald A. (1985) "Disclosure of nonproprietary information." *Journal of Accounting Research* 23(1), 123–145.

——(1990) "Mandatory versus voluntary disclosures: the cases of financial and real externalities." *The Accounting Review* 65(1), 24.

——(2001) "An evaluation of 'essays on disclosure' and the disclosure literature in accounting." *Journal of Accounting and Economics* 32(1–3), 181–235.

Einhorn, Eti, and Amir Ziv (2012) "Biased voluntary disclosure." *Review of Accounting Studies* 17(2), 420–442.

Fischer, Paul E. (1999) "Managing employee compensation risk." *Review of Accounting Studies* 4(1), 45–60.

Gao, Pingyang (2010) "Disclosure quality, cost of capital, and investor welfare." *The Accounting Review* 85(1), 1–29.

Gao, Pingyang, and Robert Verrecchia (2012) "Economic consequences of idiosyncratic information in diversified markets." Chicago Booth Research Paper.

Gigler, Frank, Chandra S. Kanodia, Haresh Sapra, and Raghu Venugopalan (2009) "Accounting conservatism and the efficiency of debt contracts." *Journal of Accounting Research* 47(3), 767–797.

Goex, Robert F., and Alfred Wagenhofer (2009) "Optimal impairment rules." *Journal of Accounting and Economics* 48(1), 2–16.

Grossman, Sanford J., and Joseph E. Stiglitz (1980) "On the impossibility of informationally efficient markets." *American Economic Review* 79(3), 393–408.

Guttman, Ilan, Ohad Kadan, and Eugene Kandel (2006) "A rational expectations theory of kinks in financial reporting." *The Accounting Review* 81(4), 811–848.

Hakansson, Nils H., J. Gregory Kunkel, and James A. Ohlson (1982) "Sufficient and necessary conditions for information to have social value in pure exchange." *Journal of Finance* 37(5), 1169–1181.

Heinle, Mirko S, and Robert E Verrecchia (2012) "Idiosyncratic risk, systematic risk, and firm welfare." Wharton School Working Paper.

Hirshleifer, Jack (1971) "The private and social value of information and the reward to inventive activity." *American Economic Review* 61(4), 561–574.

Hughes, John S., Jing Liu, and Jun Liu (2007) "Information asymmetry, diversification, and cost of capital." *The Accounting Review* 82(3), 705–729.

Johnstone, David (2013) "The effect of information on uncertainty and the cost of capital." Conference of Contemporary Accounting Research, Fall 2013.

Jorgensen, Bjorn, and Michael Kirschenheiter (2003) "Discretionary risk disclosures." *The Accounting Review* 78(2), 449–469.

——(2009) "Voluntary disclosure of sensitivity." Columbia GSB Working Paper.

Jung, Woon-Oh, and Young K. Kwon (1988) "Disclosure when the market is unsure of information endowment of managers." *Journal of Accounting Research* 26(1), 146–153.

Kanodia, Chandra, Haresh Sapra, and Raghu Venugopalan (2004) "Should intangibles be measured: what are the economic trade-offs?" *Journal of Accounting Research* 42(1), 89–120.

Kirschenheiter, Michael T., and Ram Ramakrishnan (2009) "Prudence demands conservatism." UIC Working Paper.

Lambert, Richard, and Robert Verrecchia (2014) "Information, illiquidity and cost of capital." *Contemporary Accounting Research*, forth.

Lambert, Richard, Christian Leuz, and Robert E. Verrecchia (2007) "Accounting information, disclosure, and the cost of capital." *Journal of Accounting Research* 36(2), 385–420.

——(2012) "Information asymmetry, information precision, and the cost of capital." *Review of Finance* 16(1), 1–29.

Laux, Volker, and Phillip C. Stocken (2012) "Managerial reporting, overoptimism, and litigation risk." *Journal of Accounting and Economics* 53(3), 577–591.

Levitt, Arthur (1998) "The importance of high quality accounting standards." *Accounting Horizons* 12(1), 79–82.

Liang, Pierre J. (2004) "Equilibrium earnings management, incentive contracts, and accounting standards." *Contemporary Accounting Research* 21(3), 685–718.

Mehra, Rajnish, and Edward C. Prescott (1985) "The equity premium: a puzzle." *Journal of Monetary Economics* 15(2), 145–161.

Modigliani, Franco, and Merton H. Miller (1958) "The cost of capital, corporation finance and the theory of investment." *American Economic Review* 48(3), 261–297.

Rubinstein, Mark (1975) "The strong case for the generalized logarithmic utility model as the premier model of financial markets." *Journal of Finance* 31(2), 551–571.

Stiglitz, Joseph E., and David Cass (1970) "The structure of investor preferences and asset returns, and separability in portfolio allocation: a contribution to the pure theory of mutual funds." *Journal of Economic Theory* 2(2), 122–160.

Strobl, Günter (2013) "Earnings manipulation and the cost of capital." *Journal of Accounting Research* 51(2), 449–473.

Suijs, Jeroen, and Jacco L. Wielhouwer (2014) "Disclosure regulation in duopoly markets: proprietary costs and social welfare." *European Accounting Review* 23(2), 227–255.

Tseng, Ayung (2015) "Investors' demand for disclosures: the case of the bellwether firms." PhD Dissertation, Columbia University.

Verrecchia, Robert E. (2001) "Essays on disclosure." *Journal of Accounting and Economics* 32(1), 97–180.

Zhang, Guochang (2013) "Accounting standards, cost of capital, resource allocation, and welfare in a large economy." *The Accounting Review* 88(4), 1459–1488.

15

A Bayesian understanding of information uncertainty and the cost of capital

D.J. Johnstone

This chapter has been assisted by seminar participants at the University of Graz and the University of Lancaster.

1 Introduction

Lambert et al. (2007, p. 386) describe the connection between information and the cost of capital as one of the most fundamental issues in markets. They quote a former Chairman of the Securities and Exchange Commission (SEC) who held that 'more information always equates to less uncertainty', and that better accounting disclosure (e.g. higher 'earnings quality') results in a lower cost of capital. Whilst this claim points to a potentially valuable role for financial reporting, Lambert et al. (2007) call for a deeper theoretical understanding of the benefits of improved accounting information in asset pricing.

The purpose of my chapter is to specify probabilistic notions of 'information' and 'information quality' and to clarify from a general Bayesian perspective how the attributes of financial information influence rational asset prices. My results are fundamentally contrary to conventional wisdom, especially in regard to the mechanics of information reducing the cost of capital.

Following the finance literature on estimation risk (e.g. Klein and Bawa 1976, 1977; Barry 1978; Brown 1979; Barry and Brown 1985; Coles and Lowenstein 1988; Lewellen and Shanken 2002), users of financial information are depicted as rational Bayesian decision makers whose task is portfolio choice under uncertainty. Consistent with this literature, and by generally the same approach as Lambert et al. (2007), information is understood not merely Bayesianly but specifically in terms of its effects on the decision maker's subjective estimates of the capital asset pricing model (CAPM) parameters (means and covariances) of future asset payoffs.

1.1 Information uncertainty

'Information risk' or 'information uncertainty' is defined in one of two ways. The first involves the quality of information available to the decision maker and the second concerns the possibly asymmetric distribution of information across different decision makers. In this chapter, I follow

Francis et al. (2004, 2005), who define 'information risk' as the risk of observing a wrong or misleading signal (my paraphrase).

To avoid the difficulties of blending Bayesian decision analysis with game-theoretic decision models, I follow Coles and Lowenstein (1988), Lambert et al. (2007) and most of the finance literature on parameter risk by adopting a strictly information-theoretic rather than game-theoretic (adverse selection) understanding of information risk. The latter framework is developed in Lambert et al. (2011).

Francis et al. (2008, p. 54) adopt the same stance as others in the accounting and noisy rational expectations literatures by focussing only on signal precision (variance), thus suppressing the common issue of accounting bias or misstatement: 'By earnings quality, we mean the precision of the earnings signal emanating from the firm's financial reporting system' (Francis et al. 2008, p. 54). Rather than precluding possible bias, it will assist our understanding of information uncertainty if we establish a mathematical characterization of information that is sufficiently general to encompass notions of signal 'strength', 'reliability', 'precision', 'noise', 'ambiguity' and the like, along with bias and any other relevant parameter of a sample observation.

Consider signal S in relation to uncertain state or parameter ϕ. Signal quality is defined Bayesianly in terms of the likelihood function, $f(S \mid \phi)$. Ideally, $f(S \mid \phi)$ is very spiked in the region of the true ϕ. By corollary of Bayes theorem, $f(\phi \mid S) \propto f(\phi) f(S \mid \phi)$, the likelihood function $f(S \mid \phi)$ is a sufficient (exhaustive) summary of S with respect to parameter ϕ. Two signals S_1 and S_2 for which $f(S_1 \mid \phi) \propto f(S_2 \mid \phi)$ carry the same information with respect to ϕ (conditional on the underlying model or model family). This is known in Bayesian theory as the 'likelihood principle' (Berger and Wolpert 1988) and is the root of logical inconsistency between frequentist and Bayesian statistics (Bernardo and Smith 1994; Robert 2007; Shanken 1987).

2 The decision model

The following decision model assumes all the normative principles of subjectivist Bayesian expected utility theory (often abbreviated to SEU). The hallmarks of SEU are strict adherence to Bayes theorem and its corollaries – particularly the likelihood principle – and recognition of 'everything being personal', most importantly the decision maker's utility function and probability assessments.

From a SEU perspective, all uncertainty is of an homogeneous subjective character, in the sense that it is impossible to differentiate between uncertainty that exists in nature and uncertainty introduced by the observer's own human or technological limitations. Analogously, Francis et al. (2007) and Zhang (2006) emphasize that 'fundamental risk' and 'information risk' are inseparable. SEU is widely accepted as the model of individual rationality in portfolio theory. This endorsement dates to Markowitz in the 1950s.[1]

2.1 Log utility CAPM

In the following derivation I assume log utility for its simplicity, in the same way as Easley et al. (2002). The analytical advantage of log wealth is that like all CRRA utility functions, the investor's optimal portfolio weights do not change with wealth or with her investment horizon (log utility is myopic, implying a one period horizon in all periods). Also, conveniently, unlike more general power utility functions, log utility does not require specification of a risk aversion parameter.

The log utility CAPM was developed by Litzenberger and Budd (1971) and Rubinstein (1976). My exposition extends Luenberger (1998, pp. 417–443) and repeats Johnstone (2012). Satchell (2012) extends my log CAPM to power (CRRA) utility functions generally.

Consider a rational (SEU) investor who is endowed at time $t = 0$ with wealth W_0 and utility function $\log(W)$ of wealth W. The investor has a one-period horizon and must allocate her wealth between the risk-free asset and a finite set of risky assets $i = 1, 2, \ldots, n$. The return from asset i over the period is defined as $R_i = V_i/P_i$, where V_i is the uncertain terminal value of asset i at $t = 1$ and P_i is the price of asset i at $t = 0$. Assume also that the risk-free asset has unit price $P_{rf} = 1$ at $t = 0$ and is certain to be worth V_{rf} at $t = 1$. The risk-free return is then a known constant $R_{rf} = V_{rf}/P_{rf} = V_{rf}$.

The investor's expected utility can be written as

$$E\left[\log\left(\{w_1 R_1 + \ldots + w_n R_n\} + \left(1 - \sum_{i=1}^{n} w_i\right) R_{rf}\right) + \log(W_0)\right],$$

where w_i is the weight or proportion of initial wealth W_0 allocated to risky asset i (there are n such assets available).

To maximize this expectation with respect to each asset weight w_i, the first order condition is

$$E\left[\frac{R_i - R_{rf}}{\{w_1 R_1 + \ldots + w_n R_n\} + \left(1 - \sum_{i=1}^{n} w_i\right) R_{rf}}\right] = 0. \tag{1}$$

The return factor on the resulting optimal (under log utility) portfolio of all available securities, including the risk-free security is then

$$R_{opt} = \left(w^\star_1 R_1 + \ldots + w^\star_n R_n\right) + \left(1 - \sum_{i=1}^{n} w^\star_i\right) R_{rf}, \tag{2}$$

where $w^\star_i$ satisfies (1) for all i. Accordingly, the unit price of this log optimal portfolio is the weighted average unit price

$$P_{opt} = \left(w^\star_1 P_1 + \ldots + w^\star_n P_n\right) + \left(1 - \sum_{i=1}^{n} w^\star_i\right),$$

since $P_{rf} = 1$.

Implicitly there is either no supply constraint on any of the securities or they are available in exactly the same number of units. If one security is in greater or less supply than another, then the respective security prices must be determined not on a 'per unit' basis but for the whole of the supply of each security.

The optimality condition (1) can now be written more simply as

$$E\left[\frac{R_i - R_{rf}}{R_{opt}}\right] = 0,$$

and then by expanding as

$$E\left[\frac{R_i}{R_{opt}}\right] - R_{rf} E\left[\frac{1}{R_{opt}}\right] = 0.$$

By definition $R_i = V_i/P_i$, hence

$$E\left[\frac{V_i}{P_i}\frac{P_{opt}}{V_{opt}}\right] - R_{rf}E\left[\frac{P_{opt}}{V_{opt}}\right] = 0. \tag{3}$$

Recognizing the identity $E\left[\frac{V_i}{P_i},\frac{P_{opt}}{V_{opt}}\right] = cov\left(\frac{V_i}{P_t},\frac{P_{opt}}{V_{opt}}\right) + E\left[\frac{V_i}{P_i}\right]E\left[\frac{P_{opt}}{V_{opt}}\right]$ and noting that

$$cov\left[\frac{V_i}{P_i},\frac{P_{opt}}{V_{opt}}\right] = cov\left(V_i,\frac{1}{V_{opt}}\right)\frac{P_{opt}}{P_i}, \quad (3) \text{ becomes}$$

$$\frac{E[V_i]}{P_i} - R_{rf} = \frac{-cov\left(V_i,1/V_{opt}\right)P_{opt}/P_i}{P_{opt}E\left[1/V_{opt}\right]}$$

$$= \frac{-cov\left(V_i,1/V_{opt}\right)}{P_iE\left[1/V_{opt}\right]}.$$

Multiplying through by the constant P_i and rearranging gives an expression defining the 'price' or ex ante worth of risky security i

$$P_i = \frac{1}{R_{rf}}\left\{E(V_i) + \frac{cov\left(V_i,1/V_{opt}\right)}{E\left[1/V_{opt}\right]}\right\} \qquad (i = 1,2,...,n), \tag{4}$$

which can be written even more simply as

$$P_i = \frac{1}{R_{rf}}\left\{\frac{E\left[V_i/V_{opt}\right]}{E\left[1/V_{opt}\right]}\right\},$$

since $cov\left(V_i,1/V_{opt}\right) = E\left[V_i/V_{opt}\right] - E[V_i]E\left[1/V_{opt}\right]$. This is the log utility CAPM applicable to investments in discrete time, and regardless of the joint distribution of $V_i (i = 1, \ldots, n)$.

There are two possible philosophical interpretations of the unit prices P_i. When the P_i are calculated using just one investor's subjective probabilities, they represent that individual's 'coherent' (i.e. mutually consistent) prices. The more conventional objectivist interpretation requires that all investors possess the same probabilities, meaning that they have the same estimates of the expected values and covariances of each of the available securities. Under these circumstances, the P_i are equilibrium prices that would emerge in rational exchange between log utility investors. Pricing models in finance are usually interpreted in the objectivist way as if investors share the same probabilities.

Under either interpretation, a log utility investor maximizes expected utility by spreading her wealth W_0 over all assets in proportion to price. Hence, from (2) the return factor on a log optimally weighted portfolio is

$$R_{opt} = \left[P_1\left(\frac{V_1}{P_1}\right) + ... + P_n\left(\frac{V_n}{P_n}\right) + P_{rf}\left(\frac{V_{rf}}{P_{rf}}\right)\right]\frac{1}{P_1 + ... + P_n + P_{rf}} \tag{5}$$

$$= \frac{V_1 + ... + V_n + V_{rf}}{P_1 + ... + P_n + 1}.$$

D. J. Johnstone

This expression is found from (2) by substituting the optimal security weights $w_i^* = P_i/\left(\sum_1^n P_i + P_{rf}\right)$ and $w_{rf}^* = P_{rf}/\left(\sum_1^n P_i + P_{rf}\right)$, where $\sum_1^n P_i + P_{rf} = \left(P_1 + \ldots + P_n + 1\right)$ is the normalizing constant required to make those weights sum to one (given $P_{rf} = 1$).

By definition $R_{opt} = V_{opt}/P_{opt}$ and P_{opt} is a constant. Hence

$$\mathrm{cov}\left(V_i, \frac{1}{V_{opt}}\right) = \mathrm{cov}\left(V_i, \frac{1}{R_{opt}}\right)\frac{1}{P_{opt}}$$

$$= \mathrm{cov}\left(V_i, \frac{1}{V_1 + \ldots + V_n + V_{rf}}\right)\frac{\left(P_1 + \ldots + P_n + 1\right)}{P_{opt}},$$

and

$$E\left[\frac{1}{V_{opt}}\right] = E\left[\frac{1}{R_{opt}}\right]\frac{1}{P_{opt}} = E\left[\frac{1}{V_1 + \ldots + V_n + V_{rf}}\right]\frac{\left(P_1 + \ldots + P_n + 1\right)}{P_{opt}}.$$

Substituting these equalities in (4) gives an empirical or usable form of the log utility CAPM

$$P_i = \frac{1}{R_{rf}}\left\{E[V_i] + \frac{\mathrm{cov}\left(V_i, 1/\left(V_1 + \ldots + V_n + V_{rf}\right)\right)}{E\left[1/\left(V_1 + \ldots + V_n + V_{rf}\right)\right]}\right\}. \tag{6}$$

Writing $V_M = \left(V_1 + \ldots + V_n + V_{rf}\right)$ and $P_M = \left(P_1 + \ldots + P_n + 1\right)$, and noting that $\mathrm{cov}\left(V_i, 1/V_M\right) = E[V_i/V_M] - E[V_i]E[1/V_M]$, the log CAPM (6) can be written very simply as

$$P_i = \frac{1}{R_{rf}}\left\{\frac{E[V_i/V_M]}{E[1/V_M]}\right\}.$$

The difference between expression (4) and expression (6) is that (4) is written in terms of the (as yet) indeterminate optimal portfolio value V_{opt}, whereas (6) is in terms of the empirical asset values V_i and V_{rf}. Equation (6) is thus an operational re-expression of (4).[2]

In what follows, the log CAPM equation (6) is employed to illustrate how the decision maker's subjective estimate of the ex ante 'worth' or price of asset i is affected by information.

3 Information and asset prices

The mechanics by which information moves asset prices are examined in the following numerical illustration. For simplicity, suppose that all n risky assets are binaries with unknown $V_j \in \{1,0\}$ and that rational asset prices are defined by the log utility CAPM equation (6). I assume this most elementary asset form for the same reasons of simplicity recognised by Easley and O'Hara (e.g. 1987) in their information economics market microstructure models. The resulting rational asset prices are always between 0 and 1 and hence are easy to relate to their underlying probabilities.

The terminal value V_j of each risky asset is generated by a simple two-step stochastic process, pictured in Figure 15.1. Note that this model extends the Easley and O'Hara (1987) model by allowing for the general case of n dependent binary assets.

400

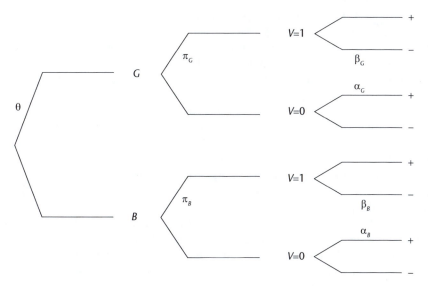

Figure 15.1   Stochastic process generating asset value $V \in \{1,0\}$ and signal $S \in \{+,-\}$ with probabilities conditioned on the market state $M \in \{$ Good, Bad$\}$

Step 1: A binary 'market factor' $M \in \{$ Good, Bad$\}$ is drawn from a Bernoulli distribution with probabilities $\theta = p$ (Good $\equiv$ G) and $(1-\theta) = p$ (Bad $\equiv$ B).

Step 2: V_j is drawn independently from another Bernoulli distribution with conditional probability $\pi_G = p$ ($V_j 1 \mid$ G) when $M=$ Good or alternatively $\pi_B = p$ ($V_j 1 \mid$ B) when $M=$ Bad. The second stage of this random process is repeated independently for each risky asset $j = 1, 2, \ldots ,$ n while holding the market state M constant. The role of M is to introduce a common or 'systematic' factor into the causation of all V_j.

For numerical illustration, let $\theta = 0.5$ and let $\pi_G = 0.8$ and $\pi_B = 0.3$ for all $j = 1, 2, \ldots , n$. Similarly, let $n = 30$ and $V_{rf}= (1+ rf) = 1.10$ (the unit price of the risk free asset is $P_{rf= 1}$). Under these assumptions, all risky assets have the same parameters and hence the same price P_j. Specifically,

$$E\left[V_j\right] = p\left(V_j = 1\right) = \theta\pi_G + \left(1-\theta\right)\pi_B$$
$$= 0.5\left(0.8\right) + 0.5\left(0.3\right) = 0.55$$

and by Monte Carlo simulation (100,000 repeats)

$$E[1/V_M] = E\left[1/\left(\Sigma_j V_j + V_{rf}\right)\right] = 0.07098$$
$$\mathrm{cov}\left(V_j, 1/V_M\right) = \mathrm{cov}\left[V_j, 1/\left(\Sigma_j V_j + V_{rf}\right)\right]$$
$$= -0.009233.$$

Hence from the log CAPM equation (6)

$$P_j = \frac{1}{R_{rf}}\left\{E\left[V_j\right] + \frac{\mathrm{cov}\left(V_j, 1/V_M\right)}{E[1/V_M]}\right\} = 0.382,$$

implying an expected return factor of $E[R_j] = E[V_j]/P_j = 0.55/0.382 = 1.44$ (and thus a market required return of 44 percent in usual terms).

Note that simulation is necessary to perform the calculations that involve the ratio $1/V_M$. Unlike V_M, its reciprocal $1/V_M$ is not amenable to the standard statistical mathematics of variance and covariance. While the need for simulation is unfortunate, the log CAPM equation has the great advantage that it has a closed form, unlike most equilibrium pricing models which require numerical search routines to solve systems of equations.

Also note that P_j is quite a bit lower than $E[V_j]/R_{rf} = 0.55/1.10 = 0.5$, the price that a risk–neutral investor would pay for asset j. This discount for risk is tempered by diversification across all $n = 30$ stocks in the market, which makes each individual asset more valuable,[3] and also by the assumption of log utility. A log utility investor has many well-documented characteristics, one of which is that, among all risk-averse CRRA (myopic) utility functions, log utility lies towards the more risk-tolerant end of the spectrum.

Now consider one particular risky asset, say asset k. Suppose that our log utility investor receives information $S_k \in \{+,-\}$ regarding asset k with error characteristics $p(+ \mid V_k = 0) = \alpha$ and $p(- \mid V_k = 1) = \beta$. For the sake of example and without loss of generality, let $S_k = +$.

The Bayesian posterior probability of $V_k = 1$, $p(V_k = 1 \mid S_k = +)$, denoted more conveniently by $p(1 \mid +)$, is given by

$$p(G \mid +)p(1 \mid +,G) + p(B \mid +)p(1 \mid +,B)$$

where

$$p(1 \mid +,G) = p(1 \mid G)p(+ \mid 1,G)/p(+ \mid G)$$

$$= \frac{\pi_G(1-\beta)}{\pi_G(1-\beta)+(1-\pi_G)\alpha}$$

$$p(1 \mid B,+) = \frac{\pi_B(1-\beta)}{\pi_B(1-\beta)+(1-\pi_B)\alpha}$$

$$p(+ \mid G) = p(1 \mid G)p(+ \mid 1,G)+p(0 \mid G)p(+ \mid 0,G)$$
$$= \pi_G(1-\beta)+(1-\pi_G)\alpha$$

$$p(+) = p(G)p(+ \mid G)+p(B)p(+ \mid B)$$
$$= p(G)\left[p(1 \mid G)p(+ \mid 1,G)+p(0 \mid G)p(+ \mid 0,G)\right]$$
$$+ p(B)\left[p(1 \mid B)p(+ \mid 1,B)+p(0 \mid B)p(+ \mid 0,B)\right]$$
$$= \theta\left[\pi_G(1-\beta)+(1-\pi_G)\alpha\right]+(1-\theta)\left[\pi_B(1-\beta)+(1-\pi_B)\alpha\right]$$

$$p(G \mid +) = p(G)p(+ \mid G) / p(+)$$
$$= \theta\, p(+ \mid G) / p(+).$$

It is assumed in these equations that $p(+ \mid G, 0) = p(+ \mid B, 0) = p(+ \mid 0) = \alpha$ and $p(- \mid G, 1) = p(- \mid B,1) = p(- \mid 1) = \beta$, implying that the probability of signal $S_k \in \{+,-\}$ is dependent only on the state of V_k and not on the state of the market M. This is a strong assumption and raises the fundamental question of whether signal quality is entirely idiosyncratic (asset-specific) rather than partly dependent on the systematic or market factor $M \in \{G,B\}$. The likely instance of systematic market-driven (cross-sectionally correlated) error characteristics has been raised by Lambert et al. (2007, pp. 402–403) and is discussed in the next section of this paper.

To observe the effect of signal S_k on the asset price P_k, assume for simplicity that no signal is observed for any other asset $j \neq k$. Simulation is used again to find the updated CAPM parameters $\text{cov}(V_k, 1/V_M \mid S_k)$ and $E[(1/V_M) \mid S_k]$ and finally the asset price conditioned on signal S_k

$$P_k \mid S_k = \frac{1}{R_{rf}} \left\{ E[V_k \mid S_k] + \frac{\text{cov}(V_k, 1/V_M \mid S_k)}{E[(1/V_M) \mid S_k]} \right\}.$$

It is important to note for this calculation that a signal $S_k = +$ has been received, and hence coherence requires that the market condition M must be generated from $p(G \mid +)$, not $p(G)$. The values of all the other assets $j \neq k$ are then generated based on state M, as per step 2 above. This is entirely logical. The observation $S_k = +$ tells decision makers something about the likely state of M and therefore changes the probability distribution of V_j for all assets j, not just $j = k$.

The results of these calculations are displayed in Figures 15.2–15.5 over the range of possible values of the signal error characteristics $\{\alpha_k, \beta_k\}$. Figure 15.2 is a contour plot of the posterior probability $p(1 \mid +)$, remembering that $p(1) = \theta \pi_G + (1+\theta)\pi_B = 0.55$. Note how the evidential effect of signal S varies simultaneously with α and β. Note also that a signal with $\{\alpha = 0.5; \beta = 0.5\}$ has likelihood ratio $p(+ \mid 1)/p(+ \mid 0)$ equal to one and is completely uninformative. Any other signal has likelihood ratio greater or less than one and is therefore informative. Perversely, a 'perfectly bad' signal with $\{\alpha = 1, \beta = 1\}$ is just as informative as an error free signal with $\{\alpha = 0, \beta = 0\}$. For example, if $\beta = 1$, a positive signal $S_k = +$ proves that $V_k = 0$ since $S_k = +$ has zero probability under $V_k = 1$ (i.e. $p(+ \mid 1) = 1 - \beta = 0$).

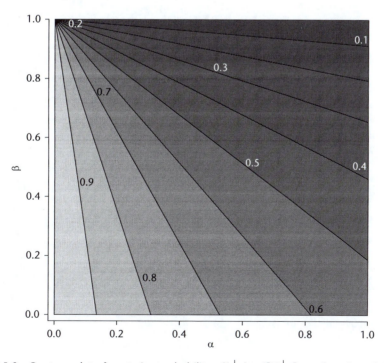

Figure 15.2 Contour plot of posterior probability $p(1 \mid +) = E[V_k \mid +]$ as a function of signal error characteristics $\{\alpha, \beta\}$

It is essential not to ignore signals with very high error probabilities. When understood in reverse, by reading $S = +$ as $S = -$ and vice versa, these become good signals with increasingly good error characteristics as $\alpha, \beta \rightarrow 1$. Comfortingly, Bayes theorem does this implicitly, which is why there is no loss of generality in assuming a nominally 'positive' signal $S = +$ in our example. In effect, by allowing both α and β to vary across the full range from 0 to 1, it becomes unnecessary to analyse the effect of a 'positive' (favourable) signal and then separately the effect of a 'negative' (unfavourable) signal. Both analyses are completed at once and represented in a single graph.

Indeed, it is not justifiable to limit the domain of possible $\{\alpha, \beta\}$ to some segment of the unit square, because there is no inherent boundary on either error probability within that square. It might be tempting for example to admit only $\alpha, \beta < 0.5$, but that would preclude a signal with say $\alpha = 0.01$ and $\beta = 0.9$, which is potentially a very informative signal. To see this, note that the likelihood ratio of $S = +$ is then $p(+|1)/p(+|0) = 0.1/0.01 = 10$, which is an extremely strong indication of $V = 1$. Note also that signals with such oddly disproportionate error probabilities can sometimes arise in practical applications. Suppose for example that the signal source is highly conservative in the sense that it nearly always reports a negative signal $S = -$ when $V = 0$ (e.g $p(-|0) = 0.95$, implying $\alpha = 0.05$), but it also reports $S = -$ with high probability when $V = 1$ (e.g. $p(-|1) = \beta = 0.7$). This signal has $\{\alpha, \beta\} = \{0.05, 0.7\}$ but cannot be excluded as either uninformative or unrealistic.

Figure 15.3 reveals the effect of signal $S_k = +$ with error characteristics $\{\alpha, \beta\}$ on the investor's assessment of the covariance of asset k with the market, $\text{cov}(V_k, 1/V_M | \cdot)$. Note how this estimate can increase or decrease depending on $\{\alpha, \beta\}$. The posterior covariance equals the

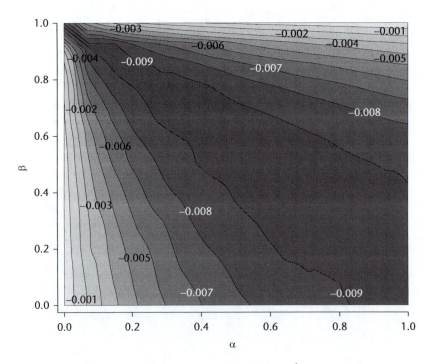

Figure 15.3 Contour plot of posterior covariance $\text{cov}(V_k, 1/V_M | +)$ as a function of signal error characteristics $\{\alpha, \beta\}$

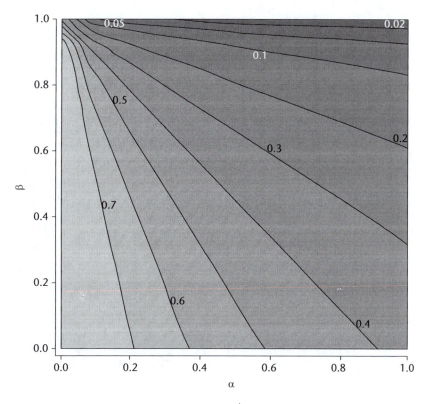

Figure 15.4 Contour plot of posterior asset price $P_k | S = +$ as a function of signal error characteristics $\{\alpha, \beta\}$

prior covariance only under a Bayesianly uninformative signal $\{\alpha = 0.5, \beta = 0.5\}$. Maximum posterior covariance $cov(V_k, 1/V_M |.)$ occurs under $S = +$ with error probabilities $\{\alpha, \beta\}$ both between 0.5 and 0.55. This signal is logically equivalent to $S = -$, with error probabilities slightly less than 0.5.

It is important to recognize that signal S leads to simultaneous reassessment of both CAPM parameters, $E[V_k |.]$ and $cov(V_k, 1/V_M |.)$, and that depending on $\{\alpha, \beta\}$ both parameters can rise or fall, not necessarily in the same direction, based on a given signal (here $S = +$). The resulting asset price might therefore also move up or down when conditioned on S. Figure 15.4 plots the updated price $P_k | S$. Note that the direction in which P_k moves from its prior value of $P_k = 0.382$ (calculated above, and shown in Figure 15.4 at the point of an uninformative test $\alpha, \beta = 0.5$) depends not only on the value of the signal $S \in \{+, -\}$ observed, positive or negative, but also on the error characteristics of that observation.

Figure 15.5 is a contour plot of the expected return $E[R_k | S_k = +]$ as a function of $\{\alpha, \beta\}$. Note especially how this rational required return increases greatly as $\alpha, \beta \to 1$. As explained above, the signal $S = +$ is understood by Bayes as a strongly negative signal when α and β both take high values. The posterior probability $p(1|+)$ therefore approaches zero with increasing $\{\alpha, \beta\}$, and takes the expectation $E[V_k | s]$ with it. An interesting connotation is that although

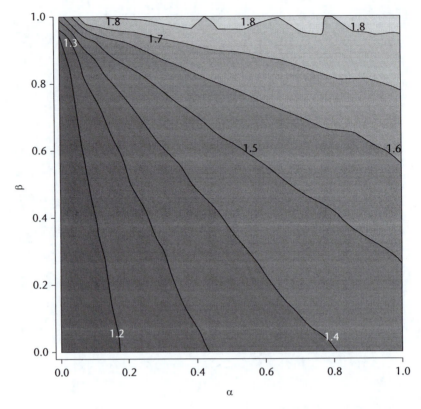

Figure 15.5 Contour plot of posterior expected return $E[R_k \mid +]$ as a function of signal error characteristics $\{\alpha, \beta\}$

certainty increases when $p(1 \mid +)$ becomes very small, the required return on the asset does not decrease, but in fact increases very markedly. This is easily explained. Although increasing certainty pushes the CAPM covariance term towards zero, and therefore pushes the required return downwards, this downward influence is swamped by the upward influence of the lower expected value. In net effect, the cost of capital increases strongly with increasing $\{\alpha, \beta\}$ until a discontinuity is reached at $\beta = 1$, where $E[V_k \mid +] = p(1 \mid +) = 0$ and $cov(V_k, 1/V_M \mid +) = 0$, at which point the asset becomes a 'risk free' source of zero payoff.

This result, which contradicts much of the literature, was foreshadowed by Lambert et al. (2007, p. 392), who showed that in the case of (i) a negative exponential utility CAPM, and (ii) a typical asset k with positive covariance with the market V_M, the required return on investment, $E[R_k \mid \cdot]$, is decreasing in expected return $E[V_k \mid \cdot]$. It is easily verified that this same negative relationship between $E[R_k \mid .]$ and $E[V_k \mid \cdot]$ holds for both my log utility CAPM, and also the usual quadratic utility CAPM. Writing $E[R_k]$ as $E[V_k]/P_k$ and substituting for P_k in the log CAPM equation (6), it is immediately evident that for typical assets k (for which $cov(V_k, 1/V_M)$ is negative) $E[R_k]$ is decreasing in $E[V_k]$. And similarly for the quadratic utility CAPM where the covariance term is $cov(V_k, V_M)$ rather than $cov(V_k, 1/V_M)$, in which case the usually realistic kind of asset has positive covariance.

A good way to sum up is to say that the widely held inverse relationship between certainty and cost of capital tends to apply in reverse when the information giving rise to that newfound certainty is negative (i.e. unfavourable), thus causing a reduction in $E[V_k \mid .]$. By comparison, when the signal bringing greater certainty is sufficiently positive, that information not only tends to push the CAPM covariance term towards zero but also pushes the expectation term $E[V_k | .]$ higher, both of which drive the required return $E[R_k | .]$ downwards.

Figure 15.5 is demonstration enough that increasing certainty does not necessarily reduce the cost of capital. This plot exhibits the interplay between the two CAPM valuation parameters, $E[V_k | .]$ and $\text{cov}(V_k, 1/V_M | .)$. The conventional wisdom that expected (required) return reduces with certainty is corroborated when the signal is positive, and the decision maker becomes more certain of a good or perhaps still better positive payoff V_k. However, when the signal is negative, so much so that the investor becomes quite certain of a payoff with expectation approaching zero, the mean's effect outweighs the covariance, and the CAPM required return on capital tends quickly upwards. In the Figure 15.5 illustration, the highest required return contour is shown at 80 percent (i.e. $E[R_k] = 1.8$).

Note that the wobbles in the contours are produced by small approximation errors inherent in simulation. The simulation was run with $\{\alpha, \beta\}$ between $\{0.01, 0.01\}$ and $\{0.99, 0.99\}$ in two-way steps of 0.07. Results for each $\{\alpha, \beta\}$ pair were produced by 300,000 repeats.

Philosophically, the investor's objective in seeking new information such as signal S is to make more accurate probability and price assessments, so as to arrive at more profitable (higher expected utility) portfolio weights. This objective does not imply that the investor's assessment of a given asset price P_k or its underlying parameters $E[V_k | .]$ and $\text{cov}(V_k, 1/V_M | .)$ should shift in any particular direction. The only requirement is that these assessments are conditioned on all available relevant information, which of itself is expected to bring about the best (most accurate) possible probability assessments.

4 Systematic error characteristics

It is possible that the error characteristics of signal S depend on the market state, as depicted in Figure 15.1 (Clarkson and Thompson 1990). In these circumstances, where S_k is dependent not only on V_k but also on $M \in \{G,B\}$, the signal quality of S is governed by four error probabilities rather than two

$$\begin{cases} \alpha_G = p(+|0,G) & \alpha_B = p(+|0,B) \\ \beta_G = p(-|1,G) & \beta_B = p(-|0,B) \end{cases}.$$

The joint probability distribution $p(V_1, V_2, \ldots, V_n | .)$ is conditioned on all available signals $(S_1, S_2, \ldots, S_n)$. If one or more of the observed signals has error probabilities that depend on the market state M, Bayesian probability revision must build in this systematic error process when interpreting what the sum of available information $(S_1, S_2, \ldots, S_n)$ implies about any given asset price P_k. It is possible to alter the price of asset k conditioned on $(S_1, S_2, \ldots, S_n)$ by changing the properties of any of the signals in $(S_1, S_2, \ldots, S_n)$.

For example, if signal S_j has systematic error probabilities such that a particular observation, say $S_j = +$, is strongly indicative of $M = G$, then in general the price of any asset k which has a relatively high probability of doing well under $M = G$ will tend to increase when conditioned on S_j. In typical market environments, it is likely that some signals have strongly systematic error probabilities, implying that price P_k can be greatly influenced by $S_j \neq k$ (cf. Leuz and Wysocki 2008).

The Bayesian requirement of conditioning each asset price P_k on all information $(S_1, S_2, \ldots, S_n)$ is illustrated as follows. Consider a simplified market offering $n = 2$ risky assets and a risk-free asset with $P_{rf} = 1$ and $V_{rf} = 1.10$. The value V_i of each risky asset i ($i = 1, 2$) is generated by the stochastic process depicted in Figure 15.1. As above, $\theta = 0.5$, $\pi_G = 0.8$ and $\pi_B = 0.3$. For simplicity, assume

Table 15.1 Asset parameters $E[V_1|++]$ and $cov(V_1, 1/V_M|++)$, price $P_1(=P_2)$ and expected return $E[R_1|++] = E[V_1|++]/P_1$ for different systematic error probabilities $\{\alpha_G, \alpha_B, \beta_G, \beta_B\}$

$\{\alpha_G, \alpha_B, \beta_G, \beta_B\}$	$\{0.2, 0.2, 0.2, 0.2\}$
$E[V_1]$	0.868
$cov(V_1, 1/V_M)$	−0.02879
Price $P_1(=P_2)$	0.7185
$E[R_1]$	1.207 (20.7%)
$\{\alpha_G, \alpha_B, \beta_G, \beta_B\}$	$\{0.0083, 0.2, 0.3603, 0.2\}$
$E[V_1]$	0.868
$cov(V_1, 1/V_M)$	−0.03398
Price $P_1(=P_2)$	0.7067
$E[R_1]$	1.2277 (22.8%)
$\{\alpha_G, \alpha_B, \beta_G, \beta_B\}$	$\{0.38, 0.2, 0.0083, 0.2\}$
$E[V_1]$	0.868
$cov(V_1, 1/V_M)$	−0.02612
Price $P_1(=P_2)$	0.725
$E[R_1]$	1.1971 (19.7%)

that the two risky assets have identical signal error properties $\{\alpha_G, \alpha_B, \beta_G, \beta_B\}$. The decision maker observes $\{S_1, S_2\}$ and prices both assets based on this full information. Suppose that the two independent (given M) signals are both positive, $S_1 = +$ and $S_2 = +$. Because the two assets are the same and have the same signal $S_1 = S_2 = +$, they must by symmetry have the same price $P_1 = P_2$.

Prices and related results are shown in Table 15.1. For convenience, the joint signal $S_1 = S_2 = +$ is denoted by $++$. There are three sets of results, each based on a different set of error probabilities $\{\alpha_G, \alpha_B, \beta_G, \beta_B\}$. These are chosen specifically so as to hold the likelihood ratio $p(++|V_1=1)/p(++|V_1=0)$ constant and, therefore, to hold the posterior expected value $E[V_1|++]$ of both risky assets constant (V_2 can be interchanged with V_1 since the two assets are really the same apart from their different names). The related probability equations are shown in the Appendix. Because there are just two risky assets, numerical results are calculated longhand, without requiring simulation (the Excel probability tree and pricing model is available from the author).

Table 15.1 reveals that changes in how the error probabilities of S depend on the market M show up in rational asset prices and implied rates of return. Generally, any change in the error probabilities of signals (S_1, S_2) causes changes in both the expected value $E[V_1|S_1, S_2]$ and expected return $E[R_1|S_1, S_2]$, for any given signal pair (S_1, S_2). The first set of results in Table 15.1 assumes non-systematic error probabilities, $\alpha_G = \alpha_B$ and $\beta_G = \beta_B$. The remaining two sets of results assume error probabilities that depend on the market state M, while nonetheless leading to the same Bayesian posterior probability $p(V_1 = 1 | ++)$. By holding this probability constant, any increase (decrease) in asset price translates to a decrease (increase) in the expected return on capital. In the first instance shown in Table 15.1, $P_1(=P_2)$ decreases and the expected cost of capital increases from 20.7 percent to 22.8 percent. In the second instance, the asset price $P_1(=P_2)$ increases and the expected cost of capital decreases to 19.7 percent.

5 Signal quality and ex ante value

Signal quality makes a great difference to how a signal is interpreted and to what effect signal observations have on the investor's assessments of an asset's expected value, covariance and price. This is shown above from an ex post perspective, where we assume that the signal has already arrived and calculate new probabilities and required returns on capital conditional on (i) what was observed, and (ii) the error characteristics of the mechanism by which that observation was generated.

A related concern addressed by Christensen et al. (2010) is whether signal quality makes a difference to the assessed asset price ex ante. Specifically, how does the quality of a future signal come into the decision maker's assessments before that signal arrives, and more broadly, is there an ex ante preference or premium for assets with higher future signal quality?

The Bayesian answer to this question is that future signal characteristics make no difference to the decision maker's prior assessments of mean and covariance. This seems intuitively obvious since the prior mean and covariance are based on existing information rather than future information.[4]

The following analysis formalises the mathematical relationship between prior and posterior means and covariances. By the law of iterated expectations, $E[E[V_j | S]] = E[V_j]$, the expected posterior (i.e. post S) asset value equals the ex ante (prior to S) expectation of V_j. This means that although it is understood that $E[V_j | S]$ can differ greatly from the current expectation $E[V_j]$, and that the calculation of $E[V_j | S]$ upon observing S hinges on the error characteristics of S, the current (prior) expected value of $E[V_j | S]$ is unaffected by the error characteristics of S. Put another way, the maths of Bayes theorem are such that whatever the error characteristics of S, the different possible values of $E[V_j | \Sigma]$ based on different signal observations S are constrained such that they must on average equal $E[V_j]$. Or, in other words, it is not true that the error characteristics of S affect $E[V_j]$, but it is true that $E[V_j]$ affects how much signal S with its given error characteristics affects the posterior $E[V_j | S]$.

The less obvious but equivalent point is that the ex ante covariance assessment is also unaffected by the attributes of the future signal. This follows immediately from the fact that the covariance can be written in terms of expectations, and, as has just been seen, prior expectations are not affected by future signal error characteristics.

Another way to prove this point is to write the prior (ex ante) covariance in terms of the expected posterior (conditional) covariance. For notational convenience, the value V_j of the given asset j is written without the subscript.

$$\text{cov}\left(V, \frac{1}{V_M}\right) = E\left[\text{cov}\left(V, \frac{1}{V_M}\right)\middle| S\right] + \text{cov}\left(E[V|S], E\left[\frac{1}{V_M}\middle| S\right]\right) \tag{7}$$

Each of the two terms on the right of this equation is influenced by signal quality, but this influence is cancelled out when the two terms are added together.

More specifically, these two terms are

$$E\left[\text{cov}\left(V, \frac{1}{V_M}\right)\middle| S\right] = E\left[E\left(V\frac{1}{V_M}\middle| S\right) - E(V|S)E\left(\frac{1}{V_M}\middle| S\right)\right]$$

$$= E\left[V\frac{1}{V_M}\right] - E\left[E(V|S)E\left(\frac{1}{V_M}\middle| S\right)\right],$$

and

$$\text{cov}\left(E[V|S], E\left[\frac{1}{V_M}\middle| S\right]\right) = E\left[E(V|S)E\left(\frac{1}{V_M}\middle| S\right)\right] - E\left[E(V|S)\right]E\left[E\left(\frac{1}{V_M}\middle| S\right)\right]$$

$$= E\left[E(V|S)E\left(\frac{1}{V_M}\middle| S\right)\right] - E[V]E\left[\frac{1}{V_M}\right].$$

Table 15.2 Price parameters assuming $n = 2$ risky assets for different possible signal error probabilities $\{\alpha, \beta\}$ (with $\theta = 0.5$, $\pi_G = 0.8$, $\pi_B = 0.3$, and $V_{rf} = 1.1$)

$\{\alpha, \beta\}$	$\{0.5, 0.5\}$	$\{0.1, 0.4\}$	$\{0.4, 0.1\}$	$\{0.1, 0.1\}$
$p(+)$	0.5	0.375	0.675	0.54
$\mathrm{cov}(V_1, 1/V_M \mid +)$	−0.0883	−0.0377	−0.0698	−0.0273
$\mathrm{cov}(V_1, 1/V_M \mid -)$	−0.0883	−0.0814	−0.0502	−0.0376
$E\,[\mathrm{cov}(V_1, 1/V_M \mid -)]$	−0.0883	−0.0650	−0.0634	−0.032
$\mathrm{cov}\left(E[V|S], E\left[\dfrac{1}{V_M}\Big| S\right]\right)$	0	−0.0233	−0.0249	−0.0563
$\mathrm{cov}\left(V, \dfrac{1}{V_M}\right)$	−0.0833	−0.0833	−0.0833	−0.0883
$E[V|+]$	0.55	0.88	0.7333	0.9167
$E[V|-]$	0.55	0.352	0.1692	0.1196
$E[E(V| S) = E[V]$	0.55	0.55	0.55	0.55
$E\,[(1/V_M \mid +)]$	0.5348	0.4171	0.4694	0.4040
$E\,[(1/V_M \mid -)]$	0.5348	0.6055	0.6707	0.6885
$E\left[E[1/V_M|S]\right] = E[1/V_M]$	0.5348	0.5348	0.5348	0.5348
Ex Ante Asset price P	0.35	0.35	0.35	0.35

Hence, from (7) the covariance is

$$\mathrm{cov}\left(V, \frac{1}{V_M}\right) = E\left[V\frac{1}{V_M}\right] - E[V]E\left[\frac{1}{V_M}\right],$$

and is unaffected by the error characteristics of S.

5.1 Numerical illustration

Consider the case again of $n = 2$ identical and conditionally independent risky assets, with $\theta = 0.5$, $\pi_G = 0.8$, $\pi_B = 0.3$ and $V_{rf} = 1.1$. For either asset, the ex ante probability of receiving signal $S = +$ is then

$$p(+) = \theta\,[\pi_G(1-\beta) + (1-\pi_G)\alpha] + (1-\theta)[\pi_B(1-\beta) + (1-\pi_B)\alpha].$$

Results for some arbitrary values of α and β are provided in Table 15.2. These are calculated analytically (in a spreadsheet available from the author). Their main purpose is to demonstrate how the two terms on the right of (7) change with $\{\alpha, \beta\}$ yet their sum is constant. The other log utility CAPM terms $E[V]$ and $E[1/V_M]$ shown in Table 15.2 are also unaffected by the error probabilities of S, implying that signal quality has no effect ex ante on the asset price P ($= P_1 = P_2$).

6 Financial information

Examples of good information and analysis that unfortunately add to doubts rather than eliminating them are commonplace and just as inevitable in financial reporting as in other fields. Observed monthly sales volumes or costs or cash receipts may sometimes cast great doubt over the sustainability of a firm or product. This does not mean that these figures are inaccurate or imprecise. Rather, provided that measurement is rigorous, even the most common types of accounting data may shake investor confidence, while at the same time leaving investors more accurately informed about fundamentals and therefore likely to make more profitable or less costly portfolio management decisions.

Activity-based costing (ABC) proponents have long made this kind of argument. They hold that a more refined costing system might expose previously unseen doubts over a firm's or product's economic sustainability. Any similar enhancement that leads to more timely loss recognition is likely to dent investor confidence. Firms may wish not to divulge information of this ilk, which is why nondisclosure is often viewed as a negative signal (Verrecchia 1983, 2001). At a more macro level, aspects of market value accounting might reveal the full exposure of the firm to derivative markets, suggesting jointly that (i) the probability distribution of its future profits has a peak in the far left tail that was not previously recognized and (ii) that the firm's beta or dependence on market-wide factors is higher than previously understood.

These examples are simplistic but sufficient to suggest that even very 'good' accounting may not assist the firm by lowering its cost of capital. To the contrary, better disclosure or measurement systems can produce signals that lead an analyst to simultaneously downgrade expected earnings and raise the required return on equity, thus bringing about a big price fall. This point is well made by Leuz and Wysocki (2008) in relation to accounting restatements, which are Bayesianly just a further mechanism for transmission of accounting information. Similarly, Rogers et al. (2009) explain how some earnings forecast releases, particularly those bringing unexpected negative news, can 'create uncertainty' rather than resolve it.

Yet contrary to these ideas, it has become almost axiomatic in accounting theory, and noisy rational expectations theory in general, that better information (e.g. better earnings quality) implies more certainty and a lower cost of capital.

> The intuition is straightforward. A firm's cost of capital is the riskless interest rate plus a risk premium. Releasing more information and, in particular, more public information through .financial reports and other public disclosures by firms reduces the uncertainty about the size and the timing of future cash flows and, therefore, also the risk premium.
>
> *(Christensen et al. 2010, p. 817)*

> . . . we propose that poor earnings quality represents imprecise information about firms' future cash flows and thereby increases the cost of equity capital.
>
> *(Bhattacharya et al. 2012, p. 455)*

> The link between corporate disclosure, investor information and the cost of capital is one of the most fundamental relations in finance and accounting. Understanding this link is of substantial interest to firms that provide information to capital markets as well as to financial market regulators who mandate disclosures. Various theoretical models predict that an increase in information quality is negatively related to the cost of capital . . . Similarly, the estimation risk literature suggests that higher quality information should manifest in lower systematic risk and expected returns.
>
> *(Leuz and Schrand 2009, p. 1)*

> . . . we show that higher quality accounting information and financial disclosures affect the assessed covariances with other firms, and this effect unambiguously moves a firm's cost of capital closer to the risk-free rate.
>
> *(Lambert et al. 2007, p. 387)*

Taking these quotes at face value, accounting practice has the unique advantage over other information sources that the better the accounting method, the more certain that market predictions become. This contradicts the archetypal Bayesian analysis of the expected value of imperfect information (EVII) laid out by Raiffa and Schlaifer (1961) in contexts such as oil exploration. Standard EVII calculations show that a technically sound or even ideal geological sample can leave the oil company either more or less certain of oil after observing the actual test result.

The same is true of accounting information. Realistically, the accountant, like the geologist, does not have the capacity to produce signals that by necessity make uncertain outcomes (oil or cash flows) more predictable. Sometimes the most technically advanced indicator (e.g. a geological test) leaves an expert analyst significantly less certain of the underlying state of nature. This is not to say of course that such information is not worth paying for ex ante. Rather, it merely acknowledges that a test or signal with high expected information value, and hence clearly worth its cost ex ante, will not always bring about greater certainty ex post.

The precept that information resolves uncertainty is almost lawlike in economics but is not always operational. Suppose that risky V is driven by factor or parameter F, and that signal S is indicative of F. The predictive distribution of V is then $\int_F p(V|F)p(F|S)dF$, assuming that V is independent of S when given F. Hence, any signal S that shifts the investor's probability distribution of F towards states under which V is highly uncertain must add to investor uncertainty about V, and conversely.

Take the hypothetical case of oil exploration. Imagine that credible drill sites are in nature of two types, A and B, where testing is required to identify the nature of a given site. In A-type sites the known frequency of oil is 0.5, and in B-type sites this relative frequency is 0.95. The population average frequency of oil is therefore $\rho(0.5) + (1 - \rho)0.95$, where ρ is the proportion of A-type sites. If from experience or theory the geologist establishes that $\rho = 0.7$, then his prior probability of oil in a 'random' site is 0.635. Now suppose that the technically ideal geological test reveals with certainty the type of site he is looking at. It follows that in 70 percent of such tests, the probability of oil will fall from a prior of 0.635 to a posterior of 0.5, thus leaving greater uncertainty post-test than pre-test.

In this simple but realistically uncertain world, the market will of course want to know every possible geological test result and will price each drill site accordingly, leaving A-type sites trading at a much reduced price and higher risk premium and B type sites trading at a much higher price and reduced cost of capital.[5] The same bivalent outcome might be expected from redesigned technically 'better' accounting measurements. Such enhanced accounting methods will ideally show all firms more clearly for what they 'really are', leaving some firms to face higher costs of capital and others with lower costs of capital. A priori, the accounting equivalent of the geologist's ρ is unknown, and thus it is unclear whether a new accounting regime would spawn more winners than losers.

In scientific fields like geology, it is possible to design a test or signal with technical specifications that ensure good error characteristics (or a sharply peaked likelihood function). Accounting theory and practice faces the same signal design (optimization) task, however there is generally less theory and laboratory technique by which to work. This inherent difficulty is reflected in decades of academic and professional dispute about accounting standards and fundamental questions such as how to value assets in the balance sheet (historical cost, current cost, 'fair value' etc.). Similarly, there are many unresolved issues in the empirical literature regarding how to explicate and measure 'earnings quality' (Dechow and Schrand 2010; Dechow et al. 2010; DeFond 2010). In medicine, tests exist that tell the technician whether cells are infected or not, generally with very low error rates, but the same technology is not available, to accountants when the unknown quantity is whether a firm is a 'going concern' or not, or whether a merger, a product or a new management strategy will succeed or not. The innate technical limits to conceiving and implementing qualitatively or even incrementally 'better' accounting measures counteracts any presumption that markets can benefit mechanically from better accounting.

7 Choice of models

How is it that segments of both the accounting and finance literatures have arrived at the position expressed in passages like those quoted in the section above? Part of the answer appears to be that the Bayesian probability models on which this position is constructed are too narrow in their assumptions to yield truly general results, especially when interpreted literally rather than in the light of all that is widely understood in accounting and finance to the contrary.

7.1 Unbiasedness, known σ and iid

The Lambert et al. (2007) model is a Bayesian standard. An uncertain payoff V has a normal prior distribution $N(\mu_0, \sigma_0)$. A sample of n iid observations $(x_1, x_2, \ldots, x_n)$ is drawn from a normal distribution $N(V^*, \sigma_x)$, where V^* is the true payoff and σ_x is a known constant. Each draw x is thus an unbiased estimate of V^* with known precision $1/\sigma_x^2$. The posterior belief distribution of V is $N(\mu_1, \sigma_1)$, where

$$\mu_1 = \frac{\left(1/\sigma_0^2\right)\mu_0 + \left(n/\sigma_0^2\right)\bar{x}}{\left(1/\sigma_0^2\right) + \left(n/\sigma_x^2\right)} \quad \text{and} \quad \frac{1}{\sigma_1^2} = \frac{1}{\sigma_0^2} + \frac{n}{\sigma_x^2}.$$

It follows that no matter how weak the sample evidence, the posterior variance of V is always less than its prior variance, that is $\sigma_1^2 < \sigma_0^2$ for any n. Lambert et al. (2007, p. 395) conclude that this result 'formalizes the notion that accounting information and disclosure reduce the assessed variance of the firm's end-of-period cash flow'. By this way of thinking, certainty can be accumulated monotonically, simply by generating more data.

A more general model-free understanding can be gleaned from the law of conditional variance

$$\text{var}(V) = E\left[\text{var}(V/S)\right] + \text{var}(E\left[V \mid S\right]),$$

where S is the signal or data. This identity implies that the average variance after observing S is lower than the prior variance, that is $E\left[\text{var}(V/S)\right] < \text{var}(V)$, but not that the posterior variance is always lower (Gelman et al. 2004, p. 37). That data like S produce an 'average' gain in certainty is consistent with the theoretical property of Bayes that enough data concerning V will 'in the long run' make V certain. Importantly for portfolio theory, it follows from (7) that (imperfect) information S brings no necessary reduction in covariance, not even on average.

The tractable but narrow model of signal quality applied by Lambert et al. (2007) is widely adopted but is fundamentally at odds with other parts of accounting theory.

(i) It is assumed that signals are unbiased and that their quality is represented fully by signal variance or precision.[6] To the contrary, there are theoretical and empirical suggestions of innate or intentional bias (e.g. conservatism, misstatement) in earnings reports (cf. Core 2001; Dechow 1994; Dechow and Schrand 2010; Dechow et al. 2010; Fischer and Verrecchia 2000). Overlooking or assuming away bias is clearly no way to think of the needs of a decision maker who must estimate $E[V \mid .]$ accurately. The diversion of fixating on variance and covariance is made worse by the finding that mean–variance optimal portfolio weights are generally far more sensitive to the estimated mean than variance or covariance (e.g. Best and Grauer 1991).

> Investors have limited resources available to spend on obtaining estimates of necessarily unknowable future parameters of risk and reward. . . . the bulk of these resources should be spent on obtaining the best estimates of expected [mean] returns . . . . For investors with moderate to high risk tolerance, the cash equivalent loss for errors in means is an order of magnitude greater than that for errors in variances or covariances. . . .
>
> *(Chopra and Ziemba 1993, p. 10)*

(ii) Signals are assumed to have constant precision (variance) independent of the true parameter. In an unconstrained Bayesian model, the likelihood function $f(S \mid \phi)$ can take arbitrarily different shapes for different signals. Suppose, for example, that ϕ is the parameter in question – ϕ represents 'true' earnings say, and $S = S^*$ is the reported estimate of earnings. The subjective likelihood function $f(S^* \mid \phi)$ might then be taken as quite flat over all ϕ when S^* is high (i.e. high reported earnings). This would capture an accounting propensity to overstate earnings when actual or true earnings are low. The more standard setup in the literature of $S \sim N(\phi^*, \sigma)$, with ϕ^* denoting the true parameter value and σ constant, assumes zero bias ($E[S \mid \phi^*] = \phi^*$) and does not allow the accounting signal to possess attributes that change with ϕ^*. It is not possible therefore to reflect in this model an accounting regime that can be aggressive or conservative depending on underlying 'true' earnings.

A less familiar but still standard Bayesian alternative to the model adopted by Lambert et al. (2007) and many others is to assume that uncertain payoff V has known mean and unknown variance (Gelman et al. 2004, pp. 50–52). This is a plausible theoretical depiction when the investor is interested in what the sample data reveal about the variance (risk) associated with V, although not as plausible as the more complicated model where both parameters are unknown. In either case, the posterior distribution for the unknown variance can shift toward higher values, thus implying greater risk. The common generalization that information always adds to certainty is thus easily overturned by choosing a different model.

7.2 Nonstationarity and model risk

The literature on estimation risk in portfolio theory makes the Bayesian argument that empirical (sample) point estimates of mean and covariance parameters cannot be taken as 'true parameters'. Rather, to calculate optimal (maximum SEU) portfolio weights, the investor must come to a subjective assessment of the Bayesian predictive joint distribution $f(V_1, V_2, \ldots, V_n \mid .)$ of the uncertain firm values V_j, using all available objective and subjective information (e.g. Barry and Brown 1985; Coles and Lowenstein 1988; Kalymon 1971; Klein and Bawa 1976; Lewellen and Shanken 2002). This distribution can then be used to find the implicit means $E[V_j \mid .]$ and covariances $\text{cov}(V_i, V_j \mid .)$.

The statistical models developed in the parameter risk literature in finance are more diverse than in the information risk literature in accounting. In particular, there are Bayesian models allowing for typical situations where both the firm's mean and variance or covariances are unknown, and where empirical returns data are informative about both parameters at the same time, causing the decision maker to revise her probabilities for both parameters at once. Moreover, under standard Bayesian models these parameters are dependent, so information must alter beliefs about both at once (Gelman et al. 2004).

The greatest difference between the two literatures is that the finance literature includes models that assume nonstationary payoff processes. There is no guarantee under nonstationarity that certainty will ever be reached, no matter how much data is collected (Barry 1978; Barry and Winkler 1976; Lewellen and Shanken 2002). Indeed, it is possible that the most recent (i.e. most relevant) empirical observations might indicate that a jump has occurred in the natural volatility of the returns or pay off process, in which case a Bayesian observer may become far less certain about the future value of the firm than she was beforehand.

Assumptions of stationarity are often disparaged as unrealistic in the estimation risk literature (e.g. Avramov and Zhou 2010; Barry and Winkler 1976; Barry 1978). However, this literature is itself relatively narrow in that it rests on models designed primarily for their mathematical tractability rather than descriptive validity. This point was emphasized by Winkler (1973, p. 402) and Barry and Winkler (1976), who noted that standard closed form models involve certain tractable forms of prior and likelihood distributions rather than capturing factors such as fat tails and other subtleties that analysts believe or suspect. It is possible that this caveat has often been ignored, however it remains valid in the sense that the complexity and apparent changeability of the processes by which firm values are generated are unlikely to capture adequately all the structure, signs, intuitions and concerns that professional analysts possess or sense at any moment.

Bayesian methods require subjective prior distributions. Perhaps more critical is the choice of likelihood function (i.e. the model or function that generates the sample observations), which is just as subjective and is not a uniquely Bayesian input. The risk of getting this part of the inference process wrong is called 'model risk' (Draper 1995) and is handled Bayesianly in the same way as parameter risk by averaging over a probability distribution of all possible models and model parameters. Bayesian calculations of $f(V_1, V_2, \ldots, V_n | .)$ thus mathematically 'integrate out' all uncertain parameters (or other uncertain inputs such as the model), thereby incorporating all known sources of uncertainty into the choice of optimal portfolio. Kadane (2011, pp. 342–345) describes this method as a way of 'keeping all models in play'.

Contrary to the narrow view, it does not follow that introducing a new source γ of uncertainty into the calculations will always add to the uncertainty in the posterior distribution for V_j. In the non–Bayesian setup we simply estimate γ and plug that value into the calculations as though it were true. But what if the estimated value is $\gamma = 1$ and yet we are much more certain about V under $\gamma = 0$. In this case, the Bayesian analysis, which averages over all possible values of γ, weighted by their subjective posterior probabilities (Avramov 2002), will come to a probability distribution for V with lower variance or uncertainty than the classical analysis. Adding a new source of uncertainty γ within a more coherent Bayesian analysis can thus sometimes reduce posterior uncertainty.

It should be conceded however that hierarchical Bayesian modelling that makes explicit allowance for all known sources of uncertainty, including model risk and even higher order risks concerning political and social factors, cannot rule out events that upset the foundations of market beliefs. New information can negate all previous structural thinking concerning the firm's or market's prospects, sending investors back to a state of primitive uncertainty about not only parameters and priors, but also about models and likelihood functions.

The simple model of information flows as akin to draws from a stationary urn does not fit this reality. This was noted in the early parameter risk literature: 'dramatic events may occur that can have so significant effect upon security price behavior as to require a complete reevaluation of one's opinions and can render historical data nearly useless' (Barry 1978, p. 422). Barry (1978) extended his argument on the ups and downs in market certainty by noting that many changes to firms' business prospects are products of slow evolution rather than of abrupt shock and are best modelled as random parameter changes over time. Their effect nonetheless is that historical information, including previous years' earnings results, loses relevance, and subjective forecasts based on technical and instinctive readings of contemporary conditions and predictions concerning future economic and social events become paramount.

If we view Barry's two levels of nonstationarity as realistic, the first involving occasional 'crises' and the second caused by continual gradual evolution of both firms and markets, then it is a black mark against any market information source, including accounting earnings reports and earnings forecasts, if such information is unable to alter our forecasts in ways which sometimes leave us much less certain about future events and payoffs than we were when less well informed.

8 Diversifying information risk

The arch subjectivist de Finetti famously (among Bayesians) said that 'probability does not exist'. We might think that the coin has a probability 0.5 of coming up heads, but this is not a physical property akin to the weight of the coin or its metallic content. It is a subjective assessment based on a blend of observation and various bits of thinking, just like the probability we attach to the stock market going up tomorrow. The probability of heads is of course generally 'more objective' in the sense, for example, that there is more sample data or physics on which to assess it, but that is a matter of degree rather than a qualitative difference between the two assessments. To de Finetti and most Bayesians, any categorical distinction between risk and uncertainty is illusory (Cyert and DeGroot 1987).

In the same vein, we can say that information uncertainty does not exist as a physical entity, or as separate from all other uncertainty. Rather, we have a subjective joint distribution $f(V_1, V_2, \ldots, V_n \mid .)$ of asset payoffs that subsumes all uncertainty as an homogeneous whole, and which is based on a myriad of subjective considerations blended together, including confidence or otherwise in our information sources. It is confusing, therefore, from a Bayesian standpoint to speak of 'diversifying information risk'. Rather, all risk is diversified as one, as best as possible, by choosing the optimal SEU portfolio based on that subjective belief distribution $f(V_1, V_2, \ldots, V_n \mid .)$.

As an example, a portfolio of two binary assets A and B is well diversified under information Ω if we assess that both $p(V_A=1 \mid V_B=0, \Omega)$ and $p(V_B=1 \mid V_A=0, \Omega)$ are high, but these probabilities are conditioned on what we know or can infer about the reliability of information within Ω (its error properties), and hence we cannot diversify 'fundamental' risk independently of information risk, or vice versa.

It is often proposed that investors prefer stocks about which they have more information, all else equal. Barry and Brown (1985) make standard assumptions on which a Bayesian predictive distribution $f(V_1, V_2, \ldots, V_n)$ gives lower covariance (beta) to those stocks with larger sample sizes of past observations (holding the prior distribution and historical sample estimates of mean and covariance constant). They conclude, however, only that investors 'may' perceive that firms with less information are more risky, regardless of how the amount of information available about the firm (from all its multiple sources) is measured.

Barry and Brown's use of the word 'may', repeated in their related (1984) empirical paper, is crucial to their maintaining strict Bayesianism. The point is that a Bayesian can know very little at all about an investment and still regard it as low beta. Suppose for example that as far as the investor knows, the investment amounts to a 'coin toss' with some subjective expected (mean) payoff. That would still be a zero beta asset, just like casino betting. Alternatively, the investor might know very little about the firm and yet still be sure that its success hinges on market factors such as interest rates, making it very high risk in a CAPM covariance sense. The point of these examples is to show intuitively that there is no necessary relationship between the amount of information available about a firm and its weight in a rational SEU portfolio. Put another way, investors do not necessarily 'diversify away' from low information stocks, although obviously that can be the case when the lack of information makes it impossible to believe strongly that the stock has either a sufficiently high expected payoff or sufficiently low covariance with the market (or both).

Proposition. For a given set of beliefs, the rational portfolio is not affected by how much information underlies those beliefs.

Consider two posterior predictive distributions $f(V_1, V_2, \ldots, V_n | \Omega_1)$ and $f(V_1, V_2, \ldots, V_n | \Omega_2)$, where Ω_1 and Ω_2 are different information sets. Portfolio theory makes use of only the probability distribution $f(V_1, V_2, \ldots, V_n | .)$ and does not take any account of the information set Ω upon which that distribution rests. It follows therefore that if $f(V_1, V_2, \ldots, V_n | \Omega_1) = f(V_1, V_2, \ldots, V_n | \Omega_2)$, the rational portfolio is the same under both information sets. In other words, the application of portfolio theory leaves information gathering to the user and does not reduce asset prices or portfolio weights when the investor has less information.

This proposition overrides the common intuition that, all else equal, we invest more when we have more information and we invest more in stocks about which we know more. Its proof is self-evident, apart perhaps from the assumption that two information sets Ω_1 and Ω_2 can have very different ingredients and yet still lead investors to the very same beliefs (posterior probabilities). Simple examples where different Ω_1 and Ω_2 have the same effect on beliefs are easy to imagine. There is a well known demonstration in the work by Easley and O'Hara (1987) in which the market maker's probability $p(V=1 | \Omega)$ conditional on an observed sequence Ω of trades (Buys and Sells) goes up and down depending on the trades observed and can take the same value for two very different trade sequences, of which one can be a much longer series than the other.

It is true that on average, or in the long run, 'more' or 'better' information leads asymptotically to less dispersion in Bayesian posterior distributions, but as explained above this may be a long time happening and is not guaranteed.

8.1 Dependent signal errors

One of the dangers in investment arises when signal errors tend to occur together rather than independently of one another, resulting in overinvestment in 'losing' assets and underinvestment in 'winning' assets, all at once. To avoid this risk as far as is rational, Bayesian coherence requires that $f(V_1, V_2, \ldots | .)$ takes account not merely of the individual error probabilities $\{\alpha, \beta\}$ or likelihood functions of each signal, but of their joint likelihood under each possible state of $(V_1, V_2, \ldots)$. One effect of allowing for dependence between signals is that an apparently strong set of signals, such as $(+,+,+, \ldots)$ or $(-,-,-, \ldots)$ may be given little weight, much less than if individual signals are seen as independent. This point has been much discussed in the Bayesian literature on combining expert forecasts, where experts' stated forecasts and forecast errors are often not statistically independent (e.g. Clemen and Winkler 2007).

When signal errors are believed to be dependent, in the sense that an error in signal S_i increases the investor's probability of S_j also being false, coherent Bayesian inference ensures that the SEU portfolio is adjusted accordingly. This adjustment does not always lead to a portfolio weighted more towards cash. Rather, it can happen for example that predominately negative signals S_i are regarded as being driven by a professional culture of conservatism, rather than being driven independently by their respective underlying 'true' asset values V_i. After discounting for this shared bias and consequent dependence, the Bayesian predictive distribution $f(V_1, V_2, \ldots | .)$ is located more heavily in the region of high asset values, and hence the SEU investor carries a greater weight of stocks.

Dependence between signals can stem from any number of common influences. The stochastic process described in Figure 15.1 shows one possibility. In this process, the Type I and Type II error probabilities can each change across the two possible market states; that is, $\alpha_G = p(+ | 0, G)$ may not equal $\alpha_B = p(+ | 0, B)$) and similarly for β_G and β_B. So, for example, $\alpha_G < \alpha_B$

would imply a more 'aggressive' or lax signalling regime under '*bad*' market conditions. In this case, assuming $\pi_G > \pi_B$, observation of a Type I error increases the probability of the market being '*bad*', in which case the probability of Type I errors in other positive signals also increases. Signal errors are thus not independent.

To be most informative, and thus have maximum influence on $f(V_1, V_2, \ldots \mid .)$, each S_i should 'say something' that is not largely implied in $S_{j \neq k}$. Accounting principles such as 'decision usefulness', and 'audit independence' are supported by this logic, but others, such as 'conservatism' and 'objectivity' (i.e. avoiding subjectivity) work against it. Realistically, however, even if all sources of dependence (e.g. herding) are removed, the job of designing accounting signals with low error probabilities remains difficult in the extreme – which helps explain why accountants might resort to safety first mechanisms such as explicit 'conservatism'.

9 Conclusion

A characteristic of better information is that it can reveal previously unseen negative signals and grounds for either greater uncertainty or greater certainty in a negative direction, thus driving the market down and the cost of capital up. Struggling firms will be reticent to divulge better information for two reasons: (i) the market will downgrade their expected cash flows, and (ii) the CAPM will apply a higher discount rate to those low expectations. The resulting price fall is thus twofold, with a lower numerator being magnified by a simultaneously higher denominator.

Any increase in the cost of capital brought about by 'better' information is not necessarily a bad thing. It is taken for granted within the decision-usefulness ethos of financial reporting that rational investors want accurate information rather than misplaced certainty. If better information leads to generally greater uncertainty, or lower expected cash flows, the price of stocks might fall. But if that price drop implies that investors are no longer too heavily weighted in stocks, and no longer misled by accounting misrepresentation or noise into false confidence, then their investments will on average be more profitable (higher realized utility) after their portfolios are reweighted towards cash.

The methodological stance underlying this discussion is that more information is good because in general it leads to more 'accurate' probabilities (cf. Johnstone 2011; Johnstone et al. 2011; Jose et al. 2008). Importantly, however, more accurate probabilities are not always closer to zero or one, so users are not always left with greater certainty. More accurate probabilities are desirable nonetheless because on average they lead to higher realized payoffs and thus utility. This second point has been demonstrated elegantly in the theory of economic Darwinism, which underpins efficient markets. See, for example, Blume and Easley (2006) and Sandroni (2000).

Any information about firm j that leads to a reassessment of the joint probability distribution $f(V_j, V_k, \ldots \mid .)$ of all asset values will surely involve a change in $E[V_j \mid .]$ and thus involve both numerator and denominator effects. The second of these points was put succinctly by Kasznik (2004) and was elaborated upon by Lambert et al. (2007, pp. 393–394). As an instrument, accounting disclosure may help to add value to the firm directly and indirectly (Lambert et al. 2007), but from a 'value relevance' perspective its primary role is not to increase the value of the firm but to help users to value the firm (cf. Bath et al. 2001; Holthausen and Watts 2001).

For this reason, accounting theory should not focus over much on the denominator (cost of capital) and neglect the numerator (expected cash flow), when both are essential to valuation and both are affected simultaneously by earnings announcements and other relevant information releases. An accounting emphasis on both numerator and denominator is logically consistent with corporate finance theory, where the commonly accepted objective of the firm is not to minimize the cost of capital per se but to maximize firm value or stock price. Finance is concerned with the cost of capital only as one means to an end, or as one input in determining the value of the business.

Appendix

The expected value of asset 1 is $E[V_1 \mid +_1, +_2] = p(V_1{=}1 \mid +_1, +_2)$ where $+_1$ and $+_2$ denote positive signals $S_1 = +$ and $S_2 = +$. For greater convenience, the joint observation $(+_1, +_2)$ is denoted by $++$ where possible. It is also helpful to abbreviate $V_1 = 1$ to 1_1 and similarly $V_1 = 0$ to 0_1, and likewise for V_2.

To find $p(1_1 \mid +,+)$ and for other related calculations, it is sufficient to find the likelihood ratio as follows

$$\frac{p(+,+ \mid 1_1)}{p(+,+ \mid 0_1)} = \frac{p(+,+,1_1)\,p(0_1)}{p(+,+,0_1)\,p(1_1)}$$

where

$$p(1_1) = p(G)\,p(1_1 \mid G) + p(B)\,p(1_1 \mid B)$$
$$= \theta\,\pi_G + (1-\theta)\,\pi_B$$
$$p(0_1) = 1 - p(1_1)$$

$$p(+,+ \mid 1_1) = p(G)p(1_1|G)p(+_1|G,1_1)p(+_2|G,1_1,+_1) + p(B)p(1_1|B)p(+_1|B,1_1)p(+_2|B,1_1,+_1)$$
$$= p(G)p(1_1|G)p(+_1|G,1_1)\big[p(1_2|G)p(+_2|G,1_2) + p(0_2|G)p(+_2|G,0_2)\big]$$
$$+ p(B)p(1_1|B)p(+_1|B,1_1)\big[p(1_2|B)p(+_2|B,1_2) + p(0_2|B)p(+_2|B,0_2)\big]$$
$$= \theta\pi_G(1-\beta_G)\big[\pi_G(1-\beta_G)+(1-\pi_G)\alpha_G\big] + (1-\theta)\pi_B(1-\beta_B)\big[\pi_B(1-\beta_B)+(1-\pi_B)\alpha_B\big]$$

$$p(+,+ \mid 0_1) = p(G)p(0_1|G)p(+_1|G,0_1)\big[p(1_2|G)p(+_2|G,1_2) + p(0_2|G)p(+_2|G,0_2)\big]$$
$$+ p(B)p(0_1|B)p(+_1|B,0_1)\big[p(1_2|B)p(+_2|B,1_2) + p(0_2|B)p(+_2|B,0_2)\big]$$
$$= \theta(1-\pi_G)\alpha_G\big[\pi_G(1-\beta_G)+(1-\pi_G)\alpha_G\big] + (1-\theta)(1-\pi_B)\alpha_B\big[\pi_B(1-\beta_B)+(1-\pi_B)\alpha_B\big].$$

Notes

1 "Of course, none of us know probability distributions of security returns. But I was convinced by Leonard J. Savage, one of my great teachers at the University of Chicago, that a rational agent acting under uncertainty would act according to 'probability beliefs' where no objective probabilities are known; and these probability beliefs or 'subjective probabilities' combine exactly as do objective probabilities." (Markowitz 1991, p. 469)

2 By using (6) to find the unknown P_i, we can find the price-weighted price $P_{opt} = \dfrac{P_1(P_1) + \ldots P_n(P_n) + 1}{P_M}$, $(P_f = 1)$

since each optimal security weight w^*_i is proportional to P_i. Then, using (5), $V_{opt} = P_{opt}R_{opt} = P_{opt}\left(\dfrac{V_M}{P_M}\right)$

3 If $n = 2(10)[100]$, $P_j = 0.350(0.358)[0.390]$. The simulation result for $n = 2$ was verified analytically by longhand calculation in a spreadsheet available from the author.

4 Remember, however, that in forming the prior probability distribution $f(V_j \ldots)$, the decision maker may take account of beliefs regarding the possible signal observations that can arise and how probable each observation is based on available indications. For example, perhaps an insider within an accounting firm has intimated that the forthcoming firm j profit figure will be bad, i.e. $S = $ 'bad'. In this case, the

investor's prior belief (i.e. prior to actually receiving S) will be formed Bayesianly and will incorporate his beliefs based on what the insider has indicated about the likely value of S, and the perceived error properties of both that indication and of S. Put simply, if the investor is basically assured by a reliable insider that the yet unreleased accounting profit S is going to be 'bad', then his prior beliefs may change greatly, especially if he perceives both the informant and S, or at least the specific value $S = $ 'bad', as highly reliable indicators.

5 See Johnstone (2013) for a numerical illustration of pricing relevant subsets of assets.

6 Similarly, in the literature on adverse selection, Verrecchia (2001, p. 174) notes that theoretical models 'commonly characterize information asymmetry as a second moment effect'.

References

Avramov, D. (2002) Stock Return Predictability and Model Uncertainty. *Journal of Financial Economics*. 64: 423–458.

Avramov, D. and Zhou, G. (2010) Bayesian Portfolio Analysis. *Annual Review of Financial Economics*. 2: 25–47.

Barry, C.B. (1978) Effects of Uncertain and Nonstationary Parameters Upon Capital Market Equilibrium. *Journal of Financial and Quantitative Analysis*. 13: 419–433.

Barry, C.B. and Brown, S.J. (1984) Differential Information and the Small Firm Effect. *Journal of Financial Economics*. 13: 283–294.

——— (1985) Differential Information and Security Market Equilibrium. *Journal of Financial and Quantitative Analysis*. 20: 407–422.

Barry, C.B. and Winkler, R.L. (1976) Nonstationarity and Portfolio Choice. *Journal of Financial and Quantitative Analysis*. 11: 217–235.

Bath, M., Beaver, W.H. and Landsman, W.R. (2001) The Relevance of the Value Relevance Literature for Financial Accounting Standard Setting: Another View. *Journal of Accounting and Economics*. 31: 77–104.

Berger, J.O. and Wolpert, R.L. (1988) *The Likelihood Principle*. 2nd ed. Haywood, CA: IMS Lecture Notes – Monograph Series.

Bernardo, J.M. and Smith, A.F.M. (1994) *Bayesian Theory*. New York, NY: Wiley.

Best, M.J. and Grauer, R.R. (1991) On the Sensitivity of Mean-Variance Efficient Portfolios to Changes in Asset Means: Some Analytical and Computational Results. *The Review of Financial Studies*. 4: 315–342.

Bhattacharya, N., Eecker, F., Olsson, P. and Schipper, K. (2012) Direct and Mediated Associations Among Earnings Quality, Information Asymmetry, and the Cost of Equity. *The Accounting Review*. 87: 449–482.

Blume, L. and Easley, D. (2006) If You're So Smart, Why Aren't You Rich? Belief Selection in Complete and Incomplete Markets. *Econometrica*. 74: 929–966.

Brown, S.J. (1979) The Effect of Estimation Risk on Capital Equilibrium. *Journal of Financial and Quantitative Analysis*. 14: 215–220.

Chopra, V.K. and Ziemba, W.T. (1993) The Effect of Errors in Means, Variances, and Covariances on Optimal Portfolio Choice. *Journal of Portfolio Management*. 19: 6–11.

Christensen, P.O, de la Rosa, L.E. and Feltham, G.A. (2010) Information and the Cost of Capital: An Ex Ante Perspective. *Accounting Review*. 85: 817–848.

Clarkson, P. and Thompson, R. (1990) Empirical Estimates of Beta When Investors Face Estimation Risk. *Journal of Finance*. 45: 431–453.

Clemen, R.T. and Winkler, R.L. (2007) Aggregating Probability Distributions. In Ward, E., Miles, R.F. and von Winterfeldt, D. (eds.) *Advances in Decision Analysis: From Foundations to Applications*. pp. 154–176. Cambridge: Cambridge University Press.

Coles, J.L. and Lowenstein, U. (1988) Equilibrium Pricing and Portfolio Composition in the Presence of Uncertain Parameters. *Journal of Financial Economics*. 22: 279–303.

Core, J.E. (2001) A Review of the Empirical Disclosure Literature: Discussion. *Journal of Accounting and Economics*. 31: 441–456.

Cyert, R.M. and DeGroot, M.H. (1987) *Bayesian Analysis and Uncertainty in Economic Theory*. New York, NY: Rowman and Littlefield.

Dechow, P.M. (1994) Accounting Earnings and Cash Flows as Measures of Firm Performance: The Role of Accounting Accruals. *Journal of Accounting and Economics*. 18: 3–42.

Dechow, P.M. and Schrand, C.M. (2010) *Earnings Quality*. Research Foundation of CFA Institute.

Dechow, P.M., Ge, W. and Schrand, C.M. (2010) Understanding Earnings Quality: A Review of the Proxies, Their Determinants and Their Consequences. *Journal of Accounting and Economics*. 50: 344–401.

DeFond, M.L. (2010) Earnings Quality Research: Advances, Challenges and Future Research. *Journal of Accounting and Economics*. 50: 402–409.

Draper, D. (1995) Assessment and Propagation of Model Uncertainty. *Journal of the Royal Statistical Society, Series B.* 57: 45–97.

Easley, D. and O'Hara, M. (1987) Price, Trade Size, and Information in Securities Markets. *Journal of Financial Economics.* 19: 69–90.

Easley, D., Hvidkjaer, S. and O'Hara, M. (2002) Is Information Risk a Determinant of Asset Returns? *Journal of Finance.* 57: 2185–2221.

Fischer, P. and Verrecchia, R.E. (2000) Reporting Bias. *The Accounting Review.* 75: 229–245.

Francis, J., Olsson, P. and Nanda, D.J. (2008) Voluntary Disclosure, Earnings Quality, and Costs of Capital. *Journal of Accounting Research.* 46: 53–99.

Francis, J., LaFond, R., Olsson, P. and Schipper, K. (2004) Costs of Equity and Earnings Attributes. *The Accounting Review.* 79: 967–1010.

―――― (2005) The Market Pricing of Accruals Quality. *Journal of Accounting and Economics.* 39: 295–327.

―――― (2007) Information Uncertainty and Post-Earnings Announcement Drift. *Journal of Business Finance and Accounting.* 34: 403–433.

Gelman, A., Carlin, J.B., Stern, H.S. and Rubin, D.B. (2004) *Bayesian Data Analysis.* 2nd ed. Boca Raton, FL: CRC Press.

Holthausen, R.W. and Watts, R.L. (2001) The Relevance of the Value-Relevance Literature for Financial Accounting Standard Setting. *Journal of Accounting and Economics.* 31: 3–75.

Johnstone, D.J. (2011) Economic Interpretation of Probabilities Estimated by Maximum Likelihood or Score. *Management Science.* 57: 308–314.

―――― (2012) Log Optimal Economic Evaluation of Probability Forecasts (with discussion). *Journal of the Royal Statistical Society, Series A.* 175: 661–689.

―――― (2013) Information, Uncertainty and the Risk Premium in a Mean-Variance Efficient Market. http://papers.ssrn.com/sol3/papers.cfm?abstract_id=2220544.

Johnstone, D.J, Jose, V.R.R. and Winkler, R.L. (2011) Tailored Scoring Rules for Probabilities. *Decision Analysis.* 8: 256–268.

Jose, V.R., Nau, R.F. and Winkler, R.L. (2008) Scoring Rules, Generalized Entropy, and Utility Maximization. *Operations Research.* 56: 1146–1157.

Kadane, J.B. (2011) *Principles of Uncertainty.* Boca Raton, FL: Chapman and Hall.

Kalymon, B.A. (1971) Estimation Risk in the Portfolio Selection Model. *Journal of Financial and Quantitative Analysis.* 6: 559–582.

Kasznik, R. (2004) Discussion of 'The Effect of Accounting Restatements on Earnings Revisions and the Estimated Cost of Capital'. *Review of Accounting Studies.* 9: 357–367.

Klein, R.W. and Bawa, V.S. (1976) The Effect of Estimation Risk on Optimal Portfolio Choice. *Journal of Financial Economics* 3: 215–231.

―――― (1977) The Effect of Limited Information and Estimation Risk on Optimal Portfolio Diversification. *Journal of Financial Economics* 5: 89–111.

Lambert, R., Leuz, C. and Verrecchia, R.E. (2007) Accounting Information, Disclosure, and the Cost of Capital. *Journal of Accounting Research.* 45: 385–420.

―――― (2011) Information Asymmetry, Information Precision, and the Cost of Capital. *Review of Finance.* 16: 1–29.

Leuz, C. and Schrand, C. (2009) Disclosure and the Cost of Capital: Evidence from Firms' Responses to the Enron Shock. NBER Working Paper No. w14897.

Leuz, C. and Wysocki, P. (2008) Economic Consequences of Financial Reporting and Disclosure Regulation: A Review and Suggestions for Future Research. http://papers.ssrn.com/sol3/papers.cfm?abstract_id=1105398.

Lewellen, J. and Shanken, J. (2002) Learning, Asset-Pricing Tests, and Market Efficiency. *Journal of Finance.* 57: 1113–1145.

Litzenberger, R.H. and Budd, A.P. (1971) A Note on Geometric Mean Selection and the Market Prices of Equities. *Journal of Financial and Quantitative Analysis.* 6: 1277–1282.

Luenberger, D. (1998) *Investment Science.* New York, NY: Oxford University Press.

Markowitz, H. (1991) Foundations of Portfolio Theory. *Journal of Finance.* 46: 469–477.

Raiffa, H. and Schlaifer, R. (1961) *Applied Statistical Decision Theory.* Boston, MA: Harvard University.

Robert, C. (2007) *The Bayesian Choice: From Decision-Theoretic Foundations to Computational Implementation.* 2nd ed. New York, NY: Springer.

Rogers, J.L., Skinner, D.J. and Buskirk, A.V. (2009) *Journal of Accounting and Economics.* 48: 90–109.

Rubinstein, M. (1976) The Strong Case for the Generalized Logarithmic Utility Model as the Premier Model of Financial Markets. *Journal of Finance.* 31: 551–571.

Sandroni, A. (2000) Do Markets Favor Agents Able to Make Accurate Predictions? *Econometrica*. 68: 1303–1342.

Satchell, S. (2012) Log Utility Pricing. *Journal of the Royal Statistical Society, Series A*. In press.

Shanken, J. (1987) A Bayesian Approach to Testing Portfolio Efficiency. *Journal of Financial Economics* 19: 195–215.

Verrecchia, R.E. (1983) Discretionary Disclosure. *Journal of Accounting and Economics*. 5: 179–194.

———— (2001) Essays on Disclosure. *Journal of Accounting and Economics*. 32: 97–180.

Winkler, R.L. (1973) Bayesian Models for Forecasting Future Security Prices. *Journal of Financial and Quantitative Analysis*. 8: 387–405.

Zhang, X.F. (2006) Information Uncertainty and Analyst Forecast Behavior. *Contemporary Accounting Research*. 23: 565–590.

16

Controlling for risk in accounting research

Nuno Soares and Andrew W. Stark[1]

1 Introduction

In this chapter we discuss the different methods for risk control that are used in accounting-based research, focusing on particular implementation issues and the associated limitations of these methods in the context of (i) markets with small amounts of data relative to that found in the USA, (ii) markets which are relatively unexplored in identifying firm characteristics that explain the cross-section of firm expected returns, or (iii) both. Given that to fully discuss such implementation issues an illustration is useful, we use UK market and accounting data for this purpose. Nonetheless, any general conclusions we reach are potentially applicable to other markets and, indeed, to the USA.

The need to control for risk occurs in a number of settings in accounting research. For example, one setting is 'anomalies' research, whereby the mispricing of accounting numbers is studied. A particular example would be the 'accruals anomaly' (Sloan, 1996), which asserts that the US market systematically misjudges the persistence of the accruals and cash components of earnings, and as a consequence, the market reaction to earnings announcements is biased. Such a biased reaction then predicts that firms with low accruals will be under-priced, whereas those with high accruals will be over-priced. Taken together, these predictions suggest that a hedge portfolio strategy of going long on low accruals firms and selling short high accruals firms should generate positive risk-adjusted returns. Should such be the case, and given the ease of forming the portfolios in information processing terms, this outcome could pose a substantial challenge to the notion of efficient markets.[2]

The accruals anomaly is not the only accounting-information-based anomaly. Another example is the Ball and Brown (1968) post-earnings announcement drift phenomenon whereby, after a firm earnings announcement, the future abnormal returns tend to follow the sign of the earnings surprise. Further, fundamental analysis is concerned with whether financial statement analysis can be used to generate a sufficient return on the costs of such analysis. Examples include Ou and Penman (1989), who, *via* data-intensive information processing methods, developed a model of the likelihood of a firm experiencing an earnings increase. They developed and tested their model, with the results suggesting that a portfolio strategy based upon their model is able to generate positive risk-adjusted returns.

At the heart of such studies is the issue of adjusting, or controlling, for risk in generating estimates of risk–adjusted returns for firms and portfolios. Essentially, to assess whether a firm or portfolio is making an 'abnormal' return once risk effects are taken into account, the research has to be able to come up with a reliable estimate of the appropriate expected 'normal' risk–adjusted return to which the achieved return can be compared. How to do this is one of the most problematic methodological issues that researchers have to deal with in this context. If risk is not properly controlled for in the assessment of the 'normal' risk–adjusted return, it can lead to erroneous conclusions that firms or portfolios constructed upon accounting (or other) characteristics are incorrectly priced when in fact they are not, or vice versa. Furthermore, every approach of which we are aware has an underlying bad-model problem, as the approaches chosen are generally incomplete representations of expected 'normal' risk–adjusted returns (Fama, 1998).

We start this chapter by providing a description of the most common approaches to risk control that are currently followed in the accounting literature. We then provide an empirical description of the relationship between individual firm stock returns and various firm characteristics, using UK listed firms as a basis for analysis. In so doing, we do not attempt to draw on any particular theory or theories that might relate the tested firm characteristics to firm stock returns, although we do provide commentary on some possible theoretical links. Further, we assume that the results of our empirical description reflect rational pricing, and as a consequence, the relationship between firm returns and firm characteristics implies that these characteristics do indeed capture risk. Hence, we attempt to show how, if at all, the firm characteristics empirically relate to future returns.

Having provided the empirical description, we conclude that there is evidence that the ratios of research and development expense and cash flow to market value, the log of share price, the book-to-market ratio, past stock returns, the earning-price ratio, firm size and leverage all jointly help explain firm returns. There is weak evidence that dividend yield also helps explain firm returns. We then discuss the implications of these results for controlling for risk in the particular case of the UK, and by so doing, we highlight potential difficulties in implementing the various risk control methods identified in smaller or relatively unexplored markets.

The next section describes the most common options followed by researchers when trying to control for risk. The third section describes our approaches to providing an empirical description of the properties of UK firm returns, the data employed to run our tests, and the results. The fourth section discusses the methods of risk control available to empirical researchers and their applicability in the particular case of the UK, given the results of our tests. The final section summarises the chapter.

2 Possibilities for controlling for risk

Consider the problem of an empirical researcher attempting to investigate whether a particular portfolio strategy (for example, based upon ranking firms by total accruals or by earnings surprises) is profitable over some significant period of time once risk has been taken into account.

First, individual realised firm returns can be matched with the return on a benchmark portfolio formed on the basis of firm characteristics thought to capture risk. Here, the purpose is to match firms with portfolios consisting of other firms with firm characteristics as 'similar' as possible to those of the firms being studied. In the US, such characteristics might include firm size, the firm book-to-market ratio, and the prior stock returns for the firm, all of which have been found to have a relationship with future returns. The difference between the realised firm return and the benchmark portfolio return is treated as an estimate of the risk-adjusted, or abnormal, return for the firm over the portfolio holding period. An estimate of the portfolio abnormal return can then be constructed as the weighted average of the individual firm abnormal returns, using the portfolio weights as the weights in the weighted averaging process. Such an approach has been popular in the US, where size-matched abnormal returns, for example, have often been estimated in the context of tests of the accruals anomaly.[3]

Within such an approach, it is crucial to be able to identify firm characteristics, in any given jurisdiction, that capture cross-sectional differences in firm expected returns and, hence, risk differences across firms. Whether relationships between firm characteristics and the cross-section of stock returns in countries outside the US will mimic those found in the US is a matter of empirical evidence. Further, we should emphasise that, in countries without large amounts of data, the approach depends upon the existence of a parsimonious empirical description of the cross-section of returns (i.e., one with relatively few firm characteristics). Otherwise, the process of matching firms to portfolios with 'similar' firm characteristics could become very difficult.

Second, an asset pricing model can be specified. For example, such a model could be the Capital Asset Pricing Model (CAPM), in which the expected firm excess return (the difference between the firm expected return and the risk-free rate of return over the period) is a multiple (the CAPM β) of the expected excess return on the market portfolio (the difference between the expected return on the market portfolio and the risk-free rate of return over the period).

There are two basic ways in which such an approach can be used. One way starts with regressing the firm excess returns for a period prior to the portfolio formation period, for each of the individual firms making up the specified portfolio, on the excess return on the market portfolio to get an estimate of the CAPM β for each firm.[4] The estimated β's can then be multiplied by the realised excess market return for the period over which the portfolio is held. The multiples then are estimates of the expected excess returns for each firm over the portfolio holding period (adjusted for general market movements) and can be subtracted from the realised firm excess returns to produce estimates of the abnormal returns for each firm. Using specified portfolio weights, these abnormal returns can then be used to create a weighted average abnormal return for the portfolio.[5]

A second way creates a time series of realised portfolio excess returns by using a specified set of portfolio weights covering successive holding periods, with new portfolios constructed at the start of each holding period. These portfolio excess returns are then regressed on realised excess market returns.[6] Should a statistically significant constant term emerge, this is seen as evidence of under-pricing if the estimated constant term is significantly positive, or of over-pricing if the estimated constant term is significantly positive.[7, 8]

Other, more empirical, asset pricing models extend the CAPM. For example, the Fama-French (1993) three factor model adds in two factors to the CAPM. These factors reflect that, as mentioned above, firm size and the book-to-market ratio seem to help explain the cross-section of firm returns in the US. The Carhart (1997) four factor model adds a prior return factor to the Fama-French (1993) model to reflect the fact that, again as mentioned above, prior returns appear to help explain the cross-section of firm returns in the USA. If chosen, these models can be used in exactly the way described above for the CAPM.

As with the portfolio matching approach, the specification of which factors to add in to the CAPM is crucially dependent upon an understanding of firm characteristics that can explain the cross-section of firm expected returns in the jurisdiction being studied. It is from such an understanding that the process of constructing factors begins. A further issue that will be discussed below, however, is the construction of factors that reflect the relationship between firm characteristics and first returns.

Finally, individual firm returns can be regressed on firm characteristics known (or thought) to be associated with the cross-section of returns, together with additional variables designed to identify effects that capture some possible portfolio strategy (for example, accruals decile ranks or earnings surprise ranks). Depending on the outcomes with respect to the coefficients of the additional variables, it can be identified whether there is an 'anomaly', or returns effect, associated with the additional variables. Examples of the implementation of this technique can be found in Teoh and Zhang (2011) and Sloan (1996). Again, such an approach crucially depends upon an understanding of firm characteristics that can explain the cross-section of firm expected returns in the jurisdiction being studied.

Overall, there is no consensus in the literature about which approach is best suited to proxy for 'normal' risk-adjusted returns and, hence, control for risk. Furthermore, the standard methods used for implementing these approaches in the US might not apply well to different countries where, for example, data limitations could constrain their implementation or different firm characteristics could better capture the cross-section of firm expected returns. What can be said, however, is that the starting point for all the approaches to controlling for risk requires, in the jurisdiction studied, an understanding of the determinants of firm expected returns. In the next section, we aim to contribute to such an understanding in the UK.

3 An empirical description of UK stock returns

In sub-section 3.1 we present our approach to providing empirical descriptions of the determinants of individual firm expected stock returns. The application of this method to the UK, including data sources and variable definitions, is presented in sub-section 3.2. The results of the analysis are presented in sub-section 3.3.

3.1 Determinants of stock returns

We follow a relatively standard approach of analysing firm realised excess annual returns, where an excess stock return is the excess of the firm's annual stock return (over the risk-free rate of return for the year). We defined *Firm excess return* as $(r_{it} - r_{ft})$, where r_{it} is the realised return for firm i for period t and r_{ft} is the risk-free rate of return for the same period t. The realised firm excess annual return is used as an unbiased estimate of the 'normal' risk-adjusted excess return for the period. Using a panel of data, we initially regress individual firm excess returns on the excess return on the market $(r_{mt} - r_{ft})$, the *Market factor*, where r_{mt} is the realised return on the market for the annual period t that is matched to the period over which the annual firm return is measured. Thus, we run the following regression:

$$(r_{it} - r_{ft}) = \beta_0 + \beta_1 (r_{mt} - r_{ft}) + \varepsilon_{it} \qquad (1)$$

where r_{it} is the annual return for firm i for annual period t. By running this regression, we can see to what extent the excess return on the market affects individual firm excess returns across time, which is captured by β_1. Note, however, that this is not an application of the CAPM, because we do not allow the coefficient of the independent variable to vary across firms.

To equation (1), we then add independent variables capturing firm size $(Size_{it})$ and the firm book-to-market ratio (BM_{it}) for firm i prior to time t. We do this to see if, over the period we study, and given the role that firm size and the firm book-to-market ratio have played in the construction of factor models (e.g., the Fama-French (1993) three factor model), these characteristics help explain annual returns. Hence, we estimate:

$$(r_{it} - r_{ft}) = \beta_0 + \beta_1 (r_{mt} - r_{ft}) + \beta_2 Size_{it} + \beta_3 BM_{it} + \varepsilon_{it} \qquad (2)$$

The third model we estimate adds in a variable that captures the impact of past returns on future returns, or momentum, which we refer to as Mom_{it}.[9] As the second model links to the Fama–French (1993) three factor model, the third model links to the Carhart (1997) model. Again, we would expect that, in particular, the past returns variable ought to have a (positive) relationship with firms returns if including a 'momentum' factor in UK factor-based asset pricing models makes sense. Therefore, we estimate:

$$(r_{it} - r_{ft}) = \beta_0 + \beta_1 (r_{mt} - r_{ft}) + \beta_2 Size_{it} + \beta_3 BM_{it} + \beta_4 Mom_{it} + \varepsilon_{it} \tag{3}$$

We also estimate versions of equations (2) and (3) in which $Size$, BM and Mom are replaced by their respective yearly decile ranks, as a way of further investigating the relationship between these variables and firm returns.[10]

Our fourth model adds in firm characteristics that have been found to have relationships with firm returns, either in prior UK empiricism or elsewhere. Therefore, we add in the following variables: (i) the earnings-to-price ratio (EP_{it}) for firm i prior to period t; (ii) the dividend yield (DY_{it}) for firm i prior to period t; (iii) the ratio of research and development expenditures to market value (RD_{it}) for firm i prior to period t; (iv) leverage (Lev_{it}) for firm i prior to period t; and (v) the cash flow to average total assets ratio (CF_{it}) for firm i prior to period t.[11] By estimating this model, we investigate whether firm characteristics other than the 'standard' ones used to justify the construction of factors in 'standard' asset pricing models are able to describe the pattern of UK stock returns. Hence, we estimate:

$$(r_{it} - r_{ft}) = \beta_0 + \beta_1 (r_{mt} - r_{ft}) + \beta_2 Size_{it} + \beta_3 BM_{it} + \beta_4 Mom_{it} + \beta_5 EP_{it} + \beta_6 DY_{it} + \beta_7 RD_{it} + \beta_8 Lev_{it} + \beta_9 CF_{it} + \varepsilon_{it} \tag{4}$$

Finally, our fifth model adds in a variable that is thought to be a proxy for liquidity – the share price for firm i prior to period t (SP_{it}).[12] By including this variable, we intend to capture the impact of liquidity on future returns. Our fifth model, then, is

$$(r_{it} - r_{ft}) = \beta_0 + \beta_1 (r_{mt} - r_{ft}) + \beta_2 Size_{it} + \beta_3 BM_{it} + \beta_4 Mom_{it} + \beta_4 Mom_{it} + \beta_5 EP_{it} + \beta_6 DY_{it} + \beta_7 RD_{it} + \beta_8 Lev_{it} + \beta_9 CF_{it} + \beta_{10} SP_{it} + \varepsilon_{it} \tag{5}$$

3.2 Data sources, variable definitions and estimation methods

Having presented our general models, we now specifically describe how we estimate them. For data sources, Datastream and Worldscope are used to retrieve market and accounting data, respectively. Additionally, delisting reasons are obtained from the 2012 version of the London Share Price Database.[13] The sample is comprised of all non-financial firms listed at the London Stock Exchange for the financial years 1990–2010. Only those firms that have complete information in Datastream and Worldscope for all the variables are used in the analysis, with the sample totalling 25,197 firm-years.

Taking into account UK market specificities, we define our variables as follows:

r_{it} is the annual return for firm i associated with financial year-end t, which starts being accumulated six or four months after the financial year-end, depending on the date of the financial year-end;[14]

r_{ft} is the annual risk-free rate, determined as the cumulative one-month UK Treasury discount bill rate, for the return accumulation period associated with financial year-end t;

r_{mt} is the annual realised return on the FTSE All Shares index for the return accumulation period associated with financial year-end t;

$MktCap_{it}$ is the market value for firm i, measured at the start of the return accumulation period for financial year-end t;

$Size_{it}$ is the natural log of $MktCap_{it}$;

BM_{it} is the ratio of common equity (Worldscope item wc03995) to $MktCap_{it}$ at the financial year-end t;

Mom_{it} is the prior annual return for firm i for financial year-end t, the accumulation period for which starts one year before the return accumulation period for r_{it};

EP_{it} is the ratio of operating income (Worldscope item wc01250) for firm i for the year ending in financial year-end t to $MktCap_{it}$;

DY_{it} is the ratio of dividends (Worldscope item wc04551) for firm i for the year ending in financial year-end t to $MktCap_{it}$;

RD_{it} is the ratio of research and development expenses (Worldscope item wc01201) for firm i for the year ending in financial year-end t to $MktCap_{it}$;[15]

Lev_{it} is the ratio of total debt (Worldscope item wc03255) for firm i at the financial year-end t to $MktCap_{it}$;

CF_{it} is the ratio of operating cash flows determined using the balance sheet approach (implemented in Soares and Stark, 2009) for firm i for the year ending in financial year-end t to the average of beginning and end of period total assets for that period;

SP_{it} is the natural log of the share price for firm i, measured at the start of the return accumulation period for financial year-end t and, hence, six or four months after the financial year-end t.

Our models are estimated using the Fama and MacBeth (1973) approach.[16] Annual cross-sectional regressions are run and we then report the averages for the coefficients of the independent variables across the annual cross-sections, together with associated t-statistics for the null hypothesis that the true coefficient is zero. An annual cross-section is created by pooling all financial year-ends t ending in a specific calendar year. We estimate all models on a common sample in which all variables are winsorized at the top/bottom 1 per cent, to reduce the impact of outliers on the coefficient estimates.

3.3 Results

We start this section with a brief analysis of the descriptive statistics of the variables that are the basis of the study. The descriptive statistics can be found in Table 16.1. Starting with Panel A, the average firm excess return is positive (0.047), although its median is negative (−0.010), suggesting skewness in realised excess returns. The market factor yields a positive mean (median) of 0.045 (0.099), and there is a wide dispersion in firm size, with a mean (median) log of market capitalization of 10.780 (10.562), a minimum of 6.492 and a maximum of 16.301. *BM* has a minimum of −0.969 and a mean (median) of 0.764 (0.523). The negative minimum for *BM* is capturing firms with negative book values that are likely to be highly distressed and could fail in the future. A positive mean (median) of 0.090 (0.019) is reported for *Mom*, implying that sample firms on average exhibit positive cumulative returns in the twelve months before future returns start being accumulated. Positive average and median *EP*s are reported, with some loss firms in the sample resulting in a value of −0.006 for the twenty-fifth percentile. Both *DY* and *RD* report positive averages of 0.027 and 0.017, respectively. More than 50 per cent of the firms, however, do not report any research and development expense, resulting in a reported *RD* median of 0.000. *Lev* has an average of 0.461, but a median of only 0.160, suggesting that the measure is skewed and that some highly leveraged firms are found in the UK stock market. Furthermore, while average (median) cash flow (*CF*) is 0.064 (0.105), there are firms with extremely negative *CF*, which could be further evidence of some distressed firms existing in the sample. Finally, we report an average of 4.455 for *SP*, with some extreme values of −0.248 and 8.106 being reported for the minimum and maximum, respectively.

Table 16.1, Panel B, reports on the correlations between the variables. For brevity, we will focus only on the most relevant relationships. Starting with the *Market factor*, a positive relation is found with *Firm excess return*, as is expected. Although *Size* has been found in the US literature to be negatively related to returns, we find either no relationship (using the Pearson correlation coefficient) or a positive correlation (using the Spearman correlation coefficient) between it and *Firm excess return*. All the remaining variables are positively correlated with *Firm excess return*, with the exception of *SP* which reports a negative Pearson coefficient and a positive Spearman coefficient. Finally, investigating the correlations between all the independent variables suggests that there are no correlations high enough to induce multicollinearity problems. The highest Pearson correlation coefficient is 0.626, between *SP* and *Size*. There are no other Pearson correlation coefficients higher than 0.5.

To further explore the basic characteristics of our data, Panel A of Table 16.2 provides the average winsorized annual excess returns for each rank decile for the variables *Size*, *BM*, *Mom*, *EP*, *Lev*, *CF* and *SP*. We rank by firm characteristics on an annual basis. For the variables with zero as the lower bound (*DY* and *RD*), we calculate the average winsorized annual excess returns for all firms with zero values for these variables and then rank the remaining firms into quintiles.

In Panel A, we observe that there are fairly strong positive (negative) relationships between *EP* and *CF* (*SP*) with average annual firm excess returns. We also find less strong positive (negative) relationships between *BM* and *Mom* (*Lev*) and average firm excess returns. Further, contrary to what is implied in most of the literature, the relationship between *Size* and annual excess returns is positive for the top nine deciles, with an average firm excess return of the first decile of similar size to that for the tenth decile.

Table 16.1 Descriptive statistics and correlations

Panel A: Descriptive statistics	N	mean	sd	p25	median	p75	min	max
Firm excess return	25,197	0.047	0.598	−0.313	−0.010	0.292	−1.036	2.651
Market factor	25,197	0.045	0.162	−0.078	0.099	0.153	−0.342	0.361
Size	25,197	10.780	2.132	9.207	10.562	12.163	6.492	16.301
BM	25,197	0.764	0.881	0.265	0.523	0.986	−0.969	5.271
Mom	25,197	0.090	0.590	−0.279	0.019	0.325	−0.881	2.649
EP	25,197	0.020	0.287	−0.006	0.077	0.134	−1.642	0.595
DY	25,197	0.027	0.036	0.000	0.018	0.038	0.000	0.213
RD	25,197	0.017	0.050	0.000	0.000	0.005	0.000	0.337
Lev	25,197	0.461	0.964	0.021	0.160	0.466	0.000	6.937
CF	25,197	0.064	0.226	0.014	0.105	0.177	−0.998	0.506
SP	25,197	4.455	1.573	3.555	4.659	5.525	−0.248	8.106

(continued)

Table 16.1 (continued)

Panel B: Pearson/Spearman correlations in the lower/upper diagonal

	Firm excess return	Market factor	Size	BM	Mom	EP	DY	RD	Lev	CF	SP
Firm excess return	1	0.313	0.085	0.068	0.085	0.143	0.139	0.021	0.015	0.143	0.021
		(0.000)	(0.000)	(0.000)	(0.000)	(0.000)	(0.000)	(0.001)	(0.017)	(0.000)	(0.001)
Market factor	0.304	1	−0.026	0.036	−0.016	0.056	0.054	0.004	0.038	0.026	−0.031
	(0.000)		(0.000)	(0.000)	(0.014)	(0.000)	(0.000)	(0.501)	(0.000)	(0.000)	(0.000)
Size	0.000	−0.024	1	−0.313	0.321	0.247	0.241	0.119	−0.033	0.342	0.657
	(0.995)	(0.000)		(0.000)	(0.000)	(0.000)	(0.000)	(0.000)	(0.000)	(0.000)	(0.000)
BM	0.064	0.039	−0.311	1	−0.308	0.194	0.244	−0.088	0.312	−0.173	−0.260
	(0.000)	(0.000)	(0.000)		(0.000)	(0.000)	(0.000)	(0.000)	(0.000)	(0.000)	(0.000)
Mom	0.020	−0.006	0.226	−0.270	1	0.072	−0.036	−0.023	−0.202	0.223	0.316
	(0.002)	(0.345)	(0.000)	(0.000)		(0.000)	(0.000)	(0.000)	(0.000)	(0.000)	(0.000)
EP	0.042	0.030	0.310	−0.059	0.181	1	0.597	−0.080	0.320	0.484	0.247
	(0.000)	(0.000)	(0.000)	(0.000)	(0.000)		(0.000)	(0.000)	(0.000)	(0.000)	(0.000)
DY	0.057	0.044	0.057	0.290	−0.190	0.297	1	−0.026	0.258	0.353	0.281
	(0.000)	(0.000)	(0.000)	(0.000)	(0.000)	(0.000)		(0.000)	(0.000)	(0.000)	(0.000)
RD	0.042	0.002	−0.121	0.055	−0.133	−0.257	−0.053	1	−0.092	−0.030	0.038
	(0.000)	(0.701)	(0.000)	(0.000)	(0.000)	(0.000)	(0.000)		(0.000)	(0.000)	(0.000)
Lev	0.005	0.039	−0.189	0.345	−0.212	−0.095	0.219	0.029	1	0.005	−0.056
	(0.438)	(0.000)	(0.000)	(0.000)	(0.000)	(0.000)	(0.000)	(0.000)		(0.448)	(0.000)
CF	0.084	0.046	0.308	−0.021	0.129	0.459	0.222	−0.203	−0.003	1	0.328
	(0.000)	(0.000)	(0.000)	(0.001)	(0.000)	(0.000)	(0.000)	(0.000)	(0.678)		(0.000)
SP	−0.048	−0.026	0.626	−0.242	0.230	0.325	0.108	−0.146	−0.191	0.315	1
	(0.000)	(0.000)	(0.000)	(0.000)	(0.000)	(0.000)	(0.000)	(0.000)	(0.000)	(0.000)	

The sample is comprised of 25,197 non-financial firm-year observations for the period 1990–2010. Firm excess return is the difference between the annual firm return (r_{it}) and the associated risk-free return (r_{ft}); *Market factor* is the difference between the annual market return (r_{mt}) and the associated annual risk-free return (r_{ft}); *Size* is the natural log of *MktCap*; *BM* is the ratio of common equity at the financial year-end to *MktCap Mom* is the prior annual return for each firm; *EP* is the ratio of operating income to firm market value; *DY* is the ratio of annual dividends to *MktCap*; *RD* is the ratio of research and development expenses to *MktCap*; *Lev* is the ratio of total debt to *MktCap*; *CF* is the ratio of cash flows to average total assets; *SP* is the natural log of price for the firm. *p*-values in parentheses.

In Panel B, the relationships between *RD* and *DY* and average annual firm excess returns are generally positive for firms with positive values, although the effect is concentrated in the upper two quintiles for *RD* and is fairly small for *DY*. Firms with zero values for *RD* have similar average annual excess returns to the lower three quintile positive *RD* firms, whereas firms with zero *DY* have much lower average excess returns than those possessed by firms with positive values.

We now consider the results with respect to the relationship between firm future excess returns, the market factor, and the firm characteristics. The results are reported in Table 16.3.

Table 16.2 Average annual firm excess returns for groups of firms ranked by firm characteristics

Panel A								Panel B		
				Ranking variables					Ranking variables	
Portfolio	Size	BM	Mom	EP	LEV	CF	SP	Portfolio	DY	RD
1	0.067	−0.016	0.016	−0.005	0.071	−0.040	0.072			
2	0.023	0.030	0.023	0.016	0.083	−0.024	0.082			
3	0.028	0.035	0.026	0.027	0.083	0.059	0.070	0	0.000	0.040
4	0.031	0.050	0.007	0.021	0.056	0.023	0.078			
5	0.039	0.060	0.028	0.034	0.061	0.038	0.058			
6	0.052	0.040	0.053	0.051	0.051	0.061	0.052	1	0.056	0.044
7	0.059	0.057	0.075	0.061	0.044	0.085	0.044	2	0.070	0.034
8	0.046	0.053	0.070	0.077	0.031	0.077	0.022	3	0.074	0.045
9	0.061	0.080	0.096	0.082	0.008	0.078	0.030	4	0.076	0.069
10	0.065	0.082	0.076	0.107	−0.012	0.115	−0.039	5	0.080	0.119

The table reports the average annual excess returns of firms ranked on deciles (quintiles) based on the specific characteristic. Firm excess return is the difference between the annual firm return (r_{it}) and the associated risk-free return (r_{ft}); *Size* is the natural log of *MktCap*; *BM* is the ratio of common equity at the financial year-end to *MktCap*; *Mom* is the prior annual return for each firm; *EP* is the ratio of operating income to firm market value; *DY* is the ratio of annual dividends to *MktCap*; *RD* is the ratio of research and development expenses to *MktCap*; *Lev* is the ratio of total debt to *MktCap*; *CF* is the ratio of cash flows to average total assets; *SP* is the natural log of price for the firm.

Table 16.3 suggests that the market factor has a strong and positive relationship with returns, irrespective of the variables included in the model. When *Market factor*, *Size* and *BM* are included as explanatory variables (column (2), neither *Size* nor *BM* exhibits a significant relationship with returns, however. When *Mom* is added to these three variables (column (3), the relationship is positive and statistically significant at the 1 per cent level, with *BM* now exhibiting a positive relationship that is significant at the 10 per cent level and the coefficient of *Size* remaining insignificant.

In untabulated regressions, we transform the *Size*, *BM* and *Mom* variables into decile rank dummies and re-run the different models. While the conclusions for *Size* remain broadly unchanged, the lowest-size decile portfolio exhibits positive and statistically significant results. No significant evidence of an association between *Size* decile affiliation and future excess returns is found for the remaining deciles, however, with the lowest- and highest-size portfolios exhibiting coefficients of a similar size. For *BM*, a monotonic relationship is found, with lower (higher) *BM* portfolios exhibiting lower (higher) estimated coefficients. However, statistical significance (at levels of 5 per cent or better), is found only for decile ranks nine and ten and, perhaps surprisingly, decile five. Hence, although more evidence of a *BM* effect can be found in the UK when transforming *BM* into decile rank dummy variables, it seems to be mainly confined to the highest *BM* firms. Stronger evidence of a significant relationship with excess returns can be detected for *Mom*, with significant coefficients found for portfolios six to ten.

Column (4) reports the results of adding in *EP*, *DY*, *RD*, *Lev* and *CF* to the more 'conventional' risk variables, followed by also adding in *SP* to capture the impact of liquidity restrictions in explaining future excess returns (column (5). The inclusion of the additional variables in column (4), strengthens the relationship between *BM* and firm excess returns, in the sense that the coefficient of *BM* is now significant at the 5 per cent level. Further, four of the additional variables have coefficients that are statistically significant at the 5 per cent level or better: *EP*, *RD*, *Lev* and *CF*.

Table 16.3 Estimates of various relationships between firm excess returns, the market factor, and firm characteristics

	(1)	(2)	(3)	(4)	(5)
Market factor	0.704***	0.685***	0.686***	0.696***	0.689***
	(3.363)	(3.324)	(3.099)	(3.271)	(3.217)
Size		0.006	0.002	−0.003	0.012**
		(1.002)	(0.371)	(−0.621)	(2.298)
BM		0.019	0.026*	0.024**	0.023**
		(1.424)	(2.027)	(2.304)	(2.202)
Mom			0.071***	0.068***	0.079***
			(3.268)	(3.124)	(3.594)
EP				0.056**	0.060**
				(2.189)	(2.428)
DY				0.249	0.329*
				(1.307)	(1.750)
RD				0.760***	0.694***
				(3.863)	(3.654)
Lev				−0.020**	−0.027***
				(−2.262)	(−3.157)
CF				0.160***	0.163***
				(3.913)	(4.030)
SP					−0.046***
					(−6.388)
Constant	0.060**	−0.021	0.008	0.045	0.093
	(2.313)	(−0.244)	(0.084)	(0.581)	(1.088)
Observations	25,197	25,197	25,197	25,197	25,197
Average R^2	0.028	0.042	0.054	0.080	0.091

There are 25,197 firm-year observations for the period 1990–2010. Firm excess return is the difference between the annual firm return (r_{it}) and the associated risk-free return (r_{ft}); Market factor is the difference between the annual market return (rm_t) and the associated annual risk-free rate (rf); Size is the natural log of MktCap; BM is the ratio of common equity at the financial year-end to MktCap. Mom is the prior annual return for each firm; EP is the ratio of operating income to firm market value; DY is the ratio of annual dividends to MktCap; RD is the ratio of research and development expenses to MktCap; Lev is the ratio of total debt to MktCap; CF is the ratio of cash flows to average total assets; SP is the natural log of price for the firm. Mean coefficients of 21 annual regressions are reported. t-statistics are provided in parentheses. *,**,*** denote 10%, 5% and 1% levels of significance, respectively.

The addition of SP in column (5) produces two effects on the existing variables in the model. Size, in the presence of SP, now has a *positive* and significant (at the 5 per cent level) estimated relationship with firm excess returns. DY acquires a coefficient which is statistically significant at the 10 per cent level. The statistical significance of the relationships between EP, RD, Lev and CF and firm excess returns is largely unchanged, with all of them other than EP significant at the 1 per cent level. Finally, SP has a highly significant (at the 1 per cent level) negative relationship with excess returns.

To summarise, a number of firm characteristics appear to have strong evidence in their favour as explanatory variables for the cross-section of firm excess returns, in addition to the market factor. These are Size, BM, Mom, EP, RD, Lev, CF and SP. DY has only moderate evidence in its favour.

4 Empirical approaches to capturing risk in the UK, and their likely effectiveness

Taking the results from the previous section at face value, we now discuss issues surrounding how risk can be captured in the UK. As above, in so doing, we initially assume that the results in the previous section reflect rational pricing, and as a consequence, the relationship between firm returns and firm characteristics implies that these characteristics do indeed capture risk. We also comment on the possible implications of our results for other jurisdictions, especially those with less data than the UK or which are less well explored in terms of understanding the properties of firm returns.

First, the results do not suggest that factors controlling for market, size, book-to-market, and past return effects are likely to be sufficient to control for risk in the UK, if only because of the other effects identified. On these grounds, and ignoring other relevant evidence, it seems likely that tests employing the Fama-French (1993) three factor model or the Carhart (1997) model will be mis-specified, leading to unreliable results. If such is the case in the UK, it is not clear why these factor models can be assumed to be suitable for use in other jurisdictions, even if they are an accepted tool of risk control in the US.[17]

Notwithstanding the justifications for these models in the US, recent work in the UK does indeed question the effectiveness of these factor models in explaining asset returns and controlling for risk in the UK. Michou et al. (2014) perform this analysis using a *variety* of three factor models which attempt to mimic the Fama-French (1993) three factor model that reflects market, firm size and firm book-to-market ratio effects on returns. Gregory et al. (2013) adopt a similar investigation strategy with respect to both three and four factor models. Both papers conclude that the models studies are mis-specified with respect to the pricing of chosen test portfolios.

The results above for the UK suggest why this might be so: the factors used in the models are based on firm characteristics that are an incomplete set in explaining returns. As a consequence, one possibility for improving the performance of factor models in the UK is to add more factors into the models to reflect the additional firm characteristics identified as explanatory variables for the cross-section of firm excess returns.

Of relevance here is that Michou et al. (2014) and Gregory et al. (2013) study a *variety* of three factor models for the UK because researchers estimate the factors related to firm size and firm book-to-market ratio effects in a variety of ways. As a consequence, even when UK researchers have evaluated the Fama-French (1993) model (for example, Miles and Timmerman (1996) and Fletcher (2001), it has been for a *specific* implementation of the model.[18] This suggests that the construction of factors is as much an empirical art as it is an empirical science. Put another way, even if there is evidence that a firm characteristic helps explain returns, to construct a factor that performs well in a factor-based asset pricing model is a non-trivial task.

Overall, the construction and testing of such expanded factor-based asset pricing models is needed before their use as controls for risk can be regarded as providing reliable evidence in accounting research using UK data. More importantly, similar problems of this nature are quite possible in countries other than the UK.

If we now consider the portfolio matching approach, we can identify clear difficulties. The previous section identifies eight firm characteristics which help explain excess returns. If only two are chosen (for example, *Size* and *BM*, as in Soares and Stark (2009)), it is likely that incomplete controls for risk are in place. If more firm characteristics are used to match a studied firm with a benchmark portfolio, it is not clear that the matching process can be at all precise, if only because of the number of firms available for benchmark portfolio construction in the UK. For example, if firms are split into above- and below-median on each of the eight firm characteristics, the number of possible combinations is $2^8 = 256$. Given that there are around one thousand listed non-manufacturing firms in the UK, it is clear that (i) there will be a small number of firms in most portfolios, and (ii) some portfolios will contain no firms. Further, splitting such firms into above- and below-median will achieve only an imprecise matching on each firm characteristic. Nonetheless, a more precise matching is clearly impossible.

Suppose an alternative application of the matched portfolio process is employed with only, say, two firm characteristics being used to match firms. Suppose also that a set of portfolios is being compared (constructed by ranking firms by accruals or by earnings surprises, for example). First, the evidence above suggests that it is not at all clear that making *Size* and *BM* the two matching firm characteristics is likely to achieve strong risk control – they attain statistically significant relationship with firm excess returns only *in combination with* other firm characteristics. Second, the question of which two firm characteristics to choose to match on does not have a clear answer. Further, if matched portfolio-adjusted returns are to be compared across the set of portfolios, comparisons are going to provide robust evidence of differences between portfolios only if it is assumed that the other firm characteristics that are not controlled for are jointly identically distributed in each of the portfolios studied. As a consequence, such a form of (restricted) risk control needs to report on the validity of this assumption.

Overall, the portfolio matching approach is going to be limited in its ability to generally provide reliable evidence in accounting research when UK data are used. More importantly, similar or even more acute problems of the nature reported above are likely to apply in countries with stock markets smaller than the UK if it is identified that a large number of firm characteristics help explain firm returns.

Finally, the general approach described in this paper can be adopted. That is, to regress firm (excess) returns on firm characteristics known to explain the cross-section of returns, together with variables that capture the phenomenon of interest (e.g., accruals or accruals rank dummies, or earnings surprise or earnings surprise rank dummies) to find out if the additional variables also help explain the cross-section of returns. If they do, then we can interpret the results as suggesting either the identification of further firm characteristics that capture risk or that a portfolio strategy could exist, based upon the new additional variables, that could be profitable.

This approach, although primarily empirically based, would appear to be the best approach to use in the UK, given data availability and the constraints on current technology in developing successful factor-based asset pricing models. It allows more firm characteristics to be used compared to the other approaches and is also simpler to implement. This is especially so until better factor model-based asset pricing models can be developed.

The results arising from the regression approach can be interpreted in more than one way, however. Remember that we assume that the results in the previous section reflect rational pricing, and as a consequence, the relationship between firm returns and firm characteristics implies that these characteristics do indeed capture aspects of priced risk. Alternatively, if it is not clear why, from a theoretical perspective, the chosen firm characteristics capture risk, the regression approach has the potential to identify whether one anomaly (e.g., the accruals anomaly) is distinct from other anomalies (e.g., a book-to-market anomaly).

5 Summary and conclusions

In this chapter, we consider the issue of controlling for risk in the particular case of the UK stock market. We demonstrate the need to first provide an empirical description of UK stock returns and their determining characteristics before any of the risk control methods typically used in the accounting research literature can be employed. Our description suggests that a wide variety of firm characteristics are candidates for jointly explaining firm excess returns in the UK. Further, the conventionally accepted firm characteristics that tend to be used in UK asset pricing factor models – firm size, book-to-market ratio, and past stock returns – are not the strongest amongst such candidates, although there is evidence in their favour.

Our results suggest that risk control methods need to be carefully thought through, as is made clear by the UK application; we would argue that importing conventional wisdoms from other jurisdictions is likely to result in low-power, mis-specified, tests. We suspect that this conclusion might well apply in other countries, too. For example, according to the World Federation of Exchanges (2012), the London Stock Exchange was the fourth largest exchange in the world (based on market capitalization) at the end of 2012. Nevertheless, as demonstrated, data limitations on the implementation of some risk control methods are already present in the UK, which casts doubt on the viability of using such methods. Hence, if smaller exchanges are to be studied, these limitations are likely to be even more acute. If factor models are to be employed, the evidence above suggests that variables used to construct factors need, at least, to be expanded relative to a list derived from conventional wisdom in other jurisdictions. It is also true that some of the factors on that list might need to be removed. Until such factor models are constructed and tested, however, it might well be better for researchers to use other methods of controlling for risk.

Given the state of the art and the empirical evidence on the topic of risk control, we would advise use of a regression approach where variables that have been proven to explain future excess returns are included as proxies for risk control. Such an approach is likely to provide the most useful insights on the phenomena being studied, particularly in countries with a limited number of firms available for constructing control portfolios or with under-developed factor models.

At the heart of our approach, however, is the need to thoroughly understand the determinants of firm returns in any jurisdiction before developing methods of controlling for risk in accounting research. Importing the specifics of approaches from other jurisdictions (e.g., controlling for size and/or book-to-market and/or momentum effects commonly found in the US) without such a thorough understanding could well result in misleading results in the absence of additional analysis. Further, as demonstrated above, it is not difficult to provide an empirical description in any jurisdiction, given the availability of data.

Notes

1 Contact author: Andrew W. Stark, Coutts Professor of Accounting and Finance, Manchester Business School, Booth Street West, Manchester, M15 6PB. Email: andrew.stark@mbs.ac.uk. Nuno Soares would like to thank the Fundação para a Ciência e Tecnologia (FCT-Portugal) financial support under the grant PTDC/EGE-GES/122976/2010.

2 Strictly speaking, to challenge the notion of efficient markets in the presence of trading cost frictions requires that portfolios should not only provide positive risk-adjusted returns, but they should also be of sufficient size to cover such trading costs as stamp duty, bid-ask spreads, shorting costs, price disturbance effects and standard variable transactions costs. Further, information processing costs (including payments for technical capabilities in the analysis of accounting information and acquiring and analysing information) should also be covered by the portfolio return. One of the points about anomalies such as the 'accruals anomaly' is that these latter costs are likely to be minimal.

3 Sloan (1996) and Xie (2001) are examples of the implementation of this method.

4 An underlying assumption of this approach is that the CAPM β is stable over time.

5 Kothari and Warner (1997) is an example using this methodology.

6 An underlying assumption of this approach is that the sensitivities of the portfolio returns to changes in the factors are constant over time. More complicated approaches could allow the sensitivities to vary over time, although modelling the manner in which the sensitivities change could be difficult.

7 When the CAPM is used as the basis of the asset pricing model, researchers often use the market model to specify the benchmark return.

8 This option, for instance, is followed by Joos and Plesko (2005), Balakrishnan et al. (2010) and Li (2011) in different research contexts.

9 Berk (1995) and Berk et al. (1999) provide analyses that suggest theoretical rationales for why size, book-to-market and prior returns might have a relationship with expected returns. Empirical evidence of UK momentum effects can be found in, for example, Liu et al. (1999).

10 Michou *et al.* (2014), using decile portfolio analysis, find that a size effect does exist in their UK data, but the effect is confined to the lowest three deciles. Hence, any relationship between firm size and returns might not be monotonic and could be captured better by using decile ranks as explanatory variables.

11 Earnings-to-price and cash-flow-to-price effects in UK stock returns have been identified in single-dimensioned portfolio sorts by, for example, Gregory *et al.* (2001). Soares and Stark (2011) identify both effects operating simultaneously using a regression approach. Both ratios are likely to capture both expected growth and cost of capital effects. Dividend yield effects in UK stock returns are identified in Chan and Chui (1996). Similarly, this ratio is likely to capture both expected growth and cost of capital effects. Research and development effects have been identified by Al-Horani *et al.* (2003) and Dedman *et al.* (2009), using both single-dimensioned portfolio sorts and regression approaches. Leverage effects, in which leverage has a *negative* relationship with returns, have been found by Muradoglu and Sivaprasad (2012), using regression approaches.

12 Following Ball *et al.* (1995).

13 This relates to calculating a firm's realised return when it delists. Following previous UK literature (e.g. Liu *et al.* (2003) and Soares and Stark (2009)), when a firm delists and the London Share Price Database (LSPD) assigns a delisting code of 7, 14, 16, 20 or 21, it is assumed that the delisting return is −100 per cent. In all the other cases, it is assumed that the delisting return is the last return provided by Datastream. Also, it is assumed that the delisting proceeds are reinvested at the risk-free rate.

14 Listed firms with financial years starting on or after 20 January 2007 have until four months after the end of the financial year to publish their financial statements (http://fsahandbook.info/FSA/html/handbook/DTR/4/1). Before this ruling, UK listed firms had until six months after the financial year-end to publish their financial statements.

15 Given the high number of firms with missing RD expenses being reported by Worldscope, it is assumed that in these cases there is no RD expense, and thus RD_{it} is 0.

16 Following Petersen (2009) and Gow *et al.* (2010), we also use two-way clustered standard errors to estimate the different models. The results remain robust to the different techniques used.

17 That we get the results we do in the UK suggests that either (i) the UK is an anomaly with respect to factor pricing models in an otherwise global sea of uniformity or (ii) that other countries might also need empirically optimal factor models to be locally developed, should such exist, as opposed to using those parachuted in as a consequence of US evidence. Artmann *et al.* (2012) suggest the latter is the case in Germany.

18 See Michou *et al.* (2014) for a description of the variety of ways in which UK researchers have estimated factors related to firm size and the firm book-to-market factor.

References

Al-Horani, A., P. F. Pope, and A. W. Stark (2003), 'Research and Development Activity and Expected Returns in the United Kingdom', *European Finance Review*, Vol. 7, No. 1, pp. 161–181.

Artmann, S., P. Finter, and A. Kempf (2012), 'Determinants of Expected Stock Returns: Large Sample Evidence from the German Market', *Journal of Business Finance & Accounting*, Vol. 39, Nos 5–6, pp. 758–784.

Balakrishnan, K., E. Bartov, and L. Faurel (2010), 'Post Loss/Profit Announcement Drift', *Journal of Accounting and Economics*, Vol. 50, No. 1, pp. 20–41.

Ball, R., and P. Brown (1968), 'An Empirical Evaluation of Accounting Income Numbers', *Journal of Accounting Research*, Vol. 6, No. 2, pp. 159–178.

Ball, R., S. P. Kothari, and J. Shanken (1995), 'Problems in Measuring Portfolio Performance: An Application to Contrarian Investment Strategies', *Journal of Financial Economics*, Vol. 38, No. 1, pp. 79–107.

Berk, J. (1995), 'A Critique of Size-related Anomalies', *Review of Financial Studies*, Vol. 8, No. 2, pp. 275–286.

Berk, J., R. C. Green, and V. Naik (1999), 'Optimal Investment, Growth Options, and Security Returns', *Journal of Finance*, Vol. 52, No. 1, pp. 57–82.

Carhart, M. M. (1997), 'On Persistence in Mutual Fund Performance', *Journal of Finance*, Vol. 52, No. 1, pp. 57–82.

Chan, A., and A. P. L. Chui (1996), 'An Empirical Re-examination of the Cross-section of Expected Returns: UK Evidence', *Journal of Business Finance & Accounting*, Vol. 23, Nos 9–10, pp. 1435–1452.

Dedman, E., S. Mouselli, Y. U. N. Shen, and A. W. Stark (2009), 'Accounting, Intangible Assets, Stock Market Activity, and Measurement and Disclosure Policy – Views From the UK', *Abacus*, Vol. 45, No. 3, pp. 312–341.

Fama, E. F. (1998), 'Market Efficiency, Long-term Returns, and Behavioral Finance', *Journal of Financial Economics*, Vol. 49, No. 3, pp. 283–306.

Fama, E. F., and K. R. French (1993), 'Common Risk Factors in the Returns on Stocks and Bonds', *Journal of Financial Economics*, Vol. 33, No. 1, pp. 3–56.

Fama, E. F., and J. D. MacBeth (1973), 'Risk, Return, and Equilibrium: Empirical Tests', *Journal of Political Economy*, Vol. 81, No. 3, pp. 607–636.

Fletcher, J. (2001), 'An Examination of Alternative Factor Models in UK Stock Returns', *Review of Quantitative Finance and Accounting*, Vol. 16, No. 2, pp. 117–130.

Gow, I. D., G. Ormazabal, and D. Taylor (2010), 'Correcting for Cross-sectional and Time-series Dependence in Accounting Research', *Accounting Review*, Vol. 85, No. 2, pp. 483–512.

Gregory, A., R. D. F. Harris, and M. Michou (2001), 'An Analysis of Contrarian Investment Strategies in the UK', *Journal of Business Finance & Accounting*, Vol. 28, Nos 9–10, pp. 1192–1228.

Gregory, A., R. Tharyan, and A. Christidis (2013), 'Constructing and Testing Alternative Versions of the Fama-French and Carhart Models in the UK', *Journal of Business Finance & Accounting*, Vol. 40, Nos 1–2, pp. 172–214.

Joos, P., and G. A. Plesko (2005), 'Loss Firms', *Accounting Review*, Vol. 80, No. 3, pp. 847–870.

Kothari, S. P., and J. B. Warner (1997), 'Measuring Long-horizon Security Price Performance', *Journal of Financial Economics*, Vol. 43, No. 3, pp. 301–339.

Li, K. (2011), 'How Well Do Investors Understand Loss Persistence?', *Review of Accounting Studies*, Vol. 16, No. 3, pp. 630–667.

Liu, W., N. Strong, and X. Xu (1999), 'The Profitability of Momentum Investing', *Journal of Business Finance & Accounting*, Vol. 26, Nos 9–10, pp. 1043–1091.

—— (2003), 'Post-earnings-announcement Drift in the UK', *European Financial Management*, Vol. 9, No. 1, pp. 89–116.

Michou, M., S. Mouselli, and A. Stark (2014), 'On the Differences in Measuring SMB and HML in the UK – Do They Matter', *British Accounting Review*, Vol. 46, No. 3, pp. 281–294.

Miles, D., and A. Timmermann (1996), 'Variation in Expected Stock Returns: Evidence on the Pricing of Equities from a Cross-section of UK Companies', *Economica*, Vol. 63, No. 251, pp. 369–382.

Muradoglu, Y. G., and S. Sivaprasad (2012), 'Capital Structure and Abnormal Returns', *International Business Review*, Vol. 21, No. 3, pp. 328–341.

Ou, J. A., and S. H. Penman (1989), 'Financial Statement Analysis and the Prediction of Stock Returns', *Journal of Accounting and Economics*, Vol. 11, No. 4, pp. 295–329.

Petersen, M. (2009), 'Estimating Standard Errors in Finance Panel Data Sets: Comparing Approaches', *Review of Financial Studies*, Vol. 22, No. 1, pp. 435–480.

Sloan, R. G. (1996), 'Do Stock Prices Fully Reflect Information in Accruals and Cash Flows about Future Earnings?', *Accounting Review*, Vol. 71, No. 3, pp. 289–315.

Soares, N., and A. W. Stark (2009), 'The Accruals Anomaly: Can Implementable Portfolios Strategies be Developed That Are Profitable in the UK?', *Accounting and Business Research*, Vol. 39, No. 4, pp. 321–345.

—— (2011), 'Is There an Accruals or a Cash Flow Anomaly in UK Stock Returns?', Available at SSRN: http://ssrn.com/abstract=1734507 or http://dx.doi.org/10.2139/ssrn.1734507.

Teoh, S. H., and Y. L. Zhang (2011), 'Data Truncation Bias, Loss Firms, and Accounting Anomalies', *Accounting Review*, Vol. 86, No. 4, pp. 1445–1475.

World Federation of Exchanges (2012), 'WFE 2012 Market Highlights', *World Federation of Exchanges*.

Xie, H. (2001), 'The Mispricing of Abnormal Accruals', *Accounting Review*, Vol. 76, No. 3, pp. 357–373.

17

Financial measurement and financial markets

Mike Dempsey and Stewart Jones

The chapter is structured as follows. We commence by reviewing the understanding of asset pricing and market efficiency that is upheld in modern finance theory. This leads to a discussion of the Global Financial Crisis (GFC) and the destruction of individual and corporate wealth that had relied on price discovery in orderly markets. We then highlight the adverse reaction to the concept of efficient markets as an outcome of the GFC. This is followed by a review of economic theory that had warned of the innate dynamic of unsustainable bubbles and dysfunctional cycles in the economy, warnings that modern finance theory has chosen to ignore. The final section of this chapter concludes with a consideration of the implications for accounting measurement seeking to avail of market pricing as an arbiter of value in corporate financial reports.

Financial markets and the concept of rational asset pricing

Whereas historical cost accounting (HCA) posits the definition of the value of a firm's physical assets as their value at historical cost with allowance for subsequent depreciation, the concept of 'mark-to-market' valuation or fair-value accounting (FVA) accords with the adage that 'something is worth what somebody is prepared to pay for it'. The issue is observed in the initiatives of the International Accounting Standards Board (IASB) and the US Financial Accounting Standards Board (FASB) towards attaining a consensus of the application of FVA reporting in which *market* prices might be employed as opposed to principles of HCA.

The issue of insolvency as a condition of legal corporate failure – when the value of assets must be compared with the value of liabilities – brings into sharp relief the question of how to measure the value of assets and liabilities. So, also, does the question of whether the exit of a firm would add to efficiency – when the present value of assets must be compared with their value in an alternative use. The inclination of the accounting bodies is sometimes equivocal. Thus, for a financial loan held to maturity, the essential notion of HCA appears relevant. For a stock share, however, such a notion appears unacceptable. The value of the share, we are inclined to agree, is its market value.

Proponents of mark-to-market accounting argue that FVA reflects the true (and relevant) value of the balance sheets of financial institutions, which in turn should allow investors and policy makers to better assess their risk profile and undertake more timely market discipline and corrective actions. The method reflects the amount at which that asset or liability can be bought or sold between knowledgeable willing parties in an arm's length transaction. As reasonable as FVA might appear, however, it carries with it the assumption that the market's valuations are in some sense 'reliable'. If, for example, market prices are held to be given to fickle mood swings of sentiment or to be capable of spiralling in progressions of self-fuelling ascents or descents, the case for FVA is compromised.

A capital market where prices provide meaningful signals for capital allocation is, in effect, an assumption of the marked-to-market belief system. In such a system, when firms issue securities to finance their activities, they can expect to get fair prices, and, equally, when investors choose among the securities that represent ownership of firms' activities, they can do so under the assumption that they are paying fair prices given what is known about the firm. The foundations of modern finance theory embrace such a view of capital markets. The underlying paradigm asserts that in financial systems in equilibrium, financial capital circulates to achieve those rates of return that are most attractive to its investors, and that in accordance with this principle, prices of securities observed at any time fully reflect all information available at that time, so that it is impossible to make consistent economic profits by trading on such available information (for example, Fama, 1976).

The 'efficient market hypothesis' – the notion that market prices react rapidly to new information (weak, semi-strong or strong form) – is claimed to be the most extensively tested hypothesis in all the social sciences. Jensen (1978) went as far as to claim that 'there is no other proposition in economics which has more solid empirical evidence supporting it than the efficient market hypothesis'. Consistent with the hypothesis, detailed empirical studies of stock prices indicate that it is difficult to earn above-normal profits by trading on publicly available data because the profits are already fully incorporated into security prices. Fama (1976) reviews much of this evidence, though the evidence is not completely one-sided (for example, Jensen, 1978).

Yet, allowing that empirical research has succeeded in broadly establishing that successive share price movements are systematically uncorrelated, thus establishing that we are unable to reject the efficient market hypothesis, this does not describe *how* markets respond to information and *how* information is impounded to determine share prices. That is to say, the much-vaunted efficient market hypothesis does not in itself enable us to conclude that capital markets allocate financial resources efficiently from an economic perspective. If we wish to claim *allocative* efficiency for capital markets, we must show that markets not only rapidly impound new information, but that they also meaningfully impound that information.

Thus, while the efficient market hypothesis states that at any time, all available information is imputed into the price of an asset so that it is impossible to trade profitably on public information, the 'capital asset pricing model' (CAPM) gives content to how such information should be imputed. The CAPM has dominated financial economics to the extent of being labelled 'the paradigm'. Since its inception in the early 1960s, it has served as the bedrock of capital asset pricing theory and its application to practitioner activities. It is based on the concept that for a given exposure to uncertain outcomes, investors prefer higher rather than lower expected returns. This tenet appears highly reasonable, and following its inception, a good deal of empirical work was performed aimed at supporting the prediction of the CAPM that an asset's excess return over the risk-free rate should be proportional to its exposure to overall market risk, as measured by beta. In *Fisher Black and the Revolutionary Idea of Finance*, Mehrling (2007) considers the CAPM as the 'revolutionary idea' that runs through finance theory. If the first major step in the development of modern finance theory is the efficient markets hypothesis, the second step is the CAPM.

Simply stated, the CAPM says that investors can expect to attain a risk-free rate plus a 'market risk premium' multiplied by their exposure to the market, as

$$E(R_j) = r_f + \beta_j [E(R_M) - r_f]$$

where $E(R_j)$ is the expected return on asset j over a single time-period, r_f is the riskless rate of interest over the period, $E(R_M)$ is the expected return on the market over the period, and β_j identifies the exposure of asset j to the market.

The intuition is that if the market of all assets offers investors a 'risk premium' – $[E(R_M) - r_f]$ – in compensation for bearing risk exposure, then, all else being equal, each individual stock, j, must rationally offer a risk premium equal to $\beta_j[E(R_M) - r_f]$, since β_j measures the asset's individual exposure to market risk. Market frictions (limited access to borrowing at the risk-free rate, for example) might imply adjustments, but at the core, the CAPM must maintain. For this reason, validation of the CAPM was seen at the time as a validation of the effective efficiency of capital markets. Mehrling captures the sense of discovery back in the late sixties and early seventies as researchers believed that they were at the forefront of significant discovery as they moved to understand financial markets in relation to rational models that would advance how such markets might be manipulated and improved.

Accordingly, over the decades following its inception, the industry of writing papers in support of the CAPM has grown vibrantly. Notwithstanding, the evidence from the very beginning has been squarely *against* the notion that investors set stock prices in accordance with beta. The work of Black, Jensen and Scholes (1972), while demonstrating that stocks of higher beta appeared on aggregate to earn higher returns than stocks of lower beta, nevertheless pointed out that the relation was far too weak to support application of the CAPM. To make the model work required a risk-free rate significantly higher than the rate actually observed. The outcome was a statistical fudge in search of a theoretical explanation. Other work at the time had also highlighted the deficiencies of the CAPM.[1]

We suspect that a 'blind' eye was purposefully turned to the evidence. At a time when researchers were convinced that markets could and should be made subject to something like scientific inquiry, evidence against the CAPM was not what researchers were willing to hear. Such a revelation would have fundamentally undermined the determination of finance to be accepted as a domain of economics with its study of 'efficient markets' made susceptible to econometric techniques. Lo and Mueller (2010) – themselves advocates of this kind of research – observe that up to the early 1990s, any challenge to the notion of market efficiency was anathema, and papers claiming to have discovered departures in the data from what was predicted by the CAPM were 'routinely rejected from the top economics and finance journals, in some cases, without even being sent out to referees for review' (p. 18). In the introduction to their paper, they explain:

> The quantitative aspirations of economists and financial analysts have for years been based on the belief that it should be possible to build models of economic systems – and financial markets in particular – that are as predictive as those in physics.
>
> *(p. 13)*

In 1992, Eugene Fama and Kenneth French – while continuing to hold to the principle of market efficiency – introduced their paper in the prestigious *Journal of Finance* with the pronouncement that beta had effectively no explanatory power in regard to asset pricing: 'When the tests allow for variation in β that is unrelated to size, the relation between β and average return is flat, even when β is the only explanatory variable.' Not only was Eugene Fama something of an icon of academic finance, but he had consistently and resolutely defended the efficiency of markets. So his pronouncements with Kenneth French were not short of attention.[2]

Fama and French (FF) introduced two variables in addition to beta, which they claimed administered most of the 'heavy work' in explaining historical share price movements. These variables were the market equity *(ME)* value or size of the underlying firm, and the ratio of the book value of its common equity to its market equity value *(BE/ME)*, which 'provide a simple and powerful characterization of the cross-section of average stock returns for the 1963–1990 period' (FF, 1992, p. 429). The authors concluded that 'if stocks are priced rationally, the results suggest that stock risks are multidimensional' (p. 428).

Although not actually the first to do so, Fama and French in the early 1990s were particularly aggressive in pronouncing the ineffectiveness of the relation between historical average returns and beta. Like others before them, Fama and French nevertheless realised the necessity of retaining a risk-based model of asset pricing. In the absence of such a model, the rational integrity of markets is undermined. Thus, in their 1996 paper, Fama and French place their model squarely in the tradition of the CAPM, stating that 'this paper argues that many of the CAPM average-return anomalies are related, and that they are captured by the three-factor model in Fama and French (1993)'.

Their model says that the expected return on a portfolio in excess of the risk-free rate $[E(R_j) - r_f]$ is explained by the sensitivity of its return to three factors:

i   the excess return on a broad market portfolio $(R_M - r_f)$,
ii   the difference between the return on a portfolio of small firm stocks and the return on a portfolio of large firm stocks ($E(R_{SMB})$, small minus big), and
iii the difference between the return on a portfolio of high-book-to-market stocks and the return on a portfolio of low-book-to-market stocks ($E(R_{HML})$, high minus low).

Specifically, the expected return on portfolio j is

$$E(R_j) - r_f = b_j [E(R_M) - r_f] + s_j E(R_{SMB}) + h_j E(R_{HML})$$

where $E(R_M) - r_f$, $E(R_{SMB})$, and $E(R_{HML})$ are expected premiums, and the factor sensitivities or loadings, b_j, s_j, and h_j, are the slopes in the time-series regression:

$$R_j - r_f = \alpha_j + b_j(R_M - r_f) + s_j R_{SMB} + h_j R_{HML} + \varepsilon_j$$

where α_j and ε_j represent, respectively, the intercept and error terms of the regression.

Fama and French interpret their model as *extending* the structure of the CAPM. Thus, whereas $[E(R_M) - r_f]$ is the CAPM risk premium, which is identified as the expected return on the market portfolio of all risky stocks $E(R_M)$ minus the return on non-risky Treasury bonds r_f; in analogy, $E(R_{SMB})$ is the risk premium for stocks of small firms, which is identified as the expected return on a portfolio of stocks of the smallest firms (Fama and French choose the 30 per cent of stocks with the smallest firm size) minus the return on a portfolio of stocks of the largest firms (Fama and French choose the 30 per cent of stocks with the largest firm size); and, similarly, $E(R_{HML})$ is the risk premium for a portfolio of stocks of the highest book-to-market value minus the return on a portfolio of those stocks of the lowest book-to-market value.

In seeking to establish their model as a strictly risk-based model, Fama and French argue that the size of the underlying firm (ME) and the ratio of the book value of equity to market value *(BE/ME)* are 'risk-based' explanatory variables, with the former a proxy for the required return for bearing exposure to small stocks, and the latter a proxy for investors' required return for bearing 'financial distress', neither of which are captured in the market return (FF, 1995). They also claim that their model provides both a resolution of the CAPM (FF, 1996) and a resolution of prior attempts to generalise a risk-based model of stock prices.[3]

There is, however, an obvious inherent contradiction between, on the one hand, Fama and French's repeated denouncement of β, and, on the other hand, their inclusion of β as an explanatory variable in their model. In fact, in the formal test of their model, Fama and French do not even trouble to allow for a beta effect. Thus, in FF (1996), they form 25 (5 × 5) portfolios on 'book-to-market value' and 'firm size', but not on β, with the outcome that the b_j coefficients of the 25 portfolios are all very close to 1.0 (none diverge by more than 10 per cent, as shown in Table 1 of FF (1996)). The Fama and French three-factor model has simultaneously included β and made it redundant as an explanatory variable.

We thereby have a disconnect between the FF three-factor model and the CAPM. Whereas the CAPM states that all assets have a return equal to the risk-free rate 'as a base' plus a market risk premium multiplied by the asset's exposure to the market, the FF three-factor model states that all stocks have the market return 'as a base' plus or minus an element that depends on the stock's sensitivity to the differential performances of high and low book-value-to-market-equity *(BE/ME)* stocks and big and small firm size *(ME)* stocks. The FF model is more truthfully (and parsimoniously) expressed as a 'two-factor' rather than a 'three-factor' model:

$$E(R_j) = E(R_M) + s_j\, E(R_{SMB}) + h_j\, E(R_{HML})$$

But to express it thusly would be to concede that investor rationality, as captured by the CAPM, is now abandoned, whereas by allowing the loading of b_j coefficients on the excess market return $[E(R_M) - r_j]$ to remain in the model, a formal continuity with the CAPM and the illusion that the three-factor model can be viewed as a refinement of the CAPM is maintained.

Conceptually, the Fama and French model leaves a good deal to be desired. Ultimately, the model derives from a fitting of data rather than from theoretical principles. The model states that US institutional and retail investors (a) care about market risk but (b) do not appear to care about how such risk might be magnified or diminished in particular assets as captured by their beta (thereby contradicting the CAPM), while (c) simultaneously appearing to care about the book-to-market equity ratio and the firm size of their stocks. But if sensitivity to market risk as captured by beta does not motivate investors, it is, on the face of it, difficult to envisage how the book-to-market equity and firm size variables can be expected to motivate them. Black (1993) considered the then fledgling Fama and French three-factor model as 'data mining'.

There is a correspondence here with the observation of the scientific philosopher Thomas Kuhn (1962), who states that facts always serve to justify more activity without ever seriously being allowed to threaten the paradigm core. In Kuhn's view, 'normal science' generally consists of a protracted period of adjustments to the surrounding framework of a central paradigm with 'add-on' hypotheses aimed at defending the central hypothesis against various 'anomalies'. The continued defence of the CAPM – adding more factors to the CAPM to explain more anomalies – has led the single-factor CAPM model to become the three-factor model of Fama and French. To this model, additional factors for idiosyncratic volatility, liquidity, momentum and so forth have subsequently been added, which accords with Kuhn's articulation of 'normal science'.

Lakonishok, Shleifer and Vishny (1994) argue that the Fama and French risk premiums are not risk premiums at all, but rather the outcome of mispricing. They argue that investors consistently underestimate future growth rates for 'value' stocks (captured as high market-to-book equity value) and therefore underprice them. This results in value stocks outperforming growth stocks. From another perspective, Daniel and Titman (1997) provide evidence against the premiums as risk premiums by finding that the return performances of the Fama and French portfolios do not relate to covariances with the risk premiums as the Fama and French model dictates, but rather they relate directly to the book-to-market and size of the firm as attributable 'characteristics' of the stock. Nevertheless, the three-factor model of Fama and French (1993, 1996) and the Carhart model (1997), which adds momentum exposure as a fourth factor, are now academically mainstream.

The anatomy of the Global Financial Crisis

The term 'Global Financial Crisis' (GFC) refers to the near collapse of the global financial system from the later part of 2007 and the ensuing contagion effects to the wider economy that played out to the European sovereign debt crisis and a global recession from 2008–2012. Writing at the onset of the GFC, legendary hedge fund manager George Soros (2009) explained:

> Cheap money engendered a housing bubble, an explosion of leveraged buyouts, and other excesses. When money is free, the rational lender will keep on lending until there is no one else to lend to. Mortgage lenders relaxed their standards and invented new ways to stimulate business and generate fees. Investment banks on Wall Street developed a variety of new techniques to hive credit risk off to other investors, like pension funds and mutual funds, which were hungry for yield. They also created structured investment vehicles (SIVs) to keep their own positions of their balance sheets.
>
> *(p. xv)*

The US Government's *Financial Crisis Inquiry Commission* (FCIC, 2011) would reach similar conclusions. At the core of the GFC was the sub-prime lending market, which had expanded rapidly on the back of an unsustainable housing bubble. Between 2000 and 2005, US housing prices had grown over 50 per cent, aided by the use of interest only and 'low doc' loans. Typically an adjustable rate mortgage was used with a low 'teaser' rate for a two-year period and a much higher rate at the end of the honeymoon period. Speculative activity supported the assumption that mortgages could be refinanced after this period to take advantage of rising housing prices. Mortgage originators were incentivised on sales volume, not loan quality, and lending standards deteriorated rapidly. Loans were referred to pejoratively as 'Ninja' loans – No Income, No Job or Assets – and many mortgage defaults were associated with customers who had failed to make their first loan instalment. However, by mid-2007, mortgage default rates had risen to 11 per cent (double the previous year), and on 4 August of that year, the American Home Mortgage Investment Corporation was bankrupt.

The FCIC (2011) concluded that the situation had been exacerbated by skilful financial engineering by investment banks and hedge funds. The rapid development of structured credit products, particularly those products with significant exposure to the sub-prime lending market, contributed to the deterioration in underwriting standards. As noted by Soros (2009), banks repackaged their riskiest mortgages and sold them as mortgage-backed securities (MBSs) to investors, thereby effectively transferring the risk (including the risk of lax underwriting standards) to investors. The growing collateralised debt obligation (CDO) market – securities backed by, or linked to, a diversified pool of credits – contributed to the sub-prime market collapse. By dividing or slicing up the MBSs into series of tiered or tranched bonds with different risk and yield profiles, reflecting different investment grades, sub-prime mortgages (the 'toxic waste') were repackaged with higher-grade debt. The CDO cash flows were then channelled to investors on a 'waterfall' model: the top-tier tranches, which comprised the majority of the bonds, had first call on the underlying mortgage cash flows and were sold to investors with a triple-A rating, with lower tiers absorbing the first dollar risks with higher promised yields.

From 2005, securitisation simply grew on itself. Variations of CDOs, such as synthetic CDOs, were created and were 'merely bets on the performance of real mortgage-related securities. They amplified the losses from the collapse of the housing bubble by allowing multiple bets on the same securities and helped spread risk throughout the financial system' (FCIC, 2011, p. xxiv). Credit default swaps (CDS) – also a type of synthetic CDOs – were designed to protect investors against default or decline in the value of mortgage-related securities backed by risky loans, and they were duly fed into the 'securitization pipeline'. The American International Group alone, prior to its near collapse and bailout, had written $79 billion in CDSs into the pipeline, which had worked to inflate the housing bubble and expand the synthetic CDO market.

The value of the CDOs were obligingly 'marked up' while housing prices were increasing in the US, allowing them to be used as collateral with banks to raise further cheap debt. Hedge funds – which were particularly active in trading equity and mezzanine tranches of high yield CDOs – were able to exploit this opportunity to lever more heavily into the CDO market. A 'securitization pipeline' was created 'that transported toxic mortgages from neighbourhoods across America to investors around the globe' (FCIC, 2011, p. xxiii).

However, when the mortgages underlying the CDOs collateral began to spiral downward, banks and investment institutions holding CDOs experienced a significant deterioration in the value of their CDO holdings. Their problems were compounded by the increasingly illiquid market for CDOs and the difficulties faced by hedge funds in pricing their losses in a rapidly declining market. The atmosphere of panic in the market resulted in banks calling in their original collateral. With rising congestion and panic in CDO sales, markets simply dried up. Unsustainable book losses were delivered to a number of hedge funds and investment banks. With no active market, the equity and mezzanine tranches literally had no value. As delinquencies and defaults on sub-prime mortgages escalated, CDOs backed by equity and mezzanine sub-prime collateral were experiencing dramatic downgrades of their ratings. As an example, on 10 July 2007, Moody's – which between 2000 and 2007 had rated nearly 45,000 mortgage-related securities as triple-A – cut ratings on more than 400 securities that relied on sub-prime loan exposures. Around the same time, Standard & Poor's announced that 612 securities were on review, of which the majority were downgraded (Jones and Peat, 2008). These belated actions by the ratings agencies served to highlight their shortcomings in the first place. Their actions were described as 'the equivalent of slapping food-safety warnings on meat that's already rotting in the aisles' (Jones and Peat, 2008). The erratic shifts in ratings worked to compound nervousness in financial markets. A raft of criticism was levelled at the ratings agencies for reacting too slowly to the crisis, for failing to downgrade mortgage bonds and related structured products in a timely manner, and for failing to anticipate the escalating default rates on sub-prime mortgages in the first place (Jones and Peat, 2008). The FCIC (2011, p. 118) used Moody's as a case study of how the ratings agencies contributed to the meltdown, particularly noting their flawed formulas, pressure from clients that paid for the ratings, the drive for market share, and lack of appropriate public oversight.[4] The FCIC (2011) stated:

> From the speculators who flipped houses to the mortgage brokers who scouted the loans, to the lenders who issued the mortgages, to the financial firms that created the mortgage-backed securities, collateralized debt obligations (CDOs), CDOs squared, and synthetic CDOs: no one in this pipeline of toxic mortgages had enough skin in the game. They all believed they could off-load their risks on a moment's notice to the next person in line. They were wrong. When borrowers stopped making mortgage payments, the losses – amplified by derivatives – rushed through the pipeline. As it turned out, these losses were concentrated in a set of systemically important financial institutions.
>
> *(p. xxiv)*

As a relatively latecomer to the CDO market, Bear Stearns Asset Management Inc. acquired many CDOs at the height of the US property market (explaining why the firm was inflicted with heavy losses). When two hedge funds managed by Bear Stearns faced cash or collateral calls from lenders that had accepted CDOs backed by sub-prime loans as loan collateral, it was unable to deliver, and the market at that point had begun to collapse. AIG, which carried large positions in CDSs, faced default, forcing a bailout by the US government. The big game changer then came with the failure of Lehman Brothers on 15 September 2008, the consequences of which were 'disastrous' (Soros, 2009, p. 161). Lehman Brothers was a major market-maker in commercial paper and a major issuer, and its failure precipitated a run on market money funds. The contagion soon spread to global stock markets. In growing desperation, the US Federal Reserve extended guarantees to all market money funds and then suspended short selling of all financial stocks, before launching the $700 billion Emergency Economic Stabilization legislation. However, it appeared that the costs of various government bailouts might not be curtailed. In 2010, the International Monetary Fund estimated that the cost of the GFC to financial institutions alone was US$2.3 trillion.

Aftermath of the GFC

The GFC has brought into sharp relief the question of whether the US financial system had been operating under an exaggerated belief in efficient markets. As noted by Ball (2009): 'The Efficient Market Hypothesis (EMH) – the idea that competitive financial markets ruthlessly exploit all available information when setting security prices – has been singled out for particular attention' (p. 8). Thus, the ethos of laissez-faire and free markets, and market efficiency which grew out of the culture of free market principles, has been singled out for particular scrutiny.[5] Much of the criticism concerns the failure of the efficient markets hypothesis (EMH) to acknowledge the potential for such asset bubbles.

A fundamental premise of the EMH is that rational investors price assets on expectations of their risk-adjusted future cash flows (as discussed in the first section of this chapter). However, such rational investment patterns appear to break down in bubbly markets when prices and fundamentals depart from reality and markets do not appropriately price risk.

The FCIC (2011) concluded that 'widespread failures in financial regulation and supervision proved devastating to the stability of the nation's financial markets' (p. xviii). Alan Greenspan, former Chairman of the Federal Reserve, acknowledged in congressional testimony on 23 October 2008 that he was 'partially' wrong in opposing regulation and stated: 'Those of us who have looked to the self-interest of lending institutions to protect shareholders' equity – myself especially – are in a state of shocked disbelief.' And Greenspan duly conceded: 'A critical pillar to market competition and free markets did break down.'

Very much capturing the anger at government and frustration with establishment complacency surrounding theories of efficient markets, respected fund manager Jeremy Grantham was quoted in the *New York Times* from one of his investor newsletters:

> The incredibly inaccurate efficient market theory was believed in totality by many of our financial leaders, and believed in part by almost all. It left our economic and government establishment sitting by confidently, even as a lethally dangerous combination of asset bubbles, lax controls, pernicious incentives and wickedly complicated instruments led to our current plight. 'Surely, none of this could be happening in a rational, efficient world,' they seemed to be thinking. And the absolutely worst part of this belief set was that it led to a chronic underestimation of the dangers of asset bubbles breaking.[6]

While it can be difficult to determine the existence of a bubble as it develops and to know when prices are too high or too low, the FCIC (2011, p. xvii) nevertheless concluded that the GFC could have been avoided, citing many warning signs and red flags that were ignored or discounted by regulators and market participants, including a rapid escalation in risky sub-prime lending and the unregulated derivatives market, the housing bubble and associated sharp increases in household mortgage debt, evidence of extensive predatory lending practices and so on.

Back to earlier theories of markets

The bull market leading up to the GFC was prime-pumped by easy borrowing, with soaring levels of debt on both corporate and individual balance sheets. The cycle began in 2003, with Fed chief Alan Greenspan's decision to reduce short-term interest rates to 1 per cent, combined with an influx of foreign money, particularly Chinese money, into US Treasury bonds, which further made money plentiful. As we saw, the low cost of borrowing – mortgage rates, in particular – had encouraged a speculative real-estate boom, until the ever rising roller coaster of the economy turned and plummeted into the bear market that was the GFC, as debt was withdrawn from the system and markets froze.

An economist who had articulated the importance of debt in the cycle was Hyman Minsky, whose theories emphasised the macroeconomic dangers of speculative bubbles in asset prices (*Stabilizing an Unstable Economy,* 1986). Minsky proposed theories linking financial market fragility in the economy with speculative investment bubbles endogenous to financial markets. There are basically five stages in Minsky's model of the credit cycle: displacement, boom, euphoria, profit taking, and panic. His theories, however, were not incorporated into central bank policy. Rather, as the famous Modigliani and Miller irrelevancy propositions articulated, debt was allowed to be 'irrelevant'.

Following Minsky, when times are good, investors take on debt (and risk); and the longer times stay good, the more debt they take on. In prosperous times, when corporate cash flow rises beyond what is needed to pay off debt, a speculative euphoria develops, until, inevitably, a point is reached where the cash generated by the assets acquired is no longer sufficient to pay off the mountains of debt that were taken on to acquire the assets. At this point, losses on such speculative assets prompt lenders to call in their loans. This leads to a collapse of asset values as investors are forced to sell off even their safer positions to make good on their loans. Markets spiral downward and create a severe demand for cash. The global financial crisis was similarly triggered as banks, under pressure from shareholders in the good times to increase returns, operated with minimal equity, leaving them exposed when the downturn occurred.[7]

Shleifer's (2000) concept of a bubble resonates with Minsky's. It is based on positive feedback mechanisms and strategies, stimulated by 'smart money' or arbitrageurs, whose anticipatory actions fuel the bubble even further. He envisages six steps in the creation and bursting of an asset bubble:

1   Initial good news or 'displacement', which generates substantial profits for some particular asset class.
2   Smart money response to rising asset prices, as 'smart money' or arbitrageurs begin by increasing the supply of both the desirable physical asset and claims on the asset.
3   Sustaining the bubble, particularly at the later stages of the bubble, as smart money, seeking to sustain noise trader enthusiasm in maintaining price trends, takes early positions in assets and attempts organised front running in bubbly markets.
4   Authoritative endorsement when authoritative blessing (such as government support) is sought to sustain the bubble.

5   Crash, when steps 1–4 are followed by a crash, with losses to noise traders who held on to their investments, usually followed by recession.
6   Political reaction.

Even though Shleifer was writing well before the GFC, the sequence of events of the GFC conforms to his descriptions. The displacement effect was the rising US housing market and the general buoyancy of the US stock market. Rapidly rising house prices attracted investors to the market. Smart money (in the form of investment banks and hedge funds) recognised the emerging trend and fuelled credit expansion into the housing market (particularly the sub-prime market), augmented by the creation of complex derivatives such as synthetic CDOs and CDSs, which facilitated further leveraging into mortgage markets and further overheated the housing market. At the same time, smart money reduced its risk exposure by using CDSs and other instruments, which transferred counter-party risk to noise traders (the securitisation pipeline effect). Smart money was well aware that market conditions were very bubbly, and in some cases it even took short positions against its own clients positions. Authoritative endorsement came from the Federal Reserve, which kept interest rates low and failed to provide regulatory oversight despite the warning signs (FCIC, 2011). Credit ratings agencies also provided a level of 'authoritative endorsement' by issuing credit ratings which failed to reflect the real underlying risk of many structured investment products. After the crash ensued (with huge losses to noise traders), the political fallout duly followed.

George Soros (2009) proposes the concept of reflexivity in financial markets as an explanation of the emergence of asset bubbles. He states: 'Every bubble consists of a trend that can be observed in the real world and as misconception relating to that trend. The two elements interact with each other in a reflexive manner' (p. x). Soros is among those who reject the rational expectations theory underpinning efficient market theory, which posits that markets are inherently self-correcting and tend towards price equilibrium, displaced only by random exogenous shocks to the system. Following Soros, market prices are distorted because markets operate with a good deal of bias. Distorted prices affect fundamentals, which they are assumed to reflect, thus reinforcing biased expectations in a 'self-reinforcing and eventually self-defeating way'. Thus, market prices do not passively reflect fundamental values, particularly in bubble conditions:

> . . . bubbles are not the only form in which reflexivity manifests itself in financial markets, but they are the most dramatic and they can have disastrous consequences. Bubbles are often responsible for financial crises and play an important role in the evolution of the regulatory regime . . .

> *(p. x)*

Of course, the notion that the instincts, emotions and proclivities of human beings, such as greed and fear, have a significant influence on markets is not new and has been recognised by several leading economists over the past hundred years. For instance, John Maynard Keynes famously stated (1936):

> Even apart from the instability due to speculation, there is the instability due to the characteristic of human nature that a large proportion of our positive activities depend on spontaneous optimism rather than mathematical expectations, whether moral or hedonistic or economic. Most, probably, of our decisions to do something positive, the full consequences of which will be drawn out over many days to come, can only be taken as the result of animal spirits – a spontaneous urge to action rather than inaction, and not as the outcome of a weighted average of quantitative benefits multiplied by quantitative probabilities.

> *(pp. 161–162)*

The fickleness of markets is highlighted by Huberman and Regev (2001), who in a rare case study analysis, demonstrate a contagious speculation effect in the presence of what is effectively 'no information'. A *Sunday New York Times* article on the *potential* development of a new cancer drug resulted in a biotech company (EntreMed) seeing its share price soar from $12 on 1 May 1998 to $85 on Monday, 4 May, before remaining above $30 through the following weeks. Contagion was felt by other biotech companies, whose share prices also increased. Actually, the potential breakthrough in cancer research had been published in the leading science journal *Nature,* and indeed in many leading newspapers five months earlier (with virtually no stock price reaction at the time). Such observations contradict market efficiency, which predicts that prices reflect an asset's risk-adjusted expected cash flows, with expectations changing as a result of new information. The authors conclude that 'capital markets may allocate funds in a somewhat arbitrary fashion' (p. 396). Sornette (2003) confirms that industries such as information technology, biotechnology, healthcare and the Internet are particularly susceptible to sensational stories that lead to 'enthusiasm, contagion, herding, and speculative bubbles' (p. 96).

Keynes (1936) used the abstraction of a beauty contest to explain fluctuations in equity prices. If one wanted to win a contest which picked the prettiest face in a beauty contest, a naive strategy would be to select the prettiest face based on one's own opinion or perception of beauty. A more sophisticated strategy would be to work out what the consensus opinion would be, or even what the consensus would be of the consensus opinion:

> It is not a case of choosing those (faces) that, to the best of one's judgment, are really the prettiest, nor even those that average opinion genuinely thinks the prettiest. We have reached the third degree where we devote our intelligences to anticipating what average opinion expects the average opinion to be. And there are some, I believe, who practice the fourth, fifth and higher degrees.
>
> *Keynes, General Theory of Employment Interest and Money, 1936, Chapter 12*

In other words, rather than picking stocks based purely on fundamental value, one needs to understand the mood of the crowd and how this psychology can affect future prices.

Conclusions and implications for financial measurement

The contrasting view of market activity, entirely denied by the efficient market academics, is – as Keynes put it – not that market players are *independently* assessing fundamental values, but that they are 'anticipating what average opinion expects the average opinion to be'. This essential insight provides the basis by which markets are capable of self-fulfilling forces of growth and decline, as each successive upward (downward) movement of prices motivates additional endogenous optimism (pessimism) and yet further upward (downward) movements. Such insights, however, appear to have been discarded by modern finance theory with its assertion of 'market efficiency' and a near religious belief in the superior wisdom of markets left to self-regulation.

The outcome, as has been observed, is that fair-value accounting (FVA) allowed banks to increase their leverage in the boom times, which made the financial system vulnerable at the outset of the financial crisis. Additionally, FVA provoked contagion in financial markets as banks sold assets at a price below the fundamental value in fire sales, and the price of the forced sales became relevant to other institutions that were required by FVA to mark their assets to market.

When assets are priced according to market values, low prices can lead to contagion from the insurance sector to the banking sector. Banks are then declared insolvent by regulators and forced to sell their long-term assets. This worsens the illiquidity problem in the market and reduces prices even further. As liquidity dries up, the price of an asset becomes a function of the amount of liquidity available in the market. So, again, marking to market leads to contagion between the banking sector and the insurance sector. In effect, in times of financial crisis, the interaction of institutions and markets can lead to situations where prices in illiquid markets do not reflect future payoffs, but rather reflect the amount of cash available to buyers in the market.

Following the global financial crisis, there has been intense debate about using market prices to value the assets of financial institutions, which may not be beneficial when financial markets are illiquid. The level of liquidity in such markets is endogenously determined and is ultimately priced. When accounting values are based on historic costs, the problem seems to be avoided, as the accounting value of assets need not be affected. In contrast, when accounting values are based on market prices, the volatility of asset prices directly affects the value of banks' assets, leading to distortions in banks' portfolio and contract choices and to contagion. Banks can become insolvent even though they would be fully able to cover their commitments if they were allowed to continue until the assets matured.

Following the political fallout of the GFC, the FASB relaxed its FVA reporting require-ments, allowing reporting entities more flexibility with the application of FVA where markets are illiquid.[8] However, the problem is that 'flexibility', by allowing managers to introduce their own assumptions into FVA determinations, leads to the potential for creative accounting, which is always likely to be exploited. For example, Enron's indebtedness and earnings were concealed to flatter the performance being achieved by the company's assets in their current use. In the savings and loan crisis of the 1980s, the regulatory authorities themselves responded to the potential bankruptcies of institutions with changes in accounting rules which redefined insolvent businesses as solvent.

A potential solution to the problem of asset and liability valuation might be to recognise that while markets are capable of fluctuating quite wildly on market sentiment, they have – over the long haul – shown themselves capable of meaningfully assessing asset valuations. Thus, we might propose the possibility of a formula that marks assets to the market's price determination over a set period prior to either an upturn or downturn that exceeds some allocated severity. This is, in fact, the recommendation of Walter Bagehot,[9] who, as far back as 1873 in his publica-tion *Lombard Street,* discussed how central banks should respond to crises, arguing that collateral should be valued by weighting panic and pre-panic prices.

Notes

1 For example, empirical work as far back as Douglas (1969) confirms that the average realised stock return is significantly related to the variance of the returns over time, but not to their covariance with the index of returns, thereby contradicting the CAPM. Douglas also summarises some of Lintner's unpublished results that also appear to be inconsistent with the CAPM (reported by Jensen, 1972). This work confirms that asset returns appear to be related to the idiosyncratic (non-market) volatility that is diversifiable.

2 Eugene Fama's contributions earned him a Nobel Prize for Economics in 2013. His co-recipients were Robert Shiller and Lars Peter Hansen.

3 Nevertheless, the model does not work entirely satisfactorily. As Fama and French (1996) concede, there are large negative unexplained returns on the stocks in their smallest size and lowest BE/ME quintile portfolios, and large positive unexplained returns for the stocks in the largest size and lowest BE/ME quintile portfolios.

4 See the section of the Commission's report on 'Moody's: "Given a Blank Check"', from p. 118.

5 Examples include "The Myth of the Rational Market" (2009) by Justin Fox, "The Crash of 2008 and What It Means" (2009) by legendary hedge fund manager George Soros, "A Failure of Capitalism: The Crisis of '08 and the Descent into Depression" (2009) by Richard Posner, and "After the Music Stopped: The Financial Crisis, The Response, and the Work Ahead" (2013) by Alan Blinder. There were also

several critiques of the EMH prior to the GFC. Notable examples are Shiller (2000) and Shleifer (2000); both books were published on the eve of the dot com crash.

6 Nocera, J., 'Poking Holes in a Theory of Markets', *New York Times* (5 June 2009), p. 1.

7 This slow movement of the financial system from stability to fragility, followed by crisis, means that we inevitably arrive at what has become known as a 'Minsky moment'. Similarly, the Asian tiger economies in the 1990s enjoyed the experience of high levels of debt fuelling a sense of wealth (escalating house prices, for example) and exuberance as the banks made possible ever higher debt levels to fund asset purchases (as opposed to new investments), up to point of unsustainability and collapse.

8 Bowing to political pressure from the Securities and Exchange Commission and Congress, on 10 October 2008 the FASB backed down from its more stringent FVA requirements by releasing Financial Accounting Standard 157-3, 'Determining the Fair Value of a Financial Asset When the Market for That Asset Is Not Active'. In this Statement, the FASB acknowledged that in circumstances of illiquid markets and distressed/forced asset sales, a reporting entity can use its assumptions determining future cash flows and appropriately risk-adjusted discount rates where appropriate.

9 Walter Bagehot was one of the earliest editors of *The Economist* (he was related to the newspaper's founder). Bagehot continues as the pen name of a weekly contribution in *The Economist*.

References

Ball, R. 2009. 'The Global Financial Crisis and the Efficient Market Hypothesis: What Have We Learned?' *Journal of Applied Corporate Finance*, vol. 21: 8–16.

Black, F. 1993. 'Beta and Return'. *The Journal of Portfolio Management*, vol. 20: 8–18.

Black, F., M. Jensen and M. Scholes. 1972. 'The Capital Asset Pricing Model: Some Empirical Tests'. In *Studies in the Theory of Capital Markets*. Praeger Publishers, New York.

Blinder, A. 2013. *After the Music Stopped: The Financial Crisis, The Response, and the Work Ahead*. Penguin, New York.

Carhart, M. M. 1997. 'On Persistence in Mutual Fund Performance'. *Journal of Finance*, vol. 52: 57–82.

Daniel, K. and S. Titman. 1997. 'Evidence on the Characteristics of Cross Sectional Variation in Stock Returns'. *Journal of Finance*, vol. 52: 1–33.

Douglas, G. 1969. 'Risk in the Equity Markets: An Empirical Appraisal of Market Efficiency'. *Yale Economic Essays*, vol. 9: 3–45.

Fama, E. 1976. *Foundations of Finance*. Basic Books, New York.

Fama, E. and K. French. 1992. 'The Cross-Section of Expected Stock Returns'. *Journal of Finance*, vol. 47: 427–466.

Fama, E. and K. French. 1993. 'Common Risk Factors in the Returns on Stocks and Bonds'. *Journal of Financial Economics*, vol. 33: 3–56.

Fama, E. and K. French. 1995. 'Size and Book-to-Market Factors in Earnings and Returns'. *Journal of Finance*, vol. 50: 131–155.

Fama, E. and K. French. 1996. 'Multifactor Explanations of Asset Pricing Anomalies'. *Journal of Finance*, vol. 51: 55–84.

Financial Crisis Inquiry Commission. January 2011. *Final Report of the National Commission on the Causes of the Financial and Economic Crisis in the United States*. US Government Printing Office, Washington.

Fox, J. 2009. *The Myth of the Rational Market: A History of Risk, Reward, and Delusion on Wall Street*. Harper Business, New York.

Huberman, G. and T. Regev. 2001. 'Contagious Speculation and a Cure for Cancer: A Nonevent that Made Stock Prices Soar'. *The Journal of Finance*, vol. 56: 387–396.

Jensen, M. C. 1972. 'The Foundations and Current State of Capital Market Theory'. In *Studies in the Theory of Capital Markets*. Praeger Publishers, New York.

Jensen, M. C. 1978. 'Some Anomalous Evidence Regarding Market Efficiency'. *Journal of Financial Economics*, vol. 6: 95–101.

Jones, S. and M. Peat. 2008. 'Credit Derivatives: Current Practices and Controversies'. In S. Jones and D. A. Hensher, editors, *Advances in Credit Risk Modelling and Corporate Bankruptcy Prediction*. Cambridge University Press, Cambridge.

Keynes, J. M. 1936. *General Theory of Employment Interest and Money*. Harcourt, New York.

Kuhn, T. 1962. *The Structure of Scientific Revolutions*. University of Chicago Press, Chicago.

Lakonishok, J., A. Shleifer and R. W. Vishny. 1994. 'Contrarian Investment, Extrapolation and Risk'. *Journal of Finance*, vol. 49: 1541–1578.

Lo, A. W. and M. T. Mueller. 2010. 'Warning: Physics Envy May be Hazardous to Your Health'. *Journal of Investment Management*, vol. 8: 13–63.

Mehrling, P. 2007. *Fisher Black and the Revolutionary Idea of Finance*. John Wiley and Sons, New Jersey.

Minsky, H. 1986. *Stabilizing an Unstable Economy*. Yale University Press. More recent: McGraw-Hill, New York.

Posner, R. A. 2009. *A Failure of Capitalism: The Crisis of '08 and the Descent into Depression*. Harvard University Press, Boston.

Shiller, R. J. 2000. *Irrational Exuberance*. Princeton University Press, Princeton.

Shleifer, A. 2000. *Inefficient Markets: An Introduction to Behavioral Finance*. Oxford University Press, New York.

Sornette, D. 2003. *Why Stock Markets Crash: Critical Events in Complex Financial Systems*. Princeton University Press, Princeton.

Soros, G. 2009. *The Crash of 2008 and What It Means: The New Paradigm for Financial Markets*. Perseus, New York.

18

Social theorisation of accounting

Challenges to positive research

*Trevor Hopper, Junaid Ashraf, Shahzad Uddin
and Danture Wickramasinghe*

Introduction

Trying to delineate the relevance of social theory (broadly defined as an attempt to explain and predict behaviour under certain circumstances) to accounting often provoke responses of despair. A common reaction is to state that accounting has no theory. This has foundation. Apart from those who argue that double entry book-keeping is a theory in itself (a view not shared by the authors, who see it as an equation), accounting lacks a unique theoretical basis. It is often taught and practised as techniques and systems created through trial and error and the experience and pragmatism of practitioners. However, techniques implicitly rest on theory, be it of causes and effects or an understanding of what clients want or need. Given the absence of a distinct accounting theory, one must turn to other social science disciplines to make sense of practices (Hopper and Powell, 1985; Sutton and Staw, 1995).

This invites the retort that accounting consists of practical techniques to resolve financial problems – hence theory is irrelevant. This view is unfortunately widely held, as an inspection of syllabuses for degrees and professional qualifications will reveal. This raises questions about the status of accounting knowledge. Theory is essential to understanding why, how and for whom accounting works. Without the underpinnings of a theory, accounting is little other than folk wisdom or 'magic', which renders its claims to constitute a corpus of knowledge warranting academic or professional status questionable (Smith, 1998; Sutton and Staw, 1995). The etymology of theory derives from 'truth': given that accounting aspires to 'true and fair' views, ignoring theory is perilous. Without theory it is difficult to design effective systems for regulation, accountability, decision making or control. For example, early engineers often over-compensated structures (and sometimes under-compensated with disastrous consequences), as engineering science then could not accurately calculate loads in advance. The lack of theory raises similar problems for accounting.

Another common response is that social theory is unnecessary because methods used in the physical sciences serve accounting well. Here the researcher is portrayed as a neutral and detached observer of an objective and external reality (Abbott, 2004). Knowledge is created by identifying key characteristics of empirical phenomena, measuring them, and through statistical techniques testing whether hypothesised associations, sometimes in causal chains, exist. The aim is to create a 'fact net' that mirrors reality and predicts outcomes. A popular area in accounting in this vein is testing market reactions to accounting announcements, but it is used extensively elsewhere. For example, contingency theory tries to link types of controls to environmental factors, whereas other researchers relate variations in accounting practices to national cultures (Chow et al., 1999; Otley, 1980). An extreme version of 'scientism' that dominates much accounting research is positive accounting theory. This claims to be descriptive, non-normative, and justified because its statistical empirical studies predict events (Watts and Zimmerman, 1978). Leaving aside claims by philosophers of science that this inaccurately reflects how much scientific discovery occurs, 'scientific' work within accounting has value. Our concern is that its claims to be exclusively the correct and appropriate means for theorising accounting fails to recognise that 'scientism' is an artefact (as are competing theories) and cannot deliver the universal truths it promises (Baxter and Chua, 2003; Chua, 1986; Hopper and Powell, 1985). The consequence is a stultifying denial of interesting and valuable alternative modes of inquiry.

The depiction of neutral, detached researchers in positive accounting theory, as elsewhere, is a myth. (This does not imply that researchers should not try to reduce bias or not follow established research protocols.) Human beings are inevitably subject to cognitive biases. Thus what we see and select for study and how we interpret results is mediated by personal and contextual factors (Alvesson and Karreman, 2011; Alvesson and Skoldberg, 2009). Moreover, reality is socially constructed through interaction with others and through communication mediums such as texts or the media. This gives rise to issues of power, ideologies, interpretation and meaning, and language (Boland, 1993). Claims to be merely descriptive are spurious. The problems, concepts and attributes to be studied must be chosen. Such decisions are clouded by issues of interests, language and culture and entail, even if unconsciously, normative judgements. Theory makes some things visible and potentially controllable, but it also renders other issues and parties invisible: it not only reflects particular understandings of the world but also creates them (Marshall, 1990). Given that the accounting profession has been granted status and privileges premised on its claims to serve the public interest, this cannot be ignored. For example, much accounting research and practice promotes the economic interests of investors but neglects the public interest. Its claims to be neutral and descriptive and its denial of other modes of inquiry open up allegations that it sustains the status quo and dominant world view at the expense of the views of employees, customers, or civil society (Hopper et al., 1987).

Much 'scientific' accounting research analyses static or short-run data. Often the meaning of its constructs is debatable and subject to interpretation, and the analysis can include contentious judgements, for example about causality or establishing 'outliers'. Often it is assumed that self-equilibrating economic equilibriums occur, oiled by accounting data. This may have some immediate validity, but it ignores major discontinuities stemming from social conflicts, economic crises, or technological change. Lastly, the depiction of human behaviour is overly deterministic: it is seen as a response to external forces or, occasionally, innate psychological properties. This denies the potential of human agency and choice (Hopper et al., 1987).

A frequent complaint is that accounting research employing social theory is difficult to understand and lacks practical application. Unfortunately, this can be so. However, given that the professional status and privileges of accountants rest on claims that they possess expertise beyond the comprehension of the layman, it is difficult to understand why accountants should expect their theory to be simple and immediately discernible – although better written and more accessible material would undoubtedly help. Given the youthfulness of social theory applications to accounting, its under-resourcing relative to other avenues of inquiry, and its challenge to prevailing interests and approaches, it is unsurprising that fruitful applications remain sparse. However, this need not be so.

Concerns about conventional theory have spurred some accounting researchers, largely from beyond the USA (where academic gatekeepers police and prohibit academics from pursuing research beyond a 'scientific' and often positivist paradigm), to investigate accounting through the lenses of social, sometimes critical, theories (Baxter and Chua, 2003). This chapter outlines the basis and achievements of work in this genre. Since constraints of space preclude a detailed and full exposition, the aim is to outline the main features as a prelude to deeper investigation by the reader should they so wish, which we hope they will. Work has been put into four categories according to the perceived commonality of central themes and potential contributions. The attribution of different (though arguably overlapping) theories to each category is undoubtedly cavalier: it cannot fully represent each theory and their differences, overlaps, achievements and potential. However, this formulation is offered as a heuristic device to assist further understanding and investigation.

The categories are the micro creation and interpretation of accounting; accounting discourses and text; the political economy of accounting; and institutional analyses. Each is examined with respect to its ontology (assumptions about how reality is constituted, and its form and nature); epistemology (beliefs about how knowledge is created); methodology (what tools and techniques should be applied to acquire knowledge); and its relevance to furthering socio–economic change and stability. To illustrate these facets and their relevance to accounting, a small number of studies within each category are drawn upon. Where possible, studies by the authors are used, not because they are the best but because they are familiar and we can trace their underlying assumptions, intentions and conclusions with more confidence. They are largely on management accounting, but the theories elucidated are relevant to financial accounting.

The micro creation and interpretation of accounting includes ethnographic, grounded, structuration, and social studies of science theories (Boland, 1993). Researchers normally conduct detailed case studies to establish how the form, meaning and employment of accounting systems and data are derived. They assume that common understandings of reality derive from our social interactions with others. These understandings may vary across time, space and persons. This belief that people actively construct the external world challenges conventional views that reality exists prior to and independent of the actors involved. It has provoked debates over how notions of an objective and subjective reality might be reconciled; for example, some have turned to the structuration theory of Giddens to resolve this (Roberts and Scapens, 1985). More recently, researchers have turned to studies in the sociology of science, especially actor network theory, which is suspicious of attempts to distinguish between levels of analysis, and the social and technical, to identify how accounting technologies and practices emerge.

In contrast to the above studies' focus on social interaction, postmodern (e.g. Derrida, 1978) and post-structural (e.g. Baudrillard, 1975; Foucault, 1972) research focus on discourses conveyed by texts, and how diverse subcultures and modern communications, often associated with consumerism and the media, relate to accounting. They are suspicious of claims that knowledge can be singular and emanates from a single source; rather, it is seen as relative, dispersed and pluralistic. This research seeks to demonstrate that any text, including accounting reports and academic papers, has multiple interpretations and relies on tautologies, self-referential logic and often paradoxical and contradictory circular reasoning. Their interest is in analysing not just what is *in* the text but also what it *excludes*. By subversively puncturing claims of texts purporting to represent the truth, they seek to enable the emergence of alternative explanations.

The theoretical approaches above are primarily inductive – theory is constructed bottom up from the data, whether textual or based on observations of social behaviour. They tend to focus on micro rather than macro analyses. In contrast, political economy and institutional theory research is more deductive, more inclined to examine events from a predetermined theoretical stance and to lay greater emphasis on macro analyses of structural factors, although micro activities are not ignored (Ashraf and Uddin, 2011).

Much work within political economy derives from or is influenced by Marxism, especially variants from its classical form. This approach tries to reveal how political and economic institutions within specific cultures and economic systems interact with and reproduce socio-economic outcomes, particularly regarding distributions of wealth and power. It critiques the accounting profession, relates accounting measurement to the creation of surplus value, and describes how systems seeking to extract effort from labour have been changed by conflicts and crises caused by labour and capital differences. Neo-Marxist approaches question the economic and political determinism of classical Marxism. Instead, greater attention is paid to ideology and culture and the contingent nature of political outcomes. In this vein, the work of Bourdieu has attracted much interest because economic capital is studied alongside social and cultural capital (Craib, 1992).

Theoretical debates about macro social theory often reflect differences between Marxist and Weberian approaches, but they are not invariably dichotomous. Institutional theory flows from Weber: it is less normative than Marxist work and more oriented towards determining how social consensus is reached rather than how social conflicts and contradictions wreak social transformations. Institutional theory rejects economic attributions of organisational forms to competitive pressures and efficiency. Whilst it is sympathetic to interpretive work attributing behaviour to shared cultures and beliefs, institutional theory emphasises how schemes, rules, norms and routines emanating from higher level organisations, such as government departments, competitors, and experts, govern the behaviour of organisations. A basic premise is that to survive, organisations must conform to prevailing external rules and beliefs rooted in cultures, politics and history. Institutional isomorphism (the process of conforming) gains legitimacy for the organisation and thence institutional support. Often this owes much to habit, coercion and mimicry rather than efficiency and competitiveness.

The micro creation and interpretation of accounting: interpretivism

An early interpretive study of accounting is that of the UK National Coal Board by Berry et al. (1985). The research team studied how and why managers constructed, interpreted and used accounting information. The aim was to understand accounting from the perspective of preparers and users. The ontology did not rest on a belief that accounting consisted of 'hard' visible and tangible facts independent of subjects, but rather on an assumption that accounting is socially constructed and is given meaning according to people's beliefs and claims, which are neither stable over time nor consistent across populations. However, knowledge is not random or without form: patterns or structures, sometimes enduring, are created and sustained during personal interactions. Hence, considerable time was spent not only interviewing managers but also observing workers and supervisors at and returning from the coal face and above ground in control rooms and during accountability meetings. No prior hypotheses were made; instead, rich descriptions and explanations were built bottom up using qualitative coding methods (Straus and Corbin, 1990).

They found that collieries were profit centres formally controlled through budgets that fed an accountability system from the pit, through the region, and ultimately to the headquarters (HQ) in London. Senior managers at HQ emphasised financial criteria when discussing results with regional managers, but elsewhere, accounting data were little used and viewed with suspicion. Why was this so? First, mines dominated local communities that were often relatively isolated and notoriously close and cohesive. Even managers, normally mining engineers, often came from mining families, lived alongside miners, and expected to work in the Coal Board for life, since it was a nationalised monopoly. A strong mining culture emphasised production, technology and safety rather than profits. Secondly, financial forecasting was notoriously fraught because of the uncertainties attached to estimating future workable coal reserves, the cost of extracting them, and volatile world coal prices. There was a widespread belief that short-run financial plans and reports (relying heavily on arbitrary apportionments of costs and revenues at pit level and beyond) were unreliable guides for decisions about the scale and location of future mining. The worry was that external agents, such as government ministers and civil servants, would see financial data as objective and reliable and would make incorrect decisions if they relied on it. Decisions therefore prioritised engineering and physical criteria over financial ones; that is, accounting became decoupled from operations. Accounts were deliberately 'smoothed' to reinforce an appearance of financial continuity and stability and to protect the industry from unwarranted and possibly erroneous external interventions. Formally, future budgets and budget achievements were a cornerstone of accountability, but they were adapted to the mining engineers' management culture. In deep mines, management cannot observe operations and the geology can be complex and uncertain, so managers must rely on information transmitted upwards. A central tenet of management was 'the need to know'; managers must be well informed about operations by whatever means necessary. Hence, budgets were not interrogated in accountability meetings to assess performance; rather, superiors would seize upon details to test whether subordinates had a detailed knowledge of operations and whether their information was reliable and had been cross-checked.

What does such work contribute to the theory and practice of accounting? First, it shows how community, industry and occupational cultures influence perceptions of the social and economic value of accounting information, its construction, and the meanings attached to it, which may be at odds with the rational and technical depiction in textbooks. In the National Coal Board study, meanings attached to accounting were derived during socialisation into occupational groups and during social interactions with colleagues. Second, technical accounting representations of activities rest on subjective and arbitrary choices. Those with agency and power may influence these choices according to their interests and shared beliefs. The aura of objectivity and neutrality often attached to accounting data may be mythical – not least when applied to highly uncertain future decisions – and may be only marginally relevant to managing immediate operations.

Such interpretive work emphasises the cultural interpretations of accounts. However, scant attention is paid to how accounting systems are created. Actor network theory (ANT) has become prominent in efforts to understand this phenomenon. We use two papers to illustrate this theory: Quattrone and Hopper (2005) and Hopper et al. (2008). The first study analyses implementations of Enterprise Resource Planning systems (ERPs), namely SAP, in two large multinational organisations (MNOs), Japanese and USA owned. The second examines how consultants helped a UK quasi-governmental regional development agency, the North West Training and Education Council (NWTEC), create and apply a training programme for small and medium sized businesses (SMEs) based on World Class Manufacturing (WCM) principles. Special attention was paid to accounting.

ANT traces how scientific achievements and artefacts are (or are not) realised. Machines, scientific discoveries and, likewise, accounting systems are not presumed to evolve in a linear, deterministic manner but are posited to be a product of contingent, socially negotiated processes of knowledge creation. ANT opens up the 'black box' of technology to show how it evolves within a network of actors (or actants) that can include governments, technologies, prior knowledge, money and people. Ontologically, ANT is 'flat': it does not construct 'nested' hierarchical structures akin to 'Russian dolls' (e.g. individuals embedded in groups embedded in organisations embedded in society). Each actor may have influence, though some prove more powerful than others. Thus in the ERP study, local managers and computer technicians were as significant as senior managers at HQ, and in the WCM research, consultants and council managers were not subordinate to national government officials. ANT is similar to social constructivist or interpretive approaches[1] in that it sees knowledge as created in social processes, but it places greater focus on outcomes (e.g. the design of a machine or accounting system) and attendant practices rather than subjective beliefs. A major ontological feature of ANT is its contentious claim that technologies are actants, while critics argue that inanimate objects cannot influence translations without human intermediation. The claim of ANT about the impact of technologies gives it an element of realism beyond interpretive theory. In the USA company, SAP initially reconfigured time (e.g. real-time rather than periodic results) and space (porous rather than clear boundaries around subsidiaries), but its impact upon control brought local modifications incorporating Excel spread-sheets, which frustrated the desire of HQ to gain greater central control.

Translation, which covers how actors exercise authority over and cooperate with other elements in a network, how issues are problematised, getting others to recognise this (interessement), enrolling and mobilising allies, and mediation of means and ends to keep the project alive, is central to ANT epistemology. Technologies are not necessarily stable; they may fail or be resisted, modified or replaced because networks are dynamic and porous. New or discarded actors, whether people or technologies, may enter and effect changes. Thus in the USA company in the ERP study, HQ managers initially saw SAP as a real-time integrated information system that would reinforce a coordinated global strategy and enable the centre to control its global operations. However, the implementation proved chaotic, and local managers no longer felt in control because the new system eliminated distances between them and HQ and destroyed previous conventional accounting controls that had distinguished between the controller and those controlled. Accounting data often failed to meet local needs, and multiple postings of data within and without the subsidiary could create unexpected results. Consequently, local managers adapted SAP by incorporating other technologies and restricting postings. This frustrated the centralised, real-time control sought by HQ. Instead, multiple changing loci of control and perceptions of reduced accountability emerged. Visibility and control relied on accounting inscriptions and translations that were never complete. In contrast, the Japanese MNO did not use ERP to globally integrate activities. It helped implement some best practices, but it left hierarchical controls with gaps for local discretion intact. Thus it reproduced previous structures of time and distance by retaining conventional accounting controls, and changes towards more integrated information systems were incremental, consensual and gradual. For example, subsidiaries ran parallel information systems alongside SAP. The results cast doubt on common beliefs that ERP systems invariably enhance integration, real-time communications and centralised control; implementation was not a straightforward application of 'off the shelf' systems but involved unpredictable and contingent processes of choice and translation.

Likewise, in the WCM study, concepts like WCM, accounting and competiveness were products of translation within complex and extended networks. The ANT concept of 'boundary objects' (this occurs when concepts lacking consistent definition amongst actors become the focus of translation and mediation within the network and thence labels for practices) became apparent. For example, the concept of WCM varied across actors and sites: consultants created it from previous formulations by others (which often varied) and added fashionable accounting systems like activity-based costing (despite original formulations of WCM seeing accounting as anathema) to enrol other consultants and potential clients. After initial WCM training for local SMEs, NWTEC and the consultants secured central government funding for further interventions by linking WCM to national 'competitiveness' programmes for British industry. The government department's delineation of competitiveness embraced programmes advocated by other ministries to gain their support, and during implementation, each SME translated WCM differently and sometimes at odds to NWTEC's WCM principles. (For example, some adopted activity-based costing, but in others institution of WCM amounted to little more than the use of conventional, traditional accounting controls.) We are often sceptical of poorly or inconsistently defined concepts, but boundary objects like WCM, accounting and competiveness provided a focus for discourse and were sufficiently flexible in concept and practice to retain allies. Rigid definition of technologies may render them defunct because they may be unable to be modified to gain support.

ANT research methods are similar to those of interpretative theory, especially ANT's mantra of 'follow the network'. This is the employment of cascading research methods to identify how processes between various actors, resources, knowledge and technologies shape the object under consideration and associated practices. It constructs events and explanations bottom up. For example, ANT makes no prior delineation of networks, which can bring interesting and surprising results. In the WCM research, for example, the research question unexpectedly switched from assessing the effectiveness of WCM in local SMEs to 'How did WCM reach a small engineering shop in the backstreets of Bolton?' However, like much ANT research, the data analysis was relatively unsystematic compared to the protocols of interpretive research employing coding.

So what does such work contribute to the theory and practice of accounting? Interpretive work concentrates on identifying people's shared understanding and meanings attributed to accounting systems but tends to ignore how they are constructed. We are taught that accounting systems are given techniques built on a series of principles and rules, and therefore they are relatively determinate and fixed. ANT challenges this view by illustrating that technologies are inherently unstable and are a product of complex processes of translation within extended networks, not only of people and organisations but also of other technologies, money and knowledge. Accounting rules and principles are not irrelevant but are potentially just one amongst many potential actors. How a system evolves is contingent, unpredictable and dynamic – there is no endpoint. ANT views systems as a set of practices rather than as faithful applications of predetermined blueprints and official manuals. The practice of accounting thus becomes the object of study. Those involved in designing and implementing systems can learn much from ANT.

Accounting discourse and texts: post-structuralism

As Hopper et al. (1995) show using dialectical critique, the privileging of positive accounting theory and the exclusion of alternative theories by important gatekeepers such as editors and deans maintains a market-based hegemony in accounting. Some researchers with similar concerns have turned to postmodern (c.f. Derrida) and post-structural (c.f. Foucault and Baudrillard, *inter alia*) theories that challenge the modernism that emerged in Western Enlightenment thought of the seventeenth and eighteenth centuries and continues today. Modernism spawns singular, grand narratives of history rooted in notions of progress through science, be they class-based narratives as in Marxism or market-based as in neo-classical economics. Postmodernists are sceptical of this idea and endeavour to puncture grand narratives, whether about the arts, politics or the economy. Their ontology rejects models of reason founded on social unity and cohesion and models that construct realities based on universal relations within markets or between classes or national cultures. They see society as fragmented, localised, contingent and multifaceted. Rather than examining how, say, networks or social interaction produce meanings, systems and practices, they explore how diverse texts, languages and discourse associated with subcultures, modern communications, consumerism and the media construct localised perceptions of reality. Accounting is seen as a textual practice that affects meanings and behaviour at increasingly diverse and fragmented micro levels of society rather than reproducing social (class) or market relations. Grand theorisations of how and why accounting policies emerge are avoided.

Jacques Derrida (1978) subverts mainstream approaches to knowledge advancement and tries to create intellectual space to question them. He argues that the world is governed by texts which can be deconstructed to question their fundamental reasoning and reveal alternative meanings inside and outside the texts. Derrida's desire is to deconstruct frameworks, especially those that privilege a single version of truth. Within this ontology, accounting cannot represent a universal truth: its language is disordered and unstable because different contexts give rise to different meanings and practices.

Arrington and Francis (1989), pioneers of textual and discourse analysis of accounting, reject beliefs in 'objective knowledge' grounded in either positivism's faith in observation and scientific methods or Marxist historical determinism. Instead, they argue that rhetoric and language bolsters a particular political creed. They use Derrida's 'deconstruction' principles to analyse Jensen's (1983) positivistic accounting 'text', 'Organization Theory and Methodology', to show how its claim to a value-free epistemology based on 'scientifically' testing hypotheses using descriptive data privileges positive accounting theory ontologically and dismisses alternative notions of reality contingent upon human consciousness or situations, events and circumstances. Arrington and Francis demonstrate how Jensen's arguments rely on linguistic and rhetorical devices that in turn rely on particular values or moral codes and, ultimately, tautologies. The work violates the premises upon which it rests. It is as normative as the work it decries.

Post-structuralists deny that accounting (systems) follow universally accepted laws that predict outcomes; rather, they claim that they can be deconstructed to reveal how they are contextually determined. For example, Malaysia adopted universal corporate governance codes recommended in the Cadbury Report, but closer textual analysis reveals how practices were bounded by local ethnic politics, especially *Bumiputera* political ideology (Yusof et al., 2013). Graves et al. (1996) concentrate on accounting as signs, claiming that information and design technologies now dominate the business world. US accounting reports may report numbers, but they also incorporate aesthetic visual designs that anesthetise any material reality represented by the numbers and accounting policies. These authors argue that colour pictures, gloss, novelty formats and television media technologies construct an alternative visual reality and 'truth claims' that mask business functions and generate legitimacy for corporations.

Baudrillard (1975) advocates an ontology (a 'code of production') similar to that of Derrida and Foucault. He focuses on how signs and systems generated by electronic media, information processing, computers and cybernetic models dominate our understanding. Baudrillard sees the modern world as operating in a hyper-reality where time and space implode and texts produced by electronic mediums no longer reflect material or economic reality. Some researchers claim that accounting is similar in that it no longer represents material or economic realities but rather produces signs that become organising principles of contemporary society (Graham, 2008). Macintosh et al. (2000) argue that accounting income and capital have become free floating signs representing a hyperreal global financial economy that exists only as an abstraction. For example, the accounting sign of capital is nothing but 'the capacity to earn the current market rate of return' (International Accounting Standards Committee, 1997, p. 128, cited in Macintosh et al., 2000), and accounting policy that endeavours to construct concepts that represent truth or fair value are doomed to fail. Graham (2008) also examines accounting signs, claiming that accounting numbers, though merely textual images, are powerful in contemporary societies. For example, pension accounting signs, widely used by investors, creditors and government agencies, blur the boundaries between the private and the public, the legal identity of organisations, and the actual functioning of their supply chains.

Michel Foucault also emphasises the importance of texts, discourses and local circumstances for understanding power and control. However, his ontology emphasises how thought and knowledge systems ('epistemes' or 'discursive formations') governed by rules (beyond those of grammar and logic) delineate thought at particular locations or times. Power-knowledge patterns ('genealogies of knowledge') determine what people believe is right and wrong, what is possible, and, ultimately, how they unconsciously discipline themselves. Power is everywhere: it does not emanate from a particular point or person or creed, but originates in mundane, taken-for-granted local practices best studied through archaeological methods that identify 'a set of rules of formation that determine the conditions of possibility' (Foucault, 1972).

Hoskin and Macve (1986, 1994) utilise Foucault's genealogical ontology and archaeological epistemology to link rational accounting calculations and controls, such as budgets and performance measurement, to educational developments. For example, in the late eighteenth century, examinations that assessed and ranked West Point Military Academy cadets in the USA rendered them calculable by numerically scoring their academic attainments, information which was used to assess future performance. West Point graduates filled many senior accounting positions in leading US companies where they developed similar management controls, for example in railroad companies (Chandler, 1977) and the Springfield Armory, the primary manufacturer of US military firearms since 1777. Today, such disciplinary practices are evident in surveillance techniques such as budgeting and Balanced Scorecards, which provide information about outlying subordinates that enables HQ to maintain control despite being distant from operations. For example, Hopper and Macintosh (1993) trace how the CEO of a large US conglomerate created penal management controls akin to Foucault's delineation of panopticon controls to discipline and render managers obedient. At the time, this was lauded by financial markets as a model management system.

Miller and O'Leary (1987) attribute standard costing's emergence in the USA to discourses of progress prominent in political debates on stemming national decline and labour–capital conflicts in the early twentieth century. They argue that standard costing's language of variances, based on 'scientifically' determined performance measures of 'efficiency', 'normalised' people as passive, programmed and atomised individuals. The rise of standard costing was related to an 'Efficiency Movement' that incorporated proposals for the rational, scientific study of the social, which spawned social programmes such as work study, mental testing and eugenics. Miller and O'Leary's (1993, 1994) Foucauldian study of Caterpillar's Decatur, Illinois, plant examines how economic and political discourses in the 1980s re-conceived the worker as an 'economic citizen' of the corporation and the nation. Caterpillar was problematised (by senior management) as unprofitable and internationally uncompetitive, and its problems were attributed to traditional accounting methods such as overhead recovery rates and discounted cash flow. They invested in technology and adopted WCM techniques focusing on product quality, re-conceptions of the customer, cellular manufacture, just-in-time production and electronically coordinated supply chains. These brought new financial representations and calculations, such as activity-based costing, value-added analysis of supply chains, customer costing, predictive costing and investment bundling, which Miller and O'Leary claim created new forms of visibility and governance. Work cells financially reproduced production activities as a chain of customers serving one another, thereby creating a 'myriad of little businesses'. Each cell became a calculable space monitored against targets for costs, quality and throughput, benchmarked against best practice levels. Workgroups had to continuously reduce costs and improve operations and products; that is, they became 'cell proprietors'. This group-based individualism tapping workers' intellectual and manual skills was portrayed as reinforcing American ideals of entrepreneurship, involvement, equality and progress. Miller and O'Leary saw the managerial discourse of economic citizenship as inverting organisational hierarchies and increasing accountability to customers (see also Vaivio, 1999).

The research described in this section rejects claims that a single unitary reality can be identified. Rather, multiple 'realities' contained in texts and discourse exist, though not all receive equal prominence. The epistemological implication of this ontology is that accounting practices and accounting reports are discursive practices governed by texts or discourses that produce 'a particular truth' as opposed to 'the universal truth' in grand meta-theorisations. They re-read accounting texts to reveal how their language and discourse contain 'incoherence', 'fluidity', 'fragmentation', 'discontinuity' and 'contradictions' as circumstances change (Cooper and Burrell, 1988). Foucauldian analyses are often historical inquiries utilising archaeological and genealogical methods, which differ radically from traditional historical archival methods seeking cause and effect relationships. Instead they study texts, documents, statements, archives and life stories to illustrate how accounting produces surveillance, discipline and controls associated with particular knowledge and power relations. The analysis is often literary. Critics find that their failure to adopt conventional historical methods renders their findings unconvincing or sometimes just wrong.

Post-structural research provides a fresh view on accounting masked by conventional accounting research that depicts it as essentially independent and technical. Instead it reveals how accounting creates and sustains particular images of the world and reproduces knowledge that unconsciously entraps individuals. In this regard, post-structural approaches are similar to interpretive ones, but the former emphasises analyses of accounting texts and language rather than observing how meanings of accounting are socially constructed and then acted upon. Post-structural approaches reveal how accounting constitutes a disciplinary practice embedded in taken-for-granted knowledge systems that render people governable, and they question 'truth' claims produced by the accounting profession or accounting procedures.

Critics argue, however, that post-structural theories, and Foucauldian ones in particular, neglect the role of resistance, depict power-knowledge systems as totalising and unconsciously accepted, are unduly pessimistic about the possibilities of enacting reform, and are reluctant to make normative recommendations beyond the need to promote debate. They accuse these practitioners of relativism (i.e. anything goes). If material truth claims cannot be produced by 'postmodern' accounting, then should critical researchers abandon accounting policy-making efforts? Should we see the accounting world as governed by texts, rhetoric, discourses, signs and design technologies and abandon conventional modes of operation in accounting education and professional training? Post-structuralists would respond by arguing that deconstruction of texts and discourse reveals what actually accounting does, assumes and reproduces as a prelude to developing alternative accounting policies more congruent with the public interest. Although the criteria and narratives cannot be ultimately proven, this approach facilitates informed choice rather than imposed solutions.

Post-structural research in accounting is growing, possibly because of growing academic and popular disbelief in totalising political ideologies, the replacement of class allegiances with fragmented social groupings associated with particular lifestyles, and the growing influence of images in the media, corporate reports and new information technology mediums over shared work, family and community experiences. Considering these changes, more emphasis on knowledge creation, language and discourse is necessary and understandable. However, political economy researchers criticise such work for neglecting structural and wider issues such as class analysis, economic conditions and resistance. For example, see critiques of the Caterpillar studies (Arnold, 1998; Froud et al., 1998). If the ontology of post-structuralism cannot capture all aspects of accounting controls in action, then it may need to be supplemented by a political economy approach (Hopper and Macintosh, 1993).

Political economy of accounting

Political economies of accounting draw largely but not exclusively on Marxist ideas. Their central theme is how accounting practices create and perpetuate inequality by enabling a privileged capitalist class to exploit labour and expand and globalise capital accumulation. In classical Marxism, human actions and institutions are economically determined: declining rates of profits and inherent socio-economic contradictions will precipitate class struggle and, eventually, the superseding of capitalism by communism. This deterministic ontology and realist 'scientific' epistemology has been heavily criticised for its predictions not materialising, its depictions of class identity no longer being valid, and its underestimation of capitalism's capacity, aided by the state, to cope with crises. Classical Marxism, however, does not ignore subjectivity: ideology and consciousness are seen to be in a dialectic relationship with the socio-economic superstructure. More recent neo-Marxist work, including that of the Frankfurt School (Habermas, 1968, 1979), labour process theory (Braverman, 1974; Burawoy, 1979), and Gramsci (2001) on hegemony and civil society, is less deterministic, sceptical of a socialist endpoint, and more attendant to individual agency, but it remains critical of capitalism and inequality. Such work often employs interpretive research methods to identify how worker resistance, subjectivity and identity, contingent factors, and developments within firms are central to accounting changes and practices. However, such micro analyses cannot reveal how they are also linked to the international division of labour and global restructuring, such as when production is shifted to low-wage cost economies, for example.

An early Marxist study, Tinker (1980), relates accounting measurement to the creation of surplus value and socio-economic conflicts and crises, and it questions the validity of neo-classical economic theorising about capital and profit distribution. His alternative analysis of a mining company in Sierra Leone links changing strategies of corporate capital accumulation to socio-economic and historical contingencies. Cooper and Sherer (1984) claim that accounting is a technology of mystification reflective of a capitalist mode of production and state policies that sustain labour exploitation, capital accumulation and, ultimately, unequal wealth distribution and social inequality. Important Marxist analyses of accounting measurement and income determination have subsequently been conducted by Bryer (2006, 2012) and Toms (2010).

Peter Armstrong (1985), a leading Marxist accounting scholar, claims that the dominance of accounting controls in UK firms was not merely capitalists' response to failures of engineering controls associated with Scientific Management, but was a product of interprofessional rivalries amongst engineers, personnel managers and accountants to provide capital with techniques to control labour. The success of UK accountants and the power of the UK accounting profession are attributed to their appropriation of an abstract body of (engineering) knowledge and making it more congruent with capitalist interests. Armstrong argues that accounting controls were influential in Britain because they endorsed the favoured British mode for extracting and appropriating surplus value, but the dominance of accountants and accounting techniques was not inevitable – in Germany, for example, engineers were more powerful. Armstrong (1987) attributed the pre-eminence of accountants and financial control in British companies to the British capital market's stress on audits. This established a power base from which the accounting profession could sponsor its preferred modes of internal control. State intervention during World War II favoured financial controls because they avoided direct industrial intervention and helped maintain *laissez faire* capitalism. This and widespread mergers further strengthened the position of accountant.

Many contemporary political economy analyses of accounting take issue with classical Marxism's economic determinism and focus more on ideology/hegemony, culture, individual agency and subjectivity, and contingent political outcomes. Three studies of the authors that pursue more sociological approaches to political economy illustrate this. Hopper and Armstrong (1991) and Uddin and Hopper (2001) adopt a labour process theory approach, and the third (Wickramasinghe and Hopper, 2005), a (cultural) political economy approach. All examine how accounting practices at the point of production are linked not only to power, societal institutions (notably the state) and conflicts over economic surplus, but also to local cultures and organisational dynamics. They try to link micro processes of control to broader socio-economic factors.

Hopper and Armstrong (1991) apply labour process theory from Braverman (1974) to trace the development of controls and cost accounting in USA corporations, starting from subcontracting in the nineteenth century to direct controls by foremen to the large-scale multi-division bureaucracies of today. They question Johnson and Kaplan's (1987) history of management accounting in the USA. Drawing from labour history, they argue that accounting techniques and calculations were not driven by economic or technological imperatives but were rooted in labour–capital struggles associated with different strategies by firms to control labour in various epochs of capitalistic development. For example, cost accounting developments helped destroy internal subcontracting and craft control in early factories.

Uddin and Hopper (2001) and Wickramasinghe and Hopper (2005) explore why management accounting controls changed in a Bangladeshi and a Sri Lankan company. Given the ontological desire to combine how modes of production relate to controls of labour processes, and the influence of the state and transnational financial institutions on local actors' agency, indigenous culture and historical context, the research methods were based on an interpretive epistemology within a political economy framework.

Uddin and Hopper (2001) found that controls were the outcome of production and state politics. Nationalisation of firms after independence marked state attempts to manufacture consent by constructing a modern democratic state based on socialism, central planning, rational-legal governance, bureaucracy and recognised trade unions, but in practice control was secured by political interventions, often at the behest of trade unions, for party political rather than commercial ends. Comprehensive accounting systems for control and accountability were maintained but became marginal, ritualistic and decoupled from operations. Economic crises led external financial agencies, especially the World Bank, to advocate and finance wholesale privatisations, including that of the firm studied. Controls over labour became coercive when an indigenous family bought the company. In their haste to privatise, governments and advisory bodies paid insufficient attention to creating effective regulatory structures and open, transparent capital markets. Thus, majority shareholders could operate relatively unfettered and ignore statutory rules on auditing, annual reports, accountability to shareholders and taxation. Financial information became a prerogative of the family rather than of market players. Little consideration was paid to protecting workers, and the new owners could thus abandon previous labour agreements negotiated by trade unions and reduce wages and benefits, segment labour markets, make redundancies and introduce coercive controls.

Wickramasinghe and Hopper (2005) identify how cultural and political factors shaped budgeting in a Sri Lankan textile mill. Imported Western management accounting controls repeatedly tried to reproduce capitalist modes of production in the mill, which was situated in a village habituated to a traditional culture and a non-capitalist mode of production. Repeated attempts by governments to introduce modern financial controls to meet financier demands and market pressures failed due to complex interactions between state organs, political ideologies, trade unions, ethnic divisions, local culture and internal organisational dynamics. Employees from the village were normally passive, but there was little internalisation of capitalist values of efficiency and improvement. Because real incomes increased little, workers remained antagonistic to the management controls that they believed threatened their 'way of life'. The workers' ethnocentrism was difficult for senior, non-local management to appreciate, as workers invariably presented a respectful, co-operative face in their presence whilst behaving differently when outside their gaze. Class, ethnic and cultural differences between senior managers and shop floor operators prevented problems from being addressed bottom up, whilst local managers from a similar cultural background as the workers often sympathised with local grievances. For over forty years, waves of rational budgeting initiatives failed to penetrate to the shop floor or eradicate non-capitalist beliefs and behaviour. Each initiative was eventually relaxed to allow managers to incorporate slack to buffer workers against budget pressures and enable them to fulfil traditional village obligations. Despite the government changing policies and bringing in new managers and owners, budgets failed to establish themselves as meaningful forms of control at any level. The mill eventually went bankrupt after new foreign owners disappeared, taking much of the new machinery, funded by state banks, with them.

Both papers examine how management accounting control practices changed as material structural conditions altered (e.g. from politicised state capitalism to politicised market capitalism). They also note how labour resistance, political interventions and, in the Sri Lankan case, local culture affected controls. The cases helped the authors build a typology of how and why management accounting controls are enacted and diffused in developing countries based on close observation of practices but linked to broader structural factors including markets, international financial institutions and political regimes (Hopper et al., 2009). Following colonialism, newly independent countries imported idealised regimes of control, initially through state central planning and then through market-based mechanisms that ended up reinforcing politically despotic regimes. The expectations of accounting reformers failed to materialise because of indigenous politics and neo-patrimonial leadership.

What does such work contribute to the theory and practice of accounting? Importantly, it critiques accounting controls from the perspective of labour and civil society and reveals how accounting is implicated in political struggles. Accounting reports do not impartially mirror economic events: they reproduce and legitimise dominant power relations in society. Political economy research explicitly adopts a normative stance by advocating reforms to coercive controls and governance. Like post-structuralism, political economy research endeavours to make 'hidden scripts' of accounting and governance 'public' in order to precipitate debate and critical reflection and trigger policy and accounting reforms for the establishment of a fairer society with more participative and collaborative forms of social accountability. This is not an abstract aspiration. For example, development programs in poor countries by non-governmental organisations and aid providers now often promote greater civil society involvement through new forms of accountability and governance to induce redistributions of wealth and power. Hopefully, managers and researchers habituated to operating in the interest of capital can develop more flexible and bottom-up management controls that empower the grassroots; are more humane and flexible; and diminish undue bureaucracy, hierarchical subordination and exploitation. Proponents of 'beyond budgeting', participative budgeting, flexible organisation and empowerment of the grassroots can learn from political economy accounting research.

Unlike interpretive and post-structural research, political economy research contains a broader historical meta-narrative of events within a normative stance which is primarily but not exclusively materialistic. Its ontology is different. Issues of language, discourse and social creation of meaning are not ignored, but social interactions and texts are not the principal objects of study. The emphasis is on macro rather than micro studies; single rather than multiple narratives; materialism and realism over subjectivity, discourse and language; and normative judgments over relativism. However, like post-structuralism, it seeks self-determination of controls after informed debate and dialogue.

Institutional theory research in accounting

Institutional theory, which also researches accounting in a macro context, has three strands: new institutional economics based on the transaction cost theory of Williamson (not examined here); new institutional sociology (NIS); and old institutional economics (OIE) (Roberts and Scapens, 1985). NIS examines how institutions are created, sustained and diffused (creating social objects is institutionalisation, and the end products are institutions). Meyer and Rowan (1977) and DiMaggio and Powell (1983) link the work of post–World War Two institutional sociologists on how the social and political milieu shapes local events to how organisations gain legitimacy by responding to prevalent social beliefs. It extends the subjective ontology of interpretive theory to a societal and organisational level and creates a distinct theory that challenges individualistic and materialistic neo-classical economic theories. Rather than attributing organisational practices and structures to efficiency and competition, NIS argues that they are responses to rules, beliefs and conventions within their social and political environment; that is, institutional forces, including myths, educational and professional knowledge, public opinion and the law shape practices. Organisations must comply to be judged as successful, gain resources, and ultimately survive.

The quest for legitimacy drives behaviour: organisations become isomorphic with external institutional environments (an isomorphism is a 'constraining process that forces one unit in a population to resemble other units that face the same set of environmental conditions' (Powell and DiMaggio, 1991, p. 66). Three 'pillars' of institutional order – regulative, normative and cultural-cognitive – are associated with coercive, normative and mimetic isomorphisms. The *regulative* pillar encompasses rules ranging from informal customs to formal systems of *coercive isomorphism*, often exercised through state laws and sanctions. This promotes organisational convergence. The *normative* pillar defines goals and appropriate means of attaining them. *Normative isomorphism* occurs when institutions with moral legitimacy, especially educational and professional ones, make pronouncements perceived as binding social obligations – recommendations by professional accounting bodies, for example. The *cultural-cognitive* pillar rests on common beliefs and logics of action. Here, behaviour is mimetic: taken-for-granted understandings, often unconscious, give structure, meaning and predictability to human life. *Mimetic isomorphism* is driven by imitation, particularly when, for example, uncertainties abound and businesses adopt techniques with widespread cultural support and copy successful companies. Thus NIS identifies how organisations gain legitimacy by complying with legal sanctions, moral obligations and cultural expectations. A recent interest in path dependency argues that organisations often follow solutions and paths that appeared to work in the past. Case studies and other qualitative research methods are often preferred by NIS researchers, though quantitative contributions are not precluded.

Some accounting researchers have analysed how the accounting choices of organisations are strategic responses to institutional pressures and the interests of powerful agents. For example,

Carpenter and Feroz (2001) examined how institutional pressures influenced the adoption of generally accepted accounting principles (GAAP) in financial reporting by four US state governments. The institutional factors were conditioned by the financial position of the states, professional acclimatisation of decision makers, and interests of key agents. States that resisted early GAAP adoption had a strong financial position and their bureaucrats were less exposed to professional associations promoting GAAP, while states where key decision makers' interests were threatened were also more likely to resist early adoption. Agents confronting strong institutional pressures pursued different strategies, illustrating that institutional actors negotiating within institutional environments can be proactive. The study reveals that decisions are not a function of economic considerations alone but an outcome of the prevailing economic and institutional environment and institutionalised beliefs. Agents with different cognitive and normative beliefs based on their exposure to different institutional pressures (training, membership in professional associations, etc.) must interpret and reconcile these factors. Adopting accounting principles is therefore a 'complicated' phenomenon affected by the historical, economic and social pressures confronting decision makers.

Some accounting researchers have kept pace with advancements in institutional theory, but there is a need for more pro-activity here (Lounsbury, 2008). NIS research, especially in accounting, has traditionally concentrated on how external pressures upon organisations influence accounting choices. However, much contemporary work incorporates internal factors; conflict, not just compliance; issues of power and change; normative judgements; and creative ways actors not only respond to but also shape the institutional environment. A more nuanced and sophisticated analysis of institutional environments and how actors manage conflicting expectations of multiple institutions is an important area of contemporary accounting research (Greenwood et al., 2011). Examining this work is beyond the scope of this chapter, but an illustration is Greenwood and Suddaby's (2006) analysis of how Canadian accounting firms changed the institutions in which they were embedded. Specialist accounting firms became multidisciplinary practices providing multiple services spanning various professions, especially law, accounting and consulting, despite the disapproval of the local institutional environment in Canada (the accounting profession and local regulators). 'Big Five' accounting firms championed the change, and their size enabled them to challenge institutions and expose them to alternative ideas about organisational forms. During the 1980s and 1990s, economic pressures and the demands of large international clients forced Big Five accounting firms to become large international entities, and their institutional environment became different from that of smaller accounting firms. The Big Five firms and their large clients now look to each other for legitimacy cues rather than to the 'local profession', and their strong financial power enables them to create multidisciplinary practices. The paper explains how elite players at the centre of an institutional field rather than at the peripheries can bring about institutional change.

Nevertheless, NIS has neglected change, agency and factors within organisations. OIE focuses on such matters. Concepts of value and the interest-laden nature of organisational routines are used to explain stability and changes in accounting rules and practices. The most cited example lies in Burns and Scapens (2000), which derives its basic assumptions and methods from the philosophy of economic pragmatism associated with economists like Veblen and Commons. Burns and Scapens model how an organisation's accounting practices (formal and informal) become institutionalised over time, or how they become taken-for-granted institutionalised routines shaped by and shaping organisational members' actions. They explicitly recognise the role of power and conflict vis-à-vis these routines, noting that organisational actors with hierarchical powers can introduce accounting routines. Less powerful organisational actors may resist the routines, but the continuous re-enactment of accounting routines may inhibit attempts to modify them. Radical change in institutionalised practices occurs when there is a shock, either internal or external, which makes organisational members question taken-for-granted institutionalised practices. Losing a major client or a source of revenue are examples of external shocks, and rifts between groups within an organisation or a new managerial regime are examples of internal shocks. Incremental changes in accounting routines are attributed to the inquisitive nature of humans: their innovations can tacitly and unintentionally alter organisational routines when consistently enacted. Stability and change are therefore endemic to social systems and organisations.

Burns (2000) illustrates this in an exploration of accounting change in the product development department of a small chemicals manufacturer in Northern England. Following a cash flow crisis, the managing director (MD) and sympathetic departmental managers developed 'results-orientated' controls based on routines stemming from new accounting practices. Crises over loss of customers and liquidity led staff to accept and implement these financial practices – that is, they were institutionalised. However, they did not penetrate the physically and culturally distant product development department that still pursued scientific rather than commercial results. The MD imposed the results-based systems there by exerting the power of his office over the head of product development, the Chief Chemist. Eventually, after many trials and tribulations, the Chief Chemist accepted the need to prepare the necessary accounting reports, but these were produced 'mechanically' and he acted as a 'buffer' between the MD and his staff, who carried on as previously. Power alone failed to institutionalise the new culture and its supporting routines. Eventually the new accounting systems in the product development department were abandoned, the department was disbanded, and its head demoted. The OIE framework of accounting and power mobilisation enabled the dynamics of change processes to be teased out. It identified how power over resources, decision making and meanings facilitated accounting change, barriers to change, and conflicts that emerge when accounting routines fail to permeate practices.

Dillard et al. (2004) present a model of institutional change that combines both NIS and OIE. Hopper and Major (2007) apply this model when investigating why a Portuguese telecommunications company, Marconi, adopted activity-based costing (ABC). Marconi's decision lay in a complex, interrelated chain of institutions, including the parent company, management consultants, national and European Union regulators, financial markets and consumer associations, during a period of market liberalisation and technological change. European Union regulators' directives recommended firms to adopt ABC following recommendations from 'expert' consultants (who subsequently gave similar advice when hired by larger telecommunication firms and then by Marconi). The diffusion and adoption of ABC throughout European telecommunications and eventually the Marconi company involved mimetic, coercive and normative isomorphisms. However, ABC was a means and symbol for all to demonstrate improved competitiveness and efficiency: in regulated environments, external legitimacy and efficiency are intertwined. The results confirmed criticisms that early NIS research treated isomorphisms as mutually exclusive and dichotomising economic and institutional pressures. However, demonstrating efficiency by using accounting symbols proved problematic due to conflicts within Marconi (Major and Hopper, 2005). Production engineers were reluctant to use ABC because they were sceptical about its accuracy and usefulness. Workers resisted ABC by inputting inaccurate data late, and production managers tolerated this. Production personnel had difficulty understanding ABC and relating it to their jobs, and they feared it would add to work intensification and redundancies. In contrast, commercial managers, responsible for pricing and investment, and senior managers were satisfied with ABC. They believed it was more accurate than previous systems, met the requirements of regulators and financial markets, and eased consolidation of accounts. They used ABC data for decisions despite its technical problems associated with joint and common costs. The ABC system did not meet the stringent conditions for providing valid data laid down by Noreen (1991) and others. Hopper and Major (2007) conclude that whilst the Dillard et al. (2004) model accommodates many features of institutionalisation, it needs extending to incorporate the public interest, the role of boundary spanners across social levels, and the part played by intra-organisational factors and properties of the technology following translation and praxis. To enrich their observations and extend the model of Dillard et al., Hopper and Major (2007) employed theoretical triangulation to incorporate aspects of economic, labour process, and actor network theories.

Institutional theory generally and in accounting is a vibrant area with increasingly various formulations being applied. Consequently (as with the other approaches discussed), it is difficult to specify with exactitude. However, it is important to remember that its antecedents lie in, and arguably remain in, the subjective ontology of Weberian sociology and interpretivism. Despite studies employing traditional scientific research methods, the epistemology should and usually does lie in social construction, not realism. Thus quantitative studies must be judged by how convincing they are rather than by protocols of absolute proof as in conventional scientific methods. As indicated, institutional theory has limitations and difficulties: it is descriptive rather than normative, neglects issues of power and conflict within and without organisations, and is an allegedly inadequate theorisation of social and economic transformation. However, contemporary research is addressing these issues, and it may be premature to judge whether they are successful. Nevertheless, institutional theory represents a major challenge to mainstream accounting research rooted in the assumptions and methods of neo-classical economics. Its growing focus on integrating macro structural factors and processes within organisations gives it an ontology akin to many political economy approaches.

Conclusions

This chapter has endeavoured to give a flavour of accounting research employing social theory. It is not definitive or exhaustive, and it often over-simplifies; for example, the categorisation of schools may infer mutual exclusivity, whereas they often overlap significantly. Hopefully the chapter will make readers more aware of the concerns and findings of branches of accounting research often neglected in accounting courses. With the exception of some classical Marxism, the theories share common beliefs in subjective ontology, a social constructivist epistemology, and research methods based on intensive case studies. These ideas lie in sharp contrast to positive accounting theory, which has tended to dominate accounting research, especially in North America. There is considerable scope for advancing social research in accounting through theoretical triangulation, but given the fundamentally different assumptions between the theories, the methodology of doing so needs careful consideration. A common criticism of social theory research is that it has provided interesting insights on accounting but is weak on prescription. This critique has justification, but it must be recognised that social theory research is often aimed at enhancing understanding, serving a broad range of constituencies, and puncturing claims to absolute truth by those in privileged positions of power. Thus the research is often offered as a prelude and contribution to better informed, more democratic debate and choice, rather than prescribing predetermined technical solutions. It is process oriented rather than output oriented.

So which theory is right? The authors counsel caution here. The answer may be philosophically impossible to determine, but this does not mean that anything goes – logical argument remains necessary. However, the question reveals the perils of absolutism and the impossibility of divorcing theoretical choices from values, beliefs and the context in which the researcher operates. Nevertheless, choice of theory is important: it not only helps identify the issues and factors deemed important, but it can also render others invisible. The choice of theory may depend on the problem being studied. In several studies the authors chose political economy because they wished to study poverty and embrace a wider view of development than merely economic growth and profitability. Lastly, researchers have agency – we are not merely dupes of our environment. Reflexivity is vital here, not least with regard to iterating theory and data and, if necessary, abandoning or modifying the theories now in use. The final plea is for researchers to be bold but humble. Boldness requires being willing to consider and engage with theories beyond the mainstream. Humbleness refers to the need to be aware of the dangers of making absolute truth claims about a theoretical approach and associated findings. Rather than being informative, this stance merely reveals the philosophical ignorance of the professors and their mistaken attempts to privilege their chosen approach.

Note

1 'Interpretive' research is an umbrella term for several different and sometimes violently conflicting theories (e.g. ethnomethodology, symbolic interactionism and phenomenology). Accounting research has paid little attention to these debates as it tends to be oriented towards symbolic interactionism.

References

Abbott, A. (2004) *Methods and Discovery: Heuristics for the Social Sciences*, Norton, New York.

Alvesson, M. and Karreman, D. (2011) *Qualitative Research and Theory Development: Mystery as Methods*, Sage, London.

Alvesson, M. and Skoldberg, K. (2009) *Reflexive Methodology (2nd edition)*, Sage, London.

Armstrong, P. (1985) 'Competition between the organizational professions and the evolution of management control strategies', *Accounting Organizations and Society*, 10(2): 129–148.

—— (1987) 'The rise of accounting controls in British capitalist enterprises', *Accounting, Organizations and Society*, 12(5): 415–436.

Arnold, P. J. (1998) 'The limits of postmodernism in accounting history: the Decatur experience', *Accounting, Organizations and Society*, 23: 665–684.

Arrington, C. E. and Francis, J. R. (1989) 'Letting the chat out of the bag: deconstruction, privilege, and accounting research', *Accounting, Organizations and Society*, 14: 1–25.

Ashraf, M. J. and Uddin, S. N. (2011) 'Review of management accounting change research with special reference to the public sector and less developed countries', in *Review of Management Accounting Research*, edited by Magdy Abdel-Kader, Palgrave Macmillan, Basingstoke.

Baudrillard, J. (1975) *The Mirror of Production* (M. Poster, Trans.), Telos Press, St. Louis.

Baxter, J. and Chua, W. (2003), 'Alternative management accounting research – whence and whither', *Accounting, Organizations and Society*, 28: 97–126.

Berry, A. J., Capps, T., Cooper, D., Ferguson, P., Hopper T., and Lowe, E. A. (1985) 'Management control in an area of the NCB: rationales of accounting practices in a public enterprise', *Accounting, Organizations and Society*, 10: 3–28.

Boland, R. J (1993) 'Accounting and the interpretative act', *Accounting, Organizations and Society*, 18(2/3): 125–46.

Braverman H. (1974) *Labor and Monopoly Capital: The Degradation of Work in the Twentieth Century*, Monthly Review Press, London.

Bryer, R. A. (2006) 'Accounting and control of the labour process', *Critical Perspectives on Accounting*, 17: 551–598.

—— (2012) 'Americanism and financial accounting theory. Part 1: was America born capitalist?' *Critical Perspectives on Accounting*, 23: 511–555.

Burawoy, M. (1979) *Manufacturing Consent*, University of Chicago Press, Chicago.

Burns, J. (2000) 'The dynamics of accounting change inter-play between new practices, routines, institutions, power and politics', *Accounting, Auditing & Accountability Journal*, 13(5): 566–596.

Burns, J. and Scapens, R. (2000) 'Conceptualising management accounting change: an institutional framework', *Management Accounting Research*, 11: 3–25.

Carpenter, V. L. and Feroz, E. H. (2001) 'Institutional theory and accounting rule choice: an analysis of four US state governments' decisions to adopt generally accepted accounting principles', *Accounting, Organizations and Society*, 26(7/8): 565–596.

Chandler, A. D. (1977) *The Visible Hand: Managerial Revolution in American Business*, Harvard University Press, Boston.

Chow, C. W., Shields, M. D. and Wu, A. (1999) 'The importance of national culture in the design of and preference for management controls for multinational operations', *Accounting, Organizations and Society*, 24: 441–461.

Chua, W. F. (1986) 'Radical developments in accounting thought', *The Accounting Review*, 61(4): 601–632.

Cooper D. J. and Sherer M. J. (1984) 'The value of corporate accounting reports: arguments for a political economy of accounting', *Accounting, Organizations and Society*, 9(3/4): 207–232.

Cooper, R. and Burrell, G. (1988) 'Modernism, postmodernism and organizational analysis: an introduction', *Organization Studies*, 9: 91–112.

Craib, I. (1992) *Modern Social Theory: From Parsons to Habermas (2nd edition)*, Pearson Education, London.

Derrida, J. (1978) *Writing and Difference*, University of Chicago Press, Chicago.

Dillard, J. F., Rigsby, J. T. and Goodman, C. (2004) 'The making and remaking of organization context: duality and the institutionalization process', *Accounting, Auditing & Accountability Journal*, 17(4): 506–542.

DiMaggio, P. J. and Powell, W. W. (1983) 'The iron cage revisited: institutional isomorphism and collective rationality in organizational fields', *American Sociological Review*, 48(2): 147–160.

Foucault, M. (1972) *The Archaeology of Knowledge*, Tavistock, London.

Froud, J., Williams, K., Haslam, C., Johal, S. and Williams, J. (1998). 'Caterpillar: two stories and an argument', *Accounting, Organizations and Society*, 23(7): 685–708.

Graham, C. (2008) 'Fearful asymmetry: the consumption of accounting signs in the Algoma Steel pension bailout', *Accounting, Organizations and Society*, 33: 756–782.

Gramsci, A. (2001) *Selections from the Prison Notebooks of Antonio Gramsci*, Electric Book Company, London.

Graves, O. F., Flesher, D. L. and Jordan, R. E. (1996) 'Pictures and the bottom line: the television epistemology of US annual reports', *Accounting, Organizations and Society*, 21(1): 57–88.

Greenwood, R., Raynard, M., Kodeih, F., Micelotta, E. R. and Lounsbury, M. (2011) 'Institutional complexity and organizational responses', *The Academy of Management Annals*, 5(1): 317–371.

Greenwood, R. and Suddaby, R. (2006) 'Institutional entrepreneurship in mature fields: the Big Five accounting firms', *Academy of Management Journal*, 49(1): 27–48.

Habermas, J. (1968) *Towards a Rational Society*, Heinemann Educational Books, London.

—— (1979) *Communication and the Evolution of Society*, Heinemann Educational Books, London.

Hopper, T. and Armstrong, P. (1991) 'Cost accounting, controlling labour and the rise of conglomerates', *Accounting, Organizations and Society*, 16(5/6): 405–438.

Hopper, T. and MacIntosh, N. (1993) 'Management accounting as disciplinary practice: the case of ITT under Harold Geneen', *Management Accounting Research*, 4: 181–216.

Hopper, T. and Major, M. (2007) 'Extending institutional analysis through theoretical triangulation: regulation and activity-based costing in Portuguese telecommunications', *European Accounting Review*, 16(1): 59–97.

Hopper, T. and Powell, A. (1985), 'Making sense of research into the organizational and social aspects of management accounting: a review of its underlying assumptions', *Journal of Management Studies*, 22: 429–465.

Hopper, T., Storey, J. and Willmott, H. (1987) 'Accounting for accounting: towards the development of a dialectical view', *Accounting, Organizations and Society*, 12(5): 437–456.

Hopper, T., Westrup, C. and Jazayeri, M. (2008) 'World Class Manufacturing and accountability: how companies and the state aspire to competitiveness', *Journal of Accounting and Organisational Change*, 4(2): 97–135.

Hopper, T., Annisette, M., Dastoor, N., Uddin, S. and Wickramasinghe, D. (1995) 'Some challenges and alternatives to positive accounting research', in *Accounting Theory: A Contemporary Review*, edited by S. Jones, J. Ratnatunga and C. Romano, Harcourt-Brace, Sydney, 515–550.

Hopper, T., Tsamenyi, M., Uddin, S. and Wickramasinghe, D. (2009). 'Management accounting in less developed countries: what we know and needs knowing', *Accounting, Auditing and Accountability Journal*, 22(3): 469–514.

Hoskin, K. and Macve, R. (1986) 'Accounting and the examination: a genealogy of disciplinary power', *Accounting, Organizations and Society*, 11(2): 105–136.

—— (1994) 'Reappraising the genesis of managerialism: a re-examination of the role of accounting at the Springfield Armory', *Accounting, Auditing and Accountability Journal*, 7(2): 4–29.

Jensen, M. C. (1983). 'Organization theory and methodology', *Accounting Review*, 58(2): 319–339.

Johnson, H. T. and Kaplan R. S. (1987) *Relevance Lost: The Rise and Fall of Management Accounting*, Harvard Business School Press, Boston.

Lounsbury, M. (2008) 'Institutional rationality and practice variation: new directions in the institutional analysis of practice', *Accounting, Organizations and Society*, 33: 349–361.

Macintosh, N. B., Shearer, T., Thornton, D. B. and Welker, M. (2000), 'Accounting as simulacrum and hyperreality: perspectives on income and capital', *Accounting, Organizations and Society*, 25(1): 13–50.

Major, M. and Hopper, T. (2005) 'Managers divided: implementing ABC in a Portuguese telecommunications company', *Management Accounting Research*, 16(2): 205–229.

Marshall, G. (1990) *In Praise of Sociology*, Unwin & Hyman, London.

Meyer, J. W. and Rowan, B. (1977) 'Institutionalized organizations: formal structure as myth and ceremony', *The American Journal of Sociology*, 83(2): 340–363.

Miller, P. and O'Leary, T. (1987). 'Accounting and the construction of the governable person', *Accounting, Organizations and Society*, 12(3): 235–266.

—— (1994). 'Accounting, "economic citizenship" and the spatial reordering of manufacture', *Accounting, Organizations and Society*, 19(1): 15–43.

Noreen, E. (1991). 'Conditions under which activity-based cost systems provide relevant costs', *Journal of Management Accounting Research*, 3: 159–168.

Otley, D. T. (1980). 'The contingency theory of management accounting: achievement and prognosis', *Accounting, Organizations and Society*, 5(4): 413–428.

Powell, W. W. and DiMaggio, P. J. (1991) *The New Institutionalism in Organizational Analysis*, University of Chicago Press, Chicago.

Quattrone, P. and Hopper, T. (2005). 'A "time-space odyssey": management control systems in multinational organisations', *Accounting, Organizations and Society*, 30(7/8): 735–764.

Roberts, J. and Scapens, R. W. (1985). 'Accounting systems and systems of accountability: understanding accounting practices in their organisational context', *Accounting, Organizations and Society*, 10: 443–456.

Smith, M. (1998) *Social Science in Question*, Sage, London.

Straus, A. and Corbin, J. (1990) *Basics of Qualitative Research*, Newbury Park, Sage.

Sutton, R. and Staw, B. (1995) 'What theory is not', *Administrative Science Quarterly*, 40: 371–384.

Tinker, T. (1980) 'Towards a political economy of accounting', *Accounting, Organizations and Society*, 5(1): 147–160.

Toms, S. (2010) 'Calculating profit: a historical perspective on the development of capitalism', *Accounting, Organizations and Society*, 35(2): 205–221.

Uddin, S. and Hopper, T. (2001) 'A Bangladesh soap opera: privatisation, accounting, and regimes of control in a less developed country', *Accounting, Organizations and Society*, 26(7/8): 643–672.

Vaivio, J. (1999) 'Exploring a "non-financial" management accounting change', *Management Accounting Research*, 10: 409–437.

Watts, R. and Zimmerman, J. (1978) 'Towards a positive theory of the determinants of accounting standards', *The Accounting Review*, 53: 112–134.

Wickramasinghe, D. and Hopper, T. (2005) 'A cultural political economy of management accounting controls: a case study of a textile mill in a traditional Sinhalese village', *Critical Perspectives on Accounting*, 16(4): 473–503.

Yusof, N., Wickramasinghe, D. and Zaman, M. (2013) 'Historical analysis of Bumiputere institution and corporate governance in Malaysia', *Asia Pacific Interdisciplinary Research in Accounting Conference*, July, Kobe, Japan.

19

True and fair

A business ethos 'par excellence'

Frank Clarke and Graeme Dean

Introduction

From the four cardinal virtues of temperance, courage, justice and practical wisdom flows the major business virtue of honesty, engendering the necessary trust for sustained business engagement (Malloch, 2011). Through much of the annals of finance, it is clear that those cardinal virtues have not attended business actions the way they should, for business misbehaviour at times has been rampant, especially since World War II. This is manifested by accounting and audit failure leading to the often poor, frequently misleading disclosure of corporate financial progress or regress that has frustrated informed investment, produced inept regulation, seen dishonest motives driving business decisions and distorted perceptions of managers' responsibilities. The earlier works of Valance (1955), Haldane (1970), Chambers (1973a, 1978) and Briloff (1972, 1976), and more recently Jones (2011), Clikeman (2013) and the trilogy of Clarke *et al.* (1997, 2003), Clarke and Dean (2007) and Clarke *et al.* (2014), provide substantial evidence to support this claim.

This paper first addresses Malloch's notion of business ethics to derive the basis of the commercial ethos underpinning commerce. Following, amongst others, Chambers (1973a) and West (2003), it identifies in particular accounting's assumed role in business to be 'telling the truth'. Malloch shows that business dealing is based on an assumed trust that is supported, when markets are demonstrated to have failed, by legislation. Commercial legislation generally entails a mix of principles and related rules. There is an overarching ethos in many commercial areas – such as 'truth in securities' legislation, the assumed 'fair game' in the securities market, 'fair trading' generally in commerce, and the concept of 'fair and reasonable' underpinning specific areas, such as in mergers and takeovers; wage negotiations; and the sale of goods legislation wherein it is assumed that goods are serviceable and 'fit for the purposes' specified in the product warranty statements. An exemplar of this ethos is the criterion of 'true and fair view' (TFV). Application of this ethos results in a TFV of an entity's statements of its affairs, primarily its financial position and performance. Recent articles (Bayou *et al.*, 2011; Smeliauskas *et al.*, 2008 and the related commentary by Alexander, 2010) have suggested that the current reporting system is unable to effectively operationalize this ethos as the cornerstone. We reject this conclusion, and through an historical and current analysis of how the TFV ethos has endured in legislation (notwithstanding these and myriad other criticisms), show how it can be operationalized. The analysis reinforces that the TFV criterion should continue to be the cornerstone of corporate publicity obligations.

I Honesty: truth and fairness in accounts revisited

All too frequently, the issue of business ethics is addressed in a negative way. Usually, we are told what not to do, what not to use to undergird business actions. This is frequently expressed metaphorically in terms of Pope Gregory the Great's *seven deadly sins* (lust, gluttony, greed, wrath, sloth, envy and pride) or their equivalents, before we are barraged with rules of what amounts to good business behaviour. The transition from condemning the unethical to advocating the ethical is usually made without a logical explanation of why unethical procedures should not be followed. Often, there is no explanation of what is in it for the business person who decides to act ethically. Accordingly, mostly it suffices in argument for ethical and legal behaviours to coincide.

In contrast, Malloch, in his *Doing Virtuous Business: The Remarkable Success of Spiritual Enterprise* (2011), approaches ethics from the opposite direction. He internalizes ethical behaviour, describing it as the source of inner happiness. He proceeds to explain how from four cardinal virtues of 'temperance, courage, justice and practical wisdom' there flows the major business virtue of honesty, engendering the necessary trust for sustained business engagement. It is accepted that without trust in the system, commercial affairs will be shackled.[1]

It is reasonable to suggest that Malloch's cardinal virtues are roughly antonyms for the seven deadly sins. Despite obvious overlap, we can substitute the positive temperance for the negative lust and gluttony; courage for sloth, greed and envy; justice for wrath; and practical wisdom for pride.

Malloch's (2011) thesis is drawn from tradition and injects the wisdom of experience. He posits that whether one is happy with one's actions dictates in the end whether the action is ethical. He pleads for what he refers to as 'spiritual capital'. Now, whereas he claims the source of ethical behaviour lies in Judaeo-Christian beliefs and teaching, he draws heavily upon the works of Socrates and Aristotle (see Malloch, 2011, Chapter 2). Clearly, neither could have had any perception of modern day commerce, though the eighteenth-century iconoclastic economist-cum-philosopher Adam Smith may well have. Accordingly, Malloch opines:

> Smith asked a question that had been overlooked by Descartes, Thomas Aquinas, Aristotle, and every other great thinker before him: 'What is the nature and the cause of [Smith's] the wealth of nations?' . . . [he sought] a world from which poverty could be banished . . . that was his goal.

For Malloch, such a world is achievable by undertaking his form of virtuous business.

Virtuous behaviour and 'business political correctness'

Without *courage*, Malloch suggests, we often fail to recognize the inherent limitations we all have, especially those failings revealed in the recent excesses of capitalism that featured in the fallout of the Global Financial Crisis (GFC). Business education has been assailed for years for its promotion of the Calvinistic work ethic (particularly in most MBA curricula) as an essential underpinning of the way to commercial success. Although it was not perhaps intended, as the world continues to reel more than five years after the peak of the GFC, this has gradually spawned a convenient patsy in the 'anything goes' approach to designing business curricula – whatever the cost. A consideration of business ethics puts flesh on the myriad do-it-yourself management and finance books explaining how successful individuals built their financial empires. This success was generally achieved without giving any credit to luck or to the humility that equips one to know good fortune when it comes along.[2]

By *temperance* Malloch means the facility to take a balanced view and to not be over-whelmed by momentary success or the failure to produce a desired outcome. A gambler who doubles up on a losing bet is intemperate. A business manager who abandons a product merely because initial sales are down relative to the target acts intemperately if it is truly believed that the product is something the public ought to have. Enron's response to its success when named several times in succession as 'business of the year' was intemperate. It set out to out-do itself – it acted as if it could do anything and successfully enter into any kind of deal in every kind of business it chose. Some have characterized such actions of Enron as getting 'too big for its boots'; others applauded it for seeking 'continuous improvement'. But irrespective of labels, Enron lacked a balanced view of its ability to perform in particular settings and of its skills relative to those of its competitors. That is, it lacked the necessary humility to acknowledge where it ranked in the pecking order. If we emulate Enron executives, we almost certainly will act intemperately.

Similarly, those who agree to participate in organizational ranking exercises must always acknowledge the prospect that some will rank ahead of them. However, under the 'continuous improvement' goal, it is suggested that by acknowledging constraints, one should always strive to be the best. It is courageous to be competitive, fully knowing that the chance of winning the laurel wreath is remote. Although this attribute is often referred to as being 'a good loser', such a characterization ignores the inner motives of courage that drive success. Many organizations such as universities currently offend this principle when they provide incentives that encourage staff to publish only in the leading so-called 'A*' or 'A' journals and barely recognize publications in lower-ranked journals or in the reputable practitioner journals for the applied disciplines. It is counterproductive for staff to be discouraged, by university promotion or financial reward systems, from publishing where they can expose false doctrines in practice, and it is contrary to the academic pursuit of spreading the truth as they reason and observe it to be.

It takes courage to admit to one's errors. BP appears to have lacked such courage when its Deepwater Horizon oil spilled into the Gulf of Mexico in 2010. So also did Barclays Bank executives lack courage in not immediately admitting it when they became aware that employees intentionally erred in their London Interbank Offered Rate (Libor) 'calculations'. US rating agencies Standard & Poor's, Moody's, and Fitch lacked courage when they AAA-rated parcels of derivatives without (as hindsight has shown) any sound basis. Fabrice Tourre, who reportedly emailed his girlfriend boasting that he had sold derivatives to 'widows and orphans' for Goldman Sachs, lacked courage when not disclosing that his firm had 'bet against' the deal.[3] In sum, a lack of courage has often facilitated deception and wrongdoing.

In *The End of Ethics and a Way Back* (2013, Chapter 1), Malloch and Mamorsky explain how '[Libor] Regulators were reduced to accomplices' and the Bank of England, the Financial Services Authority, and the Securities and Exchange Commission were 'knowingly asleep at the wheel'. Further, that they relied on written notes by a senior Bank of England regulator indicates that officials were concerned Barclays was reporting above average borrowing costs – that 'in the summer of 2007, the Federal Reserve Bank of New York was questioning Libor's accuracy'. Notwithstanding, 'officials met in April and May 2008 to address the falsehoods of Libor, however they did nothing other than talk . . . [N]o action was taken to publicize the fraud'. Barclays acknowledged to the Fed that untrue Libor rates had been submitted (*In the Matter of Barclays PLC, Barclays Bank PLC, and Barclays Inc, CFTC Docket 12–25*, 2012). A Barclays whistleblower is said

[to] have known in December 2007 that Barclays was proactively manipulating the Libor Index. . . . Libor's manipulation is not just another financial scandal . . . [O]ver time the values that helped found the Libor rate – faith, accountability and cooperation – became so substantially eroded that systemic fraud became the new normal. In a selfish game of deceit, lies, and greed, no one dared to care about the outcome for investors [and contractors using Libor] . . . The Libor crisis is hard evidence that we are approaching the end of ethics.

(Malloch and Mamorsky, pp. 15–16)

For Aristotle, *justice* entailed giving each person his due. Malloch notes (in his Chapter 2) that Aristotle argued that '[a]ll rational beings need justice . . . since all need the cooperation of their fellows and the trust on which this depends'. Trust is the root source of friendship, Malloch explains, because friends both 'give' and 'receive'. In contrast with modern day perceptions, Aristotle's notion was an 'individual characteristic' rather than a 'community virtue', as is evident in the modern notion of social justice. Justice was a matter of self-governance – the basis for societal leadership. As such it currently enjoys a strong position in Catholic theology, with its primary aim of the earlier notion of social justice for all. But social justice has morphed into the anti-capitalism feature of the 'occupy Wall Street' movement. It underpinned socialism and must take its share of the blame for the worst aspects of communism. As such, social justice has likely severed individual responsibility from the traditional notion of justice.

Such a severance undergirds the notion of corporate social responsibility (CSR) residing in institutions rather than in the persons managing them. CSR in that manifestation cannot flourish. It manifests itself as rules capable of being ticked off rather than as principles necessarily to be embraced by individual practitioners.

What is in essence a virtuous ideal becomes a form of 'corporate political correctness' through the tick-a-box activity. Enron, for example, had a complete CSR manifesto. Kenneth Lay and Andrew Fastow were able to tick off each item in Enron's list and were lauded for years because *their* Enron was a model of social responsibility. Yet at the time, Enron, with the cooperation of some utility company employees, had engaged in activities (highlighted in the movie, *The Smartest Guys in Town*) that illegally rigged power prices for customers in California. They used accounting gimmicks (some arguably in compliance with prescribed accounting and legal rules, as noted in Salter, 2008) to misguide the public's views of its corporate profitability, thereby ensuring continued financing and extending the charade.

Likewise, in the credit boom and crisis leading up to the GFC, Bear Stearns and Lehman Brothers were top runners in the so-called 'financial engineering' of derivative products (like CDOs and CDSs) and the unjustified mortgages that funded housing for low-income earners through the operation of relevant US legislation. Bear Stearns and Lehman Brothers are classic examples of the inoperable external tests of CSR. Like Enron, they too could tick – and, what is more serious, would have been required to tick by their auditors – all the usual CSR boxes. Shareholders reaped high returns, and the low-income stakeholders were ecstatic. Those who exited both Bear Stearns and Lehman before the low point were lucky, for when the engineered derivatives went belly-up, the internal nature of ethical virtue became obvious. The rest, like Bear Stearns and Lehman Brothers, is history. Such 'grotesquely'[4] complex and risky financial instruments, with their arguably misleading and deceptive AAA ratings, brought on the financial world's stumbling and near meltdown. Up to then, both companies were rated as highly socially responsible, with high returns for shareholders being the major enablers of a demand that few frowned upon.

A feature of the GFC is the number of circumstances in which those benefiting from the distinct exercise of CSR were happy until things turned sour. Lehman Brothers' exploitation of repurchasing arrangements called Repos 105 is a case in point.

Lehman Brothers collapse in September 2008 is now a bell-weather point in GFC history, but its use of deceit to hide from the public in general and the public gatekeeper, the Securities and Exchange Commission (SEC), is now the stuff of legend. By its contestably illegal use of Repos105 technology, Lehman misled those perusing its quarterly and annual filings with the SEC during 2007 and 2008 regarding the level of its financial leveraging. Repos 105 is a legitimate technology used in everyday investment banking, where financial instruments (such as bonds) are sold under an arrangement in which the purchaser acquires the instruments at a discount – that is, for a price less than their present value. Usually the seller bank agrees to buy back the instrument within a short term (ten days) at the inflated price. The deal means that, should the bank have financial difficulties before that repurchasing, the purchaser has the bond to recover the amount paid.

Lehman used Repos 105 extensively during 2007 and 2008. Together presumably with their auditors Ernst & Young, Lehman perceived a loophole in the relevant accounting rule which required the Repos to be considered not as sales but as a 'financing arrangement'. To many, the accounting rule required Lehman to book the cash received as a *loan* and to retain the asset on its books. Yet at balance date, Lehman Brothers borrowed, pledging its illiquid assets comprising CDOs and similar securities as collateral, and accounted for the transactions as 'sales' and the cash inflow as 'revenues' (not as a loan). This had the effect of removing the illiquid assets from its balance sheet immediately before accounts were due for lodgement at the SEC. Lehman used the cash to pay down its borrowings. For a brief period (until the transaction was reversed), this had the effect of decreasing its borrowings by an amount larger (relatively) than the decrease in its assets – and it thus lowered its leverage ratio. Immediately after the filings' lodgement date, Lehman repurchased the illiquid assets and renewed its borrowings. The impact of such financial deceit amounted to US$38.6 billion in the final quarter of 2007, and to US$49.1 billion and US$50.4 billion in the first and second quarters of 2008.

The counterparties to the repurchasing deals were quite happy with their guaranteed quick profit. Contemporaneously, nor were Bernie Madoff's clients complaining initially about the higher than normal (and as the financial analyst-cum-whistleblower Harry Markopolos pointed out to the SEC on many occasions, 'unrealistically regular') returns they received. Clients benefiting from returns that are 'too good to be true' in some instances have nearly as much to answer for as the arch perpetrator. Clearly, temperance is in short supply when this occurs.

In a sense, the CSR ideal has been hijacked by it morphing into an external feature of companies, not an inner virtue of those who manage them. It has been relegated to something to be reported on by accountants. But accountants have no trouble with an ethical code that is enunciated as a list of accounting rules (standards) to be ticked off. They follow lists of standards that prohibit them from disclosing, except by accident, the wealth and progress of their employer companies. And once the rules are ticked off, they then believe that the accounts will automatically show a true and fair view to all who see them. Indeed, accountants stand at the epicentre of business ethics, yet they generally fail to treat their obligations in accord with internal virtues by which to judge right or wrong in their external observations of business at work.

Practical wisdom is acquired by the accumulation of experience. It possibly irks younger individuals to be harangued by hearing the 'life experience' argument, but there is no substitute for observing first-hand what goes on around oneself. Observing what works and what does not is essential. Oscar Wilde captured this quirk of human behaviour so eloquently in his *An Ideal Husband*, where he notes that perhaps many have 'had all the experience' but not the privilege of 'making' the 'observations'.

The filtering mechanism by which observations are sorted into those that are considered worthwhile to repeat in similar settings and those that are not is inevitably based on values regarding what is *right* and what is *wrong*. Too often, the filtering process appears to have been monitored by values of greed and deceit – that is, by mores that betray the trust upon which orderly commerce relies. Deceit inevitably leads to one individual benefiting at the expense of another's unwilling loss. Greed inevitably feeds on either deceit or the manipulation of rules of disclosure to deny to the aggrieved party a level playing field. The point at which commercial transactions turn from profit making to greed is often a matter of judgment. Those who risk capital certainly deserve a reasonable return. What is *reasonable* no doubt is a sticking point for many. But clearly we know when the return is obscene, beyond the pale. Profit gouging is properly frowned upon. In wartime, for example, agencies are set up to seek out and prosecute those earning excessive profits from their war effort. In normal times, excessive loan charges by money lenders are also scrutinized. Meanwhile, banks seem to earn profits well above what others can earn because of their protected position in business affairs. However, their basis for charging fees, such as when cheques are dishonoured, is being tested currently in courts in Australia. Whether those fees are 'fair and reasonable' is under the microscope. Whether the banks deserve super profit-making capacities because of their lynchpin role in capitalistic economies is also contestable.

Perhaps their interest-charging capacity should be brought more in line with Islamic competitors. Under Islamic mores, interest, *riba*, is forbidden, and banking business is undertaken more on a partnership basis, with individuals' deposits allocated to business projects on an agreed profit and loss sharing basis. The bank depositors provide the financial capital, and the entrepreneurs, the management. But of course that arrangement does not prevent greed, even though it is outlawed under Islamic law. Greed is not, however, outlawed under Western commercial law.

Rather, Wall Street now appears to side with the words of the infamous 1990s *Wall Street* film character Gordon Gecko that 'greed is good'. Greed played a major role in the GFC, as was depicted hypothetically in the actions of John Belfort in the 2013 movie *The Wolf of Wall Street*; it underpins the enduring excessive executive remuneration packages – the golden, welcoming 'hellos'; yearly remuneration and bonuses; and golden parachutes – negotiated when executives join a company's management. Normal commerce appears to feed on greed. Greed appears to have been the primary motive behind Tyco CEO Dennis Kozlowski's extremely extravagant lifestyle, lived at his company's expense. It motivated WorldCom's Bernie Ebbers' private (at the expense of the public) actions more than a decade prior to the GFC. According to Malloch (2013), Kozlowski was infected with the greed gene as the high-flying CEO of Tyco Laboratories. But high flying had appealed to Kozlowski earlier, when he was in charge of the Fire Protection section of the Tyco empire. There, his acquisition program was designed to grow the ambit of Tyco, its share price, and his personal wealth 'at the expense of due diligence, governance, and corporate accountability' (p. 119). Such actions were often claimed by Kozlowski to be legal. An internal auditing book written several years earlier by Russell, *Foozles and Frauds* (1978), captured this commercial action. The notion of a financial 'foozle' was coined to describe any financial and managerial manoeuvre that might be thought to sit on the grey line between legal and fraudulent.

According to Malloch, the four virtues together make up an *honest* businessperson. For to be honest in business requires *temperance* to judge between right and wrong, *courage* to do what is right notwithstanding the cost to oneself, *justice* in all dealings, and the accumulation of *practical wisdom* by observing the world of business.

Clearly, those cardinal virtues have not attended business the way people like Malloch suggest they should, for business misbehaviour has been rampant, especially since World War II.

Deal-a-day actions by Dennis Kozlowski throughout the 1990s raised the book value of Tyco's assets from US$40 million to US$40 billion. By then he had a salary of US$170 million a year, qualifying him to participate in Tyco's 'top hat' deferred compensation arrangement – a scheme organized primarily during the 1990s. Lavish Fifth Avenue apartments were acquired by Kozlowski, with US$16.8 million and another US$14 million spent on restyling and furnishing in 2001. By then, Kozlowski's greed gene was certainly active.

Bernie Ebbers, like Kozlowski, seemingly was more concerned with the growth of his personal wealth than with the wealth of WorldCom's shareholders. His acquisitions while CEO of WorldCom were driven by a desire to acquire personal wealth by the consequential upwards movements in WorldCom's share price as the group grew and obtained the largest proportion of US internet bandwidth. In Malik's *Broadbandits* (2003), Ebbers emerges as not having the knowledge necessary to enter in such a large manner the electronic communication industry. His acquisitions binge necessitated his guessing on the demand for broadband. As luck would have it, he guessed incorrectly. It may well be that WorldCom and Ebbers were merely before their time, but greed certainly played its part in the antics of the ever-growing Ebbers empire facilitated by the internet bubble created by the 1996 US Telecommunications Act.

When asked why the broadband bubble burst, Malik suggested (p. xvi) that the cause was the 'fear of falling stock'. Ebbers *was* fearful of having to tell the market that the broadband demand had not materialized. He engaged in what he regarded as a short-term foozle. He borrowed in order to buy WorldCom shares in the hope that a demand recovery would prop up their price and save WorldCom. It did not. Nor did it save WorldCom's competitor, Global Crossing. Both were bankrupted. 'CEOs forgot that they served the shareholders and not their own bank accounts', Malik also noted. CEOs like Ebbers were made 'the new American hero. We put him on the cover of magazines, we celebrated his lifestyle' (p. xvi). Citing *Business Week*, Malik also points to executive remuneration being blown out with stock options. Even so, without counting in stock options, executives made 42 times the pay rate of average hourly workers in 1980, 85 times in 1990, and by 2000 they were paid 531 times ordinary workers' rates. Understandably, no executive could admit to failure to meet Wall Street's expectations or the public's expectation of hypergrowth of 20 per cent annual returns 'in an economy that typically grows at 3 percent' (p. xvi). All of which fits nicely into Macey's (2013) reputational thesis (see next section).

Unvirtuous behaviour – a long history

Practical wisdom is frustrated by deceit. Greed feeds on deceit; it provides the information fed to those who are misled and leads to the provider gaining. Bernie Madoff's deceit gave him the reputation and respect of a master investor, which in turn brought investors flocking for his assistance to make them rich. This was critical to his Ponzi scheme. Once the information is shown to be false, the system and the reputation it spawns are doomed. Madoff's empire crumbled immediately, as had Carlo Ponzi's 80 years earlier – and as had, only a decade earlier than Madoff, that of Barings' Nick Leeson. The GFC is replete with such examples. However, while the GFC currently receives the notoriety, few seem willing to accept that the annals of finance are full of reported cases of companies failing unexpectedly, and of many where deceit or unsolicited greed was a motivator for the worst of commercial characteristics (see Valance, 1955; Haldane, 1970; Clarke and Dean, 2007; Jones, 2011; Clikeman, 2013; Margret and Peck, 2014).

Valance and Haldane both describe well the 1920s UK Royal Mail case, while the other monographs above refer to the collapses of the Maxwell and Polly Peck empires in the 1980s that gave the impetus for the corporate governance movement, the Lloyds of London affair, the failure of Rolls-Royce, the BCCI debacle, and the collapse of Allied Irish Bank. The accounts suggest that each case was underpinned by greed, generally assisted by deceit. There has been more of the same recently – Northern Rock's problems in the early part of the GFC and the Libor scandal at Barclays Bank and other banks. And, were the allegations proven, the following also would then be shown to have involved deceit regarding information disclosures: Standard Chartered Bank's alleged engagement in money laundering and gun running, HSBC's alleged foreign dealings in the rorting of its 'Oil for Food' transactions, and the Australian Wheat Board's alleged illegal bribes surreptitiously paid to Iraqi officials in its UN-sanctioned transactions in the Oil for Food Programme.

Much earlier, the contestable dealings of the US Robber Barons at the turn of the twentieth century epitomized business greed and deceit, as did the long-life asset accounting of 1920s US electricity utility king, Samuel Insull, and the 1930s reporting of non-existent inventory in its Canadian warehouse by McKesson and Robbins. The Enron affair should not have surprised, nor the bankrupting of Tyco, Global Crossing and WorldCom, or the problems at Waste Management, Disney, Cisco, Vivendi and Parmalat. In the 1990s, the downfall of one of Australia's largest-ever companies, Bond Corporation, is possibly the best internationally known of several large, unexpected local company collapses in the last few decades (see Clarke and Dean, 2007).

Since World War II, the Australian corporate scene has witnessed several booms and busts with consequent high-profile failures, including the conglomerate Adelaide Steamship Company; national electrical retailer H.G. Palmer; investment company Stanhill Consolidated; property developers and related financiers Reid Murray, Cambridge Credit Corporation, Associated Securities Limited, Estate Mortgage Trust (and more recently, Westpoint, Fincorp, Baycorp, LM Investment, Banksia); construction company Mainline; investment advisers in the 1960s, Latec Investments and Neon Signs and, more recently, Opes Prime and Trio; the insurer HIH, and telecommunications company One.Tel in the 2000s.

While greed is not always evident, dishonesty and gross breach of trust are. Embarrassingly for the Australian government, eight officers of two subsidiaries of the Reserve Bank of Australia (RBA) – Note Printing of Australia (then wholly owned) and Securency (then half-owned) – are on trial for their alleged part in encouraging some Asian central banks to purchase the rights to use RBA's innovative anti-forgery currency note process. Significantly, this highlights complications of corporate governance, risk management and reporting when groups of companies are involved, irrespective of whether they are wholly owned or a part-owned subsidiary. The directors of RBA (the holding company in this case) have become embroiled in the matter, as there are mounting allegations that they were aware of the alleged bribery approaches being used by the note-printing subsidiaries and should have notified police earlier.[5]

The GFC and the spate of collapses and corporate misdemeanours means it is doubtful whether there is much worth observing and accumulating as 'practical wisdom'! There is certainly not a lot to trust regarding corporate disclosures. That is the message in Clarke and Dean's *Indecent Disclosure* (2007) and Clarke et al.'s *The Unaccountable and Ungovernable Corporation* (2014). Few of those perpetrating the misleading disclosures mentioned in those accounts appear conscious of the loss of any *reputation* for integrity they may have built. 'Reputational theory' has it that business growth, indeed the survival of a business enterprise, depends on the reputation of its managers for honest, fair dealing (see Jonathan Macey's *The Death of Corporate Reputation: How Integrity Has Been Destroyed on Wall Street*, 2013). Macey suggests that modern business fails miserably to build its reputation for integrity. Regulation has been deemed the solution, but it equally fails to engender trust.

Reputational theory suggests that because investors would ordinarily prefer to deal with those with a reputation for truthful dealing rather than with those without, the rewards of earning and maintaining a good reputation outweigh the costs. Macey (2013, p. 18) proposes that an ordinary cost-benefit analysis over the long term would show that it is not in companies' interests to act dishonestly. Of course the catch is 'over the long term', for dishonest behaviour is likely to reap huge short-term rewards. For this reason it is now more common for executive packages to include bonuses payable for average performances over periods of five years or more rather than on yearly outcomes.[6]

Short-term benefits were certainly also prevalent during the GFC when Standard & Poor's, Fitch, and Moody's rated pools of derivatives AAA on what were later revealed to be flimsy bases, seemingly to meet market demands. Similarly, short-term benefits were to the fore when investment banks Lehman Brothers, Goldman Sachs, Washington Mutual, Wachovia, Bear Stearns, Wells Fargo, J.P. Morgan and the like bought and then on-sold derivatives to unsuspecting clients worldwide. Likewise, J.P. Morgan underwrote the 2012 Facebook IPO at US$38 per share, issued at US$42.50, only to have the shares price drop to US$16 within months. But nowhere was short-termism as evident as in the Timberwolf derivative deal Goldman's made. It was described by Goldman officer Thomas Montag to Mortgage Department Head Daniel Sparks in an internal email at the time as 'one *shitty* deal' (US Senate Permanent Subcommittee on Investigations, 2011, p. 394), when Goldman Sachs bet on the stock price falling without advising clients who purchased the stock. Goldman would eventually agree to a multi-million dollar settlement (on a no fault, no liability basis). Other major financiers such as J.P. Morgan have subsequently agreed to similar payments for similar deals. J.P. Morgan, for example, agreed to in excess of US$14 billion, a record settlement with the US government, for having sold what were described by the regulators as dodgy securities to its customers during the lead-up to and during the GFC.[7]

With this evidence, Macey (2013) concludes that reputation theory no longer holds sway. This is because the compulsory regulatory agencies' monitoring imposed on companies 'to keep them honest' actually increases the costs of companies otherwise seeking to enhance their reputations themselves. Misplaced regulation, Macey argues, is a major reason for the lack of companies' attempts to build business trust based on individual customers' experiences. Although likely with the best of intentions, regulation has been presented as a substitute for a corporation's efforts to build a reputation for good dealing. Several regulatory issues arise. Although the SEC is used to illustrate them here, each could be applied to regulators in other jurisdictions. Macey's description particularly meshes with Australian experience over several decades (Clarke *et al.*, 2014, especially Chapter 3).

The origins of the SEC in the early days of President Roosevelt's first term, at the beginning of the 1930s, was by far more dramatic than the gradual emergence in the 1970s of Australia's National Companies and Securities Commission, the antecedent body to the Australian Securities and Investments Commission (ASIC). But Roosevelt's 1932 pledge to put 'truth in securities' is no more effective in the US now than it is in contemporary Australia. According to Macey (2013), the SEC's performance is judged by Congress in accord with how many actions it has brought, fines collected and settlements achieved. His description of SEC behaviour complains:

> Longstanding criticism that the SEC has largely failed to prosecute cases against corporate executives, opting for quick settlements with companies . . . quick settlements because it is judged on the number of cases it wins . . . [C]ompanies don't defend themselves as vigorously as individuals . . . [so it] makes sense . . . to register large numbers of cases brought and fines collected.

(p. 272)

Not pursuing individuals because of the poor statistic they contribute to the efficiency and effectiveness metric may well explain why Bernie Madoff was not pursued as vigorously as companies were by the SEC, even when Harry Markopolos provided good grounds for the SEC to do so. He was unsuccessful for a decade in his attempts to have the SEC pursue Madoff (Markopolos *et al.*, 2011). Likewise, Australian regulator ASIC's performance is assessed similarly by the Australian government. Getting high-profile corporate heads on poles appears to be ASIC's main objective. It quickly courted praise when it jailed HIH CEO Ray Williams and FAI's Rodney Adler and secured a conviction against James Hardie directors, banning their director activities for various periods. But ASIC was remarkably quiet when it failed miserably in the quest to see off One. Tel's co-founder, Jodee Rich (then managing director), and finance director Mark Silberman.

The UK, the US and Australia have demonstrated similar knee-jerk regulatory responses to spates of corporate wrongdoing. In the US, the Enron affair and the repetitive occurrence of early 2000s financial restatements presaged the Sarbanes Oxley Act, while the shenanigans during the GFC produced the Dodd-Frank Act and spawned the Financial Protection Bureau. In the UK, following the GFC, the new coalition government was quick to plan the scrapping of the Financial Services Authority, to give its gate-keeping responsibility to the Bank of England, and to create two new bodies – a new Financial Regulatory Authority and the Financial Conduct Authority. In Australia, the collapses of the pre-GFC era brought on the mid-2000s Corporate Legal and Economic Reform Program, a raft of contestable corporate governance rules and a new focus on ASIC. Yet, curiously, despite the increased regulation and formalizing governance rules, unexpected corporate failures, accounting misstatements and audit failure have continued. The essential business ethos, honesty, remains missing.

II Post–World War II corporate chaos

Since World War II, unexpected, often large, company collapses and corporate crises have occurred repeatedly. These crises place the loss of corporate ethics in an everyday perspective. While the companies involved may represent only a relatively small percentage of companies, their size and the repeated occurrence of crisis is indicative of a major market failure. In our previous works, audited accounting, especially company (and in particular consolidation) accounting has been the main focus. With that and the obvious consequences of a lack of integrity as background, consider the following in the context of the problematic future of the corporation and its accounting as we know it.

Business in the British tradition enjoys a unique heritage from the 1841 Gladstone inquiry and report examining numerous insurance and other financial scandals, followed by reforms allowing companies to be created through mere registration under the UK companies Act of 1844.[8] There, bestowed through legislation, was the requirement that generally incorporated entities were to prepare accounts that were *full and fair*. That is a business ethos par excellence – an overriding ethical reporting obligation. Moreover, apart from changes in actual wording to *full and correct* (in several nineteenth-century UK Companies Acts), *true and correct* (1946 UK Companies Act), *true and fair* (1960 Australian Companies [now Corporations] Act), this general ethical criterion has survived for 170 years. Accountants arguably are the custodians of the oldest uninterrupted professional ethic enshrined in legislation.[9] West (2003, p. 172) makes apposite observations about truth and accounting: 'It is on grounds of its claimed expertise that the accounting profession has been granted an exclusive responsibility for independently pronouncing on the truth and fairness of financial reports.'

Of course, the setting in which such a unique ethos emerged in the 1844 Select Committee on Joint Stock Companies report has changed greatly (Maltby, 1998). So has the way commerce is conducted. Companies were necessary in the first half of the nineteenth century to amass the large capital outlays needed to fund the transportation systems (the railways and canals) and the associated industrial revolution by then in full swing. The accounts of Hunt (1936) and Shannon (1932) confirm the substantial numbers of registered companies at that time. Whereas such an imperative may no longer exist to kick-start industry, large capital inputs are necessary to fund business affairs on the global basis and scale that now is the norm for everyday commerce. Globalization is the catch-cry of the twenty-first century. Likewise, it is necessary for tradable shares to persist. For that to occur it is paramount that investors are continuously informed of the financial wealth and progress of the companies they fund. That is, companies' accounts must be full and fair – that is, trustworthy and unequivocally honestly prepared and audited. They must inform all who are interested in a company's wealth and progress of the best *approximation* of its exact financial position *as it is!* For only by doing so can investors properly assess myriad risk/return options.

Despite the obvious necessity outlined above, there appears a curious doubt in accounting circles as to both what the full and fair (or modern equivalent) wording means and, as a consequence, what the ethos is. The numerous concerns in the accounting literature, expressed prior to the papers addressed below, focus on matters such as the problematic nature of truth and fairness, or whether the phrase was a portmanteau. At issue has been whether the words 'truth' and 'fairness' are to be considered as isolates; whether the phrases full and fair, full and correct, true and correct, and ultimately true and fair, are of similar intent; and whether there are several true and fair views because of the foci of differing users. Notably, 'users' is a primary focus in those analyses. In contrast, members of the Sydney School of Accounting have proposed 'uses' rather than 'users' to be the focus (see especially, Chambers, 1973a; Clarke and Dean, 2007; Clarke *et al.*, 2012; Clarke *et al.*, 2014).

Most importantly, prior to the latter part of the twentieth century, there appears to have been neither doubt nor any general unease that such a full and fair view of a company's financial state of affairs could easily be obtained by a 'professional' acting honestly. Nor was there any unease originally (1844) with the appointment of one of the shareholders as an auditor; presumably an intimate knowledge of the company's business outranked today's obsession with independence. Nor was it contemplated (or so it seems) that either *full* and *fair*, separately or in conjunction with one another, had been or were to be attributed anything other than their ordinary meaning in ordinary, everyday English language dialogue under statutory interpretation (Chambers, 1973b).

In Australia presently, Part 2M.3 of the Corporations Act 2001 requires company directors to prepare financial statements that comply with the approved accounting standards (ss. 296 and 304) and show a true and fair view of its financial performance and financial position (ss. 297 and 305). But these requirements are modified by the caveats in sections 297 and 305 that where a true and fair view does not emerge from complying with the accounting standards, such additional information as is necessary is to be shown in the *notes to and forming part of the accounts*. Similar, albeit not identical, situations apply in the UK, US and many Commonwealth countries.

True and fair – a turbulent history

Arguably underscoring all the debate and concerns about true and fair in various British colonies in the 1960s and beyond (footnote 9 provides some sources of that debate), was a virulent form of the rewriting of the history of true and fair and what it was intended to achieve. The phrase or its stronger equivalents had survived continuously in the legislation for nearly 150 years before the allegation that it had passed its use-by date was made in the early 1990s. This followed nearly two decades of press and practitioner rumblings in many countries. Table 19.1 and related discussion provides a snapshot of that history and some more recent events.

Table 19.1 Selected dates in the history of the true and fair quality criterion

1844	UK Companies Act – accounts required to show a *full and fair* balance sheet; focus on *investor* and *creditor* protection
1855	Limited liability introduced into the UK Companies Act
1856	UK Companies Act requires a *full and fair* balance sheet, *just and correct view* of the company's financial affairs(as part of a voluntary Table A)
1900+	UK Companies Act requires accounts and audited balance sheet; profit and loss eventually was prescribed in the 1929 UK Companies Act
Mid-1930s	Some Australian states adopt the 1929 UK Act as own legislation
1940s	*Fair* substituted for *correct* after 1945 UK Cohen Committee Inquiry and 1948 UK Companies Act
1961	Australian Uniform Companies Act adopts *true and fair* nomenclature
1970s–1980s	125+ years without equivocation (perhaps the longest uninterrupted professional ethos in legislation)
	Accountants' and regulators' uncertainty increases; deviations irk regulators' angst; accounts must comply with standards *and* show a *true and fair* view
1988	UK QC Arden confirms that true and fair view is operative as a quality criterion
Early 1990s	The explicit override is said to be deleted from Australia's corporate legislation – described in textbooks in early 1990s as an 'anachronism' and contestably suggested by regulators as 'inapplicable'
	Profession presses the *technical interpretation* – that compliance with the standards leads to true and fair view; the *override* actually remains, in different wording, the explicitly final disclosure criterion; Notes to Accounts disclosures if standards compliance does not provide a true and fair view
2002	Mark Leibler's submission to JCPAA; Walker's and Clarke and Dean's suggestion that 'true and fair view' still applies as the override in Australia's corporate reporting legislation
June 2005	UK FRC PN 85 and similar August 2005 UK FRC PN 119 dictum retain true and fair and professional judgment
May 2008	UK QC Martin Moore's opinion and the June 2008 UK FRC PN 222 dictum – true and fair is confirmed to be the cornerstone of British financial reporting
November 2011	UK FRC PN 338 reiterates true and fair's primacy

The antecedent to this table was a smaller version prepared for a University of Sydney Business and Professional Ethics Group seminar.

In a contemporary publication, Clarke *et al.* (2014, p. 43) observe:

> For the most part of a century and a quarter there appears to have been general content-ment with the true and fair (or its equivalent) format. . . . [B]ut by the late1960s through to the mid-1970s, in Australia at least, 'true and fair' produced considerable uneasiness. Likely this arose by virtue of the use of the override as justification for deviations from the accounting conventions of the day. Corporate Affairs Commissioner for New South Wales, F.J.O. Ryan, was an early antagonist, as his *Abacus* piece (1967) reveals. Calls for change had increased by the early to mid-1970s when, for example, [it was evident that] the professional accounting standard prescribing depreciation on land and buildings was not being complied with by many companies. During 1975–77 thousands of corporates' finan-cial accounts reviewed by the New South Wales Corporate Affairs Commission revealed

the following annual percentage deviations from one or more prescribed standards – 25%, 55% and 85%. In the next four years another regulatory review found an average annual deviation of 41%. It was claimed by preparers that following the standards, especially the depreciation on land and buildings standard, would result in untrue and unfair accounts. This continued into the early 1990s with other standards being in focus. Despite the rhetoric, there was nonetheless little prosecution to prove the allegations that the override was being abused. Bearing in mind the differences between the approved accounting practices then and those under the post-2005 AIFRS, the abandonment of the former in favour of the latter suggests that the prior practices were faulty. Unless, of course, we accept the untenable situation – that the financial position, financial performance and state of affairs are different now from what they were then. So, the likelihood is that those who deviated from the standards may, perversely, have been closer to disclosing a reliable view of a company's state of affairs – its financial position – than were those complying.

But as that quote implies there clearly is a call for change underway. Since the early 1970s in Australia and the UK, there have been suggestions that the true and fair view criterion is faulty and inoperable and that it should be supplanted by mere compliance with rules (standards).[10] During 2013 and early 2014, the UK Financial Reporting Council (FRC) again revisited the suitability of the override in the context of European Legislative Directives and the International Financial Reporting Standards (IFRS) setting following concerns raised by a major group of investors, including the Universities' Superannuation Scheme, Threadneedle Asset Management, UK Shareholders Association and the Local Authority Pension Fund Forum. They had sought legal advice from leading QC George Bompas (2013) because they felt that some IFRS were so flawed that they distorted the financial statements of banks from 2005 onwards. The FRC responded, seeking another opinion from QC Martin Moore. The main issues addressed by the QCs were in essence the status of true and fair in British compliance with the IFRS, whether the true and fair override existed, and whether the reporting standards had to be complied with when doing so did not result in the accounts showing a true and fair view. After reviewing the argument and counterargument by the QCs, the FRC produced a 2014 'True and Fair' paper which reiterated its 2008 and 2011 view about the primacy of the true and fair view.

Now we focus on some more recent critiques of TFV which address some similar, but also some additional, concerns. They also provide different solutions to those noted earlier.

Recent observations about accounting 'telling the truth'

Articles by Bayou, Reinstein and Williams (2011; hereafter BRW), Smeliauskas, Craig and Armenic (2008; hereafter SCA), and the related Alexander (2010) have suggested that the current reporting system is unable to operationalize effectively with this TFV ethos as the cornerstone of financial reporting. We reject this, as has the UK FRC on numerous occasions (see Table 19.1 for details). Indeed, here and elsewhere (e.g. Clarke *et al.*, 2014), analysis shows how and why the TFV ethos has been and should continue to be the cornerstone of corporate financial reporting.

BRW (2011, p. 109) suggest that:

> the assertion of a false or misleading financial report implies some belief that there could exist a true or not-misleading report. Accounting-standard setters have finessed this issue by suggesting that 'decision usefulness', not truth, is financial reporting's ultimate objective.

Over time they have gravitated to a coherence notion of truth to provide rationales for accounting policy. The result has been a serious conflict between the content of financial accounting and the auditing of that content. [Here] we describe this conflict and its consequences and, relying on John McCumber's work, provide an argument about how accounting scholars and practitioners might begin to think more cogently about what a truthful type of corporate reporting might be. [A]ccounting-standard setters have too narrowly construed what accounting's role in democratic society is and how the contradictions of current standard-setting jeopardize the essential professional franchise of accountants, the audit function.

There is much to agree with in this perspective, which covers a plethora of issues, including some of those addressed by Malloch and others in the first part of this paper. We agree, however, with West (2003; following Chambers and others) that the legal verification aspects of auditing as it interfaces with accounting in its accountability and decision usefulness function are crucial. There are, however, several points of disagreement with BRW (2011). One is the overlap in the notions of accountability/stewardship and decision usefulness. We have demonstrated elsewhere that, contrary to the understanding of BRW and others, there is a major overlap. In this regard, it is important to note that accounting is a technology. As a 'technology', what is important are accounting's 'uses', not its 'users'. Accepting this mitigates much of the BRW critique about standards setters' extreme focus on decision usefulness and its incompatibility with truth and fairness. Our previous works have distinguished 'uses' from 'users', noting also that the legislative qualitative criterion 'true and fair view' has a qualifier – namely, the law requires directors (with the assistance of the accounting technology) to provide a true and fair view of an entity's financial position and performance (in sum, its financial condition or state of affairs). Chambers (1973b) showed that the phrase 'statutory interpretation' could be interpreted (unless the legislation stated explicitly otherwise) through the ordinary use of the words, while Chambers and Wolnizer (1990) demonstrated through an historical review of the TFV criterion that there needs to be recourse to external referents when determining an entity's financial affairs. All of this is independent of who the 'users' are. Assuming compliance with the accounting standards *per se* will rarely suffice. As shown below, in preparing financial statements, directors need to step back from automatically complying with professional accounting standards, as do auditors in their attestation task, and consider whether in their professional judgment such compliance produces a true and fair view of an entity's financial position and performance.

SCA's (2008) contribution

> examines argumentation factors which affect the truth of an audit opinion. . . . [They] propose that the auditor's report be revised to replace the words 'true and fair view' with 'acceptable risk of material misstatement'. [They suggest] . . . this would better align the communication of auditors with the characteristics of accounting information upon which they report. Adoption of the wording 'acceptable risk of material misstatement' will facilitate a better appreciation by users of financial statements of the accounting estimates in financial statements.

> *(p. 225)*

Further, SCA show that fundamental to their concerns about true and fair are the inherent risks in accounting estimates.

As with the BRW (2011) piece, again there is plenty to agree with in SCA (2008). Consider the starting point, where they observe:

> Audit reform proposals, such as those contained in the Sarbanes–Oxley Act, 2002 (SOX) give insufficient attention to the intrinsically important underlying logic (or *logos*) of the auditor's report and to improving the truthfulness (or epistemic probability) of the audit opinion. Rather, the principal focus of audit reform has been directed to inspire stronger confidence in the reputation (or *ethos*) of auditors.
>
> *(p. 225)*

Elsewhere (Clarke and Dean, 2007, especially in Chapter 5), it is suggested that audit reforms in many jurisdictions have been observed to be much more concerned with audit input and processing procedures than with the outputs of the audit process, specifically the effectiveness (read, usefulness) of the audit opinion. Our view is also consistent with the SCA (2008) analysis that raises concerns that reported data emanating from mere compliance with IFRS fail (generally) to have any external referents: specifically, they observe that they are not estimates of realizable amounts of assets and liabilities. In the subsequent Alexander (2010) commentary, concerns are raised about the SCA (2008) proposal. Criticisms expressed (as in many earlier discussions about TFV) are underpinned by a belief that the phrase 'true and fair view' cannot accommodate the 'user' needs of a variety of different types of shareholders, let alone other types of investors (to which it is not too large a leap to add other users, like employees). This also misses the point about accounting being a technology, and therefore, as noted in our observations on BRW (2011), the focus should be on uses, not users.

We depart further from SCA (2008) when they assert that a change is needed because 'the meaning of "true and fair" is unclear and controversial' (p. 226). There is some similar discussion in SCA (2008) and BRW (2011), namely that there are (i) problems in accounting adequately addressing the inherent risks in accounting estimates, and (ii) communicating the results of the current audit process, because mentioning true and fair in the report necessarily means that there is recourse to the problematic notion of what is meant by economic reality. As noted, SCA (2008) propose that the solution is to replace in the audit report 'true and fair view' with 'acceptable risk of material misstatement'.

In the substantial argy-bargy between SCA (2008) and Alexander (2010) (and similarly in BRW, 2011), there is no recognition that in at least the British and Australian companies legislation, and the related professional audit standards, the term 'true and fair view' has the qualifier 'of financial position and performance'. Those and many earlier debates are thus vacuous and miss a critical aspect of what an audit opinion seeks to warrant. This legislative specification of external referents – financial position and financial performance – identifies a major component of an entity's current financial state. While this may not always be immediately apparent, nevertheless auditors are able to draw on their professional wisdom acquired from years of observations to complete their audit task to provide an opinion on how the directors report this state. This is the *differentia specifica* for which auditors obtain a service premium. What appears in the accounts can be warranted against their adjudged best assessment of that financial position and performance.

In sum – accounting's unique ethos

Our view accords with West (2003), who, having observed that the 'accounting profession has been granted an exclusive responsibility for independently pronouncing on the truth and fairness of financial reports' (following the earlier ideas of Chambers, 1973a, 1973b, 1978, 1991, and reiterated subsequently by, amongst others, Clarke, 2006), argues that the '[r]esponsibility to define "true and fair" runs parallel to this privilege' (p. 172). Elsewhere, members of the

Sydney School of Accounting have attempted to show how this may be achieved. Consider this proposed definition:

> *True and fair view:* the true and fair view of financial position and performance of a company, as it is at a specific date, meaningfully refers to the *serviceability* of the data in its financials – that is, the effectiveness with which the data in its financial statements can be used in determining the company's financial characteristics. This notion of true and fair uniquely links the nature and composition, and the individual money's worths of a company's assets and the amounts of its liabilities, and the aggregates and sub-aggregates of various classes of each, with the significant financial characteristics habitually used to distinguish different companies. For habitually, a company's financial strengths and constraints are compared to assess its wealth and progress. These include indicators of earnings and notions of earnings (underlying EBITA, etc), rate of return, solvency, liquidity, leverage, asset backing, interest cover, dividend cover and corporate earnings per share are calculated. The worth of one asset or class of assets is compared with that of another, and the amount owing by one liability or class of liabilities is compared with that of another (or with those due to be paid at a particular time). All that is a matter of financial commonsense, nothing special – other than it is not the way accountants appear to understand financial matters.
>
> *(Clarke et al., 2014, p. 45)*

Defining true and fair in this way is consistent with Malloch's thesis that the onus for ensuring trust in accounting should return to individual accounting practitioners. They should be bound not by rules (standards) capable of being ticked off but rather by a principled approach that ensures that reported accounting data are serviceable. 'Serviceability' encompasses the much contested qualitative characteristics of relevance, reliability, neutrality, verifiability and understandability. Importantly, it provides an operational meaning based on audit and financial outputs, not inputs or processes.

Finally, there is indirect support for the type of serviceability notion just outlined. BRW (2011) in fact allude to several US instances where the actions of businessmen and judges are *as if* commercial parties perceive it is *not* too difficult to operationalize TFV. There are likely many similar instances in other jurisdictions. In this respect, we are heartened by two recent high-level Australian judicial decisions following disputes about the misleading disclosures made during the GFC about derivative instruments.

The first relates to the single judge Federal Court of Australia Act (Cth) class action by several local councils against Grange Securities, a unit of Lehman Brothers. The ruling and settlement by the Hon. Justice Steven Rares upheld the action brought under the 'misleading and deceptive conduct' (i.e. untrue and unfair) provisions of a morass of legislative consumer protection provisions (thousands of pages), including the Corporations Act. Evidence was adduced that in promoting the sale to those local councils of the so-called innovative synthetic and other financial investment products (that the judge in obiter described as a 'speculative bet'), there had been a lack of transparency by representatives of Grange regarding the riskiness of those assets. More generally, the judge recommended that in order to better protect investors, the government should bring simplified legislation, such as the former s. 51 (all of two pages) of the Trade Practices Act, before the parliament.[11] This simplified approach accords with our view that the ethical code approach of the current legislative TFV override is better than recourse to various prescribed rules (like accounting standards).

Similarly, the Hon. Justice James Jagot ruled, in a related class action case also brought in a single judge of the Federal Court of Australia (FCA) by twelve councils against their local government financial services adviser, that Standard & Poor's and several financial institutions had misled investors and breached their duty of care when they gave 'grotesquely' complex and risky assets (described as proportionate CDOs) a AAA rating – a rating subsequently found on the basis of evidence to be untrue and unfair.[12] Seemingly along the lines of the FCA case, the US Department of Justice has issued a civil lawsuit against the ratings agency Standard & Poor's, claiming it inappropriately rated a particular CDO as AAA, causing investors to be misinformed about the CDO's risk. The lower court rulings were upheld on appeal in 2014 by a FCA (Full Court) judgement.[13] Such judgements show that, ultimately, in order for there to be a workable order, the law will expect operationalization of what many (especially accounting academics) view as problematic norms, such as the enforcement of truth and fairness reporting obligations, so that financial statements are not 'misleading and deceptive'. The law has no qualms about the existence of such norms. Regulators and some standards setters also seem to accept this. In the words of Australian Accounting Standards Board Chairman Roger Armstrong and Audit Practices Board Chairman Richard Fleck in July 2011:

> [O]ur Boards expect preparers, those charged with governance and auditors: Always to stand back and ensure that the accounts as a whole do give a true and fair view; to be prepared, albeit in extremely rare circumstances, to consider using the true and fair override; and to ensure that the consideration they give to these matters is evident in their deliberations and documentation. This will help ensure that accounts in the UK continue to demonstrate the high quality that users have come to expect.

Nearly identical wording in support of the override proposition concludes the abovementioned June 2014 FRC document on 'True and Fair'.

In Australia, it is contestable whether the override applies, while in the USA it appears not to apply (see Clarke *et al.*, 2014, pp. 41–57). As championed by proponents of the IFRS regime, whither international reporting comparability?

Reiterating the points made, business in the British tradition following the 1844 joint stock companies legislation thus enjoys a unique heritage. For there was bequeathed, ultimately, the requirement that incorporated entities were to prepare accounts that were *full and fair*. Apart from changes in actual wording to *full and correct* (several nineteenth-century UK Companies Acts), *true and correct* (1948 UK Companies Act) and *true and fair* (1960, Australian Companies [now Corporations] Act), this general ethical criterion has survived for 170 years. Moreover, in 2008, when the wording in the UK legislation had to be changed to 'presents fairly' to accord with EU law, UK advocate Martin Moore, QC, determined the new wording the equivalent of the former and that true and fair undeniably remained 'the cornerstone of British accounting'(Martin Moore Opinion, 2008). This was confirmed in the July 2011 FRC PN 338, and again in the June 2014 FRC 'True and Fair' paper.

Arguably, accountants in the British tradition are the custodians of the oldest surviving and uninterrupted professional ethic enshrined in legislation. 'True and fair' is a business ethos par excellence, one that we have sought to show here is the province of individual practitioners to determine based on their accumulated knowledge and wisdom.

Notes

1 A similar point is made by the Hon. Justice Steven Rares (obiter) in *Wingecarribee Shire Council v. Lehman Brothers Australia*. The lack of trust in the financial sector is shown by Chamley *et al.* (2012) to have been integral to the Global Financial Crisis.

2 Some examples include Peters and Waterman's *In Search of Excellence* (1982) and Miller's critique of their excellence thesis in *The Icarus Paradox* (1990). In 2007, Nicholas Taleb made a similar point about the role of luck in his *Black Swan*. It should be noted that many corporate case exemplars are discussed below – they are primarily, following Malloch, US examples. But, importantly, other countries have had similar instances, as demonstrated in the earlier works by Valance (1955) and Haldane (1970) and in the more recent works of (say) Clarke and Dean (2007), Jones (2011), Clikeman (2013) and Margret and Peck (2014) that discuss many of the cases noted in this article.

3 *The Financial Times*, 26 July 2013; accessed online on 8 July 2014 at http://www.ft.com/intl/cms/s/0/4798ae22-f552-11e2-b4f8-00144feabdc0.html?siteedition=intl#axzz2a69QO7I.

4 In the Federal Court of Australia case *Bathurst Regional Council v. Local Government Financial Services Pty Ltd (No. 5)* [2012] FCA 1200, Honourable Justice James Jagot in obiter used the 'grotesque' metaphor.

5 Daniel Flitton, 'Investigative process shown to be flawed', *Sydney Morning Herald*, 13 August 2012; accessed online on 28 September 2012. See also: Geoff Winestock, 'Stevens admits failure on Securency', *Australian Financial Review*, 9 October 2012, pp. 1, 4. In October 2013, the scandal widened with allegations aired in an ABC TV *Four Corners* program that there was knowledge by members of the boards of the subsidiaries of bribery practices to secure the note technology sales.

6 There are recent claims of Australian instances of managerial short-termism. Reports of Leighton Holdings' alleged $42 million kickback paid to the Iraq officials for the $750 million pipeline construction contract, if proven, is one such case that would further illustrate that a lack of trust in the leaders of Australian corporates (and their regulator) is justified. Indeed, the text under the Fairfax press editorial, 'Foreign bribery a stain on our reputation', complained: 'The bribery scandal surrounding Leighton holdings reflects an arrogant corporate culture absence of regulatory zeal, and weak legislation screaming for reform' (Nick McKenzie and Richard Baker, 'The Leighton Files', *Sydney Morning Herald*, 3 October 2013, pp. 1 and 8; Chanticleer *Australian Financial Review*, 2 October 2013, p. 52). Leighton refutes the claim. Another instance involves the actions of one of Australia's major banks, the CBA, and its financial planners. A major parliamentary enquiry concluded that poor incentive schemes by the CBA led to conflicted actions by its financial planners. The bank's CEO subsequently apologized to customers in an attempt to repair the long-term implications of such short-term actions.

7 A table of the GFC-related settlements by financial institutions appeared in the *Frankfurter Allgemeine Zeitung*, 7 June 2014, p. 22. It reveals that since 2009 those settlements have exceeded US$94 billion, mostly on a no fault, no liability settlement basis!

8 Joint Stock Companies Registration and Regulation Act, 1844, (7 & 8 Vict. c.110).

9 There have been numerous articles discussing true and fair view, over many decades. For example, Chambers (1973a) and Chambers and Wolnizer (1990, 1991). The last two articles are reproduced in Parker *et al.* (1996), which contains a compendium of articles on TFV. An article by Nobes (2009) provides some contrasting views about whether the override currently applies. It and two others are discussed in detail below.

10 Footnote 9 lists several papers included in that ongoing debate.

11 Federal Court of Australia, *Wingecarribee Shire Council v. Lehman Brothers Australia Ltd (in liq)* [2012] FCA 1028.

12 Federal Court of Australia, *Bathurst Regional Council v. Local Government Financial Services Pty Ltd (No. 5)* [2012] FCA 1200.

13 Federal Court of Appeal (Full Court), *AEN-Ambro Bank NV v. Bathurst Regional Council* [2014] FCAFC 65, 6 June 2014.

References

Alexander, D. (2010), 'Material Misstatement of What? A Comment on "A Proposal to Replace 'True and Fair View' with Acceptable Risk of Misstatement"', *Abacus*, Vol. 46, No. 4, pp. 447–454.

Bayou, M.E., A. Reinstein and P.F. Williams (2011), 'To Tell the Truth: A Discussion of Issues Concerning Truth and Ethics in Accounting', *Accounting, Organizations and Society*, Vol. 36, No. 2, pp. 109–124.

Bompas, A.G. (2013), *International Financial Reporting Standards (Issues arising in relation to the Companies Act 2006)*, QC Opinion 8 April.

Briloff, A. (1972), *More Debits than Credits*, Harper & Row, New York.

—— (1976), *Truth About Accounting*, Harper & Row, New York.

Chambers, R.J. (1973a), *Securities and Obscurities: A Case for Reform of the Law of Company Accounts*, Gower Press, Melbourne; reissued in 1986 as *Accounting in Disarray*, Garland Publishing, New York.

—— (1973b), 'Accounting Principles and the Law', *Australian Business Law Review*, June, pp. 113–129.

—— (Chairman) Accounting Standards Review Committee (1978), *Company Accounting Standards*, Government Printer, Sydney.

—— (1991), 'Accounting and Corporate Morality: The Ethical Cringe', *Australian Journal of Corporate Law*, September, pp. 9–21.

Chambers, R.J. and P.W. Wolnizer (1990), 'A True and Fair View of Financial Position', *Company and Securities Law Journal*, December, pp. 353–368.

—— (1991), 'A True and Fair View of Position and Results: The Historical Background', *Accounting, Business and Financial History*, April, pp. 197–203.

Chamley, C., J. Laurence, L.J. Kotlikoff and H. Polemarchakis (2012), 'Limited-Purpose Banking: Moving From "Trust Me" to "Show Me" Banking', *American Economic Review*, Vol. 102, No. 3, pp. 113–119.

Clarke, F. L. (2002), 'Submission 11 to JCPAA Inquiry', Review of Independent Auditing by Registered Company Auditors; http://www.aph.gov.au/Parliamentary_Business/Committees/House_of_Representatives_Committees?url=jcpaa/indepaudit/contents.htm, accessed on 19 January 2014.

—— (2006), 'Introduction: True and Fair: Anachronism or Quality Criterion Par Excellence?', *Abacus*, Vol. 42, No. 2, pp. 129–131.

Clarke, F.L. and G.W. Dean (2007), *Indecent Disclosure: Gilding the Corporate Lily*, Cambridge University Press, Melbourne.

Clarke, F.L., G.W. Dean and M. Egan (2014), *The Unaccountable and Ungovernable Corporation: Corporates' Use-By Dates Close In*, Routledge, London.

Clarke, F.L., G.W. Dean and K.G. Oliver (1997), *Corporate Collapse: Regulatory, Accounting and Ethical Failure*, Cambridge University Press, Cambridge.

—— (2003), *Corporate Collapse: Accounting, Regulatory and Ethical Failure*, 2nd revised edn, Cambridge University Press, Cambridge.

Clarke, F.L., G.W. Dean and M.C. Wells (2012), *The Sydney School of Accounting: The Chambers Years*, University of Sydney, Sydney.

Clikeman, P.M. (2013), *Called to Account: Financial Frauds that Shaped the Accounting Profession*, 2nd edn, Routledge, London.

Federal Court of Australia, *Wingecarribee Shire Council v Lehman Brothers Australia Ltd* (in liq) [2012] FCA 1028.

FRC (UK Financial Reporting Council) (2005), PN 85, 'Financial Reporting Review Panel publishes legal opinion on the effect of the IAS Regulation on the requirement for accounts to give a True and Fair View', 24 June 2005; http://www.frc.org.uk/News-and-Events/FRC-Press/Press/2005/June/Financial-Reporting-Review-Panel-publishes-legal-o.aspx, accessed on 24 April 2013.

—— (2005), PN 119, 9 August 2005; http://www.frc.org.uk, accessed on 24 April 2013.

—— (2008), PN 222, 'Relevance of "True and Fair" concept confirmed', 19 May 2008; http://www.frc.org.uk/News-and-Events/FRC-Press/Press/2008/May/Relevance-of-True-and-Fair-concept-confirmed.aspx, accessed on 24 April 2013.

—— (2011), PN 338, 'Relevance of "True and Fair" concept confirmed'; https://frc.org.uk/News-and-Events/FRC-Press/Press/2011/July/Importance-of-true-and-fair-view-in-both-UK-GAAP-a.aspx, accessed on 24 April 2013.

—— (2014), *True and Fair*; https://frc.org.uk/Our-Work/Publications/Accounting-and-Reporting-Policy/True-and-Fair-June-2014.pdf, accessed on 24 April 2013.

Haldane, A. (1970), *With Intent to Deceive*, William Blackwood, Edinburgh.

Hunt, B.C. (1936), *The Development of the Business Corporation in England 1800–1867*, Harvard University Press, Cambridge, MA.

Jones, M. (2011), *Creative Accounting: Fraud and International Accounting Standards*, John Wiley & Sons, Chichester.

Macey, J.R. (2013), *The Death of Corporate Reputation: How Integrity Has Been Destroyed on Wall Street*, Pearson Education, Singapore.

Malik, O. (2003), *Broadbandits: Inside the $750 Billion Telecom Heist*, John Wiley & Sons, Hoboken, NJ.

Malloch, T.R. (2011), *Doing Virtuous Business: The Remarkable Success of Spiritual Enterprise*, Thomas Nelson, Wheaton, IL.

Malloch T.R. and J.D. Mamorsky (2013), *The End of Ethics and a Way Back*, John Wiley & Sons, Singapore.

Maltby, J. (1998), 'UK Joint Stock Companies Legislation 1844–1900: Accounting Publicity and "Mercantile Caution"', *Accounting History, NS*, Vol. 3, No. 1, pp. 3–27.

Margret, J. and G. Peck (2014), *Fraud in Financial Statements*, Routledge, London.

Markopolos, H., with F. Casey, N. Chelo, G. Kachroo and M. Ocrant (2011), *No One Would Listen: A True Financial Thriller*, John Wiley & Sons, Hoboken, New Jersey.

Miller, D. (1990), *The Icarus Paradox: How Successful Companies Bring About Their Own Downfall*, Harper Business, New York.

Moore, M. (2008), 'The True and Fair View Requirement Revisited', QC Opinion for Financial Reporting Council, Erskine Chambers, 21 April 2008.

—— (2013), *International Accounting Standards and the True and Fair View*, QC Opinion for Financial Reporting Council, Erskine Chambers, 8 October.

Nobes, C. (2009), 'The Importance of Being Fair: An Analysis of IFRS Regulation in Practice: A Comment', *Accounting and Business Research*, Vol. 39, No. 4, pp. 415–427.

Parker, R., P. Wolnizer and C. Nobes (1996), *Readings in True and Fair*, Garland Publishing, New York.

Peters, T.J. and R.H. Waterman Jr. (1982), *In Search of Excellence: Lessons from America's Best-Run Companies*, Harper & Row, Sydney.

Russell, H.F. (1978), *Foozles and Frauds*, Institute of Internal Auditors, Altamonte Springs, Florida.

Ryan, F.J.O. (1967), 'A True and Fair View', *Abacus*, Vol. 32, No. 2, pp. 95–108.

Salter, M.S. (2008), *Innovation Corrupted: The Origins and Legacy of Enron's Collapse*, Harvard University Press, Cambridge, MA.

Shannon, H.A. (1932), 'The First Five Thousand Companies and Their Duration', *Economic History, NS*, Vol. 3, No. 7, pp. 396–424.

Smeliauskas, W., R. Craig and J. Amernic (2008), 'A Proposal to Replace "True and Fair View" with "Acceptable Risk of Misstatement"', *Abacus*, Vol. 44, No. 3, 225–250.

Taleb, N.N. (2007), *The Black Swan*, Penguin, New York.

The Matter of Barclays PLC, Barclays Bank PLC, and Barclays Inc, CFTC Docket 12–25.

US Senate Permanent Subcommittee on Investigations (2011), *Wall Street and the Financial Crisis: Anatomy of a Financial Collapse*, Cosimo Reports, New York.

Valance, A. (1955), *A Very Private Enterprise*, Thames and Hudson, London.

Walker, R.G. (2002), Submission 41 to JCPAA Inquiry, Review of Independent Auditing by Registered Company Auditors, http://www.aph.gov.au/Parliamentary_Business/Committees/House_of_Repre sentatives_Committees?url=jcpaa/indepaudit/contents.htm, accessed on 19 January 2014.

West, B. (2003), *Professionalism and Accounting Rules*, Routledge, London.

20

Accounting for the carbon challenge

Janek Ratnatunga and Stewart Jones

Introduction

The balance of scientific evidence indicates that the world is facing significant risks associated with the potentially damaging consequences of climate change (Garnaut Report, 2008). The international responses have been the 1992 *United Nations Framework Convention on Climate Change (UNFCCC)* and the 1997 *Kyoto Protocol*. The UNFCCC classified its ratifying countries into two major groups: Annex I countries, consisting of 41 industrially developed countries, and non-Annex I countries, comprising 151 developing countries. According to its 'common but differentiated responsibilities and capabilities' principle, the UNFCCC mandates that Annex I countries take the lead in combating climate change. This principle has been used as a basic guide to construct the burden-sharing for developed and developing countries to clean up global anthropogenic pollution. The Kyoto Protocol is an international regulatory response under which almost 200 countries agreed to strive to decrease carbon dioxide (CO_2) emissions. Under the Kyoto Protocol, a country can emit more CO_2 than its assigned amount only if it can simultaneously sequester the equivalent amount in *allowable* carbon sinks, which include *afforestation* and *reforestation* activities undertaken since 1990.[1]

Although the term of the Kyoto Protocol came to an end in December 2012, it was extended for its second period from 1 January 2013 to 31 December 2020. As such, all Annex I Kyoto-ratifying countries (except Russia, Japan and Canada, which had already stated that they would not join the second period of Kyoto commitment) will continue having *mandatory* reduction targets. A future climate agreement, which is planned to come into force in 2020, will legally apply emissions reduction targets for both developed and developing countries. In addition to this, 41 developed and 48 developing countries have accepted *voluntary* carbon emission targets. To meet these mandatory and voluntary targets, countries have developed various carbon policies for reducing carbon emissions, such as (1) taxing carbon emissions, (2) putting a price on carbon sequestrations (called a carbon credit), and (3) the establishment of an *Emission Trading Scheme (ETS)* (ideally linked internationally), by which countries with surplus credits can sell them to countries with quantified mandatory or voluntary emission limitation and reduction commitments.

Under an ETS, those countries with emissions reduction targets will in turn set up a *cap and trade* scheme to pass on these pollution limits to business entities who are told how much CO_2

they can emit (the cap). If companies emit more than their cap, they can buy *Renewable Energy Credits (RECs)*[2] from other businesses that come in under their cap (the trade).[3] There are two types of RECs: (1) those issued by governments (akin to ration cards) and (2) those created by organisations internally. Governments may issue RECs free or sell them at a grant-date price. These RECs are, in fact, *permits to pollute* (i.e. to emit CO_2). Organisations can then cash these RECs in line with their pollution levels. If they do not pollute as much as the REC permits they hold, the excess permits can either be sold (income) at the prevailing market price, or held (asset) as an offset against future pollution, which is the liability.

Consider an REC issued by the government to be like a set of concert tickets purchased (or obtained free) in advance for a season of concerts that is deemed by the government as being mandatory to attend. Once a concert is attended (i.e. carbon emissions pollution happens), then a ticket must be surrendered. Excess concert tickets may be sold to those needing tickets at prevailing market (scalper) prices, and vice versa. Such government issued RECs are tangible assets like inventory. There are many accounting treatments for such tangible assets and the underlying liability, which will be overviewed later.

The second type of REC originates when governments permit some organisations (such as utility companies and forestry organisations) to issue their own RECs (called *abatement certificates*) if they can document that they have undertaken carbon sequestration activity during a period. The internally generated RECs require a very different accounting treatment to those issued by governments because the underlying assets that have the capability of creating such RECs are intangible in essence. It is the valuation and reporting of such organisational capability that is the main focus of this chapter.

The chapter will proceed as follows. The next section overviews the implications of carbon trading activity for the accounting profession, especially in terms of intangible asset valuations and corporate social responsibility reports. This is followed by a discussion of carbon emission and sequestration accounting and the resultant monetary measurements used in accounting for carbon emission trading. Next, a discussion as to why current generally accepted accounting principles (GAAP) and the traditional conceptual accounting framework are not suitable for capturing the impact of carbon trading activities on financial statement accounting is presented; this is especially so in organisations that have developed efficient carbon emissions management capabilities to internally generate RECs.

As such, the next section presents the key message of the chapter via a normative discussion on the paradigm shift required to develop a new accounting framework to capture and report the value of assets capable of absorbing carbon. First, a new metric, *Environmental Capability Value (ECV)*, is presented as underpinning the conversion of non-monetary CO_2 emission and sequestration measures to monetary values. Next, the process of bringing these monetised values within the boundaries of conventional (double-entry) GAAP is demonstrated.

The chapter concludes by suggesting three possible approaches to integrate this new measurement paradigm into current organisational financial statements.

The implications of carbon trading activity for the accounting profession

Traditionally, the monetary basis on which the various stakeholders of business entities make their investment and other commercial decisions, and evaluate the results of those decisions, has been through the framework of financial accounting. Because of the wide-ranging use of financial reports by multiple stakeholders, the profession has developed an auditing and assurance framework to ensure that the numbers reported can be relied upon. This framework provides a 'true and fair' assessment of such reports and the quantification of the economic values therein. Two major issues, however, still remain unanswered within this framework: (1) the valuation and reporting of intangibles and (2) the reporting of how an organisation is meeting its environmental and social responsibilities (Jones and Belkaoui, 2009).

Whilst there has been some (largely unfocused) discourse in the accounting profession with regard to the valuation and reporting of carbon credits and allowances, there has been little serious discourse about valuing the underlying assets that generate these allowances.

There are three main accounting issues related to carbon emissions that have been addressed in prior discussions: (1) How should the allowance be valued at the grant date and over time and when should it be reported in the income statement? (2) How should the liability be valued over time and when should it be reported in the income statement? and (3) How should the grant liability be recorded?

The state of the current discourse on these issues is summarised in the Appendix to this chapter, where it is shown that there seems to be some agreement in the accounting profession that once RECs are issued, purchased or created, a company should recognise them as a *new asset* on the *balance sheet* (akin to inventory), and that, as actual emissions occur, a *liability* should be recognised and *changes in the market price* of allowances (i.e. gains and losses on allowances) should be recognised in the *profit and loss account*. Cook (2009) argues that the allowance, the emissions liability and the grant liability should be recorded separately at fair value, and changes in the fair values should be reported in income.

There has been no specific discourse to date, however, regarding the valuation and recording of the assets (and liabilities) capable of producing (and using) the RECs that underpin a carbon trading market, especially when these are *not acquired (or obtained via a government grant)*. Some might argue that such a discourse falls within the rich literature available regarding the valuation and reporting of intangible assets generally, and that REC-creating intangible assets are no different. We hope to demonstrate in this chapter that, in fact, a special case can be made for the valuation and recording of REC-producing asset capabilities.

The intangible asset valuation issue

As with the value of the underlying asset that generates a carbon credit, it is true that valuation problems affect most intangible assets. For example, how should a customer list be valued? Should it be valued at replacement cost in terms of the marketing and advertising expenses of rebuilding it? Or should it be valued using income projections? Or by taking the incremental income attributable to the customer list? Or according to a market price, determined by how much the list would sell for if it were sold? Clearly, there are several possible responses, indicating that traditional valuation approaches of replacement costs, income projections and market valuations do not work well for intangibles. New valuation approaches have therefore been extensively considered in the literature.

These new valuation approaches are developing from two directions. First, there is a range of new approaches to performance measurement and internal corporate reporting using modified discounted cash flow techniques and accrual accounting adjustments. Second, there are the index-based measures (such as the Balanced Scorecard), which attempt to link financial performance to intangible drivers like employee quality and morale and customer satisfaction. Both these streams of development can be adapted to the valuation and reporting of carbon sequestration assets.

These approaches are not exclusive. Different kinds of measures might be more relevant to different audiences. Some are designed primarily to give managers and workers a clearer picture of the strengths and weaknesses of their business and change the way they think and act. Others may be designed to help analysts and investors assess the contribution that intangible assets make to financial performance. These valuation approaches will now be briefly summarised.

1   *Cash Flow Measures:* The future cash flow stream associated with an intangible asset is projected and discounted to the present value. Another related approach is 'shareholder value added' (SVA). This was developed by Rappaport (1986) and gained in importance during the 1980s. The SVA approach uses 'value drivers' to measure the present value of past and projected free cash flows from strategic and non-strategic investments. Although there is some general evidence that cash flow generation is better linked to share market valuations than profits and earnings, the link is far from being well established. One study found a high correlation between cash flow and market valuations (Deloitte and Touche, 1996). Another study found that between 1977 and 1996, operating cash flows were no better a guide to market value than reported earnings (Lev and Zarowin, 1998).

2   *Index-Based Measures:* These measures use coefficients to translate financial and non-financial 'key performance indicators' (KPIs) to financial values. The Balanced Scorecard is a popular approach to generating such measures, in which coefficients are obtained ex-post via statistical regression analysis (if the past is a good proxy for the future) or via managerial judgment in obtaining ex-ante consensus-based coefficients.

One such index-based measure is the *Capability Economic Value of Intangible and Tangible Assets (CEVITA™)* valuation approach, which uses some amount of expert opinion to provide valuations and performance measurements (see Ratnatunga, Gray and Balachandran, 2004).[4] The approach is to estimate the dollar value of both tangible and intangible assets by first identifying their *value-increasing* and *value-decreasing* constants, and how these constant values respond to expenditure incurred to support them. Once these constants are identified and provided by the experts, then the organisation's income generating capabilities can be valued and reported. We will demonstrate that this approach provides a key to the valuation of carbon emission and sequestration capabilities.

The corporate social responsibility (CSR) reporting issue

In addition to the financial reporting of intangible asset values, the current financial accounting information system appears to be ill-equipped to provide the framework required for reporting to multiple stakeholders as to how an organisation is meeting its environmental and social responsibilities, especially the challenge of reducing global warming (Ratnatunga, 2007; Jones and Belkaoui, 2009). While quantification in monetary terms has been accounting's sine qua non in reporting to shareholders on an organisation's economic performance, it is also well documented that monetary measurement alone can be severely limited when reporting on environmental, social and governance performance issues. This is because the actions undertaken and the resultant impacts cannot always be valued in monetary terms.[5] Thus, alternative social constructs have been proposed (and used) to report on an entity's corporate social responsibility (CSR), mostly using non-monetary measures. In fact, Bebbington and Larrinaga (2008) state that a total paradigm shift to 'non-financial reporting' is necessary to allow conditions for democratic accountability in an uncertain setting.

Despite these alternative social constructs, however, the accounting profession worldwide (using orthodox economic thinking) still seeks to parameterize the CSR discussion within a conventional accounting framework.

This chapter argues for an incremental paradigm shift in conventional accounting valuation, by leaving out of CSR reporting those non–monetary essences (i.e. the benefits of having less climatic disruption) that cannot be converted to money. The view taken in this chapter is that the existence of a carbon trading market in RECs provides a special case where the carbon emissions and sequestration transactions can be monetised and captured within the reliability and relevance requirements of accounting reporting, representing an incremental rather than total paradigm shift in reporting CSR actions as balance sheet values. This chapter deliberately focuses only on reporting the monetary consequences of a country implementing an ETS.

It could be argued that to a profession struggling to account for (1) intangible assets and liabilities such as intellectual property (IP), brand values and reputation as economic values (see Ratnatunga, Gray and Balachandran, 2004; Ratnatunga and Ewing, 2005) and (2) CSR actions as economic values (see Lantos, 2001; Orlitzky, 2005; Shank et al., 2005; Bebbington and Larrinaga, 2008), even a *minor* incremental paradigm shift required for reporting the reduction of CO_2 emissions in monetary values appears to be a hurdle too high to clear. Therefore, rather than *tinkering* with the debits and credits of a clearly *broken tool* (where intangibles are concerned), the chapter explores an alternative paradigm using a *disjointed incrementalism* approach, which produces constructs only marginally different from past practice (Quinn, 1978).

Accounting for carbon emission trading

Carbon emission and sequestration (CES) accounting

The mechanism for calculating the quantum of CO_2 either emitted by a source or sequestered in a biomass sink is referred to as 'carbon accounting'. This has very little to do with the monetary values usually associated with the term 'accounting'. Therefore, in this chapter we will refer to this mechanism as 'carbon emission and sequestration (CES) accounting'. The CES accounting mechanism must be sufficiently robust that the carbon trading market has confidence that the amount of carbon sequestered can be both measured and considered to be equivalent in its impact on global warming potential to the CO_2 released to the atmosphere from activities producing greenhouse gases.

As can be appreciated, the detailed requirements for a CES accounting system are continually being developed by organisations such as the Intergovernmental Panel on Climate Change (IPCC, 2007).[6] Any CES accounting standard developed by a country or non-governmental organisation will need to be consistent with IPCC principles before RECs generated from carbon sinks can be used in an emissions trading regime under the Kyoto Protocol.

The accounting profession would want one standardised ('one-size-fits-all') system pertaining to CES measures. Unfortunately, the current situation is that, although the interest in the carbon trading market is high, the new market is largely unregulated and lacks transparency. Government policy in countries such as the USA and Australia is in a constant state of change, and questions of measurement and pricing required for an efficient trading system are far from settled. For example, according to Tandukar (2007), business organisations and individual customers[7] have no way of discriminating between the providers who claim that their scheme is better able to measure than a competing scheme that

$$X \text{ tress} = \text{the sequestration of } Y \text{ tons of } CO_2 \text{ emissions} = \$Z \qquad (1)$$

However, without agreed CES measurements, the variation possible in the middle section of the equation (which is the domain of CES accounting measures) could lead to gross distortions of whatever dollar value was offered in a carbon trading exchange. In other words, because the sequestration or emissions measured could be a range of values (rather than a deterministic, agreed value), the dollars received or paid for such could also be a range of values.

Whatever the methodology or approach that is ultimately agreed in terms of CES measures, the issue for the accounting profession is the monetary value ($Z) of the CO_2 that these CES accounting measurements say has been either removed from the atmosphere or saved from being emitted by an organisation's products, services, equipment and processors. The existence of an efficient carbon trading market would be able to put a price on this in terms of an REC (or allowance). In addition, the traditional accounting reports would need to recognise that certain non-current assets (or liabilities) could also give rise to *future* carbon related revenues and expenses. Currently, the tangible asset (e.g. a power plant or forest) that generates the carbon credit is given a balance sheet value, but the related intangible asset or liability (i.e. the CO_2 sequestration or emissions ability of such CO_2 sinks and sources) is not. In a carbon emissions management environment, if organisations record the value of the tangible, they would need to consider the value of the related intangible.

In such instances, the accounting profession would need to obtain the services of outside consultants, such as environmental scientists and biologists, to undertake CES accounting measurements. The use of such external experts is not uncommon. The accounting profession often incorporates reports from company directors, actuaries, business analysts, engineers, quantity surveyors, and lawyers, especially in the area of balance sheet asset valuation and fair-value accounting. Using expert opinions in accounting for CO_2 flows would be no different. However, accounting standard setters have been reluctant to accept expert opinions as balance sheet values of intangible assets, and one could envisage them having concerns with values generated via CES accounting.

Carbon financial statement accounting

The current discourse in the accounting profession largely pertains to the issue of when revenue or expenses related to RECs should be recognised. This timing issue is not the focus of the chapter, as the ultimate solution can be incorporated within the conventional accounting paradigm.[8] However, for the sake of completeness, the current discourse with regard to the timing issue is overviewed in the Appendix.

This chapter focuses on the failure of conventional GAAP to recognise and measure intangible assets that are not acquired. As discussed before, whilst this failure is present in the area of intangible assets generally, this chapter puts forward a special case for the valuation of carbon sources and sinks that are not acquired (such as the internal development of assets with the capability to generate future RECs). However, a shift in conventional thinking is required for this valuation approach to be incorporated in financial reports.

The main paradigm shift is the view that a balance sheet should record 'what an organization can do' (capability) and not 'what an organization has' in monetary terms (Ratnatunga et al., 2004). This of course hinges on the definition of an asset. An asset is defined by the International Accounting Standards Board (IASB) as 'a resource controlled by the entity as a result of past events and from which future economic benefits are expected to flow to the entity'. The question then arises as to whether having the capability to reduce emissions, as opposed to having actually reduced emissions, meets the definition of an asset. There are those who would argue that having the capability to reduce emissions is less likely to provide the ability of generating tradable RECs in the future than having already reduced emissions. The issue becomes clearer if the discussion is framed in terms of a tangible (non-current) asset such as a machine.

Such a machine would fit the IASB definition of an asset, as a past event (payment of the historical purchase price) resulted in an organisation controlling this resource (machine) and its ability to produce goods (inventory) in the future that can be sold to provide future economic benefits. Using this analogy to an intangible environmental asset such as a tree (i.e. its ability to generate RECs in the future by sequestering CO_2 via growth) would be a very different asset to the inventory of RECs produced by having already reduced emissions.

It must also be noted that the unique tangible/intangible nature of carbon related assets makes their accounting treatment under conventional accounting frameworks fraught with difficulty, especially in organisations such as forestry companies that have carbon sequestration assets (sinks) such as trees. These entities may find these assets instantly becoming carbon emitting sources (liabilities) should their trees be destroyed in a forest fire. Whilst accepting that there are situations in business life in which organisational assets contain elements of contingent liability *such that in the instant the asset is wiped off the books a liability arises*, most of these contingent liabilities are litigious in nature. A plane (tangible asset) that crashes or a dangerous side effect that is discovered in a drug patent (intangible asset) may not only wipe out the assets from the balance sheet but also simultaneously give rise to a class action contingent liability.[9] However, carbon sinks such as trees are simultaneously carbon sources as well, as they shed leaves, for example, whilst growing. Thus, any metric to value the *carbon sequestration* capabilities of these assets must simultaneously capture their *carbon emission* capabilities. This type of valuation model will require a paradigm shift in how the accounting profession deals with asset valuation; such a model is presented in the next section of this chapter.

A new paradigm for the valuation of environmental capabilities

Measuring the value of assets with environmental capabilities

The earlier sections summarised the largely unfocused discourse in the accounting profession with regard to (1) intangible assets and (2) CSR initiatives in the financial reporting of carbon credits and allowances issued by governments, purchased via emissions trading schemes or created internally (i.e. abatement certificates) via emissions management schemes. Also highlighted was the virtual non-existence of any serious discourse about valuing the underlying assets that have the capability to generate these RECs in the future. The reason for this lack of guidance is that the accounting profession is constrained by an accounting framework that was originally developed to report on the economic performance of tangible 'industrial era' assets.

With carbon trading markets operating for some years in Europe (the European Union Emissions Trading Scheme, EU ETS) and trading schemes planned in many other developed countries, the accounting profession can no longer ignore the existence of such assets (and liabilities). A paradigm shift is needed to consider the valuation and recording of the assets (and liabilities) capable of producing (and using) the *Renewable Energy Credits (RECs)* that underpin a carbon trading market, especially when these are not acquired, in order to provide relevant information with regard to decisions that help reduce the impact of climate change.

It will require some revolutionary 'out of the square' thinking to effect such a paradigm shift, and this thinking will most probably be largely resisted and challenged by the accounting profession. Such resistance is not uncommon in the scientific world. Kuhn (1962) states that any conventional paradigm is challenged and replaced only when it continually fails to explain anomalies between its theorised knowledge and lived experiences. This implies that there exists an implicit social contract for practitioners to fall into line with the prevailing thinking until it is no longer palatable to do so. Thus, dissident voices would be ignored or dismissed during some interim period until the paradigm shift is finally effected. Consequently, a social contract needs to exist in the interim period between the redundant and emergent paradigms to assist practitioners in making the shift.

The following is an illustration of one such interim social contract being considered in related disciplines that could perhaps find a place in carbon financial reporting if the profession can break free of its industrial-era roots. The illustration presented is an extension of a mathematical valuation model derived in Ratnatunga et al. (2004) for valuing the capability of military assets, Ratnatunga and Ewing (2005) for valuing marketing communication capability, and in Ratnatunga and Ewing (2009) for valuing brand capabilities. In the literature referred to above, 'market consensus values' were obtained from experts within the organisation for the purpose of valuing organisational capabilities. However, in the case of RECs, the starting point of calculating the *Environmental Capability Enhancing Asset (ECEA)* values pertaining to the underlying *REC-producing assets* would need to be obtained from agreed CES accounting procedures (and the related assurances of those numbers), as discussed earlier in the chapter.[10] Once this information is obtained, then the relationship of the CES accounting measures to the ECEA values (generated, for example, via planting and maintaining trees in a forest) is demonstrated using the following equation:[11]

$$\frac{dS}{dt} = r.E.\left(\frac{M-S}{M}\right) - \delta S \tag{2}$$

The equation indicates that the change in the *economic value (dS/dt) of a capability enhancing asset* at time *t* is a function of five factors:[12]

- E the costs/expenses incurred to support the ECEA.
- r the value-increasing *carbon sequestration constant* (defined as the ECEA values generated per expense dollar when $S = 0$).
- M the maximum value of the ECEA sequestration capability, based on CES accounting and physical constraints (under best growth conditions) related to the ECEA (i.e. trees do not sequester carbon in any significant proportion after they reach maturity).
- S the current value of the ECEA sequestration capability (under current growth conditions).
- δ the value-decaying *carbon emission constant* (defined as the fraction of the ECEA value lost per time unit when $E = 0$).

The equation states that the change (increase) in the ECEA value will be higher when r, E, and the untapped ECEA value potentials $(M - S)$ are higher, and the value-decaying (emission) constant is lower.

Note that many of the equation variables and constants need to be obtained via an agreed CES accounting measure. For the purpose of our illustration, we have assumed that the science behind the CES accounting measures used is accurate and that we have confidence (via assurance) in the values generated by Equation 1 shown earlier.

The following example will illustrate the point. A newly planted forest would be both a (tangible) *Operational Capability Enhancing Asset (OCEA)*, because it has the potential to generate future cash flow by logging and selling timber, and an (intangible) ECEA (as a carbon sink) with the potential to generate future cash flow by selling internally generated RECs via carbon sequestration. The forest becomes more capable in terms of both operations and carbon sequestration (1) the more trees it has, (2) the more time it has to grow to maturity, (3) the better its growing environment (in terms of climate protection, labour provided for care and maintenance, fertilizer, etc.), and (4) the more money expended *(E)* to support, maintain and enhance the operational capability of the forest. Although the example presented focuses on the value of the forest's sequestration capability (ECEA), the same metrics can be used to value its OCEAs if agreed fair values (such as by using discounted cash flow [DCF] techniques) cannot be computed.

Any forest would have variable capability potentials, based on its growing environment (size of land, soil, climate, the maturity stage of trees, etc.), in terms of the amount of carbon it can absorb. For illustrative purposes, let us assume that CES accounting experts can estimate the *sequestration of Y tons of CO_2 emissions* (see Equation 1) over a period from the point of planting to the point of maturity under various growing conditions (within the definition of the Kyoto Protocol for fungible RECs). Based on the expected permit price of an REC in each year of sequestration[13] and an assumed discount rate, we can use DCF techniques to convert this to a present value of *$Z worth of tradable RECs* in an emissions trading market (see Equation 1).

Under steady state conditions (i.e. where future growth conditions, discount rates and REC prices are stable), this DCF computation would be the fair value of the ECEA. No further computation is necessary. However, where the growing environment of the forest can be affected by the actions of the business entity (by expending money, *E*, on care and maintenance, water, fertilizer, etc.), the ECEA values can change and should be reported under GAAP.

Let us therefore assume that by monetising the CO_2 sequestrations using agreed CES accounting computations, the present value of potential cash flows of the forest under *best growth* conditions is a *maximum* monetary ECEA value of (say) $10,000,000 *(M)*.

Currently, let us assume that the forest is still growing (and thus sequestering carbon), and that its *current* sequestration potential of CO_2 metric tons of emissions, under current growth conditions is estimated at a *present value* of $5,000,000, again based on monetizing agreed CES accounting computations.

Also assume that the environmental scientists and engineers, based on their CO_2 sequestration and emissions measurement models and experience, estimate the value-increasing carbon sequestration constant *(r)* to be 6.5 and the value-decaying carbon emission constant (δ), if no physical and environmental maintenance of the ECEA is undertaken, to be .05.

If the organisation owning the ECEA in the coming year expends $100,000 *(E)* to support the carbon sink by growing more trees within the physical constraints of the land and the climate and/or providing good care and maintenance of the existing trees to grow to their full potential (in terms of providing water, fertiliser, etc.), then the ECEA's *Environmental Capability Value (ECV)* will be enhanced as follows:

$$\left(\frac{ds}{dt}\right) = 6.5\,(100,000).\left(\frac{10,000,000 - 5,000,000}{10,000,000}\right) - 0.05(5,000,000)$$

$$\left(\frac{ds}{dt}\right) = 6.5\,(100,000)(0.5) - 250,000 = \$75,000$$

Thus, based on the expert opinions derived relating to the two carbon sequestration *(r)* and carbon emission (δ) constants, despite spending $100,000 on supporting the organisation's ECEA, the net ECV of the asset has been leveraged up by only $75,000, or a net value increase of only 0.75 of the money expended.

Let us now assume that in the early years of a carbon sink (such as a forest of fresh saplings), there is no significant value decay – that is, the *carbon emission constant* (such as via rotting vegetation, etc.) is zero. Then, expending a similar amount of $100,000, the asset's ECV will be enhanced as follows:

$$\left(\frac{dS}{dT}\right) = 6.5\ (100,000)\left(\frac{10,000,000 - 5,000,000}{10,000,000}\right) - 0.0(5,000,000)$$

$$\left(\frac{dS}{dT}\right) = 6.5\ (100,000)(0.5) - 0 = \$325,000$$

In such a case, by spending \$100,000 on supporting the ECEA via expansion and maintenance of the carbon sink, the ECV has been leveraged up by \$325,000, or a net value increase of 3.25. This is in keeping with what is observed in all types of assets, tangible and intangible (e.g. expenditure on machinery, human resource training, brand advertising campaigns, etc.) – that asset capability values are leveraged rapidly in the early years of use, with increases (if any) at a diminishing rate in the later years.

If the objective of the organisation is merely to maintain its ECEA to current ECV levels, then dS/dt will be set to zero. Thus the equation becomes

$$0 = 6.5\ (0.5)\ E - 0.05\ (5,000,000)$$

$$250,000 = 6.5\ (0.5)E$$

$$\frac{250,000}{3.25} = E = approx.\$77,000$$

Thus, a minimum of \$77,000 would need to be expended merely to maintain the capability at its current value. This approach provides an important valuation tool for an organisation dealing with combinations of tangible assets (e.g. trees for logging) and intangible capabilities (i.e. the carbon emission and sequestration capabilities of the trees), as it now is able to determine what expense levels must be included for the *maintenance* of that particular ECEA's capability at a zero-base. This concept is no different to the expenses a company would need to spend on repairs and preventive maintenance of its machines; just to keep the machines running at their current level of economic capability, a certain level of expenses would need to be incurred.

Once an asset has reached its maximum capability potential ($M = S$), then it will be of no incremental value to expend any more money on it, as the value-increasing part of the equation collapses to zero. In such a case the asset will lose its current value (S) due to the value-decay constant (δ) (i.e. the second part of the equation). Note that, other things being equal, M will then once again become greater than S (as S decays), and a small amount of expenditure (E) will be required to bring the capability back to saturation point. In the case of a tree, this point of balance where M and S values vary in close proximity to one another is at its maturity, where its CO_2 sequestrations equal it emissions.

Note that, based on the CES accounting values and constants provided earlier, if the organisation spends only \$50,000 on supporting the ECEA, by applying the above *model equation* the change in ECV (dS/dt) works out to be a *negative* \$87,500, or a net value *decrease* of 1.75. Thus an organisation would have a range of net values, some greater than 1, some between 0 and 1, and some negative. Note also that as the negative net values reduce asset values, this is conceptually very similar to the depreciation/amortisation of assets under traditional GAAP, whilst the positive net values are similar to the revaluation of asset values under traditional GAAP.

Also note that under a carbon rationing scheme, *most* tangible assets of a business entity would either have a sequestration (asset) or an emissions (liability) capability. Certain types of land could have geo-sequestration capabilities (asset); buildings could be designed (or refitted) in certain ways to reduce CO_2 emissions (asset; the reductions can be sold under the Kyoto Protocol as RECs), whilst machinery and vehicles using coal or petroleum as their energy source with significant potential to emit CO_2 would be liabilities. The equation provided above can be used in all such situations.

This chapter illustrates the capability value calculations of a tangible asset (forest, land) with an intangible CO_2 sequestration (sink) capability. The same logic will hold for the actions of entities that invest in activities that provide them with some form of *carbon offset* rather than directly reducing emissions, or those that take actions to *reduce the carbon footprint* of an asset (e.g. by making a building energy efficient). Here, *M* will be the maximum energy savings potential, and *S*, the current savings. *E* would be the amount expended in energy-saving technologies in a particular accounting period, and the sequestration *(r)* and emission (δ) constants would be provided by energy experts.

In the case of a tangible asset (machinery, motor vehicles) with an intangible CO_2 emission (liability) capability, then the maximum *(M)* and current *(S)* values would be the asset's maximum and current emission (source) capabilities. Here, the more expenses *(E)* that are incurred on the tangible asset (e.g. burning up more petroleum in running the asset), the more the intangible liability value will increase. The two constants would reverse in this case, where the emission *(r)* and sequestration (δ) constants are again provided by energy experts.

Environmental capability enhancing asset (ECEA) accounting: the recording process

This new approach to valuing the ECV of REC-producing (and REC-using) assets would also require a new approach in the financial accounting recording process. If an asset is only a 'cash generating operational asset', then it could be recorded as under current GAAP. However, it has been demonstrated that many tangible assets would also have a potential carbon sequestration capability (such as a forest) or carbon emission capability (such as a motor car) under a carbon rationing and trading scheme. In such cases, the intangible asset (or liability) must be recorded as an environmental capability. Therefore, the tangible asset has the potential of obtaining revenues from its operational capability (i.e. the tree that can be sold for logging) intertwined with revenues (or expenses) from its carbon sequestration (or emission) capability.

The following is a simple example of the types of operational and carbon-emissions-related transactions that would need to be recorded in the books to build up an organisation's *overall* ECV. Please note that this is not a calculation of an organisation's carbon footprint, although the carbon footprint CES accounting measures are incorporated in the valuation model via the value-increasing *(r)* and value-decaying (δ) constants.

It will be demonstrated that the value of both the asset's operational and environmental capability comes from three or more transaction categories: the purchase cost of the tangible asset, the cost/revenue potential of the intangible asset/liability that comes along with it, and the support costs (expenses) of the tangible/intangible asset. For reasons of brevity, in this example we will limit our discussion to only recording the transactions pertaining to a tangible operational asset with a related intangible CO_2 sequestration capability, although in the above discussion it has been shown that transactions pertaining to a tangible asset with an intangible *liability* (carbon emissions) capability can be similarly recorded.

Let us assume the organisation has an opening Capability Balance Sheet, represented in terms of financing and investments as shown in Table 20.1, clearly demarcating the operational and intangible capability assets (environmental, brands, IP, etc.) and the related *capability capital reserves* built over time.[14] The concept of capability capital reserves are similar to the *asset revaluation reserves* found in traditional financial reports. The Capability Balance Sheet shows only environmental capabilities that have the potential to be monetised, which are mainly its carbon related capabilities due to the existence of

Table 20.1 Opening capability balance sheet

	$000
Investment	
Operational assets	
Operational capability enhancing assets (OCEA) (e.g. forests)	350,000
Other capability enhancing assets (e.g. working capital)	100,000
Intangible assets	
Environmental capability enhancing assets (ECEA)	100,000
Other capability enhancing assets (brands, reputation, IP)	50,000
Total investment	**600,000**
Financing	
Accumulated surplus (equity)	250,000
Capability capital reserves	300,000
Debt	50,000
Total financing	**600,000**

a carbon rationing and trading scheme. As discussed in previous sections, this is only a disjointed incremental move towards reporting the consequences of the economically motivated behavioural responses of organisations to the existence of a carbon trading scheme. Any environmental capabilities that cannot be monetised are not shown in this version (Stage 1) of the Capability Balance Sheet.

The double-entry recording details of the impact on the Capability Balance Sheet of six transactions are now illustrated:

Transaction 1: Purchase forest for $40 million, made up of a logging asset of $30 million and the associated carbon sink capability of $10 million. The recording of this transaction is shown as a single entry, affecting operational and intangible assets, although in reality this will require the separate recording of the land, trees, access roads, buildings, and so on, as per most international accounting standards.

Table 20.2 Transaction 1: Purchase forest for logging and carbon sink

OCEA-tangible (for logging)	30,000
ECEA-intangible (for carbon sequestration)	10,000
Other assets (cash)	40,000
Capability balance sheet	

	$000
Investment	
Operational assets	
Operational capability enhancing assets (OCEA) (e.g. forests)	380,000
Other capability enhancing assets (e.g. working capital)	60,000
Intangible assets	
Environmental capability enhancing assets (ECEA)	110,000
Other capability enhancing assets (brands, reputation, IP)	50,000
Total investment	**600,000**
Financing	
Accumulated surplus (equity)	250,000
Capability capital reserves	300,000
Debt	50,000
Total financing	**600,000**

Transaction 2: Transfer timber to logging unit. The forest will essentially be written off the books as a tangible asset at this stage; this entry is similar to depreciating the asset 100 per cent in the year of purchase. The reason for this is that a Capability Balance Sheet records what an organization *can do* (capability) and not what it *has* in historical cost terms. (Note that for reasons of brevity, the profit and loss account impacts are shown only as how they ultimately affect the Capability Balance Sheet, i.e. in Accumulated Surplus.)

In the long run, it is expected that the 'asset procurement expenditure' in a particular year will be similar in value to the previously calculated 'net depreciation' of a whole host of assets purchased over a number of years. This will also avoid the problem of continuing to depreciate assets that have a 'written-down value' in the books but have no capability value in reality.

A related issue is the *physical security* of the tangible asset. It could be argued that if one does write-off 100 per cent of the asset value in the year of purchase, there will be no record of its value in the assets register, and hence it could be subject to theft and pilferage (e.g. illicit logging in the case of a forest). However, an assets register can be maintained independent of the financial accounting system with units rather than values, and most forestry operations have a reasonable record of ensuring the physical custody of tangible assets (with armed patrols) to ensure not only against theft but also against the activities of pyromaniacs.

Transaction 3: Recording timber at its fair capability value. This will be the net present value (NPV) of its capability to generate cash from operations (if the asset, in fact, does have such a capability).

Thus, the asset is essentially brought back onto the books as a capability value. Note that at the point of purchase the operational capability value of a tangible asset will, in most cases, be the purchase cost, as competitors may also have access to such assets, and thus they do not

Table 20.3 Transaction 2: Transfer timber to logging unit

Operational expense (P/L)	30,000	(Ultimately Affects Equity)
OCEA-tangible (logging)	30,000	(100% Depreciation)
Capability balance sheet		
Investment		
Operational assets	*$000*	
Operational capability enhancing assets		
(OCEA) (e.g. forests)	350,000	
Other capability enhancing assets		
(e.g. working capital)	60,000	
Intangible assets		
Environmental capability enhancing assets		
(ECEA)	110,000	
Other capability enhancing assets (brands,		
reputation, IP)	50,000	
Total investment	**570,000**	
Financing		
Accumulated surplus (equity)	220,000	
Capability capital reserves	300,000	
Debt	50,000	
Total financing	**570,000**	

Table 20.4 Transaction 3: Recording timber at its fair net present value (NPV)

OCEA-tangible (logging)	50,000	(NPV of expected future revenues)
Capability capital reserves	50,000	(Unrealised gains)
Capability balance sheet		
Investment		
Operational assets		$000
Operational capability enhancing assets (OCEA) (e.g. forests)		400,000
Other capability enhancing assets (e.g. working capital)		60,000
Intangible assets		
Environmental capability enhancing assets (ECEA)		110,000
Other capability enhancing assets (brands, reputation, IP)		50,000
Total investment		**620,000**
Financing		
Accumulated surplus (equity)		220,000
Capability capital reserves		350,000
Debt		50,000
Total financing		**620,000**

provide an organisation a competitive advantage (at that point in time). However, in the case of some environmental assets (e.g. those with access to restricted areas or requiring special permits), and also if the organisation has better-trained personnel already existing to run the operations efficiently, for synergistic reasons the capability value may well exceed the purchase cost. In this example, it is assumed that the business entity has a competitive advantage such that its present (fair) value capability to generate future net revenues (i.e. $50 million) is greater than its purchase price of $30 million.

Transaction 4: Operational cost ($2 million) of maintaining the capability values of the forest that was purchased (fertilising, thinning, labour, etc.). This is the E variable in the equation provided earlier. (Note that in this illustration, for reasons of brevity, we ignore the operational costs of maintaining the other opening ECEAs listed in Table 20.1.)

Transaction 5: Recognise the incremental intangible ECV due to expanding resources to maintain and enhance carbon sequestration capability. The intangible ECV value is derived by leveraging the expenses using the carbon sequestration *(r)* and carbon emission (δ) constants obtained by CES accounting procedures, for which the mathematics were demonstrated earlier in the chapter (Equation 2). The current capability value *(S)* is the original $10 million carbon sink capability purchased (Transaction 1). The saturation point of this capability *(M)* has been assumed as $40 million. (Again, in this illustration, for reasons of brevity, we ignore the incremental ECV of the opening ECEAs, as it is assumed that no operational costs were expended on them.)

Transaction 6: Recognise the incremental tangible *Operational Capability Value (OCV)* due to expanding resources to maintain and enhance capability of the recently purchased logging operation, with a current capability value *(S)* of $50 million (Transaction 3). It is assumed that the saturation point of this capability *(M)* is $100 million. The tangible OCV value can be derived either by using DCF techniques (if the variables are known) or by leveraging the expenses using different value-increasing *(r)* and value-decaying (δ) constants obtained by valuers of agricultural lands such as forests (Equation 2). In this illustration, the operational

Table 20.5 Transaction 4: Operational cost of maintaining the capability values of forest (fertilising, thinning, labour, etc.)

Capability support expenses (P/L)	2,000	(Ultimately affects equity)
Other assets (cash)		2,000
Capability balance sheet		
Investment		
Operational assets		*$000*
Operational capability enhancing assets (OCEA) (e.g. forests)		400,000
Other capability enhancing assets (e.g. working capital)		58,000
Intangible assets		
Environmental capability enhancing assets (ECEA)		110,000
Other capability enhancing assets (brands, reputation, IP)		50,000
Total investment		**618,000**
Financing		
Accumulated surplus (equity)		218,000
Capability capital reserves		350,000
Debt		50,000
Total financing		**618,000**

cost of $2 million was inadequate for maintaining the current capability values *(S)* of forest in terms of timber for logging, and thus the metric used indicates that the value has reduced by $1 million.

Most often, in the case of tangible operational asset capabilities, the revaluation will be a negative asset (akin to depreciation), as it is expected that capability will be diminished as the equipment ages.[15] In the case of agricultural assets such as forests and vineyards, the operational capability will initially increase as the trees grow to maturity and then diminish with age, whilst its sequestration capability will end at maturity, at which time it will be in balance as to its sequestration and emission capabilities. Most international accounting standards require a revaluation of such agricultural assets every year. Any depreciation component is to be built into this revaluation (for example if part of the forest is destroyed by fire). The OCV and ECV metrics will enable both the tangible and intangible components of this operational and environmental capability to be better assessed than existing conventional methods that only consider valuation approaches such as replacement cost and market value.

Transactions 5 and 6 would ideally be recorded as a combined journal entry, which encompasses the joint-capability components of the tangible and intangible assets working in tandem. Thus, if the organisation loses all of its (tangible) forest due to a fire, then the capability component of its carbon sequestration capability will also have its (intangible) asset value reduced to zero (and if the carbon emissions caused by the fire are recorded by the CES accounting metric used, the capability reduction would need to be recorded as a notional expense, similar to stock losses).

Note that the example above ignores the transactions that deal with the income statement side of the accounting equation (revenue and expenses) and deals almost strictly with the balance sheet equation (assets, liabilities and equity). The reason is that the example deals with only the difficulties faced by the traditional accounting framework in the valuation of non-current asset capabilities, especially when a tangible asset capability is intertwined with an intangible. As stated earlier, the accounting profession is closer to an agreement about how to record revenue and expenses related to transactions in selling and obtaining RECs (current assets and liabilities) via government grants or via carbon trading markets than on the valuation and reporting of the underlying capabilities that produce such RECs (non-current assets and liabilities).

For reasons of completeness, however, the Appendix deals with present thinking on RECs as current assets and liabilities (and their timing impact on the income statement). It is shown that in many organisations, REC inventory values (obtained, purchased or created via emissions sequestration activities that have already taken place) may be incorporated into the valuation of the emissions liability of that organisation. That is, carbon emissions valuation experts might consider that the sequestration activities would create an intangible inventory to offset the liability in their valuations. If the REC asset (i.e. sequestration inventory) is greater than the emissions liability such that netting the intangible asset from the liability results in a zero liability, two recording possibilities exist. If the REC is a tangible inventory asset obtained by government grant or purchased via an ETS (similar to a concert ticket), and if it has not expired (i.e. it can be used against future emissions liabilities [future concerts]), then it would remain in the balance sheet. If it was internally created, then it will be an intangible inventory asset that will remain off-balance sheet, unless it is 'certified' as an REC (by energy experts) and made available for trade as an abatement certificate. As stated before, this chapter does not deal with the above scenarios of accounting for REC inventory and their emission liability offsets. Instead, the chapter concentrates only on the emission management capabilities of non-current assets and liabilities.

The above discussion and example shows that the calculation metrics and transaction reporting framework being suggested requires a paradigm shift in current thinking of the accounting profession, especially with regard to balance sheet valuations. However, the shift is incremental rather than radical. The proposed model is only the first stage of the paradigm shift. This disjointed incremental shift describes the professional approach to change; not to throw out the existing model, but to try and fit new things in and change it in such a way that one can go back if it does not work.

In the reporting approach discussed above, the valuation is of capabilities (what one can do) rather than of assets in a traditional sense (what one has). The question of the effectiveness of the capability values generated by such an incremental shift will only be answered in time. If CEOs find that the value-increasing and value-decaying constants are such that they cannot control the content of the organisation's capability asset, liability, revenue and expense figures, they will be loathe to adopt them. Once the numbers are accepted, however, and the organisation makes this incremental paradigm shift, then the next question that arises is whether these environmental capability values should be integrated into its (traditional) financial statements. There are three approaches, as suggested by Leadbeater (2000), to integrate new measurement paradigms into organisational financial statements. These approaches are the fully integrated approach, the supplementary approach and the hybrid approach.

In the *fully integrated approach*, the new measures detailed above are incorporated into the financial statements, whilst in the *supplementary approach*, separate Capability Financial Statements are prepared to sit alongside the traditional statements prepared as per GAAP and international financial reporting standards. Both are intended to help investors value organisational capabilities (the intangible asset issue), including environmental capabilities (the CSR reporting issue). The *hybrid approach* is a compromise where the incorporation of tangible and intangible capability assets as balance sheet values is a gradual process, via either *half-way houses* (when an organisation 'quarantines' its tangible and intangible capability values before allowing them to migrate to the balance sheet) or *revisable rolling accounts* (where past accounts are restated as CES accounting measurements become more accepted by the mainstream stakeholders).

Table 20.6 Transaction 5: Recognise the increased intangible ECEA value due to operational costs (e.g. fertilising, thinning, labour, etc.)

ECEA-intangible	7,000	(Using equation)
Capability capital reserves		7,000
Capability balance sheet		
Investment		
Operational assets		*$000*
Operational capability enhancing assets (OCEA) (e.g. forests)		400,000
Other capability enhancing assets (e.g. working capital)		58,000
Intangible assets		
Environmental capability enhancing assets (ECEA)		117,000
Other capability enhancing assets (brands, reputation, IP)		50,000
Total investment		**625,000**
Financing		
Accumulated surplus (equity)		218,000
Capability capital reserves		357,000
Debt		50,000
Total financing		**625,000**
ECV: Net-value workings:		
dS/dt =		7,000.00
E =		2,000.00
r =		8.00
δ =		0.50
S =		10,000.00
M =		40,000.00

Whatever approach to implementation is adopted, it will be necessary to initially estimate the current capability value of all tangible and intangible capability assets and have an 'Opening Capability Balance Sheet as at a particular date' (Table 20.1), after which the double-entry accounting approach outlined in Tables 20.2 through 20.7 could be carried out.

Limitations

The validity of the arguments in this chapter rests with the practical applicability of the capability valuation equation, especially the carbon sequestration and carbon emissions constants that need to be obtained by experts in CES accounting. It has already been discussed that existing scientific knowledge on this subject is limited and the values much disputed. However, despite this, and because of the many measurement metrics available, such numbers are being computed, and the resulting RECs are being sold as certified emissions reductions (called CERs) and voluntary emissions reductions (called VERs) in emission trading markets. Another limitation is that future prices of tradable RECs cannot be determined with any certainty. However, such uncertainty is present in all trading markets including, of course, share trading markets. This has not prevented financial analysts from using valuation models that use estimations of future movements in (say) price-earnings ratios.

Another limitation, as conventional accountants will argue, is that the reason why the discourse has been limited to the impact on the financial statements of known current costs of an organisation's carbon related transactions is because the valuation of the underlying capabilities

Table 20.7 Transaction 6: Recognize the increased tangible OCEA value due to operational costs (e.g. fertilising, thinning, labour, etc.)

OCEA-tangible	(1,000)	(Using equation or NPV)	
Capability capital reserves		(1,000)	(Unrealized gains)
Capability balance sheet			
Investment			
Operational assets			*$000*
Operational capability enhancing assets (OCEA) (e.g. forests)			399,000
Other capability enhancing assets (e.g. working capital)			58,000
Intangible Assets			
Environmental capability enhancing assets (ECEA)			117,000
Other capability enhancing assets (brands, reputation, IP)			50,000
Total investment			**624,000**
Financing			
Accumulated surplus (equity)			218,000
Capability capital reserves			356,000
Debt			50,000
Total financing			**624,000**
OCV: Net-value workings:			
$dS/dt =$			(1,000.00)
$E =$			2,000.00
$r =$			4.00
$\delta =$			0.10
$S =$			50,000.00
$M =$			100,000.00

transfers the responsibility of quantifying the financial effects from accountants to scientists and engineers. However, accountants and other finance professionals such as bankers have used expert valuations as the basis for commercial transactions (such as giving loans) for a long time. Further, there is a rich literature in new valuation approaches with regard to intangibles and possible approaches to bring these values to the balance sheet (see Leadbeater, 2000). This chapter presents a valuation model that extends this literature to the valuation of capabilities, in which tangible and intangible asset are intertwined.

Summary

The concentration of greenhouse gases in the atmosphere has risen dramatically, leading to an out-of-balance greenhouse effect that most scientists believe will continue to cause a warming of the world's climate.

It has been shown that the economic decisions of organisations operating within a carbon trading scheme, and the consequences of these organisations implementing carbon emissions management schemes, will impact the accounting profession significantly. Whilst there is some discourse as to how best to report on the income statement (profit and loss) effects of CO_2 trading, there has been no discourse about how to value the underlying assets that produce or use carbon allowances on the balance sheet.

Is this approach all that different to Cook (2009), who also considered balance sheet values and argued that REC allowances, emissions liabilities and grant liabilities should be recorded separately at fair value and changes in the fair values should be reported in income? The major difference is that Cook (2009) was essentially looking at the accounting treatment within contextual situations where RECs were obtained via government grants or purchased via an ETS (the concert ticket analogy), and how these RECs should be treated in the balance sheet (as assets and liabilities) until the emission occurred (the concert was attended) and their values could be moved to the income statement. The current chapter focuses more on organisations that have the capability of generating RECs (i.e. those that have not only an emissions liability but also an emissions intangible carbon sequestration asset capability), although it is shown that the model can be used to fit into the more conventional Cook (2009) scenarios.

There is no controversy within the field of accounting and financial reporting that issuers of financial statements should provide the readers of financial statements with all material information that is both relevant and reliable. The relevance of organisational capabilities (especially via its intangibles such as carbon sequestration assets) has not usually been questioned, but the reliability of the valuations of these intangibles has often been questioned.

This chapter illustrates a technique that not only makes these valuations more relevant and contextual but also shows how tangible and intangible asset combinations provide true capability values. However, a paradigm shift from the current conceptual accounting framework is required before the profession accepts such new accounting treatments.

Appendix
Accounting treatment of carbon allowances obtained by government grant

The accounting profession has recognized at least three treatments of carbon allowances obtained by government grant (within the traditional accounting framework):

1   If the allowance is obtained as a *government grant* for a price (when allowances are allocated by governments for less than fair value), then it is first recognised as an intangible asset at cost (debit: intangible asset; credit: cash). Then, the intangible asset is increased to fair value with the difference between cost and fair value recognized as revenue on a systematic basis over the compliance period (debit: intangible asset; credit: revenue).[16] As an organisation emits carbon, the intangible asset is used up at market value (debit: expense; credit: intangible asset). Any gains or losses that result in disposing of the intangible asset are recognised in the income statement.

2   Alternatively, government grants allocated for less than fair value could be recognised as income (on the grounds that they are immediately tradable) (debit: intangible asset; credit: revenue). This argument would be applicable for government grants issued free.

3   Alternatively, government grants allocated for less than fair value could be recognised as liabilities (on the ground that all or part of these will have to be returned to the government in the settlement of an emissions liability that has not yet occurred) (debit: expense; credit: liability). If there is a shortfall, the organisation will ultimately need to purchase RECs in an open market equal to the shortfall (debit: liability; credit: cash) at market value.[17]

Instead of obtaining carbon credits as government grants, if an REC is purchased as an inventory item or cash flow hedge, then the current view is that it is recorded at fair value pertaining to the carbon allowances held (debit: intangible asset; credit: equity reserves).[18] Again, as an organisation emits carbon, the intangible asset is used up at market value (debit: expense; credit: intangible asset).

To account for such treatments in a carbon rationing scheme, a *net model* has been proposed, whereby an entity does not recognise allocated allowances (they remain off-balance sheet) and accounts for actual emissions only when it holds insufficient allowances to cover those emissions by buying RECs (debit: expenses; credit: cash) at market price.

Traditionally, however, the accounting profession prefers the separate recognition of assets and liabilities and the different treatment of such – that is, the treatment of carbon assets (i.e. allowances) independent of the liabilities (i.e. obligations). Accordingly, netting off (i.e. offsetting) of the assets and liabilities in such cases will not be permitted.

Thus, an *amortising model* has been proposed, whereby an entity recognises allocated allowances as an asset (debit: asset; credit: equity reserves as deferred income) at cost price, but then amortises the allowances as it pollutes (debit: expense; credit: asset) and simultaneously releases the deferred income to revenue (debit: equity reserves; credit: revenue). In this method, the entity recognises a liability for actual emissions only when it holds insufficient allowances to cover those emissions (debit: expense; credit: liability). The liability that the entity incurs as it emits is measured at the cost of the allowances held by the entity. However, ultimately the entity has to purchase carbon credits in an open market equal to the shortfall (debit: liability; credit: cash), and there would be an over/under provision of this liability depending on market price. Clearly, pricing and the valuation of carbon allowances (permits) is a key to this method of accounting.

Notes

1 These have to be 'incremental' (i.e. a new tree must be planted). Pre-1990 trees still existing are not considered sinks for carbon credit purposes, as they have reached maturity and are in 'balance' as to the amount of carbon sequestered and emitted.

2 Each REC represents one metric ton of CO_2 either removed from the atmosphere or saved from being emitted.

3 A scheme that permits an enterprise to trade only its excess allowances is sometimes called a *baseline and credit* scheme. Most cap and trade schemes, instead, make all allowances tradable from day 1. It is this feature that is the source of much of the accountants' difficulties in dealing with such transactions.

4 This paper won the American Accounting Association – Management Accounting Section's Impact on Management Accounting Practice Award in 2009. The award is given annually to a paper, published within the last five years in a refereed academic journal, that has the greatest potential impact on management accounting practice.

5 One cannot put a monetary value on the extinction of a species, for example, or the social cost of the use of child labour.

6 The IPCC, along with Al Gore, the former US vice president, won the 2007 Nobel Peace Prize for their work on reducing global warming.

7 Sergey Brin, the founder of Google is reported as having bought carbon credits to offset the immense amount of CO_2 emitted by his private Boeing 767, but confesses he is not sure if it really achieves anything (Krauthammer, 2007).

8 It is not an objective of this chapter to offer a solution to the timing issue. The objective instead is to consider the valuation and reporting of an organization's capability in generating future RECs.

9 The IASB is, however, considering abolishing the term 'contingent liability'.

10 As discussed earlier, these CES accounting measurements will be obtained from environmental scientists and biologists, similar to how the accounting profession currently obtains asset valuations from company directors, actuaries, business analysts, engineers, and quantity surveyors.

11 The theoretical underpinning of this model was derived from the Vidale-Wolf (1957) model employed to describe the sales response to advertising efforts.

12 Over time, and with experience, these coefficient values derived by environmental scientists should reflect the value-expense relationships that exist in most spending decisions but remain largely unquantified.

13 A permit with a face value of say $10 per metric ton of CO_2 that becomes valid at a future date will have a present value of a lesser amount today, as they are dated, single-year permits.

14 The concept of 'capability capital' is discussed in Ratnatunga et al. (2004) and Ratnatunga and Ewing (2005).

15 An exception would be, as in the case of the American B-52 bomber that is still in operation today, if expenses have been deployed to maintain/enhance a tangible asset's capability.

16 Questions as to whether such revenue is taxable or exempt from tax will be based on a specific country's tax policy.

17 Note that a 'liability' is a present obligation arising from past events. The issue of a 'carbon permit' relating to a possible future event is more a contingent liability, although the IASB is currently considering abolishing this latter term.

18 The fair value would be based on market values if a trading scheme exists. Similar questions of fair value pertain to share investments; that is, there are reporting differences if the shares are held as 'investments' or as 'inventory' in a fund management company.

References

Bebbington, J. & Larrinaga, C. (2008), Carbon Trading: Accounting and Reporting Issues. *European Accounting Review*, 17(4), 697–717.

Cook, A. (2009), Emission Rights: From Costless Activity to Market Operations. *Accounting, Organizations and Society*, 34(3–4), 456–468.

Deloitte and Touche (1996), *Value Based Measures*. London: Deloitte and Touche.

Garnaut, R. (2008), *Garnaut Climate Change Review*. Commonwealth of Australia, Canberra. http://www.garnautreview.org.au/pdf/Garnaut_prelims.pdf.

Intergovernmental Panel on Climate Change (2007), *Climate Change 2007: The Physical Science Basis*.

Jones, S. & Belkaoui, R. (2009), *Financial Accounting Theory (3rd Edition)*. Sydney, Australia: Cengage.

Krauthammer, C. (2007), Limousine Liberal Hypocrisy. *TIME Magazine*, Commentary (26 March), 16.

Kuhn, T. (1962), *The Structure Of Scientific Revolutions*. Chicago: University of Chicago Press.

Lantos, G.P. (2001), The Boundaries of Strategic Corporate Social Responsibility. *Journal of Consumer Marketing*, 18(7), 595–630.

Leadbeater, C. (2000), *New Measures for the Economy, Centre for Business Performance*. London: Institute of Chartered Accountants of England and Wales.

Lev, B. & Zarowin, P. (1998), *The Boundaries of Financial Reporting and How to Extend Them*, Working Paper, Stern School of Business, New York University, New York.

Orlitzky, M. (2005), Payoffs to Social and Environmental Performance. *The Journal of Investing*, 14(3), 48–51.

Quinn, J.B. (1978), Strategic Change: Logical Incrementalism. *Sloan Management Review*, 20 (1), 7–21.

Rappaport, A., (1986), *Creating Shareholder Value: The New Standard for Business Performance*. New York: The Free Press.

Ratnatunga, J. (2007), An Inconvenient Truth about Accounting. *Journal of Applied Management Accounting Research*, 5(1), 1–20.

Ratnatunga, J. & Ewing, M.T. (2005), The Brand Capability Value of Integrated Marketing Communication (IMC). *Journal of Advertising*, 34(4), 25–40.

Ratnatunga, J. & Ewing, M.T. (2009), Future Imperfect: An Ex-Ante Approach to Brand Capability Valuation. *Journal of Business Research*, 62(3), 323–331.

Ratnatunga, J., Gray, N. & Balachandran, K.R. (2004), CEVITA™: The Valuation and Reporting of Strategic Capabilities. *Management Accounting Research*, 15(1), 77–105.

Shank, T., Manullang, D., & Hill, R. (2005), Doing Well While Doing Good Revisited: A Study of Socially Responsible Firms' Short-Term versus Long-term Performance. *Managerial Finance*, 31(8), 33–46.

Tandukar, A. (2007), From Neutral into Drive. *BRW – Innovation*, (15–21 March), 74–75.

Vidale, M.L. & Wolfe, H.B. (1957), An Operations-Research Study of Sales Response to Advertising. *Operations Research*, 5(3), 370–381.

21

Corporate sustainability reporting

Theory and practice

Geoff Frost and Stewart Jones

Introduction

This chapter traces the development of corporate reporting of the environmental, social and sustainability performance of organisations. Over recent decades, societal expectations of organisation performance have broadened and deepened. Corporate social responsibility (CSR) and sustainability reporting are now key areas of stakeholder concern and an important and explicit underlying tenet of the relationship between society and the corporation. Public reporting has emerged from the growing need for external stakeholders to understand the underlying performance of the organisation across various dimensions. External reporting of CSR usually manifests as disclosure in the annual report or sustainability report or through an organisation's website. Indeed, there is continuous research revealing the extent and scale of uptake of voluntary sustainability reporting by corporations globally (KPMG 2011). Voluntary CSR reporting is, however, not a new phenomenon. Early research had highlighted a long history of voluntary social and environmental reporting by corporations. For instance, Hogner (1982), in a study of US Steel (1901–1980), observed that CSR was an old idea with a practical base and that the frequency of occurrence depended on a matrix of societal forces. Guthrie and Parker (1989), in a study of 100 years of reporting by BHP, concluded that CSR reporting had a long history and that it did not appear to match significant social events (with the possible exception of environmental issues in the 1970s). More recent empirical research has observed a steady increase in the level of CSR reporting, while attempting to link observed reporting practices with either internal or external factors has had mixed results (see Hahn and Kühnen 2013 or Fifka 2013 for a meta-analysis of the literature).

Social, environmental and sustainability reporting is targeted to meet the needs of general users. While CSR reporting is largely voluntary for most corporations, it is becoming increasingly systemised through the adoption of global guidelines such as the Global Reporting Initiative (GRI) and integrated reporting (IR). Increasingly, however, organisations are required to undertake mandatory reporting, to the general public but more extensively to regulatory agencies tasked with monitoring specific elements of an organisation's CSR or sustainability performance. This can result in the promulgation of increased levels of information on organisational performance for those wishing to seek such information. With an emphasis on the Australian context, this chapter seeks to examine the development of environmental, social and sustainability performance reporting and to survey the sustainability reporting landscape in which organisations now engage. Initially in this survey, we suggest the crystallisation of a social contract with respect to environmental, social and sustainability performance as a means of articulating changes in the reporting and regulatory landscape that consequentially influences the reporting practices of organisations. We also explore the engagement of accountants and accounting for environmental and CSR reporting. Finally, we survey the evolution towards more formalised reporting practices as a final step for making explicit those CSR practices that have historically been implicit and voluntary for reporting organisations.

A social contract: the firm and social and environmental performance

The social contract seeks to provide an understanding of the expectations placed upon individuals and organisations (including companies) with respect to their actions within the broader community. That is, the social contract seeks to explain the boundaries of acceptable interaction between participants within society. The social contract in its earliest theoretical development sought to explain the rightful powers and obligations of governments by conceptualising a hypothetical contract drawn up among individuals (or stakeholders) within society (Donaldson 1982). The initial concept of the social contract explored the notions of equality, the sharing of responsibility and powers, and the determination of the practices that were acceptable and unacceptable in achieving the needs of society (Rousseau 1947). Rawls (1971, p. 11) explained this notion of a social contract in the following way:

> . . . we are to imagine that those who engage in social cooperation choose together, in one joint act, the principles that are to assign basic rights and duties and to determine the division of social benefits. Men are to decide in advance how they are to regulate their claims against one another and what is to be the foundation charter of their society. Just as each person must decide by rational reflection what constitutes his good, that is, the system of ends that it is rational for him to pursue, so a group of persons must decide once and for all what is to count among them as just and unjust. The choice which rational men would make in this hypothetical situation of equal liberty, assuming for the present that this choice problem has a solution, determines the principles of justice.

Hence, the concept of the social contract was initially based upon the notion of 'justice' for individuals within society (Donaldson 1982). The social contract also recognises that there will be costs to the individual arising from such interactions, and the benefits provided must exceed the associated costs (both financial and social). Because of the implicit nature of the social contract, there are those who may disregard the boundaries of socially desirable behaviour. To counter the action of those individuals who do not remain within these boundaries, society as a whole has enabled the formation of governments with the power to regulate and restrict the individual. When an individual operates outside of these social boundaries, governments can penalise the individual, or the structure within which the individual functions, through regulatory intervention. These penalties may either be financial or in terms of the personal liberty of the individual through the restriction of the individual's activities.

The social contract has been used to explain the behaviour of firms. As stated by Donaldson (1982, p. 57), productive organisations are

. . . subject to moral evaluations which transcend the boundaries of the political systems that contain them. The underlying function of all such organizations from the standpoint of society is to enhance social welfare through satisfying consumer and worker interests, while at the same time remaining within the bounds of justice. When they fail to live up to these expectations they are deserving of moral criticism.

In other words, corporate management, via their social contract with other stakeholders within the community, seek to perform socially desirable actions in return for acceptance of their firm's objectives.[1] This concept was described by Shocker and Sethi (1974, p. 67):

Any social institution – and business is no exception – operates in society via a social contract, expressed or implied, whereby its survival and growth are based on:

a)   the delivery of some socially desirable ends to society in general, and
b)   the distribution of economic, social or political benefits to groups from which it derives its power.

In a dynamic society, neither the sources of institutional power nor the needs for its services are permanent. Therefore, an organisation must constantly meet the twin tests of legitimacy and relevance by demonstrating that society requires its services and that the groups benefiting from its rewards have society's approval. In other words, corporate management are accountable for both the entity's economic and social performance. Such accountability is considered important because certain stakeholders within the community may not be limited to financial objectives, but may also have socially orientated objectives that they desire the firm to achieve.[2]

This view of the social contract may include performance on social and environmental issues, if such issues are considered of importance to society. Hence, corporate management's responsiveness on social and environmental issues is bound by the implicit boundaries of the social contract; that is, management actions are guided by social expectations of their performance. However, failure to remain within the 'implicit' boundaries may result in the introduction of 'explicit' regulatory requirements with respect to social and environmental management and performance.

An evolving social contract

Over recent decades, society's perceptions and expectations of business in the area of corporate social responsibility and environmental performance have changed. As business, and the influence of business, has grown, so too have the expectations from society for CSR reporting.[3] Environmental and social issues and pressures are now sufficiently visible and prominent in society to influence change in corporate management behaviour, including the reporting practices of the company. For example, this ability to influence change is not driven by the physical environment itself, but it is an issue deemed important by stakeholders within the community that has resulted in an increased focus upon the interaction between business and the environment. In other words, changes in community perceptions have resulted in those entities that interact with the physical environment to be held more accountable for their actions. Corporate management have responded to increased restrictions and public scrutiny by diverting resources and technology to environmental and social management, thereby engaging in these issues and accepting accountability for performance. In other words, a change in community knowledge and responsiveness on social and environmental issues (reinforced by increased government intervention) has directly resulted in changes in corporate management responsiveness on social and environmental issues.

The impact upon business operations from government intervention with respect to environmental management can be substantial, particularly if significant economic costs result from enforced environmental control or rectification activities. However, future financial implications are often unknown or uncertain due to the inability of many organisations to place a dollar value on their current interaction with the environment. Furthermore, with the increased emphasis on the 'polluter pays' principle, which underlies much of the current legislation, environmental costs to business may be poised to escalate appreciably over coming years.

Competition is also becoming an important motivating factor for greater CSR reporting, forcing corporate management to consider a wider range of issues within their marketing frameworks and strategies. For example, many marketing strategies are now being developed around 'green' products, with the aim of gaining greater consumer acceptability. Hence, competition for community support may encourage many businesses to embrace 'best practice' environmental management principles, including more detailed accounts of relevant CSR performance.

Organisational legitimacy

From social contract theory, it is argued that corporate management seeks to comply with the expectations of society, thereby gaining organisational legitimacy. As stated by Suchman (1995): 'Legitimacy is a generalized perception or assumption that the actions of an entity are desirable, proper, or appropriate within some socially constructed system of norms, values, beliefs, and definitions.'

The social contract is not limited to economic success, but also includes social interactions. In other words, companies need to legitimise their performance not only in terms of economic indicators but also with respect to their social performance. As Patten (1992, p. 471) noted: '[U]ntil relatively recently, legitimacy was considered only in terms of economic performance. As long as a firm was successful (profitable), it was rewarded with legitimization.'

Failure to meet community expectations with respect to social performance can result in penalties or sanctions that restrict the activities of the firm. These sanctions in their most obvious form are the formalisation through legislation and regulations of previously implicit societal norms.[4,5] Sanctions can also occur in a more ad hoc form, for example through consumer boycotts, employee dissatisfaction, or restrictions on access to resources. Implicit societal expectations may also begin to crystallise through the development of community-based initiatives, guidelines and so on. Management in turn may adopt such guidelines as a means of promoting their legitimacy by acceding to these community beliefs.

Organisational legitimisation is therefore a means of describing the corporate response to changes in community expectations. In other words, it seeks to explain management's response so as to avoid further explicit restrictions (such as government regulations) or implicit restrictions (such as reputation effects) on their operations. However, legitimisation through changes in operational processes may not necessarily be the optimal outcome for the firm or an economically viable alternative. Hence, management may seek organisational legitimacy through alternate means such as the justification of current actions through communication of a commitment to improved environmental management and performance, or communication may be designed to change stakeholders' current expectations that may be seen by management as unreasonable.

Legitimisation through communication: the role of the annual report

Corporate legitimisation may involve management of the flow of information from the firm so as to meet the information demands of the community or specific stakeholders (such as the environmental

517

lobby). As argued by White and Mazur (1994, p. 9) entities not only 'have to get themselves in environmental shape, they also have to be seen to do so'. In other words, corporate legitimisation involves not only matching performance with expectations, but also the means by which corporate management can inform external parties about their responsiveness on environmental management and performance. This may in turn influence expectations of performance requirements.

Corporate legitimacy is therefore not solely a performance-orientated function but also a function of corporate image. Within this context Buhr (1998) observed that a company has choices with respect to corporate legitimacy, first, in terms of performance along a spectrum of possible behaviours and, second, in terms of the level of environmental disclosure. These two choices are not necessarily related. Laughlin (1991) noted that while the observation of social and environmental information may not accurately reflect the level of actual change in performance within the organisation, it does, however, reflect the importance management may perceive the issue has to external parties. Whether this perceived importance then results in changes to management commitment may be difficult to observe.[6] It is therefore argued that reporting is a reflection of management's legitimisation process and not necessarily an indication of actual performance. As stated by Dowling and Pfeffer (1975, p. 127), 'the organization can attempt, through communication, to alter the definition of social legitimacy so that it conforms to the organization's present practices, output and values'. The external reporting of environmental, social and now sustainability information has therefore been the subject of considerable scrutiny as a tool for legitimising firm performance (Cho and Patten 2007; Wilmshurst and Frost 2000).

The development of social and environmental accounting and reporting

> . . . the objective of accounting is to provide a fair system of information flow between the accountor and the accountee.
>
> *(Ijiri 1983, p. 75)*

Reporting of social, environmental and sustainability performance appears to be a generally accepted tenet of modern business, certainly within the academic community and more broadly within the business sector. Indeed, we are regularly updated with the next survey of practice highlighting the extent of corporate uptake of reporting on environmental issues, sustainability, carbon or the adoption of the GRI and so on (KPMG 2011). Prominent in the current debate over corporate reporting, particularly in the context of formalising processes, are the Big4 audit firms, including many of the global accounting professional bodies. The accountant's role in CSR therefore appears accepted and to some extent unquestioned. However, this has not always been the case with social and environmental accounting and the accountant's role that has been emerging over the last few decades.

As societal focus on environmental issues in Australia increased from the 1990s onwards, there was a corresponding call for accounting, and accountants, to become more involved in environmental management (Burritt and Gibson 1993). Evidence of accountants' involvement in environmental management in Australia was noted from research undertaken by Coopers and Lybrand (1993). There was, however, some confusion over what role the accountant could play within environmental management. Two issues generated this confusion: first, a lack of practical experience or training of many of the members of the accounting profession in the field of environmental management; and, second, the inability of professionals and academics to reach a consensus on what constitutes environmental accounting and, hence, how the development of appropriate measurement and reporting processes should be approached. Notwithstanding this confusion, evidence suggests that environmental accounting was developing as an integral part of the corporate response to environmental issues (Epstein 1996; Kreuze and Newell 1994; Russell *et al.* 1994; Smith and Lambell 1997).

Interest in the accountant's role in the environmental agenda was increasing in momentum by the 1990s (Gray 1994). When issues related to environmental accounting were first raised in the 1960s, the weight of argument against accountants becoming involved in so-called 'social accounting' matters outweighed the positive side of the debate (Kestigian 1991). Misconceptions that the accountant was not the most appropriate individual to report on environmental and social issues and that accounting was merely a tool to report financial information led to social issues such as environmental accounting being marginalised on the professional accounting agenda. However, the debate gradually moved from a focus of whether or not accounting should be involved to exploring what and how accounting could contribute to the management of the interaction between an organisation and the environment (Corrigan 1998; Wilmshurst and Frost 1998).

Gray (1994, pp. 9–10) attributed the increase in interest to four related factors that have provided a platform for the development of environmental accounting. In summary, these factors are:

1   The disenfranchisement of members of the accounting profession who were part of the 'greed culture' of the 1980s. On a theoretical level this was expressed through the exploration of the political economy of accounting (Cooper and Sherer 1984) and the further development of the concept of accountability (Roberts 1991).

2   The resurgence of academic interest in corporate social responsibility that had been neglected by mainstream accounting research.

3   The emergence of ethical and environmental investment trusts; the ethical and environmental consumer movement; 'new economics' in both theory and practice; the rediscovery of 'community values' and 'community organisations'; and the growth, expansion and maturation of environmental groups.

4   This development was set against a backdrop of a continuing development in and understanding of environmental (and social) accounting and related matters.

From environmental accounting's beginnings, as a subset of corporate social reporting (CSR),[7] environmental accounting has now gained its own identity. Chadwick *et al.* (1993, p. 18) described environmental accounting as

> [a]ccounting for the cost of past, present and future environmental activities (any activity which could, or will affect the natural environment) is becoming increasingly important, although there are few definitive standards. Often it is difficult or impossible to predict the actual extent of a newly discovered contamination problem, much less the cost of cleanup. Such 'fuzzy' situations do not lend themselves to easy measurement and disclosure in financial statements.

Research on social and environmental reporting has often lacked clear objectives, first due to the adoption of numerous theoretical paradigms on *what* information should be reported and, second, due to the lack of consensus as to *how* information generated should be reported.[8] Key issues to be resolved in environmental and social reporting research, as noted by Eddey (1983, p. 57), include:

1   Whether social accounting measures should all be measurement based, or is non-quantitative, narrative type reporting acceptable.

2   Whether social accounting measures should all be in financial terms, or are non-financial measurements acceptable.

3   Whether social accounting disclosures are to be audited or not, and if so, what are the appro-
     priate audit techniques.
4   Whether the accountant is adequately equipped to perform a social measurement function, or
     should others such as economists, sociologists and political scientists be involved.

Gray *et al.* (1987, p. ix) suggested the role of environmental (and social) financial reporting as
'the process of communicating the social and environmental effects of organisations' economic
actions to particular interest groups in society and society at large'.

Guthrie and Parker (1990) suggested that social (and environmental) reporting could serve
three major purposes:

1   Providing a comprehensive view of the organisation and its resources.
2   Providing a constraint upon socially irresponsible corporate behaviour.
3   Providing positive motivation for the corporation to act in a socially responsible manner.

Hence, a role for environmental reporting is the dissemination of information, particularly
financial data, to external parties. Notwithstanding the discussion on environmental reporting,
substantive progress on formal reporting standards has been slow, exacerbated by many accountants being either unprepared or unsure of how they are able to contribute, at least on a professional level, to environmental management. There are, however, a small number of regulations
that may result in the disclosure of information on social and environmental issues by Australian
companies in their annual reporting (discussed later in this chapter). Generally, however, social
and environmental reporting is a voluntary exercise, and considerable effort is being spent on
trying to understand why organisations choose to report.

Corporate responsiveness: influential disturbances on environmental reporting practices

The general causal factors that impact upon corporate management attitudes to CSR disclosure may be either implicit or explicit. From the 'minimal disclosure' perspective, application
of accounting standards and other rules on disclosure are explicit. Alternatively, full disclosure
would require complete transparency with respect to performance of activities that impact on
society or the environment. Corporate management, however, may regard full disclosure as
being too 'costly' for the organisation.[9] Conversely, compliance with the minimum requirements may result in other costs being incurred with respect to the legitimacy and reputation of
operations and performance. For example, a perceived lack of transparency may result in pressure for the minimum level of expectations of environmental management and performance to
be modified. Hence, the level at which corporate management communicates environmental
information could be interpreted as a function of the minimum reporting requirements (mandatory disclosure), and managements' need to legitimise their actions and performance to the
external social environment (voluntary disclosure). As described by Guthrie and Parker (1990,
p. 165), companies undertake voluntary social disclosures in order to

> demonstrate a constructive response to social pressure and avoid further regulation of their
> disclosures. In this way they may seek to pacify sociological demands made on business while
> attempting to win or maintain support from particular targeted constituencies. Such a disclosure
> strategy may include emphasising the corporation's positive contributions to social welfare and
> highlighting its attempts to minimise its harmful effects on various elements of society.

Reporting can therefore be used as a means of demonstrating corporate management responsiveness on social and environmental issues. From the social contract perspective, corporate management are justifying their existence and therefore 'defending' the appropriateness of the minimum boundaries of the explicit components of the social contract.

Over many years, there has been a plethora of practitioner and academic research documenting the levels of social, environmental and sustainability reporting by corporations internationally and within particular jurisdictions (see, for example, Higgins *et al.* 2014; KPMG 2011). Two general observations of this research can be made. First, the levels of CSR reporting are increasing, but there is still considerable variation in reporting levels between various organisations. Second, there has been considerable research seeking to identify and explain factors that may be influential in driving CSR reporting practices. In a recent review of the literature, Hahn and Kühnen (2013) identified 178 papers published between 1999 and 2011 from journals related to business, management and accounting that specifically focused on factors influencing the adoption, extent and quality of sustainability reporting.[10] From this meta-analysis, they observed that the only internal determinant that is consistently found to have a positive effect on sustainability reporting is company size. They observed that media exposure and stakeholder pressure as external determinants were also consistently found to have a positive influence on sustainability reporting, but this may be because the size variable may be strongly correlated with corporate visibility. Other variables that may have a positive effect on CSR reporting include capital intensity, a company's listing on the stock market, government ownership and level of foreign ownership. Interestingly, the authors find that a company's systematic risk and degree of ownership concentration may actually impede sustainability reporting.

Organisational change as represented by corporate management responsiveness is observed to be influenced by a number of disturbances (Gray *et al.* 1995; Laughlin 1991), which are associated with community values and political intervention. The framework of the social contract, however, only provides a range for corporate management responsiveness, which consequently may not explain an individual firm's level of responsiveness (as evident by the considerable variation on firm-specific disclosures observed in many studies; see for example Beck *et al.* 2013). Management may therefore be motivated to respond in two ways. First, management is influenced by changing levels of societal responsiveness on environmental issues between periods, or by inter-period disturbances on corporate management that may elicit a system-wide response.[11] Second, cross-sectional differences in levels of responsiveness by individual firms within the same period may be seen as a consequence of firm-specific factors. Uncertainty in outcomes from voluntary adoption by organisations can undermine the consistency and comparability of reporting. This in turn has led to calls for a more standardised approach to social and environmental reporting.

Towards a standardised approach for social and environmental reporting

The increasing trend in CSR reporting has also corresponded with an increasing focus on more systematic means of reporting on social and environmental performance. From earlier research where we observed ad hoc CSR disclosures, we now observe organisations reporting against well-established reporting guidelines (such as the GRI). The debate on social and environmental reporting is now entering a phase where sustainability reporting is becoming essential to provide an understanding of an organisation's performance that is complementary to the traditional financial reports (we have seen this in the development of integrated reporting). Hence, social, environmental and sustainability reporting can now be expressed against an explicit set of criteria, thus enabling external stakeholders to evaluate firm performance against a more formalised metric of expectations. Below we briefly review the GRI and IR as expressions of community expectations of firm performance reporting.

The GRI

The Global Reporting Initiative (GRI) was founded in Boston in 1997. In 2002, the GRI was formally inaugurated as a United Nations Environment Programme collaborating organisation and relocated to Amsterdam as an independent non-profit organisation. In May 2013, GRI released the fourth generation of its guidelines – G4. The stated objective of the GRI is 'to make sustainability reporting standard practice for all companies and organisations. Its Framework is a reporting system that provides metrics and methods for measuring and reporting sustainability-related impacts and performance'.[12]

Today the GRI Guidelines serve as one of the most widely adopted sets of recommendations for sustainability reporting and are increasingly seen as a *de facto* sustainability reporting standard. KPMG (2011) recently reported that '80 percent of G250 and 69 percent of N100 companies [are] now aligning to the GRI reporting standards' (p. 20).

The GRI has also proved to be a boon for researchers, with an increasing number of quantitative research papers now using the GRI as a benchmark by which to measure and evaluate sustainability reporting. McGraw and Katsouras (2010), for example, evaluated the CSR reporting levels by Australian companies in the second tier of publicly listed companies on the Australian Securities Exchange (ASX 101–200) using the Global Reporting Initiative's template, version 3 (GRI3). In a study of corporate environmental performance, Clarkson *et al.* (2011) examined both the level and the nature of environmental information voluntarily disclosed by Australian firms that was aligned with the GRI Guidelines.

More recently, the GRI and many of the global accounting professional bodies have been responding to calls to develop a set of mandatory non-financial reporting standards. Part of this response has been the establishment of the International Integrated Reporting Council (IIRC), which has been set the task of producing a standard for integrated reporting.

Integrated reporting: purpose and development

The IIRC was established in the context of calls for reporting to evolve to reflect changes in expectations towards businesses that include more than just financial measures. As the IIRC (2011, p. 9) state:

> The traditional reporting model was developed for an industrial world. Although it continues to play a valuable role with respect to stewardship of financial capital, it nonetheless focuses on a relatively narrow account of historical financial performance and of the value-creation process.

The IIRC serves as a nexus for developing this new reporting framework, garnering input from regulators, investors, companies, standard setters, the accounting profession and non-governmental organisations. It is significant to note that the IIRC has assembled financial accounting standard setters (e.g. the Financial Reporting Council, the Australian Financial Reporting Standard Setters, and stock exchanges), institutional investors and providers of voluntary guidelines for corporate responsibility disclosures (e.g. the GRI) for the purpose of developing an integrated reporting framework. The objective is then to create a reporting framework encompassing environmental, social and governance (ESG) information as required by resource allocators (mainly institutional investors as per IIRC definition) for decision making, provided the contents are relevant for creating value in the short, medium and long term:

The IIRC's mission is to create the globally accepted International Framework that elicits from organizations material information about their strategy, governance, performance and prospects in a clear, concise and comparable format. The International Framework will underpin and accelerate the evolution of corporate reporting, reflecting developments in financial, govern-ance, management commentary and sustainability reporting. The IIRC will seek to secure the adoption of by report preparers and gain the recognition of standard setters and investors.

(IIRC Press Release, 1 March 2013)

A core element in the development of a reporting framework relates to identifying the key user stakeholders. Here, the IIRC preferences capital providers as the key recipient stakeholder of IR, with the intent that reporting provides a more holistic perspective of the organisation to better inform investment decisions. IR is therefore positioned to be aligned with the traditional financial reporting paradigm of investors as the primary stakeholder; such a position however diverges from existing non-financial reporting frameworks such as the GRI that have embraced a multi-stakeholder approach. It also diverges from an established understanding of the targeted recipients of non-financial information, with prior research having observed a diverse range of stakeholders targeted as users by report preparers (Cormier and Magnan 1999; Cormier *et al.* 2005; O'Dwyer *et al.* 2005; Spence 2009; Tilt 1994).

Arriving at a position where we are debating sustainability reporting within the same context as financial reporting is an indicator that we have made considerable progress with respect to accounting and social and environmental reporting. However, there is still much to be consid-ered in the development of IR; indeed there are still questions as to the scope and development of IR from within the accounting profession. Responses were called for to a 2011 Discussion Paper, and the following are a sample of comments received:

There are many obstacles to achieving consensus on, and implementation of, global approaches to reporting. Though the IASB [International Accounting Standards Board] has been remarkably successful in its first ten years, it has been building on a long history and with the support of a significant network of domestic standard-setters and regula-tors. The IIRC would be wise to consider how this has occurred. In this regard, the IIRC should avoid any connotations that its work would replace rather than complement financial reporting requirements. On practical grounds replacement, even if agreed, would require immense time and effort to enrich existing financial reporting requirements around the world and to establish similar provisions for integrated reporting.

(Kevin Stevenson, Australian Accounting Standards Board)

We believe that the IIRC has to do even more to promote the concept of integrated reporting especially to the preparer community. The discussion paper states on page 6 that the integrated report should replace rather than add to existing reporting requirements, however, this view is not universally held especially by preparers. To alleviate the concerns of preparers that integrated reporting will be additive to existing disclosure requirements, the IIRC should explain how they anticipate that their requirements will not add to the reporting burden. To further encourage involvement from those producing reports, the IIRC needs to make a compelling case emphasising the benefits to preparers of the bet-ter quality information that is likely to flow from more integrated thinking within their organisations.

(Charles Tilley, Chartered Institute of Management Accountants)

Much progress has been made on developing comprehensive reporting guidelines, and indeed there is a significant depth in the information now being voluntarily reported by many organisations. However, there is still considerable ground to be covered before there is a universal acceptance of systematic mandatory reporting of social, environmental and sustainability performance information within the same context as financial reporting.

Putting the mandatory into reporting

Much prior research has focused on the voluntary reporting of social and environmental information and identifying causal factors that drive such disclosure. Orientating research to focus on voluntary disclosure remains a valid position given the limited level of mandated CSR reporting across various jurisdictions. However, the management of environmental and social performance does not operate in a regulatory vacuum. Indeed, many of the activities that are reported, and subsequently analysed by researchers, are subject to regulation that may result in the organisation developing management systems that collect and aggregate cohesive data sets on environmental and social performance. Whilst such regulation may not directly require reporting to stakeholders, such as investors, the data may be available to external users through other avenues. For example, Clarkson et al. (2011) examined how both the level and the nature of environmental information voluntarily disclosed by Australian firms relates to their underlying environmental performance. The environmental performance measure is based on emissions data available from the National Pollutant Inventory (NPI).

Investor focused mandatory reporting

Globally there has been progressive movement towards mandatory reporting of social and environmental performance within the annual report and other reports prepared for investors. Within the Australian context there have been a limited number of specific regulations that require firms to report on environmental and social performance. The primary legal requirement with respect to reporting in the corporate annual report is the Corporations Act 2001 s299(1)(f): '[I]f the entity's operations are subject to any particular and significant environmental regulation under a law of the Commonwealth or of a State or Territory – give details of the entity's performance in relation to environmental regulation.'

Prior research has documented a higher level of reporting that could be ascribed to the introduction of this regulation. In addition, there has been a general increase in the overall level of environmental reporting (Frost 2007). The results of the study are similar to prior research which documents higher levels of overall environmental reporting in situations where companies face adverse scrutiny from prosecution (Deegan and Rankin 1996).

The original Financial Services Reform Act 2001 was promulgated in March 2002 and required fund managers and financial product providers to state 'the extent to which labour standards or environmental, social or ethical considerations are taken into account in the selection, retention or realization of the investment'. The Australian Securities and Investment Commission (ASIC) issued Section 1013DA Disclosure Guidelines in 2003 to complement the Financial Services Reform Act and assist with disclosure about labour standards or environmental, social and ethical considerations in Product Disclosure Statements.[13]

Mandated reporting to government agencies

Greenhouse gas (GHG) emissions by firms have become a central focus of government policy seeking to combat climate change. Initially the corporate response and subsequent reporting was at the discretion of the organisation's management. However, as scientific evidence of climate change developed and public opinion crystallised, government intervention was inevitable. In Australia we have seen the introduction of a series of regulations with the purpose of providing explicit guidance as to the collection, measurement and reporting of energy and GHG emissions.

The Clean Energy Act 2011 (and taking into account amendments to Clean Energy Amendment [International Emissions Trading and Other Measures] Act 2012) includes the definition and obligations of 'covered entities' liable for purchasing carbon permits each year (according to the GRI there are approximately 400 entities currently considered 'covered entities' in Australia). Subsequent amendments to the Act since 2011 require the establishment of mechanisms to combine the Carbon Price Mechanism with existing regulatory schemes and processes including reporting under the National Greenhouse and Energy Reporting (NGER) Act, as well as other requirements for notification of significant holdings of carbon units and record-keeping obligations.[14] If you are a liable entity, you must

- be registered under the NGER Scheme;
- report your covered emissions to the Clean Energy Regulator under the NGER Scheme;
- acquire and surrender enough eligible emission units to satisfy your liability for a financial year by the 15th of June in that financial year (if you have an interim emissions number) and by the 1st of February in the following year; and
- if, at the required time, you do not surrender enough units to satisfy your liability, pay a unit shortfall charge to account for the units you do not surrender.[15]

Following the 2013 election in Australia, the new Liberal government was elected with a platform of repealing the 'carbon tax' and then implementing a Direct Action Plan designed to efficiently and effectively source low-cost emissions reductions. The Direct Action Plan is to include an Emissions Reduction Fund to provide incentives for abatement activities across the Australian economy and will complement the Carbon Farming Initiative. The government has repealed the Clean Energy Act 2011 and related legislation that establishes the carbon pricing mechanism and will shortly commence consultation on the development of the Emissions Reduction Fund. Further information on the repeal of the Clean Energy Act 2011 and related legislation and the design of the Emissions Reduction Fund will be available soon.[16]

The NGER Act was introduced in 2007 to provide a single national framework for reporting greenhouse gas emissions and energy consumption and production. The Scheme's legislated objectives are to

- inform policy-making and the Australian public
- meet Australia's international reporting obligations
- provide a single national reporting framework for energy and emissions reporting.[17]

The NGER Act requires corporations in Australia that meet specified emissions and energy use thresholds to annually report greenhouse gas emissions, energy production and energy consumption data. Information collected through the NGER Scheme provides the basis for assessing liability under the carbon pricing mechanism. There are two types of thresholds to determine which corporations are required to participate in the NGER Scheme. These are (1) facility thresholds and (2) corporate group thresholds. As a guide, businesses emitting more than 25,000 tonnes of carbon dioxide equivalent, or consuming more than 25,000 megawatt hours of electricity or 2.5 million litres of fuel, in a financial year can expect to be required to report under the NGER legislation.[18] Several legislative instruments sit under the NGER Act, providing greater detail about a corporation's obligations. The purpose of each of these legislative instruments is described below:

- The *National Greenhouse and Energy Reporting Regulations 2008* sets out the details that allow compliance with, and administration of, the NGER Act. For example, the regulations specify the information that must be provided in reports under the NGER Act and the way that provisions of the NGER Act must be applied. (Commenced on 1 July 2008.)
- The *National Greenhouse and Energy Reporting (Measurement) Determination 2008* describes the methods that reporting entities must use to estimate their greenhouse gas emissions, energy production and energy consumption. (Commenced on 1 July 2008.)
- The *National Greenhouse and Energy Reporting (Audit) Determination 2009* contains the requirements for preparing, conducting and reporting on greenhouse and energy audits. (Commenced on 7 January 2010.)
- The *National Greenhouse and Energy Reporting (Auditor Registration) Instrument 2012* specifies the qualifications that an auditor must have to be registered under the NGER Act. (Commenced on 31 November 2012.)

The National Pollutant Inventory (NPI) 1998 is an internet database that displays information about the annual emissions from industrial facilities and diffuse sources of 93 different chemical substances to air, land and water. The NPI requires industrial companies that trip certain thresholds to self-report emissions and inventories for specific substances and fuel to regulatory authorities for inclusion in a public database. Enforcement of compliance sits with State Government environment agencies.[19]

Sustainability reporting: a case analysis on positioning and hurdles for implementation

To contextualise the prior discussion on CSR reporting, the following case study is provided. The case study draws upon a series of interviews exploring sustainability reporting within an organization, Alpha. At the time the interviews were conducted, Alpha operated a portfolio of general insurance businesses in Australia, New Zealand, Asia and the UK, including some of Australia's leading general insurance brands. Alpha was an ASX 100 listed company with a market capitalization of around $8B.

Alpha had an established reputation as a leader in the sustainability field and was recognised as an industry leader in the financial modelling of the potential climate change impacts of global warming. Alpha was also well known for having adopted a number of sustainability policies and initiatives which were supported by senior executives (a 'top down' approach) as well as employees. For instance, Alpha had one of the largest fleets of hybrid vehicles in Australia. The company also claimed to be an innovator in some 'green' insurance products and services. At the time of the interviews, Alpha had published three sustainability reports on its company website and incorporated some limited sustainability information into its annual report. The company published a range of environmental and community- and employee-related sustainability indicators in its sustainability report. Within the context of a 'social contract', Alpha had clearly sought to position its business model to be perceived as encompassing sustainability, not only with respect to the performance information it reported but also with respect to the products it was providing for the broader community.

Interviews were semi-structured and participants were asked questions across a broad range of issues, taking into account the contextual background, position and experience of each respondent interviewed. Most interviews commenced with an initial explanatory overview of the research project as well as an outline of the purpose for the research. Respondents were then invited to discuss their background and specific role performed within the organisation. Several questions focused on how Alpha collected and reported sustainability information within the organisation; the types of sustainability data collected across the different divisions; how these data were measured and reported and in what formats; the types of information systems used to collect these data; the timing and frequency of the sustainability reporting; how well the internal sustainability data were integrated with other internal accounting systems; the auditing and assurance of sustainability data; and the particular hurdles that the Alpha faced with respect to the collection, integration and reporting of sustainability data within the organisation.

Public positioning through reporting

Alpha had embraced improved sustainability performance as a corporate strategy, and whilst the viewpoints of respondents differed quite sharply on some issues, the interviews revealed a strong underlying sense of enthusiasm and commitment to the concept of sustainability overall and the general strategic direction that Alpha was taking on this issue. As stated by one respondent, there seemed to be a natural fit between sustainability and the overarching business goals of an insurance company. The Consultant for Corporate Social Responsibility stated: 'Being an insurance company, we look forward, we're very future focused and sustainability is all about looking forward so there's a lovely kind of cultural fit there.'

Alpha's sustainability report had been developed around the GRI Sustainability Reporting Guidelines. Several respondents acknowledged that these guidelines are the internationally accepted best practice measurement system for social, environmental and economic reporting. The corporate website identified numerous stakeholder groups in the preparation of its sustainability report, including customers, shareholders, employees, government bodies and regulators, suppliers, unions, community partners, business organisations and industry groups. For instance, with respect to the supply chain, Alpha claimed to have delivered some 'green' products and services for customers that align with their position on sustainability. Alpha's website stated:

> First and foremost, these are customer offers that make business sense, but they also reflect a new way of thinking for the long term about how our customers respond to innovative new offers that are right for the 21st century.

Internally, most respondents appeared to recognise the importance of sustainability to the organisation as a whole. Many respondents not only supported the philosophy of sustainability but also perceived a strong business case for sustainability. For example, the Manager, Innovation and Sustainability, stated:

> I do think that things like the Dow Jones and global reporting initiative . . . are of increasing importance to us because we are starting to understand that that opens up a new set of investors who are potentially interested in Alpha.

The reporting process

Several respondents were concerned about how well Alpha was performing in terms of the underlying systems and processes that supported sustainability reporting. The Senior Manager of Sustainable Business Practices described some of these problems as follows:

Did we publish what we got last year? I don't think we did. I think we got a C or a C−. What we decided to do for this year was to clean up the problems with the systems and processes which had happened from last year's dramas and not look to too many new indicators.

Other internal problems and issues which were impacting on sustainability reporting within the organisation, included staff turnover, lack of maintenance of management systems to collect data, out-of-date guidelines and a general lack in coordination.

While Alpha had a large number of interesting and innovative sustainability initiatives, there still appeared to be a marked gap between the public image projected in the corporate reporting and the reality of sustainability within the organisation. For instance, whilst Alpha highlighted the GRI as the benchmark for best practice, it was obvious from many respondents that actual reporting against the GRI was quite limited. Respondents noted that the organisation published certain information on its environmental performance, including environmental indicators such as CO_2 emissions, electricity usage, fuel consumption, paper usage and air travel. The firm also published customer satisfaction data and employee data, such as staff turnover, absenteeism and number of women in senior management and executive positions. However, an external audit highlighted numerous areas where Alpha was not reporting or was only partially reporting. A large part of the problem was that many indicators identified in the GRI were not regarded as useful or appropriate to an insurance company. Another example of where the public image of sustainability appears to be divergent from internal perceptions is in supplier sustainability performance reporting. Notwithstanding the public statements in Alpha's sustainability report on supplier reporting, internal respondents did not believe that supplier reports were carefully or rigorously checked. Supplier reports were viewed more as 'boundary reports' than as footprints because the reports did not detail the sustainability activities of suppliers. With respect to supplier reports, the Manager, Analytics and Reporting, described the struggle to coordinate the information gathered in supplier reports:

> First of all we had to arrange with our suppliers an understanding and appreciation of sustainability. So I worked with our Category Managers at procurement to get agreements from each of our suppliers to say that sustainability now is a core component of your measurement system, to see whether you're a good or bad supplier.

While several respondents believed Alpha had made significant progress with the collection of sustainability data, in some instances there appeared to be significant problems with underlying data integrity and assurance and more broadly with the integration of sustainability information for internal decision making. We now turn to these issues.

Sustainability: data collection, measurement and reporting

Several respondents indicated that Alpha had a broad range of accounting systems to collect sustainability data. For instance, the organisation had the 'benefits tracker' system for procurement data that was expanded to include CO_2 initiatives. The Manager, Analytics and Reporting, stated:

> So, for example, if we did something that led to a cost saving, that would also be reflected as a CO_2 saving. But we haven't got anything populating there yet, but the theory is that we get that and report that to the group, just to say these initiatives led to this cost saving plus the CO_2 saving.

The Manager, Analytics and Reporting, also noted a lack of a centralised approach to management accounting systems within the organisation:

> I think we've never had a central management function ourselves in people. It's been done in each of the areas. The only area that will sort of centralise is Culture & Reputation, but they're more focussed on the communication rather than the actual management. So we don't have any form of centralised management, which is why we don't have a management database for the group.

Alpha's Consultant for Corporate Social Responsibility stated that timing of the data and the breadth of information collected were major obstacles for the integration of financial information with sustainability data:

> We would like to see the reports integrated. We have some issues around that, one being the timing. The timing is a big issue, and timing is very tight between the end of financial year and the release of an annual report. And the breadth of information that we collect for the sustainability report, the obvious one is electricity. There's always a lag.

Furthermore, many respondents noted that Alpha's international operations significantly complicated the process of integration, and presented particular problems for data quality. The Consultant for Corporate Social Responsibility stated that 'nervousness' about data quality was a major obstacle to external reporting:

> You know, we know that they have the same systems in Asia but we're not sure of everything that goes in there. . . . we are not sure of the quality of what's going in and what's coming out. . . . so group risk assurance will do a lot of work with them before we actually go out publicly.

A perhaps more fundamental problem facing the effective integration of financial and sustainability data is that the organisation had not decided on the type of sustainability information to collect and report. Conspicuous in the interviews with respondents was that the organisation did not publish lead indicators in the sustainability report, such as sustainability targets. Arguably, the sustainability report has value in a decision making sense because it is a more forward looking document than financial statements, which rely on largely historical data. However, without lead indicators, the decision usefulness of the sustainability report can be significantly reduced. For instance, when Alpha reported on CO_2 emissions, the company's sustainability report compared emissions only to last year's levels. While this is useful for determining whether emissions behaviour is changing, it is not a target per se which can drive policy and influence behaviour.

It was evident from the interviews with respondents that Alpha had previously experimented with publishing numerous sustainability targets but had recently gone to the other extreme of publishing few or no targets for external reporting purposes. The Consultant for Corporate Social Responsibility stated:

> Yes and when you look at the narrative of the report, we're very up front in saying that previously we had set ridiculous targets that we were never going to meet. And last year we set no targets at all. In the last 12 months we really concentrated on target setting and what those targets will be, particularly around environmental performance. . . . The annual report details a lot of our people targets as well. But what we've done with our

environmental targets is take a back to basics approach of where are the biggest influence and impact areas for each division, and we've assigned divisional targets which is then rolled up into an overall corporate target, which is a reduction of 3 per cent in CO_2 per FTE [Full Time Equivalent].

Data integrity

Several respondents identified concerns with the integrity of sustainability information collected within the organisation. The Manager, Workforce, Reporting and Analysis, Culture and Reputation, stated:

> . . . at the moment we know we have problems with data integrity, but we have a bigger problem with perception of data integrity and get involved in a lot of discussions and a lot of justification over the figures we produce, which sometimes are inaccurate. Sometimes that's because of the data and sometimes it's because of our manual reporting systems and somebody in my team is doing something different to somebody else in the team.

The Acting Senior Manager, Group Risk Assurance, also raised major concerns about the integrity of the data: '[W]e did actually ask, if you have the environmental data, give me the data. Let's go through it, through the correct channel. The integrity of that data was shocking.' The reliability of the data may be an important issue in explaining why senior managers are reluctant to report sustainability information externally or to integrate the information into actual economic decision making. However, on a positive note, several respondents also indicated that data capture was improving in the organisation. The Consultant for Corporate Social Responsibility stated:

> [T]hey've been quick to improve. Previously I worked for a government organisation that was producing sustainability reports and that was a challenge because they were slow to improve the systems because there wasn't seen to be the value in improving systems. Whereas a big corporate organisation that needs to move quickly, that's hungry and has an appetite for growth internationally as well as domestically, our systems really have to keep up with that. And that's been fantastic as far as the sustainability report goes. . . . we are at a stage now where we're very confident in the systems that sit behind us and our feedback from the auditor has consistently been, since that first report, that our systems are now at a very good stage.

It was also clear from respondents that the organisation was progressing with the integration of some forms of sustainability data. For instance, the Procurement Manager stated:

> We do capture the information through the financial system so, to use paper as an example, we would have various methodologies of capturing information around that and that's obviously financial dollars spent just going through your normal general ledger processing invoices and the like. . . . [W]e have interfaces with the suppliers where they provide volume information, which is then uploaded into our reporting systems. And ultimately that then flows firstly to our capture systems like SAP and then flows through into our reporting systems. It would be in those reporting systems where we're actually doing our allocation around a conversion to CO_2 equivalent.

Combining financial and sustainability reports

At the time of the interviews, Alpha did not combine their sustainability report with their annual report. Some respondents noted that separating the two reports creates the impression that the sustainability report is the 'poorer cousin' of the annual report. The Head of Group Treasury and Finance seemed to reflect the view of many respondents that the reports should be combined:

> The annual reports are so fat, what's a little bit more on it. I think it would be positive to do that. I think the sustainability report often just becomes sort of the poor cousin and the focus is on the shareholders and the financials and then the sustainability report goes out and it's probably not anywhere near as widely read.

The Group Head of Sustainable Business Practices believed that combining the reports would be highly desirable while also identifying significant dilemmas that might face the organisation if the two reports were combined, one being the potential ramifications of a qualified audit report:

> The other thing we're trying to do, but not lose the extent of information that we already report on, is to . . . crunch together our sustainability reporting into our annual report. In terms of reach, we're straight up. It would improve massively, because we have a million shareholders. So that's one reason. But the other reason is around our strong view . . . that lead indicators are far more valuable indicators of the health of a company than lag indicators. So we'd like to see them in a combined annual report. It's very complicated, in terms of audit requirements, because even something that's perfectly reasonable, but a bit peculiar, relative to the accounting standard, as you talk about, can give you a qualified audit. So that just sends our CFO into outer orbit. I mean, you know, that's the last thing a corporation can allow itself is a qualified audit, even if it's for perfectly explainable reasons. Doesn't matter. That terminology makes CFOs pass out, not to mention shareholders.

On the other hand, including the sustainability report in a few pages of the annual report (and allowing details to be searched online) has been viewed as a positive step by the organisation. The Consultant for Corporate Social Responsibility stated:

> . . . and the feedback we had from last year's concise report, which is the first year we did it, was overwhelming, 'Please keep doing it, we don't want to see a long printed version, keep the long information on the website so that we can search around it'. But overwhelmingly people were very keen to see the report produced in a concise format.

Conclusion

Over the last few decades we have seen a remarkable transformation in societal expectations of an organisation's social and environmental performance. Through a 'social contract' lens, organisations now engage more comprehensively on social and environmental performance to prove their value to society. Alpha, from a reporting perspective, presents as a model organisation for stakeholders that have called for organisations to focus more on sustainability performance and transparency through more comprehensive and formal reporting. In the case of Alpha, senior management had recognised a need to engage the community and had made a strong public commitment on sustainability. From an external perspective, this was operationalised through product development and external sustainability reporting and the delivery of socially desired services, but also through reporting.

Sustainability reporting is now at a precipice. The widespread adoption of the GRI and development of integrated reporting 'standards' has elevated the status of sustainability reporting and launched the debate to the forefront of business. Foremost is a question as to the organisation's position on sustainability performance and a corresponding commitment to external reporting. Once an organisation has made such a commitment, such as in the case of Alpha, there are considerable hurdles before we can be assured that the organisation is producing sustainability information to the same level of quality that we should expect from financial reporting. The adoption of the GRI and the discussion on integrated reporting by Alpha is an indication of a more sophisticated reporting regime where the organisation is embracing an externally 'explicit' set of criteria for CSR reporting. Once again, this aligns with the broader shift toward formal sustainability reporting that can be utilised in the same context as financial statements. The external perception of Alpha's actions can therefore fit within a social contract that arguably is expanding to incorporate sustainability as a desirable contribution to society.

Historically, social and environmental reporting has been criticised as being ad hoc and incomplete; as an 'implicit' element of an organisation's performance, such observations should be expected as management develops a deeper understanding of performance expectations. The formalisation of reporting through the development of the GRI and IR has now made more 'explicit' the performance reporting expectations of an organisation. However the existence of such guidelines will not necessarily elevate sustainability reporting to the same quality and usefulness as financial reporting. There is hesitation from many in the accounting profession to provide unqualified support for the development of IR standards which have not evolved or matured through the long-term due process that generally accepted accounting principles and accounting standards have been exposed to. The lack of comprehensive and compatible management systems in organisations (as evidenced in the Alpha case study) also underscores the reality that sustainability reporting still has some time to develop before it will be considered on par with financial reporting.

Notes

1 Corporate management are also participating members of society. As such, corporate management may be influential in the setting of the social agenda and therefore influential in the setting of the implicit (and explicit) terms of the social contract. This influence is magnified by their access to the resources of the organisation that they manage and can exist on a number of levels. They have the ability, first, to directly lobby the rule-making bodies (the government) and, second, to directly lobby the community and create the 'aura' of the socially responsible corporate citizen (a process of legitimisation of its social status with charitable donations, a perceived commitment to the community's welfare, etc.).

2 It is argued that social lobby organisations have the ability to impact upon corporate operations. In response, corporations may seek to associate with socially valuable activities.

3 Business has continued to grow; however, this growth has at times been seen as causing an unacceptable cost in terms of impact upon the natural environment. Hence, there have been increased demands for the principles of sustainable development to be adopted by the business sector (Schmidheiny 1992).

4 Once social norms have become formalised, corporate management accountability to society is enforceable through government institutions.

5 The legitimisation process may also apply to corporate reporting practices where perceived failures to provide sufficient information will result in calls for greater disclosure and the introduction of reporting standards.

6 It is, however, speculated that those organisations that adopt changes in internal processes will adopt a more in-depth external reporting process, which will be reflected in the 'quality' of the information finally disclosed (Elkington 1993).

7 Various titles have been used to describe CSR, including social accounting, social and environmental accounting, social responsibility accounting, and social auditing. These are all considered to represent the same phenomenon, that of the reporting of information on social responsibility issues.

8 A criticism of environmental reporting is that it is

> of an ad hoc, unsystematic nature, partial in terms of the range of corporate impacts addressed, lacking in the provision of comparative data against which performance may be judged, public relations driven, lacking independent attestation, and largely qualitative and descriptive with a paucity of financial data and lack of integration with main accounts.
>
> *(Owen 1994, p. 32)*

9 Costly in terms of expenditure in actual collation and distribution of all relevant data, and also in terms of competitive advantage.

10 A quick cross reference of journals such as *Accounting, Auditing & Accountability Journal* and *Accounting Forum* would suggest that the methodology employed by Hahn and Kühnen (2013) may not have captured the full population of sustainability reporting research.

11 A system-wide response is where all firms within a homogeneous social environment react to changes in community values so as to maintain the legitimacy of the system or industry.

12 https://www.globalreporting.org/information/about-gri/what-is-GRI/Pages/default.aspx

13 http://download.asic.gov.au/media/1239069/rg65-published-30-november-2011.pdf.

14 http://www.comlaw.gov.au/Details/C2013C00372.

15 www.cleanenergyregulator.gov.au.

16 This will become available and published on the Department of the Environment's website (www.cleanenergyregulator.gov.au).

17 www.climatechange.gov.au/reporting.

18 Details of exactly what type of records companies must keep can be found at http://www.cleanenergyregulator.gov.au/National-Greenhouse-and-Energy-Reporting/About-NGER/record-keeping-requirements/Pages/default.aspx.

19 www.npi.gov.au.

References

Beck, C., Frost, G., and Jones, S. (2013) *Sustainability Reporting: Practices, Performance and Potential*, CPA Australia, Melbourne.

Buhr, N. (1998) Environmental performance, legislation and annual report disclosure: the case of acid rain and Falconbridge, *Accounting, Auditing & Accountability Journal* 11, 163–190.

Burritt, R., and Gibson, K. (1993) Accounting for the environment, *Australian Accountant* 63, 17–17.

Chadwick, B., Rouse, R. W., and Surma, J. (1993) Perspectives on environmental accounting, *CPA Journal* January, 18–24.

Cho, C. H., and Patten, D. M. (2007) The role of environmental disclosures as tools of legitimacy: a research note, *Accounting, Organizations and Society* 32, 639–647.

Clarkson, P. M., Overell, M. B. and Chapple, L. (2011) Environmental reporting and its relation to corporate environmental performance, *Abacus* 47, 27–60.

Cooper, D. J., and Sherer, M. J. (1984) The value of corporate accounting reports: arguments for a political economy of accounting, *Accounting, Organizations and Society* 9, 207–232.

Coopers and Lybrand (1993) *Business and the Environment: An Executive Guide,* Coopers and Lybrand, Sydney.

Cormier, D., and Magnan, M. (1999) Corporate environmental disclosure strategies: determinants, costs and benefits, *Journal of Accounting, Auditing & Finance* 14, 429–451.

Cormier, D., Magnan, M., and Van Velthoven, B. (2005) Environmental disclosure quality in large German companies: economic incentives, public pressures or institutional conditions? *European Accounting Review* 14, 3–39.

Corrigan, J. (1998) Assessing costs and benefits: what role to play? *Australian Accountant* 68, 24–26.

Deegan, C., and Rankin, M. (1996) Do Australian companies report environmental news objectively? An analysis of environmental disclosures by firms prosecuted successfully by the Environmental Protection Authority, *Accounting, Auditing & Accountability Journal* 9, 50–67.

Donaldson, T. (1982) *Corporations and Morality*, Prentice Hall, Englewood Cliffs.

Dowling, J., and Pfeffer, J. (1975) Organizational legitimacy: social values and organizational behavior, *Pacific Sociological Review* January, 122–136.

Eddey, P. (1983) Social accounting and social disclosure: a loss of enthusiasm, *Accounting Forum* March, 55–62.

Elkington, J. (1993) Coming clean: the rise and rise of the corporate environment report, *Business Strategy and the Environment* 2, 42–44.

Epstein, M. J. (1996) *Measuring Corporate Environmental Performance: Best Practices for Costing and Managing an Effective Environmental Strategy*, Irwin, Chicago.

Fifka, M. S. (2013) Corporate responsibility reporting and its determinants in comparative perspective: a review of the empirical literature and a meta-analysis, *Business Strategy and the Environment* 22, 1–35.

Frost, G. R. (2007) The introduction of mandatory environmental reporting guidelines: Australian evidence, *Abacus* 43, 190–216.

Gray, R. H. (1994) Social and environment accounting, accountability and reporting: new wine in old skins or silk purses from sows ears? *Accounting Forum* 17, 4–30.

Gray, R., Kouhy, R., and Lavers, S. (1995) Corporate social and environmental reporting: a review of the literature and a longitudinal study of UK disclosure, *Accounting, Auditing & Accountability Journal* 8, 47–77.

Gray, R., Owen, D., and Maunders, K. (1987) *Corporate Social Reporting: Accounting and Accountability*, Prentice Hall, Hemel Hempstead.

Guthrie, J., and Parker, L. D. (1989) Corporate social reporting: a rebuttal of legitimacy theory, *Accounting and Business Research* 19, 343–352.

—— (1990) Corporate social disclosure practice: a comparative international analysis, *Advances in Public Interest Accounting* 3, 159–175.

Hahn, R., and Kühnen, M. (2013) Determinants of sustainability reporting: a review of results, trends, theory, and opportunities in an expanding field of research, *Journal of Cleaner Production* 59, 5–21.

Higgins, C., Milne, M. J., and Van Gramberg, B. (2014) The uptake of sustainability reporting in Australia, *Journal of Business Ethics*, forthcoming

Hogner, R. H. (1982) Corporate social reporting: eight decades of development at US steel, *Research in Corporate Performance and Policy* 4, 243–250.

Ijiri, Y. (1983) On the accountability-based conceptual framework of accounting, *Journal of Accounting and Public Policy* 2, 75–81.

International Integrated Reporting Council (IIRC) (2011) *Towards Integrated Reporting: Communicating Value in the 21st Century*, International Integrated Reporting Council, London.

Kestigian, M. (1991) The greening of accountancy, *Australian Accountant* 20–28.

KPMG (2011) *The KPMG Survey of Corporate Social Responsibility Reporting*, KPMG, London.

Kreuze, J. G., and Newell, G. E. (1994) ABC and life-cycle costing for environmental expenditures, *Management Accounting* 75, 38–38.

Laughlin, R. C. (1991) Environmental disturbances and organizational transitions and transformations: some alternative models, *Organization Studies* 12, 209–232.

McGraw, P., and Katsouras, A. (2010) A review and analysis of CSR practices in Australian second tier private sector firms, *Employment Relations Record* 10, 1–23.

O'Dwyer, B., Unerman, J., and Hession, E. (2005) User needs in sustainability reporting: perspectives of stakeholders in Ireland, *European Accounting Review* 14, 759–787.

Owen, D. L. (1994) The need for environmental accounting standards, *Accounting Forum* 17, 31–46.

Patten, D. M. (1992) Intra-industry environmental disclosures in response to the Alaskan oil spill: a note on legitimacy theory, *Accounting, Organizations and Society* 17, 471–475.

Rawls, J. (1971) *A Theory of Justice*, Oxford University Press, Oxford.

Roberts, C. B. (1991) Environmental disclosures: a note on reporting practices in mainland Europe, *Accounting, Auditing & Accountability Journal* 4, 62–71.

Rousseau, J. J. (1947) *The Social Contract: An Eighteenth-Century Translation (English Translation)*, Hafner Press, New York.

Russell, W. G., Skalak, S. L., and Miller, G. (1994) Environmental cost accounting: the bottom line for environmental quality management, *Environmental Quality Management* 3, 255–268.

Schmidheiny, S. (1992) *Changing Course: A Global Business Perspective on Development and the Environment*, The MIT Press, Cambridge, MA.

Shocker, A. D., and Sethi, S. P. (1974) An approach to incorporating social preferences in developing corporate action strategies, In *The Unstable Ground: Corporate Social Policy in a Dynamic Society* (Sethi, S. P., Ed.), 67–80, Melville Publishing Company, Los Angeles, CA.

Smith, R., and Lambell, J. (1997) Accounting for the environment: the role of strategic management accounting, *Management Accounting* 75, 34–35.

Spence, C. (2009) Social and environmental reporting and the corporate ego, *Business Strategy and the Environment* 18, 254–265.

Suchman, M. C. (1995) Managing legitimacy: strategic and institutional approaches, *Academy of Management Review* 20, 571–610.

Tilt, C. A. (1994) The influence of external pressure groups on corporate social disclosure: some empirical evidence, *Accounting, Auditing & Accountability Journal* 7, 47–72.

White, J., and Mazur, L. (1994) *Strategic Communications Management: Making Public Relations Work,* Addison-Wesley Publishing Company and The Economist Intelligence Unity, Workingham, UK.

Wilmshurst, T. D., and Frost, G. R. (1998) Environmental accounting: a growing concern? *Australian CPA* 68, 20–23

Wilmshurst, T. D., and Frost, G. R. (2000) Corporate environmental reporting: a test of legitimacy theory, *Accounting, Auditing and Accountability Journal* 13, 10–26.

Index